MODERN
CATHOLIC
DICTIONARY

MODERN CATHOLIC DICTIONARY

John A. Hardon, S.J.

DOUBLEDAY & COMPANY, INC. GARDEN CITY, NEW YORK 1980

ISBN: 0-385-12162-8
Library of Congress Catalog Card Number: 77-82945
Copyright © 1980 by John A. Hardon
All Rights Reserved
Printed in the United States of America
First Edition

Library of Congress Cataloging in Publication Data

Hardon, John A.
    Modern Catholic dictionary.

    1. Catholic Church—Dictionaries. 2. Theology—
Dictionaries. I. Title.
BX841.H36   282′.03

Imprimi Potest:	Michael J. Lavelle, S.J.
	Provincial
	Detroit Province
	December 3, 1979
Nihil Obstat:	William B. Smith, S.T.D.
	Censor Librorum
Imprimatur:	✠Joseph T. O'Keefe
	Vicar General
	Archdiocese of New York
	December 13, 1979

ACKNOWLEDGMENTS

The author is deeply grateful to all whose generous assistance has made the *Modern Catholic Dictionary* possible. At the editorial offices of Doubleday & Company, the co-operation of Robert Heller, Theresa D'Orsogna, and Cyrus Rogers was indispensable. Readers of the manuscript who shared their professional knowledge and made literally hundreds of incorporated recommendations included Rev. Theodore J. Cunnion, S.J., Rev. James T. O'Connor, Rev. Thomas J. O'Donnell, S.J., Rev. Joseph P. Penna, Rev. William B. Smith, and Rev. William R. Walsh, S.J. Research, editing, and clerical services were provided over a period of several years by numerous people, outstanding of whom were Sr. Mary Gertrude, H.P.B., Geraldine E. Donovan, and John F. Gonoud; also Rev. Christopher M. Buckner, Sr. Mary Roberta, D.M., Sr. Nora Bernardine, R.S.M., Margaret Aser, Marianne Breiter, Dennis Brown, Colleen Crowell, Dr. Bernard and Jane Donovan, Richard Gill, Robert Horak, Rozanne Joyce, Dr. Jorge and Deborah Juncos, Hannah Kern, Mary Lanzl, Margaret McLoughney, Sandra Munoz, and Priscilla Smith.

Special thanks are due to the editors of the *Annuario Pontificio,* the *Official Catholic Directory,* and *Le Canada Ecclésiastique—Catholic Directory of Canada* for the use of their publications; also to the Byzantine Catholic Seminary Press for the Byzantine calendar and Msgr. Eugene Kevane for the text of the Credo of the People of God.

CONTENTS

INTRODUCTION

The need for a modern Catholic dictionary seems obvious. Much has happened in the Catholic Church since the opening of the Second Vatican Council in 1962. The council itself was a historic event whose sixteen documents, confirmed by Pope Paul VI, have deeply influenced the thinking of all the faithful. As a result new words and expressions have entered the Catholic vocabulary and old terms have taken on a fresh and more profound meaning.

Moreover, the world in which the faithful live has undergone major changes, some would say among the most profound in Christianity since the apostolic age. Marxism is a stark reality. Secularism is no longer a mere theory; it is the chosen way of life of large segments of Western society. Marriage and the family are on trial for their existence; abortion and now euthanasia are being legalized in one country after another. This has placed a grave strain on Catholicism, and the effects are showing across a wide spectrum of thought and practice, again with corresponding impact on the language of people who "instead of the spirit of the world," as St. Paul says, "have received the Spirit that comes from God."

No dictionary is ever complete, and the present one makes no claim to comprehensiveness. There are too many terms in what may be called the Catholic vocabulary to even cover them all, let alone give an extensive treatment of each one. This is plainly to be a dictionary and not an encyclopedia. Yet, otherwise than in other lexicons, a Catholic dictionary should be more than a mere listing of definitions. It cannot, in the name of objectivity, remain neutral on things on which the Catholic Church has an established position. Otherwise it would not merit being called Catholic.

Many terms have been included from psychology and the social sciences, but always defined (or described) from a Catholic point of view, or because they underlie distinctively Catholic principles, or in order to indicate how the Church understands the world in which her faithful live and are working out their salvation.

All the while, however, the main focus of the dictionary and the bulk of its contents are definably, even exclusively, Roman Catholic. An effort was made to include every significant concept of the Church's doctrine in faith and morals, ritual and devotion, canon law and liturgy, mysticism and spirituality, ecclesiastical history and organization.

Special attention has been given to the Second Vatican Council, and the most important documents that implement the conciliar teaching.

Events in the life of the Church over the centuries have been screened, to include such as are necessary or at least useful for a balanced grasp of Catholic Christianity. There has endured a stable tradition that proves the Church's divine origin and guidance. But there has also been development, and therefore change. The dictionary seeks to reflect both dimensions: the Catholic, and therefore the Church's continuity, and Modern, and therefore her progress, in a marvelous paradox that is verified of no other institution in the annals of the human race.

Wherever feasible exact Scripture references or even citations have been given, to enable the reader to go back to the Bible to see the defined term in its full biblical context. So, too, precise references, often with quotations, are given for the Church's doctrines, which may then be traced to their original sources, mainly in papal documents or the canons and decrees of ecumenical councils.

Equivalent terms have not been multiplied beyond measure, but enough of them are available to help the reader find what is sought, perhaps defined under a heading different from the one that first comes to mind.

Special attention was given to Catholic shrines and prayers. With so many hallowed places of pilgrimage and forms of popular piety in the Catholic world, the author felt that these should be duly considered. They reflect one side of the Church's existence that may be overlooked, namely the people's sentiment and affections, with particular emphasis on their devotion to the Blessed Virgin Mary. Likewise the praying side of Catholicism has been highlighted with many of the better known prayers and hymns. They appear with a brief history and, in most cases, the full text of the prayer or song in question.

There are really two parts to the dictionary, of unequal length. The first and major part is the lexicon of terms, over five thousand, directly or indirectly dealing with Catholic faith, worship, morals, history, canon law, and spirituality.

The second part is the Appendix, which contains the Credo of the People of God, a listing of popes from Peter to John Paul II, updated ecclesiastical calendars of both the Roman and Byzantine rites with saints for each day of the year, and a listing of religious communities and secular institutes in the United States and Canada.

Priests and teachers, whether in the pulpit, classroom, or in the home, will find in the dictionary an invaluable aid to communicating the riches and beauty of the Catholic religion. It is the author's hope that this book will bring everyone who reads it closer to the One who is beyond all definition, and for whose honor and glory it was written.

GUIDE TO
THE USE OF THE DICTIONARY

In order to help the reader derive full benefit from this dictionary, it is worth noting certain features that the author had in mind when doing the research and assembling the data. The years of planning that went into the composition of the present volume were mainly directed to accuracy of content, conciseness of treatment, and facility of use. The following information is offered especially to facilitate the use of the *Modern Catholic Dictionary*.

Key to Sources

Most of the sources of quotations in the dictionary are self-explanatory. Some, however, call for further comment:

1. Denzinger

The full title of this source is *Enchiridion Symbolorum* (Handbook of Creeds), originally edited by Henry Denzinger and first published in 1854. The book has gone through upwards of forty editions and is the standard collection, in one volume, of the most important documents of the Catholic Church on faith and morals from the first century to the present time. The numbers following Denzinger are also standard and correspond to sections that are regularly cited in all the official statements of the popes or the organs of the Holy See. The *Enchiridion* is in Latin.

2. Second Vatican Council

Conciliar documents are quoted extensively and generally in their English titles. Numbers following a document correspond to the official subsection of the Latin original.

3. Post-Conciliar Documents

These were issued by Pope Paul VI to implement formally the sixteen basic documents of the Second Vatican Council. They cover the whole spectrum of Catholic faith, worship, and morality and range in dignity from apostolic constitutions of the Pope through the numerous directives and decrees of the Vatican congregations.

Etymology

Many of the entries are given short etymologies. Their purpose is to bring out more clearly the meaning of a term by placing it in historical context. Biblical names often symbolize the person named; Greek derivatives relate the word to its scriptural or first-century origin; and the many Latin sources indicate the role of the Church in standardizing the language of Catholicism.

Cross-References

Although this work is not an encyclopedia, every effort was made to make it as complete as limitations of space would allow. One method to achieve this was to correlate the entries. Where another entry is more or less synonymous, this is indicated by "See" after a single term. When further information is elsewhere available in the dictionary, this appears as "See also" after the entry.

Biographies

Every person named in the dictionary is somewhere given his or her biographical dates, of birth and death, and, in the case of popes, of the years of their reigns. Where the exact dates are disputed among scholars, this was shown by "c" (Latin *circa,* about) or a choice by the author of the most probable date. Some persons are given these biographical dates several times in different entries, whenever this was considered helpful to understand the subject treated.

The only biographies, as such, are those of biblical personages. This was not for lack of appreciation of the many important characters of Catholic Church history but because of the intended purpose of the volume: to concentrate on the objective faith and data of the Church's faith and practice and not enter the vast arena of her life and biographical activity.

On the other hand, biblical persons are treated at some length. Both Old and New Testament characters are given entries. In the light of the Catholic Church's new emphasis on the Scriptures, this was considered an essential part of the *Modern Catholic Dictionary.* Supporting these biblical figures are also a number of important places that belong to historic and contemporary Palestine.

Organizations and Societies

It was clearly impossible to include more than a fraction of the thousands of archaic and present-day societies within Catholic Christianity. There are, for example, some four thousand religious institutes of men and women in the Church today. In the Appendix are given the names and category of the institutes in the larger English-speaking countries. Within the dictionary itself are separate entries for about fifty institutes of Christian perfection that are of historic importance and that fairly set the pattern for similar religious communities throughout the world.

Even more limited is the number of other Catholic organizations that are given special entries. The relatively few given are those of an international character or that have particular significance for the Catholic Church in modern times.

Abbreviations

Built into the sequence of entries are several hundred standard abbreviations for Catholic use, especially for use in the liturgy, canon law, and formal writing. While most of the terms are in current use, others were included from the Church's practice before the Second Vatican Council to give the reader a handy reference source for identifying many terms that appear in print from preconciliar days.

Scholastic Philosophy and Theology

Special attention was paid to give as many basic terms from scholastic philosophy and theology as feasible. These terms are the backbone, as it were, of the Church's official teaching of faith and morals. They derive mainly from the Middle Ages, notably from St. Thomas Aquinas, and are necessary to appreciate the genius of Catholicism in its fundamental grasp of revealed and naturally knowable truth. It is impossible to understand the Catholic Church in her own deepest understanding of herself without some familiarity with this language of scholastic thought.

DICTIONARY OF TERMS

A

AACHEN (shrine). Sanctuary built by Charlemagne at Aix-la-Chapelle (Aachen), forty miles southwest of Cologne, where Charlemagne died in A.D. 814. A chapel in the main cathedral of Aachen houses four major relics believed to be from biblical times. They were never exhibited before the fourteenth century and since then only infrequently. They are the swaddling clothes of the Infant Jesus; the cloak of Our Lady; the loin cloth of Christ on the Cross; and the cloth on which lay the head of John the Baptist after his beheading. The separate reliquaries containing them are in themselves works of art. Great pilgrimages flock to Aachen to venerate these treasures in July of every seventh year, when they are on exhibition.

AARON. The founder and first head of the Hebrew priesthood for almost forty years. Son of Amram and Jochebed, he was the brother of Moses and Miriam (Exodus 6:20). He married Elisheba, and one of his sons, Eleazar, succeeded him in heading the priesthood. Aaron was associated with Moses in every enterprise (Exodus 6:23) and acted as his brother's spokesman because of his eloquence (Exodus 4:16). In the early Pentateuch narratives, his role was mentioned in connection with the Exodus, the making of the golden calf, and taunting Moses for marrying his Ethiopian wife. Apparently he was punished for doubting God's ability to cause water to spring from the rock at Meribah. After a long life he died and was buried at Mount Hor (Numbers 20:27–29).

AARON, BLESSING OF. See SERAPHIC BLESSING.

A.B. *Artium Baccalaureus*—Bachelor of Arts.

AB. *Abbas*—abbot.

ABBA. Father, transliterated from the Aramaic. St. Paul says, "It is the spirit of sons, and it makes us cry out 'Abba, Father'" (Romans 8:15).

ABBACY OF ST. JEROME. Founded by Pope Pius XI in 1933, to replace the pontifical commission created by St. Pius X in 1914 for the revision of the Vulgate. Its scope is to restore, as far as possible, the primitive Latin Vulgate translation of the Bible confirmed by the Council of Trent, to prepare editions for publication, and to engage in other pertinent studies. The abbacy belongs to the Benedictine Congregation of France, and the work on the Vulgate is under the direction of the Holy See.

ABBÉ. Originally an abbot, but more commonly the term applied to a member of the diocesan clergy in French-speaking countries. Eventually abbé came to apply to all who were entitled to similar ecclesiastical dress, which could include clerics not in holy orders and engaged as tutors or in other occupations associated with the Church. (Etym. Aramaic *abba,* father.)

ABBESS. Feminine counterpart of abbot. The spiritual and temporal superior of a community of nuns, symbolizing her role as mother of the religious women under her care. Over the centuries an abbess has enjoyed some extraordinary privileges, such as wearing a special ring and bearing the crosier as a sign of her rank. But an abbess does not have ecclesiastical jurisdiction corresponding to that of an abbot. See also ABBOT.

ABBEY. Canonically erected and independent monastery with a required minimum of religious. Occupied by monks, it is

ABB 4 **ABI**

ruled by an abbot; if by nuns, ruled by an abbess. With the exception of Carthusian abbeys, which provide cottages for individual monks, most abbey buildings are constructed around a quadrangle and comprise a novitiate, guest house, choir, conference room, infirmary, kitchen, refectory, cells, dormitory, oratory for prayer, almonry for alms distribution, cellars for storage, calefactory (or warming room), locutory (or parlor), and a chapter house for business and private meetings with the superior. Most abbeys are either Benedictine or Cistercian.

ABBEY NULLIUS. An abbey that does not belong to a diocese. It is therefore separate and juridically distinct by its own boundaries from surrounding dioceses. It is governed by an abbot who exercises active jurisdiction over the clergy and faithful living in his territory. In a document issued on December 29, 1976, Pope Paul VI declared that no more abbeys nullius would be established except for extraordinary reasons; and except for a few institutions of historic importance, present abbeys nullius would be phased out of existence.

ABBOT. Superior of a monastery of monks having a settled location; a title definitely fixed by St. Benedict. The abbot is elected, usually for life, by the professed members of the community in a secret ballot. The authority of an abbot is, first, paternal, administering the property of the abbey and maintaining discipline in the observance of rule, and, second, is quasi-episcopal in conferring a certain territorial jurisdiction. The rule of the order determines the qualifications of its abbot. His insignia are the pectoral cross and a ring. (Etym. Aramaic *abba*, father.) See also ABBESS.

ABBOT PRIMATE. Title given the abbot of the Benedictine monks resident in the Abbey of St. Anselm in Rome.

ABDICATION. The act of resigning or giving up a legitimately held ecclesiastical office, dignity, or benefice. In principle every ecclesiastical office or rank may be resigned by the one who holds it. To be valid, however, the abdication must be totally voluntary and free from simony. Papal abdication can be made into the hands of the College of Cardinals, since they have the right to elect a successor. Six popes actually abdicated: Marcellus, Liberius, Benedict IX, Gregory VI, St. Celestine V, and Gregory XII. Pope Pius VII signed a conditional abdication in 1804 before he set out for France to crown

Napoleon. The condition was that he would automatically resign the papacy if he were made a prisoner in France.

ABDUCTION. In ecclesiastical law, the forceful taking of a person for the purpose of committing a sin against chastity with the abducted victim. Abduction is an invalidating impediment to marriage between the aggressor and the abducted person. (Etym. Latin *abductio*, a leading away.)

ABEL. The second son of Adam and Eve, slain by his brother, Cain, who was jealous because Abel's offering to God was more acceptable than Cain's. Abel was a shepherd and his brother a farmer (Genesis 4:2, 4:8). During his ministry Jesus made references to Cain's offense when he warned the Scribes and Pharisees, ". . . you will draw down on yourselves the blood of every holy man that has been shed on earth, from the blood of Abel the Holy to the blood of Zechariah . . ." (Matthew 23:35).

ABIGAIL. The beautiful, intelligent wife of a rich landowner named Nabal, who raised sheep on the slopes at Carmel. Nabal, stupid and insensitive, foolishly antagonized David by refusing to share his wool, although David's soldiers had conscientiously protected Nabal's livestock. Learning that the angry David was leading his men to seek revenge, the quick-witted Abigail speedily set out with generous gifts to appease David. Her humility and eloquence in begging forgiveness moved David to abandon his intended attack. "Go home in peace," he said; "see, I have listened to you and granted your request." Within a few days, Nabal died. David promptly offered to make Abigail his wife and she accepted (I Samuel 25). Sometime later the Amalekites raided Ziklag, and among the prisoners they took were Ahinoam, David's first wife, and Abigail. David led his soldiers to battle, and, coming on the Amalekites, who were celebrating their conquest, defeated them decisively and rescued his two wives (I Samuel 30). While they were living at Hebron, Abigail bore David a son named Chileab (II Samuel 3:3).

ABIMELECH. The ruler of what later became the Philistine city-state Gerar. He made a covenant with Abraham at Beersheba to ensure friendship after a dispute about a well which the servants of Abimelech had seized (Genesis 21:22–34). A similar situation developed years later between Abraham's son, Isaac, and Abimelech, but once again the ownership of disputed wells was amicably settled (Genesis 26:19–33). Misunderstandings loomed at other times, too, involving Abimelech, Abraham, and Isaac over Sarah and Rebekah, wives of the father and son (Genesis 20 and 26:6–11). No serious consequences, however, resulted.

ABIOGENESIS. Spontaneous generation. Held by many of the ancients, its basic presupposition was that life does not precisely come from nonlife. Rather a superior power, ultimately divine, enters under certain circumstances to change inanimate matter into living organisms. In conflict with Catholic philosophy that excludes, except in miracles, divine intervention in natural causes. (Etym. Greek *a*, not + *bios*, life + *genesis*, origin.)

ABJURATION. In Church law, the formal renunciation of apostasy, heresy, or schism. While still in effect in exceptional cases, persons now entering the Catholic Church are not required to abjure their former doctrinal errors. Their positive profession of the Catholic faith implies their abjuration of whatever they may have once held contrary to this faith. (Etym. Latin *abiuratio*, a foreswearing, abjuration; from *ab*, from + *iurare*, to swear: *abiurare*, to swear away from, to deny on oath.)

ABLUTION. Liturgical washing with water. In the Latin Rite baptism is generally conferred by ablution, i.e., the pouring of water over the person's head. Also the ritual washing of the thumbs and index fingers of the celebrant at Mass; the cleansing of the chalice used during Mass; and the washing of feet in the Holy Thursday ceremony. In the Greek Church ablution refers to the public washing of newly baptized persons. (Etym. Latin *ablutio*, a washing away or cleansing; a spiritual cleaning.)

ABNEGATION. Self-denial. Voluntarily depriving oneself of some licit or even laudable experience that is pleasant, as an act of sacrifice to God. (Etym. Latin *abnegare*, to deny.)

ABOMINATION OF DESOLATION. The omen of future calamity, predicted by the prophet Daniel and referred to by Christ (Daniel 9:27, Matthew 24:15). Daniel seems to be foretelling the erection of a statue of Zeus in the Temple of Jerusalem by Antiochus Epiphanes (168 B.C.). Christ applied the prophecy to the siege of Jerusalem by the pagan enemies of Rome in A.D. 70. This was to be a sign for the Christians to flee Jerusalem.

ABORTION. In Catholic morality, abortion is either direct (induced) or indirect. Direct abortion is any destruction of the product of human conception, whether before or after implantation in the womb. A direct abortion is one that is intended either as an end in itself or as a means to an end. As a willful attack on unborn human life, no matter what the motive, direct abortion is always a grave objective evil.

Indirect abortion is the foreseen but merely permitted evacuation of a fetus which cannot survive outside the womb. The evacuation is not the intended or directly willed result, but the side effect, of some legitimate procedure. As such it is morally allowable.

The essential sinfulness of direct abortion consists in the homicidal intent to kill innocent life. This factor places the controverted question as to precisely when human life begins, outside the ambit of the moral issue; as it also makes the now commonly held Catholic position that human life begins at conception equally outside the heart of the Church's teaching about the grave sinfulness of direct abortion.

Abortion was condemned by the Church since apostolic times. *The Teaching of the Twelve Apostles*, composed before A.D. 100, told the faithful "You shall not procure abortion. You shall not destroy a newborn child" (II, 2). Direct abortion and infanticide were from the beginning placed on the same level of malice.

Hundreds of ecclesiastical documents from the first century through the present testify to the same moral doctrine, with such nuances as time, place, and circumstances indicated. The Second Vatican Council declared: "Life must be protected with the utmost care from the moment of conception," so that "abortion and infanticide are abominable crimes" (*Constitution on the Church in the Modern World*, IV, 51). Pope Paul VI confirmed this teaching in 1974. "Respect for human life," he wrote, "is called for from the time that the process of generation begins. From the time that the ovum is fertilized, a life is begun which is neither that of the father nor of the mother. It is rather the life of a new human being with its own growth. It would never be made human if it were not human already." Consequently, "divine law and natural reason exclude all right to the direct killing of an innocent human being" (*Declaration on Procured Abortion*, III, 12). (Etym. Latin *abortivus*, born prematurely, abortive; from *aboriri*, to miscarry.)

ABP. Archbishop.

ABRAHAM. Born in the twentieth or nineteenth century B.C., in Ur of the Chaldeans on the Euphrates River. His father, Terah, named him Abram. The family migrated to Haran, where Terah died (Genesis 11:26–31). At God's behest, Abram, his wife, Sarah, his nephew, Lot, and all their followers moved on to Canaan (Genesis 12:4). When Abram was ninety-nine years old, God made a covenant with him, changing his name to Abraham and promising to make him the "father of a multitude of nations . . . [Genesis 17:1–5] I will make you into nations and your issue shall be kings . . . I will give to you and your descendants the land you are living in, the whole land of Canaan, to own in perpetuity, and I will be your God" (Genesis 17:5–8). Hence he has been called the founder of the Hebrew people. Abraham's dedication to the will of God was tested when he was told to take his son, Isaac, to the land of Moriah (which later became the site of the Jerusalem temple) and sacrifice his son as a burnt offering. He obeyed without hesitation, but Isaac was spared at the last moment (Genesis 22). In his final days Abraham arranged to have his son marry Rebekah, one of his kinfolk (Genesis 24), and left Isaac all his possessions before he died at the age of one hundred seventy-five (Genesis 25).

ABRAHAM-MEN. Contemptuous name given to beggars and wanderers in Reformation days. It was derived from Lazarus, the poor man who in the Gospel passage was received into Abraham's bosom.

ABRAHAM'S BOSOM. Term used by St. Luke (Luke 16:22) to describe the abode of the just persons who died in the Old Testament, before they were admitted to the beatific vision. In patristic literature it often means heaven. It implies a return of Abraham's spiritual descendants to the embrace of the earthly father of all the faithful.

ABROGATION. In ecclesiastical law the total abolition of a law, right, duty, or privilege. (Etym. Latin *abrogare*, to repeal a law, abrogate.)

ABS. *Absens*—absent.

ABSALOM. The third son of King David, he was noted for his handsome appearance and his abundant hair (II Samuel 14:25). He fled from Jerusalem after killing his half-brother (II Samuel 13), Amnon, but returned after three years to become reconciled to his father (II Samuel 14:33). Later he organized the malcontents of Judah to make an effort to seize his father's throne, but the attempt failed (II Samuel 15). In fleeing, Absalom's horse rode under a tree and either his head or his hair became caught in a low branch. He was killed by one of his pursuers (II Samuel 18) to the dismay and sorrow of his father (II Samuel 19).

ABSAM (shrine). Marian sanctuary in the Austrian Tyrol. In January 1797 an eighteen-year-old native girl had a premonition that her father had met with an accident in the salt mines where he worked. In her anxiety she looked out the window and saw the face of the Virgin Mary appearing on the window glass. Her father reported a serious accident at the mine that afternoon but he was unhurt. The glass panel was removed, washed, and scraped in an attempt to remove the image, but all attempts to obliterate the image failed. The cherished glass was placed in a small chapel nearby, and six candles are always burning before the picture, which has become a place of pilgrimage.

ABSOLUTE. That which is independent or not related to anything else; or that which is total and complete in itself.

Applied to God, who is the Absolute, it is equivalent to the divine transcendence in two ways. He is absolutely independent of all creation for his own existence and perfections. They totally depend upon him but he is completely self-sufficient in himself, since his essence is his existence. He is the Being who cannot not be, whereas all others are contingent beings whose existence depends wholly on him who alone is necessary Being.

But God is also absolutely perfect. He is the infinite Being whose attributes are without limitation and whose perfections are without restriction. He is almighty and all good, omniscient and all holy. In a word he is the One in whom there is no potency that can be actualized and no possibility that can still be realized.

Applied to beings other than God, a thing is said to be absolute when it is considered or conceived in itself and apart from its relation to something else. Thus, absolutely speaking, sin is an unmitigated evil. But considered from the viewpoint of divine providence, sin can be the occasion of much good in the world.

ABSOLUTE GOOD. That which possesses the perfections proper to its nature. Something is good absolutely when it is what it should be. It is relatively good when it is suitable to perfect or satisfy someone or something else.

ABSOLUTELY SUPERNATURAL. A divine gift whose essence transcends nature altogether, so that it can never be due to or merited by any creature. It surpasses not only nature's powers but its rights and its needs or exigencies. Given to a creature, it is finite but beyond the exigency of anything created. It is a divine thing communicated and shared in a finite way. The Incarnation and Sanctifying Grace are the sole instances of the absolutely supernatural, the latter in a lesser degree because, unlike Christ, other human beings are not divine persons.

ABSOLUTE MIRACLE. An effect produced by God in the visible world which totally surpasses all the forces of created nature, e.g., raising a certainly dead person back to life.

ABSOLUTE POWER. The power of God to act or to make, considering only his sovereign authority and unlimited ability as Creator, or abstracting from his other perfections and from the present order of divine providence.

ABSOLUTE TUTIORISM. A rigorist moral system for resolving practical doubts which holds that in every difference of opinion one must choose what is certain and thus decide in favor of compliance with the law. Only full certainty of the opposite frees a person from observance of the law. This theory is not acceptable in Catholic morality.

ABSOLUTION. In the sacrament of penance, the act by which a qualified priest, having the necessary jurisdiction, remits the guilt and penalty due to sin. The new formula of absolution, since the Second Vatican Council, is: "God, the Father of mercies, through the death and resurrection of His Son, has reconciled the world to Himself and sent the Holy Spirit among us for the forgiveness of sins; through the ministry of the Church may God give you pardon and peace, and I absolve you from your sins in the name of the Father, and of the Son, and of the Holy Spirit." To which the penitent answers, "Amen." In this formula the

essential words are: "I absolve you." For centuries, the Church used the deprecatory form of absolution, e.g., "May God absolve you from your sins." This was really declarative in meaning, as is clear from the fact that in the whole of tradition the priest who absolved was looked upon as a judge who actually absolved, even though he used the subjunctive mood to express his affirmative judgment. (Etym. Latin *absolvere,* to free from; to absolve, acquit.)

ABSOLUTION FROM CENSURE. Removal of an ecclesiastical penalty by one who is authorized to do so. The absolution can be in the internal (private) forum only, or also in the external (public) forum, depending on whether scandal would be given if a person were privately absolved and yet publicly considered unrepentant.

ABSOLUTION OF THE DYING. Special faculties conferred by the Church's common law, for any priest, even though laicized or not approved for confessions, can validly and licitly absolve any penitent in danger of death. The absolution covers any sin and censure, even in the presence of a priest who is approved for confessions.

ABSOLUTISM. Government in civil society in which the authority is totally vested in the ruler. In theory it is unlimited sovereignty that has no checks or balances either within the political system or from the people who are governed. In practice it is reflected in the Pharaohs of ancient Egypt and the tyrants of pre-Christian Greece and Rome. The governments of Louis XIV in France and the czars of Russia were absolute monarchies. Modern dictatorships under Communism are forms of absolutism. (Etym. Latin *absolutus,* completed, unfettered, unconditional, from *absolvere,* to free from, complete: *ab-,* away from + *solvere,* to loosen.)

ABST. Abstinence day.

ABSTENTION. See ABSTINENCE.

ABSTINENCE. The moral virtue that inclines a person to the moderate use of food or drink as dictated by right reason or by faith for his own moral and spiritual welfare.

As commonly understood, abstinence refers to refraining from certain kinds of food or drink and may be undertaken by a person spontaneously or it may be prescribed by ecclesiastical law, whether for the universal Church or for certain territories.

Institutes of Christian perfection may also have special provisions for abstinence according to their rule of life.

The Jewish law contained elaborate food prohibitions which, however, were abrogated by the New Dispensation, the only apparent exceptions being blood and things strangled (Acts 15:20). From early Christian times, other kinds of abstinence were practiced, especially among the hermits. Thus St. Antony of Egypt and his followers abstained from all food except bread, water, and salt, and many contemplative orders still observe a severe abstinence for all or most of the year. (Etym. Latin *abstinere*, to refrain from, to keep away.) See also FASTING.

ABSTRACTION. A mental act by which the mind attends to one aspect of a thing without attending to other aspects naturally present in the same object. On the first level of abstraction, the mind disregards individual material things and concentrates on some universal material nature such as water or color. On the second level, the mind concentrates on abstract quantity, such as circle, plane, or square. On the third level, proper to metaphysics, the mind disregards all matter and grasps its object without any necessary relation to matter, arriving at the knowledge of being, existence, substance, unity, and the like. It is by means of abstraction that human reason, apart from revelation, can arrive at the knowledge of God's existence, and his attributes of infinite wisdom, goodness, and power. Abstraction is, therefore, the underlying principle of natural theology.

ABSURD. In existentialist philosophy the meaninglessness of human life and activity. An absurdist is one who positively affirms the absence of purpose in man's existence on earth. Linked to a denial of God's existence, absurdism sees no finality at work in the universe and reduces all events in the world, including man's deepest thoughts and affections, to a blank irrationality. (Etym. Latin *ab*, from + *surdus*, deaf, inaudible, harsh: *absurdus*, inharmonious, foolish.)

ABULIA. In Catholic morality an emotional disorder that either totally or at least partially prevents a person from making decisions.

ABYSSINIAN CHURCH. Popular name of the Catholic Church in Ethiopia following the Ethiopian Rite, with its metropolitan bishop in Addis Ababa. Its origins go back to the fourth century, when Christianity was first introduced into Abyssinia by St. Frumentius and Edesius of Tyre. The liturgy and canon law are adapted from the traditions of the old Church of Abyssinia.

A.C. *Auditor Camerae*—Auditor of the Papal Treasury.

A.C. *Ante Christum*—Before Christ.

ACACIANS. Heretical sect named after Acacius of Caesarea (d. 366), who refused to accept the Nicene term *homoousios* (one in being with) the Father in reference to Christ. They claimed that Christ was merely *homoios* (like) the Father. Also called Semi-Arians and Homoeans. According to St. Jerome the leader of the Acacians was nominated Felix, the antipope, in 358. In the next century another Acacius, who was Patriarch of Constantinople (471–89), provoked the Acacian Schism with Rome by his compromise with the monophysites.

ACCEPTANTS. The Catholics who accepted Unigenitus (1713), the bull of Clement XI condemning the Jansenism of Pasquier Quesnel (1634–1719), in contrast to the appellants who appealed against the Pope.

ACCESS. In ecclesiastical law, the right that a person has to a certain benefice in the future. In the meantime, it is held in abeyance because of some impediment.

ACCESSION. In Catholic moral philosophy the title by which one comes into the ownership of the natural or artificial increment accruing to his property. New trees in a forest, new births in a herd are examples of natural increment. Artificial increment occurs when the property of two or more people becomes inseparably mixed without a previous agreement, as when someone in good faith makes wine out of someone else's grapes. In general the property should go to the one who contributed most to the combined value, with compensation to the other. (Etym. Latin *accessus*, a coming unto, approach.)

ACCIDENT. That which is not of the essence of something. In logic a predicable accident is a predicate incidentally attributed to a subject. In metaphysical philosophy, a predicamental accident is a category of being whose nature is not to exist in itself but in another as in a subject. It is not a thing but the mode of a thing. Of the nine categories of accident, relation, quality, and quantity are the most important. (Etym. Latin *accidens*, a happening; something that is added; chance; nonessential quality; from *accidere*, to come to pass, happen, befall.)

ACCIDENTS. Things whose essence naturally requires that they exist in another being. Accidents are also called the appearances, species, or properties of a thing. These may be either physical, such as quantity, or modal, such as size or shape. Supernaturally, accidents can exist, in the absence of their natural substance, as happens with the physical properties of bread and wine after Eucharistic consecration.

ACCIDIE (acedia). One of the seven capital sins. Sloth or laziness as a state of mind that finds the practice of virtue troublesome. It is not so much a repugnance of conviction as of indifference to God and to the practice of one's religion.

ACCLAMATION. 1. One of the ways of electing a pope in which the cardinals unanimously, without consultation or balloting, proclaim one of the candidates Supreme Pontiff. 2. Liturgical acclamations at the coronation of a pope or the election of a bishop.

Acclamations were sent as compliments to the emperors from the early Church councils and were found in the coronation rites of secular princes and kings. Sepulchral monuments carried them as inscriptions. Brief liturgical formulas such as *"Deo gratias"* (thanks to God) may be classified as acclamations. (Etym. Latin *ac-*, to + *clamare*, to cry out: *acclamare:* proclaim, declare, invoke.)

ACCOMMODATION. In moral matters, the legitimate adjustment of a law to meet the circumstances in which a person finds himself. In biblical usage, it is the application of a passage in Scripture, because of a similarity or analogy, to something not intended by the sacred writer.

ACCOMPLICE. Anyone who actively helps or abets a lawbreaker in a sinful act. In ecclesiastical law, the term specially applies to the person with whom a priest has committed some sin of unchastity. The same priest cannot validly absolve his accomplice of this sin except in danger of death. (Etym. Latin *cum-*, together + *plicare*, to weave, join, fold together.)

ACCULTURATION. The process or fact of accommodating religious belief and practice to the dominant culture of a society. It may be either praiseworthy or blameworthy, depending on whether a religion, notably Catholicism, is strengthened or weakened by the adaptation. It is strengthened when Catholic faith and morality become more effective in transforming the culture. It is weakened when Catholic principles are compromised to make them more acceptable to the people.

A.C.N. *Ante Christum Natum*—Before the Birth of Christ.

ACOLYTE. A ministry to which a person is specially appointed by the Church to assist the deacon and to minister to the priest. His duty is to attend to the service of the altar and to assist as needed in the celebration of the Mass. He may also distribute Holy Communion as an auxiliary minister at the Eucharistic liturgy and to the sick. An acolyte may be entrusted with publicly exposing the Blessed Sacrament for adoration but not with giving benediction. He may also, to the extent needed, take care of instructing other faithful who by appointment assist the priest or deacon by carrying the missal, cross, candles, and similar functions. The ministry of acolyte is reserved to men and conferred by the bishop of the diocese or, in clerical institutes of religious, by the major superior, according to liturgical rites composed for the purpose by the Church. Women may be delegated to perform some of the functions of an acolyte. (Etym. Greek *akolouthos*, attendant follower.) See also ALTAR BOY.

ACOSMISM. Denial of the world's existence. The theory borrowed from Oriental pantheism, taught by Hegel and others, claiming that the external world (cosmos) does not exist because it is really absorbed into God. It is the opposite of God disappearing in the world, which would be atheism. (Etym. Greek *a*, not + *kosmos*, the world.)

ACQUIRED CONTEMPLATION. The prayer of simple recollection, in which acts of the mind and will are the result of a person's own effort aided by grace, and helped by the gifts of knowledge, wisdom, and understanding coming from the Holy Spirit, so that the mind and will remain fixed on God.

ACQUIRED HABIT. Disposition obtained by one's own activity through the repetition of certain actions. Contrasted with infused habit.

A CRUCE SALUS. Salvation comes from the Cross. No less than Christ redeemed the world by his cross, so are the faithful redeemed by patiently bearing their cross.

ACTA APOSTOLICAE SEDIS. Acts of the Apostolic See. An official journal, published periodically. Established September 29, 1908, it contains all the principal decrees, encyclical letters, decisions of Roman congregations, and notices of ecclesiastical appointments. The contents are to be considered promulgated when published, and effective three months from date of issue.

ACTA SANCTAE SEDIS. Monthly publication in Rome, but not officially by the Holy See, from 1865 to 1908. It contained the principal declarations of the Pope and the Roman congregations. In 1904, its contents were declared official and authentic. By the end of 1908, it was superseded by the *Acta Apostolicae Sedis.*

ACTA SANCTORUM. Acts of the Saints. The lives of the saints based on extensive research and published by the Bollandists. Although many volumes have been issued, the series is not yet complete. It is the standard source for Catholic hagiography.

ACTION. In philosophy, the opposite of passion. It is an accident by which a cause is actually producing an effect. When the effect is outside the agent, such as speech or writing, the action is transient. When the effect remains within the producing agent, such as thinking or growing, it is an immanent action. (Etym. Latin *actio,* a doing, performing, action.)

ACTION FRANÇAISE. French political movement begun in 1899 by the freethinker Charles Maurras to re-establish the monarchy. It held that Catholicism is essential to French civilization. Its paper, *L'Action Française,* was put on the Index by Pope Pius XI in 1926.

ACTIVE LIFE. Human life insofar as it is occupied with created things, as distinct from the contemplative life. That aspect of a person's life which is necessarily concerned with external activity, in contrast with the internal concerns of prayer and the worship of God.

ACTIVE UNITIVE WAY. See SIMPLE UNITIVE WAY.

ACTIVE VIRTUES. Term used by Pope Leo XIII in his condemnation of Americanism in 1899. It refers to such practices as humanitarianism, eugenic reform, and democracy, which proponents of Americanism said were to be fostered in preference to such virtues as humility and subjection to authority. In general, active virtues correspond to what is commonly associated with American activism.

ACTIVISM. Preoccupation with activity instead of mental reflection. As a philosophical theory, it emphasizes the active character of the mind. The principal value of thinking is to serve man and society outside the mind. Activism is part of the philosophy of Marxism-Leninism, which holds that the main purpose of thought is not to discover and contemplate the truth but to change reality, especially social reality, in the world.

ACT OF CHARITY. A deliberately expressed love of God, based on divine faith. The act may be either perfect or imperfect, depending on whether the motive is God's goodness in himself or in relation to the person who benefited or hopes to benefit from his love of God.

ACT OF CONTRITION. The prayer of the penitent in the sacrament of penance, by which he expresses sorrow for the sins confessed before receiving absolution. In general, an act of repentance for having offended God.

ACT OF FAITH. A voluntarily expressed assent of the mind to some truth revealed by God. The assent may be purely internal, or it may be vocalized, as in the recitation of the Apostles' Creed, or it may be implied, as in genuflecting before the Blessed Sacrament. It must always be assisted by divine grace.

ACT OF GOD. An accident that arises from a cause beyond the control of man, and therefore attributed to God. Cyclones, hurricanes, and lightning are typical acts of God.

ACT OF HOPE. A voluntarily expressed trust in God's goodness, based on faith, whereby a person declares his confidence that what God promised he will also fulfill. As a supernatural act, it can be made only with the help of divine grace.

ACTS OF MAN. Action performed by a human being but without reflection and free consent, e.g., digesting food, instinctive reaction to some external stimulus.

ACTS OF THE APOSTLES. The book of the New Testament, written by St. Luke, which narrates some of the important events in the lives of Sts. Peter and Paul and, to a lesser degree, of the Apostles John, the two James, and Barnabas. The Acts are a historical narrative which describes the founding of the Church on Pentecost, the influence of the Holy Spirit on the early Christians, the persecution of the faithful, the miracles worked in confirmation of their faith, and the rapid expansion of Christianity throughout the eastern Mediterranean world. The Acts were written about A.D. 63, in Greek, and most probably while Luke was in Rome.

ACTS OF THE MARTYRS. Actual accounts of early Christian martyrdoms. The most reliable are those that follow the official shorthand reports of the trials and executions. Among the best known are the Acts of St. Ignatius, St. Polycarp, the Martyrs of Lyons, and the Passions of Sts. Perpetua and Felicitas, and St. Irenaeus. In the Western Church the Acts of the Martyrs were carefully collected and used in the liturgy from the earliest times, as witnessed by St. Augustine.

ACTS OF THE PENITENT. The necessary actions of a person who receives the sacrament of penance. He must be sorry for his sins, confess them to the priest, and make due satisfaction for having offended God.

ACTUAL. That which is not potential, i.e., that which is not in potency but in act. The existent as distinct from the merely possible.

ACTUAL GRACE. Temporary supernatural intervention by God to enlighten the mind or strengthen the will to perform supernatural actions that lead to heaven. Actual grace is therefore a transient divine assistance to enable man to obtain, retain, or grow in supernatural grace and the life of God. See also EFFICACIOUS GRACE, GRACE, GRATUITOUS GRACE, HABITUAL GRACE, JUSTIFYING GRACE, SACRAMENTAL GRACE, SANATING GRACE, SANCTIFYING GRACE, SUFFICIENT GRACE.

ACTUAL INTENTION. The intention that a person freely makes to perform a given action, and that exists and influences him at the time he is doing the action, e.g., administering a sacrament. See also HABITUAL INTENTION, INTENTION, INTERPRETATIVE INTENTION, VIRTUAL INTENTION.

ACTUALITY. The state of being in act or of being real and complete. The opposite of potentiality.

ACTUAL SIN. Any thought, word, deed, or omission contrary to God's eternal law. All actual sins are classified on the basis of this division, where sinful thoughts are essen-

tially desires, the words may either be spoken or otherwise articulated, the deeds involve some external manifestation, and omissions are failures to do what should have been done by a person in a given set of circumstances.

Sin is a human act that presumes three elements: objective malice in the action performed, or at least the person considers it wrong; actual advertence of mind by which the sinner is at least confusedly aware of the malice of his conduct; and consent of the will, which formally constitutes actual sin and without which the sin is said to be only material.

Every sin is a genuine offense against God. There is consequently no such thing as merely philosophical sin, which offends against right reason but is not at the same time a deliberate transgression of the divine law. Sin is theological by its very nature.

ACTUS DEI. An act of God. Some fortuitous event occurs for which no human being can be held responsible; it must be attributed simply to the positive or permissive providence of God.

A.D. *Anno Domini*—Year of Our Lord.

A.D. *Ante diem*—the day before.

ADAM. The first man. Created in the image of God. His wife was Eve and his sons Cain, Abel, and Seth. They lived in the Garden of Eden but were expelled because Adam and Eve disobeyed God's command not to eat the fruit of a certain tree (Genesis 1, 2). In early accounts of Adam's life he is referred to, not by a specific name, but as "the man" (Genesis 3). Not until his descendants were given (Genesis 4:25) was the proper noun "Adam" applied to him. Many doctrines in the New Testament are traced back to the life of the first man, notably original sin and the concept of Jesus as the second Adam bringing redemption to the human race.

ADAMITES. A Christian sect in the early Church whose adherents sought to return to man's primitive innocence by the practice of nudity. Opposed by St. Epiphanius (c. 310–403) and St. Augustine (354–430), [they] also advocated community of wives and sexual promiscuity. More recently, groups like the Waldenses also called themselves Adamites and held similar views.

AD APOSTOLORUM PRINCIPIS. Decisive encyclical of Pope Pius XII issued in 1958, declaring the Church's innocence of the charges made against Catholics in Red

China, and denouncing the persecution of Christians because of their religious beliefs and practices.

ADAPTATION. Legitimate adjustment of basic principles to time, place, and circumstances. Used by the Second Vatican Council to distinguish external accommodation from internal renewal. Adaptation is secondary to renewal and corresponds to updating in accidentals for the sake of greater effectiveness. (Etym. Latin *adaptatio;* from *adaptare,* to fit to.)

ADDICTION. The state of being physically dependent on something, generally alcohol or drugs, but it can be any material object or experience. Addiction means increased tolerance, but also greater difficulty in withdrawal. In fact, the fear of withdrawal symptoms is the main obstacle even in persons who are convinced on moral grounds that they should overcome an addiction. The study of addiction has contributed to a major development in Catholic moral theology, through a better understanding of subjective guilt and a more effective pastoral care of persons with bad moral habits. (Etym. Latin *addicere,* to give one's consent to a thing.)

AD DIEM ILLUM. Encyclical of Pope Pius X, issued in 1904, explaining that Mary is the mediatrix of all graces. The union of her will with Christ in suffering now makes her "the principal agent in distributing graces."

ADDOLORATA. Our Lady of Sorrows. Popular title of the Blessed Virgin, and object of special devotion among the faithful.

ADDOLORATA INSTITUTES. The title of several religious institutes of men and women in the Catholic Church who have a special devotion to the Sorrowful Mother. Best known are the Servites or Servants of Mary, established by the Seven Holy Founders at Florence in 1253, under the Rule of St. Augustine, with a distinctive constitution.

ADEQUATE REPARATION. The full expiation of man's sin required by divine justice and offered by a lawful representative of mankind. This required that God become man in the person of Jesus Christ. Being infinite as God, Christ satisfied for the malice against an infinite God. Being capable of suffering and offering himself as man, he made reparation for man as the Second Adam and supernatural head of the human race.

ADESTE FIDELES. Christmas hymn of anonymous origin, most likely written in France or Germany in the eighteenth century. There are some forty translations; the one most commonly used in English is by Canon Oakeley, "O come, all ye faithful, joyfully triumphant."

AD GENTES DIVINITUS. Decree of the Second Vatican Council on the Church's missionary activity. The Church's mission is defined as "the evangelization and the implanting of the Church among peoples or groups in which it has not yet taken root." Among the surprising recommendations is that the young churches of the newly evangelized take part "in the universal mission of the Church as soon as possible" and send "missionaries to preach the Gospel throughout the whole world, even though they are themselves short of clergy." Special stress is placed on adequate training of missionaries, their sanctity of life, and co-operation among themselves in the apostolate (December 7, 1965).

AD HOMINEM. In scholastic philosophy an argument that appeals to a person's emotions rather than to his intellect. Also said of a personal attack on someone's character, and thus obscuring the real issue under discussion.

ADJURATION. Using the name of God or of a saint or the mention of some holy thing to confirm a command or a request. At the trial of Jesus the high priest said to him, "I put you on oath by the living God to tell us if you are the Christ, the Son of God" (Matthew 26:63). Many of the liturgical prayers of the Church end with the adjuration "through our Lord Jesus Christ, your Son, who lives and reigns with you and the Holy Spirit, one God for ever and ever."

To be licitly employed, an adjuration must be made in the name of the true God or of some truly sacred person or object; there must be a lawful purpose in mind; and the occasion should be of some importance to warrant the solemn invocation of God or some sacred name.

AD LIBITUM. At one's choice. Term applied to the various options in the Eucharistic liturgy and the Liturgy of the Hours, when there is a choice of prayer or ritual.

AD LIMINA APOSTOLORUM. A pilgrimage to the tomb of the Apostles Sts. Peter and Paul, canonically required of every bishop every three to ten years. On this visit he renders an account of the complete condition of his diocese to the Pope. If unable to go on this visit for lawful reasons, a delegate may be sent in the bishop's place. Often abbreviated to "ad limina" visit.

ADM. REV. *Admodum Reverendus*—Very Reverend.

AD MAJOREM DEI GLORIAM. For the greater glory of God, abbreviated A.M.D.G. The motto of the Society of Jesus, but commonly used by Christians everywhere. See also A.M.D.G.

ADMINISTRATION. The care and government of ecclesiastical property by persons who are qualified to do so by the laws of the Church. In countries where the Church is hindered in the possession, sale, or transfer of her own property, the administration is at least partially handled by persons who are not clerics or religious. When the laity are appointed administrators of Church property, this assumes they are responsible to the hierarchy or the superiors of religious institutes.

AD NUTUM SANCTAE SEDIS. A term that means "at the disposition of the Holy See." It refers to any circumstance involving a conflict of ecclesiastical jurisdiction, where Rome decides to take the matter under its own jurisdiction and reserves to itself the right to make a final judgment on the matter.

ADOLESCENCE. Physiologically the period of development from puberty to full adulthood. But theologically the operations of divine grace are quite independent of this physical process. Not only can adolescents live a deep life of faith, but they are capable of reaching a high degree of sanctity, as testified by the Church's canonization of such young persons as St. Stanislaus Kostka (1550–68), St. Dominic Savio (1842–57), and St. Maria Goretti (1890–1902). (Etym. Latin *adolescentia,* time of youth; from the fifteenth year to the thirtieth, between the *puer* and the *iuvenis.*)

ADONIJAH. The fourth son of David and an older brother of Solomon. He aspired to succeed his father as king, even though he knew that his brother had been promised the throne. Sensing his ambition, friends of Solomon urged the latter's mother, Bathsheba, to persuade David to forestall the conspiracy. David readily agreed and arranged to have Solomon escorted to Gihon, where he was anointed, proclaimed king, and seated on the throne. He took no immediate steps to punish Adonijah for conspiring against him, but when he learned from Bathsheba that his brother was seeking marriage with Abishag, a union that would threaten Solomon's sovereignty, he promptly ordered his brother's death (I Kings 1, 2).

ADOPTION, CANONICAL. The act by which a person, with the approval of public authority, takes as his own the child of another. Where the civil law considers adoption an impediment to marriage, the Church accepts this provision and prohibits the marriage accordingly, either as invalid or illicit, depending on the civil law. Dispensations, however, are granted for just reasons.

ADOPTION, SUPERNATURAL. The act of God's goodness by which he takes us as his own children to make us heirs to the happiness of heaven. Unlike legal adoption, supernatural adoption transforms the persons adopted by transforming them into the likeness of Christ and making them by grace coheirs with Christ to the kingdom of heaven.

ADOPTIONISM. The heretical teaching that claims that Christ as man is only the adoptive Son of God. It was advocated by Elipandus of Toledo and Félix of Urgel, but condemned by Pope Adrian I in 785 and again in 794. When Peter Abelard (1079–1142) renewed a modified form of this teaching in the twelfth century, it was condemned by Pope Alexander III in 1177 as a theory proposed by Peter Lombard.

ADORATION. The act of religion by which God is recognized as alone worthy of supreme honor because he is infinitely perfect, has supreme dominion over humans, and the right to human total dependence on the Creator. It is at once an act of mind and will, expressing itself in appropriate prayers, postures of praise, and acts of reverence and sacrifice. (Etym. Latin *ad-,* to + *orare,* to pray; or *os,* oris, mouth, from the pagan custom of expressing preference for a god by wafting a kiss to the statue: *adoratio,* worship, veneration.)

ADORATION OF THE EUCHARIST. Acknowledgment that, because the whole Christ is really present in the Blessed Sacrament, he is to be adored in the Eucharist as the incarnate God. The manner of showing this homage differs among countries and has varied through the ages. The postconciliar legislation for the Latin Rite requires that the Blessed Sacrament, whether in the tabernacle or exposed on the altar, is to be venerated by genuflecting on one knee.

ADORO TE DEVOTE. Hymn to the Holy Eucharist, written by St. Thomas Aquinas. Unlike the other hymns by St. Thomas, it was not originally composed for the feast of Corpus Christi. Until the liturgical revision after the Second Vatican Council, it was among the optional prayers in the Missal and the Breviary for recitation by the priest after Mass. There are some twenty-five English translations, of which one popular version begins, "Lord and God, devoutly you I now adore; Hidden under symbols, bread and wine no more."

AD PASCENDUM. Apostolic letter of Pope Paul VI establishing the new norms for the order of deacon, for men vowing celibacy and going on to the priesthood, and for those, whether celibate or married, who enter the permanent diaconate. Provisions were also made for the ministries of reader and acolyte, also reserved to men, August 15, 1972.

AD TOTAM ECCLESIAM. Directory published by the Secretariat for Promoting Unity among Christians. Its main purpose is to delineate in specific norms some of the more critical areas of ecumenical effort and communication, summarily identified by the Second Vatican Council. Sixty-three norms are given, some through numerous paragraphs, on: 1. establishment of ecumenical commissions in the dioceses; 2. the validity of baptism by ministers of non-Catholic Christian denominations; 3. spiritual ecumenism in the Catholic Church; 4. co-operation with our separated Christian brethren, May 14, 1967 (Pentecost Sunday).

ADULT. A person who has reached the age of maturity. In ecclesiastical terms the age varies; e.g., sixteen years is adult for men and fourteen for women to marry. But adult baptism means that one has reached the age of reason. A person is a canonical minor (Canon 88) until the completion of the twenty-first year.

ADULTERY. Sexual intercourse of a married person and another who is not the wife or husband. Forbidden by the sixth commandment of the Decalogue, it was extended in meaning by Christ, who forbade divorce with the right to remarry during the lifetime of one's legitimate spouse. (Etym. Latin *adulterium,* adultery, carnal or spiritual.)

ADV. *Adventus*—Advent.

ADVENT. A period of prayer in preparation for Christmas, including four Sundays, the first nearest the feast of St. Andrew, November 30. It is the beginning of the Church's liturgical year. The use of the organ and other musical instruments is restricted in liturgical functions. However, it is allowed 1. in extraliturgical functions, 2. for exposition of the Blessed Sacrament, 3. to support singing, and 4. on Gaudete Sunday, feasts and solemnities, and in any extraordinary celebration. Altars may not be decorated with flowers. In the celebration of matrimony, the nuptial blessing is always imparted. But the spouses are advised to take into account the special character of the liturgical season. Masses for various needs and votive Masses for the dead are not allowed unless there is a special need. (Etym. Latin *adventus,* a coming, approach, arrival.)

ADVENT WREATH. A band or circle of green foliage, surrounding four candles that may be enclosed in glass and are lighted successively in the four weeks of the Advent season. They symbolize the coming celebration of Christmas, when Christ the Light of the World was born in Bethlehem. The wreath originated in Germany, and in some countries there is a special ceremony, with prayers and hymns, associated with the lighting of the candles on the Sundays of Advent.

ADVOCATE. A title of Christ, who is called "our Advocate with the Father" (I John 2:1). Also the title of the Holy Spirit, sometimes translated Paraclete, whom Christ promised to send to his followers (John 14:16). Christ is our Advocate who defends the cause of Christian believers against their accuser, the devil (Revelation 12). The Holy Spirit is our Advocate as "the person called to one's side" to strengthen and plead our cause, implying that we effectually seek his aid. (Etym. Latin *advocatus,* an advocate, one "called upon" to plead.)

ADVOCATUS DEI. Advocate of God. The one authorized to examine the virtues and reported miracles of a person whose cause for beatification has been introduced with the Holy See. Also called the promoter of the cause.

ADVOCATUS DIABOLI. See DEVIL'S ADVOCATE.

AEON. A long period of time. In Gnosticism it was one of the spiritual beings evolved from the Divine Being by emanation and constituting the *pleroma* (plenitude) or invisible spiritual world as distinct from the *kenoma* (chaotic world), which is material and visible. Familiar term for Christ among some early heresies of Gnostic origin. (Etym. Greek *aiōn*, age.)

AFFABILITY. The virtue of approachableness. It partakes of justice in that a person adjusts to other people, giving each one the respect he or she deserves. But charity also enters into affability, since being friendly to others often requires the practice of selfless love, and not only of justice. (Etym. Latin *affabilitas*, affability, friendliness, kindness, courtesy.)

AFFECTED IGNORANCE. In ecclesiastical law, directly willed ignorance of a law or of its penalty, or both. Such ignorance does not excuse a person from automatic penalties (*latae sententiae*), i.e., those which follow immediately on breaking the law.

AFFECTIONS. A broad variety of human sentiments that are distinguished from strictly mental or cognitive experiences. Affections pertain to the will, desires, and feelings, i.e., the outgoing activities. In the spiritual life they are identified with those movements of the soul that reach out to God and with the invisible world of angels and saints. Affections are acts of the infused virtues of hope and charity. (Etym. Latin *affectus*, condition, situation; affectionate state or inclination; faculty of desire.)

AFFILIATION. In ecclesiastical law, the association of a smaller or lesser group or society with a larger or greater one. All affiliation must be approved by the proper Church authority and, in the case of religious institutes, by the Holy See. (Etym. Latin *filiatio*, filial relationship, sonship, filiation.)

AFFINITY. An invalidating impediment to marriage with certain blood relatives of a deceased husband or wife, unless a dispensation is granted. No dispensation is given for marriage in the direct line, that is, with any of his or her ancestors or descendants. In the collateral line, the impediment extends to the second degree—first cousin, uncle or aunt, nephew or niece—and dispensations are granted for both the first and second degrees of affinity. (Etym. Latin *affinitas*, relationship, nearness; from *affinis*, bordering on, nearby family relationship.)

AFFIRMATION. Judgment that declares some objective identity between subject and predicate, or between evidence and conclusion. All statements of divine faith are affirmations that what God has revealed is true.

AFFUSION. Baptism administered by the pouring of water, practiced already in the first century of the Christian era, as testified by the Didache.

AFRICA, OUR LADY OF. Ancient shrine at Algiers, dedicated to the Immaculate Conception. It was originally a small statue of the Madonna, set in a frame of shells at a spot often visited by Barbary robbers. Fishermen came there to pray for safe voyages. In time, the grotto became a chapel and eventually a large church. A great miracle made the revered chapel even better known. Archbishop Lavigerie of Algiers was on his way to Rome accompanied by seven hundred soldiers, priests, and a Trappist abbot when their ship was caught in a violent storm. The crew despaired of the ship's safety. The archbishop had promised the Mother of God a pilgrimage to the shrine of "Our Lady of Africa" if she would save them. The ship was saved and the promise was kept. In 1872 an impressive cathedral was consecrated and now houses the crowned statue of Mary. Pope Pius IX donated the golden diadem with precious stones that Mary, "Consolation of the Afflicted," now wears. At the shrine there are as many Moslem pilgrims as Christian. To the faithful Moslem she is "Lala Meriem," who bestows her favors. The Holy See has entrusted the care of the sanctuary to the congregation of White Sisters of Africa.

AGAPE. The most distinctively Christian form of love. Used by Christ to describe the love among the persons of the Trinity, it is also the love he commanded his followers to have for one another (John 13:34–35). It is totally selfless love, which seeks not one's own advantage but only to benefit or share with another.

As a proper noun, Agape is the so-called love feast celebrated in the early Church (I Corinthians 11:20–22, 33–34). At first these were often joined with the Eucharistic liturgy but in time were separated from the Mass because of the disorder and scandal they provoked. Legislation against the Agape was passed by the Council of Carthage (397), and by the eighth century the practice disappeared. Since the Second Vatican Council a limited use of the Agape has been encouraged (*Decree on the Apostolate of Lay People*, 8). (Etym. Greek *agapē*, love.)

AGE, CANONICAL. The age of reason, fixed by canon law, when a person is permitted or required to receive the sacraments. It differs for various sacraments. For penance and the Eucharist it is commonly assumed to be at the age of reason. For religious profession and holding certain ecclesiastical offices the canonical age is further specified and widely varies.

AGENT. In scholastic philosophy and theology, an efficient cause, namely that which by its activity produces existence or change in another. (Etym. Latin *agens,* doing, active, effecting; also cause, agent; from *agere,* to do, drive, conduct.)

AGENT INTELLECT. In the philosophy of St. Thomas Aquinas, the intellect in its operation of abstracting from the imagination to produce intelligible ideas.

AGE OF AQUARIUS. Expression derived from astrology to describe the new age of freedom in all areas of human life and of peace without war among men. The term is partly derived from the medieval belief that the conjunction of certain planets was the sign of a new era in human history. It is also associated with the claim among astrologers that the Aquarian personality is warm and friendly, hence the Age of Aquarius (just dawned) is to be an epoch of universal brotherhood.

AGE OF DISCRETION. Sometimes refers to the age at which a person reaches adulthood and can make lifetime decisions, especially regarding one's state of life. But more commonly it is the age when a child is capable of making free acts of the will and therefore becomes morally responsible for his actions. This was St. Pius X's understanding as regards the age for receiving the sacraments of penance and Holy Communion. In general, it is about seven years of age.

AGE OF REASON. The time of life at which a person is assumed to be morally responsible and able to distinguish between right and wrong. It is generally held to be by the end of the seventh year, although it may be earlier. With the retarded it will be later. See also AGE, CANONICAL.

AGE QUOD AGIS. Do what you are doing. An imperative phrase in ascetical writers to point up the value of not scattering one's moral forces but of concentrating on one responsible task at a time.

AGERE CONTRA. To act against. A term in ascetical literature to describe the deliberate effort one must make to strive to overcome his evil tendencies by doing the opposite of that to which he is sinfully inclined.

AGGEUS. See HAGGAI.

AGGIORNAMENTO. Updating. The term entered common Catholic usage under Pope John XXIII, and it has two quite distinct meanings. It means internal spiritual renewal, and external adaptation of the Church's laws and institutions to the times.

AGILITY. Quality of the glorified human body, which St. Paul says is sown in weakness and is raised in strength (I Corinthians 15:42). This is commonly understood to mean that the body is totally submissive to spirit, in movement through space, with the speed of thought. (Etym. Latin *agilis,* nimble; lit., easily driven about.)

AGLIPAYANISM. A schism in the Philippine Islands started in 1902 by Gregorio Aglipay (1860–1940), a native priest of Manila. Reacting against the Spanish-dominated Church and taking advantage of the American acquisition of the Philippines, Aglipay proclaimed himself pope of the Philippine Independent Catholic Church with about a million followers. When Aglipay died in 1940, reconciled with the Church, the movement began to decline. But it is still influential in that country. There are now two main types of Aglipayans: the Unitarians, who deny the Trinity; and the Trinitarians, who entered into full communion with the Protestant Episcopal Church of the United States.

AGNOETES. A sect of Monophysites who held that Christ was subject to positive ignorance. The leading exponent of its error was Deacon Themistios of Alexandria. He was condemned by the Church, which declared that Christ's humanity cannot be ignorant of anything of the past or of the future. To attribute ignorance to Christ's human nature is to profess Nestorianism (Denzinger 474–76).

AGNOSTICISM. The theory that either knowledge or certitude about ultimates is impossible. In practice, it stresses uncertainty about the nature or substance of things, the existence of an immortal soul, the origin of the universe, life after death, and the existence and perfections of a personal God. (Etym. Greek *agnōstos,* unknown, unknowable.)

AGNUS DEI. A sacramental consisting of a small piece of wax, blessed by the Pope, stamped with the figure of a lamb on one side and with the coat of arms of the Pope on the reverse side. It is a symbol of the Lamb of God as the Savior. It is used as a protection against Satan, sickness, temptations, fire, tempests, and sudden death, and, for pregnant women, safe delivery. Its use is not indulgenced. Except as minute particles of the one blessed by the Pope on the Wednesday of Holy Week in the first year and every succeeding seventh year of his pontificate, no other Agnus Deis are to be distributed among the faithful.

AGNUS DEI (liturgy). The invocation Lamb of God is sung or recited at Mass during the breaking of the bread and the commingling. It may be repeated as often as necessary, but the conclusion is always "Grant us peace."

AGONY. Extreme suffering. In Gethsemane, Christ's agony was so severe that his sweat fell to the ground like great drops of blood (Luke 22:44). (Etym. Greek *agōnia*, struggle, anguish.)

AGONY IN THE GARDEN. The bloody sweat of Christ in the Garden of Gethsemane, described by the third Evangelist (Luke 22:43). Although Matthew and Mark also narrate the event, only Luke mentions the sweat of blood and the visitation of the angel. Catholic tradition has understood the bloody perspiration literally. Medical testimony indicates that, although rare, the phenomenon is neither impossible nor, by itself, miraculous. Commemoration of the event forms the first of the sorrowful mysteries of the Rosary. (Etym. Latin *agonia;* from Greek, contest, anguish, from *agōn*, contest, from *agein*, to drive.)

AGRAPHA. Sentiments attributed to Christ but not appearing in the Gospels. Some are probably apocryphal. (Etym. Greek *agraphos*, unwritten.)

AHAB. The son of Omri, Ahab succeeded his father as King of Israel, ruling for twenty-two years during the ninth century before Christ (I Kings 16:29). He antagonized ardent Israelites by allowing his wife's religion, the Baal cult, to flourish during his reign in Samaria, even participating in the pagan worship himself (I Kings 16:31–33). The prophet Elijah accurately foretold a drought afflicting the kingdom which lasted for three years (I Kings 17:1). Moreover, his wife, Jezebel, had many of Yahweh's prophets murdered (I Kings 18:4). Subsequently, in a battle against the Assyrians, Ahab was fatally wounded (I Kings 22:34–35).

AIN KARIM. A small town west of Jerusalem believed to be the home of Zechariah and Elizabeth, John the Baptist's parents.

AISLE. An architectural division of a church separated from the nave by rows of pillars or columns. In Gothic buildings the roof of the aisle is lower than that of the nave. Sometimes the aisles stop at the transepts, but often they are continued around the apse. Confusing *ala* (wing) with the French *allée* (alley), the word aisle is popularly used to describe the passage between rows of pews or chairs. (Etym. Latin *ala*, wing.)

AIX-LA-CHAPELLE. See AACHEN.

AKATHISTOS HYMN. Office hymn in honor of the Blessed Virgin, always sung standing, used on some days in Lent in the Byzantine Liturgy. It is available in several translations for use in the Latin Rite and was indulgenced by Pope Benedict XIV. (Etym. Greek *a* not, + *kathistis*, a sitting down.)

AKEDAH. Literally "binding," it is the willingness of Abraham to sacrifice his son Isaac (Genesis 22). The prophet's readiness to kill his own son represents to the Jewish people their ideal of martyrdom, if need be, for what is called "the sanctification of God's name."

AL., ET AL. *Alii, alibi, alias*—others, elsewhere, otherwise.

ALB. *Albus*—White.

ALB. A full length white linen vestment secured with a cincture used at Mass. An adaptation of the undertunic of the Greeks and Romans of the fourth century. It is blessed before being worn. It symbolizes the garment in which Christ was clothed by Herod and the purity of the soul with which the Sacrifice of the Mass should be offered. "Make me white O Lord and cleanse my heart that, made white by the Blood of the Lamb, I may be able to serve Thee" is said by the priest as he puts on the alb. It is also the white garment worn by the newly baptized person from Holy Saturday to the Sunday after Easter, Low Sunday, sometimes called the "Sunday in white." (Etym. Latin *albus*, white.)

ALBIGENSIANISM. A modified form of the Manichaean heresy that flourished in Southern France in the twelfth and thirteenth centuries. It claimed that a good deity created the world of the spirit, and an evil god the material world, including the human body, which is under its control. The good deity sent Jesus Christ, as a creature, to deliver human souls from their imprisonment. Albigensians favored suicide and advocated abstaining from marriage. A crusade was organized against them as a menace to society, and was opposed by Raymond of Toulouse. In Belgium, France, and Germany the war against them continued even after their defeat, contrary to the wishes of Pope Innocent III. By the fifteenth century they had disappeared as a political force, but their Manichaean ideas reappeared in the Reformation.

ALCOHOLISM, MORALITY OF. Habitual excessive consumption of alcoholic beverages. It is characterized by an abnormal and persistent desire to drink ethyl alcohol to excess; and also describes the condition that results from such drinking. Chronic alcoholism may have begun as a moral weakness or disorder, but in time it produces psychic instability. It causes psychological and structural changes. One of its most serious effects is to lessen the willpower that is needed to stop. In time all higher faculties are impaired and, not infrequently, undoubted insanity results. Overcoming alcoholism is a major social problem in many societies. Treatment is effective only if a person is sufficiently motivated to practice total abstinence.

ALEXANDRIAN THEOLOGY. Dominant theology in the early Church of Alexandria. It favored a Platonic view of the universe, with a stress on the dualism between God and the world, between spirit and matter. In its view of Christ, it stressed his divinity. In the interpretation of the Bible, it favored a mystical or allegorical exposition, in contrast with the literal and historical approach of the Antiochene theology.

ALEXIANS. Religious institute of brothers, founded in the fourteenth century in Brabant and re-established in 1854. Their apostolate is to care for the sick, direct hospitals and homes for the aged and poor, and administer cemeteries. There are also Alexian Sisters doing similar work. The patron is St. Alexis of Edessa (d. 430).

ALIENATION. The transfer, sale, or reduction of value of Church property. Ecclesiastical law regulates the alienation and sets down specific conditions under which it is to be done. (Etym. Latin *alienus,* of another, foreign.)

ALITURGICAL DAYS. The days on which Mass may not be celebrated. Formerly there were two such days in the Roman Rite: Good Friday and Holy Saturday. Since the Second Vatican Council only Good Friday is an aliturgical day.

ALLEGORICAL SENSE. Form of biblical interpretation. An actual accomplished fact is understood to be a figure of something else. The literal meaning is expressed in a sustained metaphor. Commonly applied to giving a mystical explanation to any part of the Bible.

ALLEGORY. A long or complicated story with an underlying meaning that differs from the literal or surface meaning. The greatest biblical allegory is the Canticle of Canticles. (Etym. Latin *allegoria;* from Greek *allēgoria,* a description of one thing under the image of another.)

ALLELUIA. Hebrew *hallelujah* "praise Yahweh." Ancient liturgical form of jubilation especially in the Psalms, now in the Divine Office and Eucharistic liturgy. Best known in the Easter chant and in the Alleluia verse at Mass. (Etym. Hebrew *halelu jah,* praise ye Yahweh; praise to him who is.)

ALLOCUTION. Solemn form of address delivered by the Pope to the cardinals in private consistory on a matter of importance. If it is considered of general interest to the faithful, it may later be published. (Etym. Latin *al-,* to + *locutio,* a speaking: *allocutio,* a speaking, an address.)

ALL-POWERFUL. Omnipotent. An attribute of God that enables him to do anything good and not self-contradictory. See also AL-MIGHTY.

ALL SAINTS. A feast now celebrated on November 1 as a holy day of obligation. It originated in the West in 609, when Pope Boniface IV dedicated the Pantheon to the Blessed Virgin Mary. At first celebrated in Rome on May 13, Pope Gregory III (731–41) changed the date to November 1, when he dedicated a chapel in honor of All Saints in the Vatican Basilica. Gregory IV later extended the feast to the whole Church.

ALL SOULS. A feast commemorating on November 2, the faithful departed. Begun by Abbot Odo of Cluny in his monasteries in 998, it was gradually adopted by the whole Church. Pope Benedict XV granted all priests the privilege of offering three masses on this day: one for all the poor souls, another for the Pope's intentions, and a third for the intentions of the priest. When the feast falls on Sunday, it is observed on November 3.

ALMA REDEMPTORIS MATER. "Loving Mother of the Redeemer." One of the three seasonal antiphons sung at the end of Compline in the Liturgy of the Hours. Its four verses have been translated into many languages and sung to a variety of melodies. The author is believed to have been the eleventh-century Benedictine monk Herman the Cripple, in the German monastery at Reichenau, Baden.

ALMIGHTY. All-powerful (*Pantokrator*), referring to God. The title is used many times in the Bible, in combination with God (*El, theos*) and Lord (*Kurios*), for identification, invocation, praise, or simple description. (Etym. Anglo-Saxon *aelmihtig*, all strength.) See also ALL-POWERFUL.

ALMONER. An official appointed to distribute alms. Often the chaplain in an orphanage or convent, or a social worker in a hospital or clinic. (Etym. Anglo-Saxon *almaesse*, alms; Greek *eleēmosynē*, compassionateness, pity, alms.)

ALMS. Material or financial assistance given to a needy person or cause, prompted by Christian charity. Almsgiving is recognized by the Church as one of the principal forms of penance, especially since the mitigation of the laws on fast and abstinence.

ALMS BOX. Or alms chest. Permanent receptacle in a church for the donations that are prompted by charity and given to the poor by the parishioners or worshipers. See also POOR BOX.

ALOES. Spices brought by Nicodemus to Jesus' tomb (John 19:39). His body was wrapped in linen with a mixture of myrrh and aloes.

ALPHA AND OMEGA. A symbol witnessing to the divinity of Christ. Words spoken by Jesus of himself: "I am the Alpha and the Omega, the beginning and the end, who is, who was, and who is to come, the Almighty" (Apocalypse 1:8). This combined symbol is often used in conjunction with the cross and together are favorite symbols in ecclesiastical decorations on altars, walls, and vestments.

ALPHABETIC PSALMS. So called because their verses, in sequence or in parallel series, begin with the successive letters of the alphabet. The best known is Psalm 118, which begins each of its twenty-two stanzas (each of eight verses) with a succeeding letter of the Hebrew alphabet. The Lamentations of Jeremiah are another example of alphabetic arrangement in Hebrew poetry. This feature is not discernible in vernacular translations except that the Hebrew letter name precedes each verse.

ALTAR. A table or stand on which sacrifice is offered. In Catholic churches the table on which the Sacrifice of the Mass is offered. One or more relics of martyrs are commonly set into the altar. In the primitive church and in the catacombs, the altar was usually a niche covered with a slab over the tomb of a martyr. Altar in the Greek Rite is synonymous with sanctuary in the Latin Rite. It may also refer to a secondary side space or section in the transept of the church dedicated to a saint.

With the liturgical changes introduced by the Second Vatican Council, the Holy See has issued detailed directives on the construction and adornment of the altar:

"In a consecrated building the altar on which the Eucharist is celebrated may be fixed or movable; in any other place, especially if Mass is not normally celebrated there, a convenient table may be used, but it must be covered with a cloth and a corporal.

"An altar is said to be fixed if it is in fact fixed to the floor so that it cannot be moved; it is said to be movable if it can in fact be moved.

"The main altar should be freestanding, away from any wall, so that the priest can walk all around it and can celebrate facing the people. It should be in a position such that the entire congregation will naturally focus their attention on it. Normally the main altar should be both fixed and consecrated.

"The table of a fixed altar should be made of natural stone; this accords with age-long practice of the Church and its own symbolic meaning. Nevertheless the Bishops' Conference may authorize the use of some other generally accepted and solid material susceptible of good workmanship. The structure supporting the table may be of any material so long as it is solid and durable.

"A movable altar may be made from any material which is solid and dignified, suitable for liturgical use and acceptable to local traditions and culture.

"Both fixed and movable altars should be consecrated by the rites provided in the Roman Pontifical, but it suffices merely to bless an altar if it is movable. There is no obligation to incorporate a consecrated stone in a movable altar or to place such a stone on a table used for celebrating Mass in a non-consecrated building.

"The custom of putting relics of saints, whether martyrs or not, into or underneath consecrated altars is to be commended. But it is important to verify the authenticity of the relics.

"Minor altars should be few in number; in new churches they should be located in chapels somewhat apart from the nave of the church.

"Out of reverence for the Mass which is both sacrifice and sacred meal the altar must be covered with at least one cloth. Its shape, size and ornamentation should be in keeping with the structure of the altar.

"In all liturgical celebrations candles are required to express reverence and to indicate the various degrees of solemnity. These may be put on the altar or placed near it as may best suit the structure of the altar and the character of the sanctuary. The candles must not impede the people's view of the altar or of anything placed on it.

"A cross, easily visible to the people, should be on the altar or somewhere not far from it" (*Institutio Generalis Missalis Romani,* 1969, Nos. 260–70). (Etym. Anglo-Saxon *altare,* altar; Latin *altar* or *altare,* an altar, high place.)

ALTAR BELL. A small bell, originally kept at the epistle side of the altar, rung at the Sanctus and Elevation during Mass as an invitation to those present to alert them to the solemnity of the Eucharistic consecration. In some countries, the bell was also rung first before the Consecration, and before the Communion of priest and the faithful. Although no longer prescribed by the rubrics, it is a laudable and approved practice to ring the altar bell at least at the Elevation of the Host and the chalice.

ALTAR BOY. Server at the altar at the Mass, Vespers, and other liturgical functions. Also called acolyte.

ALTAR BREAD. Round wafers of wheaten bread, unleavened in the Latin, Maronite, and Armenian Rites, used at Mass for consecration.

ALTAR CARDS. Printed or manuscript cards placed on the altar and facing the priest during Mass. They were to help the memory of the celebrant when it was inconvenient to use the Missal. Three cards, center and two sides, were commonly used, though only one was prescribed. Still in use in some places, they are no longer required by the rubrics.

ALTARPIECE. See REREDOS.

ALTAR RAIL. Horizontal bar of wood, marble, or metal, supported by vertical posts and generally ornamented. Its immediate purpose is to separate the sanctuary from the body of the church. It also serves as a communion rail when the Eucharist is given to kneeling communicants (*Eucharisticum Mysterium,* 1967, No. 34).

ALTAR STEPS. Wood, stone, or brick steps extending around an altar on three sides. High altars commonly had three, five, or seven steps; side altars were required to have at least one.

ALTAR STONE. A small flat stone, consecrated by a bishop, that contains in a hollowed out cavity relics of two canonized martyrs. The stone is usually inserted in the center of an altar that is not entirely consecrated. It constitutes the altar proper and can be moved from one altar table to another. The host and chalice during the Sacrifice of the Mass are placed on it. See also PORTABLE ALTAR.

ALTÖTTING (shrine). An ancient pilgrimage center in the heart of Bavaria; its original shrine has never been destroyed. One of the richest sanctuaries in the world. It is the site where, in 680, St. Rupert baptized Otto the pagan in a temple built in pre-Christian times. It is now a Catholic chapel to which the people make pilgrimage from May until November to venerate Our Lady and her Son. The larger church built around the first octagonal chapel has been enlarged repeatedly for the crowds that come and need accommodation. The center of attention is an ancient wooden statue of Mary and her Son. They are robed in heavily embroidered white and black mantles. On Good Friday both are draped with black veils. Mother and Child wear costly crowns, and she holds a scepter of jeweled lilies. The walls around the statue and the altar are nearly all of solid silver. The many lamps that burn constantly in thanksgiving for the miraculous cures and favors received here have so blackened the faces of the statue that Mary is often referred to as the Smiling Black Madonna of Altötting. Pope Pius IX's special lamp still burns before Mary's statue as he requested. This shrine has long been considered the heart of Catholic Marian devotion in Southern Germany.

ALTRUISM. A theory of conduct claiming that only actions directed toward the happiness of other people have any moral value. In fact, the supreme end of all action is to be found only in devotion to the welfare of others. The theory was first propounded by Auguste Comte, a French philosopher, in the early nineteenth century. It ignores, on principle, man's primary duty toward the Creator and inverts the teaching of Christ by making love of one's neighbor more important than the love of God.

ALTRUISTIC HEDONISM. See UTILITARIANISM.

ALUMBRADOS. A loosely organized group of spiritual persons in sixteenth-century Spain, condemned many times by the Inquisition, who taught that once a person attains the vision of God's essence in this life he can dispense with all external means of sanctification. Vocal prayer, the use of the sacraments, the practice of justice and charity, penance and bodily mortification become unnecessary. Perfect souls need give themselves only to mental prayer and ecstatic contemplation, which unite them so intimately with God that they lose personal liberty and individuality. In the state of perfection a man becomes incapable of sin, and what might be grave crimes in others are not even venial faults in the *iluminados*.

Consistent with these principles, the Alumbrados often gave themselves over to unrestrained indulgence of the passions. In less extreme forms, Spanish illuminism for a while affected not only the simple people but also members of the clergy and nobility. Repressive measures by the Inquisition finally crushed the movement, which persisted in the Diocese of Cádiz and Seville into the late seventeenth century. Later on the same ideas were revived in Italy under Miguel de Molinos (1640–97) as quietism.

A.M. *Anno mundi*—year of the world.

A.M. *Artium Magister*—Master of Arts.

AMADEANS. A reform of the Friars Minor in Lombardy led by Amadeus of Portugal about 1740. Pope Pius V suppressed the movement, for the sake of unity, by distributing its members among other Franciscan communities.

AMBITION. Inordinate seeking of recognition or honor. Ambition is morally good when the recognition sought is not selfish and the means used are not evil. It becomes sinful when motivated by pride or pursued without concern for justice or charity. (Etym. Latin *ambitio*, a going around, especially used of going around to solicit votes; hence a seeking for preferment, strive after, seek; from *ambire*, to go about.)

AMBO. Elevated pulpit with a flight of stairs on each side, from which the Epistles and Gospels were read and sermons preached in the early Church. Later two ambos were used, one for the Epistle reading, the other on the right side of the altar for the Gospel. Generally, now, one ambo or lectern suffices for the entire Liturgy of the Word.

In the Greek Church the ambo is a table in front of the iconostasis, or screen where baptisms, confirmations, and marriages are celebrated. In the Russian Church the ambo is a flight of stairs in front of the iconostasis. (Etym. Greek *ambo*, an elevation.)

AMBROSIAN RITE. The liturgical rite used in the Church of Milan, Italy, so called from St. Ambrose (340–97), Bishop of Milan. Most probably he is responsible for its principal characteristics. It is also called the Milanese Rite. Some features are: a procession with the oblations of bread and wine before the Offertory; the litany chanted by the deacon; the Creed said after the Offertory. The ritual is also used elsewhere.

AMBRY. A box in which the holy oils are kept in Catholic churches. It is either affixed to the wall or inserted in the wall of the sanctuary. (Etym. Latin *armarium*, a chest or safe.)

AMBULATE IN DILECTIONE. Brief of Pope Paul VI, covering the removal of the memory of the excommunications between Rome and Constantinople. There are really two documents in one: the first is in French, entitled *Pénétrés de Reconnaisance*, and the second is the papal brief. Both were dated December 7, 1965.

AMBULATORY. A covered passage, with one side open to the air, around the apse of a church or cloister. The former often has radiating altars or chapels. (Etym. Latin *ambulare,* to walk, go about.)

A.M.D.G. Abbreviation of *Ad Majorem Dei Gloriam* (for the greater glory of God), meaning to strive to give God more glory by always doing what is more pleasing to him. It is the motto of the Society of Jesus.

AMEN. Solemn prayerful affirmation, taken over by the Christians from the synagogue for scriptural and liturgical use in apostolic times. It was often spoken by Christ, and is given as one of his names (Revelation 3:14). Now used as an acclamation of assent or religious confirmation of the speaker's own thoughts. (Etym. Latin *amen;* Greek *amen,* verily; Hebrew *amen,* verily, sobeit; from *aman,* to confirm.)

AMENDE HONORABLE. Public form of satisfaction formerly inflicted on condemned criminals. With candle in hand, stripped to the waist and barefoot, they appeared before the ecclesiastical judge, begging pardon of God, the king, and justice. It was used as late as the seventeenth century.

A MENSA ET TORO. From bed and board. Separation in which husband and wife are not living together, although not legally divorced.

AMERICANISM. The movement propagated in the United States in the late nineteenth century which claimed that the Catholic Church should adjust its doctrines, especially in morality, to the culture of the people. Emphasizing the "active" virtues of social welfare and democratic equality, it underrated the "passive" virtues of humility and obedience to ecclesiastical authority. Americanism was condemned by Pope Leo XIII in an apostolic letter, *Testem Benevolentiae* (January 22, 1899), addressed to Cardinal Gibbons.

AMICE. A short, oblong vestment of white linen, worn beneath the alb to cover the shoulders of the priest while celebrating Mass. Now optional in the Latin Rite. When putting on the amice, the priest says, "Put on my head, O Lord, the helmet of salvation in order to repel the assaults of the devil." (Etym. Latin *amictus,* garment, mantle, cloak; from *amicire,* to throw around.)

AMMONIAN SECTIONS. Divisions marked in the margins of nearly all the ancient manuscripts of the Gospels. Their purpose was to illustrate the parallelism between corresponding parts in the four evangelists. They were the forerunners of our present chapters and verses.

AMNIOCENTESIS. A medical technique sometimes used during pregnancy (after the fourteenth to sixteenth weeks) whereby a hollow needle is inserted through the abdomen and into the mother's womb to pierce the amniotic sac (the so-called "bag of waters" that surrounds the fetus) in order to withdraw some of the liquid to examine it for chromosomal evidence of the sex of the unborn child as well as evidence of certain diseases or defects of the developing infant. The risk to the unborn child is statistically low, but the damage that may be induced is grave. Moreover, it is often used as a prenatal screening. When performed for such reasons, amniocentesis is forbidden on Catholic moral principles. But even for a good purpose it is morally questionable because of the risk to the life of the unborn child.

AMORAL. See UNMORAL.

AMOS. Third among the minor prophets. He describes Israel as steeped in national prosperity and reveling in sin. The central theme of his book is a threefold prophecy that extends through nine chapters. The first part (1–2) foretells God's judgment on the nations surrounding Israel and then on Israel itself. The second part (3–6) develops the divine judgment against Israel in three separate discourses. The third part (7–9) records five visions, of which the fifth describes the glorious anticipation of messianic blessings. Amos is the prophet of God's sovereign lordship over all creation.

AMPHORA. Tall, two-handled vessel, usually of clay, for holding wine for the Eucharistic sacrifice. Those found in the catacombs were inscribed with Christian symbols. (Etym. Latin *amphora,* a vessel; Greek *amphi,* on both sides + *phero,* to carry.)

AMPULLAE. Two-handled jars used for holding holy oils or burial ointments. Found in the catacombs, they usually bore the symbol of a saint. Filled with oil from the lamps at a martyr's shrine, they were often carried by pilgrims in the Middle Ages.

AMRA. An elegy or panegyric on a native saint in Ireland. Best known is that of St. Columba, attributed to Dallan Mac Forgaill.

AMULET (animism). A lifeless object that is carried on one's person and that others credit with secret and innate power to preserve from misfortune or to cause an undertaking to prosper.

AN. *Annus*—year.

ANABAPTISTS. Protestant groups that appeared at Zwickau in Switzerland as early as 1521. Their principal tenets were that: 1. the baptism of infants is unbiblical, 2. only adults should be baptized as a sign of Christian belief, 3. primitive Christianity should be restored, notably through the abolition of oaths, capital punishment, and the magistracy, 4. a new kingdom of God on communitarian grounds should be founded. The Anabaptist principles were later adopted by the Baptists, their lineal descendants.

ANACEPHALAEOSIS. A summary or recapitulation, applied in theology to explain St. Paul's statement that God will "bring everything together under Christ, as head, everything in the heavens and everything on earth" (Ephesians 1:10). It means that the whole of creation is related to the Incarnation. Christ is indeed the highest descendant of Adam's race; he is also the goal of creation. But even more, as the one who redeemed mankind from sin, he literally transformed every phase of human history and reconstituted the whole of creation, which until he came had been subjected to vanity.

ANAGOGICAL SENSE. Teachings of the Bible that relate to or lead to eternal life, including blessings hoped for and related to that future life, e.g., Jerusalem in its anagogical sense typifies the Church triumphant.

ANALECTA BOLLANDIANA. Quarterly publication, since 1882, by the Bollandists. It is devoted to research on the lives of the saints.

ANALEPSIS. The feast of the Ascension of Christ into heaven, in the Eastern Churches.

ANALOGY. Similarity without identity, or any imperfect likeness between two or more beings or things that are compared. The two basic forms are the analogy of attribution and of proportionality. In the analogy of attribution some property that belongs to one being is attributed to other beings because of a real or apparent connection between them, as health in a living body and health in the climate. In the analogy of proportionality there is a resemblance between things because of a complex set of relations (proportions) between them, as goodness in food and goodness in an act of kindness. (Etym. Latin *analogia*, comparative likeness; from Greek *analogia*, equality of ratios.)

ANALOGY OF FAITH. The Catholic doctrine that every individual statement of belief must be understood in the light of the Church's whole objective body of faith.

ANAMNESIS. After the consecration at Mass, the prayer of remembrance in which the Church calls to mind the Lord's passion, resurrection, and ascension into heaven. This is the high point of the Mass as a memorial of what occurred during Christ's visible stay on earth as a pledge of what he continues to do invisibly through the Eucharist. (Etym. Greek *anamnesis*, calling to mind, recollection.)

ANANIAS. A member of the early Christian community with his wife, Sapphira. In obedience to the ideal that the community owned everything in common, Ananias sold his property but connived with his wife to turn over to the Apostles only part of the proceeds. Peter rebuked him for his deception: "It is not to men you have lied but to God." Ananias dropped dead. His wife arrived later and, not knowing her husband's fate, repeated the lie. She, too, died on the spot. This incident originated the familiar use of the name Ananias to represent a liar (Acts 5:1–10).

ANAPHORA. 1. the part of the Mass in the Greek Rite corresponding to the Latin canon; 2. the offering of the Eucharistic bread; 3. aer (veil); 4. the procession in which the offerings are brought to the altar.

ANARCHISM. The theory that laws are an invasion of the rights of free, intelligent beings; that individuals have the right to unlimited self-expression; and that the self-interest of the individual, if intelligently pursued, will best serve the common good. Its origins are traceable to the French Revolution, and to Pierre Joseph Proudhon (1809–65). Some anarchists are evolutionary, believing that propaganda and the ballot will gradually eliminate (or make obsolete) most laws. Others are revolutionary, urging the establishment of anarchism by violence. Nihilists are extreme revolutionary anarchists. The basis of anarchism is an unreasoning optimism about the goodness of unrestrained human nature. Anarchism has been more than once condemned by the Catholic Church, e.g., in the *Syllabus of Errors* of Pope Pius IX in 1864. (Etym. Latin *anarchia*; from Greek *anarchos*, having no ruler.)

ANASTASIMATARION. A book containing text with music of the various compositions sung during the Sunday offices of the Greek Church. (Etym. Greek *anastasia,* resurrection.)

ANATHEMA. Solemn condemnation, of biblical origin, used by the Church to declare that some position or teaching contradicts Catholic faith and doctrine.

"If anyone," Paul wrote to the Galatians, "preach to you a gospel besides what you have received, let him be anathema" (Galatians 1:9). Reflecting the Church's concern to preserve the integrity of faith, the Fathers anathematized heretics in a variety of terms. Polycarp called Marcion the firstborn of the devil. Ignatius saw in heretics poisonous plants, or animals in human form. Justin (c. 100–65) and Tertullian (160–220) called their teachings an inspiration of the Evil One. Theophilus compared them to barren and rocky islands on which ships were wrecked, and Origen said they were pirates placing lights on cliffs to lure and destroy vessels in search of refuge. These primitive views were later tempered in language, but the implicit attitudes remained and were crystallized in solemn conciliar decrees. The familiar *anathema sit* (let him be anathema, or excommunicated) appears to have been first applied to heretics at the Council of Elvira (Spain) in 300–6, and became the standard formula in all the general councils of the Church, as against Arius (256–336) at I Nicaea (325), Nestorius at Ephesus (431), Eutyches at Chalcedon (451) and the Iconoclasts at II Nicaea in 787. (Etym. Greek *anathema,* thing devoted to evil, curse; an accursed thing or person; from *anatithenai,* to set up, dedicate.)

ANATHEMA MARANATHA. An expression of hope in anticipation of the coming of the Lord (I Corinthians 16:22).

ANCHOR. An ancient symbol of the Church signifying hope and security. It was found among the catacomb inscriptions of the first century. Before the fourth century the anchor was often represented with a dolphin or two fishes suspended from the crossbar, as a symbol of Christ. The anchor early signified the cross to be known to the Christians but to be kept in secret from the unbelievers. St. Paul (Hebrews 6:18–19) writes "hold fast the hope set before us which we have as anchor for the soul." In religious art this emblem indicated courage, safety, and confidence and appeared in conjunction with certain saints, notably St. Clement, whose martyrdom was by drowning weighed down

by an anchor. It is a symbolic prayer for aid to mariners in danger of shipwreck.

ANCHOR-CROSS. A sacred symbol found in the catacombs; the combination of a cross and an anchor was emblematic of faith and hope.

ANCHORESS. In medieval language a woman hermit. Also called ancress, it is commonly applied to women who have renounced the world to spend their lives in penance, prayer, and solitude. (Etym. Latin fem. of *anchorita,* variant of *anchoreta;* from Greek *anakhōrētēs,* "one who withdraws [from the world]," from *anakhōrein,* to withdraw: *ana-,* back, + *rhōrein,* to make room.)

ANCHORITE. A hermit. One who separates himself from the world in order to give himself more completely to prayer and penance. Women, doing the same, are known as anchoresses.

ANCIENT OF DAYS. Title applied to God by the Prophet Daniel, comparing his eternal power with the frail existence of the empires of earth (Daniel 7, 9, 13, 22).

ANDACOLLO (shrine). The national sanctuary of Our Lady of the Rosary in Chile. Devotion at the shrine grew up around the three-foot cedar statue of the Madonna and Child. It is said that the Spaniards brought the statue with them when they discovered Chile in the sixteenth century. Nearby Indians revolted and killed the newcomers and the statue disappeared. Many years later the Spaniards returned and converted the Indians. One of them, named Collo, cutting trees in the mountains, found the discarded statue after his ax blade had hit it and he had heard a voice say, "You are hurting me." He took the wooden image home. Later a shrine was made and people came for devotions to pray to the Virgin, who still bears the scars of the ax. A privileged citizen is appointed at the annual celebration, December 24, 25, 26, to make a public apology to the Virgin Queen in Collo's name for the injury his ax caused her. It symbolizes the people's sorrow for their sins.

ANDREW. A fisherman and follower of John the Baptist. He was in John's company when he saw Jesus for the first time and stayed with him for the rest of the day. Convinced that Jesus was the Messiah, he took his brother, Simon Peter, to meet him the next day. This was the occasion on which Jesus told Andrew's brother that from being called Simon his name would be changed to Cephas, meaning the Rock (John 1:35–42). The two brothers were the first apostles chosen by Jesus; they accepted his summons to become fishers of men and abandoned their fishing nets (Mark 1:16–18). The miracle of the loaves which Jesus performed at Tiberias followed Andrew's report of a boy with five loaves and two fishes (John 6:5–10). According to tradition, Andrew was crucified in Achaea on a *crux decussata* (x), which thereafter was called St. Andrew's cross. His feast day is November 30. (Etym. Greek *andreas,* manly.)

ANGEL. A pure, created spirit, called angel because some angels are sent by God as messengers to humans. An angel is a pure spirit because he has no body and does not depend for his existence or activity on matter. The Bible tells us that the angels constitute a vast multitude, beyond human reckoning. They differ in perfection of nature and grace. Each is an individual person. According to Christian tradition, they form three major categories in descending order. The word "angel" is commonly applied only to those who remained faithful to God, although the devils are also angels by nature. Moreover, "angel" is the special name for the choir of angelic spirits, from whom guardian angels are sent to minister to human needs. The existence of angels has been twice defined by the Church: at the Fourth Lateran Council (Denzinger 800) and the First Vatican Council (Denzinger 3002). (Etym. Latin *angelus,* an angel; Greek *angelos,* messenger.)

ANGELIC SALUTATION. First part of the Hail Mary, repeating the words of the archangel Gabriel to the Blessed Virgin, up to and including the name "Jesus."

ANGELISM. A theory of human existence that minimizes concupiscence and therefore ignores the need for moral vigilance and prayer to cope with the consequences of original sin. In general, the tendency to regard human affairs with casual optimism, as though human beings were angels without bodily needs and without proneness to sin.

ANGELS (symbols). Depicted in various forms to express the will of God, of which they are the mediators. Shown as messengers, in worship, and in executing justice, they appeared in Western art before A.D. 600. Before Constantine their appearance without wings was mainly with a staff indic-

ative of their office as messengers. The nine choirs are distinctively represented. Angels in art are represented with a variety of articles, musical instruments, thuribles, shields, scrolls, and in a few instances emblems of the Passion, though they are usually represented in worship before the Blessed Sacrament on earth and before the throne of God in heaven. Archangels are variously depicted: Michael driving Satan into hell; Gabriel announcing the Incarnation to Mary; Raphael healing the blind Tobit. The thrones are shown kneeling in adoration. Seraphim symbolize fire and love with their six red wings and eyes; cherubim, with four-eyed wings of blue and holding a book, indicate their great knowledge; dominations, in royal robes, are crowned for authority; virtues, two-eyed, are charged with dispensing celestial miracles; the powers, holding swords, indicate their conquest of the evil spirits shown under their feet; the principalities carry scepters to assist in their direction of God's commands. The emblem of St. Frances of Rome is her guardian angel, whom she saw daily in visible form.

ANGELUS. Devotion in honor of the Incarnation, commemorating the angel Gabriel's annunciation to the Blessed Virgin. Recited approximately at 6 A.M., noon, and 6 P.M., it is the opening word of the prayer *"Angelus Domini nuntiavit Mariae"* (the angel of the Lord declared unto Mary). The evening Angelus probably owes its origin to the curfew bell, a signal for evening prayer. The morning recital began as a prayer for peace. The noon Angelus was first said only on Friday. It is replaced by the prayer *Regina Coeli Laetare* (Queen of Heaven, Rejoice) during the Easter season. The text of the Angelus follows:

The Angel of the Lord declared unto Mary.
And she conceived by the power of the Holy Spirit. (Hail Mary)
Behold the handmaid of the Lord.
Be it done to me according to your word. (Hail Mary)
And the Word was made flesh.
And dwelled among us. (Hail Mary)
Pray for us, O Holy Mother of God.
That we may be made worthy of the promises of Christ.
Let us Pray.
Pour forth, we beseech you, O Lord, your grace into our hearts; that we, to whom the Incarnation of Christ your Son was made known by the message of an angel,

may by His passion and cross, be brought to the glory of His Resurrection; through the same Christ our Lord. Amen.

ANGELUS BELL. Consists of three strokes of a bell followed each by a pause, then by nine strokes while the Angelus prayer is being finished.

ANGER. An emotional sense of displeasure and usually antagonism, aroused by real or apparent injury. The anger can be either passionate or nonpassionate, depending on the degree to which the emotions are excited, strongly in one case and mildly in the other.

ANGLICAN COMMUNION. The churches in communion with the See of Canterbury. It originated with Henry VIII's Act of Supremacy, 1534, declaring "the king's majesty justly and rightfully is and ought to be the supreme head of the Church of England." But the complete rupture with Catholicism did not come until 1563, when the Elizabethan Parliament made the Thirty-nine Articles of Religion obligatory on all citizens under heavy penalties.

Since then the Thirty-nine Articles have played a major role in shaping the doctrine of Anglicanism. Among typical features, the Bible is declared to contain all that is necessary for salvation, general councils are said not to be infallible, transubstantiation is denied, and the civil ruler is given authority over the Church. To this day the Church of England retains its State Establishment.

Even more influential has been the Book of Common Prayer. This is the official service book of the Church of England and contains, among other things, the forms for the administration of the sacraments and the Ordinal. Mainly the creation of Thomas Cranmer, Archbishop of Canterbury, the Book of Common Prayer has been the single most cohesive force in shaping world Anglicanism. Recently the subject of much controversy, a revised edition was issued in 1928 but, because it failed to get the approval of Parliament, has no formal authority.

ANGLICAN RELIGIOUS ORDERS. Religious communities recognized and approved by the Church of England or one of its national Episcopalian branches in other countries. Their existence in Anglicanism began with the Oxford Movement, under Keble, Pusey, and Newman. The first community was started by Edward Pusey, who in 1841 received the vows of Marian Rebecca

Hughes, superior of the Convent of the Holy Trinity at Oxford. There are now many communities of men and women in the Anglican Communion, monastic, contemplative, and active. Among the best known for men are the Society of St. John the Evangelist, known as the Cowley Fathers, the Community of the Resurrection, the Benedictines at Caldey, and the Franciscans at Dorset. Women's institutes include the Community of St. Mary the Virgin, of All Saints, of St. Margaret, and the contemplative Order of the Love of God.

ANGLO-CATHOLICISM. Popular name of most Catholic sections of the High Church movement among Anglicans or Episcopalians. It stresses some form of acceptance of the papacy, the seven sacraments, and a sacrificing (not merely functional) priesthood.

ANIMA CHRISTI (soul of Christ). A hymn written in the fourteenth century by an unknown author. There are numerous translations in all the modern languages. It was a favorite prayer of St. Ignatius Loyola. The translation of Cardinal Newman reads:

> Soul of Christ, be my sanctification;
> Body of Christ, be my salvation;
> Blood of Christ, fill all my veins;
> Water of Christ's side, wash out my stains;
> Passion of Christ, my comfort be;
> O good Jesu, listen to me;
> In Thy wounds I fain would hide,
> Ne'er to be parted from Thy side;
> Guard me, should the foe assail me;
> Call me when my life shall fail me;
> Bid me come to Thee above,
> With Thy saints to sing Thy love,
> World without end. Amen.

ANIMISM. A form of religious belief and practice that attributes the human qualities of mind, will, and emotions to material objects or to nonhuman living creatures. These objects, considered as animated and endowed with a *mana,* can in certain circumstances enter into direct relation with human beings in their personal and social activities. Since the power attributed to the objects is extraordinary and even superhuman, they are invoked to obtain favors and are propitiated to prevent evils. Ritual ceremonies, appeasing or placating these hidden forces, are an essential part of animism. (Etym. Latin *anima,* soul, principle of life, life.)

ANN. *Anni*—years.

ANNA. This woman was a prophetess who spent all her time, day and night, in the Temple. She was present when Jesus was brought to the Temple by his parents in accordance with the Law of Moses. She "began to praise God" on seeing him, "and she spoke of the child to all who looked forward to the deliverance of Jerusalem" (Luke 2:36–38).

ANNAS. The high priest before whom Jesus was taken when the chief priests and scribes sought evidence in order to condemn him to death. Actually Annas had finished his time as high priest in A.D. 15 and had been succeeded by his son-in-law, Caiaphas, but the older man's prestige was such that Jesus was brought before him. Having questioned Jesus, without significant results, about his disciples and teaching of them, Annas then sent Jesus to Caiaphas for further questioning (John 18:13–24).

ANNIHILATION. The act of wiping out the existence of something. According to the Christian faith, as God has freely created the whole universe, he is also free to annihilate any or all of it through withdrawing of his preserving influence and so allow it to relapse into nothingness. However, revelation teaches that, in point of fact, God has no intention of annihilating what he made. Even the material universe, it is believed, will not be put out of existence but will only be drastically changed.

ANNIHILATIONISM. A school of thought that considers immortality of the soul to be a grace and not the natural attribute of every human spirit. It also professes that those impenitent at death will merely cease to exist. (Etym. Latin *annihilare*, to reduce to nothing.)

ANNO DOMINI. In the year of our Lord. Abbreviated A.D., it is based on the supposed year of Christ's birth devised by Dionysius Exiguus (d. 550). Modern scholarship agrees that the actual birth was several years earlier, either between 7 and 4 B.C., based on the death of Herod the Great (Matthew 2:19) in 4 B.C., or at A.D. 6, based on the great taxation under Quirinius (Luke 2:1–2).

ANNO HEGIRAE (A.H.). In the year of Hegira, i.e., since the historic flight of Mohammed from Mecca to Medina. The Hegira occurred in A.D. 622 and is considered the beginning of the Moslem era.

ANNO INEUNTE. Letter of Pope Paul VI to Patriarch Athenagoras of Constantinople, on the co-operative efforts of the Roman Catholic Church and the Eastern Orthodox Church in the interests of ecclesiastical unity (July 25, 1967).

ANNUAL CONFESSION. The duty to receive the sacrament of penance at least once a year. First decreed by the Fourth Lateran Council in 1215, it has been reconfirmed many times since, especially by Pope St. Pius X in 1910 and Pope Paul VI since the Second Vatican Council. It is binding by ecclesiastical law on "everyone of the faithful of both sexes, after he has reached the age of discretion," and therefore also children or those with only venial sins. It is also binding by divine law on those with mortal sins committed since their last worthy confession and sacramental absolution.

ANNUARIO PONTIFICIO. Annual publication of the Holy See as an official directory of the Roman Catholic Church. It contains all the essential information about the Pope, Roman congregations, residential and titular sees, religious and secular institutes of men and women, rites in the Catholic Church, prelates, curial officials, and a historical summary of the principal offices and activities of the Church's central administration. Originally published unofficially as the *Annuaire Pontifical Catholique*, begun in 1898, it is now under the direction of the papal secretary of state.

ANNULMENT. Official declaration by competent authority that, for lawful reasons, a previous act or contract was invalid and consequently null and void. In ecclesiastical law, annulments mainly apply to marriage contracts over which the Church has the right to determine their validity. (Etym. Latin *an-*, to + *nullus*, none; *anullare*, to annihilate, to annul.)

ANNUNCIATION. The feast, observed on March 25, commemorating the announcement of the Incarnation by the angel Gabriel to the Virgin Mary. There are references to the feast as early as the fifth century. Its date was finally determined by the date of Christmas on December 25. It is considered a feast of the Blessed Virgin and, in the revised liturgy, is a solemnity. (Etym. Latin *annuntiatio*, an announcing, announcement.)

ANOINTED. The meaning of "Christ," derived from the Greek *Christos*, corresponding to the Hebrew *Mashijah* (Messiah). (Etym. Latin *inunctio,* besmearing, an anointing.)

ANOINTING. Literally the pouring of oil on someone or some thing in a religious ceremony. Its biblical purpose was to make sacred the object anointed. Thus kings were anointed (I Samuel 10:1), priests (Exodus 28:41), and prophets (I Kings 19:16). The reference to anointing in the New Testament as a sacred rite pertains to the sacrament of anointing the sick, but the verb here used (James 5:14), *aleipho,* is unique. It therefore has a different meaning from "to make sacred," as elsewhere in the Bible. In the Catholic Church, holy oils are used in the administration of the three sacraments, which impart a permanent character (baptism, confirmation, and holy orders) and with a different purpose, in the anointing of the sick. Oil is used in the blessing of altars, bells, and sacred vessels. There are also a number of blessed oils, e.g., in honor of St. Serapion (fourth century), that are used as sacramentals. (Etym. Latin *inunguere; in-,* upon + *unguere,* to smear, anoint.)

ANOINTING OF THE SICK. Sacrament of the New Law, instituted by Christ to give the sick spiritual aid and strength and to perfect spiritual health, including, if need be, the remission of sins. Conditionally it also restores bodily health to Christians who are seriously ill. It consists essentially in the anointing by a priest of the forehead and the hands, while pronouncing the words "Through this holy anointing and His most loving mercy, may the Lord assist you by the grace of the Holy Spirit, so that, freed from your sins, He may save you and in His goodness raise you up." In case of necessity, a single anointing of the forehead or of another suitable part of the body suffices. Olive oil, blessed by a bishop, is normally used for the anointing, but any vegetable oil may be substituted in case of emergency.

The institution of anointing by Christ is an article of the Catholic faith, defined by the Council of Trent (Denzinger 1716). The Church further teaches that this sacrament is implied in Gospel reference to Christ sending out the disciples, who "anointed many sick people with oil and cured them" (Mark 6:13); moreover that the sacrament was promulgated by the Apostle James when he wrote, "Is anyone among you sick? Let him bring in the presbyters of the Church and let them pray over him, anointing him with oil in the name of the Lord. And the prayer of faith will save the sick

man and the Lord will raise him up and if he be in sins, they shall be forgiven him" (James 5:14–15).

ANSELMIAN ARGUMENT. The famous argument of St. Anselm (1033–1109) of Canterbury (1033–1109) for the existence of God. It is an argument a priori, drawn from the idea of God rather than a posteriori, from the works of God. Anselm used it to refute the fool who says there is no God (Psalm 13). He argues as follows: We call God a being so great that nothing greater can be conceived. This definition is accepted even by the atheist, who admits that God exists at least in the mind of the believer. But that which is so great that one cannot imagine anything greater, cannot exist only in the mind. Why not? Because on this supposition one *could* think of something greater, namely, the same being existing outside the mind, i.e., in reality. Therefore, God exists both in mind and reality. Anselm's argument depends on the realistic metaphysics of Plato and has been the subject of learned discussion over the centuries.

ANT. Antiphon.

ANT. The insect that is mentioned twice in the Old Testament as a symbol of what man ought to be. The ant is a rebuke to laziness, "Idler, go to the ant; ponder her ways and grow wise" (Proverbs 6:6). It is an example of prudence, the first among "creatures little on the earth, though wisest of the wise; the ants, a race with no strength, yet in the summer they make sure of their food" (Proverbs 33:25).

ANTECEDENT CONSCIENCE. The judgment of a person deciding on a moral matter prior to acting on it. Antecedent conscience either commands or forbids, counsels or permits the performance of an act. See also CONSEQUENT CONSCIENCE.

ANTECEDENT GRACE. The actual grace that precedes and affects a deliberate act of the will. Also called *prevenient*—arousing, calling, and operating grace—it is grace considered prior to or independent of man's free co-operation.

ANTE CHRISTUM. Before Christ; sometimes abbreviated A.C. as the equivalent of B.C.

ANTE MORTEM. Before death. Refers to the need for a priest to make sure that he administers the last sacraments to persons before they die.

ANTEPENDIUM. The curtain or hanging covering the front of the altar from the tabletop to the floor. It is often decorated or richly embroidered. (Etym. Latin *ante-*, before + *pendens,* hanging, suspended.)

ANTHEM. A hymn of acclamation and loyalty, it may be a musical composition set to a sacred text, or a patriotic song expressing celebration and praise. (Etym. Latin *antiphona,* an anthem; Greek *antiphona,* sounding in response to; from the alternate singing of the half-choirs.)

ANTHROPOCENTRISM. The belief that the human race is the center of the universe, on whom all else depends and from whom everything derives. As such it is only a variant of pantheism. There is, however, a valid anthropocentrism that recognizes creation of human beings by God and total dependence on him. But it also views the universe as having been created to serve human beings and, by being rightly used, to help them attain the heavenly destiny for which they were made. A distorted form of anthropocentrism has become a feature of the "New Christianity," in which the love and service of God are reduced to the love and service of humankind. The first commandment, "You must love the Lord your God with all your heart," is transformed into the second commandment, "You must love your neighbor," which becomes not the second but the only commandment. (Etym. Greek *anthrōpos,* man + *kentron,* center: centering in man.)

ANTHROPOLOGICAL EVOLUTION. A view of human origins that believes that the human species gradually evolved from a lower animal organism. This view may or may not be part of a larger hypothesis, e.g., monistic or cosmic evolution. If separated from such hypotheses, it is tenable on Catholic grounds provided that: 1. divine providence is recognized as having specially directed the evolutionary process, 2. the human soul is held to have been uniquely created by God.

ANTHROPOMORPHISM. The attribution of human form and qualities to the Deity, a common literary method in the Bible to depict or dramatize God's dealings with humanity. Some of the early Christians, interpreting such texts in Genesis literally, held that God had human form. To obviate this error, the Church teaches that God is an infinitely perfect spiritual being who has no body or spatial dimensions. (Etym. Greek *anthrōpomorphos,* of human form.)

ANTHROPOSOPHY. A religious philosophy developed by Rudolf Steiner (1861–1925) of Germany, by revising Hindu theosophy through the substitution of the human for God as the center of the new system. The method is essentially disciplined meditation that leads to one's lower self arriving at a vision of the higher self, not unlike the discovery of the Atman, or divine Self, characteristic of Vedanta Hinduism. Its doctrine includes belief in various epochs of the human race, reincarnation, Christ as the *Sonnenwesen* (sun being) of the universe, and karma. Anthroposophy was condemned in 1919 by the Holy Office, which declared that its tenets could not be reconciled with Catholic doctrine.

ANTICAMERA. The private room adjoining the quarters where the Pope works. In the anticamera he meets cardinals and other persons of distinction. (Etym. Latin *anti,* against + *camera,* room, chamber; i.e., private room.)

ANTI-CATHOLICISM. Concerted and coordinated opposition, on principle, to the Roman Catholic Church. Its origins are lost in obscurity, but its modern development was one of the fruits of the Reformation. The rise of the modern secular state has intensified the conflict. The Catholic Church's insistence on operating her own schools and welfare institutions, and her uncompromising position on such issues as abortion and marital morality are logically opposed by those who disagree with the Church and have the power to enforce their views.

ANTICHRIST. The chief of Christ's enemies. The New Testament specifically names him only in I John 2:18, 2:22; 4:3, and II John 7, where he is identified with unbelievers who deny the Incarnation. Over the centuries the Antichrist has been variously associated with historical persons, e.g., Caligula, Simon Magus, and Nero, or again with organized movements such as Arianism. The more common Catholic interpretation says that he is not merely symbolic or an embodiment of the anti-Christian. The Antichrist is a real person. (Etym. Greek *antichristos,* against Christ.)

ANTICIPATION. To privately read part of the Liturgy of the Hours before the time usually assigned for its recitation. Thus the Office of Readings may be anticipated after 2 P.M. for the following day.

ANTICLERICALISM. A popular name for

a variety of modern movements, especially in Catholic cultures such as France, Italy, and Spain. Its prominent features are opposition to any doctrinal form of Christianity, removal of all privileges of the clergy and religious, and a total separation of the Church from any influence on the public life of the citizens.

ANTICONCEPTION. An explicit synonym for contraception to bring out the morally culpable intention of interfering with the human life process.

ANTIDICOMARIANITES. The name given to those opposed to Mary's divine maternity and consequently her perpetual virginity. They were led by Epiphanius in the fourth century.

ANTIDORON. In the Greek Rite those remains of loaves from which portions have been cut for consecration. Sometimes blessed, it is then distributed after Mass for consumption by the faithful. (Etym. Greek *anti*, instead of + *doron*, a gift.)

ANTIMORALISM. A theory that claims there are no absolutes in morality and therefore no certain criteria in human conduct. (Etym. Greek *anti*, against + Latin *moralis*, relating to conduct.)

ANTINOMIANISM. The doctrine that claims that a person's faith in God and in the person of Christ frees him from the moral obligations of the law, whether natural or positive, biblical or ecclesiastical. It is a logical consequence of any theory that so stresses the work of the Holy Spirit as to exclude the need for co-operation with divine grace. The most authoritative condemnation of Antinomianism was by the Council of Trent, which saw in the Reformation principle of faith without good works the source of Antinomian conclusions. Hence among other anathemas of Trent was the censure of anyone who says that "God has given Jesus Christ to men as a redeemer in whom they are to trust, but not as a lawgiver whom they are to obey" (Denzinger 1571). (Etym. Greek *anti*, against + *nomos*, law.)

ANTINOMIES. Contradictions or inconsistencies that seem to exist in the Catholic Church. Thus the Church appears in opposition to material civilization and yet fosters it; appears to oppose and yet supports the state; represents a religion of suffering and yet of happiness; is full of scandals and yet is all holy; proclaims a law at once difficult and yet easy; upholds religious freedom and yet opposes unrestrained liberty of conscience; upholds the equality of men and yet the inequality of power and property; is one and yet Christendom has always been divided; is ever the same but ever changing; is ever defeated yet is always victorious.

ANTINOMY. Some real or apparent self-contradiction of laws or principles. Commonly applied to alleged contradictions between human reason and such divine attributes as goodness in God and evil in the world.

ANTIOCHENE RITE. A ritual used throughout the Patriarchate of Antioch. The pure Antiochene, in its oldest form, eliminated the Pater Noster and the names of the saints in the Mass. This form was early displaced by the Liturgy of St. James from Jerusalem, which became the ritual of all Western Syria. Originally Greek, the Liturgy of St. James was later translated into Syriac. The Greek version is now used twice a year by the Orthodox; the Syriac version by the Jacobites in Syria and Palestine and by the Syrian Catholics. A Romanized form of this liturgy is used by the Maronites.

ANTIOCHENE THEOLOGY. The dominant theology of the early Church in Antioch. It was generally in contrast with and sometimes opposed to the theology of Alexandria. Its underlying philosophy, favoring the historical rather than the speculative, was from Aristotle (384–322 B.C.). In Christology it stressed the humanity of Christ, sometimes to the extreme of denying the hypostatic union.

ANTIPASCH. Low Sunday, the first after Easter in the ecclesiastical year of the Greek Orthodox Church.

ANTIPHON. Alternate chanting. A psalm or hymn alternately sung by two choirs. A form of chant introduced in the West about A.D. 500, displacing the responsorial form. Antiphons are also short verses sung before and after a psalm or canticle to determine its musical mode or to provide the key to the liturgical or mystical meaning. Antiphons may be from the psalm that follows, or from the mystery or feast, or mixed from both. A "double" antiphon is using the entire antiphon before and after a psalm; "announcing" the antiphon is using it only at the beginning of the psalm in choral singing or recitation. (Etym. Greek *anti*, opposite of + *phone*, voice: *antiphona*.)

ANTIPHONARY. A liturgical book for choir use containing the music and texts of all sung portions of the Roman breviary. The Gregorian antiphonary, attributed to Pope Gregory I, was the official codification of the collection of antiphons occurring in the Divine Office.

ANTIPHONER. A book containing the Gregorian chants in the Divine Office.

ANTIPOLO (shrine). Church of Our Lady near Manila, Philippines, dating from 1632. It is the national shrine of the island group, and hundreds of pilgrims come here to pay homage to Mary every day. The little wooden statue of the Virgin stands atop a beautiful silver shrine. It is not unusual to see twenty thousand worshipers on a feast day, while a hundred thousand may attend the May crowning that follows a candlelight procession in that month each year.

ANTIPOPE. A false claimant to the Holy See in opposition to the Pope canonically elected. There have been more than thirty in the Catholic Church's history. (Etym. Latin *antipapa;* Greek *anti,* against + *papas,* father.)

ANTIPOPES

The following claimed or exercised the papal office in an uncanonical manner. The list includes names, birthplaces, and dates of alleged rule. An alphabetical list of antipopes and a similar list of antipopes of the Western Schism follow this chronological list.

ST. HIPPOLYTUS: Rome; 217–35; reconciled before his death.
NOVATIAN: Rome; 251.
FELIX II: Rome; 355 to November 22, 365.
URSINUS: 366–67.
EULALIUS: December 27 or 29, 418 to 419.
LAWRENCE: 498; 501–5.
DIOSCORUS: Alexandria; September 22, 530 to October 14, 530.
THEODORE: ended alleged rule 687.
PASCHAL: ended alleged rule 687.
CONSTANTINE: Nepi; June 28 (July 5), 767, 769.
PHILIP: July 31, 768; retired to his monastery on the same day.
JOHN: ended alleged rule January 844.
ANASTASIUS: August 855 to September 855; d. 880.
CHRISTOPHER: Rome; July or September 903 to January 904.
BONIFACE VII (Boniface Franco): Rome; June 974 to July 974; August 984 to July 985.
JOHN XVI (John Philagathus): Rossano; April 997 to February 998.
GREGORY: ended alleged rule 1012.
BENEDICT X (John Mincius): Rome; April 5, 1058 to January 24, 1059.
HONORIUS II (Pietro Cadalous): Verona; October 28, 1061 to 1072.
CLEMENT III (Guibert of Ravenna): Parma; June 25, 1080 (March 24, 1084) to September 8, 1100.
THEODORIC (Theodoric of Rufina): ended alleged rule 1100; d. 1102.
ALBERT (Alberic): ended alleged rule 1102.
SYLVESTER IV (Maginulf): Rome; November 18, 1105 to 1111.
GREGORY VIII (Maurice Bourain): France; March 8, 1118 to 1121.
CELESTINE II (Teobaldo Boccadipecora): Rome; ended alleged rule December 1124.
ANACLETUS II (Pietro Pierleone): Rome; February 14 (23), 1130 to January 25, 1138.
VICTOR IV (Gregorio Conti): March 1138 to May 29, 1138; submitted to Pope Innocent II.
VICTOR IV (Octavian of Monticello): Montecelio; September 7 (October 4), 1159 to April 20, 1164; he did not recognize his predecessor Victor IV (above).
PASCHAL III (Guido di Crema): April 22 (26), 1164 to September 20, 1168.
CALLISTUS III (John of Struma): Arezzo; September 1168 to August 29, 1178; submitted to Pope Alexander III.
INNOCENT III (Lando dei Frangipani): Sezze; September 29, 1179 to 1180.
NICHOLAS V (Pietro Rainalucci): Rieti; May 12 (22), 1328 to August 25, 1330; d. October 16, 1333.

ANTIPOPES OF THE WESTERN SCHISM:

CLEMENT VII (Robert of Geneva): September 20 (October 31), 1378 to September 16, 1394.
BENEDICT XIII (Pedro de Luna): Aragon; September 28 (October 11), 1394 to May 23, 1423.
ALEXANDER V (Pietro Filargo): Crete; June 26 (July 7), 1409 to May 3, 1410.
John XXIII (Baldassare Cossa): Naples; May 17 (25), 1410 to May 29, 1415.
FELIX V (Amadeus, Duke of Savoy): Savoy; November 5, 1439 (July 24, 1440) to April 7, 1449; d. 1451.

Antipopes Listed in Alphabetical Order

Albert	Honorius II
Anacletus II	Innocent III
Anastasius	John
Benedict X	John XVI
Boniface VII	Lawrence
Callistus III	Nicholas V
Celestine II	Novatian
Christopher	Paschal
Clement III	Paschal III
Constantine	Philip
Dioscorus	Sylvester IV
Eulalius	Theodore
Felix II	Theodoric
Gregory	Ursinus
Gregory VIII	Victor IV
Hippolytus, St.	Victor IV

Antipopes of the Western Schism Listed in Alphabetical Order

Alexander V	Felix V
Benedict XIII	John XXIII
Clement VII	

ANTI-SEMITISM. Feelings of prejudice and hostility toward the Jews. The term was used in 1879 in a pamphlet attacking the Jews as descendants of the biblical Shem. On this subject the Second Vatican Council stated that the Catholic Church "deplores all hatreds, persecutions, displays of antisemitism leveled at any time or from any source against the Jews" (*Decree on the Relation of the Church to Non-Christian Religions*, 4). (Etym. Greek *anti*, against + Hebrew *Shēm*, son of Noe.)

ANTISEXUAL. A term of reproach often leveled at Christian morality for its stand on sexual misconduct and its prohibition of sexual activity outside of marriage. Antisexuality then becomes antagonism toward sex and is equated with ferocious conservatism in matters of sexual behavior.

ANTISTES. The title in liturgical language sometimes given to a bishop. It identifies him as the chief priest of the diocese.

ANTITYPE. A person or thing typified or prefigured by a biblical person or object. Christ is the antitype of the Old Testament figures of Noah, Moses, David; the Blessed Virgin is the antitype of Eve. (Etym. Greek *anti*, corresponding to + *typos*, a mold, type.)

ANTONIANS. Several religious communities tracing their descent from St. Anthony of Egypt (251–356). Among others are: 1. the original disciples of St. Anthony with whom the present-day Maronites claim continuity; 2. the group founded by Gaston de Dauphine in 1095 and known as the Hospital Brothers of St. Anthony, who survived until the French Revolution; 3. an order in the Armenian Church founded in the seventeenth century; 4. Chaldean and Maronite groups; 5. the Orthodox monastery of Mount Sinai; 6. a congregation established in Flanders in 1615. The *Annuario Pontificio* gives four religious orders of Antonians of pontifical status.

ANULUS ET BACULUS. Ring and staff. These are symbols of a bishop's episcopal authority. During the controversy over lay investiture they were emblems of dependence of bishops on civil power.

ANXIETY. A general feeling of apprehension about the immediate or eventual future, without discernible cause for the fear. The moral evaluation of anxiety begins with the exercise of prudence, to discover if there are valid grounds for the apprehension. If there are not, to act on the anxiety or fail to act because of it would be a lack of trust in God's providence.

APATHY. A lack of feeling in circumstances that call for a show of emotion. Apathy may be temperamental, but it can also be morally culpable, as when a situation demands strong and decisive action that an apathetic person is not prepared to take. (Etym. Greek *apatheia*, want of feeling.)

APOCALYPSE. The Book of Revelation, commonly attributed to St. John the Apostle. It was written to encourage the persecuted Christians by foretelling the fall of Rome and the final victory of Christ and his church. It is also a prophetical work, describing in anticipation the many trials of the followers of Christ and their eventual triumph over Satan and the forces of Antichrist. It is also eschatological, in predicting the glories of the Heavenly Jerusalem in the City on High. The Apocalypse is the most image-laden book of the New Testament, rich in allegory, and subject to numerous, legitimate interpretations. (Etym. Latin *apocalypsis*, a disclosing, revelation; Greek *apokalypsis*, a revelation.)

APOCALYPTIC NUMBER. The mystical number 666 in the Apocalypse (Revelation). The Greek letters of the word *Lateinos*, i.e., Pagan Rome, are also numerals that when added amount to 666. Antichrist is another interpretation.

APOCREAS. In the Greek Rite corresponds to the Sunday before Ash Wednesday (Sexagesima) and formerly was the last day on which meat might be eaten before Lent.

APOCRYPHA. Originally writings that claimed a sacred origin and were supposed to have been hidden for generations; later, a well-defined class of literature with scriptural or quasi-scriptural pretensions, but lacking genuineness and canonicity, composed during the two centuries before Christ and the early centuries of our era. Protestants apply the term improperly to denote also Old Testament books not contained in the Jewish canon but received by Catholics under the name of deuterocanonical. The following is a list of the Apocrypha:

Apocrypha of Jewish Origin: *Jewish Apocalypses:* Book of Henoch; Assumption of Moses: Fourth Book of Esdras; Apocalypse of Baruch; Apocalypse of Abraham. *Legendary Apocrypha of Jewish Origin:* Book of Jubilees, or Little Genesis; Third Book of Esdras; Third Book of Maccabees; History of Maxims of Ahikar the Assyrian. *Apocryphal Psalms and Prayers:* Psalms of Solomon; Prayer of Manasses. *Jewish Philosophy:* Fourth Book of Maccabees.

Apocrypha of Jewish Origin with Christian Accretions: Sibylline Oracles; Testaments of the Twelve Patriarchs; Ascension of Isaias.

Apocrypha of Christian Origin: *Apocryphal Gospels of Catholic Origin:* Protoevangelium Jacobi, or Infancy Gospel of James, describing the birth, education, and marriage of the Blessed Virgin; Gospel of the Pseudo-Matthew; Arabic Gospel of the Infancy; History of Joseph the Carpenter; Transitus Mariae, or Evangelium Joannis, describing the death and assumption of the Blessed Virgin. *Judaistic and Heretical Gospels:* Gospel according to the Hebrews; Gospel according to the Egyptians; Gospel of Peter; Gospel of Philip; Gospel of Thomas; Gospel of Marcion; Gospel of Bartholomew; Gospel of Matthias; Gospel of Nicodemus; Gospel of the Twelve Apostles; Gospel of Andrew; Gospel of Barnabas; Gospel of Thaddeus; Gospel of Philip; Gospel of Eve; Gospel of Judas Iscariot. *Pilate Literature and Other Apocrypha Concerning Christ:* Report of Pilate to the Emperor; Narrative of Joseph of Arimathea; Pseudo-Correspondence of Jesus and Abgar, King of Edessa. *Gnostic Acts of the Apostles:* Acts of Peter; Acts of John; Acts of Andrew; Acts and Martyrdom of Matthew;

Acts of Thomas; Acts of Bartholomew. *Catholic Apocryphal Acts of the Apostles:* Acts of Peter and Paul; Acts of Paul; Acts of Paul and Thecla; Acts of Philip; Acts of Matthew; Acts of Simon and Jude; Acts of Barnabas; Acts of James the Greater. *Apocryphal Doctrinal Works:* Testamentum Domini Nostri Jesu; Preaching of Peter, or Kerygma Petri. *Apocryphal Epistles:* Pseudo-Epistles of Paul; Pseudo-Epistles to the Laodiceans; Pseudo-Correspondence of Paul and Seneca. *Christian Apocryphal Apocalypses:* Apocalypse of Peter; Apocalypse of Paul. (Etym. Latin *apocryphus,* uncanonical, apocryphal; from Greek *apokryphos,* hidden.)

APOCRYPHAL GOSPELS. See GOSPELS, APOCRYPHAL.

APODICTIC. Absolutely certain and conclusive. The term is used in philosophy to describe a method of reasoning from premises that are evident. Opposed to dialectical reasoning, which is argumentation with probability and consistency on open questions. (Etym. Greek *apodeiktikos,* from *apodeiknynai,* to demonstrate.)

APODOSIS. The last day on which the prayers in commemoration of a feast are said in the Greek Church. (Etym. Greek *apo,* back + *didomi,* to give.)

APOKATASTASIS. See UNIVERSALISM, DOCTRINAL.

APOLLINARIANISM. Heretical doctrine of Apollinaris the younger (310–90), Bishop of Laodicea, that Christ had a human body and only a sensitive soul, but had no rational mind or free human will. His rational soul was replaced by the divine logos, or word of God. The theory was condemned by Roman councils in 377 and 381, and also by the Council of Constantinople in 381. Apollinarianism practically disappeared by the early fifth century, with some of its adherents returning to the Church, and others becoming Monophysites believing that Christ had only a divine will but no human will.

APOLLOS. An Alexandrian Jew mentioned in the Acts of the Apostles as an enthusiastic convert whose eloquence in Ephesus and Achaea won a great following. His continued success in preaching Christ in Corinth created a problem for St. Paul on his arrival. He was disturbed to learn that Christian cliques were forming, each responding to the personal appeal of different disciples. Paul's emphasis on the importance of unity is instructive (Acts 18:24–28): "It is clear that there are serious differences among you. What I mean are all those slogans that you have, like: 'I am for Paul,' 'I am for Apollos,' 'I am for Cephas,' 'I am for Christ.' Has Christ been parceled out?" (I Corinthians 1:11–12). And again a short time later: "What could be more unspiritual than your slogans, 'I am for Paul,' 'I am for Apollos?' After all, what is Apollos and what is Paul? They are servants who brought the faith to you" (I Corinthians 3:4–5). (Etym. Greek *apollos,* destroyer.)

APOLOGETICS. The science that aims to explain and justify religious doctrine. It shows the reasonableness of such doctrine in the face of the objections offered by those who refuse to accept any religion, especially Christianity and more particularly Roman Catholicism. Also called fundamental theology as the science that establishes the credibility of Christian revelation on the evidence of miraculous phenomena and the testimony of unbiased history. (Etym. Greek *apologetikos,* a defense.)

APOLOGIA PRO VITA SUA. The autobiography of John Henry Newman, published in 1864. It is a history of his religious opinions down to his entrance into the Roman Catholic Church, October 9, 1845. It is one of the great books on modern religious thought, its purpose being to defend his sincerity in becoming a Catholic.

APOLYSIS. The blessing by the Greek priest at the end of Mass, Matins, or Vespers. Called a Great Apolysis after the liturgy, baptisms, and marriages; a Little Apolysis at other times. (Etym. Greek *apolysis,* dismissal.)

APOST., AP., APP. *Apostolus*—apostle, apostles.

APOSTASY. The total rejection by a baptized person of the Christian faith he once professed. The term is also applied in a technical sense to "apostates from religious life," who without authorization leave a religious institute after perpetual vows with no intention of returning. (Etym. Latin *apostasia,* falling away or separation from God; from Greek *apostasis,* revolt, literally, a standing-off.)

APOSTASY (biblical). In general, a desertion from a solemn commitment. In the Old Testament apostasy meant a rebellion against the Lord (Joshua 22:22) or abandonment of the Jewish religion (I Mac-

cabees 2:15). The two passages in the New Testament where the term occurs refer to giving up the Mosaic law (Acts 21:21) and the mysterious religious revolt that is to precede the second coming of Christ (II Thessalonians 2:3).

APOSTASY (clerical). Desertion by a man in major orders from his clerical state. The earliest discipline of the Church forbade clerics to leave the clerical state even in time of war. The Council of Chalcedon (451) threatened all deserting clerics with excommunication. Innocent III (1160–1216) modified the centuries old custom and gave permission for clerics in minor orders (below the subdiaconate) to leave the clergy of their own will. Before the Second Vatican Council, those in minor orders who, after being admonished by the bishop, failed for a month thereafter to resume the clerical garb were reduced to the lay state. In current practice those in major orders—priests and deacons who apostatize—are subject to supervision and, if they remain contumacious, may be deposed from office.

APOSTASY (ecclesiastical). One of three kinds of desertion recognized by the laws of the Roman Catholic Church; from Christianity, when a baptized person entirely gives up his Christian faith; from orders, when a cleric abandons the ecclesiastical state; and from religion, when a man or woman leaves the religious life without dispensation from public vows.

APOSTASY IN FAITH. The complete abandonment of the Christian religion and not merely a denial of some article of the creed. Since apostolic times, it was classified among the major crimes, along with murder and adultery, whose remission in the sacrament of penance carried severe censures and, among certain rigorists, even remission of the sin was denied. St. Cyprian (d. 258), Bishop of Carthage, defended the Church's right to remit apostasy before the hour of death, and the practice was supported by Pope Cornelius (d. 253). Under the Christian Roman Empire, apostates were punished by deprivation of civil rights, including the power to bequeath or inherit property. During the late Middle Ages, Christians who apostatized were subject to trial and punishment by the Inquisition.

The code of canon law of 1918 declared that apostates from the faith (as also heretics and schismatics) incur *ipso facto* excommunication, are deprived, after warning, of any benefice, dignity, pension, office, or any position they may have in the Church, and are declared under infamy. After a second warning, clerics are to be deposed, and members of a religious community automatically dismissed.

A POSTERIORI. From what is after, that is, from effect back to cause. Reasoning from experience or inductively. Opposite of a priori. This is the only valid proof for the existence of God, from creatures as effects to the Creator as their First Cause.

APOSTLE. A messenger and authorized representative of the sender. Broadly used in Scripture, it refers to many followers of Jesus who spread his message. More precisely, however, it applies to the original twelve men chosen by Jesus to be his immediate aides. They are referred to as disciples during the period in which he was instructing them, but following his ascension they are always called Apostles. After Pentecost they spoke and acted with confidence and assurance in teaching others what he had taught them and in assuming leadership roles in the early church. They were ordained priests by Christ at the Last Supper and were commissioned by him to preach the Gospel to all mankind (Matthew 28:19–20). (Etym. Latin *apostolus,* an apostle; Greek *apostolos,* one who is sent off.)

APOSTLES' CREED. A formula of belief, in twelve articles, containing the fundamental doctrines of Christianity, whose authorship (in substance if not in words) tradition ascribes to the Apostles. Its full text reads: "I believe in God the Father Almighty, Creator of heaven and earth. And in Jesus Christ, His only Son our Lord, who was conceived by the Holy Spirit, born of the Virgin Mary, suffered under Pontius Pilate, was crucified, died, and was buried. He descended into hell. The third day He arose again from the dead. He ascended into heaven, and sits at the right hand of God the Father Almighty. From thence He shall come to judge the living and the dead. I believe in the Holy Spirit, the holy, catholic Church, the communion of saints, the forgiveness of sins, the resurrection of the body, and life everlasting. Amen." Eastern Christians do not use the Apostles' Creed in their liturgy. At a very early date the Western Church required catechumens to learn and recite the Apostles' Creed before admission to baptism.

APOSTLESHIP OF PRAYER. Worldwide organization, founded at Vals, France, in 1844, to promote devotion to the Sacred Heart of Jesus. Basic requirements for membership are the recitation of the Daily Offering and inscription of one's name in the Apostleship. The members are asked to pray for the particular intentions of the Holy Father, which are specified each month in two forms. There is a general and a mission intention, and both are made publicly known a year ahead of time. The Apostleship publishes *The Messenger of the Sacred Heart* in many countries.

APOSTLESHIP OF THE SEA. International Catholic organization, founded in 1920 in Glasgow, Scotland, for the spiritual and social welfare of seafarers and persons involved in serving the maritime industry. Formally approved by the Holy See in 1922, it is under the direction of the Pontifical Commission for Migrants and Tourism.

APOSTOLATE. The work of an apostle, not only of the first followers of Christ but of all the faithful who carry on the original mission entrusted by the Savior to the twelve to "make disciples of all the nations" (Matthew 28:19). The apostolate belongs essentially to the order of grace. Its purpose is not temporal welfare, however noble, but to bring people to the knowledge and love of Christ and, through obedience to his teaching, help them attain life everlasting.

APOSTOLICAE CURAE. Encyclical of Pope Leo XIII, issued on September 13, 1896, in which Anglican orders were declared invalid because of defect in both the form (rite) and intention.

APOSTOLICAM ACTUOSITATEM. Second Vatican Council's Decree on the Apostolate of Lay People (November 18, 1965). The document is a practical expression of the Church's mission, to which the laity are specially called in virtue of their baptism and incorporation into Christ. One of its important provisions is the recognition that, while preserving the necessary link with ecclesiastical authority, the laity have the right to establish and direct associations and to join existing ones. In effect the decree provides for three kinds of corporate lay apostolates: 1. those which "owe their origin to the free choice of the laity and are run at their own discretion," but always having "the approval of legitimate ecclesiastical authority"; 2. those specially chosen by the bishops and "without depriving the laity of their rightful freedom" nevertheless have received a "mandate" from the hierarchy; 3.

those so closely associated with the hierarchy that they are "fully subject to the superior ecclesiastical control in regard to the exercise of these charges."

APOSTOLICA SOLLICITUDO. Apostolic Letter of Pope Paul VI, establishing the synod of bishops for the universal Church, September 15, 1965.

APOSTOLIC CAMERA. The Vatican agency in charge of temporal goods and rights of the Holy See, especially during a vacancy in the papacy. It is under the presidency of the Cardinal Camerlengo of the Holy Roman Church. The office, powers, and privileges of the priest-clerics of the Apostolic Camera were determined by Pope Pius XI in 1934, but the institution itself goes back to the eleventh century.

APOSTOLIC CANONS. A set of eighty-five canons, forming a part of the Apostolic Constitutions and attributed to the Apostles. Dating from the late fourth century, they represent the Church's early tradition on ordination, moral conduct of the clergy, and the duties of Christians. They became part of the Church's early canon law.

APOSTOLIC CHANCERY. Also called the papal chancery. Originating in the eleventh century, it was mainly responsible for issuing papal bulls and briefs. It was abolished in 1973, and its functions have been absorbed in the papal secretariat of state.

APOSTOLIC CHURCHES. A name used from the second to the fourth centuries to designate a diocese originally founded or ruled by an Apostle. Thus Rome was founded by St. Peter, Alexandria by St. Mark, Jerusalem by St. James the Less, and Athens by St. Paul. Later on "Apostolic Church" referred to the whole Catholic Church, whose apostolicity is especially identified with the apostolic see of Rome.

APOSTOLIC CONSTITUTIONS. Collection of ecclesiastical laws from the fourth century. Their most important part is the set of eighty-five canons, attributed to the Apostles, dealing with ordinations, official responsibilities, and the moral behavior of bishops and priests. They eventually became the basis for canon law in the West.

APOSTOLIC DELEGATE. A papal representative who has the right and duty of supervising the status of the Church in the area assigned to him and keeping the Pope informed of the same. He has certain faculties delegated to him by the Holy See. Where established relations exist with a civil government, he is a papal representative with diplomatic status; otherwise his role is purely ecclesiastical. His duties do not interfere with the jurisdiction of local ordinaries but rather strengthen the general condition of the Church throughout the territory by unifying and facilitating the work of the bishops. He does not constitute a tribunal of justice but he may decide certain conflicts according to Church law. The delegate takes precedence in honor over the bishops not cardinals in his territory. He also enjoys other concessions of an honorary nature.

APOSTOLIC FATHERS. Christian writers of the first centuries thought to have had personal relations with the Apostles or been directly influenced by their writings. Sts. Clement of Rome, Ignatius of Antioch, and Polycarp of Smyrna were the most important of these fathers. Their writings covered the last twenty years of the first century to mid second century, and were concerned mostly with the guidance of individuals or local churches in some pressing need.

APOSTOLIC INDULGENCES. Those attached to pious articles, rosaries, crucifixes, or medals when the Pope or his authorized representative blesses them. Fragile material or printed pictures are excluded.

APOSTOLICITY. That quality of the Catholic Church by which she is derived from the Apostles. There is an apostolicity of origin, since the Church was first organized by the apostles chosen by Christ; of teaching because what the Church teaches now is essentially what was taught by the Apostles; and of succession in office, since there has been an unbroken historical transmission of episcopal powers, through ordination, from the Apostles to all the bishops in communion with the Bishop of Rome today.

APOSTOLIC LETTERS. Generally speaking, all documents issued by the Holy See. Formerly papal bulls and briefs were apostolic letters. Since St. Pius X, only documents in brief form used for lesser appointments, erecting or dividing mission territory, designating basilicas, and approving religious congregations are so designated.

APOSTOLIC PENITENTIARY. A papal tribunal, whose origins go back to the twelfth century, delegated by the Pope to grant absolution from censures and certain dispensations reserved to the Holy See. In 1967, Pope Paul VI confirmed the competence of this tribunal over all that embraces the internal forum, even nonsacramental and to the use of indulgences, while reserving the right of the Congregation for the Doctrine of the Faith to examine the doctrinal aspects of indulgences.

APOSTOLIC PREACHER. Originally the office of procurator generals of the four mendicant orders (Dominicans, Franciscans, Augustinians, and Carmelites), it is now reserved to the Friars Minor. Sermons are preached in the throne room on the Fridays of Lent and four times in Advent. The apostolic preacher resides at the generalate of the Capuchins.

APOSTOLIC PROCURATORS. Originally counselors for cases to be tried before the Pope, and for the gratuitous defense of the poor. They are official legal advocates of the Holy See.

APOSTOLIC SCHOOLS. Schools for boys or young men of insufficient means who desire to become missionary priests or brothers or who wish to become secular priests and labor in missionary lands. These schools are supported by the faithful augmented by voluntary contributions of parents and friends. The first such school was opened by the Jesuits in France in 1865. Within ten years more apostolic schools were opened, not only in France but elsewhere.

APOSTOLIC SECULARITY. The erroneous theory that the primary apostolate of the priesthood does not consist in ecclesiastical ministerial functions, i.e., the Mass and administration of the sacraments, but in the social and economic development of the people.

APOSTOLIC SEE. Title given to Rome since the first Christian centuries. It applies to the Pope and the persons and offices directly under his authority. It implies that, as successor of St. Peter, the Prince of the Apostles, he has the primary duty of extending the Christian faith to all the world. See also HOLY SEE.

APOSTOLIC SIGNATURA. See SEG-NATURA APOSTOLICA.

APOSTOLIC SUCCESSION. The method by which the episcopacy has been derived from the Apostles to the present day. Succession means successive consecration by the laying on of hands, performing the functions of the Apostles, receiving their commission in a lineal sequence from the Apostles, suc-

cession in episcopal sees traced back to the Apostles, and successive communion with the Apostolic See, i.e., the Bishop of Rome. The Eastern Orthodox and others share in the apostolic succession in having valid episcopal orders, although they are not in collegial union with the Roman Catholic hierarchy.

APOSTOLIC VICAR. See VICAR APOSTOLIC.

APOTHEOSIS. A human being elevated to the rank of deity, especially among the ancient Greeks and Romans. Also applied to the transition of a person upon death, from this life to one of sainthood in eternal glory. (Etym. Greek *apotheosis*, deification.)

APPARENT GOOD. That which merely seems good; that which satisfies some appetite or desire sufficiently to become an object of choice. But it is not the true good because it is not morally right, since it does not conform to the purpose of man as a whole.

APPARITION. Supernatural vision. It is a psychical experience in which a person or object not accessible to normal human powers is seen and ordinarily also heard. When apparitions are claimed, the Church's policy is to require proof of the fact, since illusions and hallucinations are so common, and the influence of the evil spirit is also to be taken into account. Yet from the Scriptures on there have been numerous, well-attested apparitions that were certainly of divine origin.

APPEAL. Application for judgment from lower to a higher judicial authority in connection with ecclesiastical courts. There is no appeal from a decision by the Pope, but below him every Catholic has the right to appeal if one considers oneself wronged by a judgment in a lower tribunal. The term "appeal" also refers, especially in modern times, to taking an ecclesiastical matter to the civil courts on the ground that the Church had encroached on the rights of the state.

APPELLANTS. Various groups who appealed against certain decisions or doctrines of the Holy See. The best known were the appellants in Elizabethan England who protested the alleged use of political means to bring the country back to the Catholic faith; and the appellants in France, led by the Archbishop of Paris, who opposed Pope Clement XI's condemnation of Jansenism in

1713. (Etym. Latin *appellare,* to address, call upon, appeal to one.)

APPETITE. The spontaneous movement of a faculty to a good, naturally suitable to itself, or away from something evil to it. When the movement is toward an object, the appetite is called concupiscible and corresponds to desire; when movement is away from an object, it is irascible and becomes some form of resistance. (Etym. Latin *appetitus,* a striving, desire.)

APPIAN WAY. Highway constructed in 312 B.C. by Appius Claudius from Rome to Capua, later to Brindisi. Often mentioned in the Roman martyrology as the site of burial of the Christians who died for the faith in persecutions in the Eternal City.

APPLICATION. A term used for the practice of applying the satisfactory (expiatory) and impetratory (intercessory) value of one's prayers and good works for others, including the souls in purgatory.

APPRECIATION. The moral judgment that recognizes the value of someone or something. It differs from an ordinary judgment that merely defines or describes what is known. Appreciation adds the notion of purpose or why.

APPROBATION. The act by which a legitimate ecclesiastical superior authorizes a cleric actually to exercise his ministry.

APPROPRIATION. A manner of speaking in which the properties and activities of God, though common to the three divine persons, are attributed to an individual person. The purpose of appropriation is to manifest the differences in the divine properties and persons. Four kinds of appropriations are known from Scripture and sacred tradition: 1. substantive names of God (*Theos*), applied to the Father, and of Lord (*Kurios*), applied to the Son; 2. absolute attributes of God, namely power, unity, and eternity applied to the Father; wisdom, equality, and beauty applied to the Son; goodness, harmony, and happiness applied to the Holy Spirit; 3. works of God, namely efficient cause (Father), exemplary cause (Son), and final cause (Holy Spirit); 4. worship of God, with the Father as recipient of adoration and sacrifice, and the Son and Holy Spirit as mediators between God and man. (Etym. Latin *appropriatio,* ascribing, the attributing of a special characteristic.)

APRIL. Month of the Holy Eucharist. The reason for this association is that the Eucharist is the risen Christ, and at least part of the Easter season regularly comes during April.

A PRIORI. From what is before, that is, from cause to effect. Reasoning from principles to conclusions, or from prior knowledge to consequences; therefore deduction. A basic premise of Catholic morality in reducing general norms to specific practice.

A.P.S.A. *Administratio Patrimonii Sedis Apostolicae*—Administration of the Patrimony of the Apostolic See.

APSE. Semicircular polygonal termination to the choir or nave of a church, in which the altar is placed. The term was applied variously to the arched roof of a room; canopy over an altar; or any semicircular recess with a roof. The apse is solid below, generally with windows above; the roof is vaulted. The term was first used in the Roman basilicas where the apse was an important feature, later retained when the basilica was transformed into a Christian church. The chevet is an apse enclosed by an open screen of columns leading into an aisle, then into several apsidal chapels. The apse as described was retained in Byzantine churches, also in Germany and Italy. In France they are polygonal in shape with chevets; in England the square apse is preferred. (Etym. Latin *apsis,* a bow, turn; Greek *apsis,* curve, bow, arch.)

AP. SED. *Apostolica Sedes*—Apostolic See.

AP. SED. LEG. *Apostolicae Sedis Legatus*—Legate of the Apostolic See.

AQUILA. A Jewish tentmaker married to Priscilla. They evidently traveled considerably, for they are mentioned as having been in Asia Minor, Rome, Corinth, and Ephesus. Paul made their acquaintance in Corinth, working with them in their common trade, and lodged with them (Acts 18:1–2). When Paul's preaching took him to Syria, Aquila and Priscilla accompanied him. Evidently they aided his work with their hospitality (Acts 18:18); in the final greetings that Paul wrote in his Epistle to the Corinthians, he included "Aquila and Priscilla, with the church that meets at their house" (I Corinthians 16:19). And in his Epistle to the Romans, he spoke warmly of these two devoted followers "who risked death to save my life" (Romans 16:3). (Etym. Latin *aquila,* eagle.)

ARA COELI. A church and shrine of the Blessed Virgin on the Capitoline Hill in Rome, one of the most ancient sites in the city's three thousand years of history. Atop one of the Capitoline stairways of one hundred twenty-four marble steps, a votive offering for Rome's deliverance from the black plague, is the church of Ara Coeli. It was built in the seventh century. One of its side chapels, dedicated to St. Helena (255–330), is where Emperor Augustus is said to have had a vision of a beautiful lady standing on the altar of heaven, hence the church's name. The church's most cherished possession is an olive wood statue of the Christ Child brought from the Holy Land during the sixteenth century. The base of the ornately decorated statue is covered with votive offerings of gratitude from all parts of the world, thanking the Bambino for his favors. In extreme cases of illness the cherished image is taken by private car, attended by two Franciscans, to the sick patient hoping for a miraculous recovery.

ARAMAIC. Named from Aram, a country in Southwestern Asia. A Semitic language spoken by the Jews during and after the Babylonian exile (606–536 B.C.). It was spoken by Christ and the Apostles, since in New Testament times Hebrew was cultivated only by the learned. To meet the needs of the Jewish faithful, the Hebrew Bible was made available in Aramaic paraphrases called Targums.

ARCA. A box in which the Eucharist was kept by the early Christians in their homes. It was also a chest for the safekeeping of church moneys, endowment funds for churches, schools, or other pious uses. The term is now used to describe the investments for some ecclesiastical purpose, e.g., *arca seminarii*, seminary fund. (Etym. Latin *arca*, chest, coffer.)

ARCANA. Secrets or mysteries. Hence an "ark" that holds secret objects, said of a secluded area used for occult practices.

ARCANUM DIVINAE SAPIENTIAE. Encyclical of Pope Leo XIII, published in 1880, on the sacrament of matrimony. Its main thesis is that the marriage contract and the sacrament cannot be separated.

ARCH. A prefix forming compounds signifying a unit, an institution or a person that has pre-eminence over other institutions or persons, e.g., archbishop, archchaplain, archdiocese. Arch (in architecture), a structure built of rigid blocks, shaped like wedges and put together in variously modified curved lines so that, when supported at its ends, it keeps its position by mutual pressure. The separate blocks are called arch stones; the lowest members of the arch are termed springers; the uppermost, when a single stone is used, is called the keystone. The supports of the arch are called piers and pillars, which receive vertical pressure, and abutments or buttresses, which resist lateral thrust or outward pressure. Of all types of arches the pointed arch is the strongest. (Etym. Latin *arcus*, bow, arch, vault, arc.)

ARCHABBOT. An honorary title bestowed on the head of a monastery noted for its pre-eminence and antiquity.

ARCHANGEL. A chief or ruling angel. The term occurs twice in the New Testament (Jude 5:9; I Thessalonians 4:16) and has two meanings in the Catholic vocabulary. In its wider sense, an archangel is any angel of higher rank, so that St. Michael is an archangel although he is the prince of the Seraphim. But more strictly, archangels are those angelic spirits who belong to the eighth or second last of nine choirs of angels. As distinct from guardian angels, archangels are messengers of God to men in matters of greater significance. Thus Raphael delivered Tobias' wife from demonic obsession (Tobit 12:6, 15) and traditionally is identified with the angel who moved the waters of the pool, where Christ worked his miracle (John 5:1–4). Gabriel was the angel of the Annunciation. St. Michael is the leader of the heavenly host, who fought and won against the rebellious spirits (Revelation 12:7–9).

ARCHBISHOP. A bishop who presides over one or more dioceses. He may call the bishops to a provincial council, having the right and duty to do so, and he may act as first judge of appeal over a decision of one of his bishops. His immediate jurisdiction, however, pertains solely to his own diocese. He is often styled "metropolitan" because of the importance of his see city or ecclesiastical province.

ARCHCONFRATERNITY. A confraternity that has developed to the point where similar associations are affiliated with it and adopt its structure and rules.

ARCHDEACON. An official who formerly administered part of a diocese, in virtue of jurisdiction delegated to him by his bishop. Today similar duties are performed by auxiliary bishops, vicar-generals and others. In the Anglican Church the assistants to the bishops are still called archdeacons.

ARCHETYPE. The original form or pattern according to which existing things are made. Commonly applied to the divine ideas of the Creator by which he made the universe and guides the world by his providence. (Etym. Latin *archetypus,* the original pattern, original, typical; Greek *archetypon,* a model.)

ARCHID. *Archidiaconus*—archdeacon.

ARCHIEP. *Archiepiscopus*—archbishop.

ARCHIEPISCOPAL CROSS. A cross with two horizontal crossbars; it forms a part of the heraldic arms of an archbishop. It is carried before him in processions and solemn liturgical functions within his own ecclesiastical province.

ARCHIMANDRITE. Superior of a monastery in one of the Eastern Churches, notably the Melchites and Catholic Greeks. It is also a title of honor attached to the chancery of the leading Oriental patriarchates. (Etym. Greek *arkhos,* chief, ruler + *mandra,* monastery.)

ARCHIPRB. An archipresbyter—archpriest.

ARCHITRAVE. In classic church architecture the lowermost part of an entablature or superstructure on top of a column. In the case of a square opening, it may be any molded or similarly ornamented band framing a square window or door, or projecting from it.

ARCHIVES. A repository of public records and historical documents. Diocesan archives are a compartment in a safe place containing all the pertinent written material regarding the material and spiritual affairs of a diocese. Within these archives are certain confidential documents. Keeping the archives up to date and catalogued is required by Church law. The provincial and generalate houses of religious institutes also have archives, some of them going back many centuries. (Etym. Latin *archivum;* Greek *archeion,* a public building, residence of magistrates.)

ARCHIVES, VATICAN. Collections of documents pertaining to the affairs of the Holy See. Since apostolic times, the popes preserved writings of importance, but most of the material before Pope Innocent III (1161–1216) has been destroyed or has disappeared. Pope Paul V (1552–1621) established a central repository of documents of the Holy See. In 1881, Pope Leo XIII opened these archives to scholars for consultation. The Vatican Archives are connected with the Archivist School, which before 1968 was the annual Archivist Institute, first established by Pope Pius XI in 1923. The archives of the Holy See contain tens of thousands of documents and are the most important center of historical research in the world.

ARCHPRIEST. The head of a college of presbyters as special representatives of a bishop. The union of several archpriests constituted an archdiaconate whose individual archpriests were subject to the archdeacon. Since the Council of Trent the duties of archpriests have been assumed by deans and other diocesan officials.

ARCOSOLIUM. An arched recess used as a burial place in the catacombs. Sometimes the marble slab placed horizontally over the opening was decorated with symbolic frescoes and used as an altar for the celebration of the Mass. (Etym. Latin *arcus,* bow, arch + *solium,* a throne, royal seat; a seat.)

ARCULAE. Small boxes made of gold or other precious metal used by the faithful to carry the Blessed Sacrament. They were usually worn suspended from the neck.

AREA. An open-air cemetery of the early Christians, especially in Africa, as distinct from the catacombs for burial.

AREOPAGUS. A public court at Athens in ancient Greece that had jurisdiction to hear charges brought against lecturers and teachers. Paul was summoned before this august group on the allegation that his teaching was "startling" (Acts 17:19–34). He preached with customary eloquence; one of the court members, Dionysius, became a Christian. (Etym. Greek *areios pagos,* hill of Ares; English Mars Hill.)

ARGUMENT AD IGNORANTIAM. An argument directed at a person's factual ignorance or his inability either to prove the facts he presents or disprove those presented against him.

ARGUMENT AD POPULUM. An appeal to the people; hence an argument directed at the emotions of the masses.

ARGUMENT EX SILENTIO. An argument from the absence of information or data, concluding to a person's death from the fact that nothing has been heard from or concerning the person, by anyone, for many years.

ARIAN CHURCHES. Religious bodies, forming Arianism, that trace their origin to bishops who did not accept the First Council of Nicaea (325). After Nicaea, Arianism entered on its ecclesiastical phase. Different formulas of doctrine became current, generally ambiguous and susceptible of an orthodox interpretation, which the civil authorities frequently sanctioned and even imposed under heavy penalties of law.

The Arians themselves broke into several factions. Strict Arians (Anomoeans) claimed that the Son is unlike (*anomoios*) the Father. Semi-Arians said that the Son is only similar (*homoios*) but not identical in essence with the Father. Both forms persisted longer among the Goths than elsewhere. Ulfilas (311–83), an Arian Goth educated in Constantinople and consecrated bishop by Arius' friend, Eusebius (d. 371), organized missionary work among the Visigoths and made most of them Arians after the middle of the fourth century. After the Battle of Adrianople (378), the great body of Visigoths settled within the Roman Empire, where Arianism became the national religion of Visigoths, Ostrogoths, Burgundians, Suevi, Vandals, and Lombards. For almost two centuries they kept it alive in the West.

ARIANISM. A fourth-century heresy that denied the divinity of Jesus Christ. Its author was Arius (256–336), a priest of Alexandria, who in 318 began to teach the doctrine that now bears his name. According to Arius there are not three distinct persons in God, co-eternal and equal in all things, but only one person, the Father. The Son is only a creature, made out of nothing, like all other created beings. He may be called God but only by an extension of language, as the first and greatest person chosen to be divine intermediary in the creation and redemption of the world.

In the Arian system, the logos or word of God is not eternal. There was a time when he did not exist. He is not a son by nature, but merely by grace and adoption. God adopted him in prevision of his merits, since he might have sinned but did not. In a word, instead of being God he is a kind of demiurge who advanced in virtue and merit and thus came to be closely associated with the Father. But his nature is not of the same substance as the Father's.

Boldly anti-Trinitarian, Arianism struck at the foundations of Christianity by reducing the Incarnation to a figure of speech. If the logos was created and not divine, God did not become man or redeem the world, and all the consequent mysteries of the faith are dissolved.

The First Council of Nicaea was convoked in 325 to meet the Arian crisis. Since the signature lists are defective, the exact number of prelates who attended the council is not known. However, at least two hundred twenty bishops, mostly from the East but also from Africa, Spain, Gaul, and Italy, signed the creed that affirmed the divinity of Christ and condemned Arius as a heretic. "We believe," the formula read, "in one God, the Father Almighty, Creator of all things visible and invisible. And in one Lord Jesus Christ, the Son of God, the only-begotten of the Father, that is, of the *substance of the Father;* God from God, light from light, true God from true God; begotten, not created, consubstantial [Greek *Homo ousion*] with the Father." The soul of the council was St. Athanasius (296–373), Bishop of Alexandria, whose resolute character and theological insight were the main obstacle to the triumph of Arianism in the East.

Since the fifth century, Arian churches have remained in existence in many countries, although some of them were absorbed by Islam. A principal tenet of these churches is the recognition of Christ as Messiah but denial that he is the natural Son of God.

ARIDITY. In ascetical theology, the state of a soul devoid of sensible consolation, which makes it very difficult to pray. It may be caused by something physical, such as illness, or voluntary self-indulgence, or an act of God, who is leading a person through trial to contemplation. (Etym. Latin *ariditas,* dryness, drought, meagerness, aridity; dullness, flatness.)

ARISTOTELIANISM. The system of thought of the Greek philosopher Aristotle (384–322 B.C.) and his followers. Aristotle divided human knowledge into three categories: the theoretical, conceived with the truth for its own sake; the practical, directed to the guidance of conduct; and the productive, to be used in the cultivation of the arts. This division has ever since affected what may be called Christian Aristotelianism, through Thomas Aquinas (1225–74), who built on Aristotle an impressive philosophy of the Christian faith. On this level, Aristotle's main contributions include: 1. a clear analysis of the foundations of human reasoning, through induction and deduction; 2. the theory of the four causes, material, formal, efficient, and final; 3. hylomorphism, or the theory of matter and form; 4. the principle of teleology that every being has a purpose; 5. the postulate that every living being has a principle of life, which in man is the rational soul; 6. the proof of an eternal unmoved Mover, to explain the existence of a world that is changeable, and the identification of this eternal unmoved First Mover with the god or gods of popular religion; 7. the conclusion that this First Cause is pure thought, who is pure actuality, the only being with no extension, who is the supreme object of all knowledge and the ultimate object of all desire; 8. the definition of the ethical good as that which corresponds to man as rational being and consists in the subordination of the senses to reason and in the exercise of reason to search for and contemplate the truth.

ARK. The chest containing the tables of the law. God ordered Moses to construct it of acacia wood, telling him the exact dimensions. "Inside the ark you must place the Testimony I shall give you" (Exodus 25:10–22). This Ark of the Covenant became a dramatic symbol in Israelite history, accompanying the people on their wilderness journeys and throughout Joshua's rule. Later it was seized by the Philistines but surrendered in fear to Israel. David brought the ark to Jerusalem, where it remained until the first temple was destroyed. At that point it disappeared from history. See also SANCTUM SANCTORUM.

ARMAGH, BOOK OF. Famous eighth- to ninth-century manuscript containing two lives of St. Patrick (389–461), a life of St. Martin of Tours (315–97), and a non-Vulgate text of the New Testament. Used for centuries in giving testimony and administering oaths of office. Now in Trinity College, Dublin. (*Ard-Macha*, Hill of Macha, a legendary queen.)

ARMENIAN RITE. Used by the Armenian Church, it is substantially the Greek Liturgy of St. Basil (329–79). It includes some elements of the Antiochene Rite, and originally used the Syriac language, but now the Armenian. Both Catholic and dissident Oriental Christians follow this rite.

ARMINIANISM. Doctrine held by certain Calvinists in the Netherlands in the seventeenth century. Originally taught by the Dutch Reformed theologian Jacobus Ar-

minius (1560–1609). His followers were called Remonstrants. They opposed Calvin's teaching that grace benefits only the elect, that Christ died for the elect only, and, in general, his doctrine of selective salvation and absolute predestination, independent of human merit. Condemned by the Reformed Synod of Dort (1618–19), it paved the way for permanently dividing the followers of Calvin (1509–64) and the churches derived from the theory of predestination.

ARROWS. Single symbols, with the heart, to emphasize the wounding for love, of the Sacred Heart of Jesus and the suffering heart of Mary. St. Augustine (354–430) holds his heart pierced by a single arrow to indicate his great love for Christ. St. Edmund the Martyr (841–70) also has an arrow as emblem. Arranged in a bundle, grasped in the hand, arrows identify St. Sebastian (d. 288), whose attempted martyrdom is represented by the many darts shot at him by the hired archers.

A.R.S. *Anno Reparatae Salutis*—in the year of our redemption.

ARS ANTIQUA. Music of the twelfth and thirteenth centuries.

ARS ARTIUM. Logic, since every other exercise of the human mind depends on logical reasoning.

ARS MORIENDI. The art of dying, said to be acquired only by the practice of right living.

ARS NOVA. Treatises by Philippe de Vitry (1291–1361); music of the first half of the fourteenth century.

ARS (shrine). A basilica on the site of the parish of St. John Vianney (1786–1859), who labored as pastor of the village church of Ars in central France. The Byzantine structure is next to the original church, where the Curé of Ars was pastor and confessor to thousands for forty years, and in 1929 was declared by Pope Pius XI the heavenly patron of parochial clergy. At the shrine are kept the saint's modest possessions, including the half-burned bed, said to have been set afire by the devil in one of the obsessions to which the Curé was often subjected.

ARTICLE OF FAITH. A term used by the catechism of the Council of Trent, speaking of the Apostles' Creed: "The chief truths which Christians must hold are those which the holy Apostles, the leaders and teachers of the faith, inspired by the Holy Spirit have divided into the twelve Articles of the Creed." But the term "article" has a long history and designates whatever a Catholic must believe, whether defined by the Church as revealed or commonly held by the Church's ordinary and universal magisterium as revealed in Scripture or sacred tradition. (Etym. Latin *articulus,* a joint, member, part; literally, a small joint.)

ARTIFICIAL INSEMINATION. Any process by which the male spermatozoa and the female ovum are brought together apart from and wholly distinct from an act of natural intercourse. Long used in animal husbandry, the practice presents no moral problem in the lower forms of life. The Catholic Church teaches that among humans artificial insemination constitutes such a violation of the dignity of the person and the sanctity of marriage as to be contrary to the natural and divine law. Catholic teaching on artificial insemination (among humans) was summed up by Pope Pius XII in an address to Catholic physicians (September 29, 1949). The various dimensions of the immorality involved include: in donor insemination (insemination with the active element of a donor); the third-party invasion of the exclusive marriage covenant in a kind of mechanical adultery; the irresponsibility of the donor fathering a child for which he can fulfill no paternal responsibility; and the deordination of his masturbation in order to thus donate his paternal seed. Even if insemination could be artificially achieved with the husband's semen properly collected (without masturbation) the papal teaching still points out that any process that isolates the sacred act of human generation from the beautiful and intimate conjugal union of the marriage act itself is inconsistent with the holiness and intimate personalism of that two-in-one-flesh union which alone is appropriate for the generation of a child. As long, however, as the integrity of the marriage act is preserved, various clinical techniques designed to facilitate the process are not to be condemned.

ARTOPHORION. A receptacle for the reserved Blessed Sacrament in the Byzantine Rite. Among the dissident Oriental Christians no special reverence is given to the reserved Eucharist, except when Holy Communion is being brought to the sick.

ASCENSION. Christ's going up to heaven forty days after his resurrection from the dead. All the creeds affirm the fact, and the Church teaches that he ascended into heaven in body and soul (Denzinger 801). He ascended into heaven by his own power, as God in divine power and as man in the power of his transfigured soul, which moves his transfigured body, as it will. In regard to the human nature of Christ, one can also say, with the Scriptures, that it was taken up or elevated into heaven by God (Mark 16:19; Luke 24:51; Acts 1:9, 11).

Rationalism has denied the doctrine since the earliest times, e.g., Celsus in the second century. It tries to explain the Ascension as a borrowing from the Old Testament or from pagan mythology, but in doing so omits the basic differences.

Doctrinally the Ascension means the final elevation of Christ's human nature into the condition of divine glory. It is the concluding work of redemption. According to the Church's common teaching, the souls of the just from the pre-Christian era went with the Savior into the glory of heaven. Christ's Ascension is the archetype and pledge of our own ascension into heaven. (Etym. Latin *ascensio,* an ascending, ascent.)

ASCENT OF MOUNT CARMEL. The earliest work of St. John of the Cross (1542–91) on the spiritual life, written between 1578 and 1580. Its intended readers are persons interested in the direction of souls. Its theme is the necessary purification of will, mind, and senses for union with God.

ASCETERION or ASCETERY. A monastery for monks; also a house of retreat or a place of retirement for spiritual exercises, especially those of St. Ignatius (1491–1556). This name was given to the first of such houses erected by St. Charles Borromeo (1538–84) at Milan. (Etym. Latin *asceteria,* hermitage; from Greek *askētēs,* one that exercises, hermit.)

ASCETICAL THEOLOGY. The science of the saints based on a study of their lives. It is aimed to make people holy by explaining what sanctity is and how to attain it. It is the science of leading souls in the ways of Christian perfection through growth in charity and the practice of prayer leading to contemplation. It is that part of spiritual theology which concentrates on man's cooperation with grace and the need for human effort to grow in sanctity.

ASCETICISM. Spiritual effort or exercise in the pursuit of virtue. The purpose is to grow in Christian perfection. Its principles and norms are expanded in ascetical theology. (Etym. Greek *askētikos*, literally, given to exercise; industrious; applied to hermits who strictly exercised themselves in religious devotion.)

ASEITY. The divine attribute of uncaused existence. Creatures exist as effects of other beings and ultimately of God; they are therefore "from another" (*ab alio*). But God exists of himself (*a se*); he is wholly self-actualized. (Etym. Latin *a*, from + *se*, self.)

ASHES, BLESSED. A sacramental of the Church used mainly on Ash Wednesday to remind the faithful of death and the necessity of penance and contrition especially during the Lenten season. The use of ashes, expressing humiliation and sorrow, was common in ancient religions and is frequently mentioned in the Old Testament. Introduced into the early Church by converts from Judaism, for many centuries ashes were imposed only on public penitents, those who had given public scandal. The ashes were used to sprinkle the penitential garb, which they wore on Ash Wednesday as they stood at the church door. Catholics, including priests, now receive ashes that are placed on the head of the penitent accompanied by the words "Turn away from sin and be faithful to the Gospel," or "Remember, man, you are dust and to dust you will return." Unused palms from the previous Palm Sunday, burned, furnish the ashes for use on Ash Wednesday.

ASH WEDNESDAY. The first day of Lent. Named from the custom of signing the foreheads of the faithful with blessed ashes. Its date depends on the date of Easter. In the early Church, public penitents were liturgically admitted to begin their penance on this day. And when this fell into disuse, from the eighth to the tenth centuries, the general penance of the whole community took place. This was symbolized by the imposition of ashes on the heads of the clergy and laity alike.

ASKESIS. A term in Eastern monastic tradition for all the forms of discipline, community prescription, sacramental practice, and participation in the divine liturgy whereby a religious grows in the spiritual life.

ASPERGES. The first word in the Latin of the Psalm "Thou shall sprinkle me with hyssop" gave its name to the ceremony of sprinkling the people with holy water before the principal Mass on Sunday. During the

paschal season the "Asperges" is replaced by the hymn *"Vidi Aquam."* (Etym. Latin *asperges*, thou wilt sprinkle; from *aspergere*, to sprinkle.)

ASPERGILL. A small brush or instrument used for sprinkling holy water during the liturgical services.

ASPERSION. Administration of baptism, in exceptional circumstances, by merely sprinkling the head of the person being baptized. The expression is also used to describe any sprinkling with holy water.

ASPIRATION. Short formalized prayer of about a dozen words. It is expressed in choice language, sometimes poetic, its purpose being to help one maintain a spirit of recollection in God's presence during the day. Such prayers are generally indulgenced by the Church. (Etym. Latin *aspirare*, literally, to breathe upon.)

ASSENT. The mental acceptance of a particular judgment as true. Assent is essentially internal, but it may also be manifested externally by some verbal expression or sign. Since the Church is a visible institution, her members must give not only internal but also external assent to her teachings. And in the reception of some of the sacraments, external assent must be given, for example, some sensibly perceptible sign of accepting one's partner in matrimony. (Etym. Latin *assensus*, agreement, assent, especially on the part of the mind, approval.)

ASSISI. The city of St. Francis in central Italy. One of Christianity's most fervent centers of spirituality. A shrine within a shrine, the Porziuncula was the ancient chapel given to the Franciscans by the Benedictines and restored by St. Francis (1181–1226) himself, where he received the call from Christ and founded the Order of Friars Minor. Here St. Clare (1194–1253) received her habit and began the Order of the Poor Clares, and here in 1216 St. Francis in a vision received from Christ the "Pardon of Assisi," which any pilgrim may gain on the conditions decreed for all plenary indulgences. In 1569 Pope St. Pius X ordered the large church to be built, of which the Porziuncula is but a shrine. It is named St. Mary of the Angels and was elevated in 1909 by St. Pius X to the rank of basilica with a papal chapel. An earthquake in 1832 destroyed the major part of the interior; only the original dome and the Porziuncula were saved. It was rebuilt in 1840. The venerable church of St. Damian, where the first

Poor Clares dwelled until 1260, dates in part from the eighth century. Here are the small choir and the dormitory where the Pope visited St. Clare before her death. Above the altar in the rough stone long chapel is a copy of the crucifix from which Our Lord spoke to St. Francis, telling him to "go repair my House." The original was brought to the more recent basilica of St. Clare when the former was abandoned. Numerous Franciscan relics are in St. Clare's basilica, including her tomb in the crypt. The basilica dedicated to St. Francis towers the hill—a monumental church where in the crypt is entombed the body of "Il Poverello." The upper part of the cathedral is enhanced by the frescoes of Cimabue. The lower basilica has numerous chapels honoring various saints, with paintings by Giotto (1266–1337), Cimabue (1240–1302), and Lorenzetti (fourteenth century). In the transept is the famous painting with its gold background of Our Lady and the Divine Infant with St. Francis and St. John, the Virgin indicating by her finger that she is telling her son about the saintly friar. The habit, the hood, and the worn sandals of the saint are preserved here, his first rule, and his own handwritten script of the blessing he gave to Brother Leo.

ASSISTANTS AT THE THRONE. Originally patriarchs, archbishops, and bishops who, since the eleventh century, were thus specially honored by the Pope. During liturgical ceremonies they were seated near the Pope. Assistants at the throne are now also domestic prelates (*antistites urbani*). They do not lose their rank with the death of the Sovereign Pontiff.

ASSUMPTION. The doctrine of Mary's entrance into heaven, body and soul. As defined by Pope Pius XII in 1950, the dogma declares that "Mary, the immaculate perpetually Virgin Mother of God, after the completion of her earthly life, was assumed body and soul into the glory of heaven."

While there is no direct evidence of the Assumption in the Bible, implicitly the Church argues from Mary's fullness of grace (Luke 1:28). Since she was full of grace, she remained preserved from the consequence of sin, namely corruption of the body after death and postponement of bodily happiness in heaven until the last day.

The Church does not rely on the Scriptures for belief in Mary's Assumption. The doctrine is rather part of the oral tradition, handed down over the centuries. It was therefore certainly revealed because, in reply

to the questions, the Catholic bishops of the world all but unanimously expressed the belief that this was part of the divine revelations. In explaining the grounds for the Church's belief, Pius XII singled out the fact that Mary was the Mother of God; as the body of Christ originated from the body of Mary (*caro Jesu est caro Mariae*); that her body was preserved unimpaired in virginal integrity, and therefore it was fitting that it should not be subject to destruction after death; and that since Mary so closely shared in Christ's redemptive mission on earth, she deserved to join him also in bodily glorification.

ASSUMPTION CHAPEL. A shrine dedicated to Our Lady of the Assumption, constructed in gratitude for Mary's help in ridding the area of locusts during the summer of 1877. It is located in Cold Spring, Minnesota, northwest of Minneapolis.

ASSUMPTIONISTS. The Augustinians of the Assumption, founded at Nîmes in 1845 by Emmanuel Daudé d'Alzon. Encouraged by a brief of Pope Pius IX in 1864, and formally approved in 1923. Dispersed by state decree in France in 1909, the congregation has done extensive work in teaching, writing, and the pastoral ministry. Its publication *Echos d'Orient* was begun in 1897, and among its writers were the patrologist F. Cayre and the specialist in Eastern Christianity M. Jugie. Six congregations of Assumptionist Sisters have pontifical status.

ASTERISK. A liturgical utensil in the Greek Rite. It is made of two curved bands of silver or gold, crossing each other to form a double arch; and placed over the blessed bread in the early part of the Mass to prevent contact with the veil.

ASTROLOGY. A form of divination based on the theory that the planets and stars influence human affairs. Until Copernicus (1473–1543), much of the lore of astrology was a partial basis for astronomy. Since Copernicus, astrology and astronomy separated. In astrology a horoscope is a map of the heavens at the time of birth, using the chart of the zodiac. The "house," or sign in the ascendancy at the time of one's birth, is said to determine one's temperament, tendencies to disease, and liability to certain fortunes or calamities.

It is normally wrong to believe in astrology or to direct one's life and conduct according to its supposed predictions. The reasons are that astrology involves contradictions, since it claims uniform influence on persons born on the same day and in the same place, and who later on prove to be unmistakably different; it claims to predict accurately the free future, i.e., happenings that depend on the exercise of man's free will, whereas such knowledge is unknown to anyone except God; it is against the doctrine of free will, for it leads to fatalistic views of man's destiny; and it is against belief in divine providence, which includes the influence of divine grace and the value of intercessory prayer.

Astrology has been more than once formally condemned by the Church, as at the Council of Trent, which expressly forbade the faithful to read books on astrology dealing with "future contingent achievements, with fortuitous events and such actions as depend on human freedom, but daring to claim certitude about their occurrence" (*Regulae Tridentinae*, 9). Those who believe in astrology expose themselves to a weakening of their Christian faith. (Etym. Greek *astron*, star + *logia*, science, knowledge.)

ATHANASIAN CREED. Profession of faith dating from the late fourth century and attributed to St. Athanasius (296–373). It differs from the other standard creeds in its extraordinary length and in embodying anathemas against those who would deny the doctrines it professes. Its opening word *Quicumque* is also the Latin title of the creed, whose first sentence declares, "If anyone wishes to be saved, before everything else he must hold the Catholic faith."

ATHEISM. Denial of a personal God who is totally distinct from the world he created. Modern atheism has become so varied and widespread that the Second Vatican Council identified no less than eight forms of disbelief under the single term *atheismus:* "Some people expressly deny the existence of God. Others maintain that man cannot make any assertion whatsoever about Him. Still others admit only such methods of investigation as would make it seem quite meaningless to ask questions about God. Many, trespassing beyond the boundaries of the positive sciences, either contend that everything can be explained by the reasoning process used in such sciences, or, on the contrary, hold that there is no such thing as absolute truth. With others it is their exaggerated idea of man that causes their faith to languish; they are more prone, it would seem, to affirm man than to deny God. Yet others have such a faulty notion of God that when they disown this product of the imagination their denial has no reference to the God of the Gospels. There are also those who never enquire about God; religion never seems to trouble or interest them at all, nor do they try to see why they should bother about it" (*Church in the Modern World*, I, 19). In the light of this array of infidelity, it was only logical for the Council to declare that atheism is one of the greatest problems facing mankind in the world today. (Etym. Greek *atheos*, denying the gods, without a god.)

ATHOS. The famous "Holy Mountain" or peninsula that projects into the Aegean Sea from the coast of Macedonia and terminates in Mount Athos. Some twenty Orthodox monasteries have been situated on the peninsula, containing valuable manuscripts and works of art.

ATONEMENT. The satisfaction of a legitimate demand. In a more restricted sense it is the reparation of an offense. This occurs through a voluntary performance that outweighs the injustice done. If the performance fully counterbalances the gravity of the guilt, the atonement is adequate. And if the atonement is done by someone other than the actual offender, but in his stead, it is vicarious.

Applied to Christ the Redeemer, through his suffering and death he rendered vicarious atonement to God for the sins of the whole human race. His atonement is fully adequate because it was performed by a divine person. In fact, it is superabundant because the positive value of Christ's expiation is actually greater than the negative value of human sin. (Etym. Middle English *at one*, to set at one, to reconcile; of one mind, in accord.)

ATONEMENT, CHAPEL OF. See POINTE AUX TREMBLES.

ATTACHMENT. An emotional dependence, either of one person on another, or of a person on some real or illusory object. Attachments play an important role in spiritual development, since the first condition for progress in sanctity is some mastery over one's inordinate attachments.

ATTENTION. Deliberate concentration on some act or occupation, such as prayer or the administration of the sacraments. Regarding attention in prayer, although it is a quality of the mind, it is mainly an attitude of the affections and will. The mental attention is necessary only insofar as the will requires some intellectual awareness of whom we are praying to or in whose presence we are. What is more important is the disposition of heart.

ATTITUDE. Habitual predisposition to think or act in a certain way. It is the sum total of a person's moral character responding to a given person, idea, or situation. (Etym. Latin *aptitudo,* suitability, fitness, inclination.)

ATTRIBUTION. See ANALOGY.

ATTRITION. Imperfect contrition, which is sorrow for sin, based on faith, from motives that are self-interested and not the perfect love of God. (Etym. Latin *ad,* to + *terere,* to rub: *attritio,* rubbing, imperfect grinding; incomplete compunction of heart.) See also IMPERFECT CONTRITION.

ATTRITIONISM. The doctrine that imperfect contrition, i.e., sorrow for sin not from perfect love, is sufficient for valid absolution in the sacrament of penance. Luther (1483–1546) attacked it as "repentance of the gallows" out of fear of God. But the Council of Trent declared that attrition is a morally good preparation for the sacrament of penance.

A.U. Alma Urbs—Beloved City (Rome).

AUCTION. A public sale in which commodities are offered and sold to the highest bidder. Catholic morality teaches that any price arrived at by auction will be a just price provided that no unfair means are used either to run up the bid or to keep it down.

AUCTOREM FIDEI. The bull of Pope Pius VI, in 1794, that condemned eighty-five propositions of the Italian Jansenist Synod of Pistoia, led by the Bishop Scipione de' Ricci (1741–1810). Among other views condemned was the theory that national councils of bishops have binding power independent of the Holy See.

AUDIENCES, PAPAL. Receptions given to interested persons, clerical or lay, who have business with the Holy See. Audience requests are presented to the Maestro di Camera, even for bishops, ambassadors, or heads of religious institutions. Religious orders are received on stated days. Cardinal prefects of the sacred congregations are received regularly by the Pope, at which time counsel is given and decrees are signed. Rulers of nations are received in formal audience. Special or private audiences for groups of individuals follow a definite order. Generally a letter of recommendation from the bishop of a home diocese is received by some responsible personage in Rome, who transmits the request to the Master of the Chamber. If the audience is granted, the required ticket for admission, with specified date and time, is communicated to the one(s) working on the request. Public and general audiences are a recent development. They are held in the Audience Hall, built in 1971, in the Basilica or Piazza of St. Peter's, or at the papal summer residence, Castel Gondolfo.

AUDITOR. One who prepares the acts of a trial in ecclesiastical procedure. He summons and presents witnesses, prepares judicial documents, and summarizes acts. He never pronounces final judgment unless specifically authorized to do so. He is appointed by a bishop, either permanently or for a specific case or cases. The auditor of His Holiness is in charge of the department that deals with the appointment of bishops.

AUGUSTINE, RULE OF ST. Name popularly applied to the *Regula Sancti Augustini,* drawn up by one of the disciples of St. Augustine (354–430) but based on St. Augustine's directives to two groups of consecrated persons: clerics whom Augustine formed into a monastic community, and nuns to whom he wrote a famous letter outlining their way of life (A.D. 423). Not much used after Augustine's death, the rule was resuscitated in the late eleventh century and has since been adopted by many monastic and contemplative bodies, including the Dominicans, the Servites, and the Visitation nuns.

AUGUSTINIANISM. The thought of St. Augustine and his followers. In a more technical sense, the theological explanation of St. Augustine, approved by the Church, of man's fall, divine grace, and the freedom of the will in co-operating with the grace of God. Within Augustinianism, there are numerous schools of thought, all part of the Church's theological pluralism.

AUGUSTINIANS. A general name for a number of religious institutes of men and women who base their way of life on the Rule of St. Augustine. Among the men are Augustinian canons, since the eleventh century; Augustinian hermits or friars, to whom Martin Luther had belonged; Augustinian recollects, or discalced hermits; and Augustinians of the Assumption, better known as Assumptionists. There are fourteen distinct communities of Augustinian religious institutes.

AUGUSTINUS. The treatise of Cornelius Jansenius (d. 1638), published after his death, in which were expounded the main principles of Jansenism. Based on St. Augustine's anti-Pelagian works, *Augustinus* denied the existence of a supernatural order and the resistibility of grace. It was condemned as heretical by Pope Innocent X in five propositions.

AUREOLA. The special reward in heaven for three classes of persons who struggled and won victories on earth in their service of God. The aureola is given to virgins for their victory over the flesh (Revelation 14:4); to martyrs for their victory over the world (Matthew 5:11–12); and to faithful teachers of the truth for their victory over the devil, the father of lies (Daniel 12:3; Matthew 5:19). The essential feature of the aureola is the distinctive enjoyment for having conquered the enemies of human salvation. (Etym. Latin *aureola,* corona, a golden wreath or halo; from *aurum,* gold.)

AUREOLE. Oval rays of light visible at times about the sun or moon. Adopted in the Middle Ages as a symbol of the heavenly honor of the saints, it represented the glory attached to their persons. It is to be distinguished from a halo or nimbus. In early times it was used only with representations of God.

AUREOLE OF THE SAINTS. Special heavenly rewards over and above the essential happiness of seeing God. They correspond to one or more victories gained by a saint while on earth, notably victory over the flesh in virginity, over the world in martyrdom, and over the devil in preaching the truth.

AURICULAR CONFESSION. The obligation by divine law of confessing one's grave sins, committed after baptism, to a qualified priest. It is called auricular confession because normally the manifestation of sins is done by word of mouth and heard by the priest before he gives absolution. (Etym. Latin *auricula,* the external ear.)

AURIESVILLE. Shrine of the North American Martyrs, near Albany, New York, on the Mohawk River. In 1642 Father Isaac Jogues (1607–47) and a Jesuit lay brother, René Goupil (1606–42), newly arrived from France and trying to run supplies to the famished Huron Indians, were captured by the Iroquois tribe and cruelly tortured at Ossernenon, present Auriesville. René Goupil died as a result. Jogues recovered and was persuaded to return to France, but 1646 saw him back again in the same place with John La Lande, a nineteen-year-old French boy. Both received the crown of martyrdom in 1647. Auriesville, as the original Ossernenon, has been verified by documentary evidence and excavations on the six hundred acres of rolling land. The first pilgrimage was made in 1885. The small oratory soon became too small to care for the crowds. The second church seated five hundred, to be replaced in 1931 by a vast amphitheater built to accommodate sixteen thousand. Four altars facing the points of the compass are in the center of this buff-colored brick building, and during the summer and fall the rising tiers of seats are often filled to capacity for Mass and benediction. Auriesville is a year-round retreat center. A museum adjacent to the church houses some important relics of the missionaries and their Indian converts. Jogues, Goupil, and La Lande were canonized in 1930 together with Brébeuf (1593–1649), Lallemant (1610–49), Garnier (1643–1730), Chabanel (1613–49), and Daniel (1601–48), their companions who died as martyrs trying to convert the Canadian Indians. Their composite feast day is commemorated on October 19. See also MARTYRS' SHRINE.

AURI SACRA FAMES. The accursed greed for gold. An expression that voices St. Paul's dictum that the desire of money is the root of all evil (I Timothy 6:10).

AUSCULTA FILI. "Listen, my son." The opening words of the Rule of St. Benedict. Motto of the Church's solicitude for the faithful, urging them to sanctity of life.

AUSTERITY. The quality of being severe in one's demeanor or way of life. More commonly in the plural, austerities. These are vigorous forms of bodily penance that persons impose on themselves in order to bring the passions under control, expiate one's own or other people's sins, and help the spirit to more effectively respond to the will of God. Austerities are only a means to perfection and not an end in themselves. They are to be undertaken only under competent spiritual direction. (Etym. Latin *austerus;* from Greek *austeros,* harsh, severe.)

AUTHENTIC INTERPRETATION. See INTERPRETATION.

AUTHENTIC INTERPRETER. In Church

law the person or persons who are authorized to interpret an ecclesiastical law. They are the legislator himself, or his successor, or someone to whom they have given the right to give the interpretation.

AUTHENTICITY. Genuineness as applied to various objects or aspects of the Christian religion. The opposite of spurious or questionable, as authentic prophecy, revelation, relic, and especially inspired books of the Bible. More recently, especially since the Second Vatican Council, authenticity refers to the official teachings of the Church's hierarchy. They are authentic because, and insofar as, they are authorized and therefore binding on the consciences of the faithful to accept and obey. (Etym. Latin *authenticus,* what comes from the author, original, genuine; from Greek *authentikos,* from *authentēs,* perpetrator, master.)

AUTHENTIC TEACHING. Official teaching of the hierarchical Church. Its authenticity depends on its authorization, which means the assurance of divine guidance, as vested in the duly ordained successors of the Apostles united with the Bishop of Rome. Authentic teaching is also infallible when the hierarchy (Pope or bishops with the Pope) intends it universally to bind the consciences of the faithful.

AUTHORITARIANISM. A theory of knowledge that favors acceptance of authority in preference to use of one's own reason. Also the tendency to subject people to authority as opposed to allowing them individual freedom. The term "authoritarian" is commonly used by those who dislike the Church's exercise of her teaching authority, especially in moral matters.

AUTHORITY. The right of a society to direct and compel the members to co-operate toward the attainment of the end of that society. Ultimately all authority in a society comes from God but in different ways, depending on the kind of society.

In a conventional society, founded by the free agreement of men and women who set its purpose and choose its means, God is the final source of authority, but indirectly, in the sense that he is the source of everything. He created the persons who form the society and gave them the faculties by which to direct the society.

In natural societies, such as the family and state, God is the source of authority directly and immediately. He established the natural law that requires that people organ-

ize themselves. The authority passes from God directly to the society and not through the personalities of the founders.

In theocratic societies, such as the Catholic Church, God founded a particular society by supernatural revelation. He specified its structure and determined its leaders. Here God is most directly and immediately the source of authority, not only in governing but also in teaching the faithful who belong to the society. (Etym. Latin *auctoritas,* source, authorship; authority, weight, might, power.)

AUTOCEPHALI. Certain bishops in early Christian times who were not subject to any patriarch or metropolitan. They were dependent solely and directly on a triennial provincial synod of bishops or on the Holy See.

AUTO-DA-FÉ. The public ceremony celebrating the official final pronouncement of a sentence of the Inquisition. Features of the ceremony included: 1. participation of those to be condemned of heresy and those to be publicly reprimanded in a procession to a designated place; 2. a religious discourse followed by swearing in of secular authorities who vowed obedience to the inquisitor in matters pertaining to putting down heresy; 3. the "decrees of mercy" relative to sentences previously imposed on those who had become reconciled with the Church; 4. pronouncement of sentence on the guilty, who were then surrendered for punishment to the civil powers. This ceremony was at its height in Spain in the sixteenth century.

AUTONOMOUS MORALITY. The theory that each person imposes the moral law on himself. It is opposed to heteronomous morality, which holds that the moral law is imposed from outside of man by another, and ultimately by the divine Other, who is God, which makes the moral law theonomous.

Developed into a system by Immanuel Kant (1724–1804), autonomous morality in effect deifies each person's free will. In the Kantian understanding of freedom, liberty means not only freedom of choice but freedom of independence, on the assumption that one cannot retain free will and still be under the command of another's law. To save freedom, Kant demanded autonomy, but by demanding autonomy he destroyed all real obligation and therefore all real law. (Etym. Greek *autonomos,* free, living by one's own laws; Latin *moralis,* relating to conduct.)

AUTOTELIC. Term applied to any absorbing activity in which a person engages for its own sake (Greek *autos*, self, and *telos*, end), such as philosophical speculation or beholding a work of art. From a Catholic viewpoint no human action should be totally autotelic; since everything should somehow be referred to God.

AUX. *Auxilium, auxilio*—help, with the help of.

AUXILIARY BISHOP. One deputed by the Holy See to assist a diocesan bishop in the performance of pontifical functions. As such, he does not have ordinary jurisdiction in a diocese, nor does he have the right of succession to a diocesan see.

AVARICE. An excessive or insatiable desire for money or material things. In its strict sense, avarice is the inordinate holding on to possessions or riches instead of using these material things for some worthwhile purpose. Reluctance to let go of what a person owns is also avarice.

Of itself, avarice is venially sinful. But it may become mortal when a person is ready to use gravely unlawful means to acquire or hold on to his possessions, or when because of his cupidity he seriously violates his duty of justice or charity. (Etym. Latin *avaritia*, greediness, covetousness, avarice.)

AVE MARIA. The title for the Hail Mary in Latin, which reads: *Ave Maria, gratia plena. Dominus tecum. Benedicta tu in mulieribus, et benedictus fructus ventris tui Jesus. Sancta Maria, Mater Dei, ora pro nobis peccatoribus, nunc et in hora mortis nostrae. Amen.*

AVE MARIS STELLA. The hymn "Hail, Star of the Sea," which dates from the ninth century, written by an unknown author. For centuries part of Divine Office at Vespers on feasts of the Blessed Virgin Mary.

AVE REGINA CAELORUM. The hymn "Hail, Queen of the Heavens," used since the twelfth century. Part of Compline in the Divine Office.

AVERROISM. The philosophy of the Moslem writer Averroës (1126–98) and his followers. His commentaries on Aristotle (384–322 B.C.) were used, but also criticized, by Albert the Great (1200–80) and St. Thomas Aquinas (1225–74). The points of Averroism mostly opposed by Catholic scholars were: the co-eternity of the created world, the numerical identity of the intellect in all human beings, the theory that a proposition may be philosophically true but theologically false.

AVERSION. Spontaneously turning away from something unpleasant. The aversion may be spontaneous and morally indifferent, or it may be an interior movement that should be controlled. Growth in the spiritual life requires mastery of one's natural aversions. (Etym. Latin *aversio*, a turning away.)

AVIGNON POPES. The legitimate popes who lived at Avignon in France from 1309 to 1377. They were Clement V, John XXII, Benedict XII, Clement VI, Innocent VI, Urban V, and Gregory XI. The Pope became temporal ruler of Avignon in 1348 and later on the territory was governed by a papal legate. All were French, and their absence from Rome contributed substantially to the Western Schism and later to the Protestant Reformation. The period of the Avignon Papacy is often referred to as the Babylonian Captivity. Moreover, the antipopes Robert of Geneva (Clement VII) and Peter of Luna (Benedict XIII) resided at Avignon from 1379 to 1411.

A VINCULO MATRIMONII. From the bond of matrimony. Said of a person who is freed of matrimonial responsibilities by the death of his or her spouse.

AVOIDING SIN. The moral responsibility of not exposing oneself unnecessarily to occasions of sin. Three principles are standard in Catholic moral teaching: 1. no one is obliged to avoid the remote occasions of sin. This is true because the danger of sin is slight and otherwise it would be impossible to live in the world; 2. everyone is obliged to avoid voluntary proximate occasions of sin, where "voluntary" means that it can easily be removed or avoided; 3. anyone in a necessary proximate occasion of sin is obliged to make the occasion remote. An occasion is necessary when the person's state of life or profession or circumstances make it morally impossible to avoid exposure to certain enticements. What is a proximate danger to sinning can be rendered remote by such means as prayer, the sacraments, and custody of the senses, especially of the eyes.

AX. The emblem of St. Thomas of Canterbury (1118–70), who was martyred by an ax, as were also St. Justin (c. 100–65) and St. Barnabas. St. Boniface (675–755) is shown with the ax recalling his role in the destruction of the great oak dedicated to the pagan Thor, which contributed to the Christianizing of Germany.

AXINOMANCY. Divination by ax heads.

AXIOLOGY. A theory that studies the nature, norms, and meaning of value as that which is desired for being good. Axiology has in modern times sought to replace the traditional ethics and aesthetics, and has sought to lay new foundations for both. The object of ethics is said to be the subjective realization of value, whereas aesthetics is the representation of values. (Etym. Greek *axios,* worth, worthy + *logia,* science, knowledge.)

AXIOM. Self-evident truth that serves as an established norm of law. It states a universal principle whose self-evidence is not questioned within a given system of philosophy or religious doctrine. (Etym. Greek *axioma,* honor; from *axios,* of like value, worthy, worth.)

AZYMITES. A term of reproach used by dissenting Byzantines after 1053 in speaking of Catholics, Armenians, and Maronites, because of the celebration of the Eucharist with unleavened bread by the Maronites. It remains one of the principal grievances against the Church of Rome.

B

B.A. *Baccalaureus Artium*—Bachelor of Arts.

BABEL, TOWER OF. On the plain of Shinar the people decided to build a town and erect a tower so high it would reach heaven. Yahweh distrusted their motives (Genesis 11:1–9). He confused their language so that they could not understand each other. Then he scattered the people over the earth.

BABYLONIAN CAPTIVITY. A term used by Petrarch and later writers of the exile of the popes at Avignon, France, from 1309 to 1377. Seven French popes—so called Clement V, John XXII, Benedict XII, Clement VI, Innocent VI, Blessed Urban V, and Gregory XI—were involved. Pope Gregory, the last one, yielded to the entreaties of St. Catherine of Siena (1347–80) to return to Rome in spite of the protests of the King of France and most of the cardinals.

BAD EXAMPLE. The external performance of some morally evil action that scandalizes other people and encourages them to do the same. Bad example refers especially to leaders in the Church or human society who are expected to practice above ordinary virtue and whose conduct is under constant public scrutiny. Their misconduct, therefore, inevitably gives a bad example to people who look to them for guidance and inspiration.

BAD FAITH. The condition of a person who either acts against the dictates of his or her conscience or who has not sought to enlighten conscience before making a moral decision. The term is also applied to one who has acquired another person's property and does not take reasonable means either to find the owner or to restore the owner's possessions. People are likewise said to be in bad faith when they do not embrace Catholicism although convinced of its truth, or when they do not take appropriate measures to learn what is the true faith.

BAIANISM. A system of grace developed by Michael Baius (1513–89) at Louvain and condemned in seventy-nine propositions by Pope St. Pius V in 1567. Its main principles were: 1. man's original state was not a supernatural gift of God; 2. original sin is the same as habitual concupiscence; 3. as a result of the fall, man's will is not really interiorly free; 4. all human actions proceed either from cupidity (evil concupiscence) or from the charity infused by God. The former actions are morally bad, the latter morally good. Baianism was the direct forerunner of Jansenism and gave it the logical premises derived from the Protestant reformers, on which it was built.

BALAAM. A heathen soothsayer who makes contradictory impressions in Scripture. Invited urgently by Balak, King of Moab, to come into the Jordan Valley and curse the invading Israelites, Balaam showed a surprising willingness to obey Yahweh, despite the fact that he was not a believer. All of Balak's pleas and bribes were futile; instead of cursing the Israelites, Balaam repeatedly blessed them (Numbers 22–24). Later, however, Moses became aware that Balaam had betrayed his people by inducing them to sin grievously by eating food sacrificed to idols. He ordered Balaam's death (Numbers 31:8–16). Even in the New Testament reference is made to Balaam's iniquity. Jude classifies him with the rebellious Cain and Korah (Jude 11), and John denounces certain evildoers as "followers of Balaam" (Revelation 2:14).

BALDACHINO. A dome-shaped canopy, made of wood, stone, or metal, over a high altar. It is either suspended by chains or supported by columns. Also called a ciborium. The most famous is that of St. Peter's in Rome, designed by Bernini (1598–1680) for Pope Urban VIII. Its name comes from Baldacco, Italian for Baghdad, which furnished the precious materials for these canopies. The term is also applied to the canopies used in processions or to those placed over an episcopal throne.

BALM, BALSAM. Aromatic viscous fluid from the terebinth tree and other plants. In cathedral-churches on Holy Thursday blessed balm is mixed with olive oil and then poured into the oil of the holy chrism. In the administration of some sacraments and for other blessings in the Church, this holy chrism is used.

BALSAM. An aromatic resin obtained from certain trees and used in some medicines and perfumes. It is one of the ingredients of chrism, along with olive oil, for the administration of the sacrament of confirmation and in ceremonies of public baptism. Balsam symbolizes the reception of grace to preserve oneself from the corruption of the world, and to send forth by a devout life the fragrance of Christian virtue.

BALTIMORE CATECHISM. Originally the "Cathechism of Christian Doctrine, Prepared and Enjoined by Order of the Third Council of Baltimore." It was the Plenary Council of 1884 that authorized this manual, first published in 1885, after a committee of six bishops were entrusted with the composition. The question of a uniform textbook of Catholic doctrine had been considered by the American hierarchy since their First Provincial Council in 1829, but it took fifty years to see the project to completion. After the catechism was issued, various editions were published, with word meanings, explanatory notes, and even different arrangements, so that in a few decades there was great diversity in the books that were called the Baltimore Catechism.

BALTIMORE, COUNCILS OF. Series of thirteen councils of American bishops, three plenary (1852–84) and ten provincial (1829–69), by which the Catholic Church in the United States was organized. The last of these councils, in 1884, decreed the preparation of the Baltimore Catechism, legislated Catholic education in Catholic schools, established the Catholic University of America, and determined the six holy days of obligation for the ecclesiastical year.

BAMBINO. A figure of the Infant Jesus, usually of wax, represented as in the Crib at Bethlehem. It is exposed in Catholic churches from Christmas to Epiphany. This devotion owes its origin in the thirteenth century to St. Francis of Assisi (1181–1226). A jeweled wooden figure of the Divine Infant, "Santissimo Bambino," is in the Franciscan Church of Ara Coeli in Rome. Brought from the Holy Land, it is carried in procession on Christmas and Epiphany and is reputed to have miraculous powers.

BANNEUX. The shrine of Our Lady of the Poor, near the city of Liège in the Flemish village of Banneux. Devotion to Mary began as a result of an apparition to a poor twelve-year-old Belgian child in the garden of her home on January 16, 1933. Our Lady told her that she had come to relieve the ills and sufferings of the poor of all nations. A painting on the wall of the village's chapel made according to the child's description shows Mary robed in white with a blue sash and with a rosary over her right arm. On January 18, 1933, the child's father, an avowed atheist, accompanied his daughter to the garden, and although he did not see the Virgin he was instantly converted, overwhelmed in the presence of an unseen power. After years of investigation, the Holy See authorized public devotion to Our Lady of Banneux, patroness of the poor, in 1942. Formal approval was given by the Bishop of Liège in 1949, and a statue of that title was solemnly crowned in 1956. Pilgrims from many countries came to worship at the shrine. Over one hundred shrines throughout the world are dedicated to Our Lady of Banneux.

BANNEZIANISM. Theory of the relationship of divine grace and human freedom, developed by Dominic Banez

(1528–1604), Spanish Dominican philosopher and theologian. In this theory, God foresees futuribles (hypothetical future events depending on human freedom) and free futures (actual future events determined by the human will) in his predetermining decrees. He physically premoves the free created will to one course of action. This physical predetermination concurs naturally with a person's natural use of the will. In the supernatural order, it is actual efficacious grace for the human will. Without this premotion, the will cannot act in this way. Consequently what we fail to do and our sins are also known in God's predetermining decrees. The principal rival theory is known as Molinism, which originated with the Jesuit Louis Molina.

BANNS. Public announcements of an intended marriage. Their purpose is to discover matrimonial impediments if any exist. Unless a dispensation has been secured, three publications are required on three Sundays or holy days in the churches of the marrying parties. Anyone knowing of such impediments is bound in conscience to make the same known to the clergy concerned. Similar announcements are required for those about to receive holy orders. (Etym. Anglo-Saxon *gebann,* a proclamation.)

BAPTISM. The sacrament in which, by water and the word of God, a person is cleansed of all sin and reborn and sanctified in Christ to everlasting life. (Etym. Latin *baptisma;* from Greek *baptisma,* a dipping.)

BAPTISM, MATTER AND FORM. Natural water that is poured or sprinkled on a person, or in which a person is immersed, is the matter or material element necessary for baptism. The pronouncing of the words is the form of baptism, namely: "I baptize you in the name of the Father, and of the Son, and of the Holy Spirit." It is a disputed question whether in the early Church, besides the foregoing, baptism was also administered in the name of the Lord Jesus. What is certain is that the Catholic Church early declared the necessity of using the Trinitarian formula for valid baptism.

BAPTISMAL COVENANT. An agreement made by the person being baptized, either personally or through one's sponsor, to belong entirely to Christ, who in turn promises the new Christian to bless him or her with a lifetime of divine grace.

BAPTISMAL FONT. A stone, metal, or wooden receptacle, usually ornamented, for holding baptismal water used in the solemn administration of the sacrament. According to common law, every parish church must have a baptismal font.

BAPTISMAL GRACES. The supernatural effects of the sacrament of baptism. They are: 1. removal of all guilt of sin, original and personal; 2. removal of all punishment due to sin, temporal and eternal; 3. infusion of sanctifying grace along with the theological virtues of faith, hope, and charity, and the gifts of the Holy Spirit; 4. incorporation into Christ; and 5. entrance into the Mystical Body, which is the Catholic Church; 6. imprinting of the baptismal character, which enables a person to receive the other sacraments, to participate in the priesthood of Christ through the sacred liturgy, and to grow in the likeness of Christ through personal sanctification. Baptism does not remove two effects of original sin, namely concupiscence and bodily mortality. However, it does enable a Christian to be sanctified by his struggle with concupiscence and gives him the title to rising in a glorified body on the last day.

BAPTISMAL NAME. The name that a person receives at baptism. It is prescribed by the Church's newest ritual, as when the celebrant asks the parents or sponsors at infant baptism, "What name do you wish to give the infant?" According to the Church's tradition, the baptismal name "should be taken from some person whose eminent sanctity has given him a place in the catalogue of the saints. The similarity of name will stimulate each one to imitate the virtues and holiness of the Saint and, moreover, to hope and pray that the one who is the model for one's imitation will also be his advocate and watch over the safety of his body and soul" (*Catechism of the Council of Trent,* Baptism).

BAPTISMAL REGISTER. The record of baptism to be made by the priest who performs the baptism. It is kept in the parish archives. To be listed in the register are the names of those who are baptized, of the one who administers the baptism, of the parents, and of the sponsors; also the place and date of the baptism. Special provisions are made for recording the parents of children born out of wedlock. The mother's name is to be recorded if her maternity is public or if she spontaneously requests it in writing or in the presence of witnesses. Also the father's name is to be recorded if he spontaneously requests it in writing or in the presence of witnesses, or if he is recognized as the father in some authentic public document. In other cases, the child is recorded as born of parents unknown. The pastor has custody of the baptismal register.

BAPTISMAL VOWS. Profession of the Christian faith by an adult candidate for baptism or by the sponsor in the name of the infant to be baptized. The solemn renewal of these promises is a widespread act of piety usually at the close of a mission or retreat or when receiving First Communion or the sacrament of confirmation. It is a part of the Eucharistic liturgy at the Easter Vigil and on the Feast of the Baptism of the Lord.

BAPTISMAL WATER. The water used for the administration of the sacrament of baptism. For the valid conferral of baptism any ordinary natural water may be used. But for licit administration of solemn baptism, the water should be ritually blessed. Normally, the water is blessed for this purpose during the Easter Vigil on Holy Saturday. But it may be blessed at each baptism by the one who confers the sacrament. Three ritual blessings of the water are provided by the Roman ritual, two of which include a symbolic touching of the water by the priest and alternate responses by the people.

BAPTISM OF BLOOD. Martyrdom in the case of a person who died for the Christian faith before he or she could receive the sacrament. The effects of martyrdom of blood are the complete remission of all sin and the title to immediate entrance into heaven. The expression entered the Christian vocabulary during the first three centuries when many catechumens awaiting baptism and pagans suddenly converted to the Christian faith were martyred before they could receive formal baptism of water.

BAPTISM OF DESIRE. The equivalent of sacramental baptism of water, which in God's providence is sufficient to enable a person to obtain the state of grace and to save his or her soul. According to the Church's teaching, "Those who through no fault of their own, do not know the Gospel of Christ or His Church, but who nevertheless seek God with a sincere heart, and, moved by grace, try in their actions to do His will as they know it through the dictates of their conscience—those too may achieve eternal salvation" (Second Vatican Council, *Constitution on the Church,* I, 16).

BAPTISM OF MARTYRDOM. Also called baptism of blood. It is the patient endurance of fatal torture inflicted out of hatred for Christ or the Christian faith or Christian virtue.

BAPTISTERY. A portion of a church or separate building set apart for the administration of baptism. It is often placed in the open entrance court to signify the need of baptism for entrance into the Church. As separate buildings, baptisteries are mainly octagonal or circular in shape, are surrounded by an ambulatory, have an anteroom and a central chamber that contains a pool. The finest such buildings are in Palma on Mallorca; Florence and Pisa in Italy; and Cranbrook in England.

BAPTISTS. The name for a variety of Protestant groups originally stressing the duty of adult baptism. They were started in England by John Smyth (1554–1612), a Cambridge graduate and Anglican minister early in the seventeenth century. His nonconformism forced his flight to Holland, where under Mennonite influence he preached against infant baptism. Early divisions in Europe and America have separated the Baptists into numerous denominations, notably the General Baptists, who believed in a general redemption of all men, and the Particular Baptists, who claimed that only a few would be saved. Strongly congregational in church organization, they have no prescribed confessions of faith. The Baptists have divided mainly into the extremely liberal in matters of belief and the fundamentalists who adhere to a literal interpretation of the Bible. The latter believe in the Trinity; divinity of Christ; original sin; need for redemption; salvation through Christ; eternal heaven or hell; Scripture as divinely inspired; the Bible as the sole standard by which creed, opinion, and conduct are measured; all humankind are sinners inclined to evil and under condemnation to eternal perdition, utterly unholy; justification is bestowed solely through faith.

Doctrinally the Baptists commonly regard the visible Church as a congregation of baptized believers covenanted in faith and fellowship; observing Christ's laws and governed by them and exercising the rights and privileges assured them by his Word. Faith with baptism is required for church membership. They admit two ordinances, not sacraments; baptism, which does not remit sin; and the Lord's Supper, which is a purely symbolic presence of Christ. The church is organized by consent of the group, who agree in worshiping under a pastor of their own choice.

BAR. A prefix in Aramaic meaning "son," e.g., Bar-Jonah, son of Jonah; Bartholomew, son of Tolmai.

BARABBAS. "A notorious prisoner," Matthew described him (Matthew 27:16–17). John called him "a brigand" (John 18:40–41). Mark and Luke both said that he was in prison as a rioter and a murderer (Mark 15:7–15; Luke 23:19–25). When Pilate questioned Jesus at his trial and could find him guilty of nothing, he offered the people the choice of freeing Christ or Barabbas, hoping that the latter's notorious reputation would induce them to release Christ. But, whipped into fury by their chief priests, they insisted that the guilty man be freed and the innocent die. (Etym. Aramaic *bar' abba,* son of the father.)

BAR-JONAH. Simon Peter's surname. Peter was the son of Jonah. Jesus hailed him by his family name at the time he bestowed on him his new name. "You are Peter and on this rock I will build my Church" (Matthew 16:18). (Etym. Greek *bar ionas,* from Aramaic *bar yonah,* son of Jonah; Hebrew *yonah,* dove.)

BARNABAS. Otherwise known as Joseph, a Levite of Cyprus (Acts 4:36–37). He became a member of the primitive Church. Paul's acceptance by the Christians in Jerusalem was largely due to Barnabas' eloquence in persuading them of Paul's sincerity and the miraculous conversion at Damascus. The two traveled together in the work of the Church in obedience to the Holy Spirit: "I want Barnabas and Saul set apart for the work to which I have called them" (Acts 13:2). They were especially successful in the year they spent together in Antioch, converting many (Acts 11:25–26). The team of Paul and Barnabas was finally disrupted by a "violent quarrel." On Paul's next projected journey Barnabas wanted his nephew, Mark, to accompany them, but Paul disagreed. The consequence was that Paul chose Silas to accompany him, while Barnabas and Mark traveled to Cyprus (Acts 15:36–40). This new partnership paved the way for Mark's development as Peter's disciple and the second Evangelist. (Etym. Greek *barnabas,* from Aramaic word, popular meaning "son of consolation.")

BARNABITES. A religious order founded in Milan in 1530 by St. Antonio Maria Zaccaria (d. 1539). Also known as the Clerks Regular of St. Paul, their name is derived from the mother church of St. Barnabas in Milan. Their monastic life includes the special study of St. Paul's letters and the prohibition of accepting ecclesiastical dignities. They also engage in missionary work and education.

BAROQUE. The ornate form of ecclesiastical art and architecture that began in Italy in the seventeenth century and eventually spread throughout the Continent. Its purpose was to infuse new life into the cold style of the later Renaissance. Purity of form, however, was sometimes sacrificed to a love of ornament.

BARRETTINI. See HUMILIATI.

BARSABBAS. One of the two candidates nominated to succeed Judas as the twelfth Apostle (Acts 1:23–26). Tradition holds that Barsabbas and Matthias were among the seventy-two disciples chosen by Christ (Luke 10:1). Lots were drawn and Matthias was chosen. (Etym. Aramaic *bar sa'ba',* son of Sabbas.)

BARTHOLOMEW. One of the twelve Apostles mentioned each of the four times they are listed in the New Testament (Matthew 10:3; Mark 3:18; Luke 6:14; Acts 1:13). Otherwise his name does not appear. Writers speculate that he may be the Nathanael discussed in John's Gospel (John 1:45–48), but there is no definite proof. (Etym. Greek *bartholomaios,* from Aramaic *bar talmai,* son of Tolmai.)

BARTIMAEUS. A blind beggar who was sitting at the side of the road when Jesus passed with his disciples after visiting Jericho. The beggar attracted his attention by shouting and begged him to cure his blindness. Jesus did so on the spot and Bartimaeus joined the crowd following him (Mark 10:46–52). (Etym. Greek *bartimaios,* from Aramaic *bartimai,* son of Timaeus.)

BARUCH. Trusted friend and amanuensis of the prophet Jeremiah, living in the seventh century B.C. God delivered lengthy warnings to Jeremiah about the Israelites. Chapter 36 in the Book of Jeremiah describes in detail how he dictated these messages to Baruch and ordered him to read them to the people in the temple. King Jehoiakim listened to the warnings with displeasure and ordered them destroyed. Jeremiah repeated the dictation of the messages, so determined was he that the people be enlightened. Both Jeremiah and Baruch fled the kingdom. The Book of Baruch is in the Catholic Bible. Its first five chapters are the prophecy with which Baruch consoled the Jewish exiles. Chapter 6 is the Epistle of Jeremiah, which seems to have been authored by Jeremiah rather than Baruch.

BASILIANS. A general name for various religious institutes. Orthodox monks are sometimes called Basilians because they have inherited the spirit of St. Basil (329–79), although they have no uniform rule. There are five Catholic Basilian orders of men and four congregations of women, all of pontifical status. A congregation of the Priests of St. Basil was founded in 1822 at Annonay in France for educational and parochial work.

BASILICA. A lengthy oblong religious edifice, rectangular in shape with an apse at one end. This name was originally given to certain ancient churches in Rome, the Holy Land, and elsewhere that were converted from pagan edifices to Christian use. The width of a basilica building is never greater than one half of its length. It is divided by rows of columns into a central nave and a surrounding aisle, or ambulatory. The upper part of the nave is lighted by clerestory windows overlooking the roof over the aisles. Similar lower windows light the aisle sections. The altar is placed within or before the apse arching from the nave and opening into the transept, or cross hall. At the main entrance to the basilica is the narthex, beyond which the early neophytes were not admitted. St. John Lateran, the Mother Church, is the archbasilica for the patriarch of the West, the Pope; St. Peter's for the patriarch of Constantinople; St. Paul's Outside the Walls for the patriarch of Alexandria; St. Mary Major for the patriarch of Antioch; St. Lawrence Outside the Walls, for the patriarch of Jerusalem. Each of these major basilicas has an altar exclusively for the Pope's use, and by others only with his permission. Adjoining their basilicas were the former residences of the various patriarchs when they were in Rome. St. Francis of Assisi's church is also a major basilica with a papal altar and a throne. Eleven churches in Rome and many others throughout the world have been designated by the Pope as minor basilicas, e.g., at Loreto and Padua in Italy, Lourdes in France, Lough Derg in Ireland. The clergy who serve in them enjoy a title of honor that gives them certain ceremonial rites. (Etym. Latin *basilicus*, royal.)

BASILICA OF ST. PETER. The patriarchal church adjoining the Vatican Palace of the Pope. In A.D. 67, St. Peter was executed in the circus of Nero near the foot of the obelisk that was brought from Egypt and that stands in the center of the piazza in front of St. Peter's Basilica. In A.D. 90, Pope St. Anacletus marked the grave by building a small oratory over the spot that Constantine, destroying the old circus, hoped to place within the foundations of the new cathedral. This first basilica had lasted for 1100 years when Pope Nicholas V determined to build a more pretentious edifice. Work progressed very slowly. Successive popes engaged Rosselino (1439–1507), Alberti (1474–1515), Bramante (1444–1514), Michelangelo (1475–1564), Maderna (1556–1629), and Bernini (1598–1680). The basilica was finally finished after being in process of construction for 176 years. It was dedicated with great ceremony by Pope Urban VIII in 1626. The famed colonnade surrounding the piazza, four columns deep, was designed by Bernini. The top is surmounted by 126 statues of saints each twelve feet in height. Over the front entrance is the Loggia della Benedizione, from which the Pope imparts benediction. From the portico five entrances lead into the basilica—the first is the Porta Santa, opened only during the Holy Year. The central entrance has the noted bronze doors from the first cathedral depicting the life of Christ and the Virgin. The nave is the longest in the world, flanked by fluted pillars with the niches that contain the huge sculptured statues of the founders of the religious orders. This leads to the high altar, with its bronzed and gilt-ornamented canopy done by Bernini in 1633. In front of it is the circular marble balustrade, with its ninety-five lamps burning day and night, leading below to the bronze sarcophagus above which is the gold cross of St. Peter. At the left as one ascends from the Confessio is the fifth-century bronze statue of the first Pope from the first basilica of A.D. 445. The right foot of bronze has been worn and polished by the millions who, passing by, have kissed Peter's foot. Beyond the transept is the tribune that contains the bronze reliquary enclosing the ancient episcopal wooden chair of the first Vicar of Christ. Numerous papal tombs are in the tribune and aisles, notably Pope Paul III's, considered the finest of the monuments in St. Peter's. The world famous Michelangelo *Pietà* is in the first chapel of the right aisle with the youthful Mother and her dead Son. In the crypt, in the thirteen feet between the pavement of the new and old cathedrals, are the tombs of many popes, including Pope Adrian IV, the only Englishman to be a successor of Peter, and St. Pius X, best known as the Pope of the Blessed Sacrament. St. Peter's body lies in a vault beneath the high altar. Recent scientific excavations have established authenticity of his remains.

BASIL, RULE OF SAINT. A rule of life drawn up, from 358 to 364, by St. Basil the Great (329–79). It is still the basis for monasticism in the Eastern Church. There are two forms of the rule, in question and answer form, with 55 and 313 items respectively. Although austere, it consciously avoids some of the extremes of Eastern monasticism before Basil's time. Hours of liturgical prayer were prescribed. Manual and other work were required. Children were to be trained in classes attached to the monastery and given an opportunity to test their vocation to the religious life. The monasteries were to care for the poor. The present rule owes its form to the revision of St. Theodore of Studion (759–826).

BASIN (ecclesiastical). An ornamental metal bowl used for ablutions especially at the lavabo of the Mass and in ceremonial ablutions of bishops.

BATH-SHEBA. The wife of Uriah the Hittite. She was coveted by King David, who connived with his military leader, Joab, to send Uriah into such a dangerous part of the battlefield that he would be killed. His plot succeeded, and then he made Bath-Sheba his queen. A child resulted from this unholy union, but Yahweh was angered by the king's shameful conduct (II Samuel 11:14–27). The prophet Nathan appeared in David's court and delivered a stinging rebuke. David's repentance was expressed eloquently in Psalm 51, and he willingly offered penance for his crime, but the child died within a week. Later Bath-Sheba bore him another child. This was Solomon, destined to become the famous successor to David (II Samuel 12:1–25). Years later the rivalry of Solomon's half-brother, Adonijah, impelled Bath-Sheba to persuade the aging king to have Solomon secretly anointed and crowned (I Kings 1:25–40).

B., BB., B1. *Beatus, beati*—blessed.

B.C. Before Christ.

B.C.L. *Baccalaureus Civilis* (or *Canonicae*) *Legis*—Bachelor of Civil (or Canon) Law.

B.D. Bachelor of Divinity.

BEADLE. A minor church officer whose duties have varied over the centuries and in different localities. Under Gregory the Great a beadle was the "guardian of the church," who was to light the lamps or candles. Later he came to be an usher who led people into their seats, or an announcer who read messages to the congregation, or something of a bodyguard who preceded a bishop or other prelate to clear the way for his passage through a crowd. (Etym. Anglo-Saxon *bēodan,* to command, to bid.)

BEADS. Small pellets or bits of wood, stone, or glass arranged on a chain, wire, or string according to a kind, order, or number of prayers in certain forms of devotion. They are in common use among Catholics as a simple way to ensure accuracy in the count of prayers said in frequent repetition. The rosary, sometimes referred to as a "pair of beads," consists of five units of ten beads each and is in common use. The device of using beads for counting prayers is very ancient and is a common practice among Hindus, Buddhists, and Moslems.

BEARD. In the Eastern Church the wearing of beards has remained the practice since apostolic times as a sign of virility. From the fifth century on, the West gradually had its clerics clean-shaven. By the twelfth century there were many decrees by Western Church councils against clerics wearing beards. In the sixteenth and seventeenth centuries the contrary practice prevailed, and beards were worn by popes. Then there was a return to the earlier practice, and most recently some priests in the West conform to the prevalent custom of long hair and a beard.

BEATA VIRGO MARIA. Blessed Virgin Mary, often simply *Beata Virgo* or *Beata Maria.*

BEATIFICATION. A declaration by the Pope as head of the Church that one of the deceased faithful lived a holy life and/or died a martyr's death and is now dwelling in heaven. As a process, the beatification consists of a years-long examination of the life, virtues, writings, and reputation for holiness of the servant of God under consideration. This is ordinarily conducted by the bishop of the place where he or she resided or died. For a martyr miracles worked through the person's intercession need not be considered in this primary process. The second, or Apostolic, process is instituted by the Holy

See when the first process reveals that the servant of God practiced virtue in a heroic degree or died a martyr for the faith. Beatified persons are called "Blessed" and may be venerated by the faithful but not throughout the universal Church. (Etym. Latin *beatificatio,* the state of being blessed; from *beatus,* happy.)

BEATIFIC VISION. The intuitive knowledge of God which produces heavenly beatitude. As defined by the Church, the souls of the just "see the divine essence by an intuitive vision and face to face, so that the divine essence is known immediately, showing itself plainly, clearly and openly, and not mediately through any creature" (Denzinger 1000–2). Moreover, the souls of the saints "clearly behold God, one and triune, as He is" (Denzinger 1304–6). It is called vision in the mind by analogy with bodily sight, which is the most comprehensive of human sense faculties; it is called beatific because it produces happiness in the will and the whole being. As a result of this immediate vision of God, the blessed share in the divine happiness, where the beatitude of the Trinity is (humanly speaking) the consequence of God's perfect knowledge of his infinite goodness. The beatific vision is also enjoyed by the angels, and was possessed by Christ in his human nature even while he was in his mortal life on earth. (Etym. Latin *beatificus,* beatific, blissful, imparting great happiness or blessedness; from *beatus,* happy.)

BEATI POSSIDENTES. Blessed are the possessors, meaning that possession is nine tenths of the law. The law favors the possessor, whereas anyone else must prove his claim.

BEATITUDE. Happiness or blessedness as the enduring possession of perfect good. Supernatural beatitude is the perfect happiness enjoyed by a nature raised by grace and the light of glory to the eternal vision of God. (Etym. Latin *beatitudo,* felicity; a state of being happy; an object, the attainment of which will make one happy; from *beatus,* happy.)

BEATITUDES. The promises of happiness made by Christ to those who faithfully accept his teaching and follow his divine example. Preached in the Sermon on the Mount, they are recorded in St. Matthew (5:3–11) and in St. Luke (6:20–22). In Matthew there are eight (or nine) blessings of a spiritual nature, applicable to all Chris-

tians; in Luke there are four blessings of a more external character, addressed to the disciples. Luke's version also includes four maledictions threatened on those who do the opposite. In both versions, the beatitudes are expressions of the New Covenant, where happiness is assured already in this life, provided a person totally gives himself to the imitation of Christ.

IN THE GOSPEL OF MATTHEW
"How happy are the poor in spirit: theirs is the kingdom of heaven.
Happy the gentle: they shall have the earth for their heritage.
Happy those who mourn: they shall be comforted.
Happy those who hunger and thirst for what is right: they shall be satisfied.
Happy the merciful: they shall have mercy shown them.
Happy the pure in heart: they shall see God.
Happy the peacemakers: they shall be called sons of God.
Happy those who are persecuted in the cause of right: theirs is the kingdom of heaven.
Happy are you when people abuse you and persecute you and speak all kinds of calumny against you on my account. Rejoice and be glad, for your reward will be great in heaven; this is how they persecuted the prophets before you" (Matthew 5:3–12).

IN THE GOSPEL OF LUKE
"How happy are you who are poor: yours is the kingdom of God.
Happy you who are hungry now: you shall be satisfied.
Happy you who weep now: you shall laugh.
Happy you when people hate you, drive you out, abuse you, denounce your name as criminal, on account of the Son of Man. Rejoice when that day comes and dance for joy, for then your reward will be great in heaven. This was the way their ancestors treated the prophets.
But alas for you who are rich: you are having your consolation now.
Alas for you who have your fill now: you shall go hungry.
Alas for you who laugh now: you shall mourn and weep.
Alas for you when the world speaks well of you! This was the way their ancestors treated the false prophets" (Luke 6:20–26).

BEATTY PAPYRI. Manuscript of thirty

leaves from the Gospels and Acts, dating from the third century, together with twenty more leaves from St. Paul and Revelation. Old Testament manuscripts in the same collection amount to 180 leaves from nine books, dating to the second century. The Beatty papyri substantiate the essential soundness of the existing biblical texts. No striking or fundamental variant is shown either in the Old or New Testament. The papyri were found near Hermopolis in Egypt, most of which were acquired by A. Chester Beatty (1875–1968) in 1931.

BEAUPRÉ, ST. ANNE DE. World famous shrine to the mother of the Blessed Virgin in Quebec, Canada. Its origins are dated from the reported miraculous cure of the cripple Louis Grimont, March 16, 1658. The small chapel was gradually enlarged, and the present structure was declared a minor basilica in 1888. In the north transept of the church is a golden reliquary containing an authenticated wristbone of St. Anne. Many miracles are reported annually, with thousands of pilgrims praying there the year round, but especially on July 26, the feast day of the saint.

BEAURAING (shrine). Scene of the apparition of the Immaculate Virgin. She revealed herself to five Belgian children aged nine to fifteen years on thirty-three occasions in the small village of Beauraing in the Vallon part of Belgium. On November 29, 1932, the children walking over the railway viaduct saw a lady with arms outstretched dressed in white, veiled with a crown of golden rays around her head and a golden heart on her breast. In a later apparition she admonished the children to always be good. On January 1, 1933, at her last appearance she told the oldest boy, "If you love my Son and me, sacrifice yourself for me." At first all public recognition in the way of processions was forbidden. Ten years of investigation followed. Numerous miracles were reported by those who had visited the shrine by then built to honor Mary and who had been cured. Finally, on July 2, 1949, Bishop Charue of Namur authorized public devotion to "Our Lady of Beauraing."

BEAUTY. That which instinctively appeals. According to St. Thomas Aquinas, "Beauty relates to the cognitive faculty; for beautiful things are those which please on being seen. Hence beauty consists in due proportion" (*Summa Theologica*, I, 5, 4). There is, consequently, beauty not only in things material but also, and especially, in things spiritual.

"Union in distinction makes order; order produces agreement; and proportion and agreement, in complete and finished things, make beauty" (St. Francis de Sales, *Treatise on the Love of God,* I).

BECOMING. To change; to go from one definiteness to another. Becoming is opposed to being, in the sense of a being in the process of becoming something other than what it had been. The terms "become" and "becoming" are current features of process philosophy and theology, which deny that any being, including God, simply exists, but claim that everything is in constant flux and change.

BEEHIVE. The emblem of several saints, generally symbolizing their great eloquence. St. Ambrose (340–97) is considered patron of the beekeepers. Bees are likewise symbols of St. John Chrysostom (347–407), the golden-tongued patron of orators, and also of St. Bernard of Clairvaux (1090–1153).

BEELZEBUL (also Baalzebub, Beelzebub). Under whichever spelling the name appears, it designates a demonic deity or influence. In the New Testament, Jesus denied vigorously that he performed miracles through the power of Beelzebul (Matthew 12:24, Luke 11:19–20). In the Old Testament, King Ahaziah attempted to consult the god of Ekron under the spelling Baalzebub (II Kings 1:3). The name carries the contemptuous connotation of "the lord of flies."

BEFORE CHRIST (B.C.). The era of human history from the origin of man to the coming of Christ. Sometimes called "Before the Christian Era" (B.C.E.).

BEGHARDS. Groups of lay persons in the Middle Ages, dedicated to living an above-ordinary life of prayer and mortification in the world. They were founded in the twelfth century in the Netherlands, mostly among the craft guild workers of the day. Each community had a common purse, property, and one house for shelter. After two centuries of edifying behavior, abuses crept in and heretical policies were adopted. Censured by the Pope and their bishops and warned by the Inquisition, they would not relent and so were condemned. After the French Revolution they practically disappeared.

BEGUINES. Communities of lay women founded in the Netherlands in the twelfth century. Devoting themselves to the care of the disabled and poor, they lived a semi-monastic life, free to own property and return to the world at their pleasure. Each residence of two or three persons was called a *béguinage,* a self-supporting unit with a chapel in the enclosure for general use. Without a common rule or superiors, some adopted the regulations of the third order of St. Francis. They greatly influenced the lives of the people for good, especially in educational and charitable works, but became involved in the errors and heresies current at the time and were condemned by the Council of Vienne. They almost disappeared during the French Revolution. Those who remain today care for the sick and make lace for profit and support. (Etym. French *Béguine,* after founder, Lambert le Bègue.)

BEHAVIOR. In moral theology all the activity of a human being. More specifically, it is the way a person acts under given circumstances, with the implication that he or she might have acted differently and therefore chose to do what was done or not done. Behavior is observable human activity.

BEING. Whatever in any way is, whether it exists or is possible, whether in the mind, in the imagination, or in a statement. Philosophically being is the real, and corresponds to essence or thing. Its opposite is the unreal and finally that which implies an inner contradiction.

BEING IN TIME. A term in the philosophy of Martin Heidegger (1889–1976) to redefine man as *Dasein in Zeitlichkeit,* i.e., "being in temporality." On these premises human beings have no stable essence or nature. Rather they are constantly changing with the passage of time. Heideggerian philosophy has been applied to both the Gospels and to Catholic Church documents. When applied to the Gospels, their real meaning can be found only by stripping the story of Christ's life of its time-conditioned mythology. Applied to Church documents, Heideggerianism calls for a reappraisal in modern terms of every Catholic doctrine from the past.

BEL. The tutelary god of Babylon, occasionally called Merodach. The Hebrews gloried in a victory over the Babylonians by proclaiming: "Babylon is captured, Bel disgraced, Merodach shattered (Her idols are disgraced, her obscenities shattered)" (Jeremiah 50:2).

BELIAL. Wickedness, lawlessness. The word is personified in the New Testament. Paul says, "Light and darkness have nothing in common. Christ is not the ally of Belial" (II Corinthians 6:14–15). (Etym. Greek *belial;* from Hebrew *bĕlīyaʻal,* worthlessness.)

BELIEF. The acceptance of something as true on a trustworthy person's word. It differs from faith only in the stress on confidence in the one who is believed. Moreover, belief emphasizes the act of the will, which disposes one to believe, where faith is rather the act of the mind, which assents to what is believed.

BELL-BOOK-CANDLE. Symbols used in an old form of excommunication in the Church. The sentence of greater excommunication having been read, these accessories, carried by the priests attending, were also used symbolically: the book was closed, the candle extinguished, and the bell tolled as for the dead.

BELLS. Hollow metal cups that make a ringing sound when struck or rung. When blessed, they are sacramentals of the Church. The Mass bell is a small handbell rung at the elevation of the Sacred Host and Chalice to direct the attention of the congregation to this most solemn part of the Mass. In many churches and in some convents and monasteries the tower bells are rung at dawn, noon, and night, and also in the elevation in the Mass so that people nearby are made aware of the service and can join in prayer. A priest carrying the Blessed Sacrament to the sick in a convent or Catholic hospital is accompanied by a person carrying a bell announcing the presence of the Holy Eucharist. Bells are not rung at Divine Services from the Gloria on Holy Thursday until the Gloria on the Easter Vigil, denoting the Church's sorrow at the Passion and the death of Christ.

BELLS, BLESSING OF. A special solemn ceremony by a bishop or by a priest delegated by him to bless the bells in church belfries. First washed with holy water, they are then anointed inside and outside with holy oils, and prayers are offered that at the sound of these bells the evil spirits may be put to flight and the people of God called to prayer. A simple blessing is used for less important bells.

BEN. Son of; e.g., Ben-hadad, the son of Hadad. In the plural, clan members descended from a common ancestor.

BEN., BD. *Benedictio*—blessing.

BENEDICITE. Canticle of Tobit, whose opening words are "Praise [Benedicite] the Lord, all you His chosen ones" (Tobit 13:10).

BENEDICTINES. The men and women religious who follow the Rule of St. Benedict (480–547). Founded about 529 at Monte Cassino, some eighty miles south of Rome, the Benedictine Order early included both monks and nuns. The latter were separately established by St. Benedict with the help of his sister, St. Scholastica (480–543). Originally each monastery was an independent and self-sustaining unit, and this principle remains substantially in effect to the present day.

It is customary to distinguish four stages in the history of the Benedictines: 1. from St. Benedict to St. Gregory the Great who died in A.D. 604. The latter as monk who became pope extended the Benedictine ideal into other countries and through his *Dialogues* developed the ascetical principles of the founder; 2. from the sixth century to the foundation of the Cistercians at Cîteaux, St. Bernard of Clairvaux (1090–1153) began a form of Benedictinism that was more austere; 3. from Cîteaux to the Council of Trent. During this period a grouping of monasteries and a development of the monastic way of life took place, affecting the whole of Western Europe. There was also decadence due to the inroads of the pagan renaissance; 4. from Trent to the Second Vatican Council. The Council of Trent passed decrees regulating monastic life, e.g., election of superiors, administration of property, prescriptions on poverty and common life. These had the salutary effect of joining autonomous monasteries into confederations and thus giving the Benedictine way of life a co-ordinated unity that St. Benedict assumed was necessary to grow in sanctity and the love of God.

BENEDICTION OF THE BLESSED SACRAMENT. A Eucharistic devotion in the Catholic Church of the Latin Rite. In its traditional form, a priest, vested in surplice, stole, and cope, places on the altar or in the niche above it the consecrated Host in the ostensorium, or monstrance, and then incenses it. *O Salutaris Hostia* or similar hymn is usually sung at the beginning of exposition, followed by a period of meditation, praise, and adoration by priest and people. At the conclusion of the ceremony the *Tantum Ergo* hymn is chanted, with another incensation, and followed by blessing the peo-ple with the raised monstrance in the form of a cross. During the blessing the priest wears the humeral veil covering his hands. A small bell is rung during the blessing. The Divine Praises are then sung or recited by priest and people, and the Blessed Sacrament is reposed in the tabernacle. Benediction is commonly held on major feasts and Sundays, also during Lent, during a mission, or retreat or during forty hours' devotions. Other days may be designated by individual bishops. Since the Second Vatican Council the Holy See has simplified the traditional ritual, allowing for a variety of options in the prayers, songs, and readings "to direct the attention of the faithful to the worship of Christ the Lord" (*Eucharistiae Sacramentum*, 1973, No. 95).

BENEDICT, RULE OF. The monastic rule of life drawn up by St. Benedict of Nursia. Originally written for the monks of Monte Cassino in the first half of the sixth century, it later became the standard not only for Benedictines but for all Western monasticism. Building on the earlier rules of St. Basil (329–79) and St. Caesarius of Arles (470–542), Benedict mitigated the practice of austerities and concentrated on obedience, self-conquest, the liturgy, and community life. The opening sentences of the rule set the tone for its whole spirit: "Listen, my son, to your master's precepts, and incline the ear of your young heart. Receive willingly and carry out effectively your loving father's advice, that by the labor of obedience you may return to Him from whom you had departed by the sloth of disobedience."

The government provided by the rule is patriarchal, giving final authority to the abbot, who is elected by vote. The monk vows to reside in one place (stability), to be obedient, and to practice monastic virtue. In the monastery the center of life is the *opus Dei*, or "work of God," consisting of prayer, private but especially liturgical in the celebration of Mass and recitation of the Divine Office. Possessions are to be held in common, and in this way the monastery is given the freedom to practice the works of mercy for which the Benedictine tradition has become famous. Manual labor, along with prescribed regularity during the day, was the focus of self-discipline not enjoyed before. It also shifted the institutes of men from a predominantly nonclerical to a growing clerical membership. There are eighteen Benedictine confederations in the world, besides the Camaldolese, Silvestrines, and the Pan-

American federation. Corresponding federations of Benedictine Sisters have been formed. Along with autonomous monasteries, they number over three hundred foundations in the Catholic Church.

BENEDICTUS. The song of thanksgiving of Zechariah at the birth of his son, John the Baptist (Luke 1:68–79). It is addressed to God in gratitude for fulfilling the Messianic promises, and to the child who is to be the forerunner of the Messiah. In the Western Church it is sung or recited liturgically at Lauds or morning prayer.

BENEDICTUS DEUS. Constitution of Pope Benedict XII, issued in 1336, in which he defined the Church's doctrine on death, judgment, heaven, and hell.

BENE ESSE. Well-being, as distinct from *esse* (being). Thus education is not necessary for a person's *esse* (existence) but is necessary for his *bene esse* (beneficial existence).

BENEFICE. A juridical entity erected in perpetuity by competent ecclesiastical authority. It consists of a sacred office and the right to receive the corresponding revenues. The revenues may arise variously from: 1. property movable or immovable owned by the benefice; 2. obligatory contributions made by a family or some moral person; 3. voluntary offerings of the faithful; 4. stole fees paid according to diocesan statute or custom; 5. choir distributions if revenues consist of such distributions. In many countries parishes are regarded as benefices according to ecclesiastical law.

BENEMERENTI AWARD. Pontifical decoration begun by Pope Gregory XVI in 1852 and conferred in recognition of distinguished service in military or civil affairs. The military medal has on one side the image of Gregory XVI and on the other an angel bearing a scroll with the word *benemerenti* (to a well-deserving person) under the papal emblems. The civil medal has *benemerenti* surrounded by a crown of oak leaves engraved on its face side. They are worn on the breast, suspended by ribbons of the papal colors.

BENE PLACITO. By your leave, or consent. Said of actions performed by an inferior with the approval, at least tacit, of his superior. Sometimes applied to the unwarranted approval that papal documents or decrees had to obtain from civil authorities

before the faithful were allowed to carry them into practice.

BENEVOL. *Benevolentia*—benevolence.

BENEVOLENCE. The virtue that disposes a person to promote the welfare of others. As the love of benevolence, it is the charity that seeks what is good for the sake of the one loved, in comparison with the love of concupiscence, whereby good is sought for the benefit of the one who loves. (Etym. Latin *benevolentia*, good-will, benevolence.) See also LOVE.

BENIGNITY. One of the fruits of the Holy Spirit, identified by St. Paul. It corresponds to kindness. (Etym. Latin *bene*, well + *gigni*, to be born: *benignitas*, kindness.)

BENJAMIN. The youngest of Jacob's twelve sons. Of these only Joseph and Benjamin were born of Rachel, Jacob's last and best-loved wife. When the brothers journeyed to Egypt for food during a famine, Joseph's great desire to see Benjamin impelled him to send the brothers back and return with Benjamin (Genesis 42–44). A happy reunion ensued. As time passed, the tribal organization developed and Benjamin's descendants formed the tribe of Benjamin, whose homeland lay west of the Jordan River. They became well known as fierce mountain warriors in defense of freedom (II Samuel 2:9, 15). St. Paul was a descendant of Benjamin's tribe (Romans 11:1–2).

BEN SIRA, BEN SIRACH. See ECCLESIASTICUS.

BEQUEST. Money or other valuables left for some religious purpose after one's death. It is in the nature of a will and normally stipulates that Masses or prayers be offered for the one who made the bequest. In certain countries bequests have been outlawed as contrary to equity.

BERENGARIANISM. The heresy of Berengarius of Tours (999–1088), French theologian who denied transubstantiation while professing some form of real presence of Christ in the Eucharist. He was required to make a profession of faith in the Real Presence by the Council of Rome in 1079. This Eucharistic creed has been frequently quoted by the popes, notably by Pope Paul VI in the encyclical *Mysterium Fidei* (1965).

BERGSONIANISM. Philosophy of Henri Bergson (1859–1941), who conceived spiritual and material vitality as a unity. The phrase *élan vital* synthesizes his doctrine that there is in existence an original, all-pervading life force that has passed from one generation of living beings to the next by way of developed individual organisms. These organisms are the connecting links between successive generations. His evolutionary theories have deeply affected modern Western thought, e.g., in the writings of Teilhard de Chardin (1881–1955).

BERNARDINES. More common name of the Reformed Congregation of St. Bernard (1090–1153) and other small foundations. The term is sometimes inappropriately used of the Cistercians, whose general chapters have consistently forbidden the name "Order of St. Bernard."

BESTIALITY. Having carnal intercourse with an animal. This is the worst of all sins against chastity, no matter how the act is performed.

BETH. The second letter of the Hebrew alphabet, used to mean "house." Numerous towns included the word in their names; e.g., Bethany, Bethanath.

BETHANY. Beyond Mount Olivet, about one mile southeast of where Christ ascended into heaven, on the side of a nearby hill, is the traditional house where Martha and Mary lived with Lazarus, and where Christ raised Lazarus from the dead. In the fourth century a crypt-chapel marked Lazarus' tomb. The original Bethany was destroyed by the Romans under Titus (A.D. 39–81) and never rebuilt. Monasteries, early Christian churches, and fairly modern shrines were built nearby, but today all are in a ruined condition. In 1187 Bethany was claimed by the Moslems, who forbade Christians to enter the tomb, but in 1614 the Franciscans by payment were allowed to open another entrance so Christians could approach the tomb without going through the mosque. (Etym. Greek *bêthania*, Hebrew *bet'aniyyah*, contraction of *bêt chananyah*, house of Ananiyah.)

BETHEL. An ancient Canaanite town, formerly called Luz, located some twelve miles from Jerusalem. It was the place where Jacob had his vision of the ladder, and where the Israelites "consulted God" (Judges 21). The Ark of the Covenant was probably kept there for a time. From the Hebrew *Beth'el*, House of God.

BETHLEHEM. Called Ephrathah to designate it as the birthplace of King David, it is one of the oldest towns in Palestine, twelve

miles southeast of Jerusalem. In the center of the village, with its thirty thousand persons, is the Church of the Nativity, whose sanctuary is directly above the traditional cave where Christ was born. Two stairways lead to it from the basilica. The large cathedral doors have been blocked to prevent Moslem desecration. Built by Constantine in A.D. 330, the Church of the Nativity is one of the oldest Byzantine structures and one of the earliest Christian churches. In the underground cave in a large niche is the altar of the Nativity. Underneath the altar table is the silver star in the marble floor whose center opening reveals the original stone floor of the cave below. Around the opening are the words "Here Jesus Christ was born of the Virgin Mary." Fifty-three lamps burn there day and night. In this grotto the Christmas Mass is celebrated every day, the faithful kneeling on the marble floor. (Etym. Hebrew *beth lechem*, house of bread or house of [the god] Lahm.)

BETROTHAL. An agreement by promise to marry. Unless written and dated, signed by both parties and by the pastor or by two witnesses, such promise, even though formally made, was not an impediment to marriage with another party. (Etym. English *troth*, a variant of truth.) See ESPOUSALS.

BETTING. An agreement in which two or more people contract to give a prize to whichever one correctly guesses some future fact or event. Betting is morally permissible by Catholic standards, but only on certain conditions. All parties to the contract must clearly understand the conditions of agreement in the same way, they must be sincerely uncertain about the outcome of what is to take place; they honestly want to pay (and can do so) in case they lose the bet; and the bet cannot be an encouragement to do something evil or sinful.

B.F. *Bona fide*—In good faith.

BIBLE. The collection of books accepted by Christian churches as the authentic, inspired record of the revelations made to mankind by God about himself and his will for men. It is divided into the Old Testament and the New Testament to distinguish between the Jewish tradition and the Christian. In the New Testament, the Old is generally spoken of as "the Scriptures" or "the sacred writings" (Matthew 21:42). Gradually the word has been used in the singular and "Scripture" has become a synonym for the Bible (Acts 8:32). "Testament" has the meaning of "covenant" with reference to the two covenants God established with his people in each period of human history.

BOOKS OF THE BIBLE
Texts, Translation, and Authenticity

The Catholic Church has more than once taught what books are to be regarded as inspired and therefore belong to the Bible. At the Council of Trent, in 1546, the biblical canon was solemnly defined and the Vulgate declared to be authentic:

"The council follows the example of the orthodox Fathers and with the same sense of devotion and reverence with which it accepts and venerates all the books both of the Old and the New Testament, since one God is the author of both, it also accepts and venerates traditions concerned with faith and morals as having been received orally from Christ or inspired by the Holy Spirit and continuously preserved in the Catholic Church. It judged, however, that a list of the Sacred Books should be written into this decree so that no one may doubt which books the council accepts. The list is here given.

"The Old Testament: five books of Moses, that is, Genesis, Exodus, Leviticus, Numbers, Deuteronomy; Joshua, Judges, Ruth, four books of Kings, two of Paralipomenon; the first book of Esdras and the second, which is called Nehemias; Tobias, Judith, Esther, Job, David's Psalter of one hundred and fifty psalms, Proverbs, Ecclesiastes, the Canticle of Canticles, Wisdom, Ecclesiasticus, Isaias, Jeremias with Baruch, Ezechiel, Daniel; the twelve minor prophets, that is Osee, Joel, Amos, Abdias, Jonas, Micheas, Nahum, Habacuc, Sophonias, Aggeus, Zacharias, Malachias; two books of Machabees, the first and the second.

"The New Testament: the four Gospels, according to Matthew, Mark, Luke, and John; the Acts of the Apostles, written by the Evangelist Luke; fourteen epistles of the Apostle Paul: to the Romans, two to the Corinthians, to the Galatians, to the Ephesians, to the Philippians, to the Colossians, two to the Thessalonians, two to Timothy, to Titus, to Philemon, to the Hebrews; two epistles of the Apostle Peter, three of the Apostle John, one of the Apostle James, one of the Apostle Jude; and the Apocalypse of the Apostle John. Moreover, if anyone does not accept these books as sacred and canonical in their entirety, with all their parts, according to the text usually read in the Cath-

olic Church and as they are in the ancient Latin Vulgate, but knowingly and willfully contemns the traditions previously mentioned: let him be anathema.

"Moreover, since the same sacred council has thought that it would be very useful for the Church of God if it were known which one of all the Latin editions that are in circulation is the authentic edition, it determines and decrees that the ancient Vulgate, which has been approved in the Church by the use of many centuries, should be considered the authentic edition in public readings, disputations, preaching, and explanations; and that no one should presume or dare to reject it under any pretext whatever" (Denzinger 1501–6).

Almost four centuries later (1943), Pope Pius XII in the encyclical *Divino Afflante Spiritu,* reconfirmed the biblical canon and the authenticity of the Vulgate. But he made some important declarations that gave the primary impetus to the publication of totally new editions of the Bible. They are new because they are based on Hebrew and Greek manuscripts beyond the Vulgate, and because new translations into the vernacular were made from the original languages and not merely from the Latin Vulgate.

According to Pius XII, "the Vulgate, as the Church has understood and does now understand, is free from all error in matters of faith and morals. Consequently, as the Church herself testifies, it can be safely quoted, without the least fear of erring, in disputations, public readings, and sermons. Its *authenticity* should not be called *critical,* but *juridical.* The authority the Vulgate enjoys in doctrinal matters does not by any means proscribe—and in modern times it fairly demands—that this same doctrine be corroborated by the original texts. Nor does it mean that the original texts cannot be continually used to help clarify and explain more and more the proper meaning of Sacred Scripture. Nor does the decree of the Council of Trent forbid that translations be made into the vernacular so that the faithful may use them and profit by them and understand more readily the meaning of the divine message. These translations may be made from the original texts" (Denzinger 3825).

A standard listing of the books of the Bible, according to the directives of Pope Pius XII, shows a number of variants in the titles of the books, their division and sequence, as follows:

BOOKS OF THE BIBLE IN BIBLICAL ORDER

Old Testament

Genesis	Gn
Exodus	Ex
Leviticus	Lv
Numbers	Nb
Deuteronomy	Dt
Joshua	Jos
Judges	Jg
Ruth	Rt
1 Samuel	1 S
2 Samuel	2 S
1 Kings	1 K
2 Kings	2 K
1 Chronicles	1 Ch
2 Chronicles	2 Ch
Ezra	Ezr
Nehemiah	Ne
Tobit	Tb
Judith	Jdt
Esther	Est
1 Maccabees	1 M
2 Maccabees	2 M
Job	Jb
Psalms	Ps
Proverbs	Pr
Ecclesiastes	Qo
Song of Songs	Sg
Wisdom	Ws
Ecclesiasticus	Si
Isaiah	Is
Jeremiah	Jr
Lamentations	Lm
Baruch	Ba
Ezekiel	Ezk
Daniel	Dn
Hosea	Ho
Joel	Jl
Amos	Am
Obadiah	Ob
Jonah	Jon
Micah	Mi
Nahum	Na
Habakkuk	Hab
Zephaniah	Zp
Haggai	Hg
Zechariah	Zc
Malachi	Ml

New Testament

Matthew	Mt
Mark	Mk
Luke	Lk
John	Jn
Acts	Ac
Romans	Rm
1 Corinthians	1 Co
2 Corinthians	2 Co
Galatians	Ga
Ephesians	Ep
Philippians	Ph
Colossians	Col
1 Thessalonians	1 Th
2 Thessalonians	2 Th
1 Timothy	1 Tm
2 Timothy	2 Tm
Titus	Tt
Philemon	Phm
Hebrews	Heb
James	Jm
1 Peter	1 P
2 Peter	2 P
1 John	1 Jn
2 John	2 Jn
3 John	3 Jn
Jude	Jude
Revelation	Rv

BOOKS OF THE BIBLE IN ALPHABETICAL ORDER

Old Testament

Amos	Am
Baruch	Ba
1 Chronicles	1 Ch
2 Chronicles	2 Ch
Daniel	Dn
Deuteronomy	Dt
Ecclesiastes	Qo
Ecclesiasticus	Si
Esther	Est
Exodus	Ex
Ezekiel	Ezk
Ezra	Ezr
Genesis	Gn
Habakkuk	Hab
Haggai	Hg
Hosea	Ho
Isaiah	Is
Jeremiah	Jr
Job	Jb
Joel	Jl
Jonah	Jon
Joshua	Jos
Judges	Jg
Judith	Jdt
1 Kings	1 K
2 Kings	2 K
Lamentations	Lm
Leviticus	Lv
1 Maccabees	1 M
2 Maccabees	2 M
Malachi	Ml
Micah	Mi
Nahum	Na
Nehemiah	Ne
Numbers	Nb
Obadiah	Ob
Proverbs	Pr
Psalms	Ps
Ruth	Rt
1 Samuel	1 S

2 Samuel	2 S
Song of Songs	Sg
Tobit	Tb
Wisdom	Ws
Zechariah	Zc
Zephaniah	Zp

New Testament

Acts	Ac
Colossians	Col
1 Corinthians	1 Co
2 Corinthians	2 Co
Ephesians	Ep
Galatians	Ga
Hebrews	Heb
James	Jm
John	Jn
1 John	1 Jn
2 John	2 Jn
3 John	3 Jn
Jude	Jude
Luke	Lk
Mark	Mk
Matthew	Mt
1 Peter	1 P
2 Peter	2 P
Philemon	Phm
Philippians	Ph
Revelation	Rv
Romans	Rm
1 Thessalonians	1 Th
2 Thessalonians	2 Th
1 Timothy	1 Tm
2 Timothy	2 Tm
Titus	Tt

The books of the Bible in alphabetical order of abbreviations

Ac	Acts
Am	Amos
Ba	Baruch
1 Ch	1 Chronicles
2 Ch	2 Chronicles
1 Co	1 Corinthians
2 Co	2 Corinthians
Col	Colossians
Dn	Daniel
Dt	Deuteronomy
Ep	Ephesians
Est	Esther
Ex	Exodus
Ezk	Ezekiel
Ezr	Ezra
Ga	Galatians
Gn	Genesis
Hab	Habakkuk
Heb	Hebrews
Hg	Haggai
Ho	Hosea
Is	Isaiah
Jb	Job
Jdt	Judith
Jg	Judges
Jl	Joel
Jm	James
Jn	John
1 Jn	1 John
2 Jn	2 John
3 Jn	3 John
Jon	Jonah
Jos	Joshua
Jr	Jeremiah
Jude	Jude
1 K	1 Kings
2 K	2 Kings
Lk	Luke
Lm	Lamentations
Lv	Leviticus
1 M	1 Maccabees
2 M	2 Maccabees
Mi	Micah
Mk	Mark
Ml	Malachi
Mt	Matthew
Na	Nahum
Nb	Numbers
Ne	Nehemiah
Ob	Obadiah
1 P	1 Peter
2 P	2 Peter
Ph	Philippians
Phm	Philemon
Pr	Proverbs
Ps	Psalms
Qo	Ecclesiastes
Rm	Romans
Rt	Ruth
Rv	Revelation
1 S	1 Samuel
2 S	2 Samuel
Sg	Song of Songs
Si	Ecclesiasticus
Tb	Tobit
1 Th	1 Thessalonians
2 Th	2 Thessalonians
1 Tm	1 Timothy
2 Tm	2 Timothy
Tt	Titus
Ws	Wisdom
Zc	Zechariah
Zp	Zephaniah

BIBLICAL ARCHAEOLOGY. The science of biblical origins, based on the study of documents, monuments, and the result of extensive excavations in Bible lands.

BIBLICAL COMMISSION. Established in 1902 by Pope Leo XIII to promote biblical studies and guard against doctrinal error. In 1904, Pope St. Pius X gave the commission the right to grant academic degrees (licentiate and doctorate) in biblical studies. In

1924 and 1931, Pope Pius XI made these pontifical degrees equal to those conferred by the pontifical universities. Pope Pius XII, in 1942, permitted the division of the matter required for the licentiate, allowing a bachelor's degree to be given after the first examination. In 1971, Pope Paul VI completely reorganized the Biblical Commission and joined it with the Congregation for the Doctrine of the Faith, whose prefect is ex officio also president of the commission.

BIBLICAL THEOLOGY. Systematic exposition of the teachings of the Bible. There are two principal forms of biblical theology. One stresses subordination to Christian dogmatics. It works through the material furnished by exegesis, correlates ideas with facts, synthesizes them on the basis of an organic principle consistent with their nature and respective value, and places them into the stream of the history of revelation.

The other form of biblical theology sees the development of exegesis into theology as the work of reason enlightened by faith. Its purpose is to enter, through grace, into more intimate contact with transcendent reality as revealed in the sacred text. In this sense biblical theology is an ideal that always tends toward a goal without stopping at the results already achieved.

The two forms of biblical theology, as auxiliary to dogma and as instrument to religious insight, are not incompatible. They are mutually conducive to heighten the value of both Scripture and dogma, by integrating two areas of religious knowledge which derive from a common, divine source.

BIBLICISM. Extreme preoccupation with the Bible. In practice, it means identifying divine revelation with the Bible to the exclusion of sacred tradition as a source of revealed truth.

BIBLIOMANCY. Divination practiced by a random passage from the Bible or other book, being given credence as a portent of future events.

BIDDING PRAYER. A list of intercessions, usually in litany form, that was read at Mass after the Gospel in pre-Reformation times. Going back to the early Church, by the ninth century the priest prayed for all conditions of persons and commemorated the faithful departed after the sermon on Sundays and feast days. In England the custom was called "bidding the beads." Such biddings formed part of the popular devotions, instructions, and notices attached to the sermon. Taken together, the practice was known in France as the *prône*. At first left to the discretion of the faithful, the bidding prayer later assumed fixed forms.

BIGAMY. Contracting a marriage while a former one remains undissolved. An older use of the term calls bigamy any valid marriage after the death of a first spouse. (Etym. Latin *bi*, double + Greek *gamos*, marriage: Latin *bigamia*.)

BIGOTRY. Obstinately adhering, through ignorance, to a social, political, or religious belief, opinion, or practice while being intolerant of the contrary views or actions of others. (Etym. French *bigot*, hypocrite, superstitious fellow.)

BILOCATION. Multiple or simultaneous presence of the same substance or soul in two places distant from each other. Bilocations have been frequently reported in the lives of the saints. (Etym. Latin *bi*, double + *locus*, location, space, place.)

BINATION. The offering of Mass twice on the same day by the same celebrant. It is permitted whenever the needs of the faithful call for the celebration of a second Mass or when a priest concelebrates on some special occasion.

BIOCIDE. Destruction of life as the result of an unreasoning drive to kill. Sometimes put forth as an explanation of the massive destruction of human life in modern times, whether by war, legalized abortion, or euthanasia. (Etym. Greek *bios*, life + Latin *-cidium*, a killing.)

BIOETHICS. The study of ethical questions arising from the development of the biological sciences. This study may be of two kinds, either resolving problems created by the rapid growth of the life sciences, or analyzing the prospects of new developments in ethical practice consistent with the Christian principles of morality. Examples of the first are genetic engineering and artificial insemination; examples of the second are organ transplantation and natural family planning. (Etym. Greek *bios*, life + *ēthos*, custom, moral nature.)

BIOGENESIS. The theory that all life has its source only in pre-existing life. Organisms, even the minutest, arise from similar organisms, never from inorganic matter. It is reasonable to affirm, and experience offers proof that "what is without life cannot generate life." Life in its origin is due to God's creative act. Opposing this theory is abiogenesis, which is without scientific basis. (Etym. Greek *bios*, life + *genesis*, origin, source.)

BIORHYTHM. The scientifically determined cycle of changes in a person, depending on his or her temperament and physical condition. The cycle basically occurs in the functions of the organs and organism, but the changes also affect a person's emotions, following various rhythms in both men and women each month. Biorhythm has considerable implications in the moral order, as a mechanism that influences one's feelings and indirectly the degree of imputability in human actions.

BIRETTA. A stiff square cap with three or four ridges on its upper side, worn by clerics when entering and leaving the sanctuary at Divine Service. The cleric's rank is indicated by the color of the biretta. It is usually black for a priest, red for a cardinal, purple for a bishop, while some monastic canons and abbots wear white.

BIRITUALISM. The temporary or permanent privilege of a priest to celebrate the liturgy and administer the sacraments in more than one rite, normally the Latin and one of the Eastern rites.

BIRTH CONTROL. A synonym for contraception, introduced into the vocabulary by professed contraceptionists in order to equate control of population by preventing conception through artificial means.

BIRTHDAY. The liturgical custom since ancient times of celebrating the death of a saint as his or her birthday in eternal life. The two exceptions are the nativity of the Blessed Virgin (September 8) and of John the Baptist (June 24).

BISHOP. A successor of the Apostles who has received the fullness of Christ's priesthood. His most distinctive power, that of ordaining priests and other bishops, belongs uniquely to a bishop. Moreover, in spite of some disputed cases in history, it is highly probable that a priest would not be authorized by the Holy See to ordain another priest. A priest certainly cannot consecrate a bishop.

In the ordination of a bishop the "matter" is the imposition of hands on the head of the bishop-elect by the consecrating bishops, or at least by the principal consecrator, which is done in silence before the consecratory prayer; the "form" consists of the words of the consecratory prayer, of which the following pertains to the essence of the order, and therefore are required for the validity of the act: "Now pour out upon this chosen one that power which flows from you, the perfect Spirit whom He gave to the apostles, who established the Church in every place as the santuary where your name would always be praised and glorified." (Etym. Greek *episkopos*, a bishop, literally, overseer.)

BLACK. A liturgical color symbolizing mourning. It was formerly used at all requiem Masses and at services on Good Friday to express grief at the death of the Savior. At the offices of the dead it is an expression of sorrow and sympathy. It is never permissible to use a black veil before the tabernacle or in the exposed presence of the Blessed Sacrament.

BLACK FAST. Abstinence from all flesh meat, with only eggs, butter, cheese, or milk allowed at the evening meal. Formerly a diet limited to bread, salt, vegetables, and water constituted a black fast during Lent.

BLACK MADONNA, THE. See OROPA.

BLACK MAGIC (animism). Invoking the lesser spirits in order to injure someone.

BLACK SCAPULAR. See SCAPULAR.

BLASPHEMOUS. Ecclesiastically censorious of a professed opinion that is not only erroneous but contemptuous of God or of holy things.

BLASPHEMY. Speaking against God in a contemptuous, scornful, or abusive manner. Included under blasphemy are offenses committed by thought, word, or action. Serious contemptuous ridicule of the saints, sacred objects, or of persons consecrated to God is also blasphemous because God is indirectly attacked. Blasphemy is a grave violation of charity toward God. Its gravity may be judged by the capital punishment in the Old Testament, severe penalties of the Church, and in many cases also of the State for blasphemous speech or conduct. In order for a person to sin gravely in this manner, he must use blasphemous expressions and realize the contemptuous meaning of what he says or does. (Etym. Latin *blasphemia*, blasphemy; from Greek *blasphēmein*, to speak ill of.)

BLESSED. In general, a person, place, or object associated with God and implying a divine favor: 1. a sacramental as a blessed article; 2. a deceased person who has been beatified by an official declaration of the Church; 3. believers in Christ who respond to his beatitudes; 4. all Christians insofar as they receive the grace of God; 5. all who are in heaven. (Etym. Anglo-Saxon *blētsian,* to consecrate by blood.)

BLESSED BREAD. Common bread presented at the Offertory of the Mass to be blessed by the priest and distributed to those present as a token of union and love. It was frequently carried home; some, however, consumed it at church. The French called it *pain bénit,* and the custom still exists in some parts of the Western church.

BLESSED SACRAMENT. The Eucharist as one of the seven sacraments instituted by Christ to be received by the faithful. Unlike the other sacraments, however, the Eucharist is not only a sacrament to be received but also a sacrament to be adored before, during, and after reception. It is therefore a permanent sacrament, since Christ remains in the Eucharist as long as the physical properties of the species of bread and wine remain essentially unchanged.

BLESSED TRINITY, SCAPULAR. A white scapular with a red and blue cross. It is the badge of the Confraternity of the Most Blessed Trinity, said to have originated in a vision given to Pope Innocent III in 1198, when an angel in this garb told him to approve the Trinitarian Order for the redemption of captives among the Moslems.

BLESSED VIRGIN MARY. Mother of Jesus Christ and greatest of the Christian saints. The title "Mary" occurs only once in the Old Testament as the name of Moses' sister (Exodus 15:20). Its etymology has been variously traced to mean beautiful, bitter, rebellion, illuminatrix, lady, and beloved of God. Scholars prefer the last meaning, derived from the Egyptian, which may be explained by the four hundred years' sojourn of the Israelites in Egypt.

The Gospel account of Mary's life begins with the appearance of the archangel Gabriel in Nazareth to announce the choice of her as mother of the Messiah. Though espoused to Joseph, she intended to remain a virgin and asked for an explanation. The angel assured her that this would be done by the power of the Most High, at which Mary gave her consent: "Be it done to me according to your word."

On her visit to Elizabeth, Mary sang the *Magnificat,* "My soul magnifies the Lord," which recalls the canticle of Anna, mother of Samuel the prophet (I Kings 2:1–10). When she returned to Nazareth, Joseph realized that Mary was pregnant and thought of putting her away privately until an angel appeared to him and revealed the mystery.

In obedience to a census decree of Augustus, Mary and Joseph, who were both of Davidic descent, went to David's city of Bethlehem, where Jesus was born in a stable. Forty days later Mary, in the company of Joseph, came to the temple in Jerusalem to be purified according to the law of Moses, and to offer her son to the Lord together with a sacrifice of a pair of turtledoves or two young pigeons. At this presentation, the old man Simeon took Jesus in his arms and foretold Mary's share in the future sufferings of her son.

During the hidden life of Christ, the Gospels are silent about Mary except for one dramatic incident when Jesus was twelve years old. Finding him in the temple in the midst of the doctors, his mother asked him why he had done this. In their first recorded dialogue, Jesus replied that he must be about his Father's business.

Mary was with Christ at the beginning of his public life, when through her intercession he changed water into wine at the marriage feast in Cana of Galilee. She was in his company at Capharnaum for a short time, and on occasion followed him in his ministry.

She stood beneath the cross on Calvary and was placed in the care of the Apostle John, being told, "Behold your son." After the Ascension of Christ into heaven, Mary waited in Jerusalem with the Apostles and disciples for the coming of the Holy Spirit. From then on there are no further biographical data about Mary in the New Testament, except for the mystical references to the "woman" in St. John's Apocalypse, and St. Paul's description to the Galatians of Christ as "made of a woman."

According to tradition, Mary lived for a time in or near Ephesus, but her permanent home after Pentecost seems to have been Jerusalem. There is no certain place or date for Mary's death, although Ephesus and twelve years after Christ's Ascension appear the most likely.

BLESSING. As found in Scripture, it means praise, the desire that good fortune go with a person or thing, dedication of a person or thing to God's service and a gift. In liturgical language a blessing is a ritual ceremony by which an authorized cleric in major orders sanctifies persons or things to divine service, or invokes divine favor on what he blesses. The Church's ritual provides for over two hundred such blessings, some of which are reserved to bishops or members of certain religious institutes.

BLISS. Intense gladness, external beatitude, perfect joy, and the happiness of heaven. (Etym. Anglo-Saxon *bliss,* akin to Anglo-Saxon *blīthe,* blithe.)

BLONDELIANISM. The "spiritual" philosophy of Maurice Blondel (1861–1949). He concentrated on analyzing the meaning of human action. Ideally every human act should include an awareness of its purpose, which is to be related to God. Human acts are more perfect as a person is conscious of why he is acting. Blondelianism has especially influenced the progressive school of Neo-Thomism.

BLOOD OF ST. JANUARIUS. A famous relic in the Cathedral of Naples. The blood of this martyr (d. about 305), preserved in a glass phial, liquifies some eighteen times each year when the reliquary is exposed and placed near the saint's head. No natural explanation has been found for the phenomenon.

BLUE. A color no longer considered liturgical but used in certain religious services at certain times. It indicates constancy, fidelity, genuineness, and aspiration. It is the color specially associated with the Blessed Virgin. A special papal indult allowed some dioceses to use blue vestments instead of white on the feast of the Immaculate Conception. Mexico and Lourdes in France enjoy this privilege. Many white vestments today are ornamented in blue for use on feast days of Our Lady.

BLUE ARMY. An organization founded in 1946 to pray and sacrifice for the conversion of Russia and for world peace. The society is a response to one of the requests made by Our Lady at Fátima, Portugal, in 1917, recommending the recitation of the rosary and urging mortification for the conversion of sinners. The Blue Army was established after Pope Pius XII in 1942 consecrated the world to the Immaculate Heart of Mary.

BLUE LAWS. Very strict legal prohibitions affecting moral conduct that originated with the Puritan adherents in England. The term "blue" was probably associated with constant and faithful persons who were considered "true blue."

BLUE SCAPULAR. See SCAPULAR.

BOAT. A boat-shaped vessel that holds incense before it is put into a censer or thurible.

BOAZ. A rich, influential Bethlehemite with a kindly interest in his workers and a strong sense of family responsibility. Ruth, widow of Mahlon, came to work in his fields and Boaz was attracted to her. They married and she bore him a son (Ruth 2, 3, 4), Obed, who was destined to be the father of Jesse and the ancestor of Jesus (Matthew 1:5–6).

BODILY IMMORTALITY. The immunity from disease and bodily death that was enjoyed by Adam and Eve before the Fall. It was a special privilege that was to have been passed on to their descendants. Since man is naturally mortal in body, this privilege was preternatural. It conferred the capacity not to die. Its purpose was to enable mankind to better use the gift of sanctifying grace in serving God.

BODILY RESURRECTION. The reunion of the soul of each human being with his own body on the last day. Christ taught the resurrection from the dead (Matthew 22:29–32; Luke 14:14; John 5:29, 6:39–40, 11:25), and the Apostles preached the doctrine as a cardinal mystery of the Christian faith (I Corinthians 15:20; Revelation 20:12). Belief in the resurrection is professed in all the ancient creeds. "The human beings that rise again are the identical persons who lived before, though their vital processes are performed in a different way. Now their life is mortal, then it will be immortal. . . . [But] they still are of the same kind and are still the same individuals as before . . . They do not assume a heavenly or ghostly kind of body. Their bodies remain truly human, though they are invested with an immortality coming from a divine strength which enables them so to dominate the body that corruption cannot enter" (St. Thomas, *Compendium Theologiae,* 155).

BODMER CODEX. A manuscript in Greek of St. John's Gospel, written in Egypt before A.D. 200, consisting of 154 pages. It is almost perfectly preserved for the first fourteen chapters of John, with the other chapters in fragmentary state. Together with the Beatty papyri, the Bodmer Codex confirms the existing text of the New Testament beyond anything comparable in any other subject or field of similar antiquity. It is the oldest, extensive manuscript of a portion of the New Testament. Published in 1956, it is named after its original owner, M. Bodmer, of Geneva, Switzerland.

BODY. The organized material part of man that is animated by his rational soul. According to the teaching of the Council of Vienne, the rational, intellectual soul is truly and by its own nature the form of the human body (Denzinger 902). Body and soul, therefore, are united into one substance and nature.

BODY OF THE CHURCH. The visible, organized commonwealth of the faithful. As the Holy Spirit is the soul of the Church, so her human members on earth are the body. One of the corollaries of this fact is that anyone who culpably remains outside the body of the Church cannot participate in the life of grace that comes to the Church from the Holy Spirit.

BOGOMILES. A dualist, heretical sect and branch of the Catharists. Originally they taught in Bulgaria, in the first half of the tenth century, but in time their influence spread through Asia Minor and the Balkans. Eventually they merged with Islam. They believed in a superior God, the Father, whose son Satanaël revolted and was driven from heaven. Satanaël created the world and Adam, but since the Father gave Adam his soul, man belongs to God as well as Satan. The latter seduced Eve and was punished by being deprived of creative power, yet entrusted with the government of the world. As man fell more and more under Satan's power, God sent his second son, Jesus, under the appearance of a man. After conquering Satan, Jesus returned to heaven and left on earth his creatures, and the Holy Spirit to carry on his work among the Bogomiles, the only true Christians, who are changed into ethereal bodies at death. Besides rejecting most of the Old Testament, they also opposed infant baptism, baptism of water, marriage, the Real Presence, and all images and prayers except the Our Father.

BOLLANDISTS. The Belgian Jesuit scholars who compile the *Acta Sanctorum.* They are named after John van Bolland, the work's first editor (1596–1665). The idea of a critical publication of the lives of the saints was conceived by Heribert Rosweyde (1569–1629), who died before any of the research was published.

BOLSHEVISM. A term derived from the Russian *bolshinstvo* (majority) and originally used to designate the radical left among the Communists. The professed aim of Bolshevism is the overthrow of existing governments and the substitution of Communism under the dictatorship of the proletariat. It has been several times condemned by name in papal documents. Pope Pius XI declared, "We have exposed the errors and the violent deceptive tactics of Bolshevistic and atheistic Communism" (encyclical *Divini Redemptoris,* III, 25).

BONA FIDE. In good faith, said of actions that may have been objectively mistaken or wrong but were done with good intentions and without culpability; also used to describe the genuine or authentic.

BONARIA, OUR LADY OF. A shrine at Cagliari, Sardinia, dedicated to the Queen of All Sailors. According to tradition, Cagliari had been a malaria-infested region. An old monk foretold that the name of the city would be changed to Bon-aria instead of "bad-air," the designation it then had. The prophecy was fulfilled on March 25, 1370, when a ship laden with merchandise ran ashore in a hurricane. Its jettisoned cargo included a heavy chest now preserved in the cathedral sanctuary. When the chest touched the sea, the storm abated; though heavy, it did not sink but drifted ashore near the church, where the priests found that it contained a beautiful figure of Our Lady carrying the Infant. The Child holds a ball in his left hand and reaches out to grasp a candle standing on a ship model held by his mother. It accurately records the wind's direction though it is in a draftless room. Our Lady of Bonaria was proclaimed patroness of Sardinia by Pope Pius X, and the unfinished church was later raised to the rank of minor basilica by Pius XI. On April 24, 1970, Pope Paul VI visited this famous shrine and celebrated an open-air Mass addressing the pilgrims on the need of veneration of the Mother of God.

BOND. The marriage bond, especially the irrevocable union in a sacramental marriage that no human authority may dissolve. (Etym. Middle-English *bond, band,* something that constricts.)

BOOK. A symbol of teaching, learning, and writing. Variously inscribed with words, the book is carried by many saints to indicate their spiritual erudition. Matthew, Mark, Luke, and John in the earlier centuries were represented carrying scrolls and books; in fact these were their first emblems. The open book represents doctrinal teaching, and St. Paul is often shown with such a book or scroll. So, too, is St. Cyril of Jerusalem, St. Brigit of Sweden, St. Ignatius Loyola, and St. Teresa of Avila for obvious reasons as founders of religious orders and teachers of the word of God. St. Anthony of Padua and St. Boniface together with Venerable Bede have the book as one of their main symbols.

BOOK OF COMMON PRAYER. See ANGLICAN COMMUNION.

BOOK OF KELLS. An ornamented manuscript of the Latin Gospels, found in the ancient monastery of Kells in Ireland. It was probably written during the eighth century. It is presently treasured in the library of Trinity College in Dublin. It is regarded as one of the finest examples of Celtic illumination.

BOOK OF LIFE. Figurative expression in the Bible (Revelation 21) for predestination. It signifies God's foreknowledge of the elect. God in virtue of his omniscience must infallibly and eternally know the elect and the lost, but this does not imply that the fate of either is sealed by God without a prevision of each person's merit. The Book of Life refers to those who will enjoy eternal happiness.

BORN AGAIN. Spiritual rebirth at baptism, as commanded by Christ: "Unless a man be born again of water and the Spirit, he cannot enter the Kingdom of God" (John 3:5). The term is used in Catholic theology to describe the spiritual change worked by divine grace, by which a person, from having been conceived and born in sin, is regenerated into a new creature, a child of God and heir of heaven. It is synonymous with supernatural regeneration. In some Protestant circles the expression refers to a new experiential knowledge in Christ, wrought by baptism or by a sudden and lasting conversion from sin to a fervent service of God.

BORROW. To receive something from a person on loan, with the understanding that it is returned to the owner. On Catholic moral principles the one who borrows assumes three main duties: proper care of the commodity loaned; keeping within the terms of the contract or even unspoken agreement; restoration of what was borrowed to the owner within a reasonable time or at the end of the term agreed upon.

BOYCOTT. Concerted refusal for just reasons to patronize a certain business establishment and persuading others to join in this refusal. On Catholic principles a boycott is morally justifiable for the same reasons and on the same conditions as a strike.

B.P. *Beatissime Pater*—Most Holy Father.

BP. Bishop.

BRAIN DEATH. A form of medical evidence of bodily death, when the death of the cerebral cortex is shown by flat tracings on an electroencephalograph. Sometimes called cerebral death or irreversible coma, it is useful as a scientific confirmation of death. The further question of how long a flat electroencephalogram must last to be sure of death is still debated, although five hours has been recommended in the case of organ transplants. On moral grounds, other proven criteria must also be used to establish clinical death.

BRANCH THEORY. The position held by some Anglo-Catholics that the one true Church of Christ is made up of three separate churches, the Anglican, Roman Catholic, and Eastern Orthodox. It assumes that episcopal and priestly orders, validly transmitted, are found only in these three churches. While admitting that these bodies differ widely in many ways, the branch theory holds that they are united in essentials. They are outgrowths, it is said, from a single ecclesiastical trunk, the original Church founded by Christ.

BREAD (liturgical use). 1. An element in the Eucharistic sacrifice of the Christian liturgy. It is made of wheaten flour, either unleavened, as in the Latin Rite, or leavened, in the other rites of the Catholic Church; 2. a symbol of union, when two loaves are presented to the celebrant at the Offertory of the Mass, while celebrating the canonization of a saint or the consecration of a bishop, or when bread blessed at the Offertory is distributed to the people for consumption at home; 3. a symbol of sacrifice when bread brought by the faithful is blessed at the Sunday parochial Mass.

BREAD (symbolic). Represents the Eucharist, especially the broken loaf reminiscent of the Disciples at Emmaus, who on Easter Sunday recognized Christ in "the breaking of the bread" (Luke 24:30). Often referred to as the staff of life, bread is the emblem of several saints noted for their feeding of the poor, e.g., St. Roch (1295–1378), the mendicant friar, and St. Geneviève (422–500), patroness of Paris, St. Elizabeth of Hungary (1207–31), whose hidden loaves were changed into roses when her benevolence needed secrecy. St. Anthony of Padua's (1195–1231) gifts were universally referred to as "St. Anthony's Bréad," soon transferred into food for the hungry.

BREAKING OF THE HOST. The liturgical breaking of the consecrated host at Mass. Its purpose is first practical, to facilitate consuming by the priest. It is also a symbol that through the body of Christ the faithful become one with him and with one another.

BREASTPLATE OF ST. PATRICK. An ancient Irish hymn attributed to St. Patrick (389–461); certainly the *Canticum Scoticum*, mentioned in the Book of Armagh as current before the ninth century. The original text survives in three ancient manuscripts. It was first published in English translation in 1839. A familiar version reads: "I bind to myself today the virtue of obedience of the angels, in the hope of the resurrection unto reward; in the preachings of the apostles, in the faith of confessors, in the purity of holy virgins, in the deeds of righteous men.

"I bind to myself today God's power to guide me, God's might to uphold me, God's wisdom to teach me, God's eye to watch over me, God's ear to hear me, God's word to give me speech, God's hand to guide me, God's shield to shelter me against the seductions of sin.

"I invoke today all these virtues against every hostile power which may assail my body and soul, against the cries of false prophets, against the black laws of heathenism, against the deceits of idolatry, against every knowledge that binds the soul of man.

"Christ, protect me today against an untimely death that I may receive abundant reward. Christ with me. Christ before me. Christ behind me. Christ within me. Christ with the soldier. Christ with the traveler. Christ in the heart of everyone who thinks of me. Christ in every eye that sees me. Christ in every ear that hears me. Praise to the Lord of my salvation. Salvation in Christ the Lord."

BREECHES BIBLE. See GENEVA BIBLE.

BREVIARY. The liturgical book containing the Divine Office of the Roman Catholic Church. Formerly the various "hours" of the office were in different books, e.g., the Psaltery, the Hymnary, and the Lectionary. But from the eleventh century they began to be combined in one book. The complete text of the Liturgy of the Hours is published in four consecutive volumes. These volumes are divided according to the following calendar year: Advent and Christmas season, Lent and Easter season, the first through the seventeenth, and the eighteenth through the thirty-fourth weeks of the year. (Etym. Latin *breviarium*, a summary, abridgment.) See also DIVINE OFFICE.

BRIBERY. The payment or promise to pay something of value to induce another to do as one wishes or prescribes. It generally refers to those pledged to the common good who act for individual profit or for the briber's benefit. The Catholic Church teaches that bribery in any form is immoral. The guilt is equally divided among all active agents, and their culpability varies with circumstances. (Etym. Middle-English *bribe;* Old French *bribe,* a piece of bread given to a beggar.)

BRIDE OF CHRIST. See SPOUSE OF CHRIST.

BRIEF. A concise papal letter prepared by the Secretary of State (formerly by the Secretary for Briefs) and stamped with an impression of the papal ring. It is a less formal document and lacks the solemnity of a bull.

BRIGITTINES. The order founded by St. Brigit of Sweden (1303–73) in 1334 and officially known as the Order of the Most Holy Savior. Based on the Rule of St. Augustine, its membership was first organized in double communities of men and women, living separately but using the same chapel. This arrangement was given up in the sixteenth century. There are also Brigittines of the Recollection, but the nuns' form of this group has disappeared.

BRO. Brother.

BROAD INTERPRETATION. See INTERPRETATION.

BROAD MENTAL RESERVATION. Speech that limits the meaning of what is said but contains a reasonable clue to the sense intended. No lie is involved, because what is said really has two meanings. The two meanings are present either by reason of the words themselves or by reason of the circumstances. One who employs a broad mental reservation expresses what he thinks and uses words according to the meaning they really have. His words have another meaning also, and the speaker foresees that in this other meaning the one listening will not understand. For a sufficient reason, it is permitted others to deceive themselves by taking the wrong meaning of what is said, and this remains true although the listener, because of his ignorance, does not know there is another meaning to what he had heard. The main reason that justifies the use of a broad mental reservation is the need for preserving secrecy, where the value to the common good is greater than would be the manifestation of something that is sure to cause harm. Such reservation must be used with great prudence, at the risk of creating suspicion and mistrust if people cannot be sure that what they are being told is what they hear.

BROTHER. A title of respect variously used in ecclesiastical documents and Catholic Church practice. The Pope regularly addresses the bishops as "venerable brothers," and among men religious the term is commonly used in correspondence and formal discourse. (Etym. Anglo-Saxon *brōthor;* akin to Latin *frater;* Greek *phratēr,* member of the same clan.)

BROTHERS. A generic name that originally referred to all members of a religious community, but is now generally used to identify those men religious who do not or will not receive holy orders. The term is also applied in some institutes to students for the priesthood who are not yet ordained.

BROTHERS' INSTITUTES. Religious institutes of men whose members are either entirely or mainly brothers who are not and do not intend to be ordained. There are more than forty such institutes of pontifical status in the Catholic Church.

BROWN SCAPULAR. See SCAPULAR.

BRUGES. A place of pilgrimage in West Flanders Province. Not far from the great market square in Bruges in the Place du Buorg is a famous Chapel of the Precious Blood. In 1150, Thierry, Count of Flanders and hero returning from the Second Crusade, brought with him a phial containing a drop of Christ's blood, which he had received from the Patriarch of Jerusalem. This precious relic is now contained in a lavish gold reliquary that is carried in solemn procession through the city with great pomp on the first Monday after May 2 each year. Pilgrims from all over the world come for the occasion, some having attended the ceremonies yearly for decades. Bruges also possesses relics of St. Basil (329–79), cherished with reverence in a chapel dedicated to him.

B. SC. *Baccalaureus Scientiarum*—Bachelor of Sciences.

B.T. *Baccalaureus Theologiae*—Bachelor of Theology.

BUGIA. A portable candle holder with a lighted candle, held beside a bishop as he celebrates certain liturgical functions. Other prelates have on occasion been given the same privilege. From *Bugia,* Latin for Bougie, Algeria, where wax was obtained.

B.U.J. *Baccalaureus Utriusque Juris*—Bachelor of Both Laws (civil and canon).

BULL, PAPAL. The most solemn and weighty form of papal letter. The name is derived from the Latin *bulla,* the disklike leaden seal attached to such a document. It is used by the Pope in appointing a bishop. Formerly all papal letters of major importance, including canonization decrees, were called bulls, but the current *Acta Apostolicae Sedis* gives some of these papal letters various names.

BULLARIUM. Various private collections of papal bulls and other pontifical documents. The authority of bullaria is simply that of the individual documents. The best known are those published by Cherubini in 1586; the "Luxembourg Bullarium," said to have been printed at Geneva (1527–30); the "Roman Bullarium," published by Mainardi (1733–62); and the "Turin Bullarium" (1857–85). (Etym. Latin *bulla,* seal.)

BURIAL, CHRISTIAN. Interment of a deceased person with the Church's funeral rites in consecrated ground. Since it is an honor granted by the Church, it follows that the Church may determine who is worthy of it. The general practice of the Church is to interpret certain prohibitions of Christian burial as mildly as possible. Doubtful cases are referred to a bishop. If the burial is to take place in a cemetery that has not been consecrated, the grave must be individually blessed before a Catholic person is interred.

BURSE. A stiff pocket about twelve inches square in which the folded corporal is carried to and from the altar. Part of a set of vestments, it is made of matching material. It is placed upon the chalice at the beginning and end of Mass and on the altar at Benediction. The leather case containing the pyx, in which the Holy Eucharist is brought to the sick, is called a burse. It is also the name for an endowment or foundation fund especially for scholarships for candidates for the priesthood. (Etym. Latin *bursa,* purse or pouch.)

BUSKINS. Liturgical stockings, sometimes ornamented, worn on occasion by the celebrant of a pontifical Mass.

B.V. *Beatitudo Vestra*—Your Holiness.

B.V. *Beata Virgo*—Blessed Virgin.

B.V.M. *Beata Virgo Maria*—Blessed Virgin Mary.

BYZANTINE RITE. Ritual and ecclesiastical policy followed by the Church of Constantinople. The second most widely used rite after the Roman, it has three forms: 1. the Liturgy of St. James the Elder, modified by St. Basil and named after him; 2. St. John Chrysostom's later modification, which became the common Eucharistic service of Constantinople. Though it did not displace the original St. Basil's, it did limit its use; 3. the liturgy of the Presanctified, essentially the distribution of the Blessed Sacrament consecrated on the preceding Sunday.

C

CABRINI SHRINE. A chapel at Fort Washington, New York, dedicated to St. Frances Cabrini (1850–1917). Founder of the Missionary Sisters of the Sacred Heart, she was asked by Pope Leo XIII to come to the United States to work among the immigrants. She arrived in New York in 1889 and died in Chicago in 1917. Canonized in 1946, she was the first naturalized American citizen so honored. Her body lies under the main altar of the shrine.

CAESAROPAPISM. The policy of kingly or civil supremacy in Catholic Church affairs. Emulating pagan priest-emperors, temporal rulers have variously meddled in ecclesiastical affairs, encroaching mainly upon the doctrinal powers of the Church; Caesar takes the place of the Pope.

CAIAPHAS. Son-in-law of Annas and his successor as High Priest of Jerusalem (A.D. 18–37) (Luke 3:2). It was his ominous observation to the chief priests and Pharisees that presaged the death of Jesus. "You don't seem to have grasped the situation at all; you fail to see that it is better for one man to die for the people than for the whole nation to be destroyed" (John 11:49–50). Jesus, after Annas had questioned him, was brought to the palace of Caiaphas (John 18:24), who sent him to Pilate for official condemnation. (Etym. Greek *kaiaphas,* rock or depression.)

CAIN. The elder son of Adam and Eve. He tilled the soil, while his brother, Abel, was a shepherd. When each offered the product of his work to Yahweh, Abel's offering was more favorably accepted. In his resentment, Cain slew his brother (Genesis 4). Condemned by Yahweh, he became "a fugitive and a wanderer over the earth" (Genesis 4:14). His wife bore him a son, Enoch, and when Cain later built a town, he named it after his son (Genesis 4:17).

CALAMUS. A pipe or reed used for the communion of the clergy and people. At a solemn papal Mass the Pope takes the consecrated wine, brought from the altar to his throne, through such a golden pipe. Of ancient origin, this custom was continued by the Cistercians until the Reformation. (Etym. Latin *calamus,* reed; stalk; Greek *kalamos.*)

CALCED. Wearing shoes or sandals. Distinguished from the discalced among the men and women religious who do not wear shoes as a form of austerity. Customs differ among religious institutes, notably the Carmelites, who have two main branches of the order, one calced and the other discalced. (Etym. Latin *calceus,* shoe.)

CALEB. One of the spies Moses sent out to make reconnaissance in Canaan before an invasion campaign that Yahweh had urged (Numbers 13:6). Despite the pessimistic estimate of some of the spies, Caleb assured Moses that the Israelites were well able to conquer Canaan. "We shall gobble them up," Caleb promised (Numbers 14:9). The assembled community quailed at the prospect, but Caleb and Joshua persisted in urging an attack (Numbers 14:1–3). Yahweh was embittered by the lack of confidence that this "perverse community" showed in him, and warned Moses of a coming catastrophe because of this cowardice (Numbers 14:27–35). Of all the leaders, only Caleb and Joshua survived (Numbers 14:38). "It is these," Yahweh promised, "I shall bring in to know the land you have disdained." Faithful to that promise, Yahweh rewarded them handsomely with rich inheritances of land in Canaan (Joshua 15:13–20).

CALENDAR, CHRISTIAN. A proposed system of regulating the sequence of the year in closer consistency with Christian feasts and seasons. The Second Vatican Council declared itself not opposed to assigning Easter to a fixed date in the Gregorian calendar, the one now popularly used in the Western world. Presently, Easter falls on the Sunday following the full moon after the vernal equinox, and it varies in date. As a result the period of Lent, together with the feasts of Pentecost, Ascension, and many others, also vary each year. This stabilization, however, is to depend on acceptance by other Christians. Furthermore, the Council declared that it would not oppose a perpetual calendar that retains a seven-day week with Sunday, without the introduction of any days outside the week, so that the succession of weeks remains intact. All of this presumes that there are no very grave reasons against the proposed change.

CALENDS. See KALENDS.

CALIFORNIA MISSIONS. The parish centers established among the American Indians by Catholic missionaries from Spain. Three sets of missions were founded, in sequence, by the Jesuits and Dominicans in Lower California (now Mexico), and by the Franciscans in Upper California (now the United States). The Jesuit missions and the years of their foundation, beginning from south to north, were: San José del Cabo (1730); Santiago de las Coras (1721); San Juan de Ligní (1705); Nuestra Señora de los Dolores del Sur (1721); Nuestra Señora del Pilar (1720); Santa Rosa or Todos Santos (1733); San Luis Gonzaga (1737); San Francisco Xavier (1699); Nuestra Señora de Loreto (1697); San José de Commundu (1708); Purísima Concepción de Cadegomó (1718); Santa Rosalía de Mulegé (1705); Nuestra Señora de Guadalupe (1720); San Ignacio (1728); Santa Gertrudis (1752); San Francisco de Borja (1759); and Santa María de los Angeles (1766). These missions remained in the care of the Jesuits until the decree of expulsion of the members of the Society of Jesus in 1767.

Dominicans arrived in California in 1772. During their long stay, which lasted to about 1846, they established the following new missions between San Fernando de Velicatá and San Diego: Rosario (1774); Santo Domingo (1775); San Vicente Ferrer (1780); San Miguel (1787); Santo Tomás (1791); San Pedro Mártir (1794); and Santa Catarina Mártir (1797). The missions were eventually secularized by the Mexican Government in 1834.

Best known are the missions established by the Franciscans. They labored in California from 1769 to 1845. Their missions from south to north, with the dates of founding, were: San Diego (July 16, 1769); San Luis Rey (June 13, 1798); San Juan Capistrano (November 1, 1796); San Gabriel (September 8, 1771); San Fernando (September 8, 1797); San Buenaventura (March 31, 1782); Santa Barbara (December 4, 1786); Santa Inez (September 17, 1804); Purísima Concepción (December 8, 1787); San Luis Obispo (September 1, 1772); San Miguel (July 25, 1797); San Antonio de Pádua (July 14, 1771); Soledad (October 9, 1791); San Carlos or Carmelo (June 3, 1770); Santa Cruz (September 25, 1791); San Juan Bautista (June 24, 1797); Santa Clara (January 12, 1777); San José (June 11, 1797); San Francisco (October 9, 1776); San Rafael (December 14, 1817); and San Francisco Solano (July 4, 1823). Mexican independence of Spain put an end to the prosperity of the Franciscan missions and the peace of some thirty thousand neophytes. With the advent of the first governor under the Mexican flag began the secularization of these monuments of Christian zeal. By 1835 the Franciscans were deprived of control and the take-over by the government completed the ruin.

After Upper California was admitted to the United States in 1850, some of the Franciscan missions were gradually restored, and in recent years public interest has further advanced the restoration. They have become an important part of tourism in California.

CALIX. A chalice, which is the term always used in the Church's official documents for the cup used in the Eucharistic liturgy. (Etym. Latin *calix,* cup, goblet, drinking vessel, chalice.)

CALIXTINES. A party of the Hussites, also called Utraquists, who contended that the laity must receive Communion under both species, i.e., under the form of bread and also from the chalice (*calix*). They received ecclesiastical approval at the Prague Compacts of 1433, eighteen years after the death of John Hus (1369–1415), a Bohemian priest who was condemned by the Council of Constance and burned at the stake for heresy. Not all Calixtines, however, were heretics. They could be Catholics who took advantage of the Church's concession to receive the chalice but also believed that Holy Communion under both forms was not necessary for salvation.

CALUMNY. Injuring another person's good name by lying. It is doubly sinful, in unjustly depriving another of his good name and in telling an untruth. Since calumny violates justice, it involves the duty of making reparation for the foreseen injury inflicted. Hence the calumniator must try, not only to repair the harm done to another's good name, but also to make up for any foreseen temporal loss that resulted from the calumny, for example, loss of employment or customers. (Etym. Latin *calumnia*, a false accusation, malicious charge; from *calvi*, to deceive.)

CALVARY. Golgotha, or the place where Jesus was crucified (Luke 23). It was so called because it resembled a head or skull. Mount Calvary was near Jerusalem and was the place where criminals were normally executed.

CALVINISM. The religious system introduced by John Calvin (1509–64), French reformer, in opposition to the doctrine of the Catholic Church on the meaning of humanity's predestination. In the Calvinist system, as a result of Adam's fall, man has no longer any internal freedom of the will; he is a slave of God. Everyone is eternally predestined, either for heaven or for hell, absolutely independent of his personal efforts. Consequently the elect cannot be lost. The basic principles of Calvinism are set forth in the *Institutes of the Christian Religion*, where Calvin argues that, since God is absolutely infinite, he is the only real agent in the universe and creatures are merely his instruments.

CAM. *Camera* (Papal Treasury).

CAMALDOLESE. A religious order founded in 1012 by St. Romuald (950–1027) at Camaldoli, near Arezzo, Italy. Branching off from the Benedictines, the Camaldolese ideal was a minimum of communal ties. Within a century, however, monasteries were established along cenobitic lines. Since St. Romuald left no written rules, the order's tradition has varied over the centuries. Long fasts, hermitages, considerable silence, and manual labor are favored. There is also an order of Camaldolese nuns.

CAM. AP., C.A. *Camera Apostolica—* Apostolic Camera (Papal Treasury).

CAMAURO. A close-fitting red velvet cap, trimmed with white fur, worn occasionally by the popes, as appears in some of their portraits.

CAMERLENGO. An Italian chamberlain. There are three ecclesiastical persons in Rome who carry this title: 1. camerlengo of the Holy Roman Church, who administers the revenue and property of the Holy See, verifies the death of the Pope, directs preparations and manages the conclave for election of a new pontiff; 2. camerlengo of the Sacred College, who is in charge of property and revenues of the college, pontificates at Mass for deceased cardinals, and registers all consistorial business; 3. camerlengo of the Roman clergy, elected by canons and parish priests of Rome, who presides over their conferences and is arbiter in questions of precedence. (Etym. Italian *camerlengo*, chamberlain.)

CAMPANILE. A form of bell tower that was developed by Lombard architects and prevails in Italy. It is usually a tall, slender tower, somewhat detached from the church, with no buttresses and topped with a turret that contains the belfry chamber. Outstanding campaniles are found in Venice, Pisa, and Florence.

CAMPO SANTO. A Catholic cemetery, especially one whose surface soil is said to have been brought from Jerusalem, where Christ was buried.

CAN. *Canonicus,* canonical.

CANA. A village in Galilee where Jesus performed the miracle of turning water into wine at the marriage feast (John 2:1–11). Later, when he returned to Cana, he performed another miracle in curing the dying son of a court official (John 4:46–53). (Etym. Hebrew *qanah*, reed; Greek *kana*.)

CANAAN. The old name for Palestine, the land on the eastern coast of the Mediterranean, which the Israelites seized, dispossessing the Canaanites, a Semitic people, who came from Arabia originally and derived their name from the descendants of Canaan, the son of Ham (Genesis 9:18, 10:6). (Etym. Hebrew *kena'an*, land of purple.)

CANC. *Cancellarius*—chancellor.

CANDELABRUM. A hanging chandelier for lamps in early Christian times. Sometimes they were not suspended but stood before the altar. In the Middle Ages the term denoted seven-branched candlesticks. Nowadays it refers to any multiple candle holder.

CANDLE. A sacramental used in the Church's liturgy. Candles were first used to dispel darkness in predawn services and in the catacombs. They have since become part of the liturgy and their symbolism part of the Church's tradition. Candles are an emblem of God, the giver of life and enlightenment. Being pure, they represent Christ's spotless body, the flame a figure of the Divine Nature. Candles are blessed solemnly on the feast of the Purification of the Blessed Virgin or Candlemas Day (February 2). Candles are required at the public administration of the sacraments, at Mass and Benediction, at funerals and at other church ceremonies.

CANDLEMAS. Synonymous with the feast of the Purification of Mary, February 2, commemorating the purification of the Blessed Virgin, according to Mosaic law, forty days after Christ's birth and the presentation of the Child Jesus in the temple. Candles are blessed on that day and a lighted candle procession held to commemorate Christ as the light of revelation to the Gentiles, and represents his entry into the temple. In Scotland it is the legal term day on which interests and rents are payable. See also PURIFICATION.

CANDLESTICK. A holder for a candle consisting of a foot, stem, knob, and bowl to receive wax drippings; in some instances it has a sharp point or pricket at the top on which the candle is fixed. In other instances the top is a cut-out cup-shaped hole into which the candle is placed. It symbolizes the Eucharist and is often represented with the Host above it. The rubrics prescribe two, four, or six candlesticks on or around the altar for Mass, with lighted candles.

CANON. An established rule for guidance, a standard, or a list of such rules: 1. in biblical usage the catalogue of inspired writings known as the Old and New Testaments, identified as such by the Church; 2. in ecclesiastical usage, a short definition of some dogmatic truth, with attached anathema, made as a rule by general councils; 3. the Eucharistic Prayer, which is the essential part of the Sacrifice of the Mass. In religious life, certain orders of men with specific duties often attached to a particular church, shrine, or ecclesiastical function; 4. in music a composition that repeats the same melody by one or more voices in turn, producing harmony; 5. in printing a size type, namely 4 line pica 48 point, used in printing church books or the Canon of the Mass; 6. catalogue of canonized saints; 7. rules of certain religious orders and the books that comprise them; 8. in art and architecture the established rule, which is periodically specified in ecclesiastical matters by Church directives or legislation; 9. a member of the clergy attached to a cathedral or other large church, with specific duties such as the choral recitation of the Divine Office. (Etym. Latin *canon*, rule, standard of conduct; summary, record; from Greek *kanōn*, rod, rule.)

CANONESS. A member of a women's religious community following the Rule of St. Augustine. Usually committed to recitation of the Divine Office, they are now distinguished into regular and secular canonesses.

CANONICAL AGE. The age required by ecclesiastical law for the valid or licit reception of the sacraments or the exercise of an ecclesiastical office.

CANONICAL DOUBT. Uncertainty whether a current ecclesiastical precept is binding because it seems to conflict with a previous law. In such cases, the former law is to be followed.

CANONICAL FORM. The requisite conditions for a valid marriage in which one or both parties are Catholic. For the marriage of a Catholic to be valid, there must be present: 1. a bishop or a parish priest in his parish or another priest duly delegated, and 2. two witnesses. A dispensation from the canonical form can be obtained for mixed marriages.

CANONICAL HOURS. The prescribed periods of prayer in the recitation or chant of the Divine Office. Also called the Liturgy of the Hours. In the revised liturgy since the Second Vatican Council, these periods are: the Office of Readings, the Morning Prayer and Evening Prayer, the Daytime Prayer and the Night Prayer. The book, in four volumes, for the canonical hours is the Breviary.

CANONICAL LIFE. A rule of life drawn up in ancient times for the clergy, mainly the cathedral assistants. Intermediate between the monastic life and secular priest-hood, they lived in community. Many later became canons regular of St. Augustine (354–430), who introduced this mode of life into his own episcopal household.

CANONICAL PENANCE. The specified penance, corresponding to the nature and gravity of the sin, prescribed by confessors in the sacrament of penance. These pen-ances were listed in penitential books. Celtic in origin, the earliest canonical lists are ascribed to St. Patrick and date from the fifth century. In time the practice spread throughout Europe. The best known peni-tential book is that ascribed to Archbishop Theodore of Canterbury (602–90).

CANONICALS. Ecclesiastical garments worn by officiating clergy. They are vest-ments ordered by Church law. (Etym. Latin *canonicus,* according to a precept; belonging to the summary or record.)

CANONICITY. The quality of a book, or part of a book of the Bible, as divinely in-spired and therefore containing the word of God.

CANONIST. An authority in ecclesiastical law, whether of its history, or interpretation, or application to individuals or institutions in the Church.

CANONIZATION. Declaration by the Pope that a deceased person is raised to the full honors of the altar, i.e., a saint after pre-viously having been beatified. Two miracles credited to the beatus (feminine: beata) are usually required before canonization to attest the heroic virtue of the saint. Beatification allows veneration of the blessed, canonization requires it. The canon-ization is celebrated at St. Peter's and is usu-ally followed by a solemn triduum in an-other church in the city or elsewhere within a limited time. (Etym. Latin *canonizare,* to canonize; from *canon,* catalogue of saints.)

CANON LAW. The authentic compilation of the laws of the Catholic Church. Two major compilations have been made in the Church's history, Gratian's Decree, as-sembled about A.D. 1140 by the Italian Ca-maldolese monk Gratian, and the Code of Canon Law, promulgated by Pope Benedict XV in 1917, and effective on Pentecost, May 19, 1918. Since the Second Vatican Council, a new compilation has been undertaken of existing Church laws.

CANONS REGULAR. Priests who are bound by religious vows and who live in community under a distinctive rule. Origi-nating in the eleventh century, in connection with the reform movement of Pope Gregory VII, they have mainly adopted the Rule of St. Augustine.

CANONS SECULAR. Priests who were canons of a cathedral or other church but took no public vows of poverty, chastity, and obedience. They sang the Divine Office but were not religious. The canons formed a cathedral chapter and determined the char-acter of the cathedral itself. Thus, if the canons were secular clergy, the cathedral was clergy diocesan; if they were religious, it was monastic. In medieval England, for example, there were two kinds of cathedrals, corresponding to the types of canons who administered the church. The nine secular foundations were those of Chichester, Ex-eter, Hereford, Lichfield, Lincoln, London, Salisbury, Wells, and York. There were eight religious foundations, namely, Canter-bury, Durham, Ely, Norwich, Rochester, Winchester, and Worcester—conducted by the Benedictines; and Carlisle, which was served by Augustinian canons.

CANOPY. An ornamental covering of cloth, wood, metal, or stone used above an altar, statue, or throne. Also called a bal-dachino. A white canopy is held above the Blessed Sacrament when carried in proces-sion. A processional canopy may be used at the solemn reception of a bishop on his first pastoral visit to any town or parish within his jurisdiction. (Etym. Latin *canopeum,* mosquito net; from Greek *konops,* mos-quito.)

CANTAT. Cantata (sung, as opposed to read).

CANTERBURY. From A.D. 597, when the Roman Benedictine who became St. Augus-tine went to England, until 1558, when Car-dinal Reginald Pole (1500–58) died, Canter-bury was the primatial Catholic see of England. With the establishment of Angli-canism as the state religion, Canterbury be-came the world center of the Anglican Communion.

CANTERBURY CATHEDRAL. A historic monument of Catholic England, in County Kent, it is the burial place of some of the Church's greatest leaders. At first it was for-bidden to bury within the cathedral pre-cincts. The rule was changed when St. Cuth-bert (d. 687), arranging his own burial, ordained that all archbishops could be buried within their own cathedral churches. St. Dunstan, St. Alphege, St. Anselm, St. Odo have their tombs within its walls. But the saint who is most responsible for Canterbury's prestige is St. Thomas à Becket, who was murdered by the agents of King Henry II (1133–89) and buried at Canterbury. Many miracles followed upon the saint's death. The son of Louis VII of France was cured when his father, risking his life to do so, visited and prayed at St. Thomas's grave. Ravaged by the Danes in 1067, the cathedral was rebuilt in Norman style. After a disastrous fire in 1174 the choir was rebuilt and St. Thomas's body was transferred to an elaborate shrine in Trinity Chapel in 1175. His head was kept in a golden reliquary there. In 1538 all pilgrimages ceased when Henry VIII (1491–1547) forbade all Catholic services. The famous shrine was despoiled and even the missals bearing the saint's name were destroyed. The saint's bones were burned by order of Lord Cromwell (1485–1540). Canterbury attracts large crowds as a witness to pre-Reformation English Catholicism.

CANTICLE. In the Divine Office a sacred chant from Scripture apart from the psalms. In the Roman Breviary there are many canticles from the Old Testament. The three evangelical canticles of the New Testament recited daily in the Divine Office are the *Benedictus* of Zechariah, *Magnificat* of the Blessed Virgin, and the *Nunc Dimittis* of Simeon. (Etym. Latin *canticulum*, a little song.)

CANTICLE OF CANTICLES. An allegorical love poem in the Bible that has several layers of meaning. Basically it expresses the special love of God for the Chosen People; prophetically the espousal of Christ with his church; universally the love of God for a devoted soul; by accommodation the delight of God with the soul of the Blessed Virgin. It was read in the Jewish liturgy on the octave of the Passover. Traditionally ascribed to Solomon, the imagery of the two lovers, united and then separated, sought and then found, reflects the changing relationships of God and his people, depending on their varying loyalty to him.

CANTICLE OF THE SUN. The best known poem of praise of St. Francis of Assisi (1181–1226). It was begun in 1225, but the final verses about Sister Death were added shortly before he died. His biographer, Thomas of Celano (1200–55), says that the saint's last words were: "Welcome,

my Sister Death." The praise in the canticle is not addressed to the creatures but to God, their Creator. The full text of this great hymn reads:

Most high, all-powerful, all good, Lord!
 All praise is yours, all glory, all honor
 And all blessing.
To you, alone, Most High, do they belong.
 No mortal lips are worthy
 To pronounce your name.
All praise be yours, my Lord, through all
  that you have made,
 And first my lord Brother Sun,
 Who brings the day; and light you give to
  us through him.
How beautiful is he, how radiant in all his
  splendor!
 Of you, Most High, he bears the likeness.
All praise be yours, my Lord, through Sister
  Moon and Stars;
 In the heavens you have made them,
  bright
 And precious and fair.
All praise be yours, my Lord, through
  Brothers Wind and Air,
 And fair and stormy, all the weather's
  moods,
 By which you cherish all that you have
  made.
All praise be yours, my Lord, through Sister
  Water,
 So useful, lowly, precious and pure.
All praise be yours, my Lord, through
  Brother Fire,
 Through whom you brighten up the night.
 How beautiful is he, how gay! Full of
  power and strength.
All praise be yours, my Lord, through Sister
  Earth, our mother,
 Who feeds us in her sovereignty and pro-
  duces
 Various fruits with colored flowers and
  herbs.
All praise be yours, my Lord, through those
  who grant pardon
 For love of you; through those who en-
  dure
 Sickness and trial.
Happy those who endure in peace,
 By you, Most High, they will be crowned.
All praise be yours, my Lord, through Sister
  Death,
 From whose embrace no mortal can es-
  cape.
Woe to those who die in mortal sin!
 Happy those She finds doing your will!
 The second death can do no harm to
  them.

Praise and bless my Lord, and give him thanks,
And serve him with great humility.

CANTOR. The chief singer of an ecclesiastical choir, who leads the singing and often selects the music. In the Divine Office the cantor intones the antiphons and starts the psalms. He is also called the precentor. (Etym. Latin *cantor*, singer.)

CANTORIAL STAFF. The staff sometimes carried as a mark of dignity by the cantor of an ecclesiastical choir in the exercise of his duties.

CAP. *Capitulum*—little chapter.

CAP. DE SEQ. *Capitulum de sequenti*—little chapter of the following feast.

CAPERNAUM. A town in Galilee somewhere along the western shore of the Sea of Galilee. Its precise location cannot be determined, though it has been identified with Tell-Hum on the north bank of the Shore of Tiberias. During Jesus' ministry in Galilee, Capernaum was the scene of many miracles and some of his most stirring sermons. It was here that the centurion's servant (Matthew 8:5–13), a paralytic (Mark 2:1–12), and a court official's son were all cured (John 4:46–54). It was here also that the five thousand were fed following his sermon (Mark 6:33–44).

CAPITAL PUNISHMENT. The death penalty imposed by the state for the punishment of grave crimes. It is certain from Scripture that civil authorities may lawfully put malefactors to death. Capital punishment was enacted for certain grievous crimes in the Old Law, e.g., blasphemy, sorcery, adultery, and murder. Christian dispensation made no essential change in this respect, as St. Paul expressly says: "The state is there to serve God for your benefit. If you break the law, however, you may well have fear: the bearing of the sword has its significance" (Romans 13:4). Among the errors of the Waldenses condemned by the Church in the early thirteenth century was the proposition that denied the lawfulness of capital punishment (Argentré, *Collectio de Novis Erroribus*, I, 86). St. Thomas Aquinas (1225–74) defends capital punishment on the grounds of the common good. The state, he reasons, is like a body composed of many members, and as a surgeon may cut off one corrupt limb to save the others, so the civil authority may lawfully put a criminal to death and thus provide for the common good.

Theologians further reason that, in receiving its authority from God through the natural law, the state also receives from him the right to use the necessary means for attaining its end. The death penalty is such a means. If even with capital punishment crime abounds, no lesser penalty will suffice.

The practical question remains of how effective a deterrent capital punishment is in some modern states, when rarely used or only after long delays. In principle, however, it is morally licit because in the most serious crimes the claims of retribution and deterrence are so demanding that the corrective value of punishment must, if necessary, be sacrificed.

CAPITAL SINS. Those sins to which man's fallen nature is mainly inclined and that are, as a result, the source of all other human failings. The name "capital" does not mean that they are necessarily grave sins. They are leading tendencies toward sin and are seven in number: pride, avarice, lust, envy, gluttony, anger, and sloth. Theology justifies the number by pointing to the goods that human nature seeks to attain or the evils it wants to avoid. The goods desired and the evils disliked can be material or spiritual, and either real or imaginary. Thus, pride and vainglory come from wanting to be held in high honor and glory, and from preening oneself in the imagination. Gluttony comes from individual high living, lust from sexuality inborn to preserve the race, and avarice from the gathering of wealth. The repulsions are about good things wrongly regarded as threatening our own proper good and that therefore are grieved over or actively combatted. Spiritual values menace our physical pleasure and ease, hence sloth or boredom about spiritual values. Envy is much the same; it resents another's good qualities because they may lower our own self-esteem. To flare out at others is anger. (Etym. Latin *capitalis*, principal, acting in the manner of a head.)

CAPITAL VIRTUES. The seven principal virtues that are contrary to the seven capital sins, namely: 1. humility (pride), 2. liberality (avarice), 3. chastity (lust), 4. meekness (anger), 5. temperance (gluttony), 6. brotherly love (envy), 7. diligence (sloth).

CAPITULATION. An agreement by which certain conditions are imposed on a candidate and accepted by him or her before election to an office subject to ecclesiastical law. Provided these conditions are just and capable of reasonable fulfillment, they are to be fulfilled. Grave moral questions, however, may arise if a candidate does not make the promises sincerely, or if the conditions are exacted as a threat and the promises are therefore made under duress. (Etym. Latin *capitulum*, a small head; division of a book; *capitulare*, to distinguish by heads or chapters.)

CAPPA CHORALIS. A long black mantle that was worn in choir during the Divine Office by the clergy of cathedral churches and by many religious. It commonly had a hood attached. The *cappa choralis* is on occasion still worn by some men religious.

CAPPA MAGNA. A cope worn by cardinals and bishops on occasions of ceremony. Formerly it had a long train requiring a train bearer, and a hood of fur or silk. Other prelates also wore an abbreviated *cappa magna* to signify their inferior dignity.

CAPPA PUERI JESU. See HOLY COAT.

CAPPEL. *Cappella*—chapel.

CAPSULA. The metal receptacle for the consecrated Host, to be reserved in the tabernacle for later exposition in the monstrance.

CAPTIOUS. See THEOLOGICAL CENSURE.

CAPUCHINS. One of three autonomous branches of the Franciscans, founded in 1525 by Matteo di Bassi of Urbano (d. 1552), an Observant friar who wished to return to the primitive poverty and simplicity of the order. Its members wear a pointed cowl (capuche), with optional sandals and beard. They were one of the most powerful instruments of the Counter-Reformation. Although the severity of the original rule has been mitigated, their life is still austere and they have gained wide respect as popular preachers, confessors, and missionaries.

CARD. Cardinal.

CARDINAL. A high official of the Roman Catholic Church ranking next to the Pope. He is a member of the Sacred College and is appointed by the Sovereign Pontiff to assist and advise him in the government of the Church. The names of newly created cardinals are usually announced at a papal consistory. They may wear a specially designed red hat and cassock. They are the ones who elect a pope, who, for centuries now, has always been a cardinal before his election. The Code of Canon Law, promulgated in 1918, decreed that all cardinals must be priests. In 1962, Pope John XXIII provided that they should all be bishops. (Etym. Latin *cardo*, hinge.)

CARDINAL BISHOP. The highest order or rank among the cardinals of the Roman Catholic Church. Originally the designation identified those members of the college of cardinals who were actually bishops, to distinguish them from cardinals who were only priests or deacons. Pope Sixtus V in 1586 determined that there should be only six cardinal bishops, among a total number of seventy cardinals. In 1962, Pope John XXIII decreed that from then on all cardinals should be consecrated bishops.

CARDINAL DEACON. The third rank of members in the college of cardinals, numbering fourteen when the full complement was seventy. The designation goes back to the early history of Christian Rome when the city was divided into seven sections, each administered by an ordained deacon. When the regional division was abandoned, the title remained and came to be applied to cardinals. In general, cardinal deacons are those who live and exercise their duties in Rome.

CARDINAL ELECTORS. Since 1179, cardinals have been the exclusive electors of the Roman Pontiff. In the twelfth century members of the electoral college were also prelates (bishops and archbishops) from outside of Rome, and by the fifteenth century (under Pope Eugenius IV in 1439) even cardinals who were only priests were given a voice in the papal election.

CARDINAL PRIEST. The second rank of members of the college of cardinals. Although now all cardinals are bishops, cardinal priests are so designated in terms of their precedence. Pope Sixtus V decreed that there should be fifty cardinal priests out of a total of seventy cardinals. Formerly, when some cardinals were simple priests, they were nevertheless eligible to vote for the Roman Pontiff. Cardinal priests represent the chief priests of the titular churches in Rome, into which the city had formerly (fifth and sixth centuries) been divided, to form quasi-parishes.

CARDINALS, RETIRED. According to the motu proprio *Ingravescentem Aetatem*, of November 21, 1970, Pope Paul VI decreed that cardinals are to retire from active duty when they have completed their eightieth year. At that age they cease to be members of the congregations of the Roman Curia, of all permanent organs of the Holy See and of Vatican City State; and they lose their right to elect the Roman Pontiff and in fact of participating in the conclave for the election of the Pope.

CARDINAL VICAR. Representative of the Pope for the city of Rome. He is also called the Vicar of the City.

CARDINAL VIRTUE. One of the four principal virtues of human morality, to which the others are necessarily related. These four central virtues are prudence, justice, temperance, and fortitude. Each of the cardinal virtues has subjective, potential, and integral parts. The subjective parts are such acts and dispositions of soul as are necessary for the full possession of that virtue, as foresight is needed for prudence and patience for fortitude. The potential parts are virtues related to the cardinal virtue but yet distinct from it, as truthfulness is a potential part of justice. The integral parts are species of a cardinal virtue, as chastity is a species of temperance.

CARDIOGNOSIS. Literally "knowledge of the heart." The special charism that God confers on some people as recorded in the lives of the saints, to know the moral and spiritual condition of a person without self-manifestation. As an extraordinary supernatural gift, it must be distinguished from the psychological phenomenon of being able to shrewdly estimate someone's minimal external evidence.

CARECLOTH. A canopy of silk or similar material of varying colors used at weddings in the Middle Ages. It was held over the bride and bridegroom if neither had previously been married.

CARMEL, MOUNT. A mountain projecting into the Mediterranean Sea along the coast of Palestine near the present-day city of Haifa. It was here that Elijah defied the hundreds of pagan prophets in the presence of King Ahab and proved to the people that Yahweh was the true God (I Kings 18:20–40).

CARMELITE ORDER. The Order of Our Lady of Mount Carmel, founded in Palestine by St. Berthold (d. 1195) about 1154. It claims continuity with hermits on Mount Carmel from ancient times, and even to the prophet Elijah. The original rule, set down in 1209 by the Latin Patriarch of Jerusalem, Albert of Vercelli (1149–1214), was very severe, prescribing absolute poverty, total abstinence from meat, and solitude. After the Crusades, the Englishman St. Simon Stock (d. 1265) reorganized the Carmelites as mendicant friars. The laxity of the sixteenth century brought reforms among the women under St. Theresa of Avila (1515–82) and the men under St. John of the Cross (1542–91). This created the two independent branches of the order, the Calced, or Shod, Carmelites (of the Old Observance) and the Discalced, or Unshod, following the Teresian Reform. The main purpose of the order is contemplation, missionary work, and theology. Carmelite nuns devote themselves to prayer, especially of intercession for priests, and to a life of hidden sacrifice. The canonization of St. Thérèse de Lisieux (1873–97) in 1925, and her designation as patroness of the missions, have done much to make the Carmelites' ideal known and imitated throughout the Catholic world.

CARNIVAL. A time of merrymaking before Lent; three or four days preceding Ash Wednesday spent in feasting and noisy unrestrained reveling. The Blessed Sacrament is exposed for adoration in many places during the time to expiate the sins of excess committed during these carnival times.

CAROL. A song of joy and praise, particularly one celebrating Christmas.

CARPENTER'S SQUARE. A symbolic emblem alone or in conjunction with other tools of the carpenter's trade. Hammer, lathe, and saw are especially symbolic of St. Joseph the Workman. St. Thomas the Apostle, patron of architects and builders, and St. James the Less are both represented in art with the carpenter's square. St. Vincent Ferrer (1350–1419), patron of the building arts, has a tool of that trade for one of his symbols.

CARTAGO. A shrine of Our Lady of the Angels in Costa Rica, near the foot of Mount Irazú. In 1635 a young Negro girl found a small black stone statue of Our Lady and the Holy Child in the woods near Cartago. She took it home with her but it returned by itself to where she had found it. After several futile attempts to keep it, she took the statue to the village priest, who tried hiding it, but to no avail. It was always found back in the woods. The Negroes nearby built a little chapel to house their treasured Mother and Child on the spot that she herself had chosen to stay. In time it became a famous place of pilgrimage for all of Costa Rica. The image of the black Madonna, gaily dressed with Jesus, was solemnly crowned in 1927.

CARTESIANISM. The principles embodied in the teaching of René Descartes (1596–1650). Its outstanding feature is the notion of universal methodical doubt. Cartesianism begins by calling into doubt whatever knowledge a person has acquired, and then seeking to find a truth so evident that it cannot be doubted. This truth it claims to find in each person's intuition of his own thought and existence. Within the Cartesian system are several principles, all at variance with the Catholic faith, which Descartes professed to believe, namely: occasionalism, which disowns free will for man; ontologism, which denies that a person can perceive ideas within his mind or objects directly in themselves; and angelism, which regards man as if he were a pure spirit within a body, as if thought must be intuitive and not deductive, and independent of things but evolved from one's own consciousness.

CARTHUSIANS. The strictly contemplative order founded by St. Bruno (1032–1101) in 1084 at the Grande Chartreuse in Dauphiné. At first there was no special rule except that the monks were expected to practice perfect mortification and renunciation of the world. Essentially hermits, the Carthusians were vowed to silence, with conventual Mass. In 1133, a form of life called the Carthusian Customs was approved by Pope Innocent II, and this has remained to the present day substantially unchanged. The Carthusian way of life is a combination of Benedictine monasticism and eremitical asceticism.

The order also includes a number of monasteries of nuns who live under a similar rule, but they have separate cells instead of cottages and are under the direction of the Carthusian monks. (Etym. French *Chartreuse*.)

CASE OF CONSCIENCE. A famous problem arising in 1701 as to the giving of absolution to a cleric who declared himself unwilling to give up certain Jansenist sentiments. Specifically, did Jansenius' book *Augustinus* contain the propositions solemnly condemned as heretical by Pope Innocent X in 1653. Forty doctors of the Sorbonne voted "yes," in favor of absolving the cleric, but this solution was condemned in the papal brief *Cum Nuper* as a denial of the Pope's power to decide whether or not a certain book contained errors against the faith. The faculties of theology at Louvain, Douai, and Paris were in agreement with Pope Clement XI's declaration.

CASES OF CONSCIENCE. Problems arising in the application of moral and canon law to various situations in daily life. The cases made specific, with detailed circumstances, have been a familiar method of preparing seminarians for hearing confessions, and of assisting priests at seminars and conferences to deal effectively with the moral problems arising in the pastoral ministry.

CASSOCK. The ecclesiastical garb of all clerics. A long, close-fitting garment that is sometimes belted. For ordinary use it is usually black in color. Cardinals may wear one of red color or with red piping, cincture and buttons; a bishop may wear purple. The Pope's is always white. (Etym. Italian *casacca*, greatcoat.)

CASTEL GANDOLFO. A papal palace begun by Pope Urban VIII in the seventeenth century. It is situated in the town of the same name about fourteen miles southeast of Rome, and is used as a summer residence by the popes. By the Law of Guarantees it has, together with the Vatican and the Lateran Palace, the right of extraterritoriality, which means that it is exempt from visitation and inspection by the Italian Government.

CASTI CONNUBII. An encyclical letter of Pope Pius XI on Christian marriage, published in 1930. Its clear, outspoken teaching on marital indissolubility and on the evil of contraception makes it a landmark in the Church's doctrine on the sanctity of matrimony. The Second Vatican Council built on this document in its treatment of Christian marriage in the Constitution on the Church in the Modern World.

CASTRATION. Surgical removal of the testicles. If the testes are seriously diseased, their removal is morally permissible according to the principle of the double effect.

CASUALISM. The theory that everything in the world exists or occurs by chance. Held by the Greek Epicurean philosophers and professed in practice by those who deny or ignore the existence of an all-wise and loving Providence. (Etym. Latin *casualis,* happening by chance.)

CASUISTRY. The theological science of applying general moral principles to particular cases of conscience. It began in the post-Apostolic age and found early expression in the penitential books, which dealt with a variety of moral failings and their appropriate forms of satisfaction. Later on came the Summas on Penance, which formed complete legal digests. St. Alphonsus Liguori (1696–1787) systematized casuistry in modern times. Although the term has taken on some unsavory meanings, due mainly to critics of Roman Catholic moral practice, casuistry is an integral part of the Church's moral tradition. Its purpose is to adapt the unchangeable norms of Christian morality to the changing and variable circumstances of human life. (Etym. Latin *casus,* case, problem to be solved.)

CATACOMBS. Subterranean galleries used as burial grounds by the Christians of the first centuries. Here, by Roman law, they were immune from disturbance. The tombs of the martyrs buried there became altars for the celebration of the divine mysteries. The disposition and maintenance of the catacombs are now reserved to the Holy See. The best known of these rediscovered cemeteries are in Rome. (Etym. Italian *catacomba,* a sepulchral vault.)

CATACOMBS, OUR LADY OF THE. Shrine in the cemetery of St. Priscilla in Rome. Beneath the basilica of St. Sylvester and above the cemetery is a fresco painting of the Blessed Virgin holding the Child Jesus on her knee. It is considered one of the first images of the Madonna, dating from about A.D. 170. Though the colors have faded and the features are blurred, it is a witness to the Church's ancient devotion to Mary. The figure standing at her left is most likely the prophet Isaiah, who foretold the Virginal conception of the Messiah.

CATAFALQUE. A stand or platform to support a coffin. At a funeral Mass the coffin contains the body of the deceased. At an anniversary Mass the absolutions are given at the catafalque as though the body were present. Sometimes it is made of wood and covered with a pall. Six candles usually burn around it during absolution services.

CATECHESIS. That form of ecclesiastical action that leads both communities and individual members of the faithful to maturity of faith. Because of varied circumstances and multiple needs, catechetical activity takes on various forms.

In regions that have been Catholic from past ages, catechesis most often takes the form of religious instruction given to children and adolescents in schools or outside a school atmosphere. Also found in those regions are various catechetical programs for adults, whether in preparation for baptism or reception into the Church, or to deepen one's understanding of the faith. Sometimes the actual condition of the faithful demands that some form of evangelization of the baptized precede catechesis.

In churches that have been established recently, special importance is placed on evangelizing in the strict sense. This becomes the well-known catechumenate for those who are being introduced to the faith in preparation for baptism.

For individuals whose minds are open to the message of the Gospel, catechesis is an apt means to understand God's plan in their own lives and in the lives of others. Having come to know this divine plan, they can more effectively co-operate with God's grace and become better instruments for the extension of Christ's kingdom. (Etym. Greek *katechizo,* to teach by word of mouth.)

CATECHETICAL SYNTHESIS. A summary of Catholic doctrine that serves as the framework for instructing the people in the essentials of faith. Numerous and varied syntheses have been in use since early patristic times. One modern summary builds on the structure of faith, hope, charity, and the sacraments, as follows:

I. FAITH
  1. As to the human race
    Its first beginning
    Its last end
  2. The belief
    In God the Father
    In Jesus Christ
    In the Holy Spirit
    In the Holy Catholic Church

II. HOPE
  1. The Our Father
    The Seven Blessings to be hoped
      for and prayed for
  2. The Hail Mary
    Assistance of the Blessed Virgin,
      of the angels and saints

III. CHARITY
  1. The Commandments of God and of
    the Church
  2. The Beatitudes

IV. THE SACRAMENTS
  Seven great means of grace corresponding

to the principal needs of the supernatural life:

1. Birth through baptism
2. Growth through confirmation
3. Nourishment through the Eucharist
4. Medicine through penance
5. Journey of the soul through anointing
6. Priesthood through ordination
7. Christian family through matrimony

CATECHISM. A popular manual of instruction in Christian doctrine. In the early Church, catechetical instruction was standardized in preparation for baptism as in the writings of St. Augustine (354–430) and St. Gregory of Nyssa (330–95). After the invention of printing, books of catechetical instruction multiplied. The best known catechisms in the Catholic Church are St. Peter Canisius' *Summa of Christian Doctrine* (1555) and the *Catechism of the Council of Trent,* or *Roman Catechism* (1566). Numerous catechisms were published in various countries authorized by their respective hierarchies, e.g., the so-called *Penny Catechism* in Great Britain and the series of Baltimore Catechisms in the United States. Since the Second Vatican Council, all catechisms published by ecclesiastical authority must also be "submitted to the Apostolic See for review and approval" (*General Catechetical Directory,* 119).

CATECHIST. In general, one who teaches the essentials of Christian faith and morals. The term also has the technical meaning of one who gives instruction in Catholic doctrine, especially in mission lands or among people who are not baptized or who are dechristianized. As one of the supernatural charisms of knowledge, it is the special gift of being able to teach the faith with extraordinary effectiveness.

CATECHUMENATE. The period of instruction in the faith before baptism and admission of converts to the Catholic Church. The Second Vatican Council set down specific directives on the catechumenate by: 1. distinguishing between the more intense and normally prolonged catechumenate in mission lands; 2. stressing the importance of not only instruction but training in the practice of virtue; 3. pointing out the responsibility of the whole Christian community to co-operate in the preparation of catechumens; and 4. directing that the catechumenate be integrated with the liturgical year and the celebration of the Paschal Mystery (*Ad Gentes Divinitus,* 13–14). (Etym. Latin *catechumenus;* from Greek

katēkhoumenos, from *katēkhein,* to catechize.)

CATECHUMEN. A learner, a person being instructed preparatory to receiving baptism and being admitted into the Church. The length of the catechumenate varies: in parts of Africa it may require a minimum of four years before the candidate is ready for baptism. (Etym. Greek *katekhouminos,* one instructed.)

CATEGORICAL IMPERATIVE. An absolute and unqualified command or prohibition of a law or of one's conscience in interpreting the law. Popularly associated with the Kantian theory of ethics, which centers on the principle "Act as if the maximum from which you act were to become through your will a universal law." It implies that, in the last analysis, each person's own will is the final legislator of what is morally right or wrong.

CATEGORY. In metaphysics one of the ten primary ways or modes in which finite being can exist, namely, substance and nine accidents: quantity, quality, relation, action (transient), passion (received), place (proper and common), time, posture (position, site, and attitude), and habit (natural adjuncts). In logic, one of the ten corresponding supreme genera to which all predicates of a subject can be referred or reduced. (Etym. Greek *katēgoria,* a predicament or class.)

CATHARI. A name applied to various Manichaean sects of the later Middle Ages. The essential tenet of their belief was philosophical dualism. There were two ultimate principles, really two creator gods, one of good and the other of evil. They denied the value of oaths and the right to punish, commended suicide, and rejected marriage. Their ideas tended to undermine the foundations of civil society, and for this reason they were opposed not only by the Church but also by the State. By the fourteenth century Catharism had practically disappeared in France, Germany, and England and by the next century in Italy and the Balkans, where it had previously flourished.

CATHARSIS. Purging or purification, especially of the emotions or conscience. The emotions can be purified by a strong affective experience in which a person identifies himself with someone else's generally tragic experience. The conscience can be purified by a sincere admission of guilt and begging

God's mercy for whatever wrong had been done. (Etym. Greek *katharsis,* purgative.)

CATHEDRA. 1. the chair or throne of a bishop in his cathedral church; 2. a liturgical term for the assuming of episcopal authority.

CATHEDRAL. The official church of a bishop, where his permanent episcopal throne is erected. It is the mother church of a diocese and its clergy have precedence. The cathedral must be consecrated, and the date of consecration and the date of its titular feast must be observed liturgically. (Etym. Latin *cathedra,* a chair, stool, throne; Greek *kathedra,* seat.)

CATHEDRAL SCHOOLS. Educational institutions since the eighth century, open to lay persons in general as well as those interested in becoming priests. They were managed by a headmaster and were similar to the episcopal schools of a few centuries before, where the bishops were the sole teachers. Chrodegang, Bishop of Metz in the mid-eighth century, is said to have been the founder of this type of school, a system later followed by the public schools of Western Europe until the eighteenth century. The cathedral schools flourished in France, Germany, and England. The curriculum of the lower schools was usually reading, writing, psalmody, and Christian doctrine; curriculum of the higher schools was grammar, dialectics, rhetoric, geometry, arithmetic, astronomy, and music, with Scripture and theology as possible additional units. They were the forerunners of the medieval universities.

CATHEDRATICUM. A moderate tax paid annually to a bishop by all the churches and benefices under his jurisdiction. Custom determines the amount; otherwise it is determined by a meeting of the bishops, subject to the approval of the Holy See.

CATHOLIC. Its original meaning of "general" or "universal" has taken on a variety of applications in the course of Christian history. First used by St. Ignatius of Antioch (A.D. 35–107) (Letter to the Smyrneans, 8, 2), it is now mainly used in five recognized senses: 1. the Catholic Church as distinct from Christian ecclesiastical bodies that do not recognize the papal primacy; 2. the Catholic faith as the belief of the universal body of the faithful, namely that which is believed "everywhere, always, and by all" (Vincentian Canon); 3. orthodoxy as distinguished from what is heretical or schis-

matical; 4. the undivided Church before the Eastern Schism of 1054; thereafter the Eastern Church has called itself orthodox, in contrast with those Christian bodies which did not accept the definitions of Ephesus and Chalcedon on the divinity of Christ.

In general, today the term "Catholic" refers to those Christians who profess a continued tradition of faith and worship and who hold to the Apostolic succession of bishops and priests since the time of Christ. (Etym. Latin *catholicus,* universal; Greek *katholikos,* universal.)

CATHOLIC ACTION. The apostolate of the laity under the guidance of the hierarchy. Since Catholic Action became an established feature of the Church in modern times, it has undergone several stages of development. The necessary role of the laity in the Church's mission of evangelization and education is one of the principal doctrines of the Second Vatican Council. They are seen as not mere supplements to make up for what is wanting among the clergy, nor even as mere assistants. Their function in the Church's mission to the world is co-ordinate with that of priests and religious, while they serve in the corporal and spiritual works of mercy in deference to the divinely established hierarchy. Consistent with the Church's development of the concept of subsidiarity, lay people are to be given every opportunity to make their own distinctive contribution to the Catholic apostolate. Moreover, with the progress in social communications they are to work co-operatively among themselves in groups and organizations that are always respectful of the local hierarchy but also conscious of their larger, even international responsibility (under the Holy See) to Christianize all of human society.

CATHOLICAM CHRISTI ECCLESIAM. An apostolic letter of Pope Paul VI, establishing the Council of the Laity and the Pontifical Commission for the Study of Justice and Peace. The function of the Council of the Laity is to promote the development of the lay apostolate as a service agency for: 1. co-ordinating apostolic works; 2. establishing liaisons between the laity and the hierarchy; 3. compiling doctrinal studies on the role of lay people in pastoral activity; and 4. establishing and maintaining a documentation center. The purpose of the Commission on Justice and Peace is to: 1. promote and develop awareness among the faithful of their mission to promote the progress of poor nations; 2. encourage international social justice; 3. seek ways and means of establishing peace in the world (January 6, 1967).

CATHOLIC CHURCH. Equivalent to the Roman Catholic Church, an earlier title by which the body of the Christian faithful were identified. It stresses the Church's universality.

CATHOLIC HERMENEUTICS. The science of interpreting the Scriptures according to Catholic tradition, notably in conformity with the Church's magisterium.

CATHOLICISM. The faith, ritual, and morals of the Roman Catholic Church as a historical reality, revealed in Jesus Christ and destined to endure until the end of time. It comprehends all that the Church teaches must be believed and lived out in order to be saved and, beyond salvation, in order to be sanctified. This system of doctrine, cultus, and practice is called Catholic (universal) because it is intended for all mankind, for all time, contains all that is necessary, and is suitable in every circumstance of human life.

CATHOLICITY. Universality of the Church founded by Christ. In the Nicene Creed the Church is said to be "one, holy, *catholic,* and apostolic." The Church's catholicity is first of all spatial, on account of her actual extension over the whole earth. This kind of catholicity may be actual, when the Church is actually extended everywhere; it is virtual in that Christ's intention was to have the Church present among all peoples. Actual catholicity is said to be physical if it embodies all persons of the earth, even if not literally every individual. It is moral if it includes only the greater part of them. Although moral catholicity suffices for the Church's universality, yet it is Christ's will that the Church constantly endeavor to extend. The ideal toward which the Church strives is physical catholicity. A common position among apologists holds that moral catholicity demands that the Church extend over the whole earth simultaneously. Thus after a certain time of development, moral catholicity will be realized and from that time on is to be perpetuated.

CATHOLICOS. Title of the two patriarchates of the Nestorian and Armenian churches, both professedly denying the hypostatic union of two perfect natures in Christ united in the one divine person of the Son of God.

CATHOLIC SCHOOL. An institution under the supervision of the Church whose corporate policy is to train the students in the Gospel message of salvation as taught by the Catholic magisterium. In the words of the Second Vatican Council, "It is the special function of the Catholic school to develop in the school community an atmosphere animated by a spirit of liberty and charity based on the Gospel. It enables young people, while developing their own personality, to grow at the same time in that new life which has been given them at baptism. Finally it so orients the whole of human culture to the message of salvation that the knowledge which the pupils acquire of the world, of life and of men is illumined by faith. Thus the Catholic school, taking into consideration as it should the conditions of an age of progress, prepares its pupils to contribute effectively to the welfare of the world of men and to work for the extension of the kingdom of God" (*Declaration on Christian Education,* 8).

CAUSALITY. The influence of a cause in the production or modification of a being. An efficient cause exercises efficacy on the effect produced; the final cause gives purpose or attraction; an exemplary cause gives guidance; and both material and formal causes communicate their being to the effect, the material supplying that from which a thing is produced and the formal giving it the specific nature it acquired.

CAUSE. A principle from which something originates with consequent dependence. It is a being that in some way directly affects the being or change of something else. It is that which gives existence in some way to another or is the reason for the existence of another being. See also EFFICIENT CAUSE, FIRST CAUSE, MORAL CAUSE, NECESSARY CAUSE, FORMAL CAUSE, MATERIAL CAUSE, FINAL CAUSE, SECONDARY CAUSE.

C.C. *Curatus*—curate (used chiefly in Ireland).

CC.VV. *Clarissimi viri*—illustrious men.

CELEBRANT. The priest or bishop who offers Mass, as distinct from those who assist at the liturgy in various ministries. When a number of priests or bishops offer Mass together, they are called concelebrants. (Etym. Latin *celebrare,* to celebrate, solemnize.)

CELEBRATION. A religious ceremony. Since the Second Vatican Council the term has come to be applied especially to the Eucharist, as the Church's principal liturgical celebration, giving the highest honor and praise to God. (Etym. Latin *celebrare,* to frequent, fill, celebrate.)

CELEBRET. A document stating that the owner is a priest in good standing and requesting that he be permitted to say Mass. It must be signed by his bishop or religious superior. Without it he may meet with a refusal to say Mass if he is a stranger locally. (Etym. Latin *celebret,* let him celebrate.)

CELESTIAL HIERARCHY. The order of superiority among the angels. Considered from the part of God, there is one celestial hierarchy with God in dominion over all the angels, but considered from their part there are three grades of superiority, the lower from the higher differing in perfection and power and where the former are subject to the latter. These subdivisions of the celestial hierarchy are often referred to as choirs.

CELESTINES. A branch of the Benedictines founded by Pope St. Celestine in 1250. It survived until 1785, when its last surviving house of Calavino near Trent was closed. First established on Monte Morrone, its spirit was one of great asceticism, favoring the solitary monastic life. At one time, it numbered one hundred fifty monasteries and exerted great influence even over the mother Benedictine community at Monte Cassino.

CELIBACY. The state of being unmarried and, in Church usage, of one who has never been married. Catholicism distinguishes between lay and ecclesiastical celibacy, and in both cases a person freely chooses for religious reasons to remain celibate.

Lay celibacy was practiced already in the early Church. The men were called "the continent" (*continentes*) and women "virgins" (*virgines*). They were also known as ascetics who were encouraged to follow this form of life by St. Paul. According to the Apostle, "An unmarried man can devote himself to the Lord's affairs, all he need worry about is pleasing the Lord . . . In the same way an unmarried woman, like a young girl, can devote herself to the Lord's affairs; all she need worry about is being holy in body and spirit" (I Corinthians 7:32, 34). Throughout history the Church has fostered a celibate life in the lay state. Towering among the means of sanctity available to the laity, declared the Second Vatican Council, "is that precious gift of divine grace given to some by the Father to devote themselves to God alone more easily with an undivided heart in virginity or celibacy. This perfect continence for love of the kingdom of heaven has always been held in high esteem by the Church as a sign and stimulus of love, and as a singular source of spiritual fertility in the world" (*Constitution on the Church,* 42).

Ecclesiastical celibacy was a logical development of Christ's teaching about continence (Matthew 19:10–12). The first beginnings of religious life were seen in the self-imposed practice of celibacy among men and women who wished to devote themselves to a lifetime following Christ in the practice of the evangelical counsels. Celibacy was one of the features of the earliest hermits and a requirement of the first monastic foundations under St. Pachomius (c. 290–346). Over the centuries religious celibacy has been the subject of the Church's frequent legislation. The Second Vatican Council named chastity first among the evangelical counsels to be practiced by religious and said that "it is a special symbol of heavenly benefits, and for religious it is a most effective means of dedicating themselves wholeheartedly to the divine service and the works of the apostolate" (*Decree on the Up-to-date Renewal of Religious Life,* 12). (Etym. Latin *caelibatus,* single life, celibacy.)

CELL. 1. a small room in a convent or monastery; 2. the separate individual room of a monk or nun; 3. the cottage of a Carthusian or the habitation of a hermit. It is usually furnished with a bed, table, chair, books, and other necessities required for decent living; 4. the name given to an outlying monastic house dependent on a great abbey. (Etym. Latin *cella,* small room, hut.)

CELLA. A small memorial chapel erected in early Christian cemeteries. It was usually built with a small nave terminating in three semicircular apses.

CELTIC CHURCH. The name originally given to the Church in the British Isles before the mission of St. Augustine of Canterbury (d. 604) from Rome (596–97). It was founded by the second century, mainly among the poor, by missions from Rome and Gaul. By the fourth century, it was sufficiently established to send delegates to the Synod of Arles in 314 and the Council of Ariminum in 359. All the evidence indicates that the Celtic Church was little affected by the major heresies of the age. It was in frequent contact with the Church of the Continent and immediately adopted the decisions of Pope Leo I in 455 about the date for Easter. It sent missions to Scotland, Wales, and Ireland. With the coming of Saxons in the fifth century, the Celtic Church was submerged along with the Celtic culture.

CELTIC CROSS. Ancient symbol originating in Ireland. It has circles indented in areas at the juncture of the crossarms. The bars are richly decorated.

CELTIC RITE. A variety of ritual forms used in churches of ancient Britain and Ireland; also in monasteries in France, Germany, Switzerland, and Italy founded by St. Columbanus (550–615) and his disciples. Their points of difference from other rites were on the date of Easter, the manner of administering baptism, and the form of tonsure. The Celtic Rite prevailed from the earliest times until the thirteenth century.

CEMETERY. A parklike enclosure reserved as a burial place. A Catholic cemetery is blessed by a bishop or by a priest deputed by him; the individual graves need no further blessing unless desecrated. The grave of a Catholic in a non-Catholic cemetery should be individually blessed. All who die in the Church have a right to ecclesiastical burial in consecrated ground. (Etym. Latin *coemeterium;* from Greek *koimētērion,* sleeping chamber, burial place.)

CENACLE. The upper room in Jerusalem where the Last Supper was celebrated (Mark 14:14; Luke 22:12) and where the Holy Spirit descended on Pentecost (Acts 1:13). St. Epiphanius (315–402) speaks of a church that had been built there during the time of Emperor Hadrian (117–38). Later on, a large basilica was erected on the same site, which eventually fell into Moslem hands and has since remained their property. The lower part of the present edifice is known as "David's tomb." (Etym. Latin *coenaculum,* dining room.)

CEN. ECCL. *Censura ecclesiastica—*ecclesiastical censure.

CENOBITE. A monk or nun living as a member in a religious group or community. Cenobitical life was instituted in the East by St. Pachomius (290–346) and modified by St. Basil (329–79). The greatest development, fitting it to Western needs, came through St. Benedict's Rule. (Etym. Latin *coenobium,* monastery; from *koinos,* common + *bios,* life.) See also HERMIT.

CENSER. A metal container in which incense is burned. It is usually shaped like a vase or cup with a cover and is suspended by chains. Also called a thurible, it is used at solemn offices of the Church. (Etym. Latin *incendere,* to burn, kindle.)

CENSOR. Clerics who, according to ecclesiastical law, are appointed by the bishop of a diocese to examine before publication those writings or other media of communication that are subject to the Church's supervision. In each case, the censor is to give his judgment in writing. If this is favorable, it should appear on the published work, usually under the phrase *"nihil obstat,"* meaning "nothing hinders [publication]," along with the name of the censor. The bishop's "imprimatur" assumes a previous censorship. In religious communities a prior censorship may be required for its members. If their institute approves, the work may then be submitted to diocesan censorship. (Etym. Latin *censor,* a taxer, valuer, critic.)

CENSORSHIP OF MEDIA. The practice in many countries of publishing the acceptability ratings of movies, plays, and television programs. The screening is done either under official Church authorization or by organized citizens' groups motivated by religious principles.

CENSURE, ECCLESIASTICAL. A penalty by which a baptized person, gravely delinquent and obstinate, is deprived of certain spiritual benefits until he gives up his obstinacy. The Church's right to inflict censure follows from her existence as a perfect society, and the main purpose of censures is corrective. Three main kinds of censures are imposed by Church law: excommunication, interdict, and suspension. Some censures take effect as soon as some grave external sin (such as professing heresy) is committed. Others take effect only on being personally imposed. Moreover, a person can be absolved from his sin through a good confession, and yet have the censure remain until removed by legitimate authority. But in the case of a censure which prevents the reception of the sacraments, the censured person cannot be absolved from the sins until he or she has first been absolved from the censure.

CENSURE, THEOLOGICAL. Doctrinal judgments of the Church by which she stigmatizes certain teachings detrimental to faith or morals. The most severe censure is to have a proposition condemned as "heretical." Other censures include, "suspect of heresy, erroneous, scandalous, seditious, harmful to Christian morals, blasphemous."

CENTURIATORS. First major publishers among the Reformers to reinterpret Christianity historically along Protestant lines. Their *History of the Church of Christ,* published in Basle (1559–74), covered the Church's life from Christ to 1440. Its main author was Matthias Flacius (1520–75), and its dominant theme was that for fourteen centuries the Church founded by Christ was suppressed and dominated by the papal antichrist, until finally liberated by Martin Luther (1483–1546). Among the earliest refutations were those of St. Peter Canisius (1521–97) and Cardinal Baronius (1538–1607), who exposed the historical inaccuracies and the liberties taken with ecclesiastical documents. (Etym. Latin *centurio,* a commander of a hundred.)

CEPHAS. The new name given to Simon Peter by Jesus at their first meeting. "You are Simon, son of John; you are to be called Cephas, meaning Rock" (John 1:42). Cephas is the Aramaic equivalent of the Greek Peter. It is interesting to note that Paul nearly always referred to him as Cephas and only once or twice as Peter (I Corinthians 1:12, 9:5, 15:5). This may indicate that his references appeared in early manuscripts (Galatians 2:7–8). The Greek usage gradually supplanted the Aramaic. (Etym. Aramaic *kepa',* the rock.)

CEREMONIAL. A book containing the order of religious ceremony and worship prescribed for ecclesiastical functions. In the Latin Rite the official publications *Ceremoniale Romanum* and *Ceremoniale Episcoporum* detail the proper ordering of ceremonies. (Etym. Latin *caerimonia,* a ceremony, rite, formal act, observance.)

CEREMONY. 1. a special form or set of acts to be done in public worship; 2. any external act, movement, or gesture accompanying the prayers and public exercises of divine worship.

CERTAIN CONSCIENCE. A state of mind when it has no prudent fear of being wrong about its judgment on some moral issue and firmly decides that some action is right or wrong.

CERTITUDE. Firm assent of the mind to a proposition without fear of error. It implies clear knowledge that the evidence for the assent excludes even the possibility of error.

CESSATION OF LAW. The termination of a positive human law in consequence of a new law replacing the old, or of legitimate custom with years of uninterrupted observance contrary to the law, or where a given law, still on the books, no longer serves its original purpose or is even harmful to the people.

CHAINED BIBLES. An institution of the medieval Church to protect copies of the Bible from thievery. Before the advent of printing, the rarity of books made them available only to the wealthy. They were often locked away in chests. The Church, wishing to make the Bible available to all the faithful and still to ensure it against loss, chained it to a desk or lectern near a window. There even poor students had its use and it was in popular demand. Bias and ignorance have interpreted this chaining as proof that the Church withheld the Bible from the laity.

CHAIN PRAYER. A superstitious practice that consists in the saying of certain prayers successively by many individuals who hope for the favors received, not so much from God's goodness as from the magic effect of this unbroken series of prayers. In its most common form a written or printed prayer is sent to the person who is to form one link in the chain and is asked to say this prayer and to continue the chain by persuading others to take up the praying where he or she leaves off. These in turn are to pass the prayer on to still others. The efficacy of the practice, therefore, is mainly in the chain and not in the prayer. All forms of chain prayer are superstition and correspondingly sinful.

CHAIR OF PETER. A portable chair preserved at the Vatican, believed to have been used by St. Peter the Apostle. The feast of the Chair of St. Peter commemorates the date of his first service in Rome. A similar feast of the Chair of St. Peter commemorates the foundation of the See of Antioch.

CHALDEAN CHRISTIANS. A popular name of the descendants of the ancient Nestorian churches that are now in communion with the Catholic Church. They are in two main groups, those in Turkey and Iran and those in Malabar. Their customs are now similar to those of the Catholic Church, and they follow the Gregorian calendar. They have preserved the use of Syriac as their official liturgical language.

CHALDEAN RITE. The ritual and canonical tradition of Catholics in Iraq and Iran, Palestine, Lebanon, Egypt, Syria, and Turkey. It is also called the Syro-Oriental Rite, and its adherents are former Nestorians who returned to Catholic unity in 1692. Catholics who follow the Syro-Malabarese Rite in India are also associated with the Chaldean Rite.

CHALICE. The cup-shaped vessel or goblet used at Mass to contain the Precious Blood of Christ. For centuries it was made of precious material; if it was not of gold, the interior of the cup was gold-plated. Since the Second Vatican Council, chalices may be of other materials. A chalice is consecrated with holy chrism by a bishop. Regilding the inside does not destroy the consecration. Sometimes the word chalice designates its contents. (Etym. Latin *calix*, cup, goblet, drinking vessel, chalice.)

CHALICE VEIL. A covering for the chalice used at Mass. According to the Church's prescription, since the Second Vatican Council "the chalice should be covered with a veil, which can always be white in color" (*Eucharistiae Sacramentum*, IV, 80).

CHALLONER'S BIBLE. A revised version of the English translation of the Douay Bible and Reims New Testament, by Bishop Richard Challoner (1691–1781). Practically speaking, it was the version of the Bible used by all English-speaking Catholics until the middle of the twentieth century.

CHAMBERLAIN. Over the centuries, the title of several classes of prelates of the Holy See, including: privy chamberlains, who compose the college of masters of pontifical ceremony; privy chamberlains to His Holiness, who are honored for special service to the Church; chamberlains of honor *extra urbem*, who are priests chosen from cities outside of Rome, who have the title of monsignor, and who in turn are subdivided into various classes; and chamberlains of honor of sword and cape, who may not be persons of distinction but nevertheless are deserving of recognition. (Etym. Latin *camera*, a chamber.)

CHANCE. That which is thought to happen without apparent purpose. But from the standpoint of the Catholic faith nothing ever merely happens; everything has a divinely ordained purpose because it is somehow part of God's universal providence. Chance, therefore, is the admission of ignorance as to why something unexplainable takes place, rather than a denial that every event has a reason for taking place. (Etym. Latin *cadere*, to fall.)

CHANCEL. That part of the choir near the altar of a church, where the clergy officiate in liturgical ceremonies. The name comes from *cancellus*, the screen that formerly divided the choir from the nave. (Etym. Latin *cancellus*, a screen.)

CHANCELLOR. In a diocese, he is the chief representative of the bishop, especially in the administration of temporal affairs. His role varies in different dioceses but may include the hearing of applications for faculties and dispensations, the preservation and arrangement of the diocesan documents, and in general acting as the bishop's secretary.

CHANCERY, APOSTOLIC. Formerly the papal office that drafted and issued the more important documents of the Holy See. It was of considerable importance in the Middle Ages, was reorganized in 1908 by Pope St. Pius X, but its functions have been absorbed by other offices of the Vatican since the Code of Canon Law in 1918, and the reorganization of the Roman Curia under Pope Paul VI after the Second Vatican Council. (Etym. Latin *cancellaria*, the record room of a chancellor.)

CHANCERY, DIOCESAN. The administrative branch of a diocese under the authority of the local ordinary; it handles the official documents pertaining to the ecclesiastical affairs of the diocese.

CHANGE. In general, any newness in a being or any origin of a difference. More properly, it is the passing from potency (or possibility) to actuality, which may be either substantial or merely accidental. Substantial change is creation, which means origin from previous nonexistence; or transubstantiation, which is complete change of a substance; or transformation, which occurs when a new living being comes into existence, when food is changed into the living organism that absorbs it, or when a living being dies. Accidental changes are all others.

CHANT. The vocal melody belonging to a liturgical office and forming an integral part of the sacred function. Liturgical chant differs from sacred music in that the latter may adorn a religious service without absolutely belonging to it. Chants are monodic, usually diatonic. Their form ranges from the simple musical recitation of a text to the most elaborate and expressive melodies. (Etym. Latin *cantare*, to sing.)

CHANTED MASS. See HIGH MASS.

CHANTRY. An endowment given to a priest requesting him to sing or say Masses for a person's soul. It may call for additional duties such as acting as chaplain or teaching gratuitously. The term was also used to designate a small chapel wherein the chantry priest said Mass. Chantries added to large churches often contained the tomb of the donor. (Etym. Latin *cantare,* to sing.)

CHANTRY SCHOOLS. Places for the education of children, in pre-Reformation times, attached to endowed chantries. In England most of the schools operated by the government after secession from Rome had been former chantry schools.

CHAOS. That which is formless, confused, totally disorderly, and absolutely lawless. Plato (427–347 B.C.) applies the term to the orderless matter before the world former (Demiurge) introduced order in the universe, changing chaos into cosmos. Chaos is also the original condition of the world as described in the Bible (Genesis 1:2). (Etym. Greek *chaos,* chaos, abyss; literally, a cleft; Latin *chaos,* chaos, confusion.)

CHAPEL. A relatively small place for liturgical worship by the members of a private or religious family. Sometimes it is an oratory in another, larger building or a small, consecrated detached room or building having an altar. Side chapels in churches often have a special purpose, as for the reservation of the Blessed Sacrament or as a shrine. (Etym. Latin *cappella,* originally a shrine in which was preserved the *capa* or cloak of St. Martin of Tours.)

CHAPEL OF EASE. A supplementary chapel built to accommodate people living at a distance from their parish church, usually in an outlying district or suburb. The clergy in charge may be vicars of the main parish. At first baptismal fonts were not found in such chapels, as certain parochial functions were reserved for the parish church, but later many chapels of ease had their own fonts. Marriages and burials were usually performed in the main church, with which the cemetery, if any, was always connected. Chapels of ease would often become independent parishes when the number of parishioners warranted the change.

CHAPLAIN. A priest who serves a chapel or oratory or is appointed to exercise the sacred ministry in an institution, such as a convent or orphanage, hospital or prison.

Also a priest or other sacred minister appointed to serve special classes of persons, such as the armed forces, or authorized to lead religious services in the assemblies of fraternal organizations, legislatures, and other bodies. (Etym. Latin *cappellanus;* from *cappella,* shrine.)

CHAPLET. Beads strung together on which prayers are counted as they are recited. The five decade rosary is the best known. Combinations of a few beads for saying aspirations honoring some saint are also called chaplets. (Etym. French *chaplet,* a headdress, wreath.)

CHAPTER, ECCLESIASTICAL. A body of clerics instituted for observing greater solemnity in divine worship, and at cathedral churches for assisting a bishop according to canon law. The name arose from the custom of reading a chapter of the rules at a prescribed periodic meeting of the members. Where there is no diocesan chapter, diocesan consultors act as a bishop's senate. Chapters can be cathedral, collegiate, secular, or regular, depending on the composition of their members. They go back to the presbytery in the early centuries and were thoroughly established by the thirteenth century. (Etym. Latin *capitulum,* literally, a little head, a chapter, a principal division.)

CHAPTER HOUSE. A building attached to a cathedral or monastery where certain meetings were held, business carried out, the martyrology read, and daily tasks assigned. The name arose from the practice of conducting the chapter of faults in this building.

CHAPTER, LEGISLATIVE. The general or regional meeting of delegates of a religious institute to discuss and decide on matters affecting the spiritual life and apostolate of the community. Chapters of religious institutes have assumed extraordinary importance since the Second Vatican Council. They were given the right to "alter, temporarily, certain prescriptions of the constitutions . . . by way of experiment, provided that the purpose, nature and character of the institute are safeguarded." (*Ecclesiae Sanctae,* 1966, II, 6).

CHAPTER, LITURGICAL. Formerly the verse that followed the Psalms at Lauds, Prime, Terce, Sext, None, Vespers, and the hymn at Compline in the Divine Office. The new name is *Lectio Brevis,* Short Reading.

CHAPTER, MONASTIC. The periodic meeting of the members of a monastic community. At this meeting, there is customarily the reading of the day's martyrology, self-accusation of external faults against the rule, the imposition by the superior of appropriate penances, and the discussion of important matters affecting the life and discipline of the community.

CHAPTER OF THE BIBLE. Divisions within the books of Holy Scripture first made by Stephen Langton (d. 1228), theologian in Paris and later Archbishop of Canterbury. Most likely he used an already existing division.

CHARACTER. Moral qualities of a person, founded on his or her temperament and developed by free choices, which distinguish one as an individual; a person's habitual virtues and failings which make one a distinct moral individual. In a praiseworthy sense, character is the integration of a person's nature and nurture in one's moral habits and the expression of these in daily living. (Etym. Latin *character;* from Greek *charaktēr,* an engraved or stamped mark.)

CHARIS. The basic term in the New Testament for "grace," especially in the letters of St. Paul. Building on the profane sense of attractiveness or charm, the biblical meaning designates the goodness of God, which is at once generous and gratuitous, undeserved by humans and sanctifying by God. *Charis* is closely identified with the whole Gospel. Ultimately it determines why the Good News is good, because God's favor raises humans to a share in God's own divine nature (Ephesians 1:6), redeems humans from sin (Romans 5:15), and enables them to practice virtue after the example of Jesus Christ (I Corinthians 1:4). In the language of St. Paul *charis* differs from *charisma* as a divine favor that sanctifies the person, differs from a spiritual gift that enables its receiver to perform some office or function in the Church for others. (Etym. Greek *kharisma,* favor, divine gift, from *kharizesthai,* to favor, from *kharis,* grace, favor.)

CHARISMA. Strong personal appeal or magnetism that is possessed by some people and that resembles the supernatural charisms known to Christian revelation. It is more often used in the form of "charismatic" to describe such persons. They can influence others almost without trying and their ability to do so seems to partake of the miraculous. (Etym. Greek *charisma,* favor, gift.)

CHARISMATIC MOVEMENT. A modern revival of Pentecostalism in many Christian churches, including Roman Catholic. The term "charismatic" is preferred in Catholic circles to "Pentecostal," which is more commonly used by Protestant leaders of the movement.

CHARISM FOR MIRACLES. One of several supernatural gifts enjoyed in the early Church for working miraculous phenomena: 1. *faith* (I Corinthians 12:9, 13:2), a special form of the infused gift of faith that leads a person to trust implicitly that, in a given situation, God will indeed manifest his miraculous power in response to prayer; 2. *performing miracles* (I Corinthians 12:10, 28), an extraordinary charism by which an individual can call upon divine power to work miraculous phenomena; 3. *miraculous healing* (I Corinthians 12:9, 30), the specialized gift of suddenly restoring the gravely sick to full bodily health.

CHARISMS. Literally "gifts of grace" (charismata), described by St. Paul as gratuitous blessings of an extraordinary and transitory nature conferred directly for the good of others. Indirectly they may also benefit the one who possesses the charisms, but their immediate purpose is for the spiritual welfare of the Christian community.

Depending on the classification, the charisms are variously numbered. The longest single enumeration is in St. Paul (I Corinthians 12:1–14, 40). Spiritual writers often list five categories, based on the Pauline writings and the Acts of the Apostles, namely charisms of instruction, administration, miracles, service, and prayer.

CHARISMS OF ADMINISTRATION. Supernatural gifts for organizing and ruling the people of God, enumerated by St. Paul: 1. *pastor* (Ephesians 4:11; Acts 20:28), formerly the special grace of office enjoyed by the presbyter-bishops to rule the Church of God, not to be confused with the priestly power conferred only by sacred orders; 2. *administrator* (Romans 12:8; I Thessalonians 5:12; I Timothy 5:17), the special charism of an official in the Church was the gift of solicitude, which maintained a wise balance between diligence for the organizational work to be done and concern for the individual person whom the administrator was to direct; 3. *minister* (I Corinthians 16:15; Romans 12:7), one who helped the presbyter-priests and assisted Church administrators, and who had the need of humility and willingness to work.

CHARISMS OF KNOWLEDGE. Extraordinary supernatural gifts for the mind to instruct others in the Christian faith. In the writings of St. Paul six classes of persons are distinguished as specially endowed to communicate the Gospel. These gifts were not limited to the original twelve Apostles and St. Paul, but refer to anyone who is sent out to proclaim the Good News: 1. *prophet* (I Corinthians 12:28), one who speaks for God and with his authorization. Among the revelations that prophets received were sometimes the prediction of future events (Acts 11:27–30, 21:10–14). They exhorted and strengthened the faithful (Acts 15:32), they edified, encouraged, and consoled (I Corinthians 14:3), and they could read men's hearts (I Corinthians 14:24–25). This gift was shared also by women (I Corinthians 11:5; Acts 21:9); 2. *evangelist* (Acts 21:8; II Timothy 4:5), not to be confused with the inspired writers of the Gospels, an evangelist was probably one appointed to strengthen new churches but not to found them; 3. *teacher* (Romans 12:7; Ephesians 4:11; I Timothy 4:13, 16), an inspired catechist who was able to bring home to his listeners the inner meaning of the Gospel; 4. *exhorter* (Romans 12:8; I Timothy 4:13; Acts 4:36), a preacher with a special gift to persuade the faithful to put the teachings of Christ into generous practice; 5. *proclaimer of wisdom* (I Corinthians 12:8), one who could explain the highest reaches of divine revelation; 6. *proclaimer of knowledge* (I Corinthians 12:8), one who could explain revealed truths by comparison with human knowledge. Most probably the last two gifts were possessed in varying degrees by all the preceding.

CHARISMS OF PRAYER. Extraordinary gifts of communing with God, as described by St. Paul. The entire fourteenth chapter of his first letter to the Corinthians is devoted to this subject, under the aspect of the gift of tongues. He distinguished two forms of the gift. There is the charism of praying to God in spirit but in words that are not intelligible to the mind. Paul tells the Christians to ask God to give them an understanding of what they are praying in spirit. They must also make sure that if they use the gift in public someone with the correlative gift of interpretation of tongues is present to explain what was said. "If there is no interpreter present, they must keep quiet in church and speak only to themselves and to God" (I Corinthians 14:28). Above all, everything must be done for the common, and not only individual, good.

CHARISMS OF SERVICE. Supernatural gifts described by St. Paul, conferred on persons in the service of the faithful: 1. *almsgiving* (Romans 12:8), the receiving of supernatural tact in service of the poor and needy with simplicity of intention; 2. *manifestation of mercy* (Romans 12:8), the quality of showing compassion for the unfortunate, the imprisoned, and the sick, along with the ability to remain always cheerful even under duress; 3. *helpfulness* (I Corinthians 12:28), the gift of simplicity in being of ready service to anyone in need; 4. *leadership* (I Corinthians 12:28), distinct from the charism of administration as a supernatural gift of taking the initiative and of directing others for the good of the Mystical Body.

CHARITY. The infused supernatural virtue by which a person loves God above all things for his own sake, and loves others for God's sake. It is a virtue based on divine faith or in belief in God's revealed truth, and is not acquired by mere human effort. It can be conferred only by divine grace. Because it is infused along with sanctifying grace, it is frequently identified with the state of grace. Therefore, a person who has lost the supernatural virtue of charity has lost the state of grace, although he may still possess the virtues of hope and faith.

CHARITY, ACT OF. A supernatural act, based on faith, wherein God is loved for himself and not for any hope of reward. An act of charity requires divine grace, either sanctifying or actual or both. It is necessary for justification in the absence of baptism, sacramental absolution, or anointing. It is also the normal way of growing in the virtue of charity. A simple and widely used act of charity says: "My God, because you are so good, I love you with all my heart, and for your sake, I love my neighbor as myself. Amen." (Etym. Latin *caritas,* love; from *carus,* dear.)

CHARM. In general, the power to allure or draw or fascinate. Specifically any object that when worn or carried on one's person is believed to ward off evil or ensure good fortune. Charms can also be words or gestures believed to have the same power. To charm, therefore, means to cast a spell upon or influence someone beyond the ordinary powers of nature. As a form of superstition, charms are sinful. As a part of animism, they are the same as amulets and belong to the same category as witchcraft.

CHARTERHOUSE. The English version of the French *maison chartreuse*, a Carthusian religious house. A famous English school also has the same name, being originally built on the site of the London Charterhouse, whose last prior was martyred with his fifteen monks, 1535–40, under Henry VIII (1491–1547). (Etym. French *Chartreuse*.)

CHARTRES. The most admired of all the French cathedrals, situated in the flat country of Beauce, forty-eight miles southwest of Paris. It is dedicated to the Blessed Virgin. In the upper church is the chapel of Our Lady of the Pillar and in the lower church one honoring "Virgini Pariturae," at which it is said the Druids paid honor to the seated virgin with a child on her knees, in the small grotto that enclosed her. Early in A.D. 300 a Christian church was built over that grotto. In 1195 the present cathedral was begun and was finally completed in A.D. 1250. The stained-glass jeweled windows represent in detail the life and perfections of Mary, Virgin and Mother. Chartres also has Mary's own veil to show pilgrims, contained in a magnificent reliquary. This relic belonged to Charlemagne (742–814), who had it transferred from Aachen to Chartres in 876. The second outstanding relic of Chartres is the statue of the Black Virgin, the "Notre Dame-du-Pilier" in the upper church, the Mother holding her Infant Son on the left while her right hand holds a gold scepter. The niche that holds them is filled with token hearts of gold, offerings for the cures wrought over the centuries through Mary's intercession.

CHASTITY. The virtue that moderates the desire for sexual pleasure according to the principles of faith and right reason. In married people, chastity moderates the desire in conformity with their state of life; in unmarried people who wish to marry, the desire is moderated by abstention until (or unless) they get married; in those who resolve not to marry, the desire is sacrificed entirely.

Chastity and purity, modesty and decency are comparable in that they have the basic meaning of freedom from whatever is lewd or salacious. Yet they also differ. Chastity implies an opposition to the immoral in the sense of lustful or licentious. It suggests refraining from all acts or thoughts that are not in accordance with the Church's teaching about the use of one's reproductive

powers. It particularly stresses restraint and an avoidance of anything that might defile or make unclean the soul because the body has not been controlled in the exercise of its most imperious passion. (Etym. Latin *castus*, morally pure, unstained.)

CHASTITY, VOW OF. See CELIBACY.

CHASUBLE. A sleeveless outer garment worn by a priest at Mass. It is worn over all other vestments and is made of silk, velvet, or other rich material usually decorated with symbols. The arms are to be free when it is worn. It symbolizes the yoke of Christ and signifies charity. (Etym. Latin *casula*, a little house; hence a mantle.)

CHEATING. Deception by trickery or fraud in order to gain materially, socially, or psychologically. Cheating is always sinful. Its gravity depends on the harm inflicted on the person defrauded or on some third party. True repentance for cheating requires at least the willingness to make restitution for the harm that may have been caused.

CHEERFULNESS. See GLADNESS.

CHERUB (plural, cherubim). Heavenly creatures mentioned in the Bible as guardians and protectors. Cherubim were the sentinels stationed at Eden (Genesis 3:24); they were golden figures erected on the Ark (Exodus 25:18). Yahweh mounted a cherub to rush to the rescue of David from his enemies (II Samuel 22:11). In Christian tradition the cherubim are identified as angels. (Etym. Hebrew *kĕrūbh*; Latin *cherub*; Greek *cheroub*.) See also CHERUBIM.

CHERUBIC CONTEMPLATION. That elevation of the mind and heart upon God and his attributes in which knowledge predominates over love. It is contrasted with seraphic contemplation.

CHERUBIM. The second of the nine choirs of angels. According to Pope St. Gregory the Great they have the "fullness of knowledge, more perfect because they may behold the glory of God more closely" (Genesis 3).

CHEVET. See APSE.

CHILDERMAS DAY. An old English name for the feast of the Holy Innocents, December 28. It is a Catholic custom for parents to formally bless their children on this day.

CHILDLIKENESS. The quality of guileless openness that Christ declared is one of the conditions for attaining salvation (Matthew

18:3). It is the virtue of humility, at once ready to do God's will and having no selfish interests of one's own.

CHILDREN. Those who have reached the age of discretion but are not yet adolescents, and for whom there are special provisions in ecclesiastical law. In general, children are those from the age of seven, when the sacraments of penance and the Eucharist are to be received, to the age of fourteen, when abstinence is to be observed. Children may also receive the sacrament of anointing and should be confirmed.

CHILDREN OF GOD. A biblical term for all who believe in Christ and strive to do God's will: "Think of the love that the Father has lavished on us, by letting us be called God's children; and that is what we are" (I John 3:1).

CHILDREN'S CRUSADE. The march of thousands of children gathered from many parts of Europe to form the Fourth Crusade and capture the Holy Land. It was current belief that the sacred places of Palestine could be secured only by the pure of heart, hence the children. Some accounts speak of three contingents: one under a shepherd boy of Vendôme, another led by a youth from Cologne, and a third got to Brindisi and met various fates. Most of the children died of hunger and exhaustion, some perished at sea, and some through the shipowners' treachery were sold as slaves to the Moors. The whole action was an example of scandalous misconception and direction.

CHILDREN'S MASS. Special Eucharistic liturgy for children of preadolescent age. In 1973 the Congregation for Divine Worship issued special guidelines for children's Masses. It provides for adaptation to their mental and spiritual level, while keeping intact the principal parts of the Mass. A *Directory for Masses with Children* was approved by Pope Paul VI on October 22, 1973.

CHILIASM. Millenarianism, or the theory that Christ's second coming will last a thousand years before the final consummation of the world.

CHIME. A set of tuned bells to make musical sounds. The term is also applied to the melody played and to a handbell used liturgically. The chimes of St. Peter's in Rome are endowed and rung in accordance with a complicated ceremonial program. The har-

monious beauty of some chimes has made them world famous.

CHIMES. A set of from five to twelve bells that are tuned to a scale and that produce a sound of harmony when struck by a hammer.

CHINA, OUR LADY OF. A Marian sanctuary in the village of Tong Lu near Peiping. In 1900 the village was attacked by about ten thousand rioters during the Boxer Rebellion. In their rage they started to shoot skyward where a woman dressed in white had appeared, but her apparition did not fade. The crazed mob was put to flight at the appearance of a strange horseman. Father Wu, a Chinese priest, admitted having prayed to Mary for help. A church was built on the site, honoring a picture of Mary and the Christ Child which was placed over the main altar. During the progress of the Red Revolution, the people had the treasured painting copied, and when the Chinese Communists destroyed the Tong Lu church the copy was burned. But the original picture known as *Our Lady of China* had been hidden and is now thought to be in the possession of some faithful priests living in disguise.

CHINESE RITES. Ancient Catholic rites practiced by the Chinese whom the Jesuits converted to Christianity in the seventeenth and eighteenth centuries. These rites allowed the honoring of ancestors and the paying of token respect to Confucius. The Jesuit missionaries, notably Matteo Ricci, S.J. (1552–1610), considered these rites essentially cultural and not religious and consequently not compromising to the purity of the Christian religion. It was also believed that their practice would make the people more tolerant of Christianity. Other missionaries objected and much misunderstanding developed. In the Apostolic Constitution *Ex illa die,* Pope Clement XI in 1715 and Pope Benedict XIV in 1742 forbade these rites to be continued among the converts on the ground that they had a basis of superstition that could not be overlooked. The Holy See, feeling that Ricci's error was one of judgment and not of faith or morals, forbade anyone from saying that the good missionary had approved idolatry.

CHI-RHO. A symbol of Christ, arranged as a monogram, comprising the first two letters, XP, of his name in Greek. First presented publicly in the fifth century, it has been found in catacomb inscriptions of the second century. The P is usually vertically rendered with a single crossbar producing the X, but sometimes an additional transverse cross is used for embellishment and the initials A and Ω are free or attached to the added bar. Emperor Constantine (d. 337) employed it as an emblem on his military standard, the labarum, and ancient Welsh and Scottish tomb monuments bear this symbol carved in stone. As a monogram denoting triumph it fell into disuse after the fall of Rome, the Cross supplanting it. (Etym. Greek *chi*, X; *rho*, P.)

CHIROGRAPHUS. A personal letter of the Pope, usually treating of an immediate event of grave concern. Several such letters were addressed to Cardinal Gasparri (1852–1934) by Pope Pius XI, e.g., on Holy Saturday, 1926, about Mexico; and on Corpus Christi, 1929, about Mussolini (1883–1945). (Etym. Greek *cheirographein*, to write with the hand.)

CHIVALRY. In its full sense the ensemble of ideals, customs, discipline, and sentiments that guided men in the Middle Ages in time of war and peace. This goes further than the traditions of medieval knighthood, although it includes the latter, and extends to all the Christian virtues that characterized a truly Christian gentleman in the ages of faith. He was to be a soldier, using his sword if necessary to uphold the cause of Christ against the Lord's enemies; he was loyal to the Church's teaching, chaste, and courageous; he was courteous and respectful to women, generous and merciful. (Etym. French *cheval*, horse; from Latin *caballus*, horse.)

CHLOE. A woman in Corinth whose "people" (servants or slaves) warned Paul of a growing spirit of divisiveness among Christians. Their loyalty to the faith was becoming subordinated to their devotion to individual leaders, e.g., Paul, Apollos, Cephas. Heeding this warning, he began his ministry in Corinth with a fervent plea for unity. Little is known about Chloe herself (I Corinthians 1:11).

CHOICE. Free judgment arising from reason; a decision to select one out of a number of available courses of action; an act of the free will choosing a particular means to some preconceived purpose or end.

CHOIR. 1. the part of a church reserved for choristers; 2. an organized body of singers who perform or lead the musical part of a church service; 3. in monasteries where the Divine Office is chanted the stalls accommo-dating the monks or nuns and separated from the sanctuary by carved low partitions; 4. one of the nine orders of angels. (Etym. Latin *chorus*, a choir; Greek *choros*, a dance, a band of dancers or singers.)

CHOIR RELIGIOUS. Members of religious institutes committed to the daily recitation of the Divine Office in common or in private even though they are not in holy orders. The term was first applied to religious in solemn perpetual vows, contrasted with those professed under simple vows.

CHOLERIC TEMPERAMENT. One of the four classic temperaments, characterized by irritability and bad temper. A familiar term to Catholic spiritual writers. Choleric personalities have to struggle with their natural tendency to anger at the least provocation. (Etym. Latin *cholera*, bile.)

CHORALE. A choral hymn or song; any part of the service sung by the choir, prevalent in early German Protestant churches.

CHORISTER. A member of a group of singers; an individual in the choir entrusted with the musical part of a church service. Choristers are organized and instructed for such an assignment.

CHRISM. A consecrated mixture of olive oil and balsam. Blessed by a bishop, it is used in the public administration of baptism, confirmation, and holy orders; in the blessing of tower bells, baptismal water, and in the consecration of churches, altars, chalices, and patens. (Etym. Middle English *chrisom*, short for chrism cloth.) See also HOLY CHRISM.

CHRISMA. A symbol of Christ. It is a monogram of the Greek letters *chi* and *rho*, shaped like an X and P, but equivalent to CH and R in Latin or English. Also called Chi Rho. (Etym. Latin *chrisma;* from Greek *khrisma*, ointment, from *khriein*, to anoint.)

CHRISMAL or CHRISMATORY. A metal jar or box for holding the holy oils and chrism. It is sometimes referred to as an oil stock. The name was formerly given to a pall or corporal covering for the altar or relics, and to the robe of the newly baptized.

CHRISMARIUM. A place in a church set aside for the administration of confirmation; a jar used for holy oils.

CHRISMATION. The act of anointing. Consequently, the use of chrism for anointing in the administration of the sacraments and in the blessing of persons and things.

CHRISMATORY. A three-compartment vessel for each of the three holy oils: chrism, oil of catechumens, and oil of the sick. The vessel is often inscribed with the Latin abbreviation for each holy oil: S.C. (*sacrum chrisma*), O.C. (*oleum catechumenorum*), and O.I. (*oleum infirmorum*). It has been in use since the Middle Ages. One set of these oils is kept on reserve in a cathedral, and smaller sets for use in a parish, hospital, or infirmary are kept locked in a cupboard in the sanctuary of each church.

CHRISOM. The white robe put on a young child at baptism as a symbol of cleansing from sin. If a child died within a month of its baptism, the garment was used as a shroud and the infant was called a "chrisom child." Its use gradually disappeared in most places, but the recent baptismal rite refers to a "white garment," which can be a full vesture similar to the ancient chrisom.

CHRIST. The word means "anointed," from the Greek *christos*. See JESUS; SACRAMENT OF GOD.

CHRIST, NEW TESTAMENT NAMES AND TITLES.
The following is a list of names and titles of Christ, together with their biblical citations, that appear in the New Testament:

I John 2:1	Advocate
Revelation 1:8; 22:13	Alpha and Omega
Revelation 3:14	Amen
Hebrews 3:1	Apostle and High Priest of our religion
Luke 2:12	Baby
Matthew 12:18	Beloved
John 6:33	Bread of God
John 6:35	Bread of life
John 6:50	Bread that comes down from heaven
John 3:29	Bridegroom
Mark 6:3	Carpenter
Matthew 13:55	Carpenter's son
I Peter 5:4	Chief shepherd
Matthew 2:20	Child
Luke 23:35	Chosen One
Matthew 16:20	Christ
I Timothy 1:15; Colossians 1:1	Christ Jesus
Luke 9:20	Christ of God
Luke 2:12	Christ the Lord
Romans 9:5	Christ who is above all
Hebrews 2:9	Crowned with glory and splendor
Romans 8:29	Eldest of many brothers
Revelation 1:5; 3:14	Faithful witness
Matthew 12:18	Favorite
Revelation 1:17; 2:8	First and the Last
Revelation 1:5	Firstborn from the dead
Colossians 1:15	Firstborn of all creation
Luke 2:7	Firstborn (Son)
I Corinthians 15:20	First fruits
Matthew 11:19	Friend of tax collectors and sinners
John 10:7	Gate of the sheepfold
John 10:11, 14	Good Shepherd
John 12:41	Glory
Luke 2:32	Glory of your people Israel
Hebrews 7:22	Greater Covenant
Hebrews 13:20	Great Shepherd of the sheep
Ephesians 4:16	Head
Colossians 1:18	Head of the Church (Now the Church is his body, he is its head)
I Corinthians 11:3	Head of every man
Colossians 2:10	Head of every Sovereignty and Power
Revelation 2:17	Hidden manna
Hebrews 3:1; 4:14; 7:26	High priest
Acts 2:27	Holy One
Mark 1:25	Holy One of God
Acts 4:27	Holy servant Jesus
I Timothy 1:2	Hope
John 8:58	I am
II Corinthians 4:5	Image of God
Colossians 1:15	Image of the unseen God
Matthew 1:23	Immanuel
II Corinthians 9:15	Inexpressible gift
I Peter 3:18	Innocent
Luke 2:25	Israel's comforting
Matthew 1:21	Jesus
I John 2:1	Jesus Christ who is just
Hebrews 6:20	Jesus has entered before us
John 18:5	Jesus the Nazarene
Acts 7:52	Just One
Matthew 21:5	King
John 1:50	King of Israel
Revelation 17:14; I Timothy 6:15	King of kings
Revelation 15:3	King of nations
Hebrews 7:2	King of righteousness
Matthew 2:2	King of the Jews
John 1:29, 37	Lamb of God
Revelation 5:12	Lamb that was sacrificed

I Peter 1:20	Lamb without spot or stain
I Corinthians 15:45	Last Adam
Matthew 2:6	Leader
Acts 5:31	Leader and Savior
Hebrews 2:10	Leader who would take them to their salvation
Romans 11:26	Liberator
John 14:6; Colossians 3:4	Life
John 12:35	Light
John 1:4	Light of men
John 8:12	Light of the world
Luke 2:32	Light to enlighten the pagans
Revelation 5:5	Lion of the tribe of Judah
John 6:51	Living Bread
I Peter 2:4	Living stone
Luke 1:25	Lord
John 20:28	Lord and my God
Romans 14:9	Lord both of the dead and of the living
Acts 7:59; I Corinthians 12:3	Lord Jesus (Jesus is Lord)
Acts 10:36	Lord of all men
I Corinthians 2:9	Lord of Glory
I Timothy 6:15	Lord of lords
II Thessalonians 3:16	Lord of peace
Ephesians 2:21	Main cornerstone
John 19:6	Man, The
I Timothy 2:5	Mediator
John 1:41; 4:25	Messiah
Hebrews 8:2	Minister of the sanctuary and of the True Tent of Meeting
II Peter 1:20; Revelation 2:29	Morning Star
Matthew 2:23	Nazarene
Hebrews 1:12	Never change
Revelation 22:16	Of David's line
Ephesians 4:5	One Lord
John 10:16	One shepherd
John 1:14	Only Son of the Father
I Corinthians 5:8	Passover
Hebrews 1:3	Perfect copy of his (God's) nature
I Corinthians 1:25	Power and the wisdom of God
Luke 1:69	Power for salvation
I Peter 2:6	Precious cornerstone
Hebrews 5:6	Priest for ever (You are a priest of the order of Melchizedek, and for ever)
Acts 3:15	Prince of life
Luke 1:76	Prophet of the Most High

Hebrews 1:3	Radiant light of God's glory
I Timothy 2:6	Ransom
Romans 3:25	Reconciliation
Hebrews 7:25	Remains for ever
John 11:25	Resurrection
II Timothy 4:8	Righteous judge
Luke 1:78	Rising Sun
Revelation 22:16	Root of David
I Timothy 6:15	Ruler of all
Revelation 1:5	Ruler of the kings of the earth
II Peter 2:20; 3:18	Savior
I John 4:14; John 4:42	Savior of the world
Romans 15:8	Servant of circumcised Jews
I Peter 2:24	Shepherd and guardian of your souls
Philippians 2:7	Slave
Galatians 4:5	Son
Matthew 1:1	Son of Abraham
Matthew 1:1	Son of David
Luke 1:36	Son of God
John 1:45	Son of Joseph
John 5:27	Son of Man
Mark 6:3	Son of Mary
Mark 14:61, 62	Son of the Blessed One
II John 3	Son of the Father
Matthew 16:17	Son of the living God
Luke 1:32	Son of the Most High
Mark 5:7	Son of the Most High God
Colossians 1:14	Son that he loves
Matthew 17:5	Son, the Beloved
I Corinthians 10:4	Spiritual rock
I Peter 2:8	Stone rejected
I Peter 2:8	Stone to stumble over
Matthew 23:11	Teacher
Hebrews 9:16	Testator
I John 5:20	True God
John 1:9	True light
John 15:1	True vine
John 14:6	Truth
Revelation 3:15	Ultimate source of God's creation
John 14:6	Way
John 12:24	Wheat grain
I Corinthians 1:25	Wisdom of God
John 1:1	Word
Revelation 19:14	Word of God
John 1:14	Word was made flesh
I John 1:1	Word who is life

CHRIST CANDLE. A white candle placed in the home and lighted on the family table during meals for the octave of Christmas. It symbolizes Christ the Light of the World, which is one of the principal themes of St. John's Gospel (John 8:12).

CHRISTE ELEISON. "Christ, have mercy." The Greek invocation for divine mercy in the Eucharistic liturgy of the Latin Mass, said or sung alternately with Kyrie Eleison, "Lord, have mercy."

CHRISTENDOM. The Christian polity insofar as the principles of Christianity governed (and still govern) the laws and civil institutions of nations. Its foundations may be traced to the Jewish traditions of a theocracy, and its history properly began with the liberation of the Church under Constantine. It developed through more than a millennium in most of the countries of Europe and with numerous setbacks remained fairly intact until the Protestant Reformation. In its best days, Christendom represented the corporate Christian social life, and its impact on world civilization through the arts and philosophy, law and the medieval universities has been great and lasting. With the changed conditions in the world, the Second Vatican Council expressed the Church's new role in civil society: "By reason of her role and competence, the Church is not identified with any political community nor bound by ties to any political system. She is at once the sign and the safeguard of the transcendental dimension of the human person" (*Church in the Modern World*, IV, 76).

CHRISTENING. Conferring the sacrament of baptism, with stress on giving the person a Christian name at baptism, or giving someone a Christian name even later on.

CHRISTIAN. A person who is baptized. A professed Christian also believes in the essentials of the Christian faith, notably in the Apostles' Creed. A Catholic Christian further accepts the teachings of the Roman Catholic Church, participates in the Eucharistic liturgy and sacraments of Catholic Christianity, and gives allegiance to the Catholic hierarchy and especially to the Bishop of Rome.

CHRISTIAN BROTHERS. Several communities of nonclerical men religious engaged in various apostolic works. The best known are the Congregation of Christian Brothers, formerly Christian Brothers of Ireland, founded in 1802 at Waterford, Ireland, by Edmund Ignatius Rice; the Brothers of Christian Instruction, founded in 1817 at Ploërmel, France, by the Abbés Lamennais and Deshayes; and the Brothers of the Christian Lamennais Schools, founded 1680 at Rheims, France, by St. John Baptist de la Salle.

CHRISTIAN CHURCH. The community of believers in Christ. Three approaches to the meaning of the Christian Church are distinguishable in Catholic teaching. Before the Eastern Schism in 1054 the accepted definition of the Church was the whole body of the faithful united under allegiance to the Pope. With the rise of Eastern Orthodoxy, which redefined the Church without obedience to the Pope, Catholicism began to stress the term Roman Catholic Church in order to emphasize the need for allegiance to the Bishop of Rome.

With the rise of Protestantism in the sixteenth century, the Catholic Church sensed the need to bring out the visible nature of the Church, challenged by the Reformers. Accordingly there entered the stream of Catholic theology the definition of the Church based on the words of St. Robert Bellarmine (1542–1621). "The one and true Church," he said, "is the assembly of men, bound together by the profession of the same Christian faith, and by the communion of the same sacraments, under the rule of legitimate pastors, and in particular of the one Vicar of Christ on earth, the Roman Pontiff." In modern times, Pope Pius XII defined the Church on earth as the mystical body of Christ, according to the teaching of St. Paul that the faithful followers of Christ are joined together in a mysterious union, of which Christ himself is the invisible head. The Second Vatican Council added the title "People of God" to describe the Christian world. Without abandoning the earlier definitions the Council offered this one to bring out the fact that all Christians belong by special title to God, who calls them to faith in Christ, and that they form a people, i.e., a chosen community, on whom God confers his special blessings for the benefit of mankind.

CHRISTIAN DECALOGUE. The Ten Commandments as part of the Christian religion. Christ on several occasions confirmed the binding character of the Decalogue (Matthew 5:21–27; Mark 7:10, 10:19; John 7:19) and even made them more stringent. He deepened and supplemented them in the Sermon on the Mount, and summed up their obligations in the double precept of loving God and one's neighbor (Matthew 12:29–31).

From the beginning the Church considered the Ten Commandments a standard way of teaching the faithful. At the Council of Trent the theory was condemned that "the Ten Commandments do not pertain at all to Christians" (Denzinger 1569).

There are two arrangements of the Decalogue in use among Christians. The Catholic Church, along with certain Protestants, e.g., Lutherans, follow the Massoretic (traditional) text in combining the two prohibitions about false worship into one. The number ten is made up by dividing the precept against covetousness into the last two commandments. See also TEN COMMANDMENTS.

CHRISTIAN EDUCATION. Development of the whole person, body, mind, and spiritual powers according to the norms of reason and revelation and with the help of divine grace, in order to prepare him or her for a happy and useful life in this world and for eternal beatitude in the world to come.

CHRISTIAN FORTITUDE. The virtue of fortitude, based on faith and motivated by the love of God. Many adversities confront those who would devoutly follow Christ, as he foretold. But they are not heavy, for the suffering, though real, is lightened by love. When someone is in love, that person does not feel overwhelmed by the sufferings endured for the sake of the beloved. One makes little of them. And so the New Law is not oppressive. "My yoke is easy," Christ promised, "and my burden light" (Matthew 11:29). It is love that makes it so.

CHRISTIANITY. The religion of Jesus Christ. It is a composite of the faith he inspired, the teachings and moral practices he communicated, the spirituality he urged on his followers, and the consequent form of civilization which for two millennia have been called Christian. It is above all the objective principles of belief, worship, and human conduct that give substance to this civilization, which is only as Christian as these principles are known and put into practice.

CHRISTIANIZATION. The gradual penetration of a society with Christian values and principles. As a world view, it sees the crisis of the modern age as the tragedy of trying to save individuals where society is dechristianized. The two are seen as inseparable. Christians are said to live in the hope of future generations developing a culture that so respects the teachings of Christ as to give people not only the promise of heavenly glory but a foretaste, in this life, of God's kingdom.

CHRISTIANIZE. To convert to Christianity, as applied to individuals, and to imbue with Christian principles, as applied to cultures, nations, and segments of society.

CHRISTIAN JUSTICE. The virtue of justice elevated to a higher plane on two counts: obligations are revealed to the mind that man's intellect would not have recognized; and grace is given to the will to enable one to give others their due beyond what a person's natural disposition inclines one to do. Moreover, Christian justice is integrated by the infused virtue of charity, which is more effective than equity in tempering what can become the harshness of justice or, as the ancient Romans used to say, the "inequity of the law."

CHRISTIAN LAW. The revealed precepts of the New Testament. There is a sense in which the Christian dispensation superseded the laws of earlier revelation, since the ceremonial and judicial practices of the Israelites have ceased to be binding on the followers of Christ. Also the moral code of pre-Christian Judaism has been greatly elevated. But all of this, as Christ was careful to explain, does not mean that he came to "abolish the Law or the Prophets. I have come not to abolish but to complete them. I tell you solemnly, till heaven and earth disappear, not one dot, not one little stroke, shall disappear from the Law until its purpose is achieved" (Matthew 5:17–18).

What Christ wished to make clear is that the morality of the New Law of the Kingdom is higher and more spiritual than that of the Old Law, especially as interpreted by the scribes and Pharisees. Above all, it is new because it is based on the example and teaching of God in human form. And it is new in the exalted demand that the law of Christ makes on human generosity in the practice of charity.

CHRISTIAN LIFE COMMUNITIES. The new name of the reorganized Sodalities of Our Lady. Groups of men and women, both adults and young people, whose purpose is to develop their Christian vocation in the world. The reorganization was done in the light of the Second Vatican Council and the new statutes promulgated by Pope Paul VI in 1971. Building on the Spiritual Exercises of St. Ignatius, Christian Life Communities are located in more than forty countries and have their World Federation office in Rome.

CHRISTIAN LOVE. The law of selfless love, which Christ said was a new commandment, by which those who are truly

Christian would be recognized. He told his followers, "Love one another as I have loved you" (John 5:12). This law is new because commanded by God himself in human form; because it is to be a mutual love, given and received, as the foundation of a new reality, i.e., the Christian community, and because its norm or measure is essentially higher than self-love (Leviticus 19:18), since it is to be patterned after the manner that Christ, who is God, loved the human race even to dying for his enemies. In practice, this means that we are to love by wishing only well to one another, by praying for one another, and by never thinking, saying, or doing anything to injure one another.

CHRISTIAN MARRIAGE. The sacrament that bestows on a baptized man and woman who have made the required contract the graces that will enable them to fulfill their marital obligations.

The marital contract is an agreement, that is freely made but that, once made, imposes a serious obligation to share the rights and duties of the married state. The agreement or consent must be internal (sincere), simultaneous with the making of the contract, externally manifested and perfectly voluntary. Moreover, the contract must be made lawfully. Both the man and woman must be baptized, and they must be free from invalidating impediments and also from illicit impediments.

Husband and wife receive actual graces to fulfill their matrimonial obligations. These duties arise from the very nature of matrimony and cannot be altered by any subjective ideas of the contracting parties. They are the procreation of children and the fostering of mutual love between husband and wife to meet their respective material and spiritual needs.

CHRISTIAN MARXISM. The theory, disavowed by the Catholic Church, that Christianity and Marxism are fundamentally compatible. Christians who favor the theory do so for a variety of reasons, among which is the claim that Marxism is not essentially atheistic.

CHRISTIAN PHILOSOPHY. The philosophy that recognizes that reason and revelation are distinct sources of human knowledge, but considers Christian revelation as an indispensable aid to enlightening reason and protecting it from error.

CHRISTIAN SCHISMS. Historic divisions in Christian unity. These divisions are differently appraised by different communions. From the Catholic standpoint, the divisions are not only schismatic but also doctrinal, even as regards the Oriental Christians who do not recognize the Roman primacy. Other churches vary in applying the term "schism" to ecclesiastical separatism. The Eastern Churches and certain Reformed and Lutheran bodies look upon the disunity as basically theological and therefore solvable only through dogmatic reconciliation, while the majority consider the divisions merely schismatic. In this theory, the reunion of Christianity primarily demands not change of belief but the exercise of charity, which is the antidote for schism and which can "make all things work together for good—even our divisions," as expressed by the Commission on Faith and Order of the World Council of Churches.

CHRISTIANS IN ISRAEL. The Christians in the State of Israel are mainly Roman Catholic and Eastern Orthodox. Their largest community is in Nazareth. Most of them speak Arabic, and their customs are similar to those of their Arab neighbors. Numerous religious orders, predominantly Catholic, have monasteries and convents on sites venerated by Christian tradition, notably in Nazareth, the scene of the Annunciation; Ein Karem, birthplace of St. John the Baptist; the Jordan; Sea of Galilee; the Mount of the Beatitudes and the Transfiguration; Cana and Capernaum. Franciscans are the most prominent, having the Custody of the Holy Land assigned to them by the Holy See.

CHRISTIAN TEMPERANCE. The supernatural virtue that moderates the desire for pleasure. It is inspired by faith and motivated by charity. Its purpose is the imitation of Christ and the pursuit of sanctity. Supernatural temperance may call for practices that are more than moderation to the natural man, such as fasting and mortification, or total abstinence and celibacy.

CHRISTMAS. Feast of the Nativity of Jesus Christ. In the early Church the feast was celebrated along with the Epiphany. But already in A.D. 200 St. Clement of Alexandria (150–215) refers to a special feast on May 20, and the Latin Church began observing it on December 25. The privilege of priests offering three Masses on Christmas Day goes back to a custom originally practiced by a pope who, about the fourth century, celebrated a midnight Mass in the Liberian Basilica (where traditionally the manger of

Bethlehem is preserved), a second in the Church of St. Anastasia, whose feast falls on December 25, and a third at the Vatican Basilica. Many of the present customs in various countries are traceable to the Church's Christianizing the pagan celebrations associated with the beginning of winter and the new year. (Etym. Anglo-Saxon *Cristes Maesse,* Christ's Mass.)

CHRISTMASTIDE. The season of Christmas, generally understood to extend from midnight of Christmas Eve to Epiphany (January 6) inclusive.

CHRISTMAS TREE. An evergreen tree decorated with lights and ornaments at Christmas time. The first known mention of a Christmas tree was made in 1605 at Strasbourg and was later introduced into France and England.

CHRISTOCENTRIC. Concentrating on Christ. The term is frequently contrasted with theocentric (centered on God, as distinct from the God-Man), and anthropocentric (centered on man). There is an absolute sense in which every action of a believer should be Christocentric, being done for Christ, like Christ, with Christ, and in Christ. (Etym. Latin *Christus;* from Greek *Christos,* "the anointed [one]," from *chriein,* to anoint + *kentrikos,* from *kentron,* center.)

CHRISTOCENTRICITY. Christ-centeredness. The quality of making the person, attributes, and redemptive work of Christ the principal focus of a system of thought or a way of life. Often distinguished from theocentricity.

CHRISTOCENTRISM. The quality of a system of thought or a mode of life in which Christ is the acknowledged center around whom everything revolves. Applied to theology, it means that even the natural world is considered as somehow affected by the Incarnation, man's state of grace before the Fall is related to Christ, the Incarnation is seen as part of God's plan even though man had not fallen, and human destiny is viewed as the consummation of Christ's Mystical Body in its heavenly glory.

CHRISTOLOGY. The scientific study of the person of Jesus Christ and especially the mystery of the union in Christ of the divine and human natures. While Christology had been widely studied since patristic times, it was mainly since the Reformation that rival Christologies have arisen in the Western world. Allowing for many variations, the Christology of Lutheranism tends to be Apollinarist, with its strong emphasis on the unity of Christ's person and its claims (since Luther's time) that Christ assumed a humanity in the sense that he rarely manifested his divinity. Calvinist or Reformed Christology tends to so stress the difference between the divine and human in Christ as to verge on Nestorianism. Outside these traditions, Protestant Christology so redefines Christ's divinity that Jesus becomes merely the "Man from Nazareth." Roman Catholic Christology, as taught by the Church's magisterium, adheres firmly to the doctrine of the early ecumenical councils of Nicaea, Constantinople, Ephesus, and Chalcedon. (Etym. Greek *Christos,* Christ + *logia,* science, knowledge.)

CHRISTOTOKOS. See THEOTOKOS.

CHRIST'S HEADSHIP. Christ as the invisible head of the Mystical Body, which is the Catholic Church. As taught by St. Paul, "He [Christ] is the head of the body, the Church" (Colossians 1:18; Ephesians 5:23). Accordingly, Christ's position in relation to the faithful is similar to the position of the head to the other members of the body.

As the head occupies the supreme position in the body, so Christ as God-man has a unique pre-eminence within the Church and, in fact, within humanity. As the head guides other members of the body, so Christ guides, controls, and governs the whole Church, immediately in each one's mind and heart and mediately through the hierarchy. As the head is the seat of all the senses, so Christ (as man), by reason of the hypostatic union, possesses the fullness of supernatural gifts, which he then passes on to the faithful.

CHRIST THE KING. A feast originally established by Pope Pius XI in 1925, to be celebrated with special solemnity on the last Sunday of October. It is now observed on the last Sunday of the liturgical year. Its object is to worship Christ's Lordship of the Universe, both as God and Man, and it was instituted to meet the crisis of faith in the Savior's authority, exercised by the Church, of which he is the invisible head.

CHRISTUS DOMINUS. Decree on the Pastoral Office of Bishops in the Catholic Church, of the Second Vatican Council. A unique document because of its extensive decrees. Its focus is on two things: to urge bishops to co-operate with one another and with the Bishop of Rome for the welfare of the universal Church, and to legislate in detail the ways in which bishops are to work together in the modern communication-conscious world (October 28, 1965).

CHRONICLES, BOOKS OF. See PARALIPOMENON.

CHURCH. The faithful of the whole world. This broad definition can be understood in various senses all derived from the Scriptures, notably as the community of believers, the kingdom of God, and the Mystical Body of Christ.

As the community of believers, the Church is the assembly (*ekklesia*) of all who believe in Jesus Christ; or the fellowship (*koinonia*) of all who are bound together by their common love for the Savior. As the kingdom (*basileia*), it is the fulfillment of the ancient prophecies about the reign of the Messiah. And as the Mystical Body it is the communion of all those made holy by the grace of Christ. He is their invisible head and they are his visible members. These include the faithful on earth, those in purgatory who are not yet fully purified, and the saints in heaven.

Since the Council of Trent, the Catholic Church has been defined as a union of human beings who are united by the profession of the same Christian faith, and by participation of and in the same sacraments under the direction of their lawful pastors, especially of the one representative of Christ on earth, the Bishop of Rome. Each element in this definition is meant to exclude all others from actual and vital membership in the Catholic Church, namely apostates and heretics who do not profess the same Christian faith, non-Christians who do not receive the same sacraments, and schismatics who are not submissive to the Church's lawful pastors under the Bishop of Rome.

At the Second Vatican Council this concept of the Church was recognized as the objective reality that identifies the fullness of the Roman Catholic Church. But it was qualified subjectively so as to somehow include all who are baptized and profess their faith in Jesus Christ. They are the People of God, whom he has chosen to be his own and on whom he bestows the special graces of his providence. (Etym. Greek *kyriakon,* church; from *kyriakos,* belonging to the Lord.) See also SACRAMENT OF SALVATION.

CHURCH AND SYNAGOGUE. A biblical distinction between Christianity and Judaism. Scriptural equivalents for the faithful in the Old Testament are *qahal,* the entire religious community of the people of Israel, and *edah,* a congregation of believers. Greek synonyms for these in the Septuagint translation are *ekklesia* and *synagoga,* respectively. In the New Testament the difference between the two became technical, the first, meaning the assembly of people called together by God, and the second an existing religious gathering of people. This is illustrated in the text of St. Matthew's Gospel, where Christ promised Peter that "on this rock I will build my Church [*ekklesia*]," and Christian tradition has since canonized the terminology by reserving *ekklesia* for the society of Christ's followers and *synagoga* for the gathering of the Jews.

CHURCH BUILDING. In ecclesiastical law a church is a sacred structure devoted to divine worship for the principal purpose of being used by all the faithful for public divine worship. An oratory is different from a church in that it is not principally destined for public worship by all the faithful even though, in the case of a public oratory, they have the right to go there. So, too, a shrine, if principally destined to honor a particular saint in a given locality, is not technically a church.

CHURCHING. A liturgical ceremony of thanksgiving by which mothers thank God for the blessing of motherhood. More appropriately the ritual is called "the blessing of a woman after childbirth," to remove any suspicion that, in giving birth, the mother incurred a legal defilement, as in ancient Judaism. The ceremony may begin at the door of a church, although it has become customary to perform the rite near the altar. Taking hold of the priest's stole, the mother is symbolically led into the church to express her gratitude. The prayer of the priest concludes with the petition that "she and her offspring may deserve to attain to the joys of eternal blessedness." In imitation of Mary at her Purification, the mother offers some gift to the church, according to her means.

CHURCHMAN. A popular term for a member of the clergy, often applied to members of the hierarchy. Generally refers to a high-ranking prelate, e.g., a cardinal, especially to distinguish him from leaders in political society.

CHURCH MILITANT. The Church on earth, still struggling with sin and temptation, and therefore engaged in warfare (Latin, *militia*) with the world, the flesh, and the devil.

CHURCH MUSIC. The music that is appropriate and authorized for use in divine worship. It is religious music that the hierarchy, and finally the Holy See, approves for the sacred liturgy. It is an exalted prayer and an expression of deep religious feeling. In common with other religions, the elements of public worship have been sacrifice, prayer, ceremonies, chanting, and instrumental music. In Catholic worship, however, these elements form an organic unity, of which music is an important but secondary part. Moreover, Catholic church music must always conform to the regulations of ecclesiastical authority.

CHURCH OF SILENCE. The Christians in Communist-controlled countries. Their condition varies, but with no exception they are restricted in their religious freedom to profess or teach their faith and to communicate with their fellow-Christians in other countries.

CHURCH PURGATIVE. See CHURCH SUFFERING.

CHURCH SUFFERING. The Church of all the faithful departed who are saved but are still being purified in purgatorial sufferings.

CHURCH SUPPORT. The duty of contributing to the support of priests, religious, and others who dedicate their whole lives to the service of the Church. The biblical foundation for this duty is the injunction of St. Paul, "The Lord directed that those who preach the Gospel should get their living from the Gospel" (I Corinthians 9:14).

CHURCH TRIUMPHANT. The Church of all those in heavenly glory who have triumphed over their evil inclinations, the seductions of the world, and the temptations of the evil spirit.

CHURCH UNITY OCTAVE. Eight days of special prayer for Christian unity, observed from January 18 to 25, i.e., closing with the feast of the conversion of St. Paul. It began in 1908 with Reverend Paul J. Francis when still an Anglo-Catholic. After he entered the Roman Catholic Church and founded the Society of the Atonement, the feast was extended by Pope Benedict XV to the universal Church in 1916.

CHURCH WARDEN. A layman hired or appointed to assist the pastor in the temporal administration of a parish. Originally quite common in some Catholic churches, it is now practically limited to the Anglicans or Episcopalians.

CHURCHYARD. Strictly speaking, the ground on which a church is built and the surrounding area. In time it came to refer to the cemetery attached to the church, along with the grounds on which trials and public meetings were held.

CIBORIUM. A covered container used to hold the consecrated small Hosts. It is similar to a chalice but covered and larger, used for small Communion hosts of the faithful. It is made of various precious metals, and the interior is commonly gold or gold-plated. Also synonymous with baldachino as the dome-shaped permanent canopy over a high altar, supported by columns and shaped like an inverted cup. (Etym. Latin *ciborium;* from Greek *kibōrion,* cup.)

C.I.C. *Codex Iuris Canonici*—Code of Canon Law.

CILICIUM. A hair shirt worn under the clothing. It is made of cloth woven from hair and has been used at all periods of the Church's history as a means of discipline and mortification. (Etym. Latin *cilicium,* a hair shirt.)

CINCTURE. A belt, girdle, or cord tied around the waist of an alb. Worn by the priest at Mass, it confines the garment. It is usually a cord with tassel of the liturgical color of the day. It symbolizes chastity. Refers also to the belt of a religious habit. (Etym. Latin *cinctura,* a girdle.)

CIRCUMCELLIONS. Extremists who joined the Donatist schism in Africa during the lifetime of Constantine. They practiced suicide, thinking it was martyrdom. Their lives were socially unprofitable, as they were spent in idleness, dissipation, and violence, hence their name, which implied that they were wandering brigands. (Etym. Latin *circa,* around + *cella,* cell.)

CIRCUMCISION. The cutting off of the foreskin as a sign of the covenant between God and Abraham. Every male, God ordered, was to be circumcised when he was eight days old (Genesis 17:12). This did not continue as an obligation in the new covenant. Gentiles were not required to submit to circumcision (Acts 15:28). (Etym. Latin *circumcisio,* a cutting around.)

CIRCUMINCESSION. See CIRCUMINSESSION.

CIRCUMINSESSION. The mutual immanence of the three distinct persons of the Holy Trinity. The Father is entirely in the

Son, likewise in the Holy Spirit; and so is the Son in the Father and the Holy Spirit; and the Holy Spirit in the Father and the Son. Circuminsession also identifies the mutual immanence of the two distinct natures in the one Person of Jesus Christ.

CIRCUMSCRIPTION. The manner in which a body is naturally present in space, being contained and measured by other material bodies. The term is especially used to distinguish the manner of Christ's presence in heaven, circumscriptively, and his manner of presence in the Eucharist, sacramentally. In heaven Christ's body occupies space and is bounded by whatever surrounding materials are present. But in the Eucharist the body of Christ is not bounded by any other material things. Yet it is present with all that makes it a real body, including the attribute of gravity.

Hence it may be said that Christ's body "lies on the altar" or "is touched" or "is raised aloft" or "carried in procession" or even that it is "broken" or "his blood is poured out." But these expressions apply to the accidents only insofar as they are perceptible signs of the reality, namely Christ himself, which they signify.

CIRCUMSTANCE. As one of determinants of morality, something that either accompanies or is missing from a human act and thereby modifies its merit or gravity or the person's responsibility.

CISTERCIANS. A strict order of monks following the Rule of St. Benedict, founded in 1098 by St. Robert of Molesme (1024–1110) at Cîteaux. Its original purpose was to establish Benedictinism on austere lines along what was considered the primitive spirit. Its most famous member, often considered its second founder, was St. Bernard of Clairvaux (1090–1153). Before the end of the twelfth century 530 Cistercian abbeys had been established and another 150 during the next century. The Cistercian way of life was to be one of silence, in a community devoted mainly to the liturgy and prayer. Monasteries were to be in secluded places, churches were to be plain, and sacred vessels not ornate. Strict rules of diet were to be followed, as also those rules relative to manual labor made by the Cistercian pioneers in agriculture, in which they gradually trained others. Their carefully structured constitutions deeply influenced other medieval orders. A period of decline after the thirteenth century was followed by a rise of new reformed groups of Cister-

cians, of which the most notable was the monastery group at La Trappe founded by Armand de Rancé (1626–1700).

CITIZEN. Member of a state or nation, who owes it allegiance by birth or naturalization. This duty is based on the teaching of Scripture (Romans 13:1). Correspondingly, a citizen is entitled by the natural law to such civil rights as voting, running for office, and protection by the state in the possession of life and property, and the worship of God according to the dictates of conscience, as declared by the Second Vatican Council (*Pastoral Constitution on the Church in the Modern World*, 73–76).

CITY OF GOD. A celebrated work by St. Augustine (354–430) and the most complete defense of Christianity against paganism in the early Church. Repeated disasters in the Roman Empire were blamed on Christianity. Augustine showed that the opposite was true. It was not Christianity but the immorality of paganism that was responsible for the disintegration. The theme of the book, published in 427, is that the natural unity of the human race was broken by the fall of Adam. Since then mankind is divided everywhere between the inhabitants of two cities: the City of the Devil (*Civitas Diaboli*), peopled by those who love self even to the contempt of God, and the City of God (*Civitas Dei*), inhabited by those who love God even to the contempt of self.

CIVIL ALLEGIANCE. Duty of respect and obedience owed by every man to the state of which he is a member. In the light of Christian principles this does not mean that one must support his country right or wrong, complying with wrong conditions solely for the sake of security. Spiritual obedience to God and the Church should not conflict with allegiance to lawfully constituted civil authority. As explained by St. Paul, "You must all obey the governing authorities, since all government comes from God, the civil authorities were appointed by God, and so anyone who resists authority is rebelling against God's decision" (Romans 13:1–2).

CIVIL LAW. Legislation promulgated by the government in a political society. In general, it is morally binding in conscience, as the Church's tradition since biblical times testifies. "For the sake of the Lord," Peter told the first-century Christians, "accept the authority of every social institution: the emperor as the supreme authority, and the governors as commissioned by him to punish criminals and praise good citizenship" (I Peter 2:13).

What is less certain is the precise nature of the moral obligation of civil laws and under what conditions they are binding in conscience. They are certainly obligatory insofar as they sanction or determine a higher law, whether natural or revealed, as when they forbid murder and stealing or specify the rights of ownership. They are certainly not obligatory when the laws are unjust, notably when they are contrary to the laws of God and of the Church, when they do not proceed from legitimate authority, when they are not directed to the common welfare, and when they violate distributive justice.

Thus a person is not permitted to obey a law that commands acts against the moral law. Yet if an unjust law does not lead one to commit illicit actions, one may in practice obey it or even be obliged to do so for reasons of general welfare beyond the immediate scope of the law. Moreover, once a law has been passed by the civil government, it should be considered just unless the contrary is clear from the nature of the law or from the declaration of ecclesiastical authority. •

CIVIL MARRIAGE. A marriage contract witnessed by a civil official authorized by the state. In some countries every marriage, although later solemnized by the Church, must first be performed before a civil functionary.

CIVIL MORALITY. The theory that makes morality the same as civil legality. Accordingly there are no acts right or wrong of their very nature, but only because commanded or forbidden by the state. Built on the ideas of Thomas Hobbes (1588–1679) and Jean Jacques Rousseau (1712–78), the theory assumes that the state is not a natural society, but the result of the social contract, a purely conventional agreement whereby men give up part of their natural rights in order to preserve the rest. Once civil society is formed, it commands and forbids certain actions for the common good, and this is the beginning of right and wrong.

CIVITAS DEI. See CITY OF GOD.

C.J.P. *Consilium "Justitia et Pax"*— Pontifical Commission "Justice and Peace."

C.L. *Consilium de Laicis*—Pontifical Council for the Laity.

CL., CLICO. *Clericus, clerico*—cleric.

CLA. *Clausula*—clause.

CLAIRVOYANCE. Seeing or knowing events occurring at a distance without the use of sensibly perceptible means of communication. As with telepathy, the available evidence indicates that this is a rare but natural phenomenon. Its exercise and evaluation should therefore be based on the same principles as other human actions.

Clairvoyance is one of the familiar physical phenomena of mysticism. But the Church's custom is to be very circumspect about admitting anything more than natural psychic powers and cautious in warning the faithful about the possibility of demonic intervention. (Etym. French *clairvoyant,* clear seeing.)

CLANDESTINITY. Illegal secrecy, especially as regards marriage. It means that a couple exchange marital consent privately, with no public evidence of their action. Unless exceptional circumstances are present, as provided in the Church's law, the ceremony is invalid, since matrimony is a social sacrament and subject to the Church's legislation.

CLAPPER. Wooden instrument, with an attachment that, when shaken, makes a knocking noise. Used on occasion instead of an altar bell, e.g., during the Liturgy of Good Friday.

CLARITY. A quality of the glorified human body in being totally free from every deformity and filled with resplendent radiance and beauty. The prototype is the transfigured body of Christ on Mount Tabor (Matthew 17:2) and after the Resurrection (Acts 9:3). The source of the transfiguration lies in the overflowing of the beauty of the beatified soul onto the body. Each person's clarity will vary according to the degree of glory in the soul, and this in turn will depend on a person's merit before God (I Corinthians 15:41–49).

CLEMENCY. Moral virtue disposing a person to moderation in inflicting punishment on the guilty. It is also leniency in passing adverse judgment on those who have done obvious wrong in their external conduct.

CLEOPAS. One of two men traveling on foot from Jerusalem to Emmaus. They were talking about the strange reports of Jesus' resurrection the day before, when he joined them, but they did not know him. He accompanied them to Emmaus, explaining at length the story of the Messiah's life and mission. Fascinated by his account, they persuaded him to remain with them for the evening meal. Not till he broke the bread and said the blessing did they recognize him, but he vanished immediately. In their excitement they immediately returned to Jerusalem and told their story to the eleven Apostles (Luke 24:13–35).

CLERESTORY. The upper part of a church wall having windows in it above the roofs of the aisles. Found in early Christian basilicas, it was beautifully developed later in Gothic cathedrals.

CLERGY. Those specially ordained for Divine Service as deacons, priests, or bishops. In this sense the clergy form the Church's hierarchy. Entrance into the clerical state now takes place when a man is ordained deacon. Formerly it was at the time he received first tonsure. (Etym. Latin *clericus;* from Greek *kleros,* lot, portion; the clergy whose portion is the Lord.)

CLERIC. A member of the clergy.

CLERICAL CELIBACY. The practice of not being married, among those in major orders in the Church. Voluntary celibacy among the clergy goes back to the first century of the Christian era. In time, two different traditions arose in the Catholic Church. In the East, the tendency was toward having a married clergy, and as early as the Council of Nicaea (A.D. 325) the proposal to make celibacy obligatory on all the clergy was not accepted. The canonical position, in general, is that priests and deacons may marry before ordination but not after. Bishops, however, must be celibate. In the West, the canonical position of the Church has remained constant from as early as the Spanish Council of Elvira (A.D. 306). In 386, Pope St. Siricius ordered celibacy for "priests and Levites." The same legislation was passed by Pope St. Innocent I (reigned 402–17). In spite of numerous failures in observance, and even concerted opposition in some quarters, the Catholic Church has remained constant in her teaching on clerical celibacy. Enacted into canon law in 1918, the legislation was not changed by the Second Vatican Council. In its *Decree on the Ministry and Life of Priests,* it declared, "Celibacy was at first recommended to priests. Then, in the Latin Church, it was imposed by law on all who were to be promoted to sacred orders. This legislation, to the extent to which it concerns those who are destined for the priesthood, this most

holy Synod once again approves and confirms" (*Presbyterorum Ordinis,* III, 16). When a man is ready for the diaconate, he is ordained either to the transient diaconate with a view to the priesthood or to the permanent diaconate. If he is going on to the priesthood, he binds himself to celibacy for life. If he is to become a permanent deacon, and is unmarried, he also binds himself to celibacy, and cannot marry in the future, although he can later become a priest. If he is a married man, he may be ordained to the permanent diaconate. Then, should his wife die, he must remain unmarried and may go on for the priesthood.

CLERICAL DRESS. The normal distinctive ecclesiastical garb of Catholic priests in the Western Church is a black cassock indoors and a clerical collar and suit for outdoors. In some countries this varies somewhat, but the Church's legislation about priests wearing a garb that distinguishes them from the laity is mandatory. The Catholic Eastern clergy in Western countries follow the pattern of the place where they reside. In other places they may wear a black gown, turban, and similar characteristic dress.

CLERICAL IMMUNITY. The privilege that exempts clerics from the jurisdiction of civil courts even in lay matters where the courts' competence is not in question. Clerics are to be tried by ecclesiastical courts unless otherwise provided for in particular places. Equivalently this means that no cleric may be summoned before a lay judge as a defendant. Only by permission of a bishop may clerics testify in criminal cases when prosecuting for a grave personal injury, but they may be cited as witnesses or act as representatives of lay persons involved. Church law also exempts clerics from military service.

CLERICALISM. The advocacy of exaggerated claims on the part of the clergy, especially in matters that belong to the jurisdiction of the state. More commonly it is used as a term of reproach by secularists and unfriendly critics of the Catholic Church who aim to banish all religious influence from public life.

CLERICS OF THE PONTIFICAL CHAPEL. A new office created in 1968 by Pope Paul VI out of the former Secret Chaplains of Honor, Pontifical Chaplains, and other offices. Their function is to assist the Holy Father under the guidance of the Pontifical Ceremoneers (*Cerimonieri Pontifici*).

CLERK. Any member of the clergy, whether diocesan or religious. Formerly a man became a cleric when he received tonsure.

CLERKS REGULAR. Religious institutes whose members are bound by vows, live in community, and engage in a variety of pastoral work. The term implies that the majority of members are priests or those studying for the priesthood, and that they follow a regulated form of life embodied in detailed constitutions. Originating in the sixteenth century, Clerks Regular became the spearhead of the Counter-Reformation in the Catholic Church's conflict with Protestantism. They included the Theatines, the Clerks Regular of the Good Jesus, and the Barnabites. The best known are the Jesuits. Since the close of the sixteenth century, there have been no official additions of Clerks Regular in the Catholic Church, but their rule and way of life have been adopted by many modern congregations of men and modified for adaptation by religious communities of women. They may be regarded as the modern equivalent of the regular canons, whose origin goes back to St. Augustine.

CLINICAL BAPTISM. Baptism given to anyone sick in bed, particularly in childbirth. Since the human fetus is animated at conception with a rational soul, clinical baptism sometimes becomes necessary in difficult parturition. (Etym. Greek *klinikos,* of a bed.)

CLOISTER. A covered walk enclosing a quadrangle around which monasteries are built. Also an enclosure for religious retirement. In canon law, restrictions to the free entry of outsiders within the limits of certain areas of the residences of men or women religious. (Etym. Latin *claustrum,* enclosure.)

CLOPAS. The husband of one of the women named Mary who stood at the foot of the Cross during Jesus' crucifixion (John 19:25).

CLOSED TIMES. Seasons of the ecclesiastical year during which there are restrictions concerning the celebration of marriage. Formerly a marriage at Mass was not allowed from the beginning of Advent until after Epiphany, and during Lent and the octave of Easter. The present legislation does not forbid a Mass at the marriage during these times but does prohibit the distinctive *Missa pro Sponsis* (Mass for the Spouses) on the Sundays of Advent, Lent, and Easter, on the last three days of Holy Week, on solemn feasts, and during the octave of Easter. Moreover, "if matrimony is celebrated during Advent, or Lent, or other days that have a penitential character, the pastor should admonish the spouses to take into account the distinctive nature of these liturgical seasons" (*Rituale Romanum, Ordo Celebrandi Matrimonium, Praenotanda*).

CLOTHING OF RELIGIOUS. Formal bestowal of the religious habit. The admission of a postulant to the canonical novitiate in a religious congregation or order is traditionally introduced by the solemn clothing in the blessed habit of that community.

CLOTHING OF THE DEAD. The Church's traditional description of how the dead should be clothed for burial. Bishops and priests should be attired in their ecclesiastical garb, in the liturgical vestments appropriate to their rank. Religious are to be laid out in their distinctive habits. Lay persons should be decently clothed and preferably with a crucifix or rosary in their hands.

CLOUD OF UNKNOWING. A famous treatise on mystical prayer, variously attributed to Walter Hilton (d. 1396), an English mystic, to an unknown contemplative monk and to the Carthusians. Its theme is that God cannot be known by reason and that there is a cloud of unknowing in the affections. Contemplative prayer is said to be not in the intellectual but in the volitional and affective part of man and therefore necessarily contains an element of ignorance. As the author explains, the work is not meant for beginners but for those already advanced in the spiritual life.

CLUNY, ORDER OF. A branch of Benedictines founded in 927 by St. Odo (879–942), who organized the reform of monasticism in France. The object of the Cluniac reform was a return to the strict rule of St. Benedict, the pursuit of personal sanctity, chanting the Divine Office in choir, solemnity in divine worship, and corresponding reduction of manual labor. The historic reforms of Pope Gregory VII, who had stayed at Cluny for a time, affected the life and discipline of the whole Catholic Church. By the later Middle Ages, the influence of the Cluniac spirit waned mainly because of interference by political powers and the confiscation by the state of monastic holdings.

C.M. *Causa mortis*—on occasion of death.

COADJUTOR BISHOP. A bishop appointed by the Pope to assist a bishop who is the ordinary of a diocese. The coadjutor may be assigned to the person of the bishop, but he may also be assigned to the episcopal see. His appointment can be with or without the right of succession.

COAT OF ARMS. The emblem of a person, place, or institution that is traditional in the Catholic Church. Cardinals, bishops, and other prelates display these emblems on their thrones and elsewhere. It is generally forbidden for the coat of arms of an ecclesiastic to be of a secular character. National Catholic directories commonly picture the coat of arms of each ordinary of a diocese. With no exceptions, episcopal coats of arms bear some short Latin, Greek, or vernacular inscription. The emblem of Vatican City is a tiara alone above two crossed keys, gold on red.

COBRE. A Cuban shrine of Our Lady of Charity. According to legend, a small statue of Mary and her Child was brought from Spain by an officer who accompanied Columbus on his second American voyage and who gave it to a native pagan chieftain. But when the crew came to claim it, both the chief and the statue had disappeared into a nearby swamp. The statue was later recovered, mysteriously floating on a wooden plank. At a later date the statue of the Madonna was on its way to Santiago de Cuba but accidentally arrived at Cobre, where a child told them that Mary had said she wanted it to be. Until the Communist takeover, Cobre was a famous place of pilgrimage with thousands of visitors, especially on December 8. Our Lady of Charity of Cobre is considered the patroness of Cuba.

COCK. The Christian emblem that stands for vigilance and diligence. Used in reference to St. Peter for his threefold denial of Christ before the cock crew. Many church towers are mounted by cocks, to symbolize the capacity of the Gospels to meet every wind of human argument.

COD. Codex—manuscript.

CODE OF CANON LAW. The collection of 2414 laws (canons) of the Catholic Church, promulgated by Pope Benedict XV to take effect on May 19, 1918. The *Codex Iuris Canonici* contains five "books" of unequal length, dealing in sequence, with General Norms; Persons (clerics, religious, and laity); Things (sacraments, sacred places and times, divine worship, teaching authority of the Church, ecclesiastical institutions, and temporal goods); Procedures (trials, beatification and canonization, and certain policies); Crimes and Penalties. The code of 1918 was the first fully authentic compilation of the Church's laws ever published. Along with the code was established a special commission for authoritatively interpreting canon law, and other provisions were made to ensure sound implementation of existing laws and the drafting of new ones. With the beginning of the Second Vatican Council, Pope John XXIII in 1963 established a Pontifical Commission for the Revision of the Code of Canon Law.

CODEX. A body of laws. Also an original parchment manuscript, e.g., one or more books of the Bible. (Etym. Latin *codex,* a tablet, book.)

CODEX, BODMER. See BODMER CODEX.

CODEX SINAITICUS. A late-fourth-century manuscript of the Greek Bible, sold by the Soviet Government to the British Museum in 1933. It contains the entire Old Testament, all the books of the New Testament along with the Epistle of Barnabas and part of the Shepherd of Hermas. It is written on vellum, with each page in four columns. Several hands took part in the writing, and the text has been revised by a number of correctors. Its name comes from the fact that the manuscript was discovered in 1844 by Tischendorf (1815–74) in the Orthodox monastery of St. Catherine on Mount Sinai. It thus found its way into the Imperial Library at St. Petersburg.

CODEX VATICANUS. A fourth-century manuscript of the Greek Bible, now in the Vatican Library, and, together with the Codex Sinaiticus, the principal source of the text of the Old and New Testaments. In the New Testament everything after Hebrews 9:14 had been lost. The sheets are of fine vellum, most probably antelope skin, with each page divided into three columns of forty lines.

COEDUCATION. The practice of educating both sexes in the same buildings at the same time. It need not mean identical methods, nor always the same classes, but what it usually implies is the identity of all educational factors without consideration of sex. Such education has become widespread in modern times. Reasons given in favor of coeducation are: economy, beneficial social relations, and in some instances improved discipline. Objections arise on psychological and physiological grounds especially in the upper grades. The Catholic Church's position has been one of reserve, pointing out the different needs of men and women and the corresponding risk of homogenizing what nature and grace intend to be complementary genders in human society.

COENOBITE. See CENOBITE.

COENOBIUM. A community of religious living in one house under one authority; the convent or monastery housing a group of religious; the basilica or church of a monastery.

COERCION. In moral and ecclesiastical law, force used by a free and external agent in order to compel someone to perform actions that are against his or her will. It is also called violence. The agent is free when it operates from voluntary choice and is not forced by some element of nature or other inanimate physical force. The agent is external when the pressure to compliance does not arise within the person as in the case of hunger, thirst, or bodily pain.

When absolute violence is used, the will resists as best it can; therefore, a person is not culpable for whatever is done under such influence. Relative violence is that which can be overcome by greater opposition, but the extra effort is not made or enough resistance is given only externally, while internal consent is actually given. As a result, relative violence diminishes free will and corresponding imputability. (Etym. Latin *coercitio,* restraint, coercion, chastisement.)

COG. LEG. *Cognatio legalis*—legal relationship.

COGNITION. Knowledge or awareness of any kind, whether in the senses or the intellect. It is the power of apprehending within oneself some reality that is outside the faculty of knowing. The result is a representation, within a person of an object, that had previously been outside the knower. (Etym. Latin *cognitio,* activity of knowing, ability of knowing, knowledge.)

COG. SPIR. *Cognatio spiritualis*—spiritual relationship.

COIF. A close-fitting headdress, usually white, worn under the veil by a woman religious. (Etym. Latin *cofea,* a cap.)

COLISEUM. A building in Rome also known as the Flavian Amphitheater. It was begun in A.D. 72 by Vespasian (9–79) and completed in A.D. 80 by Titus (39–81). It is now in ruins. Its form is elliptical, 620 feet long, 525 feet wide, built four stories 157 feet in height. A special terrace was reserved for privileged spectators, a private gallery for the emperor, seats in tiers for ordinary citizens, and standing room for all the rest. It could seat 45,000. During the Middle Ages it was used as a stronghold by the Frangipani; later it came into possession of the municipality. Much of its walls were removed for their stone until Pope Clement X declared it a shrine, sanctuary of the martyrs who gave their lives within its limits during the persecutions. It is now a place of pilgrimage for visitors to Rome. (Etym. Latin *colisseus,* huge, gigantic, colossal.)

COLLATERAL LINE. A relationship subsisting between two persons from common stock. As indirect blood relationship, it exists between brother or sister, aunt or uncle, nephew or niece, first or second cousins. It annuls marriage to the third degree, but cousins may be dispensed by permission. In certain circumstances a dispensation can also be had for an aunt and nephew or an uncle and niece. Moreover, the term collateral line can also refer to the relationship of affinity which comes from a valid marriage and exists between a man or woman and the relatives of his or her spouse to whom he or she is related in the collateral line of blood relationship (consanguinity).

COLLATION. A light meal that is allowed in addition to a full meal on fasting days. It is also the appointment of a suitable person to a vacant benefice.

COLL. CONC. *Collectio Conciliorum*—Collection of the Councils.

COLLECT. An oration by a priest which concludes the introductory rite of the Mass. The priest first invites the people to pray. They remain silent for a moment to recall that they are in the presence of God. In the Collect that follows, the special characteristics of the celebration are expressed and its sentiments are all directed to the Father through Christ and in the Holy Spirit. The people's assent is expressed with an Amen. Only one Collect is said, with variant conclusions, depending on whether it is directed to the Father, or to the Father but with mention of the Son, or to the Son. In any case, the longer conclusion is used. (Etym. Latin *collecta,* a meeting, an assembly, especially for prayer.)

COLLECTIONS. Contributions of money given by the faithful for the maintenance of clergy and church or some other worthy object. Time for taking collections generally was at the Offertory of the Mass coinciding with the time of offering of bread, wine, candles, etc., in the early Church.

COLLECTIVISM. A view of society as a collectivity to which individuals are subordinated as part to the whole. Opposite of Catholic social doctrine that views society as bound in solidarity to the person, whom it seeks to develop. As practiced in Communist countries, the social collectivity determines all the manifestations of a human's life. Until the final realization of a classless society in which the individual is fully absorbed, the proletariat meanwhile represents the collective will.

COLLEGE. In its original meaning, an organized society of persons engaged in a common pursuit. And the term has returned to this in the Church's clearer understanding of episcopal collegiality, deriving from the community of the Apostles chosen by Christ. In the fourteenth century a college meant especially a group of secular clergy living on a foundation for religious service. As some of these communities began to engage in teaching, it came to denote a society of scholars formed for the purpose of instruction. With the rise of the teaching orders of religious in the Church, the meaning of college became standardized as institution of education, though not necessarily higher education as in some Anglo-Saxon countries. (Etym. Latin *collegium*, society of colleagues or companions.)

COLLEGE, APOSTOLIC. The Apostles as a group, forming one moral hierarchical body, not a body of equals, under St. Peter as their visible head (Matthew 10, 11, 16; Luke 22). After the death of Judas, in order to remain what Christ wanted them to be, a community of immediate witnesses of the Master, they immediately (even before Pentecost) elected Matthias "to take over this ministry and apostolate" (Acts 1:25).

COLLEGE OF CARDINALS. The cardinals of the Catholic Church considered as an organized community of prelates serving the Bishop of Rome. Also the cardinals when they meet in conclave to elect a new pope.

COLLEGIALITY. The bishops of the Roman Catholic Church, united under the Pope as an episcopal community. According to the Second Vatican Council, "St. Peter and the other Apostles constitute a single apostolic college. In like manner, the Roman Pontiff, Peter's successor, and the bishops, successors of the Apostles, are linked together" (*Constitution on the Church*, III, 21). This community of Pope and bishops, and the bishops among themselves, was created by Christ and therefore belongs by divine right to the nature of the Church he founded.

COLLEGIAL PERSON. In ecclesiastical law a group of at least three persons who agree, by an absolute majority of votes, to form a society approved by competent Church authority.

COLETTINES. Poor Clares who were reformed by St. Colette (1381–1447), a native of Picardy. Seventeen convents were founded in her own lifetime. Today the Colettines are mainly in France.

COLOGNE (cathedral). A famous shrine depository of the relics of the three Magi Kings in one of the finest examples of metalcraft of medieval times. Approved as authentic early in the ninth century, these relics were brought to Milan from Constantinople and then to Cologne in 1164. They were enthusiastically venerated in Germany throughout the Middle Ages. Mystery plays were organized to present the part played by the Magi in Christ's Nativity story. Their cult was widespread, and pilgrimages were started in the twelfth century and continue to this day. Caspar, Balthasar, and Melchior have been considered patrons of travelers.

COLORS, LITURGICAL. Different colors used in Divine Services as symbols. Different truths or sentiments are symbolized by different colors. The vestments of the altar, chalice covering, and veil should match the vestments worn by the priest at Mass.

COLOSSIANS, LETTER TO THE. Written by St. Paul while he was in prison, probably in Rome or at Ephesus. The Church at Colossae, on the Lycus, was founded not by Paul but by Epaphras, yet Paul wrote to the converts there to teach them about the primacy of Christ, head of the Church and Redeemer of mankind. Faith in Christ delivers believers from the false wisdom of the world and vain observance. This letter anticipated the centuries-old conflict that the Church would have with Gnosticism.

COLUMBARIA. Dovecotes. Wall niches for support of beams. Also the niches for burial urns in tombs containing the ashes of the cremated dead. Columbaria (columbaries) are typical of the pagan catacombs in the Roman Empire.

COMFORTER. Title of the Holy Spirit in his role of strengthening the faithful against temptation or in time of trial and tribulation. (Etym. Latin *comfortare*, to strengthen: *com*, together + *fortis*, strong.)

COMITY. Association of supernatural gifts with sanctifying grace. Although really distinct from it, a variety of virtues and gifts is infused into the soul along with the vital principle of the spiritual life. They are like the powers through which the divine life is exercised. (Etym. Latin *comitas*, urbanity; *comis*, courteous, friendly.)

COMMAND. In moral theology, a rational order or directive to do something. It may be given to oneself, whenever an act of the reason prompted by the will directs a person in some human activity or in carrying out one's decisions. Or it may be an act of the reason of a lawgiver or superior requiring those under legitimate authority to take some definite action for the common good. On rare occasion, it may be an order imposed by authority on a person for his or her own private good.

COMMANDED ACT. In the philosophy of St. Thomas Aquinas, an action of some human faculty or power, directed by the free will to do or not to do what the will orders should be done or not done.

COMMEMORATION. In general, any act or practice that recalls the memory of some personage or event. In particular the liturgical memorial of a mystery of Christ or of some saint or sacred event, which the Church wants to be kept alive among the faithful. The whole Christian calendar is built around such commemorations, some pertaining to the universal Church and others to be observed according to national or local custom, as directed by the hierarchy under the authority of the Holy See. (Etym. Latin *commemorare*, to call to mind.)

COMMENDATORY ABBOT. A name formerly given to a provisional administrator of a vacant abbey. Later given to an ecclesiastic with a claim to abbatial revenues. (Etym. Latin *commendare*, to entrust to, to commit to one's charge.)

COMMERCIAL WORK. A type of work forbidden on Sundays and holy days unless required by necessity or done out of sincere Christian charity. Also called civil occupation, commercial work means buying and selling or trading in business for monetary gain.

COMMINGLING. The liturgical mixing of a particle of the Sacred Host at Mass with the Precious Blood. The priest breaks off a piece of the Host and drops it into the chalice to signify the separation of Christ's body and blood on Calvary and the effective merits of his death for all mankind.

COMMISSION FOR MIGRANTS AND TOURISM. Its full title is the Pontifical Commission for the Pastoral Care of Migrants and of Tourism. Established in 1970 by Pope Paul VI, it was placed under the jurisdiction of the Congregation for Bishops.

COMMISSION FOR RELIGIOUS RELATIONS WITH HEBRAISM. A papal commission established by Pope Paul VI in 1974 as a distinct organization associated with the Secretariat for the Union of Christians. Its purpose is to promote and encourage religious relations between Hebrews and Catholics, aimed at eventual collaboration with other Christians. The commission was founded to put into effect the directives of the Second Vatican Council's Declaration on the Non-Christian Religions, which speaks of "the people of the New Testament as spiritually related to the descendants of Abraham."

COMMISSION FOR SOCIAL COMMUNICATIONS. Originally the Pontifical Commission for Educational and Religious Motion Pictures under Pope Pius XII in 1948, it became the Motion Picture Commission in 1952 and the present commission in 1964, after the publication of *Inter Mirifica* by the Second Vatican Council. Pope Paul VI entrusted to it all aspects of social communications, including movies and radio, television, the daily and periodical press.

COMMISSION FOR THE ECCLESIASTICAL ARCHIVES. Established in 1955 by Pope Pius XII, and re-established by Pope John XXIII in 1960. Its purpose is to co-ordinate and supervise the preservation and administration of the archives of the dioceses and religious institutes of Italy.

COMMITMENT. Pledging oneself by vow, promise, or simple resolution to the performance of some action or allegiance to a cause or co-operation with a person or group of persons. The obligation is morally binding, depending on the gravity of the commitment and the formality under which it is made. (Etym. Latin *committere,* to join, connect, entrust: *com-,* together + *mittere,* to send.)

COMMITTED SECRET. The secret that one person commits or entrusts to another with the assured promise that it will be kept confidential. Generally the one to whom the secret is entrusted must make the promise explicitly. But even an implicitly committed secret may not be divulged without very serious reason.

COMMITTEE FOR THE FAMILY. A Vatican agency established in 1975 to study the spiritual, moral, and social problems of the family.

COMMON. In ecclesiastical law, pertaining to or shared by two or more persons, things, terms, or numbers of any group. What is common is not always universal, since it may not be common in precisely the same way. Thus all religious are to live a common life, yet they retain their individual rights and privileges as persons.

COMMON ERROR. Usually applied to a situation where a priest who does not have jurisdiction to hear confessions is believed by the people to have such jurisdiction. If they confess their sins to him, his sacramental absolution is valid. But the error must be founded on a reasonable conclusion from a given practical situation which is public; it cannot be just an assumption as the result of mere ignorance. (Etym. Latin *communis,* common, joint, combined; general.)

COMMON GOOD. The benefit of the community. It is the welfare of the whole community, as the proper object of a just law, and is distinguished from individual good, which looks only to the good of a single person.

COMMON LIFE. A condition of the religious life, in contrast to the private individual living of the secular clergy or to the eremetical solitary life. It means living in community, with submission to a superior and a common rule, with community of goods such as food, clothing, and shelter.

COMM. PREC. *Commemoratio praecedentis* —commemoration of the preceding feast.

COMM. SEQ. *Commemoratio sequentis—* commemoration of the following feast.

COMMUNAL PENANCE. Group celebration of the sacrament of penance in one of several different ways, authorized by Pope Paul VI in 1973. One form has a communal penitential service, with individual confession of sins with absolution. Another form is entirely communal, including general absolution. When general absolution is given in exceptional circumstances, the penitents are obliged to make a private confession of their grave sins, unless it is morally impossible, at least within a year.

COMMUNICABLE ATTRIBUTE. Divine perfection that can be shared by someone other than God, as life, goodness, and wisdom.

COMMUNICANT. One who receives Holy Communion. The term also applies to all faithful and active members of a church, as distinct from merely nominal Catholics. (Etym. Latin *communicare,* to participate in, have in common; to inform, make generally known.)

COMMUNICATE. In Christian spirituality, to share with another what one is or has, so that they are thereby united in being or possessions. Communicating material things necessarily means to be deprived of what is shared. But in things of the spirit, the one who communicates does not lose, say in teaching or loving another person, but is rather enriched by the communication.

COMMUNICATION. In ecclesiastical law the concession of a privilege to another person or institution or corporate body as an extension of a similar privilege already granted by the Church to someone else.

COMMUNICATION OF PROPERTIES. Attributing to Christ two series of predicates, one divine and one human. Since we attribute properties and activities to one person, and since Christ is one person in two natures, we may attribute either divine or human qualities and actions to the same Christ. We may correctly say that Christ is God and that he is man, that God was born of Mary and that infinite truth died on the Cross. However, only concrete names may be used in this way because abstract names "abstract" from the existence of something in a particular individual or person. It would be wrong, therefore, to say that Mary is the mother of the divinity.

COMMUNIO ET PROGRESSIO. Pastoral instruction of the Pontifical Commission for Social Communications, on the exact application of the decree *Inter Mirifica* of the Second Vatican Council. It covers in sequence: doctrinal principles; contribution of the communications media to human progress; training of recipients and communicators; opportunities and obligations of both; co-operation between citizens and civil authorities; collaboration among all believers and men of good will; the commitment of Catholics in the media; public opinion and closer communication in the life of the Church; activity of Catholics in the field of writing, movies, radio, and television, the theater, equipment, personnel, and organization; urgency of the need because forces other than Catholic or Christian are coming to dominate the media. This document is Part Two of the postconciliar teaching on the media. It complements *In Fructibus Multis* of Paul VI, May 25, 1971.

COMMUNION. In Christian parlance the most sacred expression for any one of different forms of togetherness. As communion between God and the human soul in the divine indwelling; between Christ and the recipient of the Eucharist in Holy Communion; among all who belong to the Mystical Body in heaven, purgatory, and on earth in the Communion of Saints; and among those who belong to the Catholic Church as a communion of the faithful. (Etym. Latin *communio,* sharing unity, association; participation.)

COMMUNION, FREQUENT. The daily reception of Holy Communion, as Pope St. Pius X explained the meaning of "frequent." The conditions required for daily Communion are freedom from conscious, unconfessed mortal sin, and the right intention, namely to honor God, grow in Christian charity, and overcome one's sinful tendencies. In the early Church, daily Communion was common. Later on it fell into disuse, and only in modern times is the practice being gradually restored. The Church's grounds for urging the faithful to communicate daily are based on patristic tradition. "We are bidden in the Lord's Prayer," wrote St. Pius X, "to ask for our daily bread. The holy fathers of the Church all but unanimously teach that by these words must be understood not so much the material bread to support the body as the Eucharistic Bread which should be our daily food" (*Sacra Tridentina Synodus,* December 20, 1905).

COMMUNION, SPIRITUAL. The conscious desire to receive Holy Communion, which should precede the actual reception of the sacrament. Spiritual Communion, made in acts of faith and love during the day, is highly recommended by the Church. According to the Catechism of the Council of Trent, the faithful who "receive the Eucharist in spirit" are "those who, inflamed with a lively faith that works in charity, partake in wish and desire of the celestial Bread offered to them, receive from it, if not the entire, at least very great benefits" (*On the Eucharist*).

COMMUNION ANTIPHON. The hymn that is sung during the distribution of Communion to the faithful at Mass. Besides the antiphon, other hymns approved by the Bishops' Conference may be sung. If there is no singing during the Communion procession, the antiphon is recited.

COMMUNION CLOTH. A long white linen cloth formerly suspended from the altar rail. Its purpose when held over the rail was to receive any particles of the Sacred Host that might fall by chance in its distribution to the faithful. It has been replaced in most churches by the Communion paten or plate.

COMMUNION OF CHILDREN. In ancient times in Eastern Churches children received Communion immediately after baptism; in the West little children received only when dying. The Fourth Lateran Council (in 1215) and the Council of Trent (1551) laid the precept of Easter Communion and Viaticum on children after attaining the years of discretion. After years of neglect of this legislation, St. Pius X prescribed frequent Communion, also for children (1905) and restored early Communion along with the sacrament of penance on reaching the age of reason (1910).

COMMUNION OF SAINTS. The unity and co-operation of the members of the Church on earth with those in heaven and in purgatory. They are united as being one Mystical Body of Christ. The faithful on earth are in communion with each other by professing the same faith, obeying the same authority, and assisting each other with their prayers and good works. They are in communion with the saints in heaven by honoring them as glorified members of the Church, invoking their prayers and aid, and striving to imitate their virtues. They are in communion with the souls in purgatory by helping them with their prayers and good works.

COMMUNION PATEN. A saucer-shaped plate usually of precious metal similar to the

Mass paten but having a projecting handle. It is held under the chin of the communicant to catch any particle of the Sacred Host that may fall. It is not blessed.

COMMUNION PAUSE. The period of silent prayer after Communion at Mass. As an alternative, the whole community may sing a hymn of praise during the pause.

COMMUNION RAIL. The metal, wooden, or stone railing, along the front of the sanctuary, at which the faithful receive Holy Communion while kneeling. It was also customary to have the rail covered with a Communion cloth that the communicant places under the chin at the time of receiving.

COMMUNION RITE. The celebration of the Eucharist as a paschal meal. It implies that the faithful in good dispositions should answer to the Lord's command by receiving his body and blood as their spiritual nourishment. They are prepared for the Communion and thank him afterward in a series of liturgical rites, beginning with the Lord's Prayer and ending with the Post-Communion.

COMMUNISM. The social doctrine that affirms the community of goods and denies the right to ownership of private property. As analyzed in numerous papal documents since Pope Pius IX in 1846, Communism is based on a philosophy, a theory of history, and a definable strategy or methodology. The philosophy is dialectical materialism, which claims that matter and not spirit, and least of all the infinite Spirit who is God, is the primary reality in the universe; and that material forces in conflict (dialectic) explain all the progress in the world. The Communist theory of history claims that economics is the sole basis of human civilization, making all ethical, religious, philosophical, artistic, social, and political ideas the result of economic conditions. The strategy of Communism is a shifting expediency that defies analysis but has two constants that never really change: massive indoctrination of the people and ruthless suppression of any ideas or institutions that threaten totalitarian control by the Communist Party.

COMMUNITY. A group of persons who share the same beliefs, live together under authority, and co-operate in pursuing common interests for the benefit of others besides their own members. The degree of common belief, living, and activity determines the intensity of the community and its distinctive identity as a human society. (Etym. Latin *communitas*, community, common possession; association; congregation, parish; generality.)

COMMUNITY, CLERICAL. The living and sharing together that the Church has traditionally favored and encouraged for men in the clerical state.

COMMUTATION. The substitution by legitimate authority of another work for the one to which a person is obligated by law or by vow. The work substituted must be better or equivalent to the original obligation, though not necessarily as difficult. (Etym. Latin *commutatio*, change, transformation; exchange.)

COMMUTATIVE JUSTICE. The virtue that regulates those actions which involve the rights between one individual and another individual. If a person steals another's money, he or she violates commutative justice. Any violation of commutative justice imposes on the guilty party the duty of restitution, that is, the duty of repairing the harm caused. In fact, strictly speaking, only violations of commutative justice give rise to this duty of restitution.

COMPARATIVE RELIGION. The science that compares one religion with another in order to find their common elements and to trace their development from primitive forms to their present beliefs and practices. The Catholic Church encourages such study, provided its purpose is not to disprove the unique character of Christianity or to try to prove that the Christian religion naturally evolved from previous religious systems.

COMPASSION. Pity at another person's sorrow or misfortune, with the desire to alleviate or, on occasion, even to suffer in the other's stead.

COMPATHY. A sense of compassion among people who experience in common the same sorrow or affliction. It is a with-each-other sharing of spiritual pain.

COMPENSATIONISM. A theory in moral theology for resolving practical doubts. Also called the principle of sufficient reason. It holds that when a person doubts the lawfulness of an act he or she must have sufficiently grave reason to decide in favor of the opinion that is contrary to the law. The graver the law the more probable the reasons favoring it, the greater also must be the reasons for exposing oneself to the risk of breaking the law. (Etym. Latin *compensatio,* a balancing, exchange.)

COMPL., COMP., CPL. *Completorium*—Compline.

COMPLINE. The concluding hour of the Divine Office. Its origins in the West are commonly ascribed to St. Benedict (480–547). At first it was recited after the evening meal or before retiring. It now follows Vespers. As Night Prayer it consists of a hymn, one or two psalms, a short reading from Scripture, a versicle and response, the Nunc Dimittis of Simeon, and a concluding prayer. (Etym. Latin *completorium,* complement.)

COMPOS MENTIS. Having a sound mind, being in one's right mind. A technical term in ecclesiastical law to designate a person who is capable of a free human act when making a contract or receiving a sacrament or performing some action for which he or she is therefore held morally responsible.

COMPOSTELA, SANTIAGO DE. A shrine dedicated to St. James the Apostle, in the mountain region of northwest Spain not far from the sea. After Rome and Jerusalem, Compostela is said to rank third in the order of importance of pilgrimage centers for the Christian world. It is dedicated to St. James the Greater, who is thought to have labored as a missionary in Spain and whose relics are there. Although he was beheaded in Jerusalem and buried there, tradition has it that his body was later brought to Galicia and ultimately, in A.D. 830, to Compostela. The story of his Spanish missionary efforts is disputed, but Pope Leo XIII in 1884 declared that the relics of St. James revered at Compostela are authentic. They repose in an exquisite metal casket behind and above the altar in the cathedral. The year 1976 was Holy Year for this famous shrine.

COMPUNCTION. A momentary sorrow or regret for having done, or contemplated doing, something wrong. It may also be a slight feeling of remorse, without implying either complete repentance or a firm resolve not to do the same wrong thing again. (Etym. Latin *compunctio,* remorse, the sting of conscience; from *compungere,* to prick.)

CON. *Contra*—against.

CONC. *Concilium*—council.

CONCEALMENT. As a moral issue, the act of hiding what should be kept secret, which is a virtue; or of hiding what should be disclosed, which is sinful and makes the one who conceals a sharer in the sinner's guilt.

CONCELEBRANT. A priest who offers Mass jointly with one or more other priests. The liturgy provides for three distinct parts in a concelebrated Mass: those to be said by the principal celebrant, those to be said by all the celebrants together (e.g., the words of consecration), and those that may be said by one or another concelebrant.

CONCEPTION. The beginning of human life. From the time that an ovum is fertilized a new life begins that is neither that of the father nor of the mother. It is rather the life of a new human being with his own growth. It would never become human if it were not human already (Sacred Congregation for the Doctrine of the Faith, *Declaration on Procured Abortion,* December 5, 1974).

CONCEPTUALISM. The theory that universal concepts are only subjective ideas with no objective foundation in reality. As developed by Peter Abelard (1079–1142), conceptualism denies that universals exist independently of the mind, but holds that they have an existence in the mind as concepts. Although not arbitrary inventions, they are merely reflections of similarities among particular objects.

CONCILIARISM. The theory that a general council of the Church is higher in authority than the Pope. It began in the fourteenth century, when respect for the papacy was undermined by confusion in Church and State. William of Ockham (1280–1349), in his battle with Pope John XXII (c. 1249–1334), questioned the divine institution of the primacy. Marsilius of Padua (1324) and John of Jandun (1324) declared it was only a primacy of honor. During the great Western Schism (1378–1417) many otherwise reputable theologians, such as Peter of Ailly (1394) and John Gerson (1409) saw in the doctrine of the council's superiority over the Pope the only means of once more reuniting a divided Church. The viewpoint appeared that the Church in general was free from error, but the Church of Rome could err, and in fact had erred and fallen into heresy. The Council of Constance (1414–18), in its fourth and fifth sessions, declared for the superiority of council over Pope. However, these decisions never received papal approbation. In Gallicanism the conciliarist theory lived on for hundreds of years. Conciliarism was formally condemned by the First Vatican Council (1869–70), which defined papal primacy, declaring that the Pope had "full and supreme jurisdiction over the universal Church, not only in things which belong to faith and morals, but also in those which relate to the discipline and government of the Church spread throughout the world." He therefore possesses not merely the principal part but "all the fullness of this supreme power." Moreover, this power is ordinary or constant, and immediate or direct; it extends the Pope's authority over each and all the churches, whether local or territorial, and over each and all the pastors and the faithful (Denzinger, 3063).

In more recent times, conciliarism has been renewed by those who appeal to a "magisterium of theologians" or "consensus of the people of God" against ordinary or even solemn teachings of the popes. (Etym. Latin *concilium,* council, assembly for consultation.)

CONCILIARITY. Church government by councils of bishops. In Orthodox theology this is said to be the highest form of ecclesiastical rule, excluding, on principle, the primacy of the Pope. Eastern Orthodoxy recognizes only the first seven general councils, from I Nicaea in 325 to II Nicaea in 787, as truly ecumenical.

CONCLAVE. The enclosure of the cardinals while electing a pope. To avoid interference from the outside, Pope Gregory X, in 1274, ordered the papal election to take place in conclave. Gregory's own election was preceded by a record vacancy of two years and nine months. On occasion (for example, Pope Leo XIII) popes have permitted the cardinals, by majority vote, to dispense with conclave in case of emergency. Pope Paul VI, in the apostolic constitution *Romano Pontifici Eligendo* (October 1, 1975), introduced numerous changes in the laws governing the election of the Roman Pontiff. Thus: 1. only persons who have been named cardinals of the Church may be electors of the Pope; 2. the number of electors is now limited to 120, allowing each cardinal to bring two or three assistants to the conclave; 3. while the conclave is not strictly required for validity, it is the normal way a pope is elected, during what may be called a sacred retreat made in silence, seclusion, and prayer; 4. three forms of election are allowed, i.e., by acclamation of all the electors, by compromise in which certain electors are given authority to act in the name of all, and by voting ballot; 5. if the newly elected person is a bishop, he becomes pope at once, but if he is not yet a bishop, he is to be ordained to the episcopacy immediately; 6. if no one is elected after three days, the conclave is to spend a day in prayer while allowing the electors freedom to converse among themselves; 7. secrecy is to be strictly observed under penalty of excommunication; 8. if an ecumenical council or synod of bishops is in progress, it is automatically suspended until authorized by the newly elected pontiff to proceed. (Etym. Latin *con-,* with + *clavis,* key: *conclave,* a room that can be locked up.)

CONCOMITANCE. The doctrine that explains why the whole Christ is present under each Eucharistic species. Christ is indivisible, so that his body cannot be separated from his blood, his human soul, his divine nature, and his divine personality. Consequently he is wholly present in the Eucharist. But only the substance of his body is the specific effect of the first consecration at Mass; his blood, soul, divinity, and personality become present by concomitance, i.e., by the inseparable connection that they have with his body. The Church also says the "substance" of Christ's body because its accidents, though imperceptible, are also present by the same concomitance, not precisely because of the words of consecration.

In the second consecration, the conversion terminates specifically in the presence of the substance of Christ's blood. But again by concomitance his body and entire self become present as well. (Etym. Latin *concomitantia,* accompaniment.)

CONCOMITANT GRACE. Sometimes called co-operating grace, it is assistance given in responding to a preventing grace. It has been compared to a mother who, after coaxing a child to walk, actually takes it by the arms and assists it to take a few steps. In preventing, or prevenient, grace God acts without man's co-operation; in concomitant grace God acts together with the free co-operation of man's will.

CONCORDAT. An official agreement between the Pope, in his spiritual capacity as visible head of the Catholic Church, and the temporal authority of a state. Commonly accepted as a contract between Church and State, it is a treaty governed by international laws and has been used by the Holy See since the early Middle Ages. The earliest agreement called such was the Concordat of Worms (1122), by which Pope Calixtus II and Emperor Henry V (1081–1125) put an end to the struggle over lay investiture. The best known in modern times was the Lateran Treaty of 1929. After World War II a number of concordats were abrogated by Communist regimes. (Etym. Latin *concordatus,* a thing agreed on.)

CONC. TRID. *Concilium Tridentinum.* Council of Trent.

CONCUBINAGE. The more or less permanent cohabitation of a man and woman without being married. Any continued liaison, whether there are impediments to marriage or not, is concubinage. (Etym. Latin *con-,* with + *cubare,* to lie: *concubina.*)

CONCUPISCENCE. Insubordination of man's desires to the dictates of reason, and the propensity of human nature to sin as a result of original sin. More commonly, it refers to the spontaneous movement of the sensitive appetites toward whatever the imagination portrays as pleasant and away from whatever it portrays as painful. However, concupiscence also includes the unruly desires of the will, such as pride, ambition, and envy. (Etym. Latin *con-,* thoroughly + *cupere,* to desire: *concupiscentia,* desire, greed, cupidity.)

CONCUPISCENCE OF THE EYES. Unwholesome curiosity and an inordinate love of this world's goods. The first consists in an unreasonable desire to see, hear, and know what is harmful to one's virtue, inconsistent with one's state of life, or detrimental to higher duties. As an inordinate love of money, it is the desire to acquire material possessions irrespective of the means employed, or merely to satisfy one's ambitions, or to nurture one's pride.

CONCUPISCENCE OF THE FLESH. The inordinate love of sensual pleasure, to which fallen man is naturally prone. It is inordinate when pleasure is sought as an end in itself and apart from its divinely intended purpose: to facilitate the practice of virtue and satisfy one's legitimate desires.

CONCURSUS. The divine activity in its relation to finite causes in the preservation and development of the world. Also called divine co-operation, it is immediate and universal because on it absolutely depends the continued activity of all creation. The inherent reason for the divine concursus lies in the active dependence of creatures on the Creator, not only for their being but for the power that flows from the being that they

have. (Etym. Latin *con-,* with + *currere,* to run: *concursus,* the coming together, coincidence.)

CONC. VAT. I (II). *Concilium Vaticanum I (II),* Vatican Council I (II).

CONDIGN. Due to a person for some good he has done. Generally applied to merit before God, who binds himself, as it were, to reward those who do his will. The conditions for condign merit are the state of grace and a morally good action. The beneficiary is the person who performs the good act and not someone else. Condign merit is based on the revealed fact that God has promised such a reward. Thus we condignly merit an increase of the virtue of faith by every act of faith we perform in the state of grace. (Etym. Latin *con-,* thoroughly + *dignus,* worthy: *condignus,* very worthy.)

CONDITIONAL ADMINISTRATION. Applied to the sacraments when for sufficient reason they are administered conditionally. This means that the one conferring the sacrament performs the necessary ritual and intends to confer the sacrament provided the necessary conditions are present. It is customary to express this condition verbally when conferring the sacrament: e.g., "If you are capable."

CONDITIONAL BAPTISM. The rite of baptism performed on a person who is entering the Roman Catholic Church and is not certain about previous baptism. This is not rebaptism, which is impossible, since this sacrament can be received only once. But if there is reasonable doubt about the fact or validity of one's previous baptism, the sacrament is administered conditionally, i.e., the one who performs the ritual at least mentally says, "If you are not baptized," and then proceeds to confer the sacrament.

CONDITIONAL IMMORTALITY. The belief of some Protestant groups (e.g., the Advent Christians) that immortality is a divine gift conferred on faithful Christians, who become the children of God. Only they will exist into eternity. The human soul, therefore, is not immortal by nature.

CONDITIONAL MORALITY. A system of morality based on Immanuel Kant's principle of the hypothetical imperative, namely: "If you desire this or that, you must (should or ought to) do such and such." In these cases, the obligation enjoined depends on a person's having the desire in question. From a Catholic perspective, there is an obligation prior to the hypothesis, i.e., making sure that a given desire is itself conformed to the divine law.

CONDITIONAL VOW. A promise made to God that obliges after the condition has been fulfilled. Thus a person may vow to give a certain amount of money to the poor if a favor asked of God is granted.

CONDONATION. In ecclesiastical law, the special concession to make up for Masses that have not been said and can no longer be easily said. The fruits of the Masses thus unapplied are supplied from the spiritual treasury of the Church. It is assumed that the Masses were not omitted through sinful neglect. Condonation can be granted only by the Holy See. (Etym. Latin *con-*, thoroughly + *donare*, to give: *condonare*, to remit, pardon.)

CONDUCT. The way a person behaves. It implies moral responsibility for one's behavior and is therefore open to other people's judgment whether the conduct is good or bad.

CONF. Confessor.

CONF. DOCT. *Confessor et doctor*—confessor and teacher.

CONFERENCE OF CHARITY. See SOCIETY OF ST. VINCENT DE PAUL.

CONFESSIO. A term originally applied to the tomb of a martyr. Later it came to mean the altar erected over the tomb, the underground room that contained the tomb, or even the new resting place to which the remains of the martyr were transferred, or the hollow reliquary in an altar. The most famous confessio, in the sense of a tomb, is that of St. Peter, under the high altar of St. Peter's Basilica in Rome.

CONFESSION. The voluntary self-accusation of one's sins to a qualified priest in order to obtain absolution from him. This accusation must be an external manifestation. It must be objectively complete in that the penitent confesses every mortal sin according to number and kinds that he has committed since his last worthy reception of the sacrament of penance. In extraordinary circumstances a subjectively complete confession is sufficient, that is, when circumstances prevent a person from accusing himself of all his grave sins. He is nevertheless obliged to confess all his mortal sins in a later reception of the sacrament.

When there are no mortal sins to confess, it is sufficient to confess any previous sins from one's past life or any present venial sins of which a person has been guilty, in order to obtain absolution and the grace of the sacrament of penance. (Etym. Latin *con-*, thoroughly + *fateri*, to acknowledge: *confessio*, confession.)

CONFESSIONAL. The place where the sacrament of penance is administered. In the early Church it was any kind of seat and was generally before the altar in the Middle Ages. In the sixteenth century it took the form of a separate compartment for the kneeling penitent and for the priest, furnished with a grille. This form became prescriptive until after the Second Vatican Council. The new Order of Penance does not specify for the Latin Rite what the confessional should be. It merely says: "The sacrament of penance is celebrated in the place and location [*in loco et sede*] prescribed by law" (*Ordo Paenitentiae*, IV, 12).

CONFESSIONS OF FAITH. The numerous statements of Protestant belief, composed at various times from the Reformation to the present. These creeds have been the principal cohesive and stabilizing force in world Protestantism. Each denomination or each family of denominations has its respective confession of faith. Among these the most important are the Lutheran Augsburg Confession (1530), the Calvinist Catechism of Geneva (1542–45), the Reformed Heidelberg Catechism (1563) and Belgic Confession (1561), the Anglican Thirty-nine Articles (1563), and the Presbyterian Westminster Confession (1648). Since then there have been hundreds of derivative or new confessions of faith issued, periodically revised, and regularly composed as new denominations have come into being.

CONFESSIONS OF ST. AUGUSTINE. One of the great autobiographies of Catholic Christianity. Written about A.D. 400, Augustine's life story is a masterpiece of theological synthesis woven around the theme of his conversion from unbelief and Manichaeism to the Christian faith. Its central theme is the necessity of divine grace to cope with human weakness, and the power of this grace to transform a sinner into a saint.

CONFESSOR. A priest qualified to hear the confessions of the faithful and grant sacramental absolution. A confessor is also empowered to grant certain dispensations and absolve from censures, according to the provisions of ecclesiastical law.

CONFESSOR (liturgical). A Christian in the early Church who had suffered much for the sake of Christ but did not die as a result of torture or ill-treatment. Such a person "confessed" his or her faith under trial and persecution. In present-day vocabulary all the men saints are called confessors who are not martyrs.

CONFIDENTIALITY. The quality of a verbal or written communication by which the sender wants the matter communicated to be kept secret. The moral obligation to keep the matter confidential depends on the: 1. sender's right to require confidentiality; 2. receiver's agreement; 3. nature of what is communicated; 4. difficulty of keeping the matter secret; and 5. possible harm caused by confidentiality. (Etym. Latin *confidere: con-*, together + *fidere*, to trust.)

CONFIRMATION. The sacrament in which, through the laying on of hands, anointing with chrism, and prayer, those already baptized are strengthened by the Holy Spirit in order that they may steadfastly profess the faith and faithfully live up to their profession. Confirmation is not strictly necessary for salvation, but it is eminently important in contributing to Christian perfection and there is a grave obligation to receive it in due time. (Etym. Latin *con-*, thoroughly + *firmare*, to make firm: *confirmatio*, fortification, strengthening.) See also SACRAMENT OF THE APOSTOLATE.

CONFIRMATION CHARACTER. The indelible sign imprinted on the soul by the sacrament of confirmation. Its distinctive qualities are that it assimilates a person more closely to Christ, the Teacher of Truth, the King of Justice, and the High Priest. St. Thomas Aquinas holds that the confirmation character gives a person the power and the right to perform actions that are necessary in the spiritual battle against the enemies of the faith. He distinguishes the fighters of Christ (the confirmed) from the simple members of Christ's kingdom (the baptized) and explains that confirmation empowers and entitles those who receive it to not only preserve the faith but to make public profession of what they believe and a sense of mission to extend this faith to others.

CONFIRMATION NAME. The additional name that a person assumes when receiving the sacrament of confirmation. While not strictly required, it is recommended as a sign that the one confirmed has entered on a new way of life, having received a new sacramental character as a witness of Christ.

CONFIRMATION RITE. The ceremony by which a bishop, or priest delegated by him, confers the sacrament of confirmation on a baptized person. After invoking the Holy Spirit, the bishop extends his hands over the person to be confirmed as a symbol of the coming of the Spirit. Then he traces a cross on the person's forehead with blessed oil called chrism. At the same time, he calls the person by his name (either baptismal or new) and says, "[Name] be sealed with the Gift of the Holy Spirit."

CONFITEOR. "I confess." The act of repentance that from the earliest Christian times was part of the Church's Eucharistic liturgy. In its usual form before the Second Vatican Council the confession was made to God, to the Blessed Virgin Mary, St. Michael, St. John the Baptist, Sts. Peter and Paul, and all the other saints. The present form declares: "I confess to Almighty God, and to you my brothers, that I have sinned exceedingly in thought, word, act and omission: through my fault, through my fault, through my most grievous fault. Therefore I beseech the Blessed Mary ever Virgin, all the angels and saints, and you brethren, to pray for me to the Lord our God." (Etym. Latin *confiteor*, I confess.)

CONFLICT. In moral theology the contradictory impulses within an individual. When these impulses are to be acted on, a person must apply the discernment of spirits to decide which impulse should be followed and which one rejected. The root of the conflict may be between concupiscence and conscience, or between nature and grace, or more simply between one's own will and the will of God. (Etym. Latin *con-*, with + *fligere*, to strike: *conflictus*, striking together.)

CONFLICT OF OBLIGATIONS. A situation in which two laws apparently oblige at the same time and yet only one can be observed. Actually only the more important law obliges. Thus the natural law takes precedence over a positive law. Among natural laws, the one that prohibits precedes a law that commands. Divine positive law takes precedence over human legislation; the law of a superior must be preferred to the law of a society that is subordinate to it in purpose and function.

CONFLICT OF RIGHTS AND DUTIES. The clash between one person's rights and another person's duties. Such conflict is only apparent, since all rights and duties are derived from law, and all just law is derived from the natural law based on the eternal law of God. And God cannot both command and forbid the same thing. The stronger right or duty prevails; the weaker simply ceases to be a right or duty at all.

In practice, however, it can be extremely difficult to determine which is the stronger right or duty. Certain general norms are commonly recognized in making such a determination. Thus, other things being equal, the stronger right or duty is the one that involves the *nobler person,* e.g., God before man, parents before children; *higher law,* e.g., natural law before positive law, inalienable rights before alienable rights; *more common good,* e.g., the country before the family, the family before the individual; *graver matter,* e.g., the soul before the body, life before property; *clearer title,* e.g., the certain before the doubtful, paying a debt before giving a gift; *closer relationship,* e.g., closer relatives before remote ones, friends before strangers; and *greater urgency,* e.g., fighting a fire before reading a book, saving the living before burying the dead.

What makes these norms hard to apply is that in any given situation other things are not equal. One right or duty may appear stronger according to one of these norms, and the opposite right or duty stronger for another reason. It is here especially that the virtue of prudence, both natural and supernatural, is indispensable.

CONF. PONT. *Confessor pontifex*—confessor bishop.

CONFRATERNITY. In ecclesiastical law an association of the laity whose primary purpose is the promotion of public worship. Other aims may be joined with the primary one. Over the years, as recognized by the Code of Canon Law (1918), confraternities were founded as sodalities. An archconfraternity would be a sodality with the right to aggregate other associations of the same kind. By this aggregation the affiliated society could participate in all the spiritual favors conferred by the Holy See on the archconfraternity. (Etym. Latin *con-,* with + *fraternitas,* brotherhood.)

CONGREGATIO DE AUXILIIS. A commission to settle the theological controversy on grace and free will, established by Pope Clement VIII and continued by Pope Paul V. The Dominicans and Jesuits were parties to the dispute. After nine years of ineffective discussion Pope Paul V in 1607 dissolved the commission and reserved the decision to the Holy See. A decision has never been promulgated.

CONGREGATIONALISTS. Those Protestants who believe that each local church (congregation) is to be independent and autonomous. They profess to represent the principle of democracy in church government, a policy, they hold, claiming that Christ alone is the head of the Church he founded.

Since the members of the Church are baptized Christians, they are all priests of God. No one, therefore, may claim to have priestly powers that others do not profess, or the right to teach or rule in Christ's name, except insofar as he or she is delegated by the congregation. Where two or three are gathered together in his name, he is in their midst, and the local church comes into existence as an expression and representation of the Church Universal. Congregationalists say that this system of church structure is the most primitive in Christianity and all other forms are later human additions and changes.

Although the Congregationalist principle began with Luther (1483–1546), it was not put into consistent practice until the English Reformation. With the rise of Anglicanism various separatists broke with the parent English Church to form what eventually became the Congregational Churches of Anglo-Saxon Protestantism. In the United States, most local Protestant groups of churches follow the Congregational pattern, even when they have other denominational names.

CONGREGATION FOR BISHOPS. Established in 1588 as the Sacred Consistorial Congregation by Pope Sixtus V. Its name was changed in 1967 by Pope Paul VI, and its authority clarified. In countries not subject to the Congregations for Oriental Churches or the Evangelization of Peoples, the Congregation for Bishops may erect, divide, and unite dioceses, provinces, and other ecclesiastical territories. It prepares the documentation for the choice of bishops, apostolic administrators, and prelates with personal jurisdiction. It is kept informed about and watches over whatever concerns the persons and offices of bishops and the state of their dioceses. It examines the quinquennial reports and episcopal conferences and, in general, oversees the needs of the

Church as these are to be met by the local ordinaries and their auxiliaries.

CONGREGATION FOR CATHOLIC EDUCATION. An outgrowth of three successive Roman congregations, whose work it has taken over, namely, the Congregation for Studies at the University of Rome (1588), of Studies (1824), and of Seminaries and University Studies (1915). In 1967 Pope Paul VI established the new congregation with three areas of jurisdiction over: 1. seminaries and houses of formation for religious and members of secular institutes; 2. all universities and faculties of higher education under Catholic auspices; and 3. all schools and institutes of education dependent on ecclesiastical authority. Excluded from its competence are those educational institutions and agencies depending on the Congregations for Oriental Churches and Evangelization of Peoples.

CONGREGATION FOR DIVINE WORSHIP. Established in 1969 by Pope Paul VI, it became an autonomous part of the Roman Curia, with authority over all questions of divine worship, both liturgical and extraliturgical. Its three offices were as follows: 1. approval of calendars, interpretation of liturgical norms, and the care of doctrinal, pastoral, and ritual aspects of liturgical worship; 2. communication with episcopal conferences on all questions of worship; 3. promotion of the liturgical apostolate, of sacred music and art, and maintaining contact with liturgical and pastoral institutes. In 1975 it became part of the new Congregation for the Sacraments and Divine Worship.

CONGREGATION FOR ORIENTAL CHURCHES. Originally created in 1862 by Pope Pius IX as part of the Congregation of Propaganda, it became autonomous in 1917. Its jurisdiction extends to all bishops, clergy, religious, and laity of the Oriental rites, comparable to the authority of such bodies as the Congregation of Bishops, Clergy, Religious, and Catholic Education for the Latin Rite. Moreover, it has exclusive authority in certain countries where Oriental Rite Catholics are dominant.

CONGREGATION FOR RELIGIOUS AND SECULAR INSTITUTES. Originally established by Pope Sixtus V in 1588, it was reorganized by Pope Pius X in 1908. Its competence extends to all religious orders and congregations, societies of common life, secular institutes, third orders—whether of men or women. It has no territorial limits, and no questions pertaining to a life of perfection need be remitted to other Roman congregations. It has power of dispensation and, as required, important affairs, such as the approval of constitutions, quinquennial reports and formation, are confided to various commissions. In 1967 it established a School of Practical Law for Religious. Since 1975 it has issued its own official quarterly *Informationes*, published in English as *Consecrated Life* by the Institute on Religious Life (Chicago).

CONGREGATION FOR THE CAUSES OF SAINTS. Created by Pope Paul VI in 1969, as one of two derivatives (along with the Congregation for Divine Worship) of the Congregation of Rites. Its function is to supervise the canonical process for persons whose cause for beatification and canonization has been introduced to the Holy See. It became an independent congregation in 1975.

CONGREGATION FOR THE CLERGY. The new name of the former Congregation of the Council, originally created to interpret authentically the doctrine and decrees of the Council of Trent. Re-established under its present name by Pope Paul VI in 1966, it has three main functions: to co-ordinate and initiate efforts for the spiritual, pastoral, and intellectual development of priests; to supervise the preaching of the word of God, catechetics, and the religious instruction of infants, children, and adults; to ensure the preservation and proper administration of the temporal goods of the Church.

CONGREGATION FOR THE DISCIPLINE OF THE SACRAMENTS. A temporary Roman congregation, established in 1967 and suppressed in 1975. Its functions became part of the new Congregation for the Sacraments and Divine Worship.

CONGREGATION FOR THE DOCTRINE OF THE FAITH. In its present form, established by Pope Paul VI in 1965. It began in 1542, under Pope Paul III as the Congregation of the Inquisition to defend the Church against heresy. In 1908, Pope St. Pius X reorganized the Inquisition, changed its name to the Congregation of the Holy Office, and united to it the Section for Indulgences. In 1965, Pope Paul VI once more reformed the Holy Office and changed its name to the Congregation for the Doctrine of the Faith, noting, "We now provide better for the defence of the faith by promoting doctrine." Its competence covers a wide area, including whatever concerns the Catholic faith, such as new theological theories, writings contrary to the faith, the privilege of faith in marriage cases, and the judgment of crimes against the faith. Plenary sessions of the congregation decide major questions by deliberative vote and are proposed to the Pope for approval.

CONGREGATION FOR THE EVANGELIZATION OF PEOPLES. Originally created by Popes Pius V and Gregory XIII as a commission of cardinals, it was formally re-established in 1622 by Pope Gregory XV as the Congregation for the Propagation of the Faith. This name is still used, but the new title was given in 1967, when it was reconstituted by Pope Paul VI. Its scope of activity is the whole span of missionary work throughout the Church, and the care of the whole Christian life of the faithful and the ministry of the clergy in mission territories.

CONGREGATION FOR THE SACRAMENTS AND DIVINE WORSHIP. Established in 1975, it has two sections: one to deal with the sacraments and the other with divine worship. It also has two special commissions. One of these handles dispensations from nonconsummated marriages, and the other decides on claims of doubtful holy orders.

CONGREGATION OF RITES. Established in 1967 with competence over the Roman and other Latin rites. It was suppressed in 1969; its work was divided between two new congregations, of Divine Worship and the Causes of Saints.

CONGREGATION OF THE MISSION. See VINCENTIANS.

CONGREGATION, RELIGIOUS. Institutes of Christian perfection whose members take simple vows, as distinguished from religious orders in which solemn vows are made. Congregations are a modern development in the Catholic Church, among the first being the English Ladies, approved in 1703, and the Passionists, approved in 1741. They are either diocesan or pontifical, depending on whether they are subject immediately to a local bishop or to the Holy See. Since 1908, the special approbation as a pontifical community has been given by the Vatican's Congregation for Religious.

The term "congregation" is also applied to groups of monasteries that have arisen since the Middle Ages to facilitate discipline and intercommunication. Such groups may be united under an abbot general. Examples are the Cassinese Congregation, dependent on Monte Cassino, and various national congregations.

CONGRUENT MERIT. Also called appropriate merit, it is any good deed that deserves reward on any one or more of a variety of grounds, but not in strict justice or fidelity to a promise. Thus friendship, compassion, kindness, and responding to a request are grounds for congruent merit.

CONGRUISM. The theory of man's co-operation with grace, first developed by Francisco Suárez (1548–1617) and St. Robert Bellarmine (1542–1621) and later adopted by the Jesuit order. According to congruism, the difference between efficacious and sufficient grace lies not only in the consent of the free will (Molinism), but also in the congruity or suitableness of a particular grace to the peculiar conditions of the one who receives the grace. When the grace suits the interior dispositions and external circumstances of a person, it becomes effective by the free consent of the will; otherwise it remains ineffective because it lacks free acceptance. As in Molinism, God foresees the congruity of the grace and its infallible success. Unlike Molinism, congruism places the emphasis not on man's freedom but on the supremacy of the divine will in determining salvation. (Etym. Latin *congruitas*, congruity, fitness, suitability, becomingness.)

CONGRUOUS. Equitable and proper that God should grant what is asked or expected of him. Commonly applied to merit, it is distinguished from merit strictly so called, the latter being known as condign. Congruous merit is not precisely merit, but well-founded expectation. It refers to "gaining merit" for others, obtaining from God what a person in the state of grave sin prays for, receiving the gift of final perseverance and, in general, all the blessings we are confident God will grant, without having the absolute assurance that he will do so. Congruous merit is associated with the divine goodness, where condign merit rather depends on God's fidelity to his promises.

CONJUGAL CHASTITY. The virtue of chastity to be practiced by the married. This means marital fidelity between husband and wife, which forbids adultery; mutual respect of each other's dignity, which forbids any unnatural sexual activity, or sodomy; and the practice of natural intercourse that does not interfere with the life process, which forbids contraception.

CONJUGAL LOVE. The affection of husband and wife that should be both unitive and, unless virginal, procreative. It is unitive for the married spouses and procreative from them, as potential parents of the offspring God may wish to give them. (Etym. Latin *conjugalis;* from *conjux,* husband, wife; from *conjungere,* to join, unite in marriage.

CONJUGAL RIGHTS. Principally the mutual rights to marital intercourse between husband and wife. In the words of St. Paul, "the husband must give his wife what she has a right to expect, and so too the wife to the husband. The wife has no rights over her own body; it is the husband who has them. In the same way, the husband has no rights over his body; the wife has them. Do not refuse each other except by mutual consent, and then only for an agreed time, to leave yourselves for prayer; then come together again in case Satan should take advantage of your weakness to tempt you" (I Corinthians 7:4–5). In a broader sense, conjugal rights include all that husband and wife may justly expect of one another in terms of attention, affection, co-operation, and patient forbearance.

CONOPAEUM. Veil covering the outside of the tabernacle in which the Blessed Sacrament is reserved. It may be white, gold, or the liturgical color of the priest's vestments for that day. There is normally an opening in the front of the veil, to allow the tabernacle to be opened for removing and reposing the Holy Eucharist.

CONS. *Consecratio*—consecration.

CONSCIENCE. The judgment of the practical intellect deciding, from general principles of faith and reason, the goodness or badness of a way of acting that a person now faces.

It is an operation of the intellect and not of the feelings or even of the will. An action is right or wrong because of objective principles to which the mind must subscribe, not because a person subjectively feels that way or because his will wants it that way.

Conscience, therefore, is a specific act of the mind applying its knowledge to a concrete moral situation. What the mind decides in a given case depends on principles already in the mind.

These principles are presupposed as known to the mind, either from the light of natural reason reflecting on the data of creation, or from divine faith responding to God's supernatural revelation. Conscience does not produce these principles; it accepts them. Nor does conscience pass judgment on the truths of reason and divine faith; it uses them as the premises from which to conclude whether something should be done (or should have been done) because it is good, or should be omitted (or should have been omitted) because it is bad. Its conclusions also apply to situations where the mind decides that something is permissible or preferable but not obligatory.

Always the role of conscience is to decide subjectively on the ethical propriety of a specific action, here and now, for this person, in these circumstances. But always, too, the decision is a mental conclusion derived from objective norms that conscience does not determine on its own, receiving it as given by the Author of nature and divine grace.

CONSCIENTIOUS OBJECTOR. A person who, on moral or religious grounds, refuses to perform military service. On Catholic principles, war is not necessarily and intrinsically evil. Yet a Catholic may be a conscientious objector, as when a given war is undoubtedly unjust, or when a person believes that for him, under the circumstances, participation would be morally wrong. In general, a conscientious objector must follow his sincere convictions in this matter. Hence if he cannot persuade himself of the licitness of a war to which he is being either drafted or for which he may volunteer, he must abstain from active participation in it.

CONSCIOUSNESS. Immediate awareness of something. It is the internal experience here and now of something either internally or externally present to the perceiver.

CONSECR. *Consecratus*—consecrated.

CONSECRATED ALTAR. A fixed altar or permanent structure of stone, consisting of the table and the supports liturgically consecrated together as one whole. They may not be detached without the altar losing its consecration.

CONSECRATED GROUND. Any place or space that has been liturgically blessed, or where some sacred object such as a church is built or has stood. But most commonly, consecrated ground means a single grave or several graves or a whole cemetery in which faithful Christians are buried.

CONSECRATION. The words of institution of the Eucharist, pronounced at Mass, by which is accomplished the very sacrifice that

Christ instituted at the Last Supper. The formula of consecration is uniform for all the approved canons of the Mass and reads, in literal translation: "Take and eat of this, all of you; for this is my body which will be given up for you . . . Take and drink of this, all of you; for this is the chalice of my blood, of the new and eternal testament, which will be shed for you and for many unto the remission of sins. Do this in commemoration of me." (Etym. Latin *consecratio;* from *consecrare,* to render sacred.)

CONSECRATION OF VIRGINS. A solemn rite by which a woman is constituted a sacred person, dedicating her virginity to Christ and his Church. The women on whom the consecration of virgins can be bestowed are both religious women and women living in the world who have never entered into marriage and have not publicly or openly lived in a state contrary to chastity. The one who administers the rite is the local ordinary or his delegate. There is a lifelong commitment in the consecration. Moreover, according to the norms of the Holy See, "Christian virgins, each according to her state and her charisms, must spend their time in works of penance and mercy, in apostolic activity and holy prayer."

CONSECRATION TO MARY. An act of devotion, promoted by St. Louis de Montfort (1673–1716), that consists of the entire gift of self to Jesus through Mary. It is, moreover, a habitual attitude of complete dependence on Mary in one's whole life and activity. In making the act of consecration, a person gives himself or herself to Mary and through her to Jesus as her slave. This means that a person performs good works as one who labors without wages, trustfully hoping to receive food and shelter and have other needs satisfied by the master, to whom one gives all one is and does, and on whom one depends entirely in a spirit of love. The act of consecration reads:

"I, [Name], faithless sinner, renew and ratify today in your hands the vows of my baptism; I renounce forever Satan, his pomps and works; and I give myself entirely to Jesus Christ, the Incarnate Wisdom, to carry my cross after Him all the days of my life, and to be more faithful to Him than I have ever been before.

"In the presence of all the heavenly court I choose you this day for my mother and queen. I deliver and consecrate to you, as your slave, my body and soul, my goods, both interior and exterior, and even the value of all my good actions, past, present, and future; leaving to you the entire and full right of disposing of me, and all that belongs to me, without exception, according to your good pleasure, for the greater glory of God, in time and in eternity. Amen."

CONSECRATION TO THE SACRED HEART. Formal dedication of oneself, of one's family, community, society, or even of the whole human race to the Sacred Heart of Jesus. Consecration implies a total surrender to the Savior in gratitude for his blessings in the past and as a pledge of fidelity in the future. One of the oldest known acts of consecration and reparation to the Sacred Heart dates from the fifteenth century and was popularized by the Benedictine monks at the Abbey of St. Matthias at Trier in the German Rhineland. After St. Margaret Mary, the practice of consecration to the Heart of Jesus became widespread in the Catholic world. Personal consecration of the individual can be made often and informally and, in fact, the Morning Offering of the Apostleship of Prayer is a daily act of consecration. Family consecration has been strongly recommended by the modern popes, e.g., Pope Pius XII, who declared, "It is our heartfelt desire that the love of Jesus Christ of which His Heart is the fountain, should again take possession of private and public life. May our divine Savior reign over society and home life through His law of love. That is why we make a special appeal to Christian families to consecrate themselves to the Sacred Heart." Group consecrations go back to at least 1720, when the city of Marseilles, through its bishop and civil officials, made the dedication. Pope Leo XIII consecrated the world to the Sacred Heart in 1899 in anticipation of the Holy Year at the turn of the century. In 1925, Pope Pius XI ordered a formal *Act of Consecration of the Human Race to the Sacred Heart of Jesus,* to be publicly recited annually on the feast of Jesus Christ the King. See also ENTHRONEMENT.

CONSENT. A free act in which a person agrees to do, accept, or reject something. Commonly distinguished from assent, which properly belongs in the mind. Consent of the will may be partial or total, and only when total, or complete, is a person held fully responsible for his or her actions. Thus it requires full consent for a gravely wrong action to become a mortal sin. (Etym. Latin *consentire,* to agree to.)

CONSEQUENT CONSCIENCE. The judgment of the mind on the morality of an action already performed. The conscience either approves what has been done, giving peace to the mind and spiritual joy, or disapproves of what was done, thus causing remorse and a sense of guilt. See also ANTECEDENT CONSCIENCE.

CONSERVATION. The act of preserving something in existence, activity, or any other perfection or state. Commonly applied to God's act of preserving creatures in their existence and perfections. This is positive, essential, and direct conservation inasmuch as God maintains the causal action necessary for the perdurance of the world. (Etym. Latin *conservare,* to preserve.)

CONSISTENCY. Agreement of a person's conduct with principles, hence sustained steadiness of character.

CONSISTORIAL ADVOCATES. ●Originating under Pope St. Gregory I in 598, as legal defenders of the Church, their present function is to plead cases in the Consistory and the Rota. They also have notarial functions in Vatican City and have a post in the Pontifical Chapel.

CONSISTORY. An ecclesiastical court, especially an assembly of cardinals for purposes of deliberation, presided over by the Pope. A papal consistory is secret if only cardinals are present, semi-public if bishops also participate, and public if other prelates are called to the meeting. (Etym. Latin *consistere,* to stand together.)

CONSOLATION, OUR LADY OF. A shrine at Carey, Ohio, dating from 1868, when a replica of the statue of "Our Lady of Consolation" in Luxembourg was made and brought to the parish rectory at Berwick, Ohio. Over one thousand people gathered for a solemn procession. Singing hymns, they carried the statue seven miles to the church at Carey. Reliable accounts state that none of the pilgrims were touched by the sudden downpour of rain that fell that day. In 1907 the present site was selected, and two years later the crypt of the new church was completed. Dedicated in 1925 by Bishop Stritch of the Toledo diocese, this Marian sanctuary has become a basilica and the National Shrine of Our Lady of Consolation. The Conventual Franciscans are in charge of the shrine, which is annually visited by thousands. Numerous ex-votos testify to the many cures reported by the pilgrims.

CONSTANT. Popularly, a nonvariable. In theological terms that which continues to exist while it develops. The apparent contradiction between that which remains constant while also growing is one of the phenomena of Christianity. Thus the Church remains essentially the same even as she changes in adapting to different cultures and times. And revelation stays basically what it was at the end of the apostolic age, while showing remarkable growth in depth and intelligibility over the centuries. What changes is the human, what remains constant is divine.

CONST. AP. *Constitutio apostolica*—apostolic constitution.

CONSTITUTION, CONCILIAR. A document issued by an ecumenical council and approved by the Pope, containing the positive doctrine of the Church, as distinct from the canons that formally condemn contrary teaching. Among the documents of the Second Vatican Council, the constitutions are either unqualified, on the liturgy; or dogmatic, on the Church and Divine Revelation; or pastoral, on the Church in the modern world.

CONSTITUTION, PAPAL. An authoritative document that the Pope generally issues in his own name and that is intended to affect the Universal Church. Pope Paul VI used this form to promulgate the most important postconciliar decisions affecting the administration of the sacraments.

CONSTITUTION, RELIGIOUS. The fundamental rule of life of a religious institute, containing the principles of religious life in general and as understood by a particular community, together with the basic norms by which the members are to put these principles into practice. In order to be valid, the constitutions of religious communities, whether pontifical or diocesan, must be approved by the Holy See.

CONSUBSTANTIATION. The belief, contrary to Catholic doctrine, that in the Eucharist the body and blood of Christ coexist with the bread and wine after the Consecration of the Mass. John Wyclif (1324–84) and Martin Luther (1483–1546) professed consubstantiation because they denied transubstantiation.

CONSUETUDINARIAN. A habitual sinner. One who frequently commits the same, normally grave sins over a long period of time without notable intervals during which the sins are not committed. (Etym. Latin *consuetudo*, custom.)

CONSULTOR. A member of a council in a diocese or religious institute. Consultors mainly advise, but the provisions of a given council may require a deliberative vote of the consultors for matters of greater importance.

CONSUMMATED MARRIAGE. A marriage in which after the matrimonial contract is made husband and wife have marital intercourse. Contraceptive intercourse does not consummate Christian marriage. (Etym. Latin *consummare*, to bring into one sum, to perfect.)

CONSUMMATUM EST. It is finished. Christ's words as he was dying on the Cross, in the Latin Vulgate. Often appearing on inscriptions and in sacred art.

CONTEMPLATION. The enjoyable admiration of perceived truth (St. Augustine). Elevation of mind resting on God (St. Bernard). Simple intuition of divine truth that produces love (St. Thomas). (Etym. Latin *contemplatio*, simple gazing of the mind at manifest truth; from *con-*, with + *templum*, open space for observation [by augurs]: *contemplari*, to observe, consider.)

CONTEMPLATIVE LIFE. Human life insofar as it is occupied with God and things of the spirit. Compared with the active life, it stresses prayer and self-denial as a means of growing in the knowledge and love of God. As a form of religious life, it identifies "institutes which are entirely ordered towards contemplation, in such wise that their members give themselves over to God alone in solitude and silence, in constant prayer and willing penance" (*Perfectae Caritatis*, 7).

CONTEMPLATIVE PRAYER. In general, that form of mental prayer in which the affective sentiments of the will predominate, as distinct from discursive reflections of the mind. Or again, it is that prayer which looks at God by contemplating and adoring his attributes more than by asking him for favors or thanking him for graces received.

CONTINENCE. The virtue by which a person controls the unruly movements of sexual desire or other bodily emotions. It is connected with the virtue of temperance. It generally means the chastity to be observed by the unmarried. But it may also refer to the abstinence, in marriage, voluntarily agreed upon by both parties or forced by circumstances to abstain from marital intercourse.

(Etym. Latin *continentia*, holding together, coherence; containing in itself, inclusion, restraint.)

CONTINGENT. Whatever can be or not be other than it is; that which need not exist. Thus all creatures are contingent beings, since they come into existence out of nothing, and they are changeable realities that depend totally on the sustaining power of God.

CONTINUITY. Applied to the Church's teaching, it is the uninterrupted proclamation of the mysteries of faith from apostolic times to the present. The perdurance of revealed truth, maintained by the Church's teaching authority (magisterium).

CONTRACEPTION. Deliberate interference with marital intercourse in order to prevent conception. It is the performance of the marriage act with the positive frustration of conception. Also called conjugal onanism, from the sin of Onan, referred to in the Bible (Genesis 38:8-10); Neo-Malthusianism from the name of the English sociologist Malthus (1766–1834); it is popularly termed birth control, where those concerned with high birthrates have come to equate contraception with population control.

The Catholic Church has forbidden contraception from earliest times, and the number of papal statements dealing with the subject indicates the Church's constant tradition. In modern times the most significant document was *Humanae Vitae* in 1968 by Paul VI. After referring to the long history of the Church's teaching, he declared that the "direct interruption of the generative process already begun," even though done for therapeutic reasons, is to be "absolutely excluded as a licit means of regulating birth." Equally to be excluded is direct sterilization for contraceptive reasons. "Similarly excluded is every action that, either in anticipation of the conjugal act, or in its accomplishment, or in the development of its natural consequences, purposes, whether as an end or as a means, to render procreation impossible" (*Humanae Vitae*, II, 14).

Few aspects of Christian morality in modern times have given rise to more difficulties of conscience than the Catholic doctrine on contraception. This was reflected in Paul's admission, shortly after *Humanae Vitae:* "How many times we have trembled before the alternatives of an easy condescension to current opinions."

One of the results of the Church's teaching on contraception has been to emphasize her right to teach the faithful, even to binding them gravely in conscience, in matters that pertain to the natural law. Yet the basic motivation offered to married people to live up to this difficult teaching is highly supernatural, namely the prospect of loving one another in such a way that they will share the fruits of their affection with another person whom their mutual love will bring into being.

CONTRACEPTIVE CULTURE. A society in which contraception is the accepted way of preventing the conception of unwanted offspring.

CONTRACEPTIVE INTERCOURSE. Sexual intercourse in which some physical or chemical means is used to prevent conception. Such intercourse does not consummate the sacrament of marriage.

CONTRACEPTIVE STERILIZATION. Depriving the body of its generative powers in order to prevent the conception or fetal development of undesired offspring, for the satisfaction of a person's wishes and/or the relief of an economic or social need. Its morality falls under the same category as contraception. It is forbidden by the natural law.

CONTRACT. Mutual agreement upon sufficient consideration concerning the transfer of a right. A contract is an agreement because there must be consent of at least two wills to the same object. It is mutual because the consent on one side must be given in view of the consent on the other side; it cannot be a mere coincidence that two people happen to want the same thing. The contracting parties transfer a right and so bind themsevles in commutative justice, as person to person. By natural law a tangible consideration or compensation is not necessary in all contracts, because there can be gratuitous contracts such as a gift or promise. Even here, however, some intangible consideration in the form of affection or gratitude is normally expected. Finally the obligation in justice may be on both sides or only on one side, so that contracts can be bilateral (as in marriage) or unilateral (as in the promise of a donation). In either case the consent must always be on both sides.

CONTRADICTION. The complete denial or total exclusion of the opposite. In general, the opposition between judgments or propositions that cannot simultaneously be both true and false.

CONTRADICTION, PRINCIPLE OF. The universal law of being and thought that something cannot both be and not be at the same time in the same respect.

CONTRITION. The act or virtue of sorrow for one's sins. The virtue of contrition is a permanent disposition of soul. However, only an act of contrition is required for the remission of sin, whether with or without sacramental absolution.

The act of contrition is a free decision involving a detestation of and grief for sins committed and also a determination not to sin again. This detestation is an act of the will that aims at past sinful thoughts, words, deeds, or omissions. In practice it means that a sinner must retract his past sins, equivalently saying he wished he had not committed them. The grief for sins is also an act of the will directed at the state of greater or less estrangement from God that results from sinful actions. Concretely, it means the desire to regain the divine friendship, either lost or injured by sin. There must also be a determination not to sin again, which is an act of the will resolving to avoid the sins committed and take the necessary means to overcome them.

Four qualities permeate a genuine act of contrition and affect all three constituents of the act, the detestation, the grief, and the determination not to sin again. A valid contrition is internal, supernatural, universal, and sovereign.

Contrition is internal when it is sincere and proceeds from the will, when it is not the result of a mere passing mood or emotional experience. It is supernatural when inspired by actual grace and based on a motive accepted on faith. It is universal when the sorrow extends to all mortal sins, and for valid sacramental absolution there must be sorrow for whatever sins are confessed. It is finally sovereign if the sinner freely recognizes sin as the greatest of all evils and is willing to make amends accordingly. (Etym. Latin *contritio,* grinding, crushing; compunction of heart; from *conterere,* to rub together, bruise.)

CONTROL OF PASSION. A person's sensitive and imaginative life and activity under control and ruled by reason. This means exemption from the sway of concupiscence, which makes the practice of virtue difficult. Passions controlled make one's lower faculties subservient to reason, the body to the soul's demands, and the will subject to God.

CONTROVERSIAL THEOLOGY. That

part of dogmatic theology which seeks to defend the teachings of the Church against objections to its enduring truths and binding character.

CONTUMACIOUS. In ecclesiastical law the attitude of a person who shows no regard for the authority of the Church, knowing perfectly well that he is violating its laws. (Etym. Latin *con-*, thoroughly + *tumere*, to swell, be proud: *contumacia*, insolent and stubborn perverseness.)

CONTUMACY. Obstinacy in disobeying the lawful orders of an ecclesiastical court or in refusing to follow a legitimate superior's admonitions or precepts.

CONTUMELY. The act of unjustly dishonoring another in his presence. It corresponds to what is popularly called an insult. Contumely sins against justice and charity, for it goes against one's right to the honor and marks of respect that accord with a person's character and standing. It is not merely a failure to pay due honor to a person, but a positive act of dishonor that expresses contempt. Among other forms of contumely are mimicry, lampoons, sardonic grins, caricatures, a slap in the face, and burning in effigy. Contumely is a grave sin if it does serious injury to another's honor, and restitution then is necessary. (Etym. Latin *contumelia*, insult, reproach, affront.)

CONVENT. The building or buildings in which a community of religious women live; also a monastic community in its corporate capacity. (Etym. Latin *conventus*, assembly, gathering of people; from *convenire*, to come together.)

CONVENTION. Any proposition or practice whose truth is accepted not on the basis of fact or proof, but because of social agreement or usage.

CONVENTUAL. In general, pertaining to community life, as distinct from living alone. The term is applied to all the communal aspects of monastic or religious life, as conventual Mass or conventual rules.

CONVENTUALS. The branch of the Franciscan Order that favored a mitigation of the rule of poverty. Its main provision was that property could be accumulated and held by the community. The policy of the Conventuals was approved by Pope John XXII in 1332. At first the Conventuals were strongly approved by the Observants, but a final separation between them occurred in 1517.

CONVERGENCE. A process of reasoning that leads to certainty, not because any one argument or evidence is conclusive but because of the accumulation of several arguments, all bearing on the issue.

CONVERSION. Any turning or changing from a state of sin to repentance, from a lax to a fervent way of life, from unbelief to faith, and from a non-Christian religion to Christianity. Since the Second Vatican Council the term is not used to describe a non-Catholic Christian becoming a Catholic. The preferred term is "entering into full communion with the Church." (Etym. Latin *conversio*, a turning, overturning, turning around; turning point; change.)

CONVERT. One who with the help of divine grace undergoes a significant spiritual change for the better. In all cases the change must be deeply interior and represent a change of mind and heart (metanoia) to qualify as a true conversion.

CONVULSIONARIES. Jansenist enthusiasts who opposed the papal condemnation of 1713 and exhibited supposedly miraculous phenomena in witness of their cause. The phenomena were first observed, together with cures and prophecies, at the tomb of the Jansenist François de Paris in 1731, at St. Médard, Paris. They continued in various parts of France to the end of the eighteenth century.

CO-OPERATING GRACE. Actual grace, which accompanies and supports our deliberate supernatural actions. Also called subsequent, assisting, and concomitant grace, it is grace considered in conjunction with the exercise of human freedom freely doing the will of God.

CO-OPERATION IN EVIL. The concurrence with another in a sinful action. This concurrence may be done in several ways: by acting with another in the same sin, as when a person joins another in perpetrating a robbery; by supplying a person what is helpful in performing a sinful action, such as providing a gun or other deadly weapon; and by commanding or suggesting that one do something sinful, by encouraging him or her or suggesting means of carrying it into effect.

CO-ORDINATOR. A term used instead of superior in those religious communities where the concept of real authority under obedience has been replaced by a more democratic form of government.

COPACABANA, OUR LADY OF. The principal Marian shrine of Bolivia, on the Peruvian border. This shrine to Our Lady, dating from 1592, is located in the mountains near Lake Titicaca. The site marked the location of an Inca temple to the Sun God. The legend of Mary and her Son goes back to 1576, when she appeared to some Inca fishermen and led them to safety in a violent storm on the nearby lake. In gratitude they built a small shrine in 1583 for a four-foot-high statue of wood and stucco carved by a descendant of Inca nobility. On feast days the Madonna is clothed in costly embroidered robes that scintillate with a thousand precious jewels. Her mid-August feast day pilgrimages usually last ten days, sometimes more. At these celebrations groups perform their Indian dances to drums, pipes, and flute, re-enacting events from their history. Daily processions pass along the lake roads carrying a replica of their Bolivian Queen of Heaven as she blesses the boats offshore. The original statue never leaves the basilica, for there is a popular legend that "Our Lady does not want to be outside," and when they disturb her "violent storms will always occur."

COPE. A long cape worn by priests and bishops at certain religious rites. Open in front, like a mantle, it reaches to the floor and is fastened on the breast with a clasp. It is worn in processions, at Benediction, and at other solemn offices, Mass excepted. (Etym. Latin *cappa*, cape.)

COPTIC RITE. Three forms of the Eucharistic ritual, that of St. Cyril, St. Gregory Nazianzus, and St. Basil, used by the Coptic churches united with the Holy See. The Anaphora, or canon, of St. Cyril, also called St. Mark's, together with parts common to all, duplicates the Greek St. Mark's. When translations were made into Coptic, some Greek forms were retained but were written in Coptic characters. St. Basil's ritual is used on Sundays, weekdays, and for requiems. St. Gregory's is used on certain feast days, St. Cyril's during Lent and on Christmas Eve.

CORAM POPULO. Before the people. A phrase in ecclesiastical law to describe an act performed publicly and therefore of common knowledge.

CORBAN. An offering or sacrifice to God, either bloody or unbloody (Mark 7:11).

(Etym. Hebrew *qorbān*, an offering. Arabic *qurbān*, a sacrifice.)

CORBONA. See POOR BOX.

CO-REDEMPTRIX. A title of the Blessed Virgin as co-operator with Christ in the work of human redemption. It may be considered an aspect of Mary's mediation in not only consenting to become the Mother of God but in freely consenting in his labors, sufferings, and death for the salvation of the human race. As Co-Redemptrix, she is in no sense equal to Christ in his redemptive activity, since she herself required redemption and in fact was redeemed by her Son. He alone merited man's salvation. Mary effectively interceded to obtain subjective application of Christ's merits to those whom the Savior had objectively redeemed.

CORINTHIANS, LETTERS TO THE. Two letters of St. Paul written from Ephesus to his converts at Corinth. The first was occasioned by certain problems that Paul sought to resolve. He therefore spoke of the need for unity (1:10–4:21), sins against chastity (5:1–6:20), marriage and sacrifices to idols (7:1–11:1), Christian worship and the gifts (11:2–14:40), the hymn on charity (13), the resurrection of the dead (15:1–58). In the second letter, St. Paul confronts his enemies at Corinth. He defends his apostolate, recounts the achievements God worked through him in spite of his own weakness and incompetence, asks funds for the Christians in Jerusalem, and once again defends his call as an Apostle and the extraordinary gifts the Lord conferred on him. It is very probable that St. Paul wrote four letters to the Corinthians, of which only two are extant.

CORNELIUS. A centurion of an Italian cohort stationed in Caesarea; he enjoyed good relations with the Jewish community but was considered a pagan. He received an angelic visitation, instructing him to send to Jaffa and invite Peter to visit him. His delegation of three men was readily welcomed by Peter because he in turn had been advised by a spirit that Cornelius was sending for him. On his arrival Peter was treated with reverence by the centurion and his household and friends. Peter explained that the traditional taboo against Jews mingling with non-Jews was approved by God, but the Apostle made it clear that no one should be considered profane or unclean (Acts 10). "God," he emphasized, "does not have favorites, but anybody of any nationality who fears God and does what is right is acceptable to him" (Acts 10:34–35). This was not only a welcome message to Cornelius and his friends but a startling revelation to Jewish believers, especially when Peter's explanation was climaxed by the descent of the Holy Spirit on all the listeners. Then Peter gave orders for all those well disposed to be baptized at once (Acts 10:48). Later, when he returned to Jerusalem, some Jews challenged his actions in eating with the uncircumcised and baptizing them. He explained the instructions he had received from God to spread the faith to non-Jews as well as Jews. His questioners were placated. "God," they said, "can evidently grant even the pagans the repentance that leads to life" (Acts 11:18).

CORNERSTONE. The stone in a corner of the foundation of a building. Inscribed with the name and date, a cavity in the stone may contain mementos of the time and circumstances. The cornerstone of an ecclesiastical building symbolizes Christ the Foundation of the Church and is blessed at its laying.

CORNETTE. A large, spreading white headgear. Formerly worn in France by both men and women and until recently by the Daughters of Charity of St. Vincent de Paul. (Etym. French *cornette*, headdress.)

CORONA. A Rosary of five decades, or any one of a variety of similar sacramentals for consecutive recitation of certain prayers. (Etym. Latin *corona*, a crown.)

CORONATION, PAPAL. Liturgical action by which the newly elected Pope had the tiara solemnly placed on his head by the senior cardinal-deacon. His pontificate officially began on this date, although he possesses jurisdiction from the moment he accepts the election by the cardinals. Pope John Paul I changed the custom of papal coronation with the tiara. When assuming office on September 3, 1978, he was formally invested with the pallium instead of the traditional papal tiara at a Mass he concelebrated with members of the college of cardinals. The simplicity of the ceremony symbolized the Pope's sensitivity to the pastoral needs of the Church and the world. Pope John Paul II followed the same practice when he was invested the following month, on October 22, 1978. Referring to the crowning with the tiara, he said on that occasion, "This is not the time to return to a ceremony and an object considered—perhaps wrongly—to be a symbol of the temporal power of the popes. Our time calls us, urges us, obliges us, to gaze on the Lord and to immerse ourselves in humble and devout meditation on the mystery of the supreme power of Christ himself."

CORONATION, ROYAL. The ceremony by which a monarch is crowned by the Pope or by someone in ecclesiastical authority. Early coronations in the West record that the Visigothic kings were crowned by the Bishop of Toledo in Spain. The rite of anointing was introduced in the East about the twelfth century. In Protestant regimes, where Church and State are closely united, the coronation follows the pattern of pre-Reformation times and may, as in England, include a special oath for the defense of Protestantism.

CORPORAL. A square white linen cloth on which the Host and Chalice are placed during Mass. When not in use it may be kept in a burse. It is also used under the monstrance at Benediction or under the Blessed Sacrament at any time. (Etym. Latin *corporalis*, bodily; from *corpus*, body.)

CORPORAL WORKS OF MERCY. The seven practices of charity, based on Christ's prediction of the Last Judgment (Matthew 5:3–10) that will determine each person's final destiny. They are: 1. to feed the hungry; 2. to give drink to the thirsty; 3. to clothe the naked; 4. to shelter the homeless; 5. to visit the sick; 6. to visit those in prison; and 7. to bury the dead.

CORPSE. The dead body of a human being. From the first days of Christianity the Church insisted on the respect to be paid to a corpse, because it had been the temple of the Holy Spirit (I Corinthians 6:19) and was destined to rise glorified on the last day (I Corinthians 15:39–44).

CORPUS CHRISTI. The Feast of the Blessed Sacrament, established in 1246 by Bishop Robert de Thorote of Liège, at the suggestion of St. Juliana of Mont Cornillon (1192–1258). Its observance was extended to the Universal Church by Pope Urban IV in 1264. The office for the day was composed by St. Thomas Aquinas, and the customary procession was approved by Popes Martin V and Eugene IV. Now celebrated as the solemnity of the Body and Blood of Christ on the first Thursday (or Sunday) after the feast of the Holy Trinity.

CORPUS DOMINI. The Body of the Lord,

referring to Christ's corporeal presence in the Eucharist.

CORPUS JURIS CANONICI. The body of canon law, whether codified, as in the *Codex Juris Canonici,* or simply the existing body of ecclesiastical law operative in the Catholic Church at any point of time.

CORRECT CONSCIENCE. The judgment of the mind when it concludes correctly from true principles that some act is lawful or sinful. Also called true conscience.

CORRECTION. The precept of charity, enjoined by Christ (Matthew 18:15), to admonish a person who is doing wrong or in danger of wrongdoing. Two conditions must be verified before there exists a grave obligation to correct another: 1. a person must be certain of another's grave spiritual need, which can be met only by such correction, and 2. the admonition can be given without serious trouble or harm to the one correcting. Always fraternal correction must be guided by kindness, providence, and humility. Moreover, Christ commands that it first be given secretly. Correction may have to be given publicly, in the first instance if: 1. the sin is publicly known, 2. the sin is likely to cause others harm unless the guilty person is publicly denounced, or 3. the culprit has renounced his right to private correction. (Etym. Latin *cor-,* together + *regere,* to rule: *corrigere,* to make right.)

COSMIC CHRIST. The second person of the Trinity, made man, seen as the origin or beginning and end or purpose of creation. This concept of a "world-Christ," that some have mistakenly understood in a pantheistic sense, is a favored theme of St. Paul. He describes Christ as "the image of the unseen God and the first-born of all creation, for in Him were created all things in heaven and on earth: everything visible and everything invisible, Thrones, Dominations, Sovereignties, Powers—all things were created through Him and for Him" (Colossians 1:12–14). The "Cosmic Christ" is sometimes distinguished from the "Redemptive Christ," and understood in the sense that God would have become man even though man had not sinned, out of sheer love of man and for the perfection of the universe.

The term was used by Pierre Teilhard de Chardin (1881–1955), according to whom the whole universe, with Christ as Ruler, is the true fullness of Christianity. As a result, all things are already permeated with a special presence of God, and correspondingly the whole world shares in the fruits of salvation. (Etym. Greek *kosmos,* order; the world, universe.)

COSMIC EVOLUTION. A theory of the world's origin and nature which holds that, under God, the whole visible universe, including humans, was and still is in process; it is moving toward perfection by an inner determinism that is inevitable. All humans can do is assist or accelerate the evolution but in no way resist or check its necessary development.

COSMOGONY. A theory about the origin of the universe, whether based on scientific reflection or religious belief. Catholic Christianity does not favor any particular scientific theory of the world's origins. Its concern is rather to teach on faith that God created the world in time, through the exercise of his omnipotence, and by a sovereign act of his divine will. (Etym. Greek *kosmos,* the world + *gonos,* offspring.)

COSMOLOGY. Study of the universe as an orderly creation, and of the causes that operate in the world of space and time. It presumes that the world was made according to an all-wise plan and is being directed by an infinite Mind. (Etym. Greek *kosmos,* the world + *logia,* knowledge, science.)

COSMOS. Literally "in order" or "duly." Hence good behavior, government, or rule. Commonly applied to the universe as wisely arranged and ordered. "Cosmos" is the ordinary biblical Greek term for the world as created and directed by God. (Etym. Greek *kosmos,* the world.)

COTERIE. A small circle of persons who form an intimate group, applied to the followers of some school of thought or sectarian belief.

COUNCIL FOR THE PUBLIC AFFAIRS OF THE CHURCH. Established in its present form by Pope Paul VI in 1967, the Vatican office whose principal task is to look after the Holy See's relations with civil authorities. The council, therefore, deals with the diplomatic corps attached to the Vatican, and with papal representatives to the various countries. Although distinct from the papal secretariat, its prefect is the cardinal secretary of state.

COUNCIL OF EPISCOPAL CONFERENCES OF EUROPE (C.C.E.E.). A collegial body of elected delegates from the bishops' conferences of Europe. Decreed by the Second Vatican Council (*Christus Do-*

minus) and established by Pope Paul's motu proprio, *Ecclesiae Sanctae,* the council first met in 1965. It has no juridical power and is essentially a service agency to co-ordinate and assist in communication among the episcopal conferences.

COUNCIL OF JERUSALEM. The gathering of the Apostles at Jerusalem to decide on the observance of the Mosaic precepts by the converts to Christianity. They declared: "It has been decided by the Holy Spirit and ourselves not to saddle you with any burden beyond these essentials: you are to abstain from food sacrificed to idols, from the meat of strangled animals and from fornication. Avoid these and you will do what is right" (Acts 15:28–29).

COUNCIL, PROVINCIAL. Bishops and other prelates convoked in consultative and deliberative assembly to discuss whatever is conducive to religious growth in a particular territory. Matters of faith, morals, abuses, controversies, and discipline are taken into consideration. The suffragan bishop after consultation decides on the place of meeting and presides over it. The decrees of the council oblige throughout the province. Until the creation of national and regional conferences after the Second Vatican Council, provincial councils were to be held every twenty years.

COUNCILS OF THE CHURCH. Authorized gatherings of bishops for the purpose of discussing ecclesiastical problems with a view to passing decrees on matters under discussion. In Roman Catholic terminology, if all the bishops are called to participate and actually represent the Christian world, the assembly is called ecumenical, which means universal; if only part of the hierarchy is invited, the council is particular. The latter may be plenary or provincial, depending on whether a single provincial area, e.g., the dioceses of Ohio, or a whole country sponsors the gathering. Church councils, even on a provincial basis, enjoy juridical authority in religious questions that is distinct from the legislative powers of individual bishops. In this respect also, councils differ from episcopal conferences, which are not, as such, legislative assemblies.

COUNSEL. Inquiry about the right choice of means to attain a particular end, and the advice given in response. Also a directive or recommendation by one in authority, which does not bind to its observance, as does a law or precept. (Etym. Latin *consilium,* deliberation, advice.)

COUNSELING. A general term for a wide variety of procedures for helping people cope with personal problems or adjust to difficult situations. Implicit in the Christian notion of counseling are two essential factors: that the advice given is based on the premises of faith, appealing to one's trust in divine providence; and that the counseling is joined with a prayer for light to guide the mind in discerning the will of God.

COUNSELS. Good actions that are not prescribed by any law. They are morally better than the corresponding precepts, as fasting is higher than temperance. Among the counsels the most important are the evangelical counsels of poverty, chastity, and obedience. They are called evangelical because they were taught and practiced by Christ in the Gospels. Moreover, they are especially proposed by the Church as means for attaining Christian perfection. A person can freely bind oneself to practice the evangelical counsels, as in the religious life, and then they become obligatory according to the conditions of the vows or promises assumed.

COUNTERCULTURE. The mental attitudes and customs, chiefly of the younger generation, that challenge or contradict the standards and values of established Judeo-Christian society.

COUNTER REFORMATION. A period of Catholic revival from 1522 to about 1648, better known as the Catholic Reform. It was an effort to stem the tide of Protestantism by genuine reform within the Catholic Church. There were political movements pressured by civil rulers, and ecclesiastical movements carried out by churchmen in an attempt to restore genuine Catholic life by establishing new religious orders such as the Society of Jesus and restoring old orders to their original observances, such as the Carmelites under St. Teresa of Avila (1515–82). The main factors responsible for the Counter Reformation, however, were the papacy and the Council of Trent (1545–63). Among church leaders St. Charles Borromeo (1538–84), Archbishop of Milan, enforced the reforms decreed by the council, and St. Francis de Sales of Geneva (1567–1622) spent his best energies in restoring genuine Catholic doctrine and piety. Among civil rulers sponsoring the needed reform were Philip II of Spain (1527–98) and Mary Tudor (1516–58), his wife, in England. Unfortunately this aspect of the Reformation led to embitterment between England and Scotland,

England and Spain, Poland and Sweden, and to almost two centuries of religious wars. As a result of the Counter Reformation, the Catholic Church became stronger in her institutional structure, more dedicated to the work of evangelization, and more influential in world affairs.

COURAGE. Virtue of bravery in facing difficulties, especially in overcoming the fear of consequences in doing good. As moral courage, it enables a person to pursue a course deemed right, through which one may incur contempt, disapproval, or opprobrium. As physical courage, it is simply bodily or emotional strength to withstand opposition. It differs from fortitude in being more aggressive in undertaking, whereas fortitude is more patient in undergoing what is virtuous but hard.

COVADONGA. A shrine to the "Virgin of the Battles" in the mountain region of Asturias, Spain. A national Marian place of pilgrimage. It is on the site of a historic defeat of the Moslems in 718, when their army was destroyed by a landslide while the Christian soldiers took refuge in a cave that had long been a hermitage sanctuary of Our Lady. The statue venerated there is considered an extraordinary work of art.

COVENANT, BIBLICAL. In the Old Testament an agreement between God and Israel in which God promised protection to the Chosen People in return for exclusive loyalty. "If you obey my voice and hold fast to my covenant, you of all the nations will be my very own" (Exodus 19:5). Moses presented Yahweh's offer to his people, who promptly "answered as one, 'All that Yahweh has said we will do.'" The compact was sealed (Exodus 19:8). Many years later Jeremiah prophesied that a new covenant would be offered. "Deep within them," Yahweh promised, "I will plant my law, writing it on their hearts" (Jeremiah 31:31–34). Ezekiel foresaw that God would "make a covenant of peace with them, an eternal covenant" (Ezekiel 37:26). Its universal character was foreshadowed by Isaiah, to whom it was revealed by Yahweh, "so that my salvation may reach to the ends of the earth" (Isaiah 49:6). In the New Testament, when Paul was explaining to the Corinthians the institution of the Eucharist at the Last Supper, he repeated Christ's words: "This cup is the new covenant in my blood. Whenever you drink it, do this as a memorial of me" (I Corinthians 11:25). This master idea of the New Testament is reinforced in the Letter to the Hebrews: "It follows that it is a greater covenant for which Jesus has become our guarantee" (Hebrews 7:22). Christ himself is the new covenant between God and his people. (Etym. Latin *convenire*, to agree, to come together.)

CO-VENERATION. The Nestorian theory that the man Jesus is to be venerated along with the Word of God. The Council of Ephesus (431) condemned the theory and declared that the Incarnate Word, being one person, is to be adored with one single adoration (Denzinger, 259).

COVETOUSNESS. A strong desire for possessions, especially material possessions. It implies that the desire is inordinate, with allusion to the prohibition in the Ten Commandments not to covet what belongs to someone else. Often synonymous with avarice, although referring more to the wrongfulness of the desire for possession and less (as in avarice) to its eagerness or intensity.

COWL. A hood covering the head, worn by the monastic orders. In the Middle Ages the cloak had a hood attached to it that could be drawn over the head, and the cowl became a great cloak with a hood. The Benedictine and Cistercian cowl is a large mantle with a hood that can be thrown back over the shoulders. Franciscans have a smaller hood attached to their habit. Canons wear the cowl on their mozzetta, and bishops and cardinals on the cappa. Some cowls, like those of the Augustinians and Servites, are separate hoods. The color of the cowl is that of the habit. (Etym. Latin *cuculla*, monk's hood.)

C.P.E.N. *Consilium pro Publicis Ecclesiae Negotiis*—Council for the Public Affairs of the Church.

CR. *Credo*—creed.

CRANIOTOMY. Perforation of the skull of an unborn infant and removal of its contents. It is condemned by the Church as the direct killing of an innocent human being and is never justified.

CRASS IGNORANCE. Also called supine ignorance. It is the ignorance of an ecclesiastical law, or its penalty, that a person has made no effort to enlighten. Such ignorance does not excuse one from penalties imposed by law unless some qualifying phrase to the contrary occurs in the wording of the law, e.g., "contumaciously."

CREATION. The production of material and spiritual things in their whole substance, done by God and of nothing. God creates out of nothing both because he starts with no pre-existing matter and because he parts with nothing of his own being in the act of creation. Thus creation in the proper sense (first creation) is to be distinguished from the so-called second creation described in Genesis, by which is understood the shaping of formless matter and giving it life and activity.

CREATIONISM. The Catholic doctrine that the soul of each human being is immediately created by God at the moment of conception.

CREATOR. God as Maker of all things from nothing. The earliest Latin creeds profess belief in "God the Father almighty, Creator [creatorem] of heaven and earth." Also some early Greek creeds speak of God "the Creator [ktistēn] and Maker [poiētēn]," although the Nicene Creed since the sixth century says simply "Maker" both in the Greek and Latin and now in the vernacular translations of the liturgy.

CRÈCHE. A crib or manger. Commonly applied to representations of the Nativity. (Etym. French crèche, manger, crib.)

CREDENCE. A small table or shelf in the wall at one side of the altar. On it are usually placed the cruets, basin, and finger towel. The chalice, paten, corporal, and veil used in the Mass may also be placed there until the Offertory of the Mass. (Etym. Latin credere, to believe.)

CREDENTITY. The credibility of something that is so persuasive that it morally obliges a person to believe. In theology, the credentity of Christian revelation is the convincing evidence for its truth, which imposes on a person the duty to accept it, corresponding to the decision "I must believe." It is partly the result of sincere inquiry and of proper moral dispositions, but mainly the result of God's enlightening grace. (Etym. Latin credentia, belief, trust, hence a table holding food for tasting in order to detect poison; from credere, to believe.)

CREDIBILITY. The reasonable grounds for believing something to be true. Credibility is generally applied to the evidence from experience, history, and reason for the truthfulness of Christian revelation, either in general or of a particular mystery like Christ's divinity or his resurrection. There are three logical stages for establishing the credibility of a mystery of faith: 1. the existence of God is proved by reason; 2. God's worthi-ness of being believed, if he makes a revelation, is likewise seen from reason, since a perfect God is all-knowing and trustworthy; 3. the fact that he actually made a revelation is then proved from the miracles he performs to confirm the testimony of those who claim to speak in his name. (Etym. Latin credibilis, from credere, to believe, entrust.)

CREDO. I believe. A creed or code of beliefs; also applied to any one article of faith. (Etym. Latin credo, I believe.)

CREDO QUIA ABSURDUM. I believe because it is absurd (or impossible). A phrase attributed to Tertullian (160–220), by which is meant that a Christian believer is not scandalized at the apparent absurdity or impossibility of such revealed mysteries as the Incarnation, that God became man, or the Real Presence, that Christ is truly present under the Eucharistic species.

CREDO UT INTELLIGAM. I believe in order to understand. Phrase of St. Anselm of Canterbury (1033–1109), defining one of the functions of faith as giving light to the mind. Those who believe acquire a capacity for knowledge, even in earthly terms, that unbelievers do not possess.

CREDULITY. Belief, especially religious belief, that is not based on sufficient reason. A credulous person accepts the word of someone without having established either the knowledge or honesty of the one whom he believes. Credulity is groundless faith, that believes only from instinct or habit or emotion and not on objective premises that are provable by reason. (Etym. Latin credulitas, from credulus, credulous.)

CREED. See CREDO.

CREMATION. The act of destroying the human body by fire after death. Christians followed the Jews in disposing of corpses by burial rather than by cremation, thinking of the latter as an unnatural and violent destruction of the human body, the repository of the Holy Spirit during life on earth. Since no principle of faith would be jeopardized by cremation, it has always been allowed with permission when public health required it. The Catholic Church has always opposed it, though, when it meant a defiance of belief in the resurrection of the body, and for centuries excommunicated those who ordered cremation for themselves or for others. At present, to meet changing world conditions, the Church is more lenient in her views on this method of disposal of the dead, while still preferring burial. (Etym. Latin *cremare*, to burn.)

CRESCENS MATRIMONIORUM. A decree of the Sacred Congregation for the Oriental Church, on mixed marriages between Catholics and baptized Eastern Christians who are not Catholic. Along with other provisions that make it easier for such persons to marry, the Church hereby made it only a matter of liceity, not validity, for a priest (Catholic) and witnesses to be present. Moreover, a bishop can dispense even with this regulation for grave reasons (February 22, 1967).

CRESCENT MOON. A favorite symbol of Mary under her title of the Immaculate Conception, as early as the fifteenth century. The representation is based on the passage "Who is she that comes forth as the morning rising, fair as the moon," from the Canticle of Canticles. Often the moon is represented under her feet, "a woman adorned with the sun, the moon under her feet" (Apocalypse 12:1). Combined with the crescent moon, the Cross depicted the Christian victory at Lepanto gained by Mary's intercession.

CRIB. A manger with bars. Representation of the feeding box in which the Christ Child was placed at his birth. Cribs are erected in churches at Christmas time to commemorate Jesus' birth in the Bethlehem stable. The relics of the True Crib are in St. Mary Major in Rome. See also CRÈCHE.

CRIME. An invalidating impediment to Christian marriage, arising from a grave public sin committed by one or both parties. It affects persons who, during the existence of a lawful marriage, have consummated adultery together and have mutually promised each other to marry, or have attempted marriage even by a mere civil act; those who, likewise during the existence of the same lawful marriage, have consummated adultery together, and one of whom has killed the lawful spouse; those who, even without committing adultery, have by mutual co-operation, physical or moral, killed the lawful spouse.

CRIMES OF LOGIC. A term in existentialist philosophy to identify a new phenomenon in world history: massive crimes against humanity, such as genocide and legalized abortion. They are called crimes of logic, unlike the crimes of passion, because they are done with careful planning and founded on a ready-made philosophy that legitimizes whatever those in power wish to perpetrate.

CRITERIOLOGY. The philosophical study of the first principles of human thought and their value as knowledge. It is also called epistemology and treats of the criteria or norms for determining the truth. These norms are both objective and subjective. Objective criteria are intrinsic evidence, where available, on divine or human authority, where truth is otherwise unavailable. Subjective criteria are the human faculties of knowledge, which faith tells the believer must be assisted by divine grace for the acceptance of revelation on God's authority.

CRITICISM, BIBLICAL. The scientific study and analysis of the human elements that have entered into the composition and preservation of the Scriptures. This study has been encouraged and fostered by the Church. The two outstanding papal documents urging Catholic scholars to engage in a scientific study of the Bible were Pope Leo XIII's *Providentissimus Deus* (1893), and Pope Pius XII's *Divino Afflante Spiritu* (1943). In all biblical criticism the Catholic Church insists on her scholars' recognizing that the Bible is the inspired word of God and consequently may not be treated as merely a human piece of writing. Moreover, the Church considers herself the divinely authorized custodian and interpreter of Sacred Scripture. Catholic scholars must therefore recognize that the Church's magisterium has the final word on the conclusions reached by biblical criticism. (Etym. Greek *kritikos*, able to discern or judge.)

CRITICISM, HIGHER. A term applied to the historical and literary criticism of the Bible.

CRITICISM, HISTORICAL. Regarding the Bible, it is the study that seeks to determine the historical sources, authorships, and factual contents of the Scriptures. Its focus is on the historicity of the biblical persons and events.

CRITICISM, LITERARY. Relative to the Scriptures, it is the study of the biblical text as a human, literary composition. It concentrates on this text, analyzing its style, grammatical forms and structure, with a view to better understanding of what the author meant from the internal evidence of the words themselves.

CRITICISM, LOWER. Another name for textual criticism of the Bible.

CRITICISM, TEXTUAL. Applied to the Bible, it is the study of the text of the Scriptures to determine, as far as possible, what had actually been written by the inspired authors. It deals with manuscripts, their preservation and comparison, and is the basis for all other research on the Bible.

CROSIER. An ornamental staff shaped like a shepherd's crook. It may be held or carried by bishops, mitered abbots, and other privileged prelates. It symbolizes a bishop's role as caretaker of his flock.

CROSS. Primarily the instrument of suffering on which Christ died and redeemed the world. It also stands for whatever pain or endurance that a Christian undergoes, and voluntarily accepts, in order to be joined with Christ and co-operate in the salvation of souls. The Cross is, therefore, a revealed mystery, taught by Christ when he said, "If anyone wants to be a follower of mine, let him renounce himself and take up his cross and follow me" (Matthew 16:24). The mystery of the Cross is one of the principal themes of St. Paul's writings (Romans 5:8; I Corinthians 1:17; Galatians 4:16; and Philippians 2:6–11).

CROSS ON STAFF. Symbol of St. Philip the Apostle because he was a traveling missionary who used the cross effectively in his contest with paganism and eventually died on it. St. Bridget of Sweden (1303–73) likewise has a cross-mounted staff as her emblem. The Latin style pommée cross with knoblike rounded ends is often used as a ceremonial cross.

CROWN. An emblem of royalty, honor, and victory. Found most frequently in representations of Christ as King, illustrative of his majestic power, and of Mary as Queen of Heaven, where she is crowned above all the angels and saints. A crown of glory in ecclesiastical usage symbolizes those saints who have won their race and are now reigning triumphant with Christ.

CROWN OF THORNS. A wreath of thorns mockingly placed on the head of Christ by Pilate's soldiers. St. Louis, King of France (1214–70), redeemed it from the Venetians and had constructed in its honor the magnificent Sainte-Chapelle in Paris. As a symbol of suffering in art, it is associated with martyrdom.

CRUCIFIX. A cross bearing the image of Christ. It must be placed on or over an altar where Mass is offered. Due reverence is always given to it. It is sometimes carried as a procession cross leading a line of clergy. Depicting the dead or suffering Christ, the crucifix did not come into general use until after the Reformation. The earlier ones represented Our Lord as the High Priest crowned, robed, and alive. Some men and women religious wear the crucifix as part of their habit. A crucifix is attached to the Rosary beads, and many liturgical blessings are to be given with it. A blessed crucifix is a sacramental and is commonly displayed in Catholic hospitals, homes, and institutions. (Etym. Latin *crucifixus*, the crucified.)

CRUCIFIXION. Execution of a criminal by nailing or binding to a cross. Originally used in the East, it was adopted by the Romans and was commonly inflicted on any condemned person who could not prove Roman citizenship. Normally preceded by scourging, it was later (from A.D. 69) imposed on certain lower-class citizens. Emperor Constantine abolished this method of capital punishment.

The crucifixion of Christ between two thieves is recorded by all four Evangelists. According to tradition, the cross of Christ was a *crux immissa*, with the upright extending above the transom. Also, most probably, Christ was fixed to the cross with four nails and covered with a loincloth, as prescribed by the Talmud.

CRUELTY. The vice that is the opposite of clemency. It demands and inflicts excessive punishment.

CRUELTY TO ANIMALS. Causing unnecessary pain to animals. Man has no duties toward animals because they have no independent personalities. They may therefore be used for any ethical purpose. It is sinful, however, to cause an animal needless suffering. The sinfulness does not lie in the violation of an animal's rights but in a person's irrational conduct, since reason forbids causing unnecessary pain and death. Moreover, cruelty to animals has a brutalizing effect on the tormentor.

CRUET. One of two small bottles or vessels to contain the water and wine used at the Consecration of the Mass. They are presented as offerings of the faithful at the Offertory. The cruets are also used for a priest's ablution after the Offertory, and the ablution of the chalice after Communion.

CRUSADER'S CROSS. A symbol, known also as the Jerusalem cross, that is said to have been the emblem on the coat of arms of Godfrey Bouillon (1060–1100), first ruler of the Latin Kingdom of Jerusalem. It is a Greek Cross with four equal arms having a smaller Greek cross in each of four corner fields. This cross is usually shown as red painted or appliquéd on white material.

CRUSADES. The military expeditions undertaken by Christians in the eleventh through fourteenth centuries to recover the Holy Land from the Moslems. The name comes from the cross that the crusaders bore on their clothing. There were eight principal Crusades: the first (1096–99) and the eighth (1270). However, the term is also applied in a wider sense to all expeditions blessed by the Church against heretics and infidels. (Etym. French *croisade;* Spanish *cruzada;* Latin *cruciata,* a marking with the cross.) See also CHILDREN'S CRUSADE, FIRST CRUSADE, SECOND CRUSADE, THIRD CRUSADE, FOURTH CRUSADE, FIFTH CRUSADE, SIXTH CRUSADE, SEVENTH CRUSADE, EIGHTH CRUSADE.

CRUX ANSATA. A T-shaped cross with a top loop, symbolizing eternal life.

CRUX DECUSSATA. An X-shaped cross of St. Andrew or St. Patrick (389–461). See also ST. ANDREW'S CROSS.

CRUX GEMMATA. Symbol known as the jeweled cross, suggesting a living tree with growing flowers and leaves adorning it. Jeweled, it appeared as an emblem of victory after the Edict of Milan in A.D. 313. From the ends of the crossbar were suspended the Greek letters alpha and omega.

CRYPT. A hidden recess or vault, usually underground, used as a burial room. Religious services are often held in church crypts. (Etym. Latin *crypta;* Greek *krypte,* a vault, hidden cave.)

CSIKSOMLYO-SUMULEU. Shrine of "Mary Comforter of the Afflicted" in Romania near the Transylvanian Alps. Csiksomlyo was settled by Franciscans, and the Church there dates back to the fourteenth century. The origin of the revered carved wooden statue of Our Lady is disputed. Some think she is a folk production of the native Szeklers. In the middle centuries the people, to house their statue, built an impressive Gothic cathedral, later enlarged by Baroque and Byzantine additions. Mary was working her miracles at this shrine as early as the sixteenth century. The church was burned, the worshipers were attacked, the image was mutilated, but always the shrine remained intact. Mary's crowned head is surrounded by an aureole of golden rays studded with jeweled stars. She stands upon the crescent moon. In time the church was made a basilica and enlarged to accommodate the crowds of pilgrims.

CUBICULA. Burial chambers in the Roman catacombs. Usually hewn out of rock along the passages, they were open on two sides. Horizontal tiers of such niches rose to the ceiling. Thousands of them have been excavated. (Etym. Latin *cubiculum,* apartment for residing or sleeping, a resting place.)

CUJUS REGIO, EJUS RELIGIO. The phrase "whose rule, his religion" summed up the religious peace during the Reformation. It meant that a political ruler had the right to determine the religion of his territory. His subjects had the alternative of moving to another state or country where their own religion was accepted. This principle ignored all the rights of conscience and mainly explains how entire nations, for centuries Catholic, suddenly became Protestant.

CULPA. A fault or sin, whether consciously moral or merely external. Commonly used to describe the faults against religious discipline of which religious in some communities are expected to periodically accuse themselves, either privately to the superior or publicly in a "chapter of faults."

CULPABLE. Morally responsible for an evil action. Culpability assumes sufficient awareness and (internal) consent to the evil done. It is identified with formal guilt or sin. (Etym. Latin *culpabilis,* blameworthy; from *culpare,* to blame.)

CULT. A definite form of worship or of religious observance, sometimes rendered "cultus," especially when referring to the worship of the saints. Also a particular religious group centered around some unusual belief, generally transient in duration and featuring some exotic or imported ritual and other practices. (Etym. Latin *cultus,* care, adoration; from *colere,* to cultivate.)

CULTURE. The personality of a society. As understood in Catholic social philosophy, it is the totality of a people's traditions (what they believe), attitudes (what they desire), customs (what they do) and institutions (how they live). A culture has roots that go back even centuries and may be far removed from where persons now live. Cultures differ even as individuals differ, since culture is nothing else than the divinely intended distinctiveness of a people, even as individuality is the divinely intended uniqueness of each person. But like individuals, societies have not only their own inherent characteristics but their own separate history of decisions and experiences, which further distinguish one culture from another so that no two are fully the same.

CUM ADMOTAE. Pontifical rescript of the papal secretary of state, delegating certain faculties from the Holy See to the superiors general of clerical religious communities that are pontifical, and to the presiding abbots of monastic communities (November 6, 1964).

CUPIDITY. Avarice or greed. It stresses the intensity and compelling nature of the desire for wealth or possessions. (Etym. Latin *cupiditas,* greediness, desire, covetousness; *Cupid,* god of love.)

CURATE. One who has the care (*cura*) of souls, especially a parish priest. The term is often applied to the assistant or associate pastor. (Etym. Latin *curator,* overseer; from *cura,* attention, care.)

CURÉ. A parish priest who has the care of souls under his jurisdiction. Commonly used in French-speaking countries. (Etym. French *curé;* from Latin *cura,* attention, care.)

CURIA, DIOCESAN. Technical name for a diocesan chancery, which includes a bishop and all the officials who assist him in the administration of the diocese. At times the term is used of the diocesan tribunals only, but this usage is not uniform. Each diocesan curia should have its own norms and procedure, sometimes called the constitutions.

CURIA, ROMAN. The whole ensemble of administrative and judicial offices through which the Pope directs the operations of the Catholic Church. Since the Second Vatican Council the Roman Curia has been extensively changed, with the merger of certain offices, the suppression of others, and the creation of entirely new ones. More than once in postconciliar statements the Pope has defended the Curia against critics who would distinguish between the papacy and the curial officials. Pope John XXIII spoke of the Curia as his right hand, through which the Vicar of Christ mainly exercises his primacy over the universal Church.

CURIOSITY. The natural tendency of the human mind to seek knowledge. But this tendency needs to be controlled, no less than all other urges of fallen human nature in order to conform to right reason and faith. (Etym. Latin *curiosus,* attentive, inquisitive.)

CURSE. Popularly used to describe a variety of expletives made in anger or in emphasis of one's feelings. Literally, to curse is to call down evil on someone or something. In the Bible a curse is often a prayer of imprecation. Israelites knew that they could not constrain the Almighty but only move him by prayer. Unlike the magical incantations of their neighbors, the ancient Jews believed that Yahweh could remove a curse by his blessing, preserve the pious person from an undeserved curse, change the blessing of an unworthy priest into a curse, and turn aside a curse from a humble person because of meekness. In general, the intended evil of a curse takes effect only when the just God wills it.

CURSILLO MOVEMENT. A method of Christian renewal originated by a group of laymen, assisted by Bishop Hervas y Benet, on the island of Mallorca, Spain, on January 7, 1949. The term literally means a "little course," and the program itself comes in three stages of three days each: preparation (pre-*cursillo*), the course proper (*cursillo*), and the follow-up (post-*cursillo*). Its objective is to change the world by changing one's mind according to the mind of Christ, and then reshaping one's life accordingly. The *cursillo* proper is an intensive weekend built around some fifteen talks, of which ten are given by laymen, and living together as a close Christian community. Those who participate are called *cursillistas,* who meet regularly after the initial program in what is called the *ultreya,* in small groups to pray, share their experiences, and plan apostolic action. An essential part of the *cursillo,* as conceived by Bishop Hervas, is the Spiritual Exercises of St. Ignatius, to give doctrinal foundation and spiritual structure to the movement.

CURSING. To call down evil on someone or something. To curse God or holy things or persons is a form of blasphemy. To curse rational creatures is a grave offense against justice and charity. To curse irrational creatures, such as the weather or animals, is normally a venial sin of impatience. To curse the evil spirit as the enemy of God and human beings is lawful. But exclamations that in themselves are not sinful may become unlawful for other reasons, such as the danger of scandal.

CUSTODIA. A receptacle for holding the Blessed Sacrament. A name also given to the transparent pyx in the monstrance itself or the vessel in which the Host is kept in the tabernacle. (Etym. Latin *custodia,* a keeping guard.)

CUSTODIA OF THE HOLY LAND. The principal mission of the Franciscan Order, founded by its first general chapter in 1217 and in 1263 divided into three custodias, namely, Syria, Cyprus, and Tarsus. All the houses were destroyed by the Moslems in 1291 and many religious killed. Re-established in the fourteenth century by Pope Clement VI, the Custodia now serves the faithful resident in the Holy Land, cares for certain holy places entrusted to the Franciscans, and assists the pilgrims who visit Palestine.

CUSTODY OF THE SENSES. In Christian asceticism the practice of controlling the use of the senses, especially the eyes, in order to foster union with God and preserve oneself in virtue. It is founded on the premise that "nothing is in the mind that was not first in the senses." Sense experience inevitably produces thoughts in the mind; thoughts become desires; and desires lead to actions. Morally good actions, therefore, ultimately depend on a judicious guard of sensations.

CUSTOM BOOK. A manual of practices and regulations of a religious institute, assembled or at least authorized by a general chapter. Its provisions are less permanent than the norms of the Rule or Constitutions and are subject to adaptation or revision by competent authority within the institute.

CUSTOM, ECCLESIASTICAL. A longstanding practice that takes on the force of law. No custom is ever valid that contradicts a divine law, whether natural or positive, nor does a custom abrogate ecclesiastical law unless it is reasonable and has been legitimately in practice over a period of forty full years. Where the ecclesiastical law explicitly forbids contrary customs, the latter can be valid only if they are reasonable and in legitimate existence for at least a century or from time immemorial.

CUSTOS. A superior officer among the Franciscan Order with varying duties. There are *custos provinciae,* who represents his provincial in general chapter, and *custos regiminis,* who rules a small province. Formerly the canon of a cathedral church who had the care of souls; also the treasurer of a collegiate church. (Etym. Latin *custos,* preserver, keeper, protector.)

CYRENE. The chief city in Cyrenaica, which would later become part of Libya. Simon of Cyrene was pressed into service by the soldiers on Good Friday to help Jesus carry his cross to Golgotha (Mark 15:21). Another Cyrenian mentioned in the New Testament was Lucius of Cyrene, one of the active prophets and teachers in the Church at Antioch (Acts 13:1).

CZĘSTOCHOWA. Shrine of the Black Madonna, also called Our Lady of Jasna Gora, chief Marian sanctuary of Poland. There is a legend that the picture of Our Lady and her Son at the shrine was painted by St. Luke on a tabletop made by Jesus himself when he was an apprentice carpenter to St. Joseph. Hidden during the early persecutions, it was brought by St. Helena (255–330) to Constantinople. In the troubled eighth century it was stealthily taken from that city to a forest in Eastern Poland. From there it was removed to Częstochowa. In 1430 a great Gothic cathedral was built around the precious relic, but in the war with the Hussites they stole the picture. When their horses refused to move their cargo beyond the village boundaries, they threw the picture by the roadside, where it lay broken. All attempts to repair the damage have failed. In the next three hundred years the Polish people believed that their welfare was identified with this miraculous picture. When the Turks were at the gates of Vienna, Sobieski (1624–96), the Polish king, dedicated his crusade to Mary, and the West was saved. Under Adolf Hitler (1889–1945) the people came secretly on their pilgrimages to Częstochowa, and in 1945, at the end of World War II, they came 500,000 strong to thank Mary for their liberation. In 1947 over 1,500,000 came there to beg Mary to save them from Communism. Public pilgrimages to Częstochowa are forbidden, but the shrine is still unharmed.

D

D. *Dies*—day; deacon; *Dominus,* Lord; Dame; Doctor of the Church; diocese.

D.A. *Dies assignata*—assigned day.

DAILY COMMUNION. The practice in the early Church of receiving Holy Communion by the faithful every day. This practice was restored to the universal Church, and was strongly recommended by Pope St. Pius X in his decree *Sacra Tridentina Synodus* (Denzinger 3379–83).

DAILY SINS. See VENIAL SIN.

DALMATIC. An outer liturgical garment worn by a deacon at Mass and in solemn processions. It has wide short sleeves, reaches to the knees, and is open at the sides. It is of the same material and color as the vestments of the celebrant. It was introduced from Dalmatia (hence its name) to Rome as a secular garment in the reign of Diocletian.

DAMASCUS. An ancient city in Syria, reputed to be the oldest continuously occupied city in the world. It is the capital of modern Syria. It was frequently the scene of happenings in biblical history. David captured it (II Samuel 8:5–6). Rezon, Ben-hadad, and Hazael ruled over it and lived there (I Kings 11:24; 15:18). It was near Damascus that Paul's extraordinary conversion took place (Acts 9:1–19). He later preached in the city (Acts 9:20–22). (Etym. Hebrew *dammeseq;* Akkadian *dimaski;* Egyptian *timasku.*)

DAME. The traditional title of the professed nuns of certain religious orders, e.g., Benedictine or Cistercian, corresponding to "Dom" for members of the monastic orders of men.

DAMNATION. The conscious eternal loss of the vision of God. The state of being damned by reason of one's own deliberate estrangement from God. This is the lot of the demons, and of those who die in mortal sin. It is damnation because it is the result of a just sentence pronounced by God on those who are guilty. It is eternal because it is irrevocable, being pronounced to be unending in its consequences (Matthew 25). The condemned are no longer in a state of probation, and no longer able to expiate or repent (Luke 16). (Etym. Latin *damnatio,* condemnation; from *damnum,* damage, loss, fine.)

DAMNIFICATION. Unjustly causing injury to another person's property or person, reputation or spiritual welfare. Reparation must be made as far as possible, and the willingness to undo the damage is a condition for being forgiven the offense committed.

DANCE OF DEATH. Originally a spectacular play, given in a churchyard, going back to the fourteenth century, when the Black Death and other epidemics had impressed the popular imagination. The plays opened with a sermon on death, and then a series of figures resembling skeletons appeared. The dancing movement was a later development. Traces of these plays are still found in Germany, France, England, and Italy. Pictorial representations of these plays were made on the walls of cemeteries and elsewhere. Among such engravings the most famous are those of Hans Holbein (1460–1524) and Albrecht Dürer (1471–1528).

DANCING, LITURGICAL. Moving rhythmically to music as part of a religious ceremony. Certain forms of dancing have at various times been introduced into Catholic worship, but the Church has set down two conditions. First, to the extent to which the body is a reflection of the soul, dancing has to express sentiments of faith and adoration in order to become a prayer. And second, dancing must be under the discipline of competent Church authority. "Concretely, there are cultures in which this is possible in so far as dancing is still reflective of religious values and becomes a clear manifestation of them. Such is the case among the Ethiopians. In their cultures, even today, there is the religious ritualized dance, clearly distinct from the martial dance and from the amorous dance." The same is found among Christians in the Syriac and Byzantine traditions. "However, the same criterion and judgment cannot be applied in the Western culture. Here dancing is tied in with love, with diversion, with profaneness, with unbridling of the senses; such dancing, in general, is not pure. For that reason it cannot be introduced into liturgical celebrations of any kind whatever."

What about dancing outside the liturgy? This is permissible, but only under certain conditions. Thus "if the proposal for a religious dance in the West is to be acceptable, care must be taken that this occurs *outside of the liturgy,* in assembly areas that are not strictly liturgical. Moreover, priests must always be excluded from the dance" (Sacred Congregation for the Sacraments and Divine Worship, *Notitiae,* 1975, 11, pp. 202–5). When a group of Samoans came to Rome for a missionary festival in 1971, they assisted at Mass in St. Peter's and then carried out their dance in St. Peter's Square, outside the church.

DANCING, MORALITY OF. In itself dancing is perfectly licit. It may, however, become a source of evil either because of the way in which it is done or because it is an occasion of sin for some particular individual. In general, if dancing is not a proximate occasion of sin for the dancer, then it is permissible for him or her. On occasion there may be a special prohibition of a bishop or pastor against dances held at certain times or under certain conditions. Such prohibitions must be obeyed. Ordinarily, in these cases, dancing is banned because of certain evils attendant on gatherings of this kind in that locality.

DANGEROUS OCCASIONS. Proximate occasions of sin, i.e., such people, places, or things as a person knows from experience or observation, would easily lead into sin. Dangerous occasions must be avoided, as evidence of a person's sincerity in wanting to serve God.

DANIEL, BOOK OF. A prophetic book of the Old Testament, in fourteen chapters, among which three languages are represented. The preliminary section (1, 2, and 4) is in Hebrew and describes Daniel's capture and education. The first part of his prophecies (2, 5, and 7), in Aramaic, refers to world power in relation to God's people, notably the dream of the great statue and the vision of the four beasts. The second part of Daniel's prophecies (7 to 12), in Hebrew, describes the fortunes of the Jews with respect to world power. The book concludes with the so-called deuterocanonical parts (12 to 14) that are missing in the Jewish Bible but endorsed by the Septuagint Greek translation. In this section are found the narrative of the chaste Susanna, the idol Bel, the dragon destroyed by Daniel, and a second peril in the lions' den. In telling the future the prophet is very precise. Christ quotes from Daniel, foretelling the fall of Jerusalem and the last day (Matthew 24:15–25). The Church has embodied all fourteen chapters of the book in her biblical canon.

DARING. An aspect of the virtue of courage by which a person is ready to run a risk and undergo danger. It is also a function of the gift of fortitude, which confers a sense of power, born of divine grace, to do what one would naturally dread to undertake.

DARIUS. 1. Called Darius the Great (Darius I), he ruled Persia 522–486 B.C. Many of his achievements were recorded on the limestone cliffs above Behistun (Ezra 5). He followed an exemplary policy of toleration toward the Jewish captives in Babylon and gave them practical help in their efforts to restore the Jerusalem temple. The work was completed in the early years of his reign (Ezra 6:6–12, 15); 2. Darius the Mede. Appears in the Book of Daniel as King of Babylon succeeding Belshazzar. Details of his life are contradictory (Daniel 5:31). Apparently he gave great authority early in his reign to Daniel (Daniel 6:1–3) but eventually was goaded into consigning him to the lions' den. Daniel's miraculous escape added to his prestige and his enemies' confusion (Daniel 6:22–29).

DARK AGES. The term sometimes applied to the Middle Ages, mainly by writers who erroneously believed that during the Ages of Faith (A.D. 500–1500) there was little or no progress in the arts and sciences, in government and social organization, or even in religion. Gradually the expression is being abandoned as scholars are proving that, in spite of periods of war and conflict, some of these centuries were outstanding for their enlightenment and achievement.

DARK NIGHT OF THE SENSES. The first stage of purification, through which God regularly leads souls on the way to Christian perfection. "God establishes the soul in the dark night of sense," says St. John of the Cross, "that He may purify, prepare and subdue its lower nature, and unite it to the Spirit, by depriving it of light and causing it to cease from meditation."

DARK NIGHT OF THE SOUL. General term in mystical theology to identify every form of purification through which God leads persons whom he is calling to a high degree of sanctity. It is called "night" to distinguish a person's normal spiritual condition of seeing, although dimly, by the light of faith; whereas in mystical purification a person is deprived of much of this light. There is a "groping in the night." It is called a "dark" night to emphasize the intensity of withdrawal of God's illuminating grace. The purpose of such purification is to cleanse the soul of every vestige of self-love and unite a person more and more closely with God. As the intellect is thus mortified, the will becomes more firmly attracted to God and more securely attached to his divine will. This purification, however, is only a means to an end, namely, 1. to give greater glory to God, who is thereby loved for himself and not for the benefits he confers; 2. to lead the one thus purified to infused contemplation and even ecstatic union with God; 3. to enable the mystic to be used more effectively by God for the spiritual welfare of others, since the more holy a person is the more meritorious are that person's prayers and sacrifices for the human race.

DARK NIGHT OF THE SPIRIT. The second stage of purification, through which God leads certain souls beyond meditation and ordinary contemplation to spiritual marriage. Its purpose is to detach the soul from spiritual consolations (not only sensible ones) and from all self-love (even love of one's own virtue). Its goal is to unite a person totally with God.

DATARY. The Apostolic Dataria, an office of the Roman Curia whose main function is to examine candidates for pontifical benefices, draft documents, levy charges, and satisfy claims pertaining to these benefices. The office was suppressed by Pope Paul VI on August 15, 1967, and its functions were reassigned to the Sacred Congregation for the Clergy. (Etym. Latin *datarius,* official who dated all papal letters, from data, date [time].)

DAVID. Hebrew king who ruled 1000–961 B.C. A shepherd boy, he was the son of Jesse, a Bethlehemite (Ruth 4:22). He was introduced to the court of King Saul because of his skill as a harpist. Then he achieved unexpected fame in his duel with Goliath, when he killed the gigantic soldier with a slingshot (I Samuel 17). His feats as a warrior continued to win him such admiration that Saul felt overshadowed and tried to kill David (I Samuel 18:6–11). The latter had to flee and become a roving outlaw with a band of soldiers he organized (I Samuel 19). After Saul and his sons died (I Samuel 31:6), David became King of both Judah and Israel for a period of forty years (II Samuel 5:4–5). Perhaps his most historic achievement was the capture of Jerusalem from the Philistines and its establishment as the religious capital of all Israel. The most shameful episode in David's life was his conspiracy to kill Uriah the Hittite in order to marry his widow, Bath-Sheba. Nathan, the prophet, delivered Yahweh's stern rebuke to David for this crime. As a punishment, Bath-Sheba's child died within a week of its birth. A later son of David and Bath-Sheba, however, was accepted by Yahweh and lived to become King Solomon (II Samuel 11, 12). David's life was a mixture of good and evil, but the judgment of history has been that, on balance, he was a great king, loyal to Yahweh, a great military figure, and a resourceful administrator (I Kings 2:12).

DAY. A period of time interpreted in several different ways in the Bible: 1. the period of light between sunrise and sunset (Psalms 74:16); 2. an indeterminate period of time (Genesis 1:5); 3. the span of life (John 9:4).

DAYDREAMS. Gratifying reveries usually of wish fulfillment. They are images permitted to arise and linger in one's mind for the purpose of giving oneself the illusion of living a life different from real life and to experience whatever sensations may be connected with such an illusion. A person looks for in fantasy what he or she desires in reality, or the thing is not yet attainable (as with the young) or no longer attainable (as with the old).

Daydreams are to be judged morally according to their content and the purpose one has in conjuring up these fancies. To take willful pleasure in wrong things created by the imagination is sinful, e.g., acts of revenge. But even if their content is not improper, daydreams represent a waste of time and energy; they tend to weaken one's character, diminish moral strength and will to pursue the real and possible goals of life, and they prevent the individual from becoming a more useful member of society.

DAYS OF ABSTINENCE. The days prescribed for the universal Church on which the faithful are forbidden to take flesh meat or anything made from meat. All Fridays of the year, except holy days of obligation, are days of abstinence; but since 1966 there is an option to substitute another form of penance. Abstinence must be observed on Ash Wednesday and Good Friday, and all the Fridays in Lent. Abstinence becomes binding at the age of fourteen.

D.C.L. *Doctor Civilis* (or *Canonicae*) *Legis* —Doctor of Civil (or Canon) Law.

D.D. *Doctores*—doctors.

D.D. *Donum dedit; dedicavit*—gave, dedicated.

D.D. *Doctor Divinitatis*—Doctor of Divinity (i.e., Theology).

D.D.D. *Dat, dicat, dedicat*—gives, devotes, dedicates.

DEACON. A man specially ordained to the service of the Church's ministry. In the ordination of deacons the "matter" is the imposition of a bishop's hands on individual candidates, which is done before the consecratory prayer; the "form" consists of the words of the consecratory prayer, of which the following pertain to the essence of the order and therefore are required for the validity of the act: "Lord, we pray, send forth upon them the Holy Spirit so that by the grace of your seven gifts they may be strengthened by Him to carry out faithfully the work of the ministry." The role of deacons is to assist priests in preaching, the conferral of baptism, performance of marriage, the administration of parishes, and similar duties. (Etym. Latin *diaconus;* from Greek *diakonos,* a servant, a deacon.)

DEACONESS. A woman officially charged with certain functions in the Church. St. Paul speaks of Phoebe as one who ministered to the church at Cenchrae (Romans 16:1), but the term "deaconess" did not come into use until the fourth century.

Gradually the office developed and was recognized by the Church. Among other duties a deaconess devoted herself to the care of the sick and the poor of her sex; she was present at interviews of women with bishops, priests, or deacons; instructed women catechumens and kept order in the women's part of a church. Her most important function was at the baptism of women, where she assisted the deacons. But as adult baptisms declined, deaconesses became less prominent. The decline was accelerated by the abuses that crept in where deaconesses arrogated to themselves ministerial functions, e.g., among the Monophysites and Nestorians, where they administered Holy Communion, read the Scriptures, and preached. Several regional councils abrogated the office, which was never a formal ordination, but deaconesses were found in the West until the eleventh century. In the East, where the privileges of deaconesses were more pronounced, including investiture with the state and distribution of the chalice, the decline was slower.

In Protestantism deaconesses date from the nineteenth century. And among the Anglicans they are admitted by the episcopal imposition of hands conferring lifelong status.

DEADLY SINS. Another name for the seven capital sins. They may be called deadly because they are tendencies to those basic sins which, if deliberately and fully consented to, deprive a person of the supernatural life of God in the soul.

DEAD SEA. The body of water that separated Judah and Moab. It is ten miles wide and forty-seven miles long and is more than one thousand feet below sea level. Since it has no outlet, its salt concentration is much greater than that of ocean water. As a result it was called the Salt Sea (Genesis 14:3). Some believe that the destroyed cities of Sodom and Gomorrah lie beneath its waters.

A number of references are made to the Salt Sea in the Old Testament (Numbers 34:12; II Chronicles 20:2; Ezekiel 47:18).

DEAD SEA SCROLLS. A collection of manuscripts and numerous fragments excavated in 1947 at the site of the ancient Qumran community, located close to the Dead Sea in Palestine. The principal texts include a set of rules for a monastic community, namely, *The Manual of Discipline, A Zadokite Document* (discovered earlier in Cairo), and a *Formulary of Blessings;* two collections of hymns; several commentaries on the Books of Micah, Nahum, and Habakkuk; a long oration of Moses; an epic on *The War of the Sons of Light and the Sons of Darkness;* and a manual for the future congregation of Israel, the so-called Messianic Banquet. Conservative scholarship holds that the scrolls were composed at various dates between 170 B.C. and A.D. 68. There is in the Dead Sea Scrolls no trace of any of the principal doctrines of Christianity: the Incarnation or the universality of the Messianic Kingdom. But there are many affinities that have shed much light on the meaning of the Christian faith, notably in revealing the existence of an ascetical community, similar to the Essenes, in first-century Palestine.

DEAN. An ecclesiastical official who may be the head of a cathedral or collegiate chapter; a vicar-forane or assistant to a bishop; the representative officer in a modern Catholic college or university; and in some institutions of higher learning the one in charge of student discipline. (Etym. Latin *decanus,* one set over ten [*decem*] soldiers or monks.)

DEANERY. A subdivision of a diocese, consisting of a number of parishes, over which presides a dean appointed by a bishop. The duty of the dean is to watch over the clergy of the deanery, to see that they fulfill the orders of the bishop, and observe the liturgical and canon laws. He summons the conference of the deanery and presides at it. Periodically he makes a report to the bishop on conditions in the deanery.

DEATH. The cessation of the bodily functions of a human being through the departure of the soul. It is part of revelation that, in the present order of divine providence, death is a punishment for sin. According to the teaching of the Church, death is a consequence of Adam's sin, as declared by St. Paul: "Sin entered the world through one man, and through sin death" (Romans 5:12). In the case of those justified by grace, death loses its penal character and becomes a mere consequence of sin. All human beings, therefore, are subject to death, although in the case of Christ and his Mother, because of their freedom from sin, death was neither a punishment for sin nor a consequence of sin. Yet, as they were truly human, death was natural for them.

Death is also the end of human probation or testing of one's loyalty to God. It ends all possibility of merit or demerit.

Properly speaking, only the body dies when separated from its principle of life, which is the soul. However, the Bible speaks of a second death (Revelation 20:6), referring to the souls in hell, who are separated from their principle of supernatural life, which is God.

DEATH INSTINCT. A term for the irrational desire for destruction and death and, when joined with pleasure, is a morbid drive for pain. It partly explains why some people commit suicide. It also helps to explain the nihilistic tendency in certain modern movements that exhibit a positive genius for destroying what may have taken centuries to build in religious or secular society.

DEATH WISH. The conscious and deliberate desire to die. This desire for death may be lawful, unlawful, or lacking in moral perfection. It is lawful to desire death when the hope is inspired by a good motive, such as the desire for union with God in heaven. It is unlawful when animated by an evil motive, such as boredom or disgust with life. Such a desire, however, would rarely be a grave sin for lack of serious intention to carry the desire into effect. It is a lack of moral perfection to desire death when through sheer impatience one prefers to lose one's life rather than continue to endure the hardships that God sends to one.

DE AUXILIIS. Controversy between the Dominicans and Jesuits on the relationship of divine grace and free will. The dispute mainly revolved around the relative theological soundness of the rival theories of Bannezianism (favored by Dominicans) and Molinism (favored by Jesuits). After more than a century of heated controversy, including discourses before the popes, the Holy See finally decided that both sides could hold their respective views but without condemning the opposition. Pope Clement XII, on October 2, 1733, issued the papal bull *Apostolicae Providentiae Officio,* in which he declared, "We forbid these opposing schools either in writing, or speaking or disputation or on any other occasion to dare impose any theological note or censure on the opposite school of thought or to attack their rivals in offensive or insulting language" (Denzinger 2510).

DEBITUM. Debt or that which is due. Commonly used of the conjugal rights and duties between husband and wife.

DEBORAH. A judge and prophetess who, in the highlands of Ephraim, was famous for settling disputes among Israelites. Her accomplishments indicate the significant role of leadership that noble women played during the period of the Judges. Her resentment of the harassment endured by Israelites at the hands of the Canaanites impelled her to seek the co-operation of the military leader Barak in achieving retaliation. She accompanied Barak and his army in his advance on Sisera, the Canaanite commander. Her vigorous leadership culminated in the complete destruction of the enemy and the death of Sisera. Clearly, she was a dynamic personality, gifted, resolute, and inspirational (Judges 4:4–24).

DEBT. What is due in justice to another, whether God or man, and whether to a single individual or a number of people, a community or an organization. The obligation may be in goods or services, either material or spiritual, owed by one party (the debtor) to another (the creditor). (Etym. Latin *debitum,* a sum due; from *debere,* to owe.)

DEBT, MARITAL. Sexual intercourse due by the husband to the wife and the wife to the husband, to which they have bound themselves by marital contract.

DEC. *Decanus*—dean.

DECADE. The popular name given to each of the five divisions into which each chaplet of the Rosary is subdivided. It is called a decade because each contains ten Hail Marys, together with an Our Father and, normally, a Glory be to the Father. Since each decade is a unit by itself, having its own mystery to commemorate, it may be said individually, even when the whole chaplet is not recited. In order to gain the Rosary indulgence, however, all five decades must be recited in sequence.

DECALOGUE. The Ten Commandments, given to Moses by God at Mount Sinai (Exodus 20). They were inscribed on two tablets of stone (Deuteronomy 4:13). In the New Testament Jesus accepted them as the basis of his teaching and promised to carry them to completion. "Not one dot, not one little stroke, shall disappear from the Law until its purpose is achieved" (Matthew 5:18). (Etym. Greek *deka*, ten + *logos*, a speech, saying: *dekalogos*, the Ten Commandments.)

DECEIT. A deliberate effort to conceal the truth, whether in speech, writing, or action. It is commonly said to spring from avarice, which offends against justice. But it may also be the result of pride, where a person's lack of humility leads him to act deceitfully in order to obtain or maintain a false recognition from others. In canon law, those who enter a novitiate by deceit enter invalidly. And in general an action entered into through deceit may be declared null and void and indemnity may be obtained.

DECENCY. The social aspect of the virtue of modesty. It implies due concern for what society in general or people in particular consider proper in the external practice of chastity. As the morality of a culture falls below the objective norms of Christian chastity, the standards of decency tend to be formed by the prevalent customs of the people. (Etym. Latin *decere*, to be fitting.)

DECLARATION OF NULLITY. The Church's official declaration that an apparently valid marriage is actually null and void because of: an invalidating impediment (such as a previous marriage), lack of due consent (absence of adequate knowledge or freedom), or a defect of required form (prescribed conditions for the actual celebration of marriage).

DECORATION, PAPAL. An honor conferred by the Holy See on lay people who deserve special recognition for their service to the Church. A bishop recommends a person for the honor, which, if granted, is then conferred either in Rome or in the home diocese. Papal orders of knighthood (which may also be conferred on women) are mainly, in sequence of importance: 1. Supreme Order of Christ; 2. Order of Pius IX; 3. Order of St. Gregory the Great; 4. Order of St. Sylvester; 5. Order of the Golden Militia or Golden Spur; 6. Order of the Holy Sepulcher. Other pontifical decorations include various medals, e.g., Pro Ecclesia et Pontifice, Benemerenti, and of the Holy Land. A number of offices at the papal court are accompanied by the title of count. Bishops' assistants at the papal throne have traditionally been considered Roman counts.

DECR. Decree.

DECREE. An authoritative application of a given law to a particular case. Also a decision of a superior's will, as a divine decree to give grace to those who pray. In civil matters a decree is the decision of a suit in a court of equity, and corresponds to the judgment of a court of law. Thus a judgment must be unconditionally for one or the other party in a lawsuit, whereas a decree is adaptable to the special needs of each case. Best known decrees are those given by courts of equity, which decree a divorce, deciding that a marriage is annulled and awarding alimony.

DECREE, ECCLESIASTICAL. Generally legislative enactments of the Pope, a council of the Church, or a congregation of the Holy See. Papal decrees are found in constitutions, apostolic letters, apostolic epistles, and *motu proprios*. Judicial decrees are all the rulings of an ecclesiastical court not comprised in incidental and final decisions. Nonjudicial decrees range from the regulations made in an episcopal visitation to such formal acts as removing or transferring a pastor. Roman congregations also issue decrees, but their decisions also take other forms.

DECRETALS. A letter carrying authoritative decisions on matters of discipline, or the Pope's reply when he has been appealed to on a matter of discipline. The term is also applied to a collection of certain decretals such as *Liber Sextus Decretalium*, compiled by Pope Boniface VIII (1235–1303). (Etym. Latin *decretale*, a decree.)

DECRETALS, FALSE. A collection of papal letters and council canons published around A.D. 850 by Isidore Mercator in Gaul. The first part contains sixty letters attributed to early popes (fifty-eight of them were forged); the second part is made up of canons of councils; and the third gives letters of Roman pontiffs (thirty of which were forged). David Blondel (1590–1655), and the Brothers Ballerini, in the eighteenth century, proved them to be false after they had been thought for centuries to have been authentic. The aim of this forger was to increase the authority and independence of the bishops against civil officials. He was most likely not interested in augmenting the power of the popes, which had been already well established before the ninth century.

DEDICATION. Setting aside for sacred use. This may be a person, place, or object that in whole or in part is withdrawn from its natural and secular purpose to be more or less reserved for the worship or service of God.

DEDUCTION. A reasoning process that moves from a universal premise to a less universal (or at times equally universal) conclusion; reasoning from the general to the particular, from principle to practice, from law to application of the law to an individual case or person. (Etym. Latin *deductio,* a leading down, derivation.)

DE EPISCOPORUM MUNERIBUS. An apostolic letter of Pope Paul VI setting down a series of norms to be followed by bishops in their exercise of the faculties of dispensation. Two important provisions are a reminder that the Code of Canon Law remains binding except where the Holy See has expressly abrogated some canonical directives, and that the faculty of dispensation applies only to preceptive and prohibitive laws, not to norms that establish the Church's laws. The basic thrust of the document is to spell out the dispensations reserved to the Pope (June 15, 1966).

DEF. *Defunctus*—deceased.

DE FACTO. In fact or in reality, whether something is or is not moral and lawful. The opposite of *de jure*. See also DE JURE.

DEFAMATION. Unjust injury of a person's good name. It consists in telling facts that harm another's reputation. In defamation, there is at least an implicit intention to harm the reputation of another, who is absent and therefore not a witness to being defamed.

Defamation may be committed in two ways: by spreading injurious facts that are true but not publicly known, or by saying things that are false.

Since defamation violates commutative justice, it involves the duty of making reparation for the foreseen injury inflicted. Hence the defamer must try, not only to repair the harm done to another's good name, but also to make up any foreseen temporal injury that resulted from the defamation, such as the loss of employment or of customers.

A number of reasons would release a person from the obligation of repairing the damage done to someone's good name; for example, the injury no longer exists, or reparation is physically or morally impossible to make, or the one defamed has excused the defamer, or reparation would cause the defamer a far greater injury than the one inflicted, or if there is good likelihood that a calumnious defamation was not believed by those to whom it was said.

DEFECT. A lack of something that should be present. Applied especially to human conduct, when one fails to do what should be done (as being silent when one should speak), or falls short of the perfection expected (as an employee not putting in a full day's work), or abandons responsibility undertaken, or does not fulfill promises seriously made.

DEFENDANT. In ecclesiastical law a person whose case is being tried in a Church court. Defendants must attend in person or by procurator when summoned. In criminal cases they must have an advocate. Defendants have the right to appeal, from a lower to a higher ecclesiastical court, against an adverse sentence.

DEFENDER OF THE FAITH. The title conferred on Henry VIII by Pope Leo X, in 1521, for the King's book *Assertio Septem Sacramentorum . . .* , which was a defense of the seven sacraments and the Sacrifice of the Mass against Martin Luther. The kings and queens of England still retain this title on their carriage and among their official titles.

DEFENSOR VINCULI. Latin term for "Defender of the Bond." He is the member of an ecclesiastical matrimonial court whose duty is to uphold the validity of a disputed marriage until sufficient evidence is given to prove its nullity. If he is not satisfied with the court's ruling, he must appeal to a higher tribunal.

DE FIDE. A term meaning "of faith," used to identify those doctrines of the Church which are infallibly true. Their infallible certitude derives ultimately from divine revelation, but proximately from the fact that they have either been solemnly defined by the Church's magisterium or have been taught by her ordinary universal teaching authority as binding on the consciences of all the faithful.

DEFILEMENT. The condition of uncleanness. In biblical and ecclesiastical usage it means to render unclean by contact with unclean things, by eating forbidden foods, by polluting sexually through adultery. Its most important meaning is to be stained with sin.

DEFINITION. A statement either declaring the meaning of a term or explaining what an essence is. A real definition identifies the nature of what is defined, a descriptive definition gives the characteristic properties, a causal definition tells how something comes into being, and a verbal or nominal definition merely explains the meaning of a word or of its sources and roots. (Etym. Latin *definitio*, limitation, restriction; determination.)

DEFINITION, ACCIDENTAL. Tells what something is by giving its characteristic external or changeable properties.

DEFINITION, CAUSAL. Tells what something is by identifying its causes or principles, e.g., the agent or efficient cause, purpose(s) or final cause, model or exemplary, or any combination of these.

DEFINITION, DOCTRINAL. Declaration of religious doctrine of faith or morals, or condemnation of an error, made solemnly by supreme religious authority. In the Catholic Church definitions are made by the Pope or by general councils confirmed by the Pope.

DEFINITION, ESSENTIAL. Tells what is the essence or nature of something or, in the case of material things, of what it is composed.

DEFINITION, INITIAL. A preliminary description (of something) that is stated, assumed, or conceded at the opening of a discussion or dialogue for purposes of identification or exploration of matters referred to.

DEFINITION, NOMINAL. An explanation of the meaning of a word or of its roots or sources. Verbal definition by synonym.

DEFINITION, REAL. Explanation of what something represented by a concept or word means; the statement of the nature of something.

DEFINITION, THEOLOGICAL. Explanation of one or more terms used in proving a thesis or proposition in dogmatic theology. The basic requirement in teaching sacred doctrine.

DEFINITIVE (DIFFINITIVE) PRESENCE. The way a spirit is present in space, whereby it is active in the whole of the space occupied by the body on which it acts, and yet is not limited to the "spots" or portions of that body, nor spread out in space, nor measured by the size and shape of the space occupied. This is the presence of a spirit in the whole space of the body on which it acts and wholly in each part of that space.

DEGENERATE. A person whose moral behavior is so bad that it offers little prospect of conversion. Degeneracy implies grave culpability, self-indulgence over a long period of time, and a general breakdown of character that shows positive indifference, if not hostility to the moral law. A degenerate, however, need not be notoriously criminal in external behavior, and may even appear to be a respectable person. The essence of degeneracy is internal perversion of will. (Etym. Latin *degenerare*, to fall from one's ancestral quality: *de-*, away from + *genus*, race.)

DEGRADATION. A penalty by which a cleric is reduced to the lay state; a deprivation, an abasement. Its effects may be deposition and privation of a religious habit. It is permanent unless remitted by a superior after completion of conditions required as penance. It can only be imposed for things labeled criminal by law or if one continues giving scandal after deposition. It is real if accompanied by formalities prescribed by the Roman Pontifical, and verbal when inflicted by a person authorized to sentence.

DEICIDE. Literally the killing (*cidium*) of God (Deus), and applied to those responsible for the crucifixion of Christ. This refers especially to the Jewish Scribes and Pharisees in first-century Palestine, Judas, Pilate, Annas and Caiphas, and the Roman executioners. The Second Vatican Council cautions, however, that "neither all Jews indiscriminately at that time, nor Jews today, can be charged with the crimes committed during his passion" (*Nostra Aetate*, 4). The term is permissible because, though God certainly cannot die, those who killed Christ (who is God) implicitly aimed their murderous intent against the Deity. (Etym. Latin *deicida: deus*, god + *cidium*, killing.)

DEI GRATIA. By the grace of God. Term used to attribute whatever a person has or has done by God's special providence.

DEISM. The theory that accepts the existence of God on purely rational grounds but denies (with Blount and Tindal) or doubts (with Hume) or rejects as incredible (with Voltaire and Rousseau) Christianity as a supernatural religion. Accordingly revelation, miracles, grace, and mysteries are excluded from acceptance by what is called "the rational man." Yet deism differs from rationalism in stressing its acceptance of a personal God and adherence to what is called natural religion, but with no recognition of a supernatural order. (Etym. Latin *Deus*, God.)

DEITY. God, conceived in theological terms as the divine nature or essence. Deity expresses what God is, normally the infinite Being whose essence is to exist. It therefore identifies the Trinity as one God. (Etym. Latin *deitas,* godhead.)

DEI VERBUM. Dogmatic Constitution on Divine Revelation of the Second Vatican Council. Its five sections treat of divine revelation itself; the transmission of divine revelation through the faith of believers and the custody of the Church; Sacred Scripture as God's inspired word to be interpreted under the Church's guidance; the Old Testament as fulfilled in and also shedding light on the New Testament as the completion of God's self-disclosure and the importance of Sacred Scripture in the life of the Church. Treated at length is the development of doctrine, which means the Church's ever deeper and clearer understanding of what God has once and for all revealed to the human race (November 18, 1965).

DE JURE. By right, in accordance with law, human or divine, natural or positive, juridical; therefore on the level of principle, as the opposite of *de facto.* See also DE FACTO.

DELECTATIO VICTRIX. Literally "conquering delight." In Jansenism the theory that whenever a predestined person is faced with an apparent moral option, God's grace will always make sure that what God wants that person to do will be done by reason of its overwhelming attraction. Implicit in the theory is the notion of irresistible grace. Those destined to be saved inevitably perform what God, in effect, does for them since they lack the internal freedom to either resist or co-operate with what is still called divine grace.

DELEGATION. The power of jurisdiction in spiritual matters that one person receives from another, who has ordinary jurisdiction in virtue of his office. The one delegated acts in the name of the person delegating. Before proceeding, one must wait until the power to act has been formally communicated. Ordinary jurisdiction is all that is needed to delegate, unless this power is definitely withheld. A delegate does not have the power to subdelegate, unless: 1. this power is expressly granted in his delegation; or 2. he has universal jurisdiction in certain matters, or in a specified class of matters (e.g., all marriages). Without being able to make a new delegation, he may request others to assist him with details of his work.

DELIBERATE. In moral theology, some-thing done after reflection on the motives for acting or after inquiry and advice. Opposite of what is done thoughtlessly, hastily, or impulsively. (Etym. Latin *deliberare,* to consult, to consider.)

DELILAH. The mistress of Samson; she was bribed by the Philistines to betray him. His strength was so prodigious that they knew they would be unable to subdue him unless they learned the secret of his strength. After several futile attempts Delilah wheedled him into confiding that his strength lay in his hair. "If my head were shorn, then my power would leave me and I should lose my strength" (Judges 16:4–21). She divulged the news to the Philistines, who cut off his hair while he was asleep, and readily subdued him (Judges 16:17).

DELUGE. The biblical account of God's punishment of humankind by incessant rain that finally destroyed all except those persons who were with Noah in the ark (Genesis 6–9). The Deluge need not, however, have physically covered the whole earth. (Etym. Latin *diluvium,* flood, a washing away.)

DELUSION. An erroneous belief that a person thinks is true in spite of every reasonable evidence to the contrary. A delusion is a false faith; it is fixed, persistent, and is a systematic principle for all of one's actions. More than once the Israelites were warned not to be seduced by the delusions of the false prophets (Isaiah 23:26).

DEMERIT. A voluntary misdeed that offends someone and therefore deserves some retribution or penalty. With reference to God, demerit is the effect of sin and consists in a loss of divine friendship and of the right to heaven for grave sin, and in a weakening of the supernatural life through venial sin.

DEMIURGE. Originally a craftsman working for the people, used by Plato (427–347 B.C.) to designate the Maker of the Material Universe. The Demiurge became a common term in Gnosticism and other heretical systems. He was the maker of the world, the personification of evil who caused Christ's crucifixion, at once distinct from the Supreme God and an emanation from him. Some Gnostics identified him with Yahweh of the Old Testament, from whose power man was rescued by Christ in the New Testament. (Etym. Greek *dēmos,* people + *ergon,* work: *dēmiourgos,* artisan, craftsman.)

DEMOCRACY. As defined in Catholic social philosophy, that form of civil government which is not only for the people and of the people but also by the people. Every political society, by the natural law, should be for the people, since its purpose is the common good. It should also be of the people, since it arises from their consent and with their authorization. But it need not be, unless the citizens so desire, also by the people. In a democracy, the governing heads are elected with equal right by all the people, and there exists the widest individual liberty consistent with the common good. Democracy is either limited or unlimited depending on whether all the citizens or only a part of them have equal right to public offices. Democracy may also be direct or indirect. In a direct democracy the people as a whole possess full power and exercise directly all governing functions, which is possible only in a small social community. Indirect democracy, or representative government, is that in which the people are governed through the legitimate representatives whom they elected. (Etym. Greek *dēmos*, people + *kratia*, to rule: *dēmokratia*, popular government, rule by the people.)

DEMON. Originally a spirit between the gods and men. In the New Testament a demon is the same as an evil spirit, which may be translated as "devil." It consequently means a malevolent, invisible being, which the pre-Christian word "demon" did not imply. (Etym. Latin *daemon*, evil spirit; Greek *daimōn*, a god, genius, spirit.)

DEMONIC ANGER. Anger with God, the foundation for blasphemy. It is called demonic because that is how the evil spirit is believed to react toward the divine justice for having condemned him to eternal punishment.

DEMONOLOGY. The science or doctrine concerning demons. Already in ancient times, among the Jews and outside the Judaic tradition, belief in demons was common. The modern interest in demons is partly the natural reaction of the people in societies where generations of rationalism and skepticism have ignored or ridiculed the existence of evil spirits who are permitted by God to prowl around "like a roaring lion looking for someone to devour" (I Peter 5:8).

DEMONSTRATION, A POSTERIORI. Legitimate reasoning from premises that are better known than the conclusion. Yet the premises are effects posterior (or subsequent) in being or in time to the cause in the conclusion, e.g., demonstrations of the existence of God.

DEMONSTRATION, A PRIORI. Legitimate reasoning from evident premises. The argument therefore goes from something prior in nature or in time to the being in the conclusion, e.g., from cause to effect, from the nature of something to any of its properties.

DEMYTHOLOGY. The theory that claims that the whole language and spirit of the New Testament are mythical in character. The evangelists assume that miracles occur and that the world is affected by supernatural powers. In order to discover the real facts of Christ's life and teaching, therefore, it is necessary to strip the New Testament, especially the Gospels, of this layer of mythology. (Etym. Latin *de*, reverse of + Greek *mythologein*, to relate legends, myths.)

DENIAL OF FAITH. Any word, sign, or action by which a person who is a professed Catholic denies what the Church teaches must be believed by her faithful. The denial is direct when what is said or done by its nature contains a rejection of the true faith. It is indirect when the rejection is implied under the circumstances. Every deliberate denial of one's faith is a grave sin.

DE NIHILO NIHIL. From nothing, nothing. A phrase in philosophy that states the principle of cause and effect. Every effect must have a cause, since without a cause no finite being would exist.

DENOMINATION. A legally distinct group of believers, especially among Protestants. Different denominations exist within a single Protestant tradition, e.g., Lutheran. They are not necessarily different, though they generally are, in their faith, worship, and form of church government.

DENUNCIATION. Manifestation of a crime to the proper ecclesiastical authorities. Clerics and religious who join forbidden societies are to be denounced to the Holy See. A confessor guilty of solicitation during confession should be denounced to a bishop or to Rome. A false denunciation of a confessor is a grave sin that traditionally is reserved to the Holy See.

DEO FAVENTE. God favoring, with God's favor. Said in anticipation of some enterprise whose future is entrusted to divine providence.

DEO GRATIAS. Thanks to God. One of the responses in the Eucharistic liturgy, e.g., at the end of Mass. Also a phrase used in some religious communities to begin or conclude a community exercise, such as reading or speaking at table.

DEONTOLOGISM. The theory, associated with Immanuel Kant (1724–1804), that only acts done from a motive of duty have moral value. It is a stern moral philosophy, close to Stoicism, which holds that virtue is its own reward and therefore "duty for duty's sake" is man's highest moral imperative. (Etym. Greek *deon,* that which is obligatory + *logia,* science, knowledge.)

DEONTOLOGY. A term introduced into philosophy by Jeremy Bentham (1748–1832) in 1826, to identify the science of ethics or moral duty, mainly as distinct from law or jurisprudence.

DEO OPTIMO MAXIMO. To God, who is the best and the greatest. Motto of the Order of St. Benedict. Also *Domino Optimo Maximo,* to the Lord, the best and the greatest.

DEO VOLENTE. God willing, if God wills it. A prayerful resignation to the divine will when undertaking some task whose outcome is, humanly speaking, uncertain.

DEPRESSION. A term used by spiritual writers to describe a state of despondency during which a person feels inadequate, tends to withdraw from others, lacks response to normal stimulation, and is pessimistic about the future. Theologians of asceticism warn about giving in to moods of depression, which they describe as the characteristic temptation of those who strive after sanctity.

DE PROFUNDIS. Psalm 129, "Out of the depths," which is one of the fifteen Gradual Psalms and one of the seven Penitential Psalms. It is part of the Divine Office, generally recited or sung at Vespers, and always in the Office of the Dead. In the revised *Handbook of Indulgences* there is a partial indulgence granted for every recitation of De Profundis. Its theme is a plea for divine mercy and the expression of confident trust in God. In some countries this Psalm is recited to the ringing of the bell about 9 P.M., and in Ireland it was regularly said at Mass after the Last Gospel for the victims of former religious persecutions.

DESACRALIZATION. The conscious removal or reduction of sacred symbols from religious life and worship. In Christianity it is a practical consequence of the demythology of the Bible and tradition. As the faith of a people is less concerned with revealed mysteries pertaining to God, their religious ceremonial becomes desacralized.

DESCENT INTO HELL. The coming of Christ before his resurrection to deliver the souls of the just detained in the limbo of the Fathers. The purpose of this coming of Christ's soul was to deliver all the saved who had died before then by applying the fruits of the Redemption. They were immediately given the beatific vision. The doctrine is taught in all the early creeds and was defined by the Fourth Lateran Council (Denzinger 429).

DESECRATION. The profanation of a sacred person, place, or thing. Churches are desecrated by notorious crimes committed within them, such as willful murder or use of the sacred edifice for godless and sordid purposes. A desecrated church must first be reconciled before Divine Services can be held there. (Etym. Latin *dis,* the opposite of + *sacrare,* to declare or set apart as sacred.)

DE SEQ. *De sequenti*—of the following (day's feast).

DESERT (in the Bible). An uncultivated tract of land, generally uninhabited but not necessarily without water or impossible as a place to live. The chief desert mentioned in the Bible is that in which the Israelites traveled, once they crossed the Red Sea and until they reached the Promised Land. Other deserts of biblical importance are those of Judah, west of the Jordan and the Dead Sea; of Arabia, Moab, and Idumea, east of Palestine, near the Dead Sea; of Ziph, to which King David fled from Saul, south of the Dead Sea and Hebron. John the Baptist lived and taught in the desert of Judaea, near Jericho. And Christ's temptation is believed to have taken place in the desert west of the Jordan.

DESERTION. The act of abandoning or forsaking a person or situation one has freely accepted. Parents, spouse, child, or a religious community may be the victims of desertion.

DESIRE. To wish or long for the possession or enjoyment of something that a person's appetite does not presently have. Desires are natural if they proceed from man's inborn lack of what he needs; they are supernatural when inspired by divine grace. Man's fallen nature has desires that incline to what is sinful, but, so far from being sinful, these desires of concupiscence are a source of merit provided they are controlled according to the will of God.

DESIRE FOR BEATITUDE. The natural desire for perfect happiness. It is the basic inclination of humans to be perfectly happy. This desire is universal, for it is found in all people without exception, even in morbid or abnormal persons, though with some distortion. It is also unavoidable, for it lasts throughout life. It is finally irresistible because it insistently demands satisfaction. Ceaseless human unrest, shown in its constant activity, is an expression of this innate desire in varying forms. Theologians discuss whether this instinct for perfect happiness is a natural desire for heaven. The Church's explanation is that grace builds on nature, and therefore the human will inspired by grace can have a strong desire for heaven and the vision of God. But this is already the supernatural virtue of hope and not the longing of mere human nature.

DESOLATION. A temporary darkening of the mind and disturbance of the will and emotions, permitted by God to purify the souls of his followers. It may be caused by the evil spirit or brought on by a variety of other causes, but it is always purposeful, namely to withdraw a person's affections from dwelling on creatures and bring them closer to the Creator. (Etym. Latin *de*, from + *solus*, alone: *desolatio*, devastation, loneliness.)

DESPAIR. The sin by which a person gives up all hope of salvation or of the means necessary to reach heaven. It is therefore not mere anxiety about the future or fear that one may be lost. It is rather a deliberate yielding to the idea that human nature cannot co-operate with God's grace, or that the despairing person is too wicked to be saved, or that God has cast one away. It is a grave crime against God's goodness. Experience also shows that a tendency to despair can seriously injure one's physical and mental health, and ironically can lead to all kinds of sinful indulgence. (Etym. Latin *de*, the opposite of + *sperare*, to hope: *desperatio*, hopelessness, despair.)

DESPOTISM. In scholastic philosophy a rule that is exercised like that of a tyrant, either for the sake of the ruler or at least arbitrarily and without due regard for the rights of those governed. (Etym. Latin *despoticus*, imperious, despotic; from Greek *despotēs*, a master.)

DESTINY. In general, the preordained order of events. Human destiny, therefore, is the divine ordering of all secondary causes by God leading to the goal of human existence, which is the heavenly possession of God. But always this destiny is conditional, depending on one's voluntary co-operation with divine grace. In pagan terms destiny is the fate to which a person is necessarily predestined. (Etym. Latin *de*, down + *stanare*, to cause to stand: *destinare*, to destine, resolve firmly.)

DETACHMENT. In asceticism the withholding of undue affection for creatures for the sake of the Creator. When mortal sin is involved, detachment is imperative for salvation. Detachment from creatures that are an obstacle to complete service of God is a normal condition for growth in holiness.

DETERMINANTS OF MORALITY. The factors in human conduct that determine whether it is good or bad. There are three such determinants of morality, namely the object, the end, and the circumstances.

By *object* is meant *what* the free will chooses to do—in thought, word, or deed—or chooses not to do. By *end* is meant the purpose for which the act is willed, which may be the act itself (as one of loving God) or some other purpose for which a person acts (as reading to learn). In either case, the end is the motive or the reason *why* an action is performed. By *circumstances* are meant all the elements that surround a human action and affect its morality without belonging to its essence. A convenient listing of these circumstances is to ask: *who? where? how? how much? by what means? how often?*

Some circumstances so affect the morality of an action as to change its species, as stealing a consecrated object becomes sacrilege and lying under oath is perjury. Other circumstances change the degree of goodness or badness of an act. In bad acts they are called aggravating circumstances, as the amount of money a person steals.

To be morally good, a human act must agree with the norm of morality on all three counts: in its nature, its motive, and its circumstances. Departure from any of these makes the action morally wrong.

DETERMINISM. The theory that claims that every effect is produced by necessary causes, so that nothing occurs as a result of free will, whether divine or human.

Intellectual determinism holds that the human will necessarily acts on the mind's judgment that something is better.

Natural determinism holds that the human will is impelled by nature or environment, so that people are no more free than irrational animals. As a philosophy of being, natural determinism is a form of pantheism that claims that the whole universe arose necessarily and not by the free decision of God's creative will. (Etym. Latin *determinare*, to delimit; to direct, arrange, order.)

DETERMINISM, ABSOLUTE. A philosophy that denies free will either in God or in human beings. All pantheistic theories are forms of absolute determinism.

DETERMINISM, NATURAL. The view that the human will is completely determined by nature, whether heredity, education, or environment or a combination of these. It says, in effect, that the human will is no more free than our physical bodies.

DETERMINISM, THEOLOGICAL. The theory that the human will is not free in any of its acts, but is determined by the will of God.

DETRACTION. Revealing something about another that is true but harmful to that person's reputation. It is forbidden to reveal another person's secret faults or defects, unless there is proportionate good involved. The fact that something is true does not, of itself, justify its disclosure. Detraction is a sin against justice. It robs one of what most people consider more important than riches, since a person has a strict right to his or her reputation whether it is deserved or not. (Etym. Latin *detractio*, a withdrawal.)

DEUS EX MACHINA. Literally "a god from the machine," referring to the mechanism in ancient drama whereby a god was brought on the stage to provide a miraculous solution to a dramatic difficulty. It has come to mean any idea, fact, or person artificially introduced to solve an otherwise impossible situation.

DEUS VULT. God wills (it). Motto of the Christian Crusaders.

DEUTEROCANONICAL. Referring to those books and passages of the Old and New Testaments about which there was controversy at one time in early Christian history. In the Old Testament they are Tobit, Judith, Wisdom, Ecclesiasticus, Baruch, I and II Maccabees, parts of Esther (10:4–16, 14) and Daniel (3:24–90, 13, 14). In the New Testament are Hebrews, James, II Peter, II and III John, Revelation, and Mark 16:9–20. All of these are recognized by the Catholic Church as part of the biblical canon. Among Protestants the deuterocanonical books of the Old Testament are rejected as apocryphal, along with the last twelve verses of Mark's Gospel.

DEUTERONOMY. The fifth book of the Bible. Its name (Greek *deuteros*, second; *nomos*, law) is a misnomer, since it contains no new legislation but is rather a partial repetition of previous laws with an urgent exhortation to keep them. The first discourse reviews the events that followed the promulgation of the law (1–4). The second discourse is the longest (5–26) and recalls the Covenant, covering the duties of the Jews toward God (5–11), the Lord's representatives, and their neighbors. The third discourse is a plea to observe the law, a renewal of the alliance with Yahweh, and Moses' prophetic canticle, while designating Joshua as his successor.

DEVELOPMENT OF DOCTRINE. Growth in the Church's understanding of the truths of divine revelation. Also called dogmatic progress or dogmatic development, it is the gradual unfolding of the meaning of what God has revealed. Always presumed is that the substantial truth of a revealed mystery remains unchanged. What changes is the subjective grasp of the revealed truth.

The source of this progressive understanding is the prayerful reflection of the faithful, notably of the Church's saints and mystics; the study and research by scholars and theologians; the practical experience of living the faith among the faithful; and the collective wisdom and teaching of the Church's hierarchy under the Bishop of Rome.

Implicit in the development of doctrine is the will of God that the faithful not only assent to what he revealed but also grow in the depth, clarity, and certitude of their appropriation of divine faith.

DEVIL. A fallen angel or evil spirit, especially the chief of the rebellious angels, Lucifer or Satan (Matthew 25). Adorned at his creation with sanctifying grace, he sinned by pride and along with many other angelic beings was denied the beatific vision. His abode is hell and he does not enjoy the benefits of Christ's redemption. Yet the devil remains a rational spirit, confirmed in evil, who is allowed by God to exercise some influence on living and inanimate creatures. (Etym. Greek *diabolos*, slanderer.)

DEVIL'S ADVOCATE (ADVOCATUS DIABOLI). A popular name for the advocate of God, the Vatican official who is the promoter of the cause in a process of beatification and canonization. The name arose from the fact that he is required to raise objections to a person's alleged sanctity or reputation for having worked miracles.

DEVOTION. The disposition of will to do promptly what concerns the worship and service of God. Although devotion is primarily a disposition or attitude of the will, acts of the will that proceed from such disposition are also expressions of devotion. Essential to devotion is readiness to do whatever gives honor to God, whether in public or private prayer (worship) or in doing the will of God (service). A person who is thus disposed is said to be devoted. His devotedness is ultimately rooted in a great love for God, which in spiritual theology is often called devotion. (Etym. Latin *devotio*, state, act, or expression of being devoted; from *devovere*, to vow.)

DEVOUT LIFE, INTRODUCTION TO THE. A famous spiritual treatise of St. Francis de Sales (1567–1622). Originally a small manual written for the private use of his cousin's wife, Madame de Charmoisy, it was later revised and expounded. The first edition was published in 1609 in Lyons, the final and definitive edition in 1619. Its purpose is to give practical directives for growth in holiness for people living in the world. But it has found a wide appeal among people in every state of life.

D.G. *Dei gratia*—By the grace of God.

DIABOLISM. Any form of intercourse or attempt to deal with the evil spirit by witchcraft, incantations, spiritism, and other occult practices. Strictly speaking, diabolism is the worship of the devil by invoking his assistance, depending on his guidance, and consciously choosing to honor the evil spirit in preference to God. (Etym. Greek *diabolos*, slanderer.)

DIACONATE. The ministry of service, and the lowest rank of holy orders, below the priesthood and the episcopate. (Etym. Latin *diaconus;* from *diakonos*, servant, deacon.)

DIACONATE, DEVELOPMENT OF THE. Growth in the understanding of the diaconate since Apostolic times.

From Pope St. Clement in the first century through the patristic age, the diaconate assumed a broadening variety of ministries, always under obedience to a bishop. During the celebration of the Eucharist, they read or chanted the Epistle and Gospel, received the gift offerings of the laity, inscribed the names of donors in the diptychs to be prayed for at Mass, helped the priest in distributing Holy Communion or brought the Eucharist to the homes of the sick, led the faithful in congregational prayer, gave the sign for penitents and catechumens to leave the church before the Canon of the Mass, with the bishop's permission baptized, instructed prospective converts, performed exorcisms, and in case of necessity could reconcile those who had "lapsed" during times of persecution.

The number of deacons was at first limited to seven for each diocese, and in Rome the tradition survives in the seven cardinal deacons. Their office of collecting and distributing alms made them influential in the Christian community. Archdeacons, or chief deacons of a locality, began in the East but in the West assumed greater importance as principal administrative officers of bishops. When abuses crept in, successive councils either restricted the exercise of deacons' powers (Nicaea in 325) or clarified their hierarchical inferiority to the priesthood (Toledo in 633). By the Middle Ages the diaconate was practically reduced to a temporary status, preparatory to the priesthood, although numbering in its ranks such renowned persons as St. Francis of Assisi (1181–1226).

Since the Second Vatican Council the role of the deacon has returned to something of its function in the early Church. The permanent diaconate was restored in the Western Church by Pope Paul VI.

DIADEM. In ecclesiastical art a crown or circular headband symbolic of sanctity. It may be either part of a picture or statue or be placed on the completed image as a token of special veneration. (Etym. Latin *diadema*, royal headdress; from Greek *diadema;* from *diadein*, to bind around.)

DIAKONIA. The biblical Greek word for service. As such it applies to all manner of ministry (official) or assistance (unofficial) that a person may perform or render either to the Church in general or to some private individual. In recent years the term has come to be used more technically of those services in the Church for which a person is specially ordained (as priests and deacons), or consecrated (as religious), or designated (as the faithful teaching or serving the needs of the sick or the poor).

DIALECTIC. In general, discussion between persons about matters of common interest; also a method of arguing and defending with probability and consistency on open questions, i.e., on issues that the speaker and listeners may legitimately discuss. Also the science or art of logic (Aristotle and St. Thomas Aquinas). A dialogue engaged in as a scientific method of investigation, or the science of ascertaining the real or distinct from the surface or apparent meaning of things (Plato). The logic or epistemology of appearances (Kant). The process of development of thought and of all history from thesis, or the given, through antithesis, to synthesis or the predictable result of the conflict (Hegel). The physical and political evolution of matter, to be accelerated by planned conflict in society (Marx). (Etym. Greek *dialektikos*, of conversation.)

DIALECTICAL MATERIALISM. The philosophy founded by Karl Marx (1818–83) and Friedrich Engels (1820–95), and condemned as such by the Catholic Church. It is materialism because it holds not only that matter is real but that matter is prior to mind both in time and in fact. Thus mind is said to appear only as an outgrowth of matter and must be explained accordingly. Space and time are viewed as forms of the existence of matter. It is dialectical in claiming that everything is in constant process of self-transformation. Everything is made up of opposing forces whose internal conflict keeps changing what the thing was into something else. Applied to society, the conflicts among people are essential to the progress of humanity, and to be fostered, as preconditions for the rise of the eventual classless society of perfect Communism.

DIALECTICAL THEOLOGY. A system of thought, developed by Karl Barth, which holds that the main feature of the Christian religion is an inherent opposition among its revealed mysteries. The fundamental opposition, or dialectic, is between God and man. Other oppositions, such as time and eternity, finite and infinite, creature and Creator, nature and grace, are derived from the primary conflict. Moreover, dialectical theology claims that these oppositions cannot be reconciled by the human mind. Only God can bridge the gap that separates them.

DIALOGUE MASS. Originally a Mass in which the people in the congregation made to the celebrant the responses that were commonly made by the server. Dialogue Masses were approved by the Holy See in 1922. Since the Second Vatican Council every Mass in which the faithful participate may be called a dialogue Mass because of the frequent interchange of prayers between priest and people.

DIANA OF THE EPHESIANS. Roman goddess of the moon, identified with Artemis among the Greeks who worshiped her as a virgin huntress. The Diana of the Ephesians was a combination of Artemis and the Semitic goddess Ashtoreth, patroness of the sexual instinct. An impressive statue of Diana stood inside the magnificent Temple of Ephesus, considered one of the seven wonders of the ancient world. It was a source of substantial income to the silversmiths of Ephesus to duplicate Diana's memorial as statuettes for pilgrims. St. Paul antagonized Demetrius and his fellow-silversmiths, who accused him of disparaging their statuettes as superstitions. It culminated in a riotous meeting in an assembly hall in Ephesus, and only the tact and persuasiveness of the town clerk prevented violence. With typical courage, Paul was eager to attend the meeting, but his friends dissuaded him (Acts 19:23–41).

DIASPORA. The term used to designate all those Jews who lived outside of Palestine and constituted isolated communities among Gentiles. Most of them were originally scattered as a result of extensive deportations by Assyrian and Babylonian conquerors in the centuries before Christ. By the beginning of the Christian era there were substantial numbers of Jews in Greece, Syria, Persia, Asia Minor, and Italy. Possibly 10 per cent of the population of the Roman Empire was Jewish. Most of these still considered Palestine their spiritual homeland and many made pilgrimages to Jerusalem on great feasts. Some hold that the Diaspora was the fulfillment of the warning that Moses had given his followers if they were disloyal. "Yahweh will scatter you among all the peoples" (Deuteronomy 4:27; 28:64). (Etym. Greek *diaspora*, dispersion.)

DIATESSARON. Syriac harmony of the four Gospels, compiled by Tatian about A.D. 170. It is written in one continuous narrative and was practically the only text in Syria through the fourth century.

DICASTERY. One of the official congregations of the Holy See, e.g., the Congregation for Religious and Secular Institutes, through which the Pope conducts the regular administration of the universal Church.

DICHOTOMISM. The doctrine of extreme duality, which views human beings as composed literally of two separate parts, body and soul. In this primitive understanding, all consciousness is attributed to the soul alone, and everything physical to the body alone.

In modern times, Cartesianism is a form of dichotomism. But this is not the biblical or the Christian concept, which emphasizes the unity of the human soul and body to form one substance. (Etym. Greek *dicha,* in two + *temno,* to cut.)

DICHOTOMY. In philosophy the division of a class into two mutually exclusive subclasses, as human beings into men and women.

DIDACHE. The instructional part or aspect of biblical revelation (Greek *didache,* teaching). Also refers to the Church's role as teacher and the exercise of her magisterium.

DIDACHE (Teaching of the twelve Apostles). A first-century treatise, written before A.D. 100. It was rediscovered in 1833 by Bryennios, Greek Orthodox Metropolitan of Nicomedia, in the codex from which in 1875 he had published the full text of the Epistles of St. Clement I. The *Didache* is divided into three parts: 1. the Two Ways, the Way of Life, and the Way of Death; 2. a liturgical manual treating of baptism, fasting, confession, and Holy Communion; 3. a treatise on the ministry. Doctrinal teaching is presupposed. The Way of Life is the love of God and of neighbor; the Way of Death is a list of vices to be avoided. There is a brief instruction on baptism, references to apostles, bishops, and deacons, and an exhortation to watch and be prepared for the coming of Christ.

DIDACTICS. The branch of religious education concerned with teaching and instruction (Greek *didaktikos,* apt at teaching). It is that part or aspect of catechetics which looks to training the mind to better understand and appropriate revealed truths.

DIDASCALIA APOSTOLORUM. A Greek treatise on morals and doctrine traditionally said to have been composed by the Apostles. Most probably written by a Syrian bishop in the third century. It forms the first part of the Apostolic Constitutions, i.e., the first eight books. It deals with the care of penitents, duties of clergy and laity, and the defense of the faith against heresy. Often called the first attempt at a code of canon law.

DIES IRAE. The sequence beginning "That Day of Wrath" used at Requiem Masses. It was written in the thirteenth century by Thomas of Celano, biographer of St. Francis of Assisi; there have been hundreds of translations in all the major languages. There is no record of the authorship or origin of the old ecclesiastical melody. Among others who set it to music were Cherubini, Verdi, Bruneau, Gounod, Berlioz, and Mozart.

DIETARY LAWS. Regulations governing food among practically all ancient and living religions, but especially among the Jews. In the Jewish tradition, these laws are enumerated in the Old Testament (Leviticus 11; Deuteronomy 14). They may be classified on three levels: cattle or beasts, birds, and fish. Among the cattle and beasts, they must meet two conditions to be legally edible: 1. have a divided hoof that is entirely split or cloven; 2. must chew their cud. Pigs are excluded, therefore, because they do not chew. Among birds, the Bible forbids certain ones by name and some are now impossible to identify. In general, birds of prey are prohibited. Believing Jews eat only traditionally "clean" birds, such as hen, goose, and turkey. As for fish, the general rule is that only those with fins and scales are edible; so that oysters, lobsters, crabs, and eels may not be eaten.

DIFFERENCE. In general, otherness or a lack of sameness or identity between two or more beings.

DIFFERENCE, ACCIDENTAL. Diversity among things only in some unessential property; also diversity in the mere degree or amount of some perfection, without any difference in species, as the differences among various races or nationalities.

DIFFERENCE, ANALOGICAL. Unlikeness in some perfection that is partly alike and partly unlike the other perfection with which it is being compared, e.g., the difference between knowledge in humans, which is sensible and rational, and in animals, which is merely sensible.

DIFFERENCE, ESSENTIAL. Unlikeness in kind or type of being when a certain perfection is in no way found in another type of being with which it is being compared. Thus the divine attributes of omniscience and omnipotence are unique to God alone and not verified of any creature.

DIFFINITIVE PRESENCE. See DEFINITIVE PRESENCE.

DIGNITATIS HUMANAE. Decree on Religious Liberty, of the Second Vatican Council. The scope of this document is the religious liberty to believe in God, worship him, and serve him according to one's conscience. There are two aspects of this freedom, as explained in the document: the freedom from coercion in the light of reason, based on each one's dignity as a person, and the freedom of exercise and evangelization founded on Christian revelation. The main thrust of the decree is the affirmation of a divine right, that "the Church claims freedom for herself in human society and before every public authority" (December 7, 1965).

DIGNITY. The excellence that deserves recognition and praise in a person or thing. Highest in dignity is God, whose superiority over all creation is the basis for adoration. (Etym. Latin *dignitas*, dignity, worthiness, worth.)

DILATION. To speak openly and fully, as in a canonical accusation made to proper ecclesiastical authorities. (Etym. Latin *dilatio*, a putting off, delaying; from *dilatare*, to spread wide.)

DILEMMA. Choice between two alternatives that are equally inevitable or undesirable. Christ more than once faced his opponents with a dilemma, e.g., "if it is through Beelzebub that I cast out devils, through whom do your own experts cast them out? Let them be your judges, then. But if it is through the Spirit of God that I cast devils out, then know that the Kingdom of God has overtaken you" (Matthew 12:27–28).

DIMISSORIAL LETTERS. Letters containing testimonials given to one of his subjects by a pope, bishop, or religious superior, stating that the bearer may be ordained. Such letters indicate that all the conditions required by ecclesiastical law have been satisfactorily met by the subject and the addressee is requested to ordain him.

DIOCESAN COUNCIL. A group of the faithful under a bishop's authority, co-operating with him in serving the needs of a diocese. As decreed by the Second Vatican Council, "In dioceses, as far as possible, councils should be set up to assist the Church's apostolic work, whether in the field of evangelization and sanctification, or in the fields of charity, social relations and the rest; the clergy and religious working with the laity in whatever way proves satisfactory." The authority of a diocesan council is always merely consultative with respect to the bishop, who retains the right to accept or bypass the decisions of a diocesan council. Moreover, "these councils can take care of the mutual co-ordination of the various lay associations and undertakings" of a diocese "while keeping the autonomy and par-

ticular nature of each untouched" (Decree *Apostolicam Actuositatem,* 26).

DIOCESAN PATRON. The saint, angel, or special divine attribute under whose patronage a diocese has been placed. It is the sacred title by which the persons in the diocese are identified, and in whose honor they are consecrated. The patronal feast of each diocese has specific liturgical provisions for a bishop and priests to follow.

DIOCESAN PRESBYTERIUM. See PRIESTS' COUNCIL.

DIOCESAN SYNOD. An assembly in each diocese, convoked by the local ordinary, of all the pastors and other diocesan and clerical religious administrators to deal with such matters as pertain to the clergy and faithful of the diocese. Diocesan synods, according to the Code of Canon Law (1918), were to be held at least once every ten years.

DIOCESE. The territory over which a bishop exercises ecclesiastical jurisdiction. The Pope alone, ultimately, erects dioceses, changes their limits, divides, unites, or suppresses them. (Etym. Greek *dioikēsis*, administration, administrative division.)

DIPLOMATIC CORPS. The official representatives of various countries at the court of the Sovereign Pontiff. They are most commonly ambassadors but may also be ministers, first secretaries, or persons with other special credentials.

DIPTYCH. Two tablets of metal, ivory, or wood hinged together. The inner surface was sometimes covered with wax for writing with a stylus. In the early Church one side contained the names of living persons, the other side the deceased, to be commemorated in the liturgy. Among the living were the names of the Pope, bishop, and prominent lay and ecclesiastical personages. From the diptychs of the dead originated later necrologies. Diptychs are still used in some Eastern liturgies, e.g., among the Catholic Syrians. (Etym. Greek *diptycha*, a pair of tablets.)

DIRECTION, SPIRITUAL. The guidance voluntarily sought by a person who is intent on progress in the spiritual life. The need for some spiritual direction for anyone seriously striving for sanctity is recognized in the Church's long history. In essence, spiritual direction is the positive assistance that a person receives from someone who is specially qualified by education, experience, or personal sanctity to discern the will of God in the practice of Christian virtue.

DIRECT LINE. Blood relationship as ancestry and descendants, namely great-grandparents, grandparents, parents, children, etc. Direct line can also refer to affinity, that is, in direct line from a valid marriage.

DIRECT SUICIDE. To kill oneself by intending death either as the end of one's action or as the means for attaining the end in view. It is always a grave sin, presuming that the person has sufficient use of his faculties to make a full consent of his will. Often equated with the sin of final despair.

DIRGE. A song named from the beginning word of *Dirige, Domine, Deus Meus* (Guide, O Lord, my God). It is the antiphon in the Office of the Dead, a solemn mourning hymn at funerals with its cry of lament. (Etym. Latin *dirige*, direct thou.)

DIRIMENT IMPEDIMENT. A condition, circumstance, or situation that makes an action null and void in its intended effects. Thus an existing marital bond nullifies any attempt to enter a second marriage.

DISARMAMENT. The act of disarming, or the policy of reducing a nation's production of military weapons in the interests of regional or international peace. The policy was strongly advocated by the Second Vatican Council: "True peace must be born of mutual trust between peoples instead of being forced on nations through dread of arms; all must work to put an end to the arms race and make a real beginning of disarmament, not unilaterally indeed but at an equal rate on all sides, on the basis of agreements and backed up by genuine and effective guarantees" (*Constitution of the Church in the Modern World,* 82).

DISCALCED. Barefooted. A term applied to religious congregations of men and women who are unshod or wear sandals, such as the Discalced Carmelites, Augustinians, and Clerks of the Holy Cross. It was introduced into the West by St. Francis and St. Clare as a form of austerity. (Etym. Latin *discalceatus*, unshod, barefoot.)

DISCERNMENT OF SPIRITS. The ability to distinguish whether a given idea or impulse in the soul comes from the good spirit or from the evil spirit. It may be an act of the virtue of prudence, or a special gift of supernatural grace, or both. In persons who are seriously intent on doing God's will, the good spirit is recognized by the peace of mind and readiness for sacrifice that a given thought or desire produces in the soul. The evil spirit produces disturbance of mind and a tendency to self-indulgence. An opposite effect is produced by both spirits toward sinners. (Etym. Latin *discernere*, to distinguish between, determine, resolve, decide.)

DISCIPLE. One who is learning or has learned. In the New Testament the word describes any follower of Jesus' teaching (Matthew 10:1). During his public ministry it referred as well to his twelve chosen aides, but in the Acts of the Apostles they are always referred to as Apostles (Acts 1:26). (Etym. Latin *discipulus*, pupil, follower.)

DISCIPLINE. Systematic mental, moral, or physical training under someone in authority. The term also applies to the order maintained by persons under control, whether self-determined or imposed by others. It is likewise a private means of penance, in use among ascetics since the early Church, e.g., a whip or scourge. It is the exercise by the Church of her right to administer spiritual penalty, and it may finally refer to any of the laws and directions set down by Church authority for the guidance of the faithful. (Etym. Latin *disciplina*, instruction, knowledge.)

DISCRIMINATION. In philosophy, the power of the mind clearly to distinguish between objects, whether real or conceptual, and between right and wrong in moral matters. Consequently, it is also the distinction between things that the mind recognizes, whether and how they differ. In popular usage, discrimination has come to mean acting toward someone or something with bias or prejudice. (Etym. Latin *discriminare*, to set apart as different, distinguish.)

DISCURSIVE PRAYER. That form of prayer in which the reflections of the mind are more active than the affections of the will. It is called discursive because discursion is the act of the mind that proceeds from one truth to the knowledge of another truth, either about the same object or about something else.

DISESTABLISHMENT. Depriving a given religion of its right, privileges, or position as the established religion in a certain country. Applied especially to the disestablishment of the Anglican Church, which received the support through taxation of British subjects regardless of creed. The process of disestablishment is still going on in the British Commonwealth of Nations.

DISMAS. The traditional name of the Good Thief, who was crucified with Christ and to whom Christ promised Paradise (Luke

23:39–43). A portion of the cross on which Dismas is said to have died is preserved at the Church of Santa Croce in Rome, and he is the patron of those condemned to death. See also GOOD THIEF.

DISMISSAL. Lawfully cutting off from membership in a religious institute persons who are guilty of certain grave public sins. The dismissal may be either automatic, if so provided by law, or judicial, if it follows a formal process of warnings and refusal to amend.

DISPARITY OF WORSHIP. A difference of cult. It is a diriment impediment to marriage unless dispensation is secured when one party is Catholic and the other is unbaptized.

DISPENSATION. A relaxation of the Church's law in a particular case. It is neither an abrogation of the law nor an excuse from observing the law but a release from its observance, temporarily or permanently, by competent authority, for good reasons. The Pope can dispense from all purely ecclesiastical laws. Other Church authorities can dispense from the laws that they or their predecessors have passed. Only those can dispense from the laws of a higher superior who are granted the power either by the Church's general legislation or by a special delegation. (Etym. Latin *dispensatio,* distribution, administration; freeing, release: from *dis-* + *pendere,* to weigh: *dispendere,* to weigh out.)

DISPERSION. See DIASPORA.

DISPOSITION. A quality or condition of a person necessary for the performance of some action. Commonly applied to the conditions required for the valid reception or administration of the sacraments, as the state of grace is required for the sacrament of the Eucharist or sincere contrition to receive absolution in the sacrament of penance.

DISPOSITIVE SIGN. A term especially applied to the sacramental character, insofar as it empowers the faithful in relation to certain acts of worship, and indirectly for the reception (or increase) of sanctifying grace and for lifelong actual graces.

DISPUTA, LA. A fresco in the Vatican painted by Raphael (1483–1520), considered to be one of the artist's greatest works. Representing the Church, militant and triumphant, it portrays saints, doctors, and laymen engaged in discussion. During the discussion the heavens are opened, showing Christ with the Holy Spirit hovering above him and the eternal Father blessing him as he offers himself as a sacrifice for sin.

DISPUTATION. Formal scholastic debate, originating in the medieval universities of Europe. The subject of the disputation is previously determined and the debate is conducted according to a traditional or accepted procedure. Associated for years with schools of theology, it is generally given as part of a public ceremony and often held on the occasion of some major ecclesiastical celebration.

DISPUTED QUESTION. An unsettled or debatable problem in philosophy or theology; a proposition that is seriously affirmed and denied by opposing parties. In scholasticism, disputed questions (*Quaestiones Disputatae*) were the subject of frequent disputation and formed a whole body of medieval sacred literature, e.g., among the writings of St. Thomas Aquinas.

DISSENT, DOCTRINAL. The theory that a professed Catholic may legitimately disagree with an official teaching of the Catholic Church and, in fact, should disagree in order to advance the Church's interests. It is based on one of several erroneous premises, e.g., Modernism, which denies that divine faith is an assent of the mind to God's revealed truth, or process theology, which postulates an evolving deity and therefore also an ever-changing truth. Most often the dissent applies to some doctrine of Christian morals which, though infallibly true, because taught by the Church's universal ordinary magisterium, has not been solemnly defined.

DISSENTERS. An opprobrious term mainly applied to those who disagree in matters of doctrine and practice accepted by the Established Church of England. Since about 1850 the term has been included under the more urbane title of "Non-conformists."

DISSIDENTS. A name used in theological literature to distinguish those Eastern Christians who are not in communion with Rome. Their liturgical practice, however, is often almost identical with that of Catholic Churches in the Eastern tradition.

DISSIMULATION. The act of concealing one's mind or real intention, an act that is morally permissible for a proportionally good purpose. Since secrets are to be kept, their preservation may at times require dissimulation, but of course never deception.

DISSOLUTION OF MARRIAGE. The dissolving of a natural bond in a marriage that is not a sacrament, as in the case of a Pauline Privilege when one of the parties enters a sacramental marriage union. Also the dissolving of a sacramental marriage that had not been consummated by natural intercourse after the marital contract.

DISTINCTION. Lack of identity between persons or things, ideas or terms of discourse.

DISTINCTION, LOGICAL. Difference between things that depends on thought alone and is not found in the thing itself because of no real plurality in the thing thought about. It may be a purely mental (nominal) distinction, as the difference between Christ as Savior and as Redeemer. Or it may be a virtual (metaphysical) distinction, as the differences among the divine attributes, which are really one in God but rich enough to present various aspects of this single reality to the human mind.

DISTINCTIVE SIGN. A term applied to the sacramental character insofar as it distinguishes the baptized from the nonbaptized, the confirmed from the nonconfirmed, and the ordained from the nonordained. It therefore identifies them before God and characterizes them according to each respective sacrament.

DISTRACTION. A drawing of the mind away from a predetermined subject to another. Distractions in prayer may be voluntary or involuntary. They are voluntary when not enough effort is made to keep one's mind on the presence of God. Otherwise, no matter how frequent or prolonged, they are involuntary. Voluntary distractions are venially sinful. The essence of a sinful distraction, however, is not in the mind's attention being withdrawn from any particular thought in prayer, but in not paying attention to God. (Etym. Latin *distrahere*, to draw apart.)

DISTRIBUTION OF COMMUNION. Liturgical reception of Holy Communion by the faithful. Communion is to be received either kneeling, and then "no other sign of reverence to the Blessed Sacrament is required," or standing, in which case a sign of reverence should be made before receiving.

DISTRIBUTIVE JUSTICE. The virtue that regulates those actions which involve the rights that an individual may claim from society. According to distributive justice, the state has three basic duties: to distribute the common burdens and privileges equitably; to make it possible for each citizen to exercise natural and acquired rights without undue hindrance; to foster mutual relations among the citizens for living together peacefully. Inequitable imposition of taxes, for example, would be a violation of distributive justice.

DITHEISM. The theory that there are two gods, each with a different divine nature. In Manichaeanism one god is good and the other evil. In subordinationism the Father is a higher deity than the Son, who is a second god proceeding from the first one. (Etym. Greek *di*, twofold + *theos*, god.)

DIVERSITY OF GRACE. Difference in degree and variety of the grace of justification among persons in God's friendship. As expressed by the Council of Trent, the measure of sanctifying grace varies in the individual person who is justified according to the measure of God's free distribution and the disposition or co-operation of the recipient (Denzinger 1529). Moreover, sanctifying grace is increased by good works. The various good works, done freely by co-operating with God's will, are rewarded by different grades of grace.

DIVIDE ET IMPERA. Divide and rule. Originally a policy of the Roman Empire, to rule its subject people by dividing them into provinces. These provinces were the first dioceses of the Catholic Church. The term is used in ascetical theology to describe an effective method of acquiring self-mastery by concentrating on one virtue or one failing at a time.

DIVINA COMMEDIA, LA. The Divine Comedy, written by Dante Alighieri (1265–1321). It is an allegory of life; a vision of the world of the hereafter. One hundred cantos in length, it reflects the faith of Medieval Catholic Europe and is considered one of the greatest classics of Christian literature. Composed in the vernacular the poet hoped to convert an erring world back to righteousness. The philosophy of Aristotle (384–322 B.C.) and St. Thomas Aquinas (1225–74), the mysticism of Saints Bernard (1090–1153) and Augustine (354–430) and the theology of the early Fathers are synthesized in exquisite language. The first printing of this classic was in 1472 in Italy.

DIVINATION. The art of knowing and declaring future events or hidden things by means of communication with occult forces. It is always an act of a religious nature. There is no divination if the religious element is missing, as in any scientific investigation. The occult forces in divination are always created rational powers that the Church identifies as diabolical. Implicit in this judgment is the belief that neither God nor the spiritual powers friendly to God would lend themselves to frivolous practices or subject themselves to any evoking human force. Hence, evoking these powers, whether explicitly or even implicitly, is considered an appeal to Satan's aid. It is therefore a grave offense against God to attribute to the devil a sure knowledge of the contingent future, which, as depending on free will, is known to God alone.

This explains the strong prohibition in the Bible of any divining practices. "Do not have recourse," the people were told, "to the spirits of the dead or to magicians; they will defile you. I am Yahweh your God (Leviticus 19:31). And again: "Any man or woman who is necromancer or magician must be put to death by stoning; their blood shall be on their own heads" (Leviticus 20:27).

In the history of Christianity every form of divination has been condemned by the Church. Among the more common are augury (Latin *augurare,* to predict) by the interpretation of omens such as watching the flight of birds or inspecting the entrails of sacrificed animals; axinomancy (Greek *axine,* axhead + *manteia,* divination) by means of the movements of an ax placed on a post; belomancy (Greek *belos,* dart) by drawing arrows at random from a container; bibliomancy (Greek *biblion,* book) by superstitiously consulting books, notably the Bible; capnomancy (Greek *kapnos,* smoke) by studying the ascent and descent of smoke and concluding that it was a good omen if the smoke rose vertically, especially from a sacrifice; chiromancy (Greek *cheir,* hand) by inspecting the lines of the hand, also called palmistry; necromancy (Greek *necros,* dead person) by consulting the dead or conjuring up the souls of the dead to inquire of them some secrets from the past or into the future, more commonly known as spiritualism. (Etym. Latin *devinare,* to foresee, predict, prophesy.)

DIVINE ATTRIBUTES. The perfections of God, which, according to a human way of thinking, proceed from and belong to the essence of God. In reality the divine attributes are identical among themselves and with the divine essence. Theology distinguishes the attributes from the essence because they correspond, in human language, to different properties in creatures which reflect, so to speak, the perfections of God.

DIVINE DECREE. The theory that morality finally depends on God's will and not on the divine essence. In its extreme form, it holds that good and evil are decided by God's arbitrary will. What is considered morally evil could have been morally good, and vice versa. Also God could decree that the present code of morality is not permanently binding. The modern form of this theory is some variant of process morality, which postulates an evolving and therefore changing Deity.

DIVINE ELECTION. The eternal choice by God of those whom he absolutely wills to be saved. It is a matter of Catholic faith that this divine election includes the foreknowledge of each person's merits before God. So that it does not mean, as some of the Reformers and Jansenists held, that God chooses for salvation those whom he wills independent of their free co-operation with his grace. The divine election, on Catholic principles, recognizes true human freedom in responding to the will of God.

DIVINE ESSENCE. The nature of God as mentally distinguished from the persons and the attributes of God. Thus each of the three divine persons has one and the same essence. And the different attributes of God are objectively identical with the divine essence.

DIVINE FAITH. Assent of the mind to what God has revealed, as distinct from human faith, which is the acceptance of the word of a human being.

DIVINE FRIENDSHIP. The state of grace by which a person is loved by God, becomes an heir of heaven, and on reaching the age of discretion loves God by sincerely doing the divine will. The basis of divine friendship is a sharing in the divine nature bestowed by God. There is friendship because God's love of man is reciprocated by man's love of God. The theological virtue of charity, which is inseparably connected with the state of grace, enables the justified person to love God in return for the benevolent love of God.

DIVINE GLORY. Recognition and praise of the infinite excellence of God. The fundamental glory of God is his infinite goodness and greatness in all attributes. Viewed as perfections in God, they constitute his internal fundamental glory, but viewed in their manifestation in creatures, they are the external, fundamental divine glory. The formal (actual) glory of God is the knowledge and love that he has of himself, which is called internal glory; and the knowledge, honor, and love shown him by rational creatures, which is called external, formal divine glory.

DIVINE IDEAS. The exemplary forms, not really distinct from God and existing in his mind from all eternity, according to which he created and continues to direct the universe.

DIVINE IMMANENCE. The omnipresence of God permeating all creation. It is the interpenetration of the divine essence and activity within all created beings. In the Christian faith this immanence does not deny but complements the divine transcendence. God remains God and is neither part of the world nor is perfected by the world. In pantheistic immanence God is said to be present and operating in the world, but he is also held to be somehow identical with the universe.

DIVINE JUDGMENT. An act of God affecting the life or destiny of his rational creatures. It is called judgment by analogy with the function of a human judge who weighs the pros and cons of a situation and makes his authoritative decision accordingly. During life it often refers to what are considered divine acts of retribution, such as some natural disaster. More properly, it is the decision that God renders to each human being at death, and his final judgment of mankind at the end of time.

DIVINE JUSTICE. The constant and unchanging will of God to give everyone what is due him or her. Every possible form of justice is possessed by God. He practices legal justice in that through the natural and moral law he co-ordinates creatures to the common good; distributive justice because he gives to his creatures everything they need to fulfill the purpose of their existence; remunerative justice because he rewards the good; and vindictive justice because he punishes the wicked.

DIVINE LAW. The eternal law of God, or the divine reason as governing the whole universe. God conceived as the Ruler of the Universe. The plan of government that he has in his mind bears the character of law, and because it is conceived in eternity and not in time, it is said to be the eternal law. This eternal law embraces both the physical and moral laws. Both have in common the idea of some norm to be fulfilled. In physical laws, this norm is fulfilled necessarily, as happens with gravity or the expansion of matter by heat. In moral laws, the norm may or may not be fulfilled depending on the free decision of human beings.

The eternal moral law has been manifested to the human race in two ways, naturally and supernaturally. In the first case, human beings come to know the eternal law from created nature through the light of native reason; this is natural law in the full scope of its meaning. In the second case, human beings come to know the eternal law from divine revelation to which they can respond with the help of God's grace. This is the revealed law that spans the whole ambit of God's special communication of his will "through the prophets" in times past and in our own time "through His Son" (Hebrews 1:1).

Since human beings are both individual and social beings, they are obliged by the eternal law on both levels of their existence. The duties that they have as individuals are of course never totally separable from their responsibilities as members of the human family. They are consequently always social by implication. But within the larger community of the human race are two societies that Catholicism has designated as "perfect" or "complete," in the sense that they are divinely provided with the necessary means to fulfill their respective reasons for existence. They are the civil society of the State and the ecclesiastical society of the Church.

Accordingly, each of these societies has the right to make its own laws and bind its members in conscience to obedience. Civil laws oblige all baptized persons who have reached the age of discretion and are therefore able to make rational decisions; yet the Church may also obligate children below that age in matters that pertain to the common good of the faithful.

DIVINE LOVE, OUR LADY OF. A Roman shrine on the Via Ardeatina. The sanctuary to Mary and her Divine Child was built in the mid-sixteenth century, but the image itself dates from the early fourteenth. Pilgrims and native Romans by the thousands prayed there as World War II tension mounted. Fearful for their treasured mural, the population had it removed thirteen miles away from the active fighting to the church of St. Ignatius. Pope Pius XII had Rome placed under the special protection of Our Lady of Divine Love during the war, and when hostilities ceased he declared her to have been the real savior of Rome. After the war the image was replaced in its original sanctuary.

DIVINE MERCY. The love of God beyond what humankind deserves. In one sense, every manifestation of God's love is an expression of mercy, since, absolutely speaking, God is not obligated even to create. But more properly, mercy is the exercise of divine charity toward those who have sinned. Mercy, then, is God's continued love of humans although they have sinned, his forgiving love that invites them to be reconciled with the God against whom they have sinned, his condoning love that mitigates and is even willing to remove all the punishment due to sin, and his superabundant love that mysteriously blesses the repentant sinners beyond what they might have received from God had they not sinned.

DIVINE MISSION. The sending of one divine person by another, producing a new kind of presence in the created world that corresponds to their eternal origins within the Godhead. Only those persons are sent into the world of creation who proceed within the Trinity, and they are sent only by those from whom they proceed. Hence the Father is sent by no one, the Son is sent by the Father, and the Holy Spirit is sent by the Father and the Son. The missions are either visible or invisible, depending on how the divine message comes to creatures. Thus the Incarnation of the Son of God is a visible mission of the greatest possible perfection. The visible missions of the Holy Spirit in the form of a dove and of parted tongues are mainly symbolic of his invisible mission whenever sanctifying grace is infused into a human soul.

DIVINE NOTION. An internal divine activity that characterizes the persons in the Trinity and distinguishes them, as contrasted with the essential acts that are common to the three persons. Factually the divine notions coincide with the properties. They are ungeneratedness and generation as distinctive of the Father, passive generation as the mark of identity of the Son, and passive spiration as characteristic of the Holy Spirit.

DIVINE OFFICE. The group of psalms, hymns, prayers, biblical and spiritual readings formulated by the Church for chant or recitation at stated times every day. Its origins go back to apostolic times, when it consisted almost entirely of psalms and readings from the Scriptures. Priests are obliged to say the full daily office, and religious who are not priests are obliged according to their rule of life. The latest edition of the Divine Office was promulgated by Pope Paul VI by the apostolic constitution *Laudis Canticum* in 1970. It represents a complete revision of the text and arrangement of the Hours of the Liturgy according to the directives of the Second Vatican Council (*Constitution on the Liturgy*, IV, 83–101). As contained in the Breviary, the office is divided into the Proper of the Season, with biblical readings and homilies; Solemnities of the Lord as they occur during the year; the Ordinary or normal framework of the office; the Psalter, or psalms assigned to each hour of the day on the basis of four weeks to a month; the Proper of the Saints, as their feasts occur in sequence; Common Offices, corresponding to votive Masses in the Eucharistic liturgy; and the Office of the Dead. A supplement contains canticles and Gospel readings for vigils, brief intercessory prayers, and detailed indices. See also OF-FICE, DIVINE; MORNING PRAYER, EVENING PRAYER, NIGHT PRAYER, PRAYER DURING THE DAY, OFFICE OF READINGS.

DIVINE OPERATION. God's activity outside of himself. Also called divine activity *ad extra* in contrast with divine activity within the Trinity. The Fourth Lateran Council and the Council of Florence teach that all of God's activity outside the Trinity is done simultaneously and equally by all three persons. Thus everything that God does in the world of creatures, whether naturally or supernaturally, is the operation of all three divine persons.

DIVINE PLAN. The order of the universe eternally in the mind of God, foreseeing each of its creatures, their diversity and hierarchy, activity and interrelationship, and how they serve their respective purpose in accordance with the divine will.

DIVINE POSITIVE LAW. See REVEALED LAW.

DIVINE PRAISES. A series of praises, recited for generations after the benediction of the Blessed Sacrament. They are thought to have been originally compiled in 1797 in reparation for blasphemy and profane language. Praise of the Immaculate Conception, her bodily Assumption into heaven, the Sacred Heart, St. Joseph, and the Precious Blood have been added since the middle of the nineteenth century. The present text reads:

Blessed be God.
Blessed be his holy Name.
Blessed be Jesus Christ, true God and true
  man.

Blessed be the name of Jesus.
Blessed be his most Sacred Heart.
Blessed be his most Precious Blood.
Blessed be Jesus in the most holy Sacrament of the Altar.
Blessed be the Holy Spirit, the Paraclete.
Blessed be the great Mother of God, Mary most holy.
Blessed be her holy and Immaculate Conception.
Blessed be her glorious Assumption.
Blessed be the name of Mary, Virgin and Mother.
Blessed be St. Joseph, her most chaste spouse.
Blessed be God in his angels and in his saints.

DIVINE PROCESSION. The origin of a divine person from another through the communication of the numerically one divine essence. There are two internal processions in the Trinity: the begetting of the Son from the Father, and the procession of the Holy Spirit from the Father and the Son. It is divine persons, not the divine nature, who are the subjects of the internal divine processions. The second divine person proceeds from the intellect of the first divine person by generation, and therefore is related to him as Son to a Father. The third divine person proceeds from the will or mutual love of the Father and the Son as from a single principle through spiration.

DIVINE PROPERTY. Distinctive property that belongs to one divine person in the Trinity and distinguishes it from the other two. The person-forming properties are fatherhood (first person), sonship (second person), and passive spiration (third person). The one distinguishing property is originlessness in the Father. Since active spiration is a common property of two persons, the Father and Son, it is not a property in the strict sense.

DIVINE RELATIONS. The four real relationships that exist among the persons in the Trinity. There is the relation of the Father to the Son as active generation or paternity; the relation of the Son to the Father as passive generation or filiation; the relation of the Father and the Son to the Holy Spirit as active spiration; and the relation of the Holy Spirit to the Father and the Son as passive spiration.

Although there are four real relationships within the Trinity, only three stand in contrast to one another and are therefore really distinct, namely the fatherhood, sonship, and the passive spiration. Active spiration stands in contrast only to passive spiration but not to the fatherhood and sonship. Consequently it is not really but only virtually distinct from the fatherhood and sonship. However, the relations in God are really identical with the divine nature.

DIVINE RIGHT OF KINGS. The theory that the actual rulers of states have their authority by an immediate grant from God. Not only does God give authority to the State, but he personally selects the rulers, either by positive intervention, as in the case of King Saul in the Jewish theocracy, or by tacit approval of the ruler selected by appointment, election, and especially by hereditary succession. A logical conclusion to the theory of divine right of kings was to make it immoral to unseat them no matter how badly they governed.

DIVINE TOUCHES. Spiritual sentiments, filled with consolation, that are immediately impressed on the will by a kind of divine contact and that are accompanied by a vivid illumination of the mind. Two forms of these touches are known in mystical literature. The ordinary type leaves an impression on the affective faculties along with mental enlightenment. The substantial type is so deep that they seem to occur within the very substance of the soul. Actually even in this case, it is still only the faculties that are reached by the divine visitation, but the contact produces a most intimate spiritual experience.

DIVINE WILL. The volition of God, which, like his knowledge, is purely and simply actual, and absolutely independent of all extra-divine things. Since God is infinite there is, in his willing, no transition from potency to act, no sequence of individual acts, but one single successionless act of willing. His will is actually identical with the divine essence. Things external to God are not determining reasons, but merely the goal of the divine volition. God's actual fullness of being excludes any love of acquisition. His ardent longing for the salvation of humankind (Isaiah 65:2) is an expression of his benevolent love, which shows itself in the communication of benefits to creatures, beginning with the gift of their existence.

DIVINI REDEMPTORIS. Encyclical letter of Pope Pius XI, published in 1937, condemning atheistic Communism and identifying its principal errors: dialectical materialism, utopian messianism, progress through class conflict, denial of personal liberty, and the negation of all human rights.

DIVINITY. The attribute of being divine. In an absolute sense only the infinite God is divine. But the term is sometimes loosely applied to others than God, either mistakenly or because of some relationship they have to God. (Etym. Latin *divinus,* belonging to God.)

DIVORCE. Legal separation of husband and wife, or the release by civil authority from any one or more of the bonds of matrimony between them. Imperfect divorce is the separation of husband and wife so that the duty of living together, and sometimes the support, is relaxed, but giving them no right to remarry. Also called separation from bed and board, but not the severance of the primary bond of marriage, which is the exclusive lifelong fidelity in the use of marital rights. (Etym. Latin *divortium;* from *divertere,* to part, separate, turn aside.)

D.N. *Dominus Noster*—Our Lord.

DN, DNS, D N U S. *Dominus*—Lord.

D.N.J.C. *Dominus Noster Jesus Christus*—Our Lord Jesus Christ.

DOCETISM. A heretical system of thought dating from apostolic times, which held that Christ only seemed to be a man, to be born, have lived, suffered, and risen from the dead. All the evidence indicates that Docetism was combined with some form of Gnosticism and, later on, Manichaeism. In the strict sense it was less a heresy denying a Christian doctrine than a false philosophy, claiming that there was an irreconcilable antagonism between matter and spirit, and for this reason it was thought impossible that God, who is pure spirit, would become incarnate in a material body.

DOCT. Doctor.

DOCTA IGNORANTIA. Learned ignorance. In theology it means that whatever man learns about God is infinitesimal compared to the infinity of being that is the divine essence, and must be expressed in negative terms such as in-finite, in-comprehensible, in-effable. The expression was originally the title of a treatise, *De Docta Ignorantia,* by Nicholas of Cusa (1401–64) to describe human insight into the divinity.

DOCTOR OF THE CHURCH. A title given since the Middle Ages to certain saints whose writing or preaching is outstanding for guiding the faithful in all periods of the Church's history. Originally the Western Fathers of the Church, Gregory the Great, Ambrose, Augustine, and Jerome, were considered the great doctors of the Church. But the Church has officially added many more names to the original four, including Sts. Catherine of Siena (1347–80) and Theresa of Avila (1515–82):

DOCTORS OF THE CHURCH

ST. ALBERT THE GREAT (1200–80). Dominican. Patron of natural scientists; called Doctor Universalis, Doctor Expertus.

ST. ALPHONSUS LIGUORI (1696–1787). Patron of confessors and moralists. Founder of the Redemptorists.

ST. AMBROSE (340–97). One of the four traditional Doctors of the Latin Church. Opponent of Arianism in the West. Bishop of Milan.

ST. ANSELM (1033–1109). Archbishop of Canterbury. Father of Scholasticism.

ST. ANTHONY OF PADUA (1195–1231). Franciscan Friar. Evangelical Doctor.

ST. ATHANASIUS (297–373). Bishop of Alexandria. Dominant opponent of Arianism. Father of Orthodoxy.

ST. AUGUSTINE (354–430). Bishop of Hippo. One of the four traditional Doctors of the Latin Church. Doctor of Grace.

ST. BASIL THE GREAT (329–79). One of the Three Cappadocian Fathers. Father of monasticism in the East.

ST. BEDE THE VENERABLE (673–735). Benedictine priest. Father of English history.

ST. BERNARD OF CLAIRVAUX (1090–1153). Cistercian. Called Mellifluous Doctor because of his eloquence.

ST. BONAVENTURE (1217–74). Franciscan theologian. Seraphic Doctor.

ST. CATHERINE OF SIENA (1347–80). Mystic. Second woman Doctor.

ST. CYRIL OF ALEXANDRIA (376–444). Patriarch. Opponent of Nestorianism. Made key contributions to Christology.

ST. CYRIL OF JERUSALEM (315–87). Bishop and opponent of Arianism in the East.

ST. EPHRAEM SYRUS (306–73). Biblical exegete and ecclesiastical writer. Called Harp of the Holy Spirit.

ST. FRANCIS DE SALES (1567–1622). Bishop, leader in Counter-Reformation.

Patron of Catholic writers and the Catholic press.

ST. GREGORY I THE GREAT (540–604). Pope. Fourth and last of the traditional Doctors of the Latin Church. Defended papal supremacy and worked for clerical and monastic reform.

ST. GREGORY OF NAZIANZUS (330–90). Called the Christian Demosthenes because of his eloquence and, in the Eastern Church, The Theologian. One of the Three Cappadocian Fathers.

ST. HILARY OF POITIERS (315–68). Bishop. Called The Athanasius of the West.

ST. ISIDORE OF SEVILLE (560–636). Archbishop, theologian, historian. Regarded as the most learned man of his time.

ST. JEROME (343–420). One of the four traditional Doctors of the Latin Church. Father of biblical science.

ST. JOHN CHRYSOSTOM (347–407). Bishop of Constantinople. Patron of preachers and called Golden-Mouthed because of his eloquence.

ST. JOHN DAMASCENE (675–749). Greek theologian. Called Golden Speaker because of his eloquence.

ST. JOHN OF THE CROSS (1542–91). Joint founder of the Discalced Carmelites. Doctor of Mystical Theology.

ST. LAWRENCE OF BRINDISI (1559–1619). Vigorous preacher of strong influence in the post-Reformation period.

ST. LEO I THE GREAT (400–61). Pope. Wrote against Nestorian and Monophysite heresies and errors of Manichaeism and Pelagianism.

ST. PETER CANISIUS (1521–97). Jesuit theologian. Leader in the Counter-Reformation.

ST. PETER CHRYSOLOGUS (400–50). Bishop of Ravenna. Called Golden-Worded.

ST. PETER DAMIAN (1007–72). Benedictine. Ecclesiastical and clerical reformer.

ST. ROBERT BELLARMINE (1542–1621). Jesuit. Defended doctrine under attack during and after the Reformation. Wrote two catechisms.

ST. TERESA OF AVILA (1515–82). Spanish Carmelite nun and mystic. First woman Doctor.

ST. THOMAS AQUINAS (1225–74). Dominican philosopher and theologian. Called Angelic Doctor. Patron of Catholic schools and education.

DOCTRINAIRE. Originally applied to a group of French philosophers in the early nineteenth century, the term now refers to religious and philosophical theorists who are uninterested in other views than their own. A dogmatist as one who speculates rather than acts on what he believes; an impractical visionary.

DOCTRINAL DEMYTHOLOGY. Critical evaluation of the dogma of the Catholic Church, similar to biblical demythology of the Bible. The basic premise is that doctrinal formulations are all time-conditioned. The definitions of the Councils of Nicaea, Chalcedon, and Trent are to be re-examined on the basis of what they really mean, by sloughing off what is unhistorical because mythical from what is historical and still true. On these terms nothing that the Church has ever taught in faith or morals would ever be substantially unchangeable, or at least the faithful can never be sure what this unchangeable substance is.

DOCTRINAL INTERPRETATION. See INTERPRETATION.

DOCTRINAL PLURALISM. The theory that in the Catholic Church it is permissible to hold objectively contrary positions on faith or morals. Implicit in the theory is the claim, more than once condemned by the Church, that doctrine is a subjective expression of belief on which some persons may agree, rather than the objective teaching of the Church's hierarchical authority, identifying or interpreting divine revelation.

DOCTRINAL SPIRITUALITY. A deductive method of studying Scripture, tradition, and theology, especially the Summa of St. Thomas, concerning the spiritual life. Conclusions are drawn from this deposit of faith about the nature of Christian perfection and the means to use for its attainment.

DOCTRINE. Any truth taught by the Church as necessary for acceptance by the faithful. The truth may be either formally revealed (as the Real Presence), or a theological conclusion (as the canonization of a saint), or part of the natural law (as the sinfulness of contraception). In any case, what makes it doctrine is that the Church authority teaches that it is to be believed. This teaching may be done either solemnly in *ex cathedra* pronouncements or ordinarily in the perennial exercise of the Church's magisterium or teaching authority. Dogmas are those doctrines which the Church proposes for belief as formally revealed by God. (Etym. Latin *doctrina,* teaching.)

DOGMA. Doctrine taught by the Church to

be believed by all the faithful as part of divine revelation. All dogmas, therefore, are formally revealed truths and promulgated as such by the Church. They are revealed either in Scripture or tradition, either explicitly (as the Incarnation) or implicitly (as the Assumption). Moreover, their acceptance by the faithful must be proposed as necessary for salvation. They may be taught by the Church in a solemn manner, as with the definition of the Immaculate Conception, or in an ordinary way, as with the constant teaching on the malice of taking innocent human life. (Etym. Latin *dogma;* from Greek *dogma,* declaration, decree.)

DOGMATIC FACT. A truth that, though not revealed by God, nevertheless comes under the infallible teaching authority of the Church. The reason for the Church's competence over dogmatic facts is their close connection with revealed truths. If the Church did not have authority to teach such facts infallibly, the doctrines of revelation would be jeopardized. Examples of dogmatic facts are the valid election of a pope, the validity of an ecumenical council, and the actuality of a canonized saint's presence in heaven.

DOGMATIC RELATIVISM. The theory that all the dogmas of the Christian faith are time- and circumstance-conditioned. Implied in dogmatic relativism is the denial that revelation has been completed with the apostolic age. Rather, it is claimed, revelation is still going on, and new religious insights, deriving from experience, change and even replace former doctrines of the Church's teaching authority.

DOGMATIC THEOLOGY. The science of Christian doctrine. It treats the teachings of the Church systematically as a whole, and considers each article of faith in its own right and in relation to other dogmas of Catholic Christianity. It proves the doctrines of the Church from Scripture and tradition, illustrates them by suitable comparisons, and shows that they are in harmony with reason. It answers objections from philosophy and other sciences and above all deduces theological consequences from the truths of faith.

DOGMATISM. Unqualified assertion of judgment, which has three levels of meaning: 1. the view of human knowledge which holds that the mind can attain the truth and certitudes; hence it is opposed to skepticism; 2. the position of those who are convinced about their philosophy of life but without

judicious reflection, hence opposed to intelligent belief; 3. since Immanuel Kant any metaphysical statement made without previous analysis of its justification at the bar of reason; hence opposed to rationalism.

DOLORS, SEVEN. The seven sorrows of the Blessed Virgin Mary. They are traditionally identified with the sorrows that Mary experienced in her association with Christ: the prophecy of Simeon (Luke 2:34–35), the flight into Egypt (Matthew 2:13–21), the three-day separation from Jesus in Jerusalem (Luke 2:41–50), and the four incidents related to Christ's Passion, as described or implied by the Evangelists; namely, Mary's meeting Jesus on the way to Calvary, the Crucifixion, the removal of Christ's body from the Cross, and the burial in the tomb. There were two feasts in honor of the seven sorrows: the Friday after Passion Sunday, extended to the universal Church by Pope Benedict XIII in 1727; and September 15, first granted to the Servite Order in 1668 and extended in 1814 to the whole Church by Pope Pius VII. Since the revision of the Roman calendar after the Second Vatican Council, only the feast on September 15 is observed, but its name has been changed to Our Lady of Sorrows. (Etym. Latin *dolor,* pain, sorrow.)

DOM. Traditional title of the men religious of the Benedictine and Cistercian orders. An abbreviation of *Dominus* (Lord), it originally applied to the Pope, bishops, and finally to monks. In Italy "Don" is used for all clerics except mendicant friars and clerks regular. The form "Dan" was used in medieval English, and "Monsieur" has been customary in France. (Etym. Latin *dominus,* master.)

DOM. *Dominica*—Sunday.

D.O.M. *Deo optimo maximo*—To God, the best and greatest.

DOMESTIC ORATORY. See PRIVATE ORATORY.

DOMESTIC PRELATE. See PRELATE, DOMESTIC.

DOMICILE. Permanent habitation in the eyes of the law, by which a person accepts certain responsibilities and has specified rights. To acquire domicile, one must actually take up residence in a given place with the intention of permanently living there or actually living there for ten years. Domiciles can be maintained in two places, e.g., summer and winter residences. A wife's domicile is that of her husband; a child's that of its parents or legal guardians; an ecclesiastically separated wife may maintain her own. If not ecclesiastically separated, she can have only a quasi-domicile. Temporary absence, no matter how long, does not result in loss of domicile privileges. Domicile entitles a person to ministrations from the pastor of a parish and the bishop of that diocese, to both of whom he owes spiritual obedience. By domicile one acquires a proper parish and a proper diocese. (Etym. Latin *domicilium*, abode, dwelling; from *domus*, house.)

DOMINATIONS. The highest choir of the intermediate order of angels, which includes the Powers and the Virtues, over which the Dominations have authority to direct the performance of their allotted tasks.

DOMINATIVE POWER. The right of authority over acts of persons in private societies, as husband over wife, parents over children, and master over servants. In Christianity this right is balanced by the duty to love.

DOMINICANS. The Order of Preachers, founded by St. Dominic (1170–1221), whose form took definite shape at two general chapters held in Bologna in 1220 and 1221. Also known as Friars Preachers and in England as Black Friars. Specially devoted to preaching and teaching, they were the first major order to substitute intellectual work for manual labor. At Dominic's request, the order was to practice not only individual but corporate poverty. In 1475, Pope Sixtus IV revoked the law of corporate poverty and allowed the Dominicans to hold property and have permanent sources of income.

The chief apostolate is educational. There is a carefully organized system of teaching which culminates in the *Studia Generalia*, connected with a college or university. It was especially the Dominicans who adapted Aristotle (384–322 B.C.) to the service of Christianity, following the lead of St. Albertus Magnus (1200–80) and St. Thomas Aquinas (1225–74).

The popes have used the Dominicans on many missions, including preaching the Crusades and diplomatic service. The Inquisition was regularly staffed by Dominicans, who were therefore called "watchdogs of orthodoxy." In the Age of Discovery, they established many pioneer missions in the Eastern and Western Hemispheres.

There are two orders attached to the Friars Preachers. The Second Order consists of nuns who follow a rule similar to that of the friars but are cloistered and live a con-

templative life. Most of the Third Order Sisters live an active life, with apostolic work outside the community. In 1852, Jean Baptiste Lacordaire (1802–61) founded a Third Order for priests with simple vows, which was destroyed by the French anticlerical laws of 1901.

DOMINION. Ownership of material goods, entitling the owner to proprietary rights, i.e., to use, change, keep, or dispose of what one owns. Christianity views dominion as not absolute, but always relative to the common good of society. (Etym. Latin *dominium*, dominion, might, power; from *dominus*, master.)

DOMINUS VOBISCUM. The Lord be with you. Latin greeting of the priest at Mass, addressing the people. Their response is *"Et cum spiritu tuo* [and with your spirit]."

DOM. PREL. Domestic prelate.

DONATION OF CONSTANTINE. A document forged in the eighth or ninth century, allegedly written by Emperor Constantine (c. 275–337), giving the Pope and the Church great possessions and a political privilege. It was never considered by the popes as the source of their power either in civil jurisdiction or in spiritual authority.

DONATISM. Originally a schism and then a heresy of the fourth and fifth centuries, claiming that the validity of the sacraments depends on the moral character of the minister; also that sinners cannot be members of the Church, nor can they be tolerated by the true Church if their sins are publicly known. The Donatists came into existence in Africa during the disorders following the persecution under Diocletian (245–313). A man named Caecilian was consecrated Bishop of Carthage in A.D. 311, but a group of rigorists claimed that he was not a valid bishop because his consecrator, Felix of Aptunga, had been a *traditor*, i.e., an apostate. The objectors were supported by the bishops of Numidia, who proceeded to consecrate Majorinus as a rival to Caecilian. Majorinus was soon afterward succeeded by Donatus (fourth century), from whom the movement took its name. The claims of the sect were condemned by Pope Miltiades (310–14), and by the Council of Arles (314). When civil authority also opposed the Donatists, their churches were seized and many were exiled. Yet Donatism did not disappear until the Moslem invasion of Africa in the seventh century.

DONKEY BEAD. A superstitious good luck

stone in the East. Translated from *"Khar Mohreh"* (which means "The Mark of the Donkey"), it was placed around a donkey's neck to drive away evil spirits. Over the years it has served as ornaments in jewelry, for decoration and many other purposes. However, it is still considered to bring the owner "good luck" and "long life," and is now worn also by Christians. The Donkey Bead is made from quartz that is crushed, molded, and glazed with cobalt. The traditional color is blue, with very slight variation. The entire process is done by hand, which accounts for the individuality of each piece.

DOOM. Pronouncement of sentence or judgment in the sense of condemn. Used formerly as the common term for Judgment Day and still found in such words as doomsday, also spelled domesday.

DOORS, HOLY. The doors of the basilicas of St. Peter, St. John Lateran, St. Paul, and St. Mary Major, which are not opened except during the years of a jubilee. The Pope opens the doors of St. Peter's to officially begin a Holy Year, and closes them at the end of a jubilee. Cardinals are commissioned to do the same at the three other basilicas. The custom dates back to the jubilee of 1450, under Pope Nicholas V. Between jubilees the holy doors are closed by two partitions of brick, between which are placed commemorative medals and a parchment recalling the jubilee just completed.

DORMITION. Feast of the Falling Asleep of the Blessed Virgin Mary. The Byzantine name for the Assumption, and the title of the famous Benedictine church on Mount Zion in Jerusalem. (Etym. Latin *dormitio,* a sleeping; from *dormire,* to sleep.)

DOSITHEUS, CONFESSION OF. Standard profession of Eastern Orthodox faith, drafted in 1672 to meet the challenge of Protestantism. It reads like the declarations of the Council of Trent, in defending the priesthood, Mass and seven sacraments, the episcopal hierarchy, confession of sins, Mary's divine maternity and perpetual virginity, and the necessity of man's free cooperation with divine grace to merit eternal glory.

DOUAY BIBLE. The sixteenth- and seventeenth-century English translation of the Bible, begun at the English College, Douai, Flanders. The college was later moved to Reims, where the New Testament was completed and published. The Old Testament

translation was issued some years later, when the college returned to Douai. The translation, which sought for accuracy rather than literary style, was made from the Latin Vulgate, carefully compared with the original Hebrew and Greek. It was mainly the work of Gregory Martin (d. 1582). In the eighteenth century it was considerably revised by Bishop Challoner (1691–1781) and until the mid-twentieth century was commonly used by Catholics in English-speaking countries.

DOUBLE-BARRED CROSS. See ARCHIEPISCOPAL CROSS.

DOUBLE CONSECRATION. The separate consecration of the bread and wine into the body and blood of Christ. This separate consecration constitutes the essence of the Mass as a renewal of Calvary. It symbolizes the death of Christ caused by the separation of his body and blood. All other parts of the Mass are not absolutely essential, even the priest's Communion, which, though gravely binding, belongs rather to the integrity than to the essence of the Eucharistic sacrifice.

DOUBLE EFFECT. The principle that says it is morally allowable to perform an act that has at least two effects, one good and one bad. It may be used under the following conditions: 1. the act to be done must be good in itself or at least morally indifferent; by the act to be done is meant the deed itself taken independently of its consequences; 2. the good effect must not be obtained by means of the evil effect; the evil must be only an incidental by-product and not an actual factor in the accomplishment of the good; 3. the evil effect must not be intended for itself but only permitted; all bad will must be excluded from the act; 4. there must be a proportionately grave reason for permitting the evil effect. At least the good and evil effects should be nearly equivalent. All four conditions must be fulfilled. If any one of them is not satisfied, the act is morally wrong.

An example of the lawful use of the double effect would be the commander of a submarine in wartime who torpedoes an armed merchant vessel of the enemy, although he foresees that several innocent children on board will be killed. All four required conditions are fulfilled: 1. he intends merely to lessen the power of the enemy by destroying an armed merchant ship. He does not wish to kill the innocent children; 2. his action of torpedoing the ship is not evil in itself; 3. the evil effect (the death of the children) is not the cause of the good effect (the lessening of the enemy's strength); 4. there is sufficient reason for permitting the evil effect to follow, and this reason is administering a damaging blow to those who are unjustly attacking his country.

DOUBLE STANDARD. The expressed or implied doctrine that there is no uniform code of morality for everyone, that some people have a standard different from that of the rest of humankind. The theory of a double standard is especially tempting to those in public office, whether civil or ecclesiastical. Their possession of authority and relative immunity to normal sanctions can lead them to require one level of behavior for others and another for themselves.

DOUBT. Hesitation of mind between contradictory views, accompanied by a fear of error. In methodical doubt a person is in a state of certainty but abstracts from this fact in order to critically examine the truth of some matter. It is the opposite of a real doubt. In practical doubt the mind is uncertain about a prudent course of action or the moral certitude about something to be done here and now. In speculative doubt there is uncertainty either about the mere truth or error of something or the merely abstract goodness of a course of action. Universal doubt is a state of suspended assent about any and every truth. In voluntary doubt the will enters to withhold assent even in the presence of sufficient evidence. (Etym. Latin *dubium*, doubt, deliberation; from *dubitare*.)

DOUBTFUL CONSCIENCE. A state of mind when it cannot certainly decide for or against a course of action and leaves the person unsure about the morality of what one is to do, or what one may have done. One sign of a doubtful conscience is that it gives rise to a positive judgment with a prudent fear of being wrong, or more commonly to a negative judgment in which the person does not know whether an act is lawful or not.

DOUBTING FAITH. The theory that, at least in modern times, it is quite possible to remain a good Catholic while positively doubting one or more articles of the faith. Implicit in the theory, condemned by the First Vatican Council, is the claim that "doubt is a spiritual exercise" that presupposes "permanent openness to truth." It ignores the fact that God always gives sufficient grace to believe, without either denial or doubt that what he revealed is certainly true.

DOVE. The universal symbol of the Holy Spirit. At Christ's baptism the Spirit's presence was noted by a dove descending upon Christ (Matthew 3:16; Mark 1:10, with similar passages in John and Luke). Accompanying the dove in art are the Seven Gifts of the Spirit, usually represented as parted tongues of fire. The dove with its seven flames is also emblematic of the sacrament of confirmation. Doves in numbers symbolize souls and are often portrayed with the chalice, representing their being fed with the Precious Blood of Christ. Carrying an olive branch, the dove is a symbol of peace. Surrounding the cross, twelve in orderly array, they signify the Apostles. St. Ambrose, St. Augustine, St. Gregory the Great, and St. John Chrysostom all have the dove as one of their emblems.

DOWRY. A prescribed amount of money or its equivalent brought to a community by a woman religious on her entrance into the convent. It is for her support and belongs to the community after profession. If she remains in the order, it may not be disposed of for any reason until after her death. Should she leave at any time, the dowry is returned to her but not any interest accruing from its investment. Dowry also applies to the money or property that a wife brings to her husband in marriage. (Etym. Latin *dotarium*, from *dos*, gift, marriage portion.)

DOWRY OF MARY. A title of praise given to the people of England in early times. As expressed in 1399 by Thomas Arundel (1353–1414), Archbishop of Canterbury: "We the English being the servants of her special inheritance and her own dowry, as we are commonly called, aught to surpass others in the warmth of our praise and devotion (to the Blessed Virgin Mary)." Also called Our Lady's Dowry.

DOXOL. *Doxologia*—doxology.

DOXOLOGY. A hymn or formula of praise to God. "Glory to God in the Highest," recited or sung at Mass, is known as the greater doxology. "Glory be to the Father and to the Son and to the Holy Spirit" is the lesser doxology. (Etym. Greek *doxa*, opinion, glory + *logia*, science, knowledge.)

D.R. *Decanus ruralis*—rural dean.

DRACHMA. A coin used as money; the Greeks originated the word. In the parable reported by Luke, the lost drachma was equivalent to the Roman denarius (Luke 15:8–10). Its value approximated a day's wages. (Etym. Greek *drachmē*, handful.)

DREAM INTERPRETATION. The personal or professional analysis of night (sleep) dreams, to ascertain their meaning. Night dreams are dreams in the proper sense of the term. In sleep, which is by no means a passive state, a person's sense of activity is not dominated by his higher faculties of reason and will. This sense activity, when natural, is due to a variety of traceable causes, such as the physical condition of the body, external stimuli, such as talking or the ringing of a bell, or psychical factors, such as desires, fears, past thoughts and experiences. Consequently there is some value in dream interpretation, in as much as human science may derive from dream analysis some useful data for the treatment and healing of sick individuals, especially those afflicted with some psychological abnormality or disease. If such therapy is indicated, the person should seek out a thoroughly reputable and honest therapist, who will not advise or do anything that is contrary to Christian moral teaching.

On the other hand, to believe in one's own dreams or those related by others as foretelling future events is a sin of superstition. The exceptional cases where dreams are of supernatural origin are to be judged on their own merits.

All the evidence from Scripture and the lives of the saints indicates that when God makes use of dreams as an extraordinary means of communication he also makes sure the person realizes where the dream originated. The standard rules for discernment of spirits are to be applied in case of doubt whether a dream is of supernatural origin.

DREAMS. The effect of psychic activity protracted in sleep. Their religious significance derives from many sources, not the least of which is the frequency with which the Scriptures speak of dreams, in the Old and New Testaments, and indicate that sometimes God uses this means of communicating with human beings.

Dream representations are largely expressed in visual form, but auditory, olfactory, and taste dreams also occur. Although the structure of dreams is disorganized, nevertheless dreams do contain a latent meaning. They may be considered as a symbolic transference of situations, ideas, and sentiments previously experienced by the dreamer.

DRESS, CLERICAL. See CLERICAL DRESS.

DRUG ABUSE, MORALITY OF. The use of any drug, although medicinal in original purpose, has grave moral implications, to the degree that it seriously affects a person's social adjustment, physical or mental health.

DRUNKENNESS. Overindulgence in alcoholic beverages. On Catholic moral principles, the degree of sinfulness in excessive drinking depends on how this excess is known to affect this particular drinker. It is a grave matter if it is foreseen that this drink will cause one to lose the use of one's senses or will put one in such a state that he or she is no longer able to distinguish right from wrong. It is a venial matter if one has reason for believing that this amount of drinking, though actually excessive, will neither deprive one of the use of one's senses or of the power to distinguish right from wrong.

DRUSILLA. The youngest daughter of Herod Agrippa I, the king who ordered the Apostle James beheaded and who persecuted Peter. She was the wife of Felix (Acts 24:24), the Roman procurator who presided at the trial of Paul in which Tertullus, the prosecutor, described the accused as follows: "The plain truth is that we find this man a perfect pest; he stirs up trouble among Jews the world over, and is a ringleader of the Nazarene sect" (Acts 24:5). Drusilla listened with interest to Paul explain his faith later in a private hearing before Felix. (Etym. Latin feminine form of Drusus.)

DRY MASS. A shortened form of the Mass, customary in the Middle Ages, in which the Offertory, Canon, and Communion were omitted. It was used on a variety of occasions, such as when a second Mass on the same day was forbidden; at a pilgrimage; when a priest who was still fasting was not available; on board ship in stormy weather, then called a "naval Mass"; and during hunting expeditions, called a hunter's Mass. It survives among certain priest-monks who say a Dry Mass of Our Lady, and in the ceremony for the blessing of Palms on Palm Sunday.

DS. *Deus*—God.

D.SC. *Doctor Scientiae* (*Scientiarum*)— Doctor of Science(s).

DUALISM. Any view of reality that holds there are two fundamentally and irreducibly different types of being or operations. Thus God and the world, spirit and matter, intellect and will, truth and error, virtue and sin are typical expressions of dualism. (Etym. Latin *dualis;* from *duo,* two.)

DUE. A debt; the object of justice. It is the objective right or service payable to another; the legal "debitum." Theologically the due is the good of a nature; something needed by a created nature, and sufficient for this nature either in its constitution, powers, destiny or in its means to attain its purpose of existence. In this sense, what is due is contrasted with the gratuitous character of the supernatural. Thus nature is said to be due to man, grace is freely conferred by God.

DUELING. The meeting of two parties by private agreement to fight with weapons that can cause death. A duel is undertaken to settle a real or alleged grievance between the contending parties. It is forbidden by the natural law and strictly forbidden by the Catholic Church as partaking of the malice of both suicide and homicide. Dueling is not a case of justifiable self-defense because there is no attack occurring at the time; the injured party may obtain satisfaction through legal or other channels; recourse to deadly weapons is powerless to vindicate one's honor; and dueling is not an apt means of proving one's innocence, since the guilty person may be more skillful than the aggrieved in the use of the weapons selected.

DULIA. Reverence of a disciple for his master or of a servant for his lord. It is the honor given to the angels and saints as friends of God. (Etym. Greek *douleia,* servitude, subjection.)

DURATION. Continuing existence or persistence in existence. This may be temporal if a thing finally ceases to exist, as with animals; or interrupted if a thing ceases to exist for a while but is later restored, as with a person's body; or endless if a thing, once created, will always endure, as a person's soul.

DUTY. The moral obligation to do or to omit something. This is duty taken subjectively. Understood objectively, duty is the thing that must be done or omitted. The difference is expressed in the two statements "He has a duty," meaning that a person is morally obliged, and "He does his duty," meaning that a person does the thing he is obliged to do.

Rights and duties are correlative and complementary. Thus if one person has a right, everyone else has a duty to respect that right. And if one has a duty, one also has the right to fulfill that duty and do all the things that are necessary for its fulfillment; otherwise it would not be a genuine duty. Nevertheless, while having a right, a person does not necessarily have a duty to exercise that right. In fact, no one can exercise all one's rights but must choose among them, for some of them are simultaneously incompatible, as the right to stand and the right to sit. God is the only exception to the mutual dependence of rights and duties. He has all rights and no strict duties; creatures have duties to him but no rights against him; human beings have both rights and duties toward one another.

D.V. *Deo volente*—God willing; Douay Version.

DYNAMISM. A philosophical theory that denies the reality of extended matter or mass in the world. It seeks to explain the phenomena in the universe chiefly or only in terms of force or energy, notably material energy. (Etym. Greek *dynamis,* power.)

DYSTELEOLOGY. Lack of purpose or design, either as a result of thoughtless action on someone's part or as a theory of despair that sees no providence in the world but only confusion and disorder. (Etym. Greek *dys,* apart + *telos,* end, completion + *logia,* science, knowledge.)

E

E., ECCL. *Ecclesia*—the Church.

EAGLE. The symbol of St. John the Evangelist, whose gospel emphasizes the divinity of Christ. Flying higher than any other bird, the eagle is also an emblem of John's mystical doctrine about the indwelling Trinity and the heights of prayer available to those who love Christ. The eagle is also a sign of Christ's Ascension.

EASTER. The day commemorating Christ's Resurrection from the dead. It is the greatest of all Christian festivals, having the central place in the liturgical year. It is the Christian feast linked with the Jewish Pasch. The exultant Alleluia is constantly repeated in the Mass and Divine Office, the *Vidi Aquam* replaces the *Asperges,* and the *Regina Coeli* the Angelus. The Easter season continues from Easter Sunday to Trinity

Sunday inclusive. (Etym. Anglo-Saxon *Eastre,* Teutonic goddess of dawn and spring.)

EASTER COMMUNION. Reception of the Holy Eucharist, as prescribed by the Church, during the Easter season, which differs among countries, but generally between Ash Wednesday (or the first Sunday of Lent) and Trinity Sunday. Also called "Easter Duty," it includes the reception of the sacrament of penance. Children (*puberes*) are also to make their Easter duty, and the obligation rests on parents, guardians, and the pastor to see that this duty is fulfilled.

EASTER CONTROVERSY. A protracted dispute in the second and third centuries over the date for celebration of Easter. The Eastern Church terminated Lent and began Easter celebration on the fourteenth day of Nisan regardless of the day of the week on which this date fell. The Jews celebrated Passover then, and the Pasch kept by Christ was also on that day. It was claimed that this practice was received from the Apostles Philip and John. The Western Church always celebrated the Christian Pasch on the Sunday following the fourteenth day of the full moon of the vernal equinox because it was the anniversary of Christ's resurrection. Westerners said that this tradition came from Sts. Peter and Paul. Schism was probably averted by the excommunication threat of Pope Victor I for all who would not follow the Roman custom. St. Irenaeus (130–200) pleaded with the Pope for leniency. Although the Eastern Christians did not comply, the controversy took a new direction when the Church of Antioch accepted the first Sunday after the fourteenth day of Nisan instead of after the vernal equinox. Disagreements continued until the Council of Nicaea (A.D. 325) paved the way for a final settlement by decreeing that Easter must be universally celebrated in the Christian world on the Sunday following the fourteenth day of the paschal moon, whose fourteenth day followed the spring equinox. The Roman Church adopted a cycle of ninety-five years for determining the Easter date, but the Celtic Church still followed a cycle of 532 years and the Sunday for celebration was different. By the ninth century the Celts conceded and the 95-year cycle was followed everywhere.

EASTER DUTY. The grave obligation that every Catholic has to receive Holy Communion during the Easter season, which differs in various countries. Thus, in the United States it is from the first Sunday of Lent to Trinity Sunday inclusive; in other countries the season may begin on Ash Wednesday and close on Low Sunday or Ascension Thursday.

EASTER FIRE. The fire, made of dry wood, that begins the liturgy of the Easter Vigil on Holy Saturday. It represents Christ's resurrection. While the fire is being blessed, the priest says, "Let us pray. Father, we share in the light of your glory through your Son, the light of the world. Make this new fire holy, and inflame us with new hope. Purify our minds by this Easter celebration, and bring us one day to the feast of eternal light. We ask this through Christ our Lord." To which the people answer, "Amen."

EASTERN CHURCHES. Christian churches whose members follow the Eastern rites as a body. Historically they were the Patriarchates of Constantinople, Alexandria, Antioch, and Jerusalem before the schism in the thirteenth century. They follow the ceremonies originally used by the Patriarch of Constantinople. The groups not in communion with Rome are called the separated Eastern Churches; the others are Catholic Churches of their respective Eastern rites.

EASTERN SCHISM. Separation of the Christian Churches of the East from unity with Rome. The schism was centuries in the making and finally became fixed in 1054, when the Patriarch of Constantinople, Michael Cerularius (died 1059), was excommunicated by the papal legates for opposing the use of leavened bread by the Latin Church and removing the Pope's name from the diptychs or list of persons to be prayed for in the Eucharistic liturgy. A temporary reunion with Rome was effected by the Second Council of Lyons (1274) and the Council of Florence (1439) but never stabilized.

EASTER VIGIL. The ceremonies of Holy Saturday and the most solemn memorial of the liturgical year. They consist of four parts: Service of the Light, Liturgy of the Word, Liturgy of Baptism, and Liturgy of the Eucharist. The entire celebration takes place at night, and therefore it should not begin before nightfall and should end before dawn on Easter Sunday. In the early Church the night before Easter was celebrated by the illumination of the churches and even of whole cities. The revised Easter Vigil services include ceremonies that go back to the first centuries of the Christian era and stress the Church's joy in commemorating the night that Christ rose from the dead.

EASTER WATER. The solemn blessing of water during the Easter Vigil ceremonies. The culminating point in the liturgy is the lowering of the Easter candle (representing Christ) into the water and raising it again, up to three times. This symbolizes how Christ was lowered into death and rose from the tomb. The water becomes a symbol of both death and life, of humanity's death to sin through repentance and of rising with Christ in the newness of supernatural life. The water is used for the administration of baptism, which follows during the Easter Vigil.

EASTWARD POSITION. The practice of a priest at Mass standing on the west side of the altar and facing east, which was introduced in Rome in the eighth century. In the Anglican Communion the eastward position is observed in many churches.

EBIONITES. Two early Christian sects that professed Judaistic and Gnostic errors. The Judaistic Ebionites insisted on the continued observance of the Mosaic Law, denied Christ's divinity and virginal conception, considered St. Paul an apostate, and used only Matthew's Gospel. The Gnostic Ebionites held that matter is eternal and emanates from God; that it constitutes his body; that creation is therefore only a transformation of pre-existing material; that the universe is composed of two elements, the good and the evil; that the Son of God rules over the good part of the world and the devil over the evil.

ECCL. *Ecclesiasticus*—ecclesiastic; ecclesiastical.

ECCLESIA. The unchanged Latin rendering of the Greek *ekklēsia*, meaning assembly or community. The Bible uses the term in the Septuagint translation of the Hebrew *kahal* in both a secular and a religious sense. In the New Testament the word is used of the whole community of the believers in Christ (Matthew 16:18) and of a single community of the faithful (Romans 6:5). The Catechism of the Council of Trent defines *Ecclesia* as the Church, which is the faithful of the whole world (I, 10, 2). (Etym. Latin *ecclesia*, universal or an individual Church; from Greek *ekklēsia*, assembly of people called together.)

ECCLESIA DISCENS. The learning Church. A term applied to all the faithful insofar as they are being taught by the successors of the Apostles. The basis for the expression is Christ's commission to the eleven before the Ascension, "Go, therefore, make disciples of all nations" (Matthew 28:19).

ECCLESIA DOCENS. The teaching Church. A term applied to the hierarchy, that is, the Pope and the bishops in union with him, speaking in their divinely authorized capacity of teaching the faithful in matters pertaining to salvation and sanctification.

ECCLESIAE SANCTAE. An apostolic letter issued *motu proprio* by Pope Paul VI, giving the norms by which four decrees of the Second Vatican Council are to be implemented, namely *Christus Dominus* (Pastoral Office of Bishops), *Presbyterorum Ordinis* (Ministry and Life of Priests), *Perfectae Caritatis* (Renewal and Adaptation of Religious Life), and *Ad Gentes Divinitus* (Missionary Activity of the Church). This document is the single most important postconciliar declaration of the Holy See to understand the Church's mind on the four areas of the episcopacy, priesthood, religious life, and the missions (August 6, 1966).

ECCLESIAL. Pertaining to the Church as the community of believers, with stress on their faith and union through love, and on the invisible operations of divine grace among the faithful.

ECCLESIASTES. A book of the Old Testament, called in Hebrew *Koheleth* or in English "the Preacher." Once held to have been written by Solomon, now agreed that the author is unknown. The theme of the book is the transient character of all earthly goods, compared with the true wisdom that is found in the fear of the Lord. Though sober in tone, it is not pessimistic, since hope for happiness is held out to those who direct their lives according to reason and the will of God. (Etym. Greek *ekklēsiastes*, preacher; Hebrew *Qōheleth*.)

ECCLESIASTICAL. Pertaining to the Church as an organized body, with stress on its juridical and institutional structure.

ECCLESIASTICAL LAW. An ordinance issued by legitimate authority in the Catholic Church. The legislators for the entire Church are the Roman Pontiff alone, or the Pope through the Roman Curia, or an ecumenical council together with the Pope; the bishops for their individual dioceses, or conferences of bishops for the territories under their jurisdiction; and the major superiors of institutes of perfection for their members, according to the respective constitutions.

The Catholic Church has always professed her right to pass laws that are binding on the consciences of the faithful. This right is believed to be of divine origin, since "the Church, our most prudent Mother, by the constitution received from her Founder, Christ, was endowed with all the qualities suitable to a perfect society. So, too, from her very beginning, since she was to obey the Lord's command to teach and govern all nations, she has undertaken to regulate and protect by the laws the discipline of clergy and laity alike" (Benedict XV, *Providentissima Mater Ecclesia,* May 27, 1917).

Every baptized person, even if one is not a professed Catholic, is subject to ecclesiastical laws except in such cases as are indicated in the law. The obligation stems from the fact that by the sacrament of baptism "we are made members of Christ and of his body, the Church" (*Council of Florence,* Denzinger 1314). Baptism is, in fact, the *janua Ecclesiae,* the door of the Church. Since the baptismal character is indelible, a person once baptized always remains subject to the Church into which he or she was incorporated by this sacrament of water and the Holy Spirit.

ECCLESIASTICAL OBEDIENCE. The duty of Catholics to obey the precepts of the Church. The gravity of the obligation depends on the gravity of the matter prescribed. The traditional Precepts of the Church are merely the outstanding obligations that Catholics are bound to obey. Actually the whole common law of the Church obliges the faithful in conscience, depending on their state of life and the intention of the Church in making the various prescriptions.

ECCLESIASTICAL TRADITION. The revealed word of God as entrusted to the Church to be faithfully preserved, resolutely defended, authentically interpreted, validly developed, and effectively applied in the lives of the People of God.

ECCLESIASTICAL YEAR. See LITURGICAL YEAR.

ECCLESIASTICUS. A book of the Old Testament, also known as "The Wisdom of Jesus, Son of Sirach." Originally written in Hebrew, it was highly prized by the Jews, particularly of the Dispersion, and by the early Christians, next to the Psalms and the Gospels. It is the longest didactic book of the Old Testament. After an exhortation to seek wisdom, it offers a series of practical precepts. The transition 42:15 to 43:28 is a sublime hymn extolling God's work in nature. In the second part (44 to 50:23) God is praised in the lives of the heroes of Israel. Noteworthy is chapter 24, introducing un-

created wisdom, speaking as a divine person, although the idea of a distinct substance is not expressed. New Testament references to Ecclesiasticus are numerous.

ECKHARTISM. General name for the spiritual teaching of Meister Eckhart (1260–1327), the German Dominican mystic and of his followers. In 1329, Pope John XXII condemned twenty-eight of Eckhart's sentences as heretical or dangerous, e.g.: "We are totally transformed into God and changed into Him . . . Though a person commits a thousand mortal sins, if he is rightly disposed, he should not wish not to have committed them . . . A good man is the only begotten Son of God." Investigation of his doctrine has since indicated Eckhart's personal orthodoxy, while admitting indiscretion in language and the fact that his writings have been used by persons unfavorable to the Church, as Kant to defend agnostic idealism, Hegel to defend pantheism, and Rosenberg to defend Nazism.

ECLECTICISM. The principle or practice of drawing on different religions in order to form a coherent unity, while omitting the elements in each religion that do not fit into that unity. Eclecticism is commonplace in all philosophers and many theologians. It is also part of the history of all religions, with the notable exception of Christianity. Its Founder was no mere eclectic. He did not depend on the wisdom of other religious leaders, even when he used their insight, as in building on the prophets of ancient Israel. One of the developments of the Second Vatican Council was the recognition of so many elements of truth in the non-Christian religions that the Church may legitimately cultivate in her work of evangelization without becoming eclectic and sacrificing what is essential in the proclamation of the Gospel. (Etym. Greek *eklektikos,* selecting.)

ECSTASY. In general, the state of being beside oneself through some overpowering experience. As a mystical phenomenon, it includes two elements, one interior and the other exterior. The invisible element consists in the mind being riveted on a religious subject. The corporeal aspect means that the activity of the senses is suspended, so that not only are external sensations unable to influence the soul, but these sensations become very difficult to awaken. Many saints have received ecstasies as a supernatural gift from God, although ecstasy of itself is not a criterion of holiness. (Etym. Greek *ekstasis;* from *ex,* out + *histanai,* to cause to stand: *existanai,* to derange.) See also RAPTURE.

ECUMENICAL. Literally "universal" and commonly used to identify the general councils of the Church. With the rise of the movement for Christian unity, it has become synonymous with "striving for reunification" among the separated Churches of Christendom. (Etym. Latin *oecumenicus;* from Greek *oikoumenē,* the inhabited world.)

ECUMENICAL COUNCILS

Following are the ecumenical councils of the Roman Catholic Church, with dates and a brief statement of their principal legislation.

1. Nicaea I (325)
   Condemned Arianism, defined that the Son of God is consubstantial with the Father, formulated the Nicene Creed.
2. Constantinople I (381)
   Condemned the Macedonians who denied the divinity of the Holy Spirit. Confirmed and extended the Nicene Creed.
3. Ephesus (431)
   Condemned Nestorianism, which held that there were two distinct persons in the Incarnate Christ, a human and divine. Defended the right of Mary to be called the Mother of God.
4. Chalcedon (451)
   Condemned Monophysitism or Eutychianism by defining that Christ had two distinct natures, and was therefore true God and true man.
5. Constantinople II (553)
   Pronounced against certain persons as infected with Nestorianism, notably Theodore of Mopsuestia, Theodoret of Cyrrhus and Ibas of Edessa.
6. Constantinople III (680–81)
   Defined against the Monothelites that Christ has two wills, human and divine.
7. Nicaea II (787)
   Condemned the Iconoclasts or Imagebreakers and defined that sacred images may be honored without idolatry.
8. Constantinople IV (869–70)
   Condemned Photius as Patriarch of Constantinople.
9. Lateran I (1123)
   First general council in the West, endorsed the Concordat of Worms regarding the investiture of prelates.
10. Lateran II (1139)
    Took measures against the schism of the antipope Anacletus II and issued disciplinary decrees.
11. Lateran III (1179)
    Legislated against the Waldenses and Albigensians and decreed papal elections by two-thirds majority of cardinals at conclave.
12. Lateran IV (1215)
    Made reform decrees, ordered annual confession and Easter Communion, first officially used the term "transubstantiation."
13. Lyons I (1245)
    Condemned Frederick II for his persecution of the Church.
14. Lyons II (1274)
    Effected a temporary reunion of the Eastern Churches with Rome and decreed that papal elections should begin ten days after the death of the Pope.
15. Vienne (1311–12)
    Suppressed the Knights Templar, sought aid for the Holy Land, defined the relation of the soul to the human body, and condemned the false mysticism of the Fraticelli, Dulcinists, Beghards, and Beguines.
16. Constance (1414–18)
    Issued reform decrees in "head and members," condemned Wyclif and Hus, and put an end to the Western Schism.
17. Florence (1438–45)
    Affirmed the papal primacy against Conciliarists, who said that a general council was superior to the Pope, and sought to effect a reunion of the Eastern Churches separated from Rome.
18. Lateran V (1512–17)
    Defined the relation of Pope to a general council, condemned philosophers who taught the human soul was mortal and only one for all mankind, and called for a crusade against the Turks.
19. Trent (1545–63)
    Called to meet the crisis of the Protestant Reformation; proclaimed the Bible and tradition as rule of faith, defined doctrine on the Mass, the sacraments, justification, purgatory, indulgences, invocation of saints, veneration of sacred images, issued decrees on marriage and clerical reform.
20. Vatican I (1869–70)
    Defined the nature of revelation and faith, the relation of faith and reason, and papal infallibility; condemned pantheism, materialism, deism, naturalism, and fideism.
21. Vatican II (1962–65)
    Convoked by Pope John XXIII, "mainly to more effectively preserve and present the sacred deposit of Christian doctrine." Its sixteen documents reaffirmed the principles of Catholic

faith and morality, and authorized numerous developments in the Eucharistic liturgy, the ritual of the sacraments, and in the Church's administrative structure.

ECUMENICAL THEOLOGY. Systematic reflection on the principles and postulates of the ecumenical movement, notably among Protestant and Eastern theologians. They hope to find the way that leads beyond mere co-operation to a true unity that will make it clear to the whole world that, as there can only be one Body of Christ, so there is only one Body which is the Church of his people. The basic problem, therefore, is ecclesiological.

At one extreme are theologians who believe there is strength in doctrinal divergence, for whom the ecumenical movement should lead only to a federated co-operation among the churches with no ambition to organic unity. They are "keenly sensitive to the gains in vitality" that come from Church differences. At the other extreme are Eastern churchmen for whom the unity of the Church already exists and in fact is to be found within the exclusive limits of their own communion.

Between these extremes lie the majority of Protestant and Orthodox positions in the ecumenical movement. They are undecided either on the nature of the Church or on the kind of unity it is supposed to have. Some maintain that "the unity of the Catholic (not Roman) church is an existing historic reality" within certain theoretical boundaries. Their problem is in defining these boundaries, within which the Church may be united and beyond which diversity is allowed.

Others believe that the Church is a purely invisible entity, a community known only to God. Its unity, therefore, is also known only to him, and the task of theology is to give better expression to this existent—so far mostly invisible—unity among the divided members.

Still others hold that the Church is essentially all those who profess and call themselves Christians, however diverse their belief and practice. This seems to be the majority opinion in the present World Council of Churches.

The Roman Catholic Church has not been indifferent to the efforts of scholars outside her ranks to reunite a dismembered Christian world. Catholic theologians have promoted the most extensive study of church unity since the Reformation. While holding firm to their conviction that unity is possible only through union with the See of Peter, they stress the sincerity of ecumenical efforts outside of Rome and the presence of the Holy Spirit in such deliberations.

ECUMENISM. The modern movement toward Christian unity whose Protestant origins stem from the Edinburgh World Missionary Conference in 1910, and whose Catholic principles were formulated by the Second Vatican Council in 1964. These principles are mainly three: 1. Christ established his Church on the Apostles and their episcopal successors, whose visible head and principle of unity became Peter and his successor the Bishop of Rome; 2. since the first century there have been divisions in Christianity, but many persons now separated from visible unity with the successors of the Apostles under Peter are nevertheless Christians who possess more or less of the fullness of grace available in the Roman Catholic Church; 3. Catholics are to do everything possible to foster the ecumenical movement, which comprehends all "the initiatives and activities, planned and undertaken to promote Christian unity, according to the Church's various needs and as opportunities offer" (*Decree on Ecumenism*, I, 4).

EDEN. The beautiful garden in which God put Adam and Eve. After they disobeyed him, they were expelled (Genesis 2, 3). It is a word used in Scripture to suggest an ideal place to live (Isaiah 51:3; Ezekiel 31:9).

EDICT OF NANTES. The decree that ended the French wars of religion, signed by Henry IV (1553–1610) at Nantes on April 13, 1598. The Huguenots were allowed to practice their religion, with certain restrictions. Louis XIV (1638–1715) revoked the edict in 1685.

EDIFICATION. St. Paul's term for the way Christians should behave and thus give witness by their good example, for the upbuilding of the Mystical Body of Christ (Romans 14:18; I Corinthians 14:5; II Corinthians 10:8; Ephesians 4:29). (Etym. Latin *aedificare*, to instruct or improve spiritually; from *aedes*, temple, house.)

EDUCTION. In the philosophy of nature the actualization of a form, whether substantial or accidental, out of a subject in which it had been potentially. Distinguished from infusion, whereby a human soul is specially created and united with the body.

EFFECT. Something brought about by some cause or agency; the result of some action. In morality the intended effect or purpose partially determines whether an act is good or evil. And in the principle of the double effect the morality of an action depends on whether a foreseen evil effect is merely permitted or directly willed by a person.

EFFICACIOUS GRACE. The actual grace to which free consent is given by the will so that the grace produces its divinely intended effect. In the controversy between the Dominicans [led by Báñez (1528–1604)] and the Jesuits [led by Molina (1525–1600)] there was no agreement on what precisely causes an actual grace to become efficacious. In the Báñezian theory, the efficacy of such grace depends on the character of the grace itself; in the Molinist theory, it depends on the fact that it is given under circumstances that God foresees to be congruous with the dispositions of the person receiving the grace. In every Catholic theory, however, it is agreed that efficacious grace does not necessitate the will or destroy human freedom. (Etym. Latin *efficax*, powerful, effective, efficient, *gratia*, favor freely given.) See also ACTUAL GRACE, GRACE, GRATUITOUS GRACE, HABITUAL GRACE, JUSTIFYING GRACE, SACRAMENTAL GRACE, SANATING GRACE, SANCTIFYING GRACE, SUFFICIENT GRACE.

EFFICIENT CAUSE. An agent in the production of any effect. It is that which, by its activity or exercise of power, produces existence or change in another. See also CAUSE, FINAL CAUSE, FIRST CAUSE, FORMAL CAUSE, FREE CAUSE, MATERIAL CAUSE, MORAL CAUSE, NECESSARY CAUSE, SECONDARY CAUSE.

EGO. In moral philosophy the conscious and permanent subject of one's own mental experiences and free decisions.

EGOISM. The morally sinful pursuit of one's own advantage, while ignoring the law and the interests of other people. In this it differs from egocentrism, which may be unconscious. It is, however, worse than selfishness, which need not be indifferent to others' needs.

EGYPTIAN CROSS. A pagan emblem, also known as "ankh," whose ancient meaning was "life." The top of the perpendicular bar was looped, the ends centered at the junction of the sidearms. Later the Christians made it a symbol of supernatural life that Christ merited by his cross. See also CRUX ANSATA.

EIGHTH CRUSADE. The last Crusade (1270), undertaken by St. Louis of France (1214–70), with the aid of his brother,

Charles of Anjou. After an attack on Tunis, St. Louis died there in 1270, and Charles concluded the crusade by negotiating peace with the Moslems. Soon after, the whole former Latin Kingdom of Jerusalem, established by the Christians, after the First Crusade, in A.D. 1100, passed into the hands of Islam.

EINSIEDELN, OUR LADY OF. Marian shrine in the Benedictine Abbey chapel at Einsiedeln in Switzerland. A Brother Meinrad, in 840, retired from the Benedictine monastery at Reichenau to the forest nearby, hoping to lead a more austere life. He took with him a small statue of Mary and her Son, and his cell became Our Lady's small chapel. This simple statue showed the Christ Child resting on his mother's left arm, while his little hand is raised in blessing. Twenty-three years later the old monk was murdered by bandits who thought he had hidden gold and treasure in his mountain hideout. Through the years the monk's former cell was the scene of many unusual favors and graces. It was enclosed later in a large church where it became a shrine to "Our Lady of the Hermits," as she was called. The statue is now enthroned in the abbey's splendid Chapel of Grace. Brother Meinrad has since been canonized.

EJACULATION. See ASPIRATION.

EL. *Electio, electus*—election, elect.

ELDER. See PRESBYTER.

ELDERS. The older men in a community acting as a governing body (I Samuel 16:4). The Sanhedrin, for instance, was made up of elders (Exodus 3:16). They were mentioned in Matthew as joining the chief priests in challenging Jesus during his ministry (Matthew 27:12). The traditional system carried over into Christian communities. The Apostles appointed elders to take charge of each church (Acts 14:23). According to the Council of Trent, the elders mentioned by St. James as administrators of the sacrament of anointing (James 5:14) "does not refer to the older men nor to the more influential men in the community, but to the bishops or the priests duly ordained by the bishops through the laying on of hands of the presbyterate" (Denzinger 1697).

ELEAZAR. Eleven men bore this name in the Old Testament. The best known was a son of Aaron who became a Levite leader and succeeded his father as high priest under Moses and later Joshua (Numbers

3:32; Exodus 6:23). His most significant work possibly was the apportionment of land in Canaan to the Israelites (Joshua 14:1–2).

ELECTION. The act of choice or selection of suitable means to an end, made by an intelligent being. In biblical terms the divine election is God's choice of certain people for a given mission he wanted them to fulfill. Thus Paul was a "chosen instrument" (Acts 9:15), and all Christians "have been chosen" (I Thessalonians 1:4).

ELECTION BY COMPROMISE. In ecclesiastical law an election in which the voters by unanimous and written consent agree to transfer for that one election the right of election into the hands of one or several qualified persons, either of their own body or outsiders, who shall by the power thus received hold the election in the name of all.

ELEGY. A sorrowful poem, generally commemorating the dead. The best known Christian elegy is the *Dies Irae*. (Etym. Latin *elegia*, poem in elegiac couplets; from Greek *elegos*, song of mourning.)

ELEVATION OF THE HOST. Raising of the consecrated Host for the faithful's adoration at Mass, before the consecration of the chalice, which is elevated separately for adoration immediately afterward. This separate elevation is to profess the Real Presence of Christ's Body already before the consecration of the chalice.

ELICITED ACTS. Those human acts that immediately flow from a spiritual faculty or power. They are the internal function of these faculties, by themselves, and therefore not the mere faculties, nor the preparatory stages to their operation, nor the influence of their operation on other powers. Thus an act of love, as such, is an elicited act of the will, remaining in and perfecting the will; and an act of thinking, as such, is an elicited act of the mind, which remains in and perfects the intellect.

ELIJAH. One of the greatest religious leaders of the Israelite people. He lived in the ninth century before Christ, and his influence dominated Hebrew thought for centuries although he left no writings. He was an unusual man, unconventional, physically robust, a man who survived many ordeals (I Kings 17–21). In an arduous trip across the desert to Mount Horeb, he reenacted the experiences of Moses when he received the law. His communications with God amplified the application of the Ten

Commandments in an era of more complex social life. To prove the authenticity of his God, Elijah triumphed over the prophets of Baal in a contest, a vindication that established the Hebrew religion firmly and ended the drought that had afflicted Israel (I Kings 18:22–40). In his old age Elijah chose Elisha as his successor (II Kings 2:15). Presumably he went to heaven without dying, and it was an established belief that one day he would reappear on earth to restore Israel's glory (II Kings 2:11). Many people, in fact, mistook Jesus for Elijah (Matthew 16:14). At the Transfiguration it was Moses and Elijah who appeared with Christ (Matthew 17:3). At the Jewish Passover the door is opened in anticipation of his return and a cup of wine is poured out for him. Elijah is also spelled Elias.

ELIZABETH. A descendant of Aaron, she married Zechariah and, late in life, bore him a son destined to be known as John the Baptist (Luke 1:5–13). During her pregnancy she received a visit from her kinswoman, Mary, who had received the word from the angel Gabriel that she was to be the mother of Jesus. This meeting of the two mothers-to-be was the occasion of Mary's proclamation of the Magnificat (Luke 1:46–55). Within several months Elizabeth's child was born. Her friends urged her to name him after his father, but in obedience to Gabriel's revelation to Zechariah, he was named John. "And indeed," concluded Luke, "the hand of the Lord was with him" (Luke 1:66). (Etym. Greek form of Hebrew *elishebha,* god is fullness.)

ELOHIM. The Hebrew word most frequently used for God. It appears several thousand times in the Old Testament. It was also used in a plural sense to designate heathen gods (Genesis 35:2, Exodus 18:11). When Jesus was heard to say on the Cross "Eli, Eli, lama sabachtani," he was using a modified form of Elohim (Matthew 27:46).

EL SHADDAI. Another name for God. "God said to Moses, 'I am Yahweh. To Abraham and Isaac and Jacob I appeared as El Shaddai. I did not make myself known to them by my name Yahweh!'" (Exodus 6:3). This is corroborated by reference to texts in Genesis where God used this name in speaking to Abraham and Jacob (Genesis 17:1; 35:11).

ELVIRA, COUNCIL OF. National Council of Spain, held about A.D. 306 after a period of persecution. Among the eighty-one canons it passed are severe disciplinary penalties for apostasy and adultery. Celibacy of the clergy was legislated under pain of deposition (canon 33).

E.M. *Episcopus et martyr*—bishop and martyr.

EMANATION. In the philosophy of emanationism, the flowing out of all things from the divine substance and therefore also that which has flowed out. The emanation is considered a necessary attribute of the divine substance, and that which emanates is said (like rays of light) to lose in perfection as it flows out. As a form of pantheism, emanationism was condemned by the Second Vatican Council, since God, who is absolutely simple and unchangeable, cannot pour out of his being. (Etym. Latin *emanatio,* discharge, flowing from.)

EMBALMING. The temporary or prolonged preservation of a deceased body, for practical and religious reasons. Best known ancient embalming was in Egypt, some of whose mummies are relatively intact to the present day. In modern procedure, the blood is drained from a person's veins and replaced by a fluid, such as formalin, a solution of formaldehyde in water. Embalming by arterial injection became common in Western countries since the eighteen hundreds. In the early centuries, the Church rejected any form of embalming as a pagan custom, although there were notable exceptions, like Charlemagne, whose embalmed corpse was placed in a sitting position in his tomb at Aachen where he died in A.D. 814. The chief purpose of embalming is to give the deceased person a lifelike appearance for several days after death. There is no ecclesiastical legislation on the subject.

EMBER DAYS. Three days set apart for fasting, abstinence, and prayer during each of the four seasons of the year. They were the Wednesday, Friday, and Saturday after St. Lucy (d. 304) (December 13), the First Sunday of Lent, Pentecost, and the feast of the Holy Cross (September 14). Since the revision of the Roman calendar in 1969, Ember Days are to be observed at the discretion of the National Conferences of Bishops. Moreover, their observance may be extended beyond three days and even repeated during the year. Possibly occasioned by the agricultural feasts of ancient Rome, they came to be observed by Christians for the sanctification of the different seasons of the year, and for obtaining God's blessing on the clergy to be ordained during the Embertides. (Etym. Anglo-Saxon *oēmerge,* ashes.)

EMBLEM. A device or badge associated symbolically with a person or thing suggesting some ideal or spiritual sentiment. Thus a cross is an emblem of sacrifice, an anchor of hope, a palm of victory or martyrdom. Emblems were used in the early days to express the mysteries of the Catholic faith, to give inspiration and protect spiritual doctrines from the ridicule of unbelievers. Badges distinctive of a society and banners in Church may also be classified as emblems. They should always be clearly symbolic of a religious truth and consistent with Catholic faith and practice. Emblems also give expression to certain virtues practiced by individual saints, e.g., the eagle is an emblem of the sublimity of St. John the Evangelist.

EMBOLISM. The prayer in the Canon of the Mass which begins, "Deliver us, Lord, from every evil," inserted between the Our Father and the Breaking of the Bread. Many Eastern liturgies have a similar prayer. An embolism is also the difference of days in the calendar between the lunar year of 354 days and the solar year of 365¼ days, commonly known as the "epact." (Etym. Greek *emballein,* to insert, intercalate.)

EMINENT GOOD WORKS. The three principal good works in Christianity are prayer, fasting, and almsgiving.

EMMANUEL. The biblical word for "God with us." A prophetic name used by Isaiah foreshadowing the coming of Jesus (Isaiah 7:14). The belief that the child would be born in Bethlehem and would be "the one who is to rule over Israel" is advanced by another prophet, Micah (Micah 5:2).

EMMAUS. A village about seven miles from Jerusalem. It was on the road to Emmaus that two disciples met the risen Jesus and accompanied him to the village (Luke 24:13–35). Not until he broke bread at supper did they recognize him. Then he disappeared and they hastened back to Jerusalem to tell the Apostles of the encounter.

EMOTION. In spiritual theology, any human tendency or inclination in which the senses participate. Sometimes called concupiscence, it is produced by the awareness of good or evil in the imagination. It is said to be antecedent when the emotion precedes the action of the will and induces the will to consent. This takes place, for example, in the involuntary movements of anger, hatred, or sexual arousal. The emotion is called consequent when it follows the free decision of the will and is either freely consented to or deliberately aroused.

Antecedent emotion always lessens imputability and at times may remove it entirely, depending on the degree to which it either hinders the powers of reason to think clearly or of the will to consent freely. Consequent emotion never lessens imputability, but generally increases it, especially when a person deliberately fosters certain feelings, say of anger or sex, in order to perform an action more effectively or derive greater pleasure from sinful indulgence. (Etym. Latin *emovere*, to stir up, agitate.)

EMPATHY. A function of the virtue of charity by which a person enters into another's feelings, needs, and sufferings. (Etym. Greek *en + pathein*, to suffer.)

EMPIRICISM. In moral philosophy, the system of thought that claims that experience is the only valid source of knowledge. This is more than saying that experience is a presupposition to all human knowledge or a test of that knowledge once gained. It holds that the mind can regulate only the data of experience. All so-called universal ideas and all judgments in which people speak of the nature of things, according to empiricists, are not universals or natures at all. They are merely a series of sense data drawn from experience and connected by reason in a variety of relationships, but their value remains purely hypothetical. As a result, there can be no universally true propositions for the mind to accept, and no universally binding laws for the will to obey, since all knowledge is conditioned by one's limited past experience, and unpredictable experience still to come. (Etym. Greek *empeirikos*, experienced.)

EMUS. *Eminentissimus*—Most Eminent.

ENCHIRIDION SYMBOLORUM. A manual of Catholic doctrine containing essential extracts of all the major definitions and declarations on faith and morals from the first century to the present day. Originally compiled and edited by Heinrich Denzinger (1819–83), one of the pioneers of positive theology in Catholic Germany. The Second Vatican Council relied on the *Enchiridion* for its citations, referred to as "Denzinger."

ENCLOSURE. The cloister of a religious community which reserves certain parts of the residence to the exclusive use of the members of the community. Strict enclosure, called papal, is the standard for other, less restricted forms of cloister. It pertains to religious institutes of women who are strictly contemplative. Its two main provisions, since the Second Vatican Council, are

that: 1. "the nuns, novices and postulants must live within the confines of the convent prescribed by the enclosure itself, nor may they licitly go beyond them, except in the cases provided for by the law," and 2. "the law of enclosure likewise forbids anyone, of whatever class, condition, sex or age, to enter the cloistered area of the convent, except in the cases provided for by law" (*Venite Seorsum*, 1969, VII, 5, 6).

ENCOUNTER. An existentialist term, appropriated in religious language, to describe the human being's meeting with Christ in the sacraments. The sacramental encounter is an effective communication of grace from Christ as God, through Christ as man, to the believing recipient.

ENCOUNTER WITH CHRIST. A term applied to the relation with Christ implied in every reception of a sacrament. This relation depends primarily on which sacrament is received, and therefore mainly refers to the Eucharist, where Christ is received in the fullness of his incarnate divinity. But it may be applied to all the sacraments to bring out two factors: that each sacrament is primarily administered by Christ as a continuation of his redemptive work in the world, and that the benefits derived from a sacrament also depend on the believing and trustful love of Christ with which the sacrament is received.

ENCYCLICAL. A papal document treating of matters related to the general welfare of the Church, sent by the Pope to the bishops. Used especially in modern times to express the mind of the Pope to the people. Although of themselves not infallible documents, encyclicals may (and generally do) contain pronouncements on faith and morals that are *de facto* infallible because they express the ordinary teaching of the Church. In any case, the faithful are to give the papal encyclicals their interior assent and external respect as statements of the Vicar of Christ. (Etym. Latin *encyclicus;* Greek *enkyklios,* circular, general.)

An encyclical epistle is like an encyclical letter but addressed to part of the Church, that is, to the bishops and faithful of a particular area. Its contents may be doctrinal, moral, or disciplinary matters of universal significance, but may also commemorate some historical event or treat of conditions in a certain country or locality.

The following list gives the titles and subject matter of encyclical letters and epistles from Leo XIII to Paul VI.

LEO XIII

1878: INSCRUTABILI DEI CONSILIO (crisis in society), April 21.

QUOD APOSTOLICI MUNERIS (socialism, communism, nihilism), December 28.

1879: AETERNI PATRIS (Scholastic philosophy, especially of Thomas Aquinas), August 4.

1880: ARCANUM (Christian marriage), February 10.

GRANDE MUNUS (Sts. Cyril and Methodius), September 30.

SANCTA DEI CIVITAS (three French societies), December 3.

1881: DIUTURNUM (origin of civil authority), June 29.

1882: ETSI NOS (conditions in Italy), February 15.

AUSPICATO CONCESSUM (Third Order of St. Francis), September 17.

CUM MULTA (situation in Spain), December 8.

1883: SUPREMI APOSTOLATUS OFFICIO (the Rosary), September 1.

1884: NOBILISSIMA GALLORUM GENS (religious problems in France), February 8.

HUMANUM GENUS (Freemasonry), April 20.

SUPERIORE ANNO (recitation of the Rosary), August 30.

1885: IMMORTALE DEI (the Christian Constitution of States), November 1.

QUOD AUCTORITATE (proclamation of extraordinary Jubilee Year), December 22.

1886: QUOD MULTUM (liberty of the Church in Hungary), August 22.

PERGRATA NOBIS (needs of the Church in Portugal), September 14.

1888: LIBERTAS (human liberty), June 20.

PATERNA CARITAS (recalling the dissenting Armenians), July 25.

QUAM AERUMNOSA (Italian immigrants in America), December 10.

1889: QUAMQUAM PLURIES (patronage of St. Joseph and the Blessed Virgin Mary), August 15.

1890: SAPIENTIAE CHRISTIANAE (chief duties of Christian citizens), January 10.

AB APOSTOLI (to the Clergy and people of Italy), October 15.

1891: RERUM NOVARUM (condition of the working classes), May 15.

OCTOBRI MENSE (the Rosary), September 22.

1892: AU MILIEU DES SOLLICITUDES (Church and State in France), February 16.

MAGNAE DEI MATRIS (the Rosary), September 8.

1893: AD EXTREMAS (seminaries in the East Indies), June 24.

CONSTANTI HUNGARORUM (conditions of the Church in Hungary), September 2.

LAETITIAE SANCTAE (the Rosary), September 8.

PROVIDENTISSIMUS DEUS (study of Holy Scripture), November 18.

1894: CARITATIS (conditions in Poland), March 19.

IUCUNDA SEMPER EXPECTATIONE (the Rosary), September 8.

CHRISTI NOMEN (Society for the Propagation of the Faith), December 24.

1895: ADIUTRICEM (the Rosary), September 5.

1896: SATIS COGNITUM (Church unity), June 29.

FIDENTUM PIUMQUE ANIMUM (the Rosary), September 20.

1897: DIVINUM ILLUD MUNUS (the Holy Spirit, doctrine and devotion), May 9.

MILITANTIS ECCLESIAE (third centenary of the death of St. Peter Canisius), August 1.

AUGUSTISSIMAE VIRGINIS (the Rosary), September 12.

AFFARI VOS (the Manitoba school question), December 8.

1898: CARITATIS STUDIUM (the magisterium of the Church in Scotland), July 25.

SPESSE VOLTE (Catholic Action in Italy), August 5.

1899: ANNUM SACRUM (Consecration of Mankind to the Sacred Heart), May 25.

DEPUIS LE JOUR (ecclesiastical education in France), September 8.

1900: TAMETSI FUTURA PROSPICIENTIBUS (Jesus Christ, Our Redeemer), November 1.

1901: GRAVES DE COMMUNI RE (Christian democracy), January 18.

1902: MIRAE CARITATIS (the Most Holy Eucharist), May 28.

FIN DAL PRINCIPIO (education of the clergy in Italy), December 8.

ST. PIUS X

1903: E. SUPREMI (Restoration of All Things in Christ), October 4.

1904: AD DIEM ILLUM LAETISSIMUM (jubilee of the Immaculate Conception), February 2.

IUCUNDA SANE (thirteenth centenary of the death of St. Gregory the Great), March 12.

1905: ACERBO NIMIS (teaching of Christian doctrine), April 15.

II FERMO PROPOSITO (Catholic Action in Italy), June 11.

1906: VEHEMENTER NOS (French separation law), February 11.

TRIBUS CIRCITER (condemnation of the Mariavites), April 5.

PIENI L'ANIMO (clergy in Italy), July 28.

GRAVISSIMO OFFICIO MUNERE (Forbidding Associations Cultuelles), August 10.

1907: UNE FOIS ENCORE (separation of Church and State in France), January 6.

PASCENDI DOMINICI GREGIS (modernism), September 8.

1909: COMMUNIUM RERUM (eighth centenary of the death of St. Anselm), April 21.

1910: EDITAE SAEPE (third centenary of the death of St. Charles Borromeo), May 26.

1911: IAMDUDUM (separation law in Portugal), May 24.

1912: LACRIMABILI STATU (Indians of South America), June 7.

SINGULARI QUADAM (labor organizations in Germany), September 24.

BENEDICT XV

1914: AD BEATISSIMI APOSTOLORUM (appeal for peace), November 1.

1917: HUMANI GENERIS REDEMPTIONEM (preaching), June 15.

1918: QUOD IAM DIU (Peace Congress, Paris), December 1.

1919: IN HAC TANTA (twelfth centenary of St. Boniface), May 14.

PATERNO IAM DIU (Christian charity of the children of Central Europe), November 24.

1920: PACEM, DEI MUNUS PULCHERRIMUM (peace and Christian reconciliation), May 23.

SPIRITUS PARACLITUS (Holy Scripture), September 15.

PRINCIPI APOSTOLORUM PETRO (St. Ephrem the Syrian declared Doctor), October 5.

ANNUS IAM PLENUS (child war victims), December 1.

1921: SACRA PROPEDIEM (seventh centenary of the Third Order of St. Francis), January 6.

IN PRAECLARA SUMMORUM (sixth centenary of Dante's death), April 30.

FAUSTO APPETENTE DIE (seventh centenary of the death of St. Dominic), June 29.

PIUS XI

1922: UBI ARCANO DEI CONSILIO (peace of Christ in the Kingdom of Christ), December 23.

1923: RERUM OMNIUM PERTURBATIONEM (third centenary of the death of St. Francis de Sales), January 26.

STUDIORUM DUCEM (sixth centenary of the canonization of St. Thomas Aquinas), June 29.

ECCLESIAM DEI (third centenary of the death of St. Josaphat, Archbishop of Polotsk), November 12.

1924: MAXIMAM GRAVISSIMAMQUE (French diocesan associations), January 18.

1925: QUAS PRIMAS (Feast of Christ the King), December 11.

1926: RERUM ECCLESIAE (Catholic missions), February 28.

RITE EXPIATIS (seventh centenary of the death of St. Francis of Assisi), April 30.

INIQUIS AFFLICTISQUE (persecution of the Church in Mexico), November 18.

1928: MORTALIUM ANIMOS (promotion of true religious unity), January 6.

MISERENTISSIMUS REDEMPTOR (reparation to the Sacred Heart), May 8.

RERUM ORIENTALIUM (reunion with the Eastern Churches), September 8.

1929: MENS NOSTRA (promotion of spiritual exercises), December 20.

QUINQUAGESIMO ANTE (sacerdotal jubilee), December 23.

DIVINI ILLIUS MAGISTRI (RAPPRESENTANTI IN TERRA) (Christian education of youth), December 31.

1930: AD SALUTEM (fifteenth centenary of the death of St. Augustine), April 20.

CASTI CONNUBII (Christian marriage), December 31.

1931: QUADRAGESIMO ANNO (renewal of the social order), May 15.

NON ABBIAMO BISOGNO (Catholic Action), June 29.

NOVA IMPENDET (economic crisis, unemployment, armaments), October 2.

LUX VERITATIS (fifteenth centenary of the Council of Ephesus), December 25.

1932: CARITATE CHRISTI COMPULSI (Sacred Heart and world distress), May 3.

ACERBA ANIMI (persecution of the Church in Mexico), September 29.

1933: DILECTISSIMA NOBIS (conditions in Spain), June 3.

1935: AD CATHOLICI SACERDOTII (Catholic priesthood), December 20.

1936: VIGILANTI CURA (motion pictures), June 29.

1937: MIT BRENNENDER SORGE (the Church in Germany), March 14.

DIVINI REDEMPTORIS (atheistic communism), March 19.

FIRMISSIMAM CONSTANTIAM (NOS ES MUY CONOCIDA) (conditions in Mexico), March 28.

INGRAVESCENTIBUS MALIS (the Rosary), September 29.

PIUS XII

1939: SUMMI PONTIFICATUS (role of the State in modern world), October 20.

SERTUM LAETITIAE (to the Church in the United States), November 1.

1940: SAECULO EXEUNTE OCTAVO (missions), June 13.

1943: MYSTICI CORPORIS CHRISTI (Mystical Body), June 29.

DIVINO AFFLANTE SPIRITU (biblical studies), September 30.

1944: ORIENTALIS ECCLESIAE DECUS (fifteenth centenary of the death of St. Cyril of Alexandria), April 9.

1945: COMMUNIUM INTERPRETES DOLORUM (appeal for prayers), April 15.

ORIENTALES OMNES ECCLESIAS (anniversary of the Ruthenian Reunion), December 23.

1946: QUEMADMODUM (call for intensified aid to youth), January 6.

DEIPARAE VIRGINIS MARIAE (proposing the definition of the Assumption), May 1.

1947: FULGENS RADIATUR (fourteenth centenary of the death of St. Benedict), March 21.

MEDIATOR DEI (sacred liturgy), November 20.

OPTATISSIMA PAX (peace and social disorders), December 18.

1948: AUSPICIA QUAEDAM (prayer to Blessed Virgin Mary for peace), May 1.

IN MULTIPLICIBUS CURIS (crisis in Palestine), October 24.

1949: REDEMPTORIS NOSTRI (internationalizing Jerusalem), April 15.

1950: ANNI SACRI (Holy Year call for prayer), March 12.

SUMMI MAERORIS (renewed Holy Year call for prayer), July 19.

HUMANI GENERIS (warning against errors in teaching), August 12.

MIRABILE ILLUD (crusade of prayers for peace), December 6.

1951: EVANGELII PRAECONES (call for greater missionary effort), June 2.

SEMPITERNUS REX (fifteenth centenary of the Council of Chalcedon), September 8.

INGRUENTIUM MALORUM (recitation of the Rosary), September 15.

1952: ORIENTALES ECCLESIAS (communist persecution of the Church; call for prayers for the persecuted), December 15.

1953: DOCTOR MELLIFLUUS (eighth centenary of the death of St. Bernard), May 24.

FULGENS CORONA (call to observe the Marian Year), September 8.

1954: SACRA VIRGINITAS (preeminence of evangelical chastity), March 25.

ECCLESIAE FASTOS (commemoration of St. Boniface), June 5.

AD SINARUM GENTEM (the Church in China), October 7.

AD CAELI REGINAM (Feast of the Queenship of Mary), October 11.

1955: MUSICAE SACRAE (sacred music), December 25.

1956: HAURIETIS AQUAS (the Sacred Heart), May 15.

LUCTUOSISSIMI EVENTUS (prayers for Hungary), October 28.

LAETAMUR ADMODUM (Middle East crisis), November 1.

DATIS NUPERRIME (prayers for peace), November 5.

1957: FIDEI DONUM (missionary effort, especially in Africa), April 21.

INVICTI ATHLETAE CHRISTI

(third centenary of the death of St. Andrew Bobola), May 16.

LE PELERINAGE DE LOURDES (centenary of the Lourdes apparitions), July 2.

MIRANDA PRORSUS (radio, TV and motion pictures), September 8.

1958: AD APOSTOLORUM PRINCIPIS (critical situation of the Church in China), June 29.

MEMINISSE JUVAT (prayers for peace and the persecuted Church), July 14.

JOHN XXIII

1959: AD PETRI CATHEDRAM (appeal to separated Christians to reunite with the Church), June 29.

SACERDOTII NOSTRI PRIMORDIA (centenary of the Curé of Ars), August 1.

GRATA RECORDATIO (the Rosary), September 26.

PRINCEPS PASTORUM (missions), November 28.

1961: MATER ET MAGISTRA (Christianity and social progress), May 15.

AETERNA DEI SAPIENTIA (fifteenth centenary of the death of St. Leo the Great), November 11.

1962: PAENITENTIAM AGERE (asking penance for success of the Second Vatican Council), July 1.

1963: PACEM IN TERRIS (peace on earth), April 11.

PAUL VI

1964: ECCLESIAM SUAM (Second Vatican Council themes), August 6.

1965: MENSE MAIO (prayer for success of the Second Vatican Council, peace), April 29.

MYSTERIUM FIDEI (the Real Presence), September 3.

1966: CHRISTI MATRI ROSARII (the Rosary), September 15.

1967: POPULORUM PROGRESSIO (development of peoples), March 26.

SACERDOTALIS CAELIBATUS (priestly celibacy), June 24.

1968: HUMANAE VITAE (birth control), July 25.

END. A good for the sake of which something is made, or done, or exists, or is changed. It is the purpose of an action, being, or modification; also the final cause or aim and objective to be attained by an intellect and free agent.

The "end" therefore has the primary meaning of purpose, but secondarily it also means the point at which something ceases. Yet cessation is not the real purpose of anything, but only the transition from its present condition to a further state or activity, which is the true "end" of what preceded.

END OF THE WORLD. Revealed truth that the present world of space and time will come to an end. It will be on the day when the dead will rise from the grave and Christ will appear in his majesty to judge the human race. As to the manner of the world's destruction or its time, nothing definite can be said whether from natural science or from the Christian faith. The idea of destruction by fire (II Peter 3:7, 10, 12) can be taken simply as a current mode of expression to state that the present world will be dissolved and a new world will come into existence.

ENDOMETRIOSIS. A gynecological illness caused by the abnormal presence of tissue that more or less perfectly resembles the lining of the uterus (endometrium) but growing outside of the uterus itself and distributed in other pelvic areas. Since this aberrant endometrial tissue responds to the hormone-induced changes of the woman's menstrual cycle but, unlike the true endometrial lining of the uterus, is entrapped in other tissue such as bone and muscle, its cyclic changes in response to the menstrual cycle can be the occasion of severe discomfort and pain. Pregnancy, which eliminates the cyclic changes of menstruation, causes the problem to regress, and even after the pregnancy improvement is sometimes sustained for a period up to three or four years.

Since a surgical approach to the problem is not always practical or successful, the so called "contraceptive pill" has been recommended for use over prolonged periods to eliminate the cyclic changes of the menstrual cycle and thus eliminate the periodic pain of endometriosis. It should be noted, from a moral viewpoint, that although this progestational-estrogen type therapy is, in itself, essentially the same as that used in the "contraceptive pill," it is not used in these cases as a contraceptive. The purpose of the therapy is to ameliorate a seriously abnormal and indeed pathological condition insofar as it is aggravated by hormonal changes of the menstrual cycle. Although temporary sterility is a side effect of the treatment, contraception is not the purpose, and thus the treatment in no way conflicts with Catholic teaching.

ENDS OF THE MASS. The fourfold purpose for which the Church offers the Eucharistic sacrifice; namely, adoration, thanksgiving, propitiation, and petition. The Mass is therefore a sacrifice of praise of God's eternal greatness, of gratitude for past and present goodness, of begging mercy for having offended the divine majesty, and of asking for divine favor in the future.

ENERGUMEN. A person possessed by the devil. The term was also applied to persons who were mentally deranged. Whether possessed or not, they were treated with special pity and care and, when necessary, exorcised at Mass. If not violent, they were admitted to Holy Communion. But they were debarred from ordination even after being cured.

ENERGY. Inherent power to produce a given effect. The term is commonly applied to physical or natural power, but it may also refer to the spiritual power conferred by divine grace. As supernatural power, it enables a human being to perform actions that are either beyond the capacity of human nature, weakened by sin, or totally beyond the natural capacity of any created being and leading to the possession of God in the beatific vision.

ENJOYMENT. The delight of a human appetitive power in the achievement of its proper end. The satisfaction that accompanies the attainment of a desire. The joy that a person experiences on reaching what had been hoped for.

ENLIGHTENMENT. The term used by Immanuel Kant (1724–1804) and then by others to describe man's coming of age from the state of infancy, in which he was incapable of using his own reason but depended on others, including an alleged revelation from God. The Enlightenment became a movement that has since affected much of the Western world.

ENOCH. 1. a son of Cain. We are told that the father built a town and named it after his son (Genesis 4:17); 2. in the list of patriarchs descended from Adam, Jared is named as Enoch's father and he, in turn, as father of Methuseleh (Genesis 5:18–21). In the New Testament Luke, in tracing Jesus' ancestry, repeats this succession of Jared-Enoch-Methuseleh (Luke 3:37). "Enoch walked with God. Then he vanished because God took him" (Genesis 5:24). Was he assumed into heaven without dying? Ecclesiasticus suggests this: "No one else has ever been created on earth to equal Enoch, for

he was taken up from earth" (Ecclesiasticus 49:14). This is reinforced in the Epistle to the Hebrews: "It was because of his faith that Enoch was taken up and did not have to experience death; he was not to be found because God had taken him" (Hebrews 11:5).

ENS. Being. In philosophy *ens* is the common denominator of all reality, and is variously classified according to the different kinds of reality known to the human mind. Thus *ens a se* is being from itself, or the uncaused Being who is God; *ens ab alio* is being from another, namely produced or caused being or creature; *ens in se* is being in itself, and also *ens per se* which is being through its own nature or being in an unqualified sense, and in both cases is substance; *ens entis* is being of a being, which means that it cannot have existence in itself but only in a substance, hence an accident; *ens rationis* is a "being" or creation of reason hence a purely logical or conceptual being or idea of something that does not really exist outside the mind; and *ens ut sic* is being as such, apart from its manifold and varied forms of existence, and is the object of metaphysics or the philosophy of being. (Etym. Latin *ens*, being, a being, something having existence.)

ENTABLATURE. In church architecture the wall space above a column or pillar, composed ordinarily of an architrave, a frieze, and a cornice.

ENTELECHY. The internal specifying principle that actively directs a nature to its specific good or end. In scholastic philosophy this is the substantial form. It is the vital principle that guides and co-ordinates all the activities of an organism from within, and for the benefit of the whole. More than mechanical, it is the immanent power that gives purpose and direction to all the operations of every living thing. (Etym. Latin *entelechia*, accomplishment, actuality, substantial form; from Greek *entelecheia*.)

ENTHRONEMENT OF THE SACRED HEART. The official and social acknowledgment of the sovereignty of the Heart of Jesus over a Christian family. As a religious ceremony, it consists in the formal installation of a picture of the Sacred Heart in the place of honor of a home and by an act of consecration, led by a priest. It was first promoted by Mateo Crawley-Boevey (1875–1960), member of the Fathers of the Sacred Heart, and approved by Pope St. Pius X.

ENTITATIVE HABIT. Sanctifying grace as a permanent quality added to human nature and directly modifying its being (entity) rather than its operations, as in the case of virtues.

ENTITY. In scholastic philosophy, an actual or conceivable being, with stress on its reality, as opposed to something unreal, which is a nonentity. (Etym. Latin *ens*, being, a being, something having existence.)

ENTRUSTED SECRET. A truth or fact that a person learns after an explicit or tacit agreement that secrecy would be observed. To this category belong professional secrets, as in the medical or legal profession, and other instances where it is assumed that information received will be kept confidential. Entrusted secrets bind under grave sin.

ENVOY. In Church law, a diplomatic agent; a person appointed by the Holy See to negotiate a treaty with a foreign government; anyone dispatched on a specific mission. Over the centuries papal envoys have often been sent on a variety of missions to the heads of political states. (Etym. French *envoyer*, to send.)

ENVY. Sadness or discontent at the excellence, good fortune, or success of another person. It implies that one considers oneself somehow deprived by what one envies in another or even that an injustice has been done. Essential to envy is this sense of deprivation. Consequently it is not merely sadness that someone else has some desirable talent or possession, nor certainly the ambition to equal or surpass another person, which can be laudable emulation. It is not the same as jealousy, which implies an unwillingness to share one's own possessions.

Envy is a sin against charity and, though serious in itself, allows of degrees of gravity depending on whether fully consented to and how important is the object envied. The most serious sin of envy is sadness at the supernatural gifts or graces that another has received from God, i.e., to envy sanctity. (Etym. Latin *invidia;* from *invidere*, to look askance.)

EPACT. The term applied to the surplus days of the solar year over the year of twelve lunar months, or the moon's age in days on the first day of a year. The system of epacts is used to determine the time of the ecclesiastical new moon on which the date of Easter is based.

EP., EPUS., EPS., EPISC. *Episcopus*—bishop.

EPARCHY. In the Eastern Christian Churches the name for an ecclesiastical province. It is contrasted with an exarchate or civil diocese, of which it is a subdivision. Known already in the early fourth century, its official head is an eparch, sometimes called the metropolitan, who can veto the election of the bishops of the dioceses in his eparchy. (Etym. Greek *eparchia*, province; from *eparchos*, prefect.)

EPHESIANS, EPISTLE TO THE. One of the instructional letters of St. Paul, written from Rome sometime during his first imprisonment (A.D. 61–63). Most likely it was a circular letter whose theme is the union of all the faithful with and in Christ, as members of his one Mystical Body. Its reference to matrimony as a mystery that implies the union of Christ and the Church (5:32) has made this epistle the classic source of the Church's doctrine on the sacrament of marriage.

EPHPHETA. Imperative of the "to open" in Aramaic. Part of the ceremony of baptism where accepted by the bishops' conference. The celebrant touches the ears and lips of each child baptized, while saying, "May the Lord Jesus, who made the deaf to hear and the dumb to speak, grant that you may soon be able to receive His word and profess the faith to the praise and glory of God the Father," to which all answer, "Amen." The ceremony resembles the curing of the deaf-mute (Mark 7:31–37).

EPHRAIM. Younger son of the patriarch Joseph (Genesis 41), born in Egypt during the seven years of abundance. Ephraim's superiority over his brother Manasses is seen in the blessing he receives from his grandfather, Jacob (Genesis 48). Jacob adopts Manasses and Ephraim as his sons, to make them into two tribes, but he gives the preference to the younger, by placing his right hand over Ephraim. The tribe of Ephraim became distinguished for its valor and prospered, but then became envious of the spiritual supremacy of Judah. The tribe of Ephraim provoked the rebellion and separation from the house of David. Jeroboam I (III Kings 11) became leader of the ten tribes of the north, and after the schism the story of the tribe of Ephraim is simply absorbed in the history of the northern tribes.

EPICLESIS. See EPIKLESIS.

EPIGONATION. A Eucharistic vestment of the Greek and Armenian rites. It is diamond-shaped, of stiff material, embroidered, and hangs from the waist to below the right knee. Its origin is uncertain but it now symbolizes the spiritual sword of justice. In the Western Church the Pope alone wears it. (Etym. Latin *epigonus,* successor; from Greek *epigonos* from *epigignesthai,* to be born after.)

EPIKEIA. A liberal interpretation of law in instances not provided by the letter of the law. It presupposes sincerity in wanting to observe the law, and interprets the mind of the lawgiver in supplying his presumed intent to include a situation that is not covered by the law. It favors the liberty of the interpreter without contradicting the express will of the lawgiver. (Etym. Greek *epieikes,* reasonable.)

EPIKLESIS. An invocation of the Holy Spirit said by the celebrant of the Mass after the words of Consecration. It occurs in all the liturgies of the East and is considered essential in the Orthodox Church to the validity of the Eucharistic sacrifice. Since the Second Vatican Council all the new canons of the Mass contain the epiklesis.

EPIPHANY. The feast commemorating Christ's manifestation to the Gentiles in the person of the Magi, as well as his baptism and first miracle at Cana. It began in the East in the third century and soon spread to the West, where it is identified with the visit of the Magi. In some countries it is known as Twelfth Night (after Christmas) and is the occasion for special celebrations. For centuries the Epiphany has been a holy day of obligation in many places. (Etym. Greek *epiphaneia,* appearance, manifestation.)

EPISCOPACY. Divine institution of bishops as successors of the Apostles. By virtue of divine right, therefore, bishops possess an ordinary power of government over their dioceses. The episcopal power is ordinary because it belongs to the episcopal office. It is an immediate power because it is exercised in the bishop's own name and not at the order of a superior. Thus bishops are not mere delegates or agents of the Pope, nor his mere vicars or representatives. They are autonomous pastors of the flock entrusted to them even though they are subordinated to the Pope.

The episcopal power is inherent in the bishops' ordination, though it must be activated by collegial union with the Pope and the rest of the Catholic hierarchy. It is a true pastoral power that embraces all the ecclesiastical powers belonging to the exercise of this office, namely the teaching, ruling, judging, and, when necessary, punishing re-fractory members of their diocese. It is, however, a power that is limited locally and materially, since it extends only to a definite segment of the Church and is circumscribed by the papal authority, which is superior to that of any bishop in his diocese. (Etym. Latin *episcopus,* bishop; from Greek *episkopos,* overseer.)

EPISCOPAL CONFERENCE. A form of assembly in which the bishops of a certain country or region exercise their pastoral office jointly in order to enhance the Church's beneficial influence on all men especially by devising forms of the apostolate and apostolic methods suitably adopted to the circumstances of the times (Second Vatican Council, *Christus Dominus,* III, 38). The local ordinaries and coadjutors have a deliberate vote. Each conference draws up its own statutes, which are subject to the approval of Rome. Decisions of an episcopal conference have the force of law when they have been legitimately approved by at least two thirds of the bishops who have a deliberative vote and confirmed by the Apostolic See, but then only in cases prescribed by common law, or when so declared by a special mandate of the Holy See. This mandate may come from Rome on its own initiative or in response to the conference itself.

EPISCOPAL CURIA. The group of persons who assist a bishop, or the prelate taking the place of a bishop, in the administration of a diocese.

EPISCOPALIANS. Anglicans, or members of the Anglican Communion, but called Episcopalians in certain countries such as the United States. Anglicanism came to America in 1607, with the Jamestown, Virginia, settlers, and in 1783 the American Anglicans became the Protestant Episcopal Church. They declared themselves free of all foreign authority, civil or ecclesiastical, but kept their liturgy in conformity with the Church of England. The first convention (1783) also revised the English Book of Common Prayer. Sixty-nine feast days were dropped from the Church calendar, the "Ornaments Rubric" requiring vestments was omitted, and in the catechism the reference to the Eucharist "verily and indeed taken and received by the faithful" was changed to "spiritually taken and received." One result has been that American Episcopalians reflect the whole spectrum of Anglicanism, ranging from Anglo-Catholic churches that are close to Rome in faith and liturgy, through High and Broad, to Low Church groups that are in the mainstream of evangelical Protestantism.

EPISCOPALIS POTESTATIS. An apostolic letter issued *motu proprio* by Pope Paul VI, setting the norms for granting dispensations among bishops of the Eastern Churches (May 2, 1967).

EPISCOPAL SEE. A diocese or territory over which a bishop rules. New sees are created and others divided, relocated, or suppressed by the Holy See. In early Christian times every large city was an episcopal see. Thus by the end of the first century there were one hundred dioceses around the Mediterranean world, centered in the hundred principal cities of the Roman Empire. Nowadays many sees are located in smaller towns and frequently changed to meet the needs of a changing Catholic population.

EPISCOPATE. The fullness of the sacrament of orders by which a man becomes a bishop and acquires the power to ordain other bishops and priests, to confirm, and to become part of the episcopal community with the power of jurisdiction according to the canons of ecclesiastical law and the provisions of the Holy See.

EPISTEMOLOGY. A theory of knowledge. A branch of scholastic philosophy that studies the principles underlying the acquisition of knowledge, the methods of logical reasoning, and the critical evaluation of truth, certitude, and right thinking. (Etym. Greek *epistēmē*, knowledge + *logia*, science, knowledge.)

EPISTLE. In the liturgy, before the Second Vatican Council, most frequently a selection from one of the letters of the Apostles read at Mass after the Collects, at the (priest's) right-hand side of the altar, and therefore called the Epistle side. As a rule there was only one, but on some days there were several. At solemn High Mass the Epistle was chanted in one tone by the subdeacon. In the revised liturgy the Epistle has become the First Reading and Second Reading. (Etym. Latin *epistola*, letter; from Greek *epistole*, message, letter.)

EPISTOLARIUM. A liturgical book containing the epistles that were to be said or sung by a subdeacon at a solemn High Mass.

EQUALITY. In general, the state of being equal. There are, however, two divergent interpretations of what this means. Theism, which assumes that there is a personal God, defines equality as the capacity that all men have to reach their eternal destiny, and therefore have the right to the means required for attaining the end for which they were created. Given these postulates, theism recognizes that no two people are completely equal in their possession of anything, that whatever they have is ultimately a gift from God. The nontheistic view of humanity considers man essentially earthbound with no assured destiny beyond the grave. It therefore redefines equality in this-worldly terms, as equal access to the good things of life on earth. Inequality, then, becomes any deviation from this mathematical sameness in sharing the world's available resources for giving satisfaction to mankind.

EQUIPROBABILISM. A strict moral theory for resolving practical doubts. Equiprobabilism demands that the opinion that favors freedom be equally or almost equally probable as the one favoring the law. Furthermore one may apply this principle only when the doubt concerns the existence of a law, not in a doubt as to whether an existing law has ceased to bind or has been fulfilled.

EQUITY. The wise application of positive law to particular circumstances, with due consideration for natural or revealed justice and for the spirit and not merely the letter of the law. Too strict an application of a given law, whether civil or ecclesiastical, may turn out to be inhuman although in perfect accord with what the law prescribes. (Etym. Latin *aequus*, equal, equally great; right, just, fair.)

EQUIVOCAL. A term or proposition that has two or more entirely different meanings, with mere resemblance of words or sounds. An equivocation is a disguised untruth. (Etym. Latin *aequivocus*, of like name.)

ERASTIANISM. The system of Church-State relations named after Thomas Erastus (1524–83), who was a follower of Huldreich Zwingli (1484–1531) and whose real name was Thomas Lieber. Its main thesis is the supremacy of civil rulers in matters of religion. The basis for this theory is the alleged analogy between the Jewish and the Christian dispensations. Erastianism became the theological justification for the established churches in England and elsewhere.

EROS. Originally, in Greek mythology, the god of love. In the Christian vocabulary eros is possessive love; it is the love that desires for one's own benefit. It is acquisitive love on whatever plane of self-satisfaction something is said to be loved, including learning or art, or, on a lower scale, the pleasures of sex, food, or bodily convenience. The term is most familiar in its adjective form of erotic or sexual. (Etym. Greek *erōs*, love.)

ERRONEOUS. Theological censure that the Church imposes on certain propositions. Something is said to be erroneous when it contradicts a logical conclusion derived from a revealed doctrine.

ERROR. Positive disagreement between the mind and object; a wrong judgment. Essential to an error is that what the mind conceives something to be is contrary to what it really is. Less often the notion of error is applied to a mistake in correctness or validity in reasoning. Error differs from mere ignorance in positively affirming within the mind what is objectively not so outside the mind.

ESAU. Son of Isaac and Rebekah and twin brother of Jacob (Genesis 25:24). Esau, also called Edom because of his red hair, was a rugged outdoor man, while Jacob was shrewd and calculating. This is illustrated in the familiar story of Esau selling his birthright to his brother for a meal of bread and lentil soup (Genesis 25:29–34). Jacob's duplicity was indicated in the plot that he and his mother concocted to elicit the blessing of his dying, blind father by disguising himself as Esau. Estrangement between the brothers lasted for years (Genesis 27), but when Jacob sought reconciliation, Esau was surprisingly forgiving in the light of Jacob's wretched behavior. Despite the improved relations, they settled in different sections of the country (Genesis 32, 33), "for they had acquired too much to live together" (Genesis 36:7).

ESCHATOLOGY. The branch of systematic theology that treats of the last things: death, particular and general judgments, heaven, hell, and purgatory. All the essentials of eschatology have been clearly defined by the Church, notably the Fourth Lateran Council (1215) and the constitution *Benedictus Deus* of Pope Benedict XII in 1336. (Etym. Greek *eschatos*, uttermost + *logos*, discourse on.)

ESOTERIC. Something meant for only a few experts or initiates. Applied originally to the secret doctrines held by the Stoics, or to the esoteric members of the Pythagorean brotherhoods. The opposite of exoteric. (Etym. Latin *esotericus;* from *esoterikos,* inner; hence, secret.)

ESPOUSALS. A formal contract of future marriage; a betrothal between two persons already affianced.

ESPOUSALS, SPIRITUAL. Mystical union of love between God and some chosen souls raised to the highest degree of contemplation. God reveals his greatness to these persons, adorns them with special graces, and unites himself to them as a pledge of spiritual marriage. The espousal is totally spiritual, by which the human soul is united to the Holy Spirit.

ESSE. The term "to be" used as a noun. It is the act of existence. In finite beings it is their principle of existence as distinguished from their essence or nature. Only in God are essence and existence the same. (Etym. Latin *esse,* to be; being, existence.)

ESSENCE. What a thing is. The internal principle whereby a thing is what it is and not something else. Sometimes essence is said to be the same thing as being, but being merely, affirming that a thing is, without specifying its perfections. Essence is not quite the same as nature, which adds to essence the notion of activity, i.e., nature is the essence in action. Or again essence is substance, but not all essences are substantial because accidents also have an essence. (Etym. Latin *essentia,* essence, being.) See also QUIDDITY.

ESSENES. Pre-Christian Jewish groups of ascetics, not mentioned either in the Bible or the Talmud but referred to by Philo (20 B.C.–c. A.D. 40), Josephus (A.D. 37–c. 100), and the elder Pliny (A.D. 23–79). The name probably means "the pious ones." They seem to have begun in the second century before Christ, to have gone out of existence in the second century after Christ, and to have always remained in Palestine. They numbered about four thousand, according to Josephus, in the late first century A.D. They were an exclusive society, engaged mainly in agriculture. In general they renounced marriage, without denying its value, and recruited their ranks by adopting young children. They practiced the strictest community life, and also a vigorous caste system. Along with considerable superstition, they believed in Yahweh and in immortality. They had been almost forgotten in religious history, until the discovery of the Dead Sea Scrolls in 1947. Almost certainly it was a community of Essenes that produced the treasure of literature found at Qumran, near the Dead Sea. (Etym. Greek *hosioi,* the saintly or religious; or Aramaic, the silent ones.)

ESSENTIAL HOLINESS. See HOLINESS, ESSENTIAL.

ESTHER. The adopted daughter and niece (or cousin) of Mordecai, she was also known as Hadassah (Esther 2:15). She is a traditionally heroic figure to Jews because she outwitted the anti-Semitic Agagite, Haman, a powerful official in King Ahasuerus' court. Following the banishment of Queen Vashti, the king chose Esther to be his wife (Esther 2:17). Using her beauty and intelligence to combat Haman in his attempt to wipe out the Jews, she brought about his execution on the gallows, a fate he had planned for Mordecai (Esther 3–6). The struggle emphasizes patriotic and racial devotion rather than religious aspiration (Esther 7:10). It is a lively, stirring story whose events are celebrated by Jews all over the world in the annual Feast of Purim (Esther 9:27–28). The Book of Esther was written by an unknown author, probably not later than the time of Ezra. The text of Esther has come down in two revisions, a shorter Hebrew and a longer Greek. The Catholic Bible follows the Hebrew, and then adds the missing passages (10–16) from the Greek.

ESTRANGEMENT. In general, alienating the affections of a person from someone. In theological terms, estrangement is the alienation of a sinner from God. It is caused by the deliberate commission of a sin, known to be grave, and results in the loss of the supernatural charity, and consequently the loss of sanctifying grace.

ESTREMADURA. Site of the most popular Marian sanctuary in Spain, under the title of Our Lady of Guadalupe. The Blessed Virgin is here referred to as the "Powerful Lady of Silence." The shrine statue of Our Lady with the Infant was sent by Pope St. Gregory I to St. Leander (550–600) in Spain before the Moorish conquest. To save it from capture by the enemy, it was buried in a cave together with papers telling of its origin and to whom it belonged. Centuries passed before it was unearthed in 1326 by a cowherd who said a lovely lady had appeared to him and told him where to dig for treasure. The statue he found was made of Oriental wood, unharmed by its years of underground burial. A chapel was built to house the image. Although Estremadura is almost inaccessible to travelers, the shrine has been visited by thousands of all classes including royalty. Mary possesses a vast and costly wardrobe and some of the finest altar vestments and jewels are in the shrine's treasury. The cult of Guadalupe was at its height when Mexico's Spanish missionaries were inspired to spread her devotion in the New World, so the great American shrine to Our Lady honors her under the same title.

ET. *Etiam*—also, even.

ETERNAL CITY. See ROME.

ETERNAL DEATH. The lot of the wicked who die estranged from God. It is called death because the person is deprived of the possession of God, who gives life to the soul. And it is eternal because it will never end.

ETERNAL LAW. The plan of divine wisdom, insofar as it directs all the actions and events of the universe. It is, therefore, the unchangeable effective decree of God binding the whole of creation to the fulfillment of its purpose, and to the use of such means for attaining this purpose as are adapted to each nature.

ETERNAL LIFE. The term used by Christ to describe the state of endless happiness enjoyed by the just in heaven (Matthew 25:46; Mark 9:44; Luke 18:30; John 3, 4, 5, 6, 10, 12). It means not only everlasting duration but also fullness of life, which the believer possesses already here and now through participation in the life of God.

ETERNAL PUNISHMENT. The unending penalty suffered in hell by the evil spirits and the human beings who die in mortal sin. The Church bases her teaching about the existence of eternal punishment on the words of Christ in foretelling the final judgment (Matthew 25:34, 41). He compares the sentence of the just with the condemnation of the wicked. Christ as judge will first say, "Come, you whom my Father has blessed, take for your heritage the kingdom prepared for you since the foundation of the world." But to the unjust, "Go away from me, with your curse upon you, to the eternal fire prepared for the devil and his angels." Then he repeats the two judgments with a conclusion, speaking first of the lost and then of the saved, "And they will go into eternal [*aionios*] punishment, and the virtuous to eternal [*aionios*] life" (Matthew 25:46). Since there is no question about the endless duration of heaven, the Church concludes the same about hell. The eternity of hell was defined by the Fourth Lateran Council in 1215.

ETERNITY. In its full sense, duration of being without beginning, succession, or ending. Only God possesses the fullness of eternity, since only he always existed (no beginning), has no succession (no change), and will never end (no cessation). It is defined Catholic doctrine that God possesses the divine Being in a constant undivided now. His eternity is the perfect and simultaneous total possession of interminable life.

Rational creatures share in God's eternity, but only approximate it, by participation. Angels have a beginning, and they have a succession of past, present, and future, but they have no cessation since they are pure spirits that will never die or cease to be. Human beings likewise have a beginning and they have succession, but unlike the angels they will die in body, to be later resurrected, while the souls live on forever. In God's absolute power, however, angels and human souls could be deprived of existence. Their eternity depends on the goodness and will of God.

ETHICAL DUTY. A true obligation but not binding in strict justice. It is a moral responsibility that is not also juridical.

ETHICAL HOLINESS. See HOLINESS, MORAL.

ETHICS. The science of human conduct as known by natural reason. It is a normative science because it determines the principles of right and wrong in human behavior. It is also a practical science because it does not merely speculate about moral good and evil but also decides what is right or wrong in specific human actions.

Also called moral philosophy, the purpose of ethics is to study this fact of human experience, that people distinguish right from wrong and have an instinctive sense of what they should do. The subject matter of ethics, therefore, is human conduct; its point of view is that of rightness and wrongness.

Although related to other human and social sciences, ethics is different from them by its unique point of view, namely the word *ought*. It is also different from moral theology by restricting itself to native reason as opposed to revealed religion.

Ethics is a science, not in the sense of the experimental sciences, but as a philosophical science that assumes certain postulates from philosophy and from them derives practical conclusions. It borrows three main premises from natural philosophy: the existence of a personal God, the freedom of the human will, and the immortality of the soul. Implicit in these premises is the idea that a good moral action is done freely by humans, in conformity with the mind and will of God. It is good precisely because it leads a

human to the goal or destiny set by God in a future immortality. Ethics comes from the Greek *ethos*, which denotes a fixed custom and is often used to mean a person's character.

ETHOS. The spirit of a people or culture, or, more technically, the totality of the ideas and attitudes held by a specific community in relation to behavior.

ETIOLOGY. The science of inquiring into the causes or reasons for things. It may also concentrate on a particular phenomenon, as the etiology of a mental or moral disorder, e.g., the breakdown of family life or the prevalence of contraception.

EUBULIA. Right counseling. The virtue that disposes a person to seek good counsel in human conduct, and to accept this counsel when given. It is one of the necessary conditions for prudence and is excellence in deliberation. (Etym. Latin *eubulia*, aptitude, capacity, talent; the virtue of good counsel.)

EUCHARIST. The true Body and Blood of Jesus Christ, who is really and substantially present under the appearances of bread and wine, in order to offer himself in the sacrifice of the Mass and to be received as spiritual food in Holy Communion. It is called Eucharist, or "thanksgiving," because at its institution at the Last Supper Christ "gave thanks," and by this fact it is the supreme object and act of Christian gratitude to God.

Although the same name is used, the Eucharist is any one or all three aspects of one mystery, namely the Real Presence, the Sacrifice, and Communion. As Real Presence, the Eucharist is Christ in his abiding existence on earth today; as Sacrifice, it is Christ in his abiding action of High Priest, continuing now to communicate the graces he merited on Calvary; and as Communion, it is Christ coming to enlighten and strengthen the believer by nourishing his soul for eternal life. (Etym. Latin *eucharistia*, the virtue of thanksgiving or thankfulness; from Greek *eucharistia*, gratitude; from *eu-*, good + *charizesthai*, to show favor.) See also SACRAMENT OF THE ALTAR.

EUCHARISTIAE SACRAMENTUM. A decree of the Sacred Congregation for Divine Worship, authorizing and explaining the reception of Holy Communion and the worship of the Blessed Sacrament outside of Mass. It deals with such aspects of the Eucharist as public exposition, benediction, Eucharistic processions and congresses, and the administration of Communion during and outside of Mass (June 21, 1973).

EUCHARISTIC ACCLAMATION. Mainly the Sanctus of the Mass. The entire congregation, in union with the heavenly powers, sings or says the "Holy, Holy, Holy" and concludes with the cry of praise addressed to Christ by the people on Palm Sunday. Other liturgical exclamations by the faithful are also called acclamations.

EUCHARISTIC CONGRESS. An international gathering of the faithful to foster devotion to the Blessed Sacrament of the Altar. The practice originated with a local gathering arranged through the efforts of Monsignor Gaston de Ségur, which met at Lille in France in 1881. In time the congresses developed to their present international character. The congress of 1908, which met in London, was the first occasion on which a papal legate had entered England since the Reformation. Two international Eucharistic congresses were held in the United States, the twenty-eighth at Chicago in 1926 and the forty-first at Philadelphia in 1976.

EUCHARISTIC DEVOTIONS. Pious practices in honor of the Blessed Sacrament approved and encouraged by the Church. Such are Visits to the Blessed Sacrament, the Holy Hour, Nine First Fridays, Exposition and Benediction, Eucharistic Procession, All-Night Vigil.

EUCHARISTIC DOXOLOGY. The end of the Eucharistic Prayer, which expresses the praise of God in the absolute sense of acknowledging his greatness and adoring his eternal Trinity of Father, Son, and Holy Spirit.

EUCHARISTIC ELEMENTS. The sensible matter of the Sacrament of the Eucharist, over which the words of Consecration are pronounced. They are bread, freshly made of wheaten flour, and wine as the natural uncorrupted juice of the grape. In the Latin Rite the bread is unleavened (without yeast); in the Eastern rites it is leavened.

EUCHARISTIC FAST. The abstinence from food and drink for one hour before receiving Holy Communion. Originally this meant complete abstinence even from water and medicine from midnight. Only those receiving viaticum were dispensed from this law. Pope Pius XII in 1953 reduced the fast to complete abstinence from solid food but permission for liquids (except alcohol) up to one hour before Communion. Pope Paul VI in 1964 further reduced the precept to complete abstinence up to one full hour before actually receiving Communion, but allowing water and medicine to be taken any time up to reception of the sacrament. In 1973 the Holy See further reduced the fast to fifteen minutes before Communion for the sick and advanced in age, and for those attending them if the hour's fast would be too difficult.

EUCHARISTIC INTERCESSION. Prayers of the priest at Mass, after the Consecration, which profess the belief that the Eucharist is celebrated in union with the whole Church in heaven and on earth, and that the sacrifice is offered for her and all her members living and dead.

EUCHARISTIC INVITATION. Liturgical request by a priest at Mass, while showing the people the sacred Host, asking them to receive Holy Communion. Together with him they express sentiments of humility in the words of the centurion in the Gospel.

EUCHARISTIC MEAL. Holy Communion as food of the soul. Implied in Christ's words when he told his followers to eat his body and drink his blood, the Eucharist is the principal source of sustenance of the supernatural life. Like food in the natural order, Communion nourishes this divine life, produces a sense of well-being and satiety in the soul, and protects a person from the ravages of spiritual disease or sin.

EUCHARISTIC OBLATION. After the consecration at Mass, the prayer of the Church universal and especially the congregation assembled in which the immaculate Victim is offered to God the Father in the Holy Spirit. The oblation means that the faithful offer up not only Christ but themselves in union with him. He died on his cross; they are to die to themselves on their cross and thus merit the graces that only sacrifice can merit before God.

EUCHARISTIC PRAYER. The central portion of the Eucharistic liturgy. There are eight parts to this prayer, namely the Preface, Acclamation, Epiclesis, Consecration, Anamnesis, Oblation, Intercessions, and Doxology. Its ritual history goes back to apostolic times.

EUCHARISTIC READINGS. Recitation of Bible passages at Mass during the Liturgy of the Word. By tradition the reading of extracts from the Scripture is done by an assistant. Hence the deacon, or some other priest if present, should read the Gospel; otherwise the priest celebrant. A lector reads the other extracts. Special marks of honor are paid to the reading of the Gospel, with the people standing and alternating responses with the priest at the beginning and conclusion of the Gospel reading. On solemn occasions the lectionary is incensed before the reading of the Gospel.

EUCHARISTICUM MYSTERIUM. Instruction of the Sacred Congregation of Rites on the worship of the Holy Eucharist. The document is in two parts, one dealing with principles and the other with practices. The main principle enunciated is that the Eucharist is Jesus Christ, and therefore to be honored as the heart of Catholic piety. The main practices urged on all the faithful are: 1. maintaining the spirit of oneness in the celebration of Mass; 2. restoring the centrality of Sunday, centered around the Eucharist; 3. fostering Holy Communion among the faithful; 4. reserving the Blessed Sacrament; 5. promoting devotion to the Blessed Sacrament through exposition and benediction (May 25, 1967) (Feast of Corpus Christi).

EUCHITES. See MESSALIANS.

EUDAEMONIA. Happiness as well-being, associated with Aristotle's concept of what satisfies human beings. (Etym. Greek *eudaimonia,* happiness, *eu,* good + *daimōn,* spirit.)

EUDISTS. Members of the Congregation of Jesus and Mary founded at Caen, France, in 1643, by St. John Eudes (1601–80). It is an association of priests, established to conduct seminaries. Almost extinguished by the French Revolution, it was reconstituted in 1826 and is engaged mainly in secondary education. A women's congregation, the Sisters of Our Lady of the Refuge, became an independent community in 1657. It took a fourth vow to care for fallen women.

EUGENICS. The science of hereditary and environmental influences in order to improve the physical and mental qualities of future generations. As a term, it was first used by Francis Galton (1822–1911), cousin of Charles Darwin (1809–82). There are, in general, two types of eugenics. An extreme form advocates the compulsory breeding of the select, contraception among the poor, and sterilization and euthanasia for the unfit. Moderate eugenics promotes the study of how to reduce the number of mentally and physically handicapped without resorting to coercive measures. The Catholic Church strongly supports the idea that people have a right to use suitable, licit

means to improve their own physical and mental condition and that of their children. But the Church condemns eugenicists who, in their narrow outlook, exalt eugenics as the supreme good and who, therefore, use illicit means to promote their goal. Eugenics has contributed substantially to the practice of contraception, sterilization, abortion, and euthanasia. (Etym. Greek *eugenēs,* well born.)

EUGENIC STERILIZATION. Depriving people of their generative powers in order to eliminate offspring having allegedly undesirable traits and to develop an environment more advantageous for human beings having allegedly desirable traits. The Catholic Church forbids the procedure because "public magistrates have no direct power over the bodies of their subjects. Therefore, where no crime has taken place and there is no cause for grave punishment, they can never directly harm or tamper with the integrity of the body, either for reasons of eugenics or for any other reason" (Pius XI, *Casti Connubii,* II, 68–70).

EULOGIA. Blessing or something blessed. The word was used in early Christian times for a benediction, and also for a blessed object, especially bread. It still refers to the *pain bénit* that is sometimes blessed in Church and either eaten there or taken home. Eulogia can likewise mean the Holy Eucharist. (Etym. Greek *eulogia,* praise; literally, good speaking.)

EULOGY. A formal, public address praising some person, event, or object, especially in honor of someone who recently died. St. Ambrose's eulogy of Emperor Valentinian (A.D. 392) is part of patristic history. (Etym. Greek *eulogia,* praise; literally, good speaking.)

EUNOMIANISM. The heretical teaching of Eunomius (d. 395), the Arian Bishop of Cyzicus in Mysia. It held that God is so absolutely one that the Second Person could not be generated within the divine nature. The Second and Third Persons were said to have been created. The Eunomianists also denied the value of any worship or the need for any sacraments.

EUTHANASIA. Literally "easy death," the act or practice of putting people to death because they or others decide that continued life would be burdensome. Originally the term was used for "mercy killing," which meant administration of an easy, painless death to one who was suffering from an incurable and perhaps agonizing disability or disease. Then, as mass genocide was legalized under Communism and Nazism, the term came to be applied to all forms of inflicting death on persons who are, by legal standards, permitted to take their lives or others are allowed to do so with the full protection of the civil law.

The Holy See was asked, "Is it permissible upon the mandate of public authority, directly to kill those who, although they have committed no crime deserving of death, are yet, because of psychic or physical defects, unable to be useful to the nation, but rather are considered a burden to its vigor and strength?" The reply was No, and the reason given was that "it is contrary to the natural and the divine positive law" (Pius XII, *Decree of the Holy Office*, December 1940).

The Catholic Church reprobates euthanasia because it is a usurpation of God's lordship over human life. As creatures of God, to whom human beings owe every element of their existence, they are entrusted only with the stewardship of their earthly lives. They are bound to accept the life that God gave them, with its limitations and powers; to preserve this life as the first condition of their dependence on the Creator; and not deliberately curtail their time of probation on earth, during which they are to work out and thereby merit the happiness of their final destiny.

EUTYCHIANISM. See MONOPHYSITISM.

EVANG., EVGL. *Evangelium*–Gospel, Evangelist. (Etym. Greek *eu-*, good + *angelos*, messenger: *euangelos*, bringing good news.)

EVANGELICAL OBEDIENCE. The voluntary submission of oneself to obey legitimate ecclesiastical authority beyond the demands of obedience prescribed on all the faithful. It is the free surrender of one's autonomy, according to the Church's directives, in order to better imitate Christ, and to cooperate with him in his work of redemption, who became obedient unto death, even to death on the Cross. This obedience of counsel may be given stability by a vow of obedience made to a superior in an institute of perfection or to one's confessor or spiritual director.

EVANGELICA TESTIFICATIO. Apostolic exhortation of Pope Paul VI on religious life. The most important single document on the subject since the Second Vatican Council. It recognizes that some are calling into question the very existence of the religious life. Its main focus is to urge religious to be faithful to the charism of their respective founders and to cultivate a strong spiritual life, whose center is the Eucharist (June 29, 1971).

EVANGELISM. Zealous preaching of the Gospel, commonly applied to persons or religious bodies that are dedicated to converting people to Christ. The term has this basic meaning of an outspoken proclamation of the Christian message, but it is also used in a negative sense by critics of an aggressive promotion of Christianity.

EVANGELIST. In general, a proclaimer of Gospel. The New Testament uses the term to describe a traveling missionary (Acts 21:8; Ephesians 4:11; and II Timothy 4:5). As such, it denotes a function rather than an office. Since the third century an evangelist has come to mean principally one of the writers of the Gospels: Matthew, Mark, Luke, and John.

EVANGELIST OF MARY. A title of St. Luke, whose Gospel gives us most of the facts we know about the Blessed Virgin. On two occasions, at the visit of the shepherds in Bethlehem (Luke 2:19) and after the finding of Christ in the Temple (Luke 2:51), Luke records that Mary "kept all these words, pondering them in her heart." Even the rationalist Adolf von Harnack (1851–1930) observes that "the accounts must be considered as communications from Mary." Christian tradition holds that among the sources he said he consulted in writing the Gospel (Luke 1:3) was the personal experience of the Virgin Mary.

EVANGELIUM. The Good News, the Gospel. In the Latin Vulgate it often means the New Testament, either as distinct from the Old Testament books of the Bible, or the whole New Covenant of God with His People.

EVANGELIZATION. Zealous proclamation of the Gospel in order to bring others to Christ and his Church. In the words of Pope Paul VI, "Evangelizing means to bring the Good News into all the strata of humanity, and through its influence transforming humanity from within and making it new, 'Now I am making the whole of creation new' (Revelation 21:5). But there is no new humanity if there are not first of all new persons renewed by baptism, and by lives lived according to the Gospel" (*Evangelii Nuntiandi*, 18). Evangelization, therefore, includes three distinctive elements: 1. interior conversion to Christ and his Church; 2. affecting not only the individual person but the whole culture; and 3. as a result, changing this culture and its institutions to make them Christian and Catholic. (Etym. Latin *evangelium;* from Greek *euangelion,* good news, reward for bringing good news, from *euangelos,* bringing good news: *eu-,* good, + *angelos,* messenger.)

EVANGELIZE. In general, to preach the Good News, as lived and taught by Jesus Christ. More specifically it means bringing the Christian revelation to persons and cultures to whom the Gospel has not yet been effectively proclaimed.

EVE. The first woman, wife of Adam and the mother of all the living (Genesis 3:20).

EVENING PRAYER. The fourth hour of the Divine Office, also called Vespers. It consists of a hymn, two psalms, an Old or New Testament canticle, short biblical reading, the Magnificat of the Blessed Virgin, responsories, intercessions, and a concluding prayer.

EVENSONG. The medieval name given in England for the canonical hour of Vespers. The term continued among Catholics after the Reformation but is now used quite exclusively for the Anglican service of Evening Prayer.

EVESHAM. A Marian shrine in Worcestershire, England, on the Avon River. This is an authentic place of apparition of Our Lady, who in the eighth century appeared to a swineherd named Eoves, sending him to the bishop with a request that a shrine be built to her in the forest nearby. Little is known of the first church, but Lady Godiva (c. 1010–67) rebuilt it completely and it became a favorite place of pilgrimage until the Reformation. A much frequented new shrine has been built by the Catholic people of Evesham and vicinity since World War II.

EVIDENCE. The ground or reason for knowledge, especially adequate knowledge for certitude.

EVIDENCE, CIRCUMSTANTIAL. Such convergence of facts and testimony about an event that only one conclusion can reasonably be drawn, although there has been no immediate knowledge of the event or even immediate witnesses to testify about what had taken place.

EVIDENCE, EXTRINSIC. The grounds for assenting to something on the authority of another person. It is called extrinsic evidence because it does not arise directly from the object known but from the word of someone whose credibility (authority) warrants acceptance.

EVIDENCE, INTRINSIC. The built-in grounds for the knowledge of something, and therefore not requiring the witness of authority to make it known. The object is intelligible from experience and/or reason, and not on faith.

EVIDENCE, OBJECTIVE. The reality of a thing which is so manifest to the mind that it demands assent because of the object itself and not because of any subjective grounds for acceptance.

EVIDENCE, SUBJECTIVE. The personal grounds that someone has for making a judgment or being certain about something. It is the satisfaction, actual or hopeful, that a person derives from accepting something as true.

EVIL. The privation of a good that should be present. It is the lack of a good that essentially belongs to a nature; the absence of a good that is natural and due to a being. Evil is therefore the absence of what ought to be there.

EVIL DESIRE. The wish or longing to do something forbidden. An absolute desire for what is sinful is a sin of the same moral species and gravity as the evil action desired, whether the desire is effective or not.

EVIL HABITS. Vices acquired through the repetition of bad moral actions. As a general rule, evil habits do not lessen the imputability of evil actions performed by force of habit if the habit has been recognized as evil and is freely allowed to continue. On the other hand, they do lessen the culpability of evil actions performed by force of habit if one is sincerely repentant and trying to correct the habit.

EVITERNITY. Duration with periodic or irregular intervals of change in such creatures as angels or the material universe. It is midway between the changeless duration of eternity, possessed only by God, and the constant change of time seen in individual beings. (Etym. Latin *aevum,* never-ending time.)

EVOLUTION. The theory that something was or is in a state of necessary development. Materialistic evolution assumes the eternal existence of uncreated matter and then explains the emergence of all living creatures, of plants, animals, and human beings, both body and soul, through a natural evolutionary process. This is contrary to

Christian revelation. Theistic evolution is compatible with Christianity provided it postulates the special divine providence as regards the human body and the separate creation of each human soul.

EVOLUTIONARY THEOLOGY. See PROCESS THEOLOGY.

EVOLUTIONISM. The theory that everything in the universe, including the world of spirit, is explainable by a natural and necessary development from the lower to the higher; and in Hegel's philosophy, from nonbeing to being.

EX. *Extra*—outside of.

EXAMEN, GENERAL. Prayerful daily periodic examination of one's conscience to determine what faults have been committed, which call for repentance, and what good actions were performed, for which God should be thanked.

EXAMEN, PARTICULAR. Regular prayerful examination of one's conscience by concentrating on some one particular moral failing to be overcome or virtue to be exercised. Its focus is on such external manifestations of the fault or virtue as can be remembered for periodic inventory. Particular examens are changed weekly, monthly, or otherwise in order to ensure maximum attention. They are also commonly associated with some brief invocation for divine assistance, as occasions arise for avoiding a sin or acting on a virtue. And after some time another cycle may be started of the same defects that this person has to conquer or good habits he or she needs to develop.

EXAMINATION OF CONSCIENCE. Reflection in God's presence on one's state of soul, e.g., in preparation for the sacrament of penance. See EXAMEN, GENERAL, and EXAMEN, PARTICULAR.

EXAMINER. In diocesan chanceries the priest official who was part of a board for the administrative change or removal of pastors.

EXARCH. A title originally used by civil and ecclesiastical rulers. An ecclesiastical exarch was a metropolitan with jurisdiction beyond his own province, the most important of whom were those of Ephesus and Caesarea. "Vicar Apostolic" in the West has replaced the title "Exarch." The name today is given to the heads of the Russian and Greek Catholics of the Byzantine Rite, and to the Melkite patriarchal vicar of Jerusalem. Some Ukrainian bishops in North America today

are called exarchs. (Etym. Latin *exarchus;* from Greek *exarchein,* to begin, take the lead.)

EXC. *Excommunicatus, excommunicatio*—excommunicated, excommunication.

EXCARDINATION. The perpetual release of a cleric from the jurisdiction of one bishop to another. It is not effective unless he receives absolute and permanent letters affiliating him with another diocese or vicarate. To be valid, the release must be signed by a bishop. Acceptance of a residential benefice in another diocese calls for excardination. A religious making perpetual profession is likewise excardinated from his diocese.

EX CATHEDRA. The term commonly applied to the special and explicit exercise of papal infallibility. When the Pope speaks from the chair (*cathedra*) of authority, as visible head of all Christians, his teaching is not dependent on the consent of the Church and is irreformable. (Etym. Latin *ex cathedra,* from the chair.)

EXCELLENCY. The proper title of a bishop or archbishop. It is also the correct form of address of patriarchs, instead of "His Beatitude," as decreed by the Congregation of Ceremonies in 1893.

EXCESS. More than is required. Applied especially to human conduct, when a person either indulges a bodily or spiritual appetite, as in food or knowledge, or goes beyond the limit of prudence in the way he or she practices what would otherwise be a virtue, as in showing affection.

EXCLAUSTRATION. An indult that is granted by a bishop for diocesan communities and by the Holy See for institutes of pontifical right, and that permits religious to live outside the community for a specified time. The religious remain bound by their vows and by the obligations of their profession so far as they are compatible with their status.

EXCLUSION, RIGHT OF. The alleged right of the Holy Roman emperors, and the sovereigns of France, Spain, and the two Sicilies to exclude certain cardinals from election at a papal conclave. Although the popes protested, there are on record seven occasions when the cardinals really changed their votes in order not to see the new Pope embarrassed by the disaffection of some powerful ruler. The last resistance of a successful interference was in 1903, after the death of Leo XIII. When Austria objected to Cardinal Rampolla (1843–1913), the electors on his own request ceased voting for him and concentrated on Joseph Sarto, who became Pope Pius X. Soon after his election the Pope forbade (January 20, 1904), under pain of excommunication, that any such exclusion should be expressed by any cardinal.

EXCOMMUNICATION. An ecclesiastical censure by which one is more or less excluded from communion with the faithful. It is also called *anathema*, especially if it is inflicted with formal solemnities on persons notoriously obstinate to reconciliation. Some excommunicated persons are *vitandi* (to be avoided), others *tolerati* (tolerated). No one is *vitandus* unless that person has been publicly excommunicated by name by the Holy See, and it is expressly stated that the person is "to be avoided." Anyone who lays violent hands on the Pope is automatically *vitandus.*

In general, the effects of excommunication affect the person's right to receive the sacraments, or Christian burial, until the individual repents and is reconciled with the Church. In order for an excommunication to take effect, the person must have been objectively guilty of the crime charged. (Etym. Latin *ex-*, from + *communicare*, to communicate: *excommunicatio*, exclusion from a community.)

EXCUSE. A legitimate reason that exempts a person from the observance of the law in a given instance. It corresponds to epikeia, by which one decides whether there are legitimate grounds for exemption. It may also be an alleged reason that someone adduces for not wanting to observe a law that is actually binding in the given situation. It is finally any mitigating circumstance that lessens responsibility for human acts, such as ignorance or psychological pressure.

EXCUSE FROM DUTY. Fact or circumstance that allows a person not to fulfill a certain obligation. Duty is imposed by law, which by definition is reasonable and for the common good. The purpose is not to crush men and women with unreasonable burdens. Hence there are causes that can excuse from duty, because in these cases the duty really invades a person's rights. In general, legitimate excuses are reducible to practical impossibility or disproportionate hardship. But much depends on whether the natural or a positive law is in question.

A negative duty (prohibition) arising from the natural law admits of no excuse whatever. Such a duty concerns matters forbidden by the natural law as inherently wrong. Such are blasphemy, perjury, and murder. An affirmative duty (command) arising from the natural law admits of excuse, but there must be no violation of a prohibition imposed by the natural law. For example the omission of an act of worship must not be interpreted as a denial of God. Duties arising from human positive law, whether prohibitions or commands, admit of excuse because of impossibility or excessive hardships. But here, too, there can be no excuse from a prohibition binding by the natural law.

EXEAT. The letter of excardination by which a cleric receives absolute and perpetual release from one diocese and acceptance by the bishop of another diocese.

EXEGESIS. The art and science of investigating and expressing the true sense of Sacred Scripture. Its function is to find out what exactly a given passage of the Bible says. Its rules are governed by the science of hermeneutics, whose practical application is the concern of exegesis. Given the depth and complexity of the biblical text, biblical exegesis has been practiced from pre-Christian times. (Etym. Greek *exēgēsis*, interpretation.)

EXEMPLARISM. The erroneous theory of the Atonement which holds that Christ's passion and death are salutary only by reason of the example that the Savior gave to mankind. It is a modern variant of Pelagianism, which claimed that Adam's sin was essentially the bad example he passed on to his progeny; and Christ's role would then be only to give the contrary, good example.

EXEMPLARY CAUSE. The cause that an intelligent being uses as the pattern or model, in the mind, for producing some effect. Thus the universe was created according to the Divine Plan, consisting of the ideas present in the mind of God from all eternity.

EXEMPT BISHOP. The ordinary of a diocese that does not form part of an ecclesiastical province. So called because he is exempt from the jurisdiction of a metropolitan archbishop and directly subject to the Pope.

EXEMPTION. The withdrawal of a person or place from the jurisdiction of an inferior authority and immediate subjection to a higher power. Religious orders under solemn vows and some under simple vows by papal indult are exempt or free from the jurisdiction of the local ordinary and subject immediately to the jurisdiction of the Holy See. A diocese not under the metropolitan authority of any archbishop, but under the immediate subjection of the Holy See, and any archdiocese whose archbishop is not metropolitan are both exempt. (Etym. Latin *eximere*, to take out, deliver, free.)

EXEMPTION, CLERICAL. In ecclesiastical law the privilege of being exempt from the duty of serving in the armed forces and in civil public offices enjoyed by all men in the clerical state in the Catholic Church.

EXEQUATUR. The right that civil rulers claim to examine and decide whether papal or episcopal enactments are to be accepted in their political territories. A much abused privilege, in modern times the practice is universal, in intent if not in effect, among Communist governments in their attitude toward the Catholic Church. The *Exequatur* has been formally condemned by the Church. In the Syllabus of Errors, issued by Pope Pius IX in 1864, condemned Proposition 41 reads: "The civil power, even when exercised by an infidel ruler, has an indirect and negative power over religious affairs; it therefore possesses not only the right called *exequatur*, but also the right of *appeal from an abuse*, as it is called" (Denzinger 2941). (Etym. Latin *exequatur*, let him perform.)

EXISTENCE. Whatever has reality of its own and not merely in potency or in the powers of its causes. That which really is. The fundamental actuality of any being insofar as it is being; it is the being in act. Thus the act of being as distinct from merely the capacity for being, or the act of existence by which a substance or an essence is and not only may or can be. It corresponds to the scholastic term *esse*, namely that something is, and not merely *essentia*, or what it is.

EXISTENTIAL ETHICS. The theory of conduct which stresses the personal, here-and-now aspect of human behavior; an aspect that is not covered by general laws, since every moral decision is in its way particular and even unique. Existential ethics is a useful complement to "essential ethics." But it becomes situation ethics or moral relativism when it tries to substitute for essential ethics, which is based on universal norms that apply to the human essence everywhere.

EXISTENTIALISM. In scholastic philosophy the philosophical emphasis on existence and concrete individuals rather than on essences or abstract concepts. Accordingly, it stresses the real over the speculative, the actual over the theoretical, the particular over the general, and the human over the

cosmic. It uses history as an instrument of thought and concentrates on the free actions of persons over the broad expanse of ideas or movements that shape human culture and determine human life and destiny.

EXODUS. The second book of the Bible, so named because it relates the departure of the Israelites from Egypt and their wandering through the desert up to Mount Sinai. There are five principal parts to the book: events in Egypt before the exodus (1–12), leaving Egypt and the journey to Mount Sinai (13–18), promulgation of the first precepts of the Mosaic law (19–31), apostasy of the Jews, reconciliation and renewal of the Covenant (32–34), construction of the Tabernacle (35–40).

EX OPERE OPERANTIS. A term mainly applied to the good dispositions with which a sacrament is received, to distinguish it from the *ex opere operato*, which is the built-in efficacy of a sacrament properly conferred. But it may refer to any subjective factor that at least partially determines the amount of grace obtained by a person who performs some act of piety. Thus in the use of sacramentals or in the gaining of indulgences, the blessings received depend largely on the faith and love of God with which a sacramental is employed or an indulgenced prayer or good work is performed.

EX OPERE OPERANTIS ECCLESIAE. A phrase used to distinguish the value of liturgical prayer and action, whose supernatural efficacy depends on the Church's sanctity and not, as in the sacraments, simply on the fact that the sacramental rite is performed.

EX OPERE OPERATO. A term defined by the Council of Trent to describe how the sacraments confer the grace they signify. Trent condemned the following proposition: "That grace is not conferred 'ex opere operato' by the sacraments of the New Law" (Denzinger 1608). Literally the expression means "from the work performed," stating that grace is always conferred by a sacrament, in virtue of the rite performed and not as a mere sign that grace has already been given, or that the sacrament stimulates the faith of the recipient and thus occasions the obtaining of grace, or that what determines the grace is the virtue of either the minister or recipient of a sacrament. Provided no obstacle (obex) is placed in the way, every sacrament properly administered confers the grace intended by the sacrament. In a true sense the sacraments are instrumental causes of grace.

EXORCISM. An adjuration in which the devil is either commanded to depart from a possessed person or forbidden to harm someone. Although commonly referred to as driving the evil spirit from a possessed person, exorcism is essentially the same when used in the case of obsession.

The Gospels are filled with descriptive narratives about exorcisms performed by Christ. St. Mark's Gospel is especially detailed in the number of exorcisms performed by the Master, and the effortless ease with which he delivered those who were under the influence of the evil one. In the account of these exorcisms, the contemporary idiom is unreservedly adopted: the evil spirits cry out in words found in contemporary stories where a devil about to be exorcised acknowledges the power of the exorcist: "I know you. You are . . ." Hence it is noteworthy that Jesus uses none of the contemporary exorcists' rituals and spells, but simply expels them by the power of his command. The deeper significance of these narratives is that Jesus inaugurates the final struggle against all evil and, with emphasis, against the evil spirit, and foreshadows the final victory. Significant, too, are the peace (Mark 4:39, 5:15, 6:51) and awareness of the divine presence (Mark 1:27, 2:12, 5:15) which follow Christ's expulsion of demons. (Etym. Latin *exorcismus;* from Greek *exorkizein,* to drive away by adjuration.) See also RITE OF EXORCISM.

EXORCIST. Formerly one of the minor orders leading to the priesthood, although the power to drive out evil spirits was never confined to any particular order. The office of exorcist originally included the right to lay hands on possessed persons, exorcise catechumens, and pour out the water at Mass. The office was abolished as a minor order by Pope Paul VI in 1972. But episcopal conferences may petition the Holy See to confer the ministry of exorcist if this would be useful or necessary for their territory.

EXOTERIC. Also "external," as belonging to or suited to those who are not experts or initiates. Thus exoteric arguments are forms of reasoning that the ordinary people can understand. (Etym. Latin *exotericus;* from Greek *exoterikos,* external.)

EXPERIENCE. Any form of knowledge arising from one's own immediate awareness. It is knowledge gained by a person's own contact with reality. It is a composite of the mental, volitional, and emotional activity that no one but the person himself or herself has gone through, and that, absolutely speaking, is therefore not communicable. It is the unique possession of each individual, whose self-awareness is so different from that of everyone else that it best distinguishes the individual as a person.

Experience is also the accumulated practical wisdom and skill that people acquire in their particular trade or profession. It is then contrasted with merely speculative or book knowledge and has special significance in the art and science of Christian perfection. (Etym. Latin *experientia,* act of trying, testing, becoming acquainted with.)

EXPERIMENT. An act or practice undertaken to discover, test, or illustrate some truth, principle, fact, or hypothesis. Implicit in every valid experimentation in the moral and spiritual order is: 1. the recognition of certain nonexperimental principles of faith and morality; 2. adherence to the Church's directives on the conditions for experimentation; 3. definite and clear-cut norms of time and circumstances within which the experimenting is to be done; 4. willingness to recognize the success or failure of the experimentation and take measures to implement or desist from further experimentation accordingly. (Etym. Latin *experimentum,* trial, test, experiment; learning through experience.)

EXPERIMENTAL SPIRITUALITY. A method of using knowledge gained from the observation of ascetical and mystical phenomena. It studies one's own and other people's experience in order to learn the marks peculiar to each state of soul as well as the virtues and dispositions peculiar to different persons. Carried to its full possibility, it not only tells how to practice the virtues but also discloses the principles that motivate the practice of sanctity.

EXPIATION. Atonement for some wrongdoing. It implies an attempt to undo the wrong that one has done, by suffering a penalty, by performing some penance, or by making reparation or redress. (Etym. Latin *ex-,* fully + *piare,* to propitiate: *expiare,* to atone for fully.)

EXPOSITION OF THE BLESSED SACRAMENT. The ceremony in which a priest or deacon removes the Sacred Host from the tabernacle and places it on the altar for adoration. In public exposition the Sacred Host is placed in the lunette of the monstrance and elevated so that all adorers can see it. In private expositions the tabernacle door is opened and the ciborium containing consecrated Hosts is brought forward. Any good cause is reason for private adoration. Public exposition of the Blessed Sacrament requires a period of adoration, in private or public with prescribed hymns and prayers, as well as the blessing with the monstrance. Definite days for public adoration of the Blessed Sacrament are no longer specified for the universal Church; now any days may be chosen for good reasons; and for regular exposition permissions are granted by the local ordinary. The ceremony was introduced in the fourteenth century under the influence of the newly established feast of Corpus Christi. Some religious monasteries and convents with special permission have the Sacred Host perpetually exposed for special honor and devotion with someone in attendance night and day.

EXSULTET. The Easter proclamation, sung at the Easter Vigil, beginning in Latin, *"Exsultet iam angelica turba caelorum."* In literal translation the opening words read: "Now, let the angelic host of heaven exult, exult the mysteries divine; and for the victory of so great a King, sound the trumpet of salvation." Ascribed to St. Augustine, the *Exsultet* is probably of later origin.

EXTERN. A term sometimes applied by members of a religious institute to persons who do not belong to the community. More commonly used of those women religious in cloistered communities who take care of the temporal needs of the choir sisters and are therefore in regular contact with the outside world.

EXTERNAL ACT. The physical or sensibly perceptible side of a human action. It is that which the one who performs the act and others can see or otherwise perceive by their senses. External acts, as such, are neither good nor bad, since they derive their moral value from the internal acts of the will. Nevertheless, external actions are morally good or bad by participation in what a person intends to do internally. They are the normal means for expressing, continuing, intensifying, or of repeating an internal act. Thus Catholic morality does not subscribe to the theory of Kant that morality consists solely in a good will, so that the external physical act is quite outside the scope of morals.

EXTERNAL GRACES. Those providential means that God uses as occasions for conferring interior actual graces. External graces are all creatures that are divinely intended to lead us to our eternal destiny. They are any person, place, or thing that

can help us attain the end for which we were created.

EXTRA ECCLESIAM NULLA SALUS. Outside the Church there is no salvation. Solemnly defined doctrine that says that no one who culpably refuses to become and remain a member of the Catholic Church can be saved. Positively this means that all who reach their eternal destiny are saved through the Catholic Church, of which Christ is the visible head. This is true even though they may not have lived as professed Roman Catholics (Fourth Lateran Council, A.D. 1215, Denzinger 802).

EXTRAORDINARY JURISDICTION. The right to exercise ecclesiastical authority when granted by delegation, or for a definite time or a particular function.

EXTRAORDINARY MEANS. Such means of preserving human life as cannot be obtained or used without extreme difficulty in terms of pain, expense, or other burdening factors. The burden applies either to the person whose life is at stake or to those on whom his or her welfare depends. In addition, means should be considered extraordinary if, when used, they do not offer a reasonable hope of benefit to the one for whom they are intended.

There is no general obligation to use extraordinary means to keep alive, on the premise that God does not exact what is beyond the ordinary power of humans in general. At times, however, one may be bound to employ extraordinary means to preserve life. The two conditions under which such an obligation becomes binding are that a person is necessary to one's family, to the Church, or to society, and the success of the extraordinary means is very probable.

EXTRAORDINARY MINISTER. The person who, in case of necessity, is permitted or specially delegated to administer one of the sacraments. Baptism, confirmation, and the Eucharist may have extraordinary ministers. Thus baptism is to be ordinarily administered by a priest or deacon, but in emergency any person who has reached the age of reason may validly confer the sacrament. The ordinary minister of confirmation is a bishop, but for special pastoral reasons simple priests may confirm. When they do, their power derives from the papal authorization, which the Holy See actuates in them in virtue of their priestly ordination; it is not a mere extrasacramental delegation. And the ordinary minister of Communion is a priest or deacon, but in cases of real necessity, which have been broadly interpreted since the Second Vatican Council, lay persons and religious may be authorized by a bishop to distribute the Holy Eucharist.

EXTRAVERSION. A personality trait, with moral implications, characterized by outward activity, preoccupation with people and events, and the tendency to avoid thoughtful reflection or prayer.

EXTREME NECESSITY. A very urgent need that a person has for such human goods as food or medical care in order to sustain life or even a minimum of human living. It is extreme poverty or destitution, indicating the want of basic human needs.

EXTREME UNCTION. A term used for centuries for the sacrament of the anointing of the sick. It is unction because a person is anointed with oil; it is extreme because it is conferred on those who are considered *in extremis,* i.e., in extreme physical disability with the likelihood of dying.

EXTRINSIC. The opposite of intrinsic. Something taken from the outside and having external value, without belonging essentially to the object under consideration; as the language of the liturgy is extrinsic to its efficacy as a channel of grace.

EX VOTO. Something offered by promise or vow in thanksgiving for a favor received or for one being petitioned. Plaques at shrines are *ex voto* offerings that acknowledge cures or other important favors secured. Votive candles before an altar or shrine are lighted for the same reasons.

EYE. A symbol of the omniscience of God. "The eye of Yahweh is in every place beholding the good and the evil" (Proverbs 15:3). Established about the sixteenth century, it is often represented in a triangle, the "all seeing eye" serving as an admonition against sinning. Eyes on a plate have been used in illustrations of St. Lucy, probably because her name means light and she suffered greatly from eye disability.

EZEKIEL. A prophet of the sixth century B.C. He grew up in Jerusalem and was a contemporary of Jeremiah. He was primarily a preacher profoundly concerned for the spiritual improvement of his people. He disdained the concept of the Messiah as a glorious, militant king; rather he stressed the image of the less dramatic shepherd. Some of his major themes were: reproaches addressed to unfaithful Israelites; "The guilt of the House of Israel and Judah is immense, boundless; the country is full of bloodshed, the city overflows with wickedness" (Ezekiel 9:9); occasional denunciations of foreign nations exerting evil influence on his people, and prophetic anticipation of better days ahead for Israel (Ezekiel 25, 29, 30). "Then they shall be my people and I will be their God" (Ezekiel 11:21). His book concluded on the prophetic note: "The name of the city in future is to be: Yahweh-is-there" (Ezekiel 48:35). The Book of Ezekiel is quoted extensively by St. John in the Apocalypse; in fact there are many points of similarity between the writings of the prophet and of the apostle.

EZRA. A Jewish priest during the reign of the Persian king Artaxerxes (404–358 B.C.). His chief contribution was instituting reforms in the Jewish church and state. In Greek and Latin the name is Esdras. Thanks to the generous policy of the king, Ezra was able to organize a pilgrimage of fifteen hundred families in Babylon to cross the desert to Jerusalem (Ezra 7). He was shocked on arriving to become aware of the great number of Israelites married to foreign women, a practice he described as "treachery" (Ezra 9:2). His denunciation led to the dissolution of many such marriages and considerable unhappiness among the people (Ezra 10). Aiding Ezra in his work was the layman Nehemiah. In fact the biblical report of their ministry carries the joint title "The Book of Ezra and Nehemiah." In the Vulgate, I Esdras is Ezra; II Esdras is Nehemiah. Much of Ezra's accomplishment could be called administrative. He reformed the ecclesiastical ritual, organization of the synagogue improved, and the rise of the rabbinate and eventually the development of the Sanhedrin were tributes to his ability.

F

FACULTIES. Rights granted by the Holy See to bishops and by ordinaries to their priests to enable the latter to exercise their respective powers for the faithful under their jurisdiction. The term is most commonly used in relation to the sacrament of penance, where faculties are needed for the priest to absolve not only licitly but even validly. However, faculties for licit administration are required for all the sacraments, with varying degrees of obligation. On a wider scale, faculties are also required for the exercise of ecclesiastical authority or, in general, for performance of any act of jurisdiction in the Catholic Church. In every case it is assumed that the one giving the faculties has the right to do so and the one receiving them has the power to put them into practice.

FACULTY. The power or ability to do or make something. It is an active potency and not merely a passive capacity. In human beings it is an accident that disposes a person to operate in a specific way for a specific purpose, as the faculty of thought is the intellect, which enables one to know reality outside the mind. (Etym. Latin *facultas,* facility, capacity.)

FAIRNESS. That form of justice which is practiced where no positive norms exist of what is right and just. Fairness is a disposition of will by which a person is habitually inclined to give to another his or her due, even in the absence of a specific law.

FAITH. The acceptance of the word of another, trusting that one knows what the other is saying and is honest in telling the truth. The basic motive of all faith is the authority (or right to be believed) of someone who is speaking. This authority is an adequate knowledge of what he or she is talking about, and integrity in not wanting to deceive. It is called divine faith when the one believed is God, and human faith when the persons believed are human beings. (Etym. Latin *fides,* belief; habit of faith; object of faith.)

FAITH, ACT OF. The assent of the mind to what God has revealed. An act of supernatural faith requires divine grace, either actual or sanctifying or both. It is performed under the influence of the will, which requires its own assistance of grace to render a person ready to believe. And if the act of faith is made in the state of grace, it is meritorious before God. Explicit acts of faith are necessary, notably when the virtue of faith is being tested by temptation or one's faith is challenged, or one's belief would be weakened unless strengthened by acts of faith. A simple and widely used act of faith says: "My God, I believe in you and all that your Church teaches, because you have said it, and your word is true. Amen."

FAITH AND REASON. The relationship between human response to God's revelation and use of human native intelligence. This relationship is mainly of three kinds, where the role of reason is to assist divine faith: 1. reason can establish the rational grounds for belief by proving God's existence, his authority or credibility as all-wise and trustworthy, and by proving that God actually made a revelation since he confirmed the fact by working (even now) miracles that testify to God's having spoken to human beings, especially in the person of Jesus Christ; 2. reason can further reflect on what God has revealed and thus come to an even deeper and clearer understanding of the divine mysteries; and 3. reason can both show that the mysteries of faith are in harmony with naturally known truths and can defend their validity against the charge of being contrary to reason.

FAITHFUL, THE. Believing Christians. They are faithful twice over: first by their assent to God's revelation, and again by their living up to what they profess.

FAITH HEALER. A person who claims to have extraordinary powers of healing sickness or disability. The healing is effected by the laying on of hands, quoting passages from the Bible, or calling upon God to perform the healing and generally doing so in an atmosphere charged with strong religious feeling.

Most instances of reported faith healing are cases of healing by suggestion. Because of the close relationship between mind and body, hope and courage tend to maintain and restore health, while fear and depression produce an injurious effect on the body. Strong suggestions received from one in whom a person has confidence may be beneficial to health. This is particularly true if the ailment is mainly functional or psychosomatic, or a vivid imagination has made it worse.

Although faith healing by suggestion is not sinful, provided neither superstition, scandal, nor co-operation in fraud is involved, and in serious illness there is recourse to medical help, faith healers who claim to have a divine gift and encourage people to come to them to be cured are traditionally suspect by Catholic standards. Saints are careful not to publicize their sanctity or possible gift of miraculous healing power.

FAITH VERSUS FATALISM. The phenomenon in world religious history that, as faith in a personal God recedes, fatalism takes over. Those who believe realize that there is more to human events—and therefore to history—than brute data unfolding themselves through inner necessity. There are wills, and their free exercise, in the universe: of God, who freely guides mankind, and of humans who freely reject or respond to the divine will.

FAITH, VIRTUE OF. The infused theological virtue whereby a person is enabled to "believe that what God has revealed is true —not because its intrinsic truth is seen with the rational light of reason—but because of the authority of God who reveals it, of God who can neither deceive nor be deceived" (First Vatican Council, Denzinger 3008).

FALDSTOOL. A movable folding chair used by a bishop at formal liturgical ceremonies. Other prelates who enjoy the privileges of full pontificals may also use it.

FALL. The original sin of Adam and Eve by which they lost the divine friendship and preternatural gifts for themselves and all their human progeny.

FALLACY. The violation of logical principle, disguised under the show of validity. It is a sophism and, therefore, anything illogical that is also misleading. A fallacy implies both error and the element of more or less conscious deception in the presentation of proof or argumentation. (Etym. Latin *fallere,* to deceive.)

FALLEN NATURE. Human nature since the fall of Adam. It is a nature that lacks the right balance it had originally. It is a wounded but not perverted nature. Since the fall, man has a built-in bias away from what is morally good and toward what is wrong. He is weakened in his ability to know the truth and to want the truly good. With the help of grace, however, he can overcome these natural tendencies and become sanctified in the process.

FALL OF ADAM. First sin of the father of the human race. As a result, he lost for himself and his posterity the supernatural gift of sanctifying grace and the preternatural gifts of integrity, bodily immortality, and impassibility. The fall is commonly referred only to Adam because he was appointed the juridical head of the human race, and his guilt was passed on to his progeny. However, Eve also shared in the fall of the human race because she tempted Adam after she yielded to the temptation of the devil. Adam and Eve, although specially gifted by grace, remained free to choose moral evil. They did not yet enjoy the beatific vision of God and consequently had only faith to tell them that what God forbade was truly wrong and what God threatened would really take place. It is uncertain what sin they committed. Most probably it was the disobedience of pride. They yielded to the devil's suggestion that they would become like God.

FALSE. The untrue in thought, word, or appearance. What is untrue in thought is logically false. The untrue in written or spoken word is a lie. And the misleading or deceptive in appearance is ontologically false, or false in being, and is the occasion of error in judgment.

FALSE CONSCIENCE. The judgment of the mind when it wrongly decides that something is lawful but that in fact is unlawful, or vice versa. The error may be due to the false principles used or because the mind was darkened or confused in its reasoning process.

FALSE WITNESS. In its original context in the Decalogue (Exodus 20:16) the prohibition of speaking falsely about a person before a tribunal, whether as a witness for the defense or prosecution. When a witness was found to have lied, he was subjected to the same punishment allotted for the crime for which he falsely testified against another person. In time, already before the Christian era, this commandment was understood to forbid all telling of untruth.

FAMILY. A group of persons who are related by marriage or blood and who typically include a father, mother, and children. A family is a natural society whose right to existence and support is provided by the divine law. According to the Second Vatican Council, "the family is the foundation of society" (*The Church in the Modern World,* II, 52). In addition to the natural family, the Church recognizes also the supernatural family of the diocese and of a religious community, whose members are to cooperate for the upbuilding of the Body of Christ (*Decree on the Bishops' Pastoral Office,* 34; and *Dogmatic Constitution on the Church,* 43). (Etym. Latin *familia,* a family, the members of a household; from *famulus,* a servant, attendant.)

FAMILY PLANNING. The regulation or limitation of a family by whatever means. In popular language it has become synonymous with contraception as a deliberate policy.

FAMILY ROSARY. International movement promoting recitation of the Rosary by the members of a family at home. Encouraged by the popes, the practice was singled out for special recommendation by Pope Paul VI in his Apostolic Exhortation in 1974 on devotion to the Blessed Virgin. "There is no doubt," he declared, "that after the celebration of the Liturgy of the Hours, the high point which family prayer can reach, the Rosary, should be considered as one of the best and most efficacious prayers in common that the Christian family is invited to recite" (*Marialis Cultus,* 54).

FANATICISM. A state of mind that prompts unreasonable reactions in speech or conduct, often bordering on insanity, especially in religious matters. Fanaticism differs from insanity in being concentrated on some one area of behavior; in its antecedents, which include prolonged, at least implicit, indoctrination; in the deep sense of dedication to a particular cause; in the emotional zeal with which the cause is pursued; and in the blind anger against any person or persons who stand in the way. (Etym. Latin *fanaticus,* belonging to a temple; inspired by a divinity, enthusiastic; *fanum,* a temple.)

FANTASM. Sense experience in the human imagination, out of which the intellect abstracts ideas. The sense impression may be pictorial, auditory, or any other corresponding to any of the external sensations. Divine communications often occur as fantasms, as in the biblical revelations of the New Testament, said to have taken place in a dream. Also spelled "phantasm."

FASTING. A form of penance that imposes limits on the kind or quantity of food or drink. From the first century Christians have observed fasting days of precept, notably during the season of Lent in commemoration of Christ's passion and death. In the early Church there was less formal precept and therefore greater variety of custom, but in general fasting was much more severe than in the modern Church. In the East and West the faithful abstained on fasting days from wine as well as from flesh-meat, both being permitted only in cases of weak health. The ancient custom in the Latin Church of celebrating Mass in the evening during Lent was partly due to the fact that in many places the first meal was not taken before sunset.

The modern Church regulations on fast-ing, until 1966, prescribed taking only one full meal a day, along with some food for breakfast and a collation. Days of fast and abstinence for the universal Church were Ash Wednesday, the Fridays and Saturdays of Lent, Ember days, and the vigils of certain feasts. Days of fast only were the rest of the days of Lent, except Sundays. Special indults affected different nations and were provided for by canon law.

With the constitution *Paenitemini* of Paul VI in 1966, the meaning of the law of fasting remained, but the extent of the obligation was changed. Thus "the law of fasting allows only one full meal a day, but does not prohibit taking some food in the morning and evening, while observing approved local custom as far as quantity and quality of food are concerned." To the law of fast are bound those of the faithful who have completed their twenty-first year and up until the beginning of their sixtieth year. Prescribed days of fast and abstinence for the whole Church are Ash Wednesday and Good Friday. Nevertheless, as with abstinence, so with fasting or other forms of penance, "It is up to the bishops, gathered in their episcopal conferences, to establish the norms . . . which they consider the most opportune and efficacious" (*Paenitemini,* III). In the Eastern rites it is the right of the patriarch, together with the synod or supreme authority of every rite, to determine the days of fast and abstinence in accordance with the decree of the Second Vatican Council for Eastern Churches.

FATALISM. Belief in the inevitability of all events, whether caused or uncaused. It differs from fate in that it provides for the inevitability on the basis of cause and effect relationship.

FATE. Predetermined and inevitable necessity. In the non-Christian religions, ancient and modern, it is the belief that events constitute a chain of causes and effects with absolute determinism. It differs from fortune in that the latter falls outside of determinism. (Etym. Latin *fatum,* what is spoken.)

FATHER. Theologically, a father is the principal one who produces of his own substance another person like himself. There is, consequently, a Father within the Trinity, who begets God the Son. But the triune God is himself spoken of as Father, with respect to the rational beings whom he made to share in his own possession of knowledge and love. Among human beings a father is the male parent of his own children and, ultimately, the ancestor of all his progeny. In Church usage the term is applied to the early spokesmen and defenders of Christianity, bishops who attend regional and especially ecumenical councils, and priests in general or specific priests in their role as confessors or spiritual counselors of the faithful.

FATHERS OF THE CHURCH. Saintly writers of the early centuries whom the Church recognizes as her special witnesses of the faith. Antiquity, orthodoxy, sanctity, and approval by the Church are their four main prerogatives. They are commonly divided into the Greek and Latin Fathers. It is now generally held that the last of the Western Fathers (Latin) closed with St. Isidore of Seville (560–636), and the last of the Eastern Fathers (Greek) was St. John Damascene (675–749).

LATIN FATHERS OF THE CHURCH

St. Ambrose, Bishop of Milan (340–97)
Arnobius, apologist (d. 327)
St. Augustine, Bishop of Hippo (354–430)
St. Benedict, father of Western monasticism (480–546)
St. Caesarius, Archbishop of Arles (470–542)
St. John Cassian, abbot, ascetical writer (360–435)
St. Celestine I, Pope (d. 432)
St. Cornelius, Pope (d. 253)
St. Cyprian, Bishop of Carthage (d. 258)
St. Damasus I, Pope (d. 384)
St. Dionysius, Pope (d. 268)
St. Ennodius, Bishop of Pavia (473–521)
St. Eucherius, Bishop of Lyons (d. 449)
St. Fulgentius, Bishop of Ruspe (468–533)
St. Gregory of Elvira (died after 392)
St. Gregory (I) the Great, Pope (540–604)
St. Hilary, Bishop of Poitiers (315–68)
St. Innocent I, Pope (d. 417)
St. Irenaeus, Bishop of Lyons (130–200)
St. Isidore, Archbishop of Seville (560–636)
St. Jerome, priest, exegete, translator of the Vulgate (343–420)
Lactantius Firmianus, apologist (240–320)
St. Leo the Great, Pope (390–461)
Marius Mercator, Latin polemicist (early fifth century)
Marius Victorinus, Roman rhetorician (fourth century)
Minucius Felix, apologist (second or third century)
Novatian, the Schismatic (200–62)
St. Optatus, Bishop of Mileve (late fourth century)
St. Pacian, Bishop of Barcelona (fourth century)
St. Pamphilus, priest (240–309)
St. Paulinus, Bishop of Nola (353–431)
St. Peter Chrysologus, Archbishop of Ravenna (400–50)
St. Phoebadius, Bishop of Agen (d. 395)
St. Prosper of Aquitaine, theologian (390–463)
Rufinus, Latin translator of Greek theology (345–410)
Salvian, priest (400–80)
St. Siricius, Pope (334–99)
Tertullian, apologist, founder of Latin theology (160–223)
St. Vincent of Lérins, priest and monk (d. 450)

GREEK FATHERS OF THE CHURCH

St. Anastasius Sinaita, apologist, monk (d. 700)
St. Andrew of Crete, Archbishop of Gortyna (660–740)
Aphraates, Syriac monk (early fourth century)
St. Archelaus, Bishop of Cascar (d. 282)
St. Athanasius, Archbishop of Alexandria (c. 297–373)
Athenagoras, apologist (second century)
St. Basil the Great, Archbishop of Caesarea (329–79)
St. Caesarius of Nazianzus (330–69)
St. Clement of Alexandria, theologian (150–215)
St. Clement I of Rome, Pope (30–101)
St. Cyril, Bishop of Jerusalem (315–86)
St. Cyril, Patriarch of Alexandria (376–444)
Didymus the Blind, theologian (313–98)
Diodore, Bishop of Tarsus (d. 392)
Dionysius the Pseudo-Areopagite, mystical theologian (late fifth century)
St. Dionysius the Great, Archbishop of Alexandria (190–264)
St. Epiphanius, Bishop of Salamis (315–403)
Eusebius, Bishop of Caesarea (260–340)
St. Eustathius, Bishop of Antioch (fourth century)
St. Firmillian, Bishop of Caesarea (d. 268)
Gennadius I, Patriarch of Constantinople (d. 471)
St. Germanus, Patriarch of Constantinople (634–733)
St. Gregory of Nazianzus, Bishop of Sasima (329–90)
St. Gregory of Nyssa (330–95)
St. Gregory Thaumaturgus, Bishop of Neocaesarea (213–70)
Hermas, author of *The Shepherd* (second century)
St. Hippolytus, martyr (170–236)
St. Ignatius, Bishop of Antioch (35–107)
St. Isidore of Pelusium, abbot (360–c. 450)

St. John Chrysostom, Patriarch of Constantinople (347–407)

St. John Climacus, monk (579–649)

St. John Damascene, defender of sacred images (675–749)

St. Julius I, Pope (d. 352)

St. Justin Martyr, apologist (100–65)

St. Leontius of Byzantium, theologian (sixth century)

St. Macarius the Great, monk (300–90)

St. Maximus, abbot and confessor (580–662)

St. Melito, Bishop of Sardis (d. 190)

St. Methodius, Bishop of Olympus (d. 311)

St. Nilus the Elder, priest and monk (d. 430)

Origen, head of the Catechetical School of Alexandria (184–254)

St. Polycarp, Bishop of Smyrna (69–155)

St. Proclus, Patriarch of Constantinople (d. 446)

St. Serapion, Bishop of Thmuis (died after 362)

St. Sophronius, Patriarch of Jerusalem (560–638)

Tatian the Assyrian, apologist and theologian (120–80)

Theodore, Bishop of Mopsuestia (350–428)

Theodoret, Bishop of Cyrrhus (393–458)

St. Theophilus, Bishop of Antioch (late second century)

FATHERS OF THE DESERT. The hermits and monks of the early Church who developed religious life from its Gospel origins and laid the groundwork for all future institutes of Christian perfection. Since most of them lived in the deserts of Egypt, from the third through the fourth centuries, they are called Desert Fathers. The standard collection of the lives of these Fathers is in ten volumes and contains the biographies of Sts. Paul, Anthony, and Hilarion, and of the women religious Sts. Eugenie, Euphrasia, Euphrosyne, Mary the Egyptian, and many others.

FÁTIMA, OUR LADY OF THE ROSARY OF. Shrine of the Blessed Virgin Mary in the mountain region of central Portugal near Cova da Iria. It was the scene of six apparitions of Our Lady, from May 13 to October 13, 1917, to three peasant children, Lucia Santos, Jacinta Marto, and her brother Francisco. During the apparitions Mary told the children to have processions in honor of her Immaculate Conception and to tell the faithful to do penance and pray the Rosary because otherwise the world would be chastised for its sins. During the October apparition seventy thousand people witnessed a spectacular solar phenomenon.

In 1930 the bishops of Portugal declared the apparitions to be authentic, and in 1942 Pope Pius XII, in response to Mary's request, consecrated the world to the Immaculate Heart of Mary. In 1967 Pope Paul VI personally visited and worshiped at the shrine on the fiftieth anniversary of the apparitions.

FÁTIMA INVOCATION. Prayer recommended by the Blessed Virgin to the children at Fátima (1917), to be recited by the faithful. It is often said between the decades of the Rosary and reads: "O my Jesus, forgive us our sins. Save us from the fires of hell, and bring all souls to heaven, especially those who most need your mercy."

FÁTIMA SECRET. The third part of a three-part account of the apparition of the Blessed Virgin which occurred on July 13, 1917. The account was written by Sister Lucy, a Carmelite nun and one of the three shepherd children to whom Mary appeared at what is now the famous Portuguese shrine. Part One described a vision of hell. Part Two was the promise of the conversion of the peoples of Russia through devotion to the Immaculate Heart. Part Three was the "secret" that was not to be opened until 1960, or on the death of Sister Lucy. It is reported that Sister Lucy communicated the secret to Pope John XXIII, presumably the prediction of great trials for the Church, but its contents have not been disclosed.

FEAST. Days set apart by the Church for giving special honor to God, the Savior, angels, saints, and sacred mysteries and events. Some are fixed festivals, such as Christmas and the Immaculate Conception; others are movable, occurring earlier or later in different years. Festivals are now divided, since the Second Vatican Council, into solemnity (*solemnitas*), feast (*festum*), and memorial (*memoria*) in descending order of dignity. Memorials are further classified as prescribed or optional. Below these are ferial, or week, days with no special ritual rank. And in a class by themselves are the Sundays of the year, and the various liturgical seasons, such as Advent and Lent. All of these represent what is called "sacred times," whose religious purpose is to keep the faithful mindful throughout the year of the cardinal mysteries and persons of Christianity.

FEAST OF PRECEPT. See HOLY DAYS OF OBLIGATION.

FEBRONIANISM. A system of Church-State relations developed by Johann Nikolaus von Hontheim (1701–90), Auxiliary Bishop of Trier, under the pseudonym Justinus Febronius. Influenced by Gallicanism, Hontheim advocated the subordination of ecclesiastical organizations to the State, taught that Christ entrusted Church authority not to the Pope or bishops directly but only through the body of the faithful, denied papal infallibility, and claimed that the primacy was not attached to the See of Peter. The Pope, according to Hontheim, should be subject to the bishops; and national churches, subject to the State, should be created throughout the Catholic world. Pope Clement XIII condemned Hontheim in 1764. Among civil rulers who sought to implement Febronianism were Joseph II of Austria (1741–90) and Leopold II of Tuscany (1797–1870).

FEEBLEMINDEDNESS. Condition of limited mental development. In many countries since early Christian times it has been the object of the Church's special care. The degrees of feeblemindedness are commonly distinguished on the basis of a person's intelligence quotient as follows: idiocy, with a mental age up to three years and requiring constant supervision; imbecility, with a mental age up to seven years, having the ability to learn simple tasks but seldom reading or writing; and moronic state, with a mental age from eight to twelve years, and the ability to do sometimes even complex manual labor. Less than 10 per cent show any physical deformity. Their moral responsibility depends on the mental age but especially on their religious training. It has been noted that mentally defective persons nevertheless show remarkable capacity for religious motivation and spiritual development. In ordinary usage, the technical terms for feeblemindedness are replaced with synonyms such as retardation or mentally handicapped.

FEELING. A conscious state or experience. More particularly in scholastic philosophy an experience of the external or internal senses, namely of sight, smell, touch, hearing, taste, and bodily, or somatic, sensation. Feeling is often simply equated with emotion, but emotion can also be spiritual, whereas feeling is, properly speaking, in the material order.

FELICITY. Any degree or instance or form of happiness, or whatever makes a person happy. Implies appropriateness and therefore the fulfillment of desire. (Etym. Latin *felicitas,* happiness, blessedness.)

FELIX, ANTONIUS. Procurator of Judaea (53–60). Despite a reputation for despotic rule he was uncharacteristically tolerant of Paul, who was brought before him at Caesarea, A.D. 60, accused by the Jews of disturbing the faith of their people by preaching the Christian way of life (Acts 24:1–27). Felix himself may have suffered from an uneasy conscience, because he abstained from making a judgment about Paul's guilt, even after two hearings. Eventually, he left his fate to his successor, Porcius Festus (60–62), but kept Paul in custody lest he antagonize the Jews.

FELLOWSHIP. Community, especially the Christian community, viewed as "the whole group of believers . . . united, heart and soul" (Acts 4:32). It is the body of the faithful bound together by a common faith in Christ, common worship, and common allegiance to the Church's divinely established authority. The closer these bonds of unity, the more intimate the fellowship.

FEL. MEM. *Felicis memoriae*—of happy memory.

FEL. REC. *Felicis recordationis*—of happy memory.

FEMINISM. The doctrine and movement that advocate granting to women the same social, political, and economic rights as those granted to men. On a moral and psychological level feminism is the existence of pronounced female characteristics in men.

FER. *Feria*—weekday.

FER. 2, 3, 4, 5, 6. *Feria secunda, feria tertia, feria quarta, feria quinta, feria sexta*—Monday, Tuesday, Wednesday, Thursday, Friday.

FERIA. In liturgical language any weekday on which no special ecclesiastical feast is to be celebrated. Such days are called ferial days. (Etym. Latin *feria,* weekday.)

FERIAL. In the revised liturgical calendar, a weekday on which no special feast or vigil is celebrated in the Mass or the Liturgy of the Hours. On ferial days the Mass may be that of the preceding Sunday, or an optional memorial, or a votive Mass, or a Mass for the deceased. During Advent and Lent ferial days are in a privileged category, and the same freedom in the choice of Masses is not allowed. In general, the Mondays through Fridays of each week are called ferial days (*feriae*) and are counted, in sequence, from two to six. Sunday, or the Lord's Day (*Dominica*), is always the first day, and Saturday (*Sabbatum*) is the seventh day of the week.

FERTILITY DRUG. A drug that overcomes infertility in women by stimulating ovulation. They are mainly follicle stimulating hormones (FSH) or a luteinizing hormone (LH) or their analogues. Their use, on Catholic moral principles, is normally permissible and may even be highly commendable.

FERULE (ferula). The long rod with which until recently priests of the Vatican Sacred Penitentiary lightly touched penitents. Pope Benedict XIV granted a twenty days' indulgence for observing this symbolic rite. A ferule was also the cane with a short transverse on top with which clergy and the people would support themselves during liturgical services before sitting down was allowed. Maronite monks and dissident Ethiopians and Coptics still use such a staff in choir.

FESTIVAL. See FEAST.

FESTUS, PORCIUS. Successor to Antonius Felix as Procurator of Judaea. He inherited from his predecessor the awkward charges leveled by the Jews against Paul (Acts 25:1–12). Rather than create unrest by offending the Jews, Festus offered to transfer the trial to Jerusalem. But Paul, aware of the bitter enmity of the Jews and their conspiracy to kill him, demanded his right as a Roman citizen to appeal for justice before the tribunal of Caesar. The curious King Herod Agrippa II agreed to hear the case (Acts 25:22), and the indomitable Paul described eloquently the story of his conversion and ministry (Acts 26). Festus interrupted him, shouting, "Paul, you are out of your mind; all that learning of yours is driving you mad" (Acts 26:24). But, fortunately for the accused, his sincerity impressed King Agrippa, who observed with a touch of imperial humor, "A little more, and your arguments would make a Christian of me" (Acts 26:29). Paul was judged innocent and set free.

FETICIDE. The direct killing of an unborn child. It is always murder and therefore gravely sinful. (Etym. Latin *fetus*, the young in the womb + *-cidium*, a killing.)

FIDEISM. A term applied to various theories that claim that faith is the only or ultimate source of all knowledge of God and spiritual things. The name was originally coined by followers of Kant (1724–1804) and Schleiermacher (1768–1834), both of whom denied the capacity of reason to know God or the moral law with certainty. (Etym. Latin *fides*, belief; habit of faith; object of faith.)

FIDEJUSSOR. Literally "one who testifies by faith." The term is sometimes applied to the sponsors at the baptism of an infant. They testify to the faith in place of the child and promise to ensure, as may be necessary, that the child is reared in the Catholic faith.

FIDELITY. See LOYALTY.

FIDES DIVINA. See THEOLOGICAL NOTES.

FIDES DIVINA DEFINITA. See THEOLOGICAL NOTES.

FIDES ECCLESIASTICA. See THEOLOGICAL NOTES.

FIFTEEN MARKS OF THE CHURCH. The fifteen features of the true Church developed by St. Robert Bellarmine (1542–1621), cardinal, Archbishop of Capua, and Doctor of the Church. As a contemporary of the original Protestant Reformers, he expanded the traditional four marks to fifteen, as follows: 1. the Church's *name*, Catholic, universal, and worldwide, and not confined to any particular nation or people; 2. *antiquity* in tracing her ancestry directly to Jesus Christ; 3. constant *duration* in lasting substantially unchanged for so many centuries; 4. *extensiveness* in the number of her loyal members; 5. *episcopal succession* of her bishops from the first Apostles at the Last Supper to the present hierarchy; 6. *doctrinal agreement* of her doctrine with the teaching of the ancient Church; 7. *union* of her members among themselves and with their visible head the Roman Pontiff; 8. *holiness* of doctrine in reflecting the sanctity of God; 9. *efficacy* of doctrine in its power to sanctify believers and inspire them to great moral achievement; 10. *holiness of life* of the Church's representative writers and defenders; 11. the glory of *miracles* worked in the Church and under the Church's auspices; 12. the gift of *prophecy* found among the Church's saints and spokesmen; 13. the *opposition* that the Church arouses among those who attack her on the very grounds that Christ was opposed by his enemies; 14. the *unhappy end* of those who fight against her; and 15. the *temporal peace and earthly happiness* of those who live by the Church's teaching and defend her interests.

FIFTH CRUSADE. A military expedition (1217–21) encouraged by Pope Innocent III, centered mainly in Egypt and resulted in

FIG 212 FIR

the surrender of the Holy Cross to the Christians.

FIGHTING. A general term that refers to any kind of combat or battle. The morality of fighting is to be judged by the usual norms. Not all fighting is prohibited, since self-defense may be legitimate and righteous anger is justified. Fighting is forbidden when the reason for the struggle is unjust, or the conflict could be avoided, or the means used are unreasonable, or the struggle is unnecessarily prolonged.

FILIAL FEAR. Fear of some impending evil based on love and reverence for the one who is feared. Actually filial fear is closer to love that dreads offending the one loved. Thus the filial fear of God is compatible with the highest love of God. A person, knowing his or her moral weakness, fears that he or she might displease or betray the one who is loved. It is selfless fear. (Etym. Latin *filial*, becoming of a child in relation to its parents.) See also SERVILE FEAR.

FILIOQUE. A term meaning "and from the Son," which over the centuries became the center of controversy between the Eastern Churches separated from Rome and the Catholic Church. The Eastern Christians first objected to the insertion of this phrase in the Nicene Creed, which now states that the Holy Spirit "proceeds from the Father *and the Son.*" The last three words had not been in the original creed but were added later, with the approval of Rome. After the ninth century the Eastern leaders challenged not only the addition but the doctrine itself, whether the Holy Spirit proceeded not only from the Father but also from the Son. In recent years the issue has become more historical than doctrinal, since those who believe in Christ's divinity, whether Eastern or Western Christians, all accept the fact that the Third Person proceeds from the Second as well as the First Person of the Trinity. Given this common faith, the verbal expression has become secondary.

FILMOTECA VATICANA. An agency of the Holy See, established in 1959, to collect and co-ordinate information on film and television programs that affect the life of the Church. It is administered by the Commission for Social Communications.

FINAL CAUSE. The end or purpose that an intelligent being has in performing an action or producing an effect. Strictly speaking, only created beings can have a final cause in what they do. God cannot properly be motivated by any cause, as though he

were in any way changed or modified by his actions. Yet he does act for a purpose, which is really his own infinite goodness and identified with the divine essence. See also CAUSE, EFFICIENT CAUSE, FIRST CAUSE, FORMAL CAUSE, FREE CAUSE, MATERIAL CAUSE, MORAL CAUSE, NECESSARY CAUSE, SECONDARY CAUSE.

FINAL CONSUMMATION. The end of the present world and its renewal as the final conclusion of the work of Christ. As all enemies of the kingdom of God are conquered, he will surrender the overlordship to God the Father (I Corinthians 15:24), but without losing his own dominion founded on the hypostatic union. With the end of the world there begins the perfect sovereignty of the Holy Trinity, which is the object of the whole creation and the final meaning of all human history.

FINALITY. Activity directed toward an end, or the direction of any activity toward a preconceived goal. The principle of finality states that "everyone acts for an end," i.e., no one ever acts without a purpose, whether conscious or unconscious, and whether determined by the person himself or by someone else.

FINAL PERSEVERANCE. Man's steadfastness in good up to the moment of death. It is the work of actual grace. Although man himself cannot merit the gift of final perseverance, he can, by earnest prayer and faithful co-operation with the manifold graces given him during life, secure from God's mercy this most important grace on which eternal happiness depends.

FINGER BOWL. See LAVABO DISH.

FINITE. Limited in being, perfection, operations, or dimensions. Applied to creatures, it identifies them as limited by their essence, since they are caused, ultimately, by God and depend absolutely on the divine First Cause to sustain them in existence and activity.

FIORETTI. *The Little Flowers of St. Francis,* a classic collection of stories and traditions about St. Francis of Assisi (1181–1226) and his early companions. Written in the Italian of Tuscany about 1322, it was probably translated from earlier Latin sources including the significant *Acts of the Blessed Francis and His Companions.*

FIRE OF HELL. The physical reality, outside the person, by which those in hell are punished besides their loss of the vision of

God. It is called fire in the Scriptures to emphasize the excruciating pain it causes, and to identify it as some external agent tormenting the lost. But it is not ordinary fire, since it does not consume what it burns, and, although material, it can affect the purely spiritual substance of the soul.

FIRE OF PURGATORY. The external source of suffering in purgatory besides the temporary deprivation of the vision of God. Although many sacred writers, interpreting St. Paul (I Corinthians 3:15), assume a physical fire, the Church's official teaching speaks only of "purifying punishments" and not of purifying fire (Denzinger 1304).

FIRSTBORN. The firstborn male considered as the spiritual and material heir of his father. Especially seen in the biblical account of Jacob, who persuaded his brother Esau to sell his birthright for a mess of pottage (Genesis 25:31–34). In memory of the firstborn among Jews being spared in Egypt, the fast of the firstborn was established for the fourteenth of Nisan.

FIRST CAUSE. God as the first cause of all things, because he is the first in the series of all other causes. Also, God as immediately operating in all finite causality, as the underlying cause on which all other causes constantly depend for their activity. See also CAUSE, EFFICIENT CAUSE, FINAL CAUSE, FORMAL CAUSE, FREE CAUSE, MATERIAL CAUSE, MORAL CAUSE, NECESSARY CAUSE, SECONDARY CAUSE.

FIRST CENTURY MAN. The term used by form critics of the Gospels to describe the uncultured man in the time of Jesus of Nazareth. He is said to have been a creature of his age, whose uncritical disposition to believe everything made him fall into the pattern of his society. This explains, say the critics, the naïve belief in such Gospel narratives as the virginal conception of Christ, the miracles and exorcisms and, above all, the bodily resurrection of Christ from the dead.

FIRST COMMUNION. The precept of the Church that requires children to receive Holy Communion, along with the sacrament of penance, on reaching the age of reason. First issued by the Fourth Lateran Council (1215), the practice was all but discontinued for centuries, due to the inroads of Jansenism. Pope St. Pius X restored the practice and restated the precept, while he also explained how necessarily related are the two sacraments of penance and the Eucharist. "The age of discretion," he said,

"both for confession and for Holy Communion is the time when a child begins to reason." This means that "a full and perfect knowledge of Christian doctrine is not necessary either for first confession or first Communion." Moreover, "the obligation of the precept of confession and Communion which binds the child particularly affects those who have charge of him, namely, parents, confessor, teachers, and the pastor" (*Quam Singulari*, August 8, 1910). See also SANCTUS PONTIFEX.

FIRST CONFESSION. The precept of the Church to receive the sacrament of penance on reaching the age of reason. First decreed by the Fourth Lateran Council in 1215, the law was confirmed by the Council of Trent, which condemned anyone who "denies that each and every one of Christ's faithful of both sexes is bound to confess once a year" (Denzinger 1708). The prescription was repeated and clarified by Pope St. Pius X in 1910 and again restated by the Holy See in 1973, ordering an end to experiments that postponed the sacrament of penance until after First Communion: "This precept, accepted into practice throughout the universal Church, brought and continues to bring much fruit for the Christian life and perfection of the spirit." See also SANCTUS PONTIFEX.

FIRST CRUSADE. The mainly French expedition (1096–99) inspired by Pope Urban II, which ended with the capture of Jerusalem in 1099. Godfrey of Bouillon (d. 1100), who was one of the leaders of the crusade, was elected ruler of Jerusalem. He called himself "Defender of the Holy Sepulcher," refusing to call himself king or to wear a crown, "through respect for Him who had been crowned in that place with the crown of thorns."

FIRST FRIDAYS. The customary observance of the first Friday of each month, encouraged by the Church, based on a promise made to St. Margaret Mary Alacoque (1647–90), that special favors, such as the grace of final perseverance, would be given to those who received Holy Communion on nine successive first Fridays.

FIRST FRUITS. The biblical term for the best as well as the earliest fruits or crops, both natural and prepared, taken from such sources as the threshing floor, the wine vat, and the oil press (Deuteronomy 18). They are specified in the law as offerings to God, and as prescribed on certain occasions such as the Passover and Pentecost (Deuteronomy 26).

FIRST GRACE. Sanctifying grace, conferred by certain sacraments on a person who is not in the state of grace. Thus baptism, penance, and (when needed) the anointing of the sick confer sanctifying grace, provided the minimum conditions are fulfilled.

FIRST MASS. The first Sacrifice of the Mass offered by a newly ordained priest. In the new grant of indulgences "A plenary indulgence is granted to the priest, who celebrates his first Mass with any solemnity, and to the faithful who devoutly assist at this Mass."

FIRST PARENTS. Adam and Eve as the original ancestors of the human race (Second Vatican Council, *Dogmatic Constitution on the Church*, 2, 56).

FIRST PLANK. The term used to describe the sacrament of baptism as the "first plank" flung to shipwrecked man to save him from his sins.

FIRST SATURDAYS. Devotion to the Immaculate Heart of Mary on the first Saturdays of five successive months, as part of the revelations of the Blessed Virgin at Fátima, Portugal (1917). The faithful are to go to confession and on each of the five successive first Saturdays are to receive Holy Communion, recite five decades of the Rosary, and meditate on the mysteries for at least fifteen minutes.

FISH. Symbol of Christ, seen before the fifth century. The Greek word for fish is *ichthus,* consisting also of the initial letters of Iesous, CHristos, THeou, Uios, Soter—Jesus Christ, Son of God, Savior. The fish is also emblematic of the fishermen Apostles, Andrew, Peter, and the Sons of Zebedee, whom Christ would make "fishers of men" (Mark 1:17). The archangel Raphael is often represented with a fish brought back to cure the aged Tobit of his blindness.

FISHERMAN'S RING. The Pope's signet ring, used for the sealing of important documents, such as papal briefs. It represents St. Peter fishing and bears the name of the Pope. When he dies, an official document is drawn up testifying that his ring was destroyed. This is done to prevent falsification of briefs. See also RING OF THE FISHERMAN.

FISH WITH BREAD. A symbol of the Eucharist that was early found in the catacombs and that is reminiscent of Christ feeding the multitude. Above the fish, which represented Christ, was often a basket of loaves with a glass of wine within a transparent basket, the complete elements of the Eucharistic sacrament.

FIVE SCAPULARS. Special devotion to five of the eighteen best known scapulars approved by the Church. The scapulars may be worn together. They are commonly the following: the brown scapular of Our Lady of Mount Carmel, the red of Christ's Passion, the black of the Seven Sorrows of the Blessed Virgin, the blue of Mary's Immaculate Conception, and the white of the Holy Trinity.

FIVE WAYS. The five classic arguments of St. Thomas Aquinas for the existence of God. They are proofs from the effects produced in the world, from which an unbiased mind can logically conclude to their divine source. Called the *Quinque Viae,* they reason that: 1. motion (change) in the world implies a First Mover, who is himself unmoved, i.e., unchanged; 2. a sequence of efficient causes and their effects, observed in the world, requires an uncaused First Cause; 3. the existence of things that are not self-explanatory, i.e., contingent beings that need not exist, argues to the existence of an ultimate Necessary Being who cannot not exist; 4. the universal comparisons people make (more or less "good" or "true" or "beautiful" or "holy") require that there exist a Perfect Being who has the fullness of all these qualities; 5. the tendency among all earthly things, living and nonliving, to work toward a definite purpose indicates there exists an all-wise Intelligence that is directing creatures to a predetermined end.

FIVE WOUNDS. Devotion to the Passion of Christ by concentrating on the wounds he suffered in his hands and feet and pierced side. A favorite devotion with many great saints, a Feast of the Five Wounds is celebrated in some countries on the fourth Friday of Lent. It also finds expression in the *Anima Christi,* with the invocation to Christ "Within your wounds hide me."

FIXED ALTAR. A permanent structure of stone, consisting of the table and the supports consecrated together as one whole. They may not be detached without the altar losing its consecration.

FIXED FEASTS. Festivals of greater or less importance that regularly occur on certain days in the liturgical year. Such are solemnities like Christmas, feasts of Our Lady, the Immaculate Conception, and saints' days, whether observed in the universal Church, such as those of the Apostles, or only in certain countries or localities, such as St. Elizabeth Seton in the United States and St. Andrew Bobola in Poland.

FL. *Floruit*—he, or she, flourished, i.e., lived.

FLAGELLANTS. Groups of fanatical persons who performed or administered physical penances in public. Though condemned by the popes several times, they always reappeared. Their exaggerated pretensions developed into heresy, particularly in the late Middle Ages. In modern times self-flagellation in private and in moderation is a recognized form of penance and devotion. (Etym. Latin *flagellare*, to whip, scourge, lash.)

FLATTERY. False praise. To flatter means to compliment someone insincerely. An untruth is spoken in words or actions, generally to a person but also about him or her, in order to derive some benefit or avoid some harm from the one praised. The term "flattery" may also refer to a person honored by recognition without necessarily implying that the praise was untrue.

FLESH (biblical). The body of a human being as opposed to his or her spirit. But more particularly flesh means human person in contrast to God and his spirit, and therefore stands for all that is typically human, namely mortality, weakness, and sinfulness.

FLEUR-DE-LIS. A symbol of the Blessed Virgin Mary. A medieval emblem in France representing the lily as a symbol of purity. Often seen in Annunciation representations and on wall hangings connected with Marian shrines.

FLOOD or DELUGE. The biblical term for the destruction of the human race by water as a punishment from God. All were destroyed except for a small group whom God miraculously preserved to propagate a new race of people (Genesis 6, 7, 8, 9). It is clear that God caused the deluge because "the wickedness of man was so great" that he "regretted having made him" (Genesis 6:5–7). So "I will rid the earth's face of man, my own creation." He gave Noah, "a good man, a man of integrity among his contemporaries," ample warning and detailed instructions as to how he and his family and two birds and animals of every living species would be saved by remaining in an ark for the duration of the deluge. Study of Scriptural evidence seems to indicate that the earth was in a flooded condition for approximately a year before Noah and those in the ark could safely leave and begin renewing life in the world. The account concludes with God establishing a covenant with Noah and his sons, giving them lordship over the earth and promising that never again would a flood destroy the world (Genesis 9:7–11).

FLOWERING ROD. Emblem of St. Joseph, foster father of Our Lord. Usually represented with lilies sprouting from the rod, honoring his virginity and purity. Legend has it that Mary's life partner was chosen in this way. As early as the fourth century we see Joseph represented with this emblem, while the other suitors called together by Zechariah are seen holding barren rods.

FLOWERS. Widely used in the Catholic Church to adorn altars, to place before statues, and to display in shrines or places of pilgrimage. Cut flowers are not only ornamental, they are also a form of sacrifice, as they wither and must be replaced. Floral decorations on the lampstand and on the paneling and doors of the temple are mentioned in the Bible (Exodus 25:31; I Kings 6:18).

FLOWERS (biblical). Instructive references to flowers in the Bible are mainly allusions to their striking beauty, but also to their transient nature (Psalm 103:15; Isaiah 5:24; Matthew 6:28–30). Flowers therefore symbolize the impermanent character of even the most pleasant and attractive creatures in this world, compared with the changeless and eternal beauty of God.

FONT. Receptacle for baptismal or holy water, normally made of stone, more rarely of metal or wood. Wooden fonts have stone or metal containers for the water. In the early Church, when adult baptism was more commonly administered by immersion, the font was a large basin below ground level in which the neophyte stood while the water was poured over him. For infant baptism, the font, quite large, was somewhat raised above ground so that the child could easily be immersed. As baptism by pouring became the rule, fonts became smaller and higher, often richly ornamented, and gradually took on the present shape. They are also covered by a lid. In many churches fonts either stand in a separate chapel (baptistery) or are railed off in a closed section of the church. Holy water fonts stand in the vestibule of a church, or inside the church proper, and are conveniently placed at the entrance and exit doors for people to bless themselves as they enter and leave the church.

FORBIDDEN BOOKS. Written material that Catholics are forbidden to read, except for grave reasons, because it is contrary to Christian faith or morals. Lists of forbidden books date from the earliest centuries; for example, Pope Innocent, in 417, forbade the faithful to read the apocryphal Scriptures. The first extensive list, called the *Index Librorum Prohibitorum* (List of Prohibited Books), was issued by the Congregation of the Inquisition under Pope Paul IV in 1557. In 1571 Pope St. Pius V established a special Congregation of the Index, which survived until 1917, when Pope Benedict XV transferred its responsibilities to the Holy Office. When the Code of Canon Law was published in 1918, twenty-one separate laws (1395–1405) dealt with the matter of forbidden books, and severe ecclesiastical penalties were imposed for disobedience. In 1966 the Congregation for the Doctrine of the Faith declared that the Index and its corresponding penalties were no longer binding in law. However, no basic change was made in the Church's attitude toward reading literature contrary to revealed truth. Catholics are still obliged to refrain from reading whatever would be a proximate danger to their faith and Christian virtue.

FORCE. In moral theology that which proceeds from some agent outside the victim whose will is opposed to it. It is the same thing as violence and implies an external agent and resistance on the part of the victim. Consequently no one can, properly speaking, apply force or inflict violence on himself or herself. As a basic rule, force can affect external acts only, not the internal acts of the will. It follows, then, that internal acts are morally imputable no matter how much violence a person has to endure; external acts performed under compulsion are not imputed, provided the individual has withheld internal consent.

FOREIGN MISSIONS. Places of evangelization among people outside of one's native country. The term has implied bringing the Catholic faith to people in mainly non-Christian lands. But the prefix "foreign" is now generally omitted, because of the massive dechristianization that has taken place in traditionally Christian countries and the correspondingly rapid growth of the Church among people who only recently have had the Gospel preached to them.

FORENSIC JUSTIFICATION. See IM-PUTED JUSTICE.

FOREORDINATION. That part of predes-tination which affirms that, besides foreseeing the future, God actually determines the future. Corresponds to predetermination and may also be applied to a human being's free choice to do or perform what has previously been decided on.

FORGERY. A fraudulent imitation; alteration of truth to the damage of a third person. In canon law it may be an untrue word, statement, or testimony; in writing, false words in a document; in action, spurious art work or counterfeit money. It is also the conscious use of such falsification.

FORGIVENESS. Pardon or remission of an offense. The Catholic Church believes that sins forgiven are actually removed from the soul (John 20) and not merely covered over by the merits of Christ. Only God can forgive sins, since he alone can restore sanctifying grace to a person who has sinned gravely and thereby lost the state of grace. God forgives sins to the truly repentant either immediately through an act of perfect contrition or mediately through a sacrament. The sacraments primarily directed to the forgiveness of sins are baptism and penance, and secondarily, under certain conditions, also the sacrament of anointing.

FORGOTTEN SINS. Those grave sins which a person would have confessed in the sacrament of penance but sincerely forgot. They are forgiven along with whatever sins are confessed, with the proviso that, should they later be remembered, they are then mentioned in a later confession as having been inadvertently forgotten.

FORM. The nature or essence of a thing; the internal specific principle of the distinctive nature or activities of any created being. Also, after a change, the new feature(s) in whatever has been changed. Contrasted with matter in scholastic philosophy and theology.

In reference to the sacraments, their form is the sacramental sign or the words that specify the function of the matter and confer on it the power of sanctifying. Thus in baptism the Trinitarian formula "I baptize you . . ." is the form.

FORMAL. That which pertains to the essence or nature of something. Also refers to whatever is done according to strict rules or directives.

FORMAL CAUSE. The specific element in a being which communicates itself to the indeterminate or less determinate element and together with this matter or substratum constitutes the whole being. One of the four principal causes in Thomistic philosophy. See also CAUSE, EFFICIENT CAUSE, FINAL CAUSE, FIRST CAUSE, FREE CAUSE, MATERIAL CAUSE, MORAL CAUSE, NECESSARY CAUSE, SECONDARY CAUSE.

FORMAL CO-OPERATION. The deliberate concurrence in another person's usually sinful action. The co-operation is formal and always sinful if, besides giving external help of whatever kind, one interiorly wants the evil action to be performed. Formal co-operation is at least a sin against charity by doing spiritual harm to one's neighbor; frequently it is also a sin against another virtue, especially of justice.

FORMAL EVIL. A bad human act, done with knowledge that it is morally wrong, and with consent to performing it because of some advantage to the one who does it.

FORMAL HERESY. See HERESY.

FORM CRITICISM. As a broad discipline, it studies the literary structure of historical documents that preserve an earlier tradition. Its basic assumption is that the earlier, oral use of the tradition shaped the material and resulted in a variety of literary forms found in the final written record. A critical study of these forms sheds light on the life and thinking of the people who preserved the tradition. Applied to the Bible, form criticism mistakenly assumes that the native force behind Christian tradition in the early Church was not a desire to preserve the memory of what Jesus had preached and done, but was a need to serve the religious fervor of a new community. Such necessity would tend to obscure and embellish, if not distort the facts to meet the needs of an idealistic faith.

FORMULA. The exact statement or formulation of a principle. In philosophy, there are logical formulas that state a general truth or proposition in terms of thought or speech. In ritual, there are prescribed formulas for the administration of sacraments and sacramentals. In theology, there are doctrinal formulas that express either all the essentials of the Christian faith, such as the Apostles' Creed, or certain aspects of the faith, especially when challenged or denied, such as the Berengarian formula on Christ's Real Presence in the Eucharist.

FORNICATION. An act of sexual intercourse between a man and a woman who are not validly married, although they are free to marry. It is by its nature gravely sinful. (Etym. Latin *fornicatio,* fornication; from *fornix,* a vault, arch, brothel.)

FORTITUDE. Firmness of spirit. As a virtue, it is a steadiness of will in doing good in spite of difficulties faced in the performance of one's duty.

There are two levels to the practice of fortitude: one is the suppression of inordinate fear and the other is the curbing of recklessness. The control of fear is the main role of fortitude. Hence the primary effect of fortitude is to keep unreasonable fears under control and not allow them to prevent one from doing what one's mind says should be done. But fortitude or courage also moderates rashness, which tends to lead the headstrong to excess in the face of difficulties and dangers. It is the special virtue of pioneers in any endeavor.

As a human virtue, fortitude is essentially different from what has come to be called animal courage. Animals attack either from pain, as when they are wounded, or from fear of pain, as when they go after humans because they are angered, whom they would leave alone if they were unmolested. They are not virtuously brave, for they face danger from pain or rage or some other sense instinct, not from choice, as do those who act with foresight. True courage is from deliberate choice, not mere emotion. (Etym. Latin *fortitudo,* strength; firmness of soul; courage of soul.)

FORTUNE-TELLING. The art of manifesting to another the fortune (luck), good or bad, that the future has in store for him or her. The real objective in fortune-telling is the disclosure of future events. Quite often, though, to inspire confidence, the fortune-teller will communicate bits of information about a person's past that would be naturally unknown to anyone else. As a presumed help in peering into the world of secret events they employ, for example, tea leaves, a crystal sphere, or a small pool of blood.

The Church considers it gravely wrong to consult a fortune-teller who is known to seriously claim access to the knowledge of future events. It would be a sin of formal co-operation. It is likewise wrong to consult a person who may not actually make such claims, but whom the client believes to be a fortune-teller with powers of divination. The gravity of the sin would depend on how seriously one takes the fortune-teller. If neither party takes the thing seriously and someone has a fortune told as a pastime, there is no sin. But even in this case the danger is that if what was predicted actually takes place, one's faith in fortune-telling is (or may be) aroused and there is danger that what began as amusement may become a temptation to learn about the future through forbidden means.

FORTY HOURS DEVOTION. The solemn exposition of the Blessed Sacrament during forty hours, in honor of the forty hours the body of Christ is believed to have rested in the tomb. The devotion was introduced by St. Anthony Mary Zaccaria in Milan and Vicenza in 1527, and propagated by the Jesuits under St. Ignatius. Approved by Pope Paul III in 1539, Pope Clement VIII, in 1592, in his constitution *Graves et diuturnae* and the *Clementine Instructions* of Pope Clement XI, in 1705, that were republished by Pope Clement XII in 1731 and established the correct form of the devotion. By the end of the eighteenth century, the custom had spread to many countries. St. John Neumann of Philadelphia (1811–60) was the first to hold the devotion in America with any degree of regularity. Where it is more feasible, the forty hours are interrupted during the night and the devotion extends over three days.

FORUM. The sphere within which the Church exercises her judicial authority. The external forum deals with matters that concern the public welfare of the Church and the people of God; the internal pertains to her jurisdiction in matters of conscience, notably the sacrament of penance, where sins are forgiven or retained and questions of morality are decided as to guilt, restitution, or responsibility.

FOUNDER. The person who originally establishes any institution or enterprise that continues and flourishes after his or her time. The term is commonly applied to Christ as the founder of the Church. Also refers to the man or woman who begins a religious order or congregation, either by writing the original rule, as did St. Benedict (480–547), or by establishing a specific institute, as did the numerous founders of existing communities. It is equally applicable to those who inaugurate any one of the large number of associations, societies, or institutes flourishing in the Catholic Church.

FOUNDER'S CHARISM. The distinctive spirituality of the founder or foundress of a religious institute, which then distinguishes a religious family from other forms of consecrated life approved by the Church. It is the personality of a religious community bequeathed by the one who founded the insti-

tute. According to the Second Vatican Council, this charism is "the spirit and aims of each founder [which] should be faithfully accepted and retained" (*Perfectae Caritatis*, 2).

FOUNTAIN. A symbol of the Immaculate Virgin. "Fountain sealed," from the Canticle of Canticles. Phrases applied to Mary the chosen of God and exclusively his—"my spouse a garden enclosed . . . a fountain sealed up."

FOUR HORSEMEN. Allegorical figures in the Bible, described by St. John (Revelation 6:1–8). The rider on the white horse most probably represents Christ; the rider on the red horse symbolizes war; the one on the black horse, famine; and the one on the pale horse, death.

FOUR LAST THINGS. They are death, judgment, heaven, and hell, meaning that there is no reincarnation, but that immediately after death each person is judged on his or her eternal destiny. The traditional Latin term is *novissima,* "the newest things."

FOUR TEMPERAMENTS. The four classic dispositions of human beings, traceable to Aristotle: namely, sanguine, melancholic, choleric, and lethargic or phlegmatic. While no person has exclusively any one of these temperaments, people generally have one or the other disposition as their dominant quality. Knowing this, they are better prepared to cope with their natural weaknesses and tendencies in the pursuit of spiritual perfection.

FOURTH CRUSADE. Considered the most important of the Crusades in terms of lasting results (1202–4). The crusade was preached by Pope Innocent III. Its political effect was to conquer Constantinople, but only at the cost of embittering the Eastern Christians. They mistakenly charged the Pope with responsibility for the pillage of churches and massacre of the people by the Venetian-paid crusaders' army.

FOURVIÈRES. A shrine church to Our Lady and St. Thomas of Canterbury, near Lyons, France. A basilica, crowning the hill at Fourvières, was built in thanksgiving to God for preserving the city of Lyons from invasion in the Prussian War of 1870, but it is the old sanctuary close by that is of greater interest. This very old church dedicated to Our Lady consists of just two aisles. During its reconstruction in the twelfth century Archbishop Thomas of Canterbury, an exile in Lyons, visited the church. Knowing that one aisle led to Mary's shrine, he asked the prelate in charge to whom the second aisle was to be dedicated. He was told, "To the next English martyr." Before the church was finished Thomas himself had been killed in England. Ever since, Fourvières has been identified with his name and is a place of pilgrimage, especially from England, in memory of St. Thomas à Becket (1118–70).

FR., F. *Frater, frère*—brother.

FRAGRANT ODORS. Sometimes called the odor of sanctity, they are the perfume-like scent given forth by the bodies of saints during their lifetime or after death. They are considered, as it were, symbols of the fragrance of extraordinary virtue. Thus the stigmata of St. Francis were reported occasionally to emit a sweet perfume. When St. Theresa died in 1582, the water in which her body had been bathed retained a noteworthy fragrance. During nine months a mysterious perfume rose from her grave. Both phenomena were carefully studied in the process of her canonization. Among the conditions set down by the Church to verify the phenomenon is whether any physical miracle is associated with the fragrant emanation.

FRANCISCAN CROWN. Rosary of seven decades commemorating the seven joys of the Blessed Virgin, namely the Annunciation, Visitation, Birth of Christ, Adoration of the Magi, Finding of Jesus in the Temple, the Appearance of the risen Christ to his Mother, Mary's Assumption into heaven and her Coronation as Queen of the Universe. Introduced among the Franciscans in 1422, the original crown consisted of seven Our Fathers and seventy Hail Marys. Two Hail Marys have since been added to number seventy-two, the supposed age of Mary at her Assumption.

FRANCISCANS. The numerous family of men and women religious who trace their spiritual ancestry to St. Francis of Assisi (1181–1226). The Original Rule written by St. Francis in 1209 is now lost. It was recast in 1221 and brought into final form two years later, when it was approved by Pope Honorius III. Its distinctive feature is the obligation of poverty of dispossession, not only for individual members but for each community. The friars (from *frères,* brothers) were to own no property and were to earn their livelihood by manual labor or begging.

This ideal became the focus of two divergent opinions of poverty in the order. Suc-cessive popes gave approval to the more moderate view and, when laxity crept in, favored reform along stricter lines. Eventually three major groups of Franciscans came into being: the Friars Minor, who developed from the Observants allowing no corporate property; the Conventuals, who allowed corporate ownership; and the Capuchins, who strongly emphasized poverty and austerity.

Franciscans have emphasized popular preaching and missionary activity. They have also promoted such popular devotions as the Angelus, the Way of the Cross, and the Crib. They were always strong defenders of the Immaculate Conception, long before the dogma was formally defined by the Church.

The Second Order of Franciscans is contemplative, known as the Poor Clares. There are Third Order Franciscans among men and women engaged in apostolic work and under simple vows. Third Order Secular, popularly called Tertiaries, are lay men and women in the world who follow the Rule of St. Francis according to their states of life. In 1978 Pope Paul VI approved a new Rule for the Franciscan Third Order, and changed the name to Franciscan Secular Order.

FRANKINCENSE. A white resin obtained from balsam trees and used in perfumes and medicines. One of the events related following the birth of Jesus was a visit to the manger by wise men from the East who brought him gifts of gold, frankincense, and myrrh (Matthew 2:10–11). (Etym. Old French *franc encens,* pure incense.)

FRATERNAL CHARITY. The practice of charity with a love that recognizes another person as a child of God, and therefore as brother or sister in the Lord.

FRATERNAL CORRECTION. "Brother reproving a brother." It usually involves a serious fault, either unknown as to gravity by the offender or hoped to be corrected by such admonition. It is an exercise of fraternal charity when commendably done. It should never be exercised merely for the sake of the offended, but mainly to help the offender or benefit a third party. In some religious communities it is a recognized form of fostering humility and a valuable aid to growing in Christian perfection.

FRATICELLI. In popular usage, it refers to all members of religious orders of men, especially mendicant orders, and solitaries. But in Church history it means those sectarians who in the fourteenth and fifteenth centuries separated themselves from the Franciscan

Order, which they claimed had compromised on St. Francis' original spirit of poverty. (Etym. Italian *fraticelli,* little friars.)

FRAUD. Depriving another of something to which he or she has a right. A person is defrauded either by having an object taken away or by having it withheld. Fraud implies misleading statements or deliberate perversion of the truth as a means of deprivation, which is the usual meaning in Scripture: "You must not steal nor deal deceitfully or fraudulently with your neighbor" (Leviticus 19:11).

FREE CATHOLICISM. A term used by some spokesmen for the Free Churches of England to designate a movement toward a Catholic interpretation of Christianity but without necessarily adopting Catholic beliefs and practices and without a return to Rome.

FREE CAUSE. An agent acting from knowledge and with deliberate purpose, as distinct from a necessary cause. See also CAUSE, EFFICIENT CAUSE, FINAL CAUSE, FIRST CAUSE, FORMAL CAUSE, MATERIAL CAUSE, MORAL CAUSE, NECESSARY CAUSE, SECONDARY CAUSE.

FREE CHURCHES. Protestant denominations in the Congregational tradition. They were called Free Churches originally because of their emphasis on freedom from any binding creeds, but also because they believe that each church is essentially free from any ecclesiastical authority above the local congregation.

FREEDOM. Immunity from determination or compulsion; hence the absence of all antecedent necessity, whether internal (from within a person's will) or external (from an outside source).

FREEDOM OF CONTRADICTION. The liberty to act or not to act, to perform or omit a given action. Also called the freedom of exercise.

FREEDOM OF GOD. The liberty of God relative to creatures. God loves himself of necessity, but he loves and wills outside himself with freedom. This divine liberty is the freedom to act or not to act (liberty of contradiction), for example, to create the world. And it is the freedom to choose various goods or indifferent actions (liberty of specification), for example, to create this or that world.

FREEDOM OF SPECIFICATION. The liberty to determine in which of two or more ways a person will act. It is the liberty to do this or that; the power or act of choosing any one among various possible means to an end.

FREEDOM OF SPEECH. See FREE SPEECH.

FREEDOM OF SPONTANEITY. The capacity of moving or being moved in any direction. Refers especially to the liberty a person has, under the impulse of grace, which does not coerce the action to which it invites the human will.

FREEDOM OF THOUGHT. In a correct sense, the capacity of the human mind to distinguish between truth and error. In this sense it is the foundation for freedom of the will, to choose between good and evil. But historically the term came into vogue as a motto for the Freethinkers, who were actually skeptics. Hume (1711–76) and Voltaire (1694–1778) in their day claimed to be Freethinkers, because they chose to disbelieve in divine revelation and, in fact, even to reject the basic dictates of sound moral reason.

FREEDOM OF WORSHIP. That part of religious freedom which concerns the worship of God according to the dictates of one's conscience. This refers especially to freedom from constraint by the civil law. As stated by the Second Vatican Council "the private and public acts of religion by which men direct themselves to God according to their consciences transcend by their very nature the earthly and temporal order of things. Therefore the civil authority, the purpose of which is the care of the common good in the temporal order, must recognize and look with favor on the religious life of the citizens. But if it presumes to control or restrict religious activity, it must be said to have exceeded the limits of its power" (*Declaration on Religious Liberty,* I, 3).

FREE LOVE. Uninhibited sexual relations, whether between the unmarried, or with someone else's spouse, or between persons of the same sex. All these relations are forbidden by the natural law, divine revelation, and the Church's teaching.

FREEMASONRY. The teachings and practices of a secret international organization whose modern origins date from the first quarter of the eighteenth century. It defines itself as "the activity of closely united men who, employing symbolical forms borrowed principally from the mason's trade and from architecture, work for the welfare of mankind, striving morally to ennoble themselves and others and thereby to bring about a universal league of mankind." Freemasonry began as a fraternity of Deists in Europe, and its basic orientation has been naturalistic, i.e., anti-supernatural, ever since. The hostility of Masonic lodges to the Catholic Church has evoked numerous declarations of the Holy See, notably of Popes Clement XII (1738), Benedict XIV (1751), Pius IX in several documents, especially the Syllabus of Errors (1864), and Leo XIII in the encyclical *Humanum Genus* (1884). The Code of Canon Law (1918) decreed that no Catholic may join "Masonic sects or any other similar associations which plot against the Church" (Canon 2335). Since not all Masonic lodges are professedly anti-Catholic, a decision of the Sacred Congregation for the Doctrine of the Faith mitigated the severity of the existing law, stating: "In considering particular cases, it must be remembered that penal law is always subject to strict interpretation. Therefore one may safely teach and apply the opinion of those authors who hold that Canon 2335 refers only to those Catholics who join associations which plot against the Church" (September 18, 1974). In special cases, then, a lay Catholic may belong to a Masonic lodge, but the clergy, religious, and members of secular institutes may not belong.

FREE SPEECH. The liberty to express one's beliefs or opinions in speech or writing, in accordance with the moral law and the legitimate rights and dignity of human beings. Freedom of speech is a natural right, but, like other natural rights, it is not unlimited. No one has the moral right to say things that are untrue or injurious to another person or harmful to society. Moreover, the state has the right to limit freedom of speech (and of the press) insofar as this is necessary for the common good.

FREETHINKER. Originally and still mainly one who rejects Christian revelation and professes to be agnostic in matters religious. The term is sometimes used to describe a person who claims to form his opinions independently of others.

FREE WILL. The power of the will to determine itself and to act of itself, without compulsion from within or coercion from without. It is the faculty of an intelligent being to act or not act, to act this way or another way, and is therefore essentially different from the operations of irrational beings that merely respond to a stimulus and are conditioned by sensory objects.

FRENCH REVOLUTION. The political and religious upheaval that began in France in 1789 and has influenced the whole world. Among the significant aspects that affected the Catholic Church were the oaths of allegiance to civil authority that implied denial of the faith. There were many martyrs, along with a massive dissolution of religious orders and secularization of Church property.

FREQUENT COMMUNION. The practice, dating from the first centuries of the Church, of receiving Holy Communion often, as a means of growing in union with God. Weekly reception was customary already in apostolic times. From the end of the second century many priests and laity received every day. By the thirteenth century the practice had so declined that the Fourth Lateran Council had to legislate at least annual Communion at Easter time. In the sixteenth century the Council of Trent urged the reception of Holy Communion at every Mass attended. During the centuries of Jansenist influence, Communion became rare, until 1905 when St. Pius X decreed that "Frequent and daily Communion, as a thing most earnestly desired by Christ our Lord and by the Catholic Church should be open to all the faithful" (Denzinger 3375–83). The only conditions required were the state of grace and the right intention.

FREQUENT CONFESSION. The practice, going back to the early Church, of receiving the sacrament of penance more often than just once a year, or when mortal sins have been committed. Since the beginnings of monasticism, this practice was recommended to religious even in the absence of a priest, and therefore without absolution, as a means of spiritual purification. It was increasingly used by the laity who sought to grow in Christian perfection, then it fell off until modern times, when it became commonplace in the first half of the twentieth century.

Pope Pius XII defended the practice of frequent confession, presumably of venial sins. "By it," he said, "self-knowledge is increased, Christian humility grows, bad habits are corrected, spiritual neglect and tepidity are resisted, the conscience is purified, the will strengthened, a salutary self-control is attained, and grace is increased in virtue of the sacrament itself" (*Mystici Corporis Christi*, 88). In promulgating the new rite of penance, Pope Paul VI also stressed the "great value" of "frequent and reverent recourse to this sacrament even when only venial sins are in question." This practice "is a constant effort to bring to perfection the grace of our baptism" (December 2, 1973).

FREUDIANISM. The theory and practice of psychoanalysis founded by Sigmund Freud (1856–1939). It is one of the principal challenges to Catholic moral theology. Among its distinctive features are the role of the unconscious in human motivation, the psychological harm of emotional repression, the primacy of sex in human behavior, the lifelong effect of experiences in infancy and early childhood. The position of Freudianism on religion is generally negative: 1. its presuppositions are atheist, claiming that a person's idea of God is a wish-fulfillment; 2. the spiritual life is implicitly ruled out by its preoccupation with human instinct; and 3. religion is held to be a sublimation of the libido.

FRIAR. A brother. Originally a form of address in general use among the Christian faithful, as is clear from the frequent references to "brother" and "brethren" in the New Testament writings. Later the term came to be used more exclusively by members of religious orders, and finally, since the thirteenth century, it referred to those who belonged to one of the mendicant orders, mainly the Franciscans and Dominicans, although extended to others in the monastic tradition. Strictly speaking, however, a friar differs from a monk in that his ministry engages him in work outside the monastery, whereas traditionally the prayer and labors of a monk are identified within the monastery to which he belongs. (Etym. Old French *frère, freire,* brother; Latin *frater,* brother.)

FRIARS MINOR. Part of the First Order of St. Francis, commonly called Franciscans, founded by St. Francis of Assisi (1181–1226), and canonically established in 1209. In 1517 all early reformers of the order, such as the Clareni and Coletani, were united in one body, from then on simply known as the Friars Minor of St. Francis, or Friars Minor of the Regular Observance. And in 1897, Pope Leo XIII approved another reunion when groups such as the Reformati, the Recollects, and the Discalced were rejoined with the Friars Minor.

FRIARS MINOR CAPUCHIN. See CAPUCHINS.

FRIARS MINOR CONVENTUAL. See CONVENTUALS.

FRIARS PREACHERS. See DOMINICANS.

FRIARY. A community of friars; also the residence where they live. The term especially applies to Franciscans, Dominicans, Carmelites, Augustinians, and Servites.

FRIDAY. Name derived from the Old English *frigedaeg,* day of Frig', the goddess wife of Odin, supreme Norse deity. It is the sixth day of the week that since early Christian times was specially dedicated to a commemoration of the Savior's Passion. Every Friday calls for some act of penance when abstinence from meat is not observed. This is a matter of obligation as decreed by Pope Paul VI in 1966 in the apostolic constitution *Paenitemini* (Norm II, 2).

FRIDAY ABSTINENCE. Refraining from meat on Friday in commemoration of Christ's passion and death. The custom was prevalent among Christians from the first century. It was extended to Saturday in the West at an early date. Until the apostolic constitution of Paul VI in 1966, all Fridays were obligatory days of abstinence for the whole Church, with the exception of certain territories that were exempt from the obligation. Since 1966, however, obligatory abstinence for the universal Church applies only to Ash Wednesday and the Fridays of Lent. To the law of abstinence are bound all who have completed their fourteenth year of age. The law of abstinence forbids the use of meat, but not of eggs, the products of milk, or condiments made of animal fat. The abolition of Friday abstinence is a common misapprehension. Friday abstinence was not abolished; rather the faithful now have a choice either to abstain from meat or perform some other kind of penance on Fridays. According to the Church's law, the "substantial observance" of Fridays as days of penance, whether by abstinence or in other ways, "is a grave obligation" (*Paenitemini,* Norm II, 2).

FRIENDSHIP. Reciprocal love. In philosophical terms a friend is a person whom one knows and loves well and by whom one is known and loved for virtuous reasons. The biblical notion of friendship, in the New Testament, adds the feature of total selflessness after the example of Jesus Christ, whose love was generous, forgiving, and sought only the welfare of those whom he loved. The sharing of confidences is also part of the biblical understanding of friendship (John 15:15).

FRUITS OF THE HOLY SPIRIT. Supernatural works that, according to St. Paul, manifest the presence of the Holy Spirit. The one who performs them recognizes

God's presence by the happiness he experiences, and others the divine presence by witnessing these good works (Galatians 5:22–23). They are, in other words, identifiable effects of the Holy Spirit. In the Vulgate text they are: charity, joy, peace, patience, benignity, goodness, longanimity, mildness, faith, modesty, continency, and chastity.

FRUITS OF THE MASS. The spiritual and temporal blessings obtained through the Eucharistic sacrifice. The general fruits of the Mass are applied to the whole Church, in which all the faithful share, both the living and the dead. The special fruits are applied first to the priest who celebrates Mass, then to those for whom he offers it, and finally to those who participate in the Eucharistic liturgy.

FRUSTULUM. The small portion of food, a few ounces, formerly permitted at breakfast on fast days. This was provided by canon law (Canon 1251), which permitted taking some food, morning and evening, in addition to the one full meal per day.

FULFILLMENT. The accomplishment of something promised, or the acquisition of something hoped for. Also the performance of something demanded or required. A prominent feature of modern spirituality that emphasizes the need of personal satisfaction as a motive force in achievement.

FULL OF GRACE. A term applied in the New Testament (Vulgate) to Christ, the Blessed Virgin, the Apostles, and St. Stephen. But traditionally it refers especially to Mary, as occurs in the invocation "Hail Mary, full of grace." This is the Church's official interpretation of the Greek word *Kecharitōmenē* in the angelic salutation, which all Latin translations since the earliest times render *gratia plena* (Luke 1:28). Applied to Mary, the Mother of God, it is a fullness below that of Christ but above that of all the angels and saints. Assuming that the fullness of grace in Christ was a necessary complement of the hypostatic union, and Mary's was totally gratuitous, some theologians (e.g., Francis Suarez) hold that her sanctifying grace exceeds by far the combined sanctity of all other creatures.

FUNCTION. The distinctive activity of any human power or organ, as hearing or seeing. In theology, the purpose of any specific sacrament; the duty of any particular ministry; the public celebration of an ecclesiastical ritual; the responsibilities of an approved office or position in the Church's service of the faithful.

FUNCTIONAL LOVE. The affection shown to someone not for that person's benefit but for the purpose he or she may serve or the use that can be made of the person's services.

FUND. *Fundatio*—foundation.

FUNDAMENTAL OPTION. A theory of morals that each person gradually develops in a basic orientation of his or her life, either for or against God. This fundamental direction is said to be for God if one's life is fundamentally devoted to the love and service of others, and against God if one's life is essentially devoted to self-love and self-service.

As such, the idea of a fundamental option is not new. It was reflected in St. Augustine's teaching that the human race is ultimately composed of two cities: the City of God, whose members love God even to the contempt of self, and the City of Man, whose members love themselves even to the contempt of God.

What is new is the use of this idea to explain mortal sin. In 1975 the Holy See issued a formal declaration, *Persona Humana,* in which certain theories involving the fundamental option were condemned. "There are those," the document stated, "who go so far as to affirm that mortal sin, which causes separation from God, only exists in the formal refusal directly opposed to God's call, or in that selfishness which completely and deliberately closes itself to the love of neighbor. They say that it is only then, that there comes into play the 'fundamental option', that is to say, the decision which totally commits the person and which is necessary if mortal sin is to exist."

The Holy See admitted the description of a person's basic moral disposition as a "fundamental option." What is not admissible is to claim that individual human actions cannot radically change this fundamental option. A person's moral disposition "can be completely changed by particular acts, especially when as often happens, these have been prepared for by previous more superficial acts. Whatever the case, it is wrong to say that particular acts are not enough to constitute a mortal sin" (*Persona Humana,* Congregation for the Doctrine of the Faith, December 29, 1975, number 10).

Implicit in the proscribed theory is the notion that there can be serious sins, such as murder or adultery, because the actions are gravely wrong. But no mortal sin, with the loss of sanctifying grace, is committed unless a person subjectively rejects God. This would subvert the whole moral order of Christianity, which believes that the essence of mortal sin is the deliberate choice of some creature which is known to be gravely forbidden by God.

FUNDAMENTAL THEOLOGY. That branch of theology which establishes the fact that God has made a supernatural revelation and established the Church, founded by Christ, as its divinely authorized custodian and interpreter. It is called theology because it is a science dealing with God; and it is fundamental because its role is to set forth the rational foundations of the Catholic faith. In some circles the term "fundamental theology" has taken on a derived and secondary meaning, namely the science of the fundamental doctrines of the Christian faith.

FUNERAL RITES. The liturgical functions that the Church performs at the burial of members of the Catholic Church. The Constitution on the Liturgy of the Second Vatican Council directed that the funeral services be revised to express more clearly the paschal character of Christian death, and that the rite for the burial of infants be given a special Mass. Both provisions were implemented in the new rite promulgated by Pope Paul VI, to take effect on June 1, 1970. The new emphasis is on Christian hope in eternal life and in the final resurrection from the dead.

FUTURE. In scholastic philosophy, what does not yet exist or has not taken place but will come to pass and occur. Often refers to the hereafter as "the future life" or "future happiness."

FUTURIBLE. The future free actions of rational creatures which would have occurred if certain conditions had been fulfilled. Although they will not take place, they are nevertheless known by God in what is called the divine mediate knowledge, *scientia media,* i.e., a knowledge midway between God's foreknowledge of pure possibilities and of real futures that will come to pass.

FUTUROLOGY. The art or practice of predicting future developments in society or in some phase of human endeavor, as in morals, religion, or Christianity. Borrowed from the natural sciences, futurology is based on an evolutionary concept of men and society.

G

GABBATHA. The Aramaic name of the place near Jerusalem where Pontius Pilate had his judgment seat. St. John identifies this as the site where Jesus was brought before Pilate to be condemned to death (John 9:13). (Etym. Aramaic *gabbeta,* height, knob; the name of the place called in Greek *lithostrōtos,* a flagstone pavement.)

GABRIEL. One of the seven archangels, used on a number of occasions by God as a messenger (Deuteronomy 8:15–27). He appeared to Daniel and explained a vision to him about future events, telling him, "You are a man specially chosen" (Deuteronomy 9:20–27). In the New Testament he appeared to Zechariah to announce that Elizabeth, his wife, would bear a son and he must name the child John (Luke 1:11–20). Likewise, it was Gabriel who appeared to Mary and told her that she would conceive and bear a Son whom she must name Jesus (Luke 1:26–38).

GAD. Eldest son of Jacob and the slave girl Zilpah (Genesis 30:9–11). He became the ancestor of one of the Twelve Tribes of Israel, a warlike people called Gadites (Numbers 2:14). They supported David against Saul and after Solomon's death supported the revolt of Jeroboam.

GADARENES. See GERASENES.

GAIUS. 1. a Macedonian companion of Paul who became involved in the unruly scene in Ephesus when the silversmiths rioted against Paul, who had disparaged the making of images of the goddess Diana (Acts 19:29). He is probably the same Gaius who traveled with Paul to Asia shortly thereafter (Acts 20:4); 2. a convert baptized by Paul in Corinth. He may be the same man who entertained Paul in his home in Rome (I Corinthians 1:14). The name Gaius was such a common one in

Rome that positive identification is impossible.

GALATIANS, EPISTLE TO THE. Letter of St. Paul to the Churches in Galatia, warning them against the Judaizers who wanted the Christians to be circumcised. The faithful were being told that Paul was just another disciple, so he defended his apostleship, directly from Christ. He further explained that salvation is through Christ alone, that Christ's followers are no longer under the yoke of the Old Law, that they must seek only the glory of God and avoid all self-indulgence, and that true glory is found only in the cross of Christ. St. Paul signed at least the last few lines with his own hand. (Etym. Latin name derived from Gauls who invaded Macedonia, Greece, and Asia Minor in 279 B.C.)

GALILEE. Of the three provinces that made up Palestine (Galilee, Samaria, Judaea) Galilee was the one farthest north. Approximately fifteen hundred square miles in area, it had both fertile plains and rugged mountains (Luke 4:16). Jesus grew up in Galilee, in a small village in the southern part, and most of the Apostles were Galileans (Matthew 4:18; Acts 1:11). He did much of his preaching there and many of his miracles were performed in Galilee (Matthew 4:23). (Etym. Latin *galllaea;* from Greek *galilaia,* from Hebrew *galil,* circle, district.)

GALILEO CASE. The celebrated case of Galileo Galilei (1564–1642), Italian physicist and astronomer, whose conflict with ecclesiastical authorities has become part of world history. In 1616 he was brought before the Inquisition on the charge of ignoring the implications of the Copernican (heliocentric) theory, which seemed to contradict the biblical story of the stopping of the sun in the Book of Joshua. Significantly, the Polish astronomer Copernicus in the previous century had dedicated to Pope Paul III in 1543 his published theory that the sun is the center of a great system and that the earth is a planet revolving about it. In obedience to the ruling of the Inquisition, Galileo promised not to teach Copernicus' theory as anything but a hypothesis, as in fact the proofs for the theory (on modern scientific principles) were not conclusive. In 1632, Galileo was again asked to come to Rome, this time for alleged breach of contract, since he had meantime published a satirical work, *Dialogue,* bitterly attacking his opponents. He was detained for twenty-two days in the buildings of the Holy Office, and he promised not to urge the Copernican system as a proved fact. Before he died in Florence in 1642, he received the special blessing of Pope Urban VIII. No question of papal infallibility was involved. In Galileo's case the Church defined nothing and uttered no doctrine. It made a disciplinary prohibition to protect the faithful from the disturbing effect of a then unproved hypothesis. St. Robert Bellarmine, who was involved in the Galileo affair, wrote that if a real proof were found that the sun was fixed and did not revolve around the earth, "it would be necessary to acknowledge that the passages in Scripture which appear to contradict this fact have been misunderstood." Recent scholarship has shown that the document that led to Galileo's trial in Rome (1633) was a forgery. It had been planted in the Roman Curia by an unscrupulous official. It falsely charged Galileo with having been enjoined seventeen years before from teaching the Copernican system. Galileo's famous trial, therefore, was based on this "document," which he had never before seen. In 1979, Pope John Paul II called for the formal exoneration of Galileo.

GALLICANISM. A cluster of doctrines, favored by the French Church, that tended to limit the authority of the Pope in relation to the bishops, and to subordinate the rights of the Church to the power of the State. The first exponents of Gallicanism were the Franciscans William of Ockham, John of Jandun, and Marsilius of Padua in the fourteenth century, who denied the divine origin of the papal primacy and would subject its exercise to the will of civil authority. Gallicanism became Conciliarism after the Great Western Schism, claiming the superiority of council over the Pope, and promoted by John Gerson (1363–1429) and Peter d'Ailly (1350–1420). The French Revolution drove the bishops into the arms of the Pope and dealt a mortal blow to Gallicanism, but the basic idea was still alive until the First Vatican Council formally condemned it in 1870.

GALLICAN RITE. A ritual that prevailed from the fourth to the eighth centuries in Gaul. Its origin is disputed, but the ritual was most likely introduced by the first missionaries. It differed from the Roman Rite in the arrangement of the liturgical year, the elaborate ceremonial in the offering of the bread and wine, and in the fact that all Mass prayers were variable daily. Some liturgies today at Milan and Toledo bear resemblance to the Gallican rites.

GALLIO. Roman proconsul of Achaia. The Jews brought Paul before his tribunal, accusing him of offending their religious laws, but Gallio refused to hear their complaint (Acts 18:12–17). Disagreement over religion, he maintained, was not subject to legal judgment. Even when they beat the synagogue president in front of the courthouse, he ignored them.

GAMALIEL. A Pharisee, a learned doctor of the law, and a member of the Sanhedrin. He proved the moderateness of his views when he urged the Sanhedrin to be tolerant of the Apostles when they were on trial for preaching their beliefs. "If this movement of theirs," he reasoned, "is of human origin, it will break up of its own accord, but if it does in fact come from God, you will not only be unable to destroy them, but you might find yourselves fighting against God" (Acts 5:34–41). He was the teacher of Paul before the latter's conversion and was evidently highly respected. Whether he ever became a Christian himself is debatable; there is no evidence to prove that he did.

GAMBLING. The staking of money or other valuables on a future event, chance, or contingency that is unknown or uncertain to the participants. The essential feature of gambling is wagering, or the act of hazarding as such.

The Catholic Church has never condemned gambling outright, in spite of the evident abuses to which it generally gives rise. Yet gambling may become a sin, even a serious sin, when it goes to excess that would destroy personal honesty or expose a person to loss so great as to jeopardize society and, above all, his family dependents.

GARTH. The open space enclosed by the four walks or sides of a convent or monastic cloister. In some religious communities the deceased members are buried in the garth.

GATE. A symbol of the Blessed Virgin, *"janua coeli,"* gate of heaven. Through Mary, Jesus came to us and through her and her Son her earthly children can go to heaven someday to enjoy the Beatific Vision.

GAUDETE SUNDAY. Third Sunday of Advent, so named from the opening antiphon of the Introit *Gaudete in Domino semper* (Rejoice in the Lord always). On this Sunday rose vestments are permitted in the Eucharistic liturgy. (Etym. Latin *gaudete,* rejoice.) See also LAETARE SUNDAY.

GAUDIUM ET SPES. Second Vatican Council's Pastoral Constitution on the Church in the Modern World. The longest document of the council, it has two main divisions: 1. the Church's teaching on human beings, the world they live in, and her relationship to them; 2. various aspects of life today and human society, and in particular the pressing moral issues of our day. Its treatment of the Church's role in the modern world is realistic, recognizing that "atheism must be regarded as one of the most serious problems of our time." It is also practical, noting that with all the media at work today, yet "genuine fraternal dialogue is advanced not so much on this level as at the deeper level of personal fellowship," where individuals share together in spirit. The treatment of marriage and the Christian family is the most extensive in conciliar history. And the strong position on peace and war reflects the Church's mind in the nuclear age (December 7, 1965).

GEHENNA (Hinnom). A valley southwest of Jerusalem which developed an evil reputation among Jews because of idolatrous and barbarous events that took place there during the reigns of Ahaz and Manasseh (II Chronicles 28:1–4, 33:1–6). Jeremiah deplored the superstitious excesses and renamed it the Valley of Slaughter (Jeremiah 7:32). Yahweh warned the inhabitants it would become a "city of desolation" (Jeremiah 19:8). In the New Testament the name in Hebrew acquired the meaning of Hell. Jesus used it on numerous occasions, warning sinners they would be condemned to Hell if they continued their sinful ways (Matthew 5:22, 5:29; Mark 9:43).

GELASIAN SACRAMENTARY. An ancient liturgical book, written sometime between the sixth and eighth centuries, but ascribed to Pope Gelasius I (reigned 492–96). It is the oldest known Roman Missal with the feasts arranged according to the ecclesiastical year, and certainly of pre-Gregorian origin. It contains the Roman Canon in practically its present form.

GEN. *Generalis*—general.

GENAZZANO. A shrine of Our Lady of Good Counsel in a small town thirty miles southeast of Rome. It possesses a famed picture of the Blessed Virgin and Child. The story of Genazzano goes back to 1467. A native widow, though having no funds, expressed the desire to rebuild an abandoned Church of Our Lady, dating from the fifth century. Without any means to carry out her plan, she was ridiculed by the townspeople until on St. Mark's day of that year, while the entire village was celebrating a public carnival, the town was mysteriously darkened though the sky remained clear. Before thousands of witnesses, when light returned a small picture of the Virgin Mother and Child was found on the foundation walls of the unfinished church. The bells of the village rang by themselves. Awed and in fear, the people awaited the verdict of a disinterested bishop who had been sent by Pope Paul II to verify the facts. His report stated that between April and mid August of 1467, he had witnessed one hundred seventy-one miracles at Genazzano. The picture was called *The Madonna of Paradise*. A papal committee found that the Genazzano picture had been painted on a thin layer of porcelain, of eggshell thinness, and could never have been moved by human hands. The image stands today in front of the tabernacle of the altar resting on a ledge without support. A basilica was finished in the late fifteenth century, and devotion to Our Lady of Good Counsel spread throughout the world. The day of discovery of the little picture is kept with a procession of spectacular pageantry yearly, and a feast day for Our Lady of Good Counsel is on the Church's calendar. During World War II Genazzano was bombed, the basilica hit, the roof completely crushed, the interior, including altars, paintings, and statues, completely destroyed. Only the treasured picture of the Madonna was unharmed.

GENEALOGY OF JESUS CHRIST. Matthew and Luke provide detailed genealogies of Jesus, which, though differing in some details, are substantially the same. Matthew's starts with Abraham and divides the list into three sets of fourteen generations each (Matthew 1:1–17). Luke's moves in reverse order from Jesus all the way back to Adam (Luke 3:23–38). Between Abraham and Adam, Luke's listing agrees in great part with the genealogies in Genesis and the First Chronicles (Genesis 4, 5, 10, 11; I Chronicles 1–9). Some variations may be explained by the fact that occasionally in the Old Testament family lines were based on adoptive relationships or legal heirships. It is interesting to note how both Matthew and Luke made it clear that Joseph was not the father of Jesus (Matthew 1:16; Luke 3:23).

GENERAL CATECHETICAL DIRECTORY. Document of the Sacred Congregation for the Clergy, issued by order of Pope Paul VI, "to provide the basic principles of pastoral theology—these principles having been taken from the Magisterium of the Church, and in a special way from the Second General Council of the Vatican—by which pastoral action in the ministry of the word can be more fittingly directed and governed" (April 11, 1971).

GENERAL CONFESSION. The term has two different meanings, both referring to the reception of the sacrament of penance. Most commonly, it means a private confession where the penitent (exceptionally) resolves to confess as far as he or she can all past sins, and not only those since the last confession. The practice is recommended when a person is entering on a new state of life— the priesthood, religious life, or marriage— and is required in some religious institutes by rule to be done annually. Less often, general confession is associated with the granting of general absolution. When general absolution may be validly given, the provision for general confession is that "the penitents who wish to receive absolution" are invited "to indicate this by some kind of sign." The penitents then say a general formula for confession, for example, "I confess to almighty God." However, one of the necessary dispositions for receiving valid absolution, when only a general confession was made, is that the penitent "resolve to confess in due time each one of the grave sins which he cannot confess at present."

GENERATION. In Catholic theology, the origin of a living being from a living being of its own kind or species. Most commonly applied to the conception of a human being. And in a transferred sense means the coming into being of a new substance or substantial form and especially the change of the lifeless into the living. Doctrinally the term "generation" refers to the origin of the second person of the Trinity from the Father. (Etym. Latin *generare,* to beget.)

GENERATION, DIVINE. The procession of the Second Person of the Trinity from the First, i.e., the generation of the Son by the Father. As explained by the Church, this generation is eternal and takes place in a manner similar to the intellectual activity of the human soul. "Just as our spirit knowing itself, produces an image of itself, which theologians call a 'word,' so God also, insofar as human can be compared to Divine, knowing Himself, generates the Eternal Word" (*Roman Catechism,* III, 9). Thus the generation of the Son from the Father is to be conceived purely as an intellectual generation or as an act of the Divine Intellect.

GENERATIONISM. A theory that traces

the origin of the human soul, as well as the origin of the body, back to the act of generation performed by the parents. Parents are therefore the originators of both body and soul. The cruder form of generationism, called traducianism, teaches that with the bodily semen a part of the soul substance of the parents (*tradux*) is transmitted to the child. A less crude form, taught by St. Augustine to be possible, holds fast to the spirituality of the soul but makes the soul of the child emerge from the spiritual semen of the parents. Generationism of any kind is incompatible with the simplicity and spirituality of the soul and has been several times condemned by the Church (Denzinger 1007, 3220).

GENESIS. The first book of the Bible, containing an account of the origin of the world, of the human race, and of the Chosen People. These three origins are covered as follows: the creation of the world and the early history of humanity, including the Fall, the promise of a Redeemer, and the Deluge (1–11); the early history of the Jews, including Abraham, Isaac, Jacob, and Joseph (12–50). The prophecy of Jacob (49) contains the celebrated prediction in favor of the tribe of Judah, of which will be born the Messiah.

GENEVA BIBLE. An English translation of the Bible, under Protestant auspices, published in Geneva in 1560. It was the first English edition to use verse divisions, had a strong Calvinist tone, and is popularly known as the "Breeches Bible" because of its translation of Genesis 3:7, "they . . . made themselves breeches."

GENNESARET. A fertile plain on the northwest shore of the Sea of Galilee. Sometimes the Gospel writers called the sea the Lake of Gennesaret because of its proximity to the plain. When Jesus landed on the plain, a number of sick people were brought to him and he cured them (Matthew 14:34–36; Mark 6:53–56).

GENTILES. People who were not Jews. In Old Testament accounts, relations between Jews and others were normal (Deuteronomy 10:18–19). There was even a certain amount of intermarriage. As time went on, however, Jewish teaching increasingly frowned on this (Ezra 9:11–12). Probably as a result of persecution, bitter hostility grew between Jews and Gentiles. When Jesus was teaching his disciples, he first directed them to work only among their own people: "Do not turn your steps to

pagan territory . . . go rather to the lost sheep of the House of Israel" (Matthew 10:5). But gradually he extended their apostolate to all who accepted his teaching (John 1:12–13). This wider mission continued so notably in Paul's journeys that he became known as the Apostle to the Gentiles.

GENTLEMEN OF HIS HOLINESS. An office established in 1968 by Pope Paul VI as a mark of honor to persons serving such posts as the care of the furnishings and travel arrangements for the papal household.

GENUFLECTION. Bending of the knee as an act of reverence. Customary when passing before the Blessed Sacrament in the tabernacle, entering the pew for divine worship, and during certain ceremonies to the Cross. A double genuflection of both knees simultaneously was commonly made before the Blessed Sacrament exposed in a monstrance. The new directive since the Second Vatican Council specifies: "One knee is bent before the Blessed Sacrament, whether reserved in the tabernacle or exposed for public adoration" (*Eucharistiae Sacramentum*, 1973, number 84). Genuflections are also made to the Pope, to a cardinal, and to a bishop in his own diocese.

GENUS. The qualities that are common to several species, abstracting from their distinctive differences. Thus a universal concept, like intelligent being, can be applied to angels and men. The supreme genera are called categories, of which the first (in Aristotle and St. Thomas Aquinas) expresses substance, and the nine others express accidental properties, namely quantity, quality, relation, place, time, action, passion, position, and state. (Etym. Latin *genus*, class, kind.)

G.E.R. *Generale Ecclesiae Rationarium*— General Statistics Office of the Church.

GERASENES. The inhabitants of a Decapolis city "which is opposite Galilee," according to Luke (Luke 8:26–33). Little is known about its location or history. Several of the Evangelists told the story of Jesus driving the demon out of the man "in the country of the Gerasenes" (Matthew 8:28–34; Mark 5:1–13). The word is sometimes spelled Gergesenes or Gadarenes.

GERGESENES. See GERASENES.

GERIZIM. A mountain in Samaria. When Moses was passing on to the Israelites the instructions Yahweh had given him, he told them that, as soon as they had taken over the Promised Land, they must speak the words of blessing from Mount Gerizim (Deuteronomy 11:29). In the New Testament it was on this mountain that Jesus asked the Samaritan woman for a drink of water (John 4). In the ensuing conversation she referred to the worship her people offered on Mount Gerizim to rival the Jerusalem temple. To this day certain Samaritans observe the Passover on the mountain with suitable ceremony.

GERSHOM. A son of Moses and Zipporah who was born during the period Moses sojourned in Midianite territory after fleeing from Pharaoh (Exodus 2:21–22). The name Gershom means "exile" or "stranger," which was appropriate because Moses observed ruefully, "I am a stranger in a foreign land."

GESTA. Literally "events." Sometimes applied to the stories of the life and death of the martyrs. They pertain to individual martyrs, as distinct from a martyrology, which is an official register of Christian martyrs.

GETHSEMANE. The garden lying outside Jerusalem on the Mount of Olives where Jesus spent the agonizing hours praying prior to his arrest (Mark 14:32–52, John 18:1–12). (Etym. Aramaic *gat semane,* oil press; Greek *gethsēmanei.*)

GHETTO. Originally the street or quarter of a city (*borghetto,* small borough) in which the Jewish people lived. The earliest ghettos were in Italy in the eleventh century, but they became common by the later Middle Ages. They were partly the result of legal restriction by the civil authorities, and partly the requirements of the strongly communitarian way of life of the Jews themselves. In 1556, Pope Paul IV established a ghetto in Rome, which continued until 1870. It is known that already before the time of Christ a ghetto existed in Rome, where numerous Jewish freemen (former slaves) lived in the Trastevere district.

GHOST. A disembodied spirit. Christianity believes that God may, and sometimes does, permit a departed soul to appear in some visible form to people on earth. Allowing for legend and illusion, there is enough authentic evidence, for example in the lives of the saints, to indicate that such apparitions occur. Their purpose may be to teach, or warn, or request some favor of the living.

GIANTS. Huge persons mentioned in the Bible. When Moses sent spies into Canaan to discover whether it was a suitable place for the Promised Land, the spies were frightened by "the enormous size" of the natives. "We felt like grasshoppers and so we seemed to them" (Numbers 13:32–33). These people were called Nephilim. Another group of so-called giants were the Rephaim, who lived in Moabite territory (Deuteronomy 2:10). Goliath was unquestionably the best-known gigantic figure in Scripture, because of his famous encounter with David, but he was a Philistine, not a member of a tribe of giants (I Samuel 17).

GIDEON. An inspiring religious and military leader of the Israelites during the period when the dominant worship of Baal exercised a strong pagan influence on Israel. The nomadic Midianites and Amalekites had overrun Palestine and continually destroyed the crops and flocks of the local inhabitants (Judges 6:1–6). Gideon, loyal to Yahweh and his people, organized an Israelite army, but it was not an efficient force. Inspired by Yahweh, Gideon reduced it to an aggressive force of three hundred men and achieved remarkable success in attacking the Midianites. His victory emboldened other Israelite communities and the enemy was driven out of the country (Judges 7:1–8). Gideon was offered the kingship of Israel but refused it, preferring to return to his family and agricultural life (Judges 8:22–23). His long life was distinguished by a deep faith and loyalty to Israelite beliefs and practices. (Etym. Hebrew *gide'on,* hewer, warrior.)

GIFT. As a title to ownership in scholastic philosophy, the voluntary transfer of something to another person. Gift includes two elements: alienation or giving up of the first owner's right, and acceptance or the beginning of the new owner's right. Both of these take place together and with a view to one another. The property is alienated only on condition that it can be accepted by the person to whom it is offered, so that if a gift is refused the property is not alienated and others have no claim on it.

GIFT OF COUNSEL. One of the special gifts of the Holy Spirit; it perfects the virtue of prudence. Its function is to enable a person to judge promptly and rightly, as by a sort of supernatural intuition, what should be done, especially in difficult situations. With the gift of counsel, the Holy Spirit speaks, as it were, to the heart and in an instant enlightens a person what to do. It corresponds to the promise made by Christ to his followers, "When they hand you over, do not worry about how to speak or what to say; what you are to say will be given to you when the time comes; because it is not you who will be speaking; the Spirit of your Father will be speaking in you" (Matthew 10:19).

Counsel refers primarily to prudent conduct in one's own case, and only secondarily in favor of others. Enlightened by the Spirit, a person learns what to do in a specific case and what advice to give when consulted or command to make if he is in authority.

GIFT OF FEAR. Infused gift of the Holy Spirit that confirms the virtue of hope and inspires a person with profound respect for the majesty of God. Its corresponding effects are protection from sin through dread of offending the Lord, and a strong confidence in the power of his help.

The fear of the Lord is not servile but filial. It is based on the selfless love of God, whom it shrinks from offending. Whereas in servile fear the evil dreaded is punishment; in filial fear it is the fear of doing anything contrary to the will of God.

The gift of fear comprises three principal elements: a vivid sense of God's greatness, a lively sorrow for the least faults committed, and a vigilant care in avoiding occasions of sin. It is expressed in the prayer of the Psalmist, "My whole being trembles before you, your ruling fills me with fear" (Psalm 119:120). One of its salutary effects is to induce a spirit of deep humility in dealing with others, especially with inferiors, since it makes a person aware that he or she stands constantly before the judgment of God.

GIFT OF FORTITUDE. One of the seven gifts of the Holy Spirit; it gives a person a special strength of will. This gift confers an extraordinary readiness to undergo trials for love of God or in fulfillment of the divine will; unusual courage to bear difficulties even for many years; firmness in carrying arduous tasks to their completion; perseverance in a lifetime fidelity to one's vocation in spite of heavy trials or disappointments sent by God; and gladness in being privileged to suffer persecution or humiliation in union with Christ and for the sake of his name.

GIFT OF INTEGRITY. Total exemption from the sway of concupiscence, whereby man's whole sensitive and imaginative life and activity are completely under control and ruled by reason. This preternatural gift was possessed by Adam and Eve before the Fall. It rendered their enjoyment of the pleasures of sensitive life more intense than ours because their natural faculties, being purer, were therefore keener.

GIFT OF KNOWLEDGE. One of the seven

infused gifts. By the illuminating action of the Holy Spirit it perfects the virtue of faith. It gives a person the ability to judge everything from a supernatural viewpoint. The object of this gift is the whole spectrum of created things insofar as they lead one to God. Through infused knowledge the faithful can see the providential purpose of whatever enters their lives, and they are able to put creatures to the right use according to God's will for themselves and for others. Sometimes called "the science of the saints," it enables those who have the gift to discern easily and effectively between the impulses of temptation and the inspirations of grace.

GIFT OF PIETY. A special gift of the Holy Spirit; it perfects the virtue of religion, which is the practice of justice toward God. It produces an instinctive filial affection for God and devotion toward those who are specially consecrated to God. As an infused gift of God, it is ready loyalty to God and the things of God, arising not so much from studied effort or acquired habit as from a supernatural communication conferred by the Holy Spirit.

This gift enables a person to see in God not only one's sovereign Master but a loving Father, according to the teaching of St. Paul: "Everyone moved by the Spirit is a son of God. The spirit you received is not the spirit of slaves bringing fear into your lives again; it is the spirit of sons, and it makes us cry out, 'Abba, Father!'" (Romans 8:14–15). It engenders in the soul a filial respect for God, a generous love toward him, and an affectionate obedience that wants to do what he commands because it loves the one who commands.

GIFT OF TONGUES. One of the preternatural gifts described by St. Luke. Also known as glossolalia, it was the gift of speaking so as to be understood by all (as happened on Pentecost), and the corresponding ability of the hearers to understand a person speaking in a foreign tongue. St. Paul describes a different gift of tongues in the early Church, namely talking in unintelligible speech, but he viewed it with suspicion when those who had the charism lacked the ability to explain what they were saying (I Corinthians 14:1–40). Among Pentecostals in the charismatic movement, the gift of tongues is said to be very active in modern times.

GIFTS OF THE HOLY SPIRIT. The seven forms of supernatural initiative conferred with the reception of sanctifying grace. They are in the nature of supernatural reflexes, or reactive instincts, that spontaneously answer to the divine impulses of grace almost without reflection but always with full consent. The gifts are wisdom (*sapientia*), understanding (*intellectus*), knowledge (*scientia*), fortitude or courage (*fortitudo*), counsel (*consilium*), piety or love (*pietas*), and fear of the Lord (*timor Domini*).

GIFT OF UNDERSTANDING. The infused gift of the Holy Spirit given to the mind for grasping revealed truths easily and profoundly. It differs from faith because it gives insight into the meaning of what a person believes, whereas faith, as such, merely assents to what God has revealed.

This gift produces three principal effects in those who possess it. They are enabled to penetrate to the very core of revealed truths, without ever fully understanding their meaning; they are confirmed in their belief by acquiring great certitude in the revealed word of God; and they are brought to the knowledge of a greater number of truths by drawing numerous conclusions from revealed principles.

GIFT OF WISDOM. The first and highest of the gifts of the Holy Spirit. It makes the soul responsive to God in the contemplation of divine things. Where faith is a simple knowledge of the articles of Christian belief, wisdom goes on to a certain divine penetration of the truths themselves. Built into wisdom is the element of love, which inspires contemplative reflection on these divine mysteries, rejoices dwelling on them, and directs the mind to judge all things according to their principles.

GILBERTINES. The only purely English monastic order, founded about A.D. 1130 by St. Gilbert (1083–1189) at Sempringham, England, beginning with seven women. Eventually monasteries of men were also established, all following the Rule of St. Augustine. Absolute authority was vested in a master, called "Prior of All." By the time of St. Gilbert's death, there were thirteen foundations in England. The Gilbertines were favored by the crown until Henry VIII dissolved the order, which then had twenty-five monasteries. The last master was Robert Holgate.

GILEAD. 1. father of the valiant Jephthah (Judges 11:1), who led the Israelites in their victorious wars against the Ammonites and Ephraimites; 2. part of the territory given by Moses to Gad as his inheritance when the country was apportioned among Israel's tribes. It was a grain-producing re-gion in the Jordan valley between the Yarmuk and Arnon rivers (Joshua 13:24–25).

GL. *Gloria*—glory to God; *gloria patri.*

GLADNESS. A result of interior happiness, shown in one's external disposition and even facial expression. Cheerfulness as the emotional counterpart to a person's well-being.

GLASTONBURY. Ruined abbey and shrine in County Somerset, in southwestern England, and one of the first centers of the faith in Celtic England. In 1184 the famous abbey reached the peak of its architectural glory. Now it is in ruins except for the abbot's kitchen, built in 1437, which today draws curious sightseers. St. Patrick is reported to have built the first permanent church there in 432. King Arthur and his queen are buried nearby; their tombs were recently discovered. In 943 or 944 King Edmund made St. Dunstan its abbot. From this time the abbey was organized according to the Benedictine Rule. There was a rich history of miracles at Glastonbury. In 1539 the strong Catholic enemies despoiled the entire property, stole the sapphire altar, which had been St. David's gift, and put to death Richard Whiting (1460–1539), the Benedictine abbot. He is now canonized.

GLEBE. A land permanently assigned for maintaining a parish. A glebe house is a parsonage or manse.

GLORIA. Second section of the Catholic Mass; a psalm or hymn of praise to God sung in Latin or vernacular on occasion; the opening word of the greater and lesser doxologies.

GLORIA IN EXCELSIS. The major doxology at Mass, after the Penitential Act and Appeal for Mercy. It is sung or said by the whole congregation or else by them alternately with the choir, or by the choir itself. The Gloria is used on Sundays outside of Advent and Lent, on solemnities and feast days, and at special solemn celebrations.

GLORIA PATRI. The lesser doxology, probably an early adaptation of the Jewish blessings addressed to God, as already found in the New Testament (Romans 16:27; Philippians 4:20; Revelation 5:23). Its present form was influenced by the Trinitarian formula of baptism (Matthew 28:19). The English Puritans forbade its use as unscriptural. The Latin text reads: "*Gloria Patri, et Filio, et Spiritui Sancto. Sicut erat in principio, et nunc, et semper, et in saecula saeculorum,*" and in English: "Glory (be) to the Father, and to the Son, and to the Holy

Spirit. As it was in the beginning, is now, and ever shall be, world without end. Amen."

GLORIFIED BODY. The human body after its resurrection from the dead and reunion with the soul, which beholds the vision of God. This vision is the source of the body's glorification, described by St. Paul (I Corinthians 15:42–44).

GLORIOUS MYSTERIES. The five mysteries of the Rosary on the glories of Christ and his Mother. They are: the Resurrection of Christ from the dead, Christ's Ascension into heaven, the Descent of the Holy Spirit on Pentecost, Mary's bodily Assumption into heaven, and her Coronation in heaven as Queen of the Universe. See also JOYFUL MYSTERIES, SORROWFUL MYSTERIES.

GLORY. The recognition and praise of someone's excellence. Applied to God, the divine (internal) glory is the infinite goodness that the persons of the Trinity constantly behold and mutually praise. His external glory is first of all the share that creatures have in God's goodness. Sometimes called objective glory, it is given to God by all creatures without exception, by their mere existence, insofar as they mirror the divine perfections. Formal glory is rendered to God by his rational creatures, when they acknowledge the divine goodness and praise God for who he is and what he has communicated of himself to the world. (Etym. Latin *gloria*, renown, splendor, glorification.)

GLOSSOLALIA. (Etym. Greek *glōssa*, a tongue, language, unusual word + *lalia*, chatter.) See GIFT OF TONGUES.

GLOVES. An episcopal vestment, blessed for a bishop and placed on his hands at his ordination. The practice of wearing them at liturgical functions began about the eleventh century. They are worn only at a pontifical Mass, and then only to the washing of the hands. They are made of knitted silk and ornamented on the back with a cross. They vary in color according to the Mass celebrated but are not used at Masses for the dead.

GLUTTONY. Inordinate desire for the pleasure connected with food or drink. This desire may become sinful in various ways: by eating or drinking far more than a person needs to maintain bodily strength; by glutting one's taste for certain kinds of food with known detriment to health; by indulging the appetite for exquisite food or drink, especially when these are beyond one's ability to afford a luxurious diet; by eating or drinking too avidly, i.e., ravenously; by consuming alcoholic beverages to the point of losing full control of one's reasoning powers. Intoxication that ends in complete loss of reason is a mortal sin if brought on without justification, e.g., for medical reasons. (Etym. Latin *glutire*, to devour.)

GNOSIS. Spiritual knowledge. In a valid sense it is the knowledge of divine mysteries possessed already in this life, though darkly as a "hidden wisdom" (I Corinthians 2:6–16). In a heretical sense it is the recurring error of those who claim to have knowledge of divine things exclusively from their own religious experience and even in contradiction to the Church's teaching authority. (Etym. Greek *gnōsis*, knowledge.)

GNOSTICISM. The theory of salvation by knowledge. Already in the first century of the Christian era there were Gnostics who claimed to know the mysteries of the universe. They were disciples of the various pantheistic sects that existed before Christ. The Gnostics borrowed what suited their purpose from the Gospels, wrote new gospels of their own, and in general proposed a dualistic system of belief. Matter was said to be hostile to spirit, and the universe was held to be a depravation of the Deity. Although extinct as an organized religion, Gnosticism is the invariable element in every major Christian heresy, by its denial of an objective revelation that was completed in the apostolic age and its disclaimer that Christ established in the Church a teaching authority to interpret decisively the meaning of the revealed word of God.

GOD. The one absolutely and infinitely perfect spirit who is the Creator of all. In the definition of the First Vatican Council, fifteen internal attributes of God are affirmed, besides his role as Creator of the universe: "The holy, Catholic, apostolic Roman Church believes and professes that there is one true, living God, the Creator and Lord of heaven and earth. He is almighty, eternal, beyond measure, incomprehensible, and infinite in intellect, will and in every perfection. Since He is one unique spiritual substance, entirely simple and unchangeable, He must be declared really and essentially distinct from the world, perfectly happy in Himself and by his very nature, and inexpressibly exalted over all things that exist or can be conceived other than Himself" (Denzinger 3001).

Reflecting on the nature of God, theology has variously identified what may be called his metaphysical essence, i.e., *what* is God. It is commonly said to be his self-subsistence. God is Being Itself. In God essence and existence coincide. He is the Being who cannot not exist. God alone must be. All other beings exist only because of the will of God.

GODHEAD. The divinity. When used without qualification, it refers to the divine essence or nature, with stress on God's total transcendence of creation.

GODPARENTS. Sponsors who make profession of faith for the person being baptized. Solemn baptism requires godparents. The godparent assumes an obligation to instruct the child in the event of the death or neglect of the parents, in order to fulfill the baptismal promises. Being a godparent creates a spiritual relationship that is recognized in ecclesiastical law.

GOD THE FATHER. First person of the Trinity, who is unbegotten but who eternally begets the Son; from whom and from the Son proceeds the Holy Spirit. To the Father is attributed creation.

GOD THE HOLY SPIRIT. The third person of the Trinity, who eternally proceeds from the Father and the Son and is really distinct from them yet coequal with them as God. To him are attributed all the works of the Trinity that pertain to the sanctification of the human race.

GOD THE SON. The second person of the Trinity, who is eternally the only-begotten of the Father. He is really distinct from the Father and coeternal with the Father, from both of whom proceeds the Holy Spirit. Through him all things were made. He became incarnate of the Virgin Mary by the power of the Holy Spirit and is known as Jesus Christ.

GOLDEN CALF. The image of God that Aaron made at the foot of Mount Sinai to please the Israelites, who were tired of waiting for Moses during his stay on the mountain (Exodus 32). Even if the Jews did not worship the calf as an idol, they were forbidden to make any representation of Yahweh (Exodus 20). Moreover, bovine images were associated with obscenity. That is why, on descending from the mountain, Moses was angry with the Israelites and told them, "You have committed a grave sin" (Exodus 32:30).

GOLDEN LEGEND. Called by its author,

Blessed Voragine, the "Legend of the Saints." A popular collection of biographies, stories of saints, of dubious historicity but very readable as a book of devotion. The Apocryphal Gospel of Mary's Nativity, Pseudo-Matthew, and the Protoevangelium of James are usually included.

GOLDEN MEAN. The virtue of choosing the midpoint between excess and defect in action. This midpoint is determined by reason guided by the intellectual virtue of prudence. Based on Aristotle, the golden mean assumes that too much or too little of anything, whether food, sleep, or exercise, hurts the body and the right balance promotes bodily health, so excess or defect in the habits of the soul harms the moral health of the soul because "virtue stands in the middle." Thus courage is a mean between cowardice and rashness, and generosity between stinginess and prodigality.

To be noted, however, is that the golden mean refers to the virtue objectively, as midway between opposite extremes. Subjectively a person should practice a given virtue not moderately but fully. A judge must go all out for justice, though justice itself is a mean between lenience and severity; the witness must be exactly truthful, but truthfulness itself is a mean between exaggeration and understatement.

GOLDEN NUMBER. The name of each of the nineteen numbers representing the cycle of lunar years into which Meton (432 B.C.) divided the calendar. He discovered that after nineteen solar years had elapsed the new moon would occur on the same days in the years indicated by identical numbers. They are called golden because the number for each current year was inscribed in gold on the pillar of a temple in Athens. The Golden Numbers have been adopted in the ecclesiastical calendar since the time of St. Hippolytus (A.D. 170–236).

GOLDEN ROSE. A spray of flowers made of gold, blessed by the Pope on the fourth Sunday of Lent and sent as a token of special honor to some notable person or institution. It is given in token of special services or loyalty to the Holy See. In the heart of the principal rose is a small covered cup in which musk and balsam have been placed. The Golden Rose is a symbol of spiritual joy.

GOLDEN RULE. The moral principle of treating others as one wants to be treated by them. It was expressed by Christ in his Sermon on the Mount: "So always treat others as you would like them to treat you; that is the meaning of the Law and the Prophets" (Matthew 7:12).

GOLDEN SEQUENCE. A name applied to the hymn *Veni, Sancte Spiritus, et emitte coelitus* (Come, Thou Holy Paraclete), which is sung on Pentecost Sunday.

GOLGOTHA. (Etym. Aramaic *gulgulta,* skull.) See CALVARY.

GOLIATH. A gigantic Philistine warrior from Gath, nine feet tall. Before battle lines drawn up between the Philistines and the Israelites, he challenged the latter to send forth a representative warrior and settle the battle in single combat. A young shepherd, David, volunteered to respond to the challenge, and King Saul reluctantly agreed. Without armor and equipped only with a sling and five stones, David went forth to meet the redoubtable Goliath. A single sling shot settled the combat; the stone pierced the giant's forehead and David slew him with the giant's sword. Inspired by this feat, the Israelites drove the enemy all the way back to Gath (I Samuel 17).

GOMER. Son of Japheth and grandson of Noah (Genesis 10:2). Father of an ancient people mentioned by Ezekiel as warring against Gog, King of Magog (Ezekiel 38:6). Unfaithful wife of the prophet Hosea, whose love for her symbolized the love of Yahweh for Israel in spite of its sins.

GOMORRAH. See SODOM.

GOOD. In general, whatever is suitable or befitting someone or something. Practically, however, it is that which all things tend toward or desire. The good is the desirable, and therefore the object of the natural (or supernatural) needs or tendencies of a being.

GOOD FRIDAY. Friday in Holy Week, anniversary of Christ's death on the Cross, and a day of fast and abstinence from the earliest Christian times. Black vestments were worn by the priest and Mass was not offered, except what was called the Mass of the Presanctified. A host consecrated the day before was consumed by the priest alone, although viaticum was permitted to the faithful. In the new liturgy, since the Second Vatican Council, the ceremonies consist of a reading of the Gospel according to St. John, special prayers for the Church and the people of all classes of society, the veneration of the Cross, and a Communion service at which all may receive the Eucharist. The Solemn Liturgical Action is to take place between noon and 9 P.M. Good Friday remains the only day in the year on which Mass is not celebrated in the Roman Rite.

GOOD, HIGHEST. Also the greatest, or supreme, good, the *summum bonum.* The good that transcends all other good and yet includes it. On earth it is obedience to the will of God and serving him in love; in heaven it is the possession of God in the beatific vision.

GOODNESS OF GOD. The perfect conformity of God's will with his nature (ontological goodness), and the perfect identity of God's will with the supreme norm, which is the divine essence (moral goodness).

God is absolute ontological goodness in himself and in relation to others. In himself, he is infinitely perfect and therefore his will is perfectly and infinitely happy in loving and enjoying himself as the supreme good, the *summum bonum.* He needs no one and nothing outside himself for his beatitude. God is also absolute ontological goodness in relation to others. He communicates his goodness to creatures, as the exemplary, efficient, and final cause of all created things.

God is absolute moral goodness or holiness. He is holy because he is exempt from all profaneness. He is the wholly Other whose will is not dependent on any creature. He is also holy because he is free from sin and, indeed, cannot commit sin. He is finally holy because his goodness is the norm of holiness for his creatures. They are as holy as they are like him.

GOOD NEWS. The Gospel, literally "good tidings" or "good announcement," from the New Testament term *evangelion.* This is the whole teaching of Christianity, which those who believe accept with their minds and strive to put into practice. It is "news" because what Christ revealed had previously been hidden from the foundation of the world; and it was "good" because it revealed the infinite goodness of God, who became man and because, through Christ, all the benefits of divine grace have been conferred on a fallen human race.

GOOD SHEPHERD. The title of Christ, which he gave himself, in so many words and in the Parable of the Good Shepherd (John 10:17–18; Luke 15:3–7). The theme is then taken up later in the New Testament (Hebrews 13:20; I Peter 2:25, 5:4). Implicit in the title is God's mercy on sinners and his concern for the weak and lowly. Already in the catacombs the Savior was often represented as the Good Shepherd.

GOOD THIEF. Traditionally said to be Dismas, one of the robbers crucified with Christ. He rebuked his companion for demanding that Christ should save them, prayed for a share in his Kingdom, and was assured of salvation. A portion of the cross on which he died is venerated in the Chapel of Relics in the Church of Santa Croce in Gerusalemme, in Rome. The Good Thief is the patron of persons condemned to death. See also DISMAS.

GOOD WORKS. Morally good acts that, when performed in the state of grace, merit supernatural reward. The term became highly controverted in Reformation times, when the leaders of Protestantism, notably Martin Luther (1483–1546), claimed that faith alone, and not good works, justifies. Implicit in the Catholic doctrine on good works is the belief that man's nature has not been totally depraved by reason of Adam's fall. Man is able freely to co-operate with divine grace to perform good works. His liberty is not totally enslaved by sin.

GORGIAS. A military leader in the Syrian army, ordered to invade Judah and destroy it (I Maccabees 3:38–39). Judas Maccabeus mustered an army and confronted the Syrians at Emmaus, defeating them decisively (I Maccabees 4:8–25). Gorgias regained the initiative, however, when he beat the Jews in a battle near Jamnia. Later he became the military commissioner for Idumaea and once again confronted his nemesis, Judas. He was not only defeated but barely escaped capture (II Maccabees 12:32–37).

GOSPEL. One of the four authentic accounts of the life, death, and resurrection of Jesus, which the Church teaches have been divinely inspired. They are the Gospels according to Matthew, Mark, Luke, and John. Several stages in the use of the term "Gospel" may be distinguished. In the Old Testament are predictions of the Messianic "Good News of Salvation" (Isaiah 40:9, 41:27, 61:1). The Gospels themselves speak of the "Good News" from the angelic message at Bethlehem (Luke 2:10) to the final commission to the Apostles (Mark 16:15). Beyond the four narratives of the Evangelists the entire New Testament speaks at length, in detail, and with a variety of nuances of the "Gospel of Jesus Christ." Prior to the original, inspired Gospels there was an "Oral Gospel," or tradition, on which the written narratives were based. And after the canonical Gospels were produced, numerous counterfeit Gospels were also written. There is record of twenty-one such apocryphal Gospels. (Etym. Anglo-Saxon *gōdspel: god*, good + *spel*, tale.)

GOSPEL HARMONY. See HARMONY, GOSPEL.

GOSPELS, APOCRYPHAL. Spurious narratives of the life of Christ, written between the first and third centuries. Many of these exist, and new manuscripts of some of them have been discovered in the twentieth century. These apocrypha are of different types. Some may embody at least a few trustworthy oral traditions, e.g., the Gospel of Peter, and According to the Hebrews. Others are openly heretical and sought to expound erroneous, especially Gnostic views, e.g., the Gospels of Thomas, Marcion, the Twelve Apostles, and Philip. A third group of writings are pious tales, composed to satisfy popular curiosity, and deal mainly with the childhood of Christ; such as the Childhood Gospel of Thomas, the History of Joseph the Carpenter, and the Departure of Mary. There is record of twenty-one apocryphal Gospels, some available in their full narrative text.

GOSSIP. Idle talk, especially about others. The morality of gossip is determined by the degree to which time is wasted in useless conversation, by the failure in justice or charity committed against others, and by the damage done to people's reputation by those who gossip.

GOTHIC ARCHITECTURE. Originally the style of architecture associated with the Goths; it eventually spread throughout Europe from about 1200 to 1500. It is characterized by pointed arches, ribbed vaulting, flying buttresses, and other features previously unknown in Church building. Italians of the Renaissance coined the term as a mark of contempt for the extreme of barbarism. It might be called "Catholic style" because it expressed the new civilization of the Franks, Normans, Anglo-Saxons, and Teutonic people who had become Christians after struggling with paganism. And to this day it remains the highest artistic achievement of these civilizations.

GOTHIC VESTMENTS. A name commonly given to liturgical vestments of medieval shape and pattern, with a long stole, and the chasuble actually or nearly circular when laid out flat.

GOVERNMENT. According to scholastic philosophy, the authoritative direction of a people, requiring them to use certain prescribed means for realizing a predetermined plan for the common good. Essential to the notion of government are authority vested in certain designated persons; management of things pertaining to the common good; an official plan or overview of what needs to be done to promote the welfare of the society; laws that express the will of those in authority relative to the advancement of the public good; sanctions that may be imposed on those who do not observe the laws. (Etym. Latin *gubernare*, to direct, manage, conduct, govern, guide.)

GR. *Gratia*—grace.

GRACE. In biblical language the condescension or benevolence (Greek *charis*) shown by God toward the human race; it is also the unmerited gift proceeding from this benevolent disposition. Grace, therefore, is a totally gratuitous gift on which man has absolutely no claim. Where on occasion the Scriptures speak of grace as pleasing charm or thanks for favors received, this is a derived and not primary use of the term.

As the Church has come to explain the meaning of grace, it refers to something more than the gifts of nature, such as creation or the blessings of bodily health. Grace is the supernatural gift that God, of his free benevolence, bestows on rational creatures for their eternal salvation. The gifts of grace are essentially supernatural. They surpass the being, powers, and claims of created nature, namely sanctifying grace, the infused virtues, the gifts of the Holy Spirit, and actual grace. They are the indispensable means necessary to reach the beatific vision. In a secondary sense, grace also includes such blessings as the miraculous gifts of prophecy or healing, or the preternatural gifts of freedom from concupiscence.

The essence of grace, properly so called, is its gratuity, since no creature has a right to the beatific vision, and its finality or purpose is to lead one to eternal life. (Etym. Latin *gratia*, favor; a gift freely given.) See also ACTUAL GRACE, EFFICACIOUS GRACE, GRATUITOUS GRACE, HABITUAL GRACE, JUSTIFYING GRACE, SACRAMENTAL GRACE, SANATING GRACE, SANCTIFYING GRACE, SUFFICIENT GRACE.

GRACE AT MEALS. A prayer of invocation before eating and gratitude after eating, acknowledging the divine goodness and recognizing one's total dependence, even for food and drink, on God.

GRACE OF CHRIST. The supernatural life and blessings that God bestowed and contin-

ues to bestow on mankind in view of the merits of Christ's Redemption. It goes beyond the grace of God because, in addition to raising man to the divine life, it also heals the wounds inflicted by sin.

GRACE OF GOD. The supernatural life conferred on the angels and our first parents in Paradise. It is grace because it was bestowed out of sheer love of God, leaving aside the question of the merits of Christ. The angels were not redeemed, and our first parents, before the Fall, were only negatively unworthy of the reception of grace.

GRACE OF SANCTIFICATION. The supernatural gift whose purpose is the personal sanctification of the one who receives it. It is called the grace that makes one pleasing (*gratia gratum faciens*) to God either by making the person holy (sanctifying grace), or by preparing him for sanctification, or by preserving and increasing his sanctification (actual grace).

GRAD. *Gradus*—grade.

GRADATION OF VIRTUES. The hierarchy of dignity among the virtues. Supernatural virtues rank higher than the natural. Among the supernatural virtues, the theological virtues are higher than the moral, and among the theological hope stands higher than faith, and charity stands higher than faith and hope. Yet in practice there can be no charity (or love) without hope, and neither charity nor hope without faith. The mind must first know by faith whom to trust and whom to love and why, before hope and charity are possible.

GRADUAL. The response and versicle to the Epistle formerly made at High Mass, and so named because it was sung on the step of the altar.

GRADUAL, ROMAN. A liturgical book containing the choral parts of the Mass. It belongs logically together with the sacramentary and lectionary. It was revised and the new Gradual was authorized on June 24, 1972.

GRAFFITI. Scratchings or drawings scribbled on early Christian monuments, tombs, and walls. They are of special value historically in testifying to the faith and practice of the early Church.

GRASPING. Selfish desire for possessions, especially material possessions. It implies eagerness (hence avarice) and inordinateness (hence covetousness) and lack of restraint (hence greed), but it has the added notion of ability to acquire and to use wrongful or unfair means.

GRAT. *Gratias*—thanks; or gratis—without charge.

GRATIA GRATIS DATA. See GRATUITOUS GRACE.

GRATITUDE. The virtue by which a person acknowledges, interiorly and exteriorly, gifts received and seeks to make at least some return for the gift conferred. Essentially gratitude consists of an interior disposition, a grateful heart, but when genuine it tries somehow to express itself in words and deeds. Consequently it includes three elements: acknowledgment that a gift has been received, appreciation expressed in thankfulness, and as far as possible some return for what has been freely given with no obligation on the donor's part.

GRATUITOUS GRACE. The free gift conferred on particular persons for the salvation of others. Technically called *gratia gratis data* (grace freely given), it is independent of the personal moral life or behavior of its possessor. To this class belong such gifts of grace as charismata (prophecy, gift of miracles, gift of tongues), the priestly power of consecration and absolution, and the hierarchial power of jurisdiction. See also ACTUAL GRACE, EFFICACIOUS GRACE, GRACE, HABITUAL GRACE, JUSTIFYING GRACE, SACRAMENTAL GRACE, SANATING GRACE, SANCTIFYING GRACE, SUFFICIENT GRACE.

GRAVE. An excavation in the earth for the burial of a corpse usually in a coffin and sometimes also in an outer wooden or concrete box or vault. The Church requires the blessing of all graves in which the faithful are buried.

GRAVE INCONVENIENCE. In moral theology a sufficient reason to excuse a person from fulfilling certain positive precepts of the Church, not of themselves binding by the natural or revealed law. Also sufficient reason for delaying or even not performing certain actions, otherwise obligatory, provided there is a sincere desire to do so.

GRAVE SIN. The transgression of a divine law in a grievous matter with full knowledge and consent.

The matter may be serious either in itself (as blasphemy) or because of the circumstances (as striking one's father or mother) or on account of its purpose (as telling a lie in order to destroy a person's character). Sufficient knowledge of the serious nature of a sinful action is present if one is clearly conscious that the act is mortally sinful, say because the Scriptures or the Church identify certain acts as seriously offensive to God. It is enough that one knows that what one intends to do may be a mortal sin, but does it anyhow. Indifference to the laws of God is equivalent to disobeying them.

Full consent is present when one freely wills to commit an action although one clearly knows it is gravely sinful. No sin is committed if one does not will the deed, no matter how clear one's knowledge may be. After all, the essence of sin is in the free will. Thus, too, a person does not sin who, with the best of will, cannot dispel obscene or blasphemous thoughts and desires, even though he or she well knows they are gravely sinful. The resolution to perform an action is not the same as the pleasure or satisfaction experienced in the emotions, nor the same as a compulsive idea, "I like the sin." One sign of partial knowledge or not full consent would be the fact that a person does not complete an action when this can easily be done, or is so minded that the person would rather die than commit a grave sin.

GRAVISSIMUM EDUCATIONIS. Declaration of the Second Vatican Council on Christian education. The focus of this declaration is mainly threefold. It tells all Christians that they have a right to a Christian education; it reminds parents that they have the primary duty and right to teach their children; and it warns believers of the danger of state monopoly in education. Catholic schools on every academic level, including universities, are encouraged, their teachers praised, and the right of the Church to conduct educational "institutions under their control" is defended (October 28, 1965).

GREATER ANTIPHONS. The antiphons to Vespers on the seven days before Christmas Eve, each beginning with the invocation "O," hence also called the "Great O's" as follows: O Wisdom, O Sacred Lord, O Flower of Jesse's stem, O Key of David, O Radiant Dawn, O King of all the nations, O Emmanuel.

GREATER DOXOLOGY. The *Gloria in Excelsis Deo,* recited or sung at Mass. In contrast with the lesser doxology, or *Gloria Patri.* See DOXOLOGY.

GREATER LITANIES. A procession on the feast of St. Mark (April 25) during which it has been customary to sing the Litany of the Saints. The procession and litany go back to St. Gregory the Great (d. 604), when they were introduced as a Christian replacement for the pagan Robigalia celebrated on that day.

GREAT PROMISE. The twelfth of the traditional twelve promises made by the Sacred Heart to St. Margaret Mary Alacoque (1647–90). It declares: "I promise you in the excessive mercy of my Heart that my all-powerful love will grant to all who receive Holy Communion on the First Fridays of nine consecutive months the grace of final perseverance; they shall not die in my disgrace, nor without receiving their sacraments. My divine Heart shall be their safe refuge in this last moment." Along with the other promises, the Great Promise was implicitly approved by the Church in the canonization of St. Margaret Mary (1920) and in the favorable references to her revelations in the writings of the popes, e.g., Pius XII in *Haurietis Aquas* (1956).

GREAT RELICS. The three main relics of Christ's Passion, preserved at St. Peter's in Rome and venerated on the last four days of Holy Week, Easter Sunday, and on a few other special occasions. They are a piece of the true Cross, the point of the spear that pierced the Savior's side, and the veil that, according to tradition, St. Veronica offered to Christ on his way to Calvary.

GREAT SCHISM. The Western Schism, 1378–1417, when there was controversy over the true succession to the papacy. It began with the writings of Marsilius of Padua (c. 1275–c. 1342), who claimed that a pope is subject to a council of bishops, priests, and laymen. Urban VI was elected Pope on April 8, 1378, following the seventy-year Avignon residence of the papacy. He was a stern reformer and also harsh. The French cardinals in retaliation declared that Urban had not been validly elected and proceeded to elect Robert of Geneva as the antipope Clement VII (1378–94). Clement withdrew to Avignon and the Great Schism was in full swing. France, Scotland, and Spain gave their allegiance to Clement; England, Italy, Flanders, Hungary, Poland, and most of Germany followed Urban, who died in 1389. There followed a succession of lawful popes at Rome and antipopes at Avignon. The universities of Paris, Oxford, and Prague disputed how the impasse should be resolved. Finally pope and antipope were invited to a council at Pisa (1409); both declined and were declared deposed by the council, which proceeded to elect yet another antipope, Alexander V (1409–10). In

desperation Emperor Sigismund of Germany appealed to the antipope John XXIII of Pisa, to call a general council at Constance, a German city on the Rhine. John agreed, and the council, later legitimized, was convened in 1414. It lasted four years and finally resolved the schism. The Pisan antipope John XXIII abdicated. Gregory XII, the true Roman Pontiff, having formally convoked the Council of Constance, sent his representatives, and then, for the good of the Church, freely resigned his office. The claim of Benedict XIII of Avignon was no longer worthy of serious consideration. The chair of Peter, vacant at last, was filled by the election, November 11, 1417, of Pope Martin V. The Great Schism was ended.

GREAT SILENCE. Periods of total silence observed in religious communities, usually from night prayers until next morning. The practice goes back to the beginnings of monasticism in the third century.

GREED. Avarice or cupidity. It implies a controlling passion for wealth or possessions and suggests not so much a strong as an inordinate desire and is commonly associated with the lust for power.

GREEK. The language of the New Testament and the dominant culture of the Mediterranean world in which Christianity was first established after its origins in Palestine. Its significance lay in the books of the New Testament lay in the fact that it became the primary linguistic bearer of Christian revelation and ever since has remained normative for the original meaning of the inspired text. Its importance as a civilization lay in the extraordinary intellectual development, which St. Paul calls the wisdom (*sophia*), of the Greeks and which thus became the cultural incarnation of the Church as the Messianic Kingdom. There was, then, a providential merger of the Jews, who were God's chosen people of whom the physical Christ was born in the flesh; and of the Greeks, who were the most civilized people of their age, among whom, as the society of believers, the Mystical Christ took root.

GREEK CROSS. The emblem that supplanted the Chi-Rho as a symbol of Christ. It has arms of equal length, making four equal angles. Used more in the East than in the West, especially since the Great Eastern Schism in the thirteenth century.

GREEK LOVE. A term for homosexuality among males, derived from its frequent practice among the men of ancient Greece.

Also called pederasty, especially when one of the participants is a boy.

GREEK RITES. The form and arrangement of liturgies originally celebrated in Greek in Antioch and Alexandria. Those in use today at Antioch are the pure and modified Greek St. James, Syriac St. James, Maronite, Chaldean, Malabar, Byzantine, and Armenian Rites. At Alexandria the Coptic Liturgies of Sts. Cyril, Basil, and Gregory Nazianzus, and the Ethiopian Liturgy are used.

GREEN SCAPULAR. A popular scapular of the Immaculate Heart of Mary. It is made of green felt cloth, and on the face side is a picture of the Blessed Virgin, with rays emanating from her heart. On the reverse side is an image of the Heart of Mary alone, pierced by a sword, and surrounded with the inscription, "Immaculate Heart of Mary, pray for us now and at the hour of our death." The scapular is reputed to have special efficacy in bringing people back to the Church and to the sacrament of penance even after many years of estrangement from their faith.

GREGORIAN CALENDAR. A record of the days, weeks, and months of a current year. The calendar now used is that of Pope Gregory XIII, whose decree established it in 1582. Before then the length of the year was simply the time it took for the earth to travel around the sun. Known as the Julian calendar, it was inaccurate because the earth's journey took a little less than three hundred sixty-five and a quarter days. This error amounted to ten days by Pope Gregory's time. In order to correct this it was calculated that the extra day of leap year would not occur in the century year unless it would be divisible by four hundred, hence 1600 and 2000 would be a leap year, 1700, 1800, 1900 would not be. The Pope suppressed ten days in 1582 and made the calendar obligatory on the Catholic faithful. Following the Gregorian calendar, there is an error of one day in thirty-five centuries. Two astronomers, Lilius and Clavius, had made the necessary calculations. At first Protestant countries refused to use it. England did not adopt the Gregorian calendar until 1752. Eastern Churches are gradually adopting it.

GREGORIAN CHANT. The forms of musical worship, as revised and established by Pope Gregory I. It is without definite rhythm and was probably accumulated from Jewish sources. It is accepted as the oldest chant in present day use. Its revised present form is due largely to the energy and inspiration of the monks at the Benedictine Abbey at Solesmes in northwestern France.

GREGORIANIST. One who is expert in Gregorian chant and advocates it as "the proper chant of the Roman Church, the only chant which she has inherited from the ancient Fathers, which she has jealously guarded for so many centuries in her liturgical books and which she directly proposes to the faithful as her own music" (Pope St. Pius X, *tra le Sollecitudini,* 1903).

GREGORIAN MASSES. Offering on successive days of thirty Masses said for the same deceased person, to obtain the deliverance of that soul from purgatory, through the benevolent dispensation of God's mercy. The Church has declared that the confidence of the faithful in the special efficacy of the Gregorian Masses is pious and reasonable (Sacred Congregation for Indulgences, August 24, 1888). More than one series of Gregorian Masses may be offered, but not for more than one person at a time. Also the special fruits of these Masses apply only to the deceased. But the Masses need not be said by the same priest or at the same altar. Belief in the efficacy of the Gregorian Masses is based on a private revelation made to Pope St. Gregory I.

GREGORIAN SACRAMENTARY. A liturgical book attributed to Pope St. Gregory I, sometimes called the Sacramentary of Adrian I. It contains the original text and numerous additions made by various scribes. The sacramentary has three parts: 1. the Ordinary of the Mass; 2. the Propers of the Mass for the year beginning with Christmas Eve, but with no Masses for the Sundays after Epiphany and Pentecost; and 3. the ritual prayers for ordinations.

GREGORIAN WATER. The blessed water used in the ceremony for the consecration of a church. It contains wine, salt, and ashes and requires a special formula for its blessing. The name comes from the fact that its use was prescribed by Pope St. Gregory I.

GREMIAL. The apron laid on a bishop's lap during liturgical ceremonies. The one made of silk and trimmed with embroidery, of the color of the day, for a pontifical Mass, has been abolished. A linen or other gremial may be used when really needed. (Etym. Latin *gremium,* the lap, bosom.)

GREY NUNS. The popular name of the Sisters of Charity in various countries. Best known are the Sisters of Charity of the General Hospital of Montreal, founded by Mme. d'Youville in 1739. Besides the three standard vows, the members promised to devote themselves to the relief of human suffering. Among other branches the most notable is the Grey Nuns of the Cross founded at Ottawa in 1845. In Germany a group is called the Grey Sisters of St. Elizabeth.

GRIDIRON. Symbol of St. Lawrence the deacon. Martyred in A.D. 258 by being roasted alive on a gridiron. By the fourth century venerated as one of the famous martyrs of Rome, he is included in the Canon of the Mass. St. Vincent (d. 304), a Spanish deacon martyred in the same way, also has the gridiron for his emblem.

GRIEVOUS MATTER. Moral obligations that are binding under pain of mortal sin. The gravity of the matter is determined by the object and circumstance of the action (or omission) and is known in the first place by the teaching authority of the Church, based on divine revelation. Some sins do not admit of slight matter, and these are mortal sins "from their whole nature" (*ex toto genere suo*), as lust and blasphemy. In other sins the matter is not always grave, as in theft or injustice, and these are mortal "from their nature" (*ex genere suo*). In every case, however, for a mortal sin there is also required full advertence of the mind to the fact that the matter is serious, and full consent of the will to do or not do what a person knows is a grave command or prohibition.

GRILLE. A screen or divider, sometimes an enclosure, constructed usually of metal with small spaced openings in it. For centuries it determined the extent of the cloister for nuns in papal enclosures. The use of the grille and, if used, its construction have been modified since the Second Vatican Council, but some physical symbol of enclosure is part of the Church's directives for cloistered contemplative women religious. A grille, in the form of a metal, wooden, or plastic screen, is also part of the standard equipment of a confessional. The grille separates priest from penitent; it allows them to engage in conversation without being able to see each other. Its purpose is to protect the anonymity of the penitent, since the faithful have a right not to be recognized by the confessor when they receive the sacrament of penance.

GROTESQUE. Whatever is peculiar, fantastic, or extravagant. In art it is the idealized ugly, as in some of the animal and human forms reproduced by Raphael in the Vatican.

GROTTAFERRATA. Basilian monastery, about three miles from Frascati, Italy, founded in 1004 by St. Nilus, a Calabrian Greek. Long a center of Greek ritual and learning, it became a national monument in 1874. Since then extensive catacombs belonging to the monastery have been discovered; they had been untouched since the early days of Christianity.

GROTTO. A small cave or cavern, often associated with miraculous apparitions and other supernatural experiences, as at Lourdes, France, and at Manresa, Spain.

GROUND OF BEING. A substitute for a personal God, professed by modern critics of Christianity who are sympathetic with Oriental pantheism.

GUADALUPE. A shrine of the Blessed Virgin in central Mexico, suburb of Mexico City. One of the principal shrines of Christendom. Scene of the apparition of Our Lady, in December 1531, to a native Aztec peasant, fifty-one-year-old Juan Diego. He and his wife had been recent converts to Christianity. Mary appeared on a hillside near the Aztec shrine of Tepeyac and told Juan that she wanted a church built there. When Bishop Zumarraga demanded a sign, Juan was directed by Mary to pick some roses (not in bloom then), which he took to the bishop and found that his cloak had miraculously painted on it a portrait of the Mother of God. Although the material is a coarse fabric made of cactus fiber and totally unsuitable for such painting, the portrait has remained as brilliant as ever and is the principal object of veneration at Guadalupe. The shrine church, originally dedicated in 1709, is annually visited by several million, and numerous miracles are reported to have been worked there. A new basilica was consecrated at the shrine in 1976. The central message of Our Lady of Guadalupe, expressed in the first of her five apparitions, is preserved in an ancient document. Speaking to Juan Diego, Mary says, "You must know, and be very certain in your heart, my son, that I am truly the eternal Virgin, holy Mother of the True God, through whose favor we live, the Creator, Lord of heaven and the Lord of the earth." Pope John Paul II on January 27, 1979, opened at Guadalupe the Third General Conference of the Latin American Episcopate. St. Pius X in 1910 designated Our Lady of Guadalupe patroness of Latin America, and Pope Pius

XII in 1945 declared her patroness of the Americas. Her feast is on December 12, and a holy day of obligation in Mexico.

GUARDIAN. In ecclesiastical law, a person officially responsible for the care of someone who cannot manage his own affairs, as a child during its minority or one who is emotionally or mentally handicapped. The Church now permits clerics and religious, under special circumstances, to act as guardians. The superior of a Franciscan friary is also called a guardian.

GUARDIAN ANGEL. A celestial spirit assigned by God to watch over each individual during life. This general doctrine of an angel's care for each person is part of the Church's constant tradition, based on Sacred Scripture and the teaching of the Fathers of the Church. The role of the guardian spirit is both to guide and to guard; to guide as a messenger of God's will to our minds, and to guard as an instrument of God's goodness in protecting us from evil. This protection from evil is mainly from the evil of sin and the malice of the devil. But it is also protection from physical evil insofar as this is useful or necessary to guard the soul from spiritual harm. A feast honoring the guardian angels has been celebrated in October, throughout the universal Church, since the seventeenth century. It now occurs on October 2.

GUESTHOUSE. One of the component parts of a monastery or religious institute, reserved for the reception and housing of visitors and guests.

GUEST MASTER. Also called an "obedientiary," he is the member of a monastic community whose duty is to care for the guesthouse and in general be in charge of the visitors to the monastery.

GUIDANCE. Assisting people to make the best use of their mental and moral abilities and to benefit from the opportunities available to them.

GUILT. A condition of a person who has done moral wrong, who is therefore more or less estranged from the one he offended, and who is liable for punishment before he has been pardoned and has made atonement. (Etym. Anglo-Saxon *gylt,* delinquency, trespass; also a fine for a trespass.)

GUNPOWDER PLOT. A conspiracy in English Reformation history, formed by Guy Fawkes and others, to blow up the English Parliament in London in 1605. Guy Fawkes and his co-conspirators were discovered and put to death. An attempt was made to incriminate the Catholic Church by arresting the Jesuit priests Greenway and Garnett, to whom the conspirators made their last confession. But the priests kept the seal of confession. Henry Garnett was executed in 1606. One effect of the plot was the passage of new drastic measures of persecution against Catholics.

GYNAECEUM. The part of an Eastern Rite Catholic church reserved at times for the women in the congregation. Going back to early Christian times, the separation of women worshipers is still generally common in both Catholic and dissident Eastern Churches and also practiced, though less generally, in other rites, depending on the cultural traditions of the people.

GYÖR. Marian shrine in Hungary, west of Budapest. Its main object of devotion is a picture of the praying Madonna looking at her sleeping Child. In 1649, when Oliver Cromwell went to Ireland, the Bishop of Clonfert, in the diocese of Tuam, was arrested and exiled to the island of Innisboffin. He took with him a picture that had hung in the cathedral. In 1652 he escaped and finally reached Hungary, where he was cordially received. In the city of Györ he was made auxiliary bishop for the Hungarian diocese. After his death he willed the Irish Madonna to his Hungarian friends, who felt that her presence among them had resulted in a series of military victories over the Turks and had saved them in other national disasters. In 1697 the persecution in Ireland was renewed. Simultaneously in Hungary on March 17, 1697, the hundreds praying at the cathedral Mass noticed that their Irish Madonna was shedding tears that were falling onto the head of the sleeping Christ. The miracle lasted three hours. The picture was removed from its frame and from the wall space in an attempt to discover a natural cause, but the phenomenon continued and was attested to by . many witnesses. Devotion to Our Lady of Györ has continued over the centuries. Cardinal Mindszenty (1892–1975) was photographed as he prayed publicly before the cherished Irish Madonna, asking for God's blessings on his own persecuted people.

H

HABAKKUK. The author of the eighth book of the Minor Prophets, written about 600 B.C. It is a short, philosophic book of three chapters in which he complains of the injustices of life. Evil always triumphs, as evidenced in the ruthlessness of the Chaldeans in trampling on the rights of other peoples (Habakkuk 1:6). One is startled by the insight he shows when he describes them as "A people feared and dreaded; from their might proceeds their right, their greatness" (Habakkuk 1:7). The prophet is comforted, however, by Yahweh's assurance that, in time, goodness will triumph. He concludes, "Calmly I await the day of anguish which is dawning on the people now attacking us" (Habakkuk 3:16).

HABIT. A quality that is difficult to change and that disposes a person either well or badly, either in oneself or in relations with others. Natural habits are a partial realization of our potencies. They add to nature by giving it ease of performance, where the acts intensify a habit and the habit facilitates the acts. Habits of acting are acquired by constant repetition, and lost by disuse or contrary acts. Good moral habits are virtues; evil ones are vices. (Etym. Latin *habitus*, having, possession; condition, character, from *habere*, to have.)

HABIT, RELIGIOUS. The distinctive garb of a man or woman religious, its use dating back to the beginnings of monasticism. The habit was prescribed for religious by the Second Vatican Council: "The religious habit, an outward mark of consecration to God, should be simple and modest, poor and at the same time becoming. In addition, it must meet the requirements of health and be suited to the circumstances of time and place and to the needs of the ministry involved" (*Perfectae Caritatis,* 17).

HABITUAL GRACE. Constant supernatural quality of the soul which sanctifies a person inherently and makes him or her just and pleasing to God. Also called sanctifying grace or justifying grace. See also ACTUAL GRACE, EFFICACIOUS GRACE, GRACE, GRATUITOUS GRACE, JUSTIFYING GRACE, SACRAMENTAL GRACE, SANATING GRACE, SANCTIFYING GRACE, SUFFICIENT GRACE.

HABITUAL INTENTION. A decision of the will to attain a given end, but the decision does not influence a particular act. A habitual intention implies that a person has previously intended to do something and has not retracted his intention, but the act he now performs is not done in virtue of that intention. See also ACTUAL INTENTION, INTENTION, INTERPRETATIVE INTENTION, VIRTUAL INTENTION.

HACELDAMA. The name given to the potter's field purchased with the thirty pieces of silver that Judas received for betraying Christ. It was used as a burial place for strangers (Matthew 27:3-10). (Etym. Greek *akeldamach,* Aramaic *hakel dema,* field of blood.)

HAC IN URBE ROMA. A joint statement by Pope Paul VI and Michael Ramsey, Archbishop of Canterbury, representing the Anglican Churches of the world, encouraging a continuing dialogue between the Roman Catholic Church and the Anglican Communion (March 24, 1966).

HADES. In Greek religion the god of the underworld; consequently the kingdom ruled over by Hades, or the abode of the dead. In the Bible the Greek translation of the Hebrew *sheol,* also meaning the abode of the dead, or death, or the power of destruction, or the place of the wicked after death. (Etym. Greek *Haidēs,* the nether world.)

HAGGAI. Also called Aggeus, the tenth among the Minor Prophets. About 520 B.C. he appeared among the Jews to rebuke them for apathy in building the second Temple. The book of Haggai contains four utterances: urging the rebuilding of the Temple, foretelling the glory of the new house of the Lord, threatening the Jews with misfortune until the Temple is rebuilt, and promising God's blessings on the people through Zorobabel, the representative of the royal house of David.

HAGIOGRAPHY. The writings or documents about the saints and saintly people. It began with records of the martyrs, including the dates and manner of their deaths. Later it was extended to the lives and data of all the saints. The most scientific form of hagiography is that of the Bollandists in their *Acta Sanctorum.*

HAGIOLOGY. The science of the saints. Theological investigation and interpretation of the saintly men and women whom the Church honors with public veneration. Its function is to analyze the spirituality of these persons and apply its findings to serve the needs of the faithful in their own pursuit of Christian holiness. (Etym. Greek *agios,* holy + *logos,* discourse.)

HAIL, HOLY QUEEN. See SALVE REGINA.

HAIL MARY. The Ave Maria; the most familiar of all prayers addressed to the Blessed Virgin. It contains the salutation of the angel Gabriel to Mary, and Elizabeth's greeting to Mary at the Visitation. The petition beginning "Holy Mary, Mother of God" was formulated by the Church and added to the Hail Mary in the Middle Ages. The full text reads:

"Hail Mary, full of grace, the Lord is with you.
Blessed are you among women,
And blessed is the fruit of your womb, Jesus.
Holy Mary, Mother of God, pray for us sinners,
now and at the hour of our death. Amen."

HAIR SHIRT. A garment woven of goat's hair or other coarse cloth, worn next to the skin as a matter of custom or voluntary mortification. It varies in shape and size. In some religious orders it was prescribed by rule.

HALLELUJAH. See ALLELUIA.

HALLOW. To recognize as sacred and therefore to treat as holy. In the Lord's Prayer, "Hallowed be thy name," it means to honor God's name, i.e., to reverence God and give him the respect and obedience he deserves. It is, therefore, a petition that God may be known, loved, and served by all his creatures.

HALLUCINATION. Any false perception, not deliberately induced, that makes a person accept as objectively real what are only one's own ideas. One of the functions of mystical theology is to help a spiritual director distinguish authentic supernatural phenomena from hallucinations.

HALO. In Christian art a glow of light or ornamented circle surrounding the head of Christ or one of the saints. It symbolizes holiness, the light of grace, and glory. (Etym. Latin *halos;* from Greek *halōs,* a round threshing floor; disk; halo.)

HAND. A symbol of the Presence, Will, and Providence of God. Variously expressed: open with rays; emerging from a cloud; later shown with the head of the Creator blessing his creatures. An emblem of benediction of pope, bishop, and priest.

HANDBOOK OF INDULGENCES. The official declaration of the Church's teaching on indulgences and collection of the most important prayers and good works to which indulgences are attached. Authorized by Pope Paul VI in 1968. See also RACCOLTA.

HAPPINESS. Any contentment in the possession of a good. Implies a state of well-being and not some single experience, and a relative permanence and constancy. Hence regularly used in Scripture to describe the lot of those who are blessed by God for doing his will, and the reward of the just for their faithful service on earth. Happiness is a divine gift but requires man's co-operation to be gained.

HARMONY, GOSPEL. A grouping of Gospel passages on similar subjects from various evangelists, showing points of agreement. It may also imply a satisfactory explanation of differences, especially among the Synoptics. It may finally refer to a combination of all four Gospels into one continuous narrative or simply an arrangement of passages according to historical order.

HARSHNESS. A moral defect that is shown in abruptness of manner and speech and obvious impatience with other people's defects and limitations.

HAT, ECCLESIASTICAL. Distinctive headgear worn by the clergy. A red broad-brimmed head covering with special halyards has always been a cardinal's chief insignia. It is seldom worn and in some cathedrals is suspended from the sanctuary ceiling (preferably over his tomb) on his death. In heraldry such a hat in green or black appears for a bishop or priest, but in the Catholic Church of the Latin Rite such apparel is never worn. The Pope's hat is generally white. See also RED HAT.

HATRED. A voluntary act by which someone or something is regarded with bitter aversion. On the first level hatred is directed against either God or some rational being; on the second level it is directed against some quality in another but without hatred of the individual personality.

Personal hatred of God may take the form of disgust, when a person detests God because he punishes sinners. It is a grave sin because it is contrary to the justice of God. Another form is the hatred of enmity, when a person actually wishes evil to God. Such hatred is of its nature diabolical, and is the most grievous of all sins, since it approximates the enmity that the devils have against God.

Personal hatred of a human being is the direct opposite of the virtue of love. Where love inspires a person to wish well to another, hatred arouses the desire to do harm or have harm befall the one hated, not as a source of possible good, but precisely as evil. The gravity of such sins of personal hatred depends on how serious the harm wished or intended, and on how deliberately the malicious desires are harbored.

Hatred of a quality in someone may be either sinful or not. If the hatred is directed only toward some evil quality that a person has, but does not touch that person, it is not sinful. It becomes sinful only if the hatred extends to the person who has some admittedly evil trait or sinful habit. Moreover, it becomes specially sinful when the hatred is directed at some virtue that a person possesses, even when the enmity does not extend to the individual personally.

H.B. His Beatitude or Blessedness.

H.E. His Eminence.

HEADED CROSS. A cross on which is a representation of the Savior's crucifixion.

HEALING, SACRAMENT OF. The sacrament of anointing, one of whose graces is to heal the sick, if this would be for the person's spiritual welfare. The healing may be one of several kinds: a complete recovery, partial recovery with at least an alleviation of the symptoms or pain, strength of mind and body to bear the suffering or disability with peace and resignation to God's will.

HEALING MINISTRY. Primarily refers to the ministry of Christ, who during his public life on earth healed the sick, cured the deaf-mutes, paralytics, and blind, and delivered those possessed by the devil. Also refers to the Church's care, since early Christian times, for the sick and those in physical or emotional need. But always in imitation of Christ, the Church's health or healing ministry was understood as not stopping with people's bodily needs. It is concerned with the whole person, body and soul, and seeks to alleviate every human pain or disability, whether physical, psychological, or spiritual.

Among the sacraments, penance and anointing are specially directed to healing, both primarily to heal sickness of the soul and anointing also (if it is God's will) to heal the body.

HEALTH AND APOSTOLIC BENEDICTION. Salutation in letters written by the Pope. It was first used by Pope St. Anacletus, second successor of St. Peter.

HEART. A symbol of love, showing Christ's enduring love in spite of man's ingratitude. Images representing the heart alone are to be used for private devotion only. Generally the Sacred Heart is pictured as Christ, with his heart more or less exposed, sometimes held in his hands. The love of Christ exhibited in his Passion is often represented as a flaming heart surrounded by a crown of thorns. Mary's heart, pierced by a sword, is usually shown encircled by roses. A number of saints have a heart as their emblem, e.g., St. Augustine, to symbolize his great love for God; St. Theresa of Avila, a pierced heart recalling the wound of the seraph that she received in ecstasy; St. Margaret Mary, because of the role she played in extending the devotion to the Sacred Heart in the modern world.

HEARTS OF JESUS AND MARY, SCAPULAR. A white scapular with the two hearts and the instruments of the Passion on one side and a red cross on the other. Originated in Antwerp in 1873 with the Daughters of the Sacred Heart. Approved by Popes Leo XIII and St. Pius X.

HEATHEN. Originally an unconverted member of a people, who does not acknowledge the God of Judeo-Christian revelation. Biblical translations fluctuate between "heathen" and "pagan" for unbelievers, e.g., Psalm 2:8. The term has come to mean anyone who does not believe in God, and less commonly those who are believers but are not Christians or Jews.

HEAVEN. The place and condition of perfect supernatural happiness. This happiness consists essentially in the immediate vision and love of God, and secondarily in the knowledge, love, and enjoyment of creatures. Until the final resurrection, except for Christ and his Mother, only the souls of the just are in heaven. After the last day, the just will be in heaven in body and soul. Although the same God will be seen by all and enjoyed by all, not everyone will have the same degree of happiness. The depth of beatitude will depend on the measure of God's grace with which a person dies, and this in turn will be greatly conditioned by the merits that one earns during life on earth. Heaven is eternal because it will never cease. It is continuous because its joys never stop. It is communal because the happiness is shared with the angels and saints and the company of those who were known and loved on earth.

HEBD. Hebdomad—week.

HEBDOMADARIAN. The priest or religious officiating for a week in a monastery or church. A hebdomadarian sings the conventual Mass each day, intones the various canonical hours in the Divine Office, sings the orations, and gives all the necessary blessings. (Etym. Greek *hebdomos*, seventh.)

HEBER. A nomadic Kenite who had moved to Kedesh and pitched a tent for himself and his wife Jael (Judges 4:11). Nearby a battle raged between the Canaanites, led by Sisera, and the Israelites. Inspired by Yahweh, Deborah had planned this battle to entrap the Canaanites. When the plan succeeded, Sisera fled and sought refuge in Heber's tent (Judges 4:16). Under pretense of concealing him Jael killed him while he was asleep (Judges 4:17–22).

HEBREW CALENDAR. The Jewish era, according to tradition, starts with creation and is customarily dated 3760 years added to the Christian era. There are twelve months in the Hebrew year, all of them 29 or 30 days, as follows:

1. Tishri (30) September–October
2. Heshvan (29) October–November
3. Kislev (30) November–December
4. Tevet (29) December–January
5. Shevat (30) January–February
6. Adar (29) February–March
7. Nissan (30) March–April
8. Iyar (29) April–May
9. Sivan (30) May–June
10. Tammuz (29) June–July
11. Ab (30) July–August
12. Elul (29) August–September

In every cycle of nineteen years seven are leap years. During a leap year there is added an extra month Adar B (30 days). Thus the lunar year of the Jewish calendar corresponds to the solar year of the Gregorian calendar.

HEBREWS. See JEWS.

HEBREWS, EPISTLE TO THE. A letter, ascribed to St. Paul, written in Rome about A.D. 63. It was addressed to Christians who were almost exclusively converts from Judaism. It is divided into two main parts. Part One is doctrinal (1:1 to 10:17) and tells of the dignity of Christ as the natural Son of God, the eternal priesthood of Christ, the superiority of the Sacrifice of the New Law over the sacrifices of the Old Law. Part Two is moral (10:19 to 13:17), in which the converts are exhorted to perseverance in the Christian faith and in the difficult virtues required by this faith.

HEDGE SCHOOLS. Gatherings of Catholic children and their teachers in the open fields in Ireland during the days of persecution. Due to the repression of Catholic schools by the penal laws, under the hedges along the roads was the only place where Catholic education could be continued.

HEDONISM. The doctrine that pleasure is the goal of life and is man's highest good. By pleasure, true hedonists understand the admittedly imperfect enjoyments of this life only.

It was first formulated by the Greek philosopher Aristippus (c. 435–360 B.C.). Misinterpreting the teaching of Socrates (470–399 B.C.), who said that happiness is the end of life, Aristippus identified happiness with pleasure. He held that intellectual pleasures are higher than sense pleasures, but what matters is the pleasure here and now available. An act is good, and therefore virtuous, insofar as it gives present satisfaction.

Hedonism was refined by Epicurus (c. 341–270 B.C.), who joined it to the physical theories of Democritus (c. 460–370 B.C.). It is the only ethics consistent with pure materialism. For Epicurus the goal of life is not intense pleasure but an abiding peace of mind, a state of cheerful tranquillity. Above all one must avoid fear of any kind of god and fear of death. The wise man so regulates his life that, before death, he has the greatest amount of pleasure and the least amount of pain. Moderation is counseled not on moral grounds but on one's enablement to enjoy future pleasures in this life. Desires should be restricted to the bounds within which they can be satisfied. Whatever increases pleasure or one's general peace of mind is good, and anything that decreases it is bad. Modern hedonism is the preferred moral philosophy of those who deny or doubt the existence of a future life. (Etym. Greek *hēdonē*, pleasure.)

HEGELIANISM. The doctrine and method of the German philosopher Georg Wilhelm Friedrich Hegel (1770–1831). Its main feature is the dialectic process, which postulates the universal existence of opposites, which are absorbed in a higher unity, from which in turn new oppositions generate. Hegelianism rejects identity and contradiction as grounds of thought. All thinking and all development of being follow the scheme of the "triad," thesis, antithesis, and its resulting synthesis, i.e., opposites in conflict producing a higher unity, which then becomes the source of further conflict and another unity, going on ad infinitum. In Hegelianism everything can be explained dialectically. Christianity is represented as the absolute religion of truth and freedom, as the highest so far achieved in human history. But it is neither supernatural nor final, but only a phase in the process of God's self-evaluation as the Absolute Spirit. Marxism is built on Hegelianism.

HEIDEGGERIANISM. Existentialist philosophy of Martin Heidegger (1889–1976). Its most significant influence on Christianity is through demythologists like Rudolf Bultmann, who accepted Heidegger's theory of knowledge. A human is said to be a being in time. He is *Dasein in Zeitlichkeit*, or "being in temporality," i.e., one who is constantly changing with the passage of time. What the Gospels narrate took place or was said in time, which is past history. The Christian story, therefore, is "sacred history," which means factual data that have been sacralized, overladen with nonfactual and mythological lore that belongs to a former, credulous age.

HELI. The father of Joseph, whose wife was Mary. Had Joseph been the real father of Jesus, instead of a guardian, Heli would have been Jesus' grandfather. Luke expresses it thus: "Jesus . . . the son, as it was thought, of Joseph son of Heli" (Luke 3:23).

HELL. The place and state of eternal punishment for the fallen angels and human beings who die deliberately estranged from the love of God. There is a twofold punishment in hell: the pain of loss, which consists in the deprivation of the vision of God, and the pain of sense, which consists in the suffering caused by outside material things. The punishment of hell is eternal, as declared by Christ in his prediction of the last day (Matthew 25:46), and as defined by the Fourth Lateran Council, stating that the wicked will "receive a perpetual punishment with the devil" (Denzinger 801). The existence of hell is consistent with divine justice, since God respects human freedom and those who are lost actually condemn themselves by their resistance to the grace of God.

HELLENISM. A body of classical ideals associated with ancient Greece and including reason, the pursuit of knowledge, and the application of philosophy to the study of religion. Assuming the guiding hand of Providence, Hellenism played an important role in helping to shape, on its human and cultural side, the origins and development of Christianity. The language of the New Testament writings was Greek, the Gentile civilization into which the Church entered was Greek, and the thought patterns of the educated classes in the first-century Mediterranean world were Greek.

HELP OF CHRISTIANS. Title of the Blessed Virgin Mary, established as a feast by Pope Pius VII in 1814, in gratitude for his safe return to Rome after five years of captivity in Savona. Though not in the universal calendar, it is the patronal feast of Australia. The original invocation *"Auxilium Christianorum"* was inserted in the Litany of Our Lady by Pope St. Pius V in thanksgiving for the Christian victory over the Turks at the Battle of Lepanto in 1571.

HELP OF THE SICK, SCAPULAR. The badge of a confraternity, founded in 1860, associated with the Society of St. Camillus, patron of hospitals. It is black, with a picture of the Blessed Virgin. Approved by Popes Pius IX and Leo XIII.

HENOTHEISM. Worship of one god in preference to others, while not denying a plurality of gods. In practice it means that one god is worshiped by an individual clan or nation to the exclusion of other deities belonging to other peoples. It is a form of polytheism in that even this one preferred deity is not recognized as the only true God.

HEORTOLOGY. The study of religious calendars. More specifically, the science of the history and meaning of the seasons and festivals of the Christian Church year. (Etym. Greek *heorte*, feast + *logia*, science, knowledge.)

HEPTATEUCH. The first seven books of the Bible, namely Genesis, Exodus, Leviticus, Numbers, Deuteronomy, Joshua, and Judges. They form something of a historical unity. (Etym. Latin *heptateuchos*, from Greek *hepta*, seven + *teuchos*, book.)

HERALDRY, ECCLESIASTICAL. Study of armorial bearings applied to seals and coats-of-arms of religious corporations and to emblems attributed to particular saints.

The earliest of such ecclesiastical seals bore the device of a bishop or abbot, and by the fourteenth century English religious houses were ordered to have a common seal. It developed later into an impersonal coat-of-arms for each community. The miter, the crosier, and hat appeared as emblems in the fourteenth century, and by the seventeenth century the cardinal's hat was almost universal. The rank of the prelate was shown by the number of tassels. The heraldic miter is now placed above the other symbols by those entitled to wear it. Another external ornament to the shield is the crosier, a sign of episcopal dignity. Also used armorially is the cross: two-barred for the primate, and treble traverse on the papal cross. The bourdon, or knobbed staff, often appeared behind the shield of a prior or prioress. The Armenians are the only non-Catholic Eastern ecclesiastics who use heraldic devices. The arms of Vatican City are a tiara above two crossed keys, gold on red.

HEREDITY, LAW OF. The theory that not only a person's physical characteristics but also his intellectual and moral qualities are derived from his ancestors. As such, the theory is incompatible with the Christian belief in the operations of divine grace and the role of human freedom in shaping one's personality. This does not deny that certain physical predispositions that may affect one's spiritual life can be transmitted from parents to offspring. But, besides grace and free will, a person's environment and education are also contributory factors in the making of his character.

HERESIARCH. The original expounder or promoter of a major heresy that was later condemned by the Church, e.g., Arius, Nestorius, Pelagius.

HERESY. Commonly refers to a doctrinal belief held in opposition to the recognized standards of an established system of thought. Theologically it means an opinion at variance with the authorized teachings of any church, notably the Christian, and especially when this promotes separation from the main body of faithful believers.

In the Roman Catholic Church, heresy has a very specific meaning. Anyone who, after receiving baptism, while remaining nominally a Christian, pertinaciously denies or doubts any of the truths that must be believed with divine and Catholic faith is considered a heretic. Accordingly four elements must be verified to constitute formal heresy; previous valid baptism, which need not have been in the Catholic Church; external profession of still being a Christian, otherwise a person becomes an apostate; outright denial or positive doubt regarding a truth that the Catholic Church has actually proposed as revealed by God; and the disbelief must be morally culpable, where a nominal Christian refuses to accept what he knows is a doctrinal imperative.

Objectively, therefore, to become a heretic in the strict canonical sense and be excommunicated from the faithful, one must deny or question a truth that is taught not merely on the authority of the Church but on the word of God revealed in the Scriptures or sacred tradition. Subjectively a person must recognize his obligation to believe. If he acts in good faith, as with most persons brought up in non-Catholic surroundings, the heresy is only material and implies neither guilt nor sin against faith. (Etym. Latin *haeresis,* from the Greek *hairesis,* a taking, choice, sect, heresy.)

HERESY IN PROTESTANTISM. Condemnation or censure for doctrinal deviation in a Protestant denomination. In the earlier stages of Protestantism, the concept of heresy played a major role in shaping the various churches. Doctrines like absolute predestination and practices like infant baptism were orthodox or heretical, depending on theological orientation, and the conflicting attitudes often gave rise to various denominations. Moreover, civil rulers were authorized to protect their subjects from erroneous doctrines. The duty of civil magistrates, according to the Westminster Confession of Faith, was "to take order that unity and peace be preserved in the Church, that the truth of God be kept pure and entire, that all blasphemies and heresies be suppressed" (XXIII, 3). Presbyterians and others still provide that heresy is sufficient ground for deposition from the ministry.

With some exceptions, heresy in modern Protestant Churches must be extreme and "industriously spread" before action is taken against a member of the clergy. The rule of faith in these cases is the Bible and the norm of orthodoxy, in the spirit of John Wesley, is an inclusive Christianity. "We believe," he said, "Christ to be the eternal, the supreme God. But as to all opinions which do not strike at the root of Christianity, we think and let think" (*Works,* VIII, 31). More commonly the heresy must "strike at the vitals of religion," as in agnosticism or atheism, to be officially proscribed.

A few denominations in the Lutheran and Evangelical tradition excommunicate even the laity if "convicted of denying a fundamental truth necessary to salvation—the deity of Christ, vicarious atonement, or the resurrection of the dead." This may be done only after due admonition has been given and the person shows himself or herself "to be an incorrigible sinner and unbeliever." In practice, however, the churches seldom resort to these measures.

HERETIC. A person professing heresy. Ecclesiastical law distinguishes between a formal heretic, as one who is sinfully culpable, and a material heretic, who is not morally guilty for professing what may be objectively heretical doctrine.

HERMENEUTICS. The art and science of interpreting the Sacred Scriptures and of inquiring into their true meaning. It defines the laws that exegetes are to follow in order to determine and explain the sense of the revealed word of God. It presupposes that the interpreter has a knowledge of the biblical languages and of such sciences as contribute to a better understanding of Holy Writ. (Etym. Greek *hermēneus,* interpreter.)

HERMESIANISM. Doctrinal errors of Georg Hermes (1775–1831) that were condemned by the First Vatican Council. Hermes was essentially a rationalist whose position was censured in three definitions of the council, as follows: 1. "If anyone says that the assent of Christian faith is not free, but necessarily results from arguments of human reason; or that the grace of God is only necessary for living faith, which works through charity, let him be anathema"; 2. "If anyone says that the position of the faithful and of those who have not yet reached the only true faith is the same, so that Catholics could have good reason for suspending their assent and calling into question the faith that they have already accepted under the teaching authority of the Church, until they have completed a scientific demonstration of the credibility and truth of their faith, let him be anathema"; 3. "If anyone denies that the world was made for the glory of God, let him be anathema" (Denzinger, 3039, 3040, 3025).

HERMIT. A person who dwells alone, devoting himself to prayer and meditation. Dating in Christianity from the early persecutions of the Church, hermits were already known in Old Testament times, as Elijah the Prophet and later St. John the Baptist. More numerous at first in Egypt and Asia Minor, Christian hermits soon spread to the West, where eventually monasteries arose combining the eremitical life with the cenobitical,

and isolated hermits were encouraged to form communities. (Etym. Latin *eremita,* from Greek *erēmitēs,* a dweller in the desert.) See also CENOBITE.

HERMITAGE. The residence of a hermit, which normally allows him complete privacy for prayer and, in the case of a priest, for the celebration of Mass. In some cases hermitages are clustered around a central church or monastery where the hermits meet for periodic liturgical services and community exercises. St. Francis of Assisi wrote a brief set of directives for *Religious Life in Hermitages.* In the opening paragraph he enjoined that, "Not more than three or at most four friars should go together to a hermitage to lead a religious life there. Two of these should act as mothers, with the other two or the other one, as their children. The mothers are to lead the life of Martha; the other two, the life of Mary Magdalen."

HEROD. The dynasty that ruled over Palestine and the surrounding country from about 55 B.C. to A.D. 93. None of the Herods was Jewish by birth. First in line in the dynasty was Antipater, the Governor of Idumaea, who came from Ashkelon, a Philistine city. His son, Herod the Great, received a Roman appointment during Julius Caesar's administration to rule Palestine, and his successors continued in control for approximately one hundred fifty years. Herod the Great was the one responsible for the slaughter of the Holy Innocents. (Etym. Greek *hērōdēs,* sprung from a hero.)

HEROD ANTIPAS. Son of Herod the Great. He was the Tetrarch of Galilee from 4 B.C. to A.D. 39. Since his regime roughly paralleled the life of Jesus, he is mentioned more often in the New Testament than any other Herod. Because of Herod's devious methods, Jesus referred to him as "that fox" (Luke 13:32). He broke the law by marrying his niece, Herodias, who was already married to his half-brother (the beheading of John the Baptist was the aftermath of John's denunciation of this unholy marriage). The curiosity of Herod Antipas was stirred by the accounts he received of Jesus' public ministry (Matthew 14:1–12; Luke 9:9). Pontius Pilate proposed sending Jesus to Herod, who looked forward to the meeting with anticipation. But Jesus refused to answer any questions. Contemptuously Herod sent him back to Pilate to be sentenced. In A.D. 39 Herod Antipas was banished to Gaul (Luke 23:7–11).

HERODIANS. A group of Jews who supported the dynasty of Herod and shared its loyalty to Rome. They took part in the attempt to trap Jesus over possible disloyalty to Caesar (Matthew 22:16–22). Mark accuses them of even plotting with the Pharisees to destroy him (Mark 3:6). They were a political rather than a religious group.

HERODIAS. The daughter of Aristobulus, a half-sister of Herod Agrippa. She married her uncle Philip, but left him to marry another uncle, Herod Antipas. John the Baptist denounced this marriage, and Herodias was determined to wreak vengeance. When her daughter, Salome, won the admiration of the king with her dancing, he promised to grant her whatever she asked. Her mother instructed her to demand the head of John the Baptist (Matthew 14:3–11). The king reluctantly granted the request (Mark 6:17–29). A few years later Herodias joined Herod Antipas when he was sent into exile.

HEROD PHILIP. A half-brother of Herod Antipas, he was the son of Herod the Great. He was married to Salome, the daughter of Herodias. From 4 B.C. to A.D. 34 he served as Tetrarch of Ituraea and Trachonitis. Perhaps his most notable work was rebuilding Caesarea Philippi and Bethsaida.

HEROIC ACT. An act of charity by which a person offers to God, for the benefit of the souls in purgatory, all the works of satisfaction he or she will perform during life, and all the suffrage that will come to him or her after death. It is not a vow but an offering that can be revoked at will. Its heroism consists in the readiness to undergo sufferings here and in purgatory in order to relieve others of their purgatorial pains. The Church has more than once approved such a heroic act of charity.

HEROIC VIRTUE. The performance of extraordinary virtuous actions with readiness and over a period of time. The moral virtues are exercised with ease, while faith, hope, and charity are practiced to an eminent degree. The presence of such virtues is required by the Church as the first step toward canonization. The person who has practiced heroic virtue is declared to be Venerable, and is called a "Servant of God."

HERRENMORAL. Literally the morality of the masters (*Herren*). A concept of ruthless behavior associated with the ethical theories of Friedrich Nietzsche (1844–1900), German philosopher and author of *The Antichrist*. Such ideas as the will to power, superman, master race, and the primacy of the strong-minded with no regard for Christian principles have deeply penetrated Western society.

HESYCHASM. A system of mysticism originally defended by the Orthodox monks on Mount Athos in the fourteenth century. It claims that by means of asceticism and the practice of certain prayers, a person can already in this life see the uncreated light of God. Tinged with Neo-Platonism and borrowings from pantheism, it was opposed by those Orthodox who sought reunion with Rome and who favored a more reflective approach to God. Present-day Hesychasts say that their form of mysticism is a dogma of the Orthodox Church.

HETERONOMY. The moral doctrine that man is subject to laws that are not created by himself, but by others, and ultimately by God. The opposite of autonomy. (Etym. Greek *hetero,* other + *nomos,* law.)

HEXAEMERON. The biblical six days of creation, expressed in this way by the sacred writer to declare the essential fact of faith that the whole world was created by God, and to imply two consequences of this faith for believers. They are to imitate God in working six days and resting on the seventh, and they are to work now, in co-operating with the Creator, to embellish the earth, since God made the world and now wants man to develop what has been made. (Etym. Greek *hexaemeron,* six days' work; of or in six days.)

HEXAPLA. Origen's critical edition of the Old Testament in Hebrew and Greek in the late second century. This sixfold Bible in fifty volumes is arranged in six parallel columns containing the Hebrew text in Hebrew and Greek characters, the Septuagint, and three other Greek versions. Origen wished to show the relationship of the Septuagint to the Hebrew and Greek texts. The column exhibiting the Septuagint is the only one that has survived. (Etym. Greek *hexapla,* sixfold.)

HEXATEUCH. The first six books of the Bible, from Genesis to Joshua, so called because they form a literary whole. (Etym. Greek *hex,* six + *teuchos,* case, book.)

H.H. His Holiness.

HIERARCHY. The successors of the Apostles under the Pope as successor of St. Peter. Three powers are included under the Catholic hierarchy: teaching, pastoral, and sacerdotal. They correspond to the threefold office laid on Christ as man for the redemption of the world; the office of prophet or teacher, the pastoral or royal office of ruler, and the priestly office of sanctifying the faithful. Christ transferred this threefold office, with the corresponding powers, to the Apostles and their successors. A man enters the hierarchy by episcopal ordination when he receives the fullness of the priesthood. But he depends on collegial union with the Bishop of Rome and the rest of the Catholic hierarchy for actually being able to exercise the two other powers of teaching divine truth and of legitimately ruling the believers under his jurisdiction. (Etym. Latin *hierarchia*, holy authority, from Greek *hierarchia*, power of a *hierarchēs,* a steward or president of sacred rites.)

HIERARCHY OF BEING. The scholastic concept of an ascending order of beings in the universe, comprising inanimate matter, plants, animals, and rational human beings; above them are the immaterial created spirits or angels; and finally God, whose essence is immeasurably more sublime than that of any creature. Each level in this hierarchy is complete in its own perfection, and there is no transition from one to the other, while each preceding level depends on the beings above it; and all levels totally depend upon God.

HIEROMONK. A monk in the Eastern Christian Churches, including those in union with Rome, who is ordained to the priesthood.

HIERONYMITES. Also called the Jeronymites or the Hierohymitae. Groups of hermits who followed the way of life of St. Jerome (342–420), going back to the community of men and women who gathered around him in Bethlehem. They were later given the Rule of St. Augustine. Hieronymite nuns were founded in Spain in 1426. In the sixteenth century the order was one of the channels through which the Catholic Counter-Reformation found its expression.

HIERURGIA. A sacred liturgical action, especially the Mass, in the Byzantine Rite of the Catholic Church.

HIGHER RELIGIONS. The living faiths of mankind that have been systematized into doctrines, ritual, and a moral code. They are commonly distinguished from tribal or primitive religions that have not been articulated in creeds or confessions of faith.

HIGH MASS. In Latin, *Missa Cantata,* was the popular term for a Mass that was sung by a priest without deacon or subdeacon.

HINDERING IMPEDIMENT. Also called impedient impediment, it is a condition that renders a marriage unlawful, without a dispensation, without affecting its validity. A simple vow, mixed religion, and certain legal relationships are so classified.

HINNOM. See GEHENNA.

HIRAM. A dynasty of kings in Tyre, a port near the present-day Beirut (I Kings 5:1). The best known of the Hirams was a close friend of both David and Solomon (II Samuel 5:11). He supplied them with carpenters and workmen and sent cedars and firs from Lebanese forests during the building of the Jerusalem Temple (I Chronicles 14:1). Only through Hiram's efficient co-operation was Solomon enabled to carry to completion his building program (I Kings 5:1–18). This trade alliance was made possible by the remarkable skill of the Tyrian sailors in their merchant ships (I Kings 9:11).

HIS HOLINESS. A title of honor and respect reserved in the Western Church for the Holy Father, the Pope, because of his administrative office of holy things. The term is sometimes applied to patriarchs in the East, e.g., to the Melkite patriarch in Antioch, in union with Rome, who is called "Most Holy in the Liturgy," and the Orthodox patriarch of Constantinople, who is spoken of as "His All-Holiness."

HISTORICAL DETERMINISM. A philosophy of history which claims that human actions are all determined exclusively by their antecedents. Given the same circumstances, people always behave in the same way. The task of the historian, then, is to show that the movements of nations are perfectly regular and that, like all other movements, they are solely determined by their antecedents. This conception of history as a deterministic science is at variance with Catholic Christianity, which believes in human freedom.

HISTORICISM. The theory that claims that the secular history of anything is an adequate explanation of its meaning; that the values of a movement or philosophy are adequately understood by tracing it to its origins; and that something is fully understood if its development has been historically accounted for. Prime examples of modern historicism are the philosophies of history of Georg Hegel and Karl Marx.

HISTORICITY. Applied to the Gospels, their validity as faithfully narrating the facts and events of the life of Jesus Christ, with their causes and effects explained under the inspiration of the Holy Spirit.

HISTORY OF DOGMA. The systematic presentation of the history of divine revelation since it was completed at the end of the apostolic age to the present time. This history comprehends the Church's identification of what was revealed in Sacred Scripture and tradition; formulation of God's word in creeds, definitions, and doctrinal terms; interpretation of what was revealed; growth in understanding its meaning; and defense of revealed truth against the intrusion of heresy.

H.O. Holy Day of Obligation.

HOLINESS. In the Old Testament the Hebrew *Kadosch* (holy) meant being separated from the secular or profane, or dedication to God's service, as Israel was said to be holy because it was the people of God. The holiness of God identified his separation from all evil. And among creatures they are holy by their relation to him. Holiness in creatures is either subjective or objective or both. It is subjective essentially by the possession of divine grace and morally by the practice of virtue. Objective holiness in creatures denotes their exclusive consecration to the service of God: priests by their ordination, religious by their vows, sacred places, vessels, and vestments by the blessing they receive and the sacred purpose for which they are reserved.

HOLINESS, ESSENTIAL. Also called substantial holiness, is the possession of sanctifying grace. It is present in a person from the moment of baptism and represents that person's likeness to God. As such it is independent of the person's moral conduct. It is intrinsic goodness or goodness of being and is the basic reason why the New Testament speaks of the faithful as "saints." They are holy insofar as they are pleasing to God.

HOLINESS, MORAL. Also called ethical holiness, it consists in the practice of virtue. Although closely related to essential holiness, it is nevertheless not the same. It is a person's goodness manifested in action, as distinct from his or her goodness as a person in the state of divine friendship. Sometimes God permits people to be more holy than they seem to be, morally, either to themselves or others. But insofar as holiness is shown in practice, it is moral or ethical. And the practice of virtue is, of course, necessary even to remain in God's grace, let alone to grow in sanctity.

HOLINESS, OBJECTIVE. Dedication to the service of God, whether of a person, e.g., priest or religious; or an object, e.g., a church or vestment; or an occasion, e.g., a feast day.

HOLINESS, SUBJECTIVE. The inherent sanctity of a person, as distinct from his or her position in the Church as one specially consecrated to God.

HOLOCAUST. Among the Israelites and even now among many non-Christian believers, an offering entirely consumed by fire. In Jewish tradition, only animals could be offered in holocaust, which is regarded as the most complete expression of one's reverence for God. A holocaust could either be prescribed by law or voluntarily made in fulfillment of a private vow or as an act of devotion. In the Old Testament, holocausts were vivid reminders of God's supreme dominion over his creatures. They were means of atonement for sin, and they foreshadowed the perfect sacrifice of Jesus Christ on the Cross. (Etym. Greek *holokaustos*, burned whole.)

HOLOFERNES. The leader of the powerful Assyrian army of King Nebuchadnezzar, who had the Jewish army at his mercy in Bethulia. The latter was weak in leadership and training and its water supply was exhausted. In this desperate situation Judith appeared, a beautiful, devout Jewess, who had much more confidence in God than in force of arms. She carried the battle to Holofernes, not by military prowess but by her charm and wit. He was overwhelmed by her beauty and invited her to share his tent with him for the night. At the first opportunity, she cut off his head and carried it back to the Jewish camp. In the ensuing battle the confused, leaderless Assyrians were annihilated (Judith 1–16).

HOLY ALLIANCE. A declaration, originally signed in 1815 by Russia, Austria, and Prussia and eventually by all the rulers of Europe except the Prince Regent of England, the Pope and the Sultan of Turkey. Its basic principle was that henceforth the civil powers would be guided in their relations by "the sublime truths which the Holy Religion of our Saviour teaches." Originated by the Czar and sincerely intended to foster friendship among the nations, it was never effective as a diplomatic instrument. In 1899, however, it inspired Czar Nicholas II to call the first international peace conference at The Hague.

HOLY CHILDHOOD ASSOCIATION.
Founded in 1843, it is the Catholic Church's official mission-aid society for children. It provides mission education programs and materials for Catholic elementary schools and religious education classes. Under the direction of the Holy Ghost Fathers.

HOLY CHRISM. Olive oil in which small amounts of balm or balsam have been mixed. It is one of three holy oils and is necessary for the sacrament of confirmation. It is also used in the solemn rite of baptism; consecration of churches and bishops; blessings of major church bells, baptismal water, patens, and chalices. Anointing with chrism signifies the full diffusion of grace.

HOLY COAT. The seamless garment of Christ (John 19) for which the soldiers cast lots on Calvary. Two cities both claim to possess this garment. Trier in Germany claims that its relic was sent there by St. Helena (255–330), and is substantiated by a tablet of the sixth century and several documents of the twelfth century. The coat of Argenteuil in France is mentioned in a document dating from 1156 as the *cappa pueri Jesu* (garment of the Child Jesus). Because of these two traditions the legend arose that the garment woven by the Blessed Virgin and worn by the Savior grew with him. Advocates of the Argenteuil relic say that the Trier coat is not the seamless garment mentioned in the Gospels but an outer cloak. Both relics are the object of popular pilgrimages.

HOLY COMMUNION. The Eucharist is the sacrament that preserves the soul's union with God and fosters that union by making a person more holy especially in the practice of the supernatural virtue of charity. As a sacrament of the living, to obtain the graces intended, a person must be in the state of God's friendship when receiving, otherwise the reception becomes a sacrilege (I Corinthians 11:27–29).

The union of the communicant with Christ in the Eucharist is effective in the moral order. Though physically present in the communicant, Christ is not physically united with him. Only the consecrated species, since they alone can come in contact with material things, are physically united with the communicant.

Communion aims specifically at producing a likeness to Christ in the communicants. Their acts of mind and will, as a result of Communion, are to become more conformable to the acts of Christ's mind and will. Their body, too, is to become more like Christ's sacred body.

This is the primary purpose of the sacrament, a special union of the soul with Christ. What is special about this union is that the Eucharist is extraordinarily powerful in conferring actual graces that prompt a person to make acts of love for God and one's neighbor. Moreover, these graces inspire one to live for Christ habitually, even under great difficulties, as shown by the readiness to love the unlovable, and to promote loving community in spite of great natural diversity.

The secondary purpose of Communion is to assimilate the body of the communicant to the body of Christ in two ways: it curbs or mitigates all disordered passions, especially those against chastity, and it confers a new title to the final resurrection of the body in heavenly glory.

A final effect of Communion is to remove the personal guilt of venial sins, and the temporal punishment due to forgiven sins, whether venial or mortal.

HOLY CROSS CONGREGATION. A clerical religious institute, under simple vows, engaged in home and foreign missions, retreats, educational and pastoral work, social services, and the apostolate of the press. Founded in France in 1837 by Father Basile-Antoine Moreau.

HOLY DAYS OF OBLIGATION. Feast days to be observed by attendance at Mass and rest, as far as possible, from unnecessary servile work. The number and dates of these vary among countries. In the United States there are six holy days: Solemnity of Mary on January 1; Ascension of Our Lord, forty days after Easter; Assumption of the Blessed Virgin, August 15; All Saints' Day, November 1; Mary's Immaculate Conception, December 8; and Christmas, or the birth of Christ, December 25. On holy days the pastor of every parish is required to offer or have offered a special Mass for his parishioners.

HOLY DOORS. The main doors at the Roman basilicas of St. Peter, Lateran, St. Paul Outside the Walls, and St. Mary Major; they are kept sealed except during the periodic jubilee years. The Pope personally opens and closes the doors at St. Peter's, nearest to the Vatican Palace, while cardinal legates do the same at the other churches to mark the official beginning and ending of the year of jubilee. These ceremonies symbolize the right of sanctuary, which goes back to pagan times and was actually then observed on the present site of the Lateran.

HOLY FACE, SCAPULAR. A white cloth with a picture of the Holy Face of Christ. It is a badge of the Archconfraternity of the Holy Face.

HOLY FAMILY, DEVOTION TO THE. Although the family of Jesus, Mary, and Joseph is very prominent in the Gospels, popular devotion to them on a large scale began only in the seventeenth century. General confraternities, on an international scale, were created to promote this devotion. Among modern popes Pius IX in 1847 and Leo XIII in 1892 encouraged these organizations and gave them official approval. A number of religious institutes also came into existence, specially dedicated to the apostolate of helping Christian families survive and prosper through devotion to Jesus, Mary, and Joseph. In the new revised liturgy the Sunday within the octave of Christmas is the Feast of the Holy Family, with its own special Mass and Divine Office.

HOLY FATHER. A title of the Pope, in common usage as the equivalent of *Beatissimus Pater*. Signifies the Pope's position as the spiritual father of all the Christian faithful.

HOLY GHOST. See HOLY SPIRIT.

HOLY GRAIL. The legendary cup identified with the chalice used by Christ at the Last Supper from which the Apostles received the Precious Blood. The quest for it has been the basis of many popular stories. One of the most popular was the legend that Joseph of Arimathaea brought the Holy Grail to England. This became the theme of numerous Arthurian romances.

HOLY HILL. A shrine of Mary, Help of Christians in Hubertus, Wisconsin, northwest of Milwaukee. A statue of the Madonna, arms outstretched, with the Child beside her, is the central feature of the shrine. The present edifice is the third church built since 1863, when the first log building became too small to hold the pilgrims who came to Holy Hill, where it is reputed that Jacques Marquette first planted the Cross. Now in charge of the shrine, the Carmelites have built a six-story monastery on the grounds. Discarded crutches and braces there attest to the miracles attributed to Mary, Help of Christians.

HOLY HOUR. A pious devotional exercise consisting of mental and vocal prayer with exposition of the Blessed Sacrament. It draws its inspiration from Christ's words to the Apostles in Gethsemane: "Can you not watch one hour with me?" It was taught by the Savior to St. Margaret Mary (1647–90) as one of the special practices of the Sacred Heart devotion. In the early nineteenth century a confraternity was founded at Paray-le-Monial, France, to spread the devotion, which has been highly recommended by the popes. If the hour is made publicly it is designated by a priest or the director; if made privately, any hour is suitable but preferably Thursday or Friday evening. The Passion of Christ is the theme during the hour, variously divided into meditation, vocal prayer, and singing. Many religious communities include the devotion as part of the horarium of their day.

HOLY INNOCENTS. Martyred boys under two years of age, whom King Herod ordered to be massacred. It was an attempt by Herod to kill the Babe of Bethlehem, who he feared would usurp his kingship (Matthew 2:16–18). Legends carry the numbers slain in the thousands, but it is now conceded to have been less than a hundred. The Western Church keeps their feast day on December 28. In Bethlehem it is celebrated with great solemnity.

HOLY LAND. A name given to the area that witnessed the life, death, and resurrection of Christ. The expression *terra sancta* (holy land) came into general use only in the Middle Ages, although it was found in religious literature since early patristic times.

HOLY MARY. The second part of the prayer "Hail Mary," in which the Blessed Virgin is invoked, "Holy Mary, Mother of God, pray for us sinners, now and at the hour of our death." It began as an invocation added to the *Ave Maria* in the eleventh century, and came into general use by the sixteenth century. Pope St. Pius V gave it official recognition in 1568 by including the Holy Mary in the Roman Breviary.

HOLY NAME. The name of Jesus, from the Aramaic *Yeshu* and the Hebrew *Jehoshua*, which means "Yahweh is salvation." It was given to Christ by the angel at the time of the Annunciation (Luke 1:31). It is a common name among Arabic people and is given in baptism to children in Spain and Spanish-speaking countries. A feast in honor of the Holy Name was instituted in the fifteenth century by the bishops of Belgium, England, Scotland, and Germany and extended to the universal Church in 1721. It was celebrated on the Sunday between the first and sixth of January if one occurred. Otherwise it was on January 2. The great apostle of devotion to the Holy Name was St. Bernardine of Siena (1380–1444), who would preach holding a board on which were the first three letters of the Savior's name in its Greek form—IHS—surrounded by rays, and he persuaded people to copy these plaques and erect them over their dwellings and public buildings.

HOLY NAME SOCIETY. Confraternity of men, originating at the ecumenical Council of Lyons in 1274, and promoted by the Dominicans, to whom Pope Gregory X entrusted its direction. The Spanish Friar Didacus (d. 1450) founded a confraternity of the Holy Name and drew up a rule. In time the confraternity merged with the Society of the Holy Name. World membership is several million. The purpose of the organization is twofold: to promote love and reverence for the name of God and Jesus, and to discourage profanity, blasphemy, perjury, and all improper language.

HOLY OFFICE. A Roman congregation founded by Pope Paul III in 1542. It was reconstituted in 1965 to become the Sacred Congregation for the Doctrine of the Faith, but the original functions have not substantially changed. The purpose of the Holy Office was to defend Catholic teaching of faith and morals. It censored and condemned books judged dangerous to Catholic orthodoxy, and granted permission to read such books. It could dispense priests from the midnight fast required before celebrating Mass. It had exclusive jurisdiction over questions about the Pauline privilege and the impediments of worship and mixed religion. As a tribunal, it judged heresy and all offenses leading to a suspicion of heresy. Its members were bound to the strictest secrecy, called the secret of the Holy Office.

HOLY OILS. Sacramentals blessed by a bishop. There are three kinds: oil of catechumens, holy chrism, and oil of the sick. The first and third are pure olive oil. Chrism has in the oil a mixture of balm or balsam. In 1970, the Congregation for Divine Worship declared that, if necessary, the holy oils may be from any plant and not only from olives. The holy oils are symbols of spiritual nourishment and the light of grace. They are used in the public administration of baptism, confirmation, and anointing of the sick. The blessing of the holy oils normally takes place on Holy Thursday by a bishop at a cathedral church. After distribution locally they are kept in locked boxes in the ambry. Unused oils, a year later, are burned in the sanctuary lamp.

HOLY ORDERS. See ORDERS, SACRAMENT OF.

HOLY PLACES. The places in Palestine to which the faithful make pilgrimages because of their traditional association with the persons and events recorded in the Bible. Among Jews the Holy City of Jerusalem was the object of pilgrimage centuries before Christ. Among Christians the principal places of interest since the fourth century were the sites mentioned in the Gospels, especially the Holy Sepulcher of Jerusalem.

HOLY ROOD. The Cross on which Jesus Christ died, or any representation of it. (Etym. Anglo-Saxon *rod,* a rod, pole, gallows, cross.)

HOLY ROSARY, FEAST OF THE. A special liturgical commemoration, on October 7, of the victory of the Christian naval forces over the Moslems at Lepanto (1571). The feast is now an obligatory memorial of the Blessed Virgin of the Rosary. It recalls that Our Lady was invoked under this title by the faithful who prayed the Rosary in begging for a Christian victory in spite of overwhelming odds against them. Pope St. Pius V instituted the feast.

HOLY SATURDAY. The eve of Easter, and the day that Christ remained in the tomb. In the early Church no Mass was offered, with services starting about three o'clock in the afternoon and ending with the Mass of the Resurrection on Easter morning. The present Easter Vigil is an approximation of this ancient rite.

HOLY SEE. Synonymous with Apostolic See, designating Rome. The official residence of the Pope; the power of the Supreme Pontiff; various Roman offices, especially the tribunals and congregations assisting the Pope in the government of the Church.

HOLY SEPULCHER. The tomb at Jerusalem where the body of Christ lay between his burial and resurrection. It was a new tomb, cut out of rock, closed with a big stone, and belonging to Joseph of Arimathaea. It was situated in a garden outside the city walls. Over it Emperor Constantine erected a basilica, in place of which today stands the Church of the Holy Sepulcher.

HOLY SHROUD. Relic of the winding sheet in which Christ was likely buried, and venerated in Turin, Italy. It is a strip of linen cloth, fourteen feet three inches long and three feet seven inches wide, bearing the front and back imprints of a human body. Tradition for its authenticity dates from the seventh century. Originally enshrined in France, it was transferred to Turin in 1578. It is kept in a richly decorated elaborate case behind the main altar. Recent analysis tends to verify the authenticity of this relic. The marks of the sweat and blood constitute a photographic phenomenon whose nature and preservation have not been explained naturally. An entire science, called sindonology (Latin *sindo*, shroud), has developed to study and draw theological implications from the Holy Shroud.

HOLY SOULS. The souls of those who departed in the grace of God but who are temporarily detained in purgatory for venial faults and for the unremitted punishment due to their forgiven sins. They are the object of the prayers of the faithful, especially the Sacrifice of the Mass offered for them. The feast of All Souls, November 2, and the whole month of November are designated for their remembrance by the Church. The living faithful are daily reminded in the liturgy to pray for the holy souls.

HOLY SPIRIT. The third person of the Holy Trinity, who is distinct from the Father and the Son but one in being, coequal, and coeternal with them, because, like them, he is in the fullest sense God. The Holy Spirit proceeds not only from the Father but also from the Son as from a single principle, through what is called a single spiration. He is the personal infinite term of the eternal act of mutual love of the Father and the Son; hence his name of Spirit, as the issue or term of God's eternal love or act of will. He is also called the Spirit of Truth, the Creator Spirit, the Sanctifier, as the gifts of revelation, of creation (and re-creation), and of sanctification are the outpourings of God's love, and therefore appropriated to the Spirit of Love, though whatever God does outside the Trinity (in the world of creatures) belongs to the common or united action of the three divine persons. He is called Dove, because it was in this form that he descended visibly upon Christ in the Jordan (Mark 1:10).

HOLY THURSDAY. Also called Maundy Thursday, the anniversary of the Last Supper, when Christ instituted the Eucharist, the Sacrifice of the Mass, and the sacrament of the priesthood. On Holy Thursday, since the early Church, the blessing of the holy oils

has taken place. The Church's emphasis in the revised liturgy for Holy Thursday is on the institution of the priesthood.

HOLY WATER. Sacramental blessed by a priest, invoking God's blessing on all who use it. Blessed water is a symbol of spiritual cleansing, and its use is advised in moments of physical danger and against temptations from spiritual enemies. It is common practice to dip one's fingers in holy water and reverently make the Sign of the Cross as one enters a Catholic church, and it is recommended for use in the home. Holy water is used in all blessings. There are, besides ordinary holy water, baptismal holy water, used with chrism in the conferring of public baptism, and Easter water specially blessed for use during the paschal time.

HOLY WEEK. The week preceding Easter, from Passion (Palm) Sunday through Holy Saturday inclusive. During this week the Church commemorates the Passion of Christ, and all the ceremonies reflect this attitude of sorrow, yet joined with gratitude for God's mercy in becoming man in order to suffer and die for a sinful mankind.

HOLY WELL. St. Winifride's Well in North Wales. A place of pilgrimage throughout the year but especially on November 3, the saint's feast day. The legend of St. Winifride, virgin and martyr, is authenticated by two twelfth-century documents. A daughter of a Welsh chieftain, she lived in the seventh century. When St. Beuno came to her father's house, he was hospitably received and instructed Winifride in the Christian faith. So impressed was she that she determined to become a religious. Then followed a series of extraordinary events: Winifride was beheaded, miraculously restored to life, and a spring arose in a dry region where her blood had fallen. She later founded a convent on the spot, the later Holy Well. She died in 660. In the twelfth century Winifride's bones were moved to Shrewsbury and later scattered during Henry VIII's reign of terror. All were lost except one finger, which was transferred to Holy Well. The shrine is the site of numerous miraculous cures, including those of well-known Protestants. The water from this well is also believed to have miraculous qualities. Though at one time forbidden, pilgrimages to her shrine continued. In recent decades conditions have improved and the number of pilgrims has increased.

HOLY WOMEN. A liturgical term used to designate women saints in the Bible or since biblical times in the Church's ritual. Particularly applied to the women who stood by the Cross of Christ on Calvary, and who were the first to visit the sepulcher on Easter Sunday.

HOLY WRIT. The Bible, or "Sacred Scriptures," expressed in English usage.

HOLY YEAR. Essentially, a year during which the Pope grants a special indulgence, called the Jubilee, to all the faithful who visit Rome and pray according to specified conditions. First instituted in 1300 by Pope Boniface VIII, whose original intention was that it be celebrated only every hundred years. Since then there have been three changes in the intervals. In 1343, Pope Clement VI decreed that the Holy Year be celebrated every fifty years; Urban VI in 1389 reduced it to thirty-three years in honor of the years of Christ's life; and Paul II in 1470 made it every twenty-five years, which is the period that has been kept ever since. Pope Pius XI made an exception in 1933 to commemorate the nineteenth centennial of Christ's death, resurrection, and ascension. Since 1500 the Jubilee Indulgence could be gained in one's native country, under specified conditions, after the Roman year was completed. The opening and closing of the Holy Doors at St. Peter's in Rome marks the opening and closing of each Holy Year.

HOM. *Homilia*–homily.

HOMICIDE. The killing of another human being by a person acting on his or her own initiative. The term is ambiguous because of its indiscriminate use, especially in countries where direct abortion, which is voluntary homicide, is legalized. Church law distinguishes voluntary homicide, which is murder, from other forms that may be more or less culpable but are not the unjust killing of an innocent person. (Etym. Latin *homo*, man + *-cidium*, a killing.)

HOMILETICS. The branch of theological studies that treats of the composition and delivery of sermons, homilies, and other religious discourses, and/or discussion and instruction to the faithful. It is required of all those who have prepared for the priesthood and the permanent diaconate.

HOMILY. A sermon or informal discourse on some part of the Sacred Scriptures. It aims to explain in an instructive commentary the literal meaning of the chosen text or subject and from this develop a practical application for the moral or spiritual life. The oldest extant homily is the sermon of Peter on Pentecost Sunday. Since the Second Vatican Council the homily has become an integral part of every Mass, always the Sunday Mass, but also whenever a number of the faithful are present or the occasion calls for an exposition of the Scriptures. The methods of giving a homily include: treating separately one or more parts of the biblical reading; combining the Scripture texts into a single idea; concentrating on some virtue or vice suggested by the Gospel text; paraphrasing a Bible passage as a basis for an exhortation to the people. (Etym. Greek *homilein*, to consort with, address.)

HOMOOUSIOS. A term first defined by the first general council of the Church to identify Christ's relationship to the Father. It was chosen by the council to clarify the Church's infallible teaching that the second Person of the Trinity, who became man, is of one and the same substance, or essence, or nature as God the Father. The Arians, who were condemned at Nicaea, held that Christ was "divine" only in the sense that he was from God, and therefore like God, but not that he was literally "God from God, one in being with the Father." (Etym. Greek *homousios*, of one essence, consubstantial.)

HOMOSEXUALITY. In general, some form of sexual relationship among members of the same sex. From a moral standpoint, three levels are to be distinguished: tendency, attraction, and activity. Homosexual tendencies in any person are within the normal range of human nature, whose fallen condition includes every conceivable kind of impulse that with sincere effort and divine grace can be controlled. Sexual attraction for members of the same sex may be partly due to the peculiar make-up of certain individuals or, more often, the result of indiscretion or seduction and presents a graver problem; yet this, too, is not by itself sinful and may in fact be an occasion for great supernatural merit. When the condition is pathological, it requires therapy. Active homosexuality is morally indefensible and has been many times forbidden in revelation and the teaching of the Church. The most extensive declaration on the subject was by the Congregation for the Doctrine of the Faith, approved by Pope Paul VI on November 7, 1975. See also GREEK LOVE.

HONOR. Reverence and respect given to some being, whether God or a creature, because of its recognized excellence. So, too, the reverence shown to anything because of its relation to a person who is honored.

HONORARIUM. The free-will offering given to a priest or cleric for spiritual or religious services rendered. It differs from a stipend, which is for some liturgical function, and from a fee, which is agreed upon beforehand, usually for a professional service that is not strictly religious.

HOPE. The confident desire of obtaining a future good that is difficult to attain. It is therefore a desire, which implies seeking and pursuing; some future good that is not yet possessed but wanted, unlike fear that shrinks from a future evil. This future good draws out a person's volition. Hope is confident that what is desired will certainly be attained. It is the opposite of despair. Yet it recognizes that the object wanted is not easily obtained and that it requires effort to overcome whatever obstacles stand in the way. (Etym. Latin *spes*, hope.)

HOPE, ACT OF. An act of confident expectation of possessing God in heaven and of obtaining the necessary grace to reach this destiny. Acts of hope are required in times of temptation to discouragement or despair, and are implicit in every supernaturally good work. A simple and highly authorized act of hope says: "My God, I hope in You, for grace and for glory, because of Your promises, Your mercy and Your power. Amen."

HOPE, VIRTUE OF. An infused theological virtue, received at baptism together with sanctifying grace and having the possession of God as its primary object. It belongs to the will and makes a person desire eternal life, which is the heavenly vision of God, and gives one the confidence of receiving the grace necessary to reach heaven. The grounds of hope are the omnipotence of God, his goodness, and his fidelity to what he promised. The virtue of hope is necessary for salvation. Acts of hope are also necessary for salvation and are commanded by God for all who have come to the use of reason.

HOR. *Hora*—hour.

HORIZONTALISM. The theory that holds that the only valid form of knowledge is that acquired from other human beings and not, as Christianity holds, vertically by revelation from God.

HORMISDAS, FORMULA OF. The doctrinal statement drawn up by Pope St. Hormisdas in 519, declaring the necessity of agreeing with the See of Peter to preserve the true faith. The formula condemns a series of heretics and has been used by subsequent general councils as a standard of orthodoxy. "The first condition of salvation," states the formula, "is to keep the norm of the true faith and in no way to deviate from the established doctrine of the Fathers . . . And their truth has been proved by the course of history, for in the Apostolic See the Catholic religion has always been kept unsullied" (Denzinger 363).

HOROLOGION. A liturgical book in the Byzantine Catholic Church. It is similar in part to the Roman Divine Office, containing choir parts of the antiphons for feast days, some hymns, and the ecclesiastical calendar. (Etym. Latin *horologium*, clock; from Greek *hōra*, hour + *legein*, to gather: *hōrologion*.)

HOSANNA. A Hebrew shout of joy and triumph, taken from the Psalms, and saying "Save us, we pray." During the Jewish Feast of Tabernacles it was recited or chanted daily by the priest during the procession around the altar. When certain verses were said, the trumpet sounded, palm branches were waved, and the Hoshiana was repeatedly shouted as an exultation of joy. In present day Masses it is twice proclaimed at the Sanctus, by the priest and the faithful, and either sung or recited. It is said at the distribution of palms and during Palm Sunday's solemn procession in imitation of the acclamations given to Christ as he entered Jerusalem a few days before his Passion. (Etym. Hebrew *ho shi a na*, save me; an exclamation of joy.)

HOSEA. One of the Minor Prophets, who carried on his ministry sometime between 783 and 715 B.C. in the kingdom of Israel, which seceded from Judah after the death of Solomon. The book of Hosea consists of fourteen chapters and may be divided into three parts. The first part (1–3) portrays Israel as the faithless bride, whose divine Lover remains true to her in spite of her infidelities and urges her to repent. The second part (4–9:9) is a divine reproach and a cry for vengeance. The third part (9:10–14:10) recalls God's blessings on his people, repeats the exhortation to repentance, and promises salvation. Hosea is frequently quoted in the New Testament, and twice by Christ personally (Matthew 9:13; Hosea 6:6; Luke 23:30; Hosea 10:8).

HOSPITAL. An institution for the care of the sick. The first hospitals were charitable institutions founded and directed by the Church for the aged, poor, and afflicted, and in the Middle Ages they served foundlings, orphans, and lepers as well. The oldest hospital still in existence is the Hôtel Dieu, founded under religious auspices in Paris in A.D. 660. Many religious orders have as their distinctive apostolate the service of the sick in hospitals and most Catholic hospitals are conducted by religious institutes. Hospitals have always been intimately connected with the history of Christian charity in imitation of Christ in his compassion for the sick and disabled.

HOSPITALERS. Originally Knights of the Order of the Hospital of St. John of Jerusalem. After 1310 they were also known as the Knights of Rhodes, and from 1530 as the Knights of Malta. Their beginning may be traced to the Benedictines in the eleventh century. Founded to care for the sick, during the Crusades they also gave protection to the pilgrims and in time became either soldiers (military brothers) or physicians and nurses (brother infirmarians). Eventually the military phase went out of existence. The term "hospitalers" is also applied in a wider sense to other religious institutes, e.g., the Brothers Hospitalers, founded by St. John of God, approved by Pope St. Pius V in 1572.

HOSPITALITY. The virtue of kindness and generosity toward guests. It is characterized by the spirit of welcome to visitors and strangers, and is one of the conditions for salvation, foretold by Christ: "I was a stranger and you made me welcome" (Matthew 25:36).

HOST. A victim of sacrifice, and therefore the consecrated Bread of the Eucharist considered as the sacrifice of the Body of Christ. The word is also used of the round wafers used for consecration. (Etym. Latin *hostia,* sacrificial offering.)

HOSTIA. Consecrated Bread of the Eucharist. Also, and primarily, the Victim of the Eucharistic Sacrifice, namely Christ.

HOUR. One of the five canonical hours of the Divine Office, so called because traditionally they are to be sung or recited at certain hours in the day. The hours are: the Office of Readings, Morning Prayer (Lauds), Prayer During the Day (Terce, Sext, or None), Evening Prayer (Vespers), and Night Prayer (Compline).

HOUSE BLESSING. One of several liturgical blessings of a home approved by the Church. A standard formula, which the priest recites, while sprinkling the house with holy water, begins: "We earnestly beseech You, God the Father Almighty, to bless, and sanctify and endow with every gift this home, its furnishings and those who dwell herein."

HOUSE OF GOD. The name frequently applied to a church, especially a Catholic church, where the Blessed Sacrament is reserved.

HOUSE OF GOLD. A title of the Blessed Virgin in the Litany of Loreto. It denotes her personal perfection and her privilege of divine motherhood. She was the house wherein God dwelt during the nine months in her womb, and for his sake she was a house of gold, adorned by the Creator with the most precious virtues.

HOUSE, RELIGIOUS. In general, the residence of any religious institute of men or women. It is a formal religious house (*domus formata*) if at least six professed religious dwell in it. In the case of a clerical institute four of the six must be priests.

HUGUENOTS. The term used after 1560 to designate the French Protestants in the sixteenth and seventeenth centuries. The name is derived from one of their leaders, Besançon Hugues. They owed their inspiration and organization to John Calvin, who gained acceptance in France, where the Catholic faith had been weakened by the Western Schism, the growth of Gallicanism, the Pragmatic Sanction (1438), and the opposition of the Holy League to Pope Julius II. Henry of Navarre, by the Edict of Nantes, 1598, obtained for them the freedom to exercise their religion. But, not satisfied, they sought political power, supported by arms. Their power was crushed in 1628 when La Rochelle surrendered. Louis XIV revoked the Edict of Nantes in 1685. Many Huguenots fled to England, South Africa, the Netherlands, and North America.

HUMAN ACT. Every action and the only one that proceeds from the deliberate will of a human being. Consequently it proceeds from the knowledge of the intellect and the free decision of the human will. It is an act of which a human being is the master, whether the act begins and ends in the will, i.e., elicited act (such as love), or the will affects another faculty, i.e., commanded act (such as writing). Only human acts are morally imputable to the one who performs them, unlike what are called acts of a human being performed by persons who lack the use of reason or whose freedom is totally inhibited as in sleep or under anesthesia.

Human acts are either good or bad, depending on whether they agree or disagree with the norms of morality. Morally indifferent human acts are purely theoretical. In practice all deliberate actions are somehow either morally good or bad.

Similarly the distinction between natural and supernatural actions is more speculative than real, since whatever a person does deliberately has moral significance for his or her supernatural destiny.

For juridical reasons, which may partake of divine law, human acts may be either valid or invalid, according as they fulfill the conditions required by Church law. Thus baptism administered with some liquid other than water is not valid.

HUMANAE PERSONAE DIGNITATEM. Document published by the Vatican Secretariat for Unbelievers. Its purpose is to give general principles and particular norms for Catholics who engage in private or public dialogue with unbelievers, e.g., Communist Marxists. Among the specific norms the most practical one affects public dialogues, which may be either unofficial or official, as organized by ecclesiastical authorities. Regarding the latter, "it is only rarely that conditions exist in which such dialogue can take place between Christians and unbelievers." Unofficial discussions require, above all, that the Catholic representatives "be expert in doctrine, have moral integrity, and be good speakers" (August 28, 1968).

HUMANAE VITAE. Encyclical Letter of Pope Paul VI, subtitled "The Right Order to Be Followed in the Propagation of Human Offspring." There are four parts to the encyclical: 1. new aspects of a perennial problem; 2. competence of the Church's magisterium to resolve the problem; 3. doctrinal principles to be maintained; and 4. pastoral directives. One of the major issues restated by Paul VI is the Church's right to pass final judgment in moral matters not only where these are formally revealed but also where they "pertain to the natural moral law" (July 25, 1968).

HUMANISM. Name originally given to the intellectual, literary, and scientific movements of the fourteenth century through the early sixteenth. Their aim was to base every branch of learning on the culture of classical Greek and Roman antiquity. On its pagan side, it extolled the early non-Christian writers who stressed the full development of human nature, only vaguely interested in life after death. On its Christian side, believing humanists encouraged the free use of the treasures of antiquity without compromising the truths of the Gospel. Christian humanism began with Dante (1265–1321), while pagan humanism reached its peak in Petrarch (1304–74). Popes Pius II, Sixtus IV, and Leo X favored Christian humanism and did much to promote it. St. Thomas More (1478–1535) typified its best spirit in England. After the French Revolution the extreme humanistic spirit rebelled against Christian revelation and the Church.

HUMANITARIANISM. An ethical system that places temporal welfare of the human race as an exclusive goal of human effort and basic standard of conduct. It makes the personal and social good of human beings the primary object of human existence and subordinates, if it even considers, the worship of God to the interests of human beings.

HUMANITY. Mankind taken collectively. Also the condition of being human. As a virtue, the quality of being humane and kind, understanding the weakness and limitations of being human from one's own experience and self-awareness.

HUMAN NATURE. The nature of humankind considered abstractly and apart from its elevation by grace to a supernatural state with a heavenly destiny. It is the human as such, having a body and soul, capable of rational thought and voluntary decision. Actually human nature has never existed independent either of a supernatural destiny or of free acceptance or rejection of the supernatural invitation of God's grace.

HUMAN POSITIVE LAW. Legislation imposed by human authority, implementing the natural law. It may take one of two forms, declarative or specifying. Declarative positive laws simply declare in so many words what the natural law prescribes or draw conclusions deducible from the natural law. Such are laws forbidding murder, theft, or perjury. They differ from natural law only in the manner of promulgation, say by the State, and not only by the natural light of reason. Specifying positive laws determine or establish specific ways of acting in accordance with the natural law but not directly concluding from it. Such are traffic laws, ways of collecting taxes, and the conditions for just contracts. No human law that contradicts the natural law is a true law, but it need not merely re-echo the natural law.

HUMERAL VEIL. A long oblong piece of

silk or vestment material often richly ornamented or embroidered, worn over the shoulders and covering the hands of the priest as he gives the blessing with the Sacred Host in the monstrance at benediction (*Eucharistiae Sacramentum*, 1973, III, 92). It is also used when sacred vessels with their reserved contents are carried from one tabernacle to another or in procession. (Etym. Latin *humerus*, the shoulder.)

HUMILIATI. A penitential association of the laity formed about A.D. 1150. Some of the captives taken by Emperor Henry II from Lombardy to Germany devoted themselves to works of charity and penance and were called Barrettini. When they were allowed to return to Italy, they continued their German methods of living both as to industry, calling themselves Humiliati, and also as to modes of prayer, eventually adopting the Rule of St. Benedict. In 1134 they built their first monastery at Milan. St. Charles Borromeo, attempting to eliminate some serious abuses that had crept into the group, was murderously attacked by some of them and in 1571 the order was suppressed. The wives of these Humiliati established a community under Clara Blassoni, which cared for lepers. They were known as the Hospitalers of the Observance and continued even after the Humiliati were suppressed. Some of their houses engaged in charitable nursing are in existence today in Italy.

HUMILITY. The moral virtue that keeps a person from reaching beyond himself. It is the virtue that restrains the unruly desire for personal greatness and leads people to an orderly love of themselves based on a true appreciation of their position with respect to God and their neighbors. Religious humility recognizes one's total dependence on God; moral humility recognizes one's creaturely equality with others. Yet humility is not only opposed to pride; it is also opposed to immoderate self-abjection, which would fail to recognize God's gifts and use them according to his will. (Etym. Latin *humilitas*, abasement, humility, from *humus*, ground.)

HUR. An Israelite aide to Moses. During a battle with the Amalekites, the Israelites fought bravely so long as Moses stood on the hilltop holding aloft the staff of God. But when his arms tired and the staff wavered, the efforts of his men waned. So Aaron, his brother, and Hur seated Moses on a stone to rest him, and supported his arms so that the staff remained high and steady (Exodus 17:10–12). The battle ended triumphantly for the Israelites. Further evidence of confidence in Hur: when Yahweh summoned Moses to climb the mountain to receive the law and the commandments, Moses left instructions that during his absence conflicts were to be brought to Aaron and Hur for settlement (Exodus 24:14).

HUSBAND. A man joined to a woman in lawful marriage. His responsibilities toward his wife are expressed in the nuptial prayer, which the priest invokes during the wedding Mass: "May the husband put his trust in her and recognize that she is his equal and the heir with him in the life of grace. May he always honor her and love her as Christ loves His Bride, the Church."

HUSSITES. Followers of John Hus (1369–1415), who formed a religious sect in southern Bohemia in the early fifteenth century. They professed Utraquism, i.e., the necessity of receiving Communion under both species. This was preached by Hus, who told his followers that the true followers of Christ and St. Paul must receive the chalice. The Council of Constance ordered the extirpation of this heresy. The Bohemian and Moravian nobles thought the insinuation of heresy offensive and insulting, and they formed a dissenting league. With divergent views the Hussites divided into Taborites and Calixtines. Under Jan Žiška they united to fight the imperial armies, and the papal crusaders were sent to subdue them. For fifteen years they ravaged Bohemia. Finally in 1433 peace was obtained by the Compactata, which permitted Communion under both species provided the recipient declared that the whole Christ was present both under the form of bread and under the form of wine. This was to be a retraction of the basic Hussite thesis that Communion under both forms was necessary for salvation. Some were satisfied but not the Taborites, who finally disappeared from the scene after their defeat at the Battle of Lipany in 1434. The Compactata was adopted in 1436. Trouble continued, however, with armed conflict, so that Pope Pius II had to nullify the Utraquist rite. In 1485 King Wladislau granted equal civil rights to all parties. But the seeds of discord had been sown, to be reaped in the next century with the rise of the Reformation.

HYLOMORPHISM. The theory that all physical beings are composed of two principles of being: the prime matter, which is an undefined primitive, and a substantial form, which is a definite mode of existence. The two principles are related to each other as potency and act. This theory, which St. Thomas adopted from Aristotle, is based on two features that characterize all material things: the changeableness and the different individuals of a species. Both features can be explained only on the supposition that material things in their deepest nature are composed of two ultimate elements: prime matter, which remains constant in any change and gives individuality to each being; and substantial form, which accounts for the actual existence of different things, their distinctive properties, and the profound alteration that takes place when one substance changes into another. (Etym. Greek *hylē*, matter + *morphe*, contour, form.)

HYLOTHEISM. Materialistic pantheism, which identifies the deity with the material universe of space and time. (Etym. Greek *hylē*, matter + *theos*, god.)

HYLOZOISM. An ancient Greek theory, later defended by the Stoics and, in modern times, by the French materialists, which holds that all things are in some degree alive. Without accepting pure mechanism, they reject the real distinction between matter and spirit. Closely related to this is the pantheistic hylozoism of the Renaissance, taught by such nature philosophers as Paracelsus, Cardanus and Giordano Bruno. They held that everything is animated as a radiation of the divinity. Spinoza (1632–77) combined the materialistic and pantheistic forms of hylozoism and reduced everything in the universe to attributes of the one infinite substance. (Etym. Greek *hylē*, matter + *zōē*, life.)

HYMN. A religious song of honor and praise, or of petition addressed to God or the saints. Hymns appointed for liturgical use are mainly taken from the Scriptures or based on some mystery of the faith as taught by the Church. All hymns used in the liturgy must be approved by an ecclesiastical authority. (Etym. Latin *hymnus*, song of praise.)

HYMNODY. Religious lyric poetry different from epic poetry and distinct from profane lyric poetry. Catholic hymnody is divided into liturgical and nonliturgical. The former has hymns belonging by their nature to the Sacrifice of the Mass and the canonical hours such as are found in the Breviary. The nonliturgical embrace hymns for use in private devotion or during the liturgy when they are approved by the hierarchy.

HYPAPANTE. The feast of the Purification in the Byzantine Rite. The name comes from the meeting (*hypapante*) of the Christ Child and his Mother with the holy Simeon and Anna in the Temple.

HYPERDULIA. The special veneration due to the Blessed Virgin Mary. It is substantially less than the cultus *latria* (adoration), which is due to God alone. But it is higher than the cultus *dulia* (veneration), due to angels and other saints. As the Church understands the veneration of Mary, it is to be closely associated but subordinated to that of her Son. "The various forms of piety towards the Mother of God, which the Church has approved within the limits of sound and orthodox doctrine according to the dispositions and understanding of the faithful, ensure that while the mother is honored, the Son through whom all things have their being and in whom it has pleased the Father that all fulness should dwell, is rightly loved and glorified and His commandments are observed" (Second Vatican Council, *Lumen Gentium*, VII, 66). (Etym. Latin *hyperdulia*, virtue of deep submission.)

HYPNOTISM. The phenomenon of artificially induced sleep, which renders the victim abnormally open to suggestion. The subject of hypnosis tends to be dominated by the ideas and suggestions of the hypnotist while under the induced spell and later on. According to Catholic principles, hypnotism is not wrong in itself, so that its use under certain circumstances is permissible. But since it deprives the subject of the full use of reason and free will, a justifying cause is necessary for allowing it to be practiced. Moreover, because hypnotism puts the subject's will in the power of the hypnotist, certain precautions are necessary to safeguard the subject's virtue, and to protect him or her and others against the danger of being guilty of any injurious actions. For grave reasons, e.g., to cure a drunkard or one with a suicide complex, it is licit to exercise hypnotism, given the precaution that it is done in the presence of a trustworthy witness by a competent and upright hypnotist. The consent, at least presumed, of the subject must also be had. Several documents of the Holy See set down the norms to be followed in the use of hypnotism (*The Holy Office*, August 4, 1956; July 26, 1899).

HYPOCRISY. A form of lying in which a person pretends to have virtues or moral qualities that are not possessed. Its motive is pride and its malice depends on the gravity of the pride and on the evil consequences that follow when people take one to be morally good and, perhaps, entrust one with confidences or responsibilities that are not deserved. It is not hypocrisy, however, to be on one's best behavior with those whom one justly wishes to impress favorably. Nor is it hypocrisy when a person, because of human weakness, fails to live up to his or her own principles or profession of faith. (Etym. Latin *hypocrita,* hypocrite; from Greek *hypokritēs,* actor, hypocrite.)

HYPOSTASIS. An individual, complete substance existing entirely in itself; an incommunicable substance. The term used by the Church to identify the persons in the Trinity and the union of two natures in one divine person in Christ. A person is a hypostasis endowed with reason. Moreover, hypostasis and nature are related to each other in such a manner that the hypostasis is the bearer of the nature and the ultimate subject of all being and acting, while the nature is that through which the hypostasis exists and acts. (Etym. Latin *hypostasis,* basis; single substance; rational single substance, person; Greek *hypostasis,* support, foundation, substance, sediment.)

HYPOSTATIC UNION. The union of the human and divine natures in the one divine person of Christ. At the Council of Chalcedon (A.D. 451) the Church declared that the two natures of Christ are joined "in one person and one hypostasis" (Denzinger 302), where *hypostasis* means one substance. It was used to answer the Nestorian error of a merely accidental union of the two natures in Christ. The phrase "hypostatic union" was adopted a century later, at the fifth general council at Constantinople (A.D. 533). It is an adequate expression of Catholic doctrine about Jesus Christ that in him are two perfect natures, divine and human; that the divine person takes to himself, includes in his person a human nature; that the incarnate Son of God is an individual, complete substance; and that the union of the two natures is real (against Arius), no mere indwelling of God in a man (against Nestorius), with a rational soul (against

Apollinaris), and the divinity remains unchanged (against Eutyches).

HYPOTHESIS. Conditional explanation of perceived facts or their relationship. It is therefore never in conflict with definitely established truths, nor yet to be considered as definitive or certain. Its function is to offer a tentative explanation that suggests further experiment and verification. (Etym. Greek *hypothesis,* a placing under, supposition.)

HYPOTHETICAL MORALITY. See CONDITIONAL MORALITY.

HYSSOP. A plant of unknown identity, mentioned in the Scriptures. Found in Egypt, Sinai, and Canaan, it was used to sprinkle the blood of the paschal lamb or victims of sacrifice. It is referred to in the Psalm *Miserere* and in the Church's prayers.

HYSTERECTOMY. Partial or complete removal of the uterus. In general, the operation is morally justified if the removal of the uterus is necessary for grave medical reasons. It is not justified when the purpose is direct sterilization.

HYSTERIA. An emotional disorder that may defy ready diagnosis and yet deeply affects the moral responsibility of the hysterical person. It may assume various forms, notably: 1. conversion hysteria, where conflicts in the mind become disabilities in the body, such as paralysis, blindness, or lack of feeling; 2. sleepwalking; 3. flight, where the person loses all memory of the past; 4. multiple or split personality, when the individual becomes alternately different people with no conscious connection between successive states. Hysteria has been known for centuries, and is an object of the Church's special concern in investigation of persons reputed for sanctity, and of reported miracles in order to exclude the "cure" of hysterical sickness.

HYSTERON PROTERON. Begging the question. In logic, a fallacious argument in which a person assumes what he or she is supposed to prove.

I

I. *Imperata*—ordered oration.

I.C. Jesus—first and last letters of his name in Greek, *Ihcuc.*

ICHABOD. Grandson of Eli, he ruled Israel for forty years and died when he learned that the ark of Yahweh had been captured by the Philistines. At that very time his daughter-in-law, Phinehas' wife, was giving birth to a son. The realization that Eli was dead, that Phinehas had been killed in battle, and that the ark was now in alien hands impelled her to name the newborn "Ichabod" which means "inglorious" or "dishonor" in Hebrew (I Samuel 4:17–22). Ironically, the Philistines surrendered the ark within a few months, fearful of incurring Yahweh's wrath (I Samuel 6).

ICHTHUS. See FISH.

ICON. A flat painting, sacred picture of the Eastern Church. It is generally painted on wood and covered, except the face and hands, with relief of seed pearls and gold or silver. The icon of the saint of the day is usually displayed on an analogion. Icons of Our Lord and Our Lady are reverenced with great devotion, incensed, carried in processions, and normally placed on the iconostasis screen. The icons in the Eastern Church take the place of statues in the West. (Etym. Greek *eikōn,* image.)

ICONOCLASM. A heresy that rejected as superstition the use of religious images and advocated their destruction. It was occasioned by the rise of Islam, which considers all sacred images idolatrous. Moslem pressure on those in political power precipitated the crisis, which came in two phases. The first phase began with Emperor Leo the Isaurian in 726 and closed with the seventh general council and Second Council of Nicaea in 787. The second phase started with Emperor Leo V, the Armenian, and ended when the Feast of Orthodoxy was established in 842 under Empress Theodora. Sts. John Damascene and Theodore were the principal defenders of sacred images. As defined by II Nicaea, these images may be lawfully displayed and venerated. The respect shown them really is given to the person they represent. (Etym. Greek *eikōn,* image + *klaein,* to break.)

ICONOGRAPHY. The science of the description and interpretation of the traditional representations of sacred symbols in art as found in mosaics, statues, and pictures. Many of the scenes from the Bible and legends of the saints that decorate the walls and ceilings of Christian churches have historical as well as doctrinal importance. Iconography studies this significance. (Etym. Greek *eikōn,* image + *graphia,* writing, sketch.)

ICONOSTASIS. A solid screen dividing the sanctuary, in Eastern churches, from the body of the church, shutting off the altar from the worshipers. This barrier is pierced by three doors; the central one, or royal door, has a cross on top. It must also have on it at least two icons representing Our Lord and Our Lady, though it often has many more. The Gothic builders used the reredos to beautify their altars, and the Eastern churches used this ornamental screen.

ICXC NIKA. Monogram from Greek letters Ihcuc Xpictoc Nika, "Jesus Christ conqueror."

ID. *Idus*–ides.

IDEA. Originally meant the appearance or visible form of a thing existing apart from the thing itself. Consequently, the likeness within the mind of some reality that exists outside the mind. An idea is clear when it is distinct from other ideas; it is complete when it adequately represents the nature of what is mentally conceived; it is primitive when acquired directly from the object known; and derived when arrived at from other ideas by comparison and contrast. (Etym. Greek *idein,* to see.)

IDEAL. The criterion or standard of excellence which serves as a model for moral conduct. It carries the notion of something that exists only in the imagination and is therefore visionary, and yet may serve as stimulus and inspiration for human behavior.

IDEALISM. In the philosophy of Plato it is the theory that the visible things of this world are merely copies of the perfect realities of another, supersensible world of the spirit. In St. Augustine and the Scholastics it is the doctrine that the ideal or exemplar according to which everything is made is the idea in the mind of God. In modern philosophy idealism is the theory that denies reality to the external, physical world and attributes real existence only to things as they are in the mind. In its extreme form it is pure subjectivism, denying existence to anything outside the mind of the thinking person.

IDENTITY. Quality of sameness. Absolute identity is total sameness, without any change or difference; relative identity is all other sameness, which allows of numerous differences in nature and degree. Only God is and remains absolutely identical eternally. Creatures have relative identity, inasmuch as they have already changed when first created out of nothing; they further change, depending on the relative stability of their natures and (among angels and men) their persons; and they differ among themselves in myriad ways, but mainly in that each is a separate substance and, in human beings, a distinct and incommunicable individual.

IDENTITY CRISIS. Uncertainty experienced by some people about who they really are, as human beings, and what their role in life should be in the Church or in human society. Partly created by the intrusion of ideas alien to historic Christianity. Some believers are struggling between two images of themselves: an earlier one that was supported by a friendly culture and a later one that is being challenged for validity by a culture that is hostile or at least indifferent to authentic Christian values.

IDEOLOGY. The ideas that influence a whole group or society and motivate their conduct. It is immaterial whether these ideas are true or false; they become an ideology when they move a people to action. One of the features of the modern world is its capacity for creating new ideologies, or changing former ones, through the mass communications media.

IDIORRHYTHMIC. Descriptive of a form of monastic life in the Eastern Orthodox tradition. Idiorrhythmic monasteries date from the fifteenth century, and each is directed by two annually changed trustees. A spiritual father (*pneumatikos*) has charge of the interior life of the monks, and they meet for the Divine Office and for meals on feast days. But otherwise they live on their own, either alone or in a small group, and are therefore not a coenobium or monastic community.

IDLENESS. Unwillingness to work. The reason may be physical, because a person lacks the strength; or mental, because one does not know what to do; or moral, because of laziness that will not expend the effort needed perhaps even to begin a task or at least perform it as it should be done.

IDOL. Any creature that is given divine honors. It need not be a figure or representation, and may be a person. In fact, it may be oneself, or some creation of one's own mind or will. An object becomes an idol when it is treated as an end in itself, with no reference to God. (Etym. Latin *idolum*, image, picture, idol; from Greek *eidōlon*, phantom, idol.)

IDOLATRY. Literally "the worship of idols," it is giving divine honors to a creature. In the Decalogue it is part of the first commandment of God, in which Yahweh tells the people, "You shall have no gods except me. You shall not make yourself a carved image [Greek *eidōlon*, idol] or any likeness of anything in heaven or on earth or in the waters under the earth; you shall not bow down to them or serve them" (Exodus 20:4-5).

The early Christians were martyred for refusing to worship idols, even externally, but practical idolatry is a perennial threat to the worship of the one true God. Modern secularism is a form of practical idolatry, which claims to give man "freedom to be an end unto himself, the sole artisan and creator of his own history." Such freedom, it is said, "cannot be reconciled with the affirmation of a Lord who is author and purpose of all things," or at least that this freedom "makes such an affirmation altogether superfluous" (Second Vatican Council, *Constitution on the Church*, 51).

Idolatry is always gravely sinful. Even under threat of death and without interiorly believing in the idol, a Christian may not give divine honors to a creature, thereby violating the duty of professing faith in God.

IESOUS HEMETEROS SOTER. Jesus our Savior. Greek title found in early Christian inscriptions.

IESUS HOMINUM SALVATOR. Jesus Savior of Men. Latin inscription found on early Christian monuments. Abbreviated I.H.S.

IESUS NAZARENUS REX IUDAEORUM. Jesus of Nazareth, King of the Jews. Latin inscription over the cross of Christ on Calvary. Abbreviated I.N.R.I.

IGNORANCE. Lack of knowledge that should be present. Relative to imputability, the ignorance may be either culpable or inculpable, technically called vincible or invincible. (Etym. Latin *ignorantia*, ignorance, want of knowledge or information.)

IGNORANCE OF FACT. Lack of knowledge of some person, circumstance, or event that, if it had been known, would have prevented a person from doing or saying what he or she did.

IGNORANCE OF LAW. Lack of knowledge of some provision of law, civil or ecclesiastical, of its meaning or application in a given case. Culpability, then, will depend on how morally responsible one is for one's ignorance.

IGNORANTIA JURIS. Ignorance of the law. In civil jurisprudence, ignorance of the law does not excuse a person from its observance. But in ecclesiastical law, with some exceptions, sincere ignorance may not oblige in conscience. But where the validity of an act or sacrament is involved, even sincere ignorance of prescribed essentials does not prevent the action or the sacrament from being invalid.

IGR. *Igitur*—therefore.

I.H.S. *Iesus (Jesus) Hominum Salvator* (usual interpretation), Jesus Savior of Men. Really a faulty Latin transliteration of the first three letters of JESUS in Greek (IHS for IHC). See IESOUS HEMETEROS SOTER, IESUS HOMINUM SALVATOR, JESUS.

ILLEGITIMACY. According to Church law, the birth of children born less than six months after the date of a marriage, or more than ten months after the dissolution of conjugal life. Unless otherwise specified, children legitimized by a subsequent marriage are, as far as canonical effects are concerned, held equal to legitimate children. Unless there is proof to the contrary, the husband of a woman is considered the father of her child.

ILLICIT. That which is unlawful, or contrary to established prescriptions, but not necessarily invalid. Thus, according to ecclesiastical law many elements are prescribed, but not all (or most of them) are strictly necessary for a valid act or, in the sacraments, valid administration. (Etym. Latin *illicitus,* not allowed, forbidden, unlawful; from *licere,* to be permitted.)

ILLUMINATI. The name in the early Church for catechumens after their baptism. The term is generic for members of various sects inspired by the principles of illuminism, which claims to have access to specially infused knowledge from the divinity. Sometimes the title is loosely applied to such varied groups as the ancient Gnostics, who believed that the perfect life consisted in esoteric knowledge and contemplation; the Montanists, who sought perfection in gifts of prophecy and ecstasy; and the Beghards, who held that the soul can reach an intuitive vision of God on earth. More properly Illuminati refer to the Alumbrados in the sixteenth century and a masonic society in recent times.

ILLUMINATING GRACE. Actual grace conferred by God to enlighten the mind. Its main function is to enable a person to believe with certitude in God's revelations, and to better understand the mysteries of faith and of divine providence. It is thus fundamental in the spiritual life, since moral conduct and sanctity absolutely depend on the prior convictions of faith which reside in the intellect illuminated by God's grace.

ILLUMINATION. Any manifestation of the truth, or assistance to the intellect in better understanding the truth. In Augustinian philosophy, the function of the divine light within the human mind to enable it to acquire new spiritual knowledge. In Thomistic philosophy the operation of the "active intellect" to "light up" the essence of sense perceptions so they become intelligible to the "passive intellect." In theology, the role of divine grace to illumine the intellect in order to believe what God has revealed and assist the mind to better understand what it believes.

ILLUMINATIVE WAY. The intermediary stage between purification and union on the path to Christian perfection. Also called the "Way of the Proficients," the main feature of the Illuminative Way is an enlightenment of the mind in the ways of God and a clear understanding of his will in one's state of life.

ILLUMINISM. A form of Gnosticism, it appears in the history of Christian heresy as a belief in one's own divine enlightenment, with a sense of mission to enlighten others, contrary to the express teachings of the Church's magisterium.

ILLUSION. An idea or mental state not consistent with reality, it carries the notion of being deceived and yet acting on one's erroneous concepts.

IL SASSO. A shrine of Madonna del Sasso, nine miles northeast of Florence, Italy. Sometimes called Our Lady of Grace, it is located in a fortress-like church on the top of the Rock overlooking the little village of Santa Brigida. Enfolded in her dark mantle, Mary is holding her Divine Child on her left arm, his bare feet cuddled partially in the folds. Each head is encircled with a brilliant halo. It was at this shrine that the Christian observance of May 1 began in Italy after World War II.

IMAGE. A representation or likeness of something. It corresponds to "exemplar" and implies that one thing (the image) is both a reflection and pattern of something else. In this sense the word has come to mean an attitudinal or judgmental reaction toward a person, an institution, or a people. Thus we now speak of "image makers" or "image builders" to describe the use of publicity and propaganda to create or maintain a favorable impression before the public.

(Etym. Latin *imago,* copy, likeness, image, picture; pattern, model.)

IMAGES, VEILING OF. The custom in many rites of the Catholic Church of covering all crosses, pictures, and statues with plain purple cloth from two Sundays before Easter until the liturgy on Good Friday. In the Roman Rite the custom is no longer practiced, although in the liturgy on Good Friday there is an optional unveiling of the Cross before its veneration by the celebrant and people.

IMAGES, VENERATION OF. Honor paid to representations of Christ and the saints. Their purpose is to adorn, instruct, and excite to piety those who behold, wear, or carry images on their persons. According to the Council of Trent, images of Christ, of the Mother of God, and other canonized saints are to be kept in churches and due honor paid to them not because there is any divinity or power inherent in them as images, but because the honor shown to them is referred to the prototypes they represent. Through the worship and reverence so shown, the faithful really worship Christ and honor the saints whose likenesses they display. In other words, the veneration is relative, always being referred back to the original, never absolute as though the material object is being venerated in and for itself.

IMAGINATION. The internal senses that can know absent sensible things, but not as absent from the particular sense that experiences them. There are six such internal senses: of sight, sound, taste, touch, smell, and a general somatic sense of feeling.

IMAGINATIVE VISION. Supernatural perception produced in the imagination by God or by the angels, either during sleep or during periods of being awake. Thus an angel appeared several times to St. Joseph in his sleep (Matthew 1:20, 2:13, 19). St. Teresa of Avila relates that she had imaginative visions of Christ while she was fully awake (*Autobiography,* chapter 28).

IMITATION. The conscious act or process of seeking to reproduce the desirable features or qualities of another, especially of another person. The term applies first to the field of representative art, which strives to reproduce as faithfully as possible the natural forms it is depicting. But its wider use is in Christian spirituality, where Christ is seen as the perfect exemplar for his followers to imitate. His human nature thus becomes the model for Christians to reproduce, and in the process they are becoming more God-like since Christ is also divine.

IMITATION OF CHRIST. A devotional book published anonymously in 1418. Sometimes called *The Following of Christ,* it contains counsels of perfection. The authorship is now attributed to Thomas à Kempis, a canon of the Netherlands. It was written in Latin in a familiar style and divided into four books: useful admonitions for a spiritual life; further admonitions relative to spiritual things; interior consolations; and the Blessed Sacrament. It is a popular book also outside of Catholic circles, generally with the fourth book omitted. Its basic theme is that, since Jesus Christ is true God and true man, by imitating Christ as man the Christian becomes more and more like Christ, who is God. Next to the Bible it is the most widely read spiritual book in the world.

IMITATION OF SAINTS. The practice of striving to put into practice in one's own life the virtues that the saints practiced in theirs. This is one of the reasons why the Church canonizes saints, to give the faithful secure patterns of holiness in every period of Christian history and on every level of human society.

IMMACULATE CONCEPTION. Title of the Blessed Virgin as sinless from her first moment of existence. In the words of Pope Pius IX's solemn definition, made in 1854, "The most holy Virgin Mary was, in the first moment of her conception, by a unique gift of grace and privilege of almighty God, in view of the merits of Jesus Christ the Redeemer of mankind, preserved free from all stain of original sin." This means that since the first moment of her human existence the mother of Jesus was preserved from the common defect of estrangement from God, which humanity in general inherits through the sin of Adam. Her freedom from sin was an unmerited gift of God or special *grace,* and an exception to the law, or *privilege,* which no other created person has received.

Neither the Greek nor Latin Fathers explicitly taught the Immaculate Conception, but they professed it implicitly in two fundamental ways. Mary, they said, was most perfect in purity of morals and holiness of life. St. Ephrem (c. 306–73) addressed Christ and Mary with the words "You and Your mother are the only ones who are totally beautiful in every way. For in You, O Lord, there is no stain, and in Your mother no stain." Mary was described as the antithesis of Eve. Again in Ephrem, "Mary and Eve

[were] two people without guilt. Later one became the cause of our death, the other cause of our life." While implicit in the early writers, the Immaculate Conception had to be clarified before becoming explicit dogma. Main credit for this goes to the Franciscan John Duns Scotus (c. 1264–1308), who introduced the idea of pre-redemption in order to reconcile Mary's freedom from original sin with her conception before the coming of Christ. (Etym. Latin im-, not + maculare, to stain.)

IMMACULATE CONCEPTION, SCAPULAR. A blue scapular, having on one part a picture of the Immaculate Conception and on the other the name of Mary. Established by Ursula Benincasa, foundress of the Theatine nuns, the Sisters of the Immaculate Conception of the Virgin Mary.

IMMACULATE HEART. The physical heart of the Blessed Virgin Mary as a sign and symbol of her compassion and sinlessness, and the object of devotion by the faithful. Devotion to the Immaculate Heart of Mary gained international prominence through the Fátima apparitions in 1917, and their subsequent approval by the Holy See. A widely used prayer capsulizing this devotion reads:

"Virgin of Fátima, Mother of mercy, Queen of heaven and earth, refuge of sinners, we consecrate ourselves to your Immaculate Heart. To you we consecrate our hearts, our souls, our families, and all we have.

"And in order that this consecration may be truly effective and lasting, we renew today the promises of our Baptism and Confirmation; and we undertake to live as good Christians—faithful to God, the Church and the Holy Father. We desire to pray the Rosary, partake in the Holy Eucharist, attach special importance to the first Saturday of the month and work for the conversion of sinners.

"Furthermore we promise, O most holy Virgin, that we will zealously spread devotion to you, so that through our consecration to your Immaculate Heart and through your own intercession the coming of the Kingdom of Christ in the world may be hastened. Amen."

IMMACULATE HEART OF MARY, SCAPULAR. Badge of the Sons of the Immaculate Heart of Mary. It is white, with a picture of the Heart of Mary surrounded by flames, surmounted by a lily, encircled with roses, and pierced by a sword.

IMMANENCE. Presence or operation within someone or something. Total "within-ness." As an operation, an immanent act begins within and remains within the person whom it perfects in the process. Thus acts of reflection and love are immanent acts of a human being. They may, of course, have effects outside the mind and will, but essentially they arise within and stay within the faculties by which they are produced. (Etym. Latin immanere, to remain in, hold to.)

IMMANENTIST APOLOGETICS. A method of establishing the credibility of the Christian faith by appealing to the subjective satisfaction that the faith gives to a believer. This method tends to ignore, if not deny, the corresponding value of objective criteria for accepting divine revelation, notably miracles and prophecies. The latter alone are finally demonstrative of the fact of revelation. Therefore immanentist apologetics runs the danger of leaving Christians with purely personal motives for their faith and without intellectually convincing grounds as to why they believe.

IMMANENT THEISM. The doctrine that God transcends the world as its Creator and yet is immanent in the world as its most intimate and provident First Cause.

IMMATERIAL. Not having matter or the properties of matter. Negatively it is the noncorporeal; positively the spiritual. What is immaterial has no extension in space, no size, shape, parts, or quantity, no mass or weight. It is nonmeasurable reality. Three kinds of immateriality are known to Christian thought: Some beings are partially without matter but essentially dependent on matter for their existence and operation, e.g., the power of sensation. Others are essentially spiritual and independent of matter for their existence but in this life depend on matter for their operation, e.g., the human soul in its activity of knowing and loving. Still others are totally immaterial because they are independent of matter for their existence and activity. Thus the angels, who are pure spirits, whose immateriality is a created gift, and God, who is immaterial by his essence.

IMMENSITY. The quality of being immeasurable, either because the nature of something is spiritual, such as that of angels or the human soul; or because someone is sublime and by his essence is beyond all spatial dimensions. The term was consecrated by the Fourth Lateran Council in answer to the Albigenses, who restored the Manichaean notion of deities who occupied (and were circumscribed by) the earthly and stellar regions. In the first article of a first-century creed we read: "For the first thing, believe that there is only one God . . . who encompasses everything, while He alone cannot be encompassed" (Pastor Hermae, I, 1). (Etym. Latin *immensus,* immeasurable, boundless.)

IMMERSION. The method of baptism by dipping or plunging the candidate under water while the one baptizing says, "I baptize you in the name of the Father, and of the Son, and of the Holy Spirit." It is one of the three valid forms of baptism and was the method generally used in the early Church. It is still commonly used in the Eastern Church and in certain Protestant Churches, notably in the Baptist tradition. The Catholic Church in the Latin Rite has reintroduced the practice as a permissible option, since the Second Vatican Council.

IMMODEST LOOKS. The conscious looking at a person, picture, or scene that arouses sexual feelings to which a person has no moral right or need to experience. Since sexual feelings are sacred, to which only married persons between themselves have a claim, deliberately to look at something in order to be sexually stimulated is a grave sin (Matthew 5:28).

IMMOLATION. The actual or equivalent destruction of some material object as an act of sacrifice. When the destruction is done actually, the object is radically changed, as when an animal is killed or wine is poured out. When the destruction is not done but is equivalent, it is called mystical or symbolic, as occurs in the sacrifice of the Mass, where the separate consecration of the bread and wine symbolizes the separation of Christ's body and blood on Calvary. Christ does not actually die in the Mass, but he manifests his willingness to die symbolically by the double consecration. (Etym. Latin *immolatio,* sacrifice.)

IMMORAL. Popular equivalent of licentious or dissolute, or acting contrary to established norms of behavior.

IMMORALISM. Not only moral indifference but, as in Nietzsche, positively combatting traditional Christian moral principles.

IMMORTALITY. Freedom from death or the capacity to decay and disintegrate. Absolute immortality is possessed by God alone, who has no body and whose spirit is eternal by essence. He cannot not exist; he always has been and must be. Natural immortality belongs to all spiritual beings, namely the angels and human souls, who are created indeed and therefore begin, but since they are simple by nature and have no parts, they will not die, although absolutely speaking, they could be annihilated by an act of God. Gratuitous immortality is a special grace, given originally by God to the ancestors of the human race and restored by Christ as a promise after the last day. It means freedom from bodily death and from separation of the soul from the human body.

IMMOVABLE MOVER. God as the ultimate cause of all motion or change in the universe, himself remaining unchanged. The term used by Aristotle and later by St. Thomas Aquinas, i.e., *motor immobile,* where *motor* means the one who changes, and *immobile* is unchangeable.

IMMUNITY. Freedom from something, which may be from antecedent necessity or a person's claim to liberty from interference in exercising his or her natural or conferred rights. Term commonly used to describe exemption of the Church's clergy and religious from civic duties (such as military service) regarded as incompatible with their state of life. In morality, it is applied to the condition of certain persons by which they are able to resist the pressures to conformity of a secular culture or environment.

IMMURATION. A shutting up, an enclosing. The symbolic closing of the door of a cloistered cell, voluntarily done, by a religious who attends the religious services through an opening in the chapel wall. In some cases, rare nowadays, food, light, and air are received through a window of the hermitage that is built adjoining the chapel proper. It also refers to a method of burial by which bodies are enclosed in chambers and vaults of solid masonry, for example where the native soil is impracticable for burial. Mummified bodies recovered from such places were falsely exhibited as "walled up nuns" or "victims of the Inquisition" by unscrupulous controversialists.

IMMUTABILITY IN CREATURES. Unchangeableness, which means both unchanging and not able to change or be changed. Perfect immutability is possessed only by God. Creatures participate more or less in the divine immutability as they are more perfect in being, like the soul compared with the body; or when they grow in perfection, as when the mind acquires greater certitude or the will greater fortitude.

IMMUTABILITY OF GOD. Absolute

changelessness. That is mutable which goes from one condition to another. In consequence of its finite nature, every creature is mutable. God is unchangeable because he is infinite. Mutability implies potentiality, composition, and imperfection, and is therefore not reconcilable with God as pure actuality, the absolutely simple and infinitely perfect Being. When God acts outside of himself, as in the creation of the world, he does not produce a new effect in himself, but enters on a new realization of the eternal decision of his divine will. The decree of creation is as eternal and immutable as the Divine Essence with which it is really identical; only its effect, the created world, is temporal and changeable. (Etym. Latin *immutabilis*, unchangeable; changeless.)

IMPANATION. A heretical doctrine or theory of the Eucharistic presence, taught by some of the Protestant Reformers. It claims that the words of consecration do not change bread and wine into the body and blood of Christ. Rather the substance of bread and wine remains, along with some kind of indefinable presence of Christ. Originally taught by Osiander (1498–1552), a disciple of Luther, it was one of the many attempts of the Reformers to retain some kind of "real presence" in the Eucharist while denying transubstantiation. (Etym. Latin *in-*, in + *panis*, bread.) See also CONSUBSTANTIATION.

IMPASSIBILITY. Quality of the glorified human body in being free from every kind of physical evil, such as sorrow or sickness, injury or death. It may be defined as the impossibility to suffer and to die (Revelation 21:4). The inherent reason for impassibility consists in the perfect compliance of the body and emotions to the soul. (Etym. Latin *in-*, not + *passibilis*, able to suffer; *impassibilis*, incapable of suffering.)

IMPASSIBILITY, ORIGINAL. The freedom from suffering experienced by Adam and Eve before the Fall. This gift may be defined as the possibility of remaining free from suffering. It was associated with bodily immortality.

IMPECCABILITY OF CHRIST. The absolute impossibility of Christ committing any sin. His freedom from original sin was declared by the Council of Florence (Denzinger 1347), from personal sin by the Council of Chalcedon (Denzinger 301), and the Second Council of Constantinople condemned the theory that Christ became completely impeccable only after the Resurrection (Denzinger 434). (Etym. Latin *im-*, not + *peccare*, to sin: *impeccabilitas*, freedom from liability to sin.)

IMPEDIENT IMPEDIMENT. An obstacle that affects one or both parties wishing to get married and that makes their marriage illicit unless they have received proper dispensation from the Church. Yet if they marry their marriage is valid. Also called inhibiting impediment.

IMPEDIMENT. Any obstacle to progress or activity, and in the moral order whatever hinders a person from achieving the spiritual perfection intended for him or her by God. Such would be inordinate attachments, though not sinful, to some creature that stands in the way of complete surrender to the will of God. In theology and canon law an impediment is any hindrance to the validity or legality of some action or its effects. (Etym. Latin *impedimentum*, an impediment, hindrance; from *impedire*, to entangle the feet.)

IMPENDING DEATH. Certainty of an early death due to illness or fatal disability. The moral responsibility of knowing one's own impending death is the duty of preparing oneself spiritually for entrance into eternity. On the part of the physician, he or she is obliged in charity to warn the patient or near relatives of the danger of death, so that the dying person may arrange his or her spiritual and temporal affairs. This duty would not be binding if the doctor could not give the warning without grave inconvenience. With regard to newborn babies, the doctor should see to it that they are baptized if they are in immediate danger of death, unless it is foreseen that such action would prove gravely detrimental to the doctor or to the Church.

IMPENETRABILITY. The quality of an extended body which makes it impossible for another body to penetrate it so that both occupy the same space at the same time.

IMPENITENCE, FINAL. Dying unreconciled with God, whether through loss of faith, or through despair, or through a blasphemous rejection of God's love.

IMPERFECT CONTRITION. Sorrow for sin animated by a supernatural motive that is less than a perfect love of God. Some of the motives for imperfect contrition are the fear of the pains of hell, of losing heaven, of being punished by God in this life for one's sins, of being judged by God; the sense of disobedience to God or of ingratitude toward him; the realization of lost merit or of sanctifying grace. Also called attrition, imperfect contrition is sufficient for remission of sin in the sacrament of penance. It is also adequate for a valid and fruitful reception of baptism by one who has reached the age of reason. And if a person is unable to go to confession, imperfect contrition remits even grave sin through the sacrament of anointing of the sick.

IMPERFECT DIVORCE. See DIVORCE.

IMPERFECTION, NEGATIVE. A lack of greater perfection in a human act, due to a variety of causes but not consciously willed by a person. Thus, to give a poor person alms is a morally good act. Giving that person more than one actually had given would ordinarily be a greater perfection; hence the alms, in themselves, may be considered negatively imperfect. Negative imperfections are not sinful because they are not voluntary.

IMPERFECTION, POSITIVE. A lack of greater perfection in a human act that is clearly adverted to and deliberately chosen. Positive imperfection occurs if one excludes an action that is better than another, from the standpoint of content and meaning, or more clearly suitable to the person who performs the act. This may be on the basis of a direct analysis of the action itself or a clear inspiration of the Holy Spirit. It implies the choice between doing and omitting something, or between acceptance of what is good and refusal of what is better. This refusal cannot be due to a reasonable motive. It can only be one of the many forms of egoism, and therefore makes such positive imperfections venially sinful. Some theologians argue that, in theory, even positive imperfections may not be morally wrong. In practice, however, the more common doctrine holds that there is at least some selfish, and to that extent sinful, motivation whenever a lesser good is deliberately chosen in preference to a greater one that could, then and there, be performed.

IMPERIUM. The act of command. More properly, the right of an authority in any society to make laws binding in conscience on the members of that society. It begins as an act of reason in a ruler who seeks the common good, then decides on what means are necessary to attain it, and finally orders that these means be carried into effect. (Etym. Latin *imperium*, chief, imperial power; empire, kingdom; command.)

IMPETRATION. One of the fruits of prayer and good works, especially one of the four ends of the Eucharistic Sacrifice. Impetration with right disposition and the fulfillment of prescribed conditions invariably obtains from God what is asked of him, provided it is to our spiritual advantage. It is ensured petition. (Etym. Latin *impetratio*, the action of procuring or obtaining by request or entreaty.) See also ENDS OF THE MASS.

IMPOSITION OF HANDS. The laying on of hands on a person or thing to convey the communication of some favor, power, duty, or blessing. Patriarchs in the Old Testament used it in blessing children, in consecrating priests, and in sacrifice. In the New Testament it is shown with Christ performing miracles and with the Apostles conferring the sacraments, especially the priesthood. Catholic liturgy employs it now in public baptism, confirmation, and anointing of the sick and holy orders; in other rites and blessings such as exorcisms and before the consecration of the Mass when the priest extends his hands over the bread and wine.

IMPOTENCE. Incapacity for marital intercourse. Impotence, unlike sterility, hinders the human act of generation, that is, the copula. Impotence that is prior to marriage and is permanent, whether on the part of the man or the woman, whether known to the other party or not, whether absolute or relative, invalidates marriage by the natural law. Absolute impotence prevents marital intercourse with all other persons; relative impotence prevents it only with a certain person or persons.

IMPRECATORY PSALMS. Those in which the psalmist pronounces a curse over the enemies of God and God's people, as when David prays, "May no one be left to show him kindness, may no one look after his orphans, may his family die out, its name disappear in one generation" (Psalm 109:12–13). Such imprecations should be seen as the ardent expressions of the Oriental mind, and written under divine inspiration. They were not only statements of the human author, asking God to punish evildoers, but in prophetic terms foretold the divine intention, i.e., what God was going to do to those who resisted his will. (Etym. Latin *in-* + *precari*, to pray: *imprecor*, to call upon, to invoke on a person.)

IMPRIMATUR. The Latin term for "let it be printed," which signifies the approval by a bishop of a religious work for publication. Authors are at liberty to obtain the imprimatur either from the bishop where they reside, or where the book is to be published, or where it is printed. Generally the imprimatur, along with the bishop's name and date of approval, is to be shown in the publication. According to a decree of the Sacred Congregation for the Doctrine of the Faith (1975), "the Pastors of the Church have the duty and the right to be vigilant lest the faith and morals of the faithful be harmed by writings; and consequently even to demand that the publication of writings concerning the faith and morals should be submitted to the Church's approval, and also to condemn books and writings that attack faith or morals." (Etym. Latin *imprimere,* to impress, stamp imprint.)

IMPRIMI POTEST. It can be printed. Permission that a religious receives from his major superior to publish a manuscript on a religious subject. This implies approval of the writing by the superior and clearance to receive a bishop's imprimatur.

IMPRUDENCE. Sins against prudence that are either by defect or by excess. Sins by defect against prudence are: rashness, which acts before due consideration has been given; thoughtlessness, which neglects to take the necessary circumstances into account; and negligence, which does not give the mind sufficient time for mature deliberation. Sins by excess against the virtue of prudence are: imprudence of the flesh, which eagerly seeks means that gratify self without regard for the means that are required by God; astuteness, which looks for devious means for attaining one's goal; and undue solicitude about the temporal future with resulting neglect to provide for eternity and the needs of the soul. (Etym. Latin *improvidentia,* want of foresight; *imprudentia,* lack of foreseeing in the practical order.)

IMPULSE. Any sudden, unreasonable urge to action, often induced by an emotion. Impulses are natural when explainable in terms of antecedent thoughts or feelings. They are supernatural when they incline to something good without any assignable cause, especially when the inclination arises in the context of prayer or resignation to the will of God. They can also be preternatural and demonic, as when they impel a person with a furious intensity to do something particularly offensive, such as blasphemy. (Etym. Latin *impellere,* to impel, incite, urge, instigate, stimulate, persuade, from *im-,* on + *pellere,* to drive.)

IMPURE DESIRES. Sexually oriented impulses to which a person should not deliberately yield, although the action would not be externally performed. Thus adultery, fornication, and other sexual aberrations, when fully consented to, are gravely sinful even as merely internal experiences.

IMPURE THOUGHTS. Sexually arousing thoughts that a person may not deliberately entertain because they lead to the sinful desire to commit adultery, fornication, masturbation, or homosexuality.

IMPURITY. A common term for sins of lust, whether internal or external. Internal sins of lust are interior thoughts or desires that are not carried out in practice. They may take on a variety of forms, e.g., taking pleasure in sexual imaginative representations, complacently enjoying previous sinful venereal experiences, desiring unlawful sexual pleasures. Otherwise the sins are external.

IMPUTABILITY. The moral responsibility for one's human actions. A person is accountable to God only for his or her deliberate actions. They are acts performed with knowledge of what one is doing and with the consent of the will. In order to gauge the accountability of a particular action, one must consider the degree of deliberateness involved. If a person's knowledge of the nature of the act or his or her consent is diminished, the imputability will be lessened. Catholic moral theology recognizes six chief hindrances to full imputability: ignorance, fear, passion, habits, violence, and mental disorder. (Etym. Latin *in-,* in + *putare,* to consider: *imputare,* to bring a fault into the reckoning; to ascribe.)

IMPUTATION. Attribute praise or, more generally, blame to someone whether the person is actually responsible or not. In Reformation theology the doctrine that says their sins are not imputed to those who are destined to be saved, because of the holiness of Christ. The same term is sometimes applied to Christ in the opposite sense. He allowed himself to be considered a sinner although he was innocent, and this humiliating imputation merited man's salvation.

IMPUTED JUSTICE. A Reformation theory that God ceases to impute to a sinner the guilt of one's sins because the merits of Christ are imputed to one in justification. The theory was condemned by the Council of Trent, which declared that, through justification, the sinner is not merely no longer considered sinful (because of Christ's imputed merits) but becomes a child of

God, possessed of sanctifying grace and having a right to heaven.

INALIENABLE RIGHTS. Rights that are not morally renounceable. They can be neither taken away nor given away legitimately, because they are necessary to the attainment of one's destiny or the fulfillment of a moral duty. Such is the right to life.

IN ARTICULO MORTIS. At the moment of death, or a moment before death. The phrase applies especially to some significant statement that a person consciously makes, such as an admission of guilt or a sudden act of contrition, just as he or she is about to enter eternity.

INCARDINATION. The canonical attachment of a cleric to a particular diocese, with correlative rights and duties under the local ordinary. At one time incardination took place when a seminarian for the diocesan priesthood received his first tonsure. Since the Second Vatican Council, with the elimination of minor orders and the subdiaconate, under Pope Paul VI, incardination takes place with the reception of the diaconate.

INCARNATION. The union of the divine nature of the Son of God with human nature in the person of Jesus Christ. The Son of God assumed our flesh, body, and soul, and dwelled among us like one of us in order to redeem us. His divine nature was substantially united to our human nature. Formerly the Feast of the Annunciation was called the Feast of the Incarnation. In the Eastern Churches the mystery is commemorated by a special feast on December 26. (Etym. Latin *incarnatio;* from *in-,* in + *caro,* flesh: *incarnare,* to make flesh.)

INCARNATIONAL. Like Christ, who is God become man, the adaptation of the divine to the human, the eternal to the temporal, in the preaching and teaching of the Gospel. Always without compromise of revealed truth, it is the Church's readiness to adjust her message to the culture of the people, even as Christ became incarnate not only in the human nature he assumed as God, but in the society and the times in which he lived. (Etym. Latin *incarnare,* to make flesh; Latin *in-* + *caro,* flesh.)

INCENSE. Aromatic gum or resin in the form of powder or grains that give off a fragrant smoke when they are burned. When blessed it is a symbolic sacramental. Its burning signifies zeal or fervor; its fragrance, virtue; its rising smoke, human

prayer ascending to God. It is used at Mass, for the Gospel book, the altar, the people, the ministers, and the bread and wine; before consecration; at benediction of the Blessed Sacrament; during processions; and at absolutions of the dead. When it is to be used, it is carried in a metal cup-shaped container and burned in a thurible or censer. Five large grains of it are placed in the Paschal candle at the Easter Vigil to symbolize the Five Wounds of the Risen Savior. In some countries it is placed in a stationary censer to burn slowly before the Blessed Sacrament, either exposed or reserved on the altar. (Etym. Latin *incensum,* incense; literally, something burned; from *incendere,* to kindle.)

INCENSE BOAT. A sacred vessel, oblong in shape, in which incense is kept and transferred to a censer by means of a spoon.

INCENTIVE. That which incites a person to action. It is different from motive, which is in the mind as a final cause or purpose for doing something or refraining from it. An incentive is in the will or feelings, as love or hate or disposition, and thus impelling (or appealing) one to act. Actual grace as inspiration may be described as a supernatural incentive.

INCEST. Sexual intercourse between those who are related by blood or marriage and whom the Church forbids to marry. It is a sin both against chastity and the virtue of piety or reverence due to those closely related to us. Between parent and child, or brother and sister it is also a crime against nature. (Etym. Latin *in-,* not + *castus,* chastity: *incestus,* unchastity, incest.)

IN COMMENDAM. Obtaining benefits from an ecclesiastical benefice temporarily, during a vacancy in the regular administration. Eventually the term referred to benefices that bishops or other prelates held besides their own sees, or from which lay persons might get revenue without spiritual jurisdiction or, in fact, without ever visiting or seeing. Numerous Church laws sought to restrain the practice because of the abuses to which it gave rise, from as early as the eighth century.

INCOMMUNICABLE ATTRIBUTE. Divine perfection that can be possessed by God alone, as his infinity, omniscience, or omnipresence.

INCOMPREHENSIBLE. That which cannot be fully understood. In one sense nothing is totally comprehensible by humans since they are not the first cause of anything. But, properly speaking, only God is said to be incomprehensible because only he is infinitely perfect and no finite mind can exhaustively understand the infinite. The Church teaches that God is incomprehensible (Denzinger 800). However, there is a difference between his incomprehensibility on earth and in heaven. On earth God is incomprehensible because he is known only by faith; in heaven he is still incomprehensible because he is infinite, even though in the beatific vision we shall see him in his essence as he is. Although not comprehensible, God is not unintelligible. He can be known, here by faith and hereafter by sight. But neither on earth nor in heaven can he be totally known in the fullness of his own comprehensive knowledge of himself. "God whose Being is infinite, is infinitely knowable. No created understanding can, however, know God in an infinite manner" (St. Thomas Aquinas, *Summa Theologica*, I, 12, 7).

INCONTINENCE. Failure to restrain one's sexual impulses within the legitimate bounds of marriage.

INCORRUPTIBILITY. Incapacity of decay or destruction. This may be absolute, as God, who is wholly unchangeable by nature; or natural, as the angels and souls, which, being spirits, cannot disintegrate by decomposition; or substantial, as in physical nature, whose elements can be variously recombined but in their ultimate constituents are not destroyed.

INCREASE OF MERIT. Factors that increase a person's supernatural reward for good works performed in the state of grace. There are four such factors: 1. the degree of sanctifying grace in which a person does some morally good action; 2. the intensity of will with which an act is done; 3. the sublimity of the action performed; and 4. the purity of love or selflessness that animates the performance. Difficulties of themselves do not increase supernatural merit, but, provided that a difficulty is not culpable, it normally demands additional effort of will and thus indirectly adds to the merit derived from a morally good act done in the state of grace.

INCULPABLE. Not morally responsible for some objectively evil action. It assumes that a person did something wrong but through ignorance, or because of emotional pressure or coercion, is not really guilty before God. Inculpability is identified with material, as distinct from formal, guilt, or sin.

INCUMBENT. The holder of an ecclesiastical office or benefice, such as a diocese, parish, or monastery.

IND. Index.

IND. *Indictio*—indiction.

INDEFECTIBILITY. Imperishable duration of the Church and her immutability until the end of time. The First Vatican Council declared that the Church possesses "an unconquered stability" and that, "built on a rock, she will continue to stand until the end of time" (Denzinger 3013, 3056). The Church's indefectibility, therefore, means that she now is and will always remain the institution of salvation, founded by Christ. This affirms that the Church is essentially unchangeable in her teaching, her constitution, and her liturgy. It does not exclude modifications that do not affect her substance, nor does it exclude the decay of individual local churches or even whole dioceses.

INDEPENDENCE. Freedom of being or action. It implies separateness or disconnection from another and, to that extent, does not have need or support of another. Applied to the Church, it means that she is not subordinate to the State as though dependent on the State for her existence, government, or ministry. The State, too, on its part is believed to be independent of the Church in what concerns the temporal welfare of the citizens, yet the State is not independent of the natural law or of religion.

INDETERMINISM. The principle of philosophy which holds that the human will, in some of its acts, is free; that it is not determined absolutely by heredity, education, or environment from outside of a person, nor by ideas, feelings and desires inside of a person. Human beings can, at times, act just as they please irrespective of all other factors except the one factor of their own free will.

INDEX EXPURGATORIUS. A list of books to be censored before they can be read by Roman Catholics. It was first listed separately from, but later was included in, the general *Index Librorum Prohibitorum* (Index of Forbidden Books).

INDEX OF FORBIDDEN BOOKS. A list of books that Catholics were forbidden by ecclesiastical authority to read or retain without authorization. The books so condemned were considered heretical, dangerous to morals, or otherwise objectionable. The Index was published by authority of the

Holy Office. After the Second Vatican Council its publication was discontinued, but a new set of regulations was published by the Holy See, giving specific norms on the reading of books that are dangerous to the Catholic faith or to Christian morality.

INDICTION. The fiscal period of fifteen years adopted by Emperor Constantine (c. 274–337). It is the chronological epoch used in papal and other documents. For ecclesiastical purposes Pope St. Gregory fixed January 1, 313, as the date of its having started, and it is still noted in the Roman calendar. (Etym. Latin *in-*, in + *dicere*, to say: *indictio*, declaration, appointment, especially appointment of tax.)

INDIFFERENCE. The state of not being determined to act or not act, to act in one way rather than another. Among persons, active indifference is the ability to determine oneself to a given course of action; passive indifference is the capacity to be moved or determined by someone else. In ascetical theology, indifference is the state of being freed from inordinate attachments or desires that would keep a person from total dedication to God. It is internal liberty that enables the soul to give itself unreservedly to follow Christ.

INDIFFERENT ACT. The theory that some human actions, though conscious and deliberate, are morally indifferent, that is, neither good nor bad. Defended by Duns Scotus (c. 1264–1308) and his followers, it is not commonly held by Catholic moralists. Following St. Thomas Aquinas, they admit that in the abstract a human act can be morally indifferent, but not when considered individually in the concrete. Consequently, every deliberate act performed by a definite individual is always either morally good or bad.

The controversy revolves around the question: must every human action be explicitly directed to a morally good purpose? St. Thomas answers that an implicit intention to do what is right is sufficient for a morally good action, provided it is done with some reflection and exercise of freedom.

INDIFFERENTISM. Denial that the worship of God or the practice of religion is a grave duty of human beings as creatures who are totally dependent on God. It is practical indifferentism when a person acts in this way without necessarily denying that God deserves to be honored and served. Agnostic indifferentism is the attitude that one religion is as good as another, because it is

claimed that there is no way of telling the difference.

INDIRECT SUICIDE. Allowing one's death without directly intending it. Thus a person does not want to die but permits death in the pursuit of some laudable objective that he foresees will be fatal to his life. Among the reasons considered sufficient to permit indirect suicide are the common good, e.g., soldiers fighting for their country, and the spiritual good, e.g., a priest administering the sacraments to those suffering from contagious disease. See also DIRECT SUICIDE.

INDIRECT TEMPORAL JURISDICTION. The authority of the Pope in temporal matters outside the Papal States, or now Vatican City State. Except in this territory the Pope has no mere temporal authority, possessed directly and by divine right. Yet, in virtue of his office as supreme arbiter of faith and morals, for the spiritual protection and supernatural salvation of his flock, the Pope possesses indirect temporal authority to be exercised whenever the action of secular powers threatens the eternal welfare of the faithful. In modern times the doctrine was most extensively described in the *Controversies* of St. Robert Bellarmine (1542–1621).

INDIRECT VOLUNTARY. The unintended but foreseen consequence of something that is deliberately willed. This consequence is not desired either as an end or as means, but a person sees that he cannot get something else without getting it. He wills the cause of which this is a necessary effect.

INDISSOLUBILITY. The permanence of marriage which cannot be dissolved either by the withdrawal of consent of the married partners or by civil authorities. Christian marriage is absolutely indissoluble, as defined by the Council of Trent, condemning anyone who says, "The Church errs when she has inculcated and continues to inculcate in accord with evangelical and apostolic teaching, that the bond of marriage cannot be dissolved by reason of adultery on the part of one spouse, and that both parties, even the innocent one who gave no reason for adultery, cannot contract a new marriage while the other spouse is alive; and that both the man who marries another wife after dismissing an adulterous one commits adultery and the wife who marries another husband after dismissing an adulterous one commits adultery" (Denzinger 1807).

INDISSOLUBLE MARRIAGE. Christian marriage, between two baptized persons who enter into a valid contract and consummate their marriage by natural intercourse, cannot be dissolved by any human power, whether civil or ecclesiastical.

INDIVIDUAL. Any single being, notably the human person, which cannot be divided without losing its identity. The two elements necessary to constitute an individual person are one's own identity and distinctiveness from others.

INDIVIDUALISM. The philosophy that places the interests of each person above the welfare of society. It is the subordination of the common good of many to the private good of the individual. In practice it is the sacrifice of social values to the personal desires of those who are most aggressive in demanding that society recognize their individual liberty.

INDIVIDUALITY. The quality of something which makes it precisely this being and not another. Various theories are proposed. The most common, following St. Thomas Aquinas, is to place the principle of individuality in the material component of bodily substances. Matter, then, is the basis of individuation. Others, with Duns Scotus, see it in a special "thisness," which distinguishes every single object in the created universe. For some the whole concrete being constitutes its individuality. And finally some hold that the existence of a thing, as distinct from its essence, ultimately explains the individuality of every single creature.

INDIVIDUATION. The basic philosophical reason that distinguishes a creature both from the universal or class to which he or she (or it) belongs and from every other individual in that category. Among human beings, their individuation is mainly due to the fact that each one has his own numerically distinctive, separately created immortal soul.

INDOLENCE. Habitual love of ease and comfort, and a disposition that avoids physical movement or mental or volitional activity. (Etym. Latin *in-*, not + *dolere*, to feel pain: *indolentia*, freedom from pain, insensibility.)

INDUCTION. Logical derivation of universal laws or principles from individual cases. Reasoning from particulars to a general conclusion; arriving at the definition of an essence from knowledge of features common to the instances. An argument from experience, by which we draw inferences concerning the universal subject from particular manifestations of this subject or type. It is the opposite of deduction. (Etym. Latin *in-*, in + *ducere*, to lead: *inductio*, a leading in.) See also DEDUCTION.

INDULGENCE. "The remission before God of the temporal punishment due to sins forgiven as far as their guilt is concerned, which the follower of Christ with the proper dispositions and under certain determined conditions acquires through the intervention of the Church, which, as minister of the redemption, authoritatively dispenses and applies the treasury of the satisfaction won by Christ and the saints" (Pope Paul VI, Apostolic Constitution on Indulgences).

As originally understood, an indulgence was a mitigation of the severe canonical penances imposed on the faithful for grave sins. The term "indulgence" remained, however, even after these extreme penalties were discontinued. Yet until the Second Vatican Council, the norm for determining the effectiveness of an indulgenced practice was its relationship to the ancient canonical penances, as seen in the numbers, so many years or so many days, attached to every official listing of partial indulgences.

All this was changed by Pope Paul VI. From now on the measure of how efficacious an indulgenced work is depends on two things: the supernatural charity with which the indulgenced task is done, and the perfection of the task itself.

Another innovation is that partial and plenary indulgences can always be applied to the dead by way of suffrage, asking God to remit their sufferings if they are still in purgatory.

INDULGENTIARUM DOCTRINA. Apostolic Constitution of Pope Paul VI on the Church's teaching regarding indulgences, that they are founded on divine revelation, and that the Church is now making certain changes in how they are to be gained. Twenty new norms are given, stressing that "indulgences are attached to what the faithful do, and not to things or places which are only the occasion for gaining the indulgences" (February 14, 1966).

INDULT. A temporary favor granted by the Holy See to bishops to permit them to do something not otherwise allowed. If given for a certain time, it must be renewed by competent ecclesiastical authority. Thus according to the Code of Canon Law, an indult is required for a priest to practice surgery and a cloistered nun needs an indult to travel outside the cloister.

INDWELLING. Presence of the Holy Spirit in a person who is in the state of grace. He is present not only by means of the created gifts of grace, which he dispenses, but by his uncreated divine nature. This personal indwelling does not produce a substantial but only an accidental union with the souls of the just. As the indwelling of the Holy Spirit is an operation of God outside himself and as all activity of God outside the Trinity is common to the three persons, the indwelling of the Holy Spirit implies the indwelling of the three divine persons. This indwelling as a manifestation of the love of God, the personal love of the Father and the Son, is appropriated to the Holy Spirit. St. Paul speaks of the third person: "Know you not that you are the temples of God and that the Spirit of God dwells in you" (I Corinthians 3:16). But he also says: "You are the temple of the living God" (I Corinthians 6:16), and Christ declares: "If any one loves me, he will keep my word. And my father will love him; and we will come to him and will make our abode with him" (John 14:23).

The immediate effect of the divine indwelling is sanctifying grace, which is the created result of the uncreated grace of God's presence. Its effect on the person is an experience that spiritual writers compare to a foretaste of the beatific vision; the mind is able to understand something of the mystery of God and the will is enamored of his goodness beyond anything possible by the light of reason or the natural affective powers of humans.

INEFFABLE. That which is inexpressible. Only God is ultimately ineffable because only he cannot be fully comprehended by the finite mind. Since knowledge determines expression, the divine ineffability is a result of the divine incomprehensibility. In the words of St. Augustine, "More true than our speech about God is our thinking of Him, and more true than our thinking is His Being" (*De Trinitate*, VII, 4, 7).

INEFFICACIOUS GRACES. Actual graces that are truly but merely sufficient to perform a supernatural good act. They are inefficacious because they meet with resistance from the free human will. The Protestant Reformers and Jansenists denied such graces because, according to their view, grace exercises a necessitating influence on the human will. All graces are efficacious; otherwise, Calvin said, they would not be graces.

INERRANCY. The absence of error. Commonly applied to the Bible as the revealed word of God. (Etym. Latin *in-*, not + *errare*, to err: *inerrans*, not wandering.)

IN EXTREMIS. In the last extreme. A person at the point of death, when all positive ecclesiastical laws are subordinated to the primary responsibility of preparing the one dying for entrance into eternity.

INFALLIBILITY. Freedom from error in teaching the universal Church in matters of faith or morals. As defined by the First Vatican Council, "The Roman Pontiff, when he speaks ex cathedra—that is, when in discharge of the office of pastor and teacher of all Christians, by virtue of his supreme apostolic authority, he defines a doctrine regarding faith or morals to be held by the universal Church, by the divine assistance promised to him in Blessed Peter, is possessed of that infallibility with which the divine Redeemer willed that his Church should be endowed in defining doctrine regarding faith or morals; and therefore such definitions are irreformable of themselves, and not in virtue of consent of the Church" (Denzinger 3074).

The bearer of the infallibility is every lawful Pope as successor of Peter, the Prince of the Apostles. But the Pope alone is infallible, not others to whom he delegates a part of his teaching authority, for example, the Roman congregations.

The object of his infallibility is his teaching of faith and morals. This means especially revealed doctrine like the Incarnation. But it also includes any nonrevealed teaching that is in any way connected with revelation.

The condition of the infallibility is that the Pope speaks ex cathedra. For this is required that: 1. he have the intention of declaring something unchangeably true; and 2. he speak as shepherd and teacher of all the faithful with the full weight of his apostolic authority, and not merely as a private theologian or even merely for the people of Rome or some particular segment of the Church of God.

The source of the infallibility is the supernatural assistance of the Holy Spirit, who protects the supreme teacher of the Church from error and therefore from misleading the people of God.

As a result, the ex cathedra pronouncements of the Pope are unchangeable "of themselves," that is, not because others in the Church either first instructed the Pope or agree to what he says. (Etym. Latin *in-*, not + *fallibilis*; from *fallere*, to deceive: *infallibilis*, not able to deceive, or err.)

INFALLIBILITY, EPISCOPAL. Preservation from error of the bishops of the Catholic Church. They are infallible when all the bishops of the Church are assembled in a general council or, scattered over the earth, they propose a teaching of faith or morals as one to be held by all the faithful. They are assured freedom from error provided they are in union with the Bishop of Rome and their teaching is subject to his authority. The scope of this infallibility, like that of the Pope, includes not only revealed truths but any teaching, even historical facts, principles of philosophy, or norms of the natural law that are in any way connected with divine revelation.

INFALLIBLE BOOK. A term sometimes applied to the Bible by those who criticize evangelical Protestants because they believe the Scriptures contain the inerrant word of God.

INFAMY. The stigma that is attached to a person and that debars him or her from certain rights or privileges until the source of the infamy is removed. It may be an external crime that was committed by the person and that attaches to his or her character (*infamia facti*), or it may be the result of an ecclesiastical penalty imposed by law or authority (*infamia juris*).

INFANCY. In ecclesiastical legal tradition, persons under the age of seven or before they have reached the age of reason.

INFANT BAPTISM. The Catholic Church's constant teaching is that children should be baptized soon after birth. The reason being that a child is born with original sin, which, in God's ordinary providence, cannot be removed before the age of reason except by baptism with water. Through baptism an infant receives sanctifying grace, the infused virtues of faith, hope, and charity, and the gifts of the Holy Spirit.

INFANTICIDE. Child murder. Distinguished from direct abortion, which is also murder, by the fact that the child is already born, alive, and then deliberately put to death. (Etym. Latin *infans*, a young child, a babe; literally, not yet able to speak + *-cidium*, killing: *infanticidium*.)

INFANTS. Children who have not reached the age of reason and who, although baptized, are not subject to merely ecclesiastical laws.

INFANTS, ANOINTING OF. Children may be given the sacrament of anointing of the sick even before the age of seven, provided they have reached the age of reason. The doctrinal basis for this provision is that anointing can be validly administered to any baptized person who is capable of making a moral decision and therefore of committing at least a venial sin.

INFANTS, EUCHARIST TO. In some rites of the Catholic Church, Holy Communion is given to infants after their baptism. At the Council of Trent the Church defined that this practice is not necessary. In the Latin Rite the Eucharist is given to children once they reach the age of reason, provided they can distinguish the Bread of the Eucharist from ordinary bread.

INFANTS, UNBAPTIZED. The common teaching of the Catholic Church is that unbaptized infants who die do not enjoy the beatific vision but enter into a state of perfect natural happiness, commonly called limbo.

INFERENCE. A process of reasoning by starting with a proposition as true and arriving at a conclusion as also true because it was already implicit in the original assumption. Inference may be either deductive or inductive, i.e., starting from the general and going to the particular, or vice versa.

INFIDEL. One who does not believe. Formerly applied to all non-Christians, the term is now used only of unbelievers, i.e., professed atheists or agnostics. (Etym. Latin *in-*, not + *fidelis*, true, faithful: *infidelis*, one that cannot be relied upon, faithless.)

INFIDELITY. Either a lack of faith or of faithfulness. As a lack of faith, it may be positive, privative, or negative. Positive infidelity means that a baptized person sufficiently instructed in the Christian faith rejects it by a denial of any of God's revealed truths. Privative infidelity is the culpable neglect either to examine the grounds for divine revelation or to admit one's obligation to embrace the faith once these grounds are seen to be credible. Negative infidelity is simply a lack of faith in the Christian religion by one who has some other faith and, through no fault of his or her own, has not had the Gospel adequately presented. Infidelity as a lack of faithfulness is commonly associated with marriage.

INFIDELITY, MARITAL. Unfaithfulness to one's marriage vows by having sexual relations with a person other than one's lawfully wedded spouse. It is equivalent to adultery. According to the Church's constant tradition, infidelity is sufficient grounds for separation and even civil divorce, but not for divorce with the right to remarry.

IN FIERI. In respect to change. In the state of changing or becoming, as some new organization is said to be *in fieri*, that is, in the process of coming into existence.

INFINITE. That which has no bounds or limitations. Something can be called infinite in different ways. It can be actually infinite, meaning a positive reality without limit. It can be infinitely perfect when it is unlimited in perfection of being or of operation; when it possesses every pure perfection in every way and in perfect degree. It can be potentially infinite when, as a finite reality, it is capable of actual or conceptual increase without any limit or term; thus the potentially infinite can be multiplied infinitely, but in reality it is finite and limited. On account of the indefiniteness of the limits, it is also called the indefinite. Finally, something can be either relatively or absolutely infinite. The former is infinite in some aspect or particular perfection, such as duration; the latter is infinite in every respect. Only God is actually and absolutely infinite, as only he is infinitely perfect. (Etym. Latin *in-*, not + *finis*, end: *infinitus*, indefinite; boundless.)

INFINITY OF GOD. The boundless perfection of God. According to the teaching of the Church, God is "infinite in intellect and will and in every perfection" (First Vatican Council, Session III, Chapter I). In him there is no potentiality but only pure actuality. This means more than affirming that God has no limitations. He has within himself the fullness of all perfection, whether knowledge or power or being.

INFIRMUS CUM ECCLESIA. Decree of the Sacred Congregation for Divine Worship, giving the new rite for the administration of the sacrament of anointing, authorized by Pope Paul VI on December 7, 1972.

IN FLAGRANTE DELICTO. In the very act of committing a crime. In ecclesiastical law, a person openly guilty of a grave external sin.

INFUSED CONTEMPLATION. A supernatural gift by which a person's mind and will become totally centered on God. Under this influence the intellect receives special insights into things of the spirit, and the affections are extraordinarily animated with divine love. Infused contemplation assumes the free co-operation of the human will.

INFUSED HABIT. Virtue supernaturally conferred by God without one's own effort. Good dispositions of the mind or will that are the result of divine grace rather than the effect of human effort. Some infused habits, namely the theological virtues of faith, hope, and charity, cannot be naturally acquired. Others, namely the moral virtues of prudence and justice, fortitude and temperance, can also be acquired, but when infused they elevate and perfect the naturally acquired habits.

INFUSED KNOWLEDGE. The gift of natural (secular) and supernatural (spiritual) knowledge miraculously conferred by God. Thought by some to have been possessed by Adam and Eve, who came into existence in an adult state and were to be the first teachers of the human race.

INFUSED SCIENCE. Knowledge divinely conferred on human beings without previous experience or reflection.

INFUSED VIRTUE. A good habit of the mind or will given to the soul by God, and not acquired by the action of a human being. The theological virtues of faith, hope, and charity are always infused; the moral virtues are both acquired and infused.

INFUSION. The pouring of water upon the head of a person being baptized. Practiced already in the first century, it is the most common form of baptismal ritual in the Western Church today. The term also applies to the creative act of God by which he unites the rational soul with the body at the moment of the conception of a human being. (Etym. Latin *in-*, in + *fundere*, to pour: *infusio*, a pouring into.)

IN GLOBO. All together. A term applied to a global censure or condemnation of a series of propositions that the Church considers against faith or morals.

INHERENCE. Dependence on another being for its existence. Accidents naturally inhere in the substances they modify. By divine power, in the Holy Eucharist the accidents of bread and wine exist without inhering in their substance, which has been changed through transubstantiation into the substance of Christ's body and blood.

INHERITANCE. As a title to ownership, it is the disposition of property after the death of the owner. Since property is intended not only for the good of the individual but of the family, the natural law requires that the family should be supported from the property of a deceased owner. If a person dies intestate, without declaring the heirs, the family has first claim on the property, and the civil law should reflect this primary responsibility. If there is a bequest, declaring the intention of the owner regarding his or her property to take effect at death, again one's natural heirs must first be provided for. Beyond this, a person may make any disposal of his or her property that would have been legitimate when that person was alive. Bequest is an effective way that one can take care of friends and provide for the continuance of the work in which one was chiefly interested. Implied in inheritance, therefore, is the natural right to dispose of one's property not only during life but also after death.

INHIBITING IMPEDIMENT. See IMPEDIENT IMPEDIMENT.

INHIBITIVE FEAR. Mental agitation as affecting moral responsibility. Of itself, fear does not remove the voluntary character of human actions, but it usually lessens their guilt, as also their merit. There is a distinction, however, between acting through fear or with fear. One acts through fear if it is the fear that induces one to act, as when a student cheats out of fear of failing an examination. Such actions are voluntary and imputable in most cases. One acts with fear if the emotion merely accompanies an action but does not cause it. Any significant human action involves some associated fear. Normally this reaction does not affect moral responsibility.

IN HOC SIGNO. A frequent inscription in early Christian art, after Constantine's use of the motto *"In hoc signo [crucis] vinces,"* i.e., "In this sign of the cross you shall conquer."

INITIATION OF ADULTS. Preparation of adults especially in mission countries for baptism and reception into the Church. According to the directives of the Congregation for Divine Worship (1972), the process is done in four stages: 1. initial period of inquiry, instruction, and evangelization; 2. catechumenate as a period of progressive formation in the faith, which includes being signed with the cross, blessings, exorcisms, and introduction into the Church for celebration of the Word of God; 3. immediate preparation from the beginning of Lent to Easter Vigil, when the sacraments of initiation are received, i.e., baptism, confirmation, and the Eucharist; 4. full entrance into the community of the faithful during the Easter season.

INJURIOUS WORDS. Speech that either by what is said or the manner in which it is said injures the rights or reputation of another person. Its morality is to be judged by the dignity of the person offended, the gravity of the harm done, and the malice with which the offensive language was used.

INJUSTICE. The deliberate failure to give another what is due to him or her. It may be a single act or an acquired habit (vice).

IN LOCO PARENTIS. In the place of a parent. A term applied to a person who either legally or otherwise assumes a parent's responsibility for rearing a child.

IN MEMORIAM. In remembrance of the dead. The full phrase reads, *"In memoriam fidelium defunctorum,"* in memory of the faithful departed. It implies faith in the survival of souls of the deceased, and is applied to the Masses, prayers, and good works that are offered to assist the departed if they are still in purgatory, and also refers to the cherished remembrance of the virtues and achievements of the deceased while they lived on earth.

INNATE HABIT. A tendency with which a person is supposedly born. Actually a disposition that is all but inborn, because acquired early in life, very easily and by very few acts, e.g., the habitual knowledge of the principle of contradiction.

INNATE IDEAS. The theory that spiritual ideas are not acquired from sense knowledge and reason but are part of human nature. Deriving from Plato, this theory has mainly been espoused in Christian circles regarding the knowledge of God. Since many of the Fathers of the Church characterized the knowledge of God as "not learned," as "automatic," as "implanted," or as a "gift of the soul," some mistakenly concluded that it was literally infused and not acquired. St. Thomas Aquinas explains what this means by saying that the knowledge of God is said to be innate insofar as we can easily know his existence by means of principles that are innate in us (*In Boethium de Trinitate,* I, 3, 6).

INNOCENCE. Freedom from sin or moral guilt. Applied to Adam and Eve before the Fall, to those who have just been baptized, and to persons who never lost the state of grace because they never committed a grave sin. (Etym. Latin *innocens: in-,* not + *nocere,* to harm, hurt.)

IN PARTIBUS INFIDELIUM. "In the regions of the infidels." A technical expression designating territories in which there are not now any residential episcopal sees. Used at one time to identify bishops who were not local ordinaries but to whom would be assigned a titular see in non-Christian lands.

IN PETTO. Also *in pectore*, i.e., secretly. Applied to the Pope when he announces a general decision but reserves for later publication the particular form of what he has decided. Generally refers to the choice of cardinals *in petto*, whose names are not announced.

INQ. *Inquisitio*—Inquisition.

INQUISITION. The special court or tribunal appointed by the Catholic Church to discover and suppress heresy and to punish heretics. The Roman Inquisition of the middle twelfth century, with its ecclesiastical courts for trying and punishing heretics, arose during the ravages of the anti-social Albigensian sect, whose doctrines and practices were destructive not only of faith but of Christian morality and public order. While Church authorities would condemn a person found guilty of heresy, it was the civil power that actually inflicted the penalty. The reformation of the heretic was first sought. By exhortations and minor punishments he was urged to give up his heresy. Many did. Only the relapsed heretics who were found guilty were turned over to the civil government for punishment required under civil law. The fact that secular law prescribed death must be understood in the light of those days when heresy was anarchy and treason and leniency in criminal codes was unknown. Like all institutions that have a human character abuses crept in.

The Spanish Inquisition, set up by King Ferdinand and Queen Isabella in 1478 and empowered by Pope Sixtus IV, was directed against the lapsed converts from Judaism, crypto-Jews, and other apostates whose secret activities were dangerous to Church and State. The civil government had great influence in the administration of this Inquisition, and the Spanish ecclesiastical tribunal accused of scandalous cruelty must share its condemnations with them. The latter worked during these days in defiance of the Holy See, which often condemned inquisitors because of their cruelties. Even so, these cruelties have been grossly exaggerated, and the fact that the Inquisition did tremendous good in saving the Latin countries from anarchy has been forgotten. Much falsehood surrounds the events of this period, which should be judged by the standards of those times, not by modern ideas of the human person and of religious freedom.

I.N.R.I. Symbolic rendering of the initials of the Latin words placed on the Cross as Jesus died, *Iesus Nazarenus Rex Iudaeorum,* "Jesus of Nazareth, King of the Jews." The inscription was placed on the Cross by Pilate's orders in Hebrew, Greek, and Latin. The initials have been used only since the thirteenth century. Before that the words were fully written or omitted.

IN SAECULA SAECULORUM. "Forever and ever." Customary ending of the Latin prayers of the liturgy.

INSANITY. Abnormality of the brain or nervous system producing a morbid mental condition. This condition is accompanied by loss of control of the will, rendering the individual morally irresponsible for what he does. The permanently insane may be baptized, their desire being supposed. If having lapsed into insanity and now incurable, they may be baptized if any, even implicit, desire for baptism was ever expressed by them. The sacrament of anointing of the sick may also be given, and Holy Communion may be received in sane moments or when in danger of death. A temporarily insane person upon recovery may validly receive the sacrament of confirmation and holy orders. The permanently insane may not be sponsors for baptism, nor may they marry, but, if they have contracted marriage in a period of lucidity, that marriage may be valid. The Church approves segregation for the insane and sponsors institutions for their care, but sterilization is forbidden as an infringement of their human rights.

INSCRIPTIONS. Writings or crude incisions made on the walls and tombs of the catacombs expressing the beliefs of the early Christians. These inscriptions show the people's faith in eternal life and resurrection of the dead, in purgatory, and in the joys of heaven. The word "bury" was unknown. The dead were deposited in faith, left for a time to rise on the last day.

IN SE. In itself. Term used in philosophy to identify substance, whose existence is "in itself" as distinct from an accident that exists in another (*in alio*). In theology the phrase applies to every object or situation considered in its own right and apart from its relations to other things. Thus *in se* telling the untruth is a venial sin, but circumstances (as under oath) may make it grave.

INSIGHT. A sudden enlightenment on

some subject, as of a mystery of faith, with clear understanding and the ability to explain its meaning to others.

INSIGNIA. The emblems and apparel worn by prelates when officiating in a liturgical ceremony. Although somewhat simplified since the Second Vatican Council, the traditional insignia of a bishop in the Latin Rite are, depending on the occasion, the buskins, sandals, pectoral cross, dalmatic and tunicle, miter, gloves, ring, pastoral staff, rochet, mozzetta, cappa magna, skullcap, morse, mantelletta, and gremial veil. An archbishop also has the cross and pallium. The Pope's distinctive insignia are the falda, subcinctorium, fanon, tiara, and sedia gestatoria. A Byzantine bishop has the veil, mandyas, pastoral staff, dikerion, and trikerion, sakkos, omophorion, enkolpia, and a crown or miter.

INSPIRATION, BIBLICAL. The special influence of the Holy Spirit on the writers of Sacred Scripture in virtue of which God himself becomes the principal author of the books written and the sacred writer is the subordinate author. In using human beings as his instruments in the composition, God does so in harmony with the person's nature and temperament, and with no violence to the free, natural activity of his or her human faculties. According to the Church's teaching, "by supernatural power, God so moved and impelled them to write, He was so present to them, that the things which He ordered and those only they first rightly understood, then willed faithfully to write down, and finally expressed in apt words and with infallible truth" (Pope Leo XIII, *Providentissimus Deus,* Denzinger 3293).

INSPIRING GRACE. Actual grace conferred by God to motivate and strengthen the human will and affections. Never separated in fact from illuminating grace, it is nevertheless a distinct gift to enable us not only to know the mind and will of God but also to act on the knowledge we possess.

INSTALLATION. The formal induction of an ecclesiastic in his office; it may be accompanied by certain prescribed or improvised ceremonies. Depending on the office assumed, installation also commonly means the assuming of canonical jurisdiction.

INSTINCT. According to scholastic philosophy, the natural tendency of animals and human beings to perform complex actions that are useful for the existence, development, and preservation of the individual or of the species.

INSTITUTE, CLERICAL. A religious institute of men, the majority of whose members receive the order of priesthood.

INSTITUTE, DIOCESAN. A religious institute of men or women, erected by a local ordinary, that has not as yet obtained "Pontifical Recognition" from the Holy See.

INSTITUTE, EXEMPT. A religious institute of men or women, taking either solemn or simple vows, whose members have been withdrawn from the jurisdiction of the local ordinary, according to the provisions of canon law.

INSTITUTE, LAY. Any religious institute of women, and those institutes of men in which most of the members do not receive the order of priesthood.

INSTITUTE, PONTIFICAL. A religious institute of pontifical right (*juris pontificii*), of men or women, that has received the formal approbation, or at least "Pontifical Recognition," from the Holy See.

INSTITUTE, RELIGIOUS. A society approved by legitimate ecclesiastical authority, the members of which strive after evangelical perfection according to the laws proper to their society, by the profession of public vows, either perpetual or temporary, the latter to be renewed after fixed intervals of time. The members also live in community.

INSTITUTION. The act of founding or establishing. Also that which is established, as a practice or custom. An institution is likewise an organization for the promotion of public welfare, such as a church, school, hospital, or place of residence for the aged or handicapped. Canonical institution is the act by which an ecclesiastical authority confers on someone a benefice presented by a third person who has the right of presentation, and also a bishop's approbation granted to a beneficiary for the exercise of his ministerial functions.

INSTITUTIONAL REVOLUTION. The complete change, more or less planned, of the culture of a society by transforming its institutions, e.g., marriage and family life.

INSTRUCTION. The act or practice of imparting knowledge It is that part of education which seeks to inform or develop the mind as the foundation for motivating the will. According to St. Thomas Aquinas, instruction is the primary purpose of catechesis.

INSTRUCTION, PAPAL. A document of

the Pope, or of one of the Roman congregations subject to his authority, that tells the faithful how they are to carry out or put into practice some directives in morals, worship, or spirituality.

INSTRUCTION, PARENTAL. The duty of parents to instruct their children in the faith, a grave obligation. It follows from the responsibility that parents assume when they bring children into the world. Once conceived and born, the children have a right to adequate knowledge of the means of salvation.

INSTRUMENTAL CAUSE. Anything serving as a subordinate cause. It is a cause that does not begin an action but is applied and directed as a help to its efforts and purpose by the principal agent. An instrumental cause exercises its influence chiefly according to the form and intention of the principal efficient cause. In Catholic theology the role of the priest at Mass and in the administration of the sacraments is that of instrumental cause, used by the principal agent, who is Jesus Christ.

INSTRUMENTALISM. See PRAGMATISM.

IN SYNODO EPISCOPALI. A statement of the Sacred Congregation for Catholic Education, giving the *Ratio Fundamentalis* (Basic Principles) for the formation of priests. This extensive document deals with vocations, minor and major seminary rectors, professors, spiritual formation, academic training, philosophy, theology, specialized fields, doctrinal teaching, methodology, pastoral preparation, and continuing education (January 6, 1970).

INTEGRATED PERSONALITY. The moral condition of a person whose various faculties and powers are united into a harmonious whole, resulting in easy and effective adjustment to the changing circumstances of life.

INTEGRITY. Honesty or trustworthiness. The quality of being virtuous. Wholeness of character without duplicity or internal conflict of interests. (Etym. Latin *integrare*, to make whole; to present something in its entirety.)

INTEGRITY OF CONFESSION. The duty, based on divine law, of confessing in the sacrament of penance all the certainly grave sins committed since one's last valid absolution. All mortal sins are properly confessed when their number and species (distinctive quality), together with the circumstances that change the species of the sins, are exactly indicated.

INTELLECT. The spiritual power of cognition, knowing reality in a nonmaterial way. The faculty of thinking in a way essentially higher than with the senses and the imagination. It is possessed by human beings, disembodied souls, and the angels, both good and demonic.

INTELLECTUALISM. The attitude that gives absolute priority to pursuits of the mind, before moral conduct or virtue. It cultivates the intellect as the main way, if not the only way, to ensure happiness. It respects intellectual ability and activity above every other human possession and achievement.

INTELLECTUAL MIRACLE. A divine intervention that surpasses the capacities of the human mind, such as prophecy or the mystical illumination regarding some hidden truth.

INTELLECTUAL VIRTUES. Good habits of the mind, enabling it to be a more efficient instrument of knowledge. They are distinguished from the moral virtues, since they do not, as such, make one a better person. They make one more effective in the use of what he or she knows and, to that extent, contribute to the practice of moral virtue. According to Aristotle and St. Thomas Aquinas, there are five intellectual virtues: three pertaining to the theoretical or speculative intellect concerned with the contemplation of the true; and two pertaining to the practical intellect, concerned with the two forms of action, making and doing.

The three speculative intellectual virtues are understanding, science, and wisdom. Understanding (Greek *nous,* intuitive mind) is the habit of first principles. It is the habitual knowledge of primary self-evident truths that lie at the root of all knowledge. Science (Greek *epistēmē*, knowledge) is the habit of conclusions drawn by demonstration from first principles. It is the habitual knowledge of the particular sciences. Wisdom (Greek *sophia,* wisdom) is the habit of knowing things in their highest causes. It is the organized knowledge of all principles and conclusions in the truth called philosophy.

The two practical intellectual virtues are art and prudence. Art (Greek *techne,* craftsmanship) is the habit of knowing how to make things, how to produce some external object. As a practical virtue, it includes the mechanical and fine arts and most liberal arts. Prudence (Greek *phronēsis,* practical wisdom) is the habit of knowing how to do things, how to direct activity that does not result in tangible products. It enables one to live a good human life and is the only one of the intellectual virtues that cannot exist apart from the moral virtues.

INTELLECTUAL VISION. Supernatural knowledge in which the mind receives an extraordinary grasp of some revealed truth without the aid of sensible impressions. Thus St. Ignatius Loyola (1491–1556) wrote of his seeing "the humanity of Christ with the eyes of the soul."

These visions take place either through ideas that are already acquired and that are then co-ordinated and interpreted by God, or through infused ideas, representing divine things, that are thus better perceived than a person would otherwise perceive them. At times the visions are obscure and their object is only dimly understood; at other times the perception is very clear but lasts only a moment. The mystics describe them as intuitions that leave a deep impression on the mind.

The experience of St. Paul on the way to Damascus was at once sensible, imaginative, and intellectual. He beheld the blinding light with his eyes; he saw with his imagination the personal traits of Ananias; and his mind understood the will of God (Acts 9:3–12).

INTELLIGENCE. The activity of a created intellect, or the knowledge accumulated by the mind as an acquired habit. Also refers to an intelligent being, especially a pure angelic spirit.

INTENTION. An act of the will tending effectively to some good, proposed by the mind as desirable and attainable. It differs from simply willing, which is the desire for an end without concern about the means. Intention means desiring not only some good but also the means of obtaining this good. An intention may be actual, virtual, habitual, or interpretative. See also ACTUAL INTENTION, HABITUAL INTENTION, INTERPRETATIVE INTENTION, VIRTUAL INTENTION.

INTERCESSION. Entreaty in favor of another person; hence mediation. In biblical language, "there is only one mediator between God and mankind, himself a man, Christ Jesus, who sacrificed himself as a ransom for them all" (I Timothy 2:5–6). The Blessed Virgin, Mediatrix of all graces, the angels, saints in heaven, souls in purgatory, and the faithful on earth intercede for mankind by their merits and prayers.

INTERCOMMUNION. A formal agreement between two Christian Churches that extends membership and ritual privileges between them without resolving their doctrinal differences.

INTERCOMMUNION, EUCHARISTIC. The deliberate administering of Holy Communion by a Catholic minister of the sacrament to a baptized person who is not a Catholic. Also the reception by a Catholic of Holy Communion from a non-Catholic minister of religion. According to the directives of the Holy See, "Admission to Catholic Eucharistic Communion is confined to particular cases of those Christians who have a faith in the sacrament in conformity with that of the Church, who experience a serious spiritual need for the Eucharistic sustenance, who for a prolonged period are unable to have recourse to a minister of their own community, and who ask for the sacrament of their own accord; all this provided that they have the proper dispositions and lead lives worthy of a Christian" (*In Quibus Rerum Circumstantiis,* June 1, 1972). Moreover, "It is the local ordinary's responsibility to examine those exceptional cases and to make concrete decisions" (*Dopo la Publicazione,* October 17, 1973). The question of reciprocity arises only with those churches which have preserved apostolic succession and the sacrament of orders. "Hence a Catholic cannot ask for the Eucharist except from a minister who has been validly ordained" (*Directorium Oecumenicum, 55*).

INTERDATE. The practice of dating with persons belonging to another religion, with the predictable result of entering into a mixed marriage.

INTERDICT. A censure forbidding the faithful, while still remaining in communion with the Church, the use of certain sacred privileges, such as Christian burial, some of the sacraments, and attendance at liturgical services. It does not exclude from Church membership, nor does it necessarily imply a personal fault of any individual affected by the interdict. When imposed for a fixed period, it is a vindictive penalty because of some grave act done against the common good of the Church by one or more parishes. Usual religious services are curtailed, but sacraments may be given to the dying, marriages celebrated, and Holy Communion administered if the interdict is general or local (not personal). A general interdict may be inflicted only by the Holy See. Parishes or persons may be interdicted only by the local ordinary.

INTER EA. A circular letter issued by the Sacred Congregation for the Clergy, sent to the heads of episcopal conferences, on the formation of the clergy. Three aspects of priestly formation are attended to: the spiritual, intellectual, and pastoral. One of the main concerns is the phenomenon that "Young priests often find it difficult to preserve in its fulness the deposit of faith which Jesus has committed to the Church." Twenty-six norms for training and maintaining the clergy in their loyalty to the Church are specified in detail (November 4, 1969).

INTERIORIZATION. The incorporation of other people's attitudes and moral standards to make them one's own. Also applied to so deeply assimilating a doctrine of faith, say, the Passion of Christ, that it becomes a dominant motive force in a person's spiritual life.

INTERIOR STRUGGLE. Conflict within a human person between his or her own desires and the will of God. What naturally pleases is not always good. This is the fight of the spirit versus the flesh—human will against human passions, whether bodily or spiritual. This internal struggle varies in intensity for different persons and at different times. Although often difficult, with divine grace it is always possible to overcome self in conflict with the known will of God.

INTER MIRIFICA. Decree on the Means of Social Communication of the Second Vatican Council. After defining the media as those "which of their nature can reach and influence not merely single individuals but the very masses and even the whole of human society," the Council spelled out how these are to be used. Most important, it declared that "the content of what is communicated must be true and—within the limits set by justice and charity—complete" (December 4, 1963).

INTERNAL GRACE. The supernatural life, infused virtues and divine inspirations that directly affect the human soul and elevate its being and activities to a share in the life of God. It is called internal to be distinguished from external grace that is not inherently supernatural.

INTERNAL PEACE. Quiet of soul in the absence of conflict. It is the experience of agreement between faith and reason, hope and attainment, conscience and conduct, one's own desires and those of another, and especially the sense of agreement between one's own will and the known will of God.

INTERNAL SINS. Moral failings that one experiences only by the spiritual faculties of understanding and free will and are not manifested in the external senses.

INTERNATIONAL CATHOLIC ORGANIZATIONS (ICO). Associations whose members are expert in particular areas of human concern and who witness on the international level to the Church's teachings in those fields, e.g., the International Catholic Child Bureau, International Catholic Union of the Press, International Catholic Education Office, International Catholic Union for Social Service, World Union of Catholic Women's Organizations, Pax Romana, World Federation of Catholic Youth.

The importance of the International Catholic Organizations has increased since the Second Vatican Council, which emphasized the need for the laity to participate more effectively in international affairs. Although the organizations took their origin from lay activity, priests and religious are included in their operation. According to the Church's directives, an ICO must be an organization, it must be international, and it must be Catholic. As an organization, it should be a co-ordinated legal entity whose reason for existence is clearly defined and actually operative. It must have members in different countries who communicate among themselves and develop an outlook beyond national boundaries. An ICO is to be Catholic in that its pronouncements and activities are in harmony with the magisterium of the Church. The statutes of each ICO, and any substantial amendments to them, must be approved by the Holy See. Moreover, candidates for president, general secretary, and chaplains or ecclesiastical assistants require Roman approval. Finally an ICO must be open to ecumenical co-operation with non-Catholic organizations active in the international field.

INTERNUNCIO. A papal legate whose duty is to foster good relations between the Holy See and the country to which he is accredited. He usually keeps the Pope informed on the local conditions of the Church. He is of lower rank in dignity than a nuncio, though he has similar powers and privileges.

INTER OECUMENICI. Instruction of the Sacred Congregation of Rites on the proper application of the Second Vatican Council's constitution on the liturgy. Ninety-nine areas of liturgical life and practice are given directives and specific norms (September 26, 1964).

INTER PARES. Among equals, or one's peers. Term used by those who deny the Pope's primacy of jurisdiction. They claim that he has only a primacy of honor in that he is merely held (without actually being) the first among the bishops in the Catholic Church.

INTERPRETATION. Giving the meaning or explanation of something, as of a doctrine, law, or statement of purpose. It is authentic when given by the Church's teaching authority and calls for obedient acceptance by the faithful; doctrinal when the Church exercises her magisterial right to teach the way of salvation; broad when the explanation of a law favors liberty; and narrow when the explanation limits human freedom.

INTERPRETATIVE INTENTION. An intention that has not been made but presumably would have been made if the person had been aware of the circumstances. Thus, if the literal interpretation of a law would cause more harm than good, one might interpret the mind of the lawgiver and relax the law in this particular case. See also ACTUAL INTENTION, HABITUAL INTENTION, INTENTION, VIRTUAL INTENTION.

INTERREGNUM. See SEDE VACANTE.

INTERSTICES. Periods of time required by Church law between the various grades of sacred orders. Since the abolition of the subdiaconate in the Latin Rite, the main provision is for the three-month interval between the diaconate and the priesthood. This time may be, and generally is, extended, and for exceptional reasons may also be shortened by a bishop. (Etym. Latin *inter-*, between + *stare*, to stand: *interstitium*, interval, interstice; literally, space between.)

IN THE YEAR OF THE (OUR) LORD. See ANNO DOMINI.

INTINCTION. The liturgical practice of dipping the consecrated Host into the consecrated wine in giving Holy Communion. Its use was already established by the time of Dionysius of Alexandria (d. 264). In time it became a regular method both in the East and the West. In the East, the intinction was (and is) done by means of the communion spoon (labis). An alternate form of intinction is described in the *Ordines Romani* (sixth century) and since discontinued. The consecrated Host would be dipped into unconsecrated wine. Intinction had long disappeared in the West, and has been revived since the Second Vatican Council (1969).

INTOLERANCE. A lack of reasonable patience and forbearance toward those who justly deserve recognition of their liberties. Christian charity requires tolerance even of the sinner. However, justice and charity demand intolerance of error, since the truth admits of no compromise.

INTRINSIC. That which is essential or belongs to the nature of a thing. That which is inherent to something, as freedom is intrinsic to merit, and knowledge is intrinsic to love.

INTRINSICALLY EVIL. An act or intention that of its very nature, essentially or necessarily, is not in conformity with the divine law, e.g., blasphemy.

INTRINSIC GOODNESS. The good quality of those human actions which, of their very nature, conform to the true norm of morality, e.g., love of God.

INTROIT. The entrance or introductory rite of the Mass. It consists of an opening hymn, sung or recited, while the priest approaches the altar, kisses it, and goes to the place where he will greet the people and begin the penitential rite. (Etym. French *introit*, a going in; from Latin *introitus: intro-*, within + *ire*, to go.)

INTROSPECTION. Observation and analysis of one's own mental and especially moral state; self-examination, particularly as consequent conscience judging the rightness or wrongness of a previous action.

INTROVERSION. A personality trait, with moral implications, characterized by preoccupation with one's own thoughts, avoidance of social contacts, and the tendency to turn away from extramental reality.

INTUITION. The immediate knowledge of something, especially the act of vision by divine or angelic intelligence. Among human beings, the power of insight into the meaning of primary truths, without conscious attention or reasoning. Awareness of truth without mental effort. (Etym. Latin *intuitus*, a look, view; from *intuere*, to look at, upon, or toward.)

INTUITIONISM. A doctrine that makes intuition the principal method of obtaining human knowledge. It tends to dispense with the need for abstract and reflective thinking. Favored by Plato, intuitionism has greatly influenced Christian philosophy, especially in the Augustinian tradition. (Etym. Latin *intueri*, to look at or toward, contemplate:

in-, on, toward + *tueri*, to look at, watch, see.)

INVALID. Null and void, ineffective. Applied to the sacraments, it means that something essential was missing so that a sacrament was not actually administered or conferred. In ecclesiastical law it means that some document, declaration, or jurisdiction is without effect because some necessary element was not present.

INVESTITURE. The practice in the early Middle Ages of an emperor or other lay prince to invest an abbot or bishop-elect with the ring and staff and to receive homage before consecration. Condemned by Pope Nicholas II in 1059 and in 1075 all lay investiture was forbidden by Pope Gregory VII (1021–85) and by subsequent popes. The Second Lateran Council (1139) reaffirmed the prohibition but allowed the civil ruler to bestow the temporalities. Variant forms of lay investiture remain to the present day, notably in secular states where the Church's rights are severely restricted, as in countries under Communism.

INVESTITURE, LAY. The act by which a sovereign, in the Middle Ages, granted titles, possessions, and temporal rights to bishops, abbots, and other spiritual leaders. The ritual of investiture consisted in the delivery of the spiritual emblems, ring and crosier, and sometimes the keys of the church. This privilege of secular princes and lords dates from the time of Charlemagne. So long as these princes had the Church's welfare at heart, lay investiture was tolerated. But when ecclesiastical offices were bought and sold, and free elections of bishops hindered, the Church vigorously opposed it with anti-investiture legislation, which was sporadically enforced. Pope Gregory VII, upon becoming Pope, enacted stringent measures against investiture, even to excommunicating those who continued it. The Concordat of Worms in 1122 finally ended the strife between the emperors and the Holy See. Once the major concessions were made by the emperors, the Pope agreed that all elections would be held in the emperor's presence and his bestowal of the temporalities of the bestowed office would be continued. The conflict over lay investiture reached its peak in Germany.

INVINCIBLE IGNORANCE. Lack of knowledge, either of fact or law, for which a person is not morally responsible. This may be due to the difficulty of the object of the knowledge, or scarcity of evidence, or insuffi-cient time or talent in the person, or any other factor for which he is not culpable. (Etym. Latin *in*, not + *vincibilis*, easily overcome: *invincibilis*.)

INVIOLABILITY OF LAW. See SANCTION.

INVOCATION. A prayerful appeal to a higher power. It may be God, the angels or saints, or the souls in purgatory who are invoked. Invocation implies an attitude of humility in asking for supernatural assistance. When God is invoked, the appeal is to mercy and love.

INVOCATION OF SAINTS. Asking the saints for assistance in temporal or spiritual need. Its basis is the intimate communion that exists between the blessed in heaven and the faithful on earth. The saints are invoked in order to obtain their intercession before the throne of God, and this corresponds to the familiar practice on earth of asking people to pray for us. Since the more holy a person is, the more effective his prayers, the saints in heaven are extraordinarily powerful intercessors with God. It is a matter of divine faith, implicit in Sacred Scripture and explicit in Catholic tradition, that the faithful may profitably invoke the saints in heaven. According to the Second Vatican Council, "It is not merely by the title of example that we cherish the memory of those in heaven . . . It is most fitting that we love those friends and co-heirs of Jesus Christ who are also our brothers and outstanding benefactors, and that we give due thanks to God for them, humbly invoking them, and having recourse to their prayers, their aid and help in obtaining from God through His Son, Jesus Christ, Our Lord, our only Redeemer and Savior, the benefits we need" (*Constitution on the Church*, VII, 50).

INVOLUNTARY. Not under the control of the free will, hence spontaneous or automatic. Also what is contrary to one's will or choice. What is involuntary is not morally imputable.

I.P.I. *In partibus infidelium*—among the infidels.

IPSO FACTO. By the very fact. In the very nature of the thing. Ecclesiastical law applies the term to excommunications that take effect the moment a person commits some crime, e.g., the public denial of a revealed dogma; to certain rights or privileges that a person acquires on being ordained or entrusted with a duty or elected to office; to a variety of consequences that follow by the fact that some person, place, or object is consecrated or set aside for sacred use.

IPSUM ESSE. Existence itself. Applied to God as subsistent Being, or the Being whose essence is existence, i.e., who essentially exists, or who cannot not exist, unlike creatures who cannot exist.

IRASCIBLE APPETITE. Scholastic philosophical term for the sense faculty that is aroused to resist an impending danger. The passion of anger.

IRREGULARITY. A canonical impediment, preventing one from entering the clerical state or continuing the exercise of any orders already received. Irregularities may be *ex defectu* in the subject, such as bodily deformities, epilepsy, insanity, or illegitimacy; or *ex delicto,* such as apostasy, heresy, homicide, attempted suicide, or marriage when bound by holy orders or religious vows. Ignorance of irregularities does not excuse one from them. Irregularities for the most part require papal dispensation; only in a few instances is the dispensation of a bishop sufficient.

IRREMOVABILITY. Privilege of certain ecclesiastical persons of not being liable to, or capable of, displacement. It corresponds to tenure in ecclesiastical office. Traditionally canon law has recognized that bishops in a diocese and pastors in a parish cannot be removed without a just cause determined by judicial procedure in an ecclesiastical court. Some pastors have had special privileges of tenure in exceptional cases and extraordinary circumstances.

IS. *Idus—*ides.

ISAAC. The son of Abraham and Sarah (Genesis 21:2–3). A few years after his birth, Yahweh tested Abraham's obedience by ordering him to sacrifice the growing boy as a burnt offering. Without hesitation Abraham set out with Isaac to the designated spot, built an altar, and prepared to kill his son as an offering to Yahweh. But an angel intervened, Isaac was spared, and Yahweh praised Abraham for his unquestioning obedience (Genesis 22:1–19). When Isaac was forty years old, his father arranged his marriage to Rebekah, who lived in the land of Abraham's kinfolk (Genesis 24). Eventually they had two sons, Esau and Jacob. In Isaac's old age a bitter enmity developed between the two sons because of Jacob's duplicity (Genesis 25:19–28). Isaac, blind and feeble, wanted to bestow his blessing on Esau, but Jacob, assisted by the conniving Rebekah, received it instead. Many years passed before the brothers were reconciled (Genesis 27:1–40). Isaac died at the age of one hundred eighty and was buried in Hebron (Genesis 35:28–29).

ISAIAH. Author of the longest prophetic book in the Old Testament, he was the son of Amoz, born about 760 B.C. in Jerusalem. His writing paralleled the reigns of three Judaean kings, Jotham, Ahaz, and Hezekiah. His mission was to proclaim the fall of Israel and Judah and the punishment that would befall the nation because of its sinfulness. The beauty of his style and the consistent nobility of his message made him one of the most revered of biblical writers. Constantly he pleaded with his people to place their trust in God and not in military achievements. No other prophet foreshadowed as convincingly the coming of the Messiah, who would be a descendant of David. Biblical students point out numerous incidents in Jesus' life which were foreshadowed in Isaiah's prophetic lines (Isaiah 2:1–5, 7:10–17, 9:1–6, 11:1–5).

ISHBAAL. See ISHBOSHETH.

ISHBOSHETH. This name is a deliberate alteration of the name "Ishbaal," offensive to Jews because it means "man of Baal." Ishbaal was the son of Saul, the king of Israel who was wounded and then committed suicide in the battle of Gilboa (I Samuel 31:6). Abner, Saul's commander, installed Ishbaal as successor, but David, now King of Judah, aspired to take over Israel (II Samuel 2:8–9). In the war that ensued Ishbaal antagonized Abner, who was the only one who could have kept him in power (II Samuel 3:6–11). Both Ishbaal and Abner were murdered, and the Israelites invited David to unite Judah and Israel under his rule (II Samuel 5:1–3).

ISMAEL. The son of Abraham and Hagar, a slave girl. At the time Ismael was born, it seemed unlikely that Sarah, Abraham's wife, would have a child because of her advanced age (Genesis 16:1–16). But Yahweh "dealt kindly with her" and Isaac was born (Genesis 21:1–3). Ill-feeling understandably developed between Sarah and Hagar, and the distressed Abraham was compelled to send Hagar and Ismael away. But "God was with the boy" and protected him. Following his marriage, he had twelve sons (Genesis 21:9–21). As time went on and Ismael and his sons extended their possessions in the land east of Egypt, they formed twelve tribes, each son becoming a tribal chief. Frequent references to these tribes appear in Isaiah, Ezekiel, and Jeremiah. Ismael was, at least in name, the ancestor of this widespread network (Genesis 25:12–18). Also spelled Ishmael.

ISRAEL. The name given to Jacob by an angel at the Jabbok ford. He was on a journey to hold a reunion with his estranged brother, Esau. During the night a stranger wrestled with him till daybreak and then said to him, "Your name shall no longer be Jacob, but Israel, because you have been strong against God." Was the stranger an angel? Jacob himself thought it was God. He named the place Peniel "because I have seen God face to face and I have survived" (Genesis 32:25–32). Later in Genesis, God appeared to Jacob once again and repeated the statement, "Your name is Jacob, but from now on, you shall be named not Jacob but Israel" (Genesis 35:9–10). This was enough in itself to show the unique niche he occupies in Jewish history: he is the personification of the nation of Israel.

ISSACHAR. The ninth son of Jacob and the progenitor of the tribe of Israel carrying his name. The boundaries of the tribe lay north of Manasseh and west of the Jordan River. Issachar's people were noted for their accomplishments in the field of commerce. Jacob spoke prophetically of his son thus: "He bowed his shoulders for the load, he became a slave to forced labor" (Genesis 49:15). It is significant that the name Issachar means "hired laborer."

ITALA. The pre-Vulgate Latin translation of the Bible. Praised by St. Augustine in his *De Doctrina Christiana* (II, 22), it was a literal rendering into the Latin from the Greek. It formed the basis of St. Jerome's Vulgate for the New Testament, and the books of Wisdom, Baruch, Ecclesiasticus, and Maccabees in the Old Testament. The text of the *Itala* is used by the canons of St. Peter's, in the Ambrosian Rite, and in some parts of the Roman missal.

ITE, MISSA EST. "Go, the Mass is ended." Concluding words of the priest to the people at the end of the Mass in the Latin Rite.

ITHAI. See ITTAI.

ITINERARIUM. Any prayers said before starting a journey, even a short one, asking God, Mary, the angels or saints for their protection. Before the revision of the Divine Office in 1970 it contained a lengthy form of blessing before undertaking a journey. It consisted of the *Benedictus* with corresponding antiphons, versicles, collects, and prayers. Religious communities often have their own versions of the itinerarium, a short form for ordinary trips and a more solemn form for lengthy journeys.

ITTAI or ITHAI. A gallant soldier and leader from Gath. When Absalom was conspiring to become king of Israel, David had to flee from the city. Among the supporters who loyally accompanied him were Ittai and his six hundred Gittites. Although he was a foreigner, he would not desert David (II Samuel 15:13–23).

IVIRON, OUR LADY OF (shrine). One of Russia's most famous wonder-working icons of the Blessed Virgin. Housed in a small chapel at the gate of the Red Square in Moscow was the image of the thoughtful uncrowned Blessed Virgin and her Infant Child, resting on her left arm. No czar ever thought of leaving the city without a visit to ask Mary's guidance and protection. The original of this famous painting is in the Greek monastery at Mount Athos. When Czar Alexis was seriously ill, he asked that the "Virgin of the Gate," as the Mount Athos icon was called, be brought to him. A special copy was made then and sent to him. He was cured instantly. This icon was then placed in a chapel in front of the Kremlin, the same little church that served the people as a place of refuge during the Bolshevik Revolution. During the revolution this church was destroyed, but the icon was saved and for a time received honor at the Donskoi monastery. Since the Communist take-over its present location is uncertain.

J

JABAL. One of the descendants of Cain; the writer in Genesis identifies him as "the ancestor of the tent-dwellers and owners of livestock." His brother Jubal set the pattern for traveling musicians. Tubal is described as "the ancestor of metal workers." In other words, these three are credited with having a significant part in developing the social customs of the early nomads (Genesis 4:20–22).

JACOB. The son of Isaac and Rebekah; he became the third of the Hebrew Patriarchs and one of the great figures in rabbinical literature. The account of his being renamed "Israel" by God, which thus made him the eponymous ancestor of the nation, is significant comment on his distinctive place in Jewish history (Genesis 35:9–10). In his dealings with Laban, his uncle, over a twenty-year period he acquired the latter's two daughters as wives and considerable wealth (Genesis 32:3–21). Altogether he had twelve sons, each of whom became the head of one of the tribes of Israel (Genesis 29, 30). One of the most familiar stories in Scripture is the lengthy account of the adventures of Joseph, who was the elder of the two sons of Jacob by Rachel and his father's favorite. Sold into slavery, he eventually became Governor of Egypt. During a great famine there was a family reunion and the overjoyed Jacob regained his son. Jacob and his entire family moved to Goshen in the land of Egypt, and he spent his remaining years there under Joseph's protection. He was buried at his urgent request back in Canaan, where Abraham and Isaac were buried (Genesis 37–50).

JACOBINS. Name originally given to the Dominican friars in France because their first house in Northern France was founded in Paris in 1218 on the Rue St.-Jacques. During the French Revolution, in 1789, this house was acquired by the radical club Breton, where they came to be called Jacobins. The term is now applied to all holding revolutionary views.

JACOBITES. The group of Syrian Monophysites who did not accept the teaching of the Council of Chalcedon (451) on the two natures united in one divine Person of Christ. They took their name from Jacob Baradaeus, who formed them into the national Church of Syria. One of their distinctive customs is to make the sign of the Cross with one finger to express their belief that Christ had only one nature, not two. Sometimes the term "Jacobites" is applied to the Monophysites elsewhere, e.g., in Egypt.

JAIRUS. A synagogue official in Capernaum whose daughter Jesus restored to life. Jairus appealed to Jesus to visit his home and cure her. On their way a messenger from the house of the official came to report the girl's death, but Jesus, accompanied by her parents and several disciples, entered the home and ordered the child to rise. She came back to life instantly and stood up, to the amazement of those present (Luke 8:41–42, 49–56; Mark 5:22–24, 35–43).

JAMES, EPISTLE OF. Traditionally attributed to James the Less, "the brother of the Lord." It was written in Greek, and its style and language were typically Jewish, indicating that it was originally intended for converts from Judaism. Its main stress is on the moral conduct of Christians, notably their perseverance under trial, respect for the poor, and the need to bridle one's tongue. It is especially clear on the duty of living one's faith and not merely professing it (James 2:14–26). Among the good works binding on Christians, the practice of charity and the avoidance of conflict are primary (James 4:1–12). (Etym. Anglicized form of Hebrew, *Jacob,* through Spanish *Jaime.*)

JAMES THE GREATER. The son of Zebedee and older brother of John. Both were Apostles; whenever the twelve are listed, these names are paired. Jesus called them "the Sons of Thunder" (Matthew 10:3; Mark 3:17). On one occasion he rebuked them for urging violence against some Samaritans who refused to receive him. Both were fishermen and partners with Simon Peter; the trio responded promptly to Jesus' invitation to become fishers of men (Luke 5:10–11, 9:53–56). That the brothers were especially close to him is indicated by the fact that they were present at the Transfiguration (Matthew 17:1–2) and accompanied him to Gethsemane (Matthew 26:37). James was beheaded by Herod in the early days of the Church (Acts 12:2).

JAMES THE LESS. The son of Alphaeus and Mary (the woman who was present at Calvary). The "Less" means "younger." He was one of the Twelve Apostles (Acts 1:13). He was a brother of Joset and possibly Matthew (Mark 15:40).

JANNES. An Egyptian magician named by Paul. Jewish tradition held that Jannes and Jambres had tried to outwit Moses but were proved fakers. Paul used their names in comparing them to those of his contemporaries whose "minds were corrupt and their faith spurious" (II Timothy 3:8–9).

JANSENISM. A system of grace developed by Cornelis Jansen, or Cornelius Jansenius (1585–1638), theologian at Louvain and later Bishop of Ypres. As a school of theology, it should be seen in two stages, namely the original position of Jansenius and its later development by his followers.

Jansenius' own teaching is contained in the book *Augustinus,* which he spent years in writing and was published two years after his death. According to Jansenius, man's free will is incapable of any moral goodness. All man's actions proceed either from earthly desires, which stem from concupiscence, or from heavenly desires, which are produced by grace. Each exercises an urgent influence on the human will, which in consequence of its lack of freedom always follows the pressure of the stronger desire. Implicit in Jansenism is the denial of the supernatural order, the possibility of either rejection or acceptance of grace. Accordingly those who receive the grace will be saved; they are the predestined. All others will be lost. Jansenism was condemned as heretical in five major propositions by Pope Innocent X in 1653. It was recondemned by Pope Alexander VII in 1656, when Jansenists claimed that their doctrine was misrepresented.

The later developments of Jansenism were built on the earlier foundations but went beyond them in a number of ways. Stress on God's selective salvation produced a general harshness and moral rigorism, denying God's mercy to all mankind. Disregard of papal teaching led to an arbitrary attitude toward the use of the sacraments, notably reducing the frequency of penance and the Eucharist, and giving rise to Gallicanism, which denied papal primacy and infallibility. In 1794, Pope Pius VI condemned a series of eighty-five propositions of the Italian Jansenists led by Scipione de' Ricci, Bishop of Pistoia and Prato. Among the propositions was the claim that the authority of the Church depends on the consent of its members and that the jurisdiction of a diocesan bishop is independent of the Pope.

JAPHETH. The third son of Noah, who with Shem and Ham survived the Deluge in the ark. From these three, according to Genesis, "the whole earth was peopled" (Genesis 9:18–19). Japheth was the father of Gomer, Magog, Javan, Tubal, and Meshech. Their descendants were largely Indo-European peoples who lived in the Black Sea region (Genesis 10:2–6).

JARED. The son of Mahalalel, the father of Enoch, and the grandfather of Methuselah. These names are listed in the roll of Adam's descendants in Genesis. Jared lived to be 962 years old (Genesis 5:15–21).

JASNA GORA. Polish national shrine of Our Lady of Czestochowa, which contains the famous icon of Mary holding the Child Jesus. Jasna Gora, the "Hill of Light," was the principal place of pilgrimage visited by Pope John Paul II in June 1979. There are numerous references to the shrine in the speeches and writings of the Polish Pope, referring to "Our Mother of God of Jasna Gora." The location of the image on the hill Czestochowa, in south-central Poland, was occasioned by the erection of a priory of Paulite monks there since 1382.

J.C. *Jesus Christus*—Jesus Christ.

J.C.D. *Juris Canonici Doctor; Juris Civilis Doctor*—Doctor of Canon Law; Doctor of Civil Law.

J.C.L. *Juris Canonici Licentiatus*—Licentiate in Canon Law.

J.D. *Juris Doctor*—Doctor of Law.

JECHONIAH (also spelled Jeconiah, Jeconias, Jehoiachin). The son and successor of King Jehoiakim of Judah (Jeremiah 24:1). Shortly after ascending the throne in 598 B.C., he was taken captive by Nebuchadnezzar and exiled to Babylon with his family and followers. There is no evidence that he ever returned, although he enjoyed considerable freedom (II Chronicles 36:10). After thirty-seven years of exile he was released from prison by Nebuchadnezzar's successor and was well taken care of for the rest of his life (II Kings 25:27–30).

JECONIAH. See JECHONIAH.

JECONIAS. See JECHONIAH.

JEHOIACHIN. See JECHONIAH.

JEHOSHAPHAT. King of Judah (c. 873–849 B.C.) who succeeded his father, King Asa. Apparently a prudent ruler, he took steps to strengthen peaceful relations with Israel and ensure Judah's stability (II Chronicles 17:1). He traveled through his country making wise appointments of judges and priests. "Yahweh," he reminded them, "has no part in fraud or partiality or taking of bribes" (II Chronicles 19:3–10). For nearly twenty-five years he ruled Judah without serious trouble (II Chronicles 20:31). The last years of his reign, however, were marred because he "allied himself with Ahaziah, King of Israel, who led him into evil ways" (II Chronicles 20:35). When he died, his son Jehoram succeeded him (II Chronicles 20:35).

JEHOVAH. Mistaken but common rendering of the letters JHVH or YHVH, transcribing the Hebrew letters representing the name of God. It should be Jahweh or Yahweh.

JEHOVAH-YAHWEH. Jehovah is God, the English name for the Hebrew *Yahweh*. When the latter promised Moses that he would feed Moses' people, he concluded by saying, "Then you will learn that I, Yahweh, am your God" (Exodus 16:13). Jehovah developed into the form used most commonly when he was communicating with the Israelites, whereas God was used where Gentiles were concerned. The admonition "You shall not utter the name of Yahweh your God to misuse it" (Exodus 20:7) ultimately induced the Israelites not to pronounce his name at all but to substitute for it the title "Adonai," meaning "the Lord." Other titles used in the Old Testament for God are El or Elohim or El Shaddai.

JEHU. 1. listed as one of David's many heroic supporters in battle, who are described as "champions, standbys in battle, who could handle the bow with right hand or with left, who could use stones or arrows" (I Chronicles 12:1–3); 2. a prophet, son of Hanani, who denounced King Baasha of Israel for leading his people into sin, and prophesied that the king and his family would be swept away because of Yahweh's anger (I Kings 16:1–4); 3. the son of Jehoshaphat who was inspired by Elisha to attack and kill King Jehoram of Israel because he had violated Yahweh's laws. The subsequent wholesale slaughter included Jehoram, his mother Jezebel, King Ahaziah of Judah, and all the sons and supporters of Jehoram and Ahab. Then he gathered all the devotees of the pagan deity Baal into the temple under the pretense of offering sacrifice. Unable to escape, every one of them was killed. After this bloodbath Jehu's reign over Israel lasted twenty-eight years, but it was not distinguished by virtue (II Kings 9, 10). He repeated all the offenses against Yahweh for which he had murdered his predecessor (II Kings 10:31).

JEPHTHAH. Son of Gilead. But his mother was a harlot and Gilead's other sons drove him away lest he share in his father's inheritance. He became a warrior in the land of Tob and was recognized as a valiant soldier (Judges 11:1–3). So much so that when the Israelites were attacked by the Ammonites his people begged him to return home and become their leader (Judges 11:6–11). He assumed the leadership, begged Yahweh for help, and promised to offer a human sacrifice if he won. He achieved a great victory, but tragically, his only daughter fulfilled the condition he had set for the sacrifice and he felt obliged to live up to his promise by killing her even though Israelites considered a human sacrifice a violation of Yahweh's law (Judges 11:30–40). The latter apparently approved, however, because Jephthah won another great victory against the Ephraimites (Judges 12:1–6). For the next six years he became a judge in Israel and was highly respected. When he died he was buried in his home town of Mizpah, in the region of Gilead.

JEREMIAH. One of the three Major Prophets. He lived during the seventh and sixth centuries before Christ and witnessed the capture and destruction of Jerusalem. He survived six kings of Judaea, Amon, Josiah, Jehoahaz, Jehoiakim, Jehoiachin, and Zedekiah. It was a time of intrigue and turmoil, with Assyria, Babylon, and Egypt struggling for supremacy. Tiny Judaea was caught in the middle and tried desperately to maintain its independence. Jeremiah was a reforming prophet from childhood, according to his own testimony. When he protested to Yahweh, the latter replied, "Do not say 'I am a child.' Go now to those to whom I send you and say whatever I command you" (Jeremiah 1:7). He repeatedly conveyed the anger and resentment of Yahweh to his people, deploring their apostasy and the immorality of their lives and the insincerity and superficiality of their leaders. Even his own townspeople of Anathoth were embittered by Jeremiah's denunciations and threatened him with death (Jeremiah 11:21). When he delivered Yahweh's condemnation of the pagan practices in Topheth, Pashur, who was in charge of the Temple police, had him beaten and put in the stocks at the Gate of Benjamin (Jeremiah 20:2). After he dictated a scroll to his secretary, Baruch, deploring the offenses of King Jehoiakim, the latter destroyed the scroll, unmoved by Jeremiah's reproaches. The tenacious prophet promptly dictated the entire scroll over again, even adding to his accusation (Jeremiah 36:32). During the reign of King Zedekiah, Jeremiah, acting on Yawheh's orders, advised the king to surrender to the Chaldeans, assuring him that he would be well treated. Zedekiah ignored the advice. When the Chaldeans invaded Jerusalem, as Jeremiah had prophesied, the palace was destroyed, the walls leveled, and the king's family killed (Jeremiah 39). Now, in the last year of his life, Jeremiah continued to be the voice of Yahweh until he died c. 587 B.C., probably in Egypt.

JEROBOAM I. The first king of Israel after Solomon's domain was split during the reign of his son, Rehoboam, in the tenth century B.C. Jeroboam had been a labor chief under Solomon but rebelled at the king's tyranny and fled into Egypt (I Kings 11:26–40). There was no improvement when Rehoboam came to power, so the people revolted and made Jeroboam king. Rehoboam's territory was reduced to Judah and Benjamin (I Kings 12). The schism was widened by religious differences. Jeroboam set up shrines in Bethel and Dan to offset the influence of Jerusalem in the lives of the Israelites. But Old Testament writers were unanimous in condemning "the sins of Jeroboam" and maintained that he turned Israel against the Lord by encouraging pagan ceremonies (I Kings 13).

JEROBOAM II. The son of King Joash of Israel. Jeroboam ruled the Northern Kingdom from 783 to 743 B.C., a long, prosperous reign. Several important military victories and relative instability in the Assyrian court enabled Jeroboam to extend his territory and exercise firm control. But the prophets Hosea and Amos deplored the moral and religious condition of the country (II Kings 14:23–29). His reign illustrated the oft-repeated historical phenomenon of economic prosperity corrupting the spiritual life of a people. "Yahweh indicts the inhabitants of the country; there is no fidelity, no tenderness, no knowledge of God . . . ." (Hosea 4:1–2).

JERONYMITES. See HIERONYMITES.

JERUSALEM. Ancient city in Palestine, the religious and political center of the Jewish people, situated on the crest of a chain of mountains that cross Palestine from north to south. Originally called Salem, it was the capital of King Melchizedek about 2100 B.C. (Genesis 14). First mentioned in the Book of Joshua (10, 15), the inhabitants were known as Jebusites. When the Promised Land was parceled out, Jerusalem was assigned to the tribe of Benjamin. Its most famous rulers were King David, who brought the Ark of the Covenant into the city, and his son Solomon, who built the first Temple. A second Temple was built in the sixth century B.C., and the third (and last) was the work of Herod the Great, who ruled as a vassal of Rome from 37 to 4 B.C. The Christian history of Jerusalem begins with the short ministry of the Savior, culminating in his death, resurrection, and ascension. The Apostles lived and taught there for some time after Pentecost, and met in Jerusalem for their first council about A.D. 49. The Apostle St. James the Less was the first Bishop of Jerusalem, where he was condemned by the Sanhedrin and martyred in A.D. 62.

JERUSALEM, FALL OF. Destruction of the sacred city in A.D. 70 after a siege of 143 days, in which, according to Tacitus (*Histories*, V, 13), 600,000 Jews perished, many by crucifixion. The Roman Emperor Titus razed its buildings and destroyed its temple. It is believed that the house that was the scene of Pentecost and the Last Supper was spared and became the first Christian church.

JESSE, ROOT OF. A symbol of Christ, "a shoot springs from the root of Jesse" (Isaiah 11:1). St. Ambrose explains the root as the family of the Jews, the stem as Mary, the flower as Christ. The great O antiphon of December 19 is sung "O Root of Jesse who standeth as an ensign of the people before whom kings will keep silence and unto whom the Gentiles will make supplication, come to deliver us and tarry not." Often represented as a flourishing tree, it carries the six-pointed star of Israel at its base and the Cross as its fulfilled blossom at the apex.

JESSE WINDOW. A stained-glass representation of Christ's human genealogy. The symbol is in the form of a many-branched tree and takes on a variety of forms. Christ is at the summit, with the main characters in his genealogy depicted on the branches beneath. The name is derived from Jesse, the father of King David, who is the root of the tree (I Samuel 16:18–22; Isaiah 11:1).

JESUITS. The Society of Jesus, founded by St. Ignatius Loyola and approved by Pope Paul III in 1540. As conceived by the founder, it had a twofold aim: to strengthen and where necessary to restore the Catholic faith in the wake of the Protestant Reformation, and to preach the Gospel in non-Christian lands. Typical of the first purpose was the establishment of colleges throughout Europe, and the second purpose was the development of worldwide mission enterprises in Asia, Africa, and the newly developed Americas.

The Society of Jesus grew out of the Spiritual Exercises of St. Ignatius, and its structure and discipline were embodied in the detailed Constitutions, also written by the founder.

Opposition from many quarters, but especially from the Jansenists, led to suppression of the Jesuits by Pope Clement XIV in

1773. They were restored by Pope Pius VII in 1814. Since their restoration, they grew in numbers to become the largest single religious institute in the Catholic world through their universities, colleges, and secondary schools, through scholarly publications, retreat houses, and seminaries.

The Society of Jesus is divided into assistancies, these in turn into provinces, and within the provinces are local communities. The superior general is elected for life; he appoints provincials and also the rectors of the more important local communities.

There are three kinds of finally professed members in the society: the solemnly professed and the spiritual coadjutors who are priests, and the lay brothers who are spiritual coadjutors. The solemnly professed take solemn vows of poverty, chastity, and obedience and four simple vows: special obedience to the Pope, not to mitigate the society's poverty, not to accept ecclesiastical dignitaries, actively seeking to avoid such preferments. The others take simple vows only. But all the finally professed make a total renunciation of private ownership.

JESUS. The name of Our Lord. It is the Latin form of the Greek *Iesous,* whose Hebrew is *Jeshua* or *Joshua,* meaning Yahweh is salvation. It is the name through which God the Father is to be invoked and by which the Apostles worked miracles (Acts 3, 6). In standard usage the name "Jesus" is applied to the Son of Mary, who is also the Son of God; as distinct from "Christ," which refers to his Messianic role as the fulfillment of the ancient prophecies. See also SACRAMENT OF GOD.

JESUS CHRIST THE CONQUEROR. Ancient title of Christ signifying his victory over sin, death, and the evil spirit. It appears in the familiar monogram IC XC NIKA, where I and C are the first and last letters of the Greek word *Ihcuc* (Jesus); X and C are the first and last letters of *Xrictoc* (Christ); and *nika* is the Greek word for "conquers."

JESUS MOVEMENT. A movement among fervent young people who wish to imitate Jesus, particularly as depicted in the Bible. They engage in preaching and giving instruction to their peers and, to some extent, have become involved in sexual aberrations and the use of drugs. A number have become associated with Pentecostal groups but without Church affiliation. They tend to be strongly pacifist and indifferent to accepted standards of dress and external behavior. Centered in the United States and Canada, the movement has spread elsewhere. Those who belong to the movement are often referred to as "Jesus freaks."

Also a sect of conservative Protestants, especially young people, who seek to promote faith in Jesus as Savior; they operate independently of any of the established denominations. Also called the Jesus Revolution.

JESUS PEOPLE. Also known as Street Christians, they are the promoters of the Jesus Movement. They emphasize an intense personal relationship with Jesus Christ, whom they preach everywhere and to everyone, but especially to their peers among the youth in the large cities.

JESUS PRAYER. A popular devotion among Eastern Christians. The words of the prayer are "O Lord Jesus Christ, Son of God, have mercy on me, a sinner." It is said by devout Christians at regular intervals during the day and night, and is used by them as the basis of their meditation.

JETHRO. A shepherd-priest of a tribe called Kenites. Moses tended Jethro's sheep for forty years near Mount Horeb (Exodus 3:1–6). It was during this time that Yahweh appeared to Moses and gave him the mission of leading his people out of Egypt. He married Zipporah, Jethro's daughter, who bore him two sons, Gershom and Eliezer (Exodus 18:3–4).

JEWISH DECALOGUE. The Ten Commandments as an essential part of the Jewish religion. Containing only 120 Hebrew words in all, the Decalogue has exercised more profound influence on the moral and social life of humanity than any other group of laws in history. There are two versions of the Decalogue in Scripture: the priestly version (Exodus 20:1–17) and the Deuteronomic (Deuteronomy 5:6–21). They differ mainly in two ways. In Exodus the observance of the Sabbath is based on religious motives, namely the fact that God rested on the seventh day after creation; in Deuteronomy the motive is rather humanitarian. Also in Exodus the prohibition of covetousness classes a man's wife with his other domestic property, whereas in Deuteronomy the wife is treated separately. The first four commandments (in the Catholic version the first three) refer to people's duties toward God; the last six their duties to others. In Temple times, they formed an integral part of the religious service, being recited daily just before the Shema. They are highly honored in modern Judaism. When read in the synagogue, the congregation rises and the commandments are intoned by the reader to a special solemn tone. The Jewish festival of Shavuot (seven weeks after the first day of Passover) commemorates the revelation of the Decalogue on Mount Sinai, and the solemn reading of the Ten Commandments is the highlight of the religious service on that day.

JEWS. Those who adhere to Judaism both as a religion and a people. Originally the name was restricted to the subjects of the kingdom of Judah. But after the Babylonian exile it became the common name for the race descended from Jacob and for the followers of the Mosaic religion.

JEZEBEL. The wife of King Ahab of Israel (869–850 B.C.). An ardent devotee of Baal worship, Jezebel corrupted the court of Ahab by bringing to Israel hundreds of priests of this cult from her Phoenician homeland (I Kings 18:19). She was the cause of the deaths of many faithful Israelites who protested the immoralities she fostered (I Kings 18:13). The prophet Elijah defied her and challenged the priests of Baal to a contest on Mount Carmel to prove the superiority of Yahweh over Baal (I Kings 18:21–46). He won the contest but had to flee into the wilderness. Jezebel suffered a horrible death (II Kings 9:30–37). Her name is used to symbolize wickedness.

J.M.J. Jesus, Maria, Joseph—Jesus, Mary, Joseph.

JO., JOANN. *Joannes*—John.

JOAB. The commander of David's army. He first caught David's attention when he distinguished himself in a battle against the Jebusites culminating in the capture of Jerusalem (I Chronicles 11:6). He proved to be a capable leader but bloodthirsty. He murdered Abner, a Northern Kingdom general, which shocked David into giving Abner a soldier's funeral and ovation (II Samuel 3:26–34). Joab also won great victories against the Syrians and the Ammonites. He tried to keep peace between David and his rebellious son, Absalom (II Samuel 18:14). On another occasion he brought about the death of Uriah at David's request in order to facilitate the king's marriage to the widow Bath-Sheba (II Samuel 11:6–25). Joab made a fatal decision in supporting Adonijah against Solomon. When the latter gained the throne, he had Joab executed (I Kings 2:34).

JOAKIM. A high priest in Jerusalem whose name appears in the biblical Book of Judith. While the frightened Israelites were awaiting invasion by the Assyrian general Holofernes, Joakim suggested that men be posted at certain mountain passes that the Assyrian invaders would have to use (Judith 4:5–7), but his plan was not needed. Judith's coup in killing Holofernes and bringing about a great victory for the Israelites led to a joyous scene in which Joakim hailed Judith: "You are the glory of Jerusalem! You are the great pride of Israel!" (Judith 15:10).

JOANNA. The wife of the chief steward in the household of Herod Antipas (Luke 8:3). She was converted by Jesus and was one of the women who followed him and his apostles as they traveled from town to town preaching. She was one of the three women who went to the tomb on Easter morning to anoint the body and heard the angels announce that Jesus had risen from the dead (Luke 24:1–11). (Etym. Greek *ioana*, from Hebrew *yochanan*, Yahweh is gracious.)

JOHANNINE COMMA. See THREE WITNESSES.

JOAN, POPESS. Name of a legendary person who appears in history periodically as a female pope. There was a reference to her in a chronicle about 1250, but there is no possible place in the line of popes at that time where she could be placed, nor are there any grounds to support her existence. Her picture has never been included in the papal portraits, nor does *Liber Pontificalis* mention her. She exists only as a fable in Roman folklore.

JOB. The chief character in what many critics consider the most beautifully written book in the Bible. The author is unknown. From internal evidence it is speculated that he was an Israelite who wrote sometime between 600 and 400 B.C. The Book of Job is a profound philosophic discussion of human suffering, with Job and several of his friends taking turns offering possible solutions to the problem of good and evil. Their efforts to find an answer to determine Yahweh's reasons for permitting such indignities to afflict a faithful believer were fruitless. Job and his friends realized the fatuousness of the popular belief that goodness and evil are rewarded in this life. Ultimately, there remains the dominant theme: faith in God must endure even when reason and understanding fail (Book of Job).

JOEL. 1. the older son of Samuel, the Israelite judge. He was appointed a judge in turn by his father, but failed to win public respect. He accepted bribes and perverted justice. The elders protested to Samuel and urged him to choose a king (I Samuel 8:1–5). Reluctant at first, Samuel was ordered by Yahweh to comply with their request. Saul became the new king of Israel (I Samuel 11:15); 2. the son of Pethuel who became a prophet in Judah and wrote one of the books of the Old Testament (Book of Joel). He is referred to as the prophet of Pentecost because he emphasized the future coming of the Holy Spirit (Acts 2:17). Peter quoted him in the Acts of the Apostles on Pentecost day in lines that include the familiar promise "Your young men shall see visions; your old men shall dream dreams" (Joel 3:1).

JOHN MARK. The writer of the second Gospel. Several times in the Acts of the Apostles he is referred to as John Mark (Acts 12:12, 12:25, 15:37). Twice he is referred to simply as John (Acts 13:5, 13:13). But normally readers of the Bible think of him as Mark. See MARK.

JOHN THE APOSTLE. A son of Zebedee and a brother of another Apostle, James. Both were fishermen and were among the first to be called to follow Jesus (Mark 1:19). Their mother may have been Salome, the sister of Jesus' mother—which would make the brothers the cousins of Jesus (John 19:25). It seems safe to affirm that John was "the beloved disciple," though nowhere is he specifically named. He was the closest to Jesus at the Last Supper (John 13:23), and it was to John (the only Apostle present on Calvary) that Jesus entrusted his mother (John 19:26–27). On several occasions John was accorded a special place. He was allowed to accompany Jesus to Jairus' home when the latter's daughter was brought back to life. He was present at the Transfiguration (Matthew 17:1–2). Finally, he was one of the three who went with Jesus to Gethsemane (Mark 14:33). It was appropriate that he would be the Apostle to hasten with Peter to the tomb on Easter morning and be the first to proclaim belief in the Risen Christ (John 20:1–10). Several references are made to him in the Acts of the Apostles. He was present in the upper room with the Apostles after the Ascension (Acts 1:13). He accompanied Peter when the lame man was cured in the Temple (Acts 3:1–10). Again he went with Peter to pray for the Samaritans to receive the Holy Spirit (Acts 8:14–17). The most lasting memorial of his work, of course, was his biblical writings. Three short epistles are attributed to him because in style and doctrine they are so closely akin to the fourth Gospel. The Book of Revelation, the last book of the New Testament, written during the final quarter of the century, is credited to John. Likewise, the fourth Gospel is Johannine in spirit and tone. It was obviously the work of one close to Jesus, an eyewitness of his ministry, and one who loved him intensely. The style and vocabulary are Semitic. The writer was thoroughly familiar with the customs and geography of Palestine. His close association with Peter and James is significant. John must have been the author. Some have held that he was martyred with his brother in A.D. 44, but if that is true he could not have written either the Gospel or Revelation, which were not written till some years later. In 1907 the Pontifical Biblical Commission denied that the arguments against John's authorship were valid. The weight of evidence indicates that he was the only Apostle not to be martyred. He probably died at the very end of the century. (Etym. Greek *iôannēs*, from Hebrew *yochanan*, Yahweh is gracious.)

JOHN THE BAPTIST. The son of Zechariah and Elizabeth, John was a few months older than Jesus and destined to become his forerunner (Luke 1:36). Always an austere figure, he was looked upon by the Apostles as a kind of reincarnated Elijah preparing the way for the acceptance of the Lord. Jesus himself said, "I tell you that Elijah has come already and they did not recognize him, but treated him as they pleased; and the Son of Man will suffer similarly at their hands." The disciples understood then that he had been speaking of John the Baptist (Matthew 17:12–13). John lived an ascetic life in the Judaean desert to prepare himself for his ministry in the country about the Jordan. He constantly proclaimed a baptism of penance for the forgiveness of sins (Luke 3:3), and became indeed, in the words of Isaiah, "a voice crying in the wilderness" (Isaiah 40:3). Many were so impressed that they mistook him for the Messiah. He made it clear, though, that "I baptize you with water, but someone is coming, someone who is more powerful than I am; I am not fit to undo the strap of his sandals; he will baptize you with the Holy Spirit and fire" (Luke 3:16). Jesus always spoke of him in the highest terms. "I tell you, of all the children born of women, there is no one greater than John" (Luke 7:28). The common people treated him with reverence, but the Pharisees and the lawyers showed disdain for him and refused to be baptized (Luke 7:30). Surely they had excellent precedent! Jesus himself appeared before John to be baptized. John tried to dissuade him because of his own unworthiness, but Jesus insisted and John baptized him (Matthew 3:13–15). Herod Antipas imprisoned John for boldly denouncing his unlawful marriage to Herodias. Using her daughter to trap Herod into promising her a reward, she demanded and received the head of John the Baptist (Matthew 14:3–12).

JONAH. An Israelite prophet, son of Amittai. Unlike the books of the other Minor Prophets, the short Book of Jonah (only four chapters) is narrative rather than oracular. Though he lived in the eighth century B.C., the book was not written until about the fifth century. To evade Yahweh's assignment, Jonah had fled in a ship but a terrible storm led to his being thrown overboard and being swallowed by a huge fish. After three days he was washed ashore and, properly chastened, proceeded to Nineveh to discharge his original task—to warn the people of Nineveh of their impending doom. Their contrition was so genuine that Yahweh relented and the catastrophe was averted. But now Jonah was outraged that his effective preaching was negated. He had to learn that Yahweh's compassion and love were dominant. The story uses an actual personality to teach a moral lesson: God's mercy is at hand provided man is willing to repent.

JONATHAN. Son of Saul, who was King of Israel. He is distinguished in biblical history for his unselfish, loyal friendship for David. Ironically, when the latter ultimately succeeded Saul to the throne, he was receiving what normally would have gone to Jonathan (II Samuel 5:4–5). While Saul was alive, he was so envious of David's military victories and popularity with the people that he tried repeatedly to have him killed. He sent him into battles, hoping that David would not survive (I Samuel 18:25). He attacked David himself with a spear. Yet he never succeeded (I Samuel 19:10). In all these attempts, Jonathan was caught between his father's hatred and his devoted friendship. He never wavered, however, in protecting David and warning him of Saul's schemes (I Samuel 20). Finally, the king died in the battle of Gilboa; Jonathan and his brothers were killed also (I Samuel 31:6). David paid tribute to both Saul and Jonathan, but his grief was greater for a supremely faithful friend: "Oh, Jonathan, in your death I am stricken. I am desolate for you, Jonathan, my brother . . ." (II Samuel 1:26). It was a tribute richly deserved.

JOSEPH. The youngest of Jacob's twelve sons. Because he was Jacob's favorite, his brothers were jealous of him. When his father gave him "a coat of many colors," they resented the preferential treatment. They even considered killing him, but the prudent Reuben dissuaded them (Genesis 37:3–22). Joseph was sold to the Egyptians as a slave (Genesis 37:28), but with Yahweh protecting him he rose rapidly to positions of responsibility (Genesis 39:1–6). During a severe drought that afflicted the entire region he rendered valuable service (Genesis 41:37–49). Unexpectedly he was reunited with his brothers, whom Jacob had sent to Egypt in a desperate search for food. They did not recognize him, but he knew them instantly. After subjecting them to several tests, he disclosed his identity and sent them back to Canaan to get their father. He arranged to have the family settled in Goshen in Egypt, where they would be assured a substantial living as long as they wanted (Genesis 42, 43, 44, 45). Jacob, of course, was delighted to regain his favorite son and, being assured by God that it was a safe move, he intrusted his entire family, seventy strong, to Joseph's protection (Genesis 46). Jacob lived seventeen happy years in Egypt (Genesis 47), but, when he knew that he was dying, asked to be buried in Canaan with Abraham and Isaac (Genesis 49:29–33). His son respected this dying wish. Joseph himself lived to be 110 years old and was buried in Egypt (Genesis 50:26).

JOSEPH (Barnabas). Also called Joses. He is several times referred to as Joseph or Joset (Matthew 13:55; 27:56; Mark 6:3; 15:40), but he is better known by the surname Barnabas, which was given to him by the Apostles and means "son of encouragement" (Acts 4:36), for his notable work in the early Church. (Etym. Hebrew *yoseph*, let him (the god) add; Barnabas, Aramaic, son of consolation.) See BARNABAS.

JOSEPH (Barsabbas). A disciple of Jesus. It seems likely that he was one of the seventy-two disciples Luke mentioned (Luke 10:1). When the Apostles were choosing a replacement for Judas, Barsabbas and Matthias were the candidates selected. The choice was decided by lot and Matthias became the twelfth Apostle (Acts 1:23–26).

JOSEPH, ST. Spouse of the Virgin Mary and foster father of Jesus. His name is an abbreviated form of the Hebrew *Jehoseph*, "may Jahweh give an increase." He was a descendant of David and natural relative of Mary, but the degree of kinship is not known. His father is called Jacob, though he is also said to have been the son of Heli, perhaps by some kind of adoption. Hegesippus in the second century identifies one of his brothers, Cleophas, who is called the "uncle" of Jesus. We do not know where Joseph was born. It may have been at Bethlehem, as the *Apology* of Justin the Martyr suggests, or Nazareth, where Mary lived.

According to the Evangelists, he was a workman (Greek *tekton*), which tradition has interpreted to mean carpenter, although he may have engaged in other kinds of labor, too, as circumstances in a Jewish village would require. The *Proto-Evangelium* of James and other apocrypha, wishing to safeguard Mary's virginity and explain the term "brethren of the Lord" (Matthew 13:55), present Joseph as an old man and widower with children by a previous marriage. But the exertions demanded for supporting a family and for making long journeys practically exclude old age. The "brethren" of Jesus are explained as relatives, either on the side of Cleophas or of a sister of Mary.

Joseph's marriage took place before the Incarnation, since he and Mary are called spouses before the Annunciation. When the Gospel says that Mary was a "virgin promised," this refers to Jewish matrimonial rights, which distinguished espousals (regarded as true marriage) from the bride's entering the house of her husband. When Joseph became aware of Mary's pregnancy, he thought of putting her away privately, without exposure, until an angel revealed the mystery to him. He received Mary into his home and acquired the parental right of naming the infant to be born of her.

The census decree of Emperor Augustus sent Joseph with Mary to Bethlehem, where he probably owned a small field, since the law required enrollment in the place where land was held. When the shepherds came to visit the Christ Child, they found him with Joseph and his mother. Forty days after Jesus was born, Joseph accompanied Mary and her Son at the presentation in the Temple, and through angelic direction fled into Egypt to escape the anger of Herod. Twice the Evangelist Luke says that Christ lived in Nazareth with Joseph and Mary; first after the presentation and again when Jesus, at the age of twelve, was found in Jerusalem among the doctors after being lost for three days. After this the only references to Joseph in the Gospels are to identify him as the reputed father of Jesus and a workman whose humble origins scandalized the critics of his putative Son. Very probably Joseph died before Christ finished his hidden life, since he is completely absent from the public life, whereas Christ's mother and "brethren" are mentioned more than once. The title "Son of Mary," which the people occasionally used of Christ, also intimates that Mary was a widow by the time her Son began his public ministry.

JOSEPHINISM. The Church-State policy of Joseph II (1741–90), Emperor of Austria, which advocated secular interference and state supremacy in ecclesiastical affairs. He consolidated almost the entire property of the Church and merged all the religious funds into one great *Religionsfund* for the requirements of public worship. To achieve his purpose, he suppressed all the monasteries and secularized them. For meddling in Church affairs, even to the regulation of candles, he was called the "Sacristan Emperor."

JOSEPH OF ARIMATHEA. A rich Israelite and member of the Sanhedrin. At Jesus' trial he took no part in the prosecution. That he was a secret disciple is made clear in the testimony of Matthew and Mark (Matthew 27:57; Mark 15:43). Shortly after Jesus died, Joseph appeared before Pilate and requested permission to take charge of the burial (Jewish law required that the body of the executed be removed the same day) (Deuteronomy 21:22–23). Pilate granted permission. Joseph had the body wrapped in a shroud and laid in a new tomb, one in which he intended to be buried himself. Then he had a great stone rolled across the entrance (Matthew 27:57–60).

JOSHUA. Son of Nun, an Ephraimite. A military leader and hero whose name first appeared in the Old Testament when he won a great victory for Moses against the Amalekites (Exodus 17:8–16). His prestige grew, and, obeying Yahweh's advice, Moses chose Joshua to be his successor and lead the Israelites out of Egypt and into Canaan (Numbers 27:18–23). Whereas Moses failed to reach it, Joshua succeeded in entering the Promised Land (Deuteronomy 31:2). The history of this great enterprise appears in the Book of Joshua, which relates the conquest of Canaan, the partition of the territory among the twelve tribes, and his final days (Joshua 1–12, 13–21, 22–24). Joshua was the dominating figure of the book, but he was not the author. While part of it was written during his lifetime, the writing was spread over a long period and a number of writers contributed. Hence, it is a fabric of many strands. It affords a simple overview of a long, complex historical process, idealized to ensure reverent acceptance by the Jews. Shortly before his death Joshua gathered all the elders, judges, and priests in a great assembly at Shechem. There they agreed unanimously to renounce all other deities and dedicate themselves and their people to the service of Yahweh. This was one of the great unifying actions in the history of Israel. His lifework completed, Joshua, the servant of Yahweh, died and was buried in Ephraim (Joshua 24:29–31).

JOSIAH. The son of Amon, King of Judah during the seventh century B.C. Amon was killed, while still a young man, by disloyal henchmen. Because he was respected by his people, the assassins were killed and Josiah was made king, even though he was only eight years old (II Kings 22:1). His reign lasted thirty-one years, until he died at Megiddo in a battle against the Egyptians (II Kings 23:30). One of his sons succeeded him, but he was soon ousted by strong Egyptian influence and a second son became king. This was Jehoiakim (II Kings 23:31–35). During Josiah's reign, while the Temple was being repaired, workmen found a long-lost book that was destined to be profoundly important both for Josiah and his people. It is called the Book of the Law and provided the basis for many religious reforms (II Kings 22:8). Apostasies that had developed during the years were corrected. Josiah used its teaching to clarify Jewish ideals and root out idolatrous beliefs and practices. The reformed body of work became the constitution of the state and raised the spiritual and ethical level of Judah to a height unequaled in generations (II Kings 23). "No king before him had turned to Yahweh as he did, with all his heart, all his soul, all his strength, in perfect loyalty to the Law of Moses; nor was any king like him ever seen again" (II Kings 23:25).

JOT. A trivial item or matter, a meaning derived from the fact that it was originally the smallest letter in the Hebrew alphabet. Matthew quoted the word when Jesus emphasized the fact that "not one jot, not one little stroke, shall disappear from the Law until its purpose is achieved" (Matthew 5:18).

JOY. In spiritual literature, the feeling aroused by the expectation or possession of some good. One of the fruits of the Holy Spirit. Joyful emotions affect the body, but they are essentially in the higher faculties of the soul. Differs from pleasure, which may affect the human spirit but originates in some bodily sensation. Thus joy is possessed by angels and human beings, and its source is the rational will.

JOYFUL MYSTERIES. The first chaplet of the Rosary of the Blessed Virgin consisting of: 1. the Annunication to Mary; 2. Mary's Visitation of Elizabeth; 3. the Birth of Jesus in Bethlehem; 4. the Presentation of Christ in the Temple; 5. the Finding of Christ in the Temple. See also GLORIOUS MYSTERIES, SORROWFUL MYSTERIES.

JOYS OF THE BLESSED VIRGIN MARY. Pious devotion to commemorate particular joys in the life of Blessed Mary. The numbers given are five or seven, and sometimes twelve, but most common in today's practice are the Annunciation, Visitation, Nativity of Jesus, Epiphany, Finding Jesus in the Temple, Resurrection, and Assumption. Franciscans celebrate the joys of the Blessed Virgin with a special feast and also propagate the devotion of the Rosary of Mary's Seven Joys. This devotion was very popular in old Catholic England, and today another feast on the Monday after Low Sunday celebrates the same joys in Portugal and Brazil.

JUBAL. The son of Lamech and Adah in the line descended from Cain. He is described in Genesis as "the ancestor of the lyre and the flute." In modern parlance he might be called the Patron of the Musical Arts (Genesis 4:21).

JUBILEE. In the Old Testament the Jewish celebration every fiftieth year to commemorate the deliverance of the Israelites from Egypt. It was commanded by Yahweh to Moses, "You will declare this fiftieth year sacred and proclaim the liberation of all the inhabitants of the land. This is to be a jubilee for you; each of you will return to his ancestral home, each to his own clan" (Leviticus, 25:10). In the Catholic Church the jubilee year can be traced to Pope Boniface VIII in 1300 and marked by pilgrimages to Rome, with special services then and throughout the Christian world. Since 1470 the custom has been to hold a regular jubilee every twenty-five years. However, the popes have declared extraordinary jubilees at other times, e.g., in 1933 to commemorate the nineteenth centennial of the Redemption. Jubilees are also celebrated by bishops, priests, religious, and married people to commemorate the fiftieth anniversary of their respective ordination, profession, or marriage. (Etym. Latin *jubilaeus* [*annus*], "[year] of jubilee," alteration [influenced by Latin *jubilare,* to jubilate]; of late Greek *iōbēlaios,* from *iōbēlos,* jubilee, from Hebrew *yōbhēl,* "ram's horn" [used to proclaim the jubilee].)

JUBILEE INDULGENCE. A plenary indulgence that the Pope grants every twenty-fifth year or on extraordinary occasions. During this time confessors are also granted special faculties in favor of penitents.

JUBILEES, BOOK OF. Called Little Genesis (c. 100 B.C.). A history of the world from the time of creation to the giving of the Law on Sinai. Written in Aramaic, it advocated Pharisaical rather than Hellenistic viewpoints.

J.U.D. *Juris Utriusque Doctor*—Doctor of Both Laws (civil and canon).

JUD. *Judicium*—judgment.

JUDAH. The fourth son of Jacob and Leah; his name was given to one of the Twelve Tribes (Genesis 29:35). From Judah's line Jesse and David came, and ultimately Jesus (Luke 3:23–33). Jacob evidently foresaw potential greatness in Judah, for when he gave his blessing and prophecy to each of his twelve sons, his eulogy of Judah was much more impressive than those of the others (Genesis 49:8). His tribe prospered and acquired additional territory until it was one of the most powerful kingdoms in Palestine. Of the Twelve Tribes only Judah and Benjamin remained loyal to the House of David. The kingdom lasted until Jerusalem fell in 586 B.C.

JUDAISM. The oldest living religion of the Western world, and historically the parent of Christianity and Islam. Present-day Judaism is at once a culture and a religion and should be distinguished accordingly. As a religion, Judaism is the body of a permanent moral tradition, which has its roots in the Old Testament prophets, and its hopes in a forthcoming Messiah. As a culture, it is the Jewish people, many of whom are not descendants of Abraham, and among whom is a wide spectrum of faith and worship, yet a mysterious solidarity that is quite unique in the history of mankind.

Modern Judaism may be conveniently divided along religious lines into Orthodox, Reform, and Conservative. Each of these forms builds not only on the Torah or Jewish Bible but also on the Talmud, which is the principal repository of Judaic tradition. Historically, Orthodox Jews are the oldest, reaching back to the synagogues in Palestine and Babylonia in the first century, and theologically they are the most conservative. At the other extreme, and opposed to Orthodoxy, is Reform Judaism, also called Progressive or Liberal, which began in Germany in the eighteenth century as a movement for cultural assimilation. Aroused by this break with historic Judaism, a group of English-speaking rabbis decided to create the Conservative alignment, which seeks to steer a middle course between Orthodoxy and the Reform.

Recent developments have brought all the segments of Judaism into greater unity, of which the State of Israel is their symbol of a common hope for the future.

JUDAIZERS. Early Jewish Christians who considered the Mosaic law still binding. Observance of the Sabbath instead of Sunday, circumcision, and keeping the severe dietary laws were the principal customs they wanted to keep. Some Judaizers were sincere Christians, but others were in fact heretical Gnostics. The Judeo-Christians in Antioch drew opposition from St. Peter for claiming that salvation depended upon being circumcised, and he finally separated from these so-called Christians even though at first he had refused to eat foods that by Mosaic law were held to be unclean.

JUDAS ISCARIOT. Son of Simon, the only Apostle who did not come from Galilee. His special interest was money, so he was in charge of the common fund of the Apostles (John 13:29). It was an unfortunate assignment, according to John. He referred to Judas as "a thief . . . who used to help himself to the contributions" (John 12:6). Moreover, Judas remonstrated sharply with Jesus for allowing Mary Magdalene to anoint his feet with a costly ointment, arguing that the money should have gone to the poor (John 12:1–8). His inordinate greed motivated him to betray Jesus. He knew that the high priest, Caiaphas, was anxious to arrest the Master, so he made a deal with the chief priests to identify Jesus at an opportune time for thirty pieces of silver (Matthew 26:14–16). The Apostles were startled at the Last Supper when Jesus said, "I tell you most solemnly, one of you will betray me" (John 13:21). Judas lived up to the terms of his agreement with Caiaphas by leading a number of armed men into Gethsemane and kissing Jesus as a symbol of identification, whereupon they arrested Jesus (Matthew 26:47–56). Scripture reports that when Judas learned that Jesus had been condemned to die, he was filled with remorse (Matthew 27:3–5). There is no way of knowing his motives. He returned the silver, protested that Jesus was innocent, and, when his protest was ignored, went out and hanged himself. The Gospel writers made no attempt to explore Judas' betrayal. They simply said that Satan had entered into him, and they all referred to him as the betrayer (Luke 22:3). His place in the Apostles was taken by Matthias (Acts 1:26). (Etym. Greek *ioudas* from Hebrew *yehudhah*, let him [God] be praised. Greek *iskariōtēs*.)

JUDAS MACCABEUS. Son of the priest Mattathias and leader of the Jewish army; he delivered his people from the Syrian yoke in a war of independence. He sent messengers to Rome to secure an alliance between the Jews and Romans. The alliance was successfully made, but before the news reached the east, Judas was defeated and slain in 161 B.C. on the battlefield of Elasa. When he died "All Israel wept and mourned him deeply, and for many days they repeated this dirge, 'What a downfall for the strong man, the man who saved Israel singlehanded'" (I Maccabees 9:20–21). The two books of Maccabees, so called because they contain the history of the Jews under Judas Maccabeus, are part of the Catholic canon of the Scriptures but are omitted (or considered apocryphal) in the Protestant Bible. The exploits of Judas Maccabeus are the subject of a famous oratorio by George Frederick Handel (1685–1759).

JUDE, EPISTLE OF. A letter of the Apostle Jude, surnamed Thaddaeus, written to strengthen the faith of Hebrew converts to Christianity. It is therefore a warning against false prophets. Illustrations are drawn from the Old Testament, but also from Jewish apocalyptic literature, namely the Assumption of Moses and the Book of Enoch. The evidence of previous divine punishments is a prophetic assurance that a similar punishment awaits depraved teachers. Most probably written at Jerusalem before the destruction of the city in A.D. 70, the epistle vindicates the mysterious character of the Christian faith, against those who "abuse anything they do not understand" (Jude 10).

JUDGES, BOOK OF. The seventh book of the Bible, thus called because it relates the events surrounding the temporary leaders of Israel called "Judges." This represents the period between the death of Joshua and the days of Samuel. The purpose of the author is especially to illustrate the fact of divine Providence, that apostasy is always punished and that loyalty to God is always rewarded.

JUDGMENT. In general, an act of the mind affirming or denying something. Philosophically, judgment is the mental act of combining two ideas in affirming their agreement, e.g., God is good, or separating them in denying their agreement, e.g., God is not evil. In ethics, judgment is a right decision about what is just or proper or prudent. It is also the decision of a superior in a natural society (such as the State) or a supernatural society (such as the Church), prescribing what should be done or administering justice.

JUDGMENT, GENERAL. The universal judgment of the human race at the final resurrection of the dead. It is expressed in all the creeds that affirm that Christ now "sits at the right hand of God the Father Almighty, from where He shall come to judge the living and the dead," i.e., the just and the wicked. This will be a social judgment because it will manifest to the world God's justice in condemning sinners, and his mercy in those who are saved. It will also be a total judgment by revealing not only people's moral conduct but all the accumulated blessings or injuries that resulted from each person's good or evil deeds.

JUDGMENT, PARTICULAR. The individual judgment of each human being immediately after death. It is a judgment in the sense that God irrevocably determines a person's lot for eternity, depending on his or her co-operation with grace during the stay on earth.

JUDICIAL WORK. A type of work forbidden on Sundays and holy days unless required by public necessity or permitted by legitimate custom. Judicial proceedings consist of the ordinary business of the courtroom, such as pleading cases, acting as witnesses, passing judgment. Judges and lawyers are not forbidden to do legal work privately, for example, preparing a brief or holding private consultations.

JUDITH. The name means "Jewess." She is the heroine of the Book of Judith, which is a historical romance (Judith 7). The details of a great battle are impressive, but the purpose of the book is mainly didactic. When the terrified Israelites were awaiting invasion and annihilation by Nebuchadnezzar's great army under its general, Holofernes, the beautiful, ingenious Judith, inspired by Yahweh, visited the Assyrian camp, dazzled the general with her beauty and eloquence, and during the night killed and beheaded him. In the ensuing battle, the demoralized Assyrians were vanquished and Judith became a national heroine (Judith 10–13). It is an inspiring story to teach the Israelites the importance of depending on Yahweh when catastrophe threatens.

J.U.L. *Juris Utriusque Licentiatus*—Licentiate of Both Laws.

JULIAN CALENDAR. Julius Caesar's attempt to adapt the calendar year to the time required by the earth to make a complete revolution around the sun. The Gregorian calendar, devised by Pope Gregory XIII, superseded it in 1582 and is now in almost universal use, correcting the Julian year to the astronomical year.

JUR. *Juris*—of law.

JURIDICAL DUTY. An obligation between equals binding in justice, especially under the natural law and natural commutative justice. It is a duty that corresponds to a strict right.

JURIDICAL ORDER. The whole system of rights and duties, whether civil or ecclesiastical, concerning the practice and administration of justice.

JURIDICAL POSITIVISM. The theory that, although there may be a natural law, there are no natural rights. All human rights are conferred, it claims, by civil authority, by mutual agreement, by individual freedom, or by custom that manifests the spirit of a people.

JURIDICAL RIGHTS. Those in whose defense or recovery a person may use force or might. Thus the right to life and to property is juridical because normally they are defensible by physical means. An unborn child does not have the strength to defend its right to life. But though physically violated, the right itself remains, for it is still morally inviolable, which is of the essence of right. This has grave practical implications in defending the juridical right to life of the unborn when threatened by abortion.

JURISDICTION. In ecclesiastical law, the right to exercise official and public authority in some capacity. Thus a bishop has jurisdiction in his diocese, a pastor in his parish, priests in the administration of the sacraments, priests and deacons in preaching, and religious superiors in directing the members of their respective communities. (Etym. Latin *ius*, right + *dicere*, to say: *iurisdictio*, official authority.)

JUS GENTIUM. The law of nations. International law. It comprises the norms that determine the conduct of political states in their dealings with each other.

JUS JURANDUM. A sworn oath. Any one of the oaths that the Church at times requires of the faithful, and especially of her priests. Such was the *Oath Against Modernism*, required of those teaching in seminaries, prescribed by Pope St. Pius X.

JUS PRIMAE NOCTIS. Law of the first night. In feudal times a master's "right" to spend the wedding night with a vassal's bride.

JUSTICE. As a virtue, it is the constant and permanent determination to give everyone his or her rightful due. It is a habitual inclination of the will and therefore always recognizes each one's rights, under any and all circumstances. The rights in question are whatever belongs to a person as an individual who is distinct from the one who practices justice. The essence of justice, then, as compared with charity, consists in the distinction between a person and his or her neighbor; whereas charity is based on the union existing between the one who loves and the person loved so that the practice of charity regards the neighbor as another self.

JUSTIFICATION, THEOLOGY OF. The process of a sinner becoming justified or made right with God. As defined by the Council of Trent, "Justification is the change from the condition in which a person is born as a child of the first Adam into a state of grace and adoption among the children of God through the Second Adam, Jesus Christ our Savior" (Denzinger 1524). On the negative side, justification is a true removal of sin, and not merely having one's sins ignored or no longer held against the sinner by God. On the positive side it is the supernatural sanctification and renewal of a person who thus becomes holy and pleasing to God and an heir of heaven.

The Catholic Church identifies five elements of justification, which collectively define its full meaning. The primary purpose of justification is the honor of God and of Christ; its secondary purpose is the eternal life of mankind. The main efficient cause or agent is the mercy of God; the main instrumental cause is the sacrament of baptism, which is called the "sacrament of faith" to spell out the necessity of faith for salvation. And that which constitutes justification or its essence is the justice of God, "not by which He is just Himself, but by which He makes us just," namely sanctifying grace.

Depending on the sins from which a person is to be delivered, there are different kinds of justification. An infant is justified by baptism and the faith of the one who requests or confers the sacrament. Adults are justified for the first time either by personal faith, sorrow for sin and baptism, or by the perfect love of God, which is at least an implicit baptism of desire. Adults who have sinned gravely after being justified can receive justification by sacramental absolution or perfect contrition for their sins. (Etym. Latin *justus,* just + *facere,* to make, do: *justificatio.*)

JUSTIFYING GRACE. The grace by which a person is restored to God's friendship, either for the first time, as in baptism, or after baptism, as in the sacrament of penance. See ACTUAL GRACE, EFFICACIOUS GRACE, GRACE, GRATUITOUS GRACE, HABITUAL GRACE, SACRAMENTAL GRACE, SANATING GRACE, SANCTIFYING GRACE, SUFFICIENT GRACE.

JUST WAR. Armed conflict between nations that is morally tolerated on certain conditions. These conditions, first stated by St. Augustine, have become classic in Catholic moral teaching. In order for a war to be just, it must be on the authority of the sovereign, the cause must be just, the belligerents must have a right intention, and the war must be waged by "proper means." The "just cause" means that a nation's rights are being violated by an actual or at least imminent attack; that other means of preventing aggression, e.g., diplomacy or embargo, have been tried and failed or would be useless; and that there is a proportion between the foreseen evils of conflict and the hoped for benefits of engaging in war.

K

KABBALA. A system of esoteric theosophy peculiar to Judaism in Europe after the twelfth century. When the Jews were expelled from Spain, they brought this belief to Palestine. According to the kabbalists, God, the Supreme, Endless, and Infinite One, manifests himself in ten potencies or sephiroths, which formed the first world creation, which in turn produced the second world; each world generating the next. The human was created by the sephiroth and his or her pre-existent soul returns to God through transmigration. The Messiah will be born at the end of time, and then the world will return to the Source, hell will end, and bliss will begin. To the kabbalist God is a conscious reaction to the God of Christianity. Human redemption, on kabbalist terms, is achieved through the rigid observance of the law. Kabbalism exerted a high moral influence on its members, many adherents, such as Riccio and Jacob Franck, later becoming Christians.

KAIROS. Literally a "period of time." As used in the Bible, it means time in some religiously significant sense, as "be sure you make the best use of your time" (Colossians 4:5) and "Be on your guard, stay awake, because you never know when the time will come" (Mark 13:33).

KAL. *Kalendae*—calends.

KALENDS. Also spelled "calends," the first day of each month in the ancient Roman calendar. The term is sometimes used in formal ecclesiastical documents.

KELLS, BOOK OF. See BOOK OF KELLS.

KENOSIS. The voluntary renunciation by Christ of his right to divine privilege in his humble acceptance of human status. Paul describes *kenosis* aptly to the Philippians: "His state was divine, yet He did not cling to his equality with God, but emptied Himself to assume the condition of a slave" (Philippians 2:6–7). (Etym. Greek *kenosis,* an emptying.)

KERYGMA. Preaching or proclaiming, as distinct from teaching or instruction (*didache*) in the Gospel of Christ. Before the Gospel was written, it was first preached (Romans 16:25), but beyond preaching it was also to be taught (Matthew 28:19) in order that, as far as possible, it might be understood (Matthew 13:19). (Etym. Greek *Kērygma,* proclamation; from *keryks,* herald.)

KERYGMATIC THEOLOGY. The science of theology which stresses the functional use of sacred doctrine in preaching, contrasted with a more academic or speculative study of religious truths.

KETUBIM. See WRITTEN WORD.

KEVELAER (shrine). Place of pilgrimage in North Germany, not far from the Dutch border. A Marian shrine where many disabled and sick children have been healed. In 1641 a trader on three successive nights heard a voice telling him, "Build a sanctuary in my honor here." Simultaneously his wife had an apparition of a lovely lady, and recalled an itinerant soldier selling a cheap paper picture of the Madonna. The soldier was found and the picture was bought, but because of the crowds it attracted to her small cottage she gave the picture to the village church. Repeatedly the blind, paralyzed, deaf, and mute, especially children, who came to the church were cured and the word spread that the Blessed Virgin and her Son shown in the faded picture were the merciful ones. To accommodate the crowds, it was necessary to build a larger edifice, and a new statue made of stone but resembling the paper image replaced the old picture in importance. Pope Pius IX sent the stone from Rome for the new building and in 1892 the statue was solemnly crowned. Even during the war years in Germany, thousands came to this shrine, where both the new statue and the old faded picture are centers of devotion.

KEYS. The emblem of Christ's conferral of spiritual power on St. Peter: "I will give unto you, the keys of the kingdom of heaven" (Matthew 16, 19). This distinctive power in the Church given to Peter is expressed by the two crossed keys, the first emblem to have been assigned to any saint, at the same time as the sword came to represent St. Paul. See also POWER OF THE KEYS.

K.H.S. Knight of the Holy Sepulcher.

KIDDUSHIN. Literally "sanctification," the Jewish marriage service and state of matrimony. Essential to the wedding is the ring ceremony, in which the groom places the ring on the forefinger of the bride's right hand and says, "Behold thou art consecrated unto me, according to the law of Moses and of Israel." The ceremony takes place under a *Huppah* (or canopy), symbolizing the new home to which the groom is taking the bride.

KINDNESS. One of the fruits of the Holy Spirit; the quality of understanding sympathy and concern for those in trouble or need. It is shown in affability of speech, generosity of conduct, and forgiveness of injuries sustained.

KINGS, BOOKS OF. In the Douay Bible, translation of the Vulgate, there are four Books of Kings, corresponding to Samuel and Kings in the Hebrew Bible. The two Bibles and corresponding versions compare as follows:

Original Hebrew	Vulgate and Douay
Samuel	I and II Kings
Kings	III and IV Kings

Septuagint	Recent Versions
Kingdoms A and B	I and II Samuel
Kingdoms C and D	I and II Kings

The "Kings" are rulers of a united and divided Hebrew kingdom (c. 1040–561 B.C.). I Kings deals with Samuel, the last of the judges; the origin of the monarchy, and the first King, Saul. II Kings treats the reign of David. III Kings covers the reign of Solomon and the divided kingdom up to Elijah. IV Kings tells the rest of the history of Israel, to the Assyrian captivity, and the history of Judah to the Babylonian captivity.

KIRK. Name applied to the Church of Scotland at the Western Assembly. It is also used instead of the word "church" to distinguish the Established Church of Scotland from the Catholic, Anglican, and Reformed churches. It is the form also used in parts of Northern England. (Etym. Anglo-Saxon *cirice,* circe, church.)

KISS, LITURGICAL. Touching with the lips as a mark of reverence during ceremonies of public worship. The frequency of this gesture has been reduced since the Second Vatican Council, but it is still prescribed. The priest must kiss the altar as he begins and concludes the Mass, and he is to kiss the lectionary after reading the Gospel.

KISS OF PEACE. Also known as *Pax,* it is the mutual greeting of the faithful during Mass as a sign of their union and love of Christ. Certainly in practice by the second century, it became more and more limited in the West. Since the Second Vatican Council it has been restored to being regularly given during the Eucharistic liturgy. The official text of the ritual says, "Then, depending on circumstances [*pro opportunitate*], the deacon or priest adds, 'offer each other the peace,' and all the people, according to local custom, show one another some sign of peace and charity; the priest gives the peace to the deacon or minister."

KNEELING. Resting on bent knees as a mark of reverence. The New Order of the Mass prescribes that the faithful kneel at least during the Consecration.

KNIFE AND BOOK. Emblems of St.

Bartholomew, who preached the Gospel in India, where he was martyred by being flayed alive. This is the way he is represented in Michelangelo's *Last Judgment* painting in the Sistine Chapel, Rome.

KNIGHTS OF COLUMBUS. International fraternal benefit organization of Catholic men, founded in 1882 by Rev. Michael J. McGivney, of New Haven, Connecticut. It was established on the principles of charity, unity, and patriotism, and its purpose is to provide a system of fraternal insurance benefits to the members, promote cultural relations, and engage in a variety of religious, educational, and social activities. The Knights represent the modern expression of Catholic Action. Their "purpose has meaning only insofar as they are in perfect accord with the mind of the Church." Worldwide membership is over one million.

KNOCK, OUR LADY OF. Ireland's revered Marian shrine in County Mayo, dating from 1879. On August 21 of that year, during a pouring rain, the figures of Mary, Joseph, and John the Apostle appeared over the gable of the village church, enveloped in a bright light. Beside them was an altar, with a Cross surmounting it and a Lamb at its feet. No words came from any of the figures. The parish priest was not informed until the next day, as the onlookers were too stunned to leave the scene. Twice in 1880 the apparition was repeated, but the light was too intense to clearly recognize anyone but Mary. Authenticated miracles brought hundreds to the town. The Archbishop of Tuam started an inquiry. Some fifteen testified that what they saw was no painting or illusion. The Church authorities confirmed the testimony, declaring that the apparitions were "trustworthy and satisfactory." The site is now an object of national pilgrimage. Pope John Paul II visited the shrine on September 30, 1979, to mark the centenary of Mary's apparitions and rededicate the Irish people to the Mother of God.

KNOWLEDGE. Any act, function, state, or effect of mental activity. Essential to knowledge is that some reality from outside the mind is re-presented in the mind by what is called an intentional likeness or similarity to the object known. Knowledge, therefore, is assimilation of mind with object. As a result there is an intentional (assimilative) union between knower and known. We become what we know.

KNOWLEDGE OF GOD. According to the First Vatican Council, "God, one and true, our Creator and Lord [can] be certainly known by the natural light of human reason from the things that are made" (Denzinger 3026). God's first witness of himself, therefore, is in the world of creation as declared by St. Paul: "Ever since God created the world, His everlasting power and deity—however invisible—have been there for the mind to see in the things He has made" (Romans 1:20). Moreover, the human mind "can even demonstrate" his existence and attributes by reasoning from the effects in the universe to their ultimate cause (Pope St. Pius X, *Oath Against Modernism*, Denzinger 3538). However, God has also manifested himself supernaturally in what is commonly called revelation, as found in the Bible and sacred tradition. Such revelation is morally necessary to enable everyone to know God easily, with certitude and without error. Revelation is also absolutely necessary "because God in His infinite goodness has ordained man to a supernatural end," which therefore requires man's knowledge of his destiny and of the means of getting there (Denzinger 3005).

KNOW-NOTHINGISM. A lawless anti-Catholic movement in American politics, 1852–58. All men were admittedly created equal except Catholics, foreigners, and blacks. When questioned about their philosophy, they answered, "I don't know." Their main target was Irish Catholics, whom they wished to deprive of civil and private rights. Their victims suffered from repeated acts of mob violence. In 1852 the bigots organized the "National Council of the United States of North America." They swore an oath of secrecy about their aims and promised to elect to public office only native born Americans who were not Catholic or married to Catholics. In 1855 they carried elections in nine states and had seventy-five adherents in Congress, but their defeat by the Democratic Party in 1856 and the growing feeling of anti-slavery saw their decline as a united power.

KOIMESIS. The feast of the "Falling Asleep" of the Blessed Virgin Mary, or Mary's Dormition, as celebrated in the Byzantine Liturgy.

KOINE. The popular, everyday Greek spoken by the people of the Mediterranean world in the first century of the Christian era. Also the Greek in which the New Testament was written, as distinct from Attic or classic Greek used in the Golden Age of Athens among the literati.

KOINONIA. Community, especially the community of the faithful, of whom St. Luke says they formed a fellowship (*koinonia*) of believers who worshiped together and held all their possessions in common (Acts 2:42–47). It was also the favorite term of St. Paul to identify the union of the faithful with Christ and among themselves, and it was the Church's term in the earliest creeds for the communion of saints, i.e., the believers on earth, the souls in purgatory, and the elect in glory.

KORAH. 1. Son of Esau and Oholibamah (Genesis 36:5); 2. eponymous head of the clan of Korahites, a guild of Temple musicians (Exodus 6:24). Their name appears at the head of some of the Psalms (Psalms 42); 3. son of Kohath. He led a rebellion against Moses and Aaron, demanding, "Why set yourselves higher than the community of Yahweh?" (Numbers 16:3). Yahweh supported Moses in the confrontation. The ground opened up and swallowed Korah and his company of rebels (Numbers 16:35).

K.P. Knight of Pius IX; Knight of St. Patrick.

K.S.G. Knight of St. Gregory.

K.S.S. Knight of St. Silvester.

KULTURKAMPF. A movement in Prussia, Bavaria, Hesse, and Baden to make the Catholic Church subject to the state and independent of Rome. Professor Rudolf Virchow (1821–1902), the liberal scientist who named it, called it a struggle for civilization. Bismarck and Falk, the political leaders, were actively supported by the Church's enemies in and out of the German Parliament. Their aim was to destroy papal influence and build up a national church, strengthening Protestant power. Religious orders were forced by impossible laws to secularize their schools or leave the country.

Clergy were fined or punished for practicing their ecclesiastical duties, bishops and priests were imprisoned, and religious charitable institutions were closed. With the help of the state control of education it was hoped to secure absolute power over the intellectual life of the German nation. Unity of religion, i.e., Protestantism, was considered necessary for national unity. The Catholic Church, therefore, was to be either assimilated or destroyed in the interests of political solidarity. Chancellor Otto von Bismarck expelled the Jesuits, Redemptorists, Lazarists, and other religious teachers, placing all education in secular hands, and passed the May Laws, which fined, expelled, or imprisoned all bishops and clerics who in any way opposed the secularization of Catholic schools. Catholic worship soon became virtually impossible, and civil marriages were made compulsory. But the clergy remained faithful and their power of resistance grew under the able leadership of Ludwig Windthorst (1812–91) of the Catholic Center Party and with the support of Protestants who opposed such bigotry. The Kulturkampf consolidated the Catholics into a strong political party that held socialism at bay and restored Catholics to positions of influence in government. Under Pope Leo XIII in 1878 the restoration of peace began. The militant anti-Catholic laws were gradually repealed. By 1882 Prussia had established an embassy at the Vatican.

KYRIE ELEISON. The formula of a prayer, "Lord, have mercy," said or sung and repeated in the penitential rite at the beginning of Mass in the Roman Liturgy. Used in conjunction with *Christe Eleison,* "Christ, have mercy." One of the few Greek prayers in the Latin Mass, it is most likely the remnant of a liturgical litany. It is also said in the Divine Office and in many litanies, notably the Litany of the Saints. In the Eastern Churches it may appear without *Christe Eleison.*

L

LABAN. Son of Bethuel, a descendant of Nahor from the land of the Aramaeans. When the aged Abraham sought a wife for his son Isaac, he sent a trusted servant back to his kinfolk to find a suitable wife. With Yahweh's help he chose Rebekah. Bethuel, her father, and Laban, her brother, willingly supported the choice and so Rebekah married Isaac (Genesis 24). Years later Jacob, the son of Isaac and Rebekah, was sent by his parents to live with his uncle in the hope that he would take one of Laban's daughters to be his wife (Genesis 28). For many years he worked for Laban, during which time he married both of his uncle's daughters, Leah and Rachel. Jacob prospered in spite of the trickery of Laban and finally departed from his father-in-law with his wives and his sons, returning to his own country (Genesis 29–31).

LABARUM. The imperial standard of Emperor Constantine and also his military standard after his victory at the Milvian Bridge in 312. It was a purple banner bearing in Greek "In this sign [the Cross] you shall conquer," suspended from a long gilded spear. At the top of the spear was the chi-rho, symbol or monogram of Christ. Fifty soldiers were entrusted with the care of this standard.

LACKAWANNA. National Shrine of Our Lady of Victory, in a suburb of Buffalo, New York. In 1876, Father Nelson Baker, of the Buffalo diocese, began working at an orphanage in Lackawanna, where he formed an Association of Our Lady of Victory to alert people to the needs of children. In gratitude to the Blessed Virgin for the generous response from the faithful he built what eventually became the present basilica, dedicated in 1926.

LA CONQUISTADORA. Shrine of "Our Lady of Conquest" in the Cathedral of Santa Fe, New Mexico. It has one of the oldest statues of Mary in America, brought to New Mexico in 1625. In 1680 the Indians took to the warpath, killing twenty-one Franciscans working among them. The white population fled, taking the little wooden statue of Mary with them. Thirteen years later the Spaniards in exile led by De Vargas made a vow to Mary that they would enthrone her as their Queen back in the Cathedral of Santa Fe if she would permit their taking their former property without bloodshed. In trust the Spaniards returned. The Indians for an unknown reason withdrew from their stronghold and Governor Vargas entered Santa Fe without opposition. La Conquistadora returned home. Vargas built a chapel to Mary as he had promised. This has been replaced by a Rosario chapel on the outskirts of the city, and it is to this chapel that "La Conquistadora" is taken in solemn procession on the fourteenth day after Trinity Sunday each year, leaving her ornate shrine in the cathedral for her annual fiesta.

LACTICINIA. Milk (Latin, *lac*) and milk products, e.g., butter and cheese, and eggs or animal products formerly prohibited during Lent, along with flesh meat. In the early Middle Ages lacticinia were forbidden even on Sundays during the Lenten season.

LADY DAY. Originally the feast of the Annunciation of the Blessed Virgin (March 25), although now the title is applied to other Marian feast days, e.g., the Assumption into Heaven.

LADY'S CHAPEL. A church room or building especially dedicated to Our Lady, the Virgin Mary. Within the church it was usually attached to the choir or it formed a separate small building joined to the main church. In the English cathedrals this chapel prolonged the main axis to the east: in France it was the largest and most eastern of the chevet chapels and was thought of as the crown chapel. In St. Patrick's Cathedral in New York City it is a large chapel suitable for a small congregation behind the main altar.

LAETARE SUNDAY. The fourth Sunday of Lent, when the introductory word of the Introit is *laetare*, "Rejoice O Jerusalem." As it is Mid-Lent Sunday, rose vestments are worn, flowers are permitted on the altar, and the organ is played. On this day the Golden Rose is blessed. The day is referred to also as Mediana, Mid-Lent, Mi-Carême, Mothering, Rose, or Refreshment Sunday. See also GAUDETE SUNDAY.

LAIC. *Laicus*–layman.

LAICISM. Exclusive control of Church affairs by the laity. A laicistic program, denying the value of religious ideals for civil, social, and political life, prevents the Church from functioning outside her churches and chapels. Anti-clerical proponents of separation of Church and State laicize by government supervision and control functions rightly belonging to the Church, such as education, marriage, hospitals, parishes, convents, churches, and other organizations. It appeared historically as Gallicanism, Febronianism, and Josephinism and in the anti-religious laws of France and Mexico. It is part of the political theory of Communism and prevalent in all countries where the government interprets separation of Church and State as subordination of Church to the State. (Etym. Latin *laicus*, pertaining to the people; from Greek *lāos*, people.)

LAICIZATION. The act of reducing an ecclesiastical person or thing to a lay status. The turning over of a church building to a secular purpose; the removal by a civil power of ecclesiastical control in an institution where that control and influence should be operative. In the laicization of clerics, the Holy See, for extraordinary reasons and the greater good of the Church, may laicize a bishop, priest, or deacon. In spite of the term, however, the person does not lose his sacramental powers and remains an ordained person. But he is legitimately dispensed from the ordinary duties attached to his office and, generally also, of his vow of celibacy, giving him the right to marry. In an emergency, a laicized priest can validly administer the sacraments of anointing and penance.

LAITY. The faithful who are not in holy orders and do not belong to a religious state approved by the Church.

LA LECHE, OUR LADY OF. Shrine in St. Augustine, Florida, dedicated to Nuestra Señora de la Leche, whose full title is "Our Lady, the Nursing Mother of Happy Delivery." It dates from 1565, when St. Augustine was founded by Pedro Menéndez de Avilés, who was accompanied by four diocesan priests. The shrine is part of America's oldest mission, Nombre de Dios, where the first Mass was celebrated. Central to the shrine is an image of the Madonna about to nurse her Child. The original image, from Madrid, and first chapel have been destroyed. But the new statue, in the present chapel built in 1915, is an exact replica of the original one.

LAMB. A symbol of Christ. Rendered in many forms as early as the fourth century. Various aspects show the animal balancing a staff by its right front leg, with a wound in its chest pouring blood into a chalice, representing Christ's Blood in the Passion; the staff bearing a flag signifying Christ's victory in the Resurrection; the lamb resting or standing on a closed book with its seven sealed streamers symbolizing Christ as the judge. The lamb is the emblem of docility; "harshly dealt with, he bore it humbly, he never opened his mouth like the lamb that is led to the slaughter house" (Isaiah 53:7). But the lamb triumphant is portrayed symbolically in the song ascribed to St. Ambrose, "Now at the Lamb's high royal feast," and St. John speaks of the wrath of the Lamb when the sixth seal is broken. As an emblem of St. John the Baptist, it is found in Chartres Cathedral on a banner that reads "Behold the Lamb of God," referring to Christ, "Who takes away the sins of the world." St. Agnes, the child virgin and martyr, is also symbolized by the lamb.

LAMECH. The son of Methushael and husband of Adah and Zillah. Lamech was the father of Jabal, Jubal, and Tubal-cain, who are credited in Genesis with being pioneers in the development of materials and activities among the early nomads (Genesis 4:18–24).

LAMED VAV. Talmudic tradition that the world must contain at least thirty-six (*lamed vav*) righteous people for God to keep mankind in existence. They are generally humble souls, unknown for their holiness except by God.

LAMENTABILI SANE EXITU. Decree of the Holy Office, published under Pope St. Pius X against modernism on July 3, 1907. It condemned sixty-five propositions drawn from the writings of contemporary modernists, notably Alfred Loisy and George Tyrrell. The decree was shortly after followed (September 8) by the encyclical *Pascendi Dominici Gregis*.

LAMENTATIONS. Words of the prophet Jeremiah sung on the last three days of Holy Week.

LAMENTATIONS OF JEREMIAH. In the Septuagint and Vulgate, four elegiac poems and one prayer, bewailing the fall of Jerusalem, written by the prophet Jeremiah. The elegies are acrostics, each verse starting with the consecutive letter of the alphabet. Josephus' statement that they were composed after the death of Josiah (608 B.C.) and the claim that Lamentations 4 and 5 date from the Maccabean period are without foundation. They were all composed by Jeremiah after the fall of Jerusalem (586 B.C.).

LAMP. A symbol of the Word of God. "Thy Word is a lamp to my feet." The lighted lamp is used to depict knowledge, one of the gifts of the Holy Spirit, and is sometimes shown with an open Bible to signify learning in sacred doctrine.

LANCE, THE HOLY. The instrument used to pierce the side of Christ after his death on the Cross. Said to have been found by St. Helena at Jerusalem. The broken point was brought to Constantinople and in 1241 to Paris, where it disappeared during the French Revolution. The lower, larger section was carried to Constantinople before 900 and in 1492 to Rome, where it is still preserved at St. Peter's.

LA NEGRITA. Shrine of Our Lady of the

Angels at Cartago in Costa Rica. A small black statue of the Madonna and Child was found in 1635 by a young Negro girl who took it home, but the statue returned to where it was originally. This happened several times also when the parish priest tried to keep the statue in a locked receptacle in the rectory. The citizens finally built a shrine to house the statue, which was solemnly crowned in 1927. La Negrita is a famous place of pilgrimage for Costa Ricans.

LANGUAGES, ECCLESIASTICAL. The languages used in the Church's liturgy and in her official teaching. These are two distinct meanings of an ecclesiastical language. In the liturgy there is a further distinction between the Roman Rite and other rites in communion with the Holy See. In the Roman Rite the liturgical language up to the fourth century was mainly Greek. Latin gradually took its place. And this was generally universal until the Second Vatican Council, which opened up the liturgy to the vernacular. On the doctrinal side, the Roman Rite also used Greek in the first three centuries and gradually adopted Latin. The original language of the first seven ecumenical councils, however, was Greek because all the early councils (to A.D. 787) were held in the East. Among the Eastern Christians in communion with Rome the liturgical language was and remains mainly Greek. But other languages have been used from the beginning, e.g., Coptic. The same for doctrine. Some ancient manuscripts of the Bible, including the New Testament, were in Syriac, Armenian, Coptic, and Georgian. Doctrinal statements, except those directly emanating from the Holy See, have also regularly been either in Greek or in the official language of the respective rite.

LAPSI. Third-century Christians who relapsed into heathenism by sacrificing to the gods or performing other acts of apostasy. There were three classes: *sacrificati,* who had actually offered sacrifices to idols; *thurificati,* who had merely burned incense to the gods; and *libellatici,* who certified in writing that they had offered sacrifice to idols without having actually offered sacrifice. After the edict of Decius (250–25) the lapsi who had apostasized through weakness often wished to repent and return to Christian worship. Pope Cornelius and St. Cyprian favored their return, and the synods of that time felt that after their performance of certain public penances they should be readmitted. Novatian opposed this leniency and formed a schismatic community. The Donatist schism was occasioned by a new class of lapsi, called "traditores," mostly clerics, who gave up the sacred books to the civil authorities and later repented. Several synods including the First Council of Nicaea in 325, drew up canons relative to the treatment of lapsi.

LA PURISIMA CONCEPCIÓN. Immaculate Conception mission near Lompoc, California, founded on December 8, 1787. It was originally in a lower valley, but floods and earth tremors made the site undesirable, so in 1813 a new structure was built on higher ground near Santa Barbara. Ten years were spent in constructing the church, monastery, gardens, shops, and nearby Indian dwellings. But, due to Indian uprisings, it was practically abandoned and in ruins by 1835. However, a restoration movement sponsored by the National Park Service began in 1914; the debris was cleared away and reconstruction was successful.

LA SALETTE. Shrine of the Virgin in Tears in Southern France in the diocese of Grenoble. It was there in 1846 that two illiterate children happened to meet each other while they were herding cattle. Mélanie Calvat, age nine, and Maximin Giraud, age eleven, fell asleep on the hillside. Waking up, they saw a beautiful lady sitting on a rock in the bed of a tiny dried-up stream. She was weeping but she reassured the children and told them each separately what she called a secret. The secret remains only partially revealed, although in 1851 the children told Pope Pius IX what the lady said. To others who asked them about the message, the children merely said that there was need for humility, prayer, and penance, and that a dire punishment would await the human race if it did not repent. Famine, earthquakes, epidemics of mortal illness would result. Mélanie revealed part of the secret in 1849, but the Holy See declared that no further details of La Salette's revelation would be made. Devotion to Our Lady of La Salette was approved by the Bishop of Grenoble in 1851, and by the popes since Pius X. The scene of the apparitions is marked by a large church, adjoining the monastery of the Missionaries of La Salette, who administer the shrine.

LAS LAJAS, OUR LADY OF. Colombian shrine containing a large picture of the Blessed Virgin and Child painted on a sandstone slab found in a cave high in the Andes. Its location was discovered as a result of the cures reported by Indians living nearby; even their dead children were said to have been brought back to life. Over the right arm of the Mother hangs a Rosary, while on each side stands a man, thought to be St. Francis and St. Dominic. Numerous authenticated miracles have drawn crowds numbering 150,000 yearly to this church perched on the highest spot of the nearby mountains, reached by an almost impossible climb.

LAST BLESSING. After the administration of the sacrament of anointing, the apostolic blessing that gives a plenary indulgence to the dying person. The priest says, "By the power the Apostolic See has given me, I grant you a plenary indulgence and pardon for all your sins, in the name of the Father, and of the Son, and of the Holy Spirit." To which the person, or the bystanders respond, "Amen." The indulgence is gained, not when the prayer is recited, but at the moment of death, i.e., *in articulo mortis.*

LAST GOSPEL. The Gospel formerly read in the Latin Rite at the end of Mass, usually from the first chapter of St. John (verses 1–14), except on days in Lent, vigils, and Sundays when a feast of major rank was celebrated, and the third Mass on Christmas Day.

LAST JUDGMENT. The final judgment by Christ of the human race on the last day at the resurrection of the dead (Matthew 25:34, 41).

LAST SACRAMENTS. The sacraments that the faithful receive before death, namely penance, the Eucharist (as Viaticum), and anointing of the sick.

LAST SUPPER. The last meal taken by Christ with his apostles, the night before his Passion. On this occasion he instituted the Holy Eucharist and the priesthood, and gave the apostles the long discourse on the Trinity and Christian charity, as recorded by St. John. He then proceeded to Gethsemane and the Agony in the Garden.

LAST THINGS. See ESCHATOLOGY.

LAST WILL. A formal declaration on how a person wants his or her possessions to be disposed of after death. The capacity to make a will is enjoyed by everyone who has the use of reason and the ability to bequeath according to civil or ecclesiastical law. Some of the moral issues affecting wills are: 1. the duty to make a will under certain circumstances, e.g., when serious quarrels would follow otherwise among the heirs; 2. the testator who makes a will must leave part of his possessions to his nearest kin, especially the wife and children, who need assistance; 3. on acceptance of the inheritance, heirs are obliged to pay all debts and legacies charged against the estate; 4. the details of the will are to be carried out according to the expressed or even implicit intentions of the testator. Moreover, as long as a person is alive and of sound mind, he may revoke a testament at any time, although conditioned in this matter by the provisions of the civil law.

LATENCY PERIOD. The interval between physical contact with a stimulus and a person's actual reaction. The term mainly applies to the years between five and twelve, when children do not, unless abnormally and unwisely aroused, react to sexual stimulation. The Church advises parents to cultivate this period for teaching children the principles of faith and training them in the moral habits they will need as the foundation of their adult Christian life.

LATERAN BASILICA. See LATERAN PALACE.

LATERAN PALACE. The papal edifice in Rome used as the residence of the popes from the fourth to the fourteenth centuries. It was named for Plautius Lateranus, a Roman senator, who died under Nero, and was given by Emperor Maximian in his daughter's dowry to Emperor Constantine, who gave it to the reigning pope, Miltiades, in 313. Fire destroyed it twice. Pope Sixtus V had it restored as a smaller edifice. The Church of the Most Holy Savior, commonly called St. John Lateran, adjoins it. Pius XI established the Museum of Catacomb Inscriptions and Christian Antiquities there. It was here that the Roman Question was settled by treaty in 1929, one article of which secures the Lateran to the papacy as an extraterritorial possession.

LATERAN TREATY. The agreement, signed on February 11, 1929, that finally settled the Roman Question and established Vatican City as a sovereign state under the authority of the Pope. At the same time, the Holy See recognized the Italian state with Rome as its political capital. The Italian state recognized "the Catholic, Apostolic and Roman Religion as the sole religion of the State," it declared "the sovereign independence of the Holy See in the international field," and the Holy See's "sovereign jurisdiction in the Vatican City." At the same time, a concordat was signed, providing for the teaching of the Catholic religion in the public schools, the civil recognition of marriages performed according to canon law, and the freedom of Catholic Action provided it is nonpolitical.

LATIN. Originally the Italic dialect of ancient Rome. It was the ordinary language of the Roman Empire at the time of Christ, and Latin translations of the Bible were made as early as the second century. The liturgy was also celebrated in Latin (along with Coptic, Greek, and Ethiopic) since apostolic times. Latin gradually became the official language of the Western Church, and from the time of Tertullian (c. 160–c. 220) was used extensively in theological writing. A historic change took place at the Second Vatican Council, which declared that "the use of the Latin language . . . is to be preserved in the Latin rite. But since the use of the vernacular . . . may frequently be of great advantage to the people, a wider use may be made of it" in the liturgy. (*Constitution on the Liturgy*, I, 36). Since the Council the Church continues to use Latin in her official documents, requires the study of Latin by her future priests, and encourages the use of Latin in those parts of the Mass that are sung or recited by the people, e.g., the Gloria, Credo, Sanctus, Pater Noster, and Agnus Dei. (Etym. Latin *Latinum*, district of Italy in which Rome was situated.)

LATIN AMERICAN EPISCOPAL CONFERENCE. Requested by the General Conference of the Latin American Hierarchy, it was approved by Pope Pius XII in 1955. As an organ of collaboration among the bishops of Latin America, it elects a delegate to the General Conference whose responsibility is to study the problems of common interest, work out solutions, and help co-ordinate the activity of the Catholic hierarchy. Working closely with the Holy See, the conference meets annually and has a permanent secretariat.

LATIN ARCHITECTURE. Early Christian architecture of Europe, peculiar to the Latin Church and developed among the Latin peoples of Italy. It first appeared under Emperor Constantine and was used until the eighth century. The churches so constructed had the T-shaped or basilican form and were characterized by architectural plainness. The best examples were the cathedrals of St. John Lateran, St. Peter, and St. Paul Outside the Walls, all destroyed, and only St. Paul's was rebuilt in its original form.

LATIN CHURCH. The vast portion of the Catholic Church, which uses the Latin litur-

gies and has its own distinctive canon law. Synonymous with the Latin Rite are the Western Church and Western patriarchate. The expression Latin Church is ambiguous, however. It is sometimes used in an uncomplimentary way by the Eastern Orthodox to label all Catholics "Latins" because of their allegiance to the Pope. It is also used by some Anglicans to identify what they consider one third of the whole Catholic Church, along with the Anglican and Orthodox. It is finally used, at times, by Catholics belonging to one of the Eastern (or non-Latin) Rites to distinguish this from other rites of Roman Catholicism.

LATIN CROSS. The symbol referred to as the Cross of the West. It is the crucifixion Cross with the extended lower part of the perpendicular upright, similar to the Cross in pictures on which Christ died. It is the universal symbol of self-denial as expressed by Christ, "If anyone wants to be a follower of mine, let him renounce himself, take up his cross and follow me" (Mark 8:34). See also HEADED CROSS.

LATIN RITE. See ROMAN RITE.

LATRIA. The veneration due to God alone for his supreme excellence and to show people's complete submission to him. It is essentially adoration. As absolute latria, it is given only to God, as the Trinity, or one of the Divine Persons, Christ as God and as man, the Sacred Heart of Jesus, and the Holy Eucharist. Representations of God as images connected with the Divinity may receive relative latria, which is given not to the symbol but to the Godhead, whom it signifies. (Etym. Greek *latreiā*, service, worship.)

LATROCINIUM. The "Robber Council," or "Robber Synod," held at Ephesus in August of 449. The name was given by Pope Leo I, who condemned the council for supporting the Monophysite heresy of Eutyches. Its decisions were reversed by the Council of Chalcedon in 451. (Etym. Latin *latro*, a mercenary soldier; robber + *cinium*, service: *latrocinium*: service of mercenaries; freebooting, robbery.)

LAUD. *Laudes*—Lauds.

LAUDA SION. The hymn "Praise the Savior, O Sion," composed in 1274 by St. Thomas Aquinas as the sequence for the office of the new Feast of Corpus Christi.

LAUDIS CANTICUM. Apostolic Constitution of Pope Paul VI by which the Divine Office, revised according to the decree of the

Second Vatican Council, is officially promulgated. This document gives a historical synthesis of the Divine Office from early Christian times, recalls the norms set down by the Second Vatican Council, and then declares that the new Liturgy of the Hours (*Liturgia Horarum*) is the only officially approved form of the Divine Office, confirmed by the Holy See for the universal Church in the Latin Rite (November 1, 1970).

LAUDS. One of the seven canonical hours, chanted in the Divine Office, taking its name from Psalms 148, 149, and 150. Since the Second Vatican Council it has been replaced in the breviary by "morning prayers."

LAURA. A series of hermitages clustered around a monastery. Also the type of life lived by monks in those hermitages or even the shops along a street in the neighborhood of a monastery. The monks in a laura lived in their own cells and came together at given times for special duties, which made it a combination of eremitical and community life. Although most lauras have disappeared, one of the best known in modern times is connected with the Orthodox monasteries on Mount Athos.

LAUS. Shrine of Our Lady of the Blessed Valley. Scene of a series of apparitions to a poor French shepherdess, Benoite Rencure, in 1664. In the first apparition, St. Maurice directed the girl to a nearby valley where the Virgin appeared to her over a period of two months and bade her have a church built there in her honor. The edifice was built after numerous miracles of healing had been performed on the site. Three times the shrine has been pillaged but each time rebuilt. (Etym. Latin *laus,* praise.)

LAUS DEO SEMPER. "Praise always to God," abbreviated L.D.S. The motto of many saints, especially those in the monastic tradition.

LAVABO. The liturgical washing of his hands by a priest at Mass, after the Offertory and before the Preface in the Tridentine ritual. The sixth verse of Psalm 26 (Vulgate, Psalm 25), recited by the celebrant, begins: "I will wash my hands among the innocent."

LAVABO DISH. The small flat saucer-shaped bowl that catches the water used in cleansing the fingers of a celebrant at Mass. So called from the opening words of the prayer, formerly used by a priest when ritually washing his fingers after the Offertory and before the Canon of the Mass.

LAW. An ordinance of reason for the common good, promulgated by the one who has the care of a community. As an ordinance, law is distinguished from a mere counsel or a suggestion. It is an order or command that imposes obligation or moral necessity to be obeyed. It is the imposition of the superior's will on the will of those who belong to a society, and must be expressed in a mandatory form, no matter how courteously phrased. As an ordinance of reason, though directly imposed by the will of the one in authority, it is first formulated by his intellect as the planning faculty behind the will. Since its purpose is to direct rational beings to do something, it must be reasonable. To be reasonable, a law should be consistent, just, observable, enforceable, and useful. It is consistent when it is neither self-contradictory nor in contradiction with other laws. It is just when it respects higher laws and distributes burdens equitably. It is observable when it does not demand the impossible because it is cruel or too difficult. It is enforceable when not only the law-abiding but everyone can be expected to keep it because it is supported by appropriate sanctions. And it is useful when it serves a valid purpose without needless restriction of human liberty.

A law is for the common good, and in this differs from a command, order, precept, or injunction laid on an individual person. Laws, therefore, always look to the benefit of the community as a whole, not a private or personal good. When they are territorial, they bind all who stay in a certain region, but only when they are there. Laws are relatively permanent. They are always from public authority and last until repealed, and they may bind succeeding generations, whereas personal orders cease with the death or removal from office of the one who gave them.

To promulgate a law is to make it known to those whom it binds. The way it is promulgated depends on the nature of the law, the customs of the people, and on circumstances of time and place. It is properly promulgated if the people can come to know about the law without much difficulty.

A law must be authoritative, which means that it must come from a lawgiver or legislator who has rightful jurisdiction. The lawgiver may be a physical person, which is a single individual, or a moral person, which is a body or a board passing laws by joint action. (Etym. Latin *legere,* to read; *eligere,* to choose; *ligare,* to bind; *lex,* law.)

LAW OF CONSCIENCE. The natural law as it manifests itself within each person's conscience, where its dictates are expressed by certain basic tendencies of nature, evaluated and regulated by right reason. It is binding in conscience as the fundamental source of moral duty. Human law, on the other hand, is binding only insofar as it agrees with the natural law of conscience.

All human beings are subject to the law of conscience, no matter when or where they live. It is, therefore, universal and unchangeable. No one can dispense from its observance, which becomes binding as soon as a person reaches the use of reason.

LAW OF MOSES. See MOSAIC LAW.

LAW OF NATIONS (*jus gentium*). The common element, even though unwritten, in the actual laws of various peoples. Based on the natural law, the *jus gentium* is a synthesis of the legislation enacted by different countries which reflects a basic similarity in spite of the differences of culture and political structure.

First clearly distinguished from natural law by St. Isidore of Seville (560–636), the law of nations is not the same as international law. The latter aims to regulate the mutual relations of states as states. The *jus gentium* is a general law within all nations, not between nations, and deals with individuals without considering their nationality. It is supranational rather than international.

LAW OF NATURE. The moral law as universally binding on human nature, unchangeable in its essence, and knowable to all mankind. The law of nature is universally binding no matter how many people may violate it. Its universality is not to be confused with the universality of its observance. No matter how many or flagrant the transgressions, they do not change the value or extent of the law.

The law of nature is adaptable but not essentially changeable. There have been modifications adopted at one time or another in the law. On closer study, however, they are seen to be in fact changes in circumstances or in matters to which the law is applied. What cannot change is the substance of the law itself.

Also the law of nature can be perceived, however dimly, by every human being who has the full use of his or her reason. Certain social customs, clearly in opposition to this law, do not change the fact that it can be perceived by all. What such customs prove is that fallen human nature is prone to evil and needs divine assistance as revelation even for a correct and generally available knowledge beyond the primary duties of the moral order. Obscured by passion and exposed to the moral pollution of a secularist culture, human reason is weakened in its perception of what is right and wrong. Nevertheless its light is not completely extinguished, and besides, having access to revelation, the light of grace is also always available.

LAX CONSCIENCE. An erroneous conscience when the mind decides on insufficient grounds that a sinful act is permissible or that something gravely wrong is not serious.

LAXISM. A theory in moral theology condemned by the Church. Laxism permits one to follow the opinion that favors liberty and against the law, even though the opinion is only slightly or even doubtfully probable. (Etym. Latin *laxus,* slack.)

LAY APOSTOLATE. Any form of service for the religious welfare of others practiced by the Catholic laity. More commonly refers to apostolic lay activity performed as part of an association or society. The lay apostolate, since the Second Vatican Council, may be one of three types: apostolic work done by the laity but totally supervised by the hierarchy; apostolic work conducted by the laity but officially responsible to the hierarchy; and the apostolic work totally conducted by lay men or women but approved by the hierarchy.

LAY BROTHER. A member of a clerical religious order or congregation who is not a priest and who is not preparing for the priesthood. The term was originally used to identify those men religious who were not clerics (hence brothers), and who were not bound to the chant or recitation of the Divine Office, hence lay, as distinguished from choir monks, who were also not clerics. But in modern times the term is more commonly applied to all male religious who are not, or will not be, ordained. It is customary, however, to simply call them "brothers" without the prefix "lay." The reason is that brothers are full-fledged members of the religious community to which they belong, although their rights and privileges in the community are determined by their respective rule or constitutions. The term "lay brothers" is not applied to the members of the nonclerical men's religious institutes. They are called brothers.

LAY CONFESSION. Confessing or telling one's sins to a lay person. It was prevalent during the Middle Ages as an exercise in humility or, when a person was dying, no priest was available. It was never regarded by the Church as having the sacramental efficacy of confession to a priest or as giving the lay "confessor" the right to confer absolution.

LAYING ON OF HANDS. In both the Old and New Testaments a significant symbolic action denoting various meanings. Examples: Israel giving his parental blessing to Ephraim and Manasseh (Genesis 48:18); Moses passing his authority to his successor (Numbers 27:18); Joshua receiving the spirit of wisdom to lead his people (Deuteronomy 34:9); Aaron preparing the ram for sacrifice (Exodus 29:10). In the New Testament its symbolism took on a further and deeper meaning: Jesus blessing the children (Matthew 19:15); Jesus bringing the official's daughter back to life (Matthew 9:18); Peter and John calling down the Holy Spirit on the Samaritans (Acts 8:17). After Pentecost the laying on of hands especially denoted the conferral of the powers and authority of the episcopacy, which Christ had given to the Apostles. In the Catholic Church the sacrament of orders: the diaconate, priesthood, and episcopate are administered by a bishop through the laying on of hands.

LAY INTRUSION. The unauthorized exercise of lay power or influence to affect Church policy or legislation. In the case of election to an ecclesiastical office, any such intrusion automatically renders the election invalid.

LAY SISTERS. Members of a religious institute of women who are not bound by choir duty or engaged in the distinctive apostolate of the rest of the community. Their role in a community of nuns is to serve the physical and temporal needs of those who are strictly cloistered. The term "extern Sisters" is sometimes used, but the expression is misleading. They are full members of the community and share in all its spiritual benefits. The Holy See has provided that monasteries of contemplative nuns may have "Sisters employed in the external service of the convent, in accordance with the statutes of each Institute" (Sacred Congregation for Religious and for Secular Institutes, *Venite Seorsum*, August 15, 1969). Since the Second Vatican Council, however, the Church's general policy is not to favor a division of classes in convents. Therefore, "unless conditions really suggest something else, care should be taken that there be only one class of Sisters in communities of women" (*Perfectae Caritatis*, 15).

LAZARISTS. See VINCENTIANS.

LAZARUS. 1. the brother of Mary and Martha, who befriended and entertained Jesus in their home in Bethany. While Jesus "was away," Lazarus was taken ill and died. Their faith was so strong that both Mary and Martha greeted Jesus, on his return four days later, with the same words: "If you had been here, my brother would not have died." At the tomb Jesus ordered Lazarus to rise; he came out of the tomb at once in the burial wrappings, to the amazement of the mourning family and friends. The Pharisees were so worried by Jesus' growing popularity that they decided on that day that he must die (John 11); 2. the name Jesus used to represent the poor man in the parable he related concerning the fate of Dives, the rich man who lived luxuriously, and Lazarus, the impoverished beggar, who ate the scraps from Dives' table. When they died, the rich man suffered torment in Hades, while Lazarus rested on Abraham's bosom (Luke 16:19–31). (Etym. Greek *lazaros* from Hebrew *'el'azar*, God has helped.)

LAZINESS. Disinclination or aversion to effort, whether physical, mental, or moral. It implies idleness, even when a person is supposedly at work.

L.C.D. *Legis Civilis Doctor*—Doctor of Civil Law.

L.C., LOC. CIT. *Loco citato*—in the place cited.

LD. Lauds.

LEAGUE OF THE SACRED HEART. See APOSTLESHIP OF PRAYER.

LEAH. Older daughter of Laban and first wife of Jacob. She had the dubious distinction of being the "wrong" wife. Jacob expected to marry her younger sister, Rachel, but the crafty father took advantage of the custom of keeping the bride veiled on the wedding night. Jacob had to work another seven years for Laban before he could marry Rachel, too. Leah, however, was a significant figure in Hebrew history. She was the mother of six of Jacob's sons, each of whom became the head of one of the Tribes of Israel. The Leah Tribes are distinguished from the Rachel Tribes (Genesis 29:20–30). (Etym. Hebrew *le'ah*, cow.)

LEARNING. Knowledge or skill acquired by study and practice. In the language of scholastic philosophy, learning from education, which requires another person to impart the knowledge and which involves a mental or moral development of the person educated. Learning directly pertains to what is acquired; education rather pertains to who is developed.

LEAVEN. Any substance that will cause fermentation and will raise dough; also when introduced into the Mass modifies and tempers the whole. Symbol of moral influence, whether good or bad. In the Jewish tradition unleavened bread is a sign of sinlessness. Christ spoke of the leaven of the Pharisees as harmful (Matthew 16; Mark 8). St. Paul urged the Christians to purge out the old yeast of evil and to have only the unleavened bread of sincerity and truth (I Corinthians 5:8). In one of the parables of the Gospel, the kingdom of heaven is compared to yeast that eventually leavens all who come under its influence (Matthew 13:33).

LEAVENED BREAD. The bread for the Eucharist made of fermented dough, commonly used by the Catholic Christians of the Eastern Rite except the Armenians. Natural yeast is used as the leaven. (Etym. Latin *levamen*, alleviation, "that which raises," from *levare*, to raise.)

LEAVE OF ABSENCE. Temporary absence of a religious man or woman from community life for reasons of health or otherwise, with permission of superiors and with full dependence on their authority.

LECT. *Lectio*—lesson.

LECTERN. A movable reading desk of wood or metal to support the sacred books used in liturgical ceremonies. When stationary they are sometimes elaborately decorated; those in English churches were conspicuous with eagles with outspread wings and other massive carvings. Two were frequently used, one on the Gospel and the other on the Epistle side of the sanctuary. Since the Second Vatican Council many churches have separate lecterns on either side of the sanctuary: one for the celebrant and the other for the lector of the Mass. A small folding support, sometimes called a lectern, is often placed on the altar to hold the sacramentary or gospel book during Mass.

LECTIO BREVIS. See CHAPTER, LITURGICAL.

LECTIONARY. The present lectionary was introduced March 22, 1970. It contains a three-year cycle of readings for Sundays and solemn feasts, a two-year weekday cycle, and a one-year cycle for the feasts of saints. Moreover, it contains readings for a large variety of other Masses. There are also responsorial psalms that follow the first readings for each Mass, along with Gospel or Alleluia verses to follow the second readings.

LECTOR. One of the ministries adapted to present day needs in the Latin Church, otherwise known as reader. He functions partially as the subdeacon did previously. He is appointed to read the word of God in the liturgical assembly. Accordingly he reads the lesson from Sacred Scripture, except the Gospel, in the Mass and in other sacred celebrations; recites the psalms between the readings in the absence of the psalmist; presents the intentions for general intercessions when the deacon or cantor is absent; and may also direct the congregation in the singing. If necessary he also assumes the responsibility of instructing any of the faithful called upon to read the Scriptures in any liturgical celebration. (Etym. Latin *lector,* reader; from *legere,* to read.)

LEGAL DUTY. An obligation to obey a positive law, especially civil law, but not arising from man's nature or from divine revelation. It is binding in legal justice only.

LEGAL IMPEDIMENT. An obstacle to valid marriage, determined by civil authority. According to the constant tradition of the Catholic Church, the State has no power to legislate invalidating impediments to Christian marriage. This follows logically from the Church's teaching that, since Christian marriage is a supernatural contract, the conditions for its validity are subject only to the Church, which has received this authority from her Founder. It is disputed whether the State can establish diriment impediments for marriages in which both parties are unbaptized. Yet, if even one of the parties is baptized, the Church alone has jurisdiction over the marriage, and only her invalidating impediments are binding.

LEGAL JUSTICE. The virtue that regulates those actions which society justly requires of the individual for the common good. According to legal justice, the State may institute just laws and perform such acts as further the welfare of the community. Thus import duties, fire and traffic regulations, anti-pollution laws, and similar provisions of the State concern legal justice.

LEGAL MORALITY. A term sometimes applied to those politicians who resort to the distinction between what is legal and what is moral. Morality, it is argued, is a private affair that does not pertain to the State as a religiously neutral society, no matter what it does legally. Morality is also said to belong essentially to the will. Provided the intention is good, it is immaterial what the State or the people, as citizens, do or permit juridically. A person simply dissociates his or her will from an objectively bad action (such as abortion) and thereby exempts himself or herself from any guilt or complicity. At best one should not be held guilty for allowing others, even as a legislator, the legal right of doing what one's own conscience says is wrong. "Legal morality" is a modern form of Machiavellianism.

LEGAL RELATIONSHIP. A matrimonial impediment resulting from adoption. It is classified as a nullifying or merely hindering impediment to marriage according to the existing laws of the State. The Church can dispense from both forms of impediment.

LEGATE, PAPAL. A personal representative of the Pope who has been entrusted with authority from the Holy See. There are three kinds of papal legates: legates a latere, nuncios, and legati nati.

LEGATE A LATERE. A papal legate deputed by the Holy See for important missions of a temporary character.

LEGATUS NATUS. Holder of a certain office that conferred a legatine status *ex officio,* e.g., before the Reformation the Archbishop of Canterbury, who performed some of the functions now carried out by a papal nuncio.

LEGEND OF THE SAINTS. Popular biographical stories of the saints. Not entirely fictitious, they possess a substratum of truth, usually under considerable embellishment. The Church has consistently sought to sift this substratum of truth from the legendary additions, as in the Breviary reform under St. Pius X and the total revision of the Liturgy of the Hours by Pope Paul VI, according to the directives of the Constitution on the Liturgy of the Second Vatican Council.

LEGION OF MARY. One of the largest lay organizations in the Catholic Church, founded in Dublin in 1921. Its purpose is entirely spiritual, namely, the sanctification of the members and their practice of charity toward others.

LEGIT. Legitime, *legitimus*—lawful, legitimate.

LEGITIMATE MARRIAGE. A true natural marriage between two parties, neither of whom is baptized. Such also is a marriage validly contracted by a baptized person with one who is not baptized. In this case, even the baptized party does not receive the sacrament. The marital bond is said to be a natural one.

LEGITIMATION. Removal of the irregularity due to birth out of wedlock. Ecclesiastical law presumes legitimacy even if the marriage later is found to be invalid but was reputed valid at the time of the child's birth. Illegitimacy is removed if parents marry provided they were free to marry at the time of the child's conception or birth or at some intermediate time. Legitimation does not depend on the will of the parents. The Pope and those delegated by him have the power of legitimating anyone born out of wedlock and thereby removing any irregularities that would otherwise prevent the reception of priestly orders or advancement to a higher ecclesiastical office. (Etym. Latin *legitimare,* to make lawful.)

LENT. The season of prayer and penance before Easter. Its purpose is to better prepare the faithful for the feast of the Resurrection, and dispose them for a more fruitful reception of the graces that Christ merited by his passion and death.

In the Latin Rite, Lent begins on Ash Wednesday and continues for forty days, besides Sundays, until Easter Sunday. Ash Wednesday occurs on any day from February 4 to March 11, depending on the date of Easter.

Originally the period of fasting in preparation for Easter did not, as a rule, exceed two or three days. But by the time of the Council of Nicaea (325) forty days were already customary. And ever since, this length of time has been associated with Christ's forty-day fast in the desert before beginning his public life.

According to the prescription of Pope Paul VI, in revising the Church's laws of fast and abstinence, "The time of Lent preserves its penitential character. The days of penitence to be observed under obligation throughout the Church are all Fridays and Ash Wednesday, that is to say the first days of Great Lent, according to the diversity of rites. Their substantial observance binds gravely" (*Paenitemini,* III, norm II).

Besides fast and abstinence on specified days, the whole Lenten season is to be penitential, with stress on prayer, reception of the sacraments, almsgiving, and the practice of charity. (Etym Anglo-Saxon *lengten,* lencten, spring, Lent.)

LEONINE CITY. That part of Rome situated on the right bank of the Tiber, so called in honor of Pope St. Leo IV, who between 848 and 852 surrounded it with a wall when the Moslems were threatening the city. It contains the Basilica of St. Peter and the Vatican.

LEONINE PRAYERS. Customary prayers after Mass, ordered by Pope Leo XIII for all the faithful of the Roman Rite. They consisted of three Hail Marys, the "Hail Holy Queen," and the prayer to St. Michael the Archangel. A final petition to the Sacred Heart, to be said three times, was added by Pope St. Pius X. Formally abrogated in 1964, the Leonine Prayers ceased to be recited with the revision of the liturgy after the Second Vatican Council.

LEONINE SACRAMENTARY. The oldest of the Latin sacramentaries or liturgical books. It was erroneously attributed to Pope Leo I and was in use from the fourth to the seventh centuries. It contains neither canons nor the Ordinary of the Mass, but many propers, collects, prefaces, secrets, postcommunions, and orations, together with ordination forms. Many of these prayers are still in use today.

LEPER WINDOW. A low window in the chancel wall of a church, found in medieval architecture. Often it was iron barred or shuttered. It was to enable lepers who had to remain outside the church to attend Mass.

LE PUY. French Shrine of Our Lady of the Peak. Its central interest is an ancient statue of the Blessed Virgin and Child, perhaps the oldest in Christendom. Carved of cedar, eighteen inches high, the image was given to Le Puy by King St. Louis IX when he returned from his Egyptian crusade. Devotion to Our Lady of Le Puy was at its height in 1095 at the time of the First Crusade. Pope St. Urban II knelt before her, Sts. Bernard, Dominic, Anthony, Vincent Ferrer, and John Francis Regis came to see her as pilgrims; seven popes left her rich gifts, the French Revolution saw her statue burned but directly reconstructed from memory. The early story of this shrine relates it was built about A.D. 46 in thanksgiving for a cure. Over the centuries, thousands have visited the Rock, as Le Puy is called, singing the *"Salve Regina,"* said to have been intoned the first time at this sanctuary.

LESSER DOXOLOGY. The "Glory Be to the Father," or shorter praise of the Trinity, as distinguished from the Greater Doxology, or "Glory to God in the Highest," recited or sung at Mass.

LESSER SINS. See VENIAL SIN.

LESSONS. Portions of the Scriptures to be read at Mass, now called the Readings. (Etym. Latin *lectio,* reading aloud.)

LETHARGIC TEMPERAMENT. One of the four classic temperaments, characterized by a sluggish indifference even when faced with an urgent call for action. Persons with this temperament are not easily disturbed under provocation, and they can withstand an abnormal amount of criticism or opposition. But they have to struggle against their natural tendency toward inertia.

LEVI. Third son of Jacob and Leah. He and Simeon, an older brother, were prone to violence. When their sister, Dinah, was raped by Shechem (Genesis 34:1–2), they vowed revenge and killed not only Shechem but also his father, Hamor, and all their followers, pillaged their town, and confiscated their wealth and property. Jacob was horrified by the extent of their vengefulness (Genesis 34:25–31). In the prophecies he made for each of his sons, he singled out Simeon and Levi for special condemnation. "Accursed be their rage for its ruthlessness, their wrath for its ferocity" (Genesis 49:7).

LEVITATION. Phenomenon in which a human body is raised above ground and sustained in midair without any natural support. At times the body rises to great heights; at other times it glides rapidly just above ground.

Well-documented evidence of levitation is reported in the lives of many saints, e.g., Francis Xavier, Paul of the Cross, Peter of Alcántara, Philip Neri, and Stephen of Hungary. One of the most celebrated was St. Joseph Cupertino (1603–63), Conventual Franciscan, who was treated with no little severity by his ecclesiastical superiors because of the disturbance caused by his raptures.

According to Benedict XIV, in order to verify genuine levitation it is first of all necessary to make a thorough investigation to eliminate any chance of fraud. Then he states that a well-authenticated levitation cannot be explained on merely natural grounds; that this phenomenon is not, however, beyond the power of angels or demons; and that with the saints it is a kind of anticipation of a prerogative of glorified bodies.

LEVITES. Descendants of Levi, the third son of Jacob by Leah. The whole tribe of

Levi was set apart by God for the service of the sanctuary. In place of land, they were to receive tithes and other landed property from the other tribes. Aaron and his sons were chosen for the priesthood (Exodus 8), while the subordinate offices of the temple and other public services were assigned to the rest of the tribe.

LEVITICUS. Third book of the Bible, named from its contents, which deal entirely with the service of God and the religious ceremonies to be performed by the members of the tribe of Levi, both priests and Levites. Its divisions are: the rites of sacrifice (1–7), consecration and installation of priests (8–10), the laws of purity (11–16), the law of holiness (17–22), religious institutions (23–25), blessings and curses (26). The book strongly emphasizes the divine majesty and the duty to honor and obey God as sovereign Lord.

LEX FUNDAMENTALIS. The basic law of the Roman Catholic Church, similar to a constitution for the Church, is a new feature in the history of ecclesiastical legislation. It was called forth by the decisions of the Second Vatican Council.

LEX ORANDI. Name of the axiom of Pope St. Celestine I (422–32), *"Legem credendi statuit lex orandi"* (The rule of prayer determines the rule of faith). By this is meant that the Church's liturgy is the most effective means of preserving and interpreting the true faith.

LEX SALICA. Salic law, or the legal code of the Salian Franks, which was later incorporated into French law. Also any provision of this law, notably the exclusion of women from inheritance of land or succession to the throne.

LEX TALIONIS. The law of retaliation, an eye for an eye, a tooth for a tooth. This could be understood literally and also legally. Literally it means demanding strict retribution, with no mercy shown. Legally it means inflicting punishment in kind, i.e., to suffer a penalty similar to the crime.

L.H.D. *Litterarum Humanarum Doctor*—Doctor of Literature.

LIB., LO. *Liber, libro*—book, in the book.

LIBEL. A legal term with moral implications, it means that something has been printed or written that defames a person and implicates the publication as guilty before the law.

LIBELLUS. Certificate of sacrifice, testifying that a person during the Roman persecutions had offered sacrifice to the pagan gods. The officials were required to superintend the sacrifices on a fixed day, receive in writing a statement from the person, and countersign the testimony in the name of the emperor. Many Christians apostatized; others bought certificates or had them procured by pagan friends. There seems to have been wholesale connivance by the officials. Those who refused to sacrifice were sentenced to prison or even death. A papyrus copy of a libellus, dating from A.D. 250, was discovered at Fayoum, Egypt. Its first part reads: "To the Commisioners for sacrifices in the village of Alexander's island, from Aurelius Diogenes, son of Satabus, of the village of Alexander's island, aged 72; scar on right eyebrow." The receipt of the presiding official reads: "I certify that I witnessed his sacrifice, Aurelius Syrus. Dated this first year of the Emperor Caesar Gaius Messius Quintus Trajanus Decius, Pius, Felix, Augustus, the 2nd of Epiph. (26 June 250)."

LIBERAL ARTS. Originally the program of studies in the Middle Ages, suited for free men. They had been first proposed by Plato in the *Republic* (III) and adopted by Christian educators as the foundation for more specialized study in law, medicine, and theology. There were seven liberal arts, divided into the trivium and quadrivium. See also QUADRIVIUM, TRIVIUM.

LIBERALISM. Until the eighteenth century the term generally meant whatever was worthy of a free man, e.g., as applied to the liberal arts or a liberal education. This meaning is still current, but at least since the French Revolution liberalism has become more or less identified with a philosophy that stresses human freedom to the neglect and even denial of the rights of God in religion, the rights of society in civil law, and the rights of the Church in her relations to the State. It was in this sense that liberalism was condemned by Pope Pius IX in 1864 in the *Syllabus of Errors* (Denzinger, 2977–80).

LIBERALITY. A spirit of generosity in the use of money or possessions for proper and worthy charity. (Etym. Latin *libertas*, freedom.)

LIBERATION THEOLOGY. A movement in the Roman Catholic Church that makes criticism of oppression essential to the task of theology. The forms of oppression to be criticized are mainly social and economic evils. Originating in Latin America, liberation theology has held as its main concern the exploitation of the poor, but it also seeks to defend the rights of minority and ethnic groups and to support women's liberation. It is, therefore, a theory of deliverance from the injustices caused to people by the power structures of modern society.

It is a new approach to theology, and its leaders urge a reinterpretation of the Christian faith to concentrate on the main task of the Church today, to deliver people everywhere from the inhumanity to which they are being subjected, especially by those in political power. Accordingly all the main doctrines of historic Christianity are to be reassessed and, if need be, revised. Christ becomes an inspired human deliverer of the weak and oppressed; God's kingdom centers on this world, and not on the next; sin is essentially social evil and not an offense against God; the Church's mission is mainly sociopolitical and not eschatological; and objective divine revelation is subordinated to personal experience.

Aware of both the potential and risks of liberation theology, Pope John Paul II addressed himself mainly to this subject on his visit to Mexico in early 1979. He told the bishops of Latin America, met at Puebla for their General Conference: "The Church feels the duty to proclaim the liberation of millions of human beings, the duty to help this liberation become firmly established." At the same time, ". . . she also feels the corresponding duty to proclaim liberation in its integral and profound meaning, as Jesus proclaimed and realized it." Then, drawing on Pope Paul VI's teaching, he declared that it is "above all, liberation from sin and the evil one, in the joy of knowing God and being known by him."

The Pope finally set down the norms "that help to distinguish when the liberation in question is Christian and when on the other hand it is based rather on ideologies that rob it of consistency with an evangelical point of view." Basically these norms refer to the content "of what the evangelizers proclaim" and to "the concrete attitudes that they adopt." On the level of content, "one must see what is their fidelity to the word of God, to the Church's living Tradition and to her Magisterium." On the level of attitudes, "one must consider what sense of communion they have with the bishops, in the first place, and with the other sectors of the People of God; what contribution they make to the real building up of the community; in what form they lovingly show care for the poor, the sick, the dispossessed, the neglected and the oppressed, and in what way they find in them the image of the poor and suffering Jesus, and strive to relieve their need and serve Christ in them" (address to the Third General Conference of the Latin American Episcopate, January 28, 1979).

LIBERIAN BASILICA. The patriarchal Basilica of St. Mary Major, also known as the Basilica of Our Lady of Snows and St. Mary *ad praesepe* because of the relic of the crib of Bethlehem reserved there. Originally built by Pope St. Liberius (352–66).

LIBERIUS, CASE OF POPE. In the midst of the Arian crisis Pope Liberius was banished by the Arian Emperor Constantius II in A.D. 355 for refusing to condemn St. Athanasius. Two years later he is alleged to have signed an Arian formula of faith to regain his freedom. Certain documents discrediting him are forgeries. In any event, it is certain that he signed no document freely, and so papal infallibility is not involved.

LIBER PONTIFICALIS. A collection of early biographies of the popes, from St. Peter to Pope Eugene IV (d. 1447). Each pope's life is written according to a regular formula. The earliest form of the *Liber Pontificalis* was based on the Liberian Catalogue (A.D. 354) and appears to have been the work of a Roman priest at the time of Pope Boniface II (reigned 530–32). Subsequent editions contain biographies written shortly after the death of each pope.

LIBERTY. Freedom, but with stress on the person who enjoys or exercises the freedom. Liberty, therefore, is more the subjective power of self-determination; freedom is more the objective absence of constraint or coercion, notably with reference to civil society, as freedom of religion, assembly, and education.

LIBERTY OF CONTRADICTION. See FREEDOM OF CONTRADICTION.

LIBERTY OF EXERCISE. See FREEDOM OF CONTRADICTION.

LIBERTY OF SPECIFICATION. See FREEDOM OF SPECIFICATION.

LIBER USUALIS. A liturgical book containing most of the Gregorian chants and readings in the Mass and the Divine Office of the Roman Catholic Church.

LIBIDO. Basic term in psychoanalysis for all the instinctive urges of a human person, and particularly for the sexual drive. In moral theology the libido stands for the procreative appetite, with the implication that this appetite is part of fallen human nature and therefore needs divine grace to be controlled. (Etym. Latin *libido,* desire, enjoyment; inordinate desire; lust.)

LIC. *Licentia, Licentiatus*—license, licentiate.

LICEITY. The legitimacy of a human action and its consequences, e.g., administration of a sacrament or a contract. It is commonly distinguished from validity, since an action may be valid but not licit, as a layman conferring baptism without urgent necessity. (Etym. Latin *licentia,* license, freedom to act.)

LICENTIATE. An ecclesiastical degree in theology, Sacred Scripture, philosophy, canon law, or another sacred science. It ranks above a bachelor's degree and below a doctor's degree.

LICIT. That which is permitted by law, whether civil or ecclesiastical. Often distinguished from valid, to express what the law prescribes or allows, as distinct from what is necessary to produce the desired effect. (Etym. Latin *licet,* it is lawful, it is allowed or permitted.)

LIFE. Inward activity. The essence of a being to act from within; ranging from the life of God, which is identical with his nature, on through all the forms of life in the created universe. The higher a nature the more intimate what comes from it, for its inwardness of activity corresponds to its rank of being. Life is immanent activity, which begins and terminates within the living being.

LIFE EVERLASTING. The eternal life of heavenly glory, in body and soul, promised by Christ to those who die in God's friendship.

LIGAMEN. An existing marriage acting as a deterring impediment to another marriage. It exists until the death of either party is legally attested or morally certain. Exceptions are the dissolution by the Church of a natural marital bond or a nonconsummated sacramental marriage. An apparent exception is when the Church declares a previous marital union, considered valid and sacramental, to have been no real marriage at all.

LIGHT. In revelation and sacred doctrine, a source of understanding or of insight into the truth. It may be either the truth itself, which enlightens the mind about what God wants human beings to know; or the inward supernatural power that enables the mind to grasp what is beyond its native capacity to understand; or the assistance of grace to help dispel the darkness induced by sinful passion that tends to prevent the intellect from seeing the things of God.

LIGHT SINS. See VENIAL SIN.

LILY. A symbol of purity. Virgin saints, e.g., St. Joseph, St. Anthony of Padua, St. Catherine of Siena, and St. Gertrude have a lily for their emblem. Signifying virginity, it is one of the primary symbols of Mary the Blessed Virgin, especially in the Annunciation scene.

LIMBO. The abode of souls excluded from the full blessedness of the beatific vision, but not suffering any other punishment. They enjoy the happiness that would have been human destiny if humans had not been elevated to the supernatural order.

Catholic theology distinguishes two kinds of limbo. The limbo of the Fathers (*limbus patrum*) was the place where the saints of the Old Testament remained until Christ's coming and redemption of the world. The limbo of infants (*limbus infantium*) is the permanent state of those who die in original sin but are innocent of any personal guilt.

Regarding the limbo of infants, it is an article of the Catholic faith that those who die without baptism, and for whom the want of baptism has not been supplied in some other way, cannot enter heaven. This is the teaching of the ecumenical councils of Florence and Trent. After defining justification as "a passing from the state in which man is born of the first Adam, to the state of grace and adoption as sons of God," Trent declared, "Since the Gospel was promulgated, this passing cannot take place without the water of regeneration or the desire for it, as it is written, 'Unless a man be born again of water and the Holy Spirit, he cannot enter the kingdom of God' (John 3:5)" (Denzinger 1524).

Some theologians of renown have thought that God might supply the want of baptism by some other means. St. Bernard suggested that such infants could reach heaven because of the faith of their parents (*De Baptismo* I, 4; II, 1). Cardinal Cajetan (1469–1534) espoused the same theory, but Pope St. Pius V had the passage removed from Cajetan's works.

The great majority of theologians, approved by the Church, teach that infants who die in original sin suffer no "pain of sense." They are simply excluded from the beatific vision. Do they grieve because they are deprived of heaven? St. Thomas

Aquinas answers that they do not, because pain of punishment is proportioned to personal guilt, which does not exist here. Rather, "They rejoice because they share in God's goodness and in many natural perfections" (*De Malo*, V, 3). It is believed that infants in limbo know and love God intensely by the use of their natural powers, and they enjoy full natural happiness.

The Church has never defined the existence of limbo, although she has more than once supported the fact by her authority. Those who either deny that heaven is a supernatural destiny to which no creature has a natural claim, or who deny that original sin deprives a person of a right to heaven logically also deny the very possibility of limbo. On their premises there is no need of such a place. Among others who denied the existence of limbo were the Jansenists, whose theory of selective predestination excluded the need for any mediatorial source of grace, including baptism. They were condemned by Pope Pius VI as teaching something "false, rash and injurious to Catholic education," because they claimed that it was a Pelagian fable to hold that there is a place "which the faithful generally designate by the name of limbo of children," for the souls of those who depart this life with the sole guilt of original sin (Denzinger 2626). Pope Pius XII declared that "an act of love can suffice for an adult to acquire sanctifying grace and supply for the lack of baptism; to the unborn or newly born infant this way is not open" (*Acta Apostolicae Sedis*, XLIII, 84). At stake in the traditional belief in limbo is the revealed doctrine that heaven is a sheer gift of divine goodness and that baptism of water or desire is necessary to enter heaven. (Etym. Latin *limbo*, ablative form of *limbus*, border; taken from *"in limbo patrum"* [in the border of hell reserved for the fathers (or saints)], a phrase used by the Church Fathers.)

LINUS. A Christian in Rome, evidently a companion or follower of Paul, because in the conclusion of a letter Paul sent Timothy, Linus was one of four who sent greetings (II Timothy 4:21). According to Irenaeus, Linus succeeded Peter as Bishop of Rome.

LION. A symbol of power and courage in Christian art, ascribed to Christ—"the Lion of the tribe of Judah" (Apocalypse 5:5). Credited with exceptional vigilance, the lion is portrayed as guardian before the doors of churches. St. Jerome is often shown with a lion with whom he shared his cave in Palestine.

LIQUEFACTION. The miraculous act of liquefying of solid matter, especially congealed blood, as reported of certain relics of saints. The best known liquefaction is that reported of St. Januarius (d. c. 305), Bishop of Benevento. A glass phial containing his dried blood is seen to liquefy in public eighteen times a year. This phenomenon has been recorded for 500 years, and no natural explanation has been given.

LITANY. A form of prayer, consisting of a series of petitions or biddings which are sung or said by a priest, deacon, or leader, and to which the people make fixed responses.

Litanies have a definite structure: first the invocation of the persons of the Trinity, then the petitions corresponding to a distinctive theme, followed by three invocations of the Lamb of God, and closing with a short prayer that summarizes the petitions made.

Since the Second Vatican Council, these litanies have been formally indulgenced, i.e., a partial indulgence for every recitation: the Holy Name, the Sacred Heart, the Precious Blood, the Blessed Virgin, St. Joseph, and the saints. Other litanies, approved for use by the faithful but not thus indulgenced, number over a hundred.

In the Eastern Rites, litanies are an outstanding feature of the Eucharistic liturgy, and in the Ambrosian Rite are sung every Sunday during Lent in place of the Gloria. (Etym. Latin *litania;* from Greek *litaneiā,* prayer, entreaty, supplication.)

LITANY OF LORETO. See LITANY OF OUR LADY.

LITANY OF OUR LADY. In its present form it was approved and indulgenced by Pope Sixtus V in 1587, and again by Pope Clement VIII in 1601. It is a series of invocations of the Blessed Virgin, each with the response, "Pray for us." Successive popes have added new invocations, e.g., "Mother of Good Counsel," by Pope Leo XIII, "Queen of Peace," by Pope Benedict XV, and "Queen Assumed into Heaven," by Pope Pius XII. It is a simplified version of older Litanies of Our Lady that were known already in the twelfth century.

LITANY OF ST. JOSEPH. A series of invocations of the foster-father of Jesus, approved for the universal Church by Pope St. Pius X on March 18, 1909. After the customary petitions to the Holy Trinity, and one addressed to the Blessed Virgin, the litany is composed of twenty-one invocations expressing the virtues and dignity of St. Joseph.

LITANY OF THE DYING. A series of invocations of the saints that is part of the liturgy of anointing for persons in danger of death. Also called the "commendation of a soul departing," it petitions for God's mercy on the soul that is soon to appear before him.

LITANY OF THE HOLY NAME. Invocations expressing various attributes of the Savior, with a petition for mercy repeated after each invocation. Of unknown origin, it has been commonly ascribed to St. Bernardino of Siena and St. John Capistran, zealous preachers of devotion to the Holy Name in their day. In 1588, Pope Sixtus V granted an indulgence for its private recitation. In 1862, Pope Pius IX approved it for any diocese whose bishop requested the litany, and in 1886, Pope Leo XIII extended its use to the universal Church, because of the growing devotion to the Holy Name throughout the world.

LITANY OF THE PRECIOUS BLOOD. A series of invocations of the Savior, through his Precious Blood, approved in its present form by Pope John XXIII in 1960. Each of the twenty-four petitions begins with the term "Blood of Christ," to which the response is "Save us." The Blood of Christ represents either Christ himself, as "Blood of Christ, Incarnate Word of God," or refers to the physical Blood of the Savior, as "Blood of Christ, poured out on the Cross," or spans both meanings, as "Blood of Christ, freeing souls from purgatory." The Litany of the Precious Blood is included among the official litanies of the Church in the new *Manual of Indulgences* (1968). There is a partial indulgence for each recitation.

LITANY OF THE SACRED HEART. Invocations of Jesus Christ under the title of the Sacred Heart, authorized for recitation in the universal Church by Pope Leo XIII in 1899. After the customary petitions to the Persons of the Holy Trinity, the litany contains thirty-three invocations of the Heart of Jesus. Each invocation reflects an aspect of God's love symbolized by the physical Heart of Christ, the Son of God who became man and died out of love for sinful mankind.

LITANY OF THE SAINTS. Believed to be the most ancient of the litanies used in the Church. Already prescribed by Pope Gregory the Great in 590 for a public procession of thanksgiving at the end of a plague that had devastated Rome. In a somewhat different form, it was mentioned by St. Basil in the fourth century. Called the Litany of the Saints because it is made up of petitions addressed to various saints of different classes, and to Mary, the Queen of the Saints. In its present form, after invoking forty-eight individual saints and thirteen groups of saints, the litany begs for deliverance from a dozen evils and makes some thirty intercessions, including "that you would deign to humble the enemies of Holy Church" and "grant peace and unity to all Christian people."

LITERAL SENSE. The meaning of Sacred Scripture as communicated by the words of the inspired text. It is opposed to the typical or spiritual sense, even when the literal meaning may be figurative or metaphorical. (Etym. Latin *literalis,* word for word, according to the letter.)

LITHOSTROTOS. See GABBATHA.

LITT. *Littera*–letter.

LITTLE FLOWER, NATIONAL SHRINE OF THE. Located in Chicago, Illinois, it was built by members of the Society of the Little Flower in thanksgiving for individual favors received through the intercession of St. Thérèse, and is now in the charge of the Carmelite Fathers. Outside of France, it has the most noteworthy collection of St. Thérèse's relics in the world.

LITTLE FLOWER SHRINE. Place of pilgrimage to St. Thérèse Martin, daughter of Carmel. Lisieux, a French town of some twenty-five thousand near Le Havre, is the pilgrimage center of millions. All other factors of the town are secondary to the cathedral and the Carmel, made famous by a young nun who with her "little way" captivated minds and hearts for God. She was canonized by Pope Pius XI in 1925 and declared by him to be patroness of the missions partnered with St. Francis Xavier. The magnificent cathedral was consecrated by Pope Pius XII in 1937 when he was nuncio to France. It is Romano Byzantine in style.

LITTLE FLOWERS OF ST. FRANCIS, THE. Also called *Fioretti.* A collection of stories about the life of St. Francis of Assisi and his companions. It cannot be traced to a single author, but one part at least has been attributed to a provincial of the Friars Minor, Fra. Ugolino Brunforte. The earliest manuscript dated 1390 is in Berlin. First printed at Vicenza in 1476, the vernacular translation was widely circulated and is considered a masterpiece of Italian literature. There are several English versions.

LITTLE HOURS. The shorter hours of the

Divine Office, before the revision of the Breviary since the Second Vatican Council. They were Prime, Terce, Sext, and None. In the revised office, Prime has been suppressed, while Terce, Sext, and None have become the Middle Hour (*Hora Media*), with a different closing biblical reading and prayer that is still called Terce, Sext, and None, for different times of the day, i.e., before noon, noon to three, and after three in the afternoon. Only one of the three hours is read each day, depending on the time of day it is said, i.e., midmorning, midday, or midafternoon.

LITTLE OFFICE OF OUR LADY. A shortened form of the Divine Office in honor of the Blessed Virgin. It contains seven hours, but the psalms do not vary each day. Already known in the tenth century, it originated in the monasteries and was early adopted by the Cistercians and Camaldolese. Retained after the Breviary reform of St. Pius V in 1568, but no longer binding under sin. Recited by many religious communities and used as a private devotion by the faithful.

LITURGIAE INSTAURATIONES. Instruction of the Sacred Congregation for Divine Worship, calling attention to the Church's liturgical norms and warning against abuses since the Second Vatican Council. Its most explicit directive states that "the liturgical texts composed by the Church . . . deserve the greatest respect. No one on his own authority may make changes, substitutions, additions, or deletions in them" (September 5, 1970).

LITURGICAL BOOKS. Texts approved by the Holy See, containing the orderly arrangement of the prayers, hymns, readings, and directives to be followed by the celebrant and ministers in the Church's liturgy. All the liturgical books have been revised since the Second Vatican Council, including the sacramentary and lectionary for Mass, the Liturgy of the Hours, the order for the celebration of each of the sacraments, and for religious profession.

LITURGICAL DRAMAS. Plays in medieval times developed from religious dialogues and resulting in chants about biblical characters and later in mystery plays. A few survive today as Old Testament plays without musical accompaniment.

LITURGICAL YEAR. The annual cycle of the mysteries of Christ, the Blessed Virgin, angels, and saints, which the Church commemorates in the Mass, the Divine Office, .and other forms of public worship. The liturgical year begins with the first Sunday of Advent and closes with the thirty-fourth week "through the year."

LITURGY. A public service, duty, or work. In Scripture it refers to the religious duties to be performed by priests and levites in the Temple, especially those related to the Sacrifice; in Christian use among the Eastern Churches it means the Eucharistic Sacrifice.

In present day usage liturgy is the official public worship of the Church and is thus distinguished from private devotion. It is the special title of the Eucharist, and the administration of the sacraments with the annexed use of the sacramentals.

From a theological viewpoint, the liturgy is the exercise now on earth of Christ's priestly office, as distinct from his role as teacher and ruler of his people. Christ performs this priestly office as Head of his Mystical Body, so that Head and members together offer the sacred liturgy. Its function, therefore, is twofold: to give honor and praise to God, which is worship, and to obtain blessings for the human race, which is sanctification. (Etym. Latin *liturgia;* from Greek *leitos,* of the people + *ergon,* work: *leitourgia,* public duty, public worship.)

LITURGY OF THE EUCHARIST. The most solemn part of the Mass, from the Presentation of the Gifts to the Postcommunion included. The Church has arranged this part of the Mass so that its several parts correspond to the words and actions of Christ at the Last Supper, and specifically in three stages: in the Presentation of the Gifts are brought the bread, wine, and water, even as Christ took these elements into his hands; in the Eucharistic prayer God is thanked for the whole work of redemption and the gifts become the body and blood of Christ; in the Breaking of the one Bread the unity of the faithful is signified, and in Communion they receive the same Christ who gave himself on Holy Thursday to his Apostles.

LITURGY OF THE HOURS. See DIVINE OFFICE.

LITURGY OF THE WORD. The second part of the Mass, during which the faithful are instructed in the revealed word of God. It consists of readings from Sacred Scripture and the songs occurring between them. The homily, profession of faith, and the prayer of the faithful develop and conclude the Liturgy of the Word.

LIVING WAGE. The compensation given to a worker, based on family responsibilities.

Two criteria are recognized in Catholic moral science, according to which a living wage may be either absolute or relative. These criteria are spelled out in the social encyclicals of the modern popes.

An absolute living wage is based on an average wage for family living, in which all workers who perform the same tasks receive the same pay. This is irrespective of whether they are married with children, married without children, or single. A relative living wage is based on the concrete family situation and responsibilities of each worker, in which the pay varies according to one's marital status and the number of dependents to be supported.

LL.B. *Legum Baccalaureus*—Bachelor of Laws.

LL.D. *Legum Doctor*—Doctor of Laws.

LL.M. *Legum Magister*—Master of Laws.

LOC. *Locus*—place.

LOCAL CHURCH. The parish or group of parishes in a diocese, or more generally any segment of the Catholic Church, in contrast with the universal Church throughout the world.

LOCAL CONGREGATION. The members of a single parochial community, as distinct from the diocese or the whole Catholic Church.

LOCUS CLASSICUS. Classical source, often used of biblical passages that are most cited by the Church's teaching authority as the basis in revelation for certain Catholic doctrines. Thus "You are Peter," addressed to Simon Peter by Christ, is a *locus classicus* for the papal primacy (Matthew 16:18).

LOCUTION. A supernatural communication to the ear, imagination, or directly to the intellect. The locution is supernatural in the manner of communication, that is, beyond the ordinary laws of nature. Spurious locutions may come from the evil spirit and can be recognized by their lack of coherence or clarity, the disquiet they cause in the one who receives them, and the evil effects they produce in those who listen to them. (Etym. Latin *locutio,* a speaking, speech, discourse; from *loqui,* to speak.)

LOGIA. The sayings of Jesus which are not recorded in the Bible. The Gospel of Thomas, discovered in 1945, records some of these.

LOGIC. The art or science of human reasoning. As an art, logic is the cultivated skill in reasoning with order and precision, with ease and without error. As a science, logic is the study of the first principles of knowledge, through inductive and deductive inference, and of the norms for clear thinking that leads to firm certitude. See also DEDUCTION, INDUCTION.

LOGICAL METHOD. An orderly way of making one's mental operations so as to reach the truth about any specific issue under consideration.

LOGOS. St. John's name for the second person of the Trinity, the Word of God. (Etym. Greek *logos,* word, speech, reason.)

LOLLARDISM. See WYCLIFISM.

LOLLARDS. The followers of John Wyclif (1324–84), who flourished in England in the fourteenth and fifteenth centuries, although the name was applied to certain heretics in Flanders before its use in England. The principal anti-Catholic positions of the Lollards were denial of the Church's authority and transubstantiation. They also espoused the theory of *dominium,* which claimed that the validity of the sacraments depends upon the worthiness of the one who administers them. These ideas were spread by Wyclif's "Poor Priests," whose austerity was in marked contrast to the growing luxury of the clergy. Stern measures were taken by the Church and State against the Lollards, who were, in a sense, forerunners of the Reformation in England.

LONGANIMITY. Extraordinary patience under provocation or trial. Also called long suffering. It is one of the fruits of the Holy Spirit. It includes forbearance, which adds to long suffering the implication of restraint in expressing one's feelings or in demanding punishment or one's due. Longanimity suggests toleration, moved by love and the desire for peace, of something painful that deserves to be rejected or opposed. (Etym. Latin *longus,* long + *animus,* soul, spirit, mind: *longanimitas,* long suffering, patience, forbearance.)

LONGINUS. The soldier who, according to tradition, pierced the side of Christ with a spear (John 19:34). After his conversion it is said that he returned to Cappadocia, where he was put to death by order of Pontius Pilate. His relics were preserved in the Church of St. Augustine, Rome. The Roman Martyrology mentions him on March 15.

LORD. Title commonly used of God in the Old Testament (*Adonai*), and commonly applied to Christ in the New Testament

(*Kyrios*). In the Vulgate it is used in place of Yahweh. The consistent way that St. Paul and other New Testament writers use the term of Christ indicates that they regarded him as God.

LORD'S PRAYER. See PATER NOSTER.

LORD'S PRAYER (Mass). The liturgical recitation of the *Pater Noster* at Mass. Returning to an ancient practice, the Lord's Prayer now includes five parts: an invitation by the priest; the *Pater Noster,* sung or said together with the people; the embolism, which amplifies the last petition of the Lord's Prayer; the doxology; and concluding acclamation by the faithful.

LORETO, HOUSE OF. Marian shrine at Loreto, in east central Italy near the Adriatic Sea. It is known that in 1253 St. Louis, King of France, heard Mass in Nazareth in the house where Mary, it is believed, received the Annunciation. Tradition has it that thirty-eight years later Dalmatian shepherds saw a strange house in their fields one night. The governor of Dalmatia sent to Nazareth to check the accuracy of the story and found that the holy house had disappeared. Upon examination the house in Dalmatia was found to be built of limestone, mortar, and cedar, all materials native to Nazareth and foreign to Dalmatia. Intermittently reported in various places, the house at last came to rest near the large village of Recanati at the hamlet of Loreto. Pope Boniface VIII declared that the traditions concerning the holy house were worthy of belief. December 10 was appointed the feast day of the Translation of the House. Since 1294 pilgrims from all over the world have come to Loreto, including many popes who have knelt there in prayer. The French during the Revolution removed the image of Our Lady from the holy house and took it to Paris, but Napoleon returned it and Pope Pius VII restored it to Loreto in 1802 after keeping it for a short stay at the Papal Palace on the Quirinal. The original statue was accidentally destroyed in 1921 and a new one carved from cedar grown in the Vatican gardens. Pope Pius XI enthroned the statue of Our Lady of Loreto in 1924 in the Sistine Chapel, solemnly crowned her, and with great solemnity exposed her for a day at Santa Maria Maggiore and then returned her to Loreto. The House of Loreto rests on the ground, without any foundation, yet has never evidenced any deterioration. Other remarkable aspects attend its preservation. The village of Loreto was heavily bombed in World War II, but the great church housing the House of Nazareth, with its single door, window, and fireplace, stood unshattered. Pope John XXIII made a pilgrimage to Loreto on October 4, 1962.

LOT. Son of Haran and nephew of Abraham. The most significant part of Lot's life was spent with his uncle. He accompanied Abraham from Ur to Haran and later to Canaan (Genesis 11:31). Both of them prospered. Eventually they parted, Lot settling in Sodom on the fertile Jordan plain (Genesis 13). He faced disaster when he was captured by hostile kings and his wealth confiscated, but Abraham gathered his forces, rescued his nephew, and recovered Lot's property (Genesis 14). A new crisis developed when Yahweh decided to destroy Sodom and Gomorrah because of the sinful lives of the people. Out of consideration for Abraham, Yahweh sent two angels to Lot to urge him to leave Sodom with his wife and daughters before the rain of brimstone and fire descended on the doomed cities. Lot's wife ignored the angels' warning not to look back and was turned into a pillar of salt (Genesis 19:15–29). Centuries later Jesus referred to these events when he warned his listeners that "the days of the Son of Man" would come when the good would be saved and sinners destroyed (Luke 17:26–37). Lot and his daughters were responsible for the birth of sons who were eponymous ancestors of the Moabites and the Ammonites. Occasionally they are referred to as the "Sons of Lot" (Genesis 19:31–38).

LOUGH DERG. Island shrine on a small lake in County Donegal, northwest Ireland, a place of pilgrimage since early Christian times. The principal edifice is the Basilica of St. Patrick, near the cave known as St. Patrick's Purgatory, where in answer to the saint's prayers the incredulous could experience something of the burning of hell. Penal legislation by the British Government was repealed in 1871, so that now thousands of pilgrims visit the shrine, especially between June 1 and August 15. The custom is to stay for three days, doing penance and praying. Only one meal of bread and water or sweetened tea is had on each of the three days. Shoes are removed and the pilgrim moves from station to station, where prescribed prayers are said. The sacraments are received and the whole pilgrimage is intended to be penitential, drawing people from all classes of society.

LOURDES. World famous shrine of the Immaculate Conception, in the department of Hautes-Pyrénées in France. In 1858, the

Blessed Virgin appeared eighteen times at Massabielle, at a grotto near Lourdes, to Bernadette Soubirous, a fourteen-year-old peasant girl. At the same time a spring appeared, miraculous healings were reported, and pilgrims began to come to the spot. In 1862 the apparitions received ecclesiastical approbation and a church was built above the grotto. Then beside it, from 1883 to 1901, was built the magnificent Church of the Rosary. Since then millions of people have visited the shrine, and a medical bureau has been established to investigate the character of the cures, of which hundreds have been fully authenticated by medical specialists.

The healings generally take place after the people have bathed in the waters of the spring, or during the blessing with the monstrance with the Blessed Sacrament carried in procession. Not all cures are physical, many report marvelous conversions and graces in the spiritual life. In 1891 a local feast of Our Lady of Lourdes (February 11) was established and in 1907 extended to the universal Church by Pope St. Pius X.

LOVE. To will good to someone. Also to please someone, either by sharing with that person what one possesses or by doing what someone wants. Basically there are two kinds of love. The love of concupiscence, or self-interested love, means that another is loved for one's own sake as something useful or pleasant to the one who loves. The love of friendship means selfless love of another for that person's own sake, for his or her good, to please him or her; it is the love of benevolence.

LOVE OF ENEMIES. Christ's commandment of merciful love, shown especially in loving those who are not lovable. The enemies of whom Christ speaks are "those who persecute you" (Matthew 5:44), "those who hate you . . . curse you" (Luke 6:28). This is the highest and truest test of selfless love, to "do good to . . . bless . . . pray for those who treat you badly" (Luke 6:28).

LOW MASS. A term formerly used for a Mass celebrated without music. The priest read, instead of sang, all the prayers of the Mass. Unknown in the early Church, it was also called a private Mass.

LOW SUNDAY. The first Sunday after Easter, contrasting it with the high feast a week before. In Latin it is termed *Dominica in albis* (Sunday in white) because the newly baptized set aside their white baptismal robes on that day.

LOYALTY. Constancy in allegiance to God or the things of God; steadfastness in fidelity to a person or cause, organization or enterprise. Implicit in loyalty is strong affection based on firm conviction that the object of one's fidelity deserves the allegiance. (Etym. Latin *legalis,* of or belonging to the law, legal.)

L.S. *Loco sigilli*—place of the seal.

LUCIFER. The name is sometimes applied to a king of Babylon (Isaiah 14:12), but the Fathers of the Church commonly identify Lucifer with Satan, leader of the fallen angels. In the Church's writings it is a synonym for the devil, the Prince of Darkness, who before he fell was an angel of light. In the Scriptures, Christ is also called Phosphoros—Light-Bearer (II Peter 1:19). (Etym. Latin *lucifer,* light-bearer.)

LUCIFERIANS. Early sects worshiping the devil and reviving Gnostic and Manichaean principles. They were known as Luciferites or Stedingers in the thirteenth century in North Germany. Another sectarian group in Austria in the fourteenth century was also called Luciferian.

LUCIFERITES. See LUCIFERIANS.

LUJÁN, OUR LADY OF. Argentine shrine, forty miles west of Buenos Aires. Its main object of devotion is a small doll-like statue of the Blessed Virgin; her head is surrounded by a golden aureole and is crowned with hundreds of diamonds and other precious stones. The Basilica of Our Lady of Luján is the most important pilgrimage center in Argentina. According to legend, in 1639 a peasant from Cordova, wishing to revive his neighbors' "belief in their early faith," ordered two statues from Brazil, one of the Immaculate Conception, the other the Blessed Virgin and her Son. When the caravan delivering them reached a small ranch on the outskirts of Luján, the driver could not urge the horses on until the statue of the Immaculate Conception was removed, indicating Mary's own choice of where her shrine should be. The treasured statue went through many housing vicissitudes. One Negro grew from boyhood to old age guarding her first in a small chapel, then in a church, then in a larger edifice. As the number of miracles grew, the crowds also grew larger. In 1910 an impressive cathedral was completed and today it is one of the world's famous shrines to Mary honored by papal coronation. Since 1930 the cathedral has been raised to the rank of a basilica. Argentina, Uruguay, and Paraguay now all claim

The Lady of Luján as their official protectress.

LUKE. He is described in one of Paul's epistles as "my dear friend, Luke, the doctor" (Colossians 4:14). He traveled with Paul on several of his missionary journeys, using the first person plural in giving details. One journey was a sailing from Troas to Samothrace and eventually to Phoenicia. Another was from Phoenicia to Jerusalem. Later they went to Rome together. Scholars estimate that much of his writing was done about the year 70. It seems clear that he was a Greek Gentile directing his message to Gentile Christians. During the two years Paul was imprisoned in Caesarea, Luke had ample time and opportunity to gather material and write his New Testament contributions (Acts 20, 21). He was indebted to Mark for a considerable part of the material that appears in his Gospel. (Etym. Latin *Lucas,* Greek *Loukas.*)

LUMEN GENTIUM. Dogmatic Constitution on the Church, of the Second Vatican Council. Its purpose is declared to be twofold: to explain the Church's nature as "a sign and instrument of communion with God and of unity among all men," and to clarify the Church's universal mission as the sacrament of human salvation. A unique feature of the constitution is the Explanatory Note, added to the conciliar document by order of Pope Paul VI, clarifying the meaning of episcopal collegiality, that the community of bishops have no authority without dependence on and communion with the Bishop of Rome (November 21, 1964).

LUMEN GLORIAE. The light of glory, by which a created mind is enabled to experience for eternity the immediate vision of God. It is a supernatural operative habit bestowed on the intellect to replace and perfect the virtue of faith. Thus, it confers in heaven the power of seeing God even as faith on earth gives the power of believing in God.

LUMINOUS RAYS. Phenomena of light that sometimes accompany ecstasy. They appear in a variety of forms, e.g., as a halo about the head or a glow enveloping the whole body. The norms set down to verify the supernatural character of such luminosity begin by ascertaining whether it could not be explained by natural causes. In particular inquiry should be made whether the phenomena take place in full daylight or at night and, if at night, whether the light is more brilliant than any other light; whether it is a mere spark or prolonged over a considerable length of time; whether it occurs during the course of some religious act, such as prayer, a sermon, at the altar; whether there follow provable effects of grace such as lasting conversions; and above all whether the person from whom the radiance proceeds is known to be virtuous and holy.

LUNA. A circular receptacle with glass sides, metal circled with gold or gilded metal to hold the Sacred Host upright in the monstrance. It is a sacred vessel, having received the priest's blessing. It is sometimes called a lunette. (Etym. Latin *luna,* moon.)

LUNETTE. See LUNA.

LUST. An inordinate desire for or enjoyment of sexual pleasure. The desires or acts are inordinate when they do not conform to the divinely ordained purpose of sexual pleasure, which is to foster the mutual love of husband and wife and, according to the dispositions of providence, to procreate and educate their children. (Etym. Anglo-Saxon *lut,* pleasure.)

LUSTRAL WATER. See HOLY WATER.

LUTHERANS. Those Protestants who follow the teaching of Martin Luther (1483–1546), as expressed in distinctive confessions of faith that are contained in the *Book of Concord,* published at Dresden in 1580. In the confessions the Bible is declared to be the only norm of belief, to which even the historic creeds and other traditional statements of faith are to be subordinated. Yet the Bible itself is subordinated to the single basic principle of justification by faith without good works. Since human beings lost their original innocence, which at creation was an essential part of their nature, they are no longer free to do spiritual good but are under the slavery of sin. Redemption means being justified by faith (trust) in Christ, whereby the sinner is considered pleasing to God without any cooperation on a human being's part. Lutherans have remained loyal to this belief, namely confidence that the believer has in fact been saved by the blood of Christ with no merits on a human being's part. To this day it typifies their particular form of Protestantism, which has also been remarkably constant in its allegiance to the person of Luther and to the confessions of personal faith which he inspired.

Besides Germany, where Lutheranism originated, it is the official religion in the Scandinavian countries and has numerous adherents in North America. It is most flourishing where the head of the state is, in effect, also the chief authority in the Church. As such it has contributed substantially to the development of nationalism in the modern world.

LUX IN TENEBRIS. Light in the darkness. Title of Christ, based on the prologue of St. John's Gospel, and frequently used as a motto in Christian art and architecture.

LUX MUNDI. Light of the world. Title of Christ, used of himself, and found as an inscription on monuments from early Christian times.

LUXURY. The possession and enjoyment of something that gives pleasure to the senses but is not otherwise either useful or necessary. Though not sinful in itself, luxury easily leads to sin or may itself be the result of injustice or failure in charity. As *luxuria,* it is sinful indulgence of sexual pleasure. (Etym. Latin *luxuria,* luxury, voluptuousness.)

LXX. Septuagint.

LYDIA. A woman in the purple-dye business in Philippi, and a native of Thyatira in Asia. She was deeply moved by Paul's preaching and she and her household were all baptized. Her gratitude impelled her to invite Paul and his fellow-travelers to stay in her home and enjoy her hospitality. Evidently she was a persuasive woman; Luke comments that "she would take no refusal" (Acts 16:14–15).

LYING. Speaking deliberately against one's mind. The speech is any communication of ideas to another person, and may be done by means of words, spoken or written, and by gestures. By speaking deliberately is meant that the speaker must realize what he is saying; it is not a mere matter of ignorance or misstatement. When a person tells a lie, he or she says something that is contrary to what is on that person's mind; there is real opposition between what one says and what one thinks.

LYRE. A pagan symbol meaning harmony, adopted in Christian art from the catacombs by Clement of Alexandria. It was considered an emblem of King David and appears often in angelic illustrations. Because of her representation as singing in her heart to God, St. Cecilia is sometimes shown holding the lyre, though the organ is more frequently but incorrectly considered her emblem. A lyre symbolizes St. Dunstan of England, patron of musicians, as also St. Gregory the Great, founder of the famous Roman *schola cantorum.* The harp, associated with the lyre, is an emblem of St. Patrick.

M

MAASTRICHT. Shrine of "Our Lady of the Sea," near the Belgian border in southeast Netherlands, on the Meuse River. A statue of wood about four feet high, Mary holds the Child on her left arm. He clings to her left shoulder as he reaches for a flower his Mother is holding in a vase. Both figures are gold crowned. The history of the shrine goes back to 1400 when a novice brought the statue as part of his patrimony when he came to the Franciscans at Maastricht. Since then, this most beloved sanctuary in Holland has been the object of every kind of opposition. It typifies the religious struggles of the Dutch people, who came by the thousands day and night to pay their respects to "Maris Stella."

M. Maria—Mary.

m. Memorial.

M.A. *Magister Artium*—Master of Arts.

MACCABEES. A family that controlled the course of Jewish history from 166 to 63 B.C. and secured some measure of religious freedom and political independence during those troubled years. The Seleucid king, Antiochus Epiphanes, who dominated Palestine was determined to wipe out Judaism and force Hellenistic culture on the Jews (I Maccabees 1). When he resorted to the crowning indignity of introducing pagan sacrifices to Zeus in the Temple in Jerusalem, the priest Mattathias launched open rebellion, refusing to conduct heathen sacrifices and killing an apostate Jew who agreed to do so. Mattathias and his five sons had to leave Jerusalem, but the struggle had only begun. After the father died, his son, the great Judas Maccabeus, took over leadership (I Maccabees 2) and re-entered Jerusalem victoriously and purified the Temple (I Maccabees 3–9). He eventually died in battle, but his brother, Jonathan, continued the struggle for eighteen years (I Maccabees 9–12). He was followed by a third brother, Simon, who finally achieved political freedom in 142 B.C. But intrigue and violence never ceased; both Jonathan and Simon were murdered. It was not until the reign of John Hyrcanus, Simon's son, that Judaea became the dominant power in Palestine (I Maccabees 13–16). Several other Maccabees followed (Aristobulus I, Alexander Jannaeus, Alexandra, and Aristobulus II), but increasing internal dissension weakened the government. Finally Roman legions besieged Jerusalem in 63 B.C., took over control, and the Jewish kingship was abolished. The Maccabee dynasty became extinct after a tempestuous century of violence. The history of this heroic struggle is told in detail in the First Book of Maccabees. The Second Book of Maccabees is a more rambling account that parallels the first seven chapters of the First Book but covers only fifteen years.

MACE. A short ornamental heavy staff with decorated headpiece usually of heraldic device, carried by or before certain ecclesiastical officials, e.g., a bishop, as a symbol of authority.

MACEDONIANISM. The heresy named after Macedonius, Arian Bishop of Constantinople (d. c. 362), whose followers denied the divinity of the Holy Spirit. Unlike Macedonius, most of his followers acknowledged the divinity of Christ. The heresy was opposed by Athanasius, Basil, and Gregory of Nyssa, and was condemned in 381 by the First Council of Constantinople.

MACHABEES. See MACCABEES.

MACHIAVELLIANISM. The political philosophy of Niccolò Machiavelli (1469–1527) and of those who apply his principles in the government of civil society. It is a combination of treachery and intrigue, subterfuge and tyranny, and its substance is contained in Machiavelli's *The Prince*. The basis of political morality is expediency, where any means justify whatever is good for the State. Moral law and individual virtue must give way when the interest of the State demands it. Thus a ruler or legislator may continue to profess Christian principles as an individual while denying these principles in practice as a statesman.

MADHU, OUR LADY OF. Best known shrine of Ceylon (Sri Lanka). When the Dutch conquered Ceylon and began to stamp out Catholicism, a small band of native Catholics converted by the Portuguese took to the jungle, carrying a statue of the Madonna with them. Eventually a church was built to house it. As no one can live in the jungle during the wet season, Mary is alone for months, but when the rains pass, Moslems and Hindus as well as Catholics journey to Madhu. The pilgrimage is planned to take a month. They sing hymns, chant the Rosary as they trudge through the deep tangled growth. The statue is of Our Lady of the Rosary. There is a custom that the sick must remain outside the church and chant their entreaties loud enough for Mary to hear them. The dust outside the little church is a proven cure for poisonous snakebites. During World War II daily prayers were effectively offered at Madhu that Ceylon would be saved from a Japanese invasion.

MADONNA. My lady, the Blessed Virgin Mary, either as a title or representation of the Virgin. Often combined with another title, e.g., Madonna della Strada, Our Lady of the Way. (Etym. Italian *madonna*, from *mia donna*, my lady; from Latin *mea domina*, my lady.)

MAESTRO DI CAMERA. Title of the chief chamberlain of the Vatican. He is in charge of all daily personal services of the Pope, e.g., household affairs, Vatican guards, and petitions for audiences. He makes arrangements for pontifical ceremonies and is custodian of the Fisherman's Ring.

MAG. *Magister*—master.

MAGDALENE, MARY. A woman from Galilee whose surname was probably derived from her home town, Magdala. The devotion she showed to Jesus was gratitude for the fact that he had driven seven demons out of her (Mark 16:9). According to tradition, she had been a harlot. Her faithfulness is clearly seen in that she was one of the few on Calvary at the Crucifixion (Matthew 27:56). She watched Jesus being buried and was one of the three women who went to the tomb on Resurrection morning (Mark 15:47; 16:1) and discovered that Jesus had risen (Matthew 28:1–8). The first one to whom he appeared that morning was Mary Magdalene (John 20:14–18).

MAGI. Members of the priestly caste of the Mazdean religion, with special reference to the wise men who brought gifts to Jesus at his birth. The appearance of an unusual star caused them to leave the East in search of a king of whose birth the star was a sign.

Herod asked them to return after finding the Infant. But the Magi, warned in a dream, went back to the East by another way. They are described as bringing symbolic gifts of gold, frankincense, and myrrh. Their names, Gaspar, Melchior, and Balthasar, are first mentioned in the sixth century. The Adoration of the Magi early became one of the most popular subjects of representation in art, the first extant painting being in the Cappela Greca of the Priscilla Catacomb (Rome), dating from the second century.

MAGIC. The art of making use of the forces of nature by certain occult observances that have a religious appearance, or of courting the secret influences of the invisible world. Magic may be either natural or preternatural.

Natural magic is based on the theory that nature is full of many objects whose hidden, protective or curative, properties can satisfy practically every need or drive away a host of evils. The problem is to find these objects. With their uncritical mind and animistic prejudice, tribal worshipers easily turn from a valid exploitation of the physical forces of nature to a superstitious cult of the unknown, in the form of charms, philters, auguries, omens, the art of divination, and respect for scores of sacred prohibitions and taboos.

Preternatural magic is a kind of anti-religion that has its own orders of worship, incantations, evocations, rites, fetishes, sacrifices, priests, and meeting places. It is black magic when the purpose is malevolent, and white magic when the intention is to obtain some benefit for oneself or another. The basis of preternatural magic is some form of animism, which believes that material objects or nonhuman living creatures possess preternatural powers that can be invoked or appeased by hidden or occult means. (Etym. Greek *magikos,* magician, magical, from *magos,* Magus, magician.)

MAGISTERIUM. The Church's teaching authority, vested in the bishops, as successors of the Apostles, under the Roman Pontiff, as successor of St. Peter. Also vested in the Pope, as Vicar of Christ and visible head of the Catholic Church. (Etym. Latin *magister,* master.)

MAGISTERIUM, EXTRAORDINARY. The Church's teaching office exercised in a solemn way, as in formal declarations of the Pope or of ecumenical councils of bishops approved by the Pope. When the extraordinary magisterium takes the form of papal definitions or conciliar decisions binding on the consciences of all the faithful in matters of faith and morals, it is infallible.

MAGISTERIUM, ORDINARY. The teaching office of the hierarchy under the Pope, exercised normally, that is, through the regular means of instructing the faithful. These means are all the usual channels of communication, whether written, spoken, or practical. When the ordinary magisterium is also universal, that is, collectively intended for all the faithful, it is also infallible.

MAGISTRACY. The authority of one holding civil office and having the moral right to administer laws.

MAGNANIMITY. Greatness of soul. It looks especially to honor and seeks to perform noble deeds. Its object is to perform actions that faith tells a person are great in the eyes of God, no matter what people may think of one's conduct. (Etym. Latin *magnus,* great + *animus,* mind: *magnanimitas.*)

MAGNIFICAT. The Canticle of the Blessed Virgin Mary, beginning *"Magnificat anima mea Dominum"* (My soul does magnify the Lord). Mary first recited it on her visit to Elizabeth after the Annunciation and her conception of Christ. It is included in the Roman Breviary, daily chanted at Vespers, and solemnly recited on other occasions.

MAGNIFICENCE. See MUNIFICENCE.

MAJOR BASILICA. A title of honor conferred by the Holy See on certain outstanding churches in the Catholic world, namely the patriarchal basilicas in Rome. Among the major basilicas outside of Rome the best known is St. Mary of the Angels in Assisi, Italy.

MAJOR ORDERS. The diaconate, priesthood, and episcopate. Until the Second Vatican Council and the decision of Pope Paul VI in 1973, the subdiaconate was also considered a major order.

MAJOR SACRAMENTS. A term used in some Lutheran bodies for baptism, the Lord's Supper, and the sacrament of repentance, because these three are said to have a biblical foundation. Other sacraments professed in the Catholic Church are said to be minor.

MAJOR SUPERIOR. The abbot primate, the abbot superior of a monastic congregation, the abbot of a monastery, the superior general of an entire religious institute, the provincial superior, the vicars of all the foregoing, and all others who have powers equivalent to those of provincials.

MALABAR CHRISTIANS. Also known as the "Thomas Christians," they live in southwest India, on the coast in the district of Travancore and Cochin. Tracing their spiritual ancestry to St. Thomas the Apostle, they now form three groups: the Jacobites, or Monophysites who rejected the Council of Chalcedon; the Catholics who were converted from Nestorianism by the Portuguese in 1599; and the Malankarese who reunited with Rome in 1930. Each of these groups has its special liturgy.

MALABAR RITES. The customs and practices of the natives of South India, which the Jesuit missionaries in the seventeenth century permitted their converts but which the Holy See afterward prohibited. Robert de Nobili (1577–1656) initiated these rites in order to pave the way for the hoped-for conversion of the Brahmins. Among those who observed the Malabar Rites was St. John de Britto (1647–93).

MALACHI. The name appears as the title of the last book of the Old Testament. Since the name means "messenger," it may mean that the author, the last of the Minor Prophets, is delivering a message from Yahweh. No one named Malachi is mentioned or known elsewhere in Scripture. It is a short book of three chapters and offers strong evidence of Yahweh's dissatisfaction with the performance of priests and the obedience of the people. It deplores among other evils divorce, marrying Gentiles, and failure to pay tithes. It was probably written in the fifth century before Christ (Malachi 1–3).

MALA FIDE. In bad faith. An action performed dishonestly, implying that the person is culpably responsible and therefore, in matters of justice, liable to restitution. The opposite of *bona fide*.

MALEVOLENCE. Positive ill will. The disposition to do evil to someone, characteristic of the devil. As a human vice, it is opposed to the virtue of benevolence or good will. (Etym. Latin *malevolentia*, ill will, ill disposition.)

MALICE. The evil of a conscious and deliberate transgression of the law of God. It is a contempt of the divine Author of the law, and an implicit denial of reverence toward God, who, as Creator, has a right to demand obedience of his creatures. It is the basic evil of sin.

MALIGN. Speaking evil of another for the purpose of injuring, and without regard for the truth. To malign carries the implication of doing harm to a person, group, or race by means of falsehood, even though the one who maligns may not have deliberately lied. (Etym. Latin *malignus,* ill-disposed, malicious; originally, of a bad nature.)

MALO ANIMO. With evil spirit or bad intent. An action done with malice aforethought, which increases the culpability.

MALTESE CROSS. A cross with four equal limbs of spreading or triangular form. So called because it was the badge of the military and religious order of the Knights of Malta.

MALUM IN SE. Bad in itself. Applied to human acts that are basically wrong, such as blasphemy, and not merely because of a bad intention.

MAMMON. The word in Aramaic for wealth, riches. Several times Jesus contrasted love of God and love of money as mutually exclusive goals in life (Matthew 6:24; Luke 16:13).

MAN. Latin *homo,* a human being, as distinct from *vir,* a male person. The term *homo* has no perfect English equivalent, but it is part of the Church's official vocabulary and occurs in every major document of the Catholic Church. A living substance, composed of a material body that dies and a spiritual soul that is immortal. Creature made by God to his image and likeness, to praise, reverence, and serve him in this life and thereby attain the eternal possession of God in the life to come. In philosophical terms, "man" is a rational animal, and collectively is the human species or the human race. (Etym. Anglo-Saxon *man,* a person.)

MANASSEH. 1. the older son of Joseph and Asenath. Joseph explained the name, which means "forget," as helping him forget his sufferings (Genesis 41:51). Jacob was the grandfather of Manasseh and his younger brother, Ephraim, and adopted the two boys. This was a common custom because adoption ensured inheritance. When he gave them his blessing before he died, Jacob prophesied that Ephraim would be the ancestor of a great nation. His prophecy proved accurate (Genesis 48:19). Manasseh married a Canaanite and settled in the Jordan Valley. His best-known descendant was Gilead; 2. son of Hezekiah. He succeeded his father as King of Judah and ruled from 687 to 642 B.C., the longest reign in its history. This stability, however, was not due to virtue; Jewish historians have called him the most wicked king in Judah's history, because he introduced shameful religious practices and encouraged idol worship and magic. Often he shed innocent blood and constantly defied Yahweh. His son, Amon, succeeded him but was killed within two years (II Kings 21). The Bible mentions three others named Manasseh: the husband of Judith who died of sunstroke (Judith 8:2–3); the son of Pahath-moab who married a foreign wife (Ezra 10:30); and the son of Hashum who is also rebuked for having married a foreign wife (Ezra 10:33). Both of the last two Manassehs, however, put away their wives and expiated their sin (Ezra 10:44).

MAND. *Mandamus*—we command.

MAND. AP. *Mandatum apostolicum*—apostolic mandate, e.g., for a bishop's consecration.

MANDATUM. The washing of the feet in the Liturgy of Holy Thursday. In the revised ritual the washing of the feet takes place after the Gospel, which narrates the same event at the Last Supper. The men who have been chosen are led to chairs prepared for them. Then the priest goes to each man, pours water over each one's feet, and dries them. Meanwhile the choir or congregation sings a number of antiphons from the appropriate Gospel account in St. John. The ceremony is called the *mandatum* because it was on the occasion of washing his disciples' feet that Christ gave us the new commandment (*novum mandatum*) to love one another as he has loved us (John 13:4–17). (Etym. Latin *mandatum*, commission, order.)

MANICHAEISM. A dualistic heresy initiated in the third century by a Persian named Mani, Manes, or Manichaeus (215–75). He was considered divinely inspired, and he gained a large following. In the Manichaean system there are two ultimate sources of creation, the one good and the other evil. God is the creator of all that is good, and Satan of all that is evil. Man's spirit is from God, his body is from the devil. There is a constant struggle between the forces of good and those of evil. Good triumphs over evil only insofar as spirit rises superior to the body. In practice Manichaeism denies human responsibility for the evil that one does, on the premise that this is not due to one's own free will but to the dominance of Satan's power in one's life.

MANIFESTATION OF CONSCIENCE.

Revealing the state of one's moral life to another person for spiritual guidance. It has been a practice in the religious orders since early monastic times. Ecclesiastical law respects those clerical institutes which require a manifestation of conscience. But its general attitude is to forbid superiors to demand such an account of one's interior life. On the other hand, the Church encourages all religious, men and women, to be perfectly open with their superiors and, if they wish, to freely reveal to them even their inmost thoughts and desires. In clerical communities it is assumed that superiors, who are priests, may receive such voluntary manifestations of conscience in the sacrament of penance. In nonclerical communities the Church expects religious to periodically manifest their conscience to a competent priest, in or outside of sacramental confession, as an exercise in humility and a valuable means of growing in sanctity.

MANIPLE. An ornamented small vestment, long and narrow, formerly worn over the left arm of a celebrant at Mass. Originally it was a folded handkerchief. It is no longer a required vestment. (Etym. Latin *manipulus*, that which fills the hand; from *manus*, hand.)

MANNA. The name given in Scripture for the miraculous food sent to the Israelites in the desert (Exodus 16:4–36). There are natural exudates from trees and shrubs in Arabia that yield, during two months in the fall, a minute quantity of edible substance. But their limited supply, with characteristic taste, makes them totally unlike what the Bible describes as the manna of the Exodus.

MANSE. See GLEBE.

MANTELLETTA. A sleeveless outer garment fastened at the neck, reaching to the knees, open in front, worn by cardinals, bishops, abbots, and certain prelates of the papal court. (Etym. Latin dimin. of *mantellum*, cloak, veil.)

MANUSCRIPTS, ILLUMINATED. An art in which pages of handwriting are covered with painted ornaments in initial letters, borders, marginal decorations, and even full page paintings. The most ancient examples are found on papyruses of Greek and Macedonian artists. In the fifth century a certain style of illumination spread from the Eastern Christian convents to Armenia. Byzantine illumination reached its golden age in the ninth century, with all the Slavic countries showing its influence. The Book of Kells is a famous example of the perfection of the art in Ireland. The Irish monks brought their art to England and the Continent, where it flourished in the medieval monasteries. Flemish painters used real landscapes as backgrounds, and the human figure was faithfully portrayed. The invention of printing marked the end of this art.

MANY QUESTIONS. The misleading device in discussion when a single answer is demanded to a question that is really many questions requiring separate answers. It is also the device of asking a question that contains an implicit assertion and to which an unqualified answer would give assent.

MARANATHA. An Aramaic expression occurring in St. Paul (I Corinthians 16:22) in the verse "If anyone does not love the Lord, a curse on him. Maran atha." The Christian Fathers understood the term to mean "Our Lord has come." But more probably it means what St. John has at the close of the New Testament, "Come, Lord Jesus" (Revelation 22:20).

MARCIONISM. A second-century heresy of Marcion and his followers, who rejected the Old Testament and claimed that the Apostles were wrong in claiming that the New Testament is a fulfillment of the Old. Marcion claimed to be teaching a pure Christianity, after the example of St. Paul. He wrote a mutilated revision of the New Testament, consisting mainly of the Gospel of St. Luke and ten letters of St. Paul. The Marcionists' principal doctrine was that Christianity is wholly a gospel of love to the exclusion of any law. Among their followers married people could never rise above the catechumenate. Only virgins, widows, and celibates were baptized. Marcionism disappeared after the seventh century.

MARCOSIANS. Followers of the Gnostic Marcus, who flourished in Gaul in the middle of the second century. Marcus was a magician who had women serve as his prophetesses, and whose disciples indulged in elaborate sacramental rites and fantastic speculation about numbers. Ignoring the canonical New Testament, their favorite scriptures were the Acts of St. Thomas.

MARIAN ART. The Blessed Virgin in Christian art or architecture. The most ancient image of the Blessed Virgin still extant is a painting in the Roman catacomb of Priscilla on the Via Salaria. Dating from the early second or late first century, the fresco pictures Mary seated with the Child Jesus in her arms and what appears to be a prophet standing next to her, volume in hand and pointing to a star above the Virgin. Three other Marian paintings in the same catacomb date from the second and third centuries. One image on the tomb of a Christian virgin shows Mary, as a type and model of virginity, holding the Child; another gives the scene of the wise men at Bethlehem; and a third is in the less common group of Annunciation paintings. Similar representations, all before the fifth century, are found in the Roman cemeteries of Domitilla, Callistus, Sts. Peter and Marcellus, and St. Agnes. The last mentioned is interesting for the monogram inscriptions of Christ, which are repeated on both sides of the drawing and turned toward the Child.

Paintings and sculpture of Mary in Christian antiquity featured her relations with Jesus, as virgin and mother, and generally in one of the Gospel scenes ranging from the Annunciation to the crucifixion or burial of Christ. The Council of Ephesus (431), which defined the divine maternity against Nestorius, ushered in a new artistic phase that began in the East but was soon introduced into Italy, Spain, and Gaul. Instead of the homely scenes from the Gospel, Mary was now more often depicted as heavenly queen, vestured in gold and seated in royal majesty.

Roman art adopted and propagated the "Byzantine Virgin," but in place of the Oriental posture of Mary at prayer, with hands upraised, Western painters and sculptors favored showing her as the "Seat of Wisdom." This was partly the result of cultural adaptation, but mainly an expression of real development in Marian doctrine. It verged away from the colder Asiatic lines in the direction of greater mildness, tempered by human affection. Historians of the subject have found in each of the great periods, beginning with the early Middle Ages in Europe, an artistic reflection of the dominant Marian relationship to religious thought.

In the Gothic period of architecture it was the "Mother of the Redeemer," featuring the merciful kindness of the Savior and of his mother as companion in the redemptive work of her Son. It corresponds to the "ages of faith" and the time of the Church's preoccupation with interior reformation of life and ecclesiastical discipline. During the Renaissance "Mother and Child" were the prevalent theme, graced by such names as Fra Angelico, Leonardo da Vinci, Raphael, Lippi, Botticelli, Correggio, Dolci, Perugino, Titian, and Verrocchio in Italy; Van Eyck, Memling, and Rubens in Flanders; and the Younger Holbein and

Dürer in Germany. Typical of the Baroque style was Mary's role as "Conqueror of Satan"; and in modern times as "Mediatrix of Grace," strengthened by historical association of the Blessed Virgin with authenticated revelations at La Salette, Lourdes, and Fátima, and to such mystics as Margaret Mary, Catherine Labouré, Don Bosco, and the Curé of Ars.

MARIANISTS. The Society of Mary, a congregation of men religious founded at Bordeaux in 1817 by the theologian William Joseph Chaminade (1761–1850). The society was recognized by Pope Pius IX in 1856, and again by Pope Leo XIII in 1891; the membership consists of priests and brothers. Specially engaged in education, on a secondary school and college level, they take the three customary vows plus a fourth vow of stability in their devotion to the Blessed Virgin. The Daughters of Mary (sometimes called Marianists) were established in 1816 and finally confirmed in 1888.

MARIAN LITERATURE. The Blessed Virgin theme in world literature. She has inspired the literary culture of all nations, not excepting the Oriental and Islamic, but perhaps with more accent in the Latin countries and France, and no less prominently in England and America.

It was said of Chaucer (c. 1340–1400) that he was a good servant of Mary and that in her honor he "wrote full many a line." Taking all his writings together—twenty-nine "lesser works," *Troilus and Cressida,* and the twenty-three Canterbury Tales—we find about five hundred lines that are explicitly Marian poetry, omitting incidental allusions to the Virgin. Almost half are in *The Prioress's Tale* alone. His poem *A.B.C.* (dated about 1366), where each stanza begins with a letter of the alphabet, is a collection of epithets that have survived to modern times, e.g., "But mercy, Lady, at the great assize / When we shall come before the High Justice," or "Fleeing I flee for succour to thy tent / Me for to hyde from tempestful of drede."

Among the English poets, Richard Crashaw, Francis Thompson, Coventry Patmore, and Gerard Manley Hopkins; and among essayists, John Henry Newman, G. K. Chesterton, and Hilaire Belloc have left a deep Marian impress. Many of the poems have been put into song, as Crashaw's *Gloriosa Domina* (O Glorious Lady), which begins, "Hail, most high, most humble one / Above the world; below thy Son," and ends, "O boundless hospitality / The Feast of all things feeds on thee." Newman's essay in

reply to Edward Pusey is a classic exposition of sober piety, in which he confesses that certain "devotional manifestations in honor of our Lady had been my great *crux.*" They may be fully explained and defended, he said, but sentiment and taste do not run with logic.

Writers in every tradition have described the ennobling influence of faith in Mary's dignity on the life and literature of Western thought. The first of all sentiments which they believe distinguishes an advanced civilization is that of reverence for womanhood. By this norm the honor and respect paid to Mary as the ideal of her sex have done more to elevate the status of women than any other postulate of the Christian religion. And in this sense devotion to the Madonna has ruled the highest arts and purest thoughts of creative genius for over a thousand years.

John Ruskin was persuaded that "the worship of the Madonna has been one of the noblest and most vital graces, and has never been otherwise than productive of true holiness of life and purity of character."

Wordsworth in England and Longfellow in the United States have left memorials of this inspiration. The *Virgin* of Wordsworth is addressed as "Woman, above all women glorified / Our tainted nature's solitary boast." In Longfellow's *Christus,* if Christianity gave us nothing more than "this example of all womanhood," this would be enough to prove it higher than all other religions of humankind.

MARIAVITES. A Polish sectarian group founded by Father Kowalski, a priest of Warsaw, and Felicia Kozlowska, a Tertiary sister in 1906. The group was excommunicated from the Roman Catholic Church for doctrinal reasons, based on certain revelations of Felicia Kozlowska. Professing great devotion to the Blessed Virgin, the group was for a time united with the Old Catholics, from whom the founder received episcopal ordination. They are mainly concentrated in the eastern part of the United States.

MARIAZELL (shrine). The most famous place of pilgrimage to Mary in Central Europe, high in the Austrian Alps. Its origins go back to 1154, when Magnus, a Benedictine monk, retired from the abbey at Lambrecht to live a more contemplative life. He carried with him a twenty-two-inch simple statue of Mary and her infant Son. He lost his way in the woods near Graatz, and night found him facing a high rock that he could neither climb nor go around. He placed the statue on a log while he prayed to Our Lady for direction. The high black rock suddenly split in two and light shone forth from its severed edges. He realized that Mary had led him there and wanted to be honored in that place. He built a small hermitage with a tree stump for a pedestal to hold the statue. About a century later a neighboring prince and his wife were seriously ill. Being told in a dream to go to the hermitage and pray, they were cured. In gratitude they built a church on the spot. The statue of Our Lady of Mariazell, though over eight hundred years old, has never shown any sign of wear or decay. The Madonna is seated, her dress is white, with a blue mantle. The Infant holds an apple in his hand. Mary is holding a pear. The first church replacing the small chapel was built in 1200. In 1340 the King of Hungary erected a larger church to accommodate the pilgrims. In the seventeenth century the present Baroque edifice was built. The Austro-Hungarian rulers considered it their most cherished shrine. Veneration to Mary and her Son continued under all vicissitudes until grave war dangers forced a temporary concealment of the treasured statue. This shrine has maintained its Austrian character though it has been a haven to people from many nations. In 1975 Cardinal Mindszenty was buried at Mariazell, his personally designated final resting place.

MARIOLATRY. The worship of Mary with the divine honors (*latria*) due to God alone. Adoration of the Blessed Virgin, which is absolutely forbidden by the Catholic Church. (Etym. Greek *Mariā*, Mary + *-latreiā*, service, worship.)

MARIOLOGY. The branch of theology that studies the life and prerogatives of the Blessed Virgin, and her place in the economy of salvation and sanctification. (Etym. Greek *Mariā*, Mary + *logia*, science, knowledge.)

MARISTS. The Society of Mary, founded at Lyons in 1824 by the Venerable Jean Claude Marie Colin (1790–1875), and finally approved by Pope Pius IX on March 8, 1873. The congregation consists of priests and lay brothers, and its constitutions are based on those of St. Ignatius Loyola. Its aim is to foster devotion to the Blessed Virgin and engage in missionary and educational work. The Marist Sisters were also founded by Colin in 1816 for the education of young girls, and the Third Order of the Society of Mary was established in 1850 for persons living in the world.

MARITAL RIGHTS. See CONJUGAL RIGHTS.

MARK. A Jerusalem Jew sometimes referred to in the New Testament as John Mark (Acts 12:12). He accompanied Paul and Barnabas, his cousin, to Antioch and traveled with them on their first missionary journey (Acts 12:25). At Perga, however, he left them and went home; no reason is given (Acts 13:13). This caused a split later between Paul and Barnabas when Paul refused to take Mark on their second journey. Barnabas was so incensed that he broke off his partnership with Paul and went on a voyage to Cyprus with Mark (Acts 15:36–39). Some years later, however, Paul and Mark were reunited and joined forces on another missionary trip. Mark was also closely associated with Peter, possibly acting as his interpreter. Peter referred to him affectionately as "my son" (I Peter 5:13), probably considering him a protégé. Mark's greatest contribution was the authorship of the second Gospel. Estimates vary, but it was most probably written in the decade A.D. 60–70. Mark wrote in Greek, evidently for Christians, because he uses terms meaningless to nonbelievers. His Gospel is a blend of history and theology written in simple, forceful language.

MARKS OF THE CHURCH. The four essential notes that characterize the Church of Christ, first fully enumerated in the Nicene-Constantinople Creed; one, holy, Catholic, and apostolic. Since the Eastern Schism and the Protestant Reformation they have become means of identifying the true Church among the rival claimants in Christianity. Some writers add other notes besides the traditional four, e.g., St. Robert Bellarmine with a total of fifteen, including the mark of persecution.

MARONITE LITURGY. Romanized form of the liturgy of St. James, used by the Maronite Church. Similar in some respects to the Roman Rite in using a round Host of unleavened bread and in the priest's vestments at Mass. The Maronite liturgical language is Syriac for the Epistle, Gospel, Creed, and *Pater Noster,* and Aramaic for the rest of the Mass. Maronites use incense frequently during the liturgy and have a variety of canons for Mass according to different feasts. The words of Consecration are always intoned aloud.

MARONITES. The nation and church of most Arabic-speaking Syrians living in Lebanon. The name is also given to one of the Churches in communion with Rome whose members are scattered through Syria, Palestine, Cyprus, Egypt, and the United States. The name is probably derived from St. Maron (d. 443), a Syrian hermit who remained faithful to the Catholic faith during the Monothelite heresy. From the time of the Fifth Lateran Council the Maronite communion with Rome has been uninterrupted. They use the Rite of St. James in ancient Aramaic in their liturgy.

MARRANO. A Portuguese or Spanish Jew converted to Christianity in the late Middle Ages. The conversion was sometimes under duress and the convert might have adhered to Jewish beliefs and practices in secret. (Etym. Spanish *marrano,* pig, hog; from Arabic *haruma,* was forbidden. The pig was called the "forbidden animal," since pork was forbidden by Jewish and Moslem religious law.)

MARRIAGE. As a natural institution, the lasting union of a man and a woman who agree to give and receive rights over each other for the performance of the act of generation and for the fostering of their mutual love.

The state of marriage implies four chief conditions: 1. there must be a union of opposite sexes; it is therefore opposed to all forms of unnatural, homosexual behavior; 2. it is a permanent union until the death of either spouse; 3. it is an exclusive union, so that extramarital acts are a violation of justice; and 4. its permanence and exclusiveness are guaranteed by contract; mere living together, without mutually binding themselves to do so, is concubinage and not marriage.

Christ elevated marriage to a sacrament of the New Law. Christian spouses signify and partake of the mystery of that unity and fruitful love which exists between Christ and his Church, helping each other attain to holiness in their married life and in the rearing and education of their children.

MARRIAGE BOND. The moral union between husband and wife once they have exchanged their marriage vows. It is a natural bond when either one or both parties are not baptized; it is supernatural when both are baptized.

MARRIAGE BY PROXY. An agent substituting for one of the absent parties in a marriage ceremony. It is permissible provided the agent has authentic written credentials signed by the absentee and the parish priest where the commission was given, or by two reliable witnesses.

MARRIAGE ENCOUNTER. A program of several days' intercommunication between married couples to enrich their personalmarital relationships. Marriage Encounter began in Spain through the efforts of Father Gabriel Calvo, between 1958 and 1962, co-operating with Diego and Fina Bartoneo and other married couples. From Barcelona in 1962 the movement spread rapidly throughout the Catholic world. There are variant interpretations of the movement, notably on a doctrinal understanding of such issues as contraception.

MART., M., MM. *Martyr, Martyres*—Martyr, Martyrs.

MARTHA. Sister of Mary and Lazarus of Bethany. Jesus and his companions visited their home and enjoyed their hospitality. The close friendship that developed was clearly indicated on the occasion of Jesus' raising Lazarus from the dead. The complete trust the sisters had in Jesus was shown when they both said, "If you had been here, my brother would not have died." Correspondingly, Jesus showed genuine sorrow and wept (John 11:1–44). On another occasion when Jesus visited them, Martha was preparing a meal and remonstrated with Jesus because Mary devoted her whole attention to him and failed to help her. Jesus gently rebuked her and praised Mary (Luke 10:38–42). Were these the same sisters? Martha's complaint does not seem characteristic of the Martha in the Lazarus incident, but there is no evidence to answer the question. (Etym. Aramaic *marta',* lady.)

MARTYR. A person who chooses to suffer, even to die, rather than renounce his or her faith or Christian principles. After the example of Christ one does not resist one's persecutors when they use violence out of hatred or malice against Christ, or his Church, or some revealed truth of the Catholic religion. (Etym. Greek *martyros,* witness, martyr.)

MARTYRDOM. The established fact that a person has died a martyr and is therefore eligible to have his cause introduced for eventual canonization by the Church.

MARTYROLOGIES. Lists of martyrs of certain cities or countries; catalogues of martyred saints arranged according to the occurrence of their feast days in the liturgical calendar. Originating in the early Middle Ages, they are important as sources of Church history. In some religious communities, the martyrology is read daily in the refectory. The Roman Martyrology, a catalogue of saints honored by the Church, written around the mid-sixteenth century, has been often revised and re-edited. Its total listing gives short accounts of about six thousand saints and blesseds honored by the Catholic Church.

MARTYROLOGY, ROMAN. The official martyrology of the Roman Catholic Church. Compiled by a group of scholars, it was issued by Pope Gregory XIII in 1584, to replace all other existing martyrologies. Later popes have revised the contents on the basis of historical scholarship and additional canonizations. One of the most radical revisions was made by Pope Benedict XIV in 1748.

MARTYRS, ACTS OF THE. Narrative accounts of the martyrs' trials and deaths. They include: 1. official reports of the interrogatives; 2. nonofficial records of eyewitnesses or contemporaries' reportings; 3. later documents based on 1 and 2; 4. other documents whose truth is often questionable or that are even forgeries. The studies made of these documents have contributed substantially not only to Christian hagiography but to a better understanding of world history, including modern times, as of Communism.

MARTYRS' SHRINE. Canadian shrine commemorating the Jesuit martyrs of North America who were slain for the faith between 1642 and 1649 in Ontario and the northern New York region. The shrine especially honors the memory of Sts. John de Brebeuf, Gabriel Lallemant, Charles Garnier, Noel Chabanel, and Antoine Daniel, who were martyred by the Canadian Indians. The shrine is located at Midland, Ontario, on the former site of old Forte Sainte Marie. A parallel shrine of the North American Martyrs is situated at Auriesville, New York. See also AURIESVILLE.

MARXISM. The social philosophy of Karl Marx (1818–83) as developed with his collaborator Friedrich Engels (1820–95) and later embodied in world Communism. There are five essential elements to Marxism, namely dialectical materialism, economic determinism, surplus value, progressive pauperization, and the Revolution.

Marx combined the dialectical method of Hegel with the materialism of Feuerbach. According to Marxism, nothing really exists but matter, which contains within itself the principle of its own development. Man is the spearhead of this necessary evolution.

Economic determinism holds that the underlying motive in all human history is economic. As the economy, so the civilization. The workman, according to Marx, creates

more value than he is paid for, and this surplus value goes to the employer, who exploits the worker to that extent. The employer puts this surplus value back into his business, and this constitutes capital. The lower the wages, the more capital for the capitalist.

As part of his theory of economic determinism, Marx held that the rich necessarily get richer and the poor poorer. Financial crises, inseparable from the capitalist system, accentuate the degrading process.

All the foregoing are preliminary to the Marxist hope of a classless society. Capitalism must inevitably collapse; the masses will revolt, seize the means of production, establish the dictatorship of the proletariat. After a phase of state socialism there will emerge the Communist utopia where no struggles exist because all classes of society will have disappeared.

The classic position of the Catholic Church on Marxism is the encyclical of Pope Pius XI, *Divini Redemptoris,* published in 1937.

MARY, NAME OF. Meaning "lady," "beautiful," or "well beloved." A favorite name given to Jewish women at the time of Christ. It was the name of Moses' sister. Nowadays an honored name with Catholics and one of the most popular. Christian names of women, in a variety of forms, e.g., Maria, Marie, Miriam, and in combination with other names, e.g., Marianne, Rosemary. The Irish word for Mary, "Muire," is given only to Mary the Mother of God; all other Marys are called Moira. Its special feast in the Western Church was observed on September 12, since 1684, in grateful memory of the Christian victory over the Turks at Vienna in 1683. The feast has been suppressed since the Second Vatican Council. (Etym. Greek *maria* or *mariam;* from Hebrew *miryam,* exalted one.)

MARY OF THE CRIB, ST. See SALUS POPULI ROMANI.

MARY'S DEATH. The passing from mortal life into eternity of the Virgin Mary. Although reliable records are lacking on the time, place, and circumstances of Mary's death, the fact was accepted by the early Church. Sts. Ephrem, Jerome, and Augustine take her death for granted. But Epiphanius (315–403), who had made a careful study of the documents, concluded: "Nobody knows how she departed this world." In the absence of a dogmatic pronouncement, modern theologians generally believe that Mary died. They admit that she was not bound by the law of mortality because of her exemption from sin, but it was fitting that Mary's body, by nature mortal, should conform to that of her Son, who allowed himself to die for the salvation of men.

MARY'S LENT. A period of fasting, August 1–14, observed by the Greeks, Copts, and Russians. According to custom and locality, they abstain from meat and eggs, sometimes milk and fish for two weeks preceding the feast of the Assumption of the Blessed Virgin.

MARY'S SINLESSNESS. The belief that the Mother of Jesus was never stained with any sin, original or personal, and was also free from all unruly desires or concupiscence. By itself, deliverance from original sin does not mean liberation from the defects that are the result of sin. Mary, like Christ, was not exempt from those limitations which imply no moral imperfection. She lived a normal human life, had to labor, and was subject to pain and fatigue. But concupiscence implies moral blemish because it may lead to sin by exciting the passions to act against the law of God, even when, through lack of consent, a person does not formally do wrong.

Closely tied in with her integrity or absence of concupiscence was Mary's immunity from every personal sin during life. Her sinlessness may be deduced from the Gospel title "full of grace," since moral guilt is irreconcilable with fullness of God's friendship. St. Augustine held that every personal sin must be excluded from the Blessed Virgin "because of the honor of God."

MARY'S VIRGINITY. The belief that the Mother of Jesus was always a virgin. Three stages of virginity are professed in this belief: Mary's conception of her Son without the co-operation of man, giving birth to Christ without violating her integrity, and remaining a virgin after Jesus was born.

The Church's faith in Mary's virginal conception of Jesus found its way into all the ancient professions of belief. In a text dating from the early second century, the Apostles' Creed speaks of "Jesus Christ . . . who was born by the Holy Spirit of the Virgin Mary." The biblical basis was traceable to the prophecy of Isaiah (7:14), which the first Evangelist applies to Mary: "Therefore the Lord Himself shall give a sign. Behold a virgin [*halmah*] shall conceive and bear a son and his name shall be called Emmanuel [God with us]." From the beginning, Christians understood the passage to refer to the Messiah, since the sign had been

fulfilled. Matthew thus interpreted the term in recalling the Isaian prophecy (Matthew 1:23).

All the Fathers affirm Christ's virginal conception by Mary. At the turn of the first century, Ignatius of Antioch spoke of Jesus as "truly born of a virgin." Starting with Justin the Martyr (c. 100–65), ecclesiastical writers uniformly defended the Messianic interpretation of Isaiah, as given by Matthew and confirmed in the Gospel by St. Luke.

Christian tradition went a step further. Not only did Mary conceive without carnal intercourse, but her physical virginity was also not violated in giving birth to Christ. When the monk Jovinian (d. 405) began to teach that "A virgin conceived, but a virgin did not bring forth," he was promptly condemned by a synod at Milan (390), presided over by St. Ambrose. Her integrity during the birth of Jesus is included in the title "perpetual virgin," given to Mary by the fifth general council held at Constantinople (553). Without going into physiological details, ancient writers such as Ambrose, Augustine, and Jerome employ various analogies—the emergence of Christ from the sealed tomb, his going through closed doors, penetration of light through glass, the going out of human thought from the mind.

Mary remained a virgin after Christ was born. Denied in the early Church by Tertullian and Jovinian, the doctrine of virginity *post partum* (after birth) was strenuously defended by the orthodox Fathers and crystallized in the term *aeiparthenos* (ever virgin) coined by the fifth ecumenical council (second of Constantinople). From the fourth century on, such formulas as that of St. Augustine became common: "A virgin conceived, a virgin gave birth, a virgin remained."

MARY, THE BLESSED VIRGIN (in the Bible). The mother of Jesus, the wife of Joseph, and the greatest of Christian saints. The angel Gabriel appeared to her in Nazareth, where she lived with Joseph, and announced to her that she would be the mother of the Messiah. "How can this come about," she asked in bewilderment, "since I am a virgin?" When Gabriel assured her that the Most High would overshadow her, she humbly consented (Luke 1:34). She went to visit her kinswoman Elizabeth, who had recently been told by an angel that, despite her age, she would soon bear a child who must be named John (Luke 1:39–40) (it was on this occasion that Mary sang the *Magnificat*) (Luke 1:46–55). Joseph was shocked when he became aware that Mary was pregnant. To avoid any public disgrace, he considered putting her away, but an angel comforted him by explaining God's design for Mary. At this difficult time Joseph had to take his wife to Bethlehem in obedience to the census decree of the Roman emperor. Jesus was born during this visit, and all the events familiar to us associated with the Nativity story—the inn, the stable, the manger, the star, the wise men, and the shepherds—are reverently presented (Matthew 1:18–25). After eight days the child was circumcised and given the name Jesus, in accordance with Gabriel's instructions (Luke 2). Then, after forty days, Mary and Joseph appeared at the Temple for the purification ceremonies (Luke 2:21). When the angel warned Joseph that Herod wanted to destroy Jesus, he fled into Egypt with Mary and Jesus and remained there until they learned that Herod was dead. Then they returned to their home in Nazareth (Luke 2:22–28). Only once in the next thirty years do we learn anything more about the Holy Family. When Jesus was twelve and the parents went with him to Jerusalem for the Passover, the boy was missing for three days. His parents finally found him in the Temple with the priests. The first recorded words of Jesus were given in answer to his mother's troubled inquiry: "Did you not know that I must be busy with my father's affairs?" (Luke 2:41–50). His public life began at the age of thirty. At a wedding feast in Cana, he performed his first miracle, converting water into wine at the request of Mary to aid the wedding party (John 2:1–11). Several times she appeared with him during his ministry but always remained in the background. She was present at the Crucifixion and heard her Son tell John to take care of her (John 19:25–27). She waited with the Apostles for the coming of the Holy Spirit on Pentecost. Scripture gives no further biographical information about Mary. She apparently lived in Jerusalem for some time, although there is a tradition that she may have died in Ephesus a few years after Jesus' Ascension. The two basic beliefs concerning Mary, the divine maternity and the virginal conception of Jesus, are unequivocally stated in the Gospels. But other aspects of Mariology are also important. They have a Scriptural basis but are not specifically elaborated in the Gospels.

MASOCHISM. A personality disorder that may be the result of sex indulgence in which a person derives venereal pleasure from inflicting pain on himself or herself.

MASS. The Sacrifice of the Eucharist as the central act of worship of the Catholic Church. The "Mass" is a late form of *missio* (sending), from which the faithful are sent to put into practice what they have learned and use the graces they have received in the Eucharistic liturgy.

As defined by the Church at the Council of Trent, in the Mass, "The same Christ who offered himself once in a bloody manner on the altar of the cross, is present and offered in an unbloody manner." Consequently, the Mass is a truly propitiatory sacrifice, which means that by this oblation "the Lord is appeased, He grants grace and the gift of repentance, and He pardons wrongdoings and sins, even grave ones. For it is one and the same victim. He who now makes the offering through the ministry of priests and he who then offered himself on the cross. The only difference is the manner of offering" (Denzinger 1743).

The Mass cannot be understood apart from Calvary, of which it is a re-presentation, memorial, and effective application of the merits gained by Christ.

The re-presentation means that because Christ is really present in his humanity, in heaven and on the altar, he is capable now as he was on Good Friday of freely offering himself to the Father. He can no longer die because he now has a glorified body, but the essence of his oblation remains the same.

The Mass is also a memorial. Christ's death is commemorated not only as a psychological remembrance but as a mystical reality. He voluntarily offers himself, the eternal high priest, as really as he did on Calvary.

The Mass is, moreover, a sacred banquet or paschal meal. The banquet aspect of the Mass is the reception of Holy Communion by the celebrant and the people, when the same Christ who offers himself to the Father as a sacrifice then gives himself to the faithful as their heavenly food. It was this fact that inspired the Holy See, after the Second Vatican Council, to restore the practice of receiving Communion under both kinds for all the faithful: "The entire tradition of the Church teaches that the faithful participate more perfectly in the Eucharistic celebration through sacramental Communion. By Communion, in fact, the faithful share more fully in the Eucharistic Sacrifice. In this way they are not limited to sharing in the sacrifice by faith and prayer, nor to merely spiritual communion with Christ offered on the altar, but receive Christ himself sacramentally, so as to receive more fully the fruits of this most holy sacrifice. In order that the fullness of the sign in the Eucharistic banquet may be seen more clearly by the faithful, the Second Vatican Council prescribed that in certain cases, to be decided by the Holy See, the faithful could receive Holy Communion under both species" (*Sacramentali Communione,* June 29, 1970).

Finally the Mass is the divinely ordained means of applying the merits of Calvary. Christ won for the world all the graces it needs for salvation and sanctification. But these blessings are conferred gradually and continually since Calvary and mainly through the Mass. Their measure of conferral is in proportion to the faith and loving response of the faithful who unite themselves in spirit with the Mass.

It is in this sense that the Mass is an oblation of the whole Mystical Body, head and members. Yet, among the faithful, some have been ordained priests and their role in the Mass is essentially different from that of the laity. The priest is indispensable, since he alone by his powers can change the elements of bread and wine into the body and blood of Christ. Nevertheless the role of the participants is of great importance; not as though there would be no Mass without a congregation but because the people's "full, active and conscious participation will involve them in both body and soul and will inspire them with faith, hope and charity." The more active this participation, the more glory is given to God and the more grace is bestowed not only on the Church but on all the members of the human race. (Etym. Latin *missa,* from *mittere,* to send; so called from the words of dismissal at the end of the service: *Ite, missa est,* "Go, [the congregation] is dismissed.")

MASS, CONCLUSION OF. Closing rites of the Eucharistic liturgy. The priest greets the people and gives them a blessing. On special occasions he may add a solemn form of benediction. His last action is a formal dismissal of the faithful, bidding them return to their daily lives of good works, praising and blessing God.

MASS, INTRODUCTORY RITE. The ceremonies that precede the Liturgy of the Word of the Mass. They are the Antiphon at the Entrance, the Penitential Act, the *Kyrie, Gloria,* and *Collect* and serve as an opening preparation. Their purpose is to give the faithful a sense of community and dispose them spiritually for an effective participation in the Eucharistic Sacrifice.

MASSA CANDIDA. A group of about three hundred Christians at Carthage who hurled themselves into a vat of burning lime rather than offer homage to Jupiter (c. 253). St. Augustine wrote and spoke of them, and Prudentius wrote of their courage in poetry.

MASS FOR THE PEOPLE. This is a Mass that pastors and others must celebrate, applying it for the intention of the people entrusted to their care. This Mass is to be offered on all the Sundays and holy days celebrated as feasts of obligation in a country. Among those bound by the obligation are resident bishops, abbots, and administrators of a diocese or parish when vacant.

MASS INTENTION. The object for which a priest offers the Eucharistic Sacrifice. This intention is distinct from the priest's decision to offer Mass, which is necessary for valid celebration. It is also distinct from the effects of the Mass which benefit those who take part in the sacrifice and attend the Mass. These are called the special fruits of the Mass and extensively are without limit, as are also the effects on the entire Church, called the general fruits of the Mass.

Mass intentions refer to the particular purpose for which a specific Mass is offered. This may be to honor God or thank him for blessings received. But technically a Mass intention means that the sacrifice is offered for some person(s) living or dead. Also called the application of a Mass, it pertains to the ministerial fruits of the Mass. These fruits are both extensively and intensively finite in virtue of the positive will of Christ. Other things being equal, the more often the sacrifice is offered the more benefit is conferred.

The intention for which a priest offers a Mass is determined either by the common law of the Church, or by specific precept, or, most often, by the intention of the donor of a Mass stipend, or by the priest's own devotion. Since it is not absolutely certain that the ministerial fruits of the Mass are limited, a priest may conditionally (if the one giving the stipend suffers no loss thereby) offer the Mass for several intentions. It is assumed that the priest does not intend by these second or third intentions to fulfill an obligation of justice by these conditional applications.

MASS OBLIGATION. A grave obligation of Catholics to assist at Mass on all Sundays and holy days of obligation. As expressed by the Second Vatican Council, referring to

Mass on Sunday, "On this day the faithful are bound to come together into one place. They should listen to the word of God and take part in the Eucharist, thus calling to mind the Passion, Resurrection and glory of the Lord Jesus Christ" (*Constitution on the Liturgy*, V, 106). The imperative "are bound to come together" indicates the gravity of the obligation, which, according to the Church's tradition, affects all baptized persons who have reached the age of reason. They are obliged under penalty of serious sin to hear Mass on Sundays and holy days, which means that the duty is objectively serious. Subjectively the gravity of the sin will depend on excusing circumstances, notably a person's awareness of the dignity and necessity of the Eucharistic Sacrifice.

MASS OF THE PRESANCTIFIED. The concluding service on Good Friday. The priest returns the Host consecrated on Holy Thursday from the repository to the main altar. After the recitation of several prayers, including the Our Father, the priest consumes the Host. He then gives Communion to the faithful. All the hosts received have been consecrated before, since there really is no Mass on Good Friday. The liturgy terminates abruptly after Holy Communion.

MASS PENNY. Mass offering of varying amounts given by the faithful. Presented usually at the altar rail as an offertory offering to help in the purchase of candles, wine, and bread used in the ceremonies of the Mass. The term is of Anglo-Saxon origin and was used for over three hundred years until the fifteenth century.

MASS RITUAL. The prescribed liturgy for celebrating the Sacrifice of the Eucharist in the Roman Rite. Essentially this ritual consists of two parts: the Liturgy of the Word and the Liturgy of the Eucharist. "In the Mass, both the table of God's word and the table of Christ's body are prepared, so that from them the faithful may be instructed and nourished" (Paul VI, *General Instruction on the Roman Missal*, 8). There are also some introductory and concluding rites.

Accordingly the Mass ritual is divided into four parts: Introduction, Liturgy of the Word, Liturgy of the Eucharist, Conclusion. While in general the ritual is carefully prescribed, there are also some options left to the discretion of the priest as presiding celebrant.

MASS STIPEND. Offering given to a priest as alms for his maintenance, in return for which he promises to offer a Mass for the donor's intention. The stipend is not given as a price for the Eucharistic Sacrifice. It is rather a voluntary donation whose origins go back to the early Church, when stipends were made during Mass and later on outside of Mass. Any priest who celebrates and applies Mass to a particular intention may receive a stipend. When a priest accepts a stipend he incurs a grave obligation in justice by virtue of a gratuitous contract, and he is bound to apply the Mass according to the conditions imposed and accepted. The amount of the stipend is determined by the diocesan standard, which must be observed by all priests, diocesan and religious. Nevertheless it is permissible to demand a larger amount if there are special duties attached to the Mass, such as the late hour or the appointment of a definite place.

MASTER OF CEREMONIES. A male cleric who supervises and directs the proceedings in any formal observance of a religious rite. He has complete authority within the limits of his office, especially guiding the actions of the celebrant and his assistants according to the rubrics of the Sacred Liturgy. In general the person who directs the proceedings of any observance where specific procedure is required.

MASTER OF THE SACRED PALACE. The Pope's theologian and canonist, always of the Dominican Order. St. Dominic (1170–1221) first held such an office, whose function was to develop the Palace School, which later became the Roman College. One of the duties of the position was to allow or forbid the printing of all religious books. The title now is mainly one of honor. He resides at the Vatican.

MASTURBATION. Direct stimulation of the sex organs outside of sexual intercourse. The self-stimulation can be physical, by means of some external object, or psychic, by means of thoughts and the imagination. It is a grave misuse of the procreative faculty and when done with full consent and deliberation is a serious sin. The sinfulness consists in setting in motion the generative powers while preventing them from achieving their natural, divinely intended purpose. (Etym. Latin *manu*, with the hand + *stuprare*, to defile oneself.)

MAT. *Matutinum*—Matins.

MATER DOLOROSA. Sorrowing Mother. Title of the Blessed Virgin, referring especially to her mourning Christ's death as she stood beneath the Cross.

MATERIAL CAUSE. That out of which

something is produced or made. The passive element in any change, which is united with the active element to form one physical being. The substratum in every change that itself remains unchanged. See also CAUSE, EFFICIENT CAUSE, FINAL CAUSE, FIRST CAUSE, FORMAL CAUSE, FREE CAUSE, MORAL CAUSE, NECESSARY CAUSE, SECONDARY CAUSE.

MATERIAL CO-OPERATION. Assisting in another's wrongdoing without approving it. The help given assists a person to perform the sinful action, although of itself the help is not wrong. To provide necessary information to a thief, because one is forced to, would be material co-operation. Material co-operation with another person's evil action is allowed provided certain conditions are fulfilled. Such collaboration is licit because the co-operator does not internally approve of the sin of another, nor does he or she approve of the sinful use to which the assistance is put by the other. The following principles are standard in resolving this complex moral issue:

Two kinds of material co-operation are to be distinguished: immediate and mediate.

In immediate material co-operation, one person actually does something morally wrong with another person. Thus if a surgeon and an assistant are both engaged in actually aborting a fetus, the co-operation of the assistant is immediate. Immediate material co-operation in the sinful act of another is always wrong. It is pointless to say that a person who is not under duress performs a criminal action without intending to do so.

Mediate material co-operation is concurring in the wrong action of another, but not in such a way that one actually performs the act with the other or agrees with the evil intention of the other. While doing something that is in itself good or indifferent, a person rather gives an occasion to another's sin, or contributes something by way of assistance.

The morality of mediate material co-operation is to be judged on the principle of the double effect. In applying this principle, there are four basic norms to be observed. Among these norms is the obligation not to intend the evil effect (as would really be intended in immediate material co-operation) and the need for sufficient reason to permit the evil effect. The presence of a proportionate reason is not sufficient to allow what is called material co-operation. See also DOUBLE EFFECT.

MATERIAL HERESY. See HERESY.

MATERIALISM. The theory that all reality is only matter, or a function of matter, or

ultimately derived from matter. There is no real distinction between matter and spirit; even man's soul is essentially material and not uniquely created by God. In ethical philosophy, materialism holds that material goods and interests, the pleasures of the body and emotional experience, are the only or at least the main reason for human existence. In social philosophy, the view that economics and this-worldly interests are the main functions of society.

MATERIALLY EVIL. Something that is objectively a moral evil, and therefore sinful, but a person does it either without knowing it is wrong, or under duress and without internal consent to the evil.

MATERIAL SIN. See MATERIALLY EVIL.

MATINS. The first of the canonical hours. Now replaced since Second Vatican Council by the Office of Readings, followed by Morning Prayer. Formerly chanted during the early hours shortly after midnight by enclosed monks and nuns who alone continue Matins as such, now. (Etym. French *matin*, morning.)

MATR. *Matrimonium*—marriage.

MATRIMONIAL CONTRACT. The voluntary agreement of a man and a woman to enter marriage, and recognized as such by the Church or State. Among the baptized every valid matrimonial contract is also a sacrament.

MATRIMONIAL COURT. A group of clergy attached to a diocesan chancery for reviewing and passing judgment on marriage cases submitted for study and possible decision by the bishop. Besides others, or in duplicate roles, the court consists of a judge, or judges, advocate, secretary, notary, and defender of the bond of union of the married. It meets to consider disputed cases concerning marriage, in which one or both parties are Catholic, or a marriage which must be decided so that a non-Catholic may marry a Catholic. Cases of the "decree of nullity" are the most frequently sought. All decisions to be valid must have the approval of the bishop. An appeal over the matrimonial court's decision may always be made to Rome, or such decision may be sought without recourse to the diocesan court. The ordinary of the diocese has jurisdiction over a true Pauline case. Any Catholic through an advocate has the right to bring any case to any proper Roman congregation for appraisal or decision.

MATRIMONIAL JURISDICTION. The Church's divinely authorized right to determine the conditions under which baptized persons may validly and/or licitly receive the sacrament of matrimony. Part of this jurisdiction is the right to determine who may witness the marriage and, if necessary, what dispensations are to be granted.

MATRIMONIA MIXTA. Apostolic letter of Pope Paul VI, setting down the definitive norms for mixed marriages. While allowing Catholics to marry non-Catholics, with dispensation, before a non-Catholic clergyman, they are nevertheless required to see to it that all their children are reared in the Catholic faith (March 31, 1970).

MATRIMONII SACRAMENTUM. Instruction of the Sacred Congregation for the Doctrine of the Faith on mixed marriages. The first of two historic documents that changed many aspects of the Church's attitude toward marriages in which a Catholic marries someone who is not a Catholic. Among other normative provisions, the excommunication was lifted for marrying before a Protestant minister (March 18, 1966).

MATRIMONIUM NON CONSUMMATUM. A marriage that has been validly contracted but not consummated by natural marital intercourse. Such a marriage may be dispensed for a just cause by the Pope at the request of either party or dissolved *ipso jure* (by the law itself) through a solemn vow of religious profession.

MATRIMONY. Marriage, but a more appropriate term for legal and religious use. It is the proper term for the sacrament of marriage, and refers more to the relationship between husband and wife than to the ceremony or the state of marriage.

MATTATHIAS. The father of five sons and the founder of the Maccabees family. The Greek king attempted to eliminate all traces of the Jewish religion, killing all those who stubbornly resisted. Mattathias bitterly resented these efforts and refused "to sit by, while the Holy City is delivered over to her enemies and the sanctuary into the hands of foreigners" (I Maccabees 2:7). When the king's edict was enforced in the city of Mattathias, he killed the king's commissioner and fled with his five sons. He organized a fighting force and inspired his sons to continue the campaign of defiance after his death. So successful were they that for years the Maccabee brothers preserved the religious and political liberties of Israel (I Maccabees 2).

MATTER. That which constitutes a body. That which is not spirit and manifests certain characteristics, notably gravity, extension, divisibility into parts, size, weight, mass, and volume; that which can be measured in space or time.

MATTER, SACRAMENTAL. Material elements or sensibly perceptible human actions that are necessary for the reception of a sacrament. They receive their significance from the accompanying ritual words. Valid matter must be used and is necessary for a valid sacrament.

MATTER OF A SACRAMENT. That part of a sacrament which is used to perform the sacramental rite. It is that part of a sacrament with which or to which something is done in order to confer grace, e.g., water in baptism, chrism in confirmation, bread and wine in the Eucharist.

MATTHEW. One of the Twelve Apostles and author of the first Gospel. He was a tax collector for the Roman government. Mark and Luke reported that Matthew (also known as Levi) was carrying on his work in the customhouse when Jesus called him to join the band of disciples, and Matthew promptly obeyed (Mark 2:14). Later, when he entertained Jesus and his followers at a reception in his home, it was evident how strongly the Jews resented and despised tax collectors (Luke 5:27–32). Nothing can be learned about his personal life from his writings, because he never spoke about himself in his Gospel. His purpose was to convince Christians of Jewish origin that Jesus was the Messiah and fulfilled the promises of the prophets. It is not surprising, therefore, that Matthew cites the Old Testament more frequently than either Mark or Luke. (Etym. Greek *mathhaios* or *matthaios;* from Aramaic *mattai,* a shorter form of Hebrew *mattanyah,* gift of Yahweh.)

MATTHIAS. The successor of Judas as an Apostle. Little is known about him. Possibly he was one of the seventy-two disciples Luke referred to (Luke 10:1), because Peter, in arranging the replacement, insisted that it should be someone "who has been with us the whole time that the Lord Jesus was traveling round with us." Matthias and Barsabbas were chosen as worthy candidates. Lots were drawn and Matthias was selected (Acts 1:21–26).

MAUNDY THURSDAY. See HOLY THURS-DAY.

MAURISTS. The French Benedictine monks of the Congregation of St. Maur, founded under Richelieu in 1621. From 1672 onwards, the Maurists specialized in scholarly writing and produced such outstanding men as Mabillon, Massuet, and Aubert. When some of the monks became associated with Jansenism, discipline suffered and the congregation was finally dissolved by Pope Pius VII in 1818.

MAY. Month of special devotion to the Blessed Virgin. Modern May devotions go back to the sixteenth century, occasioned by the current infidelity and immorality. Pope Pius VII approved and indulgenced the special prayers offered to Mary during May, and Popes Leo XIII and Pius XII issued a number of significant documents on Marian piety, supporting the custom throughout the Church.

MAY CROWNING. A solemn procession, during the month of May, at the close of which a statue of the Blessed Virgin is crowned with a garland of roses or other appropriate ornament. There is a special honor attached to being chosen to crown the statue. A May crowning is often the high point of public devotion to Our Lady in a diocese, parish, or Catholic institution.

MAY LAWS. A series of regulations enacted in Germany by the Prussian Landtag in 1873; they aimed to bring the Catholic Church in Germany entirely under state control, thereby detaching it from Rome. German civil authorities were to be sole arbiters of ecclesiastical discipline; clergy could leave their posts by manifesting their desire to a secular judge; church appointments depended on the state examinations solely; clergy dismissal was under state control; vacant sees became state dominated; religious communities were suppressed, nursing alone excepted. Any clergy dissenting were to forfeit all temporalities. These laws were in effect until 1887, when they were substantially modified. They were not abrogated until 1905.

M.C. Master of ceremonies.

MEAN. In general, that which is in between others. It may be the "mean term" in a comparison, or the intermediate between two extremes. In moral behavior it is the moderate and reasonable way of acting, without failing by excess or defect, as courage is a mean between rashness and coward-ice. It is therefore the mean of moral virtue, which does the right thing in the right way, in the right measure at the right time and place and by the right person. In political theory the mean condition of states is their control by the middle class. (Etym. Latin *medianus,* from *medius,* middle.)

MEANING. That which is intended in any communication of thought. In the Church's teaching it is truth conveyed in intelligible language that those who are disposed to accept do, in fact, receive from the definition, declaration, or decision of the ecclesiastical hierarchy.

MEANS. That which is intended not for its own sake but for the sake of something else. A means always supposes an end or purpose; it is called a means because it lies between the agent and the end, and its use brings the agent to the goal or end. The same thing may be both means and end, in different respects, for it may be sought both for its own sake and for the sake of something better. This is called an intermediate end, and there may be a long series of such intermediate ends, as when a person wants A in order to get B, and B in order to get C, and so on.

MEANS-END. Some good that a person seeks for its own sake, therefore end; but also as a way to acquire something else, therefore a means. Most human actions have as their object something that is both desirable in itself and useful for obtaining some other desirable end.

MEANS OF SOCIAL COMMUNICATION. All the available media for communicating ideas, facts, and experiences insofar as they affect the welfare of human society.

MEASURE. By analogy with a standard of calculating quantity, any criterion of judgment, evaluation, or comparison. Used by Christ to describe God's mercy toward us being measured by our mercy toward others. It is the basis of merit, where one's cooperation with grace determines one's supernatural reward. Used to describe a proportion, degree, or limit, e.g., "Equality is the measure of justice."

MEAT. The flesh of animals and birds eaten by human beings, as understood in Church law. Its prohibition on days of abstinence and fast has a spiritual value, going back to the Old Testament and practiced since apostolic times. "The law of abstinence forbids the use of meat, but not of eggs, the products of milk or condiments made of animal fat" (Pope Paul VI, *Paenitemini,* Norm III, 1).

MECHANISM. The theory that all living things, not excluding the human soul, are only more or less complex machines. In this view all organic life is only a function or variant of matter, following the same basic laws of physics and chemistry.

MECHITARISTS or MEKHITARISTS. A community of Catholic Armenian monks, founded at Constantinople in 1701 and living under a modified Benedictine Rule. Established by Mechitar of Sebaste, an Armenian priest who submitted to Rome, the community was driven from Constantinople and took refuge in Venetian territory, finally on the island of San Lazzaro. Another section later settled in Vienna. The Mechitarists are engaged in education and missionary work and have published many important Armenian writings. They use the Armenian Liturgy.

MEDALS. Coin-shaped metal disks bearing the image of Christ, Mary, or some saint, some shrine, or sacred event. They are blessed by the Church and are used to increase devotion. The use of medals is very ancient; many have been found in the catacombs, some with the chi-rho symbol. During the Middle Ages the pilgrims, on leaving a place of pilgrimage, were given medal tokens of the shrine. And today pilgrims to Rome, Lourdes, and elsewhere purchase medals that commemorate their visit. The efficacy of a medal depends on the faith of the person who wears or carries it, and on the Church's indulgenced blessing attached to this sacred object. There are innumerable medals approved by the Church. Among the most commonly used are the scapular and miraculous medals in honor of the Blessed Virgin.

MEDIATOR. A title of Christ as the one who reconciled God and the human race. It is based on the teaching of St. Paul, that "there is only one God, and there is only one mediator between God and mankind, Himself a man, Christ Jesus, who sacrificed Himself as a ransom for them all" (I Timothy 2:5–6). Christ is best qualified to be the mediator, i.e., one who brings estranged parties to agreement. As God, he was the one with whom the human race was to be reconciled; as a human being, he represented the ones who needed reconciliation. Christ continues his work of mediation, no longer to merit the grace of human forgiveness, but to communicate the grace already won on

the Cross. Moreover, others than Christ may also be called mediators in a totally secondary sense, "in that they co-operate in our reconciliation; disposing and ministering to men's union with God" (St. Thomas Aquinas, *Summa Theologica,* III, 48,.1). In fact every person, insofar as he or she co-operates with divine grace, is a kind of mediator between himself or herself and God. (Etym. Latin *mediator,* from *mediare,* to stand or divide in the middle.)

MEDIATOR DEI. Encyclical letter of Pope Pius XII on the Sacred Liturgy (November 30, 1947). A historic document that summarized liturgical development in the Church up to that time and laid the foundations for the liturgical reforms of the Second Vatican Council. It clearly defined the meaning of the liturgy as the Church's official public worship; stressed the primacy of interior worship; insisted on the need for the liturgy to be under the Church's hierarchical authority; traced the development of the liturgy since the Council of Trent but emphasized that to be valid this progress cannot be left to private judgment; declared that the Eucharist is the culmination and center of the Christian religion; urged the importance of the faithful actively participating in divine worship, especially in the Mass; explained how the fruits of Holy Communion are increased by better preparation and a fervent thanksgiving; praised those who are devoted to the Real Presence and promote this devotion among the faithful; placed the Divine Office next to the Eucharist as part of the Church's liturgical life; indicated that the liturgical year should revolve around the mysteries of Christ's life, Passion, and Resurrection; and recommended extraliturgical devotions to increase the piety of priests, religious, and the laity.

MEDIATRIX. A title of the Blessed Virgin as mediator of grace. There are two aspects of this mediation. It is certain in Catholic theology that, since Mary gave birth to the Redeemer, who is source of all grace, she is in this way the channel of all graces to mankind. But it is only probable, as a legitimate opinion, that since Mary's Assumption into heaven no grace is received by humans without her actual intercessory co-operation.

On the first level of mediation, Mary freely co-operated with God in consenting to the Incarnation, giving birth to her Son and thus sharing with him in spirit the labors of his passion and death. Yet Christ alone truly offered the sacrifice of atonement on the Cross. Mary gave him moral support in this action. She is therefore not entitled to the name "priest," as several Roman documents legislate. As explained by the Council of Florence in 1441, Christ "conquered the enemy of the human race alone" (Denzinger, 1347). In the same way he alone acquired the grace of redemption for the whole human race, including Mary. Her part in the objective redemption, therefore, was indirect and remote, and derived from her voluntary devotion to the service of Christ. Under the Cross she suffered and sacrificed with him, but subordinate to him in such a way that all the efficacy of her oblation depended on that of her Son.

On the second stage of mediation, Mary co-operates by her maternal intercession in applying Christ's redemptive grace to human beings, called the subjective redemption. This does not imply that the faithful must pray for all graces through Mary, nor that her intercession is inherently necessary for the distribution of divine blessing, but that, according to God's special ordinance, the graces merited by Christ are conferred through the actual intercessory mediation of his mother. Recent popes and the Second Vatican Council have spoken in favor of this type of mediation, which finds support in patristic tradition.

MEDIEVAL MUSIC. The period A.D. 600–1400 is here referred to as the medieval period. During these Middle Ages liturgical chant and secular solo public singing saw their greatest development. Polyphony reached fine artistic forms and Gregorian chant had its beginning then, as did Ambrosian chant in the north, the Gallican in France, and Visigothic in Spain. A need for a unified liturgy became most apparent as each geographical section argued its own pre-eminence over Rome until the eleventh century, when the Roman liturgy was universally enforced, with a few limited exceptions. The years between 700 and 800 saw all chants embellished with new words, preludes, and interludes. Sequences had their beginning in the twelfth century and became so elaborate that the Council of Trent felt forced to ban all of them except *Lauda Sion, Veni Creator Spiritus, Victimae Paschali Laudes,* and *Dies Irae,* admitting *Stabat Mater* a little later. A large repertory of secular melodies made their appearance in the same century, but after Rome's fall their impact, musically, was slight. Troubadour melodies appeared in the South of France, spread to the north, then to the German minnesingers. The troubadours occupied prime positions in medieval musical history, with Spain, Italy, and England producing

much devotional song composition. The thirteenth century saw the motet developed, using sacred texts, but later the liturgical aspects of the words were lost, dance tunes and troubadour melodies taking their place. Different rhythms were of great interest in the mid-thirteenth century; three-part rhythm dominating in polyphonic music. The ballad form appeared in the fourteenth century, with ornate rhythmic patterns evolving and unusual syncopations being tried. As the period closed a new musical impetus came from England—the new art exploiting thirds and sixths, very important to music.

MEDITATION. Reflective prayer. It is that form of mental prayer in which the mind, in God's presence, thinks about God and divine things. While the affections may also be active, the stress in meditation is on the role of the intellect. Hence this is also called discursive mental prayer. The objects of meditation are mainly three: mysteries of faith; a person's better knowledge of what God wants him or her to do; and the divine will, to know how God wants to be served by the one who is meditating. (Etym. Latin *meditatio,* a thinking over.)

MEDIUM. Something intermediate between two others, or that which in some way unites the extremes, or that brings influence from one to another. It is the basis for the doctrine of mediation between God and man.

In spiritualism, a medium is the one who acts as an agent between a deceased person and one or more living people with whom the disembodied soul communicates ideas and experiences from beyond the grave.

MEEKNESS. The virtue that moderates anger and its disorderly effects. It is a form of temperance that controls every inordinate movement of resentment at another person's character or behavior.

MELANCHOLIC TEMPERAMENT. One of the four classic temperaments, characterized by reflectiveness and caution. Persons with this temperament prefer to be alone, are more easily dejected, and have to struggle with overcoming their natural tendency toward pessimism.

MELANCHOLY. A permanent state of despondency. It is the result of an emotional disorder in which a person's thoughts assume a depressive character at the slightest stimulation.

MELCHIZEDEK. A king of Salem and a

priest. When Abraham returned from battle after rescuing Lot, Melchizedek greeted him and gave him a blessing in honor of his victory (Genesis 14:18–20). In return Abraham offered him tithes because of his priesthood. In a Psalm devoted to the dual role of priest and king, David exclaimed, "Yahweh has sworn an oath which he never will retract, You are a priest of the order of Melchizedek and forever" (Psalm 110:4). There are only two references to this priest-king in the Old Testament. In the New Testament the Epistle to the Hebrews associates Christ's priesthood with Melchizedek's by quoting in three successive chapters the invocation from Psalm 110: "You are a priest of the order of Melchizedek and forever." This is also the biblical basis for the Catholic doctrine that, once a man is ordained a priest, his priesthood, like Christ's "in the line of Melchizedek," is forever (Hebrews 5, 6, 7).

MELITIAN SCHISM. A division in the Church in Egypt during the fourth century. It was started by Melitius, Bishop of Lycopolis, Egypt, who objected to the conciliatory way that St. Peter, Archbishop of Alexandria, was restoring lapsed Catholics to the Church. Another schism, by the same name, occurred in Antioch during a quarrel between two orthodox claimants to the episcopal see. St. Melitius (d. 381), who had the rightful claim, suffered exile and temporary estrangement from Rome because of misrepresentation by his Arian opponents.

MELKITES. Byzantine Christians descended from those who remained faithful to the Council of Chalcedon (451) when large numbers in the Near East accepted the Monophysite heresy. They gradually became dependent on the Patriarch of Constantinople and joined him in the Greek Schism in the ninth to the eleventh centuries. They were reunited with Rome in the eighteenth century under the Patriarch Cyril VI, who, with his successors, represents the original episcopal line of Antioch. Since the twelfth century they have followed the Byzantine Rite, mainly in the Arabic language.

MEMENTO OF THE DEAD. Commemoration of the faithful departed, after the Consecration of the Mass. In the Roman Canon, the Memento is always made silently, after the brief announcement, "Remember, Lord, those who have died and have gone before us marked with the sign of faith, especially those for whom we now pray." In the other canons, there is a general Memento for all the deceased, preceded,

in Masses for the Dead, by a special prayer that includes mention by name of those for whom the Mass is being said. (Etym. Latin *memento,* remember [imperative].)

MEMENTO OF THE LIVING. Remembrance at Mass of those for whom priest and people wish to pray specially. In the Roman Canon, the Memento occurs before the Consecration, and the persons are mentioned silently by name, followed by a general remembrance of the living. In other canons, there is only a general intercession for the Church, but no silent Memento.

MEMORARE. Intercessory prayer to the Blessed Virgin, commonly ascribed to St. Bernard of Clairvaux (1090–1153), probably because it was popularized by Claude Bernard, the "Poor Priest" (1588–1641). The real author is unknown. Early texts have been known since the fifteenth century. Frequently indulgenced by the popes, there is now a partial indulgence for its recitation. A standard English version reads: "Remember, O most gracious Virgin Mary, that never was it known that anyone who fled to your protection, implored your help, or sought your intercession, was left unaided. Inspired with this confidence, I fly unto you, O Virgin of Virgins, my Mother. To you I come, before you I stand, sinful and sorrowful. O Mother of the Word Incarnate, despise not my petitions, but in your mercy hear and answer me. Amen." (Etym. Latin *memorare,* to call to mind.)

MEMORIAL. Religious commemorations, especially the Eucharistic Sacrifice. Unlike other memorials, however, the Mass is no ordinary commemoration. It does recall the mysteries of Christ's life and particularly his Crucifixion. The Mass, however, "is no more empty commemoration of the passion and death of Jesus Christ, but a true and proper act of sacrifice, whereby the High Priest by an unbloody immolation offers Himself a most acceptable victim to the eternal Father, as He died upon the cross" (Pope Pius XII, *Mediator Dei,* 68). (Etym. Latin *memorialis,* belonging to memory, from *memoria,* memory.)

MEMORIZATION. The practice of deliberately committing to memory facts and verbal expressions considered useful or necessary for future recall. Since the earliest times the Church has encouraged memorization, e.g., the directives of the American hierarchy: "The special place of memory in the transmission of the faith of the Church throughout the ages, should be valued and exercised, especially in catechetical programs for the young. Opportunities for memorization should be adapted to the level and ability of the child and presented in a gradual fashion. Among these elements of Catholic faith, tradition and practice which, through an early, gradual, flexible, and never slavish process of memorization, could become lessons learned for a lifetime, contributing to an individual's growth and development in an understanding of the Faith are the following: 1. prayers, such as the Sign of the Cross, the Lord's Prayer, the Hail Mary, the Apostles' Creed, the Acts of Faith, Hope, and Charity, the Act of Contrition; 2. factual information contributing to an appreciation of the place of the Word of God in the Church and the life of the Christian through an awareness and appreciation of: a. the key themes of the history of salvation; b. the major personalities of the Old and New Testaments; c. certain biblical texts expressive of God's love and care; 3. formulas providing factual information regarding worship, the Church year, and major practices in the devotional life of Christians: a. the parts of the Mass; b. the list of the sacraments; c. the liturgical seasons; d. the holy days of obligation; e. the major feasts of Our Lord and Our Lady; f. the various eucharistic devotions; g. the mysteries of the Rosary of the Blessed Virgin Mary; h. the Stations of the Cross; 4. formulas and practices dealing with the moral life of Christians: a. the Commandments; b. the Beatitudes; c. the gifts of the Holy Spirit; d. the theological and moral virtues; e. the precepts of the Church; f. the examination of conscience" (Amendments to the *National Catechetical Directory*, 1977).

It is assumed that what has been memorized will also be reflected on and, as far as possible, understood. But memorizing is indispensable for any sound pedagogy in the Catholic religion (*General Catechetical Directory*, 73).

MEMORY. The faculty by which a person preserves, reproduces, and identifies his or her past experiences. Training the memory is important for sound moral living. This is done by developing the habit of recalling often those ideas and states of mind which motivate good conduct, e.g., the presence of God, the example of Christ. Mental prayer, besides other benefits, helps to strengthen the memory for moral good.

MENDACITY. A personality disorder that induces habitual lying or the attempt to deceive others. (Etym. Latin *mendax*, lying, false, mendacious.)

MENDICANT FRIARS. Members of religious orders who are forbidden to own property in common, are therefore required to work or beg for their living, and are not bound to one monastery by a vow of stability. Originally the name was restricted to the Franciscans and Dominicans. Later on the name and privileges were extended to the Carmelites (1245), the Hermits of St. Augustine (1256), and the Servites (1424). Other orders received the same title later on. According to the Church law, mendicant friars are allowed to beg for alms where their houses are located, given the permission of their own superiors. In other places they must also obtain the permission of the bishop of the diocese. (Etym. Latin *mendicus*, beggar; an infirm, wretched, miserable person.)

MENOLOGY. A collection of lengthy lives of the saints in the Greek Church, arranged according to months and days; also an ecclesiastical calendar containing tables of lessons from Scriptures according to the feasts of the saints. In the East the Menology is a book for private use according to months and days, of biographies of renowned holy persons who are not canonized saints. Menologies are also compiled for individual monasteries or entire religious communities, briefly recording the lives and achievements of their outstanding deceased members. (Etym. Greek *mēnos*, month + *logos*, discourse, knowledge.)

MENSA. The flat top of a fixed or consecrated altar. The portable altar stone sometimes carries the designation of both altar and mensa. The word is also applied to that portion of church property which is set aside for the support of the prelate or the serving ministry. In a canonical sense a mensa requires that the church property be divided equitably between the part that belongs to the clergy and the part to be administered as belonging to the church community. (Etym. Latin *mensa*, table.)

MENTAL PRAYER. The form of prayer in which the sentiments expressed are one's own and not those of another person and the expression of these sentiments is mainly, if not entirely, interior and not externalized. Mental prayer is accomplished by internal acts of the mind and affections and is either simple meditation or contemplation. As meditation, it is a loving and discursive (reflective) consideration of religious truths or some mystery of faith. As contemplation, it is a loving and intuitive (immediately perceptive) consideration and admiration of the same truths or mysteries of faith. In mental prayer the three powers of the soul are engaged: the memory, which offers the mind material for meditation or contemplation; the intellect, which ponders or directly perceives the meaning of some religious truth and its implications for practice; and the will, which freely expresses its sentiments of faith, trust, and love, and (as needed) makes good resolutions based on what the memory and intellect have made known to the will.

MENTAL RESERVATION. Speech in which the common and obvious sense of one's words is limited to a particular meaning. The morality of this kind of speech depends on whether the listener can reasonably conclude from the circumstances that a mental reservation is being used.

MENTICIDE. The systematic effort to break down the beliefs and allegiances of a person by physical or psychological means, in order to substitute one's own. Also called brainwashing, it has been made possible mainly because of modern discoveries in psychology and the use of the mass media. (Etym. Latin *mens,* mind + *-cidium,* a killing.)

MERCEDARIANS. A religious order of men, founded by St. Peter Nolasco about 1220, and also called Nolascans. Its twofold purpose was originally to tend the sick and to rescue Christians who had been captured by the Moslems. Their rule derives from St. Raymond Peñafort (1175–1275). In addition to taking the usual three vows, they pledge themselves to become hostages if needed for the deliverance of Christian captives. A corresponding order of nuns was established at Seville, Spain, in 1568. The Mercedarians took their present name from their traditional devotion to Our Lady of Mercy. Hence their official name, *Orden de Nuestra Señora de la Merced.* They are currently engaged in preaching, in hospital and pastoral work.

MERCY. The disposition to be kind and forgiving. Founded on compassion, mercy differs from compassion or the feeling of sympathy in putting this feeling into practice with a readiness to assist. It is therefore the ready willingness to help anyone in need, especially in need of pardon or reconciliation.

MERCY KILLING. See EUTHANASIA.

MERIT. Divine reward for the practice of virtue. It is Catholic doctrine that by his good works a person in the state of grace really acquires a claim to supernatural reward from God. "The reward given for good

works is not won by reason of actions which precede grace, but grace, which is unmerited, precedes actions in order that they may be performed meritoriously" (II Council of Orange, Denzinger 388).

Certain conditions must be present to make supernatural merit possible. The meritorious work must be morally good, that is, in accordance with the moral law in its object, intent, and circumstances. It must be done freely, without any external coercion or internal necessity. It must be supernatural, that is, aroused and accompanied by actual grace, and proceeding from a supernatural motive. The person must be a wayfarer, here on earth, since no one can merit after death.

Strictly speaking only a person in the state of grace can merit, as defined by the Church (Denzinger 1576, 1582).

Merit depends on the free ordinance of God to reward with everlasting happiness the good works performed by his grace. On account of the infinite distance between Creator and creature, a human being alone cannot make God his or her debtor, if God does not do so by his own free ordinance. That God has made such an ordinance is clear from his frequent promises, e.g., the Beatitudes and the prediction of the Last Judgment.

The object of supernatural merit is an increase of sanctifying grace, eternal life (if the person dies in divine friendship), and an increase of heavenly glory. (Etym. Latin *merces,* hire, pay, reward.)

MESSALIANS. A pietistic mendicant sect, also called Euchites, whose name means "praying people." Originating in the fourth century in Mesopotamia, they were condemned by the Council of Ephesus in 431 but survived to the seventh century. They held that, because of Adam's sin, everyone has a devil substantially united to his soul. This demon is only partially expelled at baptism, and can be completely driven out only by ceaseless prayer and asceticism. Proof of complete deliverance is the elimination of all passions and evil desires. Those who reach this state enjoy a vision of the Trinity already in this life.

MESSIAH. The Hebrew word for "Anointed One." The equivalent word in Greek is Christos. In the Old Testament it was sometimes applied in a general sense to prophets or priests (Exodus 30:30), but more specifically it referred to the coming of one who would usher in a period of righteousness and conquer sin and evil (Daniel 9:26). In the New Testament the Evangelists made it clear that they knew Jesus was the long-anticipated Messiah (Acts 2:36; Matthew 16:17; Galatians 3:24–29). Those who refused to accept Jesus interpreted the promised kingdom to be a worldly domain and looked forward to a messiah who would be a military leader to help Israel triumph over her enemies.

MESSIANIC BANQUET. Symbolic meal described in the Dead Sea Scrolls in which bread and wine are blessed in anticipation of the forthcoming Messiah.

METANOIA. Literally repentance or penance. The term is regularly used in the Greek New Testament, especially in the Gospels and the preaching of the Apostles. Repentance is shown by faith, baptism, confession of sins, and producing fruits worthy of penance. It means a change of mind from unbelief to faith, and a change of heart from sin to the practice of virtue. As conversion, it is fundamental to the teaching of Christ, was the first thing demanded by Peter on Pentecost, and is considered essential to the pursuit of Christian perfection. (Etym. Greek *metanoein,* to change one's mind, repent, be converted, from *meta-* + *noein,* to perceive, think, akin to Greek *noos, nous,* mind.)

META-OUSIOSIS. Transubstantiation of the bread and wine at Mass into the body and blood of Christ. The Greek Fathers used this expression to identify what takes place at the Eucharistic Consecration. It is a *meta* or change of one *ousia* or being, that of bread and wine, into another *ousia* or being, that of Christ's body and blood.

METAPHYSICAL CERTITUDE. Infallible assent of the mind to a proposition. It is recognized as necessarily true because the affirmation is based on the unchangeable principles of being, e.g., the principle of contradiction.

METAPHYSICAL DUALISM. A theory of reality that claims that the coexistence of good and evil in the world postulates the pre-existence of two eternal first principles, one good and the other evil. Manichaeism is the best known form of metaphysical dualism. It is implicit, however, in every philosophy that minimizes (or eliminates) man's responsibility for his actions, especially for his misdeeds.

METAPHYSICAL EVIL. Anything finite just because it is finite. It therefore lacks the complete goodness possessed by God alone. The term was used by some philosophers

(e.g., Leibniz) to describe any limitation even though perfectly natural, as in all creatures. But the expression is not acceptable in scholastic philosophy as a correct description of evil because it implies there is something wrong in not being perfect.

METAPHYSICAL UNIT. See UNIT.

METAPHYSICS. The science of being, as being; or of the absolutely first principles of being. Also called ontology, first philosophy, the philosophy of being, the philosophy of first causes, wisdom. (Etym. Greek *meta,* after, beyond + *physika,* physics.)

METAPSYCHOLOGY. The science that deals with phenomena outside the ordinary phenomena of human experience, e.g., telepathy, clairvoyance, and psychokinesis. Also called parapsychology.

METEMPSYCHOSIS. The theory of the transmigration of human souls from one body, whether human or animal, to another. Taught by Plato (427–347 B.C.) and nowadays by theosophists, it is the single most characteristic feature of the Eastern religions, in the Vedic, mainly Hindu, and Buddhist traditions. (Etym. Greek *meta,* change + *empsychos,* animate.)

METHOD. Any planned way of doing something. In the spiritual life, it is a way of keeping order in one's moral activity so that a definite purpose is achieved. (Etym. Latin *methodus;* from Greek *methodos: meta,* after + *hodos,* a way.)

METHODICAL DOUBT. The act by which a person, in a state of certainty, abstracts from his certitude in order to examine critically and logically the truth of some matter. It is the opposite of a real doubt.

METHODOLOGY. Either a system of principles and procedures applied to a given study or discipline, or the underlying principles that govern a certain activity. Methodology is an essential part of the Christian religion, which not only teaches the faithful what they are to do to gain eternal life, but also tells them how and why they are to save their souls.

METHUSELAH. A man descended from Seth and Enoch and father of Lamech. He is remembered mostly because of the extraordinarily long life he led—969 years. So far as recorded ages are concerned, he is the oldest man in the Bible (Genesis 5:21–27).

METROPOLITAN. An archbishop who is placed over a certain section of a country, comprising a number of suffragan dioceses. However, not every archbishop is a metropolitan, because there are both titular and resident archbishops.

MGR., MSGR. *Monseigneur, Monsignore—* My Lord, Monsignor.

MICAH. A Judaean prophet, a contemporary of Isaiah, Amos, and Hosea. He was fearless in denouncing the abuses of the times, condemning the rich who defrauded the poor, usurers, swindlers, and venal judges. He warned the people that God would judge and punish them. Among his prophecies was this one: "But you, Bethlehem Ephrathah, the least of the clans of Judah, out of you will be born for me the one who is to rule over Israel" (Micah 5:1).

MICAIAH. A prophet in Israel whom King Ahab detested because he offered pessimistic prophecies when questioned. Ahab and Jehoshaphat, King of Judah, were planning a war to capture Ramoth-Gilead, and the official prophets, four hundred strong, assured Ahab that the campaign would be successful. But when Micaiah was consulted, he stubbornly insisted that the attack would be disastrous. The infuriated king had him thrown into prison and accepted the optimistic opinion of the four hundred. In the battle that followed Ahab was so badly wounded he died the same day. Micaiah was vindicated (I Kings 22).

MICHAEL. An angel sent by God to assure Daniel of God's protection against the Persians (Daniel 10). In the New Testament, Jude refers to the same Michael in contention with Satan (Jude 9), and in Revelation an account is given of Michael and his angels driving Satan out of heaven (Revelation 12:7–9).

MICHAL. The younger daughter of King Saul (I Samuel 14:49). That deceitful monarch used his daughter in a desperate attempt to have David killed. He offered to let David marry Michal provided he would kill one hundred Philistines in battle. His plan was frustrated and the two were married (I Samuel 18:20–27). In another attempt by Saul, Michal, who truly loved David, helped him escape. This did not deter her from scolding him later when she thought he weakened the dignity of the kingship by dancing before the Ark. He was unmoved; he felt that the people respected him more for participating in a religious festival (II Samuel 6:14–23).

MIDDLE AGES. The period preceding the Renaissance. Once taken to date from A.D. 476, the fall of the Roman Empire, it is now more correctly held to begin about 1100 and extend to the end of the fifteenth century. Also once viewed as a sterile period, it has come to be recognized as one of the most cultivated and productive eras of human history. It was the age that reached the highest realization of Christendom as a cultural unity built on a common faith.

MIDRASH. A homiletic interpretation of the Bible by Jewish rabbis since the beginning of the third century, and an important element in Catholic biblical exegesis. Midrashim (plural) were done for many parts of the Bible. They aimed at discovering in the sacred text a meaning deeper than the literal one, not unlike the "spiritual sense" in the Christian Bible.

MIGNE PATROLOGIA. The most comprehensive editions of the Fathers of the Church and ecclesiastical writers in existence. Jacques Paul Migne (1800–75) had been a parish priest in Orléans, France, until 1844, when he began publishing the corpus of Latin authors up to Innocent III (217 volumes, 1844–55). Then followed the Greek writers to A.D. 1439 (162 volumes, with Latin translation, 1857–66). The two collections, *Patrologia Latina* (P.L.) and *Patrologia Graeca* (P.G.), although lacking the critical perfection of modern scholarship, are still a standard source for reference and quotation.

MIGRANTS AND TOURISM, COMMISSION FOR. Its full title is the Pontifical Commission for the Pastoral Care of Migrants and of Tourism. Established in 1970 by Pope Paul VI, it was placed under the jurisdiction of the Congregation for Bishops.

MILANESE RITE. See AMBROSIAN RITE.

MILDNESS. Gentleness in disposition and behavior. As a fruit of the Holy Spirit, it is a perfection of love which tempers justice by avoiding any unnecessary action that might provoke anger or resentment.

MILITANT CHURCH. See CHURCH MILITANT.

MILITARY VICARIATE. A territory put under the care of one who has spiritual responsibility for the military personnel in that territory. It has jurisdiction over the chaplains, personnel of the armed forces and their families living with them. The jurisdiction is canonically erected by the Holy See.

MILLENNIUM. A thousand years during which Christ is to rule on earth, before the last day, based on Revelation 20:1–5. Held by some Fathers, such as Justin (A.D. 100–65) and Ireneus (130–200), the millennium is still professed by a number of Protestant denominations. The Catholic Church interprets the biblical passage as referring to Christ's spiritual reign in the Church and takes "thousand years" to mean simply an indefinitely long time.

MIND. Any state or activity of rational consciousness; also a collective name for all rationally conscious powers, states, and activities. In philosophy the mind is commonly identified with the intellect as recipient of knowledge. (Etym. Latin *mens*, mind, intellect, spirit.)

MIND DUST. A postulate of materialism that the human mind results from a combination of particles of mind that have always existed in association with material atoms. A rival theory, e.g., in Teilhard de Chardin (1881–1955), is emergent evolution, which claims that the mind is a natural product in the process of biological evolution.

MIND OF THE CHURCH. The Church's attitude or policy in matters of faith or morals not explicitly taught in official pronouncements. Where specific doctrine or direction is absent, it is the Church's intention behind her teaching or regulation. To act "according to the mind of the Church" is a mark of Catholic loyalty and frequently urged on the faithful by the modern popes.

MINIMS. The Order of Minim Friars, founded in 1435 by St. Francis of Paola (1416–1507). Their name symbolizes their desire to practice humility. Their first rule, approved by Pope Alexander VI in 1493, was based on the Rule of St. Francis of Assisi. This was revised and the second rule was more independent; it was approved by the same Pope in 1501. Its special feature is the fourth vow of complete abstinence from meat, fish, eggs, and all dairy products. Superiors are called correctors. Their purpose is contemplation and the apostolate in the parochial ministry, preaching and teaching. A community of women, also called Minims, is more popularly known as Miniams, Sisters of Charity of the Sorrowful Mother.

MINISTER. A title given to a variety of persons in the Catholic Church. Those who administer the sacraments are ministers of the sacramental rites. Persons assisting the celebrant at Mass are ministers, e.g., the lector and acolyte. The heads of certain religious orders, e.g., Franciscans, are ministers general, and among Jesuits the second in charge of a local community is the minister. Implicit in the title is the notion of service. Since the Reformation, Protestant denominations commonly speak of their ordained clergy as ministers, to distinguish them from the priesthood. (Etym. Latin *minister,* servant.)

MINISTERIAL PRIESTHOOD. The sacrament of holy orders and the permanent state of one who has been ordained a priest, as distinct from the priesthood of all believers, common to all the baptized. Essential to the ministerial priesthood is the conferral of the unique sacerdotal powers of consecrating and offering the true body and blood of Christ in the Mass, and of forgiving sins committed after baptism, through the sacraments of penance and anointing.

MINISTERIA QUAEDAM. Apostolic Letter of Pope Paul VI by which tonsure, minor orders, and the subdiaconate were suppressed in the Latin Rite of the Catholic Church (August 15, 1972).

MINISTERIORUM DISCIPLINA. Decree of the Sacred Congregation for Divine Worship, issued in 1972, giving the norms and ritual for the ministries of reader and acolyte, the admission of men to the diaconate, and the dedication to a life of celibacy (December 3, 1972).

MINISTRIES. Formerly called minor orders in the Catholic Church, namely reader, and acolyte. They may now be committed to Christian men and are no longer considered as reserved to candidates for the sacraments of orders.

MINISTRY. Authorized service of God in the service of others, according to specified norms revealed by Christ and determined by the Church. In Catholic usage the various forms of ministry include these features: 1. service of God, who is glorified by the loving service given to others; 2. authorization by the Church's hierarchy, whether the Pope directly or the local ordinary; this authorization may require ordination, as in the priestly ministry, or consecration, as in religious life; or liturgical blessing, as with lectors and extraordinary ministers of Holy Communion; 3. based on the teaching of Christ, who showed by word and example how to minister to people's spiritual and temporal needs; and 4. under the guidance of the Church in accordance with her directives and decrees.

MINISTRY OF THE WORD. The communication of the message of salvation. It brings the Gospel to the human race. The ministry of the word takes on different forms, according to the different conditions under which it is practiced and the ends that it strives to achieve.

There is the form called evangelization, or missionary preaching. This has as its purpose the arousing of the beginnings of faith, so that men will adhere to the word of God.

Then there is the catechetical form, "which is intended to make men's faith become living, conscious, and active, through the light of instruction" (Second Vatican Council, *Decree on the Bishops' Pastoral Office in the Church,* 14).

There is also the liturgical form, within the setting of a liturgical celebration, especially during the Eucharistic Sacrifice, e.g., through the homily.

Finally there is the theological form, which is the systematic and scientific investigation of the truths of faith. Theologians are ministers of the word insofar as they humbly investigate the resources of Christian revelation and present their findings to the faithful with a view to a more generous service of Christ and his Church.

MINOR BASILICA. A title given by the Pope to certain churches remarkable for antiquity, historical associations, or importance as centers of worship yet not qualifying as major basilicas. Examples of minor basilicas are St. Lawrence in Rome; Mission Dolores in San Francisco; and St. Anne de Beaupré in Quebec.

MINOR ORDERS. The present ministries of acolyte, and reader or lector which for centuries had been called minor orders. They were never considered part of the sacrament of orders and in 1973 were all reduced to Church ministries to which men can be appointed in a special liturgical ceremony presided over by a bishop or, for religious, a major superior.

MIRACLE. A sensibly perceptible effect, surpassing at least the powers of visible nature, produced by God to witness to some truth or testify to someone's sanctity. (Etym. Latin *miraculum,* miracle, marvel; from *mirari,* to wonder.)

MIRACLE OF GRACE. A sudden and unexpected conversion from ignorance to faith, from doubt to certainty, from sinfulness to holiness. It is not due to ordinary causes but to God's particular special and unmerited grace. It is an effect of divine intervention beyond the ordinary working of Providence.

MIRACLE PLAY. See MYSTERY PLAY.

MIRACLES OF CHRIST. They may be divided into five classes: nature miracles; miracles of healing; deliverance of demoniacs; victories over hostile wills; cases of resurrection.

Nature Miracles. Under this head nine miracles may be enumerated.

Changing of the water into wine at Cana (John 2).

First miraculous draught of fishes (Luke 5).

Calming of the tempest (Matthew 8; Mark 4; Luke 8).

First multiplication of loaves (Matthew 14; Mark 6; Luke 9; John 6).

Jesus's walking on the water (Matthew 14; Mark 6; John 6).

Second multiplication of loaves (Matthew 15; Mark 8).

Stater in the fish's mouth (Matthew 17).

Cursing of the fig tree (Matthew 21; Mark 11).

Second miraculous draught of fishes (John 21).

Miracles of Healing. These were numerous during the public life of Our Lord. There are references to a great many cures that are not related in detail (Matthew 4; Luke 4, 6; Mark 6), and twenty special cases are recorded.

Healing of the nobleman's son (John 4).

Cure of the mother-in-law of Peter (Matthew 8; Mark 1; Luke 4).

Cleansing of the leper (Matthew 8; Mark 1; Luke 5).

Healing of the paralytic (Matthew 9; Mark 2; Luke 5).

Healing of the sick man at Bethesda (John 5).

Restoring of the man with the withered hand (Matthew 12; Mark 3; Luke 6).

Healing of the centurion's servant (Matthew 8; Luke 7).

Healing of one blind and dumb (Matthew 12; Luke 11).

Healing of the woman with an issue of blood (Matthew 9; Mark 5; Luke 8).

Opening of the eyes of two blind men (Matthew 9).

Cure of the dumb man (Matthew 9).

Healing of the deaf and dumb man (Mark 7).

Opening the eyes of one blind at Bethsaida (Mark 8).

Healing the lunatic child (Matthew 17; Mark 9; Luke 9).

Opening the eyes of one born blind (John 9).

Restoring the woman with a spirit of infirmity (Luke 13).

Healing of the man with the dropsy (Luke 14).

Cleansing of the ten lepers (Luke 17).

Opening the eyes of the blind man near Jericho (Matthew 20; Mark 10; Luke 18).

Healing of Malchus's ear (Luke 22).

Deliverance of Demoniacs. General formulas regarding the driving out of devils (Mark 1) indicate that such acts of deliverance were very numerous during Our Lord's public life. Special cases related are as follows:

Demoniac at Capernaum (Mark 1; Luke 4).

Deaf and dumb demoniac (Matthew 12; Luke 11).

Gerasene demoniacs (Matthew 8; Mark 5; Luke 8).

Dumb demoniac (Matthew 9).

Daughter of the Syro-Phoenician woman (Matthew 15; Mark 7).

Lunatic child (Matthew 17; Mark 9; Luke 9).

Woman with the spirit of infirmity (Luke 13).

Victories over Hostile Wills. Under this heading Catholic scholars admit a greater or smaller number of miracles; it is not clear in certain cases whether the incidents in which Our Lord wielded extraordinary power over his enemies were cases of supernatural intervention of Divine Power or the natural effects of the ascendancy of his human will over that of other men. Such are the cases mentioned in John (7, 30, and 44; 8, 20, and 59), where the Jews failed to arrest him "because His hour was not yet come," or, in the fourth case, because he hid himself from them. There are two cases that appear to most Catholic commentators to involve a supernatural display of power over wills: 1. the casting out of the vendors (John 2; Matthew 21; Mark 11; Luke 19); 2. the episode of the escape from the hostile crowd at Nazareth (Luke 4).

Cases of Resurrection. Among the signs of his Messiahship which Our Lord gave to the delegates of John the Baptist, we read: "The dead rise again" (Matthew 11; Luke 7). This general statement has made some commentators think that there were cases of resurrection not described in the Gospels. This is possible because the Gospels do not aim at completeness, but the expression quoted would be justified by the three following cases of resurrection, which are related.

Raising of the daughter of Jairus (Matthew 9; Mark 5; Luke 8).

Raising of the son of the widow of Naim (Luke 7).

Raising of Lazarus (John 11).

MIRACULOUS MEDAL. A distinctive oval medal of the Blessed Virgin Mary. Its design was revealed in 1830 to St. Catherine Labouré (canonized in 1947), a Daughter of Charity of St. Vincent de Paul in Paris, in visions she had of Our Lady. On one side the medal bears an image of Mary with arms outstretched with the words "O Mary conceived without sin, pray for us who have recourse to thee," and on the reverse side the letter M with a cross and twelve stars above it and the Hearts of Jesus and Mary. The number of miracles attached to the wearing of this medal gave it the popular description of "miraculous." It shares popularity with the Scapular Medal. It is the badge of the Sodality of the Children of Mary. There are numerous special shrines and devotions dedicated to Our Lady of the Miraculous Medal and weekly devotions to her are on the agenda in thousands of Catholic churches throughout the world.

MIRACULOUS MEDAL (shrine). In the motherhouse chapel of the Daughters of Charity of St. Vincent de Paul on Rue de Bac, Paris. In 1830 the Blessed Virgin appeared three times, sitting in a chair, to a novice, Catherine Labouré, asking her to have a medal struck honoring her Immaculate Conception. The chair is now preserved as a relic there. Mary told Catherine of the terrible things that would happen unless true religious fervor among the people was revived. Catherine's first attempt to follow the Blessed Mother's request was unsuccessful, but later a medal was coined depicting the Blessed Virgin. Catherine Labouré was canonized in 1947 by Pope Pius XII, and her uncorrupted body in the motherhouse makes this shrine a most popular place of pilgrimage. A replica of the shrine brings thousands of pilgrims to novena devotions at Germantown, Pennsylvania, in America to pay tribute to the Mother of God and the humble Daughter of Charity to whom she appeared in France.

MIRAE CARITATIS. Encyclical letter of Pope Leo XIII on the Holy Eucharist (May 23, 1902). It is one of the principal modern sources of the Church's doctrine on the Blessed Sacrament, along with *Mediator Dei* of Pope Pius XII and *Mysterium Fidei* of Pope Paul VI. Its theme is mainly the marvelous effects of devotion to the Holy Eucharist in the moral and spiritual life of the faithful. The main reason for the troubles in our day, according to *Mirae Caritatis,* is the lack of charity among people because of their weakening in the love of God. On both counts, the Sacrament of the Eucharist is the most effective way to grow in selfless love.

MIRIAM. Older sister of Moses and Aaron. When Moses was born, his mother laid him in a basket and set it free on a river because of Pharaoh's edict dooming all Hebrew baby boys (Exodus 1:22). The resourceful Miriam managed to have Moses' own mother, Jochebed, assigned to care for him (Exodus 2:2–10). Later in life she was not as fortunate or as well advised. When Moses married Zipporah, both Miriam and Aaron thought he had demeaned himself by marrying a Midianite. When they criticized him, Yahweh came to his rescue and punished Miriam by inflicting her with leprosy. For a week she was forced out of the camp, until Moses interceded and begged Yahweh to heal her (Numbers 12:1–15). Years later she died and was buried in Kadesh (Numbers 20:1).

MIRROR. A symbol of the Blessed Virgin, who so thoroughly mirrored her divine Son, "the reflection of the eternal light, untarnished mirror of God's active power, image of his goodness" (Wisdom 7–26). In the Litany of Loreto, Mary is referred to as the Mirror of Justice.

MISERERE. One of three Psalms, 50, 55, and 56 (Vulgate), each of which begins, in Latin, with the invocation, *Miserere* (Have mercy), but generally the title refers only to Psalm 50, which is the most common prayer for mercy in the Christian liturgy. (Etym. Latin *miserere,* have mercy [imperative].)

MISERICORDE. Mercy, pardon. A small bar on the underside of a movable church seat to help support a person while standing in the stall while the seat is raised.

MISS. *Missa, missionarius*—Mass, missionary.

MISSAL. The book containing the prayers recited by the priest at the altar during Mass. Since the Second Vatican Council the Missal includes both the sacramentary (or ritual part of the Mass) used only by the celebrant, and the lectionary (containing readings from Scripture) for celebrant and assisting ministers. (Etym. Latin *missalis,* pertaining to Mass.)

MISS. APOST., M.A. *Missionarius apostolicus*—missionary apostolic.

MISSALE ROMANUM. Apostolic Constitution of Pope Paul VI promulgating the new Roman Missal. The most significant features of this new missal are the addition of three new canons for the Mass, and the modification of the ritual. However, in each canon the Pope decreed that there be the same formula of consecration as follows: "We want the words to be pronounced thus: over the bread, 'Accipite et manducate ex hoc omnes; Hoc est enim corpus meum, quod pro vobis tradetur'; and over the chalice, 'Hic est enim calix sanguinis mei, novi et aeterni testamenti, qui pro vobis et pro multis effundetur in remissionem peccatorum. Hoc facite in meam commemorationem.' The words 'Mysterium fidei,' taken from the context of the words of Christ the Lord, and said by the priest, serve as an introduction to the acclamation of the faithful" (April 3, 1969). Two years before *Missale Romanum,* Pope Paul VI had authorized the use of the vernacular language "even in the Canon of the Mass" (May 4, 1967).

MISSIOLOGY. That branch of theology which studies the principles and practice of the missions. It is the science of evangelization and catechesis in regions and among people where the Church is being established.

MISSION. The term literally denotes "sending" and covers a variety of meanings, all somehow expressing the idea of a going forth from one person to others in order to effect some beneficial change in their favor. At the highest level are the divine missions of the Trinity: the visible mission of the Second Person, sent by the Father in the person of Jesus Christ, and the invisible mission of the Holy Spirit, sent by the Father and the Son. Christ then sent the Apostles to make disciples of all nations. Their mission was to preach the Gospel, baptize, and teach the people "to observe all the commands I gave you" (Matthew 28:19–20). The Apostles, in turn, personally and through their successors have been sending other faithful to continue the work of the Master in evangelizing the human race. Mission, therefore, is the purpose of vocation. All who are called to follow Christ are sent by Christ, in the person of his Church, to extend the Kingdom of God. (Etym. Latin *missio,* a sending.)

MISSIONARY. A person who is sent by Church authority to preach the Gospel, or help strengthen the faith already professed, among people in a given place or region. Essential to being a missionary, whether at home or abroad, is the desire to extend the Kingdom of Christ by preaching, teaching, or other means of evangelization and catechesis.

MITER. Liturgical headdress worn by popes, cardinals, abbots, and bishops of the Latin Rite. It is a folding two-pieced stiffened cap of silk or linen, often richly ornamented with gold embroidery, united with a piece of soft material allowing the two stiffened pieces to be folded together. It usually has two fringed lappets that hang down the back. It is always removed when the celebrant prays. There are three kinds of miters to be interchanged according to the solemnity of the occasion and the liturgical season: the golden, the precious, and the simple. The last is always of white and worn on Good Friday and at funerals. Usually inferior prelates are restricted to the white miter only. (Etym. Greek *mitrā,* girdle, belt, headband, turban.)

MITIGATED TUTIORISM. A moral system for resolving practical doubts. According to this theory, a person is freed from an obligation if an opinion in favor of liberty is probable in the highest degree.

MIXED CONTEMPLATION. Active and passive contemplation alternately experienced, that is, the prayer of simplicity acquired by human effort, and mystical union freely infused by God. Sometimes called the first degree of infused contemplation. The mystical union may be of short duration, or it may last for a longer time, partly depending on a person's ability to sustain it, but mainly on the gratuitous dispensation of God's providence.

MIXED MARRIAGE. A marriage between a professed member of the Catholic Church and one who is not a Catholic. The mainstream of Roman Catholic tradition on mixed marriages is to discourage them, while recognizing that such marriages are inevitable in pluralistic societies. Two reasons are commonplace as to why the Church discourages mixed unions: the risk to the faith of the Catholic party, and the danger that the children will not be brought up in the Catholic Church. Since the Second Vatican Council the Church has drastically revised her legislation regarding mixed marriages, notably in 1966 and 1970. There is greater leniency on the permission for these marriages, but no change on the basic concern to preserve the faith of the Catholic partner and ensure that all the children are baptized and reared in the Catholic Church.

MIXED MARRIAGE PROMISES. The commitment required of the Catholic party in a marriage with a non-Catholic. As expressed in the apostolic letter of Pope Paul VI in 1970, this commitment involves two things: "The Catholic party shall declare that he is ready to remove dangers of falling from the faith. He is also gravely bound to make a sincere promise to do all in his power to have all the children baptized and brought up in the Catholic Church" (*Matrimonia Mixta,* norm 4). In many countries, e.g., the United States, the bishops' conference further specifies that, to obtain a dispensation for a mixed marriage, these promises be made orally or in writing as the Catholic prefers.

M.H. Middle Hour (Terce, Sext, None).

MINA. Biblical unit of weight in the Old and New Testaments. Equal to a hundred drachmas, or about a pound. A sum of money equal to one sixtieth of a talent.

MODALISM. A cluster of Trinitarian heresies of the second and third centuries claiming that there is only one person in God, but that this one person manifests himself in three different ways or modes, e.g., as creator (Father), redeemer (Son), and sanctifier (Holy Spirit). (Etym. Latin *modus,* way, manner, method.)

MODALITY. The way in which something has being, or any modification of something. In Christian philosophy, following St. Thomas Aquinas, modes are the transcendentals, that is, those aspects which are common to all things whatsoever, such as unity, truth, and goodness. In Cartesian thought, modes are the inseparable attributes of substance, such as thought for spirit and actual extension for body. In pantheism, modes are the appearances of the divine in the physical universe where creatures seem to have a distinct existence of their own but are only manifestations of the unique reality of the Absolute. (Etym. Latin *modalis,* from *modus,* way, manner, method.)

MODEL. The person, object, or idea in whose likeness someone or something can be made. In this sense Christ and the saints are the divinely available models of Christian perfection. As an exemplary cause, a model is the form that a person deliberately seeks to imitate.

MODERATION. The balanced use of what is naturally agreeable, whether to the body or spirit. It is the conscious control of one's desires in order to use some human power to the best advantage of oneself or someone else.

MODERN ARIANISM. Organized bodies or movements, since the Reformation, that professedly subscribe to the Arian denial that Christ is the natural Son of God. This modern Arianism is a logical though not always linear development from the ancient stock. Under the more familiar names of Unitarians, Anti-Trinitarians and Socinians, those who profess this creed believe in the Fatherhood of God, the society of the human race, the example of Jesus as a model of ethical perfection, and salvation of humankind through an evolutionary process inherent in all things.

Also in the Arian tradition are the rationalists when they deal with the person of Christ. Their system postulates the absolute rights of natural reason as the only source of religious truth. Consequently they deny the divinity of Christ, except in Arius' sense of "the most intimate to God," and for the same reason as Arius (256–336), because the Trinity and Incarnation are mysteries of faith to be accepted on the authority of God.

MODERNISM. A theory about the origin and nature of Christianity, first developed into a system by George Tyrrell (1861–1909), Lucien Laberthonnière (1860–1932), and Alfred Loisy (1857–1940). According to Modernism, religion is essentially a matter of experience, personal and collective. There is no objective revelation from God to the human race, on which Christianity is finally based, nor any reasonable grounds for credibility in the Christian faith, based on miracles or the testimony of history. Faith, therefore, is uniquely from within. In fact it is part of human nature, "a kind of motion of the heart," hidden and unconscious. It is, in Modernist terms, a natural instinct belonging to the emotions, a "feeling for the divine" that cannot be expressed in words or doctrinal propositions, an attitude of spirit that all people have naturally but that some are more aware of having. Modernism was condemned by Pope St. Pius X in two formal documents, *Lamentabili* and *Pascendi,* both published in 1907. (Etym. Latin *modernus,* belonging to the present fashion.)

MODERN WORLD. A term used in many senses but especially, among Form Critics of the Gospels, to identify today's society in contrast with that of the first century, or the time of Christ. The modern world is said to be educated; it is intelligent and therefore skeptical, and demands scientific proof for everything it even provisionally accepts as true.

MODESTY. The virtue that moderates all the internal and external movements and appearance of a person according to his or her endowments, possessions, and station in life. Four virtues are commonly included under modesty: humility, studiousness, and two kinds of external modesty, namely in dress and general behavior.

Humility is the ground of modesty in that it curbs the inordinate desire for personal excellence and inclines one to recognize his or her own worth in its true light. Studiousness moderates the desire and pursuit of truth in accordance with faith and right reason. Its contrary vices are curiosity, which is an excessive desire for knowledge, and negligence, which is remissness in acquiring the knowledge that should be had for one's age and position in life. Modesty in dress and bodily adornments inclines a person to avoid not only whatever is offensive to others but whatever is not necessary. Modesty in bodily behavior directs a person to observe proper decorum in bodily movements, according to the dictum of St. Augustine, "In all your movements let nothing be evident that would offend the eyes of another." (Etym. Latin *modestia,* moderation, modesty.)

MOKAMEH (shrine). A sanctuary of Our Mother of Divine Grace, where a church was built in 1947 about 200 miles from Calcutta on the Ganges River. The church is Hindu in style, and the statue of Mary is dressed in a sari with her eyes lowered in meditation. Organized groups of pilgrims, among whom are Christians, Moslems, and Hindus, arrive from great distances.

MOLECH. A pagan diety of certain Semitic peoples. Worship of Molech involved the sacrifice of a child by passing through a fire or a furnace, a custom reminiscent of the stories concerning Abraham and Isaac and Jephthah and his daughter. This savage ritual was forbidden by Hebrew law (Leviticus 18:21), which specified stoning to death as an appropriate punishment. The notorious King Manasseh was responsible for introducing Molech worship in the seventh century B.C., using his own son as a sacrificial offering (II Kings 21:6). One of the reforms King Josiah made was the destruction of the furnace in the Valley of Ben-hinnom to end this dreadful practice (II Kings 23:10). Also spelled Moloch.

MOLINISM. The theory on grace and free will developed by the Spanish Jesuit theologian Louis Molina (1535–1600). It teaches that there is no built-in difference, but only an external accidental difference between sufficient and efficacious grace. God gives every person sufficient grace for all supernatural actions he or she is to perform. If one freely accepts the grace offered and co-operates with it, a salutary action is produced; this co-operation automatically makes a sufficient grace an efficacious one. If the free will refuses its co-operation, the grace remains sufficient only. God from all eternity foresees the free consent of the human will by his infallible foreknowledge of what a person would do with whatever grace he or she received. Why God chooses to give the person the precise grace he does, foreseeing whether that person will accept or reject it, is left as a mystery in God.

MOLOCH. See MOLECH.

MOMENT OF TRUTH. A situation in which a person must face a challenge, make up his mind, and follow the dictates of his or her conscience at no matter what sacrifice.

MONARCHIANISM. A heretical doctrine begun in the second century, that so stressed God's unity of nature as to deny the Trinity of Persons. Three forms are distinguishable: crude monarchianism denied any distinction of persons in the Godhead and claimed that the Father became incarnate. The modalist type admitted only a distinction of functions in God, who as Father created the world, as Son redeemed, and as the Holy Spirit sanctified the world. The subordinationist variety recognized a real distinction of persons but subordinated one to the other. (Etym. Greek *monarchēs*, sole ruler, a sovereign.)

MONASTERY. The place where religious dwell in seclusion. The term applies mainly to religious men or women who live a cloistered, contemplative life and recite the entire Divine Office in common. (Etym. Greek *monastērion*, from *monazein*, live alone.)

MONASTIC CONGREGATION. A confederation or union of a number of independent (*sui juris*) monasteries.

MONASTICISM. The way of life, characterized by asceticism and self-denial, followed by religious who live more or less secluded from the world, according to a fixed rule and under vows, in order to praise God through contemplation and apostolic charity. The principal duty of those living the monastic life is to offer humble service to God within the boundaries of the monastery. Some monastic institutes dedicate themselves wholly to contemplation; others engage in some works of the apostolate or of Christian charity, in accord with the character of monastic life.

MONDAY. Second day of the week, referred to as the moon's day, dedicated customarily to the Holy Spirit.

MONISM. Any system of philosophy that substitutes a unity of substance for a unity of order in the universe. It denies all plurality of beings, considering only the One to be real and the manifold an illusion. Various philosophers have differently conceived this one reality as spirit or matter, or as spirit emanating matter, or as matter evolving into spirit. Monism is pantheism looked at from the viewpoint of being. (Etym. Greek *monos*, alone, single.)

MONISTIC EVOLUTION. A pantheistic theory that claims that all reality has always been in process, that nothing even now simply is but is still becoming, that the process includes what Christians call God. He, too, is part of the ongoing development of all being toward perfection.

MONITION. An official warning, provided by canon law, either personally or through a third person. The purpose of a monition is to warn a person that if he or she does not amend, certain formal measures will be taken against them, e.g., canonical censure; suspension of a priest from his pastoral duties; removal of a bishop from his office; dismissal of a religious from his or her institute. Monitions may be given either publicly or secretly. If public, they should be made before a notary, or before two witnesses, or by letter. (Etym. Latin *monitio*, from *monere*, to warn.)

MONK. Originally a hermit or anchorite, but already in the early Church applied to men living a community life in a monastery, under vows of poverty, chastity, and obedience, according to a specific rule, such as that of St. Basil or St. Benedict. (Etym. Greek *monachos*, living alone, solitary.)

MONOGAMY. The institution of marriage in which husband and wife may have only one marital partner, who is still living. It is the unity of marriage opposed to polygamy. (Etym. Greek *monos*, only + *gamos*, marriage.)

MONOGENISM. The doctrine that the human race derived from one original human being, identified in Scripture with Adam. This is the Church's constant traditional teaching. In the creed of Pope Pelagius I (reigned 556–61) we read: "I confess that all men until the end of time, born of Adam and dying with Adam, his wife, who themselves were not born of other parents . . . will rise and stand firm before the judgment seat of Christ, to receive each one according to his works" (Denzinger, 228a). And Pope Pius XII declared: "No Catholic can hold that after Adam there existed on this earth true men who did not take their origin through natural generation from him as from the first parent of all" (*Humani Generis*, 1950, para. 38). (Etym. Latin *mono*, one + *genus*, race.)

MONOGRAMS. Single letters intertwined to form one composite character, often used in Christian symbols.

MONOPHYSITISM. A historical system that arose in the fifth century, claiming that in Christ there was only one nature. It came as a reaction to Nestorianism, which postulated two persons in Christ. Among the early Monophysites was Eutyches (378–454), head of a monastery near Constantinople. In his effort to save the unity of the Word Incarnate, he suppressed Christ's human nature. Other Monophysites spoke of a single combined nature that was both human and divine. Condemned by the Council of Chalcedon in 451, Monophysitism still prevails in the East among the Copts and the Syrian Jacobites. (Etym. Greek *monos*, single + *physis*, nature.)

MONOTHEISM. The belief that there is only one God, who is the Creator of the universe. It is first of all theism, because it recognizes the existence of a personal God, with mind and will, who is really distinct from the world he created. It is therefore not monism, which identifies God and the universe. Moreover it affirms that this personal and transcendent God is uniquely one and not plural, hence it is opposed to polytheism and dualism. (Etym. Greek *monos*, single + *theos*, god.)

MONOTHELITISM. A heresy that began in the seventh century out of an attempt to conciliate the Monophysites. The latter confused the idea of personality with the undivided activity of a single will, claiming that there was a kind of divine-human operation in Christ. The Monothelites recognized the orthodox doctrine of Christ's two natures but taught that these two natures had a common will and a common activity. This view was urged by Sergius (d. 638), Patriarch of Constantinople, who had brought Pope Honorius to support his cause. The East was divided in controversy for over a half century, until the Sixth General Council held at Constantinople condemned Monothelitism in 681. (Etym. Greek *monos*, single + *thelein*, will.)

MONSIGNOR. A title of distinction granted by the Pope to numerous prelates. All ecclesiastical dignitaries including archbishops and bishops have a right to this title. (Etym. Italian *monsignore*, literally, my lord.)

MONSTRANCE (emblem). A symbol of the Blessed Sacrament since the monstrance is the sacred vessel which contains the consecrated Host when exposed or carried in procession. It is a well-known emblem of St. Clare, who is reported to have repulsed unbelievers who assaulted her convent of nuns by presenting to their gaze Christ in the monstrance. St. Peter Julian Eymard, founder of the Blessed Sacrament Fathers, is symbolized carrying the monstrance and blessing the people with it. St. Thomas Aquinas has the monstrance among his many emblems as the author of the famous hymns *Lauda Sion* and *Pange Lingua*, written to honor the Eucharistic Lord. St. John Neumann, who first established the forty hours' devotion in America, and St. Paschal Baylon, patron of Eucharistic Congresses, are both represented in art with the monstrance. (Etym. Latin *monstrans*, from *monstrare*, to show, point out, indicate.) See also OSTENSORIUM.

MONTANISM. A heretical movement in the second century, which professed belief in a new Church of the Spirit. Its members considered themselves specially gifted by the Holy Spirit as prophets of Christ's second coming. The substance of their doctrine was that the Holy Spirit was now supplementing the revelation of Christ, with consequent displacement of the bishops and even the Pope. The new "outpouring of the Spirit" traveled all over the Catholic world and won over the great Tertullian (160–220). Montanism was first condemned by a series of Asiatic synods and also, after some hesitation, by Pope Zephyrinus about A.D. 202.

MONTHS, DEDICATION OF THE. Traditionally each month of the liturgical year is dedicated to some mystery of the faith or special saint, as follows: January, the Holy Name of Jesus; February, the Passion;

March, St. Joseph; April, the Resurrection; May, the Blessed Virgin; June, the Sacred Heart; July, the Precious Blood; August, the Assumption; September, the Holy Cross; October, the Rosary; November, the Poor Souls; December, Advent, or the Coming of Christ.

MONTH'S MIND. A special Mass offered for the deceased on or near the thirtieth day after the person's death or burial.

MONTSERRAT (shrine). The Holy Mountain, twenty miles from Barcelona, Spain. Its central feature is a statue of the Virgin Mary and her divine Son, thirty-eight inches high, made of wood now blackened with age. It is housed in a church built on the top of the rocks where a Benedictine abbey now stands. According to tradition previous to A.D. 888, this image of Christ and his Mother was miraculously found among the rocks of Montserrat, strange lights and angelic music guiding searchers to a mountain cavern where it was hidden. All the kings of Spain came to worship at the shrine chapel, and the names of saints such as Ignatius of Loyola, Vincent Ferrer, and Joseph Calasanz have been connected with this shrine. Since the Napoleonic Wars and the more recent Spanish Civil War all the buildings have been modernized.

MORAL. Pertaining to rational beings in the use of free will; therefore pertaining to human conduct or to the science of human behavior. (Etym. Latin *moralis,* relating to conduct, *mos,* a manner, custom.)

MORAL ACT. A human act. One performed with knowledge and free will. It is called a moral act because it is always either morally good or bad. Every consciously deliberate action is therefore a moral act.

MORAL ARGUMENT. The argument for God's existence from the fact of a moral nature in human beings. Given the instinctive human awareness that some actions are good and others wrong, and the sense of peace when one does what is considered good but guilt when one does wrong, it is reasonable to conclude that there must be a God who ultimately inspires these moral sentiments because he is leading the human race to a destiny that must be gained by living a morally good life.

MORAL CAUSE. A free cause as distinguished from a necessary one. The opposite of a physical cause. One that acts as a motive for the performance of a free action or serves as an occasion that favors the action

of a free cause. See also CAUSE, EFFICIENT CAUSE, FINAL CAUSE, FIRST CAUSE, FORMAL CAUSE, FREE CAUSE, MATERIAL CAUSE, NECESSARY CAUSE, SECONDARY CAUSE.

MORAL CERTITUDE. Confident assent concerning human conduct based on people's normal and predictable responses to certain needs, abilities, and motivations.

MORAL DETERMINANTS. Conditions that need to be fulfilled to determine the morality of human conduct. In order to judge the goodness or badness of any particular human act, three elements must be weighed from which every act derives its morality. They are: the object of the act, the circumstances surrounding the act, and the purpose that the one performing the act has in mind.

The object of a human act is that which the one acting sets out to do, as distinguished from his or her ultimate purpose in doing it. It is that which the action of its very nature tends to produce. For example, the object of a suicide's act is to take his or her life; the purpose may be to escape evils that person is unwilling to bear.

Moreover, the object is not merely the act considered in its physical makeup. It is the act viewed in its moral nature, i.e., the act considered in its relationship to the moral law. It answers to the question: Does it conform or is it contrary to the standard of right conduct? The circumstances of a human act are accidental modifications that affect its morality. Circumstances are capable of changing: an ordinary indifferent act into a sinful one, such as unnecessary servile work on Sunday; an ordinarily venially sinful act into a mortal sin, such as taking even a small amount of urgently needed money from a very poor man; an ordinarily mortally sinful act into a venial sin, such as blaspheming when only half aware of what one is doing; and a sinful action into a doubly sinful, such as unjustly striking a person consecrated to God.

The end or purpose of a human act is the intention that prompts one to perform such an act, as when a person reveals some hidden failing of another in order to injure that person's reputation.

A human action is morally good only if all three elements, namely object, circumstances, and purpose, are substantially good. An action becomes morally bad if even one of these three elements is bad. The reason is that we are always obliged to avoid all evil as far as we can. If an essential part of an action is evil, we cannot avoid that evil part unless we refrain from the whole action. If, then, one does an action in spite of the substantially evil element in it, one is performing a sinful action.

MORAL EVIL. Sin, as distinct from physical evil, which is some form of suffering. It is evil because it is contrary to the will of God; it is moral evil because it is caused by a free created will acting against the law of God, who does not want moral evil as an end or as a means. The Council of Trent condemned the contrary doctrine (Denzinger 816). God simply permits moral evil because of consideration of human freedom, and because he has the wisdom and power to cause good to arise from evil. In the end, moral evil will serve the supreme purpose of the universe, the glorification of God, since it reveals his mercy in forgiving and his justice in punishing.

MORAL FORCES. Persons, places, and things that influence one's moral conduct. They may be overt or hidden, and their influence may be deliberate or unintentional, but they are moral forces insofar as they affect one's free will and contribute to the making of decisions.

MORAL FREEDOM. Immunity from obligations or binding precepts and prohibitions. Thus the permission of the moral law to act as one chooses. Moral freedom implies that many human actions are not precisely commanded or forbidden and therefore may be performed without risk of doing moral wrong; while performing them is morally good and even praiseworthy. The opposite of moral obligation or necessity.

MORAL GOOD. That which ennobles human nature because it conforms to what a person should be. Applied to human actions, it is that quality by which they lead human beings to the eternal destiny for which they were made and, already on earth, give a person the true happiness to which everyone aspires.

MORAL HOLINESS. See HOLINESS, MORAL.

MORALITY. Relation between a human act and the final destiny of a human being. It is the norm of behavior that flows from each person's ultimate end, which is the possession of God in the beatific vision.

Depending on what is conceived to be this final destiny, morality will be determined accordingly. Since Catholic Christianity believes that this destiny is heaven, a human act is either good or bad according as it leads to or detracts a person from his or her heavenly goal. The moral norm of human acts, therefore, consists in their aptitude at leading one to that end. Such an aptitude cannot be created by the human will, nor is it entirely at the disposition of some arbitrary divine freedom. It flows necessarily from the nature of God, from the human nature elevated by grace, and from the nature of the acts themselves. Hence the norm of morality contains precepts that transcend every legislative will. The acts related to them are said to have an intrinsic (essential) morality of good or evil. Extrinsic morality, on the other hand, is external to this built-in relationship between action and purpose; they depend exclusively on the free dictate of the legislator.

MORALITY IN MEDIA. Concern of dedicated citizens organized in certain countries like the United States to prevent by legal means the use of the media from morally perverting the press, movie, radio and television audience.

MORALITY OF MUSIC. The recognized fact that music and song, apart from the words used, have the ability to arouse either noble or base feelings and emotions in the persons who hear a melody. The reason for this emotional influence seems to lie deeper than the familiar association of ideas with certain music or song. It involves something inherent in all musical rhythm to evoke a human response that is either morally elevating or degrading, depending partly on the listener but also on what is heard.

MORAL LAW. The norm of human conduct, whether revealed or known by reason. The term is used to distinguish the law as binding in conscience, from mere statutes or directives intended to ensure good order.

MORAL MIRACLE. Divine intervention which enables a person to perform acts of virtue that are totally beyond the capacity of the unaided human will.

MORAL ORDER. The proper direction of human actions to a person's ultimate end, namely the eternal destiny. On a universal scale, the relationship of all human actions, under divine Providence, toward the final purpose that God has for the human race. In ecclesiastical and civil law, the legally established body of rights and duties among human beings either in general or in a given society.

MORAL POSITIVISM. The theory that claims there is no natural law, and therefore no natural right. All human rights, it holds, are derived from the state, from contracts, from each person's freedom, or from custom.

MORAL RELATIVISM. The theory that moral standards vary from one society to another, and from one period of history to another. Ethical principles are said to be social products and not universally binding or based on the objective moral order founded in human nature.

MORAL SUBJECTIVISM. The theory that the norms of human conduct are ultimately determined by each person for himself or herself. Implicit in the theory is some form of philosophical idealism, which holds that truth is not an absolute but a creation of the one who perceives it.

MORAL SYSTEM. In Catholic thought a method of handling concrete situations for solving practical doubts in moral practice. Problems of uncertainty or doubt arise when a statement asserting the lawfulness of an act and another statement denying this are more or less conflicting positions in the objective order. Several such systems are known to ethical science, of which some have been condemned by the Church and others are tenable in Catholic morality. In the pastoral ministry, confessors and spiritual directors are advised to strive to do the more perfect thing themselves and likewise to urge others to do the same. But they are not to impose their own opinions on those whom they are directing as long as the contrary view is solidly probable.

MORAL THEOLOGY. The science of human actions insofar as they are directed by natural reason and divine faith to the attainment of a supernatural destiny. The scope of moral theology, therefore, is human conduct precisely as human, that is, whatever people do under the influence of their free will. In this sense, it is the science of human freedom. It differs, however, from ethics or moral philosophy in that human destiny is supernatural twice over: once because heaven is a revealed mystery and once again because heaven cannot be reached without divine grace. On both counts, moral theology deals with the supernatural, since it takes into account a higher end than what reason alone could conceive, and it recognizes the need for God's grace to do what the human will alone could not achieve.

It differs from dogmatic theology, which it presumes, in that moral theology is concerned with the ethical imperatives of Catholic doctrine and how they are to be lived out in practice. Some authors also carefully distinguish moral from ascetical or spiritual theology, on the score that there are two levels of God's manifest will to humankind, one of precept and the other of counsel. Assuming the distinction, moral theology would then cover only the divine precepts, whether directly revealed or as taught by the Church with divine authority. Since the Second Vatican Council, however, the tendency is to include the whole spectrum of divine expectations for the human race under the single discipline of moral theology, not excluding the pursuit of sanctity.

MORAL UNIT. See UNIT.

MORAL VIRTUE. A good habit of the will whose immediate object is one of the means by which our final destiny is attained.

MORDECAI. Foster father of Esther, the Jewish heroine of the biblical story, who defended her people against the machinations of Haman, an intimate adviser of King Ahasuerus. The latter had given Haman authority to destroy all the Jews in the kingdom, beginning with Mordecai, for whom Haman had a particular hatred. But the resourceful Esther worked on the king so eloquently that Haman was hanged, Mordecai was given his post, and the Jews were saved (Esther 1–10).

MORES. Established or traditional customs of a society that have acquired the force of law. They have ethical significance not of themselves but by convention. (Etym. Latin *mos,* manner, custom.)

MORGANATIC MARRIAGE. Literally a dowry given the morning after a marriage. It is a licit and valid marital union of a prince, or other male member of royalty, with a woman of inferior rank, contracted with the understanding that the children have no right to succeed to their father's title. They are compensated by a gift or dowry to their mother.

MORISCOS. Spanish Moslems and their descendants, allowed to remain in Spain under pretense of conversion to Christianity. Hostile to their conquerors, they revolted under Philip II and, after defeat (1567–70), were first transplanted to the interior and finally expelled from Spain in 1609 by Philip III. (Etym. Spanish *moro,* Moor.)

MORNING-AFTER PILL. An oral contraceptive that would prevent pregnancy although taken one or more days after intercourse. It affects the egg after ovulation. On moral grounds, it is a contraceptive and, by intention, an abortifacient, since the woman is willing to destroy a possibly fertilized ovum.

MORNING OFFERING. Prayer of dedication of one's entire day to the Sacred Heart of Jesus, said by members of the Apostleship of Prayer (League of the Sacred Heart) since the first statutes were approved by the Holy See in 1879. A traditional form of the prayer reads: "O Jesus, through the immaculate heart of Mary I offer You all my prayers, works, joys, and sufferings of this day for all the intentions of Your Sacred Heart, in union with the holy sacrifice of the Mass throughout the world, in reparation for my sins, for the intentions of all our associates, and in particular for the intentions of the Holy Father."

MORNING PRAYER. The second hour of the Divine Office, also called Lauds. It consists mainly of a hymn, three psalms, the *Benedictus* of Zechariah, and prayers.

MOROSE PLEASURE. Deliberate complacency in a sinful object, presented by the imagination but unaccompanied by a desire for the object. Also called morose delectation (*morosa delectatio*).

MORTAL SIN. An actual sin that destroys sanctifying grace and causes the supernatural death of the soul. Mortal sin is a turning away from God because of a seriously inordinate adherence to creatures that causes grave injury to a person's rational nature and to the social order, and deprives the sinner of a right to heaven.

The terms mortal, deadly, grave, and serious applied to sin are synonyms, each with a slightly different implication. *Mortal* and *deadly* focus on the effects in the sinner, namely deprivation of the state of friendship with God; *grave* and *serious* refer to the importance of the matter in which a person offends God. But the Church never distinguishes among these terms as though they represented different kinds of sins. There is only one recognized correlative to mortal sin, and that is venial sin, which offends against God but does not cause the loss of one's state of grace. (Etym. Latin *mors*, death.)

MORTIFICATION. The practice of Christian asceticism in order to overcome sin and master one's sinful tendencies, and through penance and austerity to strengthen the will in the practice of virtue and grow in the likeness of Christ. Natural mortification is a normal part of self-discipline; supernatural mortification, based on faith, seeks to grow in holiness through merit gained by co-operating with the grace of God. (Etym. Latin *mortificatio*, a killing, a putting to death.)

MORTMAIN. The policy of claiming that land and property could be possessed in perpetuity even after the death of the owner, correctly termed a "dead man's clutch." It was invoked in order to dispute the title of charitable and religious trusts usually to misappropriate them, especially those invested by the Catholic Church. The policy was employed in England on the excuse that it discouraged property use for superstitious purposes.

MORTUARIUM. A term with several meanings, all somehow referring to the dead. It is a portion, once received by bishops, from the estate of deceased priests; or a bequest made to churches; or the fee for funerals not performed in one's own parish; or a chapel or hall for the dead, hence a morgue.

MOSAIC LAW. The body of civil, moral, and religious legislation found in the last four books of the Pentateuch and traditionally ascribed to Moses. The foundation of this law is the Decalogue (Exodus 20), and its center is the Book of the Covenant (Exodus 20–23). The civil legislation is mainly in Exodus (18–23), and Deuteronomy (16–26). The moral laws are in Exodus (20–23), supplemented by Leviticus (11–20) and Deuteronomy (5). The religious and ceremonial precepts are in Exodus (25–30) and especially Leviticus (1–27). Compared with similar laws in other nations of that time, the Mosaic code is vastly superior by reason of its strong monotheism, its proclamation of God as the only source and final sanction of all laws, and from its summation of the whole law in the love of God and of neighbor.

MOSES. The greatest figure in the Old Testament, the founder of Israel, lawgiver, leader, and proponent of monotheism. Of the tribe of Levi, he was born in Egypt during a persecution when all the Hebrew male children were to be killed. Exposed on the Nile, he was rescued by Pharaoh's daughter and educated at court. God appeared to him in a burning bush and told him to deliver his people with the help of Aaron. The plagues did not make Pharaoh relent, until the death of every firstborn forced him to yield. Moses then led the Israelites through the years' long exodus, but he is excluded from the Promised Land because of his lack of confidence at the "Waters of Contradiction." The prophet died on Mount Nebo after pronouncing the three memorable discourses preserved in Deuteronomy. He was buried in the valley of Moab, but no one knows where.

MOTET. A polyphonic musical composition, probably of secular origin but based on a sacred text. It came into liturgical use in the thirteenth century. In its classical form it is based on the Gregorian tones of the Mass, to which it belongs. For some time instrumental accompaniments were used. But Pope St. Pius X in a *motu proprio* encouraged a return to older traditions. Allegri, Bach, Handel, and Mozart have composed some of the best specimens of the motet.

MOTHER CHURCH. A term of affectionate respect found in ecclesiastical documents and especially in the writings of the saints. Thus, the first Norm of Catholic Orthodoxy in the *Spiritual Exercises* of St. Ignatius reads: "We must put aside all judgment of our own, and keep the mind ever ready and prompt to obey in all things the true Spouse of Christ, our Lord, our holy Mother, the hierarchical Church."

MOTHERHOUSE. The autonomous monastic institution that retains jurisdiction over monasteries (daughter houses) that derive from it. Also the generalate of an institute of religious women.

MOTHERING SUNDAY. The fourth Sunday of Lent, also Laetare Sunday. The name refers to the custom in some parts of England of visiting one's living mother on that day; also the practice of visiting the cathedral or mother church of the diocese.

MOTHER OF GOD. Title of the Blessed Virgin Mary as the physical parent of Jesus, who is God. Although first defined against Nestorius at the Council of Ephesus (431), the concept goes back to subapostolic times. The basis in Scripture is the twofold theme of the Gospels, that Jesus was true God and that Mary was truly the mother of Jesus. St. Ignatius of Antioch (d. 107) wrote to the Ephesians: "Our God Jesus Christ was carried in Mary's womb, according to God's plan of salvation." The title *Theotokos* (Mother of God) became current after the third century. It was used by Origen (c. 185–c. 254), and St. Gregory Nazianzen, writing about 382, said: "If anyone does not recognize the holy Mary as Mother of God he is separated from the Divinity."

The Nestorian objection that Mary could not be the Mother of God, because she gave birth to the human nature only, was met by Christian apologists who pointed out that not the nature as such but the person was conceived and born. Since Mary conceived him who was the second person incarnate, she is truly the Mother of God.

Consequent on her divine maternity, Mary transcends in dignity all created persons and stands next to her divine Son in holiness. Ancient writers stressed the relation between Mary's divine maternity and her fullness of grace, which they found asserted in the angelic greeting "Hail, full of grace" (*kecharitoméne*). Her vocation to become the Mother of God, they reasoned, demanded a special richness of divine friendship.

MOTHER OF GOOD COUNSEL SCAPULAR. A white scapular, with one part bearing a picture of the Mother of Good Counsel, and the other, the papal crown and keys. Promoted by the Augustinians, it was approved by Pope Leo XIII.

MOTHER OF THE CHURCH. A title of the Blessed Virgin, formally recognized by the Second Vatican Council (*Lumen Gentium,* 60–65) and solemnly proclaimed by Pope Paul VI at the closing address of the third session of the Council on November 21, 1964. Mary is Mother of the Church by a fivefold title: 1. she gave human life to the Son of God, from whom the whole People of God receive the grace and dignity of election; 2. Christ on the Cross explicitly extended his Mother's maternity, through the disciple John, to all the faithful; 3. the Holy Spirit came upon her, together with the Apostles, when on Pentecost Sunday the Church was born in visible form; 4. since then all generations of Christ's followers, such as John, spiritually took Mary as their Mother; 5. she continues to exercise her maternal care for the Church by her presence and powerful intercession in heaven before the throne of God.

Pope John Paul II further identified Mary's motherhood of the Church with her Immaculate Heart. "This heart," he said, "the heart of both a virgin and a mother, has always followed the work of her Son and has gone out to all those whom Christ has embraced and continues to embrace with inexhaustible love" (*Redemptor Hominis,* 22).

MOTION. In Thomistic philosophy any passage from potency to act. Therefore any change and any acquisition of perfection are motion. Every creature is by its essence subject to motion because it is finite. Only God is the immovable Mover because, while he changes all things, he remains unchanged.

MOTIVATED ERROR. A factual mistake or accident that betrays certain underlying motives or desires.

MOTIVATIONAL HIERARCHY. The theory that all human beings have an implicit hierarchy of motives in all their conscious actions. The hierarchy, it is said, ranges in ascending order as follows: physiological needs, personal security, social relations, prestige, power possession, self-actualization, and the need for knowledge, aesthetic and religious needs. Somewhat different sequences are proposed by various writers, but they agree that, unless people are morally perverse, they recognize the priority of the spiritual over the bodily and of the religious over what concerns only space and time.

MOTIVE. A conscious good that incites a rational being to perform some action. It is a motive of assent when the intellect is moved to make a judgment, and the motive of consent when the will is moved to make a decision.

MOTIVES OF CREDIBILITY. The rational grounds for accepting divine revelation in general, or of the divine establishment of the Catholic Church in particular. These grounds are also called the preambles of faith. They include the evidence from reason that God exists; that what he reveals is believable because he is all-wise and true; and that he did actually make a revelation because he performed and continues to perform verifiable miracles testifying to his having spoken.

MOTTO. A short phrase, word, or sentence that expresses a principle, goal, or ideal of some person, cause, or institution. In this sense mottoes are an integral part of Catholic history and still serve to identify and motivate the faithful, especially in their corporate enterprises. Thus "God wills it" was the motto of the Crusaders, "Pray and labor" of St. Benedict, "For the greater glory of God" of St. Ignatius, and "To restore all things in Christ" the motto of Pope Pius X.

MOTU PROPRIO. Words used in rescripts drawn up and issued by a pope on his own initiative, and not conditioned by any petitionary requests. The documents are always signed personally by a pope. See PROPRIO MOTU.

MOUNT CARMEL SCAPULAR. Badge of the Confraternity of Our Lady of Mount Carmel. It is brown in color and often ornamented with pictures, which are not essential. It originated with St. Simon Stock (1165–1265), English general of the Carmelites. The present formula for investiture was approved by Pope Leo XIII.

MOVABLE ALTAR. See PORTABLE ALTAR.

MOVABLE FEASTS. Those feasts whose dates are variable because of their dependence on the Easter date. Easter may come as early as March 22 and as late as April 25. Lent is shifted back and forth depending on the Easter date, so are Ascension Day, Pentecost, Trinity Sunday, and Corpus Christi. Other feasts are movable because they are placed in relation to certain Sundays.

MOZARABIC RITE. Also known as the Rite of Toledo. A ritual used in Spain and the territory now known as Portugal from the sixth through the eleventh centuries. It is almost identical with the Gallican Rite and is still used in the chapel services of the cathedral at Toledo by the chaplains of the college during Mass and Divine Office, and in the marriage ritual in Spanish America. At one time it was called the Gothic or Isidorian Rite because St. Isidore of Seville (560–636) revised it. The Celtic Rite, early used in the British Isles, was related to the Mozarabic.

MOZZETTA. A nonliturgical cape made of silk or wool reaching to the elbows and closed with buttons in front. At the neck there is a small hood attached. It can be worn by the Pope and as a special privilege, by cardinals, bishops, and certain abbots. It signifies jurisdiction and is worn over the rochets. Its color is red, white, purple or black depending on the wearer's status. A similar cape is worn by members of some religious orders, e.g., Dominicans and Franciscans, as part of their monastic habit. (Etym. Italian *mozzetta*, a short cape with a small hood.)

MPROP. *Missa pro populo*, Mass (said) for the people.

M.R. *Missionarius rector*—missionary rector.

MSGR. Monsignor.

MUNIFICENCE. The virtue of liberality when it involves large donations for public welfare or charitable institutions.

MURATORIAN CANON. Part of a fragmentary Roman document named after its discoverer Ludovico Muratori (1672–1760). It is the oldest known list of the canonical books of the New Testament, dating from the second century.

MURDER. The unjust killing of an innocent person. Directly to intend killing an innocent person is forbidden either to a private citizen or to the State, and this even in order to secure the common good. God has supreme and exclusive ownership over human lives, and so he is the only one who has the right to allow the taking of a human life. He confers on civil authority the right to take the life of a condemned criminal only when this is necessary for achieving the just purposes of the State. In a commentary passage on the Decalogue, divine revelation commands: "See that the man who is innocent and just is not done to death, and do not acquit the guilty" (Exodus 23:7).

MUSICAM SACRAM. Instruction on music in the liturgy of the Sacred Congregation of Rites. An extensive document giving general norms and applying them to every important aspect of liturgical music. Among other provisions there should be choirs, at least one or two properly trained singers especially in churches that cannot have even a small choir. The distinction between solemn, sung, and read Mass is retained; Gregorian chant should be given pride of place; adapting sacred music for regions having a musical tradition of their own requires "a very specialized preparation by experts"; and those instruments which are by common opinion "suitable for secular music only, are to be altogether prohibited from every liturgical celebration and from popular devotions" (March 5, 1967).

MUTILATION. An action which deprives oneself or another of a bodily organ or its use. The mutilation may be either direct or indirect. Direct mutilation is a deliberately intended act that of its very nature can cause mutilation. If the effect is not directly intended, it is called indirect mutilation.

Mutilation belongs to the category of murder. The difference is that mutilation is partial destruction, whereas murder is the total destruction of a person's physical life. Moral law is concerned with mutilation because no one has absolute dominion over the body, and the violation of this principle is an offense against God's sovereignty.

Nevertheless, a person has the right to sacrifice one or more members of the body for the well-being of the whole body. Thus it is permitted to amputate any organ of the body in order to save one's life. However, lesser reasons than danger of death also justify mutilation.

The removal or suppressing the function of any organ of reproduction is in a moral category of its own. It is never permitted when the purpose is directly to prevent conception or pregnancy. (Etym. Latin *mutilare,* to cut off, maim.)

MYRRH. Gum resin used as an ingredient in incense and oil of the sick. In ancient times it was used as a perfume, and often in embalming. Presented by one of the Magi to the Infant Jesus, it was an offering that Christian tradition has understood as a symbol of suffering.

MYSTERY. A divinely revealed truth whose very possibility cannot be rationally conceived before it is revealed and, after revelation, whose inner essence cannot be fully understood by the finite mind. The incomprehensibility of revealed mysteries derives from the fact that they are manifestations of God, who is infinite and therefore beyond the complete grasp of a created intellect. Nevertheless, though incomprehensible, mysteries are intelligible. One of the primary duties of a believer is, through prayer, study, and experience, to grow in faith, i.e., to develop an understanding of what God has revealed. (Etym. Greek *mystērion,* something closed, a secret.)

MYSTERY OF FAITH (liturgy). Title of the Holy Eucharist occurring in the Canon of the Mass. Formerly *mysterium fidei* was part of the words of Consecration. It is now spoken out loud by the priest, after the Consecration, referring not to the response by the people that follows but to the mystery of transubstantiation just enacted on the altar.

MYSTERIES OF THE ROSARY. See GLORIOUS MYSTERIES, JOYFUL MYSTERIES, SORROWFUL MYSTERIES.

MYSTERY OF THE HOLY SPIRIT. The sacrament of confirmation, especially in Eastern Christianity. It is called a mystery because it confers invisible grace through visible anointing. And it is the distinctive sacrament of the Holy Spirit as power according to the promise of Christ to his followers before Pentecost, that they would receive power to be his witnesses, i.e., martyrs, even to the ends of the earth.

MYSTERY PLAY. A religious drama during the Middle Ages, portraying some mystery of the Christian religion. These plays developed from the dramatic parts of the liturgy and joined to ideas drawn from the Bible and other sources. Biblical dramas featured the Passion of Christ, the Last Supper, the Parable of the Wise and Foolish Virgins, and the End of the World. Saints were featured in these plays, notably martyrs such as

St. Catherine and St. George. After the Reformation, mystery dramas practically disappeared, but they have since been restored in many places, notably in the Passion Play at Oberammergau, Bavaria.

MYSTERY THEOLOGY. A form of liturgical theology advocated by the Benedictine abbot Odo Casel in the early twentieth century. Its theological premise is that the Mass is a re-presentation of all the mysteries of Christ's life and not only the sacrificial death on the Cross. Its ritual stress is on such involvements of the faithful that they consider themselves real contributors to the liturgical action in which they take part.

MYSTICAL BODY. The Catholic Church established by Christ as an extension and continuation of the Incarnation.

In the words of Pius XII, "If we would define and describe the true Church of Jesus Christ—which is the one, holy, Catholic, apostolic Roman Church—we shall find nothing more noble, more sublime, or more divine than the expression 'the Mystical Body of Jesus Christ'—an expression that flows spontaneously from the repeated teaching of the sacred Scriptures and the holy Fathers."

The term "body," when referring to the Church, derives its meaning from the analogy used by St. Paul, where he speaks of Christians: "You are the Body of Christ, member for member" (I Corinthians 12:27), and of Christ: "the Head of His Body, the Church" (Colossians 1:18).

Corollary to being a body, the Church must have a multiplicity of discernible members because the possession of parts is an essential feature of anything bodily. And just as a natural body is formed of different organs with different functions arranged in due order, so the Church is bound together by the combination of structurally united parts, and has a variety of members that are reciprocally dependent. Another name for this interdependence is the hierarchy, with its graded levels of orders and jurisdiction, of superiors and subjects, beginning with the Sovereign Pontiff and terminating in the laity.

The body (*soma*) that St. Paul identifies with the Church is a living reality, and like every organism requires suitable means to enter into life, to grow and mature and prosper according to its nature. Similarly in the Catholic Church, the sacraments are available for every spiritual need and circumstance of human life.

Moreover, the Roman Catholic Church regards herself as the Body of Christ. He was the originator of the Church by his preaching and choice of the Apostles to carry on his work, by his death on the Cross when he merited the graces to be channeled through the Mystical Body, and by the descent of the Holy Spirit, whom he sent on Pentecost. He continues to rule the Church from within by supernatural means that are permanent and constantly active within the members.

The Church is called Mystical because she is a mystery, which God revealed to be true but whose inner essence must be accepted on faith and without full comprehension by the mind. Otherwise than in other societies, the end or purpose of the Church is not temporal or earthly but heavenly and eternal; its spiritual bond is the will of God; incorporation in the Church effects a profound internal change in the members; and the whole reality is called supernatural because it leads to the destiny of seeing God in the beatific vision after death. But the Roman Catholic Church is mainly said to be the *Mystical* Body of Christ because it is sacramental. The Church is the great sacrament of the New Law, instituted by Christ for the communication of invisible grace to the whole world.

MYSTICAL INTERPRETATION. The explanation of some biblical person, object, or occurrence in the past as having a divinely intended meaning or function in the future. Thus Adam prefigured Christ, the Passover anticipated the Cross and the Eucharist, and the destruction of Jerusalem in the first century of the Christian era symbolized the end of the world. To be valid, the basis for the interpretation must be found in Scripture or sacred tradition.

MYSTICAL ROSE. A traditional title given to Mary, and an invocation in the Litany of Loreto. As the rose is considered the queen of flowers, so Mary is invoked as Queen of All Saints. As described by sacred writers, she is the "mystical rose without thorn," the "rose of paradise," and the "rose bringing salvation to all who call upon her."

MYSTICAL THEOLOGY. The science of the spiritual life, with stress on the operation of divine grace. It deals with the higher forms of mental prayer and with such extraordinary phenomena as are recorded in the lives of the saints. It is the science of the study of mystic states. It is commonly distinguished from ascetical theology, which emphasizes free co-operation with and predisposition for divine grace.

MYSTICAL UNION. The union of a soul with God in deep contemplation. It is characterized by a deep awareness of the divine presence, and has a variety of grades, not necessarily successive, but distinguished by spiritual writers. They are: the two nights of the soul (senses and spirit) before mystical union, the prayer of quiet, the full union, ecstasy, and spiritual marriage or transforming union.

MYSTICI CORPORIS CHRISTI. Encyclical of Pope Pius XII, published in 1943, on the Church as the Mystical Body of Christ. The Church is a body because she is a visible, living, and growing organism, animated by the Spirit of God. She is a mystical body because her essential nature is a mystery, and all her teachings, laws, and rites are sacramental sources of grace. And she is the mystical body of Christ because he founded the Church. He remains her invisible Head and through him all blessings are communicated to her members, and through them to the rest of humankind.

MYSTICISM. The supernatural state of soul in which God is known in a way that no human effort or exertion could ever succeed in producing. There is an immediate, personal experience of God that is truly extraordinary, not only in intensity and degree, but in kind. It is always the result of a special, totally unmerited grace of God. Christian mysticism differs essentially from the non-Christian mysticism of the Oriental world. It always recognizes that the reality to which it penetrates simply transcends the soul and the cosmos; there is no confusion between I and thou, but always a profound humility before the infinite Majesty of God. And in Christian mysticism all union between the soul and God is a moral union of love, in doing his will even at great sacrifice to self; there is no hint of losing one's being in God or absorption of one's personality into the divine.

MYTH. In general, a traditional story focusing on some religious explanation of a phenomenon of nature. A parable or allegory to illustrate some truth or to prove a theory. In recent usage, a myth has come to mean a popular contemporary hope or ambition, or a social ideal. It may be described as an idea that has become a movement.

N

NAAMAN. A Syrian army commander who was afflicted with leprosy. An Israelite servant in his household spoke warmly of the cures effected by a prophet in Samaria. Hopefully Naaman traveled to Israel and sought the help of Elisha, the prophet. But when Elisha instructed him to bathe seven times in the Jordan River, Naaman was angry. The Jordan was so muddy he considered it undignified and repulsive. Nevertheless, his companions prevailed on him to obey Elisha, and after his seventh visit to the Jordan, he emerged with skin as clean "as the flesh of a little child" (II Kings 5:1–14). He returned gratefully to Elisha and said, "There is no God on all the earth except in Israel" (II Kings 5:14–15). He wanted to give the prophet a gift, but Elisha would not take it (II Kings 5:16).

NAGASAKI. Marian sanctuary at Oura, near Nagasaki, Japan. In 1865 when a French priest built a small chapel on a hill at Oura, a group of women came from nearby Urakami to tell him that they had "the same heart" that he had, which meant that they had kept the faith for two centuries without benefit of clergy. The tiny reopened church at Urakami was completely destroyed by the 1945 atom bomb, but the nearby church dedicated to Mary at Oura remained intact. It was the site hallowed by the crucifixion of twenty-six Christians in the seventeenth century. It was also the place where Catholics had preserved their faith without the sacraments, relying solely on prayer to Mary for guidance.

NAHUM. A book of the Old Testament written about 660 B.C. by an author who calls himself Elkosh, or the Elcesite. The prophet was probably a Judaean. Israel had already been destroyed, Judah humbled, and King Mannasseh probably a prisoner in Assyria (II Chronicles 33). To console the Chosen People, Nahum foretells the fall of Nineveh, hence the open line, "Oracle on Nineveh, Book of the Vision of Elkosh."

NAILS, HOLY. The nails with which Christ was fastened to the Cross, and believed to have been found by St. Helena (255–330). Many claims have been made about these relics. Some parts of these nails are said to be in different places in Europe, but at best they may be only filings of the original relics. St. Ambrose (340–97) indicated that one nail was made into a crown for Constantine (c. 274–337), which might well be preserved as the Iron Crown of Lombardy at Monza. Others are supposed to be at Santa Croce in Rome. A feast honoring the Holy Nails has been kept in certain dioceses on the second Friday in Lent.

NAME. In biblical usage, not only the title by which a person is called but the term by which the person is identified. The expressions: to profane (Amos 2:7), sanctify (Isaiah 29:23), praise (Isaiah 25:1), and love (Psalm 5:12), the name of Yahweh, all refer to God himself. In the New Testament this concept is further deepened and refined. The name of Jesus identifies his mission (Matthew 1:21), which is to redeem (Acts 10:43), to save (Acts 4:12), to confer the fullness of supernatural life (Colossians 3:17). Prayer in the name of Jesus, according to his intentions, is always heard (John 15:16), those who invoke his name will be saved (Romans 10:13), those who believe in his name form the Church (I Corinthians 1:2), so that they can be called Christians (Acts 11:26). They are consequently to pray that the name of God, who became man in the person of Christ, be sanctified (Matthew 6:9), which means honored and glorified.

NAMES, CHRISTIAN. Names given to individuals at their baptism. The custom of giving the name of a saint when a person is baptized goes back to the earliest days of the Church. It is required by ecclesiastical law and means that the saint whose name is chosen becomes a special patron to protect and guide and be the heavenly intercessor for the one who bears his or her name.

NAMES OF CHRIST. Names given to Christ in Holy Scripture and in the liturgy of the Church. Twenty-six distinct Messianic titles occur in the Old Testament, and about sixty-five in the New Testament. While teaching, he referred to himself as the Bread of Life, the Door, the Vine, Lord, Master, Son, Way, Truth, Son of Man, Good Shepherd, Light of the World, the Resurrection and the Life. These names serve to bring out specific attributes of Christ as God or qualities of the Savior as Man. Taken together, they identify all the principal mysteries in Christology and Soteriology.

N.A.N. *Nisi aliter notetur*—unless otherwise noted.

NAOMI. A Judaean woman who moved to the country of Moab with her husband and two sons. But tragedy struck the family and Naomi's husband and sons died. She returned to Judaea and Ruth, wife of one of Naomi's sons, came with her (Ruth 1). She sought a job in the fields gleaning corn, hoping that she would find another husband (Ruth 2). Now Boaz, the landowner for whom Ruth worked, was a kinsman of Naomi, and that resourceful woman worked out a plan to get Boaz interested in Ruth (Ruth 3). In due course they married and Naomi was nurse to their child (Ruth 4). Jesse and David were both members of the family line descending from Boaz and Ruth (Ruth 4:21).

NARCISSISM. See SELF-LOVE.

NARROW INTERPRETATION. See INTERPRETATION.

NATHAN. A prophet sent by Yahweh to rebuke David for his shameful conduct in deliberately planning Uriah's death in battle so that he could marry Bath-Sheba, Uriah's wife. His plan succeeded; after a period of mourning, Bath-Sheba married David and bore him a son. But Nathan prophesied that the child would die within a week. The child died despite David's sorrow and penance. Later, however, another child was born, destined to be the great King Solomon. Nathan gave this child the name Jedidiah, which meant "beloved of Yahweh," assurance that David would be punished no further (II Samuel 12:7–25). Years later Nathan played an important role in Israelite history. David, now an old man, wanted Solomon to succeed him as king. But a half-brother of Solomon, named Adonijah, attempted a coup to seize the kingship. It was Nathan who carried word of the conspiracy to David, who authorized Nathan to escort Solomon to Gihon, anoint him, and proclaim him king to succeed David immediately. This strategy worked out perfectly and Adonijah's plot was frustrated (I Kings 1). This happened before David died (I Kings 2:10). Nathan evidently lived to an old age, for he is credited with compiling a History of Nathan, in which he recorded the history of Solomon "from first to last." This suggests that he outlived Solomon as well as David (II Chronicles 9:29).

NATHANAEL. Another name for Bartholomew. Each time the Apostles are listed in the Gospels, Philip and Bartholomew are grouped together. It was Philip who brought Nathanael to see Jesus for the first time. Despite an initial skepticism, he was instantly impressed by Jesus' superhuman knowledge and became a follower (John 1:45–51). The only other reference to Nathanael was on the occasion of Jesus' appearance after his resurrection on the shore of the Sea of Tiberias, now known as the Lake of Tiberias, when a group of the Apostles, led by Peter and including Nathanael, went fishing (John 21:1–3). See BARTHOLOMEW.

NATION. A body of persons within a particular territory having their own distinctive government. Originally a nation implied ethnic unity and a certain cultural or even religious identity. But many nations are now more properly states than nations. They are politically autonomous while having a variety of racial, cultural, and religious groups under the same civil authority.

NATIONAL CONFERENCES OF BISHOPS. See EPISCOPAL CONFERENCE.

NATIONAL SYNOD. Formerly called plenary council, a deliberative meeting of the bishops of a whole country to discuss and decide on ecclesiastical matters pertaining to the Church under their jurisdiction. Their decisions become law and apply to the entire nation, even though all bishops may not have been in attendance. Since the Second Vatican Council national synods have been replaced by meetings of the national or regional episcopal conferences.

NATIV. D.N.J.C. *Nativitas Domini Nostri Jesu Christi*—Nativity of Our Lord Jesus Christ.

NATIVITY. See CHRISTMAS and CRÈCHE.

NATURAL CONTEMPLATION. In general, to look admiringly at an object with absorbing interest and affection. The term is also used to describe a religious experience of deep intensity among persons who are not Christians or may not even believe in a transcendent and personal God.

NATURAL END. A good that fulfills the natural needs of a being and that can be achieved by the proper operations of its native powers.

NATURAL FAMILY PLANNING. The controlling of human conception by restricting the marital act to the infertile periods of the wife. This practice is based on the theory that the period of a woman's ovulation can be determined with considerable accuracy. A variety of methods, or their combination, is used to determine the period of ovulation. From the moral standpoint, natural family planning is permissible. As stated by Pope Paul VI: "If there are serious motives to space out births, which derive from physical or psychological conditions of husband or wife, or from external conditions, it is licit to take account of the natural rhythms inherent in the generative functions" (*Humanae Vitae*, II, 16). See also NATURAL FAMILY PLANNING (PRACTICE).

NATURAL FAMILY PLANNING (practice). A method of determining the fertile and infertile days of a woman. There are three methods currently in use and all rely on the observation and recording of one or more signs of the body: 1. the sympto-thermal method. This is the most comprehensive and surest of the three. It involves the observation and recording of all three signs: a. mucus secreted in the cervical opening: the average menstrual period lasts from three to seven days. Toward the end of this period mucus begins to appear at the opening of the cervix. At first it is tacky and yellowish. After a couple of days it becomes stretchy and turns into a whitish color, like that of an egg white. It reaches this peak quality one to two days prior to ovulation. This indicates the time of greatest fertility; b. body temperature: this is recorded with the use of a basal thermometer, which measures body temperature in tenths of degrees. Twenty-four hours after ovulation, the body temperature will rise approximately .4–.6 degree. About the fourth day after the temperature rise it is safe to assume that the infertile days have begun, provided that the other signs concur; c. cervical opening: before ovulation, the cervix is open, soft, and high. After ovulation, the cervix is closed, firm, and lengthens. The concurrence of all three signs indicates the days on which a woman is ovulating. From this can be charted her fertile and infertile days. Differences in individual cycles must be taken into consideration; 2. the Billings, or ovulation, method relies solely on the recording of the mucus symptom; 3. the third method relies solely on the temperature symptom. The sympto-thermal method is more than 99 per cent effective for those who are willing to work with it. The Billings method is also reliable but requires a qualified instructor and somewhat more time and instruction.

NATURAL INTERNATIONAL LAW. Those fundamental elements in the law of nations that arise from the very nature of the state and are merely reaffirmations of the natural law or simple deductions from the natural law. Such would be the right of a nation to defend itself when unjustly attacked, or its duty to fulfill just contracts freely made.

NATURALISM. The view that the only reality that exists is nature, so that divine grace is either denied or ignored. There are two main forms. Philosophical naturalism claims that human beings were never elevated to a supernatural destiny; they will reach their final destiny by the sole use of their natural, individual, and social powers. Practical naturalism is human conduct that, by excluding prayer and the use of supernatural channels of grace, in effect says that the purpose of human existence is purely natural.

NATURAL KNOWLEDGE OF GOD. Man's capacity for knowing God by reason and apart from revelation. According to the First Vatican Council, "the one true God, our Creator and Lord, can be known with certainty by the light of human reason, from things that are made" (Denzinger 3004). Consequently human beings have the ability to know the one, true personal God who made the universe. The subjective means of obtaining this knowledge is human reason in the condition of fallen nature. The source of this knowledge is the world, bodily and spiritual, of created things. This knowledge can be certain and not merely probable.

The Bible, in the Old and New Testaments, also teaches that the existence of a personal God can be known from reflection on nature. Thus the Israelites were told, "Through the grandeur and beauty of the creatures, we may, by analogy, contemplate their Author" (Wisdom 13:5), and according to St. Paul, "ever since God created the world, His everlasting power and deity—however invisible—have been there for the mind to see in the things He has made" (Romans 1:20).

NATURAL LAW. As distinct from revealed law, it is "nothing else than the rational creature's participation in the eternal law" (*Summa Theologica*, 1a, 2ae, quest. 91, art. 2). As coming from God, the natural law is what God has produced in the world of creation; as coming to human beings, it is what they know (or can know) of what God has created.

It is therefore called natural law because everyone is subject to it from birth (*natio*), because it contains only those duties which are derivable from human nature itself, and because, absolutely speaking, its essentials can be grasped by the unaided light of human reason.

St. Paul recognizes the existence of a natural law when he describes the moral responsibility of those ancients who did not have the benefit of Mosaic revelation. "Pagans," he says, "who never heard of the Law but are led by reason to do what the Law commands, may not actually 'possess' the Law, but they can be said to 'be' the Law. They can point to the substance of the Law engraved on their hearts—they can call a witness, that is, their own conscience—they have accusation and defense, that is, their own inner mental dialogue" (Romans 2:14–15).

NATURAL ORDER. The built-in arrangement that belongs to things inherently, and that develops them according to the very natures they possess. Contrasted with an artificial or superimposed order. On a universal level, the sum total of all natures, their powers and activities, related to the final end or purpose they have as natural beings. Contrasted with supernatural order.

NATURAL PRECEPTS. The prescriptions of the natural law. While the object of natural law is the whole moral order as knowable by human reason, three different levels are regularly distinguished according to the ease with which the obligations of the law can be recognized. Primary precepts are most easily perceived, as for example that good must be done and evil must be avoided. Secondary precepts are also available to most people, such as the prescriptions of the Decalogue. More refined conclusions from the primary and secondary precepts are also attainable by reason but with varying degrees of difficulty, such as the evil of contraception or the fact that direct abortion is always forbidden.

NATURAL RELIGION. A composite of all those duties to God which human reason can discover by its own power and apart from supernatural revelation. Three principal truths and corresponding duties constitute natural religion: 1. God exists and is a Being of infinite excellence and worth; human beings therefore owe him special reverence; 2. God is the First Cause, as the author and provider of all that anyone is and does, everyone therefore owes him special service; 3. God is the Final Destiny and Highest Good in whom alone the human heart can find happiness; he therefore deserves special love.

NATURAL RIGHT. Human right coming from the Author of nature and directly based on the natural law. It is absolutely unchangeable and is the foundation of all positive rights. All civil laws, therefore, are only as valid as they are based on the natural rights of the citizen. Thus, e.g., the unborn child has a natural right to life that no political authority may take away.

NATURAL SECRET. A truth or fact that should be kept confidential because the obligation not to reveal arises either from the natural law or from the very nature of the case, and its disclosure would cause a grave injury to another. Revealing a serious and shameful secret sin would be the violation of a natural secret. Natural secrets bind under grave sin.

NATURAL SELECTION. The principal feature of Charles Darwin's theory of evolution. Rejecting the idea of a special creation or of supernatural influences, Darwin (1809–82) held that the variety of species among living things is explainable naturally. There is a process at work in the world whereby individual variations beneficial to an organism in a given environment naturally tend to become perpetuated in later generations. The strong (and fittest) not only survive by adapting to circumstances, but they mysteriously change species in the process of survival. Darwin's basis for natural selection has yet to be proved scientifically.

NATURAL SINS. A term used to describe those sins against chastity in which the natural purpose of the sexual act is or can be attained, but they are performed outside the legitimate bonds of matrimony. Implicit in such acts is the malice of committing a sin against some other virtue besides chastity. Thus adultery, rape, and abduction are crimes against justice; fornication sins against the justice due to the offspring, the community, and the unmarried partner; incest is opposed to familial piety; and sacrilege offends against the virtue of religion for a person vowed to celibacy.

NATURAL TEMPERANCE. The habitual moderation of one's desire for pleasure acquired by personal effort and guided by human reason, mainly in view of one's health or the good of society.

NATURAL THEOLOGY. The knowledge of God, his existence and attributes, derived from the world of nature and by the light of natural reason. Also called theodicy.

NATURAL VIRTUE. A good moral habit whose principles, object, and purpose are natural to the human person. This means any virtue whose existence is knowable by the light of natural reason and whose practice is possible (at least for a time) without the help of supernatural grace.

NATURE. The essence of a being considered as the principle of activity. Also the substance of a thing as distinguished from its properties, considered as the source of its operations. Nature is also definable in contrast to its opposites from a variety of viewpoints. In contrast with God, it is the created universe. In contrast with human activity, it is the world considered prior to or independent of the changes produced by human free will. In contrast to the life and operations of divine grace, it is that to which a human person has claim, as creature, as distinct from a share in God's own life, which is the supernatural. (Etym. Latin *natura*, the inner principle of a thing's operations and activity; from *nasci*, to be born.)

NATURE AND GRACE. The two ultimates of human existence viewed in their mutual relationship. Nature is what human beings are and have when they are born (*nati*). Grace is what they further need by divine favor (*gratia*) to reach their eternal destiny.

NATURISM. As a theory of religion, it may be: 1. ethnographic naturism, claiming that there is one animating principle in all things; 2. philosophic naturism, holding that God is the soul of the universe; or 3. scientific naturism, saying that God and nature are really the same, so that nature no less than God should be venerated as divine.

NAVE. The central open space in a church, often separated from the sanctuary or choir by a screen and from the side aisles by pillars or columns. Colloquially the nave refers to the part of the church reserved for worshipers, including the central and side aisles and crossing transepts.

NAZARENE. A New Testament title of Christ, from the place of his residence. In Matthew, John, and the Acts the spelling is Nazoraios, in Mark Nazarenos, while Luke has both forms. It is not clear to what prophecy Matthew was referring when he said that Christ should be called a Nazarene (Matthew 2:23). It may have been an oral tradition or a play on one of the two words, both applicable to the Savior, namely *nazoraios* (holy to God) or *neser* (shoot— from the stock of Jesse). (Etym. Greek *nazareth;* Hebrew *nasret.*)

NAZARENES. A Jewish and Islamic term for Christians as the followers of Jesus of Nazareth.

N.D. *Nostra Domina, Notre Dame*—Our Lady.

NEBUCHADNEZZAR. Ruler of the Babylonian Empire from 605 to 562 B.C., an autocratic but competent king who developed Babylon into one of the great cities of the world. His army besieged Judah, killed King Jehoiakim, and deported ten thousand of the finest Judaeans, including Jehoiachin, the king's son (II Kings 24:10–16). The most intelligent of these deportees were restrained for service in Nebuchadnezzar's court. Among these was Daniel, who rose rapidly in the king's estimation because of his skill in interpreting dreams (Daniel 1:1–7). In Judah, Zedekiah was installed as a puppet king, but after a few years he revolted and once again Nebuchadnezzar's forces sacked Jerusalem. Zedekiah was killed and another vast deportation took place. Finally, in the year 582 B.C., the unrest continued and a third and final invasion reduced Judah to a wilderness. "Where a thousand vines used to be," mourned Isaiah, "worth one thousand pieces of silver, all will be briar and thorn" (Isaiah 7:23). During this long period of turmoil the prophet Jeremiah incurred bitter resentment among his people because he repeatedly prophesied Nebuchadnezzar's victories and warned the people that they deserved their impending fate because of their unfaithfulness to Yahweh (Jeremiah 26: 12–15). Accordingly, Jeremiah himself was treated by the victorious Babylonians with great respect and was given his freedom (Jeremiah 39, 40).

NEBI'IM. The prophets or prophetical books of the Old Testament, as distinct from the Torah, or Law (Pentateuch), and the Ketubim, or hagiography. The Nebi'im are commonly divided into the early prophets (from Joshua to II Kings) and the later prophets, Isaiah, Jeremiah, and Ezekiel, and the twelve Minor Prophets.

NECESSARY. Whatever must be or cannot not be and should be. Various kinds of necessity are the basis for all others. Something may be necessary because it cannot not exist; its essence is to exist. It is in this sense that God is necessary Being. This is a necessity of being. Or something may be necessary in order to verify something else, as a rational soul is necessary to human nature, or four equal sides are necessary to have a square. This is a necessity of essence.

Or something may be necessary in order to attain a given purpose or achieve a given end, as it is necessary to eat in order to live. This is a necessity of means. Or something may be necessary because God wills it so and wants humanity to do it, as it is necessary to pray in order to be saved. This is a necessity of obligation or moral necessity. (Etym. Latin *necessitas, ne-*, not + *cedere,* to withdraw: that which cannot be other than it is, with respect to itself or with respect to another thing.)

NECESSARY CAUSE. An agent that acts according to compulsory tendencies of its nature, and not freely or from conscious intent. It is a naturally determined agent that cannot not act the way it does. See also CAUSE, EFFICIENT CAUSE, FINAL CAUSE, FIRST CAUSE, FORMAL CAUSE, FREE CAUSE, MATERIAL CAUSE, MORAL CAUSE, SECONDARY CAUSE.

NECESSARY FAITH. The irreducible minimum that everyone must believe as a condition for salvation. Also called the "necessity of means" to be saved, it applies to those who have reached the age of reason. It certainly includes belief that God exists and that he rewards the good and punishes the wicked: "It is impossible to please God without faith, since anyone who comes to Him must believe that He exists and rewards those who try to find Him" (Vulgate: "who seek Him") (Hebrews 11:6). Probably one must also know and believe, at least implicitly, in the Blessed Trinity and the Incarnation.

NECESSARY REVELATION. Supernatural communication of divine truth as necessary for the human race. There are two kinds of necessity corresponding to the two levels of human need, namely the absolute need of grace to reach the beatific vision and the relative need of help to overcome the limitations of fallen human nature. The human race would have needed revelation even if it had never sinned, once Christianity assumes that it has been elevated to a supernatural destiny. Otherwise how could anyone reach a destiny that is naturally impossible even to conceive? Moreover, humanity sinned. As a result the human mind is darkened, not completely but considerably. It therefore needs divine guidance, as revelation, to know what is not of itself beyond human discovery but what is difficult to attain clearly, certainly, and by everyone in the present state of the human race.

NECROLOGIES. Carefully annotated lists of those who have died in a place or up to a certain time. In many monasteries and religious orders names of deceased brethren are kept as reminders of those to be especially prayed for. Some dioceses keep necrologies of their deceased priests. Medieval necrologies were often kept in book form and became an important source for the history of the Church. The Catholic Directories of many countries, including the United States, contain abbreviated necrologies of priests for a previous year or longer. (Etym. Greek *nekros,* corpse + *eulogia,* good speaking.)

NECROMANCY. The art of divining the future through alleged communication with the dead. It was mentioned in the Bible and found in every ancient nation. It was forbidden by Mosaic law in any form, whether as alchemy, magic, or witchcraft. It is also forbidden by the Church. One reason is that the practice lends itself to dependence on the evil spirits who can pretend to foretell the future, but only to deceive and mislead the practitioners. In modern times it is called spiritism or spiritualism. (Etym. Greek *nekros,* corpse + *manteia,* divination; Latin *necromantia.*)

NECROPHILIA. Morbid love of corpses or of anything related to the dead. It is to be distinguished from the healthy attitude of some saints to meditate on death in order to strengthen their hope in the life to come. (Etym. Greek *nekros,* corpse + *philos,* dear, friendly.)

NEGATIVE ATTRIBUTE. Divine perfection that is known as a denial of some imperfection or limitation in creatures, though it is actually most positive in God, as immutability or infinity.

NEGATIVE THEOLOGY. That approach to Christian thought which rises by way of negation to the infinite and nameless One who is beyond all finite comprehension. It is the favorite approach of those who favor a mystical experience of God in preference to a rational proof of his existence and understanding of his attributes. Meister Eckhart (1260–1327), a writer in mystical theology, is the best known extremist in negative theology, claiming, for example, that all creatures are an absolute nothing: "I do not say that they are a small thing or that they are nothing but that they are an absolute nothing" (Denzinger, 976). Eckhart was condemned by Pope John XXII in 1329. There is, however, a legitimate use of negative theology to sharpen a believer's sense of God's incomprehensibility. Negative theology is sometimes distinguished from positive theology, but the latter refers rather to a branch of dogmatic theology.

NEGLECT OF PRAYER. The sinful habit of seldom or never uniting oneself, in spirit and in words, with God.

NEGLIGENCE. The conscious omission of a duty, implying mental inertia rather than malice of will. Yet it becomes morally culpable at the moment a person is even dimly aware of what he or she is doing and of the evil results that may follow. Church law distinguishes slight, ordinary, or gross negligence, and imputability differs accordingly.

NEHEMIAH. A rich, well-educated Jew in Persia who learned of the wretched conditions prevailing in Jerusalem and of the defenseless condition of the city without walls and gates. He sought the help of King Artaxerxes and was permitted to return to his homeland (Nehemiah 1–6). He found on careful inspection that the sad reports he had received were true. So he pleaded with the assembled Judaeans, "Come let us rebuild the walls of Jerusalem and suffer this indignity no longer" (Nehemiah 2:17). The Jews in great numbers responded to his plea, and volunteers labored on the repair program day and night. Their enemies ridiculed their efforts but the tremendous campaign persevered. Nehemiah proved to be an excellent organizer. Within a few months Jerusalem was like a new city. Then he concentrated on the civil and religious state of the city, enforcing marriage reform, compliance with the Mosaic laws (Nehemiah 6), insisting on competent officials, and stressing Sabbath observance. The morale of the people rose to new heights, and neighboring countries marveled at the improvements. Thousands of Jews returned from exile with new hope and pride (Nehemiah 7, 11).

NEOLOGY. In theology the introduction of new doctrine, contrary to the Church's teaching but expressed in traditional terms or phrases. (Etym. Greek *neos,* new + *logos,* discourse.)

NEO-MODERNISM. The movement attempts to reconcile modern science and philosophy at the expense of the integrity of the Catholic faith. It has its roots in the Modernism condemned by Pope St. Pius X. Like its predecessor, it rejects belief in the supernatural and considers the Church only a human society. Among the main features of Neo-Modernism are the denial of original sin, the claim that Christ was only a human person, and that dogmas of faith are only verbal formulations whose meaning substantially changes with the times. In Neo-Modernism, the philosophies of Hegel and Heidegger replace that of St. Thomas Aquinas, and faith is reduced to a purely subjective experience, apart from an objective divine revelation and independent of the magisterium or teaching authority of the Church.

NEO-ORTHODOXY. A general term applied to various movements in Protestantism to restore the faith of the people in such basic Christian mysteries as the existence of a personal God, the Incarnation and Redemption, the necessity of prayer, and life after death.

NEOPHYTE. One who has entered on a new and better state of life. Thus a newly baptized convert from unbelief or a non-Christian religion today or to Christianity from Judaism in the early Church. The name is also given to a novice or postulant in a religious community or to a beginner in studying for the priesthood. (Etym. Greek *neos*, new + *phutos*, grown: *neophutos*, lit. newly planted.)

NEO-PLATONISM. The revival of Platonism, as the dominant philosophy of the Greco-Roman world, from the middle of the third century to the closing of the philosophical schools of Athens in 529. It was given its definitive form by Plotinus (204–70). The more ardent Neo-Platonists were hostile to Christianity, but Neo-Platonist influences gradually made themselves felt in Catholic theology. Besides Synesius (370–414) and Dionysius (c. 500), Sts. Anselm and Bonaventure and other Scholastic philosophers, of the thirteenth century, were influenced by Neo-Platonism.

NEO-SCHOLASTICISM. The name given by certain Scholastic philosophers to the revival of medieval Scholasticism since the beginning of the twentieth century. These Catholic thinkers wished to revive among the public and for the people's use the teachings of the great Scholastics of the past, bringing their theories up to date and putting them in touch with modern scientific research. They do not aim to revive unchanged systems of medieval Scholasticism but rather to harmonize modern science with the fundamental doctrines and principles of this school of thought especially as related to the physical world. The movement was begun in Italy and Germany even before 1879, when Pope Leo XIII's encyclical *Aeterni Patris* gave the movement a major

impetus by his approbation. Since then it has become developed, especially in Catholic circles.

NEPOTISM. Preferment in ecclesiastical practice based on blood or family relationship rather than merit. Applied especially to the conferral of Church offices. Historically nepotism plagued the Church for centuries, was practiced by some of the popes, many bishops, and was one of the factors that led to the legislation of celibacy in the Western Church and to the Protestant Reformation. The most important legislation against nepotism was the bull *Romanum decet Pontificem* in 1692, of Pope Innocent XII. (Etym. Latin *nepos*, nephew.)

NERO. The dissolute, corrupt Emperor of Rome who ruled from A.D. 54 to 68 and ended his life by suicide when the Roman Senate replaced him on the throne and sentenced him to death. Nowhere in the New Testament is Nero mentioned by name, although the "Caesar" referred to in Acts 25 is Nero. When Paul was on trial before Porcius Festus, he stood on his rights as a Roman citizen and appealed to Caesar for justice (Acts 25:1–12). He was released after Agrippa heard his defense (Acts 26:1). Later, however, in A.D. 65, Nero was still emperor when Paul was condemned to death by Nero's deputies.

NESCIENCE. A state of ignorance, especially such as an agnostic professes. It is therefore ignorance based on a theory, notably that a human being cannot attain to any (or at least certain) knowledge of God. (Etym. Latin *ne-*, not + *scire*, to know: *nescientia*.)

NESTORIAN CHURCH. A Christian church that came into existence after the condemnation of Nestorius at the Council of Ephesus in 431. Through the efforts of Ibas, Bishop of Ephesus from 435, and Barsumas, Bishop of Nisibis from 457, Nestorianism was developed into a rounded theology and transported to Persia and Asia Minor, where a small but influential sect was founded. The Nestorian Church survives to the present day under the name of Assyrian Christians.

NESTORIANISM. A fifth-century Christian heresy that held there were two distinct persons in the Incarnate Christ, one human and the other divine, as against the orthodox teaching that Christ was a divine person who assumed a human nature. Its name was taken from Nestorius (died c. 451), a native of Germanicia in Syria, and later Bishop of Constantinople. Nestorianism was condemned by the ecumenical Council of Ephesus in 431.

Postulating two separate persons in Christ, when Nestorius came to describe their union, he could not have them joined ontologically (in their being) or hypostatically (constituting one person), but only morally or psychologically. They would be united only by a perfect agreement of two wills in Christ, and by a harmonious communication of their respective activities. This harmony of wills (*eudoxia*) and the communion of action to which it gives rise are what forms the composite personality (*henosia*) of Christ.

In the Nestorian system we cannot speak of a true communication of *idioms*, i.e., that while the two natures of Christ are distinct the attributes of one may be predicated of the other in view of their union in the one person of Christ. Accordingly it could not be said that God was born, that he was crucified or died; Mary is not the Mother of God, except in the broad sense of giving birth to a man whose human personality was conjoined to the Word of God.

Nestorian bishops continued to propagate their views, and the confusion this produced among the people contributed to the success of Islam in the seventh century.

"NE TEMERE" DECREE. A declaration of matrimonial law issued by Pope Pius X; it went into effect Easter 1908. It was the *Tametsi* decree of the Council of Trent in a modified form. It took its name from the opening words and decreed that: 1. marriages involving a Catholic are invalid unless performed by a parish priest in his parish or one delegated by him, or by a bishop or appointed delegate in his own diocese; 2. no pastor can validly perform a marriage outside the limits of his own parish without delegation of the proper pastor of the parish in which he is to perform the wedding, or the bishop in whose diocese he is to perform the wedding. A bishop cannot validly perform a wedding outside his own diocese without delegation from the pastor of the parish in which he is to perform the wedding or the delegation of the bishop of that place; 3. it is also decreed that the marriage ought to be celebrated in the parish of the bride; 4. under certain circumstances a marriage may be licit and valid without a priest; 5. all marriages must be registered in the place or places where the contracting parties were baptized. There must be at least two other witnesses for validity beside the pastor or bishop. This decree did not affect persons who had never been Catholic when they married among themselves. It applied to every marriage of a Catholic, even when marrying someone who was not of his or her faith.

NET WITH FISH. Symbol of the Church based on the text "the kingdom of heaven is like a dragnet cast unto the sea. When it is full the fishermen haul it ashore" (Matthew 13:47). Saints and sinners will fill the net to be sorted out later. Reminiscent of Christ's meeting with Peter and Andrew casting their nets into the sea as Christ bade them, "Follow me and I will make you fishers of men" (Mark 1–17).

NEUTRALISM. The policy of remaining neutral when the demands of faith or moral responsibility call for taking a stand. In philosophy, it is a type of pantheism that claims that reality is neither mind nor matter but something in between, of which mind and matter are only manifestations. This was the position of Spinoza (1632–77). (Etym. Latin *neuter*, neither the one nor the other.)

NEW CHRISTIANITY. The name given since the Second Vatican Council by spokesmen for a radically changed Catholic Christianity. Its main features are a man-centered religion, preoccupation with the present world, stress on the Bible to the exclusion of revealed tradition, a classless Church in which the hierarchy under the Pope does not have binding authority to teach and govern the people, and a Church whose purpose is to serve the world and humanity's social needs, with such an emphasis on Christ's humanity as to overshadow to the point of denying his divinity.

NEW COMMUNITY. The Church founded by Christ, corresponding to the New Testament and the New Law as compared with ancient Israel, the Old Testament and the Torah of the Jewish people.

NEW COVENANT. Essentially the same as New Testament, but with several distinct connotations. It is a sacred agreement instituted by God in the person of Christ. It is a completion of the Old Covenant that Yahweh made with the Jews. It is an eternal covenant whose fulfillment is destined for heaven. It is a promise on God's part to confer the blessings foretold in the Sermon on the Mount and at the Last Supper, provided the followers of Christ are faithful in their generosity toward God.

NEW EARTH. A term used by St. John in the Apocalypse (21:1) to describe the restored visible world after the glorious resurrection on the last day. The present earth, it implies, will not be annihilated but mysteriously renovated. Since the glorified bodies will regain their bodily faculties, it is argued, there will be in "the new earth" corporeal objects for these faculties to experience and enjoy.

NEW FIRE. A ceremony taking place outside the church door during the Easter Vigil. This does not take place inside probably because the smoke produced might be offensive. From the newly blessed flame are lighted the candles of the worshipers and later the paschal candle.

NEW HEAVEN. Like the "new earth," mentioned in the Apocalypse (21:1), the change that will take place on the last day when heaven will be occupied by the risen glorified bodies of the saints.

NEW JERUSALEM. In biblical language the Heavenly City of the angels and saints after the Last Day. As described by St. John in his prophetic vision: "I saw the holy city, and the New Jerusalem coming down from God out of heaven, as beautiful as a bride all dressed for her husband" (Apocalypse 21:2).

NEW LAW. The Law of Christ, as distinguished from the Law of Moses. It is new in its stress on the selfless love of God and the neighbor; the universality of its intent, for all mankind; the scope of its extent; and the sublimity of its motivation, i.e., the following of Christ.

NEW TESTAMENT. In the sense of new dispensation, it is the fulfillment of the Old Covenant and includes all that Christ did and said during his visible stay on earth. It also means the New Law, operative since the time of Christ and destined to remain until the last day. It most commonly means the canonical books of the Bible, beyond the Jewish Torah, namely the Gospels according to Matthew, Mark, Luke, and John; the Acts of the Apostles, the Pauline Epistles to the Romans, I and II Corinthians, Galatians, Ephesians, Philippians, Colossians, I and II Thessalonians, I and II Timothy, Titus, Philemon, and Hebrews; the Catholic Epistles of James, I and II Peter, I, II, and III John, and Jude; and the Book of Revelation of St. John.

NEW WORLD. A term used to describe the restoration of the present world on the Last Day. Its revealed basis is in the New Testament, where Christ speaks of the "regeneration," i.e., the new formation of the world (Matthew 19:28); St. Paul speaks of the

whole of creation being under a curse and awaiting redemption (Romans 8:18–25); St. Peter of a "new heaven and a new earth" concurrent with a destruction of the world, in which justice will dwell (II Peter 3:13); and St. John gives an elaborate description of the New Jerusalem, which is the tabernacle of God among men (Revelation 21:1–8). St. Augustine teaches that the properties of the future world will be just as suited to the immortal existence of the glorified human body as were the properties of the present world to corruptible existence of the mortal body (*De Civitate Dei,* 20, 16).

NICENE CREED. There are two creeds that have the same name. The original Nicene Creed was issued in A.D. 325 by the Council of Nicaea. It was composed by the Fathers of the Council in their conflict with Arianism and contains the term *homoousios* (consubstantial). It is comparatively short, ends with the phrase, "and in the Holy Spirit," and has attached to it four anathemas against Arianism. The more common Nicene Creed is more accurately the Nicene-Constantinople Creed. It came after the first ecumenical Council of Constantinople (381), is the creed now used in the liturgy, including the added phrases "and the Son," and "died," and differs from the preceding in that it: 1. has more about the person of Christ; 2. omits the phrase "from the substance of the Father" after *homoousios;* 3. says more about the Holy Spirit; 4. adds the articles on the Church, baptism, the resurrection, and eternal life; and 5. contains no anathemas. The full text reads: "We believe in one God, the Father almighty, creator of heaven and earth, of all things both visible and invisible. And in one Lord Jesus Christ, the only-begotten Son of God, born of the Father before all time; light from light, true God from true God; begotten, not created, consubstantial with the Father; through him all things were made. For the sake of us men and for our salvation, he came down from heaven, was made flesh by the Holy Spirit from the Virgin Mary, and became man; and he was crucified for our sake under Pontius Pilate, suffered, died, and was buried. And on the third day he arose according to the Scriptures; he ascended into heaven, sits at the right hand of the Father, and is going to come again in glory to judge the living and the dead. His reign will have no end. We believe in the Holy Spirit, the Lord, the giver of life; he proceeds from the Father and the Son, is adored and honored together with the Father and the Son; he spoke through the prophets. We believe in one, holy, Catholic, and apostolic Church. We profess one baptism for the forgiveness of sins. We expect the resurrection of the dead and the life of the world to come. Amen."

NICHE. A recessed space or hollow in a wall usually to hold a statue, affording it protection. With Gothic builders who introduced sculpture, incorporating it as part of the building, the canopy niche appeared, often a fine composition of light and shade, later elaborately decorated. The wall was sometimes deeply recessed and a pedestal added to elevate the statue.

NICODEMUS. A Pharisee and member of the Sanhedrin, who was intellectually in sympathy with Jesus but lacked the courage to become an avowed disciple. As recorded by the fourth Evangelist, he visited Jesus and questioned him about his teachings "by night," which suggests that it was a clandestine visit (John 3:1–2). He was a lone voice in the Sanhedrin, reminding his colleagues that they should not condemn Jesus without giving him a hearing (John 7:50). Convincing evidence that he was at least a silent disciple is the fact that, when Joseph of Arimathea was burying the crucified Christ, Nicodemus accompanied him and supplied the spices to be wrapped with the body (John 19:39–42). (Etym. Greek *nikodemos*, conqueror for the people.)

NICOLAITANS. A Christian sect in the early Church in Ephesus and Pergamum; it had a divisive influence because it encouraged pagan food practices condemned by the Church (Revelation 2:15). In Revelation, John speaks of them bitterly when he says, "It is in your favor that you loathe as I do what the Nicolaitans are doing" (Revelation 2:6). (Etym. Greek *nikolaites* [sing.], follower of Nicolaus.)

NIGHT OF THE SENSES. One of the trials that the mystics undergo in their process of spiritual purification. It is a divine action that binds the sense faculties by subjecting them to the mind, which itself is prevented from discursive reasoning on divine things. So deprived and receiving only faintly the light of contemplation, the soul feels arid and crucified, plunged into darkness. During this period of darkness and light, aridity and intense love of God, weakness and latent energy, contradictory and hard to explain, God awaits the soul's patient acceptance in love.

NIGHT OF THE SPIRIT. Purification of the soul for spiritual marriage by cleansing it of habitual imperfections. What especially needs purification is self-complacency with possible illusions of false visions, together with a loss of reverential fear resulting in an overboldness toward God. In order to facilitate the soul's reform, the mind is left in darkness immersed in aridity. With prayer almost impossible, the soul is deprived of all joy and feels itself justly forsaken by God. The night of the spirit has four happy results: 1. an increased ardent love of God; 2. a piercing light that breaks through the former mental darkness, consoling the soul; 3. a greater sense of security in God with the determination to do nothing except for his glory; and 4. a marvelous strength to climb the steps that lead to the "transforming union," which St. John of the Cross calls the ten steppingstones of divine love.

NIGHT PRAYER. The fifth and last hour of the Divine Office, also called Compline. It mainly consists of a hymn, one or two psalms, short biblical reading, the *Nunc Dimittis* of Simeon, and prayers.

NIGHT WATCH. A sacred vigil or guard. One of the four ancient divisions of the night during which official prayers were offered in the early days of the Church. The later Matins and Lauds of the Divine Office probably represented those watches.

NIHIL EX NIHILO. Nothing (comes) from nothing. A statement of the principle of causality, that every effect must have a cause; and of the principle of sufficient reason, that everything must have an adequate reason for its existence or operation. (Etym. Latin *nihil*, nothing.)

NIHILISM. Applied to various theories or systems of thought: that nothing really exists except thought; that nothing really matters, what must be, must be; that the world is an absurdity, so nothing in life is really worth struggling or even living for.

NIHIL OBSTAT. Approved by the diocesan censor to publish a manuscript dealing with faith or morals. The date of the approval and the name of the person approving (*censor deputatus*, delegated censor) are normally printed in the front of the book along with a bishop's imprimatur.

NIHIL SINE DEO. There is nothing without God. A popular Christian inscription that says all creation is the product of God's power and nothing ever happens by chance; everything is part of the providence of God.

NIMBUS. A circle or ornamented disk depicted around the head of a saint. In pre-Christian times it represented power and majesty. The Church adopted the custom and made the nimbus symbolic of virtue. The square nimbus was once used with portraits of the living as emblems of human greatness, round circles reserved for saints as a symbol of grace bestowed on them by God. Related to nimbus are the halo and aureole.

NIMROD. A descendant of Noah and son of Cush. He is impressively described in Genesis as "the first potentate on earth" and "a mighty hunter in the eyes of Yahweh." Several Babylonian cities are mentioned as being "in his empire" (Genesis 10:8–10). These phrases, brought together, seem to indicate that he was a prominent military leader respected by neighboring peoples.

NINE CHOIRS. See ANGEL.

NINE FRIDAYS. See FIRST FRIDAYS.

NINE OFFICES. A form of devotion to the Sacred Heart, originating with St. Margaret Mary Alacoque (1647–90). According to her, the Sacred Heart desires "a special union and devotion to the holy angels, who are chosen to love, honor and praise the Sacred Heart in the divine sacrament of love, so that they who are in His divine presence would love Him for us and for all those who do not love Him, and also to make up for the irreverences we commit in His holy presence." The method suggested by Margaret Mary is to take one office of special prayers for a month for nine successive months, whether assigned or chosen individually. Others prefer to take a different office each day or each week. Each office is then directed to one of the nine choirs of angels.

NO. *Nobis*—to us, for us.

NOAH. Son of Lamech and father of Shem, Ham, and Japheth. Yahweh was so embittered by the corruption and faithlessness of the world that he decided he would wipe out the human race in a flood. The one exception he made was Noah and his family. He gave Noah detailed instructions about the construction of an ark strong enough to remain intact (Genesis 6). Then he instructed him to take aboard his family and two specimens of every kind of animal and bird, male and female, so that after the flood the world could be repopulated. Noah obeyed Yahweh. Every living being outside the ark was destroyed when the flood submerged the earth (Genesis 7). After several months Noah had proof that the waters receded enough for all to leave the ark, which was now resting on Mount Ararat (Genesis 8). God promised, "Never again will I strike down every living being . . ." (Genesis 8:21). "There shall be no flood to destroy the earth again" (Genesis 9:11). Noah's sons became the eponymous ancestors of the great races in the repopulation of the world.

NOB. *Nobilis, nobiles*—noble, nobles.

NOBILITY. Moral excellence, which deserves recognition and praise, in the possession of outstanding qualities of virtue. (Etym. Latin *nobilitas*, rank; excellence, superiority, dignity.)

NOBLE GUARDS. The highest ranking corps of the papal ministry service. It originated in the light cavalry that was a mounted guard for the Pope and had been reorganized many times. Pope Leo XIII gave them their modern name. The Pope appointed the commander, who was always a Roman prince. All members were to show a sixty-year line of nobility recognized by the papacy. They appeared with the Pope at public functions and left always with him. They were privileged to convey the tidings to newly appointed cardinals of their appointments. The Noble Guards were abolished in 1970.

NOE. See NOAH.

NOMINALISM. A theory that universal ideas, like truth, goodness, and humanity, are only names. It denies that universals are true concepts, present in the mind, that correspond to and are founded on objective reality. All abstract ideas, according to the nominalists, are only useful labels. (Etym. Latin *nominalis*, belonging to a name.)

NON. *Nonae*—Nones (in the Divine Office).

NONBAPTIZED. Persons who have not received the sacrament of baptism and who are therefore not subject to merely ecclesiastical laws.

NONBELIEVER. One who professes no faith in a personal God and claims to be an atheist or agnostic.

NON-CATHOLIC. A baptized Christian believer who is not a professed member of the Roman Catholic Church.

NON-CHRISTIAN. One who is not baptized and does not profess the Christian faith.

NON-DUALISTIC ILLUSIONISM. See WORLD MIND.

NONE. The part of the Divine Office which is said about the ninth hour, that is, three in the afternoon. In the revised Liturgy of the Hours there is an option to say any one of the Middle Hours, Terce, Sext, or None, depending on the time of day when the office is being recited. (Etym. Latin *nona,* ninth.)

NON EXPEDIT. The decree of the Sacred Penitentiary of 1868 to Italian Catholics to abstain as electors or candidates from parliamentary elections. It was feared that their participation would be interpreted as approving the spoliation of the property of the Holy See by the Italian Government. The decree was modified by Pope St. Pius X, who in his encyclical *Il fermo proposito* (June 11, 1905) allowed bishops to ask for a suspension of the decree *Non Expedit.*

NONINFALLIBLE. A term coined by those who distinguish between defined doctrines, which they admit are infallible, and official doctrines not defined by the Church, which they claim are not infallible. Such use of the term is ambiguous and may be erroneous, since many doctrines of the Church in faith and morals, e.g., that contraception is gravely sinful, are infallible from the ordinary universal magisterium. Moreover, even other doctrines, just because they are taught by the Church, are to be accepted in obedience to the hierarchical authority established by Christ.

NONJURORS. Name given to Anglican clergymen who refused to take the oath of allegiance to William and Mary and their successors under the Protestant Succession Act of 1689. Since they felt that their oaths bound them to the Stuart family, they considered William and Mary as mere regents. Suspended and deprived of office, they suffered greatly. Much later some rejoined the Anglican Church. The name has been given also to the Catholic clergy of France who refused to take the oath of the Civil Constitutions in 1790. Their loyalty to the Church and the Holy See forced them to endure bitter persecution.

NON PLACET. "It does not please." A formal negative vote at an ecclesiastical council of the hierarchy. It is a simple negative.

NORM. Any criterion for determining what is true or false, good or bad. Thus we have norms of truth, to which the mind must conform in order to make correct judgments; and norms of conduct, to which the will must conform in order to perform morally good actions. (Etym. Latin *norma,* rule, pattern.)

NORMAN ARCHITECTURE. A variant of Romanesque building introduced into England by William the Conqueror (1066). The Normans retained the French style, borrowing from early Gothic. The semicircular arches are heavy and plain, the pillars are low and broad, the whole appearance massive. Canterbury Cathedral, with the churches at Lincoln, Durham, Winchester, Gloucester, and St. Paul's in London, Abbaye aux Dames at Caen, and Dunfermline Abbey are famous examples of the Norman style.

NORM OF MORALITY. A standard to which human acts are compared to determine their goodness or badness. A proximate norm is immediately applicable to the acts; the ultimate norm guarantees the validity of the proximate norm.

Human nature is the proximate norm of morality because it is common to everyone, and the rules derived from it will be applicable to all human beings. Moreover, human nature, while essentially unchangeable, is flexible enough to admit of varying applications according to circumstances. It is also constantly present and manifest to all humankind.

The ultimate norm of morality is the divine nature. This assumes that God is the Creator of the universe and the pattern of all things, that he is Being by essence and the Source of all things, so that whatever either exists or can exist is a reflection and participation of Infinite Being. This resemblance between God and creatures—including human beings—should be not only in nature (who God is) but also in action (how God acts). Consequently, the ultimate norm of human morality is the nature and activity of God. A person is as good as his or her character approximates the perfections of God; and his or her conduct is as good as it imitates the activity of God.

NORM OF TRUTH. A standard to which the mind must conform in order to make sound judgments. There are two such norms of truth: the objective evidence available in nature through the proper use of human reason; and divine revelation supernaturally communicated to humans and accessible by faith with the help of God's grace.

NORMS OF ORTHODOXY. Also called "Rules for Thinking with the Church," of St. Ignatius Loyola. They are sixteen norms that form part of the Spiritual Exercises and synthesize, in practical terms, the distinctive qualities of being a Catholic. The first norm is an epitome of the rest. It declares: "We must put aside all judgment of our own and keep the mind ever ready and prompt to obey in all things the true Spouse of Christ our Lord, and Holy Mother, the hierarchical Church."

NOSSA SENHORA APARECIDA. Shrine of Our Lady, patroness of Brazil, at the Basilica of Aparecida, near the city of São Paulo. The statue venerated here was drawn out of the water by a group of fishermen in 1717. At first housed in a small chapel, the image became the source of so many favors that eventually it was placed in the present church, declared a basilica in 1929. More than a half million pilgrims come to the shrine annually.

NOSTR. *Noster, nostri*—our, of our.

NOSTRA AETATE. Declaration of the Second Vatican Council on the Relation of the Church to Non-Christian religions. It is addressed to Christians and urges them to promote fellowship with persons and groups who do not profess the Christian faith. Singled out are tribal peoples, Hindus, Buddhists, Moslems, and Jews. The principal theme is that Catholics should "enter with prudence and charity into discussion and collaboration with members of other religions."

NOT. *Notitia*—knowledge.

NOTARIES. Authorized persons who draw up official and authentic documents that are later issued by chanceries and ecclesiastical tribunals. In the fourth century the notaries formed a group or college presided over by a chief. The best known notaries are the officials of the episcopal and Roman curiae and their secretaries. They are usually clerics and similar to registrars of the court in civil trials. (Etym. Latin *notarius*, shorthand writer; clerk, secretary.)

NOTE. In general a quality of something by which it can be identified. Applied to the Church, it is one of her attributes by which the true Church of Christ can be recognized. These are commonly understood to be the Church's unity, in doctrine and practice by being united in the same faith and sacraments; holiness in possessing the means of sanctification and producing saints; catholicism or universality, in diffusion throughout the world and acceptance of the whole teaching of Christ; and apostolicity in professing the same faith as that of the Apostles and having an episcopate, under the Pope, which derives in historical succession from the original Twelve Apostles under Peter.

NOTES OF THE CHURCH. See MARKS OF THE CHURCH.

NOTHING. That which does not exist or that cannot exist. It is therefore either what could be but is now only an imaginary possibility; or what is not even rationally possible because it is a contradiction in terms. The first is existentially nothing, the second is logically nothing. Applied to God, when we say that nothing is impossible to God, we mean the first type of nothingness.

NOTION. A concept, idea, or mental apprehension. In the Trinity, notions are the distinctive characteristics of the divine persons by which they are known. The notions of the individual persons are: 1. ungeneratedness and active generation as a mark of recognition of the Father; 2. passive generation of the Son; and 3. passive spiration as a distinctive characteristic of the Holy Spirit. The notions are internal divine activities that characterize the persons and distinguish them, as compared with the essential acts that are common to all three persons. (Etym. Latin *notitia*, a being known, knowledge.)

NOTITIAE. Official publication of the Sacred Congregation for the Sacraments and Divine Worship. Issued monthly, it contains all significant documents of the Holy See dealing with the liturgy, along with appropriate studies and commentaries. Published by the Vatican Polyglot Press.

NOTRE DAME. Our Lady. One of the most popular titles of the Blessed Virgin Mary. Corresponding to Madonna (Italian), with an equivalent in every language of Christendom.

NOUMENON. The essence of a thing. In Kantian philosophy the mind can only postulate but never know the essence of things. The essence of God, the soul, the moral law, and anything else thus become suppositions of practical reason, and people are to act on these presuppositions "as if" they really existed. This makes life livable. (Etym. Greek *nooumenon*, that which is apprehended by thought.)

NOVATIANISM. A heresy that originated with Novatian, an antipope who followed Pope Fabian in A.D. 251, in opposition to St.

Cornelius, the lawful Bishop of Rome. The schismatic church that he started adopted a form of Montanism. It claimed that people in grave sin were permanently excluded from the Church. Absolution was refused to those guilty of murder and adultery.

NOVENA. Nine days of public or private prayer for some special occasion or intention. Its origin goes back to the nine days that the Disciples and Mary spent together in prayer between Ascension and Pentecost Sunday. Over the centuries many novenas have been highly indulgenced by the Church. In modern times the one before Pentecost was prescribed for parochial churches. (Etym. Latin *novem,* nine.)

NOVICE. A person formally admitted to a religious institute to prepare for eventual religious profession. The purpose of the noviceship is also to assist superiors to better know the candidates and therefore be able to pass correct judgment on their suitability for the religious life. The noviceship is of ancient origin, and its duration varied. At present one year at least is required by common law, but many communities require more. A novice receives the religious habit, which in women's communities includes a white veil. He or she may leave or be requested to leave without stated reason during this period of probation. Before first profession the novice must testify to free consent. The minimum age for noviceship is fifteen years. (Etym. Latin *novicius,* new; newly arrived; novice.)

NOVICESHIP. See NOVITIATE.

NOVITIATE. The period of formal probation of a person in a religious community or secular institute. It follows the postulancy and precedes the first profession of vows. Also refers to the residence for novices. Sometimes called noviceship.

N.S. *Notre Seigneur, Nostro Signore*—Our Lord.

N.S. New Style.

N.T. *Novum Testamentum*—New Testament.

NTRI. *Nostri*—of our.

NULLITY. A decree or judgment by a competent ecclesiastical court that a reputed marriage is invalid and hence no marriage was contracted in the first place. Even when entered in good faith, an invalid marriage requires that it be dissolved or regulated by revalidation. The chief ground for nullity is the proved absence of free consent to enter a permanent marital union according to the teaching of the Catholic Church. Since the Second Vatican Council, local bishops have been given jurisdiction over many nullity cases previously reserved to the Holy See. (Etym. Latin *nullus,* none, not any.)

NUMBERS. The fourth book of the Bible, so named because the opening chapters deal with the census numbering of the people. It may be divided into four unequal parts: the Hebrews leave Mount Sinai (1–10); from Sinai to Cades (10, 11–12), Cades (13–20:21); from Cades to the Plains of Moab (20:22–21:35); at the Plains of Moab (22:1–36:13). The last chapter, 36, treats of the Levitical cities and the cities of refuge.

NUMBERS, RELIGIOUS. Numbers, either written or in symbolic form, associated with mysteries of the Christian faith. Drawn from Sacred Scripture, they have become part of the Church's tradition and, in varying degrees, are found everywhere in her liturgy, art, and literature. Among the more common religious numbers are the following:

One stands for the oneness of nature in God; also one divine person in Christ; one true Church founded by Christ; and there is one mortal life, one baptism, one death, and after death one judgment before eternity.

Two represents the two distinct natures in Christ, human and divine; the two covenants of God with the human race, the Old and the New; two ultimate kinds of reality, variously called heaven and earth, soul and body, spirit and matter; there are two basic commandments, to love God and one's neighbor as oneself; and the final separation on the Last Day into two groups, the saved and the lost.

Three is the number of persons in the Trinity; Christ spent three days in the tomb and rose from the dead on the third day.

Four evangelists wrote the Gospels; the heavenly City of God is perfectly square, with all its dimensions a multiple of four; and there are four cardinal virtues, prudence, justice, temperance, and fortitude.

Five wounds in Christ's two hands and feet and his side are still present in his glorified body.

Six were the days of creation, signifying completion and symbolizing the principal attributes of God, namely his power, majesty, wisdom, love, mercy, and justice.

Seven is the symbolic number of charity, grace, and the Holy Spirit. It is the term that stands for perfection. There are seven sacraments, seven gifts of the Holy Spirit, seven deadly sins, seven joys, and seven sorrows of Our Lady.

Eight is associated with joy and the resurrection. There are eight beatitudes, and Christ rose from the grave on the eighth day after his triumphal entry into Jerusalem, symbolized in the octagonal shape of many baptismal fonts.

Nine is the angelic number, since the Bible speaks of the nine choirs of angels. It is also the typical number of prayer, because the first Christian novena was the nine full days that the Disciples stayed in the Upper Room and prayed after Christ's Ascension until Pentecost Sunday.

Ten stands for the Ten Commandments that Christ confirmed for his followers; it is the basic multiple for fullness, and any number multiplied by ten (or tens) is the highest possible.

Eleven has come to mean incompleteness, as typified among the Apostles after the defection of Judas, who had to be replaced before the Day of Pentecost.

Twelve implies maturity or totality. There were Twelve Apostles, corresponding to the Twelve Tribes of Israel; and the Book of Revelation is filled with imagery built around this number. The heavenly Jerusalem will be twelve thousand furlongs on all sides, having twelve jeweled foundations, with twelve gates of twelve pearls. There are twelve fruits of the Holy Spirit.

Thirteen is the symbol of treachery, recalling the presence of the traitor at the Last Supper, beyond Christ and the faithful eleven disciples.

Forty is the biblical number for trial, testing, or waiting. The flood lasted forty days and forty nights; the Israelites wandered forty years in the wilderness; Moses remained forty days on Mount Sinai. After his baptism, Christ was forty days in the desert and there was tempted by the devil. After his Resurrection, he appeared to the Disciples for forty days before the Ascension. There are now forty days of Lent, and forty is the symbol of the Church Militant.

Fifty is related to the fulfillment of a divine promise. In later Jewish history the feast of Pentecost was celebrated on the fiftieth day after the Passover to commemorate the giving of the Law through Moses. And the Holy Spirit promised by the Savior descended on the fiftieth day after Easter.

One hundred is the scriptural number for plenitude, whether used alone or as a multiple for other numbers. Christ spoke of a hundredfold harvest and a hundredfold reward.

One thousand often means simply an immense number, too large to be counted. It has come to symbolize eternity, because all higher numbers are either an addition to a thousand or multiplications of the same. God is the Eternal One in whom there is no time element, for "with the Lord, 'a day' can mean a thousand years, and a thousand years is like a day" (II Peter 3:8).

NUMINOUS. A term used by non-Christian philosophers of religion to denote the essentially nonrational and nonmoral; it constitutes what people call "holy." It is composed of two kinds of feelings: awe and self-abasement at the Terrifying Unknown (*Mysterium Tremendum*) and enchantment (*fascinatio*), which the unknown induces in everyone who allows himself to be charmed. (Etym. Latin *numen*, the divine will, divine command.)

NUN. In general, a member of a religious institute of women, living in a community under the vows of poverty, chastity, and obedience. More accurately, nuns are religious women under solemn vows living a cloistered, contemplative life in a monastery.

NUNC DIMITTIS. The Canticle of Simeon, said by him on the occasion of the presentation of Jesus in the Temple (Luke 2:29–31). It is part of the Liturgy of the Hours, daily recited at Compline.

NUNCIO. An official prelate representing the Pope at the capital of a foreign government. He watches over the welfare of the Church in that country and handles the affairs between the Apostolic See and the civil government of the country to which he has been assigned. In Catholic countries the nuncio is the dean of the diplomatic corps. (Etym. Latin *nuntius*, messenger, envoy.)

NUNC PRO TUNC. Now for then. Intending some future effect while performing a present action. This applies especially to the administration of the sacraments, whose effects take place over a lifetime, as in baptism; or at the hour of death, as in the anointing of the sick; or with varying graces to meet different needs, as in matrimony.

NUP. *Nuptiae*—nuptials.

NUPTIAL. Usually in the plural, nuptials. A wedding, with a stress on the solemn or elaborate ceremonies with which the marriage takes place. (Etym. Latin *nuptialis*, of a marriage or wedding.)

NUPTIAL BLESSING. The formal blessing

of the newlywed couple, given at Mass after the Lord's Prayer. The priest gives the blessing with extended hands and prays for husband and wife that they may love one another, be faithful to each other, witness to others by their Christian virtue, and be blessed with children to whom they will be good parents. The nuptial blessing may also be given outside of Mass and in mixed marriages, even when the other party is not baptized; but then the wording changes.

NUPTIAL MASS. The Mass at which a Catholic is married. With a bishop's permission, a nuptial Mass may be offered in a mixed marriage when the non-Catholic partner is baptized. The ritual provides for the marriage to be performed after the Gospel and homily, with the nuptial blessing after the Lord's Prayer, and a special blessing of bride and groom at the end of the Mass.

O

O. Omit.

O ANTIPHONS. See GREATER ANTIPHONS.

OATH. The invocation of God's name to bear witness to the truth. A person, being conscious of his or her own fallibility, professes by an oath that God is omniscient and the omnipotent avenger of falsehood. For an oath to be licit, the statement sworn to must be true; there must be sufficient reason for swearing, i.e., regarding some matter of importance or because the circumstances demand an oath, as in a court of law; and the statement itself must not be sinful, e.g., not disclosing a secret that should not be revealed.

Oaths are assertive when God is invoked as witness to the truth of a past or present event, e.g., that a crime was not committed. They are promissory when God is invoked to bear witness not only to a future act but also to a person's present intention of doing or omitting something, e.g., the promise to fulfill the duties of one's office.

Oaths may also be distinguished as invocatory and imprecatory. They are invocatory when God is simply called upon as witness to the truth; they are imprecatory when, in addition, he is also invoked as the avenger of falsehood. In the Old Testament oaths of imprecation were very frequent, e.g., in the expression, "The Lord do so to me and more also." In current usage they now occur in the familiar form, "So help me God." (Etym. Greek *oetos,* a going; fate.)

OATH AGAINST MODERNISM. A solemn declaration against Modernism issued by Pope St. Pius X (September 10, 1910) and required to be taken on oath by all clergy to be advanced to major orders, pastors, confessors, preachers, religious superiors, and by professors of philosophy and theology in seminaries. The first part of the oath is a strong affirmation of the principal Catholic truths opposed to Modernism: the demonstrability of God's existence by human reason, the value of miracles and prophecies as criteria of revelation, the historical institution of the Church founded by Christ, the invariable constancy of the essentials of Catholic tradition, and the reasonableness and supernaturality of the Christian faith. The second part of the oath is an expression of interior assent to the decree *Lamentabili* and the encyclical *Pascendi.* Particular modernist errors are singled out for censure and rejection. In 1967 the Sacred Congregation for the Doctrine of the Faith issued a new Profession of the Faith to replace the longer Oath against Modernism.

OB. *Obiit*—he (or she) died.

OBADIAH. Unknown author of the shortest prophetic book in the Old Testament, only one chapter of twenty-one verses in length. He condemns the Edomites harshly for their participation in the suppression of Judah by Nebuchadnezzar and offers no hope that Yahweh will forgive a treacherous people. "For the slaughter, for the violence done to your brother Jacob, shame will cover you and you will vanish forever" (Obadiah v. 10). In contrast, Obadiah promises that Yahweh will restore the glory of the new Israel and its power will reflect the sovereignty of Yahweh.

OBED. The son of Ruth and Boaz. From Obed descended Jesse, David, and Jesus (Ruth 4:17–22).

OBEDIENCE. The moral virtue that inclines the will to comply with the will of another who has the right to command. Material obedience is merely to carry out the physical action commanded; formal obedience is to perform an action precisely because it is commanded by a legitimate superior. The extent of obedience is as wide as the authority of the person who commands. Thus obedience to God is without limit, whereas obedience to human beings is limited by higher laws that must not be transgressed, and by the competency or authority of the one who gives the orders. As a virtue, it is pleasing to God because it means the sacrifice of one's will out of love for God. (Etym. Latin *obedientia,* obedience.)

OBEDIENTIAL POTENCY. The capacity to receive either a miraculous change or a supernatural perfection that exceeds the natural capacities of a being. Thus bread and wine are in obediential potency to be changed into the body and blood of Christ by transubstantiation.

OBEDIENTIARIES. Lesser monastic officials appointed more or less permanently by their superiors with extensive powers in their designated departments. In most monasteries they included the cellarer, bursar, or procurator, sacristan, cantor, precentor, infirmarian secretary, guest master, novice master, and kitchener. Certain others, such as readers, meal servers, and hebdomadaries, received weekly appointments.

OBEDIENTIARY. See GUEST MASTER.

OBELISK, VATICAN. A giant white marble obelisk in St. Peter's Square, Rome. It was brought to Rome from Egypt by Emperor Caligula (12–41) and later stood in Nero's circus. In the sixteenth century Pope Sixtus V had the three-hundred-ton monument moved to its present location on September 10, 1586.

OBERAMMERGAU. Site of the world-famous Passion Play, in West Germany, southwest of Munich. The play is staged by the people of the Bavarian village every ten years as the result of a vow made in 1634 because of their deliverance from the black death. The oldest existing text was written about 1600 and contains parts of two older dramas. Further revisions include a Passion text by Sebastian Wild and Johann Aelbel. In the eighteenth century the Benedictine Rosner remodeled the text after the Jesuit drama, and later still the script was simplified and put into prose form. Stage and costuming are adapted to modern requirements. The music is by Rochus Dedler. Practically everyone in the village has some part to play in the production of the drama, which was interrupted in 1940 because of World War II.

OBEX. Any obstacle in the recipient that would prevent a sacrament from producing the supernatural effect for which the sacrament was instituted. These obstacles are mainly a lack of faith, or of the state of grace, or of a worthy intention. (Etym. Latin *obex,* bolt, bar, barrier; from *obicere,* to throw against.)

OBJECT. The end or purpose of something; whatever is known, as distinct from the knower. In ethics the object is that over which a person has a moral right.

OBJECTIVE. What belongs to a thing, or is grounded in reality, prior to and independent of the mind's consideration of something. Also called ontological, in contrast with the mental or psychological. Opposite of subjective. Thus objective certitude is founded on reality, and objective morality is based on divinely established standards. (Etym. Latin *obiectio,* something thrown before or presented to [the mind], from *obicere,* to throw in the way, present.)

OBJECTIVE END. The good or object that is sought, independent of the personal desires or subjective feelings of the one who seeks the end. In Christian morality the objective end that the faithful should seek is always the glory of God, i.e., to please him, irrespective of personal preference and not conditioned by one's own satisfaction.

OBJECTIVE GUILT. Sinful estrangement from God when a person deliberately does something gravely forbidden by God. Those who, with full deliberation and consent, commit adultery, murder, perjury, and similar crimes, estrange themselves from God. He sets down the conditions for human estrangements, not they. It is not up to a human being to decide subjectively whether a deliberate serious sin is also a mortal sin that deprives him or her of God's friendship. God alone has the right to determine what separates a sinner from the Creator; a creature does not have the right to stand in judgment on God and tell him what constitutes a mortal sin.

Consequently "a person sins mortally not only when his action comes from direct contempt for love for God and neighbor, but also when he consciously and freely, for whatever reason, chooses something which is seriously disordered. For in this choice there is already included contempt for the divine commandment; the person turns himself away from God and loses charity" (Paul VI, *Declaration on Sexual Ethics,* December 29, 1975).

Every serious sin, therefore, is a mortal sin when a person freely decides to do whatever he knows God forbids under penalty of exclusion from the kingdom of heaven.

OBJECTIVE HOLINESS. See HOLINESS, OBJECTIVE.

OBJECTIVE MORALITY. The conformity or nonconformity of a human act with the moral standard, but independent of the person's responsibility for the action. Thus taking what belongs to another without his or her permission is objectively wrong, even though done without awareness of its wrongness.

OBJECTIVITY. The quality of impartial reflection in which the mind considers things as they really are, and not as a person is naturally or temperamentally inclined to view them. Philosophically, it is the viewpoint that regards extramental beings as real, so that the mind is said to possess truth when its knowledge corresponds with the reality outside the mind. Opposite of subjectivity.

OBLATE, LAY. A person who is associated with a religious institute in order to grow in Christian perfection by following certain rules of the institute but living outside its community structure. Such oblates share in the merits and spiritual benefits of the order or congregation.

OBLATES. A term that has a long and varied ecclesiastical history, originally designating those children who were sent to monasteries to be brought up by religious. Some of these oblates became religious. After the early Middle Ages oblates were lay persons who were united to a religious order by a simplified rule of life, but who did not become full religious; this practice still continues. In modern times the name has been adopted by a number of fully established religious institutes, of which the best known are the Oblates of Mary Immaculate (O.M.I.), founded in France in 1816 by Bishop Charles de Mazenod, and the Oblates of St. Francis de Sales, originally founded by their namesake and re-established in 1871 by Louis Brisson, a priest of Troyes in France. (Etym. Latin *oblatus,* offered.)

OBLATIONS. The offering of the bread and wine for consecration at Mass, expressed by the offertory procession of the faithful and the offertory prayers of the priest. Also applied to any other gifts presented by the people at Mass, either symbolically on special occasions or actually when the gifts are offered for the use of the clergy, the Church, or the poor. (Etym. Latin *oblatio,* offering.)

OBLIGATION. The moral power of a law commanding obedience. Obligation is moral necessity, imposed on a free will, thus differing from physical necessity, which controls nonfree beings. Moral necessity arises from the final cause, which is from an end or good known by the intellect. This good, perceived by the mind, moves the will either to arouse or to restrain it. Since there is only one way to achieve one's last end, namely by morally good actions, a person is obliged to live what conscience tells him or her is the good life.

OBLIGATION, CLERICAL. The duty of men in sacred orders to excel in holiness above the laity and to give the laity a good example by their frequent reception of the sacrament of penance, daily mental prayer, visits to the Blessed Sacrament, recitation of the Rosary, and examination of conscience.

OBLIGATORY SIGN. A term applied to the sacramental character insofar as it imposes certain duties to carry out the Christian worship, and demands the possession of sanctifying grace for its worthy performance.

OBREPTION. The attempt to obtain, or actually obtaining, an ecclesiastical dispensation under false pretenses. If a favorable answer is received, it is considered valid provided at least one of the motive causes set forth is true. (Etym. Latin *ob-,* against + *rapere,* to seize, snatch: *obreptio,* a creeping or stealing on, deceiving.)

OBSCENITY. Whatever is sinfully calculated to arouse sexual pleasure in a person. The nature of the object that arouses the pleasure is immaterial. What is essential is the wrong intent of someone who presents, produces, or depicts something that experience shows will arouse sexual pleasure. The intention is wrong because its purpose is to unnecessarily provoke sexual pleasure outside the privileges of marriage. And the object of the intention is the person, of whatever age, whose sexual desires are inevitably excited by the obscene stimulus. (Etym. Latin *obscaenitas,* offensiveness, filthiness.)

OBSCURANTISM. Concerted opposition,

on principle and from religious motives, to justified intellectual development. A familiar charge against Christians by rationalist critics who charge the faithful with fear of enlightenment lest they weaken their beliefs. (Etym. Latin *obscurus*, dark; unintelligible.)

OBSERVANCE. The act or practice of complying with something prescribed, as a law or custom, mainly in religious matters. In the history of religious orders, the term has become normative among those who were considered "Observants," in contrast with others in the same institute who had mitigated the original rule. Thus there have been Observants among the Benedictines, Cistercians, and Franciscans.

OBSERVANTINES. Those Franciscans who professed to observe faithfully the Rule of St. Francis approved by Pope Honorius III in 1223. The observantine movement started in Italy in 1368 and gave rise to various semi-autonomous groups like the Recollects and Alcantarines, who remained subject to the minister general of the Friars Minor. In 1898, Pope Leo XIII in the document *Felicitate Quadam* abolished all the distinctions, including the name Observants, and gave the Franciscan Order its original name of Friars Minor.

OBSESSION. A compulsive idea or feeling that persistently urges the performance of some act that is often contrary to what a person knows is the rational thing to do. (Etym. Latin *obsessio*, siege.)

OBSESSION, DIABOLICAL. The exterior control by the devil of a person's actions, or of any other activity that affects human beings. The Church's ritual mentions as probable signs of obsession such things as speaking or understanding an unknown tongue or showing strength above one's natural capacity. As in the case of possession, the devil is not allowed to force a person's free will.

OBSTINACY. Unreasonable stubbornness in persisting in one's own opinion and mode of action, tenaciously insistent upon doing things in one's own way. It often shuts the mind to known truth and creates contempt by militating against divine authority. By closing the heart to promptings of grace and possible repentance, it may lead to grievous malice and flagrant error. (Etym. Latin *obstinatus*, from *ob-*, against + *stare*, to stand: *obstinare*, to set one's mind firmly on.)

OCCAMISM. Philosophical system of William of Occam (1300–49). Essentially nominalism, it maintains the basic position that universal ideas have no foundation in reality; they exist only in the thinking mind and not in individual things. Consequently all science deals not with things but with concepts, and words that convey these concepts. Since only individual things exist, the ordinary means of acquiring knowledge is not by way of abstraction from reality, but by intuition. Given this postulate, that human knowledge is essentially subjective and not derived from objective reality, Occamism led to agnosticism. Part of the Occamist theory is also the claim that the divine will is the cause of all things and its own rule, so that God did not will things because they were good, but they are good because he willed them. Martin Luther was deeply influenced by Occamism, speaking of the Franciscan philosopher as "my teacher."

OCCAM'S RAZOR. See PARSIMONY, LAW OF.

OCCASION. Any principle or circumstance that favors or expedites the present action of a free cause. Sometimes called an "accidental cause," it brings on a human action without being directly responsible for it.

OCCASIONALISM. The philosophical theory that denies that creatures are ever real efficient causes in the visible universe. God's direct intervention is said to bring about every single change in the material world. At once a theory of knowledge and of voluntary control of action, it assumes that when a human being wills a certain action this is the "occasional cause" for God to make a corresponding change in the visible world, and vice versa. The modern author of occasionalism was Arnold Geulincx (1624–69), Dutch Catholic theologian at Louvain who became a Calvinist. (Etym. Latin *occasio*, a falling down, a happening; an accidental cause.)

OCCASION OF SIN. Any person, place, or thing that of its nature or because of human frailty can lead one to do wrong, thereby committing sin. If the danger is certain and probable, the occasion is proximate; if the danger is slight, the occasion becomes remote. It is voluntary if it can easily be avoided. There is no obligation to avoid a remote occasion unless there is probable danger of its becoming proximate. There is a positive obligation to avoid a voluntary proximate occasion of sin even though the occasion of evildoing is due only to human weakness.

OCCULT. That which is hidden from most people but known to certain initiates. Also applied in ecclesiastical law to those facts or human acts that are not publicly known but only in private or in the forum of conscience. Such would be hidden impediments to marriage or sacred orders. Canon law makes special provisions for such cases. (Etym. Latin *occultus,* hidden, concealed, secret; from *occulere,* to cover over, conceal.)

OCCULTISM. The theory and practice of invoking superhuman, but not divine, powers in order to obtain results that are beyond the capacity of mere nature. In this category belong Satanism, fetishism, black and white magic, spiritism, theosophy, divination, and witchcraft.

OCCUPANCY. The taking of something that belongs to no one, with manifest intention of holding it as one's own. This implies that an object is not actually owned by anyone, as a piece of land, but is capable of being owned. It also implies that the occupant must take the thing with the purpose of making it his or her own, and moreover makes this intent known to others by some suitable sign to indicate intent of acquiring the property.

OCTAVES. The seven days following a feast with the feast day itself included. Prior to the Second Vatican Council octaves were numerous in the Latin Rite. A commemoration was offered at Mass and in the Divine Office each day of the octave, and precedence given over any other feast. The octaves now observed in the universal Church are those of Christmas and Easter.

ODIUM THEOLOGICUM. A proverbial term for the ill-feeling generated between people who differ either on deep matters of faith, or even on relatively minor issues of ritual or theological speculation.

ODOR OF SANCTITY. See FRAGRANT ODORS.

OFF. *Officium*—office.

OFFERING COMMUNION. The practice of offering the reception of Holy Communion for another person. This means asking God to transfer to someone else the satisfactory (expiatory) and impetratory (intercessory) value of one's own preparation for and thanksgiving after Communion. What cannot be transferred are the principal effects of the sacrament, namely the growth in sanctifying grace, in the love of God and neighbor, the lessening of passion, the right to a glorious resurrection, the forgiveness of venial sins, and the remission of temporal punishment due to forgiven sins.

OFFERTORY. That part of the Mass in which the unconsecrated bread and wine are offered to God. The prayers said by a priest in the new ritual are taken almost verbatim from the first-century liturgical document the Didache, discovered at Constantinople in 1873. The celebrant says, while separately offering the bread (on a paten) and the wine (in the chalice): "Blessed are you, Lord God of all things, because we have received bread [wine] from your bounty. We offer this fruit of the earth [wine] and of men's labor, that it may become for us the Bread of Life [Spiritual Drink]."

OFFICE, DIVINE. The canonical hours in the Roman Catholic liturgy. The revised Breviary since Second Vatican Council prescribes: Office of Readings, Morning Prayer, Daytime Prayer (Midmorning, Midday, Midafternoon), Evening Prayer and Night Prayer, including appropriate antiphons, orations, psalms, canticles, hymns, and responsories.

OFFICE, ECCLESIASTICAL. In general, any duty that one legitimately assumes for a spiritual purpose. More technically, it is a duty established by divine or ecclesiastical ordination, conferred according to the norms of canon law, that involves some share in ecclesiastical power, orders, or jurisdiction.

OFFICE, LOSS OF. In ecclesiastical law the cessation of the right to exercise authority in some office in the Catholic Church. An office is lost by renunciation, by deprivation, by removal, by transfer, and, where an office is for a fixed period, by the lapse of that time. An ecclesiastical office is not lost by the fact that the superior who made the appointment goes out of office in any way, unless the law or conferral ordains otherwise.

OFFICE OF READINGS. The first hour of the Divine Office, formerly Matins. It consists mainly of three psalms, and of two readings, one each from the Bible and a nonbiblical source.

OFFICIAL SECRET. Confidential information entrusted to a person holding an official position in the Church or civil society, as in the medical, legal, or counseling professions. An official secret may not be communicated, without the permission of the one who confided the information, unless very grave necessity requires it. The seal of confession arising from the sacrament of penance is a special form of official secrecy. Confessional matters may never be divulged.

OIL OF CATECHUMENS. One of the three holy oils for the administration of the sacraments. It is used in the ceremonies of baptism, from which its name is derived, the catechumen being the person about to receive the sacrament. It is also used in the consecration of churches, in the blessing of altars, ordination of priests, and has been used in the coronation of Catholic monarchs.

OIL OF SAINTS. Oily substances that are believed to flow from relics or burial places of certain saints; also the oil that burns in their shrine lamps, and water that may come from wells near their graves. These oils, used by the faithful, are said to have curative powers. Among famous oils are those of: 1. St. Walburga, abbess of Heidenheim, Bavaria, who died in 780. Her body was brought to Eichstadt, Bavaria, May 1, 870. In 893, oil was discovered flowing at intervals from her relics, which now rest at Eichstadt; 2. of St. Menas, which comes from a holy well at Mareotis in the Libyan desert near the saint's national shrine; 3. of the shrine of St. Nicholas of Myra, which is seen to exude from his relics in Bari, Italy.

OIL OF THE SICK. The olive oil blessed by the bishop of a diocese for use in the sacrament of anointing of the sick. Commonly abbreviated O.I. (*oleum infirmorum,* oil of the sick) on oil stocks used by priests. Until 1974, when Pope Paul VI published the new *Order of Anointing the Sick,* olive oil was prescribed for the valid administration of the sacrament. This is no longer necessary. Any oil from plants is permissible in case of necessity; and the blessing by a bishop, though ordinarily required, may now be supplied by a duly authorized priest and, in emergency, by any priest.

OIL STOCK. A cylindrical metal case with three compartments, each labeled for the holy oil it contains.

OLD AGE. The age at which a person qualifies for certain privileges in ecclesiastical law or becomes subject to certain juridical limitations. This is a relatively new development in the Catholic Church as a result of the general increase in longevity throughout the world. Age now affects the tenure of bishops and cardinals and pastors. The sacrament of anointing may now also be conferred "on aged who are greatly weakened in strength, even though there is no sign of a dangerous illness."

OLD CATHOLICS. General name for various national churches that at different times separated from the Roman Catholic Church. Three main segments are distinguishable.

The Church of Utrecht in Holland, which separated from Rome in 1724. The immediate occasion for the break was the Jansenism of some of the Dutch Catholics, notably their archbishop, Petrus Codde (1648–1710).

The German, Austrian, and Swiss Old Catholics were organized after certain leaders in these countries rejected the two dogmas of papal infallibility and the universal ordinary magisterium, defined by the First Vatican Council in 1870. Their principal intellectual leader was John Joseph Ignatius Döllinger (1799–1890), Bavarian priest and Church historian.

Slavic Old Catholic Churches, mainly Polish, Croat, and Yugoslav, came into existence in America and elsewhere because of alleged discrimination by Anglo-Saxon bishops, but also because of clerical celibacy.

The doctrinal basis of the Old Catholic Churches is the Declaration of Utrecht in 1889. Its main provisions are the rejection of the papal primacy and obligatory auricular confession; married clergy; and in general acceptance of the first seven ecumenical councils as adequate statements of the Christian faith.

In 1925 the Old Catholic communion formally recognized Anglican ordinations, and in 1932 entered into full communion with the Church of England, based on the Bonn Agreement of July 2, 1931.

OLD LAW. Variously known as the books of the Old Testament, the Old Covenant, or the Mosaic dispensation. The religious rites, institutions, laws, and traditional customs that prevailed among the Jews prior to the coming of Jesus Christ.

OLD TESTAMENT. A term denoting the time from the origin of the human race to Christ; also the primitive, patriarchal, and prophetic revelation; and the Old Covenant of Yahweh with the Israelites. But most commonly, the Old Testament means the collection of books that the Catholic Church believes are divinely inspired, and that are not the New Testament. In biblical order they are: Genesis, Exodus, Leviticus, Numbers, Deuteronomy, Joshua, Judges, Ruth, I and II Samuel, I and II Kings, I and II Chronicles, Ezra, Nehemiah, Tobit, Judith, Esther, I and II Maccabees, Job, Psalms, Proverbs, Ecclesiastes, Song of Songs, Wisdom, Ecclesiasticus, Isaiah, Jeremiah, Lamentations, Baruch, Ezekiel, Daniel, Hosea,

Joel, Amos, Obadiah, Jonah, Micah, Nahum, Habakkuk, Zephaniah, Haggai, Zechariah, and Malachi.

OLEA SANCTA. See HOLY OILS.

OLEUM CATECHUMENORUM (O.C.). See OIL OF CATECHUMENS.

OLEUM INFIRMORUM (O.I.). See OIL OF THE SICK.

OLIVE BRANCH. A universal symbol of peace. It is the sign of reconciliation between God and humans, shown when it was brought by the dove returning to Noah's ark after the Deluge.

OLIVETANS. The Order of Our Lady of Mount Olivet, a branch of the Benedictines founded by St. Bernard Tolomei in 1313 at Mount Oliveto near Siena. They follow a strict interpretation of the Rule of St. Benedict and for a time were total abstainers from wine. There are also Olivetan nuns, based in Switzerland.

OMEGA. The twenty-fourth and last letter of the Greek alphabet. Occurs in the Bible as Alpha and Omega (Revelation 21:6), where Christ refers to himself as the Beginning and the End. He is the Omega of the universe as the destiny of the human race and the final fulfillment of all creation. (Etym. Greek *omega,* the great [i.e., long] o., last letter of the alphabet.)

OMEN. Any chance happening or event that is supposed to be a prophetic sign. If the sign is learned by a dream, it is called a dream omen. It is morally wrong to take omens seriously and above all to guide one's life according to them, apart from such exceptional circumstances when there is clear evidence of divine intervention. (Etym. Latin *omen,* augury, foreboding.)

OMISSION. Willful neglect or positive refusal to perform some good action that one's conscience urges one to do. Such omission is morally culpable, and its gravity depends on the importance of what should have been done, on the person's willfulness, and the circumstances of the situation.

OMN. *Omnes, omnibus*—all, to (or by) all.

OMNIPOTENCE. The almighty power of God. He can do whatever does not deny his nature or that is not self-contradictory. Since God is infinite in being, he must also be infinite in power. (Etym. Latin *omnis,* all + *potentia,* power: *omnipotens,* all-powerful.)

OMNIPRESENCE. God being simultane-ously wherever he is, since he is present everywhere. The divine omnipresence is twofold, by nature and by grace.

By nature God is present in all things by essence, knowledge, and power. This is the presence of a cause in the things that share in God's goodness. By his essence, he is substantially in all things, including the created spiritual essences (angels, demons, human souls) as the immediate origin of their existence. By his knowledge, he exercises his wisdom directly in all creation down to the least details. By his power, he operates with divine activity as the First Cause of everything that creatures do.

By grace, God is further present in the souls in whom he dwells as in a temple. Hence the creature is joined, as it were, to God's substance, through the activity of mind and heart, by faith cleaving to the First Truth, and by charity to the First Good. He is therefore present by grace as the known is to the knower and the beloved is to the lover. This presence is more than a cause in an effect. It is the possession of God on earth similar to his being possessed by the angels and saints in heaven.

OMNISCIENCE. God's knowledge of all things. Revelation discloses that the wisdom of God is without measure (Psalm 146:5). And the Church teaches that his knowledge is infinite.

The primary object of divine cognition is God himself, whom he knows immediately, that is, without any medium by which he apprehends his nature. He knows himself through himself.

The secondary objects of divine knowledge are everything else, namely the purely possible, the real, and the conditionally future. He knows all that is merely possible by what is called the knowledge of simple intelligence. This means that, in comprehending his infinite imitability and his omnipotence, God knows therein the whole sphere of the possible.

He knows all real things in the past, present, and the future by his knowledge of vision. When God, in his self-consciousness, beholds his infinite operative power, he knows therein all that he, as the main effective cause, actually comprehends, i.e., all reality. The difference between past, present, and future does not exist for the divine knowledge, since for God all is simultaneously present.

By the same knowledge of vision, God also foresees the future free acts of the rational creatures with infallible certainty. As taught by the Church, "All things are naked and open to His eyes, even those things that will happen through the free actions of creatures" (Denzinger 3003). The future free actions foreseen by God follow infallibly not because God substitutes his will for the free wills of his creatures but because he does not interfere with the freedom that he foresees creatures will exercise. (Etym. Latin *omnis*, all + *scire*, to know.)

OMOPHORION. A vestment of the Greek Rite corresponding to the pallium in the Roman Church. It is a broad band often of silk or velvet, ornamented with crosses, worn around the neck and over the shoulders and breast. It is worn by Byzantine, Armenian, and Coptic bishops and archbishops. Originally made of wool, it symbolizes the duties of bishops as shepherds of their people.

OMRI. King of Israel from 885 to 874 B.C. He was a general who ascended the throne after the speedy elimination of Zimri (king for seven days). Perhaps Omri's most notable achievement was moving the seat of government from Tirzah to a hill named Samaria (I Kings 16:16). The redoubtable defenses he erected made it impregnable for years to come. By judiciously marrying his son Ahab to Jezebel and his daughter Athaliah to Jehoram, he forged useful alliances with Tyre and Judah. He is bitterly characterized in I Kings as "displeasing to Yahweh and was worse than all his predecessors" (I Kings 16:25). The prophet Micah substantiated this: "You keep the laws of Omri . . . and they force me to make a terrible example of you" (Micah 6:16).

ONAN. Son of Judah and Shua. When Onan's brother, Er, died, Judah ordered Onan to marry the widow, Tamar, and produce a son who would be Er's child, according to the levirate law (Deuteronomy 25:5–6). Onan married her but frustrated the law by withdrawal during intercourse. In punishment, Yahweh caused Onan's death (Genesis 38:8–10). In modern usage, onanism is variously used to mean contraception or masturbation. (Etym. Hebrew *Onan*.)

ONANISM. Theological term for contraception. The name is derived from Onan, son of the patriarch Judah. When Judah asked Onan to marry his (Onan's) brother's widow, in order to raise up progeny to his brother, Onan frustrated conception. "What he did was offensive to Yahweh, so He brought about his death also" (Genesis 38:8–10). The more popular terms for onanism are: birth control, contraception, planned parenthood, and Neo-Malthusianism.

ONE. That which is whole or undivided in itself, and different or distinct from every other. Only God is absolutely one, because he has no parts or composition, and as Creator of the universe he is totally unlike the world that he made. (Etym. Latin *unus*, one.)

ONESIMUS. A slave who had run away from his master, Philemon. He met Paul and was converted. This occasioned the Epistle to Philemon, a handwritten letter that reveals the gentle, affectionate side of Paul's personality. He appealed to Philemon (who was probably converted by Paul also) to show a Christian attitude toward the penitent slave, even offering to pay any debt that Onesimus owed (possible stolen valuables) (Philemon 1:8–21). Paul ended his appeal by expressing confidence that Philemon "would do even more than I ask" (Philemon 21). Tradition has it that Onesimus was not only forgiven but was given his freedom. (Etym. Greek *onesimos*, advantageous, profitable.)

ONTOGENESIS. The development of the individual living being, as distinct from the growth of a species of organisms. Applied to human beings, it is the history of each one's progress as a single person. (Etym. Greek *ontos*, being + *genesis*, origin.)

ONTOLOGISM. A theory that holds that each person has an immediate intuitive vision of God, and this vision is the source and ground of all other human knowledge. Originating with Platonic mysticism, the doctrine was first projected by Marsilio Ficino (1433–99), systematically organized by Nicolas Malebranche (1638–1715), and developed by Vincenzo Gioberti (1801–52). It was condemned in 1861 as erroneous under Pius IX by the Congregation of the Inquisition.

ONTOLOGY. The science of being. In scholastic philosophy it is the equivalent of metaphysics, or at least of that branch of metaphysics which deals with the philosophy of reality. (Etym. Greek *ontos*, being + *logia*, science, knowledge.)

OPEN PLACEMENT. The practice in some religious communities of members deciding on their own employment or apostolate, with the formality of approval by superiors but without real dependence on their authority.

OPERATING GRACE. Similar to preventing or prevenient grace, it precedes the free consent of the will or accompanies it in the performance of an act. The thought of doing a good act suggests itself with no effort on the part of the human being, as an indeliberate impulse.

OPERATIVE HABIT. A disposition either infused or acquired by which some human faculty is perfected in its activity. Thus all virtues (and vices) are operative habits, as distinguished from the entitative habit of sanctifying grace.

OPINION. Assent of the mind to a probable position, without certainly excluding its contradictory as untrue. Also a conclusion that rests on probable but not certain proof. (Etym. Latin *opinio,* from *opinari,* to think.)

OPPORTUNITY. In ethics, the positive aspect of some human right giving a person the freedom for something, in contrast to immunity, which is a freedom from something.

OPPRESSION OF THE POOR. One of sins crying to heaven for vengeance, recalling the oppression of the Jews in Egypt, "The sons of Israel, groaning in their slavery, cried out for help and from the depths of their slavery their cry came to God" (Exodus 2:23).

OPTATAM TOTIUS. Decree of the Second Vatican Council on the training of priests. Aimed at the desired renewal of the whole Church, which "depends in great part upon a priestly ministry animated by the spirit of Christ." The document centers on fostering good priestly vocations, giving more attention to spiritual training, revising ecclesiastical studies, preparing for pastoral work, and continuing studies after ordination. Special attention is given to developing priests whose sense of the Church will find expression in a humble and filial attachment to the Vicar of Christ and, after ordination, in their loyal co-operation with bishops and harmony with their fellow priests (October 28, 1965).

OPTIMA INTERPRES LEGUM. The best interpreter of laws. Expression used of custom, as the most accurate commentary on how ecclesiastical laws are to be understood.

OPTIMISM. The view that good will always prevail over evil, that there is a greater amount of good in the world than of evil, and that the world is essentially good. Various premises have been offered in support of optimism. God, who is all-good, was thought to have created the best possible world. The developments of modern science have encouraged the notion of universal evolution; what exists is good and every change is inevitable progress. Emotionally, optimists are those who consider only the pleasing and cheerful aspects of life while ignoring anything disagreeable. (Etym. Latin *optimus,* the best.)

OPTIONAL CELIBACY. A policy advocated in some Catholic circles to change the centuries-old practice of obligatory celibacy for priests in the Latin Rite of the Catholic Church. Although it was strongly promoted before the Second Vatican Council, the Council reaffirmed the Church's tradition on mandatory celibacy, declaring that "the more that perfect continence is considered by many people to be impossible in the world today, so much the more humbly and perseveringly in union with the Church ought priests demand the grace of fidelity, which is never denied to those who ask" (*Decree on the Ministry and Life of Priests, II, 16*).

OPTIONAL MEMORIAL. A feast day in the revised liturgy; it may be observed at the option of the priest in offering Mass or of those reciting the Liturgy of the Hours. The new Roman calendar has ninety-five optional memorials. They are all feast days of saints whose memory the Church encourages the faithful to celebrate, without strictly requiring their observance.

OPUS DEI. The work of God. A Benedictine name for the Divine Office, to express the idea that prayer is the human's primary responsibility to God.

OPUS DEI. An association of the Catholic faithful who dedicate themselves to the apostolate and to Christian perfection in the world. They do not, however, give up their social environment and continue in their secular profession or employment. Founded in Madrid on October 2, 1928, by Monsignor José María Escriva de Balaguer, it received its final approval from the Holy See on June 16, 1950. The full canonical name is *Societas Sacerdotalis Sanctae Crucis* (The Priestly Society of the Holy Cross). Headquarters are in Rome. There are two branches of Opus Dei, of men and of women, but each so independent of the other that they form two organizations, united only in the person of the president general. The women's branch was founded in 1930. A general council, drawn from persons in different countries, assists the general in governing the association.

Priests belong to Opus Dei and Opus Dei members have been ordained to the priesthood. Married persons also belong to Opus Dei, dedicating themselves to seeking Christian perfection in their own state of life. Co-operators, who are not official members of the association, help in its numerous apostolic activities.

O.R. Office of Readings.

OR. *Oratio*—prayer.

ORATE FRATRES. The opening words of the prayer, addressed to the people at Mass after the Offertory, "Pray, brethren, that my sacrifice and yours may be acceptable to God, the almighty Father." Their response emphasizes both the distinction and the similarity between the priest's sacrifice at the altar and that of the faithful.

ORATIO IMPERATA. An ordered prayer. The prayer for a special intention, besides the ones prescribed by the ritual, that the Pope or the bishop of a diocese may require to be said at Mass, e.g., for peace.

ORATION. A liturgical prayer, especially at Mass, and commonly identified with the collect, which is said before the Scripture reading. In general, an oration is any formal prayer of praise or petition, addressed to God, the Blessed Virgin, the angels or saints.

ORATORIANS. Members of the Congregation of the Oratory, founded by St. Philip Neri in 1564 and approved by Pope Paul V in 1612. St. Philip's Oratory is a congregation of secular priests, technically a society of common life. For years there was a variety of autonomous oratories, finally formed into a confederation in 1942. Members are priests and brothers living a common life, without public vows. The director is elected every three years. Their purpose is to promote spiritual and cultural development by pastoral work, preaching and teaching, especially among students and the young.

ORATORIO. An extended composition of dramatic type for voice and chorus with orchestral accompaniment, usually having a text based on Scripture.

ORATORY. A place of prayer other than the parish church, set aside by ecclesiastical authority for celebration of the Mass and devotional services. It may be public, semi-public, or private and not intended for the use of the general public.

ORD. *Ordo, ordinatio, ordinarius*—order, ordination, ordinary.

ORDER. A methodical arrangement of things; a body of persons, as a group united by a common bond and living under common religious or social regulations; a grade in the Christian ministry; a single choir in the angelic hierarchy; a fraternity or society; a prescribed form of service as Order in the Mass, and a group of persons of the same occupation, profession, guild membership, or confraternity. (Etym. Latin *ordo*, array, row, rank.)

ORDER, RELIGIOUS. An institute of men or women, at least some of whose members take solemn vows of poverty, chastity, and obedience.

ORDER OF CHARITY. The order to be observed in loving one's neighbor. It is determined by the neighbor's need and relationship. The need of one's neighbor may be spiritual or temporal, and both may be extreme, grave, or ordinary. In extreme spiritual necessity, we must assist the neighbor even at the risk of our life. In extreme temporal necessity, the neighbor should be helped even at great inconvenience, but not necessarily at the risk of one's own life, unless one's position or the good of society demands assistance to the threatened party. In grave spiritual or temporal need, one's neighbor should be helped as far as possible; while position, justice, or piety may even oblige a person to help another. In ordinary spiritual or temporal need, there is no obligation to help the neighbor, certainly not in every case.

Relationship, as grounds for assisting another, is to be calculated in terms of kinship on various levels. Since blood relationship is the basis for all others, relatives, at least in the first degree, should be given first preference. The classic order to be followed is husband or wife, children, parents, brothers and sisters, other relations, benefactors, friends, and acquaintances. In extreme need, one's parents are to be favored because they are the source of one's being.

ORDERS, ANGLICAN. The question of the validity of Anglican ordination to the priesthood was decided negatively by Pope Leo XIII in the document *Apostolicae Curae* (September 13, 1896). They were declared to be "absolutely null and utterly void" on the grounds of defect of form in the rite and defect of intention in the minister. Even if Rome had not made such a declaration, Anglican orders were still considered invalid in practice, since Anglican clergymen were required to be ordained to the priesthood when they entered the Catholic Church. Since Pope Leo XIII's declaration, not a few Anglicans have been ordained by bishops who had themselves been ordained by Orthodox or other prelates whose orders were held to be valid by Rome. However, the current ordinal in the Episcopal Church in the United States (and elsewhere) provides for two forms of ordination, at the choice of the candidate and the option of a bishop; one form is for the priesthood and the other for the nonsacerdotal ministry.

ORDERS, SACRAMENT OF. The sacrament that, by the imposition of a bishop's hands, confers on a man the grace and spiritual power to sanctify others. There are three forms of this sacrament, also called sacramental orders, namely diaconate, priesthood and episcopate. They are not, however, three sacraments, but only one sacrament that is separately administered with three successively higher sacramental effects. It is certain that every baptized male can be validly ordained, although it would be highly illicit to ordain him before the age of reason. It is likewise certain that every baptized male can be validly ordained a priest without previously being ordained a deacon. However, the more probable teaching is that a baptized male cannot be validly consecrated a bishop unless he has previously been ordained a priest.

ORDERS OF KNIGHTHOOD. Certain religious and secular confraternities that arose during the Middle Ages. Religious (regular) orders of knighthood were brotherhoods that combined the insignia of knighthood with the privileges of monks, and received this recognition from both Church and State. Of these the first were purely military such as the Knights Templars, Orders of Christ, Montesa, Aviz, Calatrava, and Alcántara. Second were military and hospitaler, as the Knights of Malta, Knights of Rhodes, the Teutonic Order, and the Order of St. James of Compostela. A third group was purely hospitaler, e.g., Orders of St. Lazarus of Jerusalem, of the Holy Ghost, and Our Lady of Ransom. Among lesser regular orders, the Knights of Livonia were the most important. Secular orders were fraternities of lay knights patterned on the regular orders of knighthood. In Great Britain they are all now Protestant, including the Orders of Bath, Garter, and Thistle as well as St. Patrick, St. Michael, and St. George. In Austria and Spain there is the Order of the Golden Fleece, and in Piedmont the Order of the Annunziata. There are many modern religious or fraternal organizations whose titles denote knighthood, such as the Knights of Columbus, Knights of St. John, Knights of the Cross, Knights of Father Mathew, and Knights of the Blessed Sacrament. Pontifical knighthoods are honors conferred by the papal court on laymen who are of irreproachable character, who have promoted the welfare of society, the Church, and the Holy See. These decorations are bestowed by *motu proprio* and forwarded by the Secretary of State, or when petitioned by a bishop expedited through his chancery. The papal orders of knighthood are: 1. Supreme Order of Christ; 2. Order of Pius IX; 3. Order of St. Gregory the Great; 4. Order of St. Sylvester; 5. Order of the Golden Militia or Spur; 6. Order of the Holy Sepulcher. The last may be conferred on clerics and women.

ORDINAL. Formerly a manual of directives for the recitation of the Divine Office according to the variations of the ecclesiastical year. Now the name of the book of rites and prayers for the conferring of sacred orders.

ORDINARIATE, MILITARY. See MILITARY VICARIATE.

ORDINARY. In ecclesiastical law a cleric with ordinary jurisdiction in the external forum over a specified territory; the Pope with unlimited jurisdiction; diocesan bishops and their vicars; prelates nullius; capitular vicars and administrators filling the vacancy in a diocese. Also superiors general, abbots primate, provincial abbots of exempt monasteries. Their representatives too are called ordinaries. (Etym. Latin *ordinarius,* regular, usual.)

ORDINARY CARE. The basic medical care that a physician is obliged to give in treating all cases that come under his or her charge. The fact that the patient is a mental defective or being treated out of charity does not justify the doctor in being hasty or slipshod. The doctor must always use the safer remedy. If there is a sure remedy available, he or she may not try uncertain ones on a patient with the danger of causing death or serious injury to health, even though the patient gave permission to do so. If there is no safer remedy available, the doctor may, in cases where death would otherwise result, employ such uncertain remedies, for then he or she is doing everything possible to save the patient.

ORDINARY JURISDICTION. The right to exercise authority when this right is attached to an ecclesiastical office. This is the jurisdiction enjoyed by the Pope over the entire Church, by a bishop over his diocese, and in the internal forum by the pastor over the members of his parish. Jurisdiction can be either personal or vicarious, depending on whether it is exercised by the officeholder or by someone he delegated.

ORDINARY MEANS. Whatever means are commonly considered ordinary for the preservation of human life. They are ordinary if generally accepted as such or if they are readily available to persons in the time, place, and circumstances in which they find themselves. Such means are food, shelter, and the avoidance of unnecessary bodily danger; also the use of accepted medical and health facilities. Assumed in this matter of preserving life is the sincere desire to remain alive or to keep another person alive according to the dispositions of divine providence. There is no question of directly intending to terminate one's own or another's earthly existence.

ORDINARY POWER. The moral right of the Pope or bishops to teach and govern in virtue of their office, hence by divine ordinance. It is not delegated power received for a time or periodically from a higher possessor of jurisdiction.

ORDINATION. See ORDERS, SACRAMENT OF.

ORDINEM BAPTISMI. Decree of the Sacred Congregation for Divine Worship, issued in 1969, authorizing the new ritual for the baptism of infants. Among other changes there is a special rite for conferral of baptism by a lay person and also a ceremony for presenting an already baptized child to the Church (May 15, 1969).

ORDINIS BAPTISMI ADULTORUM. Decree of the Sacred Congregation for Divine Worship, giving the norms and ritual for the reception of adult Christians into the Catholic Church. It has two main parts: first is a detailed explanation of the catechumenate, its meaning and practice; the second deals expressly with receiving validly baptized persons "into full communion with the Catholic Church" (January 6, 1972).

ORDO. One of several ritual books, published by the Holy See, for the administration of the sacraments or other liturgical offices. Since the Second Vatican Council a number of these have been issued, containing the revised rites for all the Masses and all the sacraments. An ordo is also an annual calendar containing abbreviated directions for each day's Mass and Divine Office. Every diocese, or group of dioceses, and every religious order or congregation has its own ordo, or at least a supplement to the general ordo for the Latin (or other) Rite in the Church.

ORDO CELEBRANDI MATRIMONIUM. Decree of the Sacred Congregation of Rites, revising the ritual for the celebration of marriage at Mass, outside of Mass, and between a Catholic and one who is not baptized (March 19, 1969).

ORDO SYNODI. Statement of the Council for the Public Affairs of the Church establishing the new norms for the synod of bishops, revising the former directives of December 8, 1966. Its leading provisions declare seven prerogatives of the Pope, which he alone enjoys with respect to the synod of bishops; namely, convoke, approve members, set up agenda, decide who discusses what, determine the sequence of matters for discussion, preside at the synod either personally or through a delegate, and decide on the votes of the synod (June 24, 1969).

OREMUS. "Let us pray." An invitation to pray, occurring frequently in the Roman Rite and emphasizing the people's participation with the priest in public worship.

ORGAN. A musical instrument approved and used by the Church to assist in public worship. The pipe organ, being the more popular, is used in most churches. Organs with two or more manuals or keyboards are mentioned as early as 1350. The swell with movable shutters, varying the sound volume, was invented around 1712. Modern church organs are supplied with air by electric blowers. The Roman Ordo permits its use on Gaudete and Laetare Sundays and on Maundy Thursday until the Gloria, and on Holy Saturday from the Gloria on. Though other instruments are allowed at church services, the organ's majestic tone makes it appropriate for divine service. In 1968 the Holy See authorized the use of musical instruments other than the organ in liturgical services, "provided they are played in a manner suitable to worship."

ORGANIC ARTICLES. The law regulating public worship in France, enacted under Napoleon (1769–1821). It was simultaneously published and enacted with the Concordat of 1801. Until 1905 the French Government held that the "articles" were inseparable from the Concordat, but the Holy See refused to admit their validity because Pius VII had not approved their promulgation.

ORGANIC UNIT. See UNIT.

ORIENTALIUM ECCLESIARUM. Decree of the Second Vatican Council on the Catholic Eastern Churches, whose purpose was threefold: to encourage Eastern Catholics to remain faithful to their ancient traditions; to reassure them that their distinct privileges would be respected, e.g., the patriarchates and priests administering the sacrament of confirmation; and to urge closer ties with the separated Eastern Churches with a view to fostering Christian unity. An important provision was the permission of intercommunion(along with penance and anointing) between Catholics and those Eastern Christians who have valid orders (November 21, 1964).

ORIENTATION. The custom of turning toward the East in prayer, already in practice in pre-Christian times. Christianity attached a new significance to the ritual. The East was the cradle of human civilization. Christ lived in the East while he was on earth, and from the East he will come to judge the human race. The Apostolic Constitutions (from 900 on) directed that churches be erected with the apse toward the east. This custom was observed except by Emperor Constantine, so that the churches of St. John Lateran, St. Peter, and San Lorenzo, violate that directive. Later the directions of city streets made this custom impracticable. The altar end, regardless of its situation, is always referred to as the east end, and caskets at funeral Masses are placed with a priest's head to the east and a layman's feet to the east, symbolizing the relative position of priest and people at divine services.

ORIGENISM. A number of theories either charged or attributed to Origen (A.D. 185–254), the great biblical exegete and spiritual writer. Among these theories was the preexistence of souls, denial of the personal identity of the mortal and glorified bodies, and the claim that the devil and those in hell will eventually be saved. Origenism was condemned by the second Council of Constantinople in A.D. 553.

ORIGIN. Procession of one being from another, without implying causal dependence on the other. Thus in the Trinity, the second person proceeds from the first, and the third from the first and second by way of origin. But since each of the divine persons is true God, there can be no question of any of them proceeding from the other as cause and effect. (Etym. Latin *origo*, a beginning, from *oriri*, to rise.)

ORIGINAL JUSTICE. The state of Adam and Eve before they sinned. It was the simultaneous possession of sanctifying grace, with its right to enter heaven, and the preternatural gifts. Had Adam not sinned, original justice would have been transmitted to all his descendants. Later, through repentance, he personally recovered sanctifying grace but not the other prerogatives of original justice. Since Adam, human beings are said to be deprived of original justice. Jesus Christ, the new head of the human race, by his passion and death expiated human sin and regained what Adam had lost. Sanctifying grace is restored at justification, but the preternatural gifts are returned only as capacities (such as the ability to overcome concupiscence) or only eventually (such as bodily immortality after the final resurrection).

ORIGINAL SIN. Either the sin committed by Adam as the head of the human race, or the sin he passed onto his posterity with which every human being, with the certain exception of Christ and his Mother, is conceived and born. The sin of Adam is called originating original sin (*originale originans*); that of his descendants is originated original sin (*originale originatum*). Adam's sin was personal and grave, and it affected human nature. It was personal because he freely committed it; it was grave because God imposed a serious obligation; and it affected the whole human race by depriving his progeny of the supernatural life and preternatural gifts they would have possessed on entering the world had Adam not sinned. Original sin in his descendants is personal only in the sense that the children of Adam are each personally affected, but not personal as though they had voluntarily chosen to commit the sin; it is grave in the sense that it debars a person from the beatific vision, but not grave in condemning one to hell; and it is natural only in that all human nature, except for divine intervention, has it and can have it removed only by supernatural means.

OROPA. National Shrine of Our Lady near Turin, Italy. St. Eusebius, on his way back from the Holy Land after his exile during the Arian heresy, brought to the hermitage chapel at Oropa a statue of the Madonna. Later he died there. Mary of the shrine is called the Black Madonna because the Mother and Child in the three-foot-high statue have jet black faces and hands deliberately colored by the original carver. When Biella was saved in the 1599 plague, which decimated the entire section, the commune decided to build a larger sanctuary. The main temple, or church, was to have an outer and an inner court within which the original first shrine was to be enclosed. A second coronation of the Black Madonna by Pope Clement XI took place in 1720, the centenary of the first coronation. The buildings today are as they were then. Oropa has become a veritable city of chapels, inns, hospitals, shops, offices, theater, and museum attached to the shrine. The statue shows Our Lady standing, the Holy Child seated on his Mother's left arm. Mary's head carries the triple crowns of 1620, 1720, 1820, surrounded by a hoop of gold with twelve diamond stars representing her fourth papal crowning in 1920. The list of recorded miracles here is astounding. In 1918 the Redemptorists were asked by the Holy See to take care of the shrine.

ORPHREY. The embroidered or painted symbols or images on the front and back of the chasuble and around the opening of the cope. They were perhaps originally used to cover the seams, and, though not essential, they became a prominent part of these liturgical vestments. (Etym. Latin *aurum*, gold + *Phrygian*.)

OR. ORAT. *Orator, oratorium*—petitioner, oratory.

ORTHODOXY. Right belief as compared with heterodoxy or heresy. The term is used in the East to identify those churches (not united with Rome) which accepted the ancient councils, notably Ephesus and Chalcedon, and which call themselves "the holy, orthodox, catholic, Eastern Church." In the West the word is sometimes used to describe a justifiable concern for sound doctrine in the Catholic faith. (Etym. Greek *orthos*, right + *doksa*, opinion: *orthodoksa*, having the right opinion.)

ORTHOGENESIS. The theory that all human societies are in process of evolution, and that they follow in the same direction and go through the same stages everywhere, regardless of their differences in culture. (Etym. Greek *orthos*, upright, right + *genesis*, origin.)

ORTHOLOGY. Right speech. A term used by those dissenters from Catholic teaching who claim that right doctrine (orthodoxy) is essentially a subjective experience. It should not, therefore, be identified with any formulation of dogma. Formulas of verbal doctrine, it is said, are quite changeable and unimportant.

ORTHOPHONY. Right words. See ORTHOLOGY.

ORTHOPRAXIS. Right conduct. Also used by those who minimize the importance of right doctrine (orthodoxy), claiming that behavior and not belief is primary in Christianity. (Etym. Greek *orthos*, upright, right + *praxis*, doing, action.)

O.S. Old Style.

O SALUTARIS HOSTIA. Hymn to the Blessed Sacrament, "O Saving Victim, Opening Wide," sung during Eucharistic Exposition. It forms the last two (fifth and sixth) verses of *Verbum Supernum Prodiens*, written by St. Thomas Aquinas, originally for Lauds on the feast of Corpus Christi. A standard English translation reads:

O saving Victim opening wide
The gate of heaven to man below!
Our foes press on from every side;
Your aid supply, Your strength bestow.

To Your great name be endless praise
Immortal Godhead, one in three!
O grant us endless length of days,
In our true native land to be. Amen.

OSCULATORIUM. See PEACE PLATE or TABLET.

OSEE. See HOSEA.

OSSERVATORE ROMANO, L'. The *Roman Observer*, official newspaper of the Vatican, which began publication in 1861, at first unofficially and then semi-officially under Pope Leo XIII. The editors have been laymen. It is published daily, and more recently also a special edition on Sunday. Besides news of religious interest, it publishes documents, addresses of the Pope, reports and comments on political and social events. Weekly editions in languages other than Italian are also published.

OSSUARY. A bone casket, notably that of a person buried in the Near East in the first century. Ossuaries contain inscribed names commonly used by the Jews in the time of Christ, along with rarer ones. They testify to the historical authenticity of the names used in the Gospels, as also of such titles as "master" or "teacher" (*didaskalos*), although the designation previously had been cited as evidence of a second-century date. (Etym. Latin *ossuarium*, a bone urn.)

OSTENSORIUM. A monstrance, a metal vessel usually gold- or silver-plated with a transparent section in which the Sacred Host is placed in its lunette when exposed for adoration or carried in procession. It varies in shape and ornamentation, popular models being tower-shaped or round; a metal circlet surrounded with rays or bars resting on a stem rising from a heavy base, many ornamented with jewels. The ostensorium in the Cathedral of Toledo took more than a hundred years to make and is reputed to be of gold brought by Columbus from America.

OSTIARIUS. A porter or doorkeeper, one of the minor orders, and lowest in rank. Under Pope Paul VI the order was suppressed and absorbed into the two ministries that replaced the minor orders, namely reader and acolyte. (Etym. Latin *ostium,* door, entrance.)

O.T. Old Testament.

OUR FATHER. The Lord's Prayer, taught by Christ in answer to a request by the Disciples to teach them how to pray. As recited in the Catholic Church, it says: "Our Father, who art in heaven, hallowed be thy name; thy kingdom come; thy will be done on earth as it is in heaven. Give us this day our daily bread; and forgive us our trespasses as we forgive those who trespass against us; and lead us not into temptation, but deliver us from evil. Amen." It consists of seven petitions, of which the first three are concerned with the interests of God, and the last four are requests for divine assistance to man. The single most commented on words of the Bible, the Our Father, is also the common heritage of all Christians, which synthesizes their common belief in the Fatherhood of God, the primacy of the divine over the human, the need for prayer to obtain grace, the source of morality in doing the will of God, and the struggle with evil as a condition for salvation. The longer ending, with the words "For thine is the kingdom, and the power, and the glory," used by Protestants, is a liturgical addition that found its way into some manuscripts of the New Testament but was not part of the original biblical text, either in Matthew (6:9–13) or Luke (11:2–4).

OUR LADY. The most popular title for the Blessed Virgin in Catholic piety and literature. Its first recorded use in English is in the Anglo-Saxon poet Cynewulf (c. A.D. 750) and is commonly associated with some special prerogative or office of the Blessed Virgin, e.g., Our Lady of Ransom, Our Lady of Divine Providence, Our Lady of the Way. It is equivalent to *Madonna* in Italian, and *Domina* in Latin.

OUR LADY OF RANSOM SCAPULAR. Badge of a confraternity affiliated with the Order of Our Lady of Mercy. It is white and has a picture of Our Lady of Ransom.

OUR LORD. Shortened form of Our Lord Jesus Christ, as found in the earliest liturgical prayers. Used with the prefix "Our," it stands for Christ, but alone as "Lord" or "The Lord" is also synonymous with God.

OVERPOPULATION. A theory of certain demographers that the natural resources of the earth are becoming too small to meet the needs of the world's growing population. The Church's position is that "overpopulation" is a human construct; that the same divine providence that inspired the advances in science to increase human longevity will also ensure the means of sustaining the increased human family.

OWNERSHIP. The exclusive right of disposing of a thing as one's own. It is a right because ownership is more than merely holding a thing in one's possession. The disposition means doing anything possible with what is owned, e.g., keeping, changing, giving away, selling, using, or destroying; yet though of itself ownership is unlimited, the disposition of a thing may be limited from another source, say from the rights of a higher order or from charity to the neighbor. Ownership implies disposing of an object as one's own to distinguish it from mere agency or trusteeship. And the freedom to dispose what is owned is exclusive because others are kept from the use of what is owned, which applies even in corporate ownership. No matter how large the partnership, anyone outside the owners has no claims on the property. Exclusive right to dispose of something is the most distinctive feature of ownership.

OX. An emblem in sacred art associated with St. Luke. Along with the bull, it symbolizes sacrifice and the death of Christ on the Cross.

OXFORD MOVEMENT. A concerted effort originating around 1833 at Oxford University to restore to the Church of England certain pre-Reformation principles, which through inertia and indifference had been lost. A restoration in faith and worship, with an insistence on its alleged Catholic character without any reference to union with

Rome, characterized the movement. It was begun by Dr. Keble at Oxford and was carried on by John Henry Newman, Edward Pusey, Richard Froude, Frederick Faber, Isaac Williams, Charles Marriott, Bernard Dalgairns, and William Ward. The *Tracts for the Times,* written by the leaders, was a series of doctrinal papers setting forth the aims and teachings of the movement. Many of them were censured and condemned by the Established Church, and Ward's tract cost him his status by the Convocation of the University. Several of the leaders became Catholics, among them Newman and Ward. The movement seemed then to have ended, but its influence continued. The Church of England was transformed, an Anglo-Catholic party was definitely established, and the country at large became familiar with Catholic doctrine and practice. See also TRACTARIAN MOVEMENT.

OXON. *Oxonium, Oxonienses*—Oxford, theologians or scholars of Oxford.

P

P. *Pater, Père*—Father; *Papa*—Pope.

PA. *Papa*—Pope.

P.A., PREF. AP. Prefect Apostolic.

PACHOMIUS, RULE OF ST. The first systematic rule of life for a religious community, drawn up by St. Pachomius (290–346), the Egyptian founder of cenobitic Christian monasticism. It provided for a large number of monks under one head. There were three levels of superiors: the abbot over all the monasteries, a subordinate superior (*praepositus*) over individual communities, and a leader (*hebdomadarius*) who was appointed on a weekly basis to call the monks to prayer, lead the Divine Office, and relay directives from the superior. When Pachomius died, there were nine monasteries of men and two of women under his rule. He was head of seven thousand religious, thirteen hundred of whom were at Tabennesi on the bank of the Nile, and groups of two to three hundred were in smaller foundations.

PACIFISM. The doctrine that all war is inherently wrong and, among Christians, that warfare is forbidden by the Gospels. The position of the Catholic Church is that war is, indeed, undesirable and that sinful passions give rise to war, but not all armed conflict is necessarily sinful and Christians may engage in a just war. (Etym. Latin *pacificare,* to make peace.)

PACT. *Pactum*—agreement.

PADROADO. The privilege of patronage extended by the Pope to the King of Portugal over three episcopal sees in India since 1534, which gave rise to frequent conflicts between Church and State. The *padroado* was suppressed in 1928.

PADUA (shrine of St. Anthony). Between 1232 and 1300 the first church was built by the Franciscans as a friars' mausoleum and modeled after St. Mark's in Venice. It is Romanesque in style, but many of the side chapels show Gothic influence. Six domes crown the exterior with two bell towers and two minarets. The inside is severely plain, with hundreds of tombs of military men and over sixty representations of the Blessed Virgin Mary. Within the present basilica is a statue of Our Lady in the ancient chapel that encloses her, all that is left of the ancient church of Santa Maria given to St. Anthony in 1229. Here the saint said Mass, prayed, and heard confessions. Near the Blessed Sacrament chapel is the simple oratory of the great Franciscan preacher, finished at the turn of the sixteenth century, to which many Venetian artists contributed their skill. The back wall and side panels depict in marble nine events in St. Anthony's life. The tomb of the great Paduan is in the center. To the left of the main altar is a huge bronze candlestick considered the most magnificent candelabrum in the world. Donatello's famed Crucifixion group in bronze surmounts the altar itself. Besides the tomb of St. Anthony, the most precious relic of the saint honored in the basilica is his tongue, preserved in a richly embellished reliquary.

PAENITEMINI. Apostolic constitution of Pope Paul VI, issued in 1966, by which the canonical norms of fast and abstinence were changed. While changing the norms, the Pope made it clear that divine law requires all the faithful to do penance. Accordingly the purpose of the new regulations was not to weaken the practice of penance but to make it more effective. The Church, therefore, "while preserving—where it can be more readily observed—the custom (observed for many centuries with canonical norms) of practicing penance also through abstinence from meat and fasting, intends to ratify with her prescriptions other forms of penance as well, provided that it seems opportune to episcopal conferences to replace the observance of fast and abstinence with exercises of prayer and works of charity" (*Paenitemini,* III).

PAGAN. A heathen. In general one who practices idolatry. Formerly used to describe anyone who did not profess monotheism, and still used by Christians, Jews, and Moslems to identify a person who does not believe in one God, Creator of heaven and earth. More properly a pagan is a person who has abandoned all religious belief, i.e., an irreligious person. (Etym. Latin *paganus,* countryman, villager, civilian; from *pagus,* district, province, village.)

PAIN. The experience of suffering. Pain can be physical, when the suffering is in the deprivation of some bodily want; or mental, when the mind is oppressed by uncertainty or doubt; or emotional, when the feelings are disturbed by anxiety and fear; or volitional, when desires are frustrated; or social, when a person is rejected or at least not accepted by others; and spiritual, when the soul is mysteriously tried by desolation and even a sense of abandonment by God. (Etym. Latin *poena,* punishment, penalty, pain.)

PAIN OF LOSS. The eternal loss of the beatific vision in hell. Called the *poena damni,* it is the primary punishment of the evil spirits and of the souls who die rejecting God.

PAIN OF SENSE. The suffering in hell caused by some agent called "fire" in Scripture, external to the person and secondary to the main punishment, which is the loss of God.

PALESTINE. Name originally from Philistine of the country on the east shore of the Mediterranean. In the Bible, Palestine is called Canaan before the invasion of Joshua. It was the Holy Land of the ancient Israelites because it was promised them by God and became the Holy Land of the Christians because it was the home of Jesus Christ. Its boundaries have changed many times but, in general, have included the region between the Mediterranean Sea and the Jordan River, bordering southwest on Egypt. In the fourth century B.C., Palestine was conquered by Alexander the Great. In 141 B.C., the Jews revolted under the Maccabees and established a new state, but Rome took it over seventy years later. During the time of Christ, Palestine was ruled by the puppet Herods. The Jewish revolt provoked the Romans to destroy the Temple and either kill or expel the Jews from Palestine. Then followed, in sequence, the Christian occupation of the country until the seventh century, when the Moslems took over. During the Crusades, Palestine was temporarily in Christian hands but reverted to the Moslems by the thirteenth century. Jewish colonization began around 1870, and Zionism entered in the early twentieth century. In 1920 the British, who had acquired the area in World War II as a mandate, designated Palestine as a Jewish homeland, while safeguarding the rights of non-Jews. After many Jewish-Arab clashes, Palestine became the State of Israel in 1948.

PALL. A sacred covering. Most commonly, a pall is the stiff square cardboard covered with linen, spread over the top of the chalice at Mass; also a cloth covering, ornamented or plain, placed over the coffin at funeral Masses and over the catafalque at later requiem Masses for the dead; a veil partially covering the bride and groom in marriages of the Mozarabic rite; and a veil placed over the nun at profession ceremonies in some contemplative enclosed orders. (Etym. Latin *pallium,* cloak.)

PALLIUM. A sacred vestment symbolic of the fullness of episcopal authority. It is an inch-wide white wool circular band ornamented with six small crosses with a pendant strip attached in front and another behind, worn about the neck, breast, and shoulders of the Pope and archbishops. Made from the wool of two lambs blessed in the Church of St. Agnes in Rome. When granted to a bishop the pallium is purely ornamental. In Eastern rites patriarchs alone are invested with it. It is an outward sign of union with the Holy See. Pope John Paul I was formally invested on September 3, 1978, with the pallium instead of the traditional papal tiara at a Mass he concelebrated with members of the college of cardinals. His successor, Pope John Paul II, was also invested with the pallium.

PALLOTTINES. Members of the Society of the Catholic Apostolate, founded at Rome in

1835 by St. Vincent Pallotti (1795–1850). Their purpose is to preach and teach the faith among Christians and non-Christians, and to co-operate among the faithful in the Catholic apostolate. The Pallottines, according to Pope Pius XI, were the forerunners of modern Catholic Action. There are also Pallottine Sisters, founded by St. Vincent in 1843 as a separate congregation. One of their main interests is to foster reunion of the Oriental separated Christians with Rome.

PALM. A symbol of victory. When found in the catacombs it marked a martyr's grave. It is also the emblem of many saints who suffered in the Roman persecutions. In depicting the Last Judgment, it is the symbol of final triumph (Apocalypse 7–9). Palms marked Christ's triumphal entrance into Jerusalem.

PALMS, BLESSED. A sacramental of the Church. They are blessed and distributed to the faithful on Palm Sunday, commemorating the multitude bearing palms who triumphantly led Christ in procession on that day in Jerusalem. Already palms were used in the time of St. Bede the Venerable (673–735). The Oriental date palm, when obtainable, is the most popular. But any other twig or woody outgrowth is suitable. The liturgy of Palm Sunday refers simply to branches. In the prayer of blessing, the priest says, "Almighty God, we pray you to bless these branches and make them holy." During the procession with the palms the people walk in joyous public demonstration of their loyalty to Christ.

PALM SUNDAY. The Sunday before Easter and the sixth and last of Lent, and the beginning of Holy Week. On this day the Church commemorates Christ's triumphal entry into Jersualem, when olive and palm branches were strewn in his path. In the liturgy the memorial of this event is included in every Mass, with the procession or solemn entrance before the principal Mass, and with the simple procession before the other Masses on Palm Sunday.

PANAYA KAPULU (shrine). Mary's home near Selchuk, Turkey, two hundred miles from Constantinople in western Asia Minor. The reputed house where the Blessed Virgin spent her last years on earth. Ephesus is mostly in ruins, but about ten miles from the old city Our Lady's house is a pilgrimage spot that receives five thousand or more pilgrims monthly. A Catholic priest is in constant attendance. Moslems as well as Christians have come here since 1691 to pay homage to Mary. The small house was re-built in 1951 after long years of pilgrims' feet had practically destroyed it. Pope Paul VI made a pilgrimage to this shrine in July 1967.

PANEGYRIC. An elaborate public praise given of some person or event, a formal eulogy. The most famous Christian panegyrics were those of the Fathers of the Church, e.g., St. John Chrysostom preaching on Sts. Lucian and Romanus in A.D. 387. (Etym. Greek *panēgyrikos,* for a public festival.)

PANENTHEISM. The theory that the world is part of God, though not the whole of his being. It differs from pantheism, which identifies the world as God, by saying that a part of God is the universe and a part is simply God.

PANGE LINGUA. The hymn "Sing, my tongue, the Savior's glory," from Vespers of the Feast of Corpus Christi. It is used as a processional hymn on Holy Thursday, Corpus Christi, during Forty Hours' Adoration, and generally in honor of the Blessed Sacrament. The two last verses, the *Tantum Ergo,* have long been sung at Benediction of the Blessed Sacrament. Written by St. Thomas Aquinas, it has numerous translations in all the modern languages.

PANPSYCHISM. A theory that everything in the world is animated. All things are said to be alive or even conscious. Among its proponents the best known was Gottfried Wilhelm Leibniz (1646–1716). (Etym. Greek *pan,* all + *psyche,* soul.)

PAN-SATANISM. A name given to certain forms of pantheism, or to a philosophy of pessimism, like that of Arthur Schopenhauer (1788–1860). It is the belief that the world is somehow identified with the devil, as the "prince of this world" (John 12:31). (Etym. Greek *pan,* all + Hebrew *satan,* an adversary, enemy.)

PANSEXUALISM. The view that everything in human life, both personal and social, is to be explained in terms of sexual motivation and desire. Commonly identified with Freudianism. (Etym. Greek *pan,* all + Latin *sexus,* sex.)

PANTHEISM. Any of a variety of views that claim that all things are divine, or that God and the universe are really identical, or that there is ultimately no real distinction between God and what believers in creation call the world. (Etym. Greek *pan,* all + *theos,* god.)

PANTHEON. All the gods of a polytheistic

people. Also a temple dedicated to all gods, or at least the principal deities of a nation. The Roman Pantheon was built by Agrippa in 27 B.C., rebuilt by Hadrian in the second century A.D., and converted in 609 into a Christian church. The Panthéon in Paris, originally the church of St. Geneviève, was taken over during the French Revolution as a memorial temple of unbelief; after exchanging hands several times, it finally became what it is now, a national monument and mausoleum for illustrious Frenchmen. (Etym. Greek *pantheion*, temple consecrated to all gods.)

PANTOKRATOR. Greek title of God, "the all mighty." It is also a familiar image of Christ depicted as ruling from heaven.

PAPABILE. An Italian expression denoting a prelate who, during a vacancy in the Holy See, or anticipation of a vacancy, is popularly regarded as likely to be elected the next Pope. (Etym. Italian *papabile,* qualified for the papacy.)

PAPACY. A term applied to the office and jurisdiction of the Pope as the Vicar of Christ on earth; and also to the papal authority viewed as a religious and social force in history since the beginning of the Christian era. It generally refers to the system of ecclesiastical government in the Catholic Church headed by the Pope. (Etym. Latin *papa,* father.)

PAPAL CHOIR. Going back to ancient times, the papal choir was reorganized by Pope St. Gregory the Great. It is composed of specially chosen singers under the direction of a choirmaster who is also a composer.

PAPAL CROSS. A symbol also referred to as the archiepiscopal cross, used more in art than in actual practice. Papal and archiepiscopal crosses are really crucifixes elevated on staffs.

PAPAL ELECTION. See CONCLAVE.

PAPAL FLAG. The flag of Vatican City, consisting of a ground of white and yellow divided vertically into equal parts. The white part bears the seal of Vatican State, consisting of the tiara and cross-keys, with the inscription *Stato della Città del Vaticano.*

PAPAL LETTER. A publication or announcement issued directly by the Pope or by an official delegated by him. Matters of faith and morals were generally the subjects of these letters, designated as decreta. Others of more dogmatic importance were commonly called *epistolae tractoriae.* They were incorporated in collections of canon law and ranked with canons of synods in importance. Gratian and other canonists insisted that every papal letter of general character was authoritative for the entire Church. There were many forged papal letters during the Middle Ages. From the thirteenth to the twentieth centuries a papal document was given legal form by posting it on the doors of St. Peter's, the Lateran, or the Apostolic Chancery and in the Piazza del Campo di Fiori. Now they acquire force by publication in the *Acta Apostolocae Sedis.* These papal writings are published in a variety of forms, e.g., apostolic letters, constitutions, rescripts, bulls, and briefs. The original letters are deposited in the Roman archives. Private collections of papal letters also exist.

PAPAL SECRETARY OF STATE. The closest associate of the Pope. His office came into canonical existence under Pope Innocent XII in 1692 and was totally revised by Pope Paul VI in 1967. The papal secretariat's role is to develop all the functions entrusted to it by the Sovereign Pontiff, to watch over the various congregations and commissions of the Roman Curia, with special attention to the Commission for Social Communications, and in general to help the Pope in his care for the universal Church.

PAPAL STATES. The civil territory subject to the popes as temporal rulers from 754 to 1870. They had their origins in the two donations made in 754 and 756 by Pepin, King of the Franks, to Pope Stephen II, of the Duchy of Rome, the Exarchate of Ravenna, and the Marches of Ancona. This land was enlarged by later additions, e.g., from Charlemagne in 787 and from the Countess Matilda of Tuscany in 1115. Until the French Revolution the Papal States remained substantially what they were in the time of Charlemagne. In the nineteenth century the nationalist movement to unite the principalities of Italy into one country was successful. On September 20, 1870, Rome was taken by Italian troops. However, the legal possession of the Papal States was not recognized by the Pope until the Lateran Treaty in 1929.

PAPIST. Opprobrious term used in English-speaking countries to designate a Catholic. Its origin goes back to the Protestant Reformation, when Martin Luther (1483–1546) and John Calvin (1509–64) wrote polemics against the papacy.

PAPYRI, BEATTY. See BEATTY PAPYRI.

PARABLE. A short story based on a familiar life experience used to teach a spiritual lesson. It resembles the fable and the allegory. Jesus used the parable many times in his public ministry. "Why do you teach them in parables?" his disciples asked him. "Because," he replied, "the mysteries of the kingdom of heaven are revealed to you, but they are not revealed to them" (Matthew 13:10–11). It was a means of teaching his doctrine especially to those who accepted him as Messiah. (Etym. Greek *parabolē*, comparison, parable; literally, a throwing beside, juxtaposition.)

NEW TESTAMENT PARABLES

In Matthew:

The children who play	Matthew 11:16–19
The sower	Matthew 13:3–8
The tares	Matthew 13:24–30, 36–43
Mustard seed	Matthew 13:31, 32
The leaven	Matthew 13:33
Hidden treasure	Matthew 13:44
Pearl of great price	Matthew 13:44, 45
Dragnet	Matthew 13:47, 48
The lost sheep	Matthew 18:12–14
Unmerciful servant	Matthew 18:23–35
Laborers in the vineyard	Matthew 20:1–6
Prodigal Son	Matthew 21:28–32
The wicked husbandman	Matthew 21:33–44
Great supper	Matthew 22:1–14
Marriage feast	Matthew 22:1–14
The ten virgins	Matthew 25:1–13
The pounds	Matthew 25:14–30

In Mark:

The sower	Mark 4:3–8
Seed growing secretly	Mark 4:26–29
Mustard seed	Mark 4:30–32
The wicked husbandman	Mark 12:1–11

In Luke:

The children who play	Luke 7:31, 35
The two debtors	Luke 7:41–43
The sower	Luke 8:5–8
Good Samaritan	Luke 10:25–37
Importunate friend	Luke 11:5–8
Rich fool	Luke 12:16–21
Barren fig tree	Luke 13:6–9
Mustard seed	Luke 13:18, 19
The leaven	Luke 13:20, 21
Great supper	Luke 14:16–24
Marriage feast	Luke 14:16–24
The last place at banquets	Luke 14:7–11
The tower and war	Luke 14:28–32
The lost sheep	Luke 15:4–7
Lost silver piece	Luke 15:8–10
Prodigal Son	Luke 15:11–32
The unjust steward	Luke 16:1–8

Dives, the rich man, and Lazarus	Luke 16:19–31
The unjust judge	Luke 18:1–8
Pharisee and publican	Luke 18:9–14
The pounds	Luke 19:12–27
The wicked husbandman	Luke 20:9–18

PARACHURCH. An unconventional religious assembly, generally of only a few people or of persons who are unsatisfied with any of the established churches.

PARACLETE. A title of the Holy Spirit. Christ was and remains the first advocate. When he was to leave earth in visible form, he promised "another Paraclete" so that his followers would not be orphans. That Paraclete came on Pentecost. He is the advocate of the Mystical Body, pleading God's cause for the human family, keeping the Church from error, sanctifying souls through the preaching of God's word and through the sacraments. The Holy Spirit, whose function is to teach, bear witness, and "to convince the world of sin," is the love of God producing the effects of divine grace on earth, and appropriated to the third Person of the Trinity. (Etym. Greek *para-*, beside + *kalein*, to call: *parakletōs*, advocate.)

PARADIGM. The perfect model or pattern, which demonstrates all the possible ways in which something can be imitated or done. In this sense Christ is the paradigm of Christian sanctity. (Etym. Latin *paradigma;* from Greek *paradeigma*, a pattern, model.)

PARADISE. A synonym for heaven. Jesus spoke of it in his promise to the good thief on the Cross (Luke 23:43). In only two other places in Scripture is it used in place of heaven. There is a reference to "the tree of life set in God's paradise" (Revelation 2:7). Paul wrote about a man in Christ "caught up into paradise" (II Corinthians 12:4). (Etym. Greek *paradeisos*, park, the Garden of Eden, paradise; from Persian *pairidaēza*, an enclosure.)

PARADOX. An apparent contradiction that is really true. Christianity is the religion of paradox: that God should be human, that life comes from death, that achievement comes through failure, that folly is wisdom, that happiness is to mourn, that to find one must lose, and that the greatest are the smallest. What is paradoxical about the mysteries of the faith is that reason cannot fully penetrate their meaning, so that what seems contradictory to reason is profoundly true in terms of faith. (Etym. Latin *paradoxum;* from Greek *paradoxon*, contrary to received opinion or to expectation.)

PARAENESIS. Originally meant advice or counsel (Greek *parainein*, to advise). As a form of biblical composition, it is popular preaching or exhortation, of which the Epistle of St. James is a classic example. It is exemplified in the moralizing parts of the Old Testament and is found in such Apostolic Fathers as Clement I and the Shepherd of Hermas. Besides James, it is frequently used by St. Paul, e.g., in his letters to the Galatians and Ephesians.

PARALIPOMENON. The Vulgate title for the two books of the Chronicles. St. Jerome took over the title from the Greek Septuagint, which reads, "things left out," implying that the books are supplementary to the first and second Book of Kings. The aim of the author of Paralipomenon was to encourage his fellow countrymen to be faithful to the law, especially regarding worship in the Temple of Jerusalem.

PARALITURGICAL. Form of public worship in which Catholics engage without following the official liturgy or take unauthorized liberties in removing or changing the words or actions required by Church law.

PARALLELISM. Balancing one line of a verse against another. It is distinctive of Hebrew poetry. When the second line repeats the thought of the first, the parallelism is called synonymous (Psalms 50:4). When it opposes the first thought, it is called antithetical (Psalms 1:6). When it expands the first thought, it is said to be synthetic parallelism (Psalms 7:2). If the expansion continues through several lines step by step, it is referred to as climactic or stairlike.

PARARELIGIOUS. Term applied to sects that have some religious purpose but are mainly concerned with some other pursuit, like politics, health, or social change.

PARASCEVE. In Hellenistic Judaism, the day of preparation for the Sabbath, i.e., the Friday before. With certain feasts of sabbatical rank, the preceding day was also called the Parasceve. Christ died on the eve of the Pasch. (Etym. Greek *paraskeuē*, day of preparation.)

PARAY LE MONIAL. A city in central France where Christ appeared to Margaret Mary Alacoque, a Visitation nun, on December 27, 1763, as she was praying before the Blessed Sacrament. She saw his Sacred Heart surmounted by a cross and a crown of thorns surrounding it. Many other apparitions followed. The Church approved the Communion of Reparation on the First Friday of the Month, the Holy Hour, and a special feast dedicated each year to the Sacred Heart, as a result of Our Lord's requests of Margaret Mary. In 1873 when pilgrimages were revived, English Catholics flocked to Paray le Monial, where the convent chapel became the center of attention. The Basilica of the Sacred Heart, once in the priory of the Cluniac monks and now the parish church, shares in the interest of the pilgrims, along with the Eucharistic Museum, which has a remarkable collection of books and objects of art relating to the Blessed Sacrament. Pope Leo XIII called Paray le Monial, "the town very dear to heaven."

PARDON. Any act of clemency toward a guilty person. It may be release from all or some of the punishment, or, more properly, forgiving the offense on the part of the one offended. In civil and ecclesiastical law a pardon is also the document that declares exemption from the penalties for an offense or crime. And until modern times a "pardon" was synonymous with indulgence. (Etym. Latin *per*, through + *donare*, to give: *perdonare*, to remit.)

PARDONERS. A person licensed to preach and collect alms. In the Middle Ages the name was given to preachers of indulgences who gathered alms for building churches and supporting the Crusades. So many abuses resulted from the practice that the Council of Trent forbade the granting of any indulgence that was conditioned on a money contribution for a specified object.

PARENTAL OBEDIENCE. The duty of children to obey their parents, as prescribed by the fourth commandment of the Decalogue: "Honor your father and your mother so that you may have a long life in the land that Yahweh your God has given you" (Exodus 20:12). The precept obliges children to show love, reverence, and obedience toward their parents. The love that is due should be evident in words, actions, and attitudes. The obedience concerns everything that is part of the parents' care and obliges until the children reach their majority. It does not apply, however, to the children's choice of a state of life or, when they are of age, a choice in a marriage partner.

PARENTS, DUTIES OF. Parents are to provide for the physical and intellectual well-being of their children, but they are especially bound by divine law to educate their children for God and for eternal salvation. According to the Second Vatican Council, "It is the duty of parents to create a family atmosphere inspired by love and devotion to God and their fellow men which will promote an integrated, personal and social education of their children" (*Declaration on Christian Education,* 3).

PARISH. Normally, in a diocese, a definite territorial division that has been assigned its own church, a determined group of the faithful, and its own distinct pastor who is charged with the care of souls. National parishes have also been created to meet the needs of people of a certain race or nationality, with no relation to territory. Sometimes subdivisions of vicariates and prefectures apostolic are called quasi parishes. (Etym. Greek *paroikos,* dwelling near.)

PARISH COUNCIL. Modeled on the diocesan council, a group of parishioners organized to co-operate with the pastor in the apostolic work of a parish. After describing the functions of diocesan councils the Second Vatican Council decreed that "Such councils should also be found, if possible, at parochial, inter-parochial and inter-diocesan levels, and also on the national and international plane" (decree *Apostolicam Actuositatem,* 26). As conceived by the Church, parish councils are merely advisory to the pastor and are meant to assist him. Unlike their counterparts among Protestants, a Catholic parish council does not operate under the trustee system. It does not either replace the authority of the pastor or make him juridically dependent on its decisions.

PARISHIONER. The faithful who belong to a particular parish, as indicated by their enrollment in the parish registry, regular participation in the parish activities, especially the Eucharistic liturgy, and, as far as resources permit, their support of the parish facilities.

PAROCHIAL MASS. The Mass offered on all Sundays and holy days of obligation for the parishioners of every parish. If a pastor cannot celebrate the Mass, he must have another priest do so. The obligation is a grave one. (Etym. Latin *parochialis,* pertaining to a parish.)

PAROUSIA. The second coming of Christ to the earth (I Corinthians 15:23). References to it are frequent in the New Testament, as the writers describe the ultimate triumph of Jesus and the establishment of his kingdom (I Thessalonians 4:15–17; Matthew 24:3–14; II Peter 1:16).

PARSIMONY, LAW OF. The principle of economy of thought or effort in using means to a given end. As stated by William of Occam, called "Occam's Razor," "Beings should not be multiplied beyond necessity" (*Entia non sunt multiplicanda praeter necessitatem*). In any given enterprise, whether mental or physical, only as many elements should be used (time spent, ideas expressed, or energy employed) as the purpose of the enterprise requires. (Etym. Latin *parsimonia,* sparingness, thrift.)

PARSON. In pre-Reformation times the "Person of the Church" (*Persona Ecclesiae*) or priest in charge of a parish. The term is now mainly applied to ministers of the Church of England, particularly those with a benefice. (Etym. Middle English *persone,* person, parson.)

PARSONAGE. See GLEBE.

PARTHENOS. Biblical term for "virgin," used in the pre-Christian Greek translation of the Old Testament, referring to the virginal conception of the Messiah (Isaiah 7:14). Also the term used by the Evangelists in speaking of the Blessed Virgin (Matthew 1:18–25; Luke 1:26–27). (Etym. Greek *parthenos,* virgin.)

PARTIAL INDULGENCE. An indulgence that removes part of the temporal punishment due to forgiven sin. All particularities in terms of days, months, or years are now removed from partial indulgences. The new norm is based on the dispositions of the person gaining the indulgence and the character of the indulgenced work that person performs.

PARTICLE. A consecrated Host for distribution in Holy Communion, or even a fragment of the Eucharistic species. The Catholic faith teaches as defined doctrine that "in the venerable sacrament of the Eucharist, the whole Christ is contained under each species and under each and every part of either species that is separated from the rest" (Denzinger 1653). (Etym. Latin *particula,* small part, *pars,* a part.)

PARTICULAR JUDGMENT. The individual judgment by Christ of each human being a moment after death (Hebrews 9:27).

PART. IND. Partial indulgence.

PARTNER IN SIN. See SHARING IN GUILT.

PARVITAS MATERIAE. Slightness of matter, especially in sins of unchastity. According to the teaching of the Church, "in venereal pleasures, there is no slightness of matter" (Alexander VII, *Response of the Holy Office*, 1661). This means that the sin of lust is grave by its very nature, provided full consent is given, even though full sexual satisfaction was not obtained. In pastoral practice, however, when one checks oneself in the process of sinful sexual arousal, the presumption is that there had not been full consent from the beginning.

PASCENDI. Encyclical letter of Pope St. Pius X condemning Modernism. Its full title is *Pascendi Dominici Gregis,* published September 8, 1907.

PASCH. The Jewish feast celebrated annually at God's command to commemorate the deliverance of the Jews from the bondage of Egypt. This deliverance was conditioned on the sacrifice of an unblemished lamb or kid, bones unbroken, whose blood was to be used to sprinkle the doorpost of every Hebrew house on the night before their passage. The deliverance of the Jews from Egypt was a foreshadowing of the Christian Pasch when, through the sacrifice of the Lamb of God and the application of the merits of his blood, the human race would be freed from the bondage of the devil and of sin. Good Friday in the early Church was called the Pasch of the Crucifixion, while Easter day was styled the Pasch of the Resurrection, the Sundays from Easter to Whitsunday were always referred to as "after the Pasch." Easter is the Christian Passover. See also PASSOVER.

PASCH. *Pascha*—Easter.

PASCHAL CANDLE. A large candle in which five grains of incense have been incased as a symbol of Christ's wounds. It is blessed on Holy Saturday in a special service and is symbolic of the Risen Savior, Light of the World. It is then used in the blessing of baptismal water and remains during the Paschal season in the sanctuary, where it is lighted during liturgical services.

PASCHAL LAMB. The lamb eaten at the Passover of the Jews. According to the Mosaic law, the lambs were first to be sacrificed on the afternoon of the fourteenth of Nisan and then taken to the homes, where the people ate the lamb during the night (Exodus 12). Christ as the Messiah "was sacrificed for us" (I Corinthians 5:7), "and thus became for those who believe in Him the Paschal Lamb who takes away the sins of the world" (John 1:29).

PASCHAL MEAL. Originally the Passover,

as celebrated by the Israelites. The term is sometimes used of the Eucharist as Holy Communion.

PASCHAL MYSTERY. The title of a document, *Paschalis Mysterii*, issued by Pope Paul VI on May 9, 1969. In this document he approved a reorganization of the liturgical year and calendar for the Roman Rite. Its purpose was "to permit the faithful to communicate in a more intense way, through faith, hope and love, in the whole mystery of Christ, which . . . unfolds within the cycle of a year." Paschal Mystery is a general term to describe the redemptive work of Christ, especially the events of the Last Supper and the Passion, reaching their climax on Easter Sunday. (Etym. Latin *paschalis,* from *pascha,* Passover, Easter; from Greek *pascha;* from Hebrew *pesah,* Pesach.)

PASCHAL TIME. The fifty-six days from Holy Saturday to Vespers on the Saturday following Pentecost. It corresponds to the time of rejoicing that the risen Jesus spent with his followers on earth and the nine days he told them to wait for the coming of the Holy Spirit. Liturgically it is a period of joy: white vestments are used, the Gloria is said at ferial Masses, the *Te Deum* is daily chanted, *Vidi Aquam* and the *Regina Coeli* replace the Asperges and the Angelus. Every Catholic is to receive the Holy Eucharist during this period.

PASSING BELL. The ancient custom in Catholic localities of ringing the church bell slowly when a death is imminent in a parish. When the sick person is near death, the solemn tones of the bell remind the faithful of their Christian duty to pray for the person's happy death. After the death, another bell tolls out the person's age—one short stroke for each year.

PASSION. Intense motion of a human appetite. Although commonly associated with bodily desires, such as anger or sex, passions can also arise in the spiritual faculties, as happens in envy and pride. Passions are essentially desires out of control because of fallen human nature. They are concupiscence in action. When passion arises spontaneously before the free will has acted, it is called antecedent and, as such, lessens human freedom and responsibility. When it is intentionally fostered by brooding or preoccupation, it is consequent passion because it comes after the free choice of the will. Consequent passion is morally culpable. (Etym. Latin *passio,* suffering, passion, affection.)

PASSION. The events surrounding the Suffering and Death of Jesus Christ; part of the religious rite of Holy Week in the Catholic Church.

PASSION SCAPULAR. Red, with bands of red woolen material. On one half is a picture of the crucified Savior, with the implements of the Passion and the words, "Holy Passion of Jesus Christ, Save Us." Owes its origin to a vision granted to a Sister of Charity in 1846. Promoted by the Priests of the Mission. Approved by Pope Pius IX. Another scapular of the Passion is black, and is the badge of a confraternity associated with the Passionists. It bears on the front the words, "May the Passion of Jesus Christ be always in our hearts."

PASSIONATE ANGER. A strong emotional displeasure. Even passionate anger is not necessarily sinful, provided the reaction is directed only against the guilty party and its vehemence is in proportion to the object and circumstances. Moreover, to be licit, passionate anger must not blind a person's reason or place one in danger of overstepping prudent limits of inflicting punishment. Moreover, as long as passionate anger is independent of one's will, i.e., not deliberately induced, it is not of itself sinful. There is an obligation, however, to repress a strong impulse to anger either when the passion is aroused beyond what the provocation deserves or when the emotions are so impetuous that one "loses one's temper." To consent to an immoderate outburst of anger that vents itself in the irascible words or actions is normally a venial sin. It becomes serious when what is said or done is very offensive or harmful. It is also a grave sin when the anger takes the form of conscious revenge.

PASSIONISTS. Members of the Congregation of Discalced Clerics of the Most Holy Cross and Passion of Our Lord Jesus Christ, founded at Monte Argentaro in Tuscany in 1737 by St. Paul of the Cross (1694–1775). The rule was definitely approved in 1769 by Pope Clement XIV, who conferred many privileges of the old orders on the new congregation. Passionists emphasize contemplation as the basis of their apostolic work, and take a fourth vow to promote devotion to the Passion of Christ. Their traditional apostolates are preaching missions and giving retreats. Passionist nuns, totally distinct from the clerical society, were founded as strict contemplatives.

PASSION NARRATIVE. The declamation of the Passion of Our Lord in front of the altar by different persons, one reciting the words of Christ, another the words of the Jewish tribunal or the Roman governor, and a third representing the crowd. The interrelation of their voices, pitch, and interpretation of the various roles is a part of today's Passion services. The Passion music reached its highest development under Johann Sebastian Bach and Franz Joseph Haydn.

PASSION PLAYS. The dramatic rendering of Christ's Passion in religious, artistic, and popular forms. They appeared originally as part of the ritual of the Church, first in Latin, then in German, and gradually developed in popular form until they lost their dignified character. By the seventeenth century their presentation was confined to monasteries or isolated villages. Public interest in them received new life in the nineteenth century, in the Austrian Tyrol, in southern Bohemia, and above all at Oberammergau in Bavaria, where now a world famous literary drama is enacted with appropriate music and setting. It is performed every ten years as an act of thanksgiving for the deliverance of their village from the plague.

PASSIONS. Human emotions insofar as they are inordinate in purpose, intensity or duration. They are feelings somehow out of control, and involve a notable change in a person's bodily functions or activity. Less accurately, the passions are sometimes identified with any intense movement of the sensitive appetite, e.g., sex, anger, or hunger, accompanied by some organic change.

PASSION SYMBOLS. Emblems of Christ's Passion and Death are usually found grouped in illustrations around the Cross. More than a dozen such symbols are found in stone carvings in several English cathedrals. Used alone or together they are also represented frequently in Italian and Spanish art of the sixteenth century: the thirty pieces of silver, the scourge with leaded thongs, the pillar and cord, the reed scepter, the crown of thorns, the nails, the seamless robe and dice, the sponge, the lance, the ladder, and the winding sheet. The crown of thorns is an emblem of St. John of God, St. Louis of France, and St. Rose of Lima; St. Boniface and Sts. Gervase and Protase are shown with the scourge, St. Barnabas and St. Matthias with the lance. The empty Cross, draped with the winding sheet, is the universal emblem of the Crucifixion.

PASSIONTIDE. The week before Easter from Passion (Palm) Sunday to and including the Easter Vigil. It was formerly the last two weeks before Easter Sunday.

PASSIVE RECOLLECTION. An inward recollection of the soul, not by any imaginative consideration of divine things, but by a gentle and affectionate absorption of the mind and heart in God produced by a special grace of the Holy Spirit. The senses are not suspended but remain in the soul's possession so that they can be applied to God.

PASSIVE UNITIVE WAY. Also called the mystic unitive way, it is characterized by an overpowering influence of divine grace beyond anything possible through the ordinary forms of prayer. It is called passive because the soul is, as it were, powerless to act on its own initiative but is attracted willingly by God to himself in an irresistible way.

PASSOS. A Portuguese name to designate pious Lenten exercises held at Goa and other Catholic communities in India. Originally the flagellants were active in these Friday processions, singing litanies and scourging themselves in sight of the Cross. Today the same customs are regularly held but without the scourging and other objectionable features. A presentation of a scene from the Passion is added weekly to the sermon and followed by a procession.

PASSOVER. The Jewish Pasch celebrated annually as commanded by God to commemorate the deliverance of the Israelites from the bondage of Egypt. Its main feature was the sacrificial meal, ending with eating the paschal lamb, followed by the seven-day Feast of the Unleavened Bread. At the time of Christ the Passover meal united the Jewish family from sunset to midnight on the fifteenth of Nisan. Its last celebration by the Savior was the occasion for instituting the Eucharist and the priesthood of the New Law. See also PASCH.

PASTOR. An individual priest or a corporate person (religious order or community) to whom a parish has been entrusted by a bishop, with the rights and responsibilities conferred by canon law and the statutes of the diocese. (Etym. Latin *pastor,* shepherd; literally, feeder.)

PASTOR, PAROCHIAL. The priest or moral person to whom a parish is entrusted under the authority of a bishop (or ordinary of the place), with the responsibility of caring for souls.

PASTOR AETERNUS. The title of the Dogmatic Constitution on the Church of Christ, issued by the First Vatican Council, July 18, 1870, in which four doctrines of the faith were defined: the apostolic primacy conferred on Peter, the perpetuity of the Petrine Primacy in the Roman pontiffs, the meaning and power of the papal primacy, and the infallible teaching authority (magisterium) of the Roman Pontiff.

PASTORALE MUNUS. Apostolic Letter of Pope Paul VI, conferring forty new faculties and eight special privileges on the bishops of the Catholic Church (November 30, 1963).

PASTORAL LETTERS. Official documents sent by a bishop to the clergy only or to all the faithful of a diocese. A group of bishops, of a region or of a whole country, may also issue pastoral letters for the entire territory under their jurisdiction. Pastoral letters may deal with any subject affecting the faith, practice, or worship of the people. They are often published during certain seasons, as in Lent or Advent. Over the centuries they have become expressions of the ordinary teaching authority of the Church. Nowadays important pastorals are also published in the Vatican newspaper, *L'Osservatore Romano.*

PASTORAL STAFF. See CROSIER.

PASTORAL THEOLOGY. The practical application of scientific theology to the care of souls in the sacred ministry. Its purpose is to render this ministry more effective by the use of proven methods of dealing with the spiritual needs of individuals or groups of the faithful. A relatively new discipline, it came into being to cope with the increasingly complex and changing circumstances of modern life. It draws on the principles and methodology of both the secular and the sacred sciences, with special concern to help the people live out their Christian commitments in conflict with a hostile or at least indifferent non-Christian society.

PATARINES. Also called Patarelli, they were a Catholic party in the early Middle Ages that supported the popes in their struggles for celibacy of the clergy and against simony. They ceased to exist after the death in 1075 of their leader, Erlembald. Later on the name came to be used of the Cathari, and other heretics, condemned by the Third Lateran Council in 1179.

PATEN. A saucerlike dish of the same material as the chalice—gold-plated and consecrated by a bishop or his delegate with holy chrism. It must be large enough to cover the chalice. On it rests the bread to be consecrated, and later on the Sacred Host. It was customary to have a subdeacon hold the paten, covered by the humeral veil, from the Offertory to the Pater Noster in solemn Masses. (Etym. Latin *patena,* a broad, shallow dish or pan.)

PATER NOSTER. The prayer composed and taught by Christ to the Disciples (Matthew 6:9–13; Luke 11:2–4). Named from the first two words of the prayer in the Latin, Pater Noster (Our Father). The Pater Noster has been part of the Church's liturgy since apostolic times. It was part of the profession of faith for the reception of catechumens into the Church, has more commentary by the Fathers and Doctors of the Church than any other passage in the Bible, and, after baptism, is the best known bond of unity among Christians in every tradition. Its seven petitions are a synthesis of the faith, and its balanced structure is an expression of the true hierarchy of values, first the things of God, and then the needs of man. The longer ending among Protestants, "For thine is the kingdom, and the power, and the glory, now and forever," was added in the sixteenth century. It was originally a liturgical ending, which the Catholic Church has recently incorporated into the Eucharistic Prayer of the Mass. See also OUR FATHER.

PATIENCE. A form of the moral virtue of fortitude. It enables one to endure present evils without sadness or resentment in conformity with the will of God. Patience is mainly concerned with bearing the evils caused by another. The three grades of patience are: to bear difficulties without interior complaint, to use hardships to make progress in virtue, and even to desire the cross and afflictions out of love for God and accept them with spiritual joy. (Etym. Latin *patientia,* patience, endurance; from *patiens,* suffering.)

PATR. *Patriarcha*—patriarch.

PATRIARCH. The father and ruler of a family, tribe, or race in biblical history. A name commonly applied to Abraham, Isaac, and Jacob. Also a prelate who has the honor of being called the prince of fathers but is without jurisdiction except in virtue of some particular law. He holds precedence over primates, metropolitans, and bishops. In the order of their dignity, the Patriarch of Rome leads those of Constantinople, Alexandria, Antioch, and Jerusalem. In the East there are patriarchs of the Armenian, Maronite, Melkite, and Chaldean rites, with minor patriarchs of Venice, Lisbon, the West and East Indies. The power and importance of patriarchs, except that of the Pope, have diminished since the Eastern Schism. They have the right to ordain all bishops of their patriarchate; consecrate the holy chrism; summon synods; send the omophorion (pallium) to their metropolitans, and hear appeals from lower courts. They are the highest rulers in their churches. The Sovereign Pontiff alone is over them. (Etym. Greek *patriarchēs,* father of a race.)

PATRIARCHAL BASILICA. One of major Roman basilicas of the Catholic Church. They are St. John Lateran, which is the archbasilica for the Pope as Patriarch of the West; St. Peter's for the Patriarch of Constantinople; St. Paul's Outside the Walls for the Patriarch of Alexandria; and St. Mary Major's for the Patriarch of Antioch. Although St. Lawrence's, also Outside the Walls, is the patriarchal church for Jerusalem, it is not always considered major. Originally these basilicas had adjoining residences for the respective patriarchs when they stayed in Rome.

PATRIARCHAL CROSS. Also called the archiepiscopal cross.

PATRIARCHAL THEORY. Political rulers are divinely designated leaders in civil society because of their natural endowments. The theory arose in modern times to counteract the excesses of the French Revolution and avoid the pitfalls of the divine right of kings, without admitting the democratic basis of civil government. Espoused by, among others, D'Azeglio Luigi Taparelli (1793–1862), it seems to have been more a description of how many governments are formed (from the top down) than a theoretical analysis of the origins of political authority.

PATRIARCHATE. The territory ruled ecclesiastically by a patriarch. Rome, Alexandria, Antioch were the first to enjoy patriarchal rights. The Pope as patriarch of the West holds jurisdiction over all the western lands where Latin was once the professional and liturgical language, where the Roman Rite is now used almost exclusively and Roman canon law still obtains. In the East the patriarchates have become organizations of Catholics observing different rites. The original Eastern patriarchates are now represented by a loose federation of Churches differing in liturgies and customs but united in faith, morals, and communion with the Holy See.

PATRIMONY. Any inheritance, especially

from one's father. Solemn profession in a religious order requires the renunciation of one's patrimony. The Second Vatican Council extended this practice, declaring: "Religious congregations (with simple vows) may, in their constitutions, permit their members to renounce their inheritances, both those which they have already acquired, and those which may be acquired in the future" (*Perfectae Caritatis,* 13). (Etym. Latin *patrimonium,* an estate inherited from a father, patrimony.)

PATRIMONY OF ST. PETER. The lands, properties, and revenues from various sources belonging to the Holy See. Before the Peace of Constantine (A.D. 313) the Church's properties were very limited, but after his reign, by his gifts and those of newly converted nobles, the Church found herself possessing large estates. About A.D. 600 the Pope might have been called the largest landed proprietor in the world. Large farms, forests, whole villages with their cultivators, though free, constituted a *massa.* Many *massae* formed a patrimony, almost the equivalent in extent of a Roman province. These patrimonies were mainly located in Italy, with a few in the Orient, Gaul, Dalmatia, and Africa. Sicily had the most valuable, Rome the most numerous patrimonies. Naples, Gaeta, Tivoli, Ravenna, and Genoa contributed their share. All together they were called the Patrimony of St. Peter. Hospitals, monasteries, and churches were built and maintained, the freedom of slaves was purchased, the needy of Italy and elsewhere were relieved by the revenues of Peter's Patrimony. St. Gregory called it the Patrimony of the Poor.

PATRIMONY OF THE POOR. In the early Church, after the Edict of Milan (A.D. 313), a fourth of the revenues of a diocese set aside for the relief of the poor. Its biblical basis was the strong emphasis in the New Testament on caring for the poor, and of sharing, as a condition for salvation.

PATRINI. Sponsors at baptism. So called from the Medieval Latin term, which means those taking the place of parents. They undertake the office of spiritual parents toward those whom they bring to the baptismal font.

PATRIPASSIANISM. A form of Monarchianism, which postulated that there is only one person in the Trinity, so that logically God the Father became man, as much as the Son, and suffered on the Cross for mankind. Sometimes it is called Sabellianism.

(Etym. Latin *pater,* father + *passus,* having suffered.) See also SABELLIANISM.

PATRISTIC PHILOSOPHY. The philosophy developed in Christianity during the age of the Fathers, mainly in the first five centuries. It represents the first meeting of Christian revelation with the pagan thought of antiquity. Christian intellectuals were aware that they were at the crossroads of two very different worlds, not necessarily opposed to each other. Patristic philosophy, therefore, represents the fusion of the best heritage of ancient Hellenism and the faith of Christianity, which itself had inherited much from Judaism. Three principal strains of philosophizing are discernible, of which the first two were heretical: that Christianity and paganism are utterly opposed to each other, as in Tertullian; that paganism and Christianity are totally compatible, as among the Gnostics; and that the wisdom of Christ and of pagan thought can co-operate, but always pagan philosophy is subordinate to Christianity and to be purified by the higher wisdom of revelation. Much of the conflict with heresy in the early patristic age was due to attempts by some Christian thinkers to subordinate their faith to the intellectual theories of the pagan Mediterranean world.

PATRISTICS. Originally the same as patrology, and still includes the latter. It is the study of the Fathers of the Church, their lives, writings, doctrine, and theology.

PATRISTIC THEOLOGY. Systematic reasoning on the Christian faith by the Fathers of the Church. There was scarcely any theology among the early Fathers, Clement of Rome and Ignatius of Antioch, who practically repeated the data of Scripture and the apostolic preaching with a minimum of reasoned analysis. In the second and third centuries, however, contact with the pagan world produced a reaction. Two types of apologists arose, traditionalists, such as Tatian, who rejected philosophy, and others such as Justin, who were willing to use Greek speculation in the interests of the faith. Fortunately for the latter, who were in danger of Gnostic absorption, St. Irenaeus urged the need of remaining faithful to the Church's tradition, the living depository of revealed truth.

The more speculative line of St. Justin was developed by Clement of Alexandria and Origen, with consequent influence on the great Cappadocians, Basil, Gregory of Nyssa, and Gregory of Nazianzus. Characteristics of the Alexandrian school were a marked leaning toward Platonism, an allegorical interpretation of Scripture, and a profound mysticism.

By contrast, the more positive Aristotelian school of Antioch produced St. John Chrysostom, Theodore of Mopsuestia, and Theodoret, who affected the movement of theology through the whole patristic age. The high points of subsequent controversies coincided with the first seven ecumenical councils, which profited from both the Alexandrian and Antiochian schools in defining the principal dogmas on the Trinity and the person of Christ. Among the Fathers no one contributed more to theological growth than St. Augustine. He synthesized the four centuries of tradition which preceded him, clarified and in many cases solved the most vexing dogmatic questions, and co-ordinated the ensemble of sacred knowledge which St. Thomas Aquinas and the Scholastics later organized into a unified system of Christian thought.

PATROLOGY. The study of the writings of the Church Fathers and the science of their contents. (Etym. Greek *pater,* father + *logia,* knowledge.)

PATRON. A person who supports, maintains, or protects another person, project, or enterprise. According to canon law, a patron is one who builds or maintains an ecclesiastical benefice. If church revenues constitute a benefice, then anyone donating the land, building the church, or maintaining it is a patron. Since the right of patronage is of a spiritual order, it is subject to ecclesiastical jurisdiction. (Etym. Latin *patronus,* protector.)

PATRONAGE. The act of founding a church, chapel, or religious institution, and the privileges accorded to such benefactors. Patronage also refers to the special heavenly patrons officially assigned to nations, dioceses, communities, and institutions.

PATRONAGE OF ST. JOSEPH. The role of St. Joseph, spouse of Mary and foster-father of Jesus, as patron of the universal Church. It was proclaimed by Pope Pius IX in 1847.

PATRON SAINT. A saint or blessed who, since early Christian times, has been chosen as a special intercessor with God for a particular person, place, community, or organization. The custom arose from the biblical fact that a change of personal name indicated a change in the person, e.g., Abram to Abraham, Simon to Peter, Saul to Paul; and from the practice of having churches built over the tombs of martyrs.

PAUL. The most dynamic of Christ's Apostles, even though he was not one of the original twelve. His name was Saul, changed to Paul after his conversion. He was a Jew, born in Tarsus of Cilicia and his family were Pharisees (Acts 22:3). Saul became a leader among the fanatical Pharisees and developed a reputation for ferocious enmity toward Christians (Acts 8:3). He was traveling on the road to Damascus (on an anti-Christian mission) when he was thrown to the ground and blinded by a dazzling light. Christ appeared to him and he was instantly converted. "What am I to do, Lord?" he asked (Acts 22:10). He spent a number of years in Arabia (Galatians 1:17). His status when he began to preach Christianity was awkward; the Pharisees considered him a turncoat; the Christians feared him because of his early reputation. Barnabas was especially helpful to him at this stage; he introduced him to Christian groups and vouched for his sincerity in both Antioch and Jerusalem (Acts 9:27). This association was so effective that the Church in Antioch commissioned Barnabas, as leader, and Paul and Mark as assistants to take a missionary voyage through Cyprus, Pamphylia, Iconium, Lystra, and Derbe (Acts 13, 14). This led to a dramatic confrontation. Paul, Barnabas, and Titus proceeded to Jerusalem to urge a more flexible concept of a Christian than that of a circumcised Old Law Jew (Galatians 2). Peter presided. After all viewpoints were presented, Paul's own group won the day: Gentiles did not have to become Jews to become Christians (Acts 15:5–21). Then began Paul's second missionary journey. This time the journey took Paul through Phrygia, Galatia, Philippi, Thessalonica, and Beroea (Acts 18:23). Some of these visits were the first ventures into Europe of Christian apostles. There followed a third journey, through Macedonia and Greece. Only the wariness of his followers saved him from injury or death on several occasions (Acts 19:30). Especially venomous were the Jews in Jerusalem; his Roman citizenship saved his life several times. Some of his finest epistles were written during a two-year period while he was under house arrest awaiting trial. Death came to him finally in Rome during Nero's persecution by decapitation in about 67. He is buried near the present Basilica of St. Paul. (Etym. Latin *Paul[l]us.*)

PAULICIANS. A dualistic sect that flourished from the seventh to the eleventh centuries in the Byzantine Empire. The origin of the name is uncertain, but was probably derived from the affinity to Paul of Samosata, the third-century heretical Bishop of Antioch. They held that there are two ultimate sources of creation, a good deity who is Ruler of heaven and made human souls, and an evil god who rules the material world and human bodies. Holding all matter evil, they rejected the Church's redemption through Christ's bodily death on the Cross, opposed images of Christ crucified, and substituted instead the book of the Gospels. Their dualistic doctrine led to grave moral disorders because whatever evil was committed by the body was attributed to the evil deity whose power was irresistible. Begun by Mananali in A.D. 657, the movement persisted until about 1050. Many of its ideas entered other religious groups, notably the Albigensians. In politics they were more favorable to the Saracens than loyal to Rome, and contributed to the spread of Islam.

PAULINE PRIVILEGE. Dissolution of the marriage bond between two persons who were not baptized at the time of their marriage. Its basis in revelation is St. Paul (I Corinthians 7:12–15) and its conditions are the following: both parties are unbaptized at the time of marriage and after the marriage one of the parties receives baptism; one party has embraced the faith through baptism and the other remains unbaptized; the unbaptized person departs either physically by divorce or desertion, or morally by making married life unbearable for the convert; the departure of the unbaptized party is verified by means of interpellations, i.e., being asked if he or she is willing to be baptized or at least willing to live peacefully with the convert to the faith. If the above conditions are fulfilled and are negative, the Church may grant the baptized person the right to marry another Christian.

PAULISTS. Members of the Missionary Society of the Apostle, founded in the United States in 1858 by Isaac Hecker (1819–88). It was established to further the work and interests of the Roman Catholic Church in the United States. Their rule is based on that of the Redemptorists, to which congregation the founder originally belonged.

PAULITES. Monks of St. Paul the Hermit, founded in 1225 at Gran, in Hungary, by Blessed Eusebius. Latest approval of the constitutions by the Holy See was in 1930. They are active-contemplative, concentrating on the priestly ministry in their own churches. They have charge of the Shrine of Our Lady of Czestochowa in Poland.

PAUPERISM. The state of a person who is more or less habitually without the material means of living a normal human life. Unlike poverty it implies, as a rule, dependence on regular support from the State, charitable persons or agencies. (Etym. Latin *pauper*, poor person.)

PAX. Literally "peace." In the revised liturgy the kiss of peace, which the priest celebrant at Mass gives to the ministers at the altar and announces to the congregation with the words, "Let us offer each other the sign of peace." The faithful then extend to one another some appropriate sign of peace, as approved by the national (or regional) conference of bishops. In ancient times the *pax* took place much earlier in the Mass. And for centuries, until the Second Vatican Council, it was given by the celebrant only to those immediately assisting at the altar during a solemn High Mass.

PAX ROMANA. International movement of Catholic students, founded in Switzerland in 1921. Its purpose is to instill in its members an awareness of their responsibility to exert a Christian influence on their university environment, to seek Christian solutions to contemporary world problems, and in general to prepare themselves for bringing Christ and his message to all whose lives they will later on affect. These goals are achieved through national and international seminars and through meetings with other student organizations. Another group, Pax Romana–International Catholic Movement for Intellectual and Cultural Affairs, unites Catholic university graduates to help them meet their responsibilities to the Church and to civil society. Pax Romana has a consultative status with the Economic and Social Council of the United Nations and has permanent delegates at the United Nations in New York and Geneva and with UNESCO.

P.D. *Pontificalis Domus*—Prefecture of the Papal Household.

PEACE. The tranquillity of order. Peace is first of all the absence of conflict. But it is also the serenity experienced because there is no conflict. It is the calm that accompanies agreement of human wills, and is the foundation of every well-ordered society.

PEACE OF GOD. The permanent immunity from armed hostility legislated by the Church in the early Middle Ages. It anathematized all persons who attacked noncombatants or invaded sanctuaries. *Pax Dei* laid severe penalties on those who plundered clerics, merchants, peasants, women, or children. And it was enforced by associations organized for this purpose.

PEACE OF THE CHURCH. The bestowal of privileges on the Church by Emperor Constantine, preceded by the granting of toleration to Christians in A.D. 313. As a result, religion was no longer subservient to the absolute state. Christians were given complete freedom to practice their religion, and the Church was granted possession of all previously seized property. This concession enabled the full liturgy to be resumed, the faith to be preached and proclaimed, and Christian values to infuse the public and private life of the Roman Empire.

The term "Peace of the Church" is also applied in England and Ireland to the end of persecution that followed the Acts of Catholic Emancipation (1778–1926); in Germany, after the *Kulturkampf;* and in other countries, e.g., France, Italy, and Mexico, as certain disabilities imposed on the Church were removed.

PEACE PLATE or TABLET. Also called the osculatorium. It is a plaque made of wood, metal, or ivory decorated with inscriptions and provided with a handle. It conveyed the kiss of peace from the celebrant to the faithful, each member receiving it in turn. In medieval times at a Nuptial Mass, the kiss of peace was received in this way by the bridegroom and then transmitted by him to the bride.

PEACOCK. An emblem of immortality, also of pride and vanity among men. Juno's peacock was the sacred bird of pagan Rome often represented on the tombs of the celebrated dead. When first used as a symbol by the Christians, peacocks were often seen in conjunction with the chalice, drinking from it to ensure eternal life. St. Liborius, fourth-century French bishop of Le Mans and personal friend of St. Martin of Tours, has the peacock as his emblem.

PECCATOPHOBIA. Scrupulosity, or the irrational fear of sinning or of committing some crime. (Etym. Latin *peccatum,* fault, error, sin + Greek *phobia,* panic, fear of.)

PECTORAL CROSS. A cross usually of gold and ornamented with precious stones, worn suspended from the neck by a gold chain or silken cord. It may serve as a reliquary enclosing relics of the saints or the True Cross. Although it is the badge of a bishop, other prelates may wear it during public worship. (Etym. Latin *pectoralis,* of the breast.)

PECULIUM. An allowance of money given by a superior to a religious with a vow of poverty. The money may then be spent at the prudent judgment of the religious. If the peculium is acquired and used with the knowledge and consent of the superior, it is not incompatible with religious poverty. Abuses in the practice have been discouraged by the Holy See, and the peculium itself is opposed to the ideal of evangelical poverty. (Etym. Latin *peculium,* private property.)

PEDERNEIRA. Marian shrine located in Portugal where a little statue of Mary is honored under the title of "Our Lady of Nazareth." This image is believed to have been brought from the East in the eighth century by a monk from Nazareth and enthroned in a monastery at Lerida, but soon lost. It was rediscovered in 1182 by a knight in an abandoned cave. Legend tells that on the feast of Holy Cross the knight, out hunting as usual, gave chase to a large stag. In his excitement he did not notice the steep cliff toward which the stag was leading him. The stag plunged over the cliff, and in that moment the knight discerned the animal as the devil. Realizing the imminent danger, the knight prayed to Mary and her Son for help. The horse's footprints are still visible today where they became impressed in the solid rock in the frenzied attempt to stop. In gratitude the knight built for his beloved statue a shrine that was soon replaced by a small chapel. Seventeen villages in the vicinity share the little figure as they give honor in a two-day celebration on Mary's feast, but in this case the situation is reversed— Mary takes the yearly pilgrimage, while her people remain at home to welcome her.

PELAGIANISM. Heretical teaching on grace of Pelagius (355–425), the English or Irish lay monk who first propagated his views in Rome in the time of Pope Anastasius (reigned 399–401). He was scandalized at St. Augustine's teaching on the need for grace to remain chaste, arguing that this imperiled man's use of his own free will. Pelagius wrote and spoke extensively and was several times condemned by Church councils during his lifetime, notably the Councils of Carthage and Mileve in 416, confirmed the following year by Pope Innocent I. Pelagius deceived the next Pope, Zozimus, who at first exonerated the heretic, but soon (418) retracted his decision. Pelagianism is a cluster of doctrinal errors, some of which have plagued the Church ever since. Its principal tenets are: 1. Adam would have died even if he had not sinned; 2. Adam's fall injured only himself and at worst affected his posterity by giving them a bad example; 3. newborn children are in the same condition as Adam before he fell; 4. mankind will not die because of Adam's sin or rise on the Last Day because of Christ's redemption; 5. the law of ancient Israel no less than the Gospel offers equal opportunity to reach heaven. As Pelagianism later developed, it totally denied the supernatural order and the necessity of grace for salvation.

PELICAN. A symbol of sacrifice, selflessness, and generosity. Emblem of the Eucharistic Christ, whose blood resuscitates the living soul, as the female pelican was thought to nourish her young from her own breast. In the hymn *Adoro Te*, St. Thomas Aquinas addressed the Savior, "Pelican of Mercy, cleanse me in Thy Precious Blood." As a sign of God's providence and solicitude, this sea bird is often depicted in ecclesiastical writings, painting, murals, and stained glass.

PENAL STERILIZATION. Depriving people of their generative powers as a legally authorized procedure, either to punish certain crimes or to deter a person from committing further crimes. The Church's attitude toward such procedure is one of great reserve. On the one hand it is granted that in the case of criminals the State has the objective right to inflict this kind of punishment. On the other hand penal sterilization is not considered either a real punishment or a real preventative. It does not effectively deprive a convicted person of anything precious in that person's eyes, while leaving the sex drive intact. Nor does it do anything to a would-be criminal to deter that person from sexual crimes; in fact the sterilized condition may even encourage promiscuity.

PENALTIES. A deprivation of some spiritual or temporal good by a proper authority as a corrective punishment for a criminal or delinquent act. The gravity of a penalty does not depend only on the malice of an act but also on the circumstances and consequences of what was done. Canon law states that the Church founded by Christ has the right and duty to inflict penalties for the correction of delinquent actions but recommends resorting to penal measures only when absolutely necessary, and to use them in moderation. Everyone subject to Church laws may be subject to Church penalties, and the same authority that can exempt a person from such a law may also exempt from the penalty attached to its violation.

PENALTIES, ECCLESIASTICAL. The deprivation of some good, spiritual or temporal, inflicted by lawful authority for the correction of the delinquent and the punishment of the wrongdoing. Penalties may be remedial, punitive, or penitential.

PENALTY, PENITENTIAL. A penance imposed by ecclesiastical law or superior for some wrongdoing, as a substitute for the full penalty deserved. It may be a canonical admonition or the recitation of certain prayers, and represents an indulgence motivated by mercy.

PENALTY, PUNITIVE. Also called vindictive, an ecclesiastical censure intended to chastise the offender and make reparation for the injury caused.

PENALTY, REMEDIAL. An ecclesiastical censure whose main purpose is to reform the delinquent. It is also called medicinal.

PENANCE. The virtue or disposition of heart by which one repents of one's own sins and is converted to God. Also the punishment by which one atones for sins committed, either by oneself or by others. And finally the sacrament of penance, where confessed sins committed after baptism are absolved by a priest in the name of God. (Etym. Latin *paenitentia*, repentance, contrition.) See also SACRAMENT OF CONFESSION, SACRAMENT OF RECONCILIATION.

PENETRABILITY. The capacity of a body to coincide with another body in such a way that both occupy the same space at the same time. Naturally this is impossible for ponderable matter, but is one of the qualities of a glorified body as witnessed after Christ's resurrection from the dead (John 20:19).

PENITENCE. The state of being repentant for having sinned. It is therefore a disposition of soul, arising from a realization of one's sinfulness and includes the willingness to expiate the wrongdoing.

PENITENT. In the sacrament of penance, the person who confesses sins and seeks absolution. And in general, anyone who sincerely repents of wrongdoing, resolves to amend his or her life, and by appropriate means tries to expiate the guilt and punishment incurred for offending God.

PENITENTIAL ACT. The invitation by the priest at Mass, after the opening salutation, to have the congregation acknowledge their sinfulness. This is followed by the Appeal for Mercy, the *Kyrie,* unless the plea for forgiveness was already included in the penitential act. Normally each invocation is sung (or said) twice, but there may be further repetitions and also brief text insertions (tropes) if the circumstances warrant such additions.

PENITENTIAL CHAIN. A metal chain, with sharp points piercing the flesh, worn around the waist, arms, or legs by certain religious men and women as a means of penance or mortification.

PENITENTIAL PSALMS. Seven psalms used already in the early Church to express sorrow for sin and a desire for pardon. They are Psalms 6, 31 (32), 37 (38), 50 (51), 101 (102), 129 (130), and 142 (143).

PENITENTIAL RITE. Revised ritual for the administration of the sacrament of penance, authorized by Pope Paul VI and issued by the Sacred Congregation of Divine Worship on December 2, 1973. It consists of two parts. The first contains a doctrinal section, pastoral and liturgical norms, and the revised rites for the different forms of celebration of the sacrament. The second part is offered as a help to episcopal conferences and liturgical commissions and contains eight models for nonsacramental penitential services. See also SACRAMENT OF CONFESSION, SACRAMENT OF RECONCILIATION.

PENITENTS. The members of a confraternity whose statutes prescribed penance and mercy. They flourished in Italy, France, and Spain from about the thirteenth to the sixteenth centuries. Their contributions, mostly social, were visiting the sick, dowering poor girls, assisting prisoners, and burying the dead.

PENSION. In ecclesiastical law an allowance granted to the previous holder of a benefice for some service rendered the benefice or beneficiary. As a rule, pensions cease on the death of the pensioner. (Etym. Latin *pensio,* weight, payment.)

PENT. *Pentecostes*—Pentecost.

PENTATEUCH. The first five books of the Bible taken collectively, that is, Genesis, Exodus, Leviticus, Numbers, and Deuteronomy, written from about 1400 to 1300 B.C. The name may be traced to Origen (A.D. 254). A decision of the Biblical Commission (June 27, 1906) stated that Moses was the principal and inspired author of the Pentateuch and that the books were finally

published under his name. But in 1948 the secretary of the Pontifical Biblical Commission acknowledged that "today there is no longer anyone who questions the existence of sources used in the composition of the Pentateuch or who does not admit the progressive accretion of Mosaic laws due to the social and religious conditions of later times."

PENTECOST. Feast commemorating the descent of the Holy Spirit on the Apostles. It takes its name from the fact that it comes about fifty days after Easter. The name was originally given to the Jewish Feast of Weeks, which fell on the fiftieth day after Passover, when the first fruits of the corn harvest were offered to the Lord (Deuteronomy 16:9), and later on the giving of the law to Moses was celebrated. In the early Church, Pentecost meant the whole period from Easter to Pentecost Sunday, during which no fasting was allowed, prayer was only made standing, and Alleluia was sung more often. (Etym. Greek *hē pentēkostē,* the fiftieth day.)

PENTECOSTALISM. A revivalist movement in Christianity, originally among Protestant bodies, but, since the Second Vatican Council, also among Roman Catholics. The main postulate of Pentecostalism also explains the name. Just as on the first Pentecost in Jerusalem there was an extraordinary descent of the Holy Spirit, so today there is said to be a similar effusion of spiritual gifts. No less than on Pentecost Sunday, so now the descent of the Spirit becomes clearly perceptible especially in three ways: 1. in a personally felt experience of the Spirit's presence in the one who receives him; 2. in external manifestations of a preternatural character, notably speaking in strange tongues, the gift of prophecy, the power of healing, and in fact all the charismata described in the Acts of the Apostles and the letters of St. Paul; 3. in a strong impulse to communicate these blessings to others by becoming a messenger of the Spirit in the modern world. The basic condition required to receive the charismatic outpouring is openness of faith. The only real obstacle, it is claimed, is diffidence or distrust of the Spirit to produce today what he had done in apostolic times.

PEOPLE OF GOD. A biblical term popularized by the Second Vatican Council to describe the members of the Church. The expression brings out the fact that those who belong to the Church form a visible society, that they are distinctive, specially chosen by God, and composed of all baptized believers in Christ throughout the world. Their degree of membership depends on their degree of faith, obedience to the Church's precepts, and sanctity or union with God.

PERDURANCE. The preservation of a created being in its nature and existence by the continued exercise of God's sustaining power. (Etym. Latin *per,* through + *durare,* to last.)

PEREGRINI. In ecclesiastical law those who are living outside, but without losing, the place of their domicile or semi-domicile.

PERFECT. Whole or complete. What is perfect has all the actual qualities that are proper to its nature or kind. Only God is all perfect. Creatures are more or less perfect as they are more or less what they ought to be, according to their rank or level of being, and among people, according to their age, position, or state of life. (Etym. Latin *perfectus,* finished, completed, from *perficere,* to complete.)

PERFECTAE CARITATIS. Decree of the Second Vatican Council on the Up-to-Date Renewal of Religious Life. This is intended to complement the chapter on religious life in the Council's Constitution on the Church. It is therefore a normative document on how those dedicated to Christian perfection are to renew themselves in spirit and adapt themselves to the changing times. Among the legislative provisions of the decree are community life under superiors, corporate prayer, poverty of sharing, a distinctive religious habit, and continued spiritual and doctrinal education (October 28, 1965).

PERFECT CONTRITION. Sorrow for sin arising from perfect love. In perfect contrition the sinner detests sin more than any other evil, because it offends God, who is supremely good and deserving of all human love. Its motive is founded on God's own personal goodness and not merely his goodness to the sinner or to humanity. This motive, not the intensity of the act and less still the feelings experienced, is what essentially constitutes perfect sorrow. A perfect love of God, which motivates perfect contrition, does not necessarily exclude attachment to venial sin. Venial sin conflicts with a high degree of perfect love of God, but not with the substance of that love. Moreover, in the act of perfect contrition other motives can coexist with the perfect love required. There can be fear or gratitude, or even lesser motives such as self-respect and self-interest, along with the dominant reason for sorrow, which is love for God. Perfect contrition removes

the guilt and eternal punishment due to grave sin, even before sacramental absolution. However, a Catholic is obliged to confess his or her grave sins at the earliest opportunity and may not, in normal circumstances, receive Communion before he or she has been absolved by a priest in the sacrament of penance.

PERFECT HAPPINESS. The complete possession of the perfect good. That which fully satisfies all human desires. Imperfect happiness falls short of the perfect in some way by not satisfying all human desires or, if all of them, not all of them fully. Natural happiness, when perfect, is called natural beatitude. It satisfies those cravings which spring from human nature alone. It is the kind of happiness that human beings would have been destined to, had they been left on a purely natural plane. Mere reason cannot pass beyond this point. Christian revelation adds to this the prospect of supernatural happiness. When perfect, in the life to come, it consists of the Beatific Vision, which supposes a free gift of God lifting humanity above its natural capacity and enabling it to share in the very happiness of God.

PERFECTION. That in which nothing is lacking which, according to its nature, it should possess. That is absolutely perfect, which in itself has all possible excellence and excludes all deficiencies. Only God is absolutely perfect. That is relatively perfect which has a finite nature and possesses all the advantages corresponding to its nature. The Church teaches that God is infinite in every perfection. Creatures are as perfect as they are like God, and moral perfection consists in becoming like Christ, who is infinite God in human form.

PERFECT SOCIETY. A society with a complete human purpose that is not, in its own order, subordinate to a higher good. On this level a society is perfect in its end. From another viewpoint, a society that is complete in its possession and right of control over all the means required to achieve its purpose. On this level a society is perfect in its means. The Church founded by Christ and the State are perfect societies on both levels.

PERICHORESIS. The penetration and indwelling of the three divine persons reciprocally in one another. In the Greek conception of the Trinity there is an emphasis on the mutual penetration of the three persons, thus bringing out the unity of the divine essence. In the Latin idea called *circumincession* the stress is more on the internal processions of the three divine persons. In both traditions, however, the fundamental basis of the Trinitarian *perichoresis* is the one essence of the three persons in God. The term is also applied to the close union of the two natures in Christ. Although the power that unites the two natures proceeds exclusively from Christ's divinity, the result is a most intimate coalescence. The Godhead, which itself is impenetrable, penetrates the humanity, which is thereby deified without ceasing to be perfectly human.

PERICOPE. Literally from the Greek, a "cutting around," commonly applied to a passage from the Bible to be read at Mass or in the Divine Office. Also refers to a lesson (*lectio*) from the Scriptures, Fathers of the Church, or writings of the saints read in the Liturgy of the Hours.

PERIODIC CONTINENCE. See NATURAL FAMILY PLANNING.

PERJURY. Swearing to a falsehood. Perjury is never permissible even though one swears to the truth of only a slight lie. Even in this case the sin is serious, because great dishonor is shown to God by calling upon him to witness to the truth of what is known to be false. (Etym. Latin *periurium*, false oath, broken oath.)

PERMANENT DIACONATE. The lifelong commitment to serving as deacon in the Catholic Church. Ordination to the permanent diaconate is preceded by a decision as to which form a man wishes to enter, the transitional or the permanent. If permanent, he makes the further choice of a celibate or married diaconate. The public dedication to celibacy is celebrated in a special rite, even by religious, and it is to precede ordination to the diaconate. Celibacy taken in this way is an invalidating impediment to marriage. Moreover, a married deacon who has lost his wife cannot enter a new marriage. See also SACRUM DIACONATUS ORDINEM.

PERMISSION. Authorization to act, especially to act in a way other than a particular law allows without the special permission. In philosophy, to permit is to foresee that something will occur and not intending it, yet also not preventing the occurrence although, absolutely speaking, one could have prevented that which is permitted. Thus, foreseeing certain evil effects resulting from a given action, one permits these effects for the sake of some other, equal or greater good.

PERMISSIVENESS. The attitude of those in authority which allows great latitude in the exercise of personal choice. Its underlying motives are varied, but as a philosophy of government it subordinates the common good to the primacy of individual freedom.

PERMISSIVISM. Consistently indulgent attitude toward morally wrong human behavior. It may be based on a variety of motives, including the popular view that people are not really free and therefore personally responsible for their conduct, which is rather the combined product of heredity, environment, and education.

PERPETUAL ADORATION. Prayer before the Blessed Sacrament, either reserved in the tabernacle or exposed in a monstrance, continued by successive worshipers day and night without intermission. The practice of perpetual adoration of God by psalm and prayer has been maintained by monks and nuns since early Christian times, e.g., by the *akoimetoi* in the East, and the monastery of Agaunum, founded by King Sigismund of Burgundy in A.D. 522. Similar practices were current elsewhere before the ninth century. It was in France that perpetual adoration of the Eucharist began. Mother Mechtilde of the Blessed Sacrament pioneered the custom on request of Père Picotte. The Benedictine convent, founded for this purpose, opened on March 25, 1654. Since then many religious communities have made perpetual Eucharistic adoration either the main or an essential part of their rule of life. Confraternities of the faithful have also been organized to practice the devotion, along with the religious or, in some cases, in their parish churches.

PERPETUAL HELP, OUR LADY OF. Roman shrine on Via Merulana containing the miraculous picture of Madonna and Child. The picture rests on the main altar and is painted like an icon. Two angels designated as Sts. Michael and Gabriel are flying beside the Virgin's head, carrying in their veiled hands the instruments of Christ's Passion, the Cross, the spear, and the sponge. Some think that St. Luke painted the picture, but it was more probably a Greek artist of the thirteenth or fourteenth century. It was first in the possession of a wealthy Cretan merchant, then brought to Rome and eventually enthroned in St. Matthew's Church in the Holy City after first being carried in a street procession. For three hundred years crowds of pilgrims have journeyed far to see this picture, the source of many cures. In 1812, St. Matthew's Church was razed and for fifty-four years the picture's location was not known. When it was found, Pope Pius IX gave it to the Redemptorist Fathers for their church on the spot where Mary first had been revered in this special manner as Our Lady of Perpetual Help. The American national shrine honoring her under that name is at Roxbury, Massachusetts.

PERPETUAL VOWS. Ordinarily the final vows that a person takes in an institute of Christian perfection, mainly poverty, chastity, and obedience. Other vows may be added, according to the constitutions of the institute. They are also called last vows, although some communities take perpetual vows immediately after the novitiate, and others never take what are technically perpetual vows, but they simply renew their vows regularly, according to their rule of life.

PERPLEXED CONSCIENCE. An erroneous conscience when the mind sees sin both in the performance and in the omission of some human act to be done here and now.

PER SE. Literally "by itself" or "through itself." A very common expression in scholastic philosophy and theology to describe something by reason of what it is in itself or its own nature without reference to its relationship to other things or the circumstances associated with an object or activity. Thus every human act, "per se," is a moral act because it proceeds from the free will, but it may be either morally good or morally bad. The opposite is "per accidens."

PERSECUTION. The effort by civil authority to suppress or impede the Church's liberty by physical or psychological means. Since the first days after Pentecost the Church has been persecuted by those who felt threatened by her or who sought to enforce religious conformity or who penalized dissent from the accepted or established norms of belief and behavior. Throughout the Gospels, Christ foretold that his followers would be persecuted, and at the Last Supper he predicted, "If they persecuted me, they will persecute you too" (John 15:20). This prediction has been verified in every period of the Church's history, including modern times.

PERSECUTIONS, ROMAN. The ten great persecutions of the Church from apostolic times to the Edict of Milan (A.D. 313) are generally identified by the reign of the ruling emperor: 1. Nero (54–68) accused the Christians of being haters of mankind; 2. Domitian (81–96) took his victims mainly from the Christian nobility; 3. Trajan (98–117) considered Christianity an organized menace to the empire; 4. Marcus Aurelius (161–80) confiscated the property of the faithful and tortured his victims; 5. Septimus Severus (193–211) forbade fresh conversions; 6. Maximinus Thrax (235–38) persecuted the clergy; 7. Decius (249–51) ordered all subjects who would not sacrifice to the state gods to be put to death; 8. Valerian (253–60) forbade all Christian assemblies and concentrated on clergy and nobility; 9. Aurelian (270–75) allowed the anti-Christian legislation to remain but did not seriously enforce it; 10. Diocletian (284–305) reversed Aurelian's policy and unleashed the bloodiest of all Roman persecutions.

PERSEVERANCE. Remaining in the state of grace until the end of life. The Church teaches that it is impossible, without the special help of God, to persevere in the state of grace to the end. Thus the Second Council of Orange, in A.D. 529, teaches, in opposition to the Semi-Pelagians, that the justified also must constantly pray for the help of God so that they may attain to a good end (Denzinger, 380). And the Council of Trent in 1547 calls perseverance "a great gift" and says that those in the state of grace cannot persist in God's friendship without special divine aid (Denzinger, 1572). Final perseverance cannot be strictly merited, as though a person had a claim on dying in grace because he or she had been faithful all through life. Nevertheless it can, with unfailing success, be achieved by proper prayer, offered regularly and earnestly, in the state of grace. The certainty of the prayer being heard is based on the promise of Jesus (John 16:23). Since, however, the possibility of a fall always remains, one cannot know with infallible certainty whether one will, in fact, persevere unless one receives a special revelation to that effect (*Council of Trent,* Denzinger, 1566).

PERSON. "An individual substance of a rational nature" (Boethius). Therefore every individual intellectual substance which is complete in itself, uncommunicated and existing for itself, is a person. Essential to person in theological terms are intelligence and substantiality, wholeness in oneself and especially individuality. From individuality flow such features of personhood as distinctiveness, incommunicability, and uniqueness. Among human persons there are also the elements of responsibility and possession of distinctive rights. (Etym. Latin *persona,* actor's mask; character; supposition of a rational nature.)

PERSON, ECCLESIASTICAL. In Church law a human being who has been validly baptized and who thereby acquires all the rights and duties of a Christian, except where, as regards rights, there is some impediment affecting one's communion with the Church or some censure imposed by the Church.

PERSON, MORAL. In ecclesiastical law, a group of at least three physical persons united together by their free will to form a society recognized as such by competent Church authority.

PERSONAL IDENTITY. The constant and uninterrupted substantial sameness of the human person and especially of that person's soul, throughout time and beyond bodily death into eternity.

PERSONALITY. In scholastic theology that perfection which makes an intellectual nature to be uncommunicated or unshared by another being, its individuality. In modern psychology "the dynamic organization within the individual of those psychophysical systems that determine his [or her] characteristic behavior and thought" (Allport). Others define personality in terms of their own vocabulary, e.g., for Freud it is the integration of an individual's id, ego, and superego; for Adler it is an individual's style of life or characteristic way of thinking and acting. In popular language personality is the sum total of the distinctive abilities and achievements of an individual.

PERSONAL LAW. An ecclesiastical precept binding an individual wherever he or she lives. In general, canon law is presumed not to be personal but territorial unless the opposite is evident from the nature of the precept.

PERSONHOOD. The distinctive qualities of each human being as a unique individual.

PERTINACITY. Stubborn persistence. In ecclesiastical law it occurs as an adverb, "pertinaciously," and refers to a person who firmly and culpably holds to an opinion contrary to the Church's teaching or refuses to submit to legitimate authority.

PERVERSION. Socially degenerate conduct, especially in sexual behavior. (Etym. Latin *pervertere*, to overturn, ruin, corrupt.)

PESHITTA. Ancient Syriac version of the Bible. It is the first translation of the Hebrew Bible made for and by Christians, and is also called the Syriac Vulgate. The New Testament Peshitta is still used in the Syrian Church. It was in circulation in the fourth century, and part of it was in use before A.D. 300.

PESSIMISM. An attitude of mind or philosophy of life that views the world and human life as principally or entirely evil in its nature, origin, or destiny. It is usually expressed as the view that regards the world and human existence as essentially painful, destructive, and without discernible purpose.

PETER. The first Pope and leader of the Apostles. His original name was Simon, but Jesus gave him the name "Peter," which is Greek, or "Cephas," which is the Aramaic equivalent. "Peter" and "Cephas" mean "the rock" (John 1:42). Such a name was appropriate to the strong character of the man, but the name became a supremely significant metaphor when Christ later made the dramatic assignment, "You are Peter and on this rock I will build my Church" (Matthew 16:18). What made the name distinctive as well was that neither "Peter" nor "Cephas" was ever used as a man's name. It was a career designation. There could be no question about the recognition of Peter's leadership. His name always appeared first in the listing of the Apostles (Mark 3:16). He and his brother were the first chosen. His name appears in the Gospels oftener than that of any other Apostle (Luke 5:10). He acted as their spokesman and whenever Jesus questioned them Peter responded in their behalf. He was present at the Transfiguration (Matthew 17:1–8). He was with Jesus when he raised Jairus' daughter (Luke 8:51). He was in Gethsemane during the Lord's agony (Mark 14:33). Jesus paid the temple tax for himself and Peter (Matthew 17:24–27). When Jesus disappeared from Capernaum, it was Peter who led the disciples in pursuit (Mark 1:36). It was Peter who objected to the washing of the feet (John 13:6–9). The angel in announcing the Resurrection said, "Go and tell the disciples and Peter" (Mark 16:7). Other instances from all four Gospels could be cited that make it clear that Peter's leadership was uncontested. After the Crucifixion it was Peter who directed the meeting to select a successor to Judas (Acts 1:15–26). When Paul and Barnabas attended the first council in Jerusalem, Peter presided and made the speech that silenced discussion (Acts 15:6–12). Through the early chapters of Acts he continues to exercise the leadership role. He was truly obeying the Master's valedictory injunction to "feed my lambs" and "feed my sheep" (John 21:16–17). Peter revealed human shortcomings as well as strengths. He was rebuked by Jesus for misinterpreting the Messianic mission (Mark 8:33). His impetuosity was revealed in the garden when he attacked Malchus (John 18:10). He was bitterly ashamed of the cowardice he revealed in denying Jesus in the courtyard (Luke 22:54–62). But none of these human actions reduce the significance of the assignment he received when Jesus said, "I will give you the keys of the kingdom of heaven" (Matthew 16:19). (Etym. Greek *petros*, masc. name formed from the fem. noun *petra*, rock.)

PETER, EPISTLES OF. Two letters of St. Peter the Apostle, both addressed to converts from paganism in Asia Minor. Both were sent from Rome. The second intimates his approaching death; the first contains strong admonitions to lead a Christian life, outlining the duties of citizens to civil authority, servants to their masters, wives to husbands, mutual charity, patience, and humility. The Petrine authorship of both letters has been challenged. But in the first letter the author claims to be "Peter, apostle of Jesus Christ" (I Peter 1:1), and the author of the second letter claims to be Peter who witnessed the Transfiguration of the Lord (II Peter 1:1, 1:16–18), who also wrote another letter (I Peter, II Peter 3:1), and refers to "our brother Paul, who is so dear to us" (II Peter 3:15).

PETER'S PENCE. The annual contribution from the faithful of various countries to defray the expenses of the Holy See. It seems to have started in England, where each owner of land of certain value gave a penny. It was re-established by Pope Pius IX after having lapsed since the Reformation. In some countries the contributions are gathered by various associations; in others it is an annual collection sent by the bishops to the pope.

PETITIONS TO THE HOLY SEE. The right of the faithful to petition the Holy See on any matter at any time. Requests are normally submitted through the local ordinary, who in turn communicates the petition to the appropriate Roman congregation or commission. But every Catholic may write directly to the Pope or any official at the Vatican and be assured that his or her request is given due consideration.

PEW. A seat for worshipers in a church. Pews are an early medieval innovation in the West, where they gradually developed from stone seats attached to the walls or to the piers of the nave. Many churches had elaborately carved pews, at the ends and on the back, with figures of saints and symbols of the Passion of Christ. (Etym. Middle French *puie*, prop, raised seat, balcony.)

PEW RENTS. Charges that were formerly made in some dioceses for the use of certain seats in church. In the United States the practice had been approved by the Third Council of Baltimore and endorsed by the Holy See as a source of revenue for church maintenance and the support of the clergy. Renting a pew or section entitled a person to use a given place at all or any of the divine services in that church. In some dioceses a person could receive pastoral administrations even though registered in another parish. Those unable to pay pew rent were at liberty to use the numerous unassigned seats in the Church.

PHANAR. The court of the Orthodox Patriarch of Constantinople and the name of the Greek quarter where he resided. It was the center of the Hellenistic spirit after the Turkish conquest. Orthodox Christians in European Turkey were ruled by the patriarch with the consent of the Turkish Government. The Phanar in the East corresponds to the Vatican in the West. (Etym. Greek *phānarion*, lantern.)

PHARISAICAL SCANDAL. Being disedified by the innocent actions of others. People are said to be pharisaically scandalized if they maliciously misinterpret the good or indifferent actions of a person. They are scandalized because their own extraordinary moral weakness or ignorance finds occasion to evil in what they hear or see someone doing.

PHARISAIC CONSCIENCE. An erroneous conscience when the mind minimizes grave sins but magnifies matters of little importance, in the manner of the Pharisees accused by Christ. It is also the hardened conscience, which consistently judges that all or certain grave crimes are trivial or not wrong at all, because a person has acquired the habit of sinning mortally so that his or her mind now defends as virtue what is actually vice.

PHARISEES. An active, vociferous religious Jewish sect in the centuries before and after Christ appeared on earth. They represented by and large the intellectual sector of their people, because they were avid, contentious students and teachers of Jewish religious law. Their intensity and single-mindedness resulted in a harsh and uncharitable emphasis on the legal aspects of religion at the expense of charity and loving concern. Jesus represented a threat to their intellectual security and leadership. They baited him at every opportunity. They tried to trap him into wrong answers (Matthew 22:15–22). They proposed questions, hoping to prove contradictions (Matthew 22:34–40). They deplored the company he kept. They objected to his Sabbath activities (Mark 2:15–17; Mark 2:23–26). They even plotted against his life (John 11:45–54). Indeed they worked together with the priests and the Sadducees until their plotting culminated in his arrest and crucifixion (John 18:3). Their hostility, of course, was aggravated by the accusations that Jesus leveled at the Pharisees. He called them hypocrites (Matthew 15:7). He deplored their legalisms as rendering God's word null and void (Mark 7:13). Their self-righteousness he exposed in the parable of the Pharisee and the publican (Luke 18:9–14). The entire Chapter 23 of Matthew is a lengthy, detailed indictment of Pharisee mentality. Needless to say, all Pharisees were not fanatics. Gamaliel and Nicodemus were men who kept a sense of balance and were open to the development of Judaism (John 3:1–21; Acts 5:34–39). It is likely that many Pharisees became Christians. (Etym. Hebrew *perusim;* Aramaic *perissayya',* separated, separated ones, separators.)

PH.B. *Philosophiae Baccalaureus*—Bachelor of Philosophy.

PH.D. *Philosophiae Doctor*—Doctor of Philosophy.

PHENOMENON. Something sensibly perceptible or immediately observable, as distinguished from the nature or substance to which reason must conclude. In theology, phenomena are extraordinary events whose origin may be explained by unknown natural laws, angelic or demonic intervention, or the miraculous operation of God. (Etym. Greek *phainomenon,* from *phainesthai,* to appear.)

PHILEMON. A convert of Paul who had the distinction of being the only recorded recipient of a personal letter from the Apostle. Paul had converted a runaway slave named Onesimus and learned that the master he had deserted and robbed was Philemon. He persuaded Onesimus to return to his owner with a warm, beseeching letter urging Philemon to show mercy. He offered to pay whatever the errant slave owed. It was an appeal for compassion that Philemon would not only forgive Onesimus but set him free as a Christian brother (Philemon 1–25). (Etym. Greek *philēmon,* loving.)

PHILIP. 1. the Apostle. Philip must have known Peter and Andrew, because all three came from Bethsaida. When Jesus met him, he invited Philip to join him. Philip must have been instantly impressed. He not only joined the group himself but persuaded Nathanael (better known as Bartholomew) to accompany him (John 1:43, 12:21). Generally, in the listing of the Apostles, Philip and Bartholomew are paired. Apparently Philip took care of the food supply, because it was with him that Jesus discussed the problem of feeding the crowd at the Sea of Galilee (John 6:5–7). Philip must have been painfully literal-minded in learning Jesus' relation to his Father. "Have I been with you all this time," said Jesus to him, "and you still do not know me?" (John 14:9). After the Crucifixion he was among the Apostles waiting for the Holy Spirit (Acts 1:13); 2. the Evangelist. One of the seven disciples chosen by the Apostles to supervise the food supply and relief of poor Christians as the Church was growing in numbers. The Apostles feared that preaching and converting would suffer if they consumed their energy in business matters (Acts 6:1–6). Philip himself was an able preacher and performer of miracles, as he proved in Samaria. Two instances of his zeal and eloquence are given in his conversion of Simon, the magician, and the Ethiopian court officer (Acts 8:4–40). His final appearance in Scripture took place when he entertained Paul in his home in Caesarea during his third missionary journey (Acts 21:8). (Etym. Greek *philippos,* lover of horses.)

PHILIPPIANS. One of the four letters of St. Paul written from prison to his converts. It is a letter of gratitude for the kindness the Philippians in Macedonia had shown him. The most significant passage is an exhortation to humility, based on the example of Christ, who, though "His state was divine, yet He did not cling to His equality with God but emptied Himself to assume the condition of a slave, and became as men are" (2:6–7). It is a heart-to-heart communication of Paul to his people, in which the Apostle is disarmingly frank in telling them how much he loves them and wants them to be happy, "happy in the Lord; I repeat what I want is your happiness" (4:4).

PHILOSOPHER OF PROTESTANTISM.

Immanuel Kant (1724–1804), the German philosopher who systematically analyzed and questioned the foundations of the Lutheran faith in which he was reared and died. His notion of religion was consistent with his general theory of knowledge and reality. Just as he held that phenomena are not in themselves things, "They are nothing but ideas, and cannot exist at all beyond our minds," so he believed that revelation and the Church are only "adventitious aids." Man's ultimate religious authority is his own mind. "The inner voice of reason is always his surest guide." Kantian ideas shifted the whole focus of Protestant liberal thought in the modern world, away from the Bible toward sentimentalism and dogmatic voluntarism.

PHILOSOPHICAL THEOLOGY. See DOGMATIC THEOLOGY.

PHILOSOPHICAL TRUTH. Ultimate rational explanation of an event. Specifically the reason why some historical event should be regarded as beyond the natural order of phenomena.

PHILOSOPHY. Literally the love of wisdom. It is the science in which natural reason, apart from divine revelation, seeks to understand all things by a knowledge of their first causes. (Etym. Greek *philein*, to love + *sophia*, wisdom: *philosophus*.)

PHILOSOPHY OF LIFE. A person's fundamental attitude toward human life and destiny, and the purpose of human society.

PHILOSOPHY OF MAN. The science of human nature, studied in terms of the human person's essential unity as a rational being and his or her purpose in the world as an individual and social being.

PHILOSOPHY OF RELIGION. The science of human beings as religious persons. It may take on a variety of forms, depending on the subject investigated and the premises of the investigation. Thus it may study the historic religions to determine their common denominator and account for their differences; or it may seek to establish the rational foundations of the historic religions to determine their credibility; or it may assume the validity of a given religion, as Christianity, and analyze its principal tenets and practices on philosophical grounds.

PH.M. *Philosophiae Magister*—Master of Philosophy.

PHOENIX. A symbol of Christ's Resurrection. This fabled bird, a native of Arabia, after anticipating its own death and burning itself, in three days developed into a new bird. The legend easily established the phoenix as representing Christ's three days before Easter in the tomb. Emperor Constantine made use of this symbol by representing the phoenix on the coin of the realm.

PHOTIANISM. A schism provoked by Photius (c. 815–97), Patriarch of Constantinople, that paved the way for the Eastern Schism in the thirteenth century. When Ignatius, the incumbent Patriarch of Constantinople, rebuked the vices of Bardas, co-regent under Emperor Michael III, the prelate was deposed, and Photius, a layman, was ordained priest and bishop to replace him in A.D. 857. Pope Nicholas I excommunicated Photius, who meantime charged Rome with heresy for inserting the phrase *Filioque* (and from the Son) into the Creed. When Emperor Michael died, his successor deposed Photius and restored Ignatius. Both actions were endorsed by the eighth ecumenical Fourth Council of Constantinople, 869–70, which is the first general council, no longer accepted by the Eastern Orthodox.

PHYSICAL CERTITUDE. Sure assent concerning things in physical nature without excluding the possibility of a miracle or the chance interference of some unknown natural law.

PHYSICAL EVIL. Privation of a natural good desired by a human being. Absence of some satisfaction desired by a human appetite, whether spiritual or bodily. In general, may be equated with pain. It is the loss or deprivation of what a person wants.

PHYSICAL FREEDOM. Absence of external compulsion or violence that would coerce a person to act or not act in a certain way. Lack of physical restraint or pressure compelling a given action. Corresponds to spontaneity of action.

PHYSICAL MIRACLE. An event produced by God which surpasses the powers of physical or bodily nature. Two kinds of physical miracles are known to Catholic theology: 1. those essentially supernatural, such as raising the dead, which only divine power can perform (major miracles); and 2. those relatively supernatural, such as sudden healing, which the angels can perform under divine providence (minor miracles).

PHYSICAL SOLITUDE. See SOLITUDE.

PHYSIOLOGUS. A collection of Christian allegories in which religious truths are symbolized by animals. An outstanding example is the pelican who feeds its young by shedding its own blood, as Christ saved mankind by shedding his blood. They were very popular in the Middle Ages and greatly influenced ecclesiastical art and medieval literature.

PIARISTS. An order of clerics, founded in 1597 by St. Joseph Calasanctius. The name Piarists comes from the last word of their official title, which is "Poor Regulars of the Mother of God for Schools of Piety." They began by opening free elementary schools, and ever since, their principal apostolate is teaching. They were approved as a congregation by Pope Paul V in 1617, and they take a fourth vow to devote themselves to the education of the young.

PIETÀ. A general term applied to representations of the dead Christ in art. The Blessed Virgin is usually included. Among the masters who have represented the Pietà, the best known are Bellini, Botticelli, Caravaggio, Dürer, Fra Angelico, Murillo, Raphael, Rubens, Titian, and Van Dyck. The most famous is the Pietà of Michelangelo in St. Peter's Basilica in Rome. (Etym. Latin *pietas*, duty, dutiful, piety, devotion.)

PIETISM. In general, a stress on the individual appropriation of religious truth, put into moral and spiritual action, in contrast with merely assenting to a truth with the mind. Various movements in Christianity have been called pietistic, with the implication that they are more sentimental than realistic.

PIETY. Honor and reverence given to someone in any way responsible for our existence or well-being. Thus God as our Creator and constant Provider, parents, near relatives, country, tribe, or people.

PILASTER. In church architecture a portion of a pillar or column partly inserted in a wall.

PILATE, PONTIUS. The Roman procurator of Judaea from A.D. 26 to 36, appointed by Emperor Tiberius. Several times during his administration there had been turbulent demonstrations by the Jews when their traditions were violated or their rights infringed upon. These demonstrations irritated Tiberius, and Pilate was anxious to placate the Jews so that no further Judaean unrest would be reported to Rome. This was the political situation when Pilate was confronted by the irate delegation of priests and Pharisees demanding Christ's death. All four Evangelists testify that Pilate knew full well

that the accused was innocent (Luke 23:4; John 18:38). He tried various stratagems in the hope that the charges would be reduced and the fury would abate. He offered to release Christ or Barabbas. He had Jesus flogged (Matthew 27:15–26; Luke 23:14–16). He set up the hand-washing ritual to emphasize his view of the charges in the hope that he could divert Jewish determination. But finally he capitulated and consented to the Crucifixion (Mark 15:15) rather than have the Emperor disturbed and his own administration threatened. (Etym. Latin Pontius Pilatus.)

PILGRIMAGE. A journey to a sacred place undertaken as an act of religious devotion. Its purpose may be simply to venerate a certain saint or ask some spiritual favor; beg for a physical cure or perform an act of penance; express thanks or fulfill a promise. From the earliest days pilgrimages were made to the Holy Land, and later on to Rome, where Peter and Paul and so many Christians were martyred. From the eighth century the practice began of imposing a pilgrimage in place of public penance. As a result, during the Middle Ages pilgrimages were organized on a grand scale and became the object of special Church legislation. In modern times, besides Rome and the Holy Land, famous shrines such as Lourdes, Fátima, and Guadalupe draw thousands of pilgrims each year from the Catholic world.

PILGRIM CHURCH. The Catholic Church on earth, or the Church Militant. She is said to be on pilgrimage toward the Church Triumphant in heavenly glory.

PILLAR, THE HOLY. The column at which Our Lord was scourged. A part of this original porphyry pillar is preserved in the Church of St. Praxedes in Rome, having been brought there from Jerusalem about 1223. The rest of this great relic is in the Franciscan Chapel in the Church of the Holy Sepulcher in Jerusalem.

PIOUS ASSOCIATION. In Church law, an organization of persons, approved by the local ordinary, chiefly engaged in the practice of the spiritual and corporal works of mercy. It is the usual status of a religious institute before its members are permitted to pronounce public vows in the name of the Church.

PIOUS BELIEF. A doctrinal position that, though not defined or part of the Church's universal ordinary teaching, is nevertheless acceptable in Roman Catholicism and consistent with the rest of Catholic faith and practice.

PIOUS UNION. In ecclesiastical law an association of the laity organized for the purpose of practicing some work of piety or charity. Primary unions have the right of aggregating other similar organizations. The effects are akin to the aggregation of a confraternity to an archconfraternity. The title Primary Union is sometimes conferred by the Holy See as a mark of special recognition.

PISCINA. An excavation or basin, provided with a drain directly to the earth, for the disposal of water that has been used for some sacred purpose and is no longer needed. The name is also given to the baptismal font or cistern. A sacrarium, synonymous with piscina, receives the water from the washing of the sacred vessels and linens. It is generally located in the sacristy of a church. (Etym. Latin *piscis,* fish.)

PITY. Grief or pain aroused by the suffering or misfortune of another. Pity is less than sympathy, which shares in the experience of another. It is a form of condescending sympathy.

P.K. *Pridie Kalendas*—the day before the calends,

PLACET. Literally, "it pleases," applied to many situations where someone's judgment or approval expresses or affects the teaching or jurisdiction of the Church. Commonly used of the affirmative votes at a general council, and of Rome's decisions regarding controverted issues. It also refers to juridical obligation of papal decrees depending, as in Communist countries, on the concurrence of State authorities. (Etym. Latin *placet,* it pleases.)

PLACET JUXTA MODUM. "It is not entirely pleasing." A qualified, although essentially positive vote of a bishop at a provincial or ecumenical council.

PLAGUE MEDAL. A medal specially worn to obtain God's protection during a plague or pestilence. Popular during the Middle Ages, plague medals have the image of St. Roch or St. Sebastian, but generally of the Blessed Virgin or of one of her shrines. When comets were objects of dread, medals were worn to shield the people from their supposed calamity; others commemorated important events in the Church's history.

PLAGUES, TEN. The ten calamities sent by God on the Egyptians to make Pharaoh release the children of Israel (Exodus 7, 12). Seven of the plagues were done through Moses or Moses and Aaron; the fourth, fifth, and tenth were directly worked by God. They were, in sequence: water turned to blood, multitude of frogs, swarms of gnats, pest of flies, disease that killed all the cattle, epidemic of boils, torrential hailstorm, plague of locusts, darkness for three days, death of all the firstborn among the Egyptians.

PLAIN CHANT. Sometimes inaccurately called Gregorian chant, but plain chant is a modification of the Gregorian, introduced among the Franks in the ninth century. It is unisonous and free-rhythmed and composed on a scale of four lines. The modes or scales of plain chant are limited to the natural intervals of the human voice and the melodies likewise confined to a person's natural range. Features of this chant are that the "leading note" is commonly avoided; also two choirs may be used while alternately singing the same melody. The beauty of plain chant derives from its pure melody, voice quality, and subtle rhythm.

PLAIN SONG. An ecclesiastical chant, such as Gregorian, having simple unaccompanied melody.

PLANNED PARENTHOOD. A common term for the practice of contraception or, when this fails, of abortion. Also the organized policy of governments and international cartels to coerce people by means of economic or other sanctions to practice contraception or abortion, or submit to sterilization.

PLATONISM. The system of thought originated by the Greek philosopher Plato (427–347 B.C.), pupil of Socrates. Platonism, in its influence on Christianity, is characterized by its contempt for sense knowledge and empirical studies, by a longing for another and better world, by a frankly spiritual view of life, by its method of discussion or dialogue between persons to acquire more profound insights than could be obtained by cold reasoning, and above all by an unswerving confidence in the human mind to reach absolute truth, and to rely on this inner vision for the direction of one's moral life.

PLEASURE. The satisfaction that accompanies the exercise of a human faculty. Depending on the faculty used, there are different kinds of pleasure, namely, sensuous or intellectual. In practice the two forms are never separated, since bodily satisfaction affects the rational part of a human being, and intellectual satisfaction has an influence on the body. Some writers distinguish between pleasure and joy, where pleasure refers to the satisfaction of bodily desires, such as eating and sex, and joy refers to the use of rational powers, such as thinking and loving.

PLENARY COUNCIL. A formal meeting of the archbishops and bishops of a country or region under the leadership of a papal legate, who would decide matters to be considered and ratify the council's decrees. The decrees are binding on all the faithful under the jurisdiction of the bishops assembled. In the Church's history the decisions of some plenary councils were later extended to the universal Church. (Etym. Latin *plenus*, full.)

PLENARY INDULGENCE. An indulgence that can remove all the temporal punishment due to forgiven sin. No one but God knows for certain when a plenary indulgence is actually gained, because only he knows whether a person's dispositions are adequate. One norm for such dispositions is that "all attachment to sin, even venial sin, be absent." If these dispositions are in any way less than complete, the indulgence will be only partial. The same provision applies to the three external conditions necessary to gain a plenary indulgence: sacramental confession, Eucharistic Communion, and prayer for the intentions of the Pope. If these conditions are not satisfied, an otherwise plenary indulgence becomes only partial. These conditions may be satisfied several days before or after the performance of the prescribed work, though preferably Communion should be received and the prayers offered for the Pope on the same day as the indulgenced work. A plenary indulgence can be gained only once a day.

PLEN. IND. Plenary indulgence.

PLEROMA. A Greek term used by St. Paul in the general sense of "filling up." It means the sum total of the blessings brought to the world by Christ (Romans 15:29; Ephesians 1:23, 3:19). Also applied to the fullness of divinity in Christ (Colossians 1:19), and the Church as the plenitude or complement of Christ (Ephesians 4:13). (Etym. Greek *plerōma*, fullness.)

PLOUGH MONDAY. The first Monday after Epiphany. Alms were formerly offered on that day for the needs of the Church and to receive a blessing on the land which was being plowed at that time.

PLURALISM, DOCTRINAL. The theory that a Catholic may legitimately hold a doctrinal position that is in contradiction to what the Church teaches, either as defined or by her ordinary universal magisterium. This would mean that contradictory doctrines in faith or morals could be professed by different persons, all equally in good standing in the Catholic Church. Doctrinal pluralism was condemned by the First Vatican Council, 1869–70 (Denzinger 3042, 3043).

PLURALISM, THEOLOGICAL. The multiplicity of theological positions present within the Catholic Church. These positions vary according to which premises or postulates are used in reflecting on the sources of revelation, according to the methodology employed, and according to the cultural tradition within which theology does its speculation. On the first basis, the two principal philosophical premises are the Platonic, stressed in Augustinianism; and the Aristotelian, emphasized in Thomism. On the second level, theologies differ in terms of their mainly biblical, or doctrinal, or historical, or pastoral methodology. And on the third basis, the culture of a people helps to shape the theology they develop, as between the more mystical East and the more practical West, or the more reflective Mediterranean and the more scientific Anglo-Saxon. The Church not only permits these diversities but encourages them, always assuming that theologians who are Catholic are also respectful of the rule of faith and obedient to the magisterium of the hierarchy under the Bishop of Rome.

PLURIFORMITY. Diversity in the Catholic Church's practice, reflected in the different rites, adapting the one, unchangeable faith to the different cultural traditions of the people.

PODIUM. Any elevated platform. But especially the platform on which the Pope is carried when he officiates in a procession with the Blessed Sacrament. Part of the podium is a kneeler or seat for the Pope as he adores the Holy Eucharist. (Etym. Latin *podium*, elevated place, parapet, balcony.)

POENIT. *Poenitentia*—penance.

POENIT. AP. *Poenitentiaria Apostolica*—Office of the Apostolic Penitentiary.

POINTE AUX TREMBLES. Canadian national shrine of the Sacred Heart established in 1866, an affiliation of the Sanctuary of the Sacred Heart at Montmartre in Paris.

Guardians of the shrine were successively Franciscans, Dominicans, and the Blessed Sacrament Fathers, whose Father Jean started and activated the Crusade of Atonement, which gave the shrine its present subtitle, "Chapel of Atonement." In 1921 the Capuchins were asked to care for this sanctuary; they built a nearby monastery and continued the Crusade. The number of pilgrims has steadily increased so that thousands now participate in the shrine's distinctive service, the public Way of the Cross, as a most appropriate way of atoning to the wounded Heart of Christ. The Archconfraternity of Prayer and Penance have their headquarters at Pointe aux Trembles, and the novena in preparation for the feast of the Sacred Heart is broadcast from here to Canada and the United States.

POLARIZATION. The process or state of concentrating on two contrary positions. A phenomenon that has affected many aspects of modern society, due in large measure to the influence of Hegel and Marx, with their stress on the role of conflict as a necessary condition for progress. The term is applied to the conflict, even on essentials of faith and morals, in the Catholic Church since the Second Vatican Council.

POLITICIZATION. The act or method of changing a religious issue or institution to a political one. Essential to the process is the shift of the focus from faith commitment to self-interest, and the introduction of mechanisms of political contract into a covenant relationship with God.

POLYANDRY. The simultaneous marriage of one woman with two or more men. Historically, where the practice existed, it was often accompanied by female infanticide, as a logical counterpart to a marital system in which there was a plurality of potential husbands. Polyandry was never permitted or tolerated either throughout the period of the Old Testament or among the pagan peoples of ancient times, even among those who widely condoned prostitution. (Etym. Greek *polyandros*, having many husbands.)

POLYGAMY. The status or institution of simultaneous marriage of more than one woman to one man, or of several women to several men. The two forms are polygyny and polyandry. In ordinary use, the term is restricted to polygyny, i.e., where one man is simultaneously married to more than one woman.

Polygamy as polygyny is contrary to divine positive law governing the marriage union (Genesis 2:24; Ephesians 5:31). According to the natural law, even successive polygamy (as in societies that legalize marriage after divorce) hinders the proper care and education of children. And it places an intolerable burden on practicing mutual love between the spouses.

In the Old Testament, God tolerated polygamy for a certain time, as it appears from the examples of men such as Abraham, Jacob, and David. But with the proclamation of the New Law, this concession, almost wrested from God by reason of the moral obtuseness of man, was revoked. Marriage was restored to its original unity. The language of Christ is very explicit (Matthew 19:3–9; Mark 10:1–12; Luke 16:18). Catholic tradition has consistently interpreted Christ's teaching as absolutely forbidding polygamy, and the prohibition was defined by the Council of Trent, pronouncing anathema against anyone who says that "it is lawful for Christians to have several wives at the same time, and that it is not forbidden by any divine law" (Denzinger 1802). (Etym. Greek *polygamos*, having many wives.)

POLYGENISM. The theory that, since evolution is an established fact, all human beings now on earth do not descend from one human pair (Adam and Eve), but from different original human ancestors. This theory is contrary to the official teaching of the Church, e.g., Pope Pius XII, who declared: "It is unintelligible how such an opinion can be squared with what the sources of revealed truth and the documents of the Magisterium of the Church teach on original sin, which proceeds from sin actually committed by an individual Adam, and which, passed on to all by way of generation, is in everyone as his own" (*Humani Generis*, 1950, para. 38). (Etym. Latin *poly*, many + *gen*, race + *ism*.)

POLYGLOT BIBLE. A printed rendition of Scripture text in several languages. Among the Bibles worthy of note are the Antwerp, Paris, and London polyglots. The oldest polyglot Bible is the Complutensian of the early sixteenth century. It contains printed texts of the Old Testament in Hebrew, Greek, and Latin and of the New Testament in Greek and Latin. (Etym. Greek *polyglōttos*, many tongued.)

POLYGYNY. The institution of simultaneous marriage between one man and more than one woman. More commonly (though not technically) called polygamy. (Etym. Greek *polygamos*, having many wives.)

POLYTHEISM. Belief in a plurality of gods, and the practice of worshiping them as equally divine. The biblical term is generally idolatry. (Etym. Greek *polus*, many + *theos*, god.)

POMP. Any splendor or magnificent display. It carries the notion of ostentation, as a pompous person is one who considers himself important and pretends to be more than he or she has a claim to. The expression "pomps of the devil" refers to the temptation in the desert when the evil spirit promised the Savior all the riches of this world if only Christ would worship the devil. In the rite of baptism, the catechumen is asked, "Do you renounce Satan and all his works and empty promises?" Formerly "empty promises" were called "pomps." They are literally "seductions" (*seductiones*).

PONT. *Pontifex*—pontiff, bishop.

PONT. *Pontificatus*—pontificate.

PONTIFEX MAXIMUS. Supreme Pontiff. Originally used of other bishops too, but from the fifth century practically reserved for the Pope.

PONTIFF. High priest, and therefore any bishop, as successor of the Apostles. Now reserved as the title of the Pope. In pre-Christian times, the pontifices were the chief priests of Rome and were given this name either because they were "bridge builders" (*pontem facere*), between the gods and men, or because they offered sacrifice (*puntis*). (Etym. Latin *pontifex*, high priest; literally, bridgemaker; popular original meaning: waymaker, pathfinder.)

PONTIFICAL. A liturgical book, dating from at least the eighth century and containing the prayers and ceremonies for rites reserved to a bishop. It generally contained: 1. prayers and instructions for services without Mass; 2. sacramental ceremonies with blessings and consecrations; and 3. acts of jurisdiction. Such collections were known as *Liber Episcopalis, Liber Pontificalis,* or *Ordinarium Episcopi.* The first Roman pontifical was published in 1485.

PONTIFICAL CHAPEL. A group of ecclesiastics who participate regularly in the liturgical ceremonies held by the Pope, cardinals, and prelates of the papal household.

PONTIFICAL COMMISSION FOR RUSSIA. Established in 1930 by Pope Pius XI, it deals with Catholic ecclesiastical affairs in Russia. In 1934 it was commissioned to care for the liturgical books and to concern itself with the needs of the Russian faithful of the Latin Rite.

PONTIFICAL COMMISSION FOR SACRED ART. Set up by Pope Pius XI in 1924, for the purpose of maintaining and fostering an appreciation of the Church's patrimony in art and architecture in Italy. In 1944 the commission was given the task of supervising the restoration of the churches and sacred edifices damaged during World War II. In 1967, Pope Paul VI published further directives for co-operation with diocesan liturgical commissions throughout Italy.

PONTIFICAL COMMISSION OF SACRED ARCHAEOLOGY. Established by Pope Pius IX in 1852, "to watch over the ancient sacred cemeteries, to take precautionary measures for their preservation, to provide for their further exploration, investigation and study, to safeguard the oldest memories of the first Christian centuries, the outstanding monuments and venerable basilicas in Rome, its suburbs, and the territory around Rome, and also in other dioceses, in agreement with the respective Ordinaries." Pope Pius XI in 1925 gave the commission pontifical rank and widened its authority, especially after the Lateran Treaty of 1929. This includes the Hebrew catacombs of the province of Rome. No changes can be made without the commission's authorization in the places entrusted to its care; it is in complete charge of any work to be undertaken, and it publishes the findings of such work. It sets down norms for visits of the public and of scholars to the sacred cemeteries, and determines what crypts, with what precautions, can be used for liturgical functions.

PONTIFICAL COMMITTEE FOR HISTORICAL SCIENCES. Established in 1954 by Pope Pius XII to continue the work of the Commission of Cardinals for Historical Studies, founded in 1883 by Pope Leo XIII. Its purpose is to promote the development of the historical sciences by means of international co-operation.

PONTIFICAL HOUSEHOLD, PREFECTURE OF. Established in 1967 by Pope Paul VI, it has charge of private and public audiences of the Pope, his travels, the running of the papal household, extraliturgical ceremonies, and spiritual exercises of the papal curia.

PONTIFICALIA INSIGNIA. Apostolic Letter of Pope Paul VI, decreeing who, besides bishops, may use pontifical (episcopal) vestments and ritual. There was vast reduction in such privileges regarding abbots and various prelates (June 21, 1968).

PONTIFICALIS ROMANI. Apostolic constitution approving the new ritual for the ordination of deacons, priests, and bishops. Pope Paul VI stated: "The ritual which follows, We hereby decree and establish as to the matter and form of conferring each Order. We do this by Our supreme Apostolic authority" (June 18, 1968).

PONTIFICAL MASS. Solemn Mass by a pope, cardinal, bishop, or abbot with prescribed ritual. It is celebrated with full ceremonial when said at the throne of a prelate's own cathedral.

PONTIFICAL MASTERS OF CEREMONIES. They originated in something of their present form under Pope Pius IV in 1563, and their privileges and duties were often revised. Their function is to direct the sacred ceremonies in the papal chapels and consistories. They are also in charge of the liturgy, by right or invitation, on other occasions, such as the consecration of churches, ordinations or formal visitations in and out of the city of Rome.

PONTIFICALS. The marks of dignity used by cardinals and bishops at Mass and other offices of the Church when celebrating with full solemnity. Abbots may also use pontificals, but only at the Eucharistic liturgy in their monasteries. The common pontificals have included buskins, sandals, gloves, dalmatic, tunicle, ring, pectoral cross, and miter. Among the specific pontificals for certain persons are the crosier, gremial, pallium, and archiepiscopal processional cross.

PONTIFICATE. The reign or period of reign of a pope as Roman pontiff. Once legitimately elected, and accepting the election, he immediately receives, by divine right, the full power of supreme jurisdiction over the Christian faithful.

PONTIUS PILATE. See PILATE, PONTIUS.

PONTMAIN. Shrine of Our Lady of Hope, thirty miles from Laval, in the northwest corner of Mayenne in France. The Germans had taken Paris in the Franco-Prussian War of 1870 and were on their way westward. Laval expected capture. On the eve of January 17, 1871, a vision of Our Lady appeared in the sky. She was visible for several hours to Joseph and Eugène Barbedette, aged ten and twelve. A Sister teaching at a nearby orphanage brought some children, who also saw the Lady, but the Sister did not. Babies clapped their hands when the vision appeared, but the mothers saw nothing. At the suggestion of the priest they all knelt and prayed. The smiling Lady appeared with a scroll unrolled near her feet, and a message on it read, "Pray, children, God will hear you. My Son allows Himself to be moved by compassion." The next day the news reached them that the Germans had withdrawn at the moment the Lady disappeared. Miracles sealed Our Lady's appearance. A large basilica marks the place of the vision, and a statue in it was made according to the children's description of what Mary looked like.

PONT. MAX. *Pontifex Maximus*—Supreme Pontiff.

POOR BOX. An alms box for voluntary contributions for relief of the poor. It is called in some places *corbona* (a treasure box) and has been found in churches from the earliest days of Christianity. See also ALMS BOX.

POOR CLARES. A monastic community founded by St. Clare (1194–1253) under the inspiration of St. Francis of Assisi. He first placed her in a Benedictine house, but later, when other women joined Clare, they founded a community along Franciscan lines. Clare became the first abbess (1215) and she occupied the position until her death. Several daughter houses were founded during her life, in Italy, France, and Germany. In keeping with the spirit of St. Francis, the austerity of the Poor Clares was the most severe among women religious up to that time. Some branch houses obtained dispensations from the original rule of absolute poverty not only for individuals but for the community as well. But the community of San Damiano at Assisi, with those of Perugia and Florence, obtained from Pope Gregory IX the "privilege of poverty," which enabled them to keep their primitive rule. In succeeding years modifications and reforms divided the Poor Clares into various religious institutes, mainly the Urbanists and Colettines. Their principal emphasis has been on mortification and Eucharistic adoration, with the chanting of the Divine Office.

POOR MEN OF LYONS. The original name under which the Waldenslans were condemned by Pope Lucius III in 1184.

POOR SOULS. The souls in purgatory, expiating the temporal punishment due to their sins. They are called "poor" because they cannot merit their own release or mitigation of their sufferings, but depend on the prayers and good works of the faithful on earth.

POPE. Title of the visible head of the Catholic Church. He is called Pope (Greek *pappas,* a child's word for father) because his authority is supreme and because it is to be exercised in a paternal way, after the example of Christ.

POPE, ELECTION. The choice of the Bishop of Rome, which has gone through various methods over the centuries. In 1975, Pope Paul VI issued an apostolic constitution in which he made certain changes in papal election law. In line with previous legislation, he decreed that only cardinals—a maximum of 120 under the age of eighty—may be electors. There can be no personal attendants for the cardinals during the conclave, and provisions were made for security and means for handling difficult situations that might arise during the election.

POPULAR CONSENT. A theory of civil authority which holds that God directly gives authority to the whole people civilly united, who then transfer its exercise to an individual or group to the form of government they approve. The implied contract does not establish political society as such, but only the form of government and the ruler. All government exists by the consent, at best tacit, of the governed. First clearly enunciated by St. Robert Bellarmine (1542–1621) in his *Disputationes de Controversiis,* notably in the *De Laicis,* III, 6; and Francis Suarez (1548–1617) in his *De Legibus,* III, II, 3, 4, it was later developed by John Locke (1632–1704) in England, and by Thomas Jefferson (1743–1826) in the United States, and has become the mainstay of modern political democracies.

POPULATION EXPLOSION. The notable increase in world population, resulting from improved medical care of the young and old. The term is commonly used as an argument in favor of contraception as the most effective way to prevent overpopulation.

PORNOGRAPHY. A description or portrayal of any person or activity that is consciously intended to stimulate immoral sexual feelings. (Etym. Greek *porne,* prostitute + *graphe,* writing.)

PORTABLE ALTAR. A movable altar consisting of a solid piece of natural stone, generally of a size large enough to hold the Sacred Host and the greater part of the base of a chalice. It bears on its upper surface five crosses cut into the stone, where the anointings are made when it is liturgically consecrated. Near the edge is a sepulcher or cavity that contains the relics of two martyr-saints, and sealed with a cemented stone lid. Also called an altar stone.

PORTER. Formerly one of the minor orders, the lowest in rank. Also called "doorkeeper," it was a symbolic office that in the early Church had a functional purpose. The order was abolished by Pope Paul VI in 1972, but the office may be conferred as a special ministry, with the permission of the Holy See, if an episcopal conference decides that it would be useful or necessary for their own territory.

PORT ROYAL. Benedictine abbey for women, founded in 1204, and located at Chevreuse, near Versailles. In 1609 it became a stronghold of Jansenism under Abbé St. Cyran, and in 1638 the members left Paris to found a second Port Royal near the abbey "of the Fields." In 1709 the Port Royal community was suppressed by Pope Clement XI. The buildings were razed by order of Louis XIV, but the edifice of the original monastery in Paris still stands.

PORZIUNCULA. Originally a very small church in Assisi where St. Francis received his vocation on February 24, 1208. He made it his headquarters for the rest of his life. The town has given its name to the Porziuncula Indulgence, now able to be gained by visiting certain (especially Franciscan) churches on August 2 or the Sunday following.

POSITIVE INTERNATIONAL LAW. Those aspects of the law of nations which are the result of express or tacit agreements made between nations and are not directly deducible from the natural law. Such would be the diplomatic immunity accorded ambassadors, or the internment of warships by neutrals in time of war.

POSITIVE LAW. A reasonable ordinance of a legitimate superior which becomes a general and just rule for the common good of the members of a society and is suitably promulgated by some external sign.

POSITIVE THEOLOGY. That part of theology which seeks to establish the truth of the Church's teaching from the evidence of Scripture, tradition, and the analogy of faith, i.e., consistency with the whole body of Catholic doctrine.

POSITIVISM. The view that only the sensibly perceptible is real, that only what is personally experienced is true. Thus nothing but facts can be affirmed with certitude. According to Auguste Comte (1798–1857), who coined the term "positivism," the history of humanity should be described in three stages: the first when people's minds were dominated by theology and superstition; the second when reason prevailed; and the third or final stage when dogmas and philosophies are being replaced by factual knowledge. Hence the supremacy of the physical, psychological, and social sciences in the modern age.

POSS. *Possessor, possessio*—possessor, possession.

POSSESSION, DEMONIC. The inner control by the devil of the actions of the body in a human being. The victim's liberty of soul always remains intact. Possession can be continual or intermittent, and the victim need not have culpably brought on the devil's control. There is an official exorcism provided by the Church for possessed persons. Public exorcisms must be authorized by ecclesiastical authority.

POSSESSIVE INSTINCT. The natural drive for power, or the tendency to dominate the love object. Basic urge that needs to be sublimated by divine grace in order to grow in humility, which controls the drive for power, and in charity, which seeks to sacrifice self for the one who is loved.

POSSIBLE. That which can be or can exist. In the plural, possibles are the essences of all things considered as objects of God's knowledge. (Etym. Latin *possibilis,* that which can exist or be done.)

POSTCOMMUNION. Liturgical prayer of the priest at Mass after the Communion of the faithful. In this prayer the priest asks that the celebration of the sacred mystery may bring forth its due effects. The people associate themselves with the prayer by answering Amen.

POSTCONCILIAR. A term used to describe the period since the Second Vatican Council (1962–65). It reflects the developments in Catholic doctrine, liturgy and ecclesiastical law that were authorized by the council and have been implemented by the Church's hierarchy.

POST LITTERAS APOSTOLICAS. Notification of the Sacred Congregation for the Doctrine of the Faith modifying the Church's concept of forbidden books. This document places the responsibility for avoiding such literature as would endanger the faith and morals on the conscience of each

Christian, and on the directives of bishops. But the former ecclesiastical law, concretized in the Index of Forbidden Books and in the corresponding censures, was abolished (June 14, 1966).

POSTULANT. A person taking the first step in religious life before entering the novitiate and receiving the habit. The purpose of the postulancy is to acquire some knowledge of the religious life and of the particular institute through personal experience. It enables one to become better known to the superiors of the community, and to develop such virtue as will qualify the candidate for acceptance into the novitiate. The length of the postulancy varies, but normally it is not less than six months. (Etym. Latin *postulatum,* a thing demanded; *postulatio,* supplication, intercession.)

POSTULATE. A principle or fact that is assumed to be true and that is a basis for action or argumentation. In the philosophy of Immanuel Kant, it is one of the assumptions of practical reason. The existence of God is assumed to assure a moral order in the world, and the immortality of the soul is assumed so that moral perfection might continue beyond a person's mortal life on earth. But in the Kantian system these are mere postulates; they are said to be beyond rational proof.

POSTULATION. A request for the appointment of a highly qualified candidate to an office of which he would not ordinarily be elected because of a canonical impediment. Church law recognizes this as a legitimate method of appointment.

POTENCY. The capacity of a being to be, to act, or to receive. Perfectability or capacity for perfection or change. Only creatures are in potency, since God is Pure Act and unchangeable. (Etym. Latin *potens,* power; *potentia,* power, ability to be or become or do something.)

POVERTY, EVANGELICAL. A Christian counsel by which a person voluntarily renounces all or part of his right to the ownership of material things.

POVERTY OF DISPOSSESSION. The complete renunciation of ownership and further acquisition of material possessions. The biblical foundation for such poverty is the declaration of Christ to the rich young man: "If you wish to be perfect, go and sell what you own and give the money to the poor, and you will have treasure in heaven; then come, follow me" (Matthew 19:21).

POVERTY OF SHARING. The voluntary sacrifice of one's possessions for the common good of a community. All means of support and activity are provided by the group. Practiced in the Church since apostolic times, it is described by St. Luke as one of the effects of receiving the Holy Spirit: "The faithful all lived together and owned everything in common; they sold their goods and possessions and shared out proceeds among themselves according to what each one needed" (Acts 2:44–45).

POWER. In general, the ability to do or perform something. Also called the principle of the effect, and as such is applicable to God and to creatures. More particularly, created power is the immediate principle by which a nature is directly, essentially, and permanently ordered to a definite function or specific operation. (Etym. Latin *posse*, to be able; *potentia*, power, the ability to be or become or do something.)

POWER OF JURISDICTION. The moral right to govern the faithful in the Catholic Church. Also called the power of ruling (*potestas regiminis*), which, by divine institution, belongs to the Church founded by Christ. It includes jurisdiction in the external forum (publicly known) and the internal forum (private matters of conscience), whether sacramental or nonsacramental.

POWER OF THE KEYS. Ecclesiastical authority conferred by Christ on Peter and his successors. In virtue of this authority, the popes have universal and independent jurisdiction over all the churches and all the faithful. The term is derived from Christ's promise to Peter to give him the keys of the Kingdom of Heaven (Matthew 16:19). More commonly, however, the expression refers to the Church exercise of authority to forgive or retain sins in the sacrament of penance.

POWERS. Those angels who compose the lowest choir of the second or intermediate order of the angelic host. They are called powers (*potestates*) because they have a special efficacy in restraining the assaults of the evil spirit.

POWERS OF EVIL. Satan and the fallen angels as created, invisible powers permitted by God to tempt human beings to sin, and on occasion used by God to punish people, already on earth, for their commission of sin. Also applied to those persons who are estranged from God and therefore ready instruments of the evil spirit for leading others into sin.

POWERS OF THE SOUL. The memory, understanding, and free will. They are frequently mentioned in the writings of the Fathers of the Church, who compare the Trinity of persons in one divine nature to the presence of three spiritual faculties in one human soul.

PP. *Papa*—pope; *pontificum*—of the popes.

P.P. *Parochus*—parish priest (used mostly in Ireland).

PP. AA. *Patres amplissimi*—cardinals.

P.P.P. *Propriâ pecuniâ posuit*—erected at his own expense.

PR. *Proprium*—proper.

P.R. *Permanens rector*—permanent rector.

PRACTICAL DOUBT. Uncertainty of mind concerning the prudent course of action or the moral rectitude of something to be done here and now. It is the opposite of a merely speculative doubt. (Etym. Latin *practicus*, active, acting, effective: *dubitatio*, doubt, deliberation, hesitation.)

PRAEF. *Praefatio*—Preface of the Mass.

PRAGMATISM. A theory that every truth has practical consequences that are the test of its truthfulness. Associated with the American philosopher William James, who defined the true as "only the expedient in our way of thinking." In religious terms, what justifies a creed or ritual is its ability to satisfy psychological needs and generate useful values for society.

PRAISE. To speak well of someone's good qualities or deeds. It implies awareness of someone's excellence, internal approval, and manifesting approbation of that which is praised. Strictly speaking, praise refers to activity, especially holiness in God and virtuous conduct in people. But the term is also applied to the character or nature of the one whose actions are praiseworthy.

PRAISES OF GOD. A hymn of adoration of St. Francis of Assisi. The original paper with these praises is preserved today in a reliquary in the Basilica of St. Francis in Assisi. The praises illustrate the mystical heights to which Francis had attained at the time of his stigmatization. They read: "You are holy, Lord, the only God, and your deeds are wonderful./ You are strong. You are great. You are the Most High, You are almighty. You, holy Father, are King of heaven and earth./ You are Three and One, Lord God, all good. You are Good, all

Good, supreme Good, Lord God, living and true./ You are love, You are wisdom. You are humility, You are endurance. You are rest, You are peace. You are joy and gladness. You are justice and moderation. You are all our riches, and You suffice for us./ You are beauty. You are gentleness. You are our protector, You are our guardian and defender. You are courage. You are our haven and our hope./ You are our faith, our great consolation. You are our eternal life, great and wonderful Lord, God almighty, Merciful Savior."

PRAYER. The voluntary response to the awareness of God's presence. This response may be an acknowledgment of God's greatness and of a person's total dependence on him (adoration), or gratitude for his benefits to oneself and others (thanksgiving), or sorrow for sins committed and begging for mercy (expiation), or asking for graces needed (petition), or affection for God, who is all good (love).

PRAYER, CONSTANT. The Christian practice, advocated by St. Paul, "Pray constantly" (I Thessalonians 5:17), by which a person always remains united with God. Also called the prayer of the heart, it need not be conscious awareness of God's presence. It implies that a person is constantly ready to do the will of God.

PRAYER AND PENANCE, ARCH-CONFRATERNITY OF. See POINTE AUX TREMBLES.

PRAYER BOOK. A manual of prayers for private devotion by the faithful or for communal use by members of a religious community or confraternity. There is no Catholic counterpart to the Anglican Book of Common Prayer because Catholic liturgical books of prayer and chant are totally distinct from ordinary prayer books, which may contain a variety of authorized prayers, meditations, or reflective readings.

PRAYER DURING THE DAY. The third hour of the Divine Office, also called the "Middle Hour." It consists essentially of three psalms, a short biblical reading, and prayer that vary according to the time of the day they are said.

PRAYER OF CHRIST. Formerly a liturgical feast, on the Tuesday after Septuagesima, in commemoration of Christ's prayer of agony in the Garden of Olives.

PRAYER OF QUIET. A peaceful internal repose by which the soul is captivated by the divine presence. It is the result of con-templative love and is a fruit of the gift of wisdom. During the prayer of quiet the mind is specially enlightened by divine grace and a spiritual delight pervades the whole person. Although the lower faculties and senses are free to exercise their natural activities, God makes himself felt in the subtle part of the soul obscurely as the Great Reality. At first this prayer is of short duration. Under the influence of grace it becomes longer and may eventually become habitual.

PRAYER OF RECOLLECTION. Also called the prayer of simplicity, in which the soul gathers its various faculties to concentrate the mind and will on God.

PRAYER OF SIMPLICITY. Meditation replaced by a purer, more intimate prayer consisting in a simple regard or loving thought on God, or on one of his attributes, or on some mystery of the Christian faith. Reasoning is put aside and the soul peacefully attends to the operations of the Spirit with sentiments of love.

PRAYER OF THE FAITHFUL. The General Intercession or Bidding prayer. In this the people exercise their priestly function by praying for all mankind. The prayer is normally to be included whenever there are people attending the Mass. The normal sequence of intentions recommended is for: the needs of the Church, civil authorities, and the salvation of the whole world, those oppressed by any kind of need, and the local community. On special occasions the intentions may be adjusted accordingly. It is the function of the priest to preside over this part of the liturgy by opening and concluding the Prayer of the Faithful, with an assistant reading the intentions and the congregation responding with an appropriate invocation.

PRAYER OF THE HEART. See PRAYER, CONSTANT.

PRAYER OF UNION. A most intimate union of the soul with God, accompanied by a certitude of his presence within the soul and a suspension of all interior faculties. With this prayer there is an absence of distractions because the soul is entirely absorbed in God. There is no fatigue, no matter how long the union may last, because no personal effort is involved, but rather an extraordinary experience of joy. The soul is left with an ardent zeal to glorify God; complete detachment from all created things; perfect submission to God's will; and great charity for one's neighbor.

PRAYERS OVER THE PEOPLE. Special invocation, "at the discretion of the priest," at the end of Mass or after the Liturgy of the Word, the Divine Office, and the celebration of the sacraments. It precedes the final blessing and has a variety of formulas.

PRB., PRESBIT. *Presbyter*—priest.

PREACHER APOSTOLIC. A dignitary of the pontifical household, whose duty it has been to preach to the Pope and the assembled papal court four times during Advent and weekly during Lent. A Capuchin friar has held this office since 1753, when Benedict XIV conferred it on that order.

PREACHING. Public discourse on a religious subject by one having authority to do so. Preaching, therefore, can be properly applied only to bishops, priests, and deacons in the exercise of their office of proclaiming the word of God. Speaking of priests, the Second Vatican Council places this office first among the duties of priests, who are "consecrated to preach the Gospel, shepherd the faithful, and celebrate divine worship" (*Constitution on the Church*, III, 28).

PRE-ADAMITES. The theory that there existed a human race that became extinct before Adam and Eve. A pure hypothesis, it was offered by some in an effort to avoid apparent conflict between the biblical account of man before the fall and the speculations of evolution.

PREAMBLES OF FAITH. The main premises of reason on which the act of divine faith depends as on its rational foundation. They are mainly three: 1. the existence of God; 2. his authority, or right to be believed because he knows all things and is perfectly truthful; and 3. the fact that he actually made a revelation, which is proved especially by miracles or fulfilled prophecies performed in testimony of a prophet's (or Christ's) claim to speaking in the name of God. (Etym. Latin *praeambulus*, walking in front: *prae*, in front + *ambulare*, to walk.)

PREBEND. The stipend due to a canon from the revenues of a church. According to Church law, if the revenues prove insufficient, a bishop may draw on other sources to make up the deficit.

PRECEDENCE. The right ecclesiastical arrangement of individuals according to their rank, office, and seniority, for whatever purpose they have been assembled. Canonical precedence is determined by the authority of one person over another, their rank in the hierarchy of jurisdiction and in the hierar-chy of orders, followed by priority of promotion and seniority of age. When precedence does not concern individuals, the order is: secular clergy, religious clergy, religious of nonclerical rank, and the laity—men before women. The Pope always has first place in every aspect of ecclesiastical preference. In a procession the place of honor is at the end.

PRECENTOR. See SCHOLA CANTORUM, MONASTIC.

PRECEPT. A command of God or of legitimate human authority to a definite person or a specific duty. A precept is also distinguished from the whole body of laws as any particular rule or command under the law. Affirmative precepts command a person to act or to do something. Negative precepts forbid some action. (Etym. Latin *praeceptum*, rule, maxim.)

PRECEPTS OF CHARITY. The two great commandments of divine revelation, first stated in the Old Law and confirmed by Christ in the Gospels. They are: 1. "You must love the Lord your God with all your heart, with all your soul, with all your mind and with all your strength"; and 2. "You must love your neighbor as yourself" (Deuteronomy 6:4–5; Leviticus 19:18; Mark 12:30–31). The phrase "with all your mind" is Christ's addition to the teaching of the Old Testament, as well as the observation that "there is no greater commandment than these" (Mark 12:31).

PRECEPTS OF THE CHURCH. Certain commandments of a moral and ecclesiastical nature prescribed for observance by all Catholics. Their formulation goes back to the Middle Ages, and their number has varied from four to six or more, depending on the times. A recent list of such duties "expected of Catholic Christians today" was formulated by the National Conference of Catholic Bishops in the United States, as follows:

1. To keep holy the day of the Lord's Resurrection: to worship God by participating in Mass every Sunday and Holy Day of Obligation: to avoid those activities that would hinder renewal of soul and body, e.g., needless work and business activities, unnecessary shopping, etc.

2. To lead a sacramental life: to receive Holy Communion frequently and the Sacrament of Penance regularly.

—minimally, to receive the Sacrament of Penance at least once a year (annual confession is obligatory only if serious sin is involved).

—minimally, to receive Holy Communion at least once a year, between the First Sunday of Lent and Trinity Sunday.

3. To study Catholic teaching in preparation for the Sacrament of Confirmation, to be confirmed, then to continue to study and advance the cause of Christ.

4. To observe the marriage laws of the Church: to give religious training (by example and word) to one's children; to use parish schools and religious education programs.

5. To strengthen and support the Church: one's own parish community and parish priests; the worldwide Church and the Holy Father.

6. To do penance, including abstaining from meat and fasting from food on the appointed days.

7. To join in the missionary spirit and apostolate of the Church.

PRECIOUS BLOOD. The blood of the living Christ as an integral part of human nature immediately united with the second person of the Trinity. It is called Precious Blood because, according to Pope Clement VI, "the value of the blood of Christ, on account of its union with the *Logos*, is so great that one little drop would have sufficed for the redemption of the whole human race" (*Unigenitus Dei Filius*) (Denzinger, 1025).

PRECIOUS BLOOD (worship). The blood of Jesus Christ distinctively mentioned many times in the New Testament. It is the living symbol of the Redemption and of the Savior's death on the Cross. An object of adoration as part of the Sacred Humanity, it is hypostatically united with the Second Person of the Trinity. Moreover, it is an integral part of Christ, who is really present in the Blessed Sacrament. In 1849, Pope Pius IX extended the Feast of the Precious Blood to the whole Church, assigning to it the first Sunday in July, changed by Pope St. Pius X in 1914 to July 1. Since the Second Vatican Council the feast has been merged with that of Corpus Christi, so that the new Feast of the Body and Blood of Christ (*Festum Corporis et Sanguinis Christi*) occurs on the Thursday following Trinity Sunday. In some countries it is transferred to the following Sunday.

PRECIOUS BLOOD, SOCIETY OF. Congregation of the Missionaries of the Most Precious Blood (1786–1836), founded in 1815 by St. Caspar del Bufalo. It is a society of clerics of common life, whose purpose is to promote devotion to the Precious Blood, to teach youth, evangelize, and engage in the parochial ministry. There are several communities of religious women also specially devoted to the Precious Blood.

PRECIOUS BLOOD SCAPULAR. Badge of the Confraternity of the Precious Blood. It is red, and one part usually bears a picture of a chalice adored by angels.

PRECONCILIAR. A term used to describe the period before the Second Vatican Council. It generally compares this period with the Church's development since the council.

PRECONIZATION. A public pronouncement by the Pope in consistory, solemnly confirming previous appointments to episcopal sees and other offices. At one time all new bishops were appointed by the Pope before such an assembly of hierarchy; however, today this is not always possible. Therefore, they must be given solemn proclamation in consistory. This preconization, not the former appointment, determines the precedence of bishops. (Etym. Latin *praeconizatio*, proclamation; from *praeco*, herald.)

PRECULAR. One bound by the condition of some benefaction to pray, as promised or agreed, for the benefactor. (Etym. Latin *precare*, to pray.)

PRECURSOR. As the herald of Christ, St. John the Baptist, of whom all four Evangelists wrote at length and who was described by his father, Zechariah, in the *Benedictus* "You shall be called Prophet of the Most High, for you will go before the Lord to prepare the way for Him" (Luke 1:76). (Etym. Latin *praecursor*, forerunner.)

PREDEFINITION. The idea of something in God's mind before it is created. Thus all human souls are said to be predefined before God creates them at the moment of human conception. (Etym. Latin *prae*, before + *definire*, enclose within limits.)

PREDELLA. The floor of a platform on which an altar is placed. It sometimes refers to the upper steplike shelf on the back of the altar. (Etym. Italian *predella*, altar step, footboard.)

PREDESTINARIANISM. The theory that denies that God has the will to save all mankind, since he wants only the elect to reach heaven. There is no place in this system for true internal freedom of the human will, but only for external freedom from coercion. The eternal decree of God alone predestines to glory or damnation. The elect receive irresistible grace; the others have an impulse of the will to sin and so are not given salvific grace. Predestinarianism is central to the Reformation doctrine of John Calvin. (Etym. Latin *prae,* before + *destinare,* to destine, ordain.)

PREDESTINATION. In the widest sense it is every eternal decision of God; in a narrower sense it is the supernatural final destination of rational creatures; and in the strictest sense it is God's eternal decision to assume certain rational creatures into heavenly glory. Predestination implies an act of the divine intellect and of the divine will. The first is foreknowledge, the second is predestination.

According to its efficacy in time, predestination is distinguished as incomplete or complete depending on whether it is to grace only or also to glory. Complete predestination is the divine preparation of grace in the present life and of glory in the life to come.

This doctrine is proposed by the ordinary and universal teaching of the Church as a truth of revelation. The reality of predestination is clearly attested by St. Paul: "They are the ones he chose especially long ago and intended to become true images of the Son, so that his Son, might be the eldest of many brothers. He called those he intended for this; those he called he justified and with those he justified he shared his glory." (Romans 8:29–30). All elements of complete predestination are given: the activity of God's mind and will, and the principal stages of its realization in time.

The main difficulty in the doctrine of predestination is whether God's eternal decision has been taken with or without consideration of human freedom. Catholic teaching holds that predestination by God does not deny the human free will. Numerous theories have been offered on how to reconcile the two, but all admit with St. Paul (Romans 11:33) that predestination is an unfathomable mystery. (Etym. Latin *praedestinatio,* a determining beforehand.)

PREDETERMINATION. Also called "physical premotion," to explain how God's sovereignty includes also the free actions of men. According to this theory, first developed by Dominic Bañez (1529–1604) and later adopted by the Dominican Order, God has predetermined from all eternity that certain people shall be saved. For the realization of this he bestows effective grace on these people. In this way he physically affects the free will of the elect, and so secures that they decide freely to co-operate with grace. Efficacious grace, by its inner power, therefore, infallibly brings it about that the elect freely consent to do those salutary acts which merit eternal salvation. Thus it is substantially different from sufficient grace, which merely confers the power to do a salutary act. In order that this potency may be translated into act, another new, inherently different grace (efficacious grace) must appear. From all eternity God has decreed the free assent of the human will to the efficacious grace, whereby he brings about salvation for those who fall within his decree.

PRE-EVANGELIZATION. Preparation of a person or people to receive the Gospel. The need for such preparation in the modern world arises from the massive neglect of God and things spiritual. "In the past," the Second Vatican Council explains, "it was the exception to repudiate God and religion to the point of abandoning them, and then only in individual cases; but nowadays it seems a matter of course to reject them as incompatible with scientific progress and a new kind of humanism" (*Gaudium et Spes,* 8). Through the media of social communication, this spirit of unbelief has permeated whole segments of society. Hence the need for predisposing people even to listen to the Gospel, especially in the once Christian affluent cultures of Euro-America.

PREFACE. The act of thanksgiving, which begins the Eucharistic liturgy. By it the priest, in the name of all the people of God, offers praise and gratitude to God the Father for the whole work of redemption or for some special benefits commemorated in the liturgy. (Etym. Latin *praefatio,* preface, prologue; literally, a saying beforehand.)

PREFECT APOSTOLIC. A priest with special faculties of jurisdiction in mission territory and in lands where the episcopal hierarchy has not yet been established. Subject directly to the Holy See, such a priest enjoys many rights similar to those of a resident bishop, but he cannot confer major orders. (Etym. Latin *praefectus,* overseer, chief, prefect.)

PREFECTURE OF THE PONTIFICAL HOUSEHOLD. Established by Pope Paul VI in 1967 and given the present name in 1968. It combines the former functions of the Sacred Congregation of Ceremonial and the two offices of Majordomo and Maestro di Camera. Under the direction of its prefect, it watches over the discipline of the papal household, organizes solemn audiences for eminent personages, other private, special, and general audiences, and ceremonies that are not strictly liturgical, the spiritual exercises for the Pope, cardinals, and papal prelates.

PREJUDICE. In moral philosophy a preconceived opinion formulated without consideration of known facts and usually based on erroneous knowledge. It leads to wrong judgments and renders a person blind to reason and closed to convincing argument. It often violates justice because prejudiced people tend to ignore others' rights. They are so preoccupied with their own version of persons and societies, that they prejudge adversely. Prejudice is the common basis for sinful rash judgment.

PRELATE. A dignitary having jurisdiction in external forum by right of his office. There have been prelates "nullius" who presided over the clergy and people of a certain territory not belonging to an established diocese. Thus abbots, although not bishops, have had the jurisdiction of a prelate. Such prelacies have been drastically reduced since the Second Vatican Council. In exempt religious orders, clerical superiors, such as provincials, guardians, and priors, share in the jurisdictional rank of prelate. The name and rank of prelate may also be given to priests as a mark of papal recognition of their service to the Church. (Etym. Latin *praelatus,* prelate, superior.)

PRELATE, DOMESTIC. A priest whom the Holy See honors for services rendered to the Church and who is listed in the *Annuario Pontificio* according to his proper rank, e.g., Chaplain of His Holiness or Prelate of Honor of His Holiness.

PRELATURE NULLIUS. A territory belonging to no diocese but having its own superior called a "prelate nullius," and its own clergy and congregation. If such a territory comprises a certain number of parishes, the prelate set over the area enjoys a jurisdiction similar to that of a bishop in residence.

PREMONSTRATENSIANS. Canons Regular of Prémontré, also called Norbertines. They were founded in 1120 by St. Norbert at Prémontré, near Laon, France, approved in 1126, and again in 1617–24. Their focus is on solemn liturgical worship, missions, parochial ministry, and the education of youth. Based on the Rule of St. Augustine, with some Cistercian influences, the constitutions include certain austerities, e.g., abstinence from meat.

PREPARATION OF THE GIFTS. The offertory of the Mass. It is recommended that the faithful bring up the bread and wine, which the priest or deacon receives and places on the altar. While doing this the priest says some prescribed prayers. Money and other gifts for the poor or for the Church may be collected from the faithful at this time and carried to the altar, but placed in some convenient place rather than on the altar itself. The offertory antiphon is to accompany the procession of the gifts, after which the altar may be incensed, rising like a fragrant odor in the sight of God, as a symbol of the prayers and sacrifices of the faithful. Then the priest washes his hands as a sign of his desire for inward purification. Following this he says the familiar *Orate Fratres* (Pray, Brethren), in which the faithful are invited to ask that their common sacrifice may be pleasing to God. The Prayer over the Gifts leads into the climax of the Mass.

PREPARING FOR COMMUNION. A short prayer at Mass after the *Agnus Dei* (Lamb of God), during which the priest prays privately in preparation for Holy Communion. During this time the faithful should also pray in silence.

PRESANCTIFIED, MASS OF THE. The Eucharistic liturgy on Good Friday, in which the priest and people receive the Eucharist previously consecrated or sanctified.

PRESBYTER. In the early Church a member of a group (usually of priests) who advised a bishop. Together they formed the presbytery, which, under a bishop, was the governing body of a community. The presbyter having no official duties, he was often commissioned by the bishop to teach, celebrate Mass, and baptize. Presbyters were usually of advanced age and, like a bishop, chosen by the people. Their rank was above that of deacons but inferior to that of bishops. There was no restriction on their number.

PRESBYTERATE. The priesthood, as the second rank of holy orders above the diaconate and below the episcopate. (Etym. Greek *presbyteros,* elder.)

PRESBYTERIANS. Members of various Protestant bodies, following in the tradition of John Calvin (1509–64) and his Scottish disciple John Knox (1513–72). The essential structural feature of historic Presbyterianism was that the Church's government should be in the hands of presbyters. Today, however, many Presbyterians hold that the

Church founded by Christ contained episcopal and congregational, as well as presbyterian, elements. A typical Presbyterian church is governed by a hierarchy of authorities, each in the nature of a court: session, presbytery, synod, and general assembly, having clearly defined functions and specific directors.

The substance of Presbyterian belief is contained in the Westminster Confession of Faith, drafted by the Puritan English Parliament in 1643. Its main provisions are the Calvinist predestination belief that the Church founded by Christ was essentially invisible and "consists of the whole number of the elect," a spiritual and not bodily presence of Christ in the Eucharist, and a deference to civil authority that is characteristically Presbyterian. A new confession of the faith, issued by the American Presbyterians in 1967, left the Westminster Confession essentially untouched. Added to the group of now recognized statements of faith, however, was the Theological Declaration of Barmen (1934), published under Karl Barth (1886–1968) during the Nazi regime, to defend the Church's freedom from political oppression.

PRESBYTERI SACRA. Circular letter issued by the Sacred Congregation for the Clergy, explaining the function of priests' councils in a diocese or other ecclesiastical territory. After making clear that these councils are only consultative, and that a bishop alone administers the diocese, the document spells out various ways in which such councils can be of assistance to the ordinary of a diocese (April 11, 1970).

PRESBYTERORUM ORDINIS. The Second Vatican Council's Decree on the Ministry and Life of Priests. Priests are defined as those men who "hold in the community of the faithful the sacred power of Orders, that of offering sacrifice and forgiving sins, and who exercise the priestly office publicly on behalf of men in the name of Christ." Their ministry flows from their office. It is to share with everyone the truth of the Gospel, which is "often very difficult in present-day conditions." Celibacy for priests is reaffirmed. Their sanctity is declared to be essential and to be fostered by "the double table of holy Scripture and the Eucharist" (December 7, 1965).

PRESBYTERY. Originally the senate that, in some early dioceses, assisted a bishop in the administration of his see. Later the term was applied to the part of a church reserved for the Sacrifice of Mass, now called the sanctuary, usually admitting only the clergy for services, except as ministers and in marriage ceremonies. Now occasionally used of the rectory or residence of the clergy.

PRESCIENCE. In general, foreknowledge. Specifically the foreknowledge that God has of future events whose occurrence depends on the free will of creatures. They are events that take place if certain choices are made. Prescience is also God's foreknowledge of the merits that human beings will acquire by their voluntary co-operation with divine grace. (Etym. Latin *prae,* before + *scientia,* knowledge.)

PRESCRIBED PRAYER. A special additional prayer to be said by the celebrant at Mass. It may be prescribed by the Pope or a bishop for a specific cause, e.g., drought, jubilee, persecution; or it may be prescribed by the rubrics for special feasts; or it may formerly have been required for the gaining of indulgences.

PRESCRIPTION. The obtaining of a title to something through lapse of time. One claimant has been in continued peaceful possession in good faith for a long period of time. Meanwhile the other claimant has not exercised his or her right or questioned the other's possession.

In natural law, mere lapse of time does not extinguish one's right, so that prescription is not a natural title. But there is a basis in natural law for the civil law to authorize prescription, as an exercise of eminent domain, i.e., superior dominion exerted by a sovereign state over all property within its boundaries.

PRESENCE. To be near someone or something, either actually or effectively or spiritually. Actual presence means that the object is really and substantially there; effective presence means that its influence is being exercised, although the cause of the influence may be actually somewhere else; spiritual presence is the interior response to a person who may be physically absent but is affecting the mind and will of the one to whom he or she is said to be present. (Etym. Latin *prae,* before + *ens,* being: *praesens,* being at, taking part in what goes on.)

PRESENCE OF GOD. The existence of God acting in favor of his creatures. "God is in things, first, because He is their cause, secondly because He is the object of their activity, as the known in the knower and as the desired in the lover, and this . . . which is proper to human souls, is God's special presence by grace to rational creatures who know Him and love Him, actually or habitually" (St. Thomas Aquinas, *Summa Theologica*, I, VIII, 3). Cultivating the awareness of God's presence in the soul, and in the events of divine providence, is essential for growth in the spiritual life.

PRESENT. The current and passing moment of time, the now as distinct from the past, which is gone, and the future, which is still to be.

PRESENTATION. The right of nominating a cleric to a vacant church or benefice. It is one of the privileges of the right of patronage, which may be conferred on those who endow a church or benefice. Presenting a cleric does not mean installing him in office. That belongs exclusively to an ecclesiastical superior, who must accept the nominated cleric if he is otherwise canonically suitable.

PRESENTATION, FEAST OF. See PURIFICATION.

PRESERVATION OF LIFE. The duty that every person has to use at least ordinary means like food, sleep, shelter, and available medication to sustain bodily life. If one's life is specially important for one's family, the Church or society, that person may be obliged to use proportionally extraordinary means to remain alive.

P.R.E.S.S. *Praefectura Rerum Oeconomicarum Sanctae Sedis*—Prefecture for Economic Affairs of the Holy See.

PRESTIGE MOTIVE. The desire to attain recognition by one's friends and by society in general. Identified by spiritual writers as a basic human instinct that needs to be controlled as a precondition for sanctity.

PRESUMPTION. The desire to undertake, or the actual undertaking, of what is above one's capacity. It is a result of pride, which makes a person overestimate his abilities and blinds him to his deficiencies. It also leads one to expect graces from God without doing anything to obtain them, and even when acting the opposite, as when sinning, the person presumes that forgiveness is assured. (Etym. Latin *praesumere*, to suppose, take for granted.)

PRETERNATURAL. That which is beyond the natural but is not strictly supernatural. It is preternatural either because natural forces are used by God to produce effects beyond their native capacity, or because above-human forces, angelic or demonic, are active in the world of space and time. (Etym. Latin *praeter*, beyond + *natura*, nature.)

PRETERNATURAL GIFTS. Favors granted by God above and beyond the powers or capacities of the nature that receives them but not beyond those of all created nature. Such gifts perfect nature but do not carry it beyond the limits of created nature. They include three great privileges to which human beings have no title—infused knowledge, absence of concupiscence, and bodily immortality. Adam and Eve possessed these gifts before the Fall.

PREVENTING GRACE. The grace that goes before the free consent of the will. It moves the will spontaneously, inclining it to God. A preventing grace may be a good thought or a good impulse, without human effort, to perform some action that leads to heaven.

PRIDE. An inordinate esteem of oneself. It is inordinate because it is contrary to the truth. It is essentially an act or disposition of the will desiring to be considered better than a person really is. Pride may be expressed in different ways: by taking personal credit for gifts or possessions, as if they had not been received from God; by glorying in achievements, as if they were not primarily the result of divine goodness and grace; by minimizing one's defects or claiming qualities that are not actually possessed; by holding oneself superior to others or disdaining them because they lack what the proud person has; by magnifying the defects of others or dwelling on them. When pride is carried to the extent that a person is unwilling to acknowledge dependence on God and refuses to submit his or her will to God or lawful authority, it is a grave sin. The gravity arises from the fact that a person shows contempt for God or of those who take his place. Otherwise, pride is said to be imperfect and venially wrong.

While not all sins are pride, it can lead to all sorts of sins, notably presumption, ambition, vainglory, boasting, hypocrisy, strife, and disobedience. Pride strives for perverse excellence. It despises others and, depending on its perversity, even looks down upon God. The remedies for pride are a sincere knowledge of oneself, the acceptance of daily humiliations, avoidance of even the least self-complacency, humble acknowledgment of one's faults, and prayerful communion with God.

PRIDE OF LIFE. The natural tendency to egotism, which is partly the result of original sin but mainly the mysterious desire of human beings to do their own will even when this contradicts the will of God. It is an urge to self-worship, or self-deification, and is at the root of all sin.

PRIE-DIEU. A kneeling bench used in many European churches and mainly intended for private devotions. Its present form dates from the seventeenth century. It resembles a wooden desk with a sloping shelf for resting the arms, often with a compartment for books beneath.

PRIEST. An authorized mediator who offers a true sacrifice in acknowledgment of God's supreme dominion over human beings and in expiation for their sins. A priest's mediation is the reverse of that of a prophet, who communicates from God to the people. A priest mediates from the people to God.

Christ, who is God and man, is the first, last, and greatest priest of the New Law. He is the eternal high priest who offered himself once and for all on the Cross, a victim of infinite value, and he continually renews that sacrifice on the altar through the ministry of the Church.

Within the Church are men who are specially ordained as priests to consecrate and offer the body and blood of Christ in the Mass. The Apostles were the first ordained priests, when on Holy Thursday night Christ told them to do in his memory what he had just done at the Last Supper. All priests and bishops trace their ordination to the Apostles. Their second essential priestly power, to forgive sins, was conferred by Christ on Easter Sunday, when he told the Apostles, "For those whose sins you forgive, they are forgiven; for those whose sins you retain, they are retained" (John 20–22, 23).

All the Christian faithful, however, also share in the priesthood by their baptismal character. They are enabled to offer themselves in sacrifice with Christ through the Eucharistic liturgy. They offer the Mass in the sense that they internally unite themselves with the outward offering made by the ordained priest alone.

PRIESTHOOD. Sacrament of the New Law, instituted by Christ at the Last Supper, which confers on a man the power of consecrating and offering the body and blood of Christ, and of remitting and retaining sins. There are two grades or levels of the priesthood, the presbyterate and the episcopate. Normally priesthood refers to the presbyterate and is the second rank of orders, above the diaconate. Only a bishop can ordain priests, who must first have been ordained deacons. In the ordination of priests, the "matter" of the sacrament is the imposition of the bishop's hands upon the individ-ual candidates, which is done in silence before the consecration prayer, of which the following words pertain to the nature of the order and therefore are required for the validity of the act: "We ask you, all powerful Father, give these servants of yours the dignity of the presbyterate. Renew the Spirit of holiness within them. By your divine gift may they attain the second order of the hierarchy and exemplify right conduct in their lives."

PRIESTHOOD OF CHRIST. The role of Christ as ordained to offer sacrifice and prayer for humanity to his heavenly Father. His ordination or anointing to the office of high priest took place at the moment of the Incarnation, i.e., at the moment when the Word of God assumed human flesh in the womb of Mary. During his life on earth Christ exercised his priestly office by all the acts of his will, and then at the Last Supper and on Calvary he united all these mortal acts into one supreme sacrifice to the Father. Along with the sacrifice, Christ also prayed as a priest, notably when he instituted the Eucharist and in the sacerdotal prayer recorded by St. John (17:1–26). Moreover, Christ's priesthood continues everlastingly in heaven, as revealed in the Letter to the Hebrews. Regarding the manner in which he exercises his eternal priesthood, revelation merely says: "He is always making intercession for us" (Hebrews 7:25; Romans 8:34), which is a truly sacerdotal function because, as St. Paul affirms, it bears an intimate relation to the sacrifice of the Cross. In fact, Christ's continuing priesthood is the basis in faith for the existence and efficacy of the sacrifice of the Mass.

PRIESTHOOD OF THE FAITHFUL. The share in the high priesthood of Christ received by everyone at baptism and strengthened by confirmation and the Eucharist. Essential to this priesthood is the right to receive the other sacraments, of participating in the Church's liturgy, and of being united with Christ the eternal priest as he offers himself, with the members of his Mystical Body, to the heavenly Father in the Eucharistic Sacrifice.

PRIESTS' COUNCIL. Also called a priests' senate or diocesan presbyterium. It is an elected body of priests organized to assist the ordinary of the diocese. The priests are elected according to a constitutional norm, and the council itself is directed by an executive board together with a group of officers who are elected by the members. The function of the priests' council is not to substitute for the bishop but to advise him for a more efficient and agreeable direction of the diocese.

PRIESTS' SENATE. See PRIESTS' COUNCIL.

PRIMACY. First in rank. Applied to the Pope as Bishop of Rome, it is a primacy of jurisdiction, which means the possession of full and supreme teaching, legislative and sacerdotal powers in the Catholic Church. St. Peter was promised the primacy when Christ told him that he was to be the rock on which the Savior would build his Church (Matthew 16:18). Peter received the primacy when the risen Christ told him to "feed my lambs, feed my sheep" (John 21:15–17). It follows from the dogma of the primacy that Paul, like the other Apostles, was subordinate to Peter as the supreme head of the whole Church. Pope Innocent X in 1647 rejected Jansenist teaching that Peter and Paul were joint heads of the Church (Denzinger, 1999). According to Christ's ordinance, Peter was to have successors in his primacy over the whole Church and for all time. As defined by the First Vatican Council (1869–70), it is heretical to deny that "in virtue of the decree of Our Lord Jesus Christ Himself, blessed Peter has perpetual successors in his primacy over the universal Church" (Denzinger, 3058). Following the precedent of the Second Council of Lyons (1274) and the Council of Florence (1430), the First Vatican Council further defined that the successors of Peter in the primacy are the Bishops of Rome (Denzinger, 3058). This doctrine affirms that the Bishop of Rome at any time is, in fact, the holder of the primacy. On what legal title the association of the Roman Pontiff's office with the primacy rests is not defined. The more common position is that it rests, not on the historical fact that Peter worked and died as Bishop of Rome, but on a positive ordinance of Christ or of the Holy Spirit, who revealed that the bishops of Rome should be the successors of Peter. Accordingly the fact that the bishops of Rome hold primacy over the universal Church is of divine and not merely human origin.

Like other doctrines of faith, the primacy has undergone considerable development over the centuries. Most recently, the role of the bishops to the Pope was clarified in the teaching of the Second Vatican Council on collegiality. Notwithstanding this development, the basic elements of the primacy have not changed. They are, in brief, that the Pope possesses full and supreme power of jurisdiction over the whole Church and each member in the Church, not only in

matters of faith and morals, but in Church discipline and in the government of the Church. (Etym. Latin *primus,* first, foremost, primary.)

PRIMATE. A bishop exercising authority not only over his own province, but over a national territory. His authority extends to convoking and presiding over national councils, hearing appeals, and crowning the sovereign. Today the title is one of honor only. The authority of primates was never established by canon law.

PRIME. The part of the Divine Office formerly assigned to the first hour (*hora prima*), about six in the morning in monastic communities. It is no longer part of the Liturgy of the Hours according to the Roman Rite.

PRIME MATTER. The fundamental, potential principle of all bodily substances. It is pure passive potency and therefore the completely undetermined basic material of the physical universe; the substratum of all material things remaining unchanged in every physical change that occurs in space and time.

PRIME MOVER. God as the First Cause, who originally started the world on its course of bodily and spiritual movement and continues to sustain the universe in its process of change.

PRIMER. The ordinary prayer book in use by the laity of England before the Reformation. It contained the Little Office of Our Lady, Vespers, and the Penitential and Gradual Psalms, as well as the *Pater Noster, Ave, Credo,* and other prayers. Sometimes an alphabet was placed in the book's preface so that the primer could be used in teaching children to read.

PRIMITIVE RELIGION. The religion of the early peoples. Strictly speaking, there are no genuine primitives anywhere on earth today. More accurately, the religion of the ancients was archaic, and of this there is extensive evidence in the artifacts, paintings, and symbolic writings they have left. Primitive religion, properly so-called, is that of present-day peoples whose relative isolation from the major streams of culture suggests their lineage from the chronological ancestors of the human race. Their religious condition, therefore, is on a par with other phases of conduct and knowledge, ranging from the very undeveloped, or decadent, to a fairly advanced type of civilization.

Two levels of primitive religions should

be distinguished. The lower type either has been less directly affected by one of the major religions or shows less speculative development. It corresponds to animism or fetishism, that is, more emphasis is given to attributing souls to every object and to believing in magic or sorcery. Allowing for exceptions, the following are generally held to profess a lower preliterate religion: the Negritos of the Philippine Islands, various tribes of Micronesia and Polynesia, the Papuans of New Guinea, the black Aruntas of Australia, the Andaman Islanders in the Bay of Bengal, the Kols and Pariahs of Central and Southern India, the Pygmies and Bushmen of the Central Congo Basin, the Caribs of the West Indies, and the Yahgans of the extreme south of South America. On a higher religious plane are the Samoans and Hawaiians, the Mongols in the Soviet Union, the Veddas of Sri Lanka (Ceylon), the Bantu of south central and southern Africa, and the Eskimos and Amerinds, or American Indians, in North and South America.

PRIMOGENITUS. The firstborn son. The policy in some societies of handing down property to the firstborn son in the family. Primogeniture. (Etym. Latin *primus,* first + Greek *genesis,* origin.)

PRINCE OF THE CHURCH. A cardinal of the Roman Catholic Church, so called because he is considered the ecclesiastical equal to the prince of a reigning civil society. He is responsible only to the Pope and may be deposed by him alone.

PRINCIPALITIES. The angels who belong to the highest choir in the lowest order of the angelic hosts. With the archangels and angels they form that heavenly multitude who are God's ordinary and immediate servants in what pertains to the visible world. It is probable that whole countries are assigned to the care of certain principalities.

PRINCIPLE. That from which something proceeds or on which it depends as its origin, cause, or source of being or action. In Christianity the truths of faith are principles of moral conduct. (Etym. Latin *principium,* a beginning, origin, foundation.)

PRINCIPLE AND FOUNDATION. Basic premise of Christian living and the first meditation of the Spiritual Exercises of St. Ignatius. The Principle and Foundation states two principles and two conclusions. The principles are that "Man was created to praise, reverence and serve God our Lord, and by this means to save his soul; and the other things on the face of the earth were created for man's sake, and in order to aid him in the prosecution of the end for which he was created." The conclusions are that therefore: 1. "Man must make use of creatures in so far as they help him to attain his end, and in the same way he ought to withdraw himself from them in so far as they hinder him from it;" and 2. "We should make ourselves indifferent to all created things, in so far as is left to the liberty of our free will to do so, and is not forbidden; in such sort that we do not for our part wish for health rather than sickness, for wealth rather poverty, for honor rather than dishonor, for a long life rather than a short one; and so in all other things, desiring and choosing only those which most lead us to the end for which we were created."

PRINCIPLE OF EVIL. The nonexisting source of all evil postulated by the Manichaeans and others. The immediate basis of this theory was a misconception of God's providence, as though he could not draw good out of evil or was helpless to prevent evil in the world.

PRINKNASH. A Marian shrine in Gloucestershire in the Cotswolds of western England, now a monastery of the English Benedictines. Its focus of devotion is a small statue (eighteen inches high) of Our Lady, which belonged to St. Thomas More. After the Reformation this choice possession was taken to Europe. In 1925, when the monks coming from Caldey Island, off the south coast of Wales, founded their new abbey, the statue was returned to Prinknash. Mary's shrine is now near the choir stalls of the monastery chapel.

PRIOR. A monastic superior. Before the thirteenth century the superior as prior could be an abbot, dean, provost, or just one advanced in years. The term is used in this sense in St. Benedict's Rule. Where the monastery was a dependency of an abbey, the prior was obedientiary (prior simplex). The Carmelites, Servites, and Augustinian Hermits have three grades of prior: conventual, provincial, and prior general. (Etym. Latin *prior,* former, first, superior.)

PRIORESS. Superior of a monastic community of women. She is an assistant to the abbess. Her duties are similar to the prior's in the corresponding order of men. (Etym. Latin *priorissa,* from prior, former, first, superior.)

PRIORY. Monastery of men or women governed by a prior or prioress. A conventual priory is autonomous, while one dependent upon an abbey or mother house is an obedientiary priory. In England monasteries attached to cathedral churches are termed cathedral priories.

PRISCA. See PRISCILLA.

PRISCILLA. The wife of Aquila, a Jew of Pontus and, like St. Paul, a tentmaker. She is frequently mentioned in the New Testament (Acts 18:2, 18:18, 18:26; Romans 16:3; I Corinthians 16:19; II Timothy 4:19). In the Pauline letters the more proper name is Prisca. Both she and her husband were prominent lay associates of the Apostle to the Gentiles, and in this capacity lived at Rome, Ephesus, and Corinth. They were forced to leave Rome during the persecution by Emperor Claudius. The Cemetery of Priscilla on the Via Salaria in Rome is one of the oldest catacombs but almost certainly not related to the biblical saints Aquila and Priscilla. (Etym. Latin *priscus,* old, ancient, primitive.)

PRISCILLIANISM. Fourth- and fifth-century heresy, begun by Priscillian, who as a layman and later as bishop based his ideas on a mixture of Gnosticism and Manichaeism. He and his followers taught a Modalist doctrine of the Trinity, denied Christ's divinity and his real humanity, claimed that angels were merely emanations of the Godhead, said that souls were united to bodies in punishment for their sins, so that marriage was evil, although free love was permissible. Emperor Maximus had him tried by a synod of bishops who found him guilty of practicing magic. In spite of the pleas of St. Martin of Tours, Priscillian and his followers were condemned to death.

PRISONERS OF CONSCIENCE. A term especially applied to the thousands of persons behind the Iron Curtain who have been imprisoned for their religious beliefs. Many are sent, with or without trial, for psychiatric treatment in order to change their thinking or keep them from influencing others.

PRIVATE BAPTISM. The sacrament of baptism conferred, in case of necessity, even by a person who is not a priest or deacon. It is done without the other ceremonies, by pouring water on the person's head while pronouncing the words, "I baptize you in the name of the Father, and of the Son, and of the Holy Spirit."

PRIVATE CONFESSION. The ordinary condition for receiving absolution in the sacrament of penance. It is now distinguished from communal penance, which, under extraordinary circumstances, includes general absolution. It was formerly distinguished from public penance in the early Church when, in some places, the penitents were publicly identified as guilty of certain sins. Private confession of secret sins was practiced in the early Church and, according to the teaching of the popes, was of apostolic origin.

PRIVATE MASS. Formerly the same as Low Mass. Now applied to the Mass that a priest says privately, without a congregation. The revised Roman Missal specially provides for private Masses.

PRIVATE ORATORY. A place set apart for divine worship but erected in a private dwelling for the sole benefit of some particular family or private individual.

PRIVATE REVELATIONS. Supernatural manifestations by God of hidden truths made to private individuals for their own spiritual welfare or that of others. They differ from the public revelation contained in Scripture and tradition which is given on behalf of the whole human race and is necessary for human salvation and sanctification. Although recognized by the Church and, at times, approved by her authority, private revelations are not the object of divine faith that binds one in conscience to believe on God's authority. The assent given to them, therefore, is either on human evidence or, when formally approved by the Church, on ecclesiastical authority according to the mind of the Church. Private revelations occur as supernatural visions, words, or divine touches. Often it is impossible to distinguish the three forms in practice, especially since they may be received simultaneously.

PRIVATION. The lack of something either needed for the perfection of a being, or desirable by the human will, or previously possessed. Privation is at the basis of evil, as the lack of some good that should be there.

PRIVILEGE. A concession, more or less permanent, made against or beyond the law. The popes have granted privileges at least since the eighth century. They are acquired orally or in writing, by direct concession or by communication. Personal privileges are granted to a person; real privileges are attached to things. A personal privilege need not be used and is not lost by lack of use. A real privilege is lost by destruction of the object. Privileges are perpetual unless otherwise stated.

PRIVILEGE, ECCLESIASTICAL. A special concession, not provided in the law, for persons and institutions in the Catholic Church. Privileges can be acquired by direct concession of the competent Church authority, by communication, and even by legitimate custom or prescription. Unless specified to the contrary, privileges are permanent. Typical forms are clerical privileges against violence (*privilegium canonis*), of ecclesiastical court (*privilegium fori*), of personal immunity, and benefit in case of insolvency. Since these privileges are attached to a person's state of life, they cannot be waived by the individuals who share them. They are lost by degradation, deposition, and reduction to the lay state only.

PRIVILEGED ALTAR. An altar to which the Church formerly attached a plenary indulgence in favor of the soul for whom a Mass was offered at that altar. Privileged altars were either local or personal. They were local when the favor was attached to the altar itself, so that all Masses celebrated under the prescribed conditions had a plenary indulgence attached to them. They were personal when the privilege was attached either to the priest offering the Mass or to the person for whom the Mass was offered.

PRO ARMENIS. A dogmatic decree of Pope Eugenius IV (November 22, 1439) addressed to the Armenians on the conditions for union with the Roman Catholic Church. Its most important feature is a lengthy declaration on the seven sacraments in general and on each one of them in particular. Among other provisions are the necessity of integral confession of sins for the sacrament of penance and the indissolubility of marriage.

PROBABILIORISM. A theory in moral theology for resolving practical doubts. Probabiliorism maintains that one may follow the opinion favoring liberty when the reasons for this opinion are certainly more probable than those which favor the law. (Etym. Latin *probabilior*, more likely, more credible.)

PROBABILISM. The moral theory that holds that a law against whose existence or application there stands a solidly probable argument does not bind. It is based on the principle that a doubtful law does not bind. It then excludes other theories as either too strict or too lax about the degree of doubt or probability that would exempt one from the obligation of a doubtful law. (Etym. Latin *probabilis*, likely, credible.)

PROBABILITY. Assent of the mind to something with an intellectual motive that is short of convincing evidence, and with accompanying fear in the will that the opposite may be true. A state of mind often identified with having an opinion but not a firm conviction.

PROBLEM. In general any subject on which reasoning takes place. An unsolved question in philosophy or theology about which various views are maintained, with no convincing solution as yet available or on which the Church's teaching authority has not yet made a definite judgment. (Etym. Latin *problema*, a question proposed for solution; from Greek *problēma*, something thrown forward.)

PRO-CATHEDRAL. A church used as a cathedral by a bishop until a more permanent or suitable church is built. Its rights and privileges are identical with those of a cathedral. Our Lady of Victories in Kensington, London, was the pro-cathedral for nearly thirty-six years until Westminster Cathedral in London was opened in 1903.

PROCESS. A course or method of systematic operations, as a process of inquiry into some question of doctrine or a process of investigation into some disputed issue in ecclesiastical law. In modern philosophy, process has come to mean more than method. It has entered the stream of Christian thought from Oriental pantheism to describe a concept of being that is still "in process" or becoming. Its dominant feature is that everything is in flux, everything is changing, so that nothing simply is, in any part of its nature. (Etym. Latin *processus*, a going forward, advance, procedure, method; from *procedere*, to go before.)

PROCESSION. The origin of one from another. A procession is said to be external when the terminus of the procession goes outside the principle or source from which it proceeds. Thus creatures proceed by external procession from the triune God, their Primary Origin. An internal procession is immanent; the one proceeding remains united with the one from whom he or she proceeds. Thus the processions of the Son and the Holy Spirit are an immanent act of the Holy Trinity. An internal, divine procession signifies the origin of a divine person from another divine person (Son from the Father), or from other divine persons (the Holy Spirit from Father and Son) through the communication of numerically one and the same divine essence.

PROCESSIONAL. Most commonly refers to the book containing information about church processions; also applied to the services in a religious procession, or the hymns sung during such a service, and the path of a religious procession. In medieval times processionals were the books pertaining to local churches.

PROCESSIONAL CROSS. A crucifix mounted on a staff, carried in solemn services at the head of a procession of the clergy.

PROCESSIONS. Sacred functions in which clergy and people parade from one place to another. They may be held within a church, between churches, or outside a church or shrine. Processions are public acts of homage to God, to give honor to him or his saints, to ask for divine favor, to thank him for blessings received, and to ask pardon for sins committed. Their practice goes back to Old Testament times to express the faith of a people, as distinct from the worship of a single individual, and of a people who symbolize their co-operative action, as distinct from merely their common profession of faith.

PROCESS THEOLOGY. A view of reality, including what Christianity calls God, which sees everything still in the process of becoming what it will be, but nothing really is. It is called theology because it is a form of evolutionary pantheism which postulates a finite god who is becoming perfect, but is not (as Christianity believes) infinite and all-perfect from eternity. It is called "process" because it claims that the universe (including God) is moving toward completion, without identifying what this completion is or when or whether it will be reached. On these terms nothing is stable, nothing certain, because nothing really is. There are no determined moral laws, no absolute norms of conduct, no certain principles of thought, and no means of knowing anything. There is no "thing," since what people call "things" are moving functions that keep changing in their very being. Everything, including the thinking mind, is ever becoming what it was not and ceasing to be what it was.

Not all adherents of what is called process theology are consistently evolutionary pantheists. But once they postulate a finite god who is still growing in perfection, logically all the rest follows. The main contributors to present-day process thought were the skeptic David Hume (1711–76), the philosophers Georg Hegel (1770–1831), Herbert Spencer (1820–1903), Henri Bergson (1859–1941), and Alfred North Whitehead (1861–1947), and the Marxist writer Ernst Bloch (1885–1977).

PROCLAMATION. Announcing Christ to the world, to make him known and loved by as many people as possible. The proclamation takes on as many forms as there are means of communication, by speaking and writing, and especially by reflecting the virtues of Christ in one's own life and behavior. The proclamation is also the duty of every Christian. "Jesus Christ," declared Pope John Paul II, "is the stable principle and fixed center of the mission that God has entrusted to man. We must all share in this mission and concentrate all our forces on it, since it is more necessary than ever for modern mankind" (*Redemptor Hominis,* 11).

PRO COMPERTO SANE. Apostolic letter of Pope Paul VI on the incorporation of certain diocesan bishops as members of the sacred congregations of the Roman Curia. In virtue of this document the pattern was set for making diocesan bishops of residential sees full members of the Roman Curia, while remaining shepherds in their respective sees. One provision was that the plenary sessions of the congregations, with extraordinary powers, should as a rule be held annually (August 6, 1967).

PROCREATION. Begetting children. It is a formal term for generation and stresses the role of marital intercourse with the intention of producing offspring. (Etym. Latin *procreare,* to beget.)

PROCREATIVE LOVE. The selfless love of husband with wife for the potential offspring God may wish to give them as the "procreation" of marital intercourse. This love is procreative because it evokes the creative act of God, who requires their co-operation to bring a new human being into the world.

PROCURATOR. One who manages the affairs of another by virtue of the latter's authority. The person may be employed in juridical matters or attending councils, and is often the one in charge of the domestic temporal affairs of a monastery. Religious orders have procurators as their representative permanently residing in Rome. The actions of a procurator are regarded as done by the principal when the procurator acts legally within the limits of a mandate. (Etym. Latin *procurator,* manager, overseer.)

PRODIGY. An unusual event produced by angelic power, whether good or bad, under

God's positive or permissive providence. The term is more commonly associated with the diabolical phenomena, to distinguish true, though minor, miracles performed by the good angels, from demonic interventions.

PROF. *Professus, professio, professor—*professed, profession, professor.

PROFANATION. The desecration of something holy by using or treating a sacred person, place, or thing as though it were not sacred but merely secular or profane. Thus profanity in speech is the use of God's name or of one of the saints without due regard for its sacred character.

PROFANE. The secular or merely human as compared with the sacred or divine. "Profane" does not, of itself, imply profanation, since the whole created universe, including human beings, is technically profane in contrast to the Creator, whose essence is to be holy precisely because he is the "totally other" who transcends the world that he made and continually sustains. (Etym. Latin *profanus,* lying outside the temple, ordinary, not holy.)

PROFESSED. Those persons in a religious community who have been admitted to the vows of poverty, chastity, and obedience. In some orders, however, the term is reserved for those religious who have lived in their communities for a definite period of time after the taking of their vows. The term may also apply exclusively to those who have taken final vows. But generally they are said to be "finally professed," as distinct from those who are "temporary professed" or "first professed" or "junior professed."

PROFESSION. The act of embracing the religious state by the three vows of poverty, chastity, and obedience according to the rule of an order or congregation canonically approved. For simple profession, at least a continuous year of novitiate or probation is necessary; for solemn profession, three or more years of simple profession must precede. The candidate must be of the full age required and personally at liberty to make the promises.

PROFESSIONIS RITUS. Decree of the Sacred Congregation for Divine Worship, authorizing the ritual for various kinds and levels of religious profession (February 2, 1970, and revised in 1975).

PROFESSION OF FAITH. The public acceptance of the teachings of the Church. When nonprofession would amount to a denial, the baptized Catholic must profess his faith. Under certain circumstances bishops and priests are required to make an official profession of faith according to canon law.

PRO FORMA. As a matter of formality; as should be done according to ecclesiastical protocol.

PROHIBITIVE IMPEDIMENT. A condition, circumstance, or situation that makes an act morally wrong but nevertheless valid, with varying effects according to the requirements of civil and ecclesiastical law. Thus the sacrament of confirmation, received in the state of grave sin, is received validly along with the sacramental character, but the graces are not given until the person is reconciled with God.

PRO LIFE MOVEMENT. See RIGHT TO LIFE MOVEMENT.

PROLONGED ABSTINENCE. The phenomenon of miraculously surviving without nourishment for many years. It is commonly associated with those bearing the stigmata who have lived a long time without taking food other than Holy Communion. Thus Angela of Foligno remained twelve years without any nourishment, Catherine of Siena for about eight years, Elisabeth of Reute over fifteen years, Lidwina for twenty-eight years, and Catherina Racconigi for ten years. Among the conditions looked for by the Church in verifying the phenomenon as supernatural is strict surveillance of the person at all times for a notable period, and by numerous witnesses to detect any possible fraud. The examiners must determine whether the abstinence is absolute, extending to drink as well as food, whether it is broken, and whether the individual continues to attend to customary occupations.

PROMISE. A declaration telling God or another person that one will or will not do something. A promise made to God is equivalently a vow, and it binds in conscience according to the gravity of the promise and the intention to obligate oneself under pain of sin. Promises made to people must be kept, and they oblige in justice or charity, with more or less seriousness depending on one's ability to fulfill a promise and the harm caused to another by not keeping one's word.

PROMISED LAND. The land of Canaan, generally thought to be the whole of western Palestine. It was promised to the Israelites by God after their sojourn in the desert (Exodus 12:25).

PROMISED SECRET. A truth or fact that a person has agreed to keep after the secret is revealed. The person does not have the opportunity of declining to hear the disclosure before promising to keep the matter confidential. Promised secrets bind under venial sin in ordinary circumstances.

PROMOTER OF THE FAITH. The title of the ecclesiastic advocate who takes the Church's side in various cases, particularly in the process of beatification and canonization. Popularly known as the devil's advocate, he must cross-examine those who are trying to establish a good cause.

PROMPT SUCCOR, OUR LADY OF. A Marian shrine in New Orleans, Louisiana. The story of this shrine began with an Ursuline nun, Mother St. Michel, exiled by the French Revolution. Wishing to join her American community, she was prevented by the Monsignor of Montpellier, France, who forbade her to leave a recently opened school. Mother St. Michel then prayed before a statue of Our Lady and Infant for prompt help; almost immediately she received a reply from Pope Pius VII, granting her request. The grateful nun arrived in New Orleans on January 1, 1810, with her statue and a few interested companions, and lost no time in spreading devotion to Our Lady under the title of "Prompt Help." When the Battle of New Orleans was in progress, Mother St. Michel asked people to join her in praying for an American victory. On the field of Chalmette, against great odds, the Americans won. Mary was then given her new title in a service of thanksgiving, her feast being formally approved by Pope Pius IX. Devotion spread rapidly. The Child and his Mother were crowned in 1894, and she was made patroness of Louisiana under her new title. Today the statue is in a new Gothic chapel under a stone canopy where pilgrims attest to many physical and spiritual miracles.

PROMULGATION. The act of announcing a law publicly, with the effect of obliging its observance from the date expressed. Laws enacted by the Holy See are promulgated by publication in the official *Acta Apostolicae Sedis*. They have binding force three months after the date affixed to the *Acta*. However, in a special case the Pope is free to promulgate a law in other ways.

PROPAGANDA. The deliberate and systematic attempt to influence and change the ideas, attitudes, and beliefs of others. On Catholic principles, "a propaganda campaign, with a view to influencing public opinion, is justified only when it serves the truth, when its objectives and methods accord with the dignity of humans, and when it promotes causes that are in the public interest" (*Communio et Progressio*, 1971, 29). (Etym. Latin *propagare*, to generate; to extend, increase.)

PROPAGATION OF THE FAITH. An international association for the assistance, by prayers and alms, of Catholic missionaries throughout the world. Founded in 1822 at Lyons, France, by Pauline Jaricot. It is now under the auspices of the Sacred Congregation for the Evangelization of Peoples (Propagation of the Faith).

PROPER. Those parts of the religious service (i.e., the Mass) which vary according to the feast or liturgical season. (Etym. Latin *proprius,* one's own, not common with others, special, true, real, genuine.)

PROPER CAUSE. The specific cause required to produce a particular effect. Thus, God is the proper cause of the world's existence; a human being is the proper cause of intelligible speech.

PROPER OF THE SAINTS. In the Roman Missal the feast days of the saints commemorated in the universal Church. The feasts are given in sequence, from January through December.

PROPER OF THE SEASON. In the Roman Missal the liturgical feasts of the year, as follows: Advent, Christmas season, Lent, Holy Week, Easter Sunday through Tuesday, Easter season, the season of the year, and solemnities of the Lord throughout the year.

PROPERTY. In theology and philosophy an attribute of someone or something which does not constitute its essence but necessarily follows from the essence. Hence a distinctive and characteristic quality of a being. In ethics and morality, property is either that which a person owns or the right of ownership.

PROP. FID. *Propagandâ Fide*—Congregation of the Propaganda (Rome).

PROPHECIES OF ST. MALACHY. Alleged predictions about future popes by St. Malachy (1094–1148), Archbishop of Armagh. In 1590 there was discovered in Rome a collection of 112 mystical mottoes from the time of Celestine II (reigned 1143–44) until the end of the world, when Peter the Roman will be the last pope. The authenticity of these prophecies is generally questioned, although from the eighteenth century on many of the mottoes were remarkably pertinent. The last prophecy is couched in special terms: "In the final persecution of the Holy Roman Church, there will reign Peter the Roman, who will feed his flock amid many tribulations, after which the seven-hilled city will be destroyed, and the dreadful Judge will judge the people." There may, however, be an indefinite number of popes between Peter the Roman and his predecessor *De Gloria Olivae* (from the glory of the olive tree).

PROPHECY. The certain prediction of future events that cannot be known by natural means. However, the biblical meaning of the Hebrew *hozeh* (prophecy) is more general, namely "vision" or "revelation interpreted." Those who were called upon to prophesy did, indeed, on occasion also foretell future events, but these predictions fulfilled were divine confirmations of an authentic vision rather than the vision itself. Prophecies as predictions are consequently part of God's supernatural providence. God, in whose sight all things future are ever present, is able to communicate to his creatures the knowledge that he has. He alone finally has this power, because certain foreknowledge of the contingent future is possessed only by God. Prophecies are the words of his prescience, just as miracles are the work of his omnipotence. Hence a religion supported by prophecies must be divine. (Etym. Greek *prophētēs,* one who speaks for a god, interpreter, expounder, prophet; literally, one who speaks for another.)

PROPHET. The biblical term *"nabi"* means one who spoke, acted, or wrote under the extraordinary influence of God to make known the divine counsels and will. Yet commonly associated with this primary function to proclaim the word of God, a prophet also prophesied by foretelling future events. His role, then, was to both proclaim and to make the proclamation credible.

PROPITIATION. To placate or appease an angry person. It is one of the three fruits of every good work; the others are impetration and merit. It is also one of the four ends of the Sacrifice of the Mass, whose propitiatory power extends to sin, to satisfaction and punishment for the living, and to punishment for the dead. (Etym. Latin *propitiare,* to render favorable.)

PROPORTIONALITY. See ANALOGY.

PROPOSITION. A statement that expresses a judgment by making a definite affirmation or negation. The doctrines of the Church, whether of belief or morals, are expressed by, or reducible to, propositions. They are categorical propositions because they make absolute and not merely hypothetical statements about what they affirm or deny. And they are necessary propositions because their predicate (what is said) is necessarily contained in or necessarily excluded from the nature or concept of the subject (about which something is said). (Etym. Latin *propositio,* representation, assertion; from *proponere,* to put forth.)

PROPR. *Proprium*—proper.

PROPRIO MOTU. More commonly *motu proprio.* Something done on one's own initiative or by one's own will. Said especially of certain papal documents written on the Pope's own authority, often to meet a special and urgent need in the Church.

PROSELYTE. A convert from one religion to another. In the Old Testament a proselyte to Judaism was not fully accepted until he was circumcised. When Paul and Barnabas made Christian converts in Antioch, they made no distinction between Jews and Gentiles and fought successfully at Jerusalem against the requirement of circumcision (Acts 15). Nicolaus, a proselyte from Antioch, was one of the seven deacons chosen by the Apostles (Acts 6:5).

PROSELYTIZE. Originally to convert someone from one religion to another, either by bringing a person to full acceptance of the new faith and ritual or at least sympathy with it. The more common meaning, however, is to induce people to change their religious affiliation by using unfair and even unscrupulous means. (Etym. Greek *prosēlytos,* convert to Judaism; literally, one who has arrived.)

PROSPHORA. Literally "offering" or "oblation." This is the altar bread in the Greek or Byzantine Liturgy. It is commonly a round piece of leavened bread, stamped with one or more symbols, e.g., with a cross between the Greek letters IC XC NI KA (Jesus Christ Conquers). *Prosphora* is also the third part of the Eucharistic liturgy in the Byzantine Rite, corresponding to the Offertory of the Mass.

PROSTRATION. To cast oneself down in front of anyone in adoration or contrition, petition or submission. At the services on Good Friday the ministers lie prostrate before the altar. It is also part of the ordination service for bishops, priests, and deacons. Prostration may also be required during the final profession of vows in some religious orders. Kneeling on both knees with head bowed is a form of prostration.

PROT. AP. Protonotary Apostolic.

PROTECTRESS OF ROME, OUR LADY. See SALUS POPULI ROMANI.

PROTESTANT ETHIC. The assumed set of values associated with Anglo-Saxon Protestantism. Essential to these values are a stress on personal freedom, hard work, a competitive spirit, and the profit motive in order to achieve. Modern capitalism is said to be the creation of the Protestant ethic, where the Reformation principle of private inspiration in religion was gradually transferred to rugged individualism in economics.

PROTESTANTISM. The system of faith, worship, and practice derived from the principles of the Reformation in the sixteenth century. As a name, it comes from the *Protestatio* of the Reformers at the Diet of Speyer (1529) against the decisions of the Catholic majority that no further religious innovations were to be introduced. Although now divided into hundreds of denominations, the original families of Protestantism were only five: the Lutheran, Calvinist, and Zwinglian on the Continent, and the Anglican and Free Church or Congregational in Great Britain. Three premises of Protestantism have remained fairly constant, namely, the Bible as the only rule of faith, excluding tradition and Church authority; justification by faith alone, excluding supernatural merit and good works; and the universal priesthood of believers, excluding a distinct episcopacy or priesthood divinely empowered through ordination to teach, govern, and sanctify the people of God. (Etym. Latin *protestari*, to profess one's belief in or against something, to witness to.)

PROTOCANONICAL. A term applied to those books of the Bible, especially in the Old Testament, whose inspired character had never been questioned, e.g., by any Church Father. But the expression is misleading because it was not the Church Fathers but the Church's magisterium under the Pope that was divinely authorized to decide on the canonicity of the Scriptures.

PROTOCOL. Originally the first leaf glued to papyrus rolls; later a sheet with seal affixed, containing a summary of the document's contents by a notary. Now the forms of ceremony to be observed by ecclesiastical and civil officials. In this sense the protocol for bishops and especially for Vatican dignitaries and the Pope is highly complex and carefully observed. (Etym. Greek *prōtokollon,* first leaf of a volume, containing an account of the contents.)

PROTOEVANGELIUM. The modern title of the apocryphal Gospel of the Infancy. Also known as the Book of James (the Less). Most likely of Docetist origin, it testifies to the early devotion to Mary, dating from the second century. It is the oldest known apocryphal gospel. Protoevangelium (First Gospel) is also applied to the promise of a Redeemer after the Fall. Speaking to the serpent, God said, "I will make you enemies of each other; you and the woman, your offspring and her offspring. It will crush your head and you will strike its heel" (Genesis 3:15). Traditionally the woman and her offspring have been understood to mean Mary and her Son.

PROTO-MARTYR. St. Stephen, whose martyrdom is described by St. Luke (Acts 6:8–7:60). Or anyone who is the first to suffer in any persecution after the example of St. Stephen.

PROTONOTARY APOSTOLIC. A member of the chief order of prelates attached to the papal Curia. There are four types: 1. those who sign papal documents, act in connection with the consistories and processes of canonization, examine candidates, and confer certain ecclesiastical degrees; 2. certain canons of St. Peter's, the Lateran, St. Mary Major, and a number of cathedral chapters outside of Rome; 3. those entitled to the same external insignia as the first class above; and 4. priests outside of Rome who receive the dignity.

PROTOPOPE. A priest of high rank, in the Orthodox and Byzantine Uniat Churches, who corresponds to the archpriest or dean in the Western rite. (Etym. Greek *prōto,* first, chief + *papas,* title of bishops.)

PROTOTYPE. The mind of God as the original and eternal exemplar of all creation. (Etym. Greek *prōto,* first, chief + *typos,* a blow, mark of a blow, stamp, impress, mold.)

PROV. *Provisio, provisum*–provision, provided.

PROVERB. A short statement of a universal truth written in expressive language. There are many proverbial thoughts found in Scripture, expounding spiritual truths and human aspirations. One of the best known books in the Old Testament is the Book of

Proverbs, filled with expressions of wisdom and experience.

PRO-VICAR APOSTOLIC. An appointee of the vicar apostolic to succeed him temporarily in case of his death or in the event his jurisdiction would be impeded by "captivity, exile or inability."

PROVIDENCE. God's all-wise plan for the universe, and the carrying out of this plan by his loving rule or governance. The eternal world plan and its fulfillment in time are together called divine providence. As expressed by the First Vatican Council (1869–70), "God, in His providence watches over and governs all the things that He made, reaching from end to end with might and disposing all things with gentleness" (Denzinger 3003). Divine providence is universal in that all events, even the most personal decisions of human beings, are part of God's eternal plan. It is infallibly certain because the ultimate purpose that God has for the universe will not fail. And it is immutable because God himself cannot change. (Etym. Latin *providentia,* foresight, foreknowledge.)

PROVINCE, RELIGIOUS. The union of a number of religious houses under one and the same superior, constituting a part of the same institute.

PROVINCIAL. A religious superior exercising general supervision over a number of houses that form a division of the order or congregation, called a province. The provincial superior in turn is subject to the superior general according to the constitutions of the institute.

PROVISION. Any concession of an ecclesiastical office. Thus the designation of a cleric to any office is called provision. The only legitimate ways of obtaining an ecclesiastical office are by free appointment, election, postulation, nomination, or investiture: all modes of provision. Only two conditions are necessary: fitness of the candidate in the judgment of a superior, and vacancy in an office.

PROVISION, CANONICAL. The granting of an ecclesiastical office by a competent Church authority according to the norms of canon law.

PROVISIONALISM. The theory that every form of knowledge, including religious, is merely provisional. Whatever people think now, others in a short time will probably be thinking differently and better in the future.

PROVOCATION. Exciting or stirring someone to do a certain action. It is one of the ways that a person can share in another's guilt. The provocation can be words or by actions; it can also be done by silence or inactivity. Its gravity depends on the degree of awareness that another person is being provoked to do wrong, and especially on the malice or indifference with which the incitement to evil is performed. (Etym. Latin *provocatio,* a summoning, challenging.)

PROVOST. In early Christian times the official next to the abbot in authority in a monastery, but more recently the head of an ecclesiastical chapter. The title has been appropriated in secular institutions by the heads of certain colleges. (Etym. Latin *praepositus,* a presiding official.)

PROXIMA FIDEI. See THEOLOGICAL NOTES.

PROXIMATE OCCASIONS. Situations that are likely to lead a person into sin. They are either circumstances in which any ordinary person is almost sure to sin, or those in which the individual in question as a rule sins. In general, occasions of sin looked upon as proximate for everyone are known to be such from a knowledge of human nature and the way people in general react to situations. Occasions of sin that are proximate only for certain persons are known from experience or from an honest appraisal of one's own moral frailty.

PRUDENCE. Correct knowledge about things to be done or, more broadly, the knowledge of things that ought to be done and of things that ought to be avoided. It is the intellectual virtue whereby a human being recognizes in any matter at hand what is good and what is evil. In this sense, it is the moral virtue that enables a person to devise, choose, and prepare suitable means for the attainment of any purpose or the avoidance of any evil. Prudence resides in the practical intellect and is both acquired by one's own acts and infused at the same time as sanctifying grace. It may be said to be natural as developed by us, and supernatural because conferred by God. As an act of virtue, prudence involves three stages of mental operation: to take counsel carefully with oneself and from others; to judge correctly on the basis of the evidence at hand; and to direct the rest of one's activity according to the norms determined after a prudent judgment has been made. (Etym. Latin *prudentia,* foresight in the practical order; from *providentia,* foresight, directive care, providence.)

PRUDENTIAL CERTITUDE. Assent based on sufficient evidence to justify a reasonable person acting in a certain way as regards one's own or someone else's welfare. It is high probability founded on ordinary diligence in examining the available evidence and motivated by good will in the practical affairs of daily life.

PS. *Psalmus*—psalm.

PSALM. A sacred hymn of praise, usually sung or chanted and taken in whole or in part from the Book of Psalms in the Old Testament; originally a harp song. Most of the themes used in Gregorian chant as well as the major part of the Divine Office are composed of such hymns.

PSALMODY. The chanting of psalms in divine worship; it passed over from the synagogue to the early Church, following the example of Christ.

PSALMS, BOOK OF. A collection of divinely inspired hymns or poems, also known as the "Psalter of David of 150 Psalms" (Council of Trent, Denzinger 1502). The Hebrew title of the book is *Tehilim*, hymns or songs of praise. Although David is the principal author, he is not the only author of the Psalms. They are divided into five sections, each section closing with a doxology, thus 1–40, 41–71, 72–88, 89–105, 105–50, according to the Vulgate. About 100 Psalms have titles that indicate the author, historical occasion, musical notation, or type of poetry. These titles, though not inspired, have great historical value. Each Psalm has its own theme and purpose, with eight such themes commonly distinguishable, namely: 1. hymns of praise and gratitude to God (8, 17, 102–6, 145–50); 2. petitions (29, 63, 73, 93); 3. didactic or moral instruction (1, 48, 118); 4. penitential (6, 31, 37, 50, 101, 129, 142); 5. imprecatory (17, 34, 58, 68, 78, 93, 108, 129, 142); 6. historical account of God's providential care of Israel (75, 104, 105, 113, 134, 135); 7. gradual or pilgrim songs (119–33); 8. Messianic (2, 15, 21, 44, 68, 71). Use of the Psalms for divine worship was adopted by the Church after apostolic times. Today they are the main part of the Liturgy of the Hours.

PSALM TONES. Melodies used for chanting psalms in the Catholic liturgy, especially the Divine Office. First an intonation, then a single note persisting for several syllables on the pitch of the church mode being used, then an ending tone at the half verse and the final cadence. The antiphon in whole or in part opens each psalm, the full antiphon closes it followed by the *Gloria Patri*. The opening tone of the antiphon determines the choice of the alternative endings. There are traditionally eight psalm tones.

PSALTER. Translation, often in verse, of the Book of Psalms into the vernacular for home or church use. Also an ancient stringed instrument with a soundboard, the strings being plucked.

PSALTER OF MARY. The *Palterium Marianum*. A compendium of the Psalms and Canticles applied to the Blessed Virgin Mary. It was composed by St. Bonaventure (1221–74). The Rosary, because of its one hundred fifty Hail Marys corresponding to the number of the Psalms, is sometimes called the Psalter of Mary.

PSALTERY. Any collection of the Psalms of David as used in the Divine Office. There are two principal psalteries in liturgical history: the Roman, used at St. Peter's, and the Gallican, which is a later translation by St. Jerome. The Gallican was in common use until the complete revision of the Divine Office in 1970. A psaltery is also a stringed instrument resembling a harp, used with sacred chanting.

PSYCHOANALYSIS. A form of practical psychology whose purpose is to diagnose, cure, and prevent mental disorders. Among the many schools of psychoanalysis, including those of Sigmund Freud (1856–1939), Alfred Adler (1870–1937), and Carl Gustav Jung (1875–1961), four principles seem to be agreed upon: 1. the unconscious life of a person is of main importance in determining a person's conscious and overt behavior; 2. early infancy and childhood play a determinant role in shaping one's later life; 3. conversation about one's problems, by bringing the unconscious to the surface, is an essential part of treatment; 4. a reorientation of one's philosophy of life is necessary to avoid the onset or recurrence of mental disorder. (Etym. Greek *psychē*, soul, principle of life, life + *analyein*, to loosen, break up.)

PSYCHOLOGICAL FREEDOM. See RATIONAL FREEDOM.

PSYCHOLOGISM. The theory that among all the human sciences, including ethics and theology, psychology and its findings are primary; that all other sources of knowledge about human nature and behavior are to be gauged by the principles and researches of psychology.

PSYCHOLOGY. As rational psychology,

the science of the human mind and its conscious acts, or more broadly the science of the human soul on all its levels of operation, intellectual, volitional, and emotional. Experimental psychology investigates all kinds of conscious human behavior by modern scientific methods, as an aid to rational psychology. (Etym. Greek *psychē*, soul, principle of life, life + *logia*, knowledge, science.)

PSYCHOPHYSICAL PARALLELISM. One of many theories that hold that the mental and bodily operations in human beings merely occur simultaneously but are not really unified as acts of one human being.

PSYCHOSIS. A mental illness involving emotional disturbances that prevent realistic adjustment to environment. Neurasthenia, hysteria, compulsion phenomena, hypochondria, melancholia, psychopathic inferiority are forms of psychosis. A psychosis is more severe than a neurosis that permits at least some adjustment to reality. Symptoms of psychosis may include hallucinations, severe deviations of mood, absent or inappropriate emotional response, and severe distortion of judgment. Organic psychoses are caused by structural damage of the brain; functional psychoses show no observable organic damage.

Moral imputability is reduced or removed to the extent that psychopathic ideas and fancies so take possession of a person's mind that he or she cannot at all or only with great difficulty give attention to other considerations. Consequently, depending on the degree of mental illness, freedom of choice is either altogether impeded or at least gravely impaired. In individual cases it is very difficult to determine to what extent freedom of choice and hence responsibility are nullified. In most instances this must be left to the judgment of God. (Etym. Greek *psychē*, soul + *osis*, process, abnormal condition.)

PSYCHOTHERAPY. In general, treatment of mental or emotional disorders by psychological methods. Technically it is the treatment of such disorders by means of psychoanalysis, nondirective or directive counseling, psychodrama, and the like. But in a broader sense it can include informal talks with a priest, minister, or rabbi, personal discussions with friends, and occupational therapy to help a person function more efficiently without probing into the unconscious motives of behavior. (Etym. Greek *psychē*, soul, principle of life, life + *therapuo*, to treat.)

PUB., PUBL. *Publicus, publice*—public, publicly.

PUBLICAN. In the ancient Roman Empire, usually a man of equestrian rank. In the Gospels a publican was a Jewish "tax gatherer" employed by these wealthy Roman knights. Universally detested by the Jews, publicans were regarded as traitors to their people and classed as sinners. No publican was admitted as a witness in court. Yet some of these despised men were among the earliest disciples of John the Baptist, and the Apostle and Evangelist Matthew had been the publican Levi.

PUBLIC DECENCY. See INFAMY.

PUBLIC GOOD. The common social welfare of a society, especially as a civil community, when pursued by common means under public authority.

PUBLIC ORATORY. A place set apart for divine worship if it is principally intended for the benefit of a collegiate group or even of private individuals rather than for the benefit of all the faithful in the public worship of God. Yet all the faithful have a right to enter it during the time of divine services.

PUBLIC PENANCE. The practice of requiring penitents to give public satisfaction for their sins as a condition for absolution and reconciliation with the Church. In vogue up to the early Middle Ages, public penance could be either solemn or not, depending on the gravity of the offense and the amount of scandal given.

When public penance was also solemn, the reason had to be a grave one. Among the public crimes that might be subject to solemn penance, the most common were adultery, apostasy, fornication, and murder, including abortion. A historic example of public penance was Henry II's walking barefoot in 1174 to the shrine of St. Thomas of Becket, to expiate his part in the murder of the archbishop. The more common practice was to limit solemn penance to those crimes that gave such scandal as seemed to call for proportionate expiation.

More generally, public penance was not solemn. The person would secretly confess some grave sin from which he was absolved by a priest. His satisfaction would be an external penance from which others might conclude the nature of the sin, but there was no formal identification as a public sinner.

PUBLIC PENITENTS. In the early Church, in some dioceses, persons separated from the rest of the congregation by wearing a special robe, having their hair closely cropped, and worshiping apart during the liturgy. In some places they received from the bishop a special laying-on of hands each Sunday. Only after satisfying his or her penance was the person readmitted to full communion with the Church.

PUBLIC PROPRIETY. An impediment to Christian marriage. Two forms of this impediment are commonly recognized by ecclesiastical law: invalid marriage and public or notorious concubinage. An invalid marriage here means an apparent contract between man and woman which has at least the appearance of marriage but is in fact invalid. However, a so-called civil marriage, where a Catholic is concerned, is held not to have even the appearance of marriage, and therefore does not create this impediment, in the absence of cohabitation. Concubinage means a cohabitation between a man and a woman, established on a more or less durable basis without marriage. This impediment invalidates marriage in the direct line only, to the second degree. Thus a man cannot validly marry the mother or grandmother, nor the daughter or granddaughter, of a woman who was his mistress or pseudo-wife. Dispensations are given, provided there is no danger that the second partner may be the man's daughter, which is possible if he had relations with the mother before her daughter's birth.

PUBLIC REVELATION. The supernatural manifestation of God's wisdom and will for the human race, in order to lead humanity to its heavenly destiny. It is entrusted directly to the Church for preservation and interpretation and is contained in Sacred Scripture and sacred tradition.

PULPIT. An elevated stand for preaching or reading the word of God. Pulpits became general only in the later Middle Ages. Before that a bishop preached from a cathedra; later an ambo was used, or a rood loft. Except in cathedrals, the north side of the nave is considered the most proper for the pulpit. In the new liturgy the pulpit for the priest or deacon is often balanced on the other side of the sanctuary with a reading stand for the lector at Mass. (Etym. Latin *pulpitum,* scaffold, platform.)

PUNISHMENT. Any ill suffered in consequence of wrongdoing. It has three functions, which ideally should be retributive as serving the offended person, corrective for the offender, and deterrent for the community at large. Punishment is retributive be-

cause it pays back the offender for his crime and re-establishes the balance of justice, which has been outraged. It is corrective when directed to improving the offender and rehabilitating him as a member of society. It is deterrent as a means of forestalling similar wrongdoing by others.

Some theorists hold, with Plato, that no one does wrong voluntarily. On these premises, punishment may never be retributive but only corrective or deterrent. Christianity, however, believes that because human beings are free they are responsible for their misdeeds and therefore liable to punishment that gives them their just deserts. It is therefore moral to punish the guilty even if there is no hope of correcting that person or deterring others from crime. (Etym. Latin *poena,* punishment, penalty, pain.)

PUNISHMENT, CAPITAL. Punishment by or involving death, inflicted by legitimate civil authority for crimes regarded as seriously harmful to society. The traditional doctrine of the Church is that capital punishment is not opposed to the divine law, nor is it required by this law as absolutely necessary. The grounds supporting this position are revelation, history, and reason. The Bible regularly attributes to civil authority the right to take the life of a criminal (Genesis 9:6; Exodus 21:22–25; Romans 13:4). Moreover, in all stages of civilization humanity has considered capital punishment in keeping with the moral law. And, as by now experience shows, to exclude capital punishment is to call into question the malice of even the most heinous crimes and thus expose, by implication, the lives of good citizens to the gravest danger.

PURE ACT. Simple perfection of any kind. Anything that has no imperfection. In the strictest sense, applied to God as *Actus purus,* it is the unqualified perfection of existence, which is neither present in, nor united with, nor limited by, any passive potency that could change or improve infinite being.

PURE NATURE. The theoretical condition in which humanity would possess all that, and only that, which belongs to human nature and in which a person could attain to a natural final end only. Although merely possible, the idea of a state of pure nature is defended by the Church in order to safeguard the supernatural order, denied by Luther, Calvin, and Jansen. The Church, therefore, teaches that God could have created human beings without supernatural or preternatural gifts, but not in a condition of sin.

PURGATIVE WAY. The primary stage in mental prayer, according to the teaching of Sts. Theresa of Avila and John of the Cross. The soul's chief concern in this stage of perfection is an awareness of its sins, sorrow for the past, and a desire to expiate the offenses against God.

PURGATORY. The place or condition in which the souls of the just are purified after death and before they can enter heaven. They may be purified of the guilt of their venial sins, as in this life, by an act of contrition deriving from charity and performed with the help of grace. This sorrow does not, however, affect the punishment for sins, because in the next world there is no longer any possibility of merit. The souls are certainly purified by atoning for the temporal punishments due to sin by their willing acceptance of suffering imposed by God. The sufferings in purgatory are not the same for all, but proportioned to each person's degree of sinfulness. Moreover, these sufferings can be lessened in duration and intensity through the prayers and good works of the faithful on earth. Nor are the pains incompatible with great peace and joy, since the poor souls deeply love God and are sure they will reach heaven. As members of the Church Suffering, the souls in purgatory can intercede for the persons on earth, who are therefore encouraged to invoke their aid. Purgatory will not continue after the general judgment, but its duration for any particular soul continues until it is free from all guilt and punishment. Immediately on purification the soul is assumed into heaven. (Etym. Latin *purgatio,* cleansing, purifying.)

PURG. CAN. *Purgatio canonica*—canonical disculpation.

PURIFICATION. The feast that commemorates the purifying of the Blessed Virgin according to the Mosaic Law, forty days after the birth of Christ. Also called the Feast of the Presentation of Christ in the Temple. The feast was introduced into the Eastern Empire during the reign of Emperor Justinian (527–65) and is mentioned in the Gelasian Sacramentary for the Western Church in the seventh century. Candles are blessed on this day to commemorate Simeon's prophecy about Christ as "a light to enlighten the pagans" (Luke 2:32), and a candlelight procession is held in a church to represent Christ's entry into the Temple of Jerusalem. The popular name is Candlemas Day.

PURIFICATOR. A small piece of white linen, marked with a cross in the center, used by the priest in the celebration of Mass. It is folded in three layers and used by the priest to purify his fingers and the chalice and paten after Holy Communion.

PURITY. Freedom from anything that weakens or impairs or changes the nature of a being or its activity. Purity of faith means the absence of error or what is contrary to the revealed truth; purity of intention is the exclusion of self-will in the desire to perform the will of God; purity of conscience is the absence of any sense of guilt in the performance of a moral action; purity of morals commonly refers to the virtue of chastity and therefore freedom from wrongdoing in sexual activity, but on a broader level it means the absence of misbehavior, especially in one's external or publicly recognizable conduct. (Etym. Latin *puritas,* clearness, cleanness, uprightness.)

PURITY OF BODY. The state of virginity in the unmarried and of conjugal chastity in those who are married.

PURITY OF INTENTION. The perfection of one's motive inspiring human action. An act is more or less pure depending on the degree of selfless love of God with which it is performed.

PURPLE. A color emblem of penance or sorrow used during the penitential seasons of Lent and Advent, except on saints' days and on the two Sundays when the color rose may be substituted. Purple may also be used (or white) in the Eucharistic liturgy and Divine Office for the Dead.

PURPOSE OF AMENDMENT. The firm resolution required of a penitent to receive valid absolution in the sacrament of penance. He or she must resolve to avoid, by the grace of God, not only the sins confessed but also the dangerous occasions to sin.

PURSUIVANTS. Minor officials in penal times in England who hunted and captured priests and their protectors for prosecution, resulting in imprisonment and capital punishment for ministering to Catholics. In early days pursuivants assisted the heralds and somewhat later served warrants for the king.

PUSILLANIMITY. Smallness of soul that shrinks from noble or arduous tasks. Its basis may be a lack of humility or ignorance of human dignity in co-operating with divine grace to achieve great things for God's glory. (Etym. Latin *pusillus,* very small + *animus,* mind.)

PUTATIVE MARRIAGE. A marriage that is invalid but was contracted in good faith by at least one member. Until there is positive ecclesiastical proof of nullity, such a marriage has all the effects of lawful wedlock. Children of such a marriage are legitimate, and illegitimate children are legitimatized by a putative marriage. (Etym. Latin *putare,* to trim, cleanse; to think over, consider.)

PYX. Any metal box or vessel in which the Blessed Sacrament is kept or carried. The term is more aptly applied to the small round metal case (usually gold-plated) used by a priest to carry a few hosts on his visitation to the sick. But the larger ciborium is also called a pyx. (Etym. Greek *puxis,* box.)

Q

"Q." The symbol of the hypothetical document used by the authors of the first and third Gospels, along with St. Mark, to produce the present Gospels according to Matthew and Luke. The existence of "Q" is based on the assumption that Mark and not Matthew was the first Gospel and that an unknown document (hence the German *Quelle,* source) must be supposed to account for similarities in Matthew and Luke that are not found in Mark. There are no grounds in historical tradition for the existence of such a source.

QOHELETH or KOHELETH. See ECCLESIASTES.

QUADRAG. *Quadragesima*—Lent, also the fortieth day before Easter.

QUADRAGESIMA. Any season of forty days' preparation by prayer and penance, especially Lent, whose weekdays from Ash Wednesday to Easter Sunday number forty.

QUADRAGESIMO ANNO. The encyclical of Pope Pius XI, dated May 13, 1931, published on the fortieth anniversary of Pope Leo XIII's *Rerum Novarum.* Its theme is a strong condemnation of the control of international finance and credit by a small number of financiers who thus supply "so to speak, the life blood to the entire economic body . . . so that no one can breathe against their will." As a result the State "has become a slave, bound over to the service of human passion and greed."

QUADRIVIUM. The more advanced program in medieval liberal arts education (beyond the trivium), namely arithmetic, geometry, astronomy, and music. (Etym. Latin *quatuor,* four + *viae,* ways: *quadrivium.*)

QUALITY. In philosophy an accident that essentially completes and perfects a substance either in its being or operation. It is that attribute of something which describes what kind of thing it is. In theology, the most important qualities are divine grace, both sanctifying grace, which elevates the human soul to becoming deiform (like God), and actual grace, which enables the mind and will to perform supernatural actions. (Etym. Latin *qualitas,* sort, kind; property, modification, condition.)

QUAM SINGULARI. The decree issued August 8, 1910, by the Sacred Congregation of the Sacraments, under the authority of Pope St. Pius X, stating: "The age of discretion, both for Confession and for Holy Communion, is the time when a child begins to reason, that is about the seventh year, more or less. From that time on begins the obligation of fulfilling the precept of both Confession and Communion."

QUANTA CURA. The encyclical published by Pope Pius IX on December 8, 1864, to which was attached the famous Syllabus of Errors, condemning secularism and religious indifferentism.

QUANTITY. The accident of all material substances in virtue of which they are bodies that naturally are extended in space, have dimensions of size, shape, and weight, and are divisible into integral parts. A body, therefore, has quantity, as distinct from spirit, which is a substantial being with qualities but no dimensional quantity. The body and blood of Christ in the Eucharist possesses quantity but not actual extension in space. (Etym. Latin *quantitas,* quantity, greatness, extent.)

QUARANTINE. According to the ancient Church, a rigorous fast of forty days. It was an ecclesiastical penalty imposed by a confessor. Later on it came to be applied to partial indulgences and meant that the amount of temporal punishment removed was equivalent to that remitted by the ancient canonical penalty. However, the term is no longer applied to indulgences.

QUASI-DOMICILE. Variously interpreted in ecclesiastical law, it is a less permanent and settled place of residence than a domicile. Thus the Code of Canon Law stated that a quasi-domicile was acquired by staying in a place with the intention of remaining beyond six months, and by a stay that is actually prolonged beyond six months.

QUASI PARISH. See PARISH.

QUEEN OF VIRTUES. The virtue of prudence. It gently controls all other virtues and guides all human actions, since it considers not merely generalities—for these do not really move us to achieve—but also the singular and particular things that are the objects of action. Prudence is practical, that is to say, it is the principle of acting. Because they are more experienced, some people who lack a scientific theory can be more successful with practical issues than those who possess a large fund of speculative knowledge; thus a doctor who knows what is in fact the right food is more effective than one who is merely a theoretical dietician.

QUESNELLIANISM. A theory of grace taught by Pasquier Quesnel (1634–1719) which popularized the views of Michael Baius (1513–89) and Cornelis Jansen (1585–1638). Among his doctrines condemned by Pope Clement XI in 1713 were the claims that no grace is given outside the Church, that grace is irresistible, that without grace human beings are incapable of any good, and that all acts of a sinner, even prayer and attendance at Mass, are sinful.

QUEST. The begging of alms, for support according to rule, by mendicant Friars Minor, Capuchins, and the Poor Clares; and by religious communities like the Little Sisters of the Poor, who collect food and clothing for those under their care.

QUICUMQUE. See ATHANASIAN CREED.

QUIDDITY. The essence of anything, answering to the question "What is it?" In scholastic terminology it is the definition of something. (Etym. Latin *quidditas,* what a

thing is, essence, so called because in answer to the question *"Quid est res?"* [What is a thing?], the essence of a thing is expected.) See also ESSENCE.

QUID PRO QUO. Something for something. In moral matters it is either the application of strict justice to a given situation; or the giving to someone only what he or she deserves and no more; or the inflicting of a penalty in the exact measure of a crime.

QUIETISM. General name for any view of the spiritual life that minimizes human activity and moral responsibility. But more properly it refers to the theories of Miguel de Molinos (c. 1640–97) and François Fénelon (1651–1715), Archbishop of Cambrai. Its basic position is that, to become perfect, one must be totally passive, annihilate one's will and so totally abandon oneself to God that one cares for neither heaven nor hell. In prayer, the perfect soul makes no acts of love or petition, nor even of adoration. Such* total passivity makes mortification or the sacraments useless. Sin becomes impossible to perfect souls. Quietism was condemned in the person of Molinos by Pope Innocent XI in 1687, and Fénelon by Innocent XII in 1691. (Etym. Latin *quietus,* quiet, at rest, peaceful.)

QUIETUDE. A supernatural state of prayer, partially passive, where the will is seized by God, with the other faculties active but calmed. The soul realizes that it is near to God and is completely at peace. Meanwhile, the intellect enjoys a gentle repose and experiences a keen satisfaction in God's presence.

QUINCHE, OUR LADY OF. A shrine to Mary and her Son affectionately called "La Pequeñita," at Quinche, an isolated village in the Ecuadorian Andes. In 1856 a skilled woodcarver wishing to make a statue for the neighboring Indians copied a statue of Our Lady of Guadalupe, which for some reason they refused, and he gave it to some Ecuadorians. They made a niche for their cedar Madonna and installed her at Quinche. The villagers, wanting to entertain Mary and Jesus, sang songs to them at night. Always around the little image was a bright light, and many cures were told of those who had touched the rough little mantle of coarse local fiber that had been used to clothe the Madonna. Much impressed, they built a chapel, then a church, which grew in size as the crowds increased. Many of the miracles performed by La Pequeñita have been verified, including a child brought back to life, a fatal ax victim cured, a large grain field harvested without benefit of any workers. The Ecuadorians love the "Virgin of the Rocks," as she is also called, and carry her image in procession, knowing that it will never rain on her feast days.

QUINQUAG. *Quinquagesima*—the fiftieth day before Easter.

QUINQUAGESIMA. The fiftieth day before Easter, hence the last Sunday before Ash Wednesday.

QUIRINAL PALACE. Before 1870, a papal residence where conclaves were held. Also used as a summer home. Built by Pope Gregory in 1574, it was taken over by the Italian Government at the time of the confiscation of the Papal States.

QUMRAN DOCUMENTS or SCROLLS. See DEAD SEA SCROLLS.

QUOTATIONS, IMPLICIT. Citations in the Bible from uninspired sources. The Holy See has on various occasions admitted the fact in principle but cautioned about the threat to biblical inerrancy. For if these uninspired sources are in error, it must be established that the Bible does not condone the error.

QUO VADIS? Latin words for the question that, according to legend, was asked of Christ by Peter as he was fleeing Rome during Nero's persecution. Christ is said to have answered, "I am coming to be crucified again." Peter took this as a rebuke, so he went back to be martyred. It is also the title of a famous Polish novel (1895) by Henryk Sienkiewicz on the life of the early Christians in Rome during the reign of Emperor Nero.

R

R. *Responsorium*—Responsory.

R. Roma.

RABAT. Formerly part of the clerical attire of French priests, but no longer in general use. It consists of a piece of black material attached to a rudimentary collar and resting on the upper chest. Now practically replaced by the Roman collar. Brothers of the Christian Schools wear a white rabat. The equivalent of a rabat is part of the dress of Catholic priests in other countries, as a black piece of cloth worn under the suit coat and with a clerical collar.

RABBI. In the Old Testament the title *rab* referred to any eminent holder of an office. Rabbi literally means "my master." In the New Testament it is the honorable name by which the Disciples addressed Jesus as their Master (Matthew 23:7; John 1:38). Soon after the apostolic age it became the recognized title of Jewish religious teachers, and all modern Jewish clergy are called rabbis. (Etym. Aramaic *rab*, master + first person pronomian suffix: my master.)

RACCOLTA. Formerly a book containing the prayers and exercises to which indulgences were attached by the Holy See; the conditions for gaining these indulgences; and their application to the souls in purgatory.

Translations of the official edition of the Sacred Congregation of Indulgences were authorized for national and local use. Since the Second Vatican Council, the Raccolta has become the Enchiridion of Indulgences, authorized by Pope Paul VI in 1968.

RACHEL. Daughter of Laban. Isaac was afraid that his son Jacob would marry a Canaanite, so he sent him to live with and work for Laban, his brother-in-law. Jacob fell in love with Rachel and agreed to work for his uncle for seven years in order to marry her. At the end of that time, however, Laban tricked him into marrying Leah, his older daughter (Genesis 29). Jacob had to work for seven more years in order to win Rachel as his second wife. Evidently the ordeal was worth it, for Genesis reports that the additional seven years "seemed to him like a few days, because he loved her so much" (Genesis 29:20). Of all his children Jacob loved Joseph and Benjamin most. They were the two borne by Rachel (Genesis 30:24). She died giving birth to Benjamin (Genesis 35:18) and Jacob erected a tomb in her memory (Genesis 35:20).

RAHAB. A harlot who lived in Jericho. When Joshua was planning his conquest of Jericho, two of his spies took lodging in her home. They were suspected of being Joshua's men, but Rahab risked death by hiding them on her roof and helping them escape. In gratitude the spies promised her that when Joshua had captured Jericho she and her family would be spared. Joshua abided by the promise (Joshua 2:1–24). Before the town was burned down, the two spies escorted Rahab and her family to safety (Joshua 6:22–25). Twice her name appears in the New Testament. In Matthew's genealogy of Jesus she is named as the mother of Boaz (Matthew 1:5). In the Letter to the Hebrews the writer pays tribute to her faith in protecting Joshua's spies (Hebrews 11:31).

RAPE. In ecclesiastical law the crime of forcing a woman, against her will, to have sexual intercourse. Besides the mortal sin against chastity, it is a grave sin against justice to ravish a woman. Rape can be committed by the use of physical or moral force, including fraud and deceit; likewise, in a sin committed with a woman who has not the use of reason, whether mentally deranged or under the influence of drink or drugs. A woman being ravished must offer internal resistance absolutely, in not consenting with the will; and such external resistance as is possible without endangering her life or reputation. (Etym. Latin *rapere*, to seize.)

RAPTURE. A form of ecstasy, one that is sudden and violent. This violent motion cannot, as a rule be resisted, whereas in the case of simple ecstasy, resistance is possible, at least at the outset.

RASH JUDGMENT. Unquestioning conviction about another person's bad conduct without adequate grounds for the judgment. The sinfulness of rash judgment lies in the hasty imprudence with which the critical appraisal is made and in the loss of reputation that a person suffers in the eyes of the one who judges adversely.

RAS SHAMRA. Present day site of the ancient city of Ugarit on the Syrian coast. In the fifteenth century it was a commercial center, but it was destroyed by invaders. The ruins, completely buried, were discovered in 1928. The site was fully excavated by French archaeologists between 1929 and 1933, and further explored since 1946. Extensive records of Canaanite culture and religion have been found.

RATIFIED MARRIAGE. A marriage entered into by two baptized persons, whether Catholic or not.

RATIO. The essence or nature of something intelligible to the mind. It is therefore the intelligibility of any essence. In ecclesiastical language it is the ground or reason or rationale of a thing, especially as pertaining to an organized body of knowledge, legislation, or method of performing an activity. Thus the Code of Canon Law has a fundamental ratio or set of principles on which it is based. (Etym. Latin *ratio*, reason; intelligence, mind, act of reasoning, knowledge, plan, motive, argumentation, account.)

RATIONAL FREEDOM. Immunity from determination by one's feelings, whether fears or desires, so that the will can decide for itself what the mind (enlightened by faith) judges is the right course of action. Also called psychological freedom.

RATIONALISM. A system of thought or attitude of mind which holds that human reason is self-sufficient and does not need the help of divine revelation to know all that is necessary for a person's well-being. Also the view that a priori reason can give certitude without experience or verification of facts.

RATIONALIZATION. The practice of justifying one's conduct to self or to others on rational grounds. The term implies substituting plausible or socially acceptable reasons for the real reasons in order to avoid a personal sense of guilt or loss of acceptance by others.

RAVEN. An emblem of several saints who profited by the miraculous assistance of this rapacious bird. St. Benedict (480–546), while being slandered by Florentius, had his life saved when a raven removed the poisoned loaf prepared for his meal by his enemies. St. Meinrad (d. 861), as a solitary, was murdered by two men who were after a treasure falsely reported to be hidden in the monk's cave. They were brought to justice by the croaking of two ravens who followed them from the scene of their crime. Elijah the prophet is often represented by ravens who at God's command brought food to him.

R.D. Rural dean.

READER. The ministry to which a person is specially appointed by the Church, of reading the Word of God in liturgical assemblies. He is to read the lessons from Scripture, except for the Gospel, in the Mass and other sacred functions. He is to recite the psalms between the readings when there is no psalmist. He is to present the intentions for the general intercessions in the absence of a deacon or cantor. He is to direct the singing and the participation by the faithful. He is to instruct the faithful for the worthy reception of the sacraments. He may also, insofar as necessary, take care of the faithful who by temporary appointment are to read the Scriptures in liturgical celebrations. The ministry of reader is reserved to men. Women may perform the function of readers to the degree they are delegated to do so. See also LECTOR.

REAL DOUBT. Suspension of assent or judgment of the mind because of a lack of sufficient evidence for one or the other side of opposite opinions.

REALISM. Every form of philosophy that recognizes: 1. the objective existence of God and the world and their various relationships, independently of human knowledge and desire; 2. that these beings are knowable as they are in themselves; 3. the need for one to conform his or her mind, will, and conduct to this objective reality in order to be happy and attain one's final destiny.

REALITY. That which exists objectively, and independently of the mind, as opposed to the unreal, which is merely subjective or fanciful. Reality is that to which the mind conforms when it possesses the truth. (Etym. Latin *realis,* of the thing itself; extramental.)

REAL PRESENCE. The manner of Christ's presence in the Holy Eucharist. In its definition on the subject, the Council of Trent in 1551 declared that "in the sacrament of the most holy Holy Eucharist is contained truly, really, and substantially the body and blood, together with the soul and divinity, of our Lord Jesus Christ, and consequently the whole Christ" (Denzinger 1636, 1640). Hence Christ is present truly or actually and not only symbolically. He is present really, that is objectively in the Eucharist and not only subjectively in the mind of the believer. And he is present substantially, that is with all that makes Christ Christ and not only spiritually in imparting blessings on those who receive the sacrament. The one who is present is the whole Christ (*totus Christus*), with all the attributes of his divinity and all the physical parts and properties of his humanity. (Etym. Latin *realis,* of the thing itself; extramental + *prae-esse,* to be at hand, to be immediately efficacious.) See also SACRAMENTAL PRESENCE.

REAL VOW. A promise made to God to grant or give something tangible (not a personal service). The obligation of a real vow descends to the heirs. Thus if a testator dies without having dispensed an alms he or she vowed to give, the heirs must give the alms.

REASON. In general, the mind in its function of attaining the truth. Also the basis or evidence used by the mind in its pursuit of truth. It differs from the intellect, whose proper role is to perceive the truth, whether arrived at by a reasoning process or perceived immediately as intuition. Reason, therefore, is a process, where intellect is possession.

REASONABLENESS OF FAITH. See PREAMBLES OF FAITH.

REBAPTISM. The term is inaccurate if taken literally, because baptism imprints an indelible mark on the soul, which means that it cannot, because it need not, be repeated. In the early centuries, Pope St. Stephen insisted with St. Cyprian of Carthage that not even apostasy can eradicate the sacramental character conferred in baptism. See also ABJURATION.

REBEKAH. Daughter of Bethuel and sister of Laban. Abraham did not want his son Isaac to marry a Canaanite, so he sent a trusted servant to the land of his kinfolk to choose a suitable wife. The servant prayed to Yahweh for guidance, and Rebekah proved to be the maid who met Yahweh's specifications. Rebekah's family rejoiced at the selection and she willingly returned with the servant and married Isaac (Genesis 24). In time she bore two sons, Esau and Jacob (Genesis 25:24–28). Jacob was her favorite. When the aged, blind Isaac prepared to give his blessing (which involved rights of inheritance) to Esau, Rebekah and Jacob conspired to deceive Isaac into blessing the son she favored (Genesis 27). Then, to frustrate Esau's determination to kill his brother, Rebekah prevailed on Isaac to send Jacob off to her brother's homeland (Genesis 28:1–5). This strategy paved the way for Jacob's marriage to Leah and Rachel, Laban's daughters (Genesis 29). Rebekah and Isaac were buried in Canaan in the same field with Abraham and Sarah (Genesis 49:29–31).

RECESSIONAL. A hymn sung by choir, clergy, or congregation as the celebrants leave the altar or church at the conclusion of a religious service.

RECIDIVISM. In pastoral theology, the predictable repetition of a person's misbehavior. Applied to those who have developed some vice and seem to be incapable, or unwilling, to take the means necessary to overcome their bad habit. (Etym. Latin *recidivus*, falling back, relapsing.)

RECOLLECTION. Concentration of soul on the presence of God. It calls for considerable mental discipline to avoid dissipation of mind, but is required of all who aspire after Christian perfection. See also PRAYER OF RECOLLECTION.

RECONCILIATION. The act or state of re-establishing friendship between God and a human being, or between two persons. Reconciliation with God is necessary after a person has lost the divine friendship through grievous sin. It requires repentance on the part of the sinner and forgiveness on the part of God. The willingness to be reconciled with another person is a necessary condition for obtaining God's mercy.

RECONCILIATIONEM. Decree of the Sacred Congregation for Divine Worship, issued in 1973, authorizing the revised ritual for the administration of the sacrament of penance. Unlike the decrees on the sacraments of confirmation, the Eucharist, orders, and anointing of the sick, this decree was not accompanied by an apostolic letter or constitution of the Pope (December 2, 1973).

RECTOR. The head of a religious community of men, or of an educational institution. Popularly applied to designate a pastor, and hence the term rectory. But in canonical language a rector is the priest in charge of a church that is neither parochial nor capitular nor annexed to the house of a religious community for its religious functions. (Etym. Latin *rector*, ruler, leader, director.)

RECTORY. Originally the residence of the rector of an academic or ecclesiastical institution. Now commonly used in speaking of the residence of the priest in charge of a church or a shrine and his priest assistants.

RECTO TONO. The simplest form of church music, a reciting tone. One note held for the length of a phrase.

RECUSANTS. Persons who violated the law that commanded attendance at the services of the Church of England. Penalties for violation were suffered most often by Catholics. Conviction resulted in a fine, disability to hold office, keep arms, maintain suits at law, prohibition from guardianship, practicing law, or holding military office. Three months after conviction recusants were to renounce the supremacy of the Pope over the Anglican Church or to abjure the realm. These laws were enforced with varying degrees of strictness from the reign of Elizabeth I to George III, and gave the Church many martyrs.

RED. Color symbolic of warmth and blood. Vestments of this color are used in Masses of the Holy Spirit, recalling the tongues of fire on Pentecost; on feasts commemorating the Passion of Christ; and on festivals of saints who were martyred.

REDACTION. Shortened term for the redaction-historical method of interpreting the Bible. It goes beyond form criticism in analyzing how the biblical texts underwent development and change as they were used in different Gospel contexts, e.g., the same words of Christ may be found in Matthew and Luke in different contexts, with corresponding differences in expression.

REDEMPTION. The salvation of humanity by Jesus Christ. Literally, to redeem means to free or buy back. Humanity was held captive in that it was enslaved by sin. Since the devil overcame human beings by inducing them to sin, they were said to be in bondage to the devil. Moreover, the human race was held captive as to a debt of punishment, to the payment of which it was bound by divine justice.

On all these counts, the Passion of Christ was sufficient and superabundant satisfaction for human guilt and the consequent debt of punishment. His Passion was a kind of price or ransom that paid the cost of freeing humanity from both obligations. Christ rendered satisfaction, not by giving money, but by spending what was of the highest value. He gave himself, and therefore his Passion is called humanity's Redemption. (Etym. Latin *redemptio*, a buying back, ransoming, redemption.)

REDEMPTORISTS. Members of the Congregation of the Most Holy Redeemer, founded by St. Alphonso Maria de' Liguori at Scala, Italy, in 1732. They form a clerical religious congregation engaged in the preaching and writing apostolate among the faithful, in giving parish missions and spiritual exercises and in missionary work among non-Christians.

RED HAT. The hat conferred on a cardinal. It is flat-crowned and broad-brimmed, with two clusters of fifteen tassels. A cardinal is invested with this symbolic hat in the first public consistory after the appointment has been announced, and it is not worn again. After the cardinal's death, the hat is suspended over his tomb or from the cathedral ceiling. The "red hat" is a common term for the cardinal's office. See also HAT, ECCLESIASTICAL.

RED MASS. Any Mass at which the celebrant wears red vestments. More properly, a votive Mass of the Holy Spirit offered on the occasion of a solemn opening of church councils, synods, schools, civil courts, or legislative assemblies.

RED SCAPULAR. See SCAPULAR.

REDUCTION. In ecclesiastical law, reducing the number of Masses to be said from a foundation, when the endowment no longer suffices to supply the stipends for the Masses. It is assumed that the foundation became devaluated through no fault of the administrator. Only the Holy See can authorize a reduction.

REDUCTIONS, PARAGUAY. The communal mission villages established in South America by Jesuit missionaries from 1609 to the expulsion of the Society of Jesus from Spanish colonies in 1767. The native Indians filled the villages that were chosen for their healthful climate and proximity to waterways. The plan of a village was square, with the streets running in straight lines. In the center was the church. The missionaries taught the people, managed the community, and fostered the common arts, agriculture, and cattle raising. After their destruction a fable grew up concerning their wealth, which was supposed to have been hidden by the missionaries. The reductions were never restored.

REFECTORY. The dining room of a monastery or convent. (Etym. Latin *refectorius,* refreshing.)

REFLECTION. The attention of the mind to itself, or to the knowing or willing acts of the thinker. Therefore the act or practice by which the intellect turns back on itself or its own operations.

REFORM. Change with a view to improvement. By her nature as a living organism, the Catholic Church has undertaken numerous reforms in her long history. These have been mainly concerned with the moral and spiritual life of the faithful, by the use of the elaborate legislative, administrative, and ritual means at the Church's disposal. The term "reform" occurs in the first paragraph of the first document issued by the Second Vatican Council in its Constitution on the Sacred Liturgy. And the desire "to impart an ever-increasing vigor to the Chris-

tian life of the faithful" (Introduction) runs as a theme through all the conciliar teaching and the postconciliar directives of the Holy See.

REFORMATION. A religious, social, and political upheaval (1517–1648) that divided Western Christendom and created world Protestantism. Its causes were manifold: weakening of papal authority through long residence in France and the worldliness of some popes; disloyalty to Rome of many bishops who were really temporal rulers; excessive reservation of ecclesiastical appointments to the Roman Curia; intellectual and moral unfitness of many priests; wealth of some of the monasteries and dissension in their ranks; superstition and ignorance among the laity; social unrest brought on by the disintegration of the feudal system; support given by political power to dissenters in the Church; unrest and secularism brought on by the new geographical discoveries; and the use of the printing press to propagate the new views. The effects of the Reformation have been far-reaching: Christian unity was shattered, personal liberty in religion affected every sphere of human activity, with the rise of the modern secular state, of capitalism as rugged individualism, and with the loss of the cultural solidarity, founded on a common faith, that had shaped Western civilization for almost a millennium.

REFORMATION DOGMA. The dogmatic teaching of the original Protestant reformers. They were constrained by the logic of separating from Rome to defend their new doctrinal positions. Thus we find Luther writing numerous treatises on faith, grace, and justification, and John Calvin (1509–64) producing in 1536 his *Institutes of the Christian Religion,* as the first systematic compendium of Protestant doctrine. "My design in this work," wrote Calvin in the introduction, "has been to prepare and qualify students of theology for the reading of the divine word." The beginnings of the Reformation were thoroughly dogmatic in character. The earliest Reformation dogma was biblical in the direct sense. It did not take philosophy as a basis or ally. Its first business was to know and expound the Bible. It did not claim Aristotle and Plato as friends or forerunners. It used reason, but reason derived only from the Bible and put to a biblical use. Actually there was a philosophy behind this dogmatizing, notably the nominalism of William of Ockham (1280–1349), whom Luther called "my teacher" and rated in learning far above Thomas Aquinas.

Two strains in Ockham, sometimes called "the first Protestant," became imbedded in the Reformation: a distrust of reason in dealing with religion, and a theory of voluntarism which made right and wrong depend on the will of God. The first strain appeared prominently in Lutheran or evangelical thought, with the emphasis on revelation and grace as the exclusive media of religious knowledge and salvation. The second affected Calvinism and postulated, in Calvin's words, that "God chooses some for the hope of life, and condemns others to eternal death . . . . For all men are not created on an equal footing, but for some eternal life is preordained, for others eternal damnation." The divine will, therefore, and not as in Catholic doctrine the divine wisdom, is the ultimate norm of man's existence and destiny.

REFORMATION THEOLOGY. Systematic exposition of the original principles of the Protestant Reformation. The Father of Reformation theology was Philip Melanchthon (1497–1560), professor of Greek at Wittenberg and author of two basic compendia of Reformation belief: the *Confession of Augsburg* and the *Apology for the Confession*, both compromise documents that differed from Luther and Calvin in many points and paved the way for a speculative theology. Melanchthon made important concessions on the doctrine for free will and unconditional predestination, on the power of reason to reflect on matters of faith, and on tradition as found in the Churches of Rome and the East. These concessions were more or less reconciled with the opposition in the *Formula of Concord* (1577), the last of the classical Lutheran formulas of faith, drawn up by a number of theologians, including Jakob Andreae (1528–90) and Nikolaus Selnecker (1530–92).

The latter part of the sixteenth century and most of the seventeenth were the period of Protestant scholasticism, using the *Institutes* of Calvin and the *Formula of Concord* as the base of operation. Except for an essential difference in content, the method was not unlike that of the medieval Schoolmen. Typical of the doctrines treated was the infallibility of the Bible, to which the same kind of intrinsic efficacy was attached as Catholics attached to the sacraments. Classic Protestant dogmatic theology has remained substantially unchanged to this day.

REFUGE, CITIES OF. Towns that, according to Jewish law, enjoyed the right of asylum. To justify his right to immunity, the fugitive had to prove that his crime was unpremeditated. He virtually became a prisoner in the city to which he fled. Six cities of refuge are listed in Joshua 20:7–9. The practice was carried over to Christianity in the so-called right of sanctuary.

REGENERATION. A term applied to the sacrament of baptism, following the words of Christ that no one can enter heaven who has not been reborn of water and the Holy Spirit. It implies that as there are two kinds of life, natural and supernatural, so there must be two kinds of generation, one as a human being at conception and the other as a child of God at baptism. (Etym. Latin *re*, again + *generare*, to produce.)

REGESTA, PAPAL. Copies of papal correspondence and official documents entered in special volumes. Those previous to the thirteenth century have all but disappeared, except for fragments. The British Museum and Cambridge University are the repositories of the most important of these fragments. These collections are of primary historical importance, though many have been proved not to be originals.

REGIMINI ECCLESIAE UNIVERSAE. Apostolic constitution authorizing the new constitution of the Roman Curia. This extensive document gives the juridical structure of: 1. the whole Roman Curia in general; 2. the Secretary of State and the Council for the Public Affairs of the Church; 3. the Sacred Congregations (nine); 4. the Secretariats (three); 5. the Council of the Laity and Commission "Justice and Peace"; 6. the Tribunals (three); and 7. Offices (six). Pope Paul VI hereby ratified the centuries-old curial system, which he described as "rendering the universal Church outstanding service" (August 15, 1967).

REGINA COELI. Easter anthem, of unknown authorship, dating from the twelfth century. It has been part of the Liturgy of the Hours, to be said during the Easter season at Compline. It takes the place of the Angelus in Eastertide. The prayer reads:

"O Queen of heaven, rejoice Alleluia.
For He whom you did merit to bear, Alleluia.
Has risen as He said, Alleluia.
Pray for us to God, Alleluia.
Rejoice and be glad, O Virgin Mary, Alleluia.
For the Lord has truly risen, Alleluia.
Let us pray: O God, who by the resurrection of Your Son, our Lord Jesus Christ, have been pleased to fill the world with joy, grant, we beseech You, that through the intercession

of the Virgin Mary, His Mother, we may receive the joys of eternal life, through the same Christ our Lord. Amen."

REGISTERS, PAROCHIAL. Five distinct records that the parish priest is expected to keep concerning the baptisms, confirmations, and marriages that take place in his parish, deaths among his people, and as far as possible the actual spiritual condition of the parish. At the end of the year copies of these records, except the last, are to be sent to the diocesan chancery.

REGULAE JURIS. Certain legal axioms, ninety-nine, from the Decretals of Popes Gregory IX and Boniface VIII. They were rules of canonical interpretation, for example, "once bad always presumed to be bad," i.e., if once proved guilty of perjury, a person would be excluded from giving testimony ever again.

REGULARS. Men belonging to religious institutes, whether orders or congregations. In a strict canonical sense, however, regulars are members of religious orders only. The regular clergy are priests who are also bound by the religious rule (*regula*) of their community. (Etym. Latin *regularis,* pertaining to a bar or ruler; containing rules.)

REIFICATION. The claim of certain atheist philosophers, such as Feuerbach and Nietzsche, that all religion is make-believe. Believers are said to project their subjective hopes and desires and make them into realities, such as God and heaven, which do not really exist. (Etym. Latin *res,* thing, fact + *facere,* to make.)

REINCARNATION. See METEMPSYCHOSIS.

RELATIONSHIP. Kinship between people that, according to ecclesiastical law, is the basis of mutual rights and duties and affects the validity or liceity of subsequent marriage between the related persons. The relationship may be natural by blood or consanguinity, or contractual by marriage or affinity, or legal by adoption, or spiritual by baptism or confirmation.

RELATIVELY SUPERNATURAL. A divine gift beyond the powers and needs of certain natures but not beyond all creatures. Thus infused knowledge is beyond the capacity of man but not of angels. When granted to a human person it is supernatural relatively. Natural to angels, it is called preternatural to human beings. See also ABSOLUTELY SUPERNATURAL.

RELATIVE MYSTERY. A truth whose existence had to be supernaturally revealed by God, but, once revealed, its essence or meaning can be grasped by the light of natural reason. The existence of angels is a relative mystery.

RELATIVISM. In philosophy, the view that there is no absolute truth or certitude. It is claimed that truth depends entirely on variable factors such as person, place, time, and circumstances. Moral relativism holds that there are no unchangeable principles of human behavior, either because all truth is relative or because there are no inherently evil actions, since everything depends on other factors, such as customs, conventions, or social approval.

RELATOR. The judge designated by an ecclesiastical tribunal to gather together and put into writing the data necessary for reviewing a case in law. A relator is also the one designated to assemble the data on a person whose cause has been introduced for possible beatification and canonization.

RELIC. An object connected with a saint, e.g., part of the body or clothing or something the person had used or touched. Authentic relics are venerated with the Church's warm approbation. They may not be bought or sold. Those of a martyr are placed in the altar stone at the consecration of an altar. Relics are of three classes: the first is part of the saint's body and is the type placed in the altar stone; the second is part of the clothing or anything used during the saint's life; and the third is any other object, such as a piece of cloth, that has been touched to a first-class relic. (Etym. Latin *reliquiae,* remains.) See also AACHEN.

RELIGION. The moral virtue by which a person is disposed to render to God the worship and service he deserves. It is sometimes identified with the virtue of justice toward God, whose rights are rooted in his complete dominion over all creation. Religion is also a composite of all the virtues that arise from a human being's relationship to God as the author of his or her being, even as love is a cluster of all the virtues arising from human response to God as the destiny of his or her being. Religion thus corresponds to the practice of piety toward God as Creator of the universe. (Etym. probably Latin *religare,* to tie, fasten, bind, or *relegere,* to gather up, treat with care.)

RELIGION AS FEELING. The view that Christianity is essentially a religion of feeling. It was systematically developed by Friedrich Schleiermacher (1768–1834) in his

Christian Faith, which dates an epoch in the history of modern theology. While rationalists and supernaturalists carried on their struggle, Schleiermacher took the ground from under their contention by removing its main presupposition. The Christian faith, he said, does not consist in any kind of doctrinal propositions. It is a condition of devout feeling and, like all other experience, simply an object to be described. Against the supernaturalists he maintained that Christianity is not something to be received on authority from without, but an inward condition of our own self-consciousness. Against the rationalists, he said that religion is not a product of rational thinking, but an emotion of the heart, a feeling that occurs independently of the mind. Moreover, this feeling is not merely personal but social in its Protestant form, since it is the common experience of a historical community derived from the Reformation.

RELIGIONIST. A term sometimes applied to persons professionally engaged in religious pursuits, as the clergy or theologians.

RELIGIONUM LAICALIUM. Decree of the Sacred Congregation for Religious, granting certain faculties to the superiors general of nonclerical religious communities, May 31, 1966.

RELIGIOUS APOSTASY. Desertion from the religious life. A religious apostate is one who has perpetual vows and either leaves the religious house without permission and with the intention of not returning, or leaves with permission but does not return because he intends to withdraw from religious obedience.

RELIGIOUS FUGITIVE. One who leaves a religious institute without permission but intends to return to the religious state.

RELIGIOUS INDIFFERENCE. The attitude that all religions are equally good and equally capable of leading a person to his or her eternal destiny. In its most extreme form, the theory that there is no one form of religious belief, divine worship, or moral behavior that has been revealed by God.

RELIGIOUS INSTITUTE. See INSTITUTE, RELIGIOUS.

RELIGIOUS RULE. The plan of life and discipline, approved by the Holy See, under which religious live in order to grow in Christian perfection and perform the works of the apostolate proper to their institute.

RELIGIOUS STATE. According to ecclesiastical tradition, a fixed or stable manner of life that people of the same sex live in common, and in which they observe the evangelical counsels by means of the vows of poverty, chastity, and obedience.

RELIQUARY. Any repository in which a relic is sealed and kept. Reliquaries vary in size, according to the relic, from very small ones that can be easily carried to larger caskets for whole parts of a saint's body. Relics are never exposed for public veneration unless enclosed in a reliquary. Some reliquaries are famous for their exquisite design and value.

REMARRIAGE. In general, the repetition of marriage while a married partner is still living. In the Old Testament remarriage was permitted, but, as Christ explained to the Pharisees, "It was because you were so unteachable that Moses allowed you to divorce your wives, but it was not like this from the beginning" (Matthew 19:8). Christ restored marriage to its former monogamous state and, to provide the necessary grace, raised it to the dignity of a sacrament. A valid sacramental marriage is not dissoluble by any human power, civil or ecclesiastical. Instances of remarriage, therefore, are either cases where the previous marriage was not a sacrament, or the original marriage was not valid, or the partners had not consummated their marriage by natural intercourse.

REMISSION OF SIN. The true and actual forgiveness of sin. When mortal sin is remitted, this includes pardon of the eternal punishment due to it, but temporal penalty may still remain. When venial sin is remitted, the guilt is removed and as much of the temporal punishment as the person's dispositions warrant from the grace of God.

REMORSE. Keen sense of guilt over having done something wrong. It is self-reproach coupled with a certain degree of discouragement either to undo the wrong or, more rarely, of being forgiven.

REMOTE OCCASIONS. Situations that can but will not likely lead a person into sin. They may be either circumstances in which sin for any ordinary person is possible but not at all probable, or circumstances in which the person has shown that he or she does not sin as a rule. Remote occasions exist everywhere.

REMYTHOLOGY. A theory of those biblical critics who claimed to discover the "historical Jesus" by stripping the Gospels of the miraculous, which they considered mythological. But their own premises were a form of mythology, which claimed that miracles are either impossible or unprovable.

RENEWAL. Renovation in the sense of restoring a practice, custom, or institution to its original meaning or purpose. Used by the Second Vatican Council especially of the spiritual renewal of religious communities, by a return to their Gospel foundations, the charisms of their founders, and the sacred traditions of their history.

RENEWAL OF CONSENT. The public or at least private acceptance of one's partner in the validation of a previously invalid marriage contract. The requirements and conditions for a renewal of consent are specified in ecclesiastical law.

RENOUNCING SATAN. Profession of allegiance to Christ and renunciation of the devil as the enemy of Christ, made at baptism by the person being baptized or by the sponsor. It implies the resolution to resist the devil's attempts to seduce the followers of Christ, to live in humility (contrary to Satan's pride), in obedience (contrary to Satan's disobedience), and in holiness (contrary to Satan's total estrangement from God).

RENOVATIONIS CAUSAM. Instruction of the Sacred Congregation for Religious and Secular Institutes, on the appropriate renovation of the training and preparation of persons for living the religious life. While the immediate focus of the instruction was the religious life, properly so called, persons living other forms of a consecrated life of the counsels were also affected (January 6, 1969).

RENUNCIATION. To give up something to which a person has a claim. Some renunciations are necessary by divine law; others are permitted and encouraged according to divine counsel. Everyone must renounce sin and those creatures that are proximate occasions to sin. In this category belongs the renunciation of Satan at baptism, either by the person being baptized or by the sponsor. Renunciations of counsel pertain to the exercise of such natural rights as material possessions, marriage, and legitimate autonomy or self-determination, sacrificed for love of God by those who vow themselves to poverty, chastity, and obedience.

REORDINATION. The repetition of an ordination ceremony for a bishop, priest, or deacon because there are serious grounds for doubting the validity of a previous ordi-

nation. The term is inaccurate, since sacred orders, once conferred, cannot be repeated.

REPAIRING SCANDAL. Making amends for sinful action that has scandalized others. A person is obliged to make reparation as far as he or she can. In some cases it would be impossible to make direct reparation to the people scandalized because they are too numerous or are unknown. Nevertheless the responsibility remains. Making reparation by good example to undo the harm caused others by scandal is a prominent feature of the Christian meaning of penance in expiation for sin.

REPARATION. The act or fact of making amends. It implies an attempt to restore things to their normal or sound conditions, as they were before something wrong was done. It applies mainly to recompense for the losses sustained or the harm caused by some morally bad action. With respect to God, it means making up with greater love for the failure in love through sin; it means restoring what was unjustly taken and compensating with generosity for the selfishness that caused the injury. (Etym. Latin *reparare*, to prepare anew, restore.) See also ADEQUATE REPARATION.

REPENTANCE. Voluntary sorrow because it offends God, for having done something wrong, together with the resolve to amend one's conduct by taking the necessary means to avoid the occasions of sin. To repent is to be sorry for sin with self-condemnation. (Etym. Latin *repoenitere*, to be very sorry, regret intensely.)

REPOSITORY. A side altar or secondary chapel where the Blessed Sacrament, consecrated on Holy Thursday, is reposed for adoration until Good Friday services. (Etym. Latin *repositorium*, storehouse; literally, place where things may be placed.)

REPREHENSION. Formal correction of a person, either privately or publicly, for giving scandal or disturbing good order. The reprehension may be administered either by an ordinary or through a delegate. Public reprehension should be given before an official notary or two witnesses. If done by letter, there should be some documentary evidence that the reprehension (or monition) was received and what the letter actually said. (Etym. Latin *reprehendere*, rebuke, hold back: *re-*, back + *prehendre*, to seize.)

REPROBATION. God's eternal resolve to exclude certain rational creatures from eternal happiness. As taught by the Church, God has eternally predestined certain persons, on account of their sins, to rejection from heaven. Always understood is that God wants all human beings to be saved, but he does not wish to save those who, by their abuse of divine grace, freely separate themselves from his love. (Etym. Latin *reprobare*, to reject, condemn.) See also SALVIFIC WILL.

REPUTATION. The good name that a person enjoys in the public estimation. Everyone has a right to his or her good name, even the deceased, and moral persons, e.g., a community. If one's good name is genuine, hence deserved, a person has an absolute right that no one may injure it. One's right to a reputedly good name is relative and restricted, since the greater common good requires that, at times, even secret faults may be revealed. There is no injury, however, to reputation when the faults or defects mentioned are already publicly known. An unjust injury is committed by every sin of calumny, and by revealing real faults when the disclosure serves neither the common good nor legitimate private welfare.

REQ. *Requiescat*—May he or she rest, i.e., in peace.

REQUIEM. A Mass celebrated for the dead. The name is derived from the first word of the opening hymn in the Latin Rite Mass prior to the revision since the Second Vatican Council. The invocation said, *"Requiem aeternam dona eis, Domine"* (Eternal rest give unto them, O Lord). (Etym. Latin *requies*, rest after labor, relaxation.)

REQUIESCAT IN PACE. May he or she rest in peace. Invocation of God's mercy on the soul of a deceased person. Found in some of the earliest catacomb inscriptions on the graves. A familiar prayer in the Church's liturgy to which the response is "Amen." It is customarily abbreviated R.I.P.

REREDOS. Richly painted or ornamented screen of stone or wood in back of the altar. Connected with the altar by means of the predella, it is sometimes called the altarpiece. (Etym. French *arere*, at the back + *dos*, back.)

RERUM NOVARUM. Encyclical of Pope Leo XIII, issued on May 15, 1891, on the condition of labor. It refutes the theories of the socialists and defends the rights of private ownership. It advises employers and workers to organize into both mixed and separate associations for mutual help and self-protection.

RESCR. *Rescriptum*—rescript.

RESCRIPTS. The written replies of a pope to questions, petitions, or reports generally made through curial channels. Lesser decisions are made through this form of papal document. Rescripts for dispensations may be given directly or the document may empower a bishop to grant or deny it. (Etym. Latin *rescriptum*, written reply of the emperor.)

RESERVATION OF THE BLESSED SACRAMENT. Keeping of the Blessed Sacrament in a fitting place (tabernacle) as an object of adoration or as viaticum for the sick.

RESERVED CASES. Sins or censures that only certain confessors or ecclesiastical superiors can absolve. Such cases are classified as papal, episcopal, and religious, according to whether absolution is reserved to a pope, bishop, or religious superior.

RESIDENTIAL SEE. A diocese or archdiocese over which a bishop actually presides. Technically every place in the world is under the jurisdiction of some bishop and belongs to some residential see. But sees are called residential mainly to distinguish them from titular sees, which formerly were the seats of ecclesiastical government but have since become extinct.

RESIGNATION. The acceptance of God's will in all circumstances of life, and especially during heavy trial or suffering. Also called abandonment, it has as its object the submission of one's own preferences or hopes to the dispositions of Providence. In canon law, resignation is the voluntary withdrawal of a person duly elected or appointed to an ecclesiastical office. In order to be valid, the resignation must be accepted by an authorized person or body in the Church.

RESISTING AGGRESSION. The right to use force against an unjust aggressor. This right is present when certain conditions are fulfilled, namely: 1. recourse to civil authority would be impossible. The common good demands that as a rule the State alone uses physical compulsion, for if any private citizen could at will employ force in defending his or her rights, the peace and order of the community would be disturbed; 2. the attack must be actual or immediately imminent; it is wrong to use deadly weapons before the attack, since there is grave danger that such force might be used against an innocent person; nor is it permissible to use such weapons after the attack is over, for then the defense is too late and the act of possible killing would constitute revenge; 3. the attack must be unjust, which really means that it is not provoked; aggression, therefore, is not justified; 4. the force employed must be proportionate to the loss threatened and must not exceed what is necessary; killing is not allowed if wounding would be sufficient for proper defense; wounding is not permitted if disarming the adversary or summoning help would be enough.

RESOLUTION. The firm determination to carry into effect what a person has decided should be done. It includes some decision to use the means for putting resolution into practice. In spiritual theology a resolution implies a conversion of one's moral life, arrived at after due reflection and prayer.

RESOLUTION OF AMENDMENT. The firm and sincere decision that a penitent makes to avoid the sins that person is confessing in the sacrament of penance. A true purpose of amendment includes the determination to avoid at least all grievous sins, the near occasions of them, to use the necessary means to amendment, to make due satisfaction for the sins committed, and be ready to make restitution or repair whatever injury may have been done to others.

RESP. *Responsum*—reply.

RESPECT. Esteem for someone or something, arising out of special regard for that object because of his, her, or its excellence. More properly it refers to persons, and it refers to things only because of the persons with whom they are associated. It implies a deference to the one respected and to that extent a sense of inferiority in the one who has or shows respect. (Etym. Latin *respectus*, a looking at, by or with a regard; relation, proportion; from *respicere*, to look at, look back upon.)

RESPONSE. Said or sung as a reply to the priest's words or chant, by the choir or congregation in the celebration of the liturgy.

RESPONSIBILITY. The ability to be trusted or depended on for an office or an action. It therefore adds to imputability the idea of being reliable and not merely held accountable for what is done. Responsibility may be either moral, based on imputability; or legal, based on the disposition of a law.

RESPONSORIAL. Descriptive of performance of certain musical forms in liturgical practice, vocal or instrumental with a soloist alternating with choir or congregation; priest and congregation answering each other; two choirs alternately responding usually in chant.

RESPONSORIAL PSALM. Antiphonal psalm that is said or read before the Gospel at Mass. Normally the psalm is taken from the lectionary and has some bearing on the particular text from Scripture. After the second reading and before the Gospel the Alleluia is either sung or read, followed by its appropriate verse. If the Alleluia or the verse before the Gospel is not sung, it may be omitted. Except on Easter Sunday and Whitsunday, the sequences (special festive hymns) are optional.

RESPONSORY. A psalm or part of one, sung or said between the readings at Mass and in the Divine Office.

RESSENTIMENT. A habitual feeling of resentment, at times expressed by acts of emotional violence, harbored by one group of people against another group. The source of the indignation may be envy or the memory of past injuries. It differs from prejudice in being more psychologically conditioned than founded on mistaken judgment.

RESTITUTION. Returning to its rightful owner whatever had been unjustly taken from that person. Restitution means the return to an individual of possession or dominion over something rightly owned by that person. Since dominion over certain things cannot be restored, restitution in general means making reparation for a wrong done, whether by returning what had been taken or by some other form of compensation. In this moral sense, restitution belongs to commutative justice (between person and person), whereby one restores to the rightful owner something unjustly taken or repairs damage unjustly caused. Restitution is binding in conscience because a person who does not make restitution, though able to do so, actually continues the theft or injury by depriving others of a good that belongs to them. The common good also requires restitution, since otherwise society would disintegrate if theft could be committed or injury caused with impunity. Moreover, no sin can be pardoned without sincere contrition and a firm purpose of amendment. Both elements are implied in the willingness to make restitution. (Etym. Latin *restitutio*, restoration.)

RESTORATION. The duty to give back or make up for what a person has that does not belong to him or her. It differs from restitution, which implies stealing or unjust acquisition. If something is bought rightfully from an unjust possessor, it must be returned to the rightful owner, but the buyer should be reimbursed for the price paid unless the goods were bought at a suspicious price or under dubious circumstances. Restoration is to be made to the one who suffered the damage. If one is dead, it is due to one's heirs. What must be restored is either what was borrowed or obtained or its equivalent value. And if the object was kept in bad faith, the restoration should include also the fruits accrued from the unjust possession. The obligation to restore is suspended in a physical or moral incapacity on the part of the one who possesses what belongs to someone else. But if one is able to repay gradually, one is held to the obligation, as far as it is possible to make repayment without grave injury to others who depend on him or her for their support. Among the reasons that may cancel the duty altogether are: voluntary remission on the part of one who has a right to dispose of one's own goods or a decision of the civil or ecclesiastical authorities.

RESTORED NATURE. Condition of a human being who has achieved supernatural destiny, i.e., the immediate vision of God. After the resurrection, the bodies of those in this state will also be endowed with the preternatural gifts of impeccability, bodily immortality, and inability to suffer.

RESURRECTION, BODILY. The universal return to life of all human beings, to occur soon before the last judgment by God's almighty power. Each individual soul will be reunited with the selfsame body with which it was united on earth. While all the dead will rise, only the just will have their bodies glorified.

RESURRECTION OF CHRIST. The rising from the dead of Christ on the third day after his death and burial. Christ's Resurrection is a basic truth of Christianity, which is expressed in all the Creeds and in all rules of faith of the ancient Church. He rose through his own power. The source of his Resurrection was the hypostatic union. The principal cause was the Word of God, together with the Father and the Holy Spirit; the instrumental cause was the parts of Christ's humanity, soul, and body, which were hypostatically united with the Godhead. When Scripture asserts (Acts 2:24; Galatians 1:1) that Christ was raised by God or by the Father, these statements are

to be understood as referring to his humanity. All forms of rationalism in ancient and modern times—deceit hypothesis, apparent death hypothesis, vision hypothesis, symbolism hypothesis—deny Christ's Resurrection. Yet nothing is more central in the faith as attested by Peter's sermon on Pentecost and as defended ever since by the Church's most solemn teaching authority.

The body of the risen Christ was in a state of glory, as is evident from circumstances of the appearances recorded in the Gospels and Acts, and from Christ's supremacy over the limitations of space and time. The risen Christ retained the wounds in his transfigured body as tokens of his triumph over death (John 20:27).

Theologically the Resurrection, unlike the death of Christ, is not the meritorious cause of human redemption. It is the victorious completion of redemption. It belongs to the perfection of redemption and is therefore associated in the Scriptures with Christ's death on the Cross as one complete whole. It is the model and, in the person of the risen Christ, the channel of grace for our spiritual redemption from sin and for our bodily resurrection on the Last Day.

RETALIATION. See LEX TALIONIS.

RETREAT. Withdrawal for a period of time from one's usual surroundings and occupation to a place of solitude for meditation, self-examination, and prayer, in order to make certain necessary decisions in one's spiritual life. Although the practice is older than Christianity, the example of Christ's forty days in the desert makes such retreats part of divine revelation, to be imitated, as far as possible, by his followers. As a formal devotion among all classes of the faithful, retreats were introduced with the Counter-Reformation, led by St. Ignatius of Loyola, and followed by St. Francis de Sales and St. Vincent de Paul. Retreats for a specified number of days are required of all priests and religious. "We desire," wrote Pope Pius XI, "that retreat houses, where persons withdraw for a month, or for eight days, or for fewer, to put themselves into training for the perfect Christian life, may come into being and flourish everywhere more numerously" (*Constitution Declaring St. Ignatius Patron of All Spiritual Exercises,* July 25, 1922).

RETRIBUTION. A penalty or reward that a person deserves for moral conduct. Its basis is the divine justice that repays each person according to his or her works. Retribution more generally refers to punishment for sin, but theologically it also means the merit that a person gains for free co-operation with divine grace. More often retribution is understood to belong to eternity, yet already in this life divine justice is acting, even when the punishment is tempered by God's mercy. (Etym. Latin *retributio,* recompense, restitution; from *retribuere,* to give back, restore.)

RETRIBUTISM. The view that people who commit a crime should be punished because they have done wrong. It takes on two forms, which in religious terms may be called expiatory and penal. A criminal, it is held, should expiate his or her disobedience of the law, and should suffer some penalty for the harm he or she has done to society.

RETROGRESSION. In moral theology the reaction to frustration by returning to satisfactions more important to an earlier and lower level of spiritual maturity. Also called reversion.

REUBEN. The oldest of Jacob's twelve sons (Genesis 29:32). The first incident recorded in Genesis involving Reuben was his immoral conduct with his father's concubine (Genesis 35:22). Even in his old age Jacob did not forgive this, for in the series of prophecies he made concerning his sons he described Reuben as "foremost in pride, foremost in strength, uncontrolled as a flood, you shall not be foremost, for you mounted your father's bed, and so defiled my couch to my hurt" (Genesis 49:3–4). But Reuben manifested redeeming qualities. When his jealous brothers proposed killing Joseph, it was he who dissuaded them, hoping to restore him to his father (Genesis 37:21–22). Years later he played the part of a responsible older brother in protecting Benjamin on the trip to Egypt (Genesis 42:37).

REV. Reverend.

REVALIDATION. See VALIDATION.

REVEALED LAW. Also called divine positive law, it is the sum total of all the prescriptions that God has communicated to the human race by way of supernatural revelation. It is, therefore, revealed law as distinct from the knowledge of God's will attainable by human reason alone.

Humankind needs a revealed law in addition to the divine natural law because the secondary precepts of the natural law can be obscured by evil passion, bad custom, and the allurement of sinful example. Another and higher reason why God revealed his will supernaturally is that he has elevated

human nature to a higher than natural destiny. This heavenly destiny cannot be attained without the observance of correspondingly supernatural laws, which are in the character of divine graces with which human beings must co-operate in order to reach the beatific vision.

Three periods may be distinguished in the history of God's revealed will: from the dawn of creation to the time of Moses; the Mosaic period, which spans the whole history of ancient Israel; and in New Testament time from the coming of Christ to the end of the apostolic age.

REVEALING SECRETS. Circumstances under which secrets may be revealed. A reasonable cause for revealing a secret is the urgent necessity of either the public or private good. In such necessity it would be reasonable to presume consent to the revelation of a secret. Since the public good takes precedence over the good of the individual, there are times when the latter's secret should be sacrificed for the good of society. The good of the individual that warrants disclosing a secret may refer either to the one who knows the secret, or someone who benefits from keeping the matter secret, or some third party. Where there exists a real need, it is permissible to reveal a secret for the benefit of any of these three persons. Confessional secrets, however, come under the seal of confession and may never be revealed.

REVELATION. Disclosure by God of himself and his will to the human race. The disclosure comes to human beings by way of communication, which implies the communicator, who is God; the receiver, who is the human being; and a transmitter or intermediary. Depending on the intermediary, there are in general two main forms of revelation, commonly called natural and supernatural.

If the intermediary is the world of space and time, the revelation is said to be natural. In this case, the natural world of creation is the medium through which God communicates himself to humankind. Moreover, humanity's natural use of reason is the means by which it attains the knowledge that God wishes to communicate. It is therefore natural twice over, once in the objective source from which human beings derive knowledge of God and divine things, and once again in the subjective powers that a person uses to appropriate what God is revealing in the universe into which humanity has been placed. In the Old Testament those are said to be "naturally stupid" who have "not known God and who, from the things that are seen, have not been able to discover Him-who-is or, by studying the works, have failed to recognize the Artificer" (Wisdom 13:1). And St. Paul affirmed: "Ever since God created the world his everlasting power and deity—however invisible—have been there for the mind to see in the things he has made" (Romans 1:20).

Supernatural revelation begins where natural revelation ends. It is in the character of a grace from God who has decided to communicate himself in a manner that far exceeds his manifestation through nature. The Scriptures call this form of communication a divine speech and refer to God as speaking to humankind. There are two levels of this supernatural revelation, as capsulized by the author of Hebrews: "At various times in the past and in various ways, God spoke to our ancestors through the prophets; but in our own time, the last days, he has spoken to us through his Son, the Son that he has appointed to inherit everything and through whom he made everything there is. He is the radiant light of God's glory and the perfect copy of his nature" (Hebrews 1:1–2).

The difference between these two kinds of supernatural communication lies in the fact that, before Christ, God spoke indeed but still indirectly through the prophets who were inspired to tell others what Yahweh had told them. In the person of Christ, however, it was no longer God speaking merely through human seers chosen by him; it was God himself speaking as man to his fellow members of the human race. (Etym. Latin *revelatio*, an uncovering; revelation.)

REVELATION, BOOK OF. See APOCALYPSE.

REVELATIONS, PRIVATE. Supernatural manifestations made to a particular person since apostolic times. They are distinct from visions and apparitions, properly so called, in which objects are seen but not necessarily understood. When what is seen is also understood, it becomes a revelation, although revelations can be received directly in the mind without sensory images of any kind. When the Church approves certain private revelations, as those of St. Margaret Mary (1647–90) or St. Bernadette Soubirous (1844–79), they are to be accepted on the Church's judgment, but they are not part of divine faith.

REVENGE. The act or intention of inflicting injury on someone, on one's own authority, to repay an offense committed. It is a manifestation of unjustifiable anger and is one of the most common human failings that takes on a variety of forms, from a momentary silence or frown to defamation of character or physical violence. As a form of sinful anger, it is an unruly desire for vengeance. The desire is immoderate if a person wants the undeserving to be punished, or the guilty to be punished excessively, or the punishment to be meted out in an unlawful manner or in order to vent one's own spite.

REVERENCE. The virtue that inclines a person to show honor and respect for persons who possess some dignity. There are four forms of reverence, corresponding to four forms of dignity: 1. familial reverence toward one's parents or those who take the place of parents; 2. civil reverence toward persons holding civil authority; 3. ecclesiastical reverence toward the Pope, bishops, priests, and others in the service of the Church; 4. religious reverence toward any person, place, or object related to God. (Etym. Latin *reverentia*, awe, respect.)

REVERSION. See RETROGRESSION.

REVIVIFICATION. Belief that all the sacraments, except the Eucharist and penance, confer the grace originally available, once the obstacle preventing the grace is removed. It is assumed that a person wants to receive the sacrament but lacks the proper dispositions, mainly the state of grace for sacraments of the living and adequate contrition for sacraments of the dead. When one attains the state of grace or arrives at sufficient contrition, the grace of the sacrament is "revived" without repeating the sacramental rite. The validity of baptism, confirmation, matrimony, and orders is always certain in these circumstances. Revivification pertains only to the fruitfulness of the sacraments, i.e., their conferral of sacramental grace.

REVOLUTION. A radical and generally violent effort to overthrow a civil government or constitution. Essential to a revolution is that the change of regime is not brought about by peaceful evolution or mutual agreement between the power that withdraws and the power that takes over the new government. Revolutions are caused either by the masses or by an act of high officials in the government. In the latter case it is called a *coup d'état*. In the twelfth century John of Salisbury (1115–80), followed by others, held that the murder of a tyrant was permissible even by a private citizen. The thesis was condemned by the Council of Constance in 1415 (Denzinger 1235), and by Pope Paul V in 1615 (constitution *Cura Dominici Gregis*).

REWARD. Something given in return for performing an action that either could have been left undone or at least might not have been done as well as it was. In theology the merit promised by God is a reward because the human being is physically free either to resist or co-operate with divine grace.

RHYTHM. See NATURAL FAMILY PLANNING.

RIGHT. Either opposite to wrong (adjective) or that which is just (noun). In the first sense, right means that which squares with the norm of morality, and so is morally good. In the second sense, right means that which is correlative to duty. As a noun, therefore, right is opposed to might, although both are means to achieve an end. Might is physical power, either as one's own bodily strength or as the physical (and psychological) instruments under a person's command. Physical power accomplishes its purpose by sheer force, which is indifferent to the claims of justice and can be used to help or hinder the observance of the moral law. Might becomes good or evil according to the will that directs it.

Right is moral power and works by appeal to another's will through that person's intellect. It is the moral power to do, hold or exact something. To *do* here is to be understood both affirmatively and negatively; it means either to perform or omit an action, as a person may have the right to keep silent as well as to speak. To *hold* means to own, keep, or use something, and includes metaphorical meanings, such as to hold an office or job. To *exact* means to demand that someone else perform or omit some action, such as the state requires payment of taxes or a teacher exacts attention from his or her pupils. Right is consequently a subjective moral power that resides in the subject or person possessing it. By a figure of speech, the word *right* may also be applied to the thing over which one has a moral power. Thus we may say that one has been deprived of certain rights, meaning some object that rightfully belongs to him or her. (Etym. Anglo-Saxon *riht*, right; Latin *rectus*, right: straight, upright, conformed to some measure, just, true.)

RIGHTEOUS ANGER. Justifiable indignation. It is permissible and even laudable when accompanied by a reasonable desire to inflict justifiable punishment. Christ himself was filled with righteous anger against the vendors who had desecrated the house of God. Such anger is allowable only if it tends to punish those who deserve punishment, according to the measure of their guilt, and with the sincere intention to redress what harm may have been done or to correct the wrongdoer. Otherwise the anger is sinfully excessive. The necessary provision is always that there is no tinge of hatred and no desire for revenge.

RIGHTEOUSNESS. See JUSTIFICATION, THEOLOGY OF.

RIGHT INTENTION. The motive necessary for the valid and fruitful reception of the sacraments. A person who has the use of reason must want to receive a sacrament and, at least implicitly, wish to benefit supernaturally from its reception.

RIGHT TO LIFE MOVEMENT. Organized effort in countries where direct abortion has been legalized. The movement takes on different forms in different places; from the strictly political efforts to change the existing laws of a nation that permit killing the unborn, to the exclusively spiritual promotion of crusades of prayer and penance to obtain divine assistance. The movement is not only Catholic, nor only Christian, although the Catholic Church is outstanding in her defense of the right to life of the unborn child. In the words of Pope John Paul II, "We can speak of the rights of the child from the moment of conception, and particularly of the right to life" (Address on the Rights of the Child, January 13, 1979).

RIGIDITY. A moral trait characterized by an unwillingness, or inability, to change one's attitudes or way of acting. Great difficulty in adjusting to socially justifiable change. (Etym. Latin *rigidus*, stiff, austere, rigid.)

RIGORISM. The moral theory that when there is a conflict of two opinions, one favoring the law and the other favoring liberty, the law must always be kept even if the opinion favoring liberty is more probable. Absolute rigorism, or tutiorism, taught by the Jansenists, was condemned by Pope Alexander VIII in 1690 (Denzinger 2303). See also ABSOLUTE TUTIORISM.

RING. A circular band of metal usually worn on the fourth finger. A ring is worn by the Pope, cardinals, bishops, and abbots as a sign of their espousal to the Church. Women religious and some institutes of men wear rings to remind them of their betrothal to Christ. Conferring the ring is an integral part of the marriage ceremony to signify the mutual love of husband and wife, and wearing the ring symbolizes their pledge of marital fidelity.

RING. A symbol of mystical marriage with Christ, an emblem of St. Catherine of Siena (1347–80) and St. Catherine dei Ricci (1522–90) as brides of Christ.

RING OF THE FISHERMAN. A gold seal ring with which popes are invested at the time of their election. It is used when sealing papal documents and is destroyed at the time of a pope's death by the Cardinal Camerlengo. The seal represents St. Peter fishing from a boat.

R.I.P. *Requiescat in Pace.* May he or she rest in peace. An abbreviation much used on tombstones and at the end of obituary notices.

RISUS PASCHALIS. A Bavarian custom where the priest would introduce into his sermons during Easter season some humorous story that would cause the congregation to laugh. He would then draw a moral from the story. It was prohibited by Pope Clement X when abuses arose.

RIT. *Ritus*—rite, rites.

RITE. In general, the manner and form of a religious function. Hence the words and actions to be carried out in the performance of a given act, e.g., the rite of baptism, or rite of consecration, the Roman Rite. The term in its widest ecclesiastical sense refers to the principal historic rituals in the Catholic Church, whose essentials are the same as derived from Jesus Christ. The four parent rites in Catholicism are the Antiochene, Alexandrine, Roman, and Gallican. Some religious orders have their own rites. In all cases, however, the ritual must be approved by the Holy See. (Etym. Latin *ritus*, religious custom, usage, ceremony.)

RITE OF EXORCISM. A sacramental by which a duly appointed person, generally a priest, is authorized to use the special power he receives to drive out the evil spirit. Until recently this power had been conferred in the minor order of exorcist. Nevertheless the power could not be used except by a priest who had received the special and express permission from ecclesiastical authority. The Church, in her directives to exorcists, warns them not to be too ready to assume that there is diabolical possession, since there are so many cases of hysteria or other kinds of emotional disorder that may seem to be "possession." Moreover, explicit directives are given on how to deal with ostensibly possessed persons, notably to exercise great care not to be either deceived or intimidated by the evil spirit.

Over the centuries the rite of exorcism has been long and detailed, with a variety of ritual forms, numerous signs of the cross, recitation of psalms, the Athanasian Creed, prayers to St. Michael, use of holy water, and periodic adjurations. Among other formulas, the priest declares, "I adjure you, ancient serpent, by the Judge of the living and the dead, by your Creator, and the Creator of the world, by Him who has power to send you to hell. Depart immediately with fear and with your army of terror. Depart from this servant of God [name], who takes refuge in the bosom of the Church."

Private exorcism, which is the private adjuring of the devil from harming someone, may be performed by any priest, and also by a lay person; for example, by the use of sacramentals such as holy water or by invoking the name of Jesus.

RITE OF PEACE. The sign of peace offered at Mass. After the priest has prayed for peace and unity in the Church, the people are asked to express their love for one another before they share the Eucharist. Practical details of how this should be done are determined by the national or regional Bishops' Conference in accordance with the sensibilities and conventions of the people.

RITIBUS EXSEQUIARUM. A decree of the Sacred Congregation for Divine Worship, giving the norms and ritual for Christian burial (August 15, 1969).

RITUAL. The prescribed words and ceremonies for a religious service. Refers also to the book that contains these prescriptions. In the Catholic Church these books are distinguished according to different offices, e.g., for bishops, and for different ceremonies, e.g., ordination. Ritual also means the whole body of sacred rites in use in the Church. (Etym. Latin *ritualis*, from *ritus*, rite, form.)

RITUAL, ROMAN. The book containing the prayers and ceremonies to be used by bishops, priests, and deacons in the sacred liturgy. In 1614, Pope Paul V ordered the publication of the first Roman Ritual, in order to unify what by then had become a variety of (sometimes) conflicting manuals in the Catholic Church. This was revised by Pope Benedict XIV in 1742, re-edited by Pope Leo XIII in 1884, and once more adapted by Pope Pius XI after the publication of the Code of Canon Law. The Second

Vatican Council decreed that all local rituals should be "adapted linguistically and otherwise to the needs of the different regions" and "in accordance with the new edition of the Roman Ritual" (*Constitution on the Liturgy,* III, 63).

RITUAL UNIONISM. A tendency in the ecumenical movement toward liturgical conformity among Christian churches without previous agreement on doctrine.

RIVERS OF PARADISE. Emblems of the four Evangelists whose gospels spread knowledge of the Word of God throughout the world. The symbol shows four streams of water flowing from a rock on which the Lamb of God stands mounted. Verdure is often introduced in the symbol to signify the fruitfulness of the "good news." The rivers Pison, Gihon, Tigris, and Euphrates are thought to be the streams so designated with John, Matthew, Mark, and Luke assigned to them in religious writings.

ROBBER COUNCIL OF EPHESUS. A synod held at Ephesus in 449 to vindicate Eutyches from St. Flavian's condemnation. After disgraceful scenes of violence, Eutyches was vindicated. Flavian and Theodoret then appealed to Rome. Excommunication followed for certain participants and the Pope declared all the council's actions null.

ROCAMADOUR. Near Toulouse, on a precipice above the valley, is a shrine to Mary. Legend has it that the founder of this shrine had personally known Christ. History dates it in the twelfth century, while popular belief dates it in the first. The eight-hundred-year-old statue of the seated Mother with the Child resting in her lap is made of wood. The expression on Mary's face is one of sorrow. Over two hundred steps lead from the valley to this shrine and basilica. Charlemagne, St. Louis, and Henry II of England made their way to the top, and the faithful today climb the steps as part of their devotion. Spain and France have both claimed the Mother of Rocamadour for their patroness.

ROCHET. A sleeved over-tunic of white linen, lace trimmed or embroidered, worn by bishops, abbots, and other prelates. It is an unofficial vestment. (Etym. Middle English *rochet,* red; from Latin *rubeus,* reddish.)

ROGATION DAYS. Prescribed days of prayer and penance in spring. Two sets of rogation days were kept since early Chris-

tian times: the Major Rogation on April 25, the Feast of St. Mark; and the Minor Rogations on the last three days before Ascension Thursday. They were instituted to appease divine justice, ask for protection, and invoke God's blessing on the harvest. The Litany of the Saints was chanted in procession and the Rogation Mass followed. The Feast of St. Mark, as the more ancient, was also called the Greater Litanies; it Christianized a pagan spring festival in honor of the god Robigus. The three other Rogation days were adapted in Rome under Pope Leo III (reigned 795–816). (Etym. Latin *rogatio,* inquiry, request.)

ROM. *Romanus, Romana*—Roman.

ROMAN CANON. The first Eucharistic prayer of the Mass, dating, with very slight changes, from the sixth century. It is based on the Gelasian Sacramentary, ascribed to Pope Gelasius I (reigned 492–96).

ROMAN CATACOMBS. A labyrinth of subterranean galleries where the early Christians buried their dead and held religious services. In times of persecution, besides a place to worship, they offered escape and concealment. Begun in apostolic times, they continued in use until A.D. 400. At that time there were twenty-five great catacombs and twenty lesser ones. Like all cemeteries, they were constructed from the first to the third mile outside Rome. The Christians made long recesses in the walls, not small niches for cinerary urns as did the non-Christians, to hold one to three bodies each. When filled they were hermetically sealed, and often the covering slab contained inscriptions or were decorated with various symbols; e.g., the Good Shepherd, dove, anchor, fish, and peacock. These were the first representations of Christian art. The space allotted to a burial was necessarily limited. Larger tombs were only for popes and martyrs. After 313 the catacombs were not really needed, but they remained places of pilgrimage until the seventh century. About this time the demand for relics grew and quantities of bones were taken from the catacombs to individual churches. The Church finally stopped the universal confiscation of relics. It was reported that twenty-eight cartloads were taken to the Pantheon from the catacombs for burial in the new St. Mary of the Martyrs. The old catacombs became overgrown and soon forgotten except the one under St. Sebastian's Church. In the sixteenth century interest revived and the search for other catacombs began. Today the Catacombs of Sebastian and Callistus are the most visited, with those of Sts. Domitilla, Agnes, Priscilla, and Pancratius also open to the public. The chief services in the catacombs were the Eucharistic celebration on the anniversaries of the martyrs. The inscriptions on the tomb slabs are among the earliest witnesses to the Christian faith. The 1929 concordat with Italy places the Holy See in charge of the catacombs, with responsibility for their maintenance, supervision, preservation, and expansion.

ROMAN CATHOLICISM. The faith, worship, and practice of all Christians in communion with the Bishop of Rome, whom they acknowledge as the Vicar of Christ and the visible head of the Church founded by Christ. The terms "Roman Church" and "Roman Catholic Church" date from at least the early Middle Ages, but the stress on these terms became prominent after the Protestant Reformation. The reason was to emphasize the distinctive quality of being not only a Christian, because baptized, but of being a Catholic, because in communion with the Pope.

ROMAN COLLAR. A stiff white linen neckband worn by the clergy as a distinguishing part of their public attire when outside the church or rectory. It is worn either with a black clerical shirt or attached to a breast piece called the rabat.

ROMANESQUE. An architectural style prevailing in Europe from the eleventh through the thirteenth centuries. Monastic in its origins, it is marked by thick walls, basilica or Greek cross ground plans, and vaulting of wide areas, as at Cluny and Speyer. The twelfth-century invention of rib vaults provided the basis for Gothic architecture.

ROMANIAN RITE. The rite followed by Catholics of the Byzantine, or Constantinople, Rite in Rumania.

ROMANISM. A pejorative term used of the Roman Catholic faith and practice; it came into vogue with the Protestant Reformation. Catholics are called Romanists and their religion is said to be Romish.

ROMANIZATION. A term applied to the tendency in some Protestant churches to accept Roman Catholic doctrine and adopt Catholic practices, especially in the liturgy.

ROMAN PRIMACY. The supreme and full power of jurisdiction possessed by divine right by the Bishop of Rome over the whole Church in matters of faith and in matters pertaining to the discipline and government of the Church spread throughout the world.

This power is not merely symbolic but real and truly episcopal; it is ordinary in belonging to the office; it is immediate and not dependent on any other human authority; and it affects each and every church, each and every pastor, and every single one of the faithful.

ROMAN QUESTION. See LATERAN TREATY.

ROMAN RITE. The manner of celebrating Mass, administering the sacraments and sacramentals, reciting the Divine Office, and performing other ecclesiastical functions, as authorized for the city and diocese of Rome. Its origin goes back to the more or less common but variable rite of the first three centuries. From the time of Pope St. Gregory the Great (reigned 590–604) the history was uniform, with four major stages of development. In the twelfth century the Roman Rite came to be used wherever Latin was used. During the Middle Ages it branched out into a great number of other rites, differing however only in unimportant details. In the sixteenth century (1570) Pope St. Pius V abolished most of these derived rites, but the Roman Rite by then had been deeply influenced by and received additions from the Gallican and Spanish rites. In the twentieth century, as a result of the Second Vatican Council, major revisions were again made. Yet, as Pope Paul VI declared, these revisions are not to contradict the Roman Rite, since "what is Roman is the foundation of our Catholicity" (Allocution *Facile Conicere*, October 14, 1968).

ROMAN ROTA. Originating as an extension of the Apostolic Chancery, it is essentially a tribunal of appeal for all the ecclesiastical cases in which the Roman Curia is competent and that are not reserved to other jurisdictions. It also receives cases of appeal for Vatican City State, and is a tribunal of first instance in cases reserved to the Holy See, or that the Pope has reserved for himself by means of a special rescript of the Apostolic Signature.

ROMANS, EPISTLE TO THE. Written by St. Paul at Corinth about A.D. 58, when he was about to leave for Jerusalem at the end of his third missionary journey. He was on his way to Rome. It is the only Pauline letter addressed to a church that the apostle had not personally founded, preparing the people for his visit to them. He dwells on the justification of humankind through faith in Jesus Christ, the sinfulness of the world, the meaning and fruits of justification, what faith is, and that its fruits are humility, obedience, unity, and charity. Christ, the second Adam, has more than compensated for the sin of the first Adam.

ROMAN SEE. The primatial see of Christendom, the seat of government of the universal Roman Catholic Church, the Papacy, the Apostolic See, the office of the supreme head of the Church. It was founded by St. Peter, the first Pope, in A.D. 42 and constitutes the historical foundation of the claim of the Bishops of Rome to Peter's Primacy. It was disputed by some on the ground that St. Peter never was in Rome, but it is now fully established that he was in Rome by archaeological discoveries. During the first century the Corinthian Church appealed to the Roman See to heal a schism and St. Ignatius of Antioch (d. A.D. 107) gratefully received instructions from the Roman Church. The bishops of the Roman See alone could summon councils, excommunicate from the Church, judge concerning Christian life and doctrine, and discipline offenders. In times of stress and difficulties as well as for decisions on faith and government, the first Christians regularly appealed to Rome. The Greek schismatics and the Protestants both challenged the authority of the Roman See, but by that time the unbroken succession of Bishops of Rome had established the foundations of Catholic faith and morality. Agreement with the Roman See was a test of orthodoxy according to the Fathers of the Church, e.g., St. Irenaeus (A.D. 180). Even when, during the Western Schism, the popes moved to Avignon, they were still Bishops of Rome, so that by the time of the Second Vatican Council, Pope Paul VI closed the council as the two hundred sixty-fourth bishop to rule the Roman See. Within the See's territorial limits are located the commissions, offices, and congregations that administer the affairs of the universal Church.

ROMAN VESTMENTS. A name popularly given to liturgical vestments for Mass, in contrast to the Gothic style. Roman vestments are post-Tridentine and are characterized by a broad and short stole, and a chasuble, practically rectangular in shape, and made of relatively stiff material so that the design flatly stands out.

ROME. The diocese of the Pope, also called the See of Peter, the Apostolic See, the Holy See, and the Eternal City. According to ancient tradition, St. Peter first came to Rome in A.D. 42; St. Paul arrived about A.D. 60. Both were martyred here under Nero, most probably in 64. The history of the city from that time to the present can be divided into several periods: 1. the age of persecution, to the Edict of Milan in 313; 2. freedom recognized by the empire and the building of the first churches, to the fall, in 476, of the Roman Empire in the West; 3. growing power of political rulers, in conflict with the papacy, to the coronation in 800 of Charlemagne as emperor by Pope Leo III; 4. consolidation of the Papal States, irreparably damaged by the Avignon residence of the popes, 1309–77; 5. after the Western Schism to the Reformation; 6. from the Reformation to the loss of the Papal States in 1870, until the Lateran Treaty in 1929; and 7. since the settling of the Roman Question to the present, when the Communist presence in Italy and Rome poses new challenges to the spiritual autonomy of the Holy See.

ROOD. A large crucifix with statues of Our Lady and St. John, one on either side, placed over the entrance to the choir or chancel on a screen or beam. It was often of richly carved wood, painted and gilded. The rood is also the True Cross on which Christ died. (Etym. Anglo-Saxon *rōd*, rod, pole, cross.)

ROSAC. *Rosaceus*—rose-colored (vestments).

ROSARY. A devotional prayer, mental and vocal, honoring the Blessed Mother of God. It is said on a string of beads made up of five sets each of one large and ten smaller beads, called decades. On the large beads the Pater Noster is said; on the small ones, the Hail Mary. The usual devotion is the fifteen decades, on the joyous, sorrowful, or glorious aspects of Our Lord and Our Lady's life. It is the most popular of all nonliturgical Catholic devotions and has been highly recommended by many popes. This is the standard Rosary. But there are other Rosaries also approved by the Church, notably of the Holy Trinity, Seven Dolors, Precious Blood, St. Bridget, St. Joseph, and the Rosary of the Lord. (Etym. Latin *rosarium*, rose garden.) See also GLORIOUS MYSTERIES, JOYFUL MYSTERIES, SORROWFUL MYSTERIES.

ROSE. An emblem of the Blessed Virgin, often referred to as the Mystical Rose. Mary's rose emblem is rendered as a design with five petals signifying Mary's five joys, "I was exalted like the rose plant in Jericho" (Ecclesiasticus 24:18). Mary's Rosary is symbolized by white, red, and yellow roses corresponding to the joyous, sorrowful, and glorious mysteries. St. Thérèse of Lisieux has her crucifix covered with a profusion of roses as her well-known emblem, reminiscent of the shower of roses she promised to send her friends on earth. St. Elizabeth of Hungary is also symbolized in art with roses, disguising her offerings to the poor. St. Dorothy is represented with a laden basket of roses, the miraculous gift she is reported to have sent the pagan Theophilus, who mocked her on the way to martyrdom. Rose-colored vestments may be used instead of purple on the third Sunday of Advent (Gaudete Sunday) and the fourth Sunday of Lent (Laetare Sunday). The liturgy of these Sundays is joyful.

ROSE WATER. Scented water used in certain ceremonies of the Byzantine Church, e.g., in the consecration of an altar. It is made by steeping or distilling rose petals in water. The petals of other fragrant flowers may be used to produce the equivalent of rose water.

ROSE WINDOW. A circular window, with mullions and tracery, usually radiating from the center, filled with stained glass. Characteristic of Gothic architecture, it went through various stages of development, finally becoming the center of a vast composition in a tier of lower windows.

ROSICRUCIANS. The Ancient Mystical Order Rosae Crucis (AMORC), a cultic organization that claims to unlock the secret wisdom of the ages, banish fears, and lead its followers to self-mastery. Founded at New York City in 1915 by H. Spencer Lewis, an occultist. Original Rosicrucianism is traced to a small book, *Fama Fraternitatis,* published by the Lutheran theologian Johann Andrea (1586–1654), telling the story of a fictitious person, Christian Rosenkreutz, who at sixteen made a pilgrimage to the Holy Land with an aged monk who died on the way. Rosenkreutz reputedly acquired a store of occult knowledge in Egypt, Morocco, and the Near East. Before he died he initiated eight men in his secrets. Ever since a variety of groups have claimed to be descendants of Rosenkreutz, besides the Lewis foundation. In one of its formal published statements, the Rosicrucians declared, "Because of its aggressiveness and growth, the Order Rosae Crucis of America, as well as in all other countries, has been condemned by the Pope as destructive to the principles of Roman Catholicism." The Holy Office in 1919 issued a statement forbidding Catholics to belong to theosophical societies such as the Rosicrucians.

ROSMINIANISM. A system of philosophy formulated by Antonio Rosmini-Serbati (1797–1855), founder of the Institute of Charity. Encouraged by Popes Pius VII, Gregory XVI, and Pius IX, he undertook a renewal of Italian philosophy, ostensibly following St. Thomas Aquinas. But the influence of Descartes, Kant, and Hegel shifted his thinking. He came to hold that the human mind is born with the idea of "being." In time it analyzes this basic idea to discover in it many other ideas, which are identical with those in the mind of God. Rosmini also taught that reason can explain the Trinity and that original sin is only a physical infection of the body. After his death forty of his propositions were condemned by Pope Leo XIII in 1887 and 1888.

ROTA. The Sacred Roman Rota, which for centuries has been one of the chief tribunals of the Roman Curia. Pope Innocent III gave it the right to pass sentence, and Pope Sixtus IV (1472) set its number at twelve members. Reorganized by Pope St. Pius X in 1908, it is essentially a tribunal of appeal for all cases that fall under the jurisdiction of the Roman Curia. However, it may also pass judgment on original cases reserved to the Holy See or requested by the Pope.

ROTA "STUDIUM." A program of studies in Rome for training Rota advocates, future judges, promoters of justice, and defenders of the bond in ecclesiastical courts. It is subject to the dean of the Rota. In order to obtain the title Rota Advocate from the Holy See, one must complete a three-year course.

R.P. *Reverendus Pater, Révérend Père*— Reverend Father.

RR. *Rerum*—of things, subjects; e.g., SS.RR. Ital.—Writers of Italian (historical) subjects.

R.R. Roman Ritual; *Reverendissimus*—Most Reverend.

R.R., RT. REV. Right Reverend.

R.S.V. Revised Standard Version.

RUB. *Ruber*—red.

RUBR. *Rubrica*—rubric.

RUBRICS. Originally red titles of law announcements. They are the directive precepts or liturgical provisions found in the Missal, including the Sacramentary and lectionary, and in the ritual, to guide bishops, priests, or deacons in the Eucharistic liturgy, the administration of sacraments and sacramentals, and the preaching of the Word of God. Rubrics are printed in red and are either obligatory or merely directive, as the context makes amply clear. (Etym. Latin *rubrica,* red earth; title of law written in red; hence law instruction.)

RULE. A principle or regular mode of action, prescribed by one in authority, for the well-being of those who are members of a society. It is in this sense that the organized methods of living the evangelical counsels are called rules, as the Rule of St. Augustine or St. Benedict. A rule may also be a customary standard that is not necessarily prescribed by authority, but voluntarily undertaken in order to regulate one's conduct for more effective moral living or more effective service of others. Finally rule may be distinguished from government, whether civil or ecclesiastical. Rule pertains to the possession or exercise of controlling power, whereas government refers more to actually causing another to obey one's will. (Etym. Latin *regula,* a rule; norm; measure.)

RULE OF FAITH. The norm that enables the faithful to know what to believe. The revealed Word of God in Sacred Scripture and sacred tradition is a remote rule of faith. But the teaching of the Church based on divine revelation is considered the immediate rule of faith.

RULES OF CONSCIENCE. Norms for deciding one's own course of action or advising others in following conscience. Three norms are standard in Catholic moral theology:

1. "We are obliged to use every care to have a true conscience when faced with moral decisions." Conscience is the immediate norm of morality by which a person is to guide his or her whole life and reach eternal destiny. It is imperative that this norm be suitably trained to meet the variety of circumstances that call for moral evaluation. Sound knowledge of the divine and ecclesiastical laws is primary, wise counsel should be readily available, humility of heart and sincere sorrow are necessary to remove the chief obstacles to a true conscience, namely pride and unrepentant sin. Frequent prayer is needed to obtain the light of God's grace.

2. "We must always act on the command of a certain conscience whether it commands or forbids some action, not only when it is true but also when it is in invincible error." The words "commands" and "forbids" need emphasis because if conscience permits or merely counsels some line of action there is no strict obligation to follow it. It is obvious why a true conscience must be followed. But even an invincibly erroneous conscience should be obeyed because failure to do so would mean that a person was acting contrary to the subjective norm of morality and therefore committing sin. Thus a person who is convinced that he or she ought to steal or tell lies in order to save a friend from grave danger is bound to do so. The critical term is "invincible ignorance," which means a lack of knowledge for which the person is not morally responsible. It would be vincible (removable) ignorance if it could have been removed by such reasonable care as a prudent and sincere person would use in similar circumstances.

3. "It is never permissible to act with a doubtful conscience." Thus an action that conscience does not definitely pronounce to be sinless must not be performed. The reason is that one who acts while doubtful whether his or her action is against the law or not implicitly wills what is sinful. This person says equivalently, "This action may be offensive to God, but I am going to do it anyway," freely and rashly choosing to act on an attitude of indifference to the will of God.

RUMOR. An unverified story or report that is taken seriously by others. It falls under the category of lying when circulated as though the rumor were certainly true.

RURAL DEAN. See ARCHPRIEST.

RUTH. A Moabite woman who married into a family that had left Bethlehem during a famine. The heroic mother of this family, Naomi, experienced stark tragedy during the next decade. Her husband and then both her married sons died, leaving her a widow in a foreign land. She decided in desperation to return to Judah, hoping for help from her kinfolk (Ruth 1–6). Her daughter-in-law, Ruth, refused to desert her, declaring, "Wherever you go, I will go, wherever you live, I will live. Your people shall be my people, and your God my God" (Ruth 1:16). Thus, they traveled together to Bethlehem. Ruth became a gleaner in the cornfields that were owned by Boaz, a well-to-do kinsman of Naomi's dead husband. Naomi returned Ruth's loving devotion by encouraging the friendship and protection of Boaz for her daughter-in-law. Eventually Ruth and Boaz were married and had a son named Obed, for whom Naomi acted as a nurse. Thus was the family line fostered that produced Obed, then Jesse, then David, and ultimately Jesus (Ruth 4:17).

RUTH, BOOK OF. One of the protocanonical writings of the Old Testament, narrating the story of a Bethlehem family in the time of the Judges. Its heroine is Ruth, daughter-in-law of Naomi. Although Ruth is a Moabite, she marries Boaz, a Jew, and becomes the great-grandmother of King David, of whose family Christ was born. The purpose of the book was twofold: to preserve the edifying story of David's ancestry, and to witness to the practice of extraordinary filial piety, rewarded by God.

RUTHENIAN RITE. The liturgy used by the Ruthenian Catholics in Poland, the United States, and elsewhere. Said in the Slavonic language, it differs but slightly from the Byzantine Rite in the Orthodox Church.

S

S. *Solemnis*—solemn, solemnity.

S., SACR. *Sacrum*—sacred.

SAB., SABB. *Sabbatum*—Sabbath, Saturday.

SABAOTH. A title of majesty applied mainly to God. The Hebrew word means "armies" or "hosts" and is found mainly in the expression "Lord of hosts," which occurs in the Old Testament no less than 282 times, all except 36 of which are in the prophetical books. From an early reference to Yahweh as the Lord who defended his people in battle, the term has come to mean God's dominion over the angels, good and bad, and a fortiori his power over the destinies of people. In the New Testament, except in a direct quotation from Isaiah, the name becomes "Lord of Sabaoth" (James 5:4).

SABBATH, BIBLICAL. The Jewish day of rest, with elaborate prescriptions for its observance. Failure to observe the Sabbath was one of the principal accusations of the Pharisees against Jesus. It began on Friday night at sundown and ended on Saturday at sundown. No manual labor was done on the Sabbath. This meant complete withdrawal from business and trade interests, and giving oneself to family, friends, and religion. On the preceptive side, the Sabbath was to intensify home life, deepen one's knowledge of religious history and religion, and above all concentrate on prayer and things of the spirit. Already in apostolic times (Acts 20:7) Christians transferred the Sabbath from the seventh to the first day of the week. Moreover, the Catholic understanding of Sunday as a Sabbath (rest) has never been as rigid as that of some Protestant groups, e.g., the Puritans.

SABBATICAL YEAR. The one year every seven during which the Jews were to observe a "sabbath," corresponding to the day of rest every week (Exodus 21:2-6; Deuteronomy 15:1-3). They were required to allow the land to remain fallow and have all debtors and slaves freed. The religious purpose of the sabbatical year was to teach the Israelites that God alone was the real owner of everything.

SABBATINE PRIVILEGE. The pious belief, approved by the Church, that the Blessed Virgin would be specially propitious to those who have worn the brown scapular of Our Lady of Mount Carmel and observed certain other practices. Specifically, Pope Paul V in 1613 authorized the following decree to be published: "It is permitted to the Carmelite Fathers to preach that the Christian people may believe that the Blessed Virgin will help by her continued assistance and her merits, particularly on Saturdays, the souls of the members of the Scapular Confraternity who have died in the grace of God, if in life they had worn the scapular, observed chastity according to their state of life, and recited the Office of the Blessed Virgin or observed the fasts of the Church, practicing abstinence on Wednesdays and Saturdays." There was an earlier version of the Sabbatine privilege that is now considered certainly erroneous, based on an alleged bull of Pope John XXII, supposedly published in 1322. This apocryphal document has the Pope say that Carmelites and others who wear the scapular would be delivered by the Blessed Virgin from purgatory on the Saturday after their death.

SABELLIANISM. A third-century heresy called after Sabellius, a theologian of the Monarchian school. His followers advocated belief in one Divine God, the Father who became Man in Jesus Christ and died to redeem the world. Later they modified this single belief to profess that, though only one Person, God had three modes or aspects of manifesting himself as Creator, Redeemer, and Sanctifier. This heresy, known in the East as Sabellianism, in the West was called Patripassianism. It was condemned by Pope St. Callistus I but remained in Christian history under a variety of other forms.

SACKCLOTH. Penitential garb made of a heavy, coarse-textured material or hair cloth. It is worn next to the skin as a token of sorrow for sin or simply as a form of penance.

SACRAL. That which pertains to the worship and service of God, as distinct from the profane, which pertains to the service and needs of human beings. (Etym. Latin *sacer,* sacred.)

SACRAMENT. A sensible sign, instituted by Jesus Christ, by which invisible grace and inward sanctification are communicated to the soul. The essential elements of a sacrament of the New Law are institution by Christ the God-man during his visible stay on earth, and a sensibly perceptible rite that actually confers the supernatural grace it symbolizes. In a broad sense every external sign of internal divine blessing is a sacrament. And in this sense there were already sacraments in the Old Law, such as the practice of circumcision. But, as the Council of Trent defined, these ancient rites differed essentially from the sacraments of the New Law, they did not really contain the grace they signified, nor was the fullness of grace yet available through visible channels merited and established by the Savior. (Etym. Latin *sacramentum,* oath, solemn obligation; from *sacrare,* to set apart as sacred, consecrate.)

SACRAMENTAL. Objects or actions that the Church uses after the manner of sacraments, in order to achieve through the merits of the faithful certain effects, mainly of a spiritual nature. They differ from sacraments in not having been instituted by Christ to produce their effect in virtue of the ritual performed. Their efficacy depends not on the rite itself, as in the sacraments, but on the influence of prayerful petition; that of the person who uses them and of the Church in approving their practice. The variety of sacramentals spans the whole range of times and places, words and actions, objects and gestures that, on the Church's authority, draw not only on the personal dispositions of the individual but on the merits and prayers of the whole Mystical Body of Christ.

SACRAMENTAL CHARACTER. The indelible sign imprinted on the soul when the sacraments of baptism, confirmation, and the priesthood are received. This sign is indelible because it remains even in a person who may lose the state of grace or even the virtue of faith. It perdures at least until death and most likely into eternity. It is a sign because it signifies that the one baptized, confirmed, and ordained bears a special and unique relationship to Christ. It is a character because it permanently seals the person with a supernatural quality, comparable to the character that identifies each individual as a distinct personality. It is finally a character because it empowers the one who receives with the abilities that no one else possesses. In essence the sacramental character assimilates a person to the priesthood of Christ. From this primary function, secondary functions flow, in increasing order of sublimity, from baptism through confirmation to holy orders.

SACRAMENTAL CONFESSION. The auricular confession of one's sins in the sacrament of penance. If they are mortal sins, it is required that they be confessed as to number, type, and such circumstances as affect the gravity of the sins committed.

SACRAMENTAL DISPOSITIONS. Condition of soul required for the valid and/or fruitful reception of the sacraments. The dispositions differ between minister and recipient. In the minister is required merely the faculty of conferring a given sacrament, and the willingness to carry out the intention of Christ or the Church, even just to satisfy another person's wish or desire. In the recipient who has the use of reason is required merely that no obstacles be placed in the way. Such obstacles are a lack of faith or sanctifying grace or of a right intention.

SACRAMENTAL GRACE. The grace conferred by the valid and fruitful reception of the sacraments. It may be one or more of several kinds: 1. sanctifying grace is communicated in baptism, penance and in anointing of the sick when needed; 2. sanctifying grace is always increased when a sacrament is received in the state of grace; 3. actual grace is given by all the sacraments, either actually at the time of reception or also by title as a person needs divine help; 4. the sacramental character is indelibly imprinted on the soul in baptism, confirmation, and the priesthood; and 5. a distinctive sacramental grace is imparted by each of the seven sacraments, corresponding to their respective purpose in the supernatural life of the soul. See also ACTUAL GRACE, EFFICACIOUS GRACE, GRACE, GRATUITOUS GRACE, HABITUAL GRACE, JUSTIFYING GRACE, SANATING GRACE, SANCTIFYING GRACE, SUFFICIENT GRACE.

SACRAMENTALI COMMUNIONE. Instruction of the Sacred Congregation for Divine Worship on receiving Holy Communion under both kinds. Permission is granted "in order that the fullness of sign in the Eucharistic banquet may be seen more clearly by the faithful" (June 29, 1970).

SACRAMENTAL MATTER AND FORM. The rite of each of the seven sacraments, viewed as consisting of the materials used and actions performed, which constitute the matter, and the words pronounced, which constitute the form.

SACRAMENTAL PRESENCE. The manner of presence of Christ in the Holy Eucharist. He is really, truly, and substantially "contained" under the appearances of bread and wine, in such a way that where they are and as long as they are, he is there in the fullness of his divinity and humanity. See also REAL PRESENCE.

SACRAMENTAL SEAL. See SEAL OF CONFESSION.

SACRAMENTAL SIGN. The external ritual by which a sacrament is performed and through which the distinctive graces of that sacrament are conferred. The Catholic Church believes that the essential element of each sacrament was originally determined by Christ, e.g., the pouring of water, and the Trinitarian formula in baptism. Other features of the sacramental ritual have been determined by the Church, acting under the guidance of the Holy Spirit.

SACRAMENTARY. That part of the Roman Missal which contains the prayers and directives for Mass, and a number of sacramental formulas, but does not include the readings of the Mass. In the Western Church, sacramentaries, as distinct from lectionaries, were in use down to the thirteenth century. The Leonine, Gelasian, and Gregorian Sacramentaries, the main sources for the early history of the Mass, are the best known. From the ninth century on, the advantage of having everything in one book led to combining the sacramentary, lectionary, and gradual into one book, which came to be known as the Missal. The sacramentary was restored after the Second Vatican Council.

SACRAMENT HOUSE. A method of housing the Blessed Sacrament in a tabernacle outside the sanctuary usually on the north side of the church. Sometimes it was richly canopied and the repository screened so that the Host could be dimly seen. It was widely used in Switzerland, Belgium, and Germany until the last half of the nineteenth century.

SACRAMENT OF CONFESSION. A popular name for the sacrament of penance, centering on the accusation of oneself to a priest in order to obtain absolution.

SACRAMENT OF GOD. Jesus Christ as the visible incarnation of the Son of God through whose Passion, Death, and Resurrection the human race receives the grace of salvation and sanctification.

SACRAMENT OF PENANCE. The sacrament that, by means of certain acts of the penitent and by the absolution of a qualified priest, remits sins committed after baptism. As defined by the Catholic Church, it is "truly and properly a sacrament, instituted by Christ our Lord, for reconciling the faithful to God as often as they fall into sin after baptism" (Denzinger 1701). The required acts of the penitent are contrition, confession, and the willingness to make satisfaction. These acts are called the matter of the sacrament. The priest's absolution is the form.

The sacrament of penance was instituted by Christ on Easter Sunday night, when he told the Apostles, "Receive the Holy Spirit. For those whose sins you forgive, they are forgiven; for those whose sins you retain, they are retained" (John 20:22–23). The Catholic Church interprets these words to imply that Christ conferred on the Apostles and their successors not merely the right to declare that a person's sins are forgiven but also the power of forgiving in Christ's name those who are judged worthy of remission and of withholding absolution for those who are not disposed to be absolved.

SACRAMENT OF RECONCILIATION. Another name for the sacrament of penance, focusing on the principal effect of this sacrament, namely the healing of estrangement from God caused by one's sins.

SACRAMENT OF SALVATION. The Church as the necessary means of salvation for humankind. All who are saved, therefore, receive the necessary grace somehow through the visible Church founded by Christ.

SACRAMENT OF THE ALTAR. The Eucharist viewed as the body and blood of

Christ, which are offered on the altar in the Sacrifice of the Mass. Also the Eucharist as reserved on the altar for adoration by the faithful.

SACRAMENT OF THE APOSTOLATE. The sacrament of confirmation viewed as divinely established for enabling Christians not only to preserve their own faith but to share it with others. Its effects are similar to what occurred on Pentecost Sunday, when the Holy Spirit came down on the Apostles and gave them the wisdom, zeal, and courage they needed to proclaim the Gospel and promote the Kingdom of Christ.

SACRAMENTS OF THE DEAD. Those sacraments which can be validly and fruitfully received when a person is not in the state of grace. They are baptism, penance, and, if needed, anointing of the sick. These sacraments confer or restore sanctifying grace and confer actual graces when received by one who is already in God's friendship.

SACRAMENTS OF THE LIVING. The sacraments that require the state of grace to be received fruitfully. They are confirmation, the Eucharist, matrimony, and the priesthood. Of these four, however, confirmation, matrimony, and priesthood are received validly even in the state of grave sin. So that a person is really confirmed, married, or ordained, but does not obtain the graces associated with the sacraments until the state of grace is recovered. The Eucharist is also truly received by a person not in the state of grace but who commits a grave sin of sacrilege if he or she culpably approaches Holy Communion while estranged from divine friendship. The sacrament of anointing is in a class by itself, since it can be fruitfully received even in the state of grave sin. But it is considered a sacrament of the living because it should be received in the state of grace. Under certain conditions, however, it also restores sanctifying grace.

SACRAM LITURGIAM. Apostolic letter of Pope Paul VI by which were decreed certain prescriptions of the Second Vatican Council's Constitution on the Liturgy. Among its provisions was the establishment of diocesan liturgical commissions and the requirement that all liturgical texts be formally approved by the Holy See (January 25, 1964).

SACRAM UNCTIONEM INFIRMORUM. Apostolic Constitution of Pope Paul VI, issued in 1973, revising the administration of the sacrament of anointing of the sick (No-

vember 30, 1972). The new rite took effect on January 6, 1974.

SACRARIUM. See PISCINA.

SACRED. The holy or divine. The sacred is that which pertains to God, as distinguished from what pertains to human beings; that which is eternal, in contrast with the temporal; the heavenly as opposed to the earthly; the mysterious and therefore not the rationally explainable; the infinite and not the finite. In all religions, the sacred is the Absolute, which does not change, whereas the profane is the relative, whose essence is to change. (Etym. Latin *sacrare*, to set apart as sacred, consecrate.)

SACRED COLLEGE. See COLLEGE OF CARDINALS.

SACRED CONGREGATIONS. Permanent commissions of cardinals established in Rome for handling the business of the Church. The competence of the various congregations is determined by their administrative responsibilities, although there is not in the Roman Curia a real distinction between legislation and administration. They came into existence as the work of the Apostolic Chancery grew in complexity and the Pope needed stable branches of government immediately subject to his jurisdiction. The first such commission with permanent character was the Sacred Congregation of the Inquisition, set up by Pope Paul III in 1542.

SACRED CONSISTORY. See CONSISTORY.

SACRED HEART. The physical Heart of Christ as the principal sign and symbol of the threefold love with which he loves his eternal Father and all mankind. It is, therefore, a symbol of the divine love he shares with the Father and the Holy Spirit but that he, the Word made flesh, alone manifests through a weak and perishable body, since "in Him dwells the fullness of the Godhead bodily" (Colossians 2:9). It is, besides, the symbol of that burning love which, infused into his soul, enriches the human will of Christ and enlightens and governs its acts by the most perfect knowledge derived both from the beatific vision and that which is directly infused. And finally it is the symbol also of sensible love, since the body of Christ possesses full powers of feeling and perception, in fact more so than any other human body (Pope Pius XII, *Haurietis Aquas*, II, 55–57).

SACRED HEART BADGE. A cloth or plastic emblem with a picture of Christ with his Heart on one side, and an image of the Heart of Jesus alone on the reverse. Appropriate invocations surround the picture and image. The badge may be worn inside one's clothing or carried in one's purse or wallet or, in a hospital, is often pinned to a patient's bed. It is commonly distributed by the League of the Sacred Heart.

SACRED HEART DEVOTION. The subjective response of the faithful to the objective fact of Christ's love, divine and human, symbolized in his physical Heart. Historically the Devotion to the Sacred Heart is an outgrowth of devotion to Christ's sacred humanity, which the Church has more than once defended as adorable because the human nature of Christ forms one Person with the divine nature, and that Person is divine. A series of mystics over centuries contributed to the development of this devotion, notably St. Bernard of Clairvaux (1090–1153), St. Bonaventure (1221–74), St. Mechtilde (1210–80), St. Gertrude (1256–1302), St. Frances of Rome (1384–1440), St. Francis de Sales (1567–1622), and St. John Eudes (1601–80). But it was especially St. Margaret Mary Alacoque (1647–90), whose revelations before the Blessed Sacrament gave the devotion its modern aspect and importance. Through her Jesuit spiritual director, Claude de la Colombière (1641–82), the Society of Jesus made promotion of the cultus of the Sacred Heart part of its institute, notably through the Apostleship of Prayer.

SACRED HEART OF JESUS SCAPULAR. Not the familiar badge of the Sacred Heart, the scapular is white, bearing pictures of the Heart of Jesus and the Heart of Mary. Approved by Pope Leo XIII.

SACRED HISTORY. The history of God's dealings with humanity as recorded in the Old and New Testaments. The term is sometimes used in an uncomplimentary sense to describe the Christian Gospels, which rationalist critics say are overladen with nonfactual and mythological lore that belongs to a credulous former age.

SACRED PENITENTIARY. See APOSTOLIC PENITENTIARY.

SACRIFICE. The highest form of adoration, in which a duly authorized priest in the name of the people offers a victim in acknowledgment of God's supreme dominion and of total human dependence on God. The victim is at least partially removed from human use and to that extent more or less destroyed as an act of submission to the divine majesty. Thus a sacrifice is not only

an oblation. Where an oblation offers something to God, a sacrifice immolates or gives up what is offered. In sacrifice the gift offered is something precious completely surrendered by the one making the sacrifice as a token of humble recognition of God's sovereignty. (Etym. Latin *sacrum,* holy, sacred + *facere,* to make, do.)

SACRIFICE, NEW TESTAMENT. While Christ allowed the Mosaic sacrifice in his day, he predicted the end of the Temple and its worship (Mark 13:2; John 4:20–23). At the Last Supper, when instituting the Eucharist, he declared, "This is my body which will be given up for you; do this as a memorial of me . . . This cup is the new covenant in my blood which will be poured out for you" (Luke 22:19–20). Throughout the writings of St. Paul, Christ is identified as the Sacrificial Victim (I Corinthians 5:7; Ephesians 5:2) and further confirmed by the Catholic Epistles (I Peter 1:19; I John 2:2). The eternal nature of the Lord's Sacrifice is assumed (Revelation 13:8), and the whole letter to the Hebrews is about the high priesthood of Christ, who by his perfect obedience has "offered one single sacrifice for sins, and then taken his place forever at the right hand of God" (Hebrews 10:12–13). He is, therefore, the eternal priest who even now intercedes with his heavenly Father for a sinful humanity.

SACRIFICE, OLD TESTAMENT. As described in the books of the Old Law, sacrifice essentially meant honoring God by offering him some of the creatures that are precious to human beings, in acknowledgment of God's sovereignty and human dependence on the Creator. Two kinds of sacrifice are recognized and required of humanity, the bloody and the unbloody. Four kinds of bloody sacrifices are described: 1. holocaust was the most perfect, also called the whole-burnt offering; the animal or other object was completely consumed by fire, and as the "perpetual sacrifice" it was offered twice daily, morning and evening; 2. sin offering was to expiate misdeeds committed through ignorance or inadvertence; the kind of victim depended mainly on the dignity of the person offended; 3. guilt offering was especially prescribed for sins demanding restitution; 4. peace offerings were either in gratitude or in fulfillment of a vow, or simply voluntary; part of the ceremony of this kind of sacrifice was that part of what was offered was returned to the one offering, to be eaten in a sacrificial meal.

Unbloody sacrifices were really oblations and, with the exception of incense, were offerings of articles of solid or liquid food. These food offerings accompanied every holocaust and peace offering, but never sacrifice for sin or guilt, except at the cleansing of a leper.

SACRIFICE OF THE MASS. See MASS.

SACRIFICE OF THE NEW LAW. The Sacrifice of the Mass, which is the unbloody representation of Christ's sacrifice of the Cross, in contrast to the bloody sacrifices of animals in the Old Law.

SACRILEGE. The deliberate violation of sacred things. Sacred things are persons, places, and objects set aside publicly and by the Church's authority for the worship of God. The violation implies that a sacred thing is desecrated precisely in its sacred character. It is a sin against the virtue of religion.

Personal sacrilege is committed by laying violent hands on clerics or religious of either sex; by unlawfully citing them before secular courts, i.e., without just cause and without express permission of their ecclesiastical superiors; by unlawfully demanding of them the payment of civil taxes or military service; and by the commission of acts of unchastity by or with a person bound by the public vow of chastity.

Sacred places are violated by sacrilege through defilement, e.g., serious and unjust shedding of blood, as in willful homicide or by putting the sacred place (church or shrine) to unseemly use, e.g., secular trading, acts of debauchery; by grave theft from the Church or consecrated edifice; and by violating the immunity of a place as having the right of sanctuary.

Sacred objects are desecrated by sacrilege whenever something sacred is used for an unworthy purpose. This includes the Mass and the sacraments, along with sacramentals; sacred vessels and church furnishings; and ecclesiastical property. Desecration in each of these areas includes the deliberate invalid reception of the sacraments, simulation of Mass, grave irreverence to the Eucharist; gravely profane use of sacred vessels or vestments; and the unlawful seizure of sacred things or ecclesiastical property.

Sacrilege is many times reprobated in Sacred Scripture, notably in the second book of Maccabees and in the writings of St. Paul. Grave sacrilege in the Old Testament was punishable by death, and in the Catholic Church is considered a mortal sin. (Etym. Latin *sacrilegium,* the robbing of a temple, the stealing of sacred things.)

SACRISTAN. A person appointed for the care of the sacristy, sacred vessels, vestments, and other articles required by the ceremonial for any liturgical function.

SACRISTY. A room attached to a church, usually near the altar, where the clergy vest for ecclesiastical functions. The sacristy affords storage for sacred vessels, vestments, and other articles needed for liturgical use. The sacrarium is usually located there. (Etym. Latin *sacristia,* from *sacrum,* holy, sacred.) See also PISCINA.

SACROSANCTUM CONCILIUM. The Constitution on the Sacred Liturgy of the Second Vatican Council. It was the first document issued by the Council, whose purpose was expressed in the opening paragraph: ". . . to impart an ever increasing vigor to the life of the faithful; to adapt more closely to the needs of our age those institutions which are subject to change; to foster whatever can promote union among all who believe in Christ; to strengthen whatever can help to call all mankind into the Church's fold" (December 4, 1963).

SACRUM CHRISMA. See CHRISM.

SACRUM DIACONATUS ORDINEM. Apostolic letter of Pope Paul VI setting down the general norms for restoring the permanent diaconate in the Latin Rite of the Church. This document sets down definite norms to be followed, among which are: 1. minimum age of twenty-five for the permanent diaconate; 2. obligation to celibacy for those ordained deacons as unmarried men; 3. privilege of married men "of more advanced age" being ordained permanent deacons, i.e., at least thirty-five years old; 4. rights of permanent deacons to administer the sacraments; offering Mass, giving confirmation and absolution, conferring anointing of the sick, and ordaining others are excepted; 5. all the liturgical privileges (June 18, 1967).

SADDUCEES. A small group in Jewish society, contemporaneous with Christ, who attracted to their ranks rich, educated, and conservative Jews. In religion, they supported only doctrines that they found in written law. The Pharisees indulged in constant controversy with them over oral and unwritten tradition. The Sadducees were well treated by the Roman government because they supported the established order. Because they had substantial representation in the Sanhedrin, they exercised an influence out of proportion to their numbers in Temple affairs and ceremonies. In one significant activity the Sadducees and the Pharisees were united: ridiculing and denouncing Jesus and his teaching. Frequently they challenged or baited him in his public appearances. John the Baptist called them "a brood of vipers" (Matthew 3:7). Jesus denounced both groups, warning his followers against their false teachings (Matthew 16:12). The Sadducees persisted in their anti-Christian persecution; for instance, they had Peter and John arrested for spreading word of Jesus' resurrection (Acts 4). Their numbers and influence waned as the first century moved along. Little was heard of them after the destruction of the Temple in the year 70. (Etym. Greek *saddukaioi*, popular meaning "righteous.")

SADNESS. The pain caused by the awareness of some personally experienced evil. Unlike sorrow, which implies a sense of loss or of guilt and remorse, sadness includes past, present, and especially future evils. It is nurtured by preoccupation with the dark side of one's own life, as distinct from pity, which is sorrow for another's pain or loss, and from envy, which is sorrow for another's good.

SAEC. *Saeculum*—century.

ST. ANDREW'S CROSS. Emblem assigned since the fourteenth century representing this Apostle. It resembles the letter X, Greek letter *chi*, with bars of equal length in a slanting position, sometimes called the saltire or transverse cross or crux decussata. It was the cross used in St. Andrew's crucifixion.

ST. ANN (National shrine). Founded in New Orleans in 1852 by Archbishop Antoine Blanc as St. Ann's Church. On May 18, 1926, in a papal brief, Pope Pius XI made it the national shrine of St. Ann for the United States. A shrine bureau was established, and *St. Ann's Herald* became the official publication. Upwards of seventy thousand letters asking for prayers and favors come to the shrine annually.

ST. BENEDICT SCAPULAR. Badge of a confraternity founded in England, in 1865, to give its members a share in the works of the Benedictine Order. It is black and usually bears on one part a picture of St. Benedict. Approved by Pope Leo XIII.

ST. BENEDICT'S MEDAL. A frequently indulgenced medal that bears the image of the Father of Western Monasticism. In his right hand is a cross, next to which is the inscription *"Crux Patris Benedicti"* (The Cross

of the Father Benedict). In his left hand is a copy of the Rule of St. Benedict. At his feet are images of a chalice and raven, symbols of the priesthood and the life of a hermit. Around the edge of the medal are the words *"Eius in Obitu Nostro Praesentia Muniamur,"* referring to Christ (At our death may we be strengthened by his presence). On the reverse side is a cross on whose vertical bar are the initial letters of the invocation, *"Crux Sancta Sit Mihi Lux"* (The Holy Cross be my light). On the horizontal bar are the initials of *"Non Draco Sit Mihi Dux"* (Let not the dragon be my guide), referring to Satan. Around the medal are other letters signifying other Latin sayings. At the top is usually the single word *Pax* (Peace), the characteristic motto of St. Benedict; or the monogram IHS, the first three letters in Greek of the name Jesus.

ST. BLAISE BLESSING. A special blessing of throats on the feast of St. Blaise (February 3), martyr and Bishop of Sebaste in Armenia (died c. 316). According to legend, he had been a physician who was cast into prison by the pagans in the persecution of Emperor Licinius. He performed a marvelous cure on the throat of a child who was choking on a fishbone it had swallowed. Ever since, St. Blaise has been invoked against throat troubles. He is honored as one of the Fourteen Holy Helpers. On his feast day the faithful receive the blessing of St. Blaise, given by a priest holding two candles against the throat, while saying, "Through the intercession of St. Blaise, Bishop and Martyr, may God deliver you from illness of the throat and from every other evil. In the name of the Father, and of the Son, and of the Holy Spirit. Amen."

ST. CHRISTOPHER MEDAL. One of the most popular religious medals of our day. St. Christopher is pictured carrying the Child on his shoulder. The story is told that this third-century saint as a big-bodied youth served God and his neighbor well by carrying people over a dangerous river that had taken the lives of many. Among those he carried across was Christ himself, who, on one occasion, appeared to Christopher (Greek, Christ-Bearer) in the form of a child. He is the special patron and helper of travelers, especially those who travel by plane and automobile. Hence the custom of having St. Christopher medals (or statuettes) on the dashboard of automobiles. The feast of St. Christopher is on July 25 and his name remains on the Church calendars of particular regions. It no longer appears in the universal calendar because his cultus (like that of many saints) was not originally part of the liturgical tradition of the city of Rome, unlike other early saints, e.g., Sts. Agatha, Agnes, and Cecilia. But the Church has not removed him from veneration by the faithful as a saint.

ST. DOMINIC SCAPULAR. A white scapular, usually with a picture of St. Dominic on one part and of Blessed Reginald on the other. Promoted by the Dominicans, it was approved by Pope St. Pius X.

SAINTE-ANNE-DE-BEAUPRÉ. Canadian shrine dedicated to the mother of Mary, located twenty-seven miles northeast of Quebec on the St. Lawrence River. Hundreds of thousands of ill and crippled people flock to this shrine each year, where it is said that every known disease has been cured at one time or another. Tradition says that the first chapel was built in 1658 by sailors in thanksgiving for their rescue in a storm. However, it was soon swept away, as it was too near the shore. A larger chapel was erected in 1662, but this was demolished through some error of misdirection in 1876. The present Romanesque basilica is the fourth church dedicated to St. Anne of the Meadows.

ST. JAMES, RITE OF. One of the Oriental rites of the Catholic Church, belonging to the group of the rites of Antioch, along with pure Antiochene, the Chaldean, Malabar, Byzantine, and Armenian. With the Rite of St. James are the Greek, Syriac, and Maronite Rites. The Rite of St. James is traditionally attributed to the Apostle of that name, St. James the Less, the author of the Epistle in the New Testament, first Bishop of Jerusalem, who was martyred there by being thrown down from the pinnacle of the Temple.

ST. JOHN CHRYSOSTOM, RITE OF. Sometimes loosely identified with the Byzantine Rite. Actually St. John's role in reforming the earlier Rite of St. Basil was only a later development. Specifically, Chrysostom is said to have "left out a great deal and shortened all the forms" of the liturgy of St. Basil. His motive was "so that no one would stay away from this apostolic and divine institution" (*De Traditione Divinae Missae,* PG 65:851).

ST. JOHN LATERAN. One of five great basilicas in Rome and the mother and head of all churches. It was founded by Emperor Constantine (c. 274–337) near the Lateran Palace, which he presented to Pope Sylvester as his episcopal residence and which was used by all the popes until 1309 when the papacy moved to Avignon. The church was dedicated to the Holy Savior and became the prior church of Christendom. Its canons even today take precedence over those from St. Peter's. The primitive church was destroyed by earthquake in 898. The reconstruction was partly burned in 1308 and rebuilt. The present interior is severe but rich in its proportions. Paired columns, with niches between and holding mammoth statues of the Apostles, fill both sides of the nave, while above them are reliefs taken from the Old and New Testaments. Still higher up are medallions of the Prophets leading the eye to the gorgeous ceiling with the numerous papal arms and emblems of Christ's Passion. The apse, reconstructed by Pope Leo XIII, contains precious mosaics of the thirteenth century depicting the union of the kingdom of earth and heaven as united in baptism. The high altar covers many relics including the heads of Sts. Peter and Paul, and St. Peter's small altar from the catacombs. Preserved here is the cedar table that according to tradition was used at the Last Supper. As long as the popes were in residence at the Lateran Palace, the basilica saw the coronations and entombments of the popes and was the place where four ecumenical councils were held in 1123, 1139, 1179, and 1215. Connected with the famous basilica is the Lateran Baptistery, for a long time the only one in Rome and since then the model for all others. Constantine was baptized in the year 337 shortly before his death, at the porphyry bath that is still preserved there.

ST. JOSEPH, DEVOTION TO. Manifestation of reverence for the spouse of the Virgin Mary.

In the first centuries of the Church, there was no sign of a liturgical devotion to St. Joseph, which parallels the slow development of Marian piety and is understandable in view of the need first to stabilize the Church's Christology. However, the Eastern Fathers since the fourth century, such as Ephrem, John Damascene, and John Chrysostom, often speak of Joseph and extol his purity of life as in the classic phrase of St. Ephrem (306–73): "No one can worthily praise St. Joseph." The Latin Fathers, notably Jerome and Augustine, stress the justice of Mary's spouse, in the biblical sense of his fidelity to the laws of God. The earliest public cultus of St. Joseph appeared in the East, with June 20 the commemorative feast. Later Oriental sources variously assigned December 25, 26, and the Sunday before or after Christmas as feast days honoring St. Joseph at the head of other persons associated with the birth of Christ. By the ninth century the Western martyrologies celebrated his memory on March 19. The Crusades gave great impetus to the devotion, as seen in the basilica that the Crusaders built in honor of St. Joseph at Nazareth.

From the Middle Ages on, the veneration of the foster-father of Jesus entered the full stream of Christian piety, through the writings and preaching of Sts. Peter Damian, Bernard of Clairvaux, Thomas Aquinas, and Bernardine of Siena. Before the Council of Trent, the Feast of St. Joseph (March 19) was placed in the Roman Breviary by Pope Sixtus IV in 1479. And after Trent, by a decree of 1621, Pope Gregory XV made it a day of obligatory attendance at Mass and abstention from servile work, which it still remains according to canon law, except in certain countries such as the United States.

A parallel feast to honor the patronage of St. Joseph was extended by Pope Pius IX in 1870 to the whole Christian world, and at the same time the saint was declared "Patron of the Universal Church." In 1955, Pope Pius XII instituted a new feast of St. Joseph the Worker for May 1, and March 19 now commemorates his patronage of the Church.

St. Joseph's pre-eminent sanctity, which places him next to the Blessed Virgin among the saints, was confirmed by many papal documents, especially those of Popes Leo XIII and Pius XII. He is invoked as the patron of a happy death, and by a long-standing custom the month of March and each Wednesday of the week are dedicated to him. In paintings and statues he is usually shown with the Child Jesus and a lily or staff. More recent artists picture him with a carpenter's square or other instrument of his trade in his hand.

ST. JOSEPH'S ORATORY. A shrine, located in Montreal, honoring the saint who fostered the Christ Child's care. This classic Renaissance cathedral stands near the summit of Mount Royal, overlooking Canada's largest city. Its construction is due to the efforts of Brother André (1845–1937), a member of the Holy Cross order, who had an intense devotion to St. Joseph. He served his order as a porter for many years, all the time dreaming of a monument to honor his beloved saint. The small wooden chapel was authorized in 1904, and word soon spread that the sick were being healed whenever the self-denying Brother touched their wounds.

Crutches and votive plaques marked the spot where so many physical and spiritual miracles took place. Elevators now bear the aged and infirm to the dome, and the great cathedral now houses a library where every important book or document published on St. Joseph has been collected, a radio station, and a vast tape and film collection.

ST. JOSEPH SCAPULAR. It is violet with white bands. On each half is a square of gold cloth. The one on the front has a picture of St. Joseph with the words, "St. Joseph, Patron of the Church, Pray for Us." On the other part are the papal crown and keys with the words, "The Spirit of the Lord is his guide." It is promoted by the Capuchin Fathers and was approved by Pope Leo XIII.

ST. LAWRENCE OUTSIDE THE WALLS. The fifth of the major basilicas of Rome. Emperor Constantine erected a church on this site in A.D. 330 over the graves of St. Lawrence and St. Cyriaca. It was remodeled in the sixth century and again in the thirteenth century, and the portico was added. Modern paintings looking like mosaics adorn the façade. The vestibule has many sarcophagi with high relief embellishing them, also frescoes around the walls with stories depicting St. Lawrence, St. Stephen, and Hippolytus. The campanile dates from the twelfth century. In the interior the nave and side aisles are of thirteenth-century construction—grand with their twenty-two antique columns, modern paintings of St. Lawrence and St. Stephen, and the mosaic floor. Here too is the crypt containing the bodies of Lawrence, Justin, and Stephen under the high altar, with its magnificent canopy. In the near vicinity the pilgrim sees the tall column with the martyred deacon on its top.

SAINTLINESS. The practice of such virtue as the faithful commonly associate with those whom the Church honors as saints.

ST. MICHAEL SCAPULAR. It is designed as a shield, and one part is blue, the other black, and the connecting bands are blue and black. Each part has a picture of St. Michael slaying the dragon, and the inscription, "Who is like God?" It is a badge of the Confraternity of St. Michael. It was approved by Pope Leo XIII.

ST. PAUL'S OUTSIDE THE WALLS. One of the five great basilicas of Rome. Founded in 386 by Emperor Valentinian II (372–92), it was finished by his successor, Flavius Honorius, on the site of the church built by

Emperor Constantine over the tomb of St. Paul. It was almost totally destroyed by fire in 1823. Rebuilt to the same dimensions as the original with help from many parts of the world, it was consecrated by Pope Pius IX in 1854. The interior is imposing with its broad nave, eighty columns of granite brought from Lake Maggiore, dividing the side aisles and the central area. Above the arches are the mosaic portrait medallions of every pope through Pope Benedict XV. The high altar is surmounted by the famous Arnolfo di Cambio tabernacle, the exterior reliefs on it taken from the Old Testament. Four columns of Oriental alabaster support the canopy over it. Under it in a splendid casket are the mortal remains of St. Paul. The triumphal arch, at the apse end, was saved from the conflagration along with its exquisite fifth-century mosaics of the head of Christ centered in glory and surrounded by the twenty-four elders with St. Peter and St. Paul below them.

ST. PETER'S. See BASILICA OF ST. PETER'S.

ST. PETER'S CROSS. One of St. Peter's symbols—the upside-down Latin cross on which the Apostle died at his own request; an emblem since the fourth century. This symbol, with its crossed keys, is particular to the first Pope.

SAINTS. A name given in the New Testament to Christians generally (Colossians 1:2) but early restricted to persons who were eminent for holiness. In the strict sense saints are those who distinguish themselves by heroic virtue during life and whom the Church honors as saints either by her ordinary universal teaching authority or by a solemn definition called canonization. The Church's official recognition of sanctity implies that the persons are now in heavenly glory, that they may be publicly invoked everywhere, and that their virtues during life or martyr's death are a witness and example to the Christian faithful. (Etym. Latin *sanctus*, holy, sacred.)

SAL. *Salus, salutis*—salvation, of salvation.

SALEM. A city ruled by King Melchizedek. When Abraham returned from a victorious battle against the King of Elam, Melchizedek, who was a priest as well as a king, gave his blessing to Abraham. In turn, Abraham offered tithes to the priest (Genesis 14:17–20). In this brief incident the Church finds a symbolic relationship between Melchizedek, the priest-king, and Christ, the priest-king of the New Testament.

SALESIANS. Members of the Society of St. Francis de Sales (1567–1622), founded near Turin by St. John Bosco (1815–88) in 1859. Their main purpose is to train youth in schools and professional and vocational institutes. They are also active in the missions and have entered the field of social communications. Their rule of life was approved by Pope Pius IX in 1874. St. John Bosco also founded a sister congregation of Daughters of Our Lady Help of Christians in 1872 at Mornese, Italy.

SALIC LAW. Originally the entire code of laws compiled by King Clovis (466–511), at first ruler of that part of the Salians. Eventually it referred only to that provision of the law which restricted a woman's succession to the throne. See also LEX SALICA.

SALMANT. *Salmanticenses*—theologians of Salamanca, Spain.

SALOME. 1. daughter of Herod Philip and Herodias. The historian Josephus supplied her name, because in Scripture she is identified only as "the daughter of Herodias." Her dancing at Herod's birthday celebration so delighted him that he promised on oath to give her anything she wanted. At her mother's suggestion she demanded the head of John the Baptist. Reluctantly Herod granted her request (Matthew 14:3–11); 2. named as one of the holy women who witnessed the Crucifixion of Jesus (Mark 15:40). She was probably the wife of Zebedee (Matthew 27:56). On Easter morning she accompanied the same women to Christ's tomb, only to find it empty (Mark 16:1).

SALT. Used in the liturgy in various ways. It is blessed and put into ordinary holy water and Gregorian water (of consecration). Until the revision of the ceremonies for baptism (1969), a small quantity of salt was placed on the tongue of the person to be baptized, with the words, "Receive the salt of wisdom; may it be for you a propitiation into eternal life."

SALTIRE. See CRUX DECUSSATA; ST. ANDREW'S CROSS.

SALUS POPULI ROMANI. Shrine of Our Lady Protectress of Rome, also called Santa Maria Maggiore. The original basilica of the Blessed Virgin was built about A.D. 350 and was called Santa Maria ad Nives because of the legend that the location of the church was determined by the appearance of snow on the Esquiline Hill on a summer day. The first treasure of the present church is a miraculous image of the Madonna with the Infant Jesus attributed to St. Luke and said to have been brought by St. Helena from the Holy Land. Historians rate the painting as being at least 1500 years old. The citizens of Rome flock to the basilica whenever their city is in danger. In 597, Pope Gregory I carried the painting in solemn procession to St. Peter's when Rome was being decimated by the Black Plague; and when Anzio, only twenty miles away, was being bombed in World War II, the shrine was thronged day and night by the Roman faithful. The original church was built in the fourth century. When Pope Sixtus III rebuilt it in the fifth century, he gave it the further title of Santa Maria ad Praesepe (St. Mary of the Crib) because part of the original manger from Bethlehem was in the basilica's crypt. Pope Pius XII said his first Mass before Mary's altar in this cathedral, and in 1939 he pontificated at a Mass of thanksgiving at the same altar.

SALUTARY ACT. Human action that is performed under the influence of grace and that positively leads a person to a heavenly destiny. The grace of a salutary act must be at least actual grace, whether a person is in the state of grace or not. If one is in the state of grace, the action is not only salutary but also meritorious. While the Church has not officially pronounced on the subject, it is common teaching that the justified also require actual grace for the performance of salutary acts. (Etym. Latin *salus,* health, well-being.)

SALUTATION, MASS. Greeting of the priest to the people after the opening antiphon at Mass. This greeting and the people's reply express the mystery of the Church officially gathered together.

SALVATION. In biblical language the deliverance from straitened circumstances or oppression by some evil to a state of freedom and security. As sin is the greatest evil, salvation is mainly liberation from sin and its consequences. This can be deliverance by way of preservation, or by offering the means for being delivered, or by removing the oppressive evil or difficulty, or by rewarding the effort spent in co-operating with grace in order to be delivered. All four aspects of salvation are found in the Scriptures and are taught by the Church. (Etym. Latin *salvare,* to save.)

SALVE REGINA. "Hail, Holy Queen," one of the oldest Marian antiphons in Western Christianity, used for centuries in the Divine Office. The author is not known, but was most probably Hermannus Contractus (d. 1054). The final words, "O clemens, O pia, O dulcis virgo Maria," attributed to St. Bernard, are found in manuscripts before his time and therefore seem to belong to the original prayer. The full text reads: "Hail, holy Queen, Mother of mercy; hail, our life, our sweetness and our hope. To you do we cry, poor banished children of Eve. To you do we send up our sighs, mourning and weeping in this valley of tears. Turn, then, most gracious Advocate, your eyes of mercy toward us. And after this our exile show unto us the blessed fruit of your womb, Jesus. O clement, O loving, O sweet Virgin Mary." A partial indulgence is gained for every recitation of this prayer.

SALVIFIC WILL. The desire of God that all humankind be saved. God's general or universal will is the salvation of humanity on condition that a person dies in the state of grace. It is called God's antecedent and conditioned salvific will. His special or particular will considers the moral state of each person at the time of death. Here God unconditionally desires the salvation of all those who depart this life in the state of grace. It is called God's consequent and absolute salvific will. This coincides with predestination. Insofar as the consequent, unconditional will of God refers to the expulsion of a person from heavenly happiness, it is called reprobation.

SAMARIA, DISTRICT OF. In the time of Christ, Palestine was made up of three sections, Galilee on the north, Samaria in the center, Judaea in the south. Samaria extended from the Jordan River westward to the Mediterranean Sea. In Old Testament times, when the Twelve Tribes inherited sections of Canaan, Ephraim and Manasseh occupied much of what was to become Samaria. After Solomon's time Samaria became known as the Northern Kingdom, or Israel, as distinct from the Southern Kingdom, or Judah. During several kingships— notably those of Saul, David, and Solomon— the two constituted a united kingdom. But for most of the years before the time of Christ, Samaria and Judah were hostile neighbors. Many Jews were shocked that Jesus would even speak to Samaritans (John 4:8–9). The most prosperous period in Samaria's history was the eighth century before Christ. Following this, however, Assyrian invasions led to loss of independence and the deportation of many leading Samaritans. An incursion of racially mixed foreigners took place, and Samaria never regained the stature it had enjoyed. Samaria is now the northwestern part of Jordan.

SAMARITANS. The people of Samaria, who were originally Jews but had intermarried with the pagan Assyrians, who had conquered Israel in 622 B.C. (II Kings 18:9–12). They developed a different form of Judaism, based mainly on their own Pentateuch, which was the only part of the Old Testament the Samaritans accepted. They had their own temple on Mount Gerizim and were bitterly hated by the Jews (John 4:9, 20). They were featured in three narratives of the Gospels: the Good Samaritan (Luke 10:33), the Ten Lepers (Luke 7:16), and the Samaritan Woman (John 4:5–42).

SAMPIETRINI. The permanent group of skilled workers and artisans, in every trade, who with their assistants take care of St. Peter's Basilica.

SAMSON. A hero of the Tribe of Dan. He was the son of Manoah who received a message from Yahweh's angel before the child was born that he was destined to "rescue Israel from the Philistines" (Judges 13:5). There is no evidence that he succeeded in this. A number of incidents are related of his prodigious strength. On one occasion he tore a lion to pieces with his bare hands (Judges 14:6). In fighting the Philistines he set fire to their cornfields and vineyards (Judges 15:5). But his moral strength did not match his physical strength, especially in his relations with women. A love affair with a woman named Delilah proved his undoing. The Philistines bribed her into learning the secret of his strength. They took him captive and blinded him, but in a final display of power, he destroyed the building and killed himself and his captors (Judges 16).

SAMUEL. An Ephraimite, son of Elkanah and Hannah. Deeply religious, he "grew up in stature and in favour both with Yahweh and with men . . ." (I Samuel 2:26). "All Israel from Dan to Beersheba came to know that Samuel was accredited as a prophet of Yahweh" (I Samuel 3:20). Following a disastrous defeat of the Israelites by the Philistines, Samuel rallied his humiliated people and won for himself recognition as a judge and prophet (I Samuel 7:6). He anointed Saul as Yahweh's choice as ruler, and his prestige with the people ensured Saul's elevation to the kingship (I Samuel 11:12–14). But, despite military victories, Saul disappointed Yahweh by his disobedience, and Samuel turned against him in favor of young David (I Samuel 15:10–35). Fearful of David's growing popularity, Saul tried in vain repeatedly to have the young man killed, but Yahweh protected him (I Samuel 19, 23). Samuel secretly anointed David as future king of Israel (I Samuel 16:12–13), and as soon as the insane Saul died, David succeeded him. Samuel was thus Yahweh's instrument in establishing two successive kings who ruled over a sixty-year period. An inspiring, selfless leader, Samuel was held in high regard by his people throughout his life. Two books of the Bible are named after him (I Samuel and II Samuel).

SAMUEL, BOOKS OF. The Hebrew title of what the Vulgate calls the First and Second Books of Kings. They contain the history of Samuel and the two kings, Saul and David, whom he anointed. They are the primary source for the history of Israel in the crucial years of the eleventh and tenth centuries before Christ. Three famous poems are included in these books: Hannah's prayer (I Samuel 2:1–10), David's lament (II Samuel 1:19–27), and David's song of triumph (II Samuel 22).

SANATING GRACE. Divine grace in its function of healing (*sanare,* heal) the ravages of sin, original and personal, in human nature. The healing process affects both the mind and the will. Grace heals the will by giving strength to desire and accept the known will of God, and joy in its performance.

SANATION. The canonical process by which an invalid marriage is validated retroactively, back to the time when the contract was first made. Renewal of consent is not required once the impediments are dispensed. Thus, by a sort of legal fiction, the marriage will have been considered valid from the beginning. It is especially useful in the legitimation of children already born. Sanation may also be imperfect, thus not retroactive to the time of the original contract.

SANCE BELL. The *Sanctus* bell, originally a bell hung in a small cupola over a sanctuary, rung by means of a rope that hung down near the server's place. The bell was rung three times at the *Sanctus,* once at the *Hanc Igitur* just before the Consecration, three times each at the elevation of the Host and the chalice, three times at the *Domine non sum dignus* before the priest's communion, and in some places three times also before the communion of the people, when the same words were said.

SANCTIFICATION. Being made holy. The

first sanctification takes place at baptism, by which the love of God is infused by the Holy Spirit (Romans 5:5). Newly baptized persons are holy because the Holy Trinity begins to dwell in their souls and they are pleasing to God. The second sanctification is a lifelong process in which a person already in the state of grace grows in the possession of grace and in likeness to God by faithfully corresponding with divine inspirations. The third sanctification takes place when a person enters heaven and becomes totally and irrevocably united with God in the beatific vision. (Etym. Latin *sanctificare,* to make holy.)

SANCTIFYING GRACE. The supernatural state of being infused by God, which permanently inheres in the soul. It is a vital principle of the supernatural life, as the rational soul is the vital principle of a human being's natural life. It is not a substance but a real quality that becomes part of the soul substance. Although commonly associated with the possession of the virtue of charity, sanctifying grace is yet distinct from this virtue. Charity, rather, belongs to the will, whereas sanctifying grace belongs to the whole soul, mind, will, and affections. It is called sanctifying grace because it makes holy those who possess the gift by giving them a participation in the divine life. It is *zoē* (life), which Christ taught that he has in common with the Father and which those who are in the state of grace share. See also ACTUAL GRACE, EFFICACIOUS GRACE, GRACE, GRATUITOUS GRACE, HABITUAL GRACE, JUSTIFYING GRACE, SACRAMENTAL GRACE, SANATING GRACE, SUFFICIENT GRACE.

SANCTION. In general, the inviolability of the law, whether divine or human, ecclesiastical or civil. More properly, it is the means adopted to make the law inviolable. These may be natural means and comprehend all the benefits and penalties, personal or social, that naturally follow from keeping or breaking the law. Or they may be supernatural means, which are known to exist only because they have been divinely revealed. Positive sanctions are those set up by legitimate authority in Church or State and, to be valid, must conform to right reason and revelation. Every sanction is only as effective as it is known, whether it acts as a stimulus (in promised rewards) or as a deterrent (in threatened punishments) to motivate people to observe the law. Sanctions are either temporal or eternal, depending on their duration. They are either medicinal or vindicative, depending on their purpose: to act as a remedy for violations of the law or

to restore moral order and champion justice against violators of the law. (Etym. Latin *sanctio,* the decreeing of something as sacred, decree, sanction.)

SANCTITY. In an absolute sense, the Divinity. The sanctity of God is his total transcendence or total otherness. It is in this sense that the Church prays in the *Gloria* of the Mass, "You alone are the Holy One, you alone are the Lord, you alone are the Most High." All other sanctity is by participation, so that a creature has as much sanctity as it shares in the Divinity. Essentially it consists in the possession of sanctifying grace, although the term is usually applied to persons who practice more than ordinary virtue, especially the love of God and their neighbor.

SANCTORAL CYCLE. See PROPER OF THE SAINTS.

SANCTUARY. The part of a church containing the altar. If there are several altars, the sanctuary is for the high altar. In the Byzantine tradition it is enclosed by the *iconostasis.* It is the center of liturgical ceremony, clearly distinct from the main body of the church. (Etym. Latin *sanctuarium,* holy place, shrine.)

SANCTUARY, RIGHT OF. The claim to protection for those fleeing from justice or persecution. The right of sanctuary was based on the inviolability attached to sacred things. Although generally confined to a church, it was later extended to the surrounding precincts. There was often a large ring or knocker on the church door, the holding of which gave a person the right of asylum. The privilege did not apply to sacrilege or high treason.

SANCTUARY LAMP. A wax candle, generally in a red glass container, kept burning day and night wherever the Blessed Sacrament is reserved in Catholic churches or chapels. It is an emblem of Christ's abiding love and a reminder to the faithful to respond with loving adoration in return.

SANCTUM SANCTORUM. Holy of holies. Repository for the Ark of the Covenant. Also used of any place specially dedicated to God and reserved for unassailable privacy.

SANCTUS. The fourth part of the Ordinary or fixed part of the Mass.

SANCTUS PONTIFEX. Declaration of the Sacred Congregations for the Clergy and for the Discipline of the Sacraments on First

Confession and First Communion. The document states that there should be an end to "experiments" with First Holy Communion without sacramental confession; that such practices were to end by the close of the 1972–73 school year (May 24, 1973). Four years later (March 31, 1977) another document on the same subject was issued by the Congregations for the Clergy and for the Sacraments and Divine Worship, declaring that all such experiments "should cease so that the discipline of the Church might be restored."

SANDALS. Episcopal slippers with embroidered silk or velvet tops worn by popes, bishops, and other prelates at solemn pontifical services. Sandals of leather are worn by monks, friars, and nuns, usually of the discalced orders, but also by other religious, according to their rule of life.

SANGUINE TEMPERAMENT. One of the four classic temperaments, characterized by an easy cheerfulness and optimism, even under great difficulties. People with this nature, however, have to be careful not to allow their sanguine outlook to ignore problems or fail to face up to reality.

SANHEDRIN. The highest Jewish court, which functioned from the third or fourth century B.C., until the fall of Jerusalem in A.D. 70. For several centuries earlier there were courts or councils in existence, but it was impossible to learn when a recognizable Sanhedrin took specific form. Josephus, the Jewish historian, was the first writer to name it specifically as functioning in the reign of Antiochus the Great. It was composed of seventy-one members, chosen from three classes of Jews—the elders of the chief families, the high priests, and the scribes, who were mostly lawyers from the Pharisee sect. The Sadducees were always well represented. The jurisdiction of the Sanhedrin was limited to Judaea, a fact that prevented the court from taking action against Jesus while he was preaching in Galilee. The Sanhedrin met in the Jerusalem Temple area. Any Jew could appear before it to seek clarification of the complexities of the Mosaic law. The court had the right to mete out punishment to law violators (Matthew 26:47–50; Mark 14:43–46), even to the extent of capital punishment (Mark 14:64; John 11:53). But, as it happened in the case of Jesus' Crucifixion, it had to secure the approval of the Roman procurator before such a sentence could be executed (Mark 15:1). Guilt for his unjust condemnation rested partly on the fanatical element in the Sanhe-

drin (John 18:31) and partly on the cynical Roman official willing to appease a turbulent local group (Mark 15:15). Persecution by the Sanhedrin did not end with Jesus' death. It continued after Pentecost, as in the case of Peter, John, Paul, and Stephen (Acts 4:3, 5:17–18, 5:33, 7:57–58, 23:1–10). (Etym. Greek *synedrion*, council, a sitting together.)

SANTA CLAUS. An American adaptation of the Dutch form of St. Nicholas (Sint Nikolaas), Bishop of Myra in Lycia, who lived in the time of Diocletian. He was long venerated as the patron saint of children, bringing them gifts on December 6, and his association with Christmas was popularized by the Dutch Protestants in New Amsterdam. They portrayed the saint as a Nordic magician. He is now a secularized personification of the spirit of Christmas.

SANTA CRUZ. "Holy Cross." A mission church founded on September 25, 1791, on Monterey Bay at Santa Cruz, California.

SANTA MARIA AD NIVES. See SALUS POPULI ROMANI.

SANTA MARIA AD PRAESEPE. See SALUS POPULI ROMANI.

SANTA MARIA MAGGIORE. See SALUS POPULI ROMANI.

SAPPHIRA. See ANANIAS.

SARABITES. A class of ascetics in the early Church who lived either in their own homes or in small groups near the cities and acknowledged no monastic superior. St. Benedict spoke of them critically in the first chapter of his Rule, as persons who decide on their own what is holy and what is unholy, and thus follow their own conceits. The term is still used to describe religious who follow their own ideas independently of ecclesiastical authority.

SARABAITES. See SARABITES.

SARAGOSSA (shrine). Sanctuary of Our Lady of the Pillar, near Saragossa in northeastern Spain, where Mary is said to have appeared in early Christian times, asking that a church be built there in her honor. After the vision, the jasper pillar on which she stood remained and it became a most coveted relic. A church was built as requested and the pillar was enshrined within it. It is a six-foot-high stone column almost completely unadorned, now nearly encased in silver. On top of it is an ancient black wooden statue of Mary about fifteen inches tall, covered with gold leaf. So varied is her wardrobe that she wears different attire every day. The devotion to Our Lady of the Pillar, initiated at Saragossa, was brought to the New World by the Spanish explorers, and their missions boast of many miracles worked through Mary's favor. Some of the most incredible ones at the mother shrine have been authenticated by sworn testimony. The Virgin of the Pillar is recurrent as a theme in prayer, songs, and patriotic expressions. She was often invoked in battle emergencies. The heart of Don John of Austria, the Christian victor at Lepanto, rests near the sacred pillar in this sanctuary.

SARAH. Wife of Abraham. Her original name was Sarai, but when Yahweh promised Abraham that his wife would have a son, he instructed him at the same time to change her name to Sarah (Genesis 17:15). Since she was already ninety years old, she scoffed at the promise, but Yahweh was as good as his word. The child was born and Abraham obediently named him Isaac (Genesis 21:2–3). An awkward situation developed for Abraham as Isaac grew to boyhood. Years before, Sarah had permitted her servant, Hagar, to become Abraham's second wife (a custom permitted in those days) and a son Ishmael resulted. Now that Sarah had a son of her own, she was meanly resentful of a situation she had initiated herself. "Drive away that slave-girl and her son," she said to Abraham. "That slave-girl's son is not to share the inheritance with my son, Isaac" (Genesis 21:10). Abraham was forced to do so, but Yahweh protected Hagar and Ishmael and assured them that Ishmael would head a great nation (Genesis 21:17–21). Sarah lived to be one hundred twenty-seven years old and died at Hebron in Canaan (Genesis 23:1–2). When Abraham died years later, his sons Isaac and Ishmael buried him with Sarah (Genesis 25:9–10). (Etym. Hebrew *Sārāh,* "princess.")

SARAI. See SARAH.

SARUM RITE. The regulation of the details of the Roman liturgy as they were carried out in pre-Reformation England, Scotland, and Ireland. This rite was sponsored by St. Osmund, Bishop of Salisbury (d. 1099), who incorporated into the Latin Rite certain Norman liturgical traditions. Closely resembling the present-day Dominican Rite, it was superseded by the revised Roman ritual of Pope St. Pius X.

SATAN. Chief of the fallen angels. Enemy of God and humanity and everything good.

Other names for Satan are the devil, Beelzebul, Belial, and Lucifer. The serpent that tempted Eve was identified with Satan (Genesis 3). In both the Old and New Testaments he is considered the adversary of God, bringing about evil and tempting human beings to defy God's laws (Wisdom 2:24; I Chronicles 21:1; Job 1:6–12). Even Jesus was subjected to temptation by Satan in the wilderness (Matthew 4:1–11). Later the Pharisees accused Jesus of "casting out devils through Beelzebul, the prince of devils" (Matthew 12:24). Paul warned the Corinthians against the temptations of Satan (I Corinthians 7:6). References to Satan are numerous in the Scriptures. The dominant feature of this teaching is that a personal, malign force is active in the world attempting to pervert the designs of God. (Etym. Latin *Satan;* from Greek *Satan;* from Hebrew *sātān,* devil, adversary; from *sātān,* to plot against another.)

SATANAËL. See BOGOMILES.

SATANISM. The cult of Satan or Satan worship. Known in antiquity, it has long been practiced under a different name among polytheists in their invocation and propitiation of the evil deities. But Satanism properly so called is mainly a revolt against Christianity or the Catholic Church. It rose in the twelfth century and culminated in the Black Mass, a blasphemous parody of the Eucharistic Sacrifice. Modern Satanism has become widespread in circles that venerate the devil, pray for his assistance, perform elaborate rites in his honor, including demonic caricatures of the seven sacraments, establish legally recognized "Churches of Satan," and claim to possess extraordinary power to harm those who oppose them. Philosophically, Satanists hold to a Manichaean view of the universe, that there are ultimately two creative principles in the universe, one good and the other bad. Satanists venerate what Christians call the "principle of evil."

SATISFACTION. The expiation of wrongdoing, especially the penance imposed by a priest before giving sacramental absolution. Essentially the satisfaction consists in the penitent's willingness to accept the penance imposed and its actual fulfillment. The effect of these two elements is to remove more or less the temporal punishment due to the sins confessed. In the early Church, up to the Middle Ages, the penance imposed was generally severe. Later on the severity was mitigated through what have since come to be known as indulgences. (Etym. Latin *satis-*

facere: satis, sufficient, enough + *facere,* to do, make.)

SATURDAY. Named after the Roman god Saturn, the seventh day of the week consecrated by the Church for devotion to the Blessed Virgin. Since patristic times, Saturday was observed in memory of Mary's trustful faith during the first Holy Saturday, while Christ was in the tomb. (Etym. Middle English *Saterday;* Old English *Saeterdaeg,* short for *Saeternegdaeg,* Saturn's day.)

SAUL. The son of Kish; he ruled Israel as its first king for twenty years about the year 1000 B.C. He was a tall, handsome, impressive man in appearance (I Samuel 9:2–3), but his complex personality brought him trouble. When the people of Israel begged Samuel, their highly respected prophet and judge, to get them a king in order to protect their security, Samuel consulted Yahweh, who recommended Saul (I Samuel 8–10). At first he proved very successful because of his military achievements (I Samuel 11:14–15), but he did not show respect or obedience to Yahweh, and Samuel, who had gained the kingship for him, became disenchanted. Instead, he encouraged the advancement of Saul's son-in-law, David, and even secretly anointed him as the future king (I Samuel 13:8–15). Saul became insanely jealous of David and several times tried to have him killed. Ironically, both Saul's daughter, Michal, who was married to David (I Samuel 19:11–12), and Jonathan, his son, sided with the young man against their father and did everything possible to protect David from the maddened king (I Samuel 19:1–7). Finally, in a fierce battle between the Israelites and the Philistines, all three of Saul's sons were killed. Badly wounded, the king killed himself (I Samuel 31:1–6). This cleared the way for David to become King of Israel for the next forty years.

SAVIOR. A title of Jesus Christ, arising from his sacrifice of his life for the salvation of the human race, and thus he won for sinful humanity the graces necessary to reach heaven. It is only because of his satisfaction and the invocation of his name that anyone can be saved (Acts 4:12). (Etym. Latin *salvator,* from *salvare,* to save.)

S.C. *Sacra Congregatio*—sacred congregation.

SCALA SANCTA. The twenty-eight marble steps, now covered with wood, leading to the papal chapel in the Lateran Palace. They are believed to be the steps of Pilate's praetorium, sanctified by the Savior by walking up them during his Passion. Brought to Rome by St. Helena, they are ascended by pilgrims on their knees.

SCALES. Emblem of St. Michael invoked as the patron of all who use scales in their business, because he is considered the one who carries out the decision on each person's eternal destiny on the Day of Judgment. The angelic choir of thrones have a similar symbol, based on the text "you have upheld the justice of my cause from the Thrones where you sit as righteous judge" (Psalm 9:4).

SCANDAL. Any action or its omission, not necessarily sinful in itself, that is likely to induce another to do something morally wrong. Direct scandal, also called diabolical, has the deliberate intention to induce another to sin. In indirect scandal a person does something that he or she foresees will at least likely lead another to commit sin, but this is rather tolerated than positively desired. (Etym. Latin *scandalum,* stumbling block.)

SCANDAL OF THE WEAK. Disedifying morally weak persons by permissible conduct. Circumstances determine the duty in charity to avoid giving scandal to the weak. The existence of such a duty is clear from the teaching of St. Paul, who would not eat meat that had been offered to idols lest he scandalize the weaker brethren. He warned the early Christians not to rationalize their conduct but to follow his example, lest "by sinning in this way against our brothers and injuring their weak consciences, it would be Christ against whom you sinned" (I Corinthians 8:12). This obligation in charity is such that one may licitly refrain from fulfilling even a grave positive precept that is not necessary for salvation in order to prevent serious scandal to the weak. Behind the obligation is the mandate of selfless love that seeks not only to help another in obvious need but also by self-restraint to protect another from spiritual harm.

SCANDALOUS. Ecclesiastical censure of a professed opinion that would cause spiritual harm by leading people to sin or withdrawing them from the practice of virtue. The censure is commonly applied to erroneous teaching in the moral order.

SCAPULAR. An outer garment consisting of two strips of cloth joined across the shoulders, worn by members of certain religious orders. Originating as the working frock of Benedictines, it was adopted by other religious communities and is now considered a distinctive part of the monastic habit. It symbolizes the yoke of Christ. A scapular is worn under one's secular clothes, in abbreviated form by tertiaries associated with the religious orders. Tertiary scapulars vary in size and shape; their color corresponds to that of the monastic family. As a further development, the Church has approved some eighteen blessed scapulars as two small pieces of cloth joined by strings and worn around the neck and under the clothes. Best known are the five scapulars of: Our Lady of Mount Carmel (brown), the Passion (red), Seven Dolors (black), Immaculate Conception (blue), and the Holy Trinity (white). (Etym. Latin *scapulare, scapularium,* "shoulder cloak," from Latin *scapula,* shoulder.)

SCAPULAR MEDAL. A blessed medal, worn or carried on the person, instead of one or more of the small scapulars. It was authorized as a substitute by St. Pius X in 1910. It bears on one side a representation of the Sacred Heart, and on the other an image of the Blessed Virgin. It replaces any (or all) of the small scapulars in which a person has been invested. Investing in each case must be done with the scapular and not the medal. The medal is to be blessed by a priest who has faculties for each scapular investiture.

S.C.C. *Sacra Congregatio Concilii*—Sacred Congregation of the Council, i.e. of Trent.

S.C.C. *Sacra Congregatio pro Clericis*—Sacred Congregation for the Clergy.

S.C.C.S. *Sacra Congregatio pro Causis Sanctorum*—Sacred Congregation for the Causes of Saints.

S.C.D.F. *Sacra Congregatio pro Doctrina Fidei*—Sacred Congregation for the Doctrine of the Faith.

S.C.E. *Sacra Congregatio pro Episcopis*—Sacred Congregation for Bishops.

S.C.EE.RR. *Sacra Congregatio Episcoporum et Regularium*—Sacred Congregation of Bishops and Regulars.

S.C.E.O. *Sacra Congregatio pro Ecclesiis Orientalibus*—Sacred Congregation for the Oriental Churches.

S.C.G.E. (S.C.P.F.) *Sacra Congregatio pro Gentium Evangelizatione (Sacra Congregatio de Propaganda Fide)*—Sacred Congregation for the Evangelization of Peoples (Sacred Congregation for the Propagation of the Faith).

SCHISM. A willful separation from the unity of the Christian Church. Although St. Paul used the term to condemn the factions at Corinth, these were not properly schismatical, but petty cliques that favored one or another Apostle. A generation later Clement I reprobated the first authentic schism of which there is record. Paul's exhortation to the Corinthians also gives an accurate description of the concept. "Why do we wrench and tear apart the members of Christ," he asks, "and revolt against our own body, and reach such folly as to forget that we are members of one another?" While the early Church was often plagued with heresy and schism, the exact relation between the two divisive elements was not clarified until later in the patristic age. "By false doctrines concerning God," declared St. Augustine, "heretics wound the faith; by sinful dissensions schismatics deviate from fraternal charity, although they believe what we believe." Heresy, therefore, by its nature refers to the mind and is opposed to religious belief, whereas schism is fundamentally volitional and offends against the union of Christian charity. (Etym. Latin *schisma;* from Greek *skhisma,* a split, division, from *skhizein,* to tear, rend.)

SCHISMATIC. According to Church law, a schismatic is a person who, after receiving baptism and while keeping the name of Christian, pertinaciously refuses to submit to the Supreme Pontiff or refuses to associate with those who are subject to him. The two factors, submission to the Pope and association with persons subject to him, are to be taken disjunctively. Either resisting papal authority or refusing to participate in Catholic life and worship induces schism, even without further affiliation with another religious body. Like heresy, schism is formal and culpable only when the obligations are fully realized.

SCHOLA CANTORUM. A place for teaching and training in ecclesiastical chant, or a body of singers assembled for the purpose of rendering the music in church. Pope St. Hilary (461–68) probably inaugurated the first *schola cantorum,* but it was Pope St. Gregory the Great who established the school on a permanent basis. From Rome the institution spread to other parts of the Church. See also PAPAL CHOIR.

SCHOLA CANTORUM, MONASTIC. The select group of monks who chant the more elaborate parts of liturgical music. The one in charge is called a precentor.

SCHOLASTICISM. The system of philosophy and theology first developed in the medieval schools of Christian Europe, having a scholastic or technical language and methodology, building on the writings of the Church Fathers, notably St. Augustine (354–430), using many of the philosophical principles and insights of Aristotle and Neoplatonism, and co-ordinated into a synthesis of human and divine wisdom by St. Thomas Aquinas (1225–74).

Three periods of Scholasticism are commonly distinguished: medieval period from St. Anselm to Jean Capréolus (1060–1440); Counter-Reformation or the Spanish-Portuguese Revival (1520–1640), declining after the rise of Protestantism and the spread of Cartesianism; and Neo-Scholasticism, officially recognized by Pope Leo XIII in 1879, beginning in the latter half of the nineteenth century to the present time. (Etym. Latin *schola*, place of learning, school; from Greek *scholē*, school; discussion; rest, leisure, employment of leisure time.)

SCHOOL. Any institution primarily devoted to imparting knowledge or developing skills or special aptitudes; therefore, an educational institution. However, the term is also applied to a particular system of thought, as in philosophy or theology, and a distinctive form of spirituality, as in different religious orders.

S.C.I. *Sacra Congregatio Indicis*—Sacred Congregation of the Index.

S.C.I.C. *Sacra Congregatio pro Institutione Catholica*—Sacred Congregation for Catholic Education.

SCIENCE OF FAITH. Another name for theology. It is concerned with faith in the objective sense of "that which is believed" and in the subjective sense of "that by which a person believes." Theology accepts Scripture and tradition as the remote rule of faith, and the doctrines of the Church as the proximate rule of faith. But as a science of faith, it seeks by human reason to establish the foundations of faith, to penetrate into the meaning of the mysteries of faith, to show that faith is consistent with reason, and to defend the faith against those who deny the truths of Christianity.

SCIENCE OF THE SAINTS. See GIFT OF KNOWLEDGE.

SCIOSOPHY. Any religious or quasi-religious faith that claims support from scientific data or experimentation, e.g., astrology.

SCOTISM. The system of scholastic philosophy expounded by the Franciscan philosopher Duns Scotus (1264–1308). The root difference between Scotism and the philosophy of St. Thomas Aquinas (1225–74) is that, whereas the latter gives knowledge and reason the first place in his system, Scotus gives the primacy to love and the will. Thus, in Scotism the natural law depends on the will of God and not on the divine mind. It is therefore, absolutely speaking, not immutable. Moreover, in the Scotist scheme, the essence of heavenly beatitude consists not in vision but in the love of God. The Scotist position on a number of doctrines of faith has been thought by some critics to come quite close to the double standard of truth of the Moslem Averroës (1126–98), namely, that which is true in theology may be false in philosophy.

S.C.P.F. *Sacra Congregatio de Propaganda Fide*—Sacred Congregation for the Propagation of the Faith.

SCR. Scripture.

SCRIBES. A class of well-educated Jews who studied and explained the law. Occasionally they were referred to as lawyers or rabbis (Matthew 23:7). They were not priests. Some were members of the Sanhedrin (Matthew 26:57). Because they were devoted to defending and preserving the law, they considered Jesus a threat to their security. They challenged and baited him (Mark 2:16) on numerous occasions and ultimately took part in plotting his death (Luke 22:1–2). (Etym. Latin *scriba*, official writer, clerk, scribe, from *scribere*, to write.)

SCRIPTORIUM. A room in a monastery set aside for the work of copying books and documents, illuminating manuscripts, and similar work. Artificial light was forbidden for fear of injury to the manuscripts.

SCRIPTURES. See BIBLE. (Etym. Latin *scriptura*, act of writing.)

S.C.R.I.S. *Sacra Congregatio pro Religiosis et Institutis Saecularibus*—Sacred Congregation for Religious and for Secular Institutes.

SCROLL. An ancient book in rolled-up shape. The writing was done on papyrus, animal skin, or parchment, each piece approximately six inches wide and ten inches long.

The pieces were sewn together and rolled smoothly around a stick. The reader would unroll the manuscript off the stick onto another stick. Frequently the roll would be over a hundred feet long. Much of the Old and New Testaments was written on scrolls, as were literary and scientific documents. The title was sometimes written on the outside edge of the scroll. (Etym. Middle English *scrowle;* from Old French *escro(u)e,* strip of parchment; from Frankish *skroda,* piece, shred.)

SCROLL (symbol). An emblem of wisdom and an early emblem of the Apostles. Though the crossed keys individualized St. Peter and the sword St. Paul, both of them, as well as the Evangelists, were often shown with a scroll. It is the emblem of their office of teaching. Elijah the prophet, who appeared in the Transfiguration, is also represented with a scroll.

SCRUPLE. Unreasonable doubt about the morality of an act done or to be done. Its basis is an erroneous conscience combined with a lack of control of the emotion of fear. (Etym. Latin *scrupulus,* small, sharp stone, small weight, scruple, from *scrupus,* rough stone.)

SCRUPULOSITY. The habit of imagining sin where none exists, or grave sin where the matter is venial. To overcome scrupulosity, a person needs to be properly instructed in order to form a right conscience, and in extreme cases the only remedy is absolute obedience (for a time) to a prudent confessor.

SCRUPULOUS CONSCIENCE. An erroneous conscience when the mind is unduly swayed by fear and judges that something is wrong that in fact is lawful.

SCRUTINY. A close, careful examination or study. The term is applied to the manner of electing a Pope by secret ballot in which every human precaution is taken to avoid error or dishonesty. The formal examination of candidates for sacred orders is also called a scrutiny.

SCS. *Sanctus*—saint.

S.C.S.C.D. *Sacra Congregatio pro Sacramentis et Cultu Divino*—Sacred Congregation for the Sacraments and Divine Worship.

S.C.U.F. *Secretariatus ad Christianorum Unitatem Fovendam*—Secretariat for Promoting Christian Unity.

S.D. *Sine data*—undated book.

S.D. *Servus Dei*—servant of God.

SEAL. A design impressed on wax or similar material. At first a seal was used for securing a document, but later it was attached to a document's face as a sign of validity. When authority passed to new hands, the old seal was destroyed and a new one made. This is why the Fisherman's ring, or papal seal, is immediately broken by the Cardinal Carmerlengo when the Pope dies. (Etym. Latin *sigillum,* seal, diminutive of *signum,* sign.)

SEALING. The sacrament of confirmation as a perfection of baptism, in which the confirmed person receives the indelible character or seal of a soldier of Christ, ready to undergo any hardship in the preservation and profession of his faith.

SEAL OF CONFESSION. The grave duty of keeping absolutely secret all sins that are told in sacramental confession and anything else that is told by the penitent and is related to the confession. It is an obligation binding in the natural law, the divine law of Christ, and in the positive law of the Church. It binds the confessor and any other person who in any way discovers what was confessed. Under no circumstances may any of this information be revealed unless the penitent freely gives permission.

SEAL OF CONFIRMATION. To establish or determine irrevocably, in the sacrament of confirmation, when a bishop anoints a person with chrism and says, "[Name], be sealed with the Gift of the Holy Spirit." Thus, by confirmation a baptized Christian becomes permanently marked as a witness of Christ and is enabled to preserve, profess, and communicate the faith even (if need be) with the price of his blood.

SECOND ADAM. A title given to Christ, based on St. Paul's teaching that as sin came into the world through the disobedience of the first Adam, so grace has come through the obedience of one man, Christ the Second Adam (Romans 5:12–21).

SECONDARY CAUSE. A created cause that is totally dependent on the First Cause, who is God. It is a cause that can produce a certain kind of effect but cannot produce the being or existence of the effect. See also CAUSE, EFFICIENT CAUSE, FINAL CAUSE, FIRST CAUSE, FORMAL CAUSE, FREE CAUSE, MATERIAL CAUSE, MORAL CAUSE, NECESSARY CAUSE.

SECOND COMING OF CHRIST. "I am going now to prepare a place for you and after I have gone and prepared a place for you, I shall return to take you with me" (John 14:3). This promise, which Jesus made to his Apostles the night before he died, will be the culmination of his incarnation and redemption. On the occasion of his Ascension, angels repeated the promise. "This same Jesus will come back in the same way as you have seen Him go there" (Acts 1:11). When the Second Coming will be, no one knows. Some of his devoted followers were mistaken in thinking that the return would take place in a short time, possibly in their lifetime. Nevertheless, that promise is the basis of Christian hope. As Paul wrote to Titus: "We must be self-restrained and live good and religious lives here in this present world while we are waiting in hope for the blessing which will come with the Appearing of the glory of our great God and Savior, Christ Jesus" (Titus 2:13).

SECOND CRUSADE. The expedition against the Moslems (1147–49) encouraged by Pope Eugenius III and preached by St. Bernard. It proved a failure.

SECOND ORDER. A term commonly applied to those religious orders of women whose founders had first established an order of men, notably the Franciscans and Dominicans.

SECOND PLANK. A term used to describe the sacrament of penance as the second (and further) opportunity that a sinner can grasp to save himself or herself spiritually if he or she loses God's friendship after baptism.

SECOND VATICAN COUNCIL. The twenty-first ecumenical council of the Catholic Church, first announced by Pope John XXIII, on January 25, 1959. He opened the council on October 11, 1962, and the first session ended on December 8 of the same year. After Pope John's death, June 3, 1963, Pope Paul VI reconvened the Council for the next three sessions, which ran from September 29 to December 4, 1963; September 14 to November 21, 1964; and September 14 to December 8, 1965. A combined total of 2,865 bishops and prelates took part in the Council proceedings, although 264 could not attend, mainly from Communist countries. Among the sixteen documents issued by the Council, the four constitutions—on divine revelation, the liturgy, and two on the Church—were the basis for the rest.

SECRET. A truth or fact, known to one or few persons, that should be kept concealed from others. Secrets may be natural, prom-

ised, or entrusted. The obligation to confidentiality is binding by natural or revealed law. (Etym. Latin *secretus,* separate, out of the way, secret, from *secernere,* to put apart, separate.)

SECRETARIAT FOR CHRISTIAN UNITY. Established by Pope John XXIII in 1960 as one of the preparatory commissions for the Second Vatican Council. It was reconstituted by Paul VI in 1967 and given its specific purpose, namely, the competence and duty of fostering the unity of Christians. It is also charged with dealing with the religious aspects of Judaism.

SECRETARIAT FOR NON-BELIEVERS. It was founded by Pope Paul VI in 1965, and its function is to deal with the subject of atheism in the modern world. Besides studying the causes of atheism and ways of coping with them, it is charged with promoting constructive dialogue with non-believers. The same Pope in 1967 further clarified and specified the role of the secretariat in the light of the conciliar *Constitution on the Church in the Modern World.*

SECRETARIAT OF CENTRAL AMERICA AND PANAMA (SECRETARIATO EPISCOPALE DELL'AMERICA CENTRALE, S.E.D.A.C.). An organization of the Catholic bishops of Central America and Panama, established in 1970, in accordance with the conciliar decree *Christus Dominus* and the motu proprio *Ecclesiae Sanctae* of Pope Paul VI. Its function is to exchange documents and other information and, as occasion arises, to initiate enterprises of common interest. It ordinarily meets every two years.

SECRETARY OF STATE. See PAPAL SECRETARY OF STATE.

SECRET PRAYER. One or more prayers, formerly said by the priest in a low tone, after the *Orate Fratres* and just before the Preface of the Mass. The prayer, normally only one, is now recited aloud and called the prayer *Super Oblata* (over the offerings).

SECRET SOCIETY. An organization whose members may not disclose the purposes, practices, or activities of their society to civil or ecclesiastical authorities. Because their secrecy often works to the disadvantage of nonmembers, through questionable control, and also to the detriment of the Catholic faith, the Church has for centuries forbidden Catholics to belong to secret societies and has often imposed severe canonical penalties on those who disobey. Under certain restricted conditions Catholics may retain a limited association with such organizations. Forbidden secret societies often sponsor benevolent and charitable enterprises, but they are prohibited mainly because their naturalism is a danger to the true faith. Among the secret societies forbidden by Church law are the Knights of Pythias, Odd Fellows, Sons of Temperance, and the Freemasons.

SECT, RELIGIOUS. An organized body of dissenters from an established or older form of faith, commonly applied to all religious bodies where State churches are established. In countries where many churches are recognized by law, sects are generally identified as religious groups that lack much organization or structure and that are not likely to endure. (Etym. Latin *sequi,* to follow, *secta,* a following.)

SECULAR. That which belongs to this life, in contrast with the sacred, which pertains to the life to come. The secular, therefore, is the earthly and not celestial; the human and not the divine; the created and not the uncreated; the temporal and not the eternal; the visible and not the spiritual; the humanly rational and explainable and not the mysterious and ineffable; the relative and therefore changeable with time, place, and circumstances, and not the absolute, which is immutable because and insofar as it is associated with the unchangeable God. (Etym. Latin *saecularis,* pertaining to the world, *saeculum,* the world.)

SECULAR ARM. In ecclesiastical law, the State or any lay authority when intervening in cases properly belonging to the jurisdiction of the Church. The intervention has generally been unsought and, in fact, was an intrusion that gravely interfered with the Church's right to administer her own affairs. In the Middle Ages, however, sometimes the assistance of the secular arm was sought, especially in trials for heresy or grave immorality when Church officials felt that sterner punishment was deserved than they could administer.

SECULAR CLERGY. Clergy who are engaged for the most part in pastoral work and who are not members of a religious institute. They are not bound by a vow of poverty or community life. But their celibacy, in the Latin Church, is under solemn oath and they promise obedience to a bishop as their immediate superior under the Pope.

SECULAR INSTITUTE. A society, whether clerical or lay, whose members profess the evangelical counsels in the world. Their purpose is to enable the members to attain Christian perfection and to exercise a full apostolate. They are distinguished in ecclesiastical law from other common associations of the faithful. They were first approved by Pope Pius XII on February 2, 1947, in his constitution *Provida Mater,* which still contains the guiding norms for their direction. Secular institutes differ from formal religious institutes or societies of common life because, while their members take vows or promises, these are not technically the public vows of religion, and the members do not live a common life. They are, however, states of Christian perfection, whose apostolate is in the world. The members are to work for the extension of Christ's kingdom in places and circumstances corresponding to people in the secular world.

SECULARISM. Technically the philosophy of naturalism advocated since the nineteenth century, first in England and then elsewhere. It is a closed system that affirms that human existence and destiny are fully explainable in terms of this world without reference to eternity. On its social side, secularism promotes the advancement of humanity's lot in this life, and charges Christianity with indifference to poverty and suffering because of its alleged preoccupation with God and the life to come.

SECULARITY. Legitimate concern for temporal and this-worldly interests, without denying their subordination to eternal and spiritual values.

SECULARIZATION. The act of permanent separation of men or women from their obligations to the religious life. They are released from their vows and may return to the world. Except in purely diocesan orders, secularization requires a papal indult. Another form of secularization refers to what occurs when civil power forcibly deprives the Church of the possession and use of her schools, hospitals, and welfare institutions, as happens in Communist countries.

SECUNDUM QUID. Literally "according to something," hence to some extent, or in some respect, or only in the sense noted. A standard phrase to express qualification or modification of a general principle.

SEDE VACANTE. The period during which an episcopal see or diocese is vacant, that is, without a bishop. Generally applied to the See of Rome. Procedures during this time follow the norms set down by Pope Paul VI in the apostolic constitution *Romano*

Pontifici Eligendo (1975), superseding the directives of Pope Pius XII (1945), and Pope John XXIII (1962).

SEDIA GESTATORIA. The ornamented chair serving as a portable papal throne, fastened to a small platform and carried on the shoulders of six men at solemn ceremonies in which the Pope officiates, especially in St. Peter's in Rome.

SEDILIA. Seats originally on the south side of a sanctuary for the officiating clergy during the Eucharistic liturgy. Already found in the catacombs where one stone seat was placed at the side of the altar. The new Order of the Mass prescribes: "The celebrant's chair should draw attention to his presiding over the community and leading its prayer. Hence the place for it is in the apex of the sanctuary, facing the people . . . Seats for others with special duties in the sanctuary should be in places convenient for their functions" (*Ordo Missae*, IV, 271). (Etym. Latin *sedilia*, seat, from *sedere*, to sit.)

SEDITIOUS. Ecclesiastical censure of a professed opinion that would subvert the true doctrine. It is, therefore, not only erroneous but subversive of faith or morals. (Etym. Latin *seditio*, dissension.)

SEDUCTION. The enticement of another to engage in illicit sexual activity. It is an invalidating impediment to marriage, from which the Church can give a dispensation. (Etym. Latin *seducere*, to lead away: *se*, apart + *ducere*, to lead.)

SEE. The seat (*sedes*) of the Church's papal or episcopal authority, vested in the Bishop of Rome for the universal Church and the local ordinary for each diocese. Episcopal sees have definite territorial boundaries, determined by the Holy See.

SEE OF PETER. See APOSTOLIC SEE, HOLY SEE, PAPACY, ROMAN SEE, ROME.

SEGNATURA APOSTOLICA. The highest tribunal of the Holy See; its origins go back to Pope Eugenius IV (reigned 1431–47). As reconstituted by Pope Paul VI in 1967, the Segnatura has two areas of competency, namely: 1. over tribunals already established, pilgrimages to Rome, matrimonial cases of nullity, erection of regional and interregional tribunals, handling cases involving concordats between various nations and the Holy See; 2. settling disputes arising from acts of administrative ecclesiastical power as a court of appeal, deciding on administrative controversies sent to it by the congregations of the Roman Curia, and judging on controversies submitted by the Roman Pontiff.

SELEUCIANISM. A form of Gnosticism that flourished in Galatia during the third century. It was crudely dualistic, claiming that God and matter were co-eternal, that God is the author of sin, that the human soul is made by angels out of material elements, that hell is the present world, that the resurrection is merely the generation of children. Seleucian ideas entered the stream of other heresies that tried to explain the problem of evil apart from deliberate malice in a created world.

SELF. The person considered as object of its own awareness and subject of its own acts, or, more generally, any being (including God) in relation to its own identity.

SELF-CONTROL. The act, power, or habit of having one's desires under the control of the will, enlightened by right reason and faith.

SELF-CRITICISM. The recognition that one's achievements do not fully measure up to one's moral capacity. This implies the honesty of recognizing one's weaknesses, failures, and limitations.

SELF-DECEPTION. The moral failure to recognize one's own limitations and failures or to see the real reasons for one's behavior.

SELF-DEFENSE. The right to use force against an unjust aggressor. The moral premises on which justifiable self-defense is based are the fact that the possession of life includes the right to use the means necessary to protect one's life, provided such means do not violate the rights of others. In the case of unjust aggression, the use of force and even a deathblow may be the only means of saving one's life. The rights of others are not thereby violated, for the assailant's right to live is suspended during the unjust attack. Moreover, the attacker can easily protect his or her life by merely ceasing from the attack.

SELF-DENIAL. The act or practice of giving up some legitimate satisfaction for the sake of some higher motive.

SELF-DETERMINATION. The ability to regulate one's own life from personally directed motives, rather than from a passive, although voluntary, response to social pressure.

SELF-FULFILLMENT. The realization of

one's potentialities as a human being. Since nature provides these potentialities, it is assumed that nature also intends to have them developed. Self-development, therefore, is one of the purposes of human life. From a Christian point of view, self-fulfillment is not an absolute. It presumes that God is also pleased with the sacrifice of certain powers or abilities, when this is done according to the teachings of faith and in the interest of a higher purpose, such as evangelization or the service of one's neighbor.

SELF-LOVE. Inordinate regard for self to the neglect of others and indifference to their needs. In narcissism the attention is centered on the body, especially sexual self-satisfaction.

SEMI-ARIANISM. The teaching of certain theologians who, after the Council of Nicaea (A.D. 325), sought a compromise between Arianism and the doctrine of Christ's consubstantiality with the Father. They were led by Basil, Bishop of Ancyra, and their sympathies were toward orthodoxy, although they substituted *homoiousios* (similar to) the Father. St. Athanasius treated them kindly and their influence was felt in the reaffirmation of the Nicene Creed at the ecumenical Council of Constantinople in the year 381.

SEMID. *Semiduplex*—semi-double feast.

SEMINAL PRINCIPLE. In Augustinian theology the seed or principle implanted in all creatures by God, awaiting favorable opportunity for the development of that creature. It corresponds to St. Thomas Aquinas' view, taken from Aristotle, that all creatures have potencies that are actuated in any change.

SEMINARY. A school established for the academic and spiritual training of candidates for the priesthood. The Council of Trent, July 15, 1563, ordered the establishment of a seminary in every diocese. Seminaries that are not houses of study for the regular clergy are of different kinds, depending on the authority that establishes them and has jurisdiction over them. Thus seminaries may be diocesan, regional, interdiocesan, provincial, and pontifical. The decree of the Second Vatican Council, *Optatam Totius,* issued in 1965, treats at length about the curriculum and administration of seminarians. In 1979 Pope John Paul II issued the Apostolic Constitution *Sapientia Christiana* on ecclesiastical universities and faculties. The document immediately affects all institutions of higher education, including seminaries, which have been canonically erected or approved by the Holy See with the right to confer academic degrees by the authority of the same See. Indirectly it affects all Catholic seminaries. Among other detailed provisions, the constitution requires that, "All teachers, before they are given a permanent post . . . must receive a declaration of *nihil obstat* [formal approval] from the Holy See" (Part One, III, 27).

SEMI-PELAGIANISM. Popular in Southern France, especially in the monasteries, it was formally condemned by the Council of Orange in the year 529. But the term Semi-Pelagian was later used by critics of the Molinist theory on grace and free will, accusing the Jesuits of so exalting human freedom as to deny effectively the supremacy of grace.

SEMI-PUBLIC ORATORY. A place set apart for divine worship for the benefit of a community or a group of the faithful, but without anyone else having the right to free access.

SEMITES. A race of people whose ancestral home was in Asia and Africa, and reputed descendants of Shem, son of Noah. In historic times all of Western Asia except Asia Minor was Semitic, and philologists divide the race into four main groups: Babylonian-Assyrian, Chanaanite, Aramaic, and Arabian. Their original home was probably Arabia.

SEMPITERNITY. Eternity considered as having neither beginning nor end; hence possessed only by God, who, unlike creatures, never began. Moreover, he always will be because he cannot not be, unlike creatures who may continue eternally but not by a necessity of being.

SENSATION. Consciousness of a single, specific object by means of one of the sense powers or organs in a material way. In human beings sensation therefore differs from thought in two ways: it is only of material things, whereas thought is also about spiritual things, e.g., God, love, and liberty; sensation is always a material way of knowing, whereas thought may be about material reality, e.g., the sun, a stone, or a tree, but it is a spiritual kind of knowledge. (Etym. Latin *sensatio,* knowledge through the senses, *sentire,* to feel, perceive.)

SENSE OF SIN. A salutary fear produced in the believing soul by a clear understanding of the nature and malice of sin. Its keenness depends on a person's holiness and is most sensitive among the saints. Its quality is an awareness of God's sanctity in contrast with one's own weakness, and therefore a sense of constant dependence on divine grace.

SENSISM. The philosophy that reduces all human knowledge to sense experience and all human desire to bodily appetite. Accordingly it denies universal ideas, internal freedom, the moral difference between sense and intellect, and the spirituality of the soul. (Etym. Latin *sensus,* feeling, perception; faculty of bodily perception.)

SENSUALISM. Addiction to sensual pleasures, especially carnal gratification. Also the theory that all human satisfaction is basically in the sense appetite. It corresponds psychologically to the doctrine of materialism in philosophy.

SENTENCES, BOOK OF. The classic work of the theologian Peter Lombard (1100–62). He wrote the four *Books of the Sentences* (1145–52) and is called the Master of the Sentences, or the Master. This work was the standard textbook in theology for four centuries and greatly influenced St. Thomas Aquinas. Its first part treats of God and the Trinity, Providence, predestination, and evil; Part Two, of creation, angels, the Fall, grace, and sin; Part Three, of the Incarnation, Redemption, the virtues, and commandments; Part Four, of the last things. It set the pace for all future Catholic theology by combining respect for the Church's authority with profound analysis through the right use of reason.

SENTENTIA COMMUNIS. See THEOLOGICAL NOTES.

SENTIMENT. An act of the human will consciously liking or disliking someone or something. It differs from mere feeling, which is purely sensible, and from emotion, which is normally more intense. Sentiment plays an important role in the spiritual life as a kind of supernatural impulse toward what is morally good and away from what is morally bad. (Etym. Latin *sentimentum,* from *sentire,* to feel.)

SEPARATED BRETHREN. All Christians who are baptized and believe in Christ but are not professed Catholics. More commonly the term is applied to Protestants.

SEPARATION, MARITAL. Temporary or even permanent separation of husband and wife, without the right of remarriage until the death of one of the parties. Permitted by the Church on account of adultery, loss of faith, or other grave reasons. Cohabitation ceases but the marriage bond remains.

SEPARATISM. Advocating separation from an established church. Term used especially of the Congregationalists and others who separated from the Church of England.

SEPTUAG. *Septuagesima*—seventieth day (always a Sunday) before Easter.

SEPTUAGESIMA. The seventieth day before Easter, and the third Sunday before Lent. Terminology not used in the Latin Rite since the revision of the liturgy after the Second Vatican Council.

SEPTUAGINT. The most important translation of the Hebrew Old Testament into Greek. As the story goes, the Egyptian king, Ptolemy II (309–246 B.C.), sought a copy of Jewish law for his library. Eleazer, the Jewish high priest, sent six scholars from each of the Twelve Tribes to Alexandria to work on the translation. Because of the number of the scholars involved, their joint co-operative production was called the Septuagint, abbreviated LXX. The early Christians used the Septuagint as a basis for their belief in Jesus as the Messiah. As time went on, it steadily became a Christian possession and Jews lost interest in it. (Etym. Latin *septuaginta,* seventy.)

SEPULCHER. The small cavity in an altar stone in which are placed the relics of a saint. According to the Church's provisions since the Second Vatican Council, "The custom of putting relics of saints, whether martyrs or not, into or beneath consecrated altars, is to be commended. But it is important to verify the authenticity of the relics" (*Ordo Missae,* V, 266). (Etym. Latin *sepulcrum,* tomb, from *sepelire,* to bury.)

SEQUENCE. A hymn of joy in varying meter sung or recited before the Gospel at Mass on certain feast days. Those that have survived are the Easter *Victimae Paschali,* the *Veni Sancte Spiritus* at Pentecost, and the *Lauda Sion* for Corpus Christi. The *Dies Irae* at some Masses for the Dead is not, strictly speaking, a liturgical sequence. (Etym. Latin *sequentia,* a following, sequence.)

SERAPHIC BLESSING. The blessing that St. Francis of Assisi wrote down at the request of Brother Leo at Mount Alverna in 1224. It says: "May the Lord bless you and keep you. May He show His face to you and have mercy on you. May He turn His countenance to you and give you peace.

May the Lord bless you, Brother Leo." It is based on the words of Yahweh to Moses (Numbers 6:22–27) and is now among the solemn blessings in Ordinary Time that a priest may give at the end of Mass.

SERAPHIC CONTEMPLATION. Elevation of the mind and heart, resting on God and tasting the joys of the Spirit. The soul's love is greater than its available knowledge, with the heart tending toward its object beyond what the mind understands of what the will loves.

SERAPHIM. Angels composing the highest choir of the angelic kingdom. The root meaning of their name is "to consume with fire," indicating their intense love of the Holy Trinity. (Etym. Hebrew *saraf,* plural *serafim,* burning, glowing.)

SERMON. See HOMILY.

SERMON ON THE MOUNT. The most comprehensive discourse of Jesus reported in the New Testament. It was delivered to a multitude on one of the hills near Capernaum. It extends over three chapters in Matthew's Gospel (Matthew 5, 6, 7). An abbreviated form appears also in Luke (Luke 6:20–49). The sermon outlined the kind of life that a true follower of Christ should live if he seeks the kingdom of heaven. It opens with the Beatitudes as guides to those who are to be the "salt of the earth." Jesus explained how the New Law fulfills the Old Law but carries it to a new level where love is the ultimate motive for law. He taught the Lord's Prayer as the way the disciple should approach the Father. The Golden Rule should guide people in their relations with others. Marriage is to be monogamous and the followers of Christ must be willing to carry the cross.

SERPENT, BRAZEN. A symbol of the crucified Christ. The bronze serpent entwined on the cross recalls the words of the Savior: "The Son of Man must be lifted up as Moses lifted up the serpent in the desert" (John 3:14). Though mentioned in Scripture, it became a standard symbol of the Crucifixion only in the thirteenth century.

SERPENT, COILED. The symbol of Satan, also of evil. The tempter in Eden appeared as a speaking serpent, subtle in his questioning, the easier to seduce Eve. In connection with Mary the serpent represents the fulfillment of the prophecy "I will make you enemies of each other, you and the woman, your offspring and her offspring. It will crush your head and you will strike its heel" (Genesis 3:15). A coiled serpent with an apple in its mouth, seen encircling the globe of the earth, appears as an emblem of the evil spirit being overcome by Christ through Mary in images of the Immaculate Conception.

SERRA INTERNATIONAL. An organization under Catholic leadership whose purpose is to foster vocations to the priesthood and the religious life. Aggregated since 1951 to the Pontifical Society for Priestly Vocations.

SERVER. Also called an acolyte, a server is a boy or man who assists the priest in a sanctuary, especially at the Eucharistic liturgy. In the post-conciliar directives for ministers at the altar, they are to be vested in an alb or surplice (*Ordo Missae,* 1970, III, 81).

SERVICE. In general, performing one's religious duty as a creature toward God, and fulfilling one's moral responsibility of meeting the needs of others. To serve God is the primary obligation of human beings, personally and socially, to be done in acts of worship and prayer; and in acts of virtue as prescribed by the natural and revealed laws of God. This corresponds to the first three commandments of the Decalogue, and is summarized in the precept to "love the Lord your God with all your heart, with all your soul, and with all your mind" (Matthew 22:37). To serve others is the secondary obligation of a person, deriving from the preceding duty and depending on it. This corresponds to the last seven commandments of God and is synthesized in the precept "You must love your neighbor as yourself" (Matthew 22:39). On these two commandments of service, Christ says, rest the whole law and the Prophets also. (Etym. Latin *servus,* a slave, servant, subject to the right of others.)

SERVILE FEAR. Selfish fear based on the dread of pain to oneself that would follow if another were offended. It is the fear of punishment for wrongdoing, without being motivated by honor or a sense of duty, and least of all by love. Theologically, however, servile fear may co-exist with filial fear. There is nothing incompatible in both loving and fearing God. The object of loving him is the divine goodness, of fearing him the divine justice. However, purely servile fear, with no love of God but only self-love that fears the divine punishments, is, at least in theory, inconsistent with the true love of God. See also FILIAL FEAR.

SERVILE WORK. Originally the work done by serfs from which they were freed on Sundays and holy days in order to worship God. Until recently, servile work, forbidden on Sundays, was work that was chiefly physical. At present servile work is heavy manual labor, or such work as in a given society people commonly associate with strenuous effort and do not engage in when they have the freedom to avoid it. Implicit in the Church's prohibition of servile work on Sundays is fidelity to the divine commandment to keep holy the Sabbath. This means avoiding activities that would hinder renewal of soul and body, i.e., needless work or business, unnecessary shopping or housekeeping.

SERVITES. Members of the Order of the Servants of the Blessed Virgin Mary. It was founded at Florence in 1233 by seven councilors of the city, who have since been canonized as the Seven Holy Founders, among whom the first leaders were St. Buonfiglio dei Monaldi and St. Alessio de' Falconieri, who remained a lay brother. The order was approved by the Holy See in 1249 and again in 1304. Its apostolate is among the faithful and non-Christians and includes promoting the devotion to the Blessed Virgin, especially under the title of the Sorrowful Mother. There are several institutes of women religious, pontifical and diocesan, specially devoted to Our Lady of Sorrows. The best known are the contemplative Servite nuns (Second Order) founded by two penitents of St. Philip Benizi (1233–85) about the time of his death; and the nuns of the Third Order, founded by St. Juliana Falconieri in 1306, who care for the sick and the poor and the education of children.

SERVUS SERVORUM DEI. "The servant of the servants of God." A title that the Pope sometimes uses of himself in official documents. First used by Pope St. Gregory the Great (reigned 590–604), it came into general use since the pontificate of Gregory VII (1073–85).

SETH. The third son of Adam and Eve, born after Abel's death. He became the father of a number of sons and daughters, the only one of whom named in Genesis is Enosh (Genesis 4:25). Seth lived to be nine hundred twelve years old (Genesis 5:6–8).

SEVEN CHURCHES OF ASIA. The churches in Asia Minor mentioned by St. John in the Book of Revelation. They are Ephesus, Smyrna, Pergamum, Thyatira, Sardis, Philadelphia, and Laodicea (Revelation 1:11). While on the island of Patmos, St. John was ordered by the Lord to instruct and admonish their bishops, either praising or blaming them for the way they were administering their dioceses.

SEVEN CHURCHES OF ROME. The basilicas in Rome that in ancient times were the main churches to be visited by pilgrims, especially as a form of penance for grave sins. They are St. Peter, St. John Lateran, St. Mary Major, Holy Cross in Jerusalem (within Rome proper), St. Paul, St. Lawrence, and St. Sebastian (outside the walls).

SEVEN COUNCILS. The first seven ecumenical councils of the Church, namely Nicaea (A.D. 325), Constantinople I (381), Ephesus (431), Chalcedon (451), Constantinople II (553), Constantinople III (680–81), and Nicaea II (787). They are the only councils on which the Eastern and Western Churches agree and among the Eastern Churches separated from Rome are the only test of orthodoxy.

SEVEN DEACONS. The first seven helpers ordained by the Apostles to carry on the charitable care of the poor and other material duties, so that the Twelve would not be drawn away from their primary duty of preaching the new faith. St. Stephen, the proto-martyr, was one of their number (Acts 6:1–6).

SEVEN DOLORS. See DOLORS, SEVEN.

SEVEN DOLORS SCAPULAR. Badge of a confraternity established by the Servites of Mary. It is black and often bears a picture of the Mother of Sorrows.

SEVEN GIFTS. The special gifts of the Holy Spirit infused into the soul at baptism and retained by everyone in the state of grace, namely: wisdom, understanding, counsel, fortitude, knowledge, piety, and fear of the Lord.

SEVEN HEAVENS. A popular belief, never confirmed by the Church, that heaven is divided into seven levels of beatitude, the highest being the seventh. The expression "seventh heaven" is a remnant of this belief.

SEVEN SACRAMENTS. The seven rites instituted by Christ to confer the grace they signify, namely baptism, confirmation, Eucharist, penance, orders, matrimony, and anointing of the sick. The number and names of the sacraments and their substantial institution by Christ (purpose and essential ritual) were defined on March 3, 1547, by the Council of Trent (Denzinger 1601).

SEVENTH CRUSADE. Preached by Pope Innocent IV, this expedition (1248–54) was led by St. Louis of France. But the king was captured in Egypt. On his release he returned to France.

SEVEN WORDS OF CHRIST. The last words of Christ spoken from the Cross, recorded by Mark, Luke, and John. In sequence they are "Father, forgive them for they do not know what they are doing"; "Indeed, I promise you, today you will be with Me in paradise" to the penitent thief; "Woman, this is your son," spoken to Mary; "This is your mother," Christ's bequest to John; "My God, my God, why have you deserted me?" Parched with thirst, Christ called out, "I am thirsty"; and then, "It is accomplished." When every prophecy had been fulfilled, "Father, into your hands I commit my spirit." Several oratorios interpreting them have been written.

SEXAG. *Sexagesima*—sixtieth day before Easter.

SEXAGESIMA. The sixtieth day before Easter, and the second Sunday before Lent. Terminology not used since the revision of the liturgy after the Second Vatican Council.

SEX EDUCATION. Instruction in the right use of sex, according to the teachings of the Church in the light of sound reason and the norms of Christian revelation. The Church teaches that young people should be given and adequately taught about the facts of human procreation according to their age and mental ability, more so today when they are exposed to so many perversions of sex in the media. It should always be given along with the necessary moral instruction. Parents have the primary right and duty to give this education. If they fail, it should be given by a truly qualified person. Collective or public sex education is discouraged because of the risk of incompetence in the teacher, and the practical impossibility of meeting the personal needs of each child in a mass presentation of this intimate subject.

SEXT. The part of the Divine Office that is said at the sixth hour, that is, about midday. Depending on the time of day, the one reciting the office has a choice of saying Terce, Sext, or None.

SEXTON. An official, usually a layman, who acts as sacristan, cares for a church edifice and grounds, rings the bells and serves as custodian. Sextons also care for the cemetery and dig the graves for burial, where part of a church property serves as a cemetery.

SEXUAL PLEASURE. The emotional satisfaction that arises from the movement of those organs and secretions that aid the act of procreation. This pleasure reaches its peak in a healthy man in the pleasure that accompanies the emission of seed, or in women and youths below the age of puberty in the diffusion of some secretion from the sexual glands. The Catholic Church holds that direct sexual pleasure outside marriage is gravely sinful and never admits of slight matter; indirect sexual pleasure may be either sinful or no sin at all. Direct sexual pleasure is desired and enjoyed in itself and is the privilege only of married partners between themselves. It is forbidden to the unmarried because such conduct would be contrary to the virtue of chastity. Indirect sexual pleasure is not sought for itself but arises from some other action that is performed for a good reason. If there is such a reason, the actions are not sinful, provided a person neither intends the sexual pleasure nor consents to it if spontaneously aroused.

SHADDAI. Hebrew name for God, the Almighty, the sacred name spelled out on the phylacteries that Jewish men wear when they pray.

SHALOM. Peace, used as a salutation, and found as inscriptions on Jewish and Christian graves. Also, as a greeting, *shalom aleichem* (peace be with you, *pax vobis*) has become part of the Eucharistic liturgy since Christ's greeting on Easter Sunday night.

SHAMROCK. A symbol of the Trinity. Three leaflets on one stem representing three persons in one God. Said to have been used by St. Patrick in his sermon to Laoghaire, chief of the Irish clans, who came to seize the saint for daring to light the Easter fire on the Hill of Slane. For this reason and because Patrick generally used it to illustrate the Trinity, the shamrock has become an emblem of the Apostle of Ireland and a symbol of the Irish people everywhere.

SHARING IN GUILT. Participation in another person's sin. Traditionally there are nine ways that a person may share in someone else's sin, either by causing or inciting the person to do wrong (1–4), or by approving a wrong already done (5–9), as follows: 1. by counsel; 2. by command; 3. by consent; 4. by provocation; 5. by praise or flattery; 6. by concealment; 7. by being an active partner in the sin; 8. by silence; 9. by defending the evil done.

SHEEP. Symbols of the Twelve Apostles, with Christ in the center as the Good Shepherd. A later symbol early found in the catacombs shows Our Lord either supporting a wounded sheep on his shoulder with the other sheep nearby or the Shepherd rescuing the wandering lost ewe caught in a briary thicket. The twenty-third psalm speaks of "the Lord is my shepherd, I shall not want." In song and story it is illustrative of God's providence and concern. Sheep are symbols of docility, humility, and long suffering, all attributes expected of those who follow the Lamb of God. Sheep are also an emblem of St. Germaine (c. 1579–1601), the poor abandoned child of Pibrac, near Toulouse in France.

SHEKINAH. The dwelling place of God. It is any visible manifestation of God's presence, several times alluded to in the Bible. It corresponds to God's glory in Isaiah 60:2, his glory in Romans 9:4, and the cloud that directed the Israelites on their way to the Promised Land (Exodus 14:19).

SHELL. An emblem of baptism since the twelfth century. Once pouring water was the accepted mode for baptizing, the shell became a handy accessory. Also a symbol for the pilgrim, explaining probably why the shell is an emblem of St. James the Apostle, whose shrine is a famed place of pilgrimage. It is also the emblem for St. Augustine, who had a vision of a child (believed to be Christ) who told him that he could sooner empty the ocean with a shell than understand the Trinity. The shell is likewise one of the numerous symbols of the Blessed Virgin Mary.

SHEM. The oldest son of Noah and brother of Ham and Japheth (Genesis 5:32). "From these three sons the whole earth was peopled," since they were the only survivors of the Flood (Genesis 9:19). Those descended from Shem—Hebrews, Arabs, Aramaeans (Genesis 10:22–31)—were called Shemites, the equivalent of the modern word Semites.

SHEMA. The Hebrew name for Deuteronomy, and the single most recited biblical verse among the Jewish people. In its shortest form it says, "Hear O Israel, the Lord Our God, the Lord is One" (Deuteronomy 6:4). But the regular Shema in the liturgy covers three portions—Deuteronomy 6:4–9, 11:13–21, and Numbers 15:37–41.

SHEMITES. See SHEM.

SHEOL. The Hebrew word for hell, corresponding to the Greek Hades. At first a vague, gloomy place in which departed souls lived, gradually it was looked upon as a place of terrible punishment for unworthy souls. The lesson is vividly taught in the New Testament that Sheol is the destination of souls dying in sin. Luke speaks of the "torment in Hades" (Luke 16:23). The Letter to the Hebrews warns of "the dreadful prospect of judgment and of the raging fire that is to burn rebels" (Hebrews 10:27). Revelation describes "the fire and brimstone in which they will be tortured in the presence of the holy angels and the Lamb, and the smoke of their torture will go up forever and ever" (Revelation 14:10–11).

SHEPHERD OF HERMAS. An ethical treatise of the mid-second century. It is a work of major historical importance, preaching penance and consisting of five visions, twelve mandates, and two parables. It witnesses to the high moral principles of the early Church. The authorship has been attributed to Hermas, mentioned by St. Paul in his letter to the Romans (16:14), but it was more likely written by a brother of Pope St. Pius I.

SHIP. A symbol of the Church, usually with a cross on her sails. Frequently the ship is represented in full sail plowing through turbulent waters that are testing her progress. St. Hippolytus spoke of the Church as a "boat beaten by the waves but never submerged." Fishermen saints were often represented with the ship as their emblem, so too the Apostle St. Jude. St. Brendan, the Irish navigator, and St. Francis Xavier both are symbolized by ships. St. Elmo or Erasmus is called the patron saint of sailors, and the phenomenon of St. Elmo's fire, often seen at sea, has been named after him.

SHRINE. In general, a holy place. It may be a box-shaped repository in which relics of a saint are preserved; or the sacred image or statue of Our Lord, the Blessed Virgin, or a saint in church or at home to which special devotion is given. But mainly shrines are prominent sacred localities. They may be the burial place of a saint, or where he or she lived or died, or where a heavenly apparition took place. Shrines are the focuses of pilgrimages by the faithful and often of miraculous phenomena approved by the Church. (Etym. Latin *scrinium*, box, bookcase.)

SHROUD. See HOLY SHROUD. (Etym. Middle English *sc(h)rud,* garment, clothing.)

SHROVETIDE. The few days before Ash Wednesday, particularly the day before Shrove Tuesday. It is associated with confessing one's sins and has in many places become a time for holding carnivals, as the last time for festivity before the Lenten season of penance.

SIBYL. One of the prophetesses of classical mythology, of whom there were as many as ten in different places and times. Among them the most famous was the Cumaean Sibyl, described by Vergil in the *Aeneid*. The Sibylline writings, of unknown origin, were kept at Rome in the Capitol and consulted by the state in times of emergency. They were destroyed in the burning of the Capitol in 82 B.C., and a new collection was made, also burned, in A.D. 405. In the second century B.C., Hellenistic Jews had produced, for propaganda purposes, their own version of the Sibylline Oracles. The Jewish prophecies were freely used by Christian Apologists in the second century, and further oracles from Christian sources were added by the third century. St. Augustine quotes a passage in his *City of God* (18:23). Other Fathers of the Church, e.g., Theophilus of Antioch and Clement of Alexandria, drew on the Oracles in support of Christ and the Church.

SICK CALL. The call for a priest to minister to the spiritual needs of a person who is gravely ill. Normally the sacraments administered on a sick call are penance, Holy Communion, and anointing of the sick.

SIC TRANSIT GLORIA MUNDI. Thus passes the glory of the world. Words addressed to a newly elected pope during the coronation ceremony.

SIDON. A Phoenician city that is the present site of Saida, in Lebanon, a few miles south of Beirut. It is one of the oldest cities mentioned in Scripture, dating back to the second millennium B.C. (Genesis 10:19). Sidon became an important seaport and shipbuilding center during successive regimes of Persian, Greek, and Roman domination. In the Old Testament its reputation for evildoing aroused the wrath of prophets warning Sidonians of a terrible fate. Ezekiel, for instance, quoted Yahweh as threatening, "I will send the plague to her; blood shall flow in her streets, and in her the dead will fall" (Ezekiel 28:23). In the New Testament we are told that Jesus visited Tyre and Sidon on his way to the Sea of Galilee (Mark 7:31). Sometime later Paul visited friends in Sidon on one of his journeys (Acts 27:3).

SIG. *Sigillum*—seal.

SIGILLUM. See SEAL OF CONFESSION.

SIGN. Something that leads to something else. It may be an arbitrary or conventional sign that has a connection with what is signified only by agreement among people, as a flag symbolizes a nation. Or it may be a pure sign that leads to the knowledge of something without itself being first known, as our ideas lead to the knowledge of real objects. Instrumental signs give meaning or understanding, as words lead to the knowledge of things and of mental status. Manifestative signs show the existence of something else, as a person's external behavior indicates his or her personality and training.

Each of these types of signs may be either natural or supernatural depending on whether its basis is founded on natural reason or divine revelation.

The whole of the Church's liturgy is built on the function of word, action, and object signs as symbols of the sacred. But among the sacred signs the most important are the sacraments, which not only manifest the special presence of God but actually confer the grace they signify. (Etym. Latin *signum*, mark, sign, characteristic.)

SIGN OF THE CROSS. The most popular profession of the Christian faith in action form. The cruciform sign professes one's belief in human redemption through Christ's death on the Cross. The pronunciation of the names of the Three Divine Persons professes belief in the Holy Trinity. The first of the Church's sacramentals, it has its origins in apostolic times. It is made by saying, "In the name of the Father, and of the Son, and of the Holy Spirit," and its action takes the form of a cross. One touches the forehead, the breast, and the left and right shoulders with the right hand as the words are recited. The prayer ends with "Amen" and is regularly made with holy water as a person enters a church or chapel or, in religious communities, upon entering one's room.

SIGNS OF THE TIMES. The signs predicted by Christ foretelling his second coming and the end of the world (Matthew 24:3–44). However, the term is popularly applied to any events in contemporary history that are interpreted as signs of God's providence, especially of his justice in punishing sinners and calling them to repentance.

SILAS. An active member of the first group of Christian leaders in Jerusalem. He was known also as Silvanus (I Thessalonians 1:1; II Thessalonians 1:1). He is mentioned several times as traveling with Peter or Paul and Timothy, perhaps acting as a kind of secretary or messenger (I Peter 5:12). On one occasion when Paul and Barnabas split up in disagreement, Paul chose Silas as a replacement (Acts 15:40). When the Council at Jerusalem was concluded and a message was prepared for the Christians in Antioch, assuring them that the Law of Moses was not an inflexible requirement for entrance to the Church, Silas and Barsabbas were sent with the letter to confirm its contents and assure an amicable reception (Acts 15:22–23). On Paul's trip through Galatia, he and Silas were beaten and imprisoned in Philippi (Acts 16:19–39). When the magistrates learned that they were Roman citizens, they were released—but not before the jailer and his family were converted. (Etym. Greek *silas;* from Aramaic *se'ila,* Saul.)

SILENCE. In spiritual terms, the conscious effort to communicate with God or the invisible world of faith in preference to conversation with other people. It is, therefore, not the mere absence of sound or physical stillness, except as either a precondition for recollection of spirit or the perceptible effect of being recollected. (Etym. Latin *silere,* to be still, noiseless.)

SILOAM. A water tunnel constructed in the eighth century B.C. at the direction of King Hezekiah (II Chronicles 32:30). It was primarily a defense measure in anticipation of attack by Sennacherib's army, which might cut off the main water supply of Israel (II Kings 18:17). As the water flowed into the southeast corner of the city, it emptied into a reservoir called the Pool of Siloam. It still survives, feeding water into a modern Pool of Siloam built centuries later. During his public ministry, one of Jesus' miracles was curing a blind man by having him wash in the Pool of Siloam (John 9:7).

SILUVA, OUR LADY OF. Lithuanian shrine to the Weeping Virgin, to which over a hundred thousand formerly came annually to pray to Mary for help, some to be cured. In the early sixteenth century, when much of the country was Protestant and Lithuania was fighting both Russia and Sweden, a few shepherd children saw the vision of a beautiful young woman holding a sleeping child in her arms. Dressed in white, she was crying, her tears falling on her little one. The children ran home to return with their parents and neighbors, among them a Lutheran minister serving locally. The lady told them that all the cause of her sorrow was the absence of the old church that had honored her Son and had once been on the spot where she was. An old man whose blindness was later cured at the shrine verified the lady's story. He directed the digging there and an old chest filled with altar vessels and a picture of the Virgin was brought to light. Buried records told of a church there in 1457, long since destroyed. A new church was built on the old grounds and the picture of Mary enthroned within. Pilgrims came from great distances to the hallowed spot. Since 1940, when Lithuania was incorporated into the U.S.S.R., the state of the shrine is uncertain.

SILVANUS. See SILAS.

SIMEON. 1. the second son of Jacob and Leah; he was more clearly associated with Judah than with any other of his brothers. From the final prophetic utterance of Jacob concerning his sons, it is clear that he deplored the life Simeon led. He spoke of his son's "malicious plans" and considered him "accursed" for his "ruthlessness" (Genesis 49:5–7); 2. the saintly old man who was in the Temple when Jesus was brought in by his parents to be consecrated to the Lord. The Holy Spirit had revealed to Simeon that he would not die before he set eyes on the long-promised Messiah. He recognized Jesus instantly and hailed him as "the light to enlighten the pagans and the glory of your people Israel." The event is commemorated in the fourth Joyous Mystery of the Rosary, the Presentation of the Child Jesus in the Temple (Luke 2:22–32).

SIMILITUDE. Some likeness or resemblance of one to another. Similitudes are the basis of all teaching of revealed truth. We come to know, more or less, of the meaning of the mysteries of faith by means of comparison with things that are known by reason. Every truth of revelation is communicated to the world as a similitude, e.g., grace as life, sacraments as signs, the Church as a body, heaven as a kingdom. (Etym. Latin *similitudo,* likeness.)

SIMON. 1. Simon Peter, the head of the Apostles and the first Pope (see PETER); 2. Simon the Canaanite, called the Zealot. Another one of the Twelve Apostles (Luke 6:15); 3. a leper who was cured by Jesus and who invited him to his home in Bethany for dinner (Mark 14:3); 4. a cousin of Jesus referred to as his "brother" (Mark 6:3); 5. a man from Cyrene who was compelled to help Jesus carry the Cross (Mark 15:21).

SIMON MAGUS. A magician who must have been exceedingly skillful, because many Samaritans attributed divine powers to him. He became a Christian and was astonished at the miracles performed by Philip, Peter, and John. He incurred Peter's wrath by offering money to him to learn the Apostle's secrets. Peter's angry reprimand frightened Simon, and he begged Peter to pray for him (Acts 8:9–24). See also SIMONY.

SIMONY. A sacrilege that consists in buying and selling what is spiritual in return for what is temporal. In simony the person tries to equate material things, such as money, with spiritual things, such as divine grace, and treats the latter as though he or some other human being had full ownership of what really belongs to God. The term "simony" originated with the biblical account of Simon Magus, who sought to purchase from St. Peter the spiritual power derived from the imposition of hands and the invocation of the Holy Spirit (Acts 8:18). Simony includes both agreements that are illicit by divine law and those which the law of the Church forbids as greater protection and reverence for spiritual goods. Thus to promise prayers only in exchange for a certain sum of money is simony forbidden by divine (natural) law. To confer sacred orders or obtain some position of authority in the Church in return for money or its equivalent is simony forbidden by ecclesiastical law. When simony is against the divine law, it is always a grave sin. Its gravity in other cases depends on the serious nature of what is bought or sold, and on the degree of scandal given. (Etym. Latin *simonia,* after Simon Magus.)

SIMPL. *Simplex*—simple feast.

SIMPLE. The quality of not having parts, hence undivided and not composite; also not having potency or imperfection. Spirit is simple because it is not divisible into quantitative parts. Angels are simple because they are not composed of body and soul. God is perfectly simple because he has no composition of any kind. (Etym. Latin *simplex,* simple, absolute, frank, without parts; literally, onefold.)

SIMPLE IGNORANCE. Such ignorance of an ecclesiastical law or its penalty as a person makes some effort to be enlightened on but the effort is feeble and insufficient. Nevertheless it excuses a person from automatic (*latae sententiae*) penalties.

SIMPLE INTELLIGENCE. God's knowl-edge of his own ideas and of all possibilities, by knowing all the ways in which his divine essence can be imitated in the created world.

SIMPLE UNITIVE WAY. Also called the active unitive way, it is characterized by the cultivation of the gifts of the Holy Spirit and by the simplification of prayer. Although not habitually enjoying infused contemplation, a person in the simple unitive way is intimately united with God and docile to the inspirations of the Holy Spirit.

SIMPLE VALIDATION. Making valid a previously invalid marriage by having the parties renew their marital consent. This is the preferred method and should be used whenever possible to validate a marriage that was invalid for lack of knowledge or free consent, or because of some invalidating impediment that has since been removed.

SIMPLE VOW. Every vow, whether private or public, that is not expressly acknowledged by the Church as solemn. The term came into use with the Church's recognition that religious congregations are authentic institutes of Christian perfection, as distinct from religious orders. Simple vows render actions committed against the vows illicit, unlike solemn vows that make such actions invalid.

SIMPLICITER. Simply, without limitation. In philosophy, the opposite of *secundum quid*. In canon law, a term used to describe certain, less serious cases reserved to the Holy See.

SIMPLICITY. As a character trait, the quality of not being affected; therefore, unassuming and unpretentious. A simple person is honest, sincere, and straightforward. Simplicity is single-mindedness. As a supernatural virtue it seeks only to do the will of God without regard to self-sacrifice or self-advantage.

SIMPLICITY OF GOD. The absence of any composition or divisibility in God. According to the Fourth Lateran and First Vatican Councils, God is an "absolutely simple substance or nature" (Denzinger 800). His simplicity is absolute. In him there is no composition of any kind, of substance and accidents, of essence and existence, of nature and person, of power and activity, of genus and specific difference. The theological basis of divine simplicity is that God is pure actuality, which is incompatible with any kind of composition.

SIMULATION, SACRAMENTAL. The simulation of a sacrament by changing secretly and unlawfully either the matter or the form or the necessary intention so that the sacrament becomes invalid and the recipient is led into error. One must distinguish, however, between simulation and pretense. In pretense, neither the matter nor the form of the sacrament is used; for instance, a confessor who has to deny absolution to a penitent expressly tells him of the fact, then recites some prayers and gives a blessing so that bystanders will not realize that absolution has been denied. Although it is sometimes permitted to pretend to administer a sacrament, for a sufficiently grave reason, simulation of the sacraments is never lawful.

SIN. "A word, deed or desire in opposition to the eternal law" (St. Augustine). Sin is a deliberate transgression of a law of God, which identifies the four essentials of every sin. A law is involved, implying that there are physical laws that operate with necessity, and moral laws that can be disregarded by human beings. God is offended, so that the divine dimension is never absent from any sin. Sin is a transgression, since Catholicism holds that grace is resistible and the divine will can be disobeyed. And the transgression is deliberate, which means that a sin is committed whenever a person knows that something is contrary to the law of God and then freely does the action anyway. (Etym. Old English *synn, syn,* sin; Old High German *sunta, suntea,* perhaps to Latin *sons,* guilty.)

SIN AGAINST FAITH. The deliberate withholding of assent to what God has revealed. As commonly understood, there are five principal sins against faith: profession of a false religion, willful doubt, disbelief, or denial of an article of faith, and culpable ignorance of the doctrines of the Catholic Church.

SIN AGAINST RELIGION. The deliberate refusal to give to God the honor and worship he deserves as humanity's Creator and final destiny. Sins against religion may be either explicit, as in formal contempt of God, or implicit, as in the practice of idolatry or Satanism.

SINAI. A triangular peninsula, 230 miles long, pointing down into the head of the Red Sea. It is exceptionally rugged, marked by mountain peaks thousands of feet above sea level and by wide stretches of desert land (Exodus 19:12, 18, 23; Exodus 24:16). Its biblical importance derives from the fact that one of the mountains on the peninsula, named Mount Sinai (some scholars called it

Mount Horeb), was the place where Yahweh presented the Ten Commandments to Moses (Exodus 31:18).

SINDONOLOGY. See HOLY SHROUD.

SINE COM. *Sine commemoratione*—without commemoration of other feast or feasts.

SINFUL JOY. The voluntary complacency in an accomplished evil action, whether done by oneself or by someone else. It is not sinful, however, to rejoice at the good effect of an evil deed, in the sense that God's providence draws good results even from doing things that are wrong.

SINGULAR VESSEL OF DEVOTION. Title of the Blessed Virgin in the Litany of Loreto, also rendered, "Glorious vessel of devotion" (*Vas insignae devotionis*). It refers to Mary's singular devotedness to Christ, whom, as St. Augustine says, she had already conceived by faith in her mind before she conceived him in the flesh in her womb.

SINLESSNESS. Freedom from moral offenses against God. Absolute sinlessness, including impeccability or the inability to sin, was possessed only by Christ because as a divine person he could not contradict his own divine nature. Mary was also sinless, and could not sin, but only as a unique grace because she was the Mother of God. The rest of humanity is subject to the common weakness of fallen human nature. Except for an extraordinary privilege, accorded to few saints, no one is able to avoid for his whole life at least semideliberate venial sins.

SINLESSNESS OF CHRIST. See IMPECCABILITY OF CHRIST.

SINLESSNESS OF MARY. Freedom from original and all actual sin of the Blessed Virgin. By a special privilege of grace Mary was preserved from all venial sin and, in fact, she was also impeccable. She could not sin, because of the extraordinary grace she received as the Mother of God. Moreover, she was freed from all unruly passions, concupiscence, which are the effects of sin.

SIN OF OMISSION. See OMISSION.

SINS AGAINST THE HOLY SPIRIT. Major offenses that carry a stubborn resistance to the inspirations of the Holy Spirit and a contempt of his gifts. They are despair of one's salvation, envy of another's spiritual good, opposing known truths of faith, obstinacy in sin, presumption of God's mercy, and final impenitence. Because those who sin in this way, resisting grace, do not wish to repent, we say that their sins cannot be forgiven them.

SINS CRYING TO HEAVEN. The four sins traditionally said to cry to heaven for vengeance, namely: 1. willful murder (Genesis 4:10); 2. sodomy or homosexuality (Genesis 18:20); 3. oppression of the poor (Exodus 2:23); and 4. defrauding laborers of their wages (James 5:4).

SINS OF FRAILTY. Venial sins committed through surprise, indecision, weakness, lack of vigilance or courage. Fallen human nature, without miraculous grace from God, cannot completely eradicate all venial sins of this kind, but their frequency can be diminished. Specially recommended to overcome such failings are recollection of mind, daily examination of conscience, and frequent sacramental confession.

SION. See ZION.

SIRACH. See ECCLESIASTICUS.

SISTERS. A popular term for religious women, whether cloistered nuns or members of congregations under simple vows. The title corresponds to brothers in men's religious institutes and signifies that they are all members of the same spiritual family, share possessions in common, and live together in Christlike charity.

SISTINE CHAPEL. Main chapel of the Vatican Palace, dedicated to Our Lady of the Assumption and as large as a church. It was designed by de' Dolci under Sixtus IV (reigned 1471–84), hence its name. The series of famous frescoes on the left wall of events in the life of Moses and on the right side of the life of Christ were done by Botticelli, Cosimo, Rosselli, Ghirlandaio, Perugino, and Pinturicchio. The ceiling, which is considered Michelangelo's masterpiece and the most gigantic piece of painting in existence, was begun in 1508 and finished four years later. Between sections of painted simulated vaulting, Michelangelo painted scenes from Creation, the Expulsion from Eden, and the Flood. On the lower part of this created vaulting are the famous series of the seated Prophets and Sibyls. In 1508 Julius II persuaded Michelangelo to paint the ceiling of the Sistine Chapel. It was finished in 1512. Twenty-three years later he began *The Last Judgment*, the most comprehensive painted composition in the world. It was completed in 1541. The marble screens and the choir gallery in the chapel were designed and executed by Mino da Fiesole.

The altar, which only the Pope may use, is inlaid with mother of pearl. The Sistine Chapel is the private chapel of the Pope and the place where the conclaves for papal elections take place.

SITTING. The posture prescribed liturgically for certain parts of the Mass. The faithful are to be seated during the First Reading, the Responsorial Psalm, and the Second Reading; during the Homily; during the Offertory (optional); and during the period of Silence After Communion. In other liturgical functions sitting is also part of the ceremony, e.g., during the reading or singing of the psalms in the Divine Office.

SIXTH CRUSADE. An expedition (1228 –29) against the Moslems led by Emperor Frederick II. In Jerusalem he crowned himself king, and for fifteen years the city (along with Bethlehem and Nazareth) was in the possession of Christians.

SKEPTICISM. The theory that the real truth of things cannot be known with certainty. Two kinds of skepticism are professed. One type casts doubt on the capacity of the human mind to attain to reality. Another type calls into question the existence of the real world outside the mind. The first type has been more prevalent in the Western world, notably since the writings of David Hume (1711–76) and Immanuel Kant (1724–1804). The second type is familiar in the Orient, among Hindu and Buddhist philosophers in the Vedanta tradition. (Etym. Greek *skeptikos,* thoughtful, inquiring, *skeptesthai,* consider, examine carefully.)

SKULL. A symbol of death often found in conjunction with the Cross. The Latin *calvaria* is translated "skull" (John 19:17). St. Jerome and St. Mary Magdalene are symbolized with a skull denoting their preoccupation with death, penance, and eternity. (Etym. Middle English *skulle;* of Scandinavian origin, probably from Old High German *scollo,* clod, lump, *scala,* shell.)

SKULLCAP. See ZUCCHETTO.

SLANDER. Detraction. Essentially slander is verbal defamation of a person's character, although it may be either spoken or written. It also implies suffering or positive harm done to the victim of slander. In popular language calumny is a form of slander. (Etym. Latin *scandalum,* stumbling block, offense.)

SLAVERY. The subjection of a human being to another as a captive of war, descent from such captivity, oppression by the state, or by purchase. As an institution, it existed from the earliest times, as may be seen from certain restrictions in Mosaic legislation. The New Testament accepted the fact of slavery but introduced new principles of justice and charity that gradually removed the institution from Christian nations. But slavery, as a state of servitude by which a person is the property of another human being, has by no means disappeared. It is a fact of life in countries where doctrinaire theory, e.g., Marxism, deprives people of all rights that are not consistent with the policy of the State. (Etym. Latin *sclavus*, from *Sclavus*, *Slav*, from reduction to slavery of many Slavic peoples of Central Europe.)

SLAVONIC LANGUAGE. Not a distinctive rite, but the liturgical language used in the Byzantine Rite by Catholic and Orthodox Russians, Ruthenians, Bulgars, Serbs, and others. About A.D. 866, Sts. Cyril and Methodius translated the liturgy into Old Slavonic, the language of the people in Moravia and Pannonia, and invented a new alphabet (Cyrillic) for their Slavic converts. Pope Adrian II approved the action. The Roman liturgy in Old (Southern) Slavonic dates in some territories from about the eleventh century and is still in use in Dalmatia and Croatia (Yugoslavia). The introduction of the vernacular in the liturgy since the Second Vatican Council has naturally affected the use of Slavonic among Catholics.

SLAIN IN THE SPIRIT. A phenomenon of pentecostalism and the charismatic movement, where a person is believed to be overcome by the Holy Spirit. The experience is temporary, during which the individual collapses in a faint, although the faculties of thought and volition remain intact. The "slaying" takes place when a charismatic, already possessed by the Spirit, lays his or her hands on the head of another person. It is considered one of the external signs of a special outpouring of divine grace.

SLOTH. Sluggishness of soul or boredom because of the exertion necessary for the performance of a good work. The good work may be a corporal task, such as walking; or a mental exercise, such as writing; or a spiritual duty, such as prayer. Implicit in sloth is the unwillingness to exert oneself in the performance of duty because of the sacrifice and the effort required. As a sin, it is not to be confused with mere sadness over the inconvenience involved in fulfilling one's obligations, nor with the indeliberate feelings of repugnance when faced with unpleasant work. It becomes sinful when the reluctance is allowed to influence the will and, as a result, what should have been done is either left undone or performed less well than a person is responsible for doing. Sloth may also mean a repugnance to divine inspirations or the friendship of God due to the self-sacrifice and labor needed to co-operate with actual grace or to remain in the state of grace. This kind of laziness is directly opposed to the love of God and is one of the main reasons why some people, perhaps after years of virtuous living, give up in the pursuit of holiness or even become estranged from God. (Etym. Middle-English *slowthe*, slow.)

S.M. *Sanctae memoriae*—of holy memory.

SMYRNA. An important seaport on the western coast of Turkey. The name of it now is Izmir. It was founded in the twelfth century B.C. and for years conducted a prosperous trade. But by the time of Christ it was poverty-stricken, if we can judge from the tone used by the author of Revelation delivering God's message to the people of Smyrna. He praised the Christians for their steadfast faith despite hard living conditions. "I know the trials you have had and how poor you are," he assured them, ". . . and I will give you the crown of life for your prize" (Revelation 2:8–10).

SOBORNOST. Russian term for community, used by the Catholic Eastern Christians to describe the quality needed for loving co-operation. Commonly applied to the Eucharistic liturgy as corporate worship. Among the Eastern Orthodox it describes their highest form of Church government, formed by their bishops.

S.N.C. *Secretariatus pro Non Christianis*—Secretariat for Non-Christians.

S.N.CR. *Secretariatus pro Non Credentibus*—Secretariat for Non-Believers.

SOBRIETY. The virtue that regulates a person's desire for and use of intoxicating drink. It is the virtue of temperance exercised in the practice of moderation in the use of alcoholic beverages. (Etym. Latin *sobrietas*, temperance in drinking, moderation.)

SOC. *Socius, socii*—companion, companions.

SOCIAL JUSTICE. The virtue that inclines one to co-operate with others in order to help make the institutions of society better serve the common good. While the obligation of social justice falls upon the individual, that person cannot fulfill the obligation alone, but must work in concert with others, through organized bodies, as a member of a group whose purpose is to identify the needs of society, and, by the use of appropriate means, to meet these needs locally, regionally, nationally, and even globally. Implicit in the virtue of social justice is an awareness that the world has entered on a new phase of social existence, with potential for great good or great harm vested in those who control the media and the structures of modern society. Christians, therefore, are expected to respond to the new obligations created by the extraordinary means of promoting the common good not only of small groups but literally of all humanity.

SOCIAL SIN. The sinfulness of society into which a person is born. Its premise is that modern socialization and collectivization have immersed everyone in other people's values and moral actions to an unprecedented degree.

SOCIETY FOR THE PROPAGATION OF THE FAITH. See PROPAGATION OF THE FAITH.

SOCIETY OF JESUS. See JESUITS.

SOCIETY OF ST. VINCENT DE PAUL. An association of laymen founded by the French scholar Antoine Frédéric Ozanam (1813–53). Originally called the Conference of Charity, its members are devoted to personal service of the poor through the spiritual and corporal works of mercy. The first conference was formed at Paris in 1833. Under the revised regulations, women are admitted to membership. Emphasis is also placed on opening stores and rehabilitation workshops and employing handicapped persons in the service of their neighbor. A General Council is the governing body of the society, now established throughout the world.

SOCINIANISM. The doctrine held by followers of Lelio Sozzini, or Socinus (1525–62), a priest of Siena, and of his nephew, Fausto Sozzini (1539–1604). The ideas first achieved importance in Poland. Among its main tenets are a denial of the Trinity, the Virgin Birth, and the Redemption. Socinianism is the modern forerunner of Unitarianism.

SOCRATIC METHOD. Originally used by Socrates but adopted by many Christian writers, especially in the Augustinian tradition, as a way of reaching the truth. It consists in using questions and answers in a planned series in order to understand a given subject, reach a logical conclusion, or refute a certain position. It has become the basis of catechetical instruction since early Christian times.

SODALITY. A general name for a confraternity or pious association. The term was used already in early Christian times for voluntary groups of the faithful who sought to work together with like-minded people for the strengthening of their own religious commitment and advancing the Kingdom of Christ to others. Sodalities are numerous in the Catholic Church, devoted to a variety of spiritual and corporal works of mercy. The Sodality of the Blessed Virgin was founded in Rome (1563) by Rev. John Leunis, S.J., for the students at the Roman College. At the time of its quadricentennial, the Sodality of the Blessed Virgin was established in more than one hundred countries. During the first four centuries of its existence, it had deeply influenced the lives of several million persons, through the Spiritual Exercises of St. Ignatius, Devotion to Mary, and the active apostolate in the world. Many canonized saints had been Sodalists, including St. Francis de Sales, whose *Introduction to the Devout Life* for the laity is a practical expression of the Sodality way of life. In 1971 the Sodality became a new organization, the Christian Life Communities. (Etym. Latin *sodalitas*, fellowship, brotherhood, from *sodalis*, fellow, intimate.)

SODOM. A town always coupled with Gomorrah in characterizing places of infamy and sinful living. They were probably located on land now completely covered by the southern waters of the Dead Sea. The most likely explanation for this is that about 1900 B.C. an earthquake depressed the plain on which Sodom and Gomorrah were established (Genesis 13:10). Scripture interprets this catastrophe as Yahweh's determination to punish an evil population. Abraham tried his best to dissuade Yahweh, lest innocent people be punished with guilty, but evidently the only just man who could be found was Lot, Abraham's nephew (Genesis 18:20–32). Frequently in Scripture reference is made to the destruction of the doomed cities as proverbial warnings of Yahweh's punishment of evil (Isaiah 3:9; Lamentations 4:6). Indeed, Jesus himself, in instructing his Apostles, told them that towns that refused to listen to their message would suffer the same fate as Sodom and Gomorrah (Matthew 10:15).

SODOMY. In general, unnatural sexual relations. The term is derived from the biblical city of Sodom on the Dead Sea, destroyed with the city of Gomorrah because of the wickedness of the people (Genesis 13:10). More particularly, sodomy is homosexuality between male persons or between a human being and an animal. (Etym. French *sodomie;* from Latin *Sodoma,* Sodom.)

S. OFF. *Sanctum Officium*—Congregation of the Holy Office (Inquisition).

SOLA FIDE. By faith alone, the basic principle of Reformation Protestantism. It declares that humanity is justified only by a confident trust in God through the saving merits of Jesus Christ. This confident trust, called *fides fiducialis* (trustful faith) is present in those who are predestined to be saved. It is, therefore, a work of predestination and excludes the possibility of good works that, on Catholic premises, are also necessary for salvation. Actually this "fiducial faith" is not so much a means of justification as a sure sign of a person's having been chosen to be saved. Those who have such confidence are thereby known to belong to the elect.

SOLA SCRIPTURA. In Scripture alone. One of the cardinal principles of Protestantism; it declares that all of divine revelation is contained exclusively in the Bible. It therefore denies that there is any revealed tradition.

SOLEMN BAPTISM. The sacrament of baptism, administered by a priest or deacon who performs all the ceremonies prescribed by the Church's ritual.

SOLEMN BLESSING. One of a variety of special blessings that may be used at the discretion of the priest, at the end of Mass, or after the Liturgy of the Word, the Divine Office, and the administration of the sacraments.

SOLEMNITY. The highest liturgical rank of a feast in the ecclesiastical calendar. Besides the movable feasts such as Easter and Pentecost, fourteen solemnities are celebrated in the universal Church, namely: Motherhood of God (January 1), Epiphany (January 6), St. Joseph (March 19), Annunciation (March 25), Trinity Sunday (first after Pentecost), Corpus Christi (Thursday after Trinity Sunday), Sacred Heart (Friday after the second Sunday after Pentecost), St. John the Baptist (June 24), Sts. Peter and Paul (June 29), Assumption of the Blessed Virgin (August 15), All Saints (November 1), Christ the King (Last Sunday of the ecclesi-

astical year), Immaculate Conception (December 8), and Christmas (December 25). (Etym. Latin *sollemnis,* stated, established, appointed.)

SOLEMN MASS. The Eucharistic liturgy in which the priest celebrant is assisted by a deacon and/or acolyte. Before the revision of the liturgy, a Solemn Mass was celebrated by a priest, assisted by a deacon and subdeacon; with special music, incense, and ceremonies. The practice went back to the early Church when a Solemn Mass was the typical Mass, whose liturgical texts were divided among several books to suit the convenience of those who employed them. The term Solemn Mass was also formerly applied to the liturgy celebrated by the Pope or a bishop, when assisted by other priests. The new practice of a concelebrated Mass has fairly replaced what used to be the Solemn Mass.

SOLEMN PROFESSION. The permanent and definitive embracing of the religious state in an institute recognized by the Church as a religious order. In most such orders, all those who take final vows make a solemn profession. In the Society of Jesus, only certain priest members take solemn vows.

SOLEMN VOWS. Public vows pronounced in a religious order and recognized as such by the Church. The term has become technical since the recognition of simple but public vows in religious congregations and societies of common life. In practice, a solemn vow of poverty means the actual renunciation of ownership and not merely the independent use of material possessions; and a solemn vow of chastity invalidates attempted marriage.

SOLICITATION. The crime of using the sacrament of penance, directly or indirectly, to lead a person into a grave sin against chastity. A priest who commits solicitation is to be suspended from celebrating Mass and from hearing sacramental confessions, and in more flagrant cases is to be degraded. There is a grave obligation to lodge an accusation with ecclesiastical authorities against a priest who is known to be guilty of solicitation.

SOLICITUDE. As one of the charisms of administration in the apostolic church, it was the anxious concern of a bishop about the spiritual welfare of his people. St. Paul's solicitude for the churches under his care has been the model for bishops ever since

(II Corinthians 11:28). (Etym. Latin *solli-citus,* thoroughly moved, agitated.)

SOLIPSISM. As a form of extreme subjectivism, the philosophy that holds that only the ego really exists. Everyone and everything else are said to be images of myself. Solipsism is the logical effect of idealism, which teaches that the individual ego produces the existence of thought. In practice solipsism is the attitude of people who care only for themselves. (Etym. Latin *solus,* alone + *ipse,* self + *ism.*)

SOLITARY. See HERMIT.

SOLITUDE. In Christian asceticism, the conscious and deliberate withdrawal from creatures in order to be more closely united with God. The *beata solitudo* (blessed solitude) of monasticism, praised by St. Benedict, is the best known and most widely influential in Christian history. Solitude may be physical or spiritual or both. It is physical (or exterior) insofar as a person withdraws from the company of people and worldly affairs, either permanently, as a hermit or monk; or partially, as every member of a religious institute; or temporarily, as in a retreat. Physical solitude is not escapism or isolationism, but a means to an end, the end being spiritual solitude. In spiritual solitude the soul is alone with God, attentive to him in preference to creatures, even though it has to deal with creatures. (Etym. Latin *solitudo,* from *solus,* alone.)

SOLITUDE, EXTERIOR. Withdrawal from some or most conversation with others in order to give oneself more completely to contemplation and the service of God. A certain degree of solitude is recognized as necessary for progress in the spiritual life. The example at Nazareth, the forty days in the desert, and Christ's frequent withdrawal from the company of the Disciples to spend hours and whole nights in prayer has been the inspiration of all Christian solitaries, cloistered contemplatives, and members of institutes of Christian perfection.

SOLITUDE, INTERIOR. See RECOLLECTION.

SOLLICITUDO OMNIUM ECCLESIARIUM. Apostolic letter of Pope Paul VI setting forth the duties of official representatives of the Roman Pontiff. The focus of the document is on updating the role of the numerous delegates of the Pope in various countries of the world, and in the different commissions where the Holy See is represented (June 24, 1969).

SOLOMON. The third King of Israel, son of David and Bath-Sheba, ruled his country from 961 to 922 B.C. Because it was a peaceful period in Jewish history, Solomon was able to extend Israel's borders farther than they had ever been before and to increase its prosperity and power to a level never equaled since. His accession to the throne was threatened by his brother, Adonijah, who conspired against him (I Kings 1, 2). But their father, David, preferred Solomon and had him secretly anointed. Eventually Adonijah and his military supporter, Joab, were executed for their conspiratorial efforts. Solomon displayed such remarkable intellectual qualities that his court became a center of culture (I Kings 5:14). He composed an extraordinary number of songs, and it seems certain that a great part of the Book of Proverbs had Solomon for its author (I Kings 5:12). He launched an impressive building campaign that included the Temple of Yahweh and a magnificent royal palace (I Kings 6:1, 7:1). He built a fleet of ships and extended Israel's trade to many nations. One device Solomon employed to extend his power was marrying many wives who belonged to ruling families in neighboring countries. While this was shrewd strategy, it led to his decline: he antagonized Yahweh, who resented this infiltration of pagan religions and threatened punishment (I Kings 11:1–8). During the reign of Solomon's son, Rehoboam, Yahweh lived up to his threat. "Israel has been separated from the House of David until the present day" (I Kings 12:19).

SOLO SPIRITU. One of the cardinal principles of historic Protestantism, notably in John Calvin, which holds that the Holy Spirit suffices for recognizing God's revelation and interpreting the same. There is no need of a hierarchical Church to identify or explain the meaning of the revealed word of God.

SOLOVYEVISM. Doctrine of Church and State of Vladimir Solovyev (1853–1900), Russian Orthodox theologian who became a Roman Catholic. He held that sound Christology is the basis of sound Church and State relations in society. The latter must steer a balanced middle course between two heretical extremes, Nestorianism and Monophysitism. A Nestorian approach would separate Church and State, even as it totally divides Christ into two persons, divine and human. A Monophysite approach would totally absorb the State by the Church, even as it totally absorbed Christ's human nature in his divinity. The correct attitude is to keep Church and State truly distinct, but have the Church divinize society by her doctrine and sacraments, and have the State legislate in accordance with these principles and practices.

SON. Theologically, sonship is the derivation of one person from the substance of another person who communicates the same nature to the one he produces. There is consequently a Son within the Trinity, begotten by the Father. In an analogous sense, all angels and men are sons of God because they share in the divine attributes of knowledge and freedom, and all who are in the state of grace are adopted sons (or children) of God.

SONG OF SONGS. See CANTICLE OF CANTICLES.

SON OF GOD. The Second Person of the Holy Trinity, who became man to suffer and die for the redemption of mankind. Christ is therefore the true, natural Son of God, as testified by the Father in the vision recorded at the baptism of Christ, "You are my Son, the Blessed" (Luke 3:22), and, as described by St. Paul, that "God spoke to our ancestors through the prophets; but in our own time, the last days, He has spoken to us through His Son, the Son that He has appointed to inherit everything and through whom He made everything there is" (Hebrews 1:1–2).

SON OF MAN. The most frequently used title of Christ in the New Testament, occurring eighty-two times and, all but once (Acts 7:56), in the Gospels. A messianic title (Daniel 7:2–14), it identifies the heavenly transcendence of the Savior while stressing his humanity, in contrast with the "Son of God," which emphasizes his divinity.

SONS OF GOD. A title used in Scripture for the angels, the chosen people, the prophets, and, in the New Testament, all who believe in God and do his will.

SOPHROSYNE. The virtue of temperance as moderation, avoiding either excess or defect in the exercise of some moral tendency.

SORROW. The pain or distress experienced because of some adversity that is felt personally. The sorrow may be over a loss or misfortune for which a person feels guilty, as in the case of sin; or the sorrow may be totally vicarious, out of compassion for someone else. Essential to the notion of sorrow is that it refers to what has already happened and its painful effects are still experi-

enced. (Etym. Middle English *sorge, sorow;* Old English *sorh, sorg,* anxiety, sorrow.)

SORROW FOR SIN. See REPENTANCE.

SORROWFUL MOTHER, SANCTUARY OF. This shrine to Mary was founded in 1926 in Portland, Oregon, and is constructed on two terraces, one on street level, another at the top of a high cliff. A marble Crucifixion group dominates the area. On the lower level is a cavern where under the grotto arch stands a white altar framed with flowers and vines. Above on the cliff wall is a replica of Michelangelo's *Pietà* with two bronze angels holding torches. At the western end of the amphitheater is the cross-laden Christ, whose stumbling figure leads the eye to his Mother standing at the very top of the one-hundred-fifty-foot cliff wall. The Stations of the Cross dot the base of the hill, also the praying figure of St. Philip Benizi, founder of the Servites, who are in charge of the shrine.

SORROWFUL MYSTERIES. Second chaplet of the Rosary, consisting of: 1. Christ's Agony in the Garden of Gethsemane; 2. His Scourging at the Pillar; 3. the Crowning with Thorns; 4. the Way of the Cross; and 5. the Crucifixion. See also JOYFUL MYSTERIES, GLORIOUS MYSTERIES.

SOSTHENES. The president of the synagogue in Corinth during the time of St. Paul. When Paul attempted to preach to the members of the synagogue, he was abused and reviled (Acts 18:5–8). In their wrath the frustrated Jews beat up Sosthenes, probably believing that he had not presented their case forcefully enough (Acts 18: 12–17). It is possible that Sosthenes became a Christian. Paul mentions a companion named Sosthenes in a letter he wrote later to the Corinthians (I Corinthians 1:1). (Etym. Greek *sōsthenēs,* saving strength.)

SOTERIOLOGY. That part of Christology which treats of Christ's work of salvation. It covers the study of man's fall in Adam and the sins of mankind, which needed a Savior, the doctrine of grace by which the guilt and consequences of sin are removed, and especially the twofold mystery of Christ as Redeemer and Mediator of the human race. (Etym. Greek *sōtērion,* deliverance; from *sōtēr,* savior; from *sōzein,* to save; from *saos,* safe.)

SOUL. The spiritual immortal part in human beings that animates their body. Though a substance in itself, the soul is naturally ordained toward a body; separated, it is an "incomplete" substance. The soul has no parts, it is therefore simple, but it is not without accidents. The faculties are its proper accidents. Every experience adds to its accidental form. It is individually created for each person by God and infused into the body at the time of human insemination. It is moreover created in respect to the body it will inform, so that the substance of bodily features and of mental characteristics insofar as they depend on organic functions is safeguarded. As a simple and spiritual substance, the soul cannot die. Yet it is not the total human nature, since a human person is composed of body animated by the soul. In philosophy, animals and plants are also said to have souls, which operate as sensitive and vegetative principles of life. Unlike the human spirit, these souls are perishable. The rational soul contains all the powers of the two other souls and is the origin of the sensitive and vegetative functions in the human being.

SOUL OF THE CHURCH. The Holy Spirit, who animates the Mystical Body of Christ. As Christ is the head of the Church, so the Holy Spirit is her soul. Like the soul in the human body, the Holy Spirit is the source of being and life in the Church. It is the Holy Spirit who welds together the members of the Church among themselves, with Christ their head, since the same Holy Spirit is entirely in the head and entirely in the members of the Mystical Body. It is he who by his assistance upholds the hierarchy in their exercise of the teaching, pastoral, and priestly office. It is he who by his grace arouses and fosters every solitary activity among the faithful. All the life and growth of Christianity proceed from this divine life principle indwelling in the Church.

SOURCE OF SIN. The principle or root of all sinful human actions. Two sources are commonly found in revelation, deriving from the two sides to every sin, the turning to transient satisfaction, and the turning away from everlasting good. As regards the first, the principle of all sin can be called lust, lust in its most general sense, namely, the unbridled desire for one's own pleasure. As regards the second, the principle is pride, pride in its general sense, the lack of submission to God. Lust and pride in this pervasive sense may also be called capital sins, but more properly they are the roots and sprouts of vice, as the desire for happiness is the root of all virtue.

SOUTANE. A cassock worn by the clergy. A long, fitted garment covering the body from neck to ankle, fastened by means of buttons, sash, or cord. (Etym. French; from Italian *sottana,* garment worn under [religious vestments], from *sotto,* under; from Latin *subtus,* beneath, from *sub,* under.)

SOVEREIGN PONTIFF. See PONTIFEX MAXIMUS.

S.P. *Sanctissime Pater*—Most Holy Father.

S.P. *Summus Pontifex*—Supreme Pontiff, Pope.

S.P., S. PETR. *Sanctus Petrus*—St. Peter.

S.P.A. *Sacrum Palatium Apostolicum*—Sacred Apostolic Palace, Vatican, Quirinal.

S.P.A. *Sacra Paenitentiaria Apostolica*—Sacred Apostolic Penitentiary.

SPEAR. A symbol of the Passion, usually found in conjunction with the Cross. It is an emblem also of St. Longinus, the centurion converted on Calvary after he pierced the heart of the dead Christ. St. Barnabas and St. Thomas the Apostle both have the spear as their emblems in art.

SPECIALI MODO. In a special way. Term applied to certain cases that, in the Code of Canon Law (1918), are specially reserved to the Holy See, e.g., forgery of papal documents.

SPECIALISSIMO MODO. In a most special way. Term applied in the Code of Canon Law (1918), of the first rank, reserved to the Holy See for judgment, e.g., direct violation of the seal of confession.

SPEAKING IN TONGUES. See GIFT OF TONGUES.

SPECIES. Appearances, especially those of bread and wine, after the Eucharistic consecration. The term "species" is used by the Council of Trent (Denzinger 1652) to identify the accidents, i.e., the size, weight, color, resistance, taste, and odor of bread, which remain exactly the same after transubstantiation. They are not mere appearances as though these physical properties were unreal. But they are appearances because after the consecration they lack any substance that underlies them or in which they inhere.

SPECULATION. To meditate or reflect on a subject without reducing one's reflections to practice. Speculation is thought for truth's sake. It is sometimes identified with contemplation.

SPECULATIVE DOUBT. Uncertainty of mind concerning the mere truth or error of something, or the mere abstract goodness or evil, or prudence of something. It is speculative doubt because it does not presently concern one's own personal action.

SPHRAGIS. The term originally used by the Fathers of the Church to identify the sacramental character conferred at baptism, confirmation, and orders. Literally it means a seal or identifying sign and describes the indelible and unlosable assimilation to Christ possessed by one who has the character. One is permanently and unalterably changed, so that nothing one ever does or becomes later on can eradicate this unique relationship to Christ.

SPINOZISM. Philosophy of Benedict de (Baruch d'Espinoza) Spinoza (1632–77), of Amsterdam. Because of his unorthodox ideas he was excommunicated from the Jewish synagogue. Spinozism holds that all existence is embraced in one substance, which is God or nature. On this premise it follows that mind and matter, time, and in fact everything that seems to be real is only a manifestation of the One Reality, who (or which) alone exists. Evil, whether physical or moral, exists only for finite minds and dissolves when seen as part of the divine Whole. It is not clear how Spinoza saw finite things as somehow emanating from the infinite. He held that the one divine substance becomes conscious in the infinite multiplicity of attributes. Spinozism is commonly regarded as the most thoroughgoing form of monistic idealism, and was the first of the three principal forms of pantheism condemned by the First Vatican Council.

SPIRIT. That which is positively immaterial. It is pure spirit if it has no dependence on matter either for its existence or for any of its activities. God is uncreated pure Spirit; the angels are created pure spirits. The human soul is more properly called spiritual. Although it can exist independent of the body, it nevertheless in this life depends extrinsically on the body for its operations, and in the life to come retains a natural affinity for the body, with which after the resurrection it will be reunited for all eternity. (Etym. Latin *spiritus*, breath, life, soul, mind, spirit, power.)

SPIRITISM. See SPIRITUALISM.

SPIRITUAL. In musical parlance, a Negro's religious song usually having a biblical theme and a simple melodic style similar to that of a folk song.

SPIRITUAL COMMUNION. See COMMUNION, SPIRITUAL.

SPIRITUAL DEATH. The state of the soul in mortal sin, based on the analogy with bodily death. Just as a physical body may be not only ill or suffer injury, but cease to retain its principle of life, so the soul can lose sanctifying grace through mortal sin and supernaturally cease to live. It is, therefore, spiritually dead because it is no longer united with God, who gives it supernatural life, even as a body is dead on separation from its animating principle, which is the soul. While still on earth, this union with God is both a possession and a movement. We possess him by grace and in faith, and we are moving toward him in the beatific vision of glory. When persons sin mortally, they are twice dead: once because they lose the gift of divine life they formerly had, and once again because they are no longer moving toward the consummation of that life in heaven.

Mortal sins are no longer remissible by any power within the soul itself, much as the human body, once dead, cannot be brought back to life except by a special intervention of God. In Patristic literature the restoration is compared with the resuscitation of Lazarus. The exercise of almighty power in either case is the same. "Everyone who sins, dies," says St. Augustine. Only the Lord, "by his great grace and great mercy raises souls to life again, that we may not die eternally" (*In Joannis Evangelium*, 49). Only infinite mercy can reconcile the grave sinner.

SPIRITUAL DIRECTION. Assisting persons to understand themselves and, with divine grace, to grow in the practice of Christian virtue.

SPIRITUAL EXERCISES. Any set program of religious duties, notably the prayers, meditations, and spiritual reading required of persons following a distinctive rule of life. Also the period of silence and prayerful reflection practiced annually (or more often) in a retreat. Particularly the Spiritual Exercises by St. Ignatius Loyola, drawn up as a method of arriving at the amendment of one's life and resolving on a determined way of holiness. The Exercises of St. Ignatius were first composed by him in a cave at Manresa, in Spain, after his conversion. They have been recommended by successive popes as a most effective program of spiritual renewal for priests, religious, and the laity. Their underlying principle is their opening statement that "Man was created to praise, reverence and serve our Creator and Lord, and by this means to save his soul." Given this basic purpose of human existence, the believer is told how to reach his or her destiny by overcoming sinful tendencies and imitating Christ in carrying the Cross on earth in order to be glorified with Christ in the life to come.

SPIRITUAL FATHER. The one who counsels and directs a person in the spiritual life. Generally a priest, the spiritual father is often designated by ecclesiastical authority to guide the members of a religious community or confraternity, students for the priesthood, or in general persons specially dedicated to Christian perfection or the Church's apostolate. The Pope is sometimes called the Spiritual Father of all Christians.

SPIRITUAL INDIFFERENCE. Disposition of will by which a person is totally detached from any creature that might hinder his progress toward God. The result of grace and ascetical training by which the soul is so attached to the divine will that no desire for a created good or fear of any evil can change its commitment to God.

SPIRITUALISM. Belief that the spirits of the dead in various ways communicate with the living through the agency of a person called a medium. It is also a religious movement that professes to be Christian and has been organized into several denominations, with churches, schools, and an ordained clergy.

The doctrinal position of spiritualists varies considerably, but one doctrine is common to all of them, namely: "that the existence and personal identity of the individual continue after the change called death; and that communication with the so-called dead is a fact scientifically proved by the phenomena of Spiritualism." Moreover, many adherents believe that Christ was a medium, that the Annunciation was a message from the spirit world and Christ's resurrection a proof that all human beings live on after death as disembodied spirits.

Religious services and séances are held in churches, in private homes, or in rented halls. They follow the general pattern of Protestant churches, with prayer, singing, music, reading from the *Spiritualist Manual,* a sermon or lecture, and spirit messages from the departed. Communication with the spirit world is not limited to regular church services, not even to public assemblies of professions. "Making contact" with the dead is recommended at other times, even in the privacy of one's room and without the aid of a medium.

Normally, however, spirit communications require a person who acts as a medium between the mortal audience and the world beyond. Mediums are not the ministers in a congregation; they are normally not supported by free-will offerings but through the fees that are charged for classes and séances.

The Catholic Church, through the Holy Office, has declared it is not lawful "to take part in spiritualistic communications or manifestations of any kind, whether through a so-called medium or without one, whether hypnotism is used or not, even with the best of intentions among the participants, whether for the purpose of interrogating the souls of the departed or spiritual beings, whether by listening to their responses or even in idle curiosity, even with the tacit or express protestation of not having anything to do with the evil spirits" (Denzinger 3642).

Behind the Church's attitude toward Spiritualism is the concern that a Catholic would expose himself to the risk of actually dealing with the evil spirit. The assumption is that if fraud or deception are excluded, and manifestations occur that are beyond natural explanation, the active agent in these cases is neither God nor any one of the good spirits (whether angelic or human) but demonic forces that are sure to mislead the Catholic and endanger the integrity of his faith.

SPIRITUALITY. Positive immateriality; the property of being intrinsically independent of matter at least in essence and in some activities.

SPIRITUAL LIFE. The life of the Holy Spirit, dwelling in the souls of the faithful and enabling them to praise and love God and serve him in the practice of virtue. It is called the spiritual life because: 1. its animating principle is the Spirit of God, the "Soul of the soul" in sanctifying grace; 2. it is the supernatural life of the human spirit; 3. it is mainly lived out in the spiritual faculties of intellect and will, although affecting the whole person, body and soul.

SPIRITUAL MARRIAGE. The calm, abiding, transforming union of the soul with God. Raptures and ecstasies may occur, but they are replaced by a marvelous peace and serenity enjoyed in the presence of a reciprocated love. St. Teresa describes this stage of intimacy with God as one of complete forgetfulness of self, thinking only of God and his glory, leaving her with an insatiable thirst to suffer with Christ in love and in sole conformity with his will. An ardent zeal for the sanctification of other souls follows the repose. Aridities disappear, leaving only a memory of God's tenderness.

SPIRITUAL READING. As the *Lectio Divina* prescribed in monasticism from the earliest times, it is all reading that is conducive to prayer and closer union with God. The Sacred Scriptures have always held the primacy of honor in such reading, along with writings of the Church's teachers; notably, the popes and bishops, the writings and lives of the saints, and all other forms of composition whose avowed purpose as writing is to enlighten the mind and inspire the will and affections to the worship and service of God.

SPIRITUAL REBIRTH. The transformation of soul which takes place when a person is baptized. The term was used by Christ when he said that one must be reborn of water and the Holy Spirit to enter the Kingdom of Heaven. Through baptism a person is reborn supernaturally, comparable to his or her physical birth naturally. The supernatural life of God is infused into the soul at baptism, much as human life is infused into the body at conception.

SPIRITUAL RELATIONSHIP. Religious affinity arising from active participation in the sacraments of baptism and confirmation. The sponsors in both sacraments become spiritually related to those whom they sponsor. Also the one baptizing becomes spiritually related to the person baptized. The relationship arising from sponsorship at baptism becomes an impediment to marriage with the person sponsored.

SPIRITUALS. Term popularly applied to several groups of the Friars Minor who were in opposition to the modifications of the original rule, notably in the practice of poverty during the thirteenth and fourteenth centuries. They wished to observe the rule in its primitive severity, but failed in their aim and through the errors of their leaders were led into schism and heresy. Their misguided zeal, when finally brought under control by full submission to papal authority, helped to purify the Franciscan Order and eventually to unify the Friars Minor.

SPIRITUAL SOLITUDE. See SOLITUDE.

SPIRITUAL VESSEL. A title of the Blessed Virgin in the Litany of Loreto. Mary received this title because she was the perfect vessel of the Holy Spirit, who dwelled in her by the fullness of his grace.

SPIRITUAL WORKS OF MERCY. The traditional seven forms of Christian charity in favor of the soul or spirit of one's neighbor, in contrast with the corporal works of mercy that minister to people's bodily needs. They are: converting the sinner, instructing the ignorant, counseling the doubtful, comforting the sorrowful, bearing wrongs patiently, forgiving injuries, and praying for the living and the dead. Their bases are the teaching of Christ and the practice of the Church since apostolic times.

SPIRITUS DOMINI. Ecumenical Directory, Part Two, published by the Secretariat for Promoting Unity Among Christians, dealing with ecumenical education in schools of higher learning. There is stress on proper training in the seminaries, with emphasis on sound spiritual formation and doctrinal foundation. All the while that a person is being helped to advance Christian unity, he must not lose hold of the essentials and distinctive elements of Roman Catholicism. There is also a detailed section on co-operation between Catholics and the separated Christian brethren (April 16, 1970).

SPONGE, LITURGICAL. In the Byzantine Rite the "purificator" used at Mass, to wipe the fingers of the celebrant, to convey the holy Bread from the *diskos* to the chalice, and similar liturgical functions. It is a triangular piece of sponge, covered with silk, and symbolic of the sponge offered to the Savior on the Cross.

SPONSOR. The person who presents a child at baptism and professes the faith in the child's name. A sponsor serves as the official representative of the community of faith and, with the parents, requests baptism for the child. The sponsor's function after baptism is to serve as proxy for the parents if they should be unable or fail to provide for the religious training of the child. Also called godparents, sponsors are required for baptism, even of adults. One sponsor is sufficient, of the same sex as the one baptized; but two (no more) are permitted, i.e., one man and one woman. Sponsors contract a spiritual relationship with the person baptized, but not with one another. It has been customary also to have sponsors at confirmation, but the practice is not universal. (Etym. Latin *spondere*, to make a solemn pledge.)

SPOON. The spoon used in the Eastern Rite liturgy to communicate to the faithful a part of the Host soaked in the consecrated wine. A spoon may also be used to measure a few drops of water to be mixed with wine at the Offertory of the Mass. And a spoonful of water may be given to the sick to help them swallow the Sacred Host.

SPOUSE (BRIDE) OF CHRIST. Primarily the Church, founded by Christ, which St. Paul elaborately describes as espoused to Christ. Also a woman who vows her chastity to God in order to be more like Christ and more intimately united with him. Among certain mystics, such as Sts. Teresa of Ávila and Catherine of Siena, an extraordinary union in prayer with the Savior.

SPRINKLING. The casting of water from a distance so that it falls upon the head and flows in the administration of baptism. It is the only way in which more than one person can be baptized simultaneously by one minister. It is seldom used now, but in the past was sometimes necessary, as when a large group of people were to be baptized by a single missionary.

SQUINT. A small opening in the chancel wall of a church enabling those outside to see and follow the ceremonies at the altar. Through them, the ancient anchorites were able to assist at Mass.

SR. Sister.

S.R.C. *Sacra Rituum Congregatio*—Sacred Congregation of Rites.

S.R.E. *Sancta Romana Ecclesia, Sanctae Romanae Ecclesiae*—Most Holy Roman Church, or of the Most Holy Roman Church.

S.R.R. *Sacra Romana Rota*—Sacred Roman Rota.

SS. *Scriptores*—writers.

S.S.A.T. *Supremum Signaturae Apostolicae Tribunal*—Supreme Tribunal of the Apostolic Signatura.

SS.D.N. *Sanctissimus Dominus Noster*—Our Most Holy Lord (Jesus Christ), also a title of the Pope.

S., SS. *Sanctus, Sancti*—saint, saints.

ST. Saint.

STABAT MATER. A hymn, "At the Cross her station keeping . . ." commonly attributed to Jacopone da Todi (1230–1306), Franciscan poet. It gradually came into liturgical use by the late Middle Ages and since 1727 has been part of the Eucharistic liturgy and the Divine Office for the feast of Our Lady of Sorrows. Its history in music dates largely from modern times. Another hymn, *Stabat Mater Speciosa,* apparently modeled on *Stabat Mater Dolorosa,* describing Mary's sorrows at Bethlehem, but it has never become part of the liturgy.

STABILITY. The moral quality of being relatively free from radical changes in judgment, mood, or conduct. In terms of relationship to others, it means reliability or dependability. (Etym. Latin *stabilis,* standing firm.)

STABILITY, VOW OF. Oath taken under the Rule of St. Benedict to remain attached to the monastery of one's profession. Its purpose, in the Benedictine spirit, is to foster unity under the one abbot and to ensure the continuity of each monastic institution as a religious family.

STAG. A symbol of the Christian thirsting after the living waters of Christ's Word. Usually represented in pairs, the deer are refreshing themselves from the streams of water flowing from the Cross. In the words of the Psalm, "as a hart longs for the running streams, so longs my soul for you, my God" (Psalm 42). The stag appears in representations of St. Hubert and St. Eustace, patrons of hunters, also with St. Giles shown with his pet hind, and St. Aidan noted in English hagiology.

STALLS. A term used to refer to the fixed seats in the choir of a church. They are often ornamented with face carvings on their front and back and on the misericordia, under the seat where grotesque images were sometimes depicted.

STANDING. A posture for various parts of the Eucharistic liturgy and the Divine Office. Since different countries have different customs, the episcopal conferences have given corresponding directives to the people. From time immemorial, however, standing has been customary during the reading of the Gospel and the recitation or singing of the Creed, the Preface, and Sanctus.

STAR. Emblem of the Epiphany. A second-century scene of the Magi in the catacombs displayed a star, "and in front of them was the star they had seen rising, it went forward and halted over the place where the child was" (Matthew 2:9). The star is a symbol of Christ: "I am of David's line . . . the bright star of the morning" (Revelation 22:16). "A star from Jacob takes the leadership, a sceptre rises out of Israel"

(Numbers 24:17). The eight-pointed star seen in conjunction with Mary's symbol of the "Tower of David" in the Litany of Loreto is illustrative of Christ's glory. The star is also the symbol of the Blessed Virgin Mary, whose brilliance never dims and to whom the famous titles *Ave Maris Stella* and *Stella Matutina* are addressed. In some icons Mary's mantle is studded with stars and she is often crowned with them. "A great sign appeared in the heavens, a woman adorned with the sun, standing on the moon and with twelve stars on her head as a crown" (Revelation 12:1–3). St. Dominic carries a star in his halo, and St. Nicholas of Tolentino has one on his breast—both distinctive emblems for these saints.

STATE OF BEING. The way in which a thing manifests its existence or the condition in which people find themselves under given circumstances. As such, state merely indicates a form of existence that has little or no relation to space or time. Thus the state of a person in divine grace, or in grave sin or, after death, in heaven, hell, or purgatory identifies the spiritual condition of the soul independent of matter or external factors.

STATE OF GRACE. Condition of a person who is free from mortal sin and pleasing to God. It is the state of being in God's friendship and the necessary condition of the soul at death in order to attain heaven. See also SANCTIFYING GRACE.

STATE OF NATURE. The mythical condition of human beings before they were affected by civilization. This condition was idealized by many philosophers, e.g., Jean Jacques Rousseau, as a norm of what the human situation would be except for the corrupting influence of human education and society. It was used by some (e.g., John Locke) as an argument for humanity's original rights to liberty and equality, and by others (e.g., Thomas Hobbes) as proof for the need of a state to control the social instincts of human beings.

STATES OF PERFECTION. Those stable forms of living in which some of the faithful bind themselves by vows, or promises equivalent to vows, to practice the evangelical counsels of poverty, chastity, and obedience. They are called states of perfection because those who live in these states agree to follow a particular rule of life, approved by the Church, whose faithful observance will certainly lead to Christian perfection.

STATION. A term indicating where some part of a moving or progressive liturgical celebration takes place. Thus the new Liturgy for the Dead provides for three types of function: three stations, i.e., in the home, in church, and at the cemetery; two stations, i.e., in the cemetery chapel and at the grave; and one station only, in the home of the deceased.

STATION DAYS. Appointed days on which the early Christians fasted between twelve and three. They were usually feast days on which the faithful gathered at stated churches for the celebration of Mass. These days were still marked in the Roman Missal before the Second Vatican Council, on which the Pope formerly celebrated Mass in the so-called "station churches" in Rome. Pope St. Gregory the Great is believed to have assigned a special church to each station day, which comprised all Marian feasts and the ferial days of Lent. Other days were then added so that they now total eighty-four.

STATIONS OF THE CROSS. A devotion performed by meditating on the Passion of Christ, successively before fourteen stations of the Cross. The stations are wooden crosses, normally attached to the interior walls of a church, although they may be erected anywhere, e.g., outside along a pathway. The pictures or representations depicting various scenes from Christ's *Via Crucis* are aids to devotion on the traditional stations: 1. Jesus Is Condemned to Death; 2. Jesus Bears His Cross; 3. Jesus Falls the First Time; 4. Jesus Meets His Mother; 5. Jesus Is Helped by Simon; 6. Veronica Wipes the Face of Jesus; 7. Jesus Falls a Second Time; 8. Jesus Consoles the Women of Jerusalem; 9. Jesus Falls a Third Time; 10. Jesus Is Stripped of His Garments; 11. Jesus Is Nailed to the Cross; 12. Jesus Dies on the Cross; 13. Jesus Is Taken Down from the Cross; 14. Jesus Is Laid in the Tomb. A plenary indulgence is gained, once a day, for making the Way of the Cross. But it is only necessary for a person to move from one station to the next and "nothing more is required than a pious meditation on the Passion and Death of the Lord, which need not be a particular consideration of the individual mysteries of the stations."

STATISM. A theory of society that makes the civil government totally independent of any religious principles. It is state secularism on the premise that religion is a purely private affair that the state may tolerate but in no way encourage, foster, and least of all allow to influence the policies of civil authority.

STATUE. A likeness of Christ, the Blessed Virgin, or one of the saints, or a symbolic form of an angel, sculptured, carved, or cast in a solid material, and venerated by the faithful. Its purpose is to recall the person whom the statue represents in order to inspire greater piety. Christians do not worship statues as idols.

S.T.B. *Sacrae Theologiae Baccalaureus*—Bachelor of Sacred Theology.

S.T.D. *Sacrae Theologiae Doctor*—Doctor of Sacred Theology.

STEPHEN. A zealous Jewish convert who became the first Christian martyr. He was one of the seven deacons appointed by the Apostles to take care of the needy so that they could devote their time to preaching (Acts 6:1–6). The deacons were involved in preaching as well, and this led to Stephen's tragic death. He was brought before the Sanhedrin on the ground that his preaching was inflammatory and threatened the destruction of the Temple (Acts 6:12). His eloquent defense was interpreted as blasphemy. Not waiting for Roman authorization, they took him out and stoned him to death. Among the approving witnesses was Saul, who had not yet taken his fateful ride to Damascus. Stephen's death dramatized the widening rift between orthodox Jews and the Christian Church (Acts 7).

STERILITY. The incapacity, because of physical or psychological deficiencies, to reproduce. Sterility, unlike impotence, neither invalidates marriage nor renders it illicit.

STERILITY TESTS. Examination of male semen, which is most often the main factor in sterility. Such examination requires the avoidance of illicit methods, such as masturbation, the use of a condom, or withdrawal.

STERILIZATION. Any action that deprives the body, either temporarily or permanently, of the power either to beget or to bear children. It consists in rendering the faculties of generation unfruitful. Four types of sterilization are distinguished in Catholic morality: therapeutic, contraceptive, eugenic, and penal. (Etym. Latin *sterilis,* unfruitful.)

STEWARDSHIP. In biblical usage the management of whatever a person is entrusted with, not only to preserve but profitably administer for his master, ultimately for God. Christ proposed the faithful steward as model for the responsible Christian (Luke 12:42). The Apostles are chosen stewards of the divine mysteries (I Corinthians 4:1–2), and every Christian is a steward of the mysteries of God (I Peter 4:10). Jesus praised the unjust steward of the parable, not because he was dishonest but because of his foresight, since "the children of this world are more astute in dealing with their own kind than are the children of light" (Luke 16:1–8). This is the ultimate lesson of stewardship: that a human being is not owner but only custodian of God's gifts in this world, to use them and produce with them the fruits of eternal life. (Etym. Old English *stigweard,* "keeper of the hall": *stig,* hall + *weard,* keeper.)

S. THOM. St. Thomas Aquinas.

STIGMATA. Phenomenon in which a person bears all or some of the wounds of Christ in his or her own body, i.e., on the feet, hands, side, and brow. The wounds appear spontaneously, from no external source, and periodically there is a flow of fresh blood. The best known stigmatic was St. Francis of Assisi. During an ecstasy on Mount Alvernia on September 17, 1224, he saw a seraph offer him an image of Jesus crucified and imprint upon him the sacred stigmata. Blood used to flow from these wounds until the time of his death two years later. He tried to conceal the phenomenon but not very successfully. Since that time scholarly research has established some three hundred twenty cases of stigmatization, among them more than sixty persons who have been canonized.

Authentic stigmatization occurs only among people favored with ecstasy and is preceded and attended by keen physical and moral sufferings that thus make the subject conformable to the suffering Christ. The absence of suffering would cast serious doubt on the validity of the stigmata, whose assumed purpose is to symbolize union with Christ crucified and participation in his own martyrdom.

Through centuries of canonical processes, the Church has established certain criteria for determining genuine stigmata. Thus the wounds are localized in the very spots where Christ received the five wounds, which does not occur if the bloody sweat is produced by hysteria or hypnotism. Generally the wounds bleed afresh and the pains recur on the days or during the seasons associated with the Savior's passion, such as Fridays or feast days of Our Lord. The wounds do not become festered and the blood flowing from them is pure, whereas the slightest natural lesion in some other part of the body develops an infection. Moreover, the wounds do not yield to the usual medical treatment and may remain for as long as thirty to forty years. The wounds bleed freely and produce a veritable hemorrhage; and this takes place not only at the beginning but again and again. Also the extent of the hemorrhage is phenomenal; the stigmata lie on the surface, removed from the great blood vessels, yet the blood literally streams from them. Finally true stigmata are not found except in persons who practice the most heroic virtues and possess a special love of the Cross. (Etym. Latin *stigma;* from Greek, tattoo mark; from *stizein,* to prick tattoo.)

STIPEND. Canonically speaking, a means of support for the clergy. Also a part of the revenue of a benefice to which a cleric attached to the benefice is entitled. It is popularly spoken of today as the offering made to a priest on the occasion of having him offer Mass for one's special intention.

S.T.L. *Sacrae Theologiae Licentiatus*—Licentiate of Sacred Theology.

S.T.M. *Sacrae Theologiae Magister*—Master of Sacred Theology.

STOCKINGS. Liturgical vestments worn by bishops at solemn pontifical celebrations of Mass. The stockings are of woven silk and conform in color to the vestments. They are worn with low-heeled shoes called sandals, also of the liturgical color appropriate for the occasion. Stockings and sandals are now optional.

STOLE. A liturgical vestment composed of a strip of material, several inches wide, and worn around the neck by priests and bishops; at the left shoulder like a sash by deacons, for the celebration of Mass, administration of the sacraments, and ceremonies of the Blessed Sacrament.

STORRINGTON. Shrine of "Our Lady of England," in Southern England near the Channel. Blessed by Pope Leo XIII, the uncrowned Virgin and her Son, whom she embraces, stand guard over the door leading into the garden of the Premonstratensian Canons' Monastery at Sussex. Mary holds a long scepter and Rosary in her right hand, and is said to be responsible for many remarkable conversions.

S.T.P. *Sacrae Theologiae Professor*—Professor of Sacred Theology.

STRICT INTERPRETATION. In ecclesiastical law the manner of interpreting prescriptions that inflict penalties, or limit the exercise of one's rights, or contain an exception to the law.

STRICT MENTAL RESERVATION. Speech that limits the meaning of what is said but gives no clue to the particular sense intended. This type of mental reservation is actually a lie and is never allowed. Thus if a person says that he or she is going to a distant city, meaning that this person is going there only in imagination, he or she is lying because no clue is given to the sense intended.

STRICT MYSTERY. A revealed truth that so far exceeds the capacity of a created intellect that its full meaning cannot be comprehended except by God alone. Yet strict mysteries, such as the Trinity and the Incarnation, can be partially understood, with varying degrees of insight, depending on God's grace or the believer's own effort and experience.

STRIKING THE BREAST. An ancient sign of sorrow and repentance, to strike one's breast with the hand (Luke 18:13), which has become a part of the liturgy. It is prescribed at Mass during the penitential rite.

STRIPPING THE ALTAR. The liturgical action of stripping an altar and, if possible, removing all crosses from a church after the Mass on Holy Thursday. This is to symbolize the suspension of Mass until the Easter Vigil and the stripping of Christ's garments before the Crucifixion.

STS. Saints.

STYLITES. Pillar saints. They were solitaries who dwelled on the ruins of structures surmounting columns or pillars. In this way they practiced mortification, while also preaching to the people or giving spiritual counsel. The best known were St. Simeon (390–459) of Antioch and St. Daniel (d. 493) of Constantinople.

SUAREZIANISM. Theological system of Francesco Suarez (1548–1617), Spanish Jesuit scholar and writer, named *Doctor Eximius* by Pope Benedict XIV. Building on the principles of St. Thomas Aquinas, Suarez developed a coherent system of his own. Typical of his approach is to cite extensively from the sources he uses and his stress on history as an important factor in development of doctrine. In Suarezianism, essence and existence are in the real existing things, and not distinguished as potency and act; the intellect has a certain natural intuition of the individual; prime matter has more actuality than in Aquinas, for whom it is pure potency; also the principle of individuation is not in the matter but because something exists as this being; on the relationship between grace and free will, Suarezianism favors what has come to be known as congruism, placing more stress on human freedom than in the Thomistic theory of Bannezianism. Suarez is the acknowledged source of the philosophy of natural rights, the law of nations and constitutional law as these have developed in modern times among Christian philosophers as opposed to the divine right of kings. The power to govern in civil society, on Suarezian principles, originates with God's will. But the designation of who will exercise this power is indicated, since the New Testament, by the decision of the people.

SUBAPOSTOLIC AGE. The period from the death of the last Apostle to the death of their immediate disciples, extending to about A.D. 150.

SUBCONSCIOUS. The state of marginal attention, during which a person is only dimly aware of something. It also describes the condition of a person who is not aware of a certain mental process going on within him or her, although it affects a present attitude or moral character. The subconscious is recognized in Catholic pastoral theology as an important factor in human behavior.

SUBDELEGATION. The delegation to a third party of one's right to ecclesiastical jurisdiction, originally received as a delegate from a higher authority in the Catholic Church. Thus a bishop who is delegated by the Holy See may subdelegate his jurisdiction to another bishop, priest, or even lay person. Subdelegation may pertain to a single act or a series of acts, unless ecclesiastical law or the nature of the case provides otherwise.

SUBDIACONATE. Formerly one of the major orders, although not considered a sacrament. A subdeacon assisted a deacon and had certain other auxiliary responsibilities. The subdiaconate was the normal prelude to the diaconate and priesthood. Subdeacons took the vow of celibacy before ordination. The subdiaconate was suppressed by Pope Paul VI for the Latin Church in 1973.

SUBJECT. In scholastic philosophy the term about which some declaration or statement is made. In philosophy the substance in relation to other attributes, as the subject of existence. In epistemology the conscious being as distinct from that which is known. In psychology the power that is controlled by a

habit, as the emotion of fear is the subject of the virtue of courage. In ethics either the holder of a right or the person under the authority of a ruler or superior.

SUBJECTIVE END. The personal satisfaction that one has in view as the motive for doing (or omitting) something. In Christian morality, personal satisfaction is not excluded from human behavior, but it should not be the primary or even dominant motive for the practice of virtue. The main reason should be to please God, even when what he wants may not subjectively please the one who does it.

SUBJECTIVE HOLINESS. See HOLINESS, SUBJECTIVE.

SUBJECTIVE MORALITY. Responsible human conduct, where a person knowingly and willingly performs an action that either conforms or does not conform to the moral standard.

SUBJECTIVISM. Any view of human nature and activity that denies the objective order of reality. It takes on one of three principal forms. In philosophy, it claims that a human being can have no direct knowledge or certitude about the world outside the mind. In theology, it holds that faith is essentially each person's own experience, and not the free assent of the mind to God's revelation. In morals, it admits no principles or norms of conduct except those created by each individual's autonomous will, which is then equated with conscience.

SUBLIME. That which is beautiful in the highest degree. The sublimity may be the greatest within a certain class or category, as among flowers or scenes; it may be the greatest in the physical order; or in the moral order. Among creatures the greatest beauty is spiritual. And sublime above all creatures is the Creator. His sublimity is taught by revelation, in condemning those who practice idolatry. Some have been so charmed by the beauty of creatures, "they have taken things for gods. Let them know how much the Lord of these excels them, since the very Author of beauty has created them" (Wisdom 13:3). (Etym. Latin *sublimare*, to refine, purify; from *sublimis*, uplifted, high.)

SUBORDINATION. The rank of lower to higher or of inferior to superior in any relationship, but mainly of dependence. Subordination implies that there must be a hierarchy of beings in the universe and an order of dependency among agents in order to achieve a given end.

SUBPRIOR. The appointed assistant to the prior of a monastery. He is the second superior in a priory, and the third in an abbey. A subprioress has the corresponding role and rank among nuns.

SUBREPTION. In canon law, withholding the full truth in a request for some favor. If the request is granted, it is valid provided the essentials required by law were fulfilled. (Etym. Latin *subreptio,* theft; from *subrepere,* to creep under, steal upon: *sub-,* under + *repere,* to creep.)

SUBSIDIARITY. The principle by which those in authority recognize the rights of the members in a society; and those in higher authority respect the rights of those in lower authority.

SUBSIDIES, EPISCOPAL. Taxes from a bishop's diocese to which he has a right. Positive legislation has given the bishop the right to impose certain assessments to defray expenses incurred in the exercise of his office. Best known is the *cathedraticum,* or ordinary tax accruing to the bishop in virtue of his jurisdiction over the diocesan churches. Seminary taxes levied at stated times at the bishop's discretion are also considered episcopal subsidies. Expenses incurred during an episcopal visitation are likewise to be paid by the parish. However, the contributions made to the bishop's charity appeal are not considered a direct tax but rather a voluntary gift.

SUB SIGILLO. Under the seal. The term is used to identify some absolutely confidential matter that may not be communicated because a confessor is bound by the sacramental seal.

SUBSISTENCE. The existence proper to a whole and uncommunicated substance or reality. Subsistence is that perfection whereby a nature is completed and becomes uncommunicated, that is, whereby it becomes itself and distinct from all other beings. Something, therefore, subsists when it has being and operation through itself, not through union with another. Applied to God as the being who exists essentially or by identity within his essence; the being who is completely self-sufficient for existence and activity. Also applied by the Second Vatican Council to the Roman Catholic Church, in which, it is said, subsists the fullness of the Church founded by Christ. (Etym. Latin *subsistentia,* self-contained existence; *subsistere,* to stay, abide; to stand under.)

SUBSTANCE. A being whose essence requires that it exist in itself. It is an *ens per se* (a being by itself) or *ens in se* (a being in itself). It is commonly distinguished from an accident, whose essence is to exist in another, that is, in a substance. (Etym. Latin *substantia,* that which stands under, principle, foundation.)

SUBSTANTIAL. Belonging to substance rather than to accidents, or reducible to the category of substance. Thus the Eucharistic consecration of bread and wine produces a substantial change, called transubstantiation.

SUBSTANTIAL ERROR. In contractual matters, ignorance or misjudgment about the essential nature, main terms, or principal motive of the object of a contract.

SUBSTANTIAL HOLINESS. See HOLINESS, ESSENTIAL.

SUBSTANTIAL PRESENCE. The manner of Christ's presence in the Eucharist, "according to the manner of a substance," as taught by the Council of Trent. This means that the whole Christ is present in every portion of the Eucharist, similar to the presence of the entire substance of something, e.g., the human soul, in every part of the human body.

SUBTILITY. Quality of the glorified human body which St. Paul calls "spiritualized." It is not, however, to be conceived as a transformation of the body into spirit or as a refinement into an ethereal substance. The prototype is the risen body of Christ, which emerged from the sealed tomb and penetrated closed doors. The basis for subtility lies in the complete dominion of the body by the transfigured soul.

SUCCENTOR. Assistant to the precentor, who leads the church choir in singing.

SUFFERING. The disagreeable experience of soul that comes with the presence of evil or the privation of some good. Although commonly synonymous with pain, suffering is rather the reaction to pain, and in this sense suffering is a decisive factor in Christian spirituality. Absolutely speaking, suffering is possible because we are creatures, but in the present order of Providence suffering is the result of sin having entered the world. Its purpose, however, is not only to expiate wrongdoing, but to enable the believer to offer God a sacrifice of praise of his divine right over creatures, to unite oneself with

Christ in his sufferings as an expression of love, and in the process to become more like Christ, who, having joy set before him, chose the Cross, and thus "to make up all that has still to be undergone by Christ for the sake of His body, the Church" (I Colossians 1:24). (Etym. Latin *sufferre*, to sustain, to bear up: *sub-*, up from under + *ferre*, to bear.)

SUFFICIENT GRACE. Actual grace considered apart from the supernatural effect for which it was bestowed. It may therefore mean the grace that does not meet with adequate co-operation on the part of the human recipient, and then it is merely sufficient grace. It is enough to enable a person to perform a salutary act, but who freely declines to co-operate. Or it may simply mean the grace that gives one the power to accomplish a salutary action, as distinct from an efficacious grace, which secures that the salutary act is accomplished. See also ACTUAL GRACE, EFFICACIOUS GRACE, GRACE, GRATUITOUS GRACE, HABITUAL GRACE, JUSTIFYING GRACE, SACRAMENTAL GRACE, SANATING GRACE, SANCTIFYING GRACE.

SUFFICIENT REASON. The adequate and necessary objective explanation of why something exists or why something is true.

SUFFICIENT SORROW. The adequate contrition for sins confessed to obtain valid absolution in the sacrament of penance. It is sufficient sorrow if a person repents because of the fear of God's just punishments, which for mortal sin is the fear of losing heaven and deserving hell.

SUFFR. *Suffragia*—suffrages; prayers of the saints.

SUFFRAGAN. The relationship expressed between a bishop and his archbishop. As suffragan, a bishop yields precedence of honor, even in his own diocese, to his archbishop. But in the government of his diocese a bishop is independent of archiepiscopal jurisdiction. Along with other suffragans, a bishop has equal votes in provincial councils, held under the presidency of the archbishop.

SUFFRAGES. The prayers prescribed or promised for specific intentions. More particularly, suffrages are the Masses, prayers, or acts of piety offered for the repose of the souls of the faithful departed.

SUICIDE. The direct killing of oneself on one's own authority. It is a grave sin against the natural and revealed law. The suicide offends against the divine precept "You shall not kill." One causes grave injury to the welfare of society and violates the virtue of charity to oneself. God is the supreme and exclusive owner of all things, so that exercising ownership over life is lawful only to God. He alone can take human life when he wills. The one who directly takes his or her own life violates the rights of God. (Etym. Latin *sui*, self + *cidium*, a killing.)

SUI GENERIS. Alone of its kind. Any person, event, or thing that is extraordinary or unusual. Principally said of God, who is absolutely unique.

SUI JURIS. Belonging to itself. Therefore any person or being that has its own end and rights. It has its own real and legal (juridical) independent existence, not owned by another being, except of course God.

SULPICIANS. Society of diocesan priests established in 1642 by Abbé Olier mainly to prepare men for the priesthood. The name is derived from its headquarters at St. Sulpice, in Paris, France. Their official title is Compagnie des Prêtres de Saint-Sulpice. First approved in 1664, their definitive approbation by the Holy See was in 1931. Their characteristic spirituality is to foster interior abnegation with a view to perfect "adherence" to the interior feelings of Christ.

SUMMA CONTRA GENTILES. The great apologetical work of St. Thomas Aquinas, written from 1258 to 1261. Its purpose is to convince the unbeliever of the inherent reasonableness of the Christian faith. First are set forth those truths that can be discovered by reason alone, then higher truths, beginning with morality, and finally the great mysteries, which though not provable by reason are shown to be consistent with reason and remarkably intelligible.

SUMMAE. A name of comprehensive treatises in theology and philosophy, written during the early and later Middle Ages. Their authors are called summists (Latin *summa*, compendium). Among the most famous were *Sic et Non*, by Peter Abelard (1079–1142); *Libri Quattuor Sententiarum*, by Peter Lombard (1100–60); *Summa Sententiarum*, by Hugo of St. Victor (1096–1141); *Summa Aurea*, by William of Auxerre (d. 1231); *Summa Universae Theologiae*, by Alexander of Hales (1170–1245) and his fellow Franciscans; *Summa de Creaturis*, by St. Albert the Great (1200–80); *Summa contra Gentiles* and *Summa Theologica*, by St. Thomas Aquinas (1225–74).

SUMMA THEOLOGICA. The principal doctrinal synthesis in Catholic theology, written by St. Thomas Aquinas (1225–74). The method used was the application of Aristotelian philosophy in the systematic and rational explanation of dogma and morals, without any substantial modification of the traditional teaching of the Church. Its central theme is God considered under three aspects: 1. he is studied as *Being,* not only in himself but also outside himself, as the source of all things; 2. he is then seen as the *Good,* that is, as the end of created beings and especially of angels and men; 3. he is finally studied as the *Way* of humanity to God, not humanity in the abstract, but of the fallen human being who needed an incarnate God to be saved.

SUMMUM BONUM. The supreme good. Applied to God as the object of the human being's highest aspirations and the fulfillment of all desires. It is therefore the object of perfect beatitude.

SUM. THEOL. The *Summa Theologica* of St. Thomas Aquinas.

SUNDAY. The first day of the week. Since New Testament times it replaced the Jewish Sabbath (Acts 20:7; I Corinthians 16:2). St. John called it the Lord's Day, which the Western Church later translated *Dominica.* The immediate reason for substituting Sunday for the Sabbath was to commemorate Christ's Resurrection from the dead. Eventually Sunday also became a memorial of the descent of the Holy Spirit on Pentecost. Moreover, the original purpose of the Sabbath remained as a liturgical day of rest to recall God's lordship of the universe. "On the seventh day, He rested; that is why Yahweh has blessed the sabbath day and made it sacred" (Exodus 20:8–11).

SUNDAY (biblical). The first day of the week. Jewish converts to Christianity continued to observe the seventh day as the sabbath as well as the first day in commemoration of the Resurrection and Pentecost. But, as Jewish influence waned with the spread of the Church, Sunday became the holy day. Paul's influence was strong in this change (I Corinthians 16:1–2). The name "Lord's Day" appeared first in Revelation (Revelation 1:10).

SUNDAY OBSERVANCE. The Catholic equivalent of the divine commandment to keep the Sabbath holy. In general, Sunday observance means assisting at Mass and resting from servile work.

SUNDAY REST. Abstention from servile, judicial, or commercial work on Sundays. Its religious purpose is to commemorate Christ's Resurrection on Easter Sunday and the descent of the Holy Spirit on Pentecost Sunday, allow the faithful to make the first day of each week a day of joy and of freedom from work, and enable them to celebrate the Eucharist in a fitting manner. "Other celebrations, unless they be truly of the greatest importance, shall not have precedence over Sunday, which is the foundation and center of the whole liturgical year" (Second Vatican Council, *Constitution on the Liturgy,* V, 106). Holy days of obligation are also to be days of rest.

SUNG MASS. See HIGH MASS.

SUPERCHURCH. A term applied to the projected goal within Protestantism to effect a merger of, so far, ecumenically divided religious bodies. Its basic premise is that what separates so many Protestant churches is less important than the benefits to be derived from a large-scale unification.

SUPERIOR. The person who has authority over others in the Catholic Church. There are two kinds of superior, corresponding to the two kinds of hierarchy that have authority, namely, ecclesiastical and religious. The two may coalesce in one person, but they are really distinct. (Etym. Latin *superus,* situated above, upper; from *super,* above, over.)

SUPERIOR, ECCLESIASTICAL. A member of the Catholic hierarchy who has ordinary or delegated jurisdiction in the Church. The highest ecclesiastical superior is the Pope, who has jurisdiction over the whole Church; then the cardinals, archbishops, and bishops, who have jurisdiction over the faithful in the territories under their care; and finally those in sacred orders who have been entrusted with the care of souls, in accordance with the ecclesiastical office that they hold.

SUPERIOR, RELIGIOUS. The person who governs a religious community. His or her powers are defined in the constitutions of the institute and in the common law of the Church. All religious superiors have dominative power over their subjects, i.e., they have the right of authority over the acts of the persons in their community. In a clerical exempt institute, superiors also have ecclesiastical jurisdiction.

SUPERNATURAL CONTEMPLATION. Elevation of mind to God and divine things, joined with a loving intuition of what is seen. It is the mind resting upon God and tasting the joys of his beatitude. Although still in the realm of faith and not heavenly vision, it is an intuition of Divine Truth terminating in affection and love, excluding long reasonings and a multiplicity of words as found in affective prayer. St. Teresa speaks of it as God acting on the human mind in a special way.

SUPERNATURAL COURAGE. The moral virtue of fortitude divinely infused into the soul along with sanctifying grace. As a supernatural virtue it is needed to practice what Christ commanded (precepts) or recommended (counsels) his followers to do.

SUPERNATURAL END. The purpose or good to be sought and attained beyond the needs, powers, and tendencies of nature as such. It can only be realized by divine grace, in elevating human nature above its native level of being, and in helping one's activity above its native level of operation.

SUPERNATURAL MERIT. A morally good action performed by a person in the state of grace and deserving of reward from God.

SUPERNATURAL ORDER. The sum total of heavenly destiny and all the divinely established means of reaching that destiny, which surpass the mere powers and capacities of human nature.

SUPERNATURAL REVELATION. Divine communication of truth in which either the manner of communication or its content is beyond the capacity of human nature to attain. Thus revelation may be supernatural in its objective source, which is more than the universe naturally tells about its Creator, and again supernatural in the subjective powers by which a person acquires what God desires to reveal. Revelation may also be supernatural in its very essence, as when God discloses such mysteries as the Trinity and the Incarnation. Or it may be, and always is, supernatural in the manner that God chooses to use for communicating himself to human beings. It partakes of a miraculous enlightenment of the seer who then serves as divine legate for sharing with others what God has supernaturally communicated to that person. In every case, however, the acceptance of revelation requires the influx of supernatural grace to enable a person to believe.

SUPERNATURAL THEOLOGY. The scientific exposition of the truths about God as he is known by faith in divine revelation and with the assistance of divine grace. Theology is a true science because it uses principles that are founded on God's revealed word, it draws new knowledge by reflection on these principles, and it unites the whole in a strict, scientific system.

SUPERNATURAL WORDS. Manifestations of the divine mind conveyed to the exterior or interior senses or directly to the intellect. They differ from strictly intellectual visions in that words are received and, by means of these words, certain thoughts are perceived. The words may be directed to the human ear and then the locutions are auricular, or to the ear of the imagination and they are imaginative, or directly to the mind and they are intellectual. St. John of the Cross (1542–91) distinguishes these forms of supernatural language by calling them successive, formal, and substantial (*Ascent of Mount Carmel*, II, 26–29).

SUPERSTITION. The unseemly or irreverent worship of God, or giving to a creature the worship that belongs to God. Rendering unbecoming worship to God may stem either from false devotion or from a tendency toward magic. Giving divine worship to a creature is either idolatry, divination, or vain observance. The term "superstition" more commonly means unbecoming worship to God.

When superstition arises from false devotion, it is really superfluous worship of God, which may take on a variety of forms. Their common denominator is an excessive concern that unless certain external practices, such as multiplication of prayers, are performed God will be displeased.

When superstition stems from a tendency toward magic, it reflects a false mentality that may or may not be the root of false devotion. Behind the false mentality is the notion that certain ritual practices, such as chain prayers or veneration of unapproved objects, carry with them an efficacy that is contrary to sound reason or the teaching of the Church.

SUPPLIED JURISDICTION. In ecclesiastical law, a form of delegation supplied by the Church, enabling a priest who is otherwise unauthorized to validly absolve penitents in the sacrament of penance. Thus jurisdiction is supplied in the case of common error (when people think that the priest has jurisdiction); in a doubt of law or fact, assuming that the doubt is sincere; and if a priest's jurisdiction has inadvertently expired.

SUPPORT OF RELIGION. The duty that a Catholic has to contribute to the support of the parish and other causes of religion, according to each one's means. It is an obligation more than once declared in the Scriptures (Deuteronomy 14:23; I Corinthians 9:14). Its object is that God may be duly honored and worshiped, and the kingdom of his Church extended.

SUPPOSIT. One being, complete as such, and therefore incommunicable. It is in itself and acts in itself. If the supposit is gifted with reason, it is called a person; otherwise it is called a thing. (Etym. Latin *suppositum,* something placed under, accepted, assumed, individual substance.)

SUPRALAPSARIANS. Followers of John Calvin (1509–64) who hold that God's decree of reprobation of some people to hell is absolute, and not conditioned by the Fall. God would have condemned these people to hell even though Adam had not sinned. This was Calvin's position.

SUPREME DOMINION. God's unlimited right of government over all created things, and his claim of unreserved obedience from rational creatures. His right of lordship over the universe belongs to God in virtue of his creation of the world and his redemption of mankind.

SUPREME END. The highest good to which a rational creature can aspire and, with God's grace, hope to attain. It is the *summum bonum,* which completely satisfies every legitimate aspiration of human beings, namely the possession of God in the beatific vision.

SUPREME EVIL. Whatever is regarded as the greatest loss or deprivation. Different philosophies conceive it in different ways, depending on what they consider the supreme good. In any religion or system of thought, the supreme evil is taken to mean the loss of the supreme good. In Christianity the supreme objective evil is grave sin; the supreme subjective evil is hell, or the eternal loss of the vision of God.

SURPLICE. A large-sleeved tunic of half length, made of linen or cotton, without a cincture, and occasionally embroidered at hem and sleeves. It is a liturgical garment worn by all clergy in choir, during processions, and when administering the sacraments. (Etym. Latin *superpellicium* [originally worn by clergymen of northern countries over their fur coats].)

SURROGATE. A person who functions in the place of someone's parent. The fact that such substitutions occur in real life and, for some people, in fantasy is well known. It is one of the postulates of modern atheism that God is merely a cosmic surrogate for the human race, a projection of the father image on a world people.

SURSUM CORDA. "Lift up your hearts," a phrase used by the priest when addressing the faithful at Mass during the preface. It is also used as a motto in Christian heraldry.

SUSCIPE. A prayer, composed by St. Ignatius Loyola in the Spiritual Exercises, to be said as an act of total self-sacrifice to God. It reads: "Take, O Lord, and receive all my liberty, my memory, my understanding, and all my will, all that I have and possess. You have given all of these to me; to you I restore them. All are yours, dispose of them all according to your will. Give me your love and your grace; having but these I am rich enough and ask for nothing more."

SUSPENSION. The canonical censure by which a cleric is excluded from office or from a benefice or both. A suspension from office may forbid him to exercise any or all the powers of order received through ordination, and any act of jurisdiction, whether ordinary or delegated. Suspension from benefice may, with certain exceptions, deprive a cleric of the fruit of the benefice.

SUSPICION. See RASH JUDGMENT.

S.V. *Sanctitas Vestra*—Your Holiness.

SWASTIKA. A symbol of the Cross, sometimes called the *crux gammata,* made up of four Greek gammas joined at their bases. It is of Sanskrit origin and means "good omen." It has several recognized meanings, e.g., rotation of the sun, four points of the compass. It has sometimes been referred to as the crooked cross. It was the emblem of the Nazis in World War II. Seldom used by Christians before the third century, and then only to conceal the Cross from unbelievers.

SWEET QUIETUDE. The state of soul referred to by St. Theresa of Ávila (1515–82) in her *Interior Castle* as the Fourth Mansion. She calls this the prayer of quiet or divine delights because it is here that God's presence is felt for the first time with spiritual delight. It is also called the prayer of silence and has three phases: 1. passive recollection, with grace acting directly on the faculties; 2. quietude, with the intellect and will enjoying God's presence in quiet and repose; 3. sleep of the faculties, with the intellect and will seized by God; the imagination and memory, although active, are weakened and ineffectual. This last phase is a preparation for full union of the soul with God.

SWISS GUARDS. Official police officers and bodyguards of the Pope. Going back to the Swiss soldiers in the service of the Holy See since the fourteenth century, they were formed into a distinct body by Pope Julius II in 1505. Their recruitment is based on the centuries-long agreement between the Holy See and the Catholic civil authorities of Switzerland. The most memorable event in their history was their noble defense of Pope Clement VII during the sack of Rome in 1527, when one hundred forty-seven were killed and only forty-two reached safety with the Pope in Castel Sant'Angelo. Their function is mainly to protect the person of the Pope and to guard the apostolic palaces, especially their outside entrances.

SWORD. A symbol appropriate to St. Paul because of his keen teaching and the manner of his death. The sword of the Spirit was interpreted as the Word of God (Ephesians 6:17). It is the emblem of the Holy Spirit's gift of fortitude and the symbol of St. Michael, recalling his encounter with Lucifer. It is also an emblem of St. James the Greater and St. Jude.

SWORD, FLAMING. Symbol of the angel referred to as one of the Cherubim who were sent to Eden to guard "the way to the tree of life" (Genesis 3:24) after the expulsion of Adam and Eve. Only in apocryphal writing and sometimes in art is this angel given the name of Jophiel.

SYLLABUS OF PIUS IX. A series of eighty condemned propositions listing the prevalent errors that aimed at the undermining of society, morality, and religion. Every Catholic is expected to give exterior and interior assent to the condemnation of errors expressed in this syllabus.

SYLLABUS OF PIUS X. A series of propositions condemned by the Congregation of the Holy Office and ratified by the Pope as decreed in the encyclical *Lamentabili* (July 3, 1907). It denounced the tenets of Modernism and repudiated their errors. The basis of these false doctrines was the psuedo-scientific theory of evolution on human knowledge and belief. By a subse-

quent *motu proprio* the Pope further confirmed the syllabus by publishing the *Oath Against Modernism* (September 1, 1910).

SYLLOGISM. In philosophy, an argument so arranged that if the first two statements (premise) are accepted the third (conclusion) necessarily follows. In theology, when the first statement is a revealed truth, and the second is a fact or truth knowable by reason, the third is said to be a theological conclusion. Such conclusions are frequently the object of the Church's infallible teaching authority. (Etym. Greek *syllogismos,* a reckoning together.)

SYMBOL. In general, any object that stands for or represents something else. More particularly, any conventional sign that functions as such because of an agreement, explicit or implicit, between its users. Religious symbols are also called emblems, insofar as they represent some sacred truth or mystery of the faith. (Etym. Greek *symbolon,* a token, pledge; a sign by which one infers a thing.)

SYMBOLISM. Investing outward things or actions with an inner meaning. Its effectiveness depends on the depth of personal commitment to the interior truth symbolized and the ability of a symbol to convey its inner meaning. Early Christian symbolism arose partially as a result of persecution. It was necessary to veil beliefs under emblems and figures. Another contributing factor was the instinctive religious desire to envelop the personal and collective life of the people in expressions and reminders of their faith. In time, every detail of Church art and architecture, of the liturgy and private devotion, acquired definable religious meaning. Symbolism is the universal language of every living religion. It is especially rich in Catholic Christianity because of the Church's encouragement, but mainly because the mysteries of the faith are too profound ever to fully understand. Symbols enable the mind to dwell on these mysteries with prayerful reflection and ever greater comprehension.

SYMBOLS, CHRISTIAN. Signs or emblems of religious truth. They are sensibly perceptible means by which revealed mysteries can be more or less understood. They can be written or spoken or expressed in graphic form. In a class by themselves are the sacraments, which not only symbolize a revealed truth but actually confer what they signify.

SYMPATHY. The quality of being affected by the experience of another, especially in sorrow or trial, with similar feelings in oneself. Kinship in suffering is true sympathy. (Etym. Latin *sympathia;* from Greek *sumpatheia,* from *sumpathēs,* affected by like feelings: *sun-,* like + *pathos,* emotions, feelings.)

SYN. *Synodus*—synod.

SYNAGOGUE (biblical). The Jewish community center where the study and exposition of the Old Testament was conducted. Although its main function was religious, it also served as a meeting place for other kinds of community activities—funerals, meetings, and business affairs. A staff of officials managed the synagogue, directed ceremonies, and supervised educational programs.

SYNAXIS. A meeting for any religious function in the early Church, corresponding to *synagogue,* as a Jewish religious meeting. In the Eastern Church it still means any assembly for public worship and prayer, including the liturgical synaxis, or Mass. In the Western Church it had been used for non-Eucharistic services such as the reading of Psalms or the recitation of prayers, from which the Divine Office developed. Synaxis is also the title in the Byzantine Rite of certain feasts on which people assemble in a particular church, corresponding to Roman stations in the Latin Rite. Also, in a Byzantine monastery the council of elders who assist the abbot is called a synaxis.

SYNCRETISM. The effort to unite different doctrines and practices, especially in religion. Such unions or amalgams are part of cultural history and are typical of what has occurred in every segment of the non-Christian world. Syncretism is also applied to the ecumenical efforts among separated Christian churches and within Catholicism to the attempts made of combining the best elements of different theological schools. But in recent years the term mainly refers to misguided claims that religious unity can be achieved by ignoring the differences between faiths on the assumption that all creeds are essentially one and the same. (Etym. Greek *synkrētizo,* to unite disunited elements into a harmonious whole; from *synkrētizmos,* federation of Cretan cities.)

SYNDERESIS or SYNTERESIS. The habit of knowing the basic principles of the moral law; the knowledge of the universal first principles of the practical order. Sometimes applied to conscience, which is, however, rather the mind's concrete application of known principles, judging on the moral goodness or badness of a specific human action. (Etym. Greek *synteresis,* spark of conscience.)

SYNDIC, APOSTOLIC. A lay person or procurator who administers the property used by the Friars Minor and Capuchins and owned by the Holy See. Modern social living required the Holy See to constitute itself owner in trust of property, gifts, bequests, etc., accruing to the friars or other groups forbidden by their vows to own property in common. Every friary has a syndic who is in charge and administers such goods.

SYNDICALISM. A revolutionary movement among the working class, aimed at the control of industry by the workers on a basis of organization of labor by industries. As a means to attain its end, it advocated the general strike and sabotage. Its origin is dated from 1895, when the Confédération Générale du Travail was formed in France, and the movement soon spread to other countries. Those who advocate violence in labor unions are syndicalists.

SYNOD. An assembly of ecclesiastics, not necessarily all bishops, gathered together under ecclesiastical authority to discuss and decide on matters pertaining to doctrine, discipline, or liturgy under their jurisdiction. The words *synod* and *council* were for centuries synonymous, and the terms are still interchangeable. At the Council of Trent, synod referred to a diocesan assembly, which the council decreed should be held once every year. In the Code of Canon Law, diocesan synods were legislated to be held every ten years at least, at which only a bishop was to have legislative authority, everyone else being only a consultor. (Etym. Latin *synodus;* from Greek *sunodos,* meeting: *sun-,* together + *hodos,* road, way, journey.)

SYNOD OF BISHOPS. An assembly of bishops, chosen from various parts of the world, that meets in Rome every several years to "render more effective assistance to the supreme pastor of the Church in a consultative body which will be called by the proper name of Synod of Bishops. Since it will be acting in the name of the entire episcopate, it will at the same time show that all bishops in hierarchical communion share in the solicitude for the universal Church" (*Decree on the Pastoral Office of Bishops in the Church,* I, 5). Although by its nature permanent, the synod performs its duties only for a time and when called upon. Normally operating as a consultative body, to inform and counsel the Pope, it may also have deliberative (decision-making) power, when this is conferred by the Sovereign Pontiff, who must in all cases confirm the synodal deliberations to give them validity.

SYNOPTIC PROBLEM. The problem of how the Gospels according to Matthew, Mark, and Luke are related, since large areas of these cover the same subject matter, often in similar words, and yet sometimes showing remarkable differences. There is no single solution to the Synoptic Problem. In general, Catholic scholarship favors the basic tradition, dating from the second century, that the Gospels bearing the names of Matthew, Mark, and Luke were written by Matthew the Apostle, Mark the disciple of Peter, and Luke the disciple of Paul; that Matthew's original Gospel was in Aramaic, later translated into Greek; that the similarities among the Synoptics are due to their dealing with the same historical data, and their differences due to each evangelist's perspective, personality, and distinctive purpose in writing a separate Gospel. Among Protestants the Synoptic Problem is commonly resolved by postulating Mark as the first and fundamental Gospel, on which the others built, along with other sources, notably the unknown Q whose existence is inferred purely from the textual evidence.

SYNOPTICS. The first three evangelists, Matthew, Mark, and Luke. They are so named because they follow the same general plan and reflect great similarity in the events related and even in literary expression. They offer the same comprehensive view of the life and teachings of Jesus Christ.

SYNTERESIS. See SYNDERESIS.

SYNTHESIS. The mental act by which simple ideas are combined into more complex ones. Hence the combining of separate and distinct elements to form a coherent whole on the basis of some unifying principle. (Etym. Latin *synthesis;* from Greek *synthesis,* a putting together.)

SYRIAC. A branch of the Aramaic language, spoken in Edessa (city of modern Turkey) and the surrounding region sometime before the beginning of the Christian era. It was used extensively in the early Church, e.g., in the *Diatessaron* and *Peshitta* translations of the Bible. After the religious divisions of the fifth century it continued as the language of the East and West Syrians. But once Arabic became the current vernacular, Syriac became a more or less artificial language.

SYRIAN RITE. In the East it is also known as the Chaldean, Assyrian, or Persian Rite and is used both by Catholics and dissident Oriental Christians. The language is Syriac or Aramaic. Among the Syrian Nestorians there are only five sacraments, with penance and anointing of the sick practically unknown. In the West, the Syriac Rite is also used by both Catholics and Non-Catholic Orientals, notably the Syrian Catholics, Maronites, and Jacobites. Among the last mentioned this rite is interspersed with many Arabic prayers.

SYSTEMATIC THEOLOGY. See DOGMATIC THEOLOGY.

SYSTEMS OF PROBABILITY. Theories about the degree of doubt or probability that will exempt a person from the obligation of a doubtful law. Five systems have been developed (of which the first and last are more speculative than practical), namely, tutiorism, probabiliorism, equiprobabilism, probabilism, and laxism. According to tutiorism, a person must be certain or nearly certain (*tutior,* safer) that the doubtful law does not bind; and laxism holds that even a thinly or dubiously probable reason in favor of liberty exempts one from observing a doubtful law. Probabiliorism says that the evidence against a dubious law must be more probable than the opposite. Equiprobabilism claims that the evidence must be as probable as the opposite. Probabilism holds that any solidly probable argument against the existence or application of a doubtful law is enough to keep it from binding.

T

TABERNACLE. A cupboard or boxlike receptable for the exclusive reservation of the Blessed Sacrament. In early Christian times the sacred species was reserved in the home because of possible persecution. Later dove-shaped tabernacles were suspended by chains before the altar. Nowadays tabernacles may be round or rectangular and made of wood, stone, or metal. They are covered with a veil and lined with precious metal or silk, with a corporal beneath the ciboria or other sacred vessels. According to the directive of the Holy See, since the Second Vatican Council, tabernacles are always solid and inviolable and located in the middle of the main altar or on a side altar, but always in a truly prominent place (*Eucharisticum Mysterium,* May 25, 1967, II, C). (Etym. Latin *tabernaculum,* tent, diminutive of *taberna,* hut, perhaps from Etruscan.)

TABERNACLE (biblical). A sanctuary used in Hebrew worship even before Solomon built the Temple. It represented God's presence with his people (Exodus 25:8). When they traveled from place to place, the tabernacle went with them. Yahweh gave Moses detailed instructions about the size, materials, and adornment of the tabernacle and its position in the court area set apart for religious observance (Exodus 25, 26, 27). In the New Testament the tabernacle takes on a new meaning, as described in the Letter to the Hebrews. "Christ has passed through the greater, the more perfect tent, which is better than the one made by men's hands because it is not of this created order; and he has entered the sanctuary once and for all, taking with him not the blood of goats and bull calves, but his own blood, having won an eternal redemption for us" (Hebrews 9:11–12).

TABERNACLES, FEAST OF. One of the three great feasts of ancient Israel, still commemorated by the Jews. It recalls the custom of erecting booths of branches and foliage, where all who could were to live during the feast, beginning on the fifteenth day of the month of Tishri (approximately September) and lasting seven days. Its original purpose was to thank the Lord for the harvest, but in time it became a solemn commemoration of the long sojourn in the desert, of finding a home in the Promised Land, and of building the Temple as a permanent place of worship of the one true God.

TABGHA. A place two miles from Capernaum, Palestine, is the pilgrimage spot of Christ's miracle of the multiplication of loaves and fishes. An ancient basilica was excavated nearby where a large mosaic was recovered, picturing two fishes and three loaves in a basket. In the company of a Franciscan monk and an Orthodox priest Pope Paul, in 1964, on his way to the Sea of Galilee, visited Tabgha to see the mosaic set in the floor and blessed this hallowed shrine.

TABLES OF THE LAW. The two stone tablets on which were inscribed the Ten Commandments of Yahweh (Exodus 20, 31:18). When Moses came down the mountain to his people, he found them worshiping a golden calf. He threw down the tablets and destroyed them in his anger (Exodus 32:19). Later he climbed Mount Sinai again with two new tablets and the Commandments were inscribed once more (Exodus 34:28). Moses placed them in the Ark for safekeeping (Deuteronomy 10:5).

TABOR. A mountain in Galilee, east of Nazareth. A conspicuous landmark because of its isolated location. Several military events in the Old Testament took place on Mount Tabor. Gideon's brothers were killed there by the Midianites (Judges 8:18). Barak led a dramatic charge down the mountain to defeat the Canaanites (Judges 4:14–16). There is a tradition that Jesus' Transfiguration took place on Mount Tabor rather than on Mount Hermon, but it is impossible to prove.

TABULA RASA. Clean slate or erased tablet. The term is used in scholastic philosophy to describe the human mind before it has acquired any ideas from sense experience and reasoned reflection.

TALEBEARING. Spreading malicious stories or gossip. The sinfulness of talebearing consists in being an accomplice to injuring people's reputation by the detraction or calumny involved.

TAMETSI DECREE. A ruling (1563) of the Council of Trent on matrimonial law. It stipulated that any marriage that took place outside the presence of a parish priest or his representative and two witnesses would be null. Places where priests were not available were excepted, and it was not binding where the laws of Trent were not promulgated. It was extended almost universally in a modified form by the *Ne Temere* decree (1908) of Pope Pius X.

TANT. *Tantum*—only.

TANTUM ERGO. The last two verses of the hymn *Pange Lingua,* composed by St. Thomas Aquinas and long prescribed for singing at Benediction of the Blessed Sacrament. A modern English version reads:

Down in adoration falling,
Lo, the sacred host we hail.
Lo, o'er ancient forms departing

Newer rites of grace prevail;
Faith for all defects supplying
Where the feeble senses fail.

To the everlasting Father,
And the Son who reigns on high.
With the Holy Spirit proceeding
Forth from each eternally,
Be salvation, honor, blessing,
Might and endless majesty. Amen.

TANTUM QUANTUM. So much as. The term in St. Ignatius' Principle and Foundation of the Spiritual Exercises referring to the right use of creatures: "We are to use them in so far as [*tantum quantum*] they lead us to our last end, and be rid of them in so far as [*tantum quantum*] they hinder us in the pursuit of the end for which we were created."

TARGUM. The Aramaic translations or paraphrases of the Old Testament, made by the Jews when Hebrew had ceased to be their normal medium of speech. (Etym. Mishnaic Hebrew *targūm*, translation, interpretation; from Hebrew *tirgēm*, he interpreted.)

TASTE. The bodily sense adapted to perceive flavors. The term is often used in sacred literature to describe "tasting" the Lord or "tasting" a revealed mystery. It implies the existence of a spiritual sense that can experience a sweetness on contact with divine truth similar to the savor of pleasant food or drink.

TAU CROSS. A symbol resembling the Greek letter tau or T. The standard raised by Moses to elevate the brazen serpent, and the mark made by the Israelites in blood on their doorpost is thought to have been the tau. The tau cross is also the emblem of St. Anthony of Egypt.

TE DEUM LAUDAMUS. "We praise You, O God." First words of an ancient Christian hymn of praise and thanksgiving, sometimes called the Ambrosian hymn but now believed to have been written by St. Niketas in the fourth century.

TEETOTALISM. See TOTAL ABSTINENCE.

TEILHARDISM. The evolutionary theory of the French Jesuit Teilhard de Chardin (1881–1955). He held that the universe is subject to four stages of development: 1. cosmogenesis, or evolution from the elements to organized matter; 2. biogenesis, or evolution from organized matter to life; 3. noo-genesis, or evolution from living things to rational beings; and 4. Christogenesis, or evolution from individual rational humanity to a society in which Christ was the Lord of the world. Teilhardism was the object of two critical documents from the Holy See, in 1952 and 1967, which stated that his writings abound "in such ambiguities and indeed serious errors as to offend Catholic doctrine."

TELEOLOGY. The doctrine that there is purpose or finality in the world, that nothing ever happens merely by chance, and that no complete account of the universe is possible without final reference to an all-wise God. (Etym. Greek *telos,* end, completion + *logia,* knowledge, science.)

TELEPATHY. The direct communication of ideas from one mind to another without words, signs, gestures, or any other ordinary means of communicating thought. Extensive data and years of psychical research indicate that such manner of communicating knowledge does occur in exceptional cases or with exceptional people. When verified, the phenomenon is purely natural and the use of telepathic powers by one who possesses them cannot be called divination, nor does their use pose any special moral problems. It should be judged by the general principles applicable to any other human being's behavior.

It is altogether another question whether in a given case of reputed telepathy any preternatural agency has been active. Instances of supposed communication of thought without verbal or other sensory means are reported in the lives of the saints. But the Church does not hold that such phenomena are positive signs of a person's sanctity. (Etym. Greek *tēle,* at a distance + *pathein,* to experience.)

TEMERARIOUS. Ecclesiastical censure placed on certain teaching that is, in the Church's judgment, rash and that, if consistently held, leads to doctrinal error. See also THEOLOGICAL CENSURE.

TEMP. *Tempus, tempore*—time, in time.

TEMPERAMENT. The distinctive emotional, mental, and affective qualities of each individual. A classic position holds that there are four basic temperaments: phlegmatic, or not easily aroused; choleric, or having a low threshold for anger; sanguine, or optimistic and free from anxiety; and melancholic, or given to introspection and pessimism about the future. No single person, it is agreed, has only one temperament, although one or the other trait will predominate.

TEMPERANCE. The virtue that moderates the desire for pleasure. In the widest sense, temperance regulates every form of enjoyment that comes from the exercise of a human power or faculty, e.g., purely spiritual joy arising from intellectual activity or even the consolations experienced in prayer and emotional pleasure produced by such things as pleasant music or the sight of a beautiful scene. In the strict sense, however, temperance is the correlative of fortitude. As fortitude controls rashness and fear in the face of the major pains that threaten to unbalance human nature, so temperance controls desire for major pleasures. Since pleasure follows from all natural activity, it is most intense when associated with our most natural activities. On the level of sense feeling, they are the pleasures that serve the individual person through food and drink, and the human race through carnal intercourse. Temperance mainly refers to these appetites. (Etym. Latin *temperare,* to apportion, regulate, qualify.)

TEMPLARS, THE KNIGHTS. The first and most powerful of the military orders founded in 1118 for the defense of Jerusalem. Ten years later, they were approved by the Church and placed under the Pope's immediate jurisdiction. They followed the Benedictine Rule, taking the usual three vows and an additional crusader's vow. As dauntless fighters and fervent religious, they drew many to their ranks. Many died as martyrs. Difficulties with the clergy and internal dissensions caused King Philip the Fair of France to organize a crusade against them. Pope Clement V's approval for this crusade was then dishonestly secured. The Knights were tried for heresy and sacrilege, and their grand master was burned alive by order of Philip. In 1312 the Pope decreed the dissolution of the order but without condemning its members. It was mainly the greed of Philip IV that brought on the suppression of the Templars.

TEMPLE (biblical). The world center of Jewish religion in Jerusalem. The original temple was built by Solomon in the tenth century (II Chronicles 1–5). It lasted three hundred fifty years before the Babylonians destroyed it (II Kings 25:9). In 516 B.C. a more modest temple was erected by Zerubbabel (Ezra 5:2). Herod rebuilt and improved it in 20 B.C. but again it was destroyed, this time by the Romans in A.D. 70. For over a thousand years it was the center of religious life for Jews all over the world. A number of incidents in Jesus' life took place in the Temple. His parents brought him there as an infant for the purification ceremony at which Simeon knew him to be the Messiah (Luke 2:22–35). Annually his parents visited Jerusalem for the Passover. On his twelfth birthday occurred the incident when they found him in the Temple "listening to the doctors and questioning them" (Luke 2:41–50). During his public ministry he and his disciples regularly visited the Temple and taught there. (Etym. Latin *templum,* sanctuary, space marked for observation by an augur.)

TEMPORAL. Anything that lasts only for a time, whose existence or activity will cease. In this sense, temporal is the opposite of eternal, which lasts forever. Also applied to what is of this world, or secular, as opposed to the heavenly. Or again it may refer to the material, in contrast with the spiritual. Or finally, the temporal is commonly applied to the lay or civil, as temporal power or authority; and then the opposite is ecclesiastical. In general, the temporal is everything belonging to, limited by, or characterized by time and change. (Etym. Latin *tempus,* time.)

TEMPORAL CYCLE. See PROPER OF THE SEASON.

TEMPORAL POWER. The rule of the Church in earthly possessions and the authority of the Pope over civil territories belonging to the Church, as in the Papal States. This power is in addition to his dominion in spiritual matters and becomes necessary if freedom from civil power is to be assured. It is presently exercised in relation to Vatican City or State since the Lateran Treaty of 1929. The term may also refer to the exercise of political influence by the bishops formerly through landed estates and currently through financial and other means.

TEMPORAL PUNISHMENT. The penalty that God in his justice inflicts either on earth or in Purgatory for sins, even though already forgiven as to guilt.

TEMPORARY VOW. A commitment made to God to practice poverty, chastity, obedience, or some other virtue for a specified length of time. When made in a religious institute, the vows are public, being accepted by the superior in the name of the Church The first vows of religion are generally temporary, to be renewed according to the constitutions and preliminary to perpetual vows. But they do not, therefore, imply only a temporary commitment. They are canonically temporary, so that after they expire the one who made them is free to leave the institute of Christian perfection. But intentionally, even the person who takes only temporary vows should have the desire to persevere in the vowed commitment until death.

TEMPTATION. Solicitation to sin, whether by persuasion or offering some pleasure. It may arise from the world, the flesh, or the devil. Temptation from the world is the attractiveness of bad example and the psychological pressure to conform. Temptations from the flesh are all the urges of concupiscence, whether carnal or spiritual, where man's fallen nature has built-in tendencies to the seven capital sins. Demonic temptations arise from instigations of the evil spirit, whose method is to encourage every form of avarice or selfishness, in order to lead one to pride, and through pride to all other sins.

TEMPTING GOD. An act or omission in which a person tries to test God's attributes, notably his love, power, or wisdom. It may be done either explicitly or implicitly.

God is tempted explicitly when something is demanded of him or when something is done or omitted for the actual purpose of ascertaining the extent of God's love, power, or wisdom. An example would be that of an atheist who might give God, say, five minutes to strike him or her dead, "if there is a God." To explicitly tempt God is always a grave sin.

God is tempted implicitly when, not doubting his attributes, a person rashly requires a manifestation of divine love, power, or wisdom. Examples of implicitly tempting God are needlessly risking one's life in some dangerous feat or refusing all medical aid simply because it is up to God to cure one of some grave illness or disease. Implicitly tempting God is a serious sin in grave matters, otherwise a venial sin.

TEN COMMANDMENTS. Also called the Decalogue, they are the divinely revealed precepts received by Moses on Mount Sinai. Engraved on two tablets of stone, they occur in two versions in the Bible. The earlier form (Exodus 20:1–17) differs from the later (Deuteronomy 5:6–18) in two ways. It gives a religious motive, instead of a humanitarian one, for observing the Sabbath; and in prohibiting avarice, it classes a man's wife along with the rest of his possessions, instead of separately.

With the exception of forbidding graven images and statues and the precept about the Sabbath, the Ten Commandments are an expression of the natural law. More or less extensive sections of the Decalogue are found in the laws of other ancient people. However, the Ten Commandments excel the moral codes of other religious systems in their explicit monotheism, their doctrine of God's awesome majesty and boundless goodness, and their extension of moral obligation down to the most intimate and hidden desires of the human heart. The following is a standard Catholic expression of the Ten Commandments:

1. I, the Lord, am your God. You shall not have other gods besides me.
2. You shall not take the name of the Lord, your God, in vain.
3. Remember to keep holy the sabbath day.
4. Honor your father and your mother.
5. You shall not kill.
6. You shall not commit adultery.
7. You shall not steal.
8. You shall not bear false witness against your neighbor.
9. You shall not covet your neighbor's wife.
10. You shall not covet anything that belongs to your neighbor. See also CHRISTIAN DECALOGUE.

TENDENCY. Any inclination or disposition that, in human beings, becomes a desire. It is either an attraction to some specific good or an aversion from some specific evil. Natural tendencies are inborn and are really one's natural powers or faculties seeking expression. Supernatural tendencies are the graces divinely conferred to incline the will to the practice of virtue beyond the capacity of the native will, or of virtue known only on divine faith. Both natural and supernatural tendencies may be either conscious, also called elicited, when a person actually experiences his striving toward a good or away from an evil; or they can be spontaneous, without conscious awareness of the effort used in responding to a desire. (Etym. Latin *tendentia;* from *tendere,* to stretch, extend, direct oneself, tender.)

TENDER CONSCIENCE. A conscience that forms objectively correct judgments with comparative ease even in finer distinctions between good and evil.

TENEBRAE. The public singing of part of the Divine Office, on Wednesday, Thursday, and Friday evenings of Holy Week, anticipating Matins and Lauds of Holy Thursday,

Good Friday, and Holy Saturday. A custom that went back centuries, it acquired the name because of the mourning ritual surrounding the ceremony, which included a triangular stand with fifteen candles. These were put out one by one until, after the last candle was extinguished, a prayer was said in darkness, one candle was lighted, and the assembly dispersed in silence.

TEN TRIBES. The ten social units of Israel that, after the death of Solomon (933 B.C.), separated from the two tribes of Judah and Benjamin to form the Kingdom of Israel. Those two tribes formed the Kingdom of Judah. When Israel was conquered by the Assyrians in 721 B.C., many of the more prominent Jews were exiled to Assyria, and their descendants either merged with the Gentiles or became part of the later Jewish Diaspora.

TERCE. Third hour of the Divine Office, which is to be said at about 9 A.M. The beginning hymn is in commemoration of the Holy Spirit's descent on the Apostles and is followed by three variable psalms, a short reading, versicle and response, and the collect of the day. Terce is now technically part of the *hora media* (middle hour), said after Lauds and before Vespers. (Etym. Latin *tertius*, third.)

TERMINUS AD QUEM. See TERMINUS A QUO.

TERMINUS A QUO. The starting point. In philosophy "the end from which" something begins, in comparison with *terminus ad quem*, "the end to which" something extends or is directed.

TERNA. A list of three names submitted to the Holy See as candidates for a particular episcopal see; or a similar list given to the superior general of a religious institute for appointment or approval as provincial. The term always includes reasons pro and con for each of the recommended candidates. (Etym. Latin *terni*, three each; from *ter*, thrice.)

TERRITORIAL LAW. An ecclesiastical precept binding on the faithful within a given territory, e.g., in a diocese.

TERTIAN. A religious who is going through his or her period of final spiritual formation, usually before final profession, called tertianship. (Etym. Latin *tertianus*, of the third; from *tertius*, third.)

TERTIARIES. Lay persons living in the world who are striving after Christian perfection as their station in life allows, according to the spirit of a religious order to which they are affiliated and abiding by the rules approved for their association by the Apostolic See. Secular tertiaries generally do not live in community, nor do they wear habits, but they share in the good works of their parent order.

TERTIUM QUID. A third something. An object or idea that is either intermediate between two things or is an alternative to what seems to be a dilemma.

TEST. *Testes, testimonium*—witnesses, testimony.

TESTAMENT. See COVENANT.

TESTEM BENEVOLENTIAE. The apostolic letter of Pope Leo XIII (January 22, 1899) in which he condemned Americanism.

TESTIMONIALS. Letters of recommendation required by ecclesiastical law, witnessing to a person's qualifications for the reception of a sacrament, e.g., ordination to the priesthood. Favorable testimonials are a matter of grave obligation on the one conferring the sacrament.

TESTIMONY. In ecclesiastical law the declaration or denial of something, especially by a person who has immediate knowledge of a fact and is presumed to be impartial in his or her testimony and is telling the unbiased truth.

THADDAEUS. One of the Twelve Apostles, but little is known about him. Matthew and Mark both name him in their listing of the twelve (Matthew 10:3; Mark 3:18). Luke substitutes the name "Judas son of James" (Acts 1:13). John's Gospel describes him once as "Judas, this was not Judas Iscariot" (John 14:22).

THAUMATURGUS. Miracle worker. A title given to certain saints outstanding for having performed miracles during their own lifetime or since their death. Among others are St. Gregory (213–70), Sts. Cosmas and Damian (third century), St. Nicholas (fourth century), and St. Anthony of Padua (1195–1231). (Etym. Latin *thaumaturgus*; from Greek *thaumatourgos: thauma*, wonder + *-ergos*, "working," from ergon, work.)

THEANDRIC. Literally "God human," referring to those actions of Christ in which he used the human nature as an instrument of his divinity. Such were the miracles of Christ. Other human activities of Christ, such as walking, eating, and speaking, are also theandric, but in a wider sense inasmuch as they are human acts of a divine person. The purely divine acts, such as creation, are not called theandric.

THEATINES. The Clerks Regular of the Divine Providence founded in Rome in 1524 by two members of the Roman Oratory of Divine Love, St. Cajetan (1480–1547) and Gian Pietro Caraffa (1476–1559), later Pope Paul IV. Strictly austere, they were instrumental in advancing the Counter-Reformation. Their apostolic purpose is still essentially the same: to restore in the Church of God the primitive rule of apostolic life.

THEBAN LEGION. A legion of the Roman army about A.D. 300, under Maurice, the *primicerius,* now venerated as a saint. Legend says that they refused to punish Christians and as a result were massacred in the region of Agaunum, Switzerland. Even though a great deal of controversy surrounds this story, many sources testify to its fact, notably a letter of St. Eucherius and entries in the Martyrology.

"THE FOLLOWING OF CHRIST." See "IMITATION OF CHRIST."

THEFT. The secret taking of an object against the legitimate owner's reasonable will for the purpose of gain. If secrecy is absent, the act is called robbery. If the lawful owner is not reasonably opposed to the act, no theft is committed. And if the purpose of gain is absent, the taking of an object is rather a matter of damage. Consequently it is not theft if the owner consents, expressly or tacitly, or if an object is taken for reasons of extreme necessity, or as occult compensation. Thus, if a wife takes from her husband, either absent or unreasonably opposed as an avaricious man, something necessary for herself, for the support and benefit of her children, for reasons of charity in keeping with the family's financial condition or for helping parents in grave need, it is not theft.

Generally speaking, theft is a serious sin. According to St. Paul, "Thieves, usurers . . . and swindlers will never inherit the kingdom of God" (I Corinthians 6:10). But as an owner may be opposed in different ways to the loss of property belonging to him or her, so too the sin of theft admits of degrees, even to the point of constituting only a slight sin. Moreover, opposition to a loss may be based on the value or quantity of the stolen goods. Finally, theft is more or less grave according to the manner in which it is committed. A person may be more opposed to a large theft committed at one time than to a series of small thefts although amounting to the same value. Yet repeated petty thefts—venial sins if taken separately—may become a mortal sin either because of the intention or because of the conspiracy with which they are perpetrated or because the frequency of small thefts really constitutes a single large act of thievery.

THEISM. Belief in a personal and provident God. It may, however, take on different forms, notably monotheism (one God), polytheism (several gods), or henotheism (one chief god among several). Theism is commonly distinguished from atheism, which denies the existence of a personal, transcendent deity. (Etym. Greek *theos,* god.)

THEOCENTRICITY. God-centeredness. The quality of not only being attentive to God but of making him the principal focus of a course of action or a system of thought. Often distinguished from Christocentricity.

THEOCRACY. A form of government in which God, acting usually through his priestly or prophetic representatives, is the ruler. Every civil and social act becomes religious. The Jewish nation after its return from exile was a theocracy. Until modern times Moslem nations were essentially theocratic. John Calvin sought to introduce a theocracy at Geneva in 1552. (Etym. Greek *theokratia; theo,* God + *-cracy,* strength, rule.)

THEOCRASY. Indiscriminate worship of different gods, as among polytheists who may simultaneously honor several deities in a single prayer or act of sacrifice.

THEODICY. Natural theology, or the study of God's existence and attributes as known by the light of natural reason and apart from supernatural revelation. Its main focus is to vindicate God's goodness and providence in spite of the evident evil in the universe. Gottfried Leibniz (1646–1716) is credited with giving the name to natural theology, which was already known to the ancient Greeks.

THEOL. *Theologia*—theology.

THEOLOGIAN OF THE PONTIFICAL HOUSEHOLD. Until the present title was established by Pope Paul VI, the person was called Master of the Sacred Palace. Originating in the thirteenth century and traditionally a member of the Dominican Order, from Pope Leo X to Pius XI he gave the Imprimatur to books published in Rome. He is now the Theologian of Trust of the Pope, consultor to the Congregation for the Doctrine of the Faith, prelate of the Congregation of Rites, and generally consultor of the Commission for Biblical Studies. He belongs to the Pontifical Family and lives at the Vatican.

THEOLOGICAL CENSURE. A judgment of the Church that characterizes a proposition touching on Catholic faith or morals as contrary to faith or at least doubtful. In the history of the Church's teaching there have been theological censures. A heretical proposition is opposed to a revealed dogma; proximate to heresy is opposed to a truth commonly held to be revealed; erroneous is opposed to conclusions derived from revelation; false is opposed to dogmatic facts; temerarious deviates from the accepted teaching of the Church; badly expressed is subject to misunderstanding; captious is reprehensible because of its intentional ambiguity; and scandalous because it gives rise to error among the faithful.

THEOLOGICAL COMMISSION. International group of theologians, established by Pope Paul VI in 1969 *ad experimentum*, to assist the Holy See and especially the Congregation for the Doctrine of the Faith in the examination of certain doctrinal questions of major importance.

THEOLOGICAL CONCLUSIONS. Religious truths that are derived from two premises, one of which is an immediately revealed truth, and the other a truth of natural reason. Since one premise is a truth of revelation, theological conclusions are also called mediately revealed. And they are said to call for ecclesiastical faith when such truths are proposed for acceptance by the faithful, even at times in solemn definitions of the Church. Some prefer to say that theological conclusions are virtually revealed, and their belief, then, is called mediate divine faith.

THEOLOGICAL NOTES. Degrees of certainty in the acceptance of religious doctrine. In theology several grades of certitude are recognized. The highest degree of certitude is attached to immediately revealed truths. They are to be believed with divine faith (*fides divina*) and if they are also defined by the Church, then with defined divine faith (*fides divina definita*). If the Church defines a doctrine that is not immediately revealed, it is to be believed with ecclesiastical faith (*fides ecclesiastica*). A doctrine that theologians generally regard as a truth of revelation, but that has not been finally promulgated by the Church, is said to be proximate to faith (*proxima fidei*), and if such a truth is guaranteed as the logical conclusion from a revealed doctrine, it is called theologically certain (*theologice certa*). Below this level are many grades of certainty, ranging from common teaching (*sententia communis*), when Catholic theologians responsive to the Church's authority agree on some position, to tolerated opinions that are only weakly founded but are tolerated by the Church.

THEOLOGICAL TRUTH. The explanation of some historical event as having occurred through the miraculous intervention of God.

THEOLOGICAL VIRTUE. A good habit of the mind or will, supernaturally infused into the soul, whose immediate object is God. The theological virtues are faith, hope, and charity.

THEOLOGICE CERTA. See THEOLOGICAL NOTES.

THEOLOGY. Literally "the science of God," used by the Stoics in the third century B.C. to describe a reasoned analysis of the deity. Earlier uses were more naturalistic. Thus, Plato in the *Republic* and Aristotle in his *Metaphysics* called Homer, Hesiod, and Orpheus theologians because they first determined the genealogies and attributes of the gods.

With the advent of Christianity, theology came to mean what its etymology suggested, and was defined by St. Augustine as "reasoning or discourse about the divinity." Through the patristic age to the period of the Schoolmen, this remained the acceptable generic meaning. Peter Abelard (1079–1142) is credited with first having used the term in its modern connotation. St. Thomas Aquinas (1225–74) defended theology as a science because it investigates the contents of belief by means of reason enlightened by faith (*fides quaerens intellectum*), in order to acquire a deeper understanding or revelation. He also distinguished theology proper from "natural theology" or what Gottfried Leibniz later called "theodicy," which studies God as knowable by reason alone and independent of divine authority. Since the thirteenth century the term has been applied to the whole study of revealed truth and gradually replaced its rival synonyms. (Etym. Latin *theologia;* from Greek: *theo,* God + *-logia,* knowledge.)

THEOMACHY. Literally to battle against

God. The term refers to resisting the known divine will.

THEOPHANY (biblical). A direct communication or appearance by God to human beings. Instances: God confronting Adam and Eve after their disobedience (Genesis 3:8); God appearing to Moses out of a burning bush (Exodus 3:2–6); Abraham pleading with Yahweh to be merciful to Sodomites (Genesis 18:23). These theophanies were temporary manifestations. They were not like the Incarnation, which, though it began in time, will continue for all eternity. (Etym. Latin *theophania;* from Greek *theophaneia: Theo-,* God + *phainein,* to show.)

THEOPHILUS. Possibly a government official or a person of high rank to whom Luke dedicated his Gospel. Most likely a potential convert, as may be inferred from Luke's final words in the introduction: ". . . how well founded the teaching is that you have received" (Luke 1:4). Luke also directed Theophilus' attention to the Acts of the Apostles, addressing him by name in the opening sentence (Acts 1:1). (Etym. Greek *theophilos,* beloved of God.)

THEORY OF KNOWLEDGE. The analytic study of the primary principles of human thought and their value as postulates for recognizing and attaining the truth. It is also called epistemology, criteriology, and either major or material logic.

THEOSIS. A theory of absorption of the human spirit into the Deity, as professed in some forms of Hinduism and Buddhism.

THEOTOKOS. Mother of God. A term canonized by the Council of Ephesus (A.D. 431) in defense of Mary's divine maternity, against Nestorius, who claimed that she was only the mother of the man Christ (*Christotokos*).

THERAPEUTIC STERILIZATION. The action of depriving persons of their generative powers in order to relieve some pathological condition. Its moral evaluation is based on the norms for mutilation and also the application of "double effect." The reason is that sterilization involves both the loss of bodily integrity (as mutilation) and of the procreative powers.

THESIS. In scholastic philosophy and theology, a proposition to be explained, proved, and defended. Philosophical theses are proved from established premises and a carefully structured reasoning process. Dogmatic theses are established on the testimony of Sacred Scripture and tradition, the teaching authority of the Church, the statements of the Fathers and Doctors of the Church, and theological reasoning consistent with the faith of historic Catholicism. (Etym. Latin *thesis,* from Greek *thesis,* a thing laid down, a proposition.)

THESSALONIANS, EPISTLES TO THE. Two letters written by St. Paul to the Christians of the city of Thessalonica. Both were written from Corinth about A.D. 51. In the first, St. Paul sets the people's minds at rest about the fate of the righteous dead. They are alive and at the Second Coming of Christ will rise in their glorified bodies. In the second letter, the Apostle admonishes the new converts to be steadfast in the faith in spite of false teachers who are trying to seduce them.

THING. The essence of a being, answering to the question of what it is, as distinct from the fact that it is. It is equivalent to the Latin *res,* which is the single most frequently used term in Catholic theology and in the documents of the Church. Its most common English derivatives are real, really, and reality, all referring to the objective order, e.g., in such contexts as the Real Presence or that Christ really rose from the dead.

THIRD CRUSADE. The military expedition (1188–92) led by the rulers of Germany, France, and England to recover Jerusalem. Finally Richard I of England made a three-years peace with the Moslem ruler Saladin.

THING-IN-ITSELF. See NOUMENON.

THIRD ORDERS. Associations of the faithful established by religious orders. Dating from the thirteenth century, they may be either secular or regular. If secular, they are lay persons, commonly called tertiaries. If regular, they are religious, bound by public vows and live in community. Originally, third orders were Franciscan or Dominican, but the Holy See has since approved many others, both secular and regular, e.g., the Augustinians, Carmelites, Servites, and Trinitarians.

THOMAS. One of the Twelve Apostles. In their Gospels, Matthew, Mark, and Luke mention him only once, simply in listing the names of the twelve. In John's Gospel he is named several times as "Thomas, known as the twin." The disparaging sobriquet he has borne through the centuries, Doubting

Thomas, he earned in the familiar story of his refusal to believe that the resurrected Christ had appeared to the other Apostles unless he could examine the marks of the Crucifixion (John 20:24–29). Another incident in John's Gospel reflects great credit on Thomas for strong faith and courage. When Jesus told the Apostles that he would return to Judaea despite the threats against his life, Thomas said to the others, "Let us go, too, and die with him" (John 11:16).

THOMISM. The philosophy and theology taught by St. Thomas Aquinas (1225–74) and by those who respect his ideas and follow his basic principles. The body of propositions contained in the *Twenty-four Theses* approved by Pope St. Pius X. This is the most concise and authoritative expression of Thomism as understood in the Roman Catholic Church. The term is also sometimes used to identify the Bañezian theory on the relation of grace and free will with its stress on physical predetermination to explain the efficacy of divine grace.

THOUGHT. Basically, every activity of the mind as distinguished from the operations of the external or internal senses. Also refers to the product of thinking, such as idea or judgment, reasoning or intuition, theory or system, worked out by the human mind.

THREE CHAPTERS. A sixth-century controversy involving Pope Vigilius and Emperor Justinian. The emperor had condemned three subjects: 1. the person and writings of Theodore of Mopsuestia; 2. certain writings of Theodoret against St. Cyril of Alexandria; and 3. the letter of Ibas of Edessa to Maris. Since all three were pro-Nestorian, the Emperor hoped in this way to conciliate the Monophysites. The Pope at first refused to ratify the Emperor's condemnation, but under compulsion later approved it. This was interpreted in the West as an act of weakness, and the Pope withdrew his approval. Soon after, the Second Council of Constantinople condemned the three chapters, and in 554 Pope Vigilius confirmed the council. The case of Pope Vigilius does not involve a breach of papal infallibility, but historians agree that the Pope allowed himself to be maneuvered by political powers.

THREE WITNESSES. The text in St. John which in the Vulgate reads: "There are three witnesses in heaven: the Father, the Word, and the Spirit, and these three are one; there are three witnesses on earth: the Spirit, the water, and the blood" (I John 5:7–8). These words are not found in the early Greek manuscripts of the New Testament, nor in the best manuscripts of the Vulgate. They are probably a mystical interpretation that found its way as a gloss on the original text. Called the Johannine Comma, the text has more than once been the subject of the Church's interpretation. The Holy Office declared that scholars may further investigate the authenticity of the passage but accept the Church's judgment on their findings (June 2, 1927).

THRONE. The permanent chair or seat of honor occupied by a pope, cardinal, diocesan bishop, or abbot when presiding at solemn functions. It is usually a chair with a high back, is placed on the right side of the altar and made of wood or stone resting on a dais, three steps high, covered by a square canopy.

THRONES. Those angels who compose the lowest choir of the highest angelic order. Along with the Seraphim and Cherubim, they form the court of the Heavenly King. Hence they are rarely sent as messengers to humanity.

THURIBLE. The censer or vessel in which incense is burned at liturgical services. It consists of a cup-shaped metal body for holding charcoal and incense, with a separate lid for controlling the smoke and fire, and a chain, or chains, allowing the censer to swing safely without spilling its contents. (Etym. Latin *t[h]uribulum*, from *t[h]us*, [stem t(h)ur-], incense; from Greek *thuos* [sacrificial] incense, burned offering, offering.)

THURIFER. The cleric who has charge of the thurible at church services.

THURSDAY. The fifth day of the week, usually consecrated by the Church for devotion to the Holy Eucharist, in commemoration of the Last Supper.

TIARA. The papal crown, which is a tall headdress of gold cloth ornamented with precious stones, encircled with three coronets and surmounted by a cross. Originating as a plain, helmet-like cap about A.D. 1130, it soon acquired its present form. The first circlet symbolizes the Pope's universal episcopate; the second, his primacy of jurisdiction; and the third, his temporal influence. It is placed on the Pope's head at coronation, by the second cardinal deacon, with the words: "Receive the tiara adorned with three crowns, and know that you are Father of princes and kings, guide of the world, vicar of our Savior Jesus Christ."

The tiara is worn only at nonliturgical ceremonies. Paul VI was the last Pope to be crowned with the tiara.

TIME, ECCLESIASTICAL. Calculation of periods of time in canon law. Accordingly a day is understood to consist of twenty-four continuous hours, starting from midnight; a week is seven days; a month is thirty days, and a year is 365 days, unless the month and year are specified to be taken as they are in the calendar.

TIMIDITY. A moral trait characterized by a fear of becoming involved in new situations or in meeting strangers. More generally, it is a lack of courage in shrinking from danger, difficulty, or risk. (Etym. Latin *timidus,* from *timere,* to fear.)

TIMOTHY. A companion and helper of Paul. The relationship was notably close and affectionate. Paul speaks of his young protégé as "a dear and faithful son" and as "a true child of mine" (I Corinthians 4:17; I Timothy 1:2). When they separated at Ephesus, Paul recalled the tears that Timothy shed and wrote that he longed to see him again to complete his happiness (II Timothy 1:3–4). They traveled together to many places. Timothy's name appears with Paul's in epistles sent to Corinth, to Philippi, to Thessalonica, to Colossae. They were even in prison together. In writing to Timothy, Paul constantly spurred him on to greater effort, e.g., "I am reminding you now to fan into a flame the gift God gave you" (II Timothy 1:6). Paul's confidence in Timothy was so strong that he set a very high standard of achievement for him. (Etym. Greek *timotheos,* honoring the god.)

TIMOTHY, EPISTLES TO. Two letters of St. Paul to his co-worker Timothy, whom he converted on his second missionary journey. In the first, Paul warns him against false doctrines, mainly Gnostic, and erroneous moral practices. In the second, he exhorts Timothy to be faithful to the gifts he has received and to gird himself for hardships in the apostolate and conflict with false teachers.

TIT. *Titulus, tituli*—title, titles; titular.

TITHE, BIBLICAL. The practice regulated by the Pentateuch of giving a tenth part of one's possessions as a tax to a superior. Abraham paid such a tax to Melchizedech (Genesis 14). The Levites, however, did not inherit the prescribed amount of land given to the other tribes, but rather received, as representatives of the Lord, a tenth part of all that the land produced—including flocks and cattle—from all the other tribes of Israel. They in turn were to offer to the priest a tenth part of all they received. Another kind of tithe taken from this yearly produce was to be consumed at the sanctuary (Deuteronomy 14), and the produce of every third year was to be distributed among the Levites and the poor. Tithes were offerings acknowledging the Lord's dominion and expressions of thanksgiving for blessings received from God. The sense of strong obligation to pay tithes is made clear in Leviticus (Leviticus 27:30–33).

TITHES. In canon law a tenth part of goods, computed in money, which the faithful should give for the maintenance of the clergy and religious services. The Church's common law directs that the particular laws and customs of each region or nation should determine tithing. In many countries the clergy and church edifices are supported by voluntary contributions rather than by tithing. (Etym. Middle English *tithe,* Old English *teotha, teogetha,* tenth.)

TITLE. In ecclesiastical law, a claim or right to possession of Church property or means of subsistence; a formal appellation, as of rank or office in the service of the Church; the basis on which a man is ordained to the priesthood, e.g., the title of poverty for a religious; the name of a diocese, parish, church, shrine, or any sacred edifice. (Etym. Latin *titulus,* superscription, label, title.)

TITULAR BISHOP. See TITULAR SEES.

TITULAR CHURCH. The particular ancient church in Rome over which a new cardinal receives jurisdiction on receiving the red hat. The name of the church is regularly given in all official listings of the cardinals of the Catholic Church.

TITULAR NAME. The patron of a sacred place, especially a church, whose name it bears. The patron of a church is normally chosen by the founders. Usually only one patron is chosen, or else two whose feast (if at all possible) falls on the same day. In general, the patron saint is the one under whose special protection a church has been placed. However, the titular name is a wider term, including also the persons of the Trinity, mysteries of the faith, angels, or any saint already canonized. The patron of a place is chosen by the people, and one locality may have more than one patron, principal and secondary. There cannot be more than one principal patron except by immemorial custom or special apostolic indult.

TITULAR SEES. Some two thousand ancient Catholic dioceses and archdioceses whose titles are now given to those bishops who do not occupy residential sees, e.g., auxiliary and coadjutor bishops, vicars apostolic, and officials of the Roman Curia. Most of these sees are in Asia Minor, North Africa, the Balkans, and Greece. After the Moslems had destroyed the Church in these lands, the extinct dioceses were called sees "in the lands of the infidels." But in 1882, Pope Leo XIII changed the title to "titular sees."

TITUS. A Greek who was converted to Christianity by Paul and who became one of Paul's trusted and effective assistants. Since Titus was a Gentile, Paul and Barnabas took him with them to Jerusalem to oppose the Jewish contention that, to become a Christian, a prospective convert must be circumcised. Paul "refused to yield to such people for one moment" and reported triumphantly that Titus was not obliged to be circumcised (Galatians 2:3–5). His Epistle to Titus gives the impression that Titus was a strongminded troubleshooter. Paul left him in Crete with crisp, forthright instructions to reorganize the Church, establish a stable, dependable leadership (Titus 1:9), and insist on an "unchanging message of the tradition." Paul urged him to do so "with full authority" and to be "quite uncompromising" (Titus 2:15; 3:8). On another occasion when Titus represented Paul in Corinth, he evidently won the affection and respect of the people, for Paul commented jubilantly on the success of his assistant's mission (II Corinthians 8:16–17). (Etym. Latin *titus*.)

TITUS, EPISTLE TO. A letter of St. Paul to Titus, a native of Antioch who became one of the apostle's faithful companions. Paul wrote after Titus became Bishop of Crete, and instructed him about the heresies, mainly Gnosticism, that he had to combat, and about methods of church organization. The letter was written as Paul was on his way East after his first imprisonment in Rome.

TOBIT, BOOK OF. A deuterocanonical book of the Old Testament, not recognized as part of the Bible by Jews and Protestants. It relates the story of Tobit, a pious Jew of the captivity of Nineveh, who, in the practice of charity in his old age, became blind. He sent his son Tobias on a long journey to recover a debt. Tobias' companion, the angel Raphael, rescued a family relative, Sarah, from the power of the devil, helped recover the debt, and prescribed a remedy to cure Tobit's blindness. The moral lesson of the narrative is to show God's fidelity to those who serve him, especially in the practice of charity, and to teach the special providence of the angels as ministers in the divine service.

TOLERATION. The disposition to permit, or bear with, views, actions, or teaching that differs from one's own in academic, political, and social affairs, but especially in religion. The opposite is intolerance. As stated by the Second Vatican Council, "Provided the just requirements of public order are not violated, religious groups have a right to immunity so that they may organize themselves according to their own principles." Accordingly the Catholic Church respects the rights of religious bodies other than her own to exist and "to promote institutions in which members may work together to organize their own lives according to their religious principles" (*Decree on Religious Liberty*, I, 4). (Etym. Latin *tolerare*, to bear, tolerate.)

TOMB OF MARY. The reputed burial place of the Blessed Virgin in the Valley of the Cedron, near Jerusalem. Some scholars say that she was buried at Ephesus, but the earliest tradition holds that she died in Jerusalem and was buried nearby.

TOME OF LEO. A doctrinal letter sent by Pope Leo I in the year 449 to Flavian, Patriarch of Constantinople, on the Church's teaching about the person of Christ. It affirms that Christ has two natures, human and divine, united in the one divine Person of the Son of God. Two years later, at the Council of Chalcedon, this letter was accepted with the declaration, "Peter has spoken through Leo," to define the classical Catholic doctrine on the Incarnation.

TONGRES. Shrine of Our Lady of Tongres, in Belgium, near the German border, a pilgrimage spot since the First Crusade. In February 1081 a blinded knight returning to his castle home heard angelic voices and the following morning found a statue of the Blessed Virgin in his garden. He tried to make a suitable oratory for "the lady" in his castle but after each attempt found her back in the original spot where she appeared. He then built a small outdoor chapel there to enclose the statue. In 1090 the King of France, at war with the Flemish, camped near Tongres. A voice told the blinded knight to go to the aid of the warring king. Imploring Mary's help before going into battle, he received his sight, and when the opposing Flemish army heard of the miracle they withdrew in fear before the battle hour. Much effort and money were spent in the enrichment and enlargement of this shrine that was well known throughout Christian lands. People came especially when their land was harassed by plague. During the French Revolution the original statue was hidden to prevent its destruction and a duplicate image was kept in the chapel. In 1881 the original was crowned with special papal commendation.

TONGUES, GIFT OF. See GIFT OF TONGUES.

TONSURE. For centuries, up to the Second Vatican Council, the outward visible sign of the clerical state. A lock or sometimes a circle of hair was cut, varying in size, from the top of the head. The baptized and confirmed layman so tonsured was admitted to the clerical state with all privileges in an ecclesiastical ceremony. In 1972, with the apostolic letter *Mysteria Quaedam,* Pope Paul VI decreed that "The first tonsure is no longer conferred. Entrance into the clerical state is now joined with the Diaconate." This provision applies to the Latin Rite. (Etym. Latin *tonsura,* a shearing, from *tondere,* to shear, shave.)

TORAH. 1. the first five books of the Old Testament: Genesis, Exodus, Leviticus, Numbers, and Deuteronomy; 2. the entire body of Jewish law revealed by Yahweh and interpreted and taught by priests, prophets, and sages.

TOSEFTA. Part of the Jewish Talmud, as a kind of supplement, containing passages from various Judaic schools of thought. Some scholars believe that the Tosefta is really the original Mishnah, or legal code assembled in Palestine.

TOTAL ABSTINENCE. Complete abstention from alcoholic beverages. The practice was strongly advocated by a number of Protestant leaders; notably John Wesley (1703–91), for whom the drinking of alcohol in any form was a sin. The Catholic Church does not forbid drinking in moderation, but total abstinence may be the only solution for a person with a chronic problem of alcoholism.

TOTAL GOOD. The principle that any estimate of what is morally good must be judged on the whole of human existence and purpose in life. Thus the totality of what

constitutes a human being is not body alone, but mortal body joined with immortal spirit. It is not earthly life alone, but a continuum of that life which begins as soon as a child is conceived and bridges the moment called death into eternity. It is not even human life alone, of body and soul, but human life elevated to participation in God's life because God became man in the person of Jesus Christ.

Essential to this view of totality is the value of human liberty, by which a person can freely collaborate with divine grace and thus give glory to God, although lying in bed as a "helpless" invalid; the value of enduring the Cross by patiently accepting, in oneself and in others, the ravages of disease or the heavy demands of old age; and the value of loving mercy, which does not ask why, but, like Christ, sacrifices self for others just because they are others, and knows that the self-oblation is pleasing to God.

TOTALITARIANISM. A theory of society that gives the State total control of the life and conduct of the citizens. Modern totalitarianism is a combination of five movements that were centuries in the making: Machiavellianism, which divorced the public and private morality; Protestantism, which gave princes the right to pass judgment on popes and bishops; Comtism, which favored social development and organization based on exact biological norms; Hegelianism, for which history was the march of the Absolute Idea through the world and incarnated in nineteenth-century Prussia; and Marxism, which merely changed Hegelian idealism to Communist materialism and adapted Hegel's "military class dictatorship" to "dictatorship of the proletariat." All totalitarian regimes in the recent past and the present are greater or lesser expressions of one or more of these contributing philosophies of society.

TOTAL WAR. A modern theory of warfare which claims that all the citizens of a belligerent nation are to be considered combatants. The term has entered the vocabulary of the times since massive destruction of whole segments of the population is inevitable with the use of atomic weapons. With this in mind, the Second Vatican Council declared: "Every act of war directed to the indiscriminate destruction of whole cities or vast areas with their inhabitants is a crime against God and man, which merits firm and unequivocal condemnation" (*Constitution on the Church in the Modern World,* V, 80).

Because of the totally different situation in the world today, while still maintaining that, on principle, war is justifiable, the Church holds that nuclear warfare is next to impossible to justify in practice.

TO THE GREATER GLORY OF GOD. The motto of St. Ignatius Loyola and the Society of Jesus. Often written A.M.D.G., from the Latin *Ad majorem Dei gloriam.*

TOTIES QUOTIES. "As often as." An expression formerly used for certain plenary indulgences that could be gained several times a day provided the required conditions were fulfilled. The Church's present teaching is that a plenary indulgence can be gained only once a day.

TOUCH. Physical contact produced by any one of a group of external senses whose organs respond to pressure, heat, cold, pain, or pleasure. In spiritual literature, touch is a familiar expression among mystics to describe their experience of God in terms that are similar to tactile sensations. The dominant features are an awareness of closeness to the divine, and a feeling of comfort or repose in the presence of an invisible but very real power that makes them interiorly satisfied.

TOULOUSE. Shrine Church of St. Sernin. The church of many relics, notably St. Thomas Aquinas' sacred remains. The building of the church began in the fourth century. The body of St. Sernin, Apostle of Toulouse and its first bishop, was transferred there. Soon after, the bodies of Sts. Papoul, Honestus, Sernin's disciples, and the body of St. Exuperius, who completed the church, were also placed in the shrine. Charlemagne sent the bodies of St. Susanna, St. Acisclus, and her sister St. Victoria, martyrs of Córdova, and the first crusaders returning gave the church the revered head of St. Bartholomew and the body of St. Barnabas. At the time of the French Revolution the sacred remains of St. Thomas Aquinas were transferred from the custody of the Dominicans at Toulouse to St. Sernin's, and today they repose there in a gold and silver casket. Several popes have visited the church and their gifts have enriched it. Pope Urban VIII granted the same indulgences to those who visit the seven altars of St. Sernin's as could be gained by visiting the seven altars of St. Peter's in Rome. In 1100 a special confraternity was established with the duty, accepted under oath, to care for the precious relics at St. Sernin's.

TOWEL. A cloth used at various times in the liturgy. Thus a finger towel is part of the sacred accessories at Mass, to be used by the priest after washing his hands at the offer-tory. The bishop uses a towel after washing his hands when administering the sacraments of confirmation and holy orders. In order to distinguish a finger towel a red cross is sewn at one corner of the cloth, rather than in the center, as on purificators.

TOWER OF BABEL. A biblical event symbolizing co-operative pride. Certain people living in the land of Shinar proposed building a town and a tower that would reach to heaven. "Let us make a name for ourselves," they boasted. But Yahweh distrusted their motives. He confused their language so that they could no longer understand each other. Then they scattered over the face of the earth (Genesis 11:1-9).

TOWER OF DAVID. A symbol of the Blessed Virgin occurring in the Litany of Loreto. Mary's Son recognized as the glory of the line of David, whose star often appears in conjunction with the tower when that symbol is used. Mary, too, is a tower of strength against heresy.

TOWER OF IVORY. A symbol of the purity, beauty, and strength of the Blessed Virgin Mary. The invocation occurs in the Litany of Loreto.

T.P. *Tempore paschali*—in paschal time.

TRACT. A brief treatise, commonly as a leaflet or pamphlet, on some religious subject. The term is more common in Protestant than Catholic circles. Also, in the Tridentine Mass the verse or verses recited after the Gradual and replacing the Alleluia on days of sorrow or penance, as in ferial Masses in Lent. In the revised liturgy a tract is a psalm with a responsory. (Etym. Latin *tractatus,* a discussion, treatise; from *tractare,* to pull violently, discuss.)

TRACTARIAN MOVEMENT. Synonymous with the Oxford Movement in the Anglican Church, of which it was a part. The movement's leaders published their original principles in a series of ninety pamphlets called "Tracts for the Times." In the last pamphlet, John Henry Newman tried to reconcile the Anglican *Thirty-Nine Articles* with the decrees of the Council of Trent. This was a major step in Newman's conversion to Catholicism. It also put an end to the Tractarian Movement in 1845, even though its parent, the Oxford Movement, continued.

TRADITION. Literally a "handing on," referring to the passing down of God's revealed word. As such it has two closely related but distinct meanings. Tradition first means all of divine revelation, from the dawn of human history to the end of the apostolic age, as passed on from one generation of believers to the next, and as preserved under divine guidance by the Church established by Christ. Sacred Tradition more technically also means, within this transmitted revelation, that part of God's revealed word which is not contained in Sacred Scripture. Referring specifically to how Christian tradition was handed on, the Second Vatican Council says: "It was done by the apostles who handed on, by the spoken word of their preaching, by the example they gave, by the institutions they established, what they themselves had received —whether from the lips of Christ, from His way of life and His works, or whether they had learned it by the prompting of the Holy Spirit" (*Constitution on Divine Revelation*, II, 7). (Etym. Latin *traditio*, a giving over, delivery, surrender; a handing down: from *tradere*, to give up.)

TRADITIONALISM. The theory that all human knowledge of God and religion comes from tradition. In its extreme form, it denies that reason can arrive at any certain knowledge of divine things. It proceeds from the view that God first made a comprehensive primitive revelation when the human race learned to speak. In this original revelation, God bestowed on people all the basic religious truths that have been handed down by successive generations to the present day. General reason or common sense guarantees the unfalsified transmission of its heritage. The individual receives it by oral teaching. Religious knowledge is entirely and only a knowledge of faith. The chief exponents of traditionalism in its strict form were Viscount de Bonald (1754–1840), Félicité de Lamennais (1782–1854), and Louis Bautain (1796–1867). It was represented in a more modified form by Augustine Bonnetty (d. 1879). Traditionalism is also called fideism insofar as it denies the capacity of reason to attain knowledge of divine matters and correspondingly places an excessive stress on faith.

TRADITIO SYMBOLI. "The handing over of the Creed." This was the expression used in the early Church to describe the role of priest or other teacher communicating the faith to an adult catechumen preparing for baptism, done mainly by explaining the Creed. When they were being baptized, the catechumens, in turn, were to recite and profess the Creed. This was called *redditio Symboli* (giving back the Creed).

TRADUCIANISM. The theory that holds that the soul of a child is physically transmitted from the parents. One form claims that the soul is the result of a material seed akin to the material principle of bodily generation. Another form, called spiritual traducianism, holds that a spiritual seed cast off from the souls of the parents is the germ of the new soul for the infant. The theory is in contradiction with Catholic doctrine that each person's soul is individually and separately created by God at the time of conception.

TRANSCENDENCE. Surpassing excellence, which may be either relative or absolute. It is relative when the excellence surpasses some objects below it, as human nature transcends the irrational creation. It is absolute when the excellence surpasses in being and activity all other beings. Only God is absolutely transcendent; in being because he alone is infinite and perfect Being who cannot change; in activity because he alone has existence of himself as uncreated First Cause on whom all creatures depend for their least operation.

TRANSCENDENTALS. In scholastic philosophy, those qualities that are common to all things whatsoever, and to all differences between things. They are not restricted to any category, class, or individual. The classic transcendentals are thing (*res*), being (*ens*), something (*aliquid*), the one (*unum*), the true (*verum*), the good (*bonum*), and, according to some philosophers, the beautiful (*pulchrum*).

TRANSEPT. A division of a church building which crosses the main part at right angles and includes the lofty structural part just in front of the apse.

TRANSFIGURATION OF OUR LORD. The glorification of the appearance of Jesus before his Resurrection. It took place in the presence of Peter, James, and John. While he was praying on a mountain, suddenly "his face did shine as the sun," while "his garments became glistening, exceeding white." The frightened witnesses saw Moses and Elijah appear before them and converse with Jesus and heard the voice of God. The extraordinary vision vanished as suddenly as it appeared (Luke 9:28–36; Matthew 17:1–8; Mark 9:2–8). The Church's celebration of this event occurs as a feast day on August 6. (Etym. Latin *transfigurare: trans-*, change + *figura*, figure.)

TRANSFINALIZATION. The view of Christ's presence in the Eucharist that the purpose or finality of the bread and wine is changed by the words of consecration. They are said to serve a new function, as sacred elements that arouse the faith of the people in the mystery of Christ's redemptive love. Like transignification, this theory was condemned by Pope Paul VI in the encyclical *Mysterium Fidei* (1965) if transfinalization is taken to deny the substantial change of bread and wine into the body and blood of Christ. (Etym. Latin *trans-*, so as to change + *finis*, end; purpose.)

TRANSFORMATION. A term used, especially by the Greek Fathers of the Church, to describe what happens at Mass when the bread and wine are changed into Christ's body and blood. St. Thomas Aquinas makes clear, however, that "this conversion is not according to form, but according to substance" (*Summa Theologica*, III, 75, 4). An ontological change in the substance occurs at the Eucharistic consecration. (Etym. Latin *trans-*, so as to change + *forma*, the form: *transformare*, to change in shape or form.)

TRANSIGNIFICATION. The view of Christ's presence in the Eucharist which holds that the meaning or significance of the bread and wine is changed by the words of consecration. The consecrated elements are said to signify all that Christians associate with the Last Supper; they have a higher value than merely food for the body. The theory of transignification was condemned by Pope Paul VI in the encyclical *Mysterium Fidei* (1965), if it is understood as denying transubstantiation. (Etym. Latin *trans-*, so as to change + *significatio*, meaning, sense: *transignificatio*.) See also TRANSFINALIZATION.

TRANSITIONAL DIACONATE. The temporary state of men who intend to go on for the priesthood. Before their ordination as deacons they must indicate whether they wish to enter the permanent or the transitional diaconate. They must also decide whether to marry or remain celibate. Once they are ordained deacons, they cannot marry and continue in the Church's ministry.

TRANSLATION. The solemn transporting of the relics of a saint from one shrine to another, where they have a final resting place. The former liturgical feast of the Holy House of Loreto was also called a translation. And the same term is applied to transferring a feast to another date, as when it falls on a Sunday, or a cleric is said to be transferred from one ecclesiastical office to another.

TRANSMIGRATION. See METEMPSYCHOSIS.

TRANSMUTATION. A term used by some of the Fathers of the Church, e.g., St. Gregory of Nyssa (331–?396), to describe the change that takes place at the consecration of the Mass. (Etym. Latin *transmutatio*, change; *transmutare*, to change over, shift, transmute.)

TRANSPLANTATION OF ORGANS. The transfer of an organ from one body, or body part, to another. In general, the transplant of organs from living donors is permissible when the expected benefit to the recipient is proportionate to the harm done to the donor. But always the condition is that the loss of such organ does not deprive the donor of life or of functional integrity of the body. Regarding the transplant of single vital organs, such as the heart, two problems are always involved. One is to know precisely when a person is dead. The other is the effectiveness of a transplant if a vital organ is transferred from an actually dead body. The medical temptation is to anticipate death in order to guarantee a successful transplant.

TRANSUBSTANTIATION. The complete change of the substance of bread and wine into the substance of Christ's body and blood by a validly ordained priest during the consecration at Mass, so that only the accidents of bread and wine remain. While the faith behind the term was already believed in apostolic times, the term itself was a later development. With the Eastern Fathers before the sixth century, the favored expression was *meta-ousiosis*, "change of being"; the Latin tradition coined the word *transubstantiatio*, "change of substance," which was incorporated into the creed of the Fourth Lateran Council in 1215. The Council of Trent, in defining the "wonderful and singular conversion of the whole substance of the bread into the body, and the whole substance of the wine into the blood" of Christ, added "which conversion the Catholic Church calls transubstantiation" (Denzinger 1652). After transubstantiation, the accidents of bread and wine do not inhere in any subject or substance whatever. Yet they are not make-believe; they are sustained in existence by divine power. (Etym. Latin *trans-*, so as to change + *substantia*, substance: *transubstantiatio*, change of substance.)

TRANSVERSE CROSS. See CRUX DECUSSATA; ST. ANDREW'S CROSS.

TRAPPISTINES. The women's branch of

the Trappist Order. Full title is the Cistercian Nuns of the Strict Observance (O.C.S.O.). Founded in France, at Cîteaux, in 1125. The nuns are subject to the abbot general in Rome.

TRAPPISTS. Cistercian monks who follow the rule of the abbey at La Trappe, France, as reformed in 1664. They were absorbed into the Cistercians of the Strict Observance in 1892, but the name is now commonly applied to the latter. The reformation of the Trappists, under the Abbé de Rancé in the seventeenth century, was continued by Abbé Lestrange into the early nineteenth century, emphasizing the need for a more penitential life. Separated monasteries were united into an international order in 1892 under an abbot general. Their official name is Cistercians of Strict Observance, or Reformed Cistercians. Monasteries of the order are in many countries.

TREASURE BOXES. See POOR BOX.

TREASURY OF MERITS. Also called the Treasury of the Church. It consists of the superabundant merits of Jesus Christ and his faithful ones. Such a treasury implies that good works benefit others, and that the Communion of Saints is also an intercommunication of merits, not only when a good work is performed but, under God's Providence, for all future time.

TREE OF KNOWLEDGE. A certain tree in the Garden of Eden. God forbade Adam and Eve to eat the fruit of this tree, simply to test their obedience (Genesis 2:16-17). They disobeyed his order, failed the test, and were put out of Eden (Genesis 3:23).

TREE OF LIFE. A tree that stood next to the Tree of Knowledge in the middle of the Garden of Eden (Genesis 2:9). It conferred on anyone eating its fruit the gift of immortality (Genesis 3:22). See also TREE OF KNOWLEDGE.

TRE ORE. Italian for "three hours," referring to the three hours that Christ was on the Cross on Good Friday. While no definite ritual is prescribed, the customary Tre Ore service on Good Friday from noon to three is a series of homilies on the seven last words of Christ, along with appropriate hymns, periods for silent meditation, and the Way of the Cross. The Eucharistic celebration of the Lord's Passion may follow the Tre Ore service.

TRES ABHINC ANNOS. Second instruction of the Sacred Congregation of Rites, on the exact application of the Second Vatican Council's Constitution on the Liturgy. This document is to be added to *Inter Oecumenici* (September 24, 1964). It further implements the directives of the earlier instruction and, among other important provisions, declares that "the competent territorial authority can decide" in favor of the vernacular in the liturgy, even in: 1. the Canon of the Mass; 2. the whole ritual for ordination; and 3. the recitation of the Divine Office, even the recitation in choir (May 4, 1967).

TRESPASS. To offend or go against the will of someone. In the petition of the Lord's Prayer, "forgive us our trespasses," God is asked to have mercy on us according to our mercy toward others. Literally, "to trespass" means to invade the rights of another without his or her consent; hence an act of injustice.

TRIANGLE, EQUILATERAL. Symbol of the Trinity, early used in various forms: a triangle with equal sides; three foils; three figures; the Father represented at the apex, the Son and Spirit at the bottom corners; the Hand representing the Father, the Cross the Son, the Dove the Holy Spirit, all in a triangular form. Such symbols appeared in Roman churches as late as the thirteenth century when Pope Urban VIII forbade anthropomorphic figures even as symbols of the Trinity. During the Middle Ages the triangle appeared alone with the words *Unitas, Trinitas, Pater, Filius, Spiritus* with the addition of *"Deus Est"* in the center representing the Godhead. The Catholic Church has honored the Trinity by a special feast since 1334.

TRIBES OF ISRAEL. The social units of the Jewish nation descended from Jacob through his twelve sons (Genesis 49). Strictly speaking there were thirteen tribes: Reuben, Simeon, Levi, Judah, Zebulun, Issachar, Dan, Gad, Asher, Naphtali, and Benjamin, along with the two sons of Joseph, Ephraim and Manasseh, whom Jacob adopted as his own (Genesis 48), and who therefore also became founders of tribes. But in the distribution of territory in the Promised Land, the tribe of Levi received no possession (Joshua 13) and perhaps for that reason is not counted as a tribe. Each tribe in turn was divided into clans, named after the grandsons of Jacob, and these in turn were subdivided into houses (Numbers 1, 26; Joshua 7) and the houses into families. In the family the father had complete authority over his wife (or wives) and children. The fathers, in turn, were elected or accepted by common consent, heads of families, or heads of houses whose directives they were to obey. The clan was subject to the prince of the tribe, also called a prince of Israel (Numbers 1, 7). Later, under the monarchy, the tribes became mere social units.

TRIBUNAL. Ecclesiastical court of justice, established both in Rome and in each diocese. There are three Roman tribunals: the Sacred Apostolic Penitentiary, Supreme Tribunal of the Apostolic Signatura, and the Sacred Roman Rota. Diocesan tribunals are mainly concerned with marriage cases, and their officers, judges, and members are listed in national Catholic directories.

TRICHOTOMY. Literally anything that has three parts. In the Bible, St. Paul's doctrine about the threefold division in the human beings, composed of body (*soma*), soul (*psyche*), and spirit (*pneuma*). The body is the living organism, the soul is the rational intellect and will, and the spirit is that innermost part of one's being where the Spirit of God abides.

TRICLINIUM. Originally the dining room of a Roman house which provided for nine persons to recline three each on three seats. Used of the refectory of a monastery.

TRIDENTINE MASS. The Eucharistic liturgy celebrated in the Latin Rite according to the Roman Missal promulgated by the apostolic constitution *Quo Primum* of Pope Pius V on July 14, 1570. A revised missal was decreed by the Council of Trent in order to unify what by then had become a variety of "Roman Rites" that had proliferated since the Middle Ages. "For four centuries it furnished the priests of the Latin Rite with norms for the celebration of the Eucharistic Sacrifice, and heralds of the Gospel carried it to almost all the world" (Pope Paul VI, *Apostolic Constitution,* promulgating the Roman Missal revised by decree of the Second Vatican Council, April 3, 1969). (Etym. Latin *Tridentinus,* from *Tridentum,* ancient form of Trent.)

TRIDENTINE THEOLOGY. Catholic theology affected by the Reformation and the Council of Trent. Protestant emphasis on the Bible and rejection of the Roman primacy stimulated theologians to investigate more closely the sources of revelation in Scripture and tradition and establish the grounds for a rational apologetic in support of the Catholic claims. The first need was met by developing a system of positive theology, whereby the truths professed by Catholic Christianity were shown to be found in the deposit of faith. The Jesuits, led by St. Robert Bellarmine (1542–1621), became the main expositors of this system, as they also laid the groundwork for fundamental theology, which proves from history and philosophy the credibility of the Christian religion.

The speculative side of the science began a new era, occasioned by the challenges of Protestantism on almost every position of the Catholic Church. During the eighteen years of the Council of Trent (1545–63), the combined intelligence of Roman Catholicism concentrated its efforts on so defining the nature of grace and justification, the Sacrifice of the Mass and the priesthood, the sacramental system and ecclesiastical authority, that insights were gained on which post-Tridentine writers have built an imposing theological structure. Their framework was mainly the *Summa Theologica* of St. Thomas Aquinas, with commentators in all the major schools of thought. Among the Dominicans was John of St. Thomas (1589–1644), professor at the University of Alcalá in Spain, so named from his whole-hearted devotion to the teachings of St. Thomas Aquinas; the reformed Carmelites edited a celebrated *Cursus Salmanticensis;* Franciscans published treatises of Duns Scotus, harmonized with St. Thomas; the Jesuits produced Francis Suarez (1548–1617), a dogmatic theologian famous for his works on jurisprudence, which became of paramount importance for legislators on the Continent and in America.

TRIDUUM. A period of three days of prayer, either preceding some special feast or preparing for some major enterprise. Commemorates the biblical three days that Christ lay in the tomb.

TRINITARIANS. The Order of the Most Holy Trinity, founded in 1198 at Cerfroid, France, by St. John of Matha and St. Félix of Valois, with the approval of Pope Innocent III. Their rule was based on an austere interpretation of the Rule of St. Augustine, and their purpose was especially to liberate the numerous Christian captives held by the Moslems. In 1596 a Spanish reform created the Discalced Trinitarians, who alone survive. Their present apostolate is to assist the faithful who are in special danger of losing their faith. They are engaged in missionary labors and promote devotion to the Holy Trinity.

TRINITY, THE HOLY. A term used since A.D. 200 to denote the central doctrine of the

Christian religion. God, who is one and unique in his infinite substance or nature, is three really distinct persons, the Father, Son, and Holy Spirit. The one and only God is the Father, the Son, and the Holy Spirit. Yet God the Father is not God the Son, but generates the Son eternally, as the Son is eternally begotten. The Holy Spirit is neither the Father nor the Son, but a distinct person having his divine nature from the Father and the Son by eternal procession. The three divine persons are co-equal, co-eternal, and consubstantial and deserve co-equal glory and adoration.

TRINITY SUNDAY. The first Sunday after Pentecost. Its origins go back to the Arian heresy, when an office with canticle, responses, preface, and hymns was composed by the Fathers and recited on Sundays. Bishop Stephen of Liège (903–20) wrote an office of the Holy Trinity that in some places was recited on the Sunday after Pentecost, and elsewhere on the last Sunday before Advent. St. Thomas à Becket (1118–70), consecrated Archbishop of Canterbury on the Sunday following Pentecost, obtained for England the privilege of a special feast to honor the Trinity on that day. Pope John XXII (reigned 1316–34) extended the feast to the universal Church.

TRIPLE AUTONOMY. The threefold commitment required of Catholics wherever Communism comes into full political power, e.g., Czechoslovakia and Hungary; namely, independence of Rome, self-support, and self-propagation.

TRIPLE CANDLE. The triple-branched candle formerly used in the Holy Saturday service. It was lighted by the deacon chanting three times in ascending tones, *"Lumen Christi"* (The Light of Christ), while the choir answered *"Deo Gratias"* (Thanks Be to God). From this candle the paschal candle was afterward lighted. In the revised liturgy for the Easter Vigil the triple candle is simply replaced by the paschal candle.

TRIPLE CROWN. See TIARA.

TRIPTYCH. A three-leaved hinged tablet, in contrast to the two-leaved diptych and many-leaved polytych. The names of persons to be commemorated in the liturgy were inscribed on these leaves. (Etym. Greek *triptukhos*, threefold: *tri-*, three + *ptukhē*, fold.)

TRISAGION. The invocation "Holy God, Holy and Mighty, Holy and Immortal, have mercy on us," which occurs in all the liturgies of the East at some point between the readings. In the Latin Rite it is sung on Good Friday as one of the reproaches during the veneration of the Cross. It also occurs in the Divine Office during penitential seasons.

TRITHEISM. The heresy that divides the substance of the Blessed Trinity, giving each divine person a nature that is numerically distinct from the nature of both the other persons. It was held by a group of Monophysites in the sixth century, led by two bishops, Conon of Tarus, and Eugenius of Seleucia. Later the heresy was revived by Roscellin (d. 1125) and by Oembs and Günther in the nineteenth century. Oembs was condemned by Pope Pius VII in 1804, and Günther by Pius IX in 1857.

TRIUMPHALISM. A term of reproach leveled at the Catholic Church for the claim that she has the fullness of divine revelation and the right to pass judgment on the personal and social obligations of humankind. (Etym. Latin *triumphus*, public rejoicing for a victory.)

TRIUMPHANT CHURCH. See CHURCH TRIUMPHANT.

TRIVIUM. The three primary branches in medieval education: grammar, rhetoric, and dialectic (logic). (Etym. Latin *tres*, three + *viae*, ways: *trivium*, crossroad.)

TROPE. In the Western rite a short series of words by way of antiphons added spontaneously in the liturgy of the Mass or the office sung in choir. Tropes were popular in the early Middle Ages but gradually went out of vogue and were legislated out of existence by the 1570 revision of the Roman Missal. However, the Second Vatican Council now provides for their use during the *Kyrie eleison* of the Mass.

TROPOLOGY. The figurative use of words, especially referring to the biblical interpretation that studies the figurative sense of sacred tradition.

TRUCE OF GOD. Temporary cessation of hostilities in wartime, dating from the eleventh century. It was imposed by the Church under threat of excommunication on the armed forces engaged in feudal battles. Hostilities were prohibited from Saturday night to Monday morning, and also on certain days of the week, notably on Thursday in honor of the Lord's Ascension, and on Friday, the day of his Passion, and also during Advent and Lent.

TRUE CONSCIENCE. The mind making a correct moral judgment on some action either to be performed or already done. When the conscience is true, a person's subjective judgment corresponds to the objective fact that a particular human act is morally good or morally wrong.

TRUE CROSS. The cross on which the Savior died. It was very probably discovered in A.D. 326 by St. Helena, mother of Emperor Constantine. A part of this cross is said to be preserved in the Church of Santa Croce in Rome. The feast of the Exaltation (or Triumph) of the Holy Cross is celebrated on September 14 in the Latin Rite.

TRUE GOOD. That which is really suitable to the thing or nature to which the goodness is applied.

TRULLO, COUNCIL OF. A synod held in 692 by the Eastern bishops at Constantinople to finish the work of the fifth and sixth general councils (553 and 680), also held in the same city. So called because the meetings were under the dome (Greek *troullos*) of the Emperor's palace. The disciplinary decrees were rejected by the Pope, notably because the Trullan Synod failed to repudiate the opinion that dissolution of a sacramental marriage is sometimes legitimate. Remarriage after divorce, approved by the Eastern Orthodox, is commonly traced to the decision of the bishops at Trullo.

TRUST. Reliance on someone. One has confidence in people as persons, trusts them to be faithful to their commitments, and hopes to obtain from them what they promise. Applied to God, trust is a form of hope, but with the special nuance that God will not deny his grace to one who does what one can. This means that, provided a person co-operates with divine grace according to his or her ability, that person will merit further grace from God.

TRUSTEE SYSTEM. The method used to administer diocesan property, temporalities, and parishes. A bishop usually chooses a group of responsible persons who, together with an ecclesiastical superior, form an administrative council to manage and direct possessions, property, and finances. They must account periodically for their stewardship and can in no way infringe upon the spiritual administration of the parish or diocese. The Holy See has approved their establishment, stating that the vesting of church property in a duly chosen board of trustees is a permissible procedure. What the Church forbids is to have only laymen serve as trustees, without dependence on the bishop of a diocese or pastor of a parish.

TRUTH. Conformity of mind and reality. Three kinds of conformity give rise to three kinds of truth. In *logical* truth, the mind is conformed or in agreement with things outside the mind, either in assenting to what is or in denying what is not. Its opposite is error. In *metaphysical* or *ontological* truth, things conform with the mind. This is primary conformity, when something corresponds to the idea of its maker, and it is secondary conformity when something is intelligible and therefore true to anyone who knows it. In *moral* truth, what is said conforms with what is on one's mind. This is truthfulness and its opposite is falsehood.

TRUTH, DOUBLE. See DOUBLE STANDARD.

TUESDAY. The third day of the week, day of Tiw, an ancient Teutonic deity. Liturgically it is dedicated to the angels and certain saints whose cult is usually celebrated with special devotions on that day, e.g., St. Anne and St. Anthony of Padua.

TUNIC. A long vestment formerly worn by the subdeacon who assisted the priest at solemn functions, and by cardinals, bishops, and abbots under the dalmatic at pontifical Mass. (Etym. Latin *tunica*, sheath, tunic, from a Phoenician source.)

TUTIORISM. See RIGORISM.

TWELFTH NIGHT. The evening before Epiphany, the Twelfth Day after Christmas. Once kept as a time of merrymaking and associated with taking down the Christmas decorations at home and in Church.

TWELVE FRUITS. The special graces of supernatural satisfaction in the performance of good works, infused by the Holy Spirit at baptism and possessed by everyone in the state of grace. They are: charity, joy, peace, patience, benignity, goodness, longanimity, mildness, faith, modesty, continency, and chastity. Their intensity depends on the degree of grace a person has and the generosity with which he or she performs the different virtues.

TWELVE PROMISES. The promises made by Christ to St. Margaret Mary Alacoque, a Visitation nun, in the convent chapel at Paray-le-Monial, France, between 1673 and 1675. They occurred during revelations she received on devotion to the Heart of Jesus, and have been encouraged by the Church as worthy of pious belief. They have been translated into more than two hundred languages. Although the total number is larger, the following are the most important promises made by Christ to those who are devoted to the Sacred Heart:

1. I will give them all the graces necessary in their state of life.

2. I will establish peace in their homes.

3. I will comfort them in all their afflictions.

4. I will be their secure refuge during life and above all in death.

5. I will bestow a large blessing upon all their undertakings.

6. Sinners shall find in my Heart the source and the infinite ocean of mercy.

7. Tepid souls shall grow fervent.

8. Fervent souls shall quickly mount to high perfection.

9. I will bless every place where a picture of my heart shall be set up and honored.

10. I will give to priests the gift of touching the most hardened hearts.

11. Those who shall promote this devotion shall have their names written in my Heart never to be blotted out.

12. I promise you in the excessive mercy of my Heart that my all-powerful love will grant to all those who communicate on the first Friday in nine consecutive months the grace of final penitence; they shall not die in my disgrace without receiving their sacraments; my divine Heart shall be their safe refuge in this last moment.

TWILIGHT SLEEP. A state in which awareness of pain is dulled and memory of pain is dimmed or effaced; it is produced by hypodermic injection of certain drugs. It is used chiefly in childbirth. From a moral viewpoint, twilight sleep should not be used in cases of ordinary childbirth because it creates some danger of harming the offspring. This danger is slight, however, so that twilight sleep may be resorted to in order to alleviate pains that are extreme or for some other sufficient reason, for example to facilitate the handling of a difficult delivery.

TWOFOLD EFFECT. See DOUBLE EFFECT.

TWO SWORDS. A medieval doctrine on the relation of Church and State, as explained by Pope Boniface VIII (reigned 1294–1303): "We are taught by the words of the Gospel that in this Church and under her control there are two swords, the spiritual and the temporal . . . Both of these, i.e., the spiritual and the temporal swords, are under the control of the Church. The first is wielded by the Church; the second is wielded on behalf of the Church. The first is wielded by the hands of the priest, the second by the hands of kings and soldiers, but at the wish and by the permission of the priests. Sword must be subordinate to sword, and it is only fitting that the temporal authority should be subject to the spiritual" (*Unam Sanctam,* Denzinger 873). This doctrine was not defined by the Pope but reflected the mentality of the age, when both "priests and kings" were members of the same Catholic Church in whose name Pope Boniface was speaking.

TYBURN. A small underground river of London, England. It gave its name to the famous gallows where numerous Catholics died for the faith, especially during the persecution under Queen Elizabeth I (1533–1603).

TYCHISM. A theory that chance is an objective fact in the universe and that it is not merely due to human ignorance. It is commonly associated with the idea that evolution takes place casually and without planned direction by some guiding intelligence. (Etym. Greek *tyche,* fortune, chance.)

TYPES, SCRIPTURAL. A biblical person, thing, action, or event that foreshadows new truths, new actions, or new events. In the Old Testament, Melchizedech and Jonah are types of Jesus Christ. A likeness must exist between the type and the archetype, but the latter is always greater. Both are independent of each other. God's call for the return of the Israelites from Pharaoh's bondage typifies the return of Jesus Christ from his flight into Egypt. In the New Testament the destruction of Jerusalem, foretold by Christ, was the antitype of the end of the world.

U

UBIQUITARIANISM. The doctrine of Martin Luther (1483–1546) and many of his disciples that Christ is everywhere present not only as God but also as man. It was invented by the Reformer in order to account for the real bodily presence of Christ in the Eucharist, without having to admit the priestly power of transubstantiation. (Etym. Latin *ubiquitas,* a being everywhere.)

UBIQUITY. The presence of a being in all places at once. Omnipresence of God.

ULT. *Ultimo*—last (day, month, year).

ULTIMATE. The last or final in a series, as the ultimate end or purpose of human existence to which all other goals are to be subordinated. Also that beyond which further analysis cannot be made, as the ultimate explanation of sin is God's permissive Providence. (Etym. Latin *ultimatus,* from *ultimare,* to come to an end, from *ultimus,* farthest, last.)

ULTIMATE END. The last in a series of ends for which a person strives. In terms of humanity's purpose of existence the ultimate end is final beatitude in heaven.

ULTRAMONTANE. Catholics who agreed with the Pope on matters of doctrine and policy. The name means "beyond the Alps," specifically Rome. Those who lived on the northern side of the Alps were designated as Cisalpine. (Etym. Latin *ultramontanus,* beyond the mountain: *ultra-,* beyond + *mons,* mountain.)

UNAM SANCTAM. The papal bull of Pope Boniface VIII, issued November 18, 1302, in answer to Philip IV of France, who denied the Pope's authority. Only the last sentence is irreversible doctrine, in which Boniface states: "We declare, say, define and pronounce that it is absolutely necessary for the salvation of every human creature to be subject to the Roman Pontiff" (Denzinger 875). The preceding part of the document deals at length with the relation of temporal and spiritual powers in the Church.

UNBAPTIZED INFANTS. Children, whether born or unborn, who die without baptism of water. The difficult question of whether they can attain the beatific vision in

heaven has been discussed for centuries and has become especially grave since abortion is now legalized in so many countries. There is no unqualified answer to this question from the Church's magisterium. But there are two principles of Catholic doctrine that must be reconciled.

On the one hand, the Church teaches that even those who die with only original sin on their souls cannot reach the beatific vision. The Second Council of Lyons (1274) and the Council of Florence (1438–45) explicitly define that those who die with "only original sin" (*Peccato vel solo originali*) do not reach heaven. There is also the Church's condemnation of the Jansenists, who claimed that it is a myth to hold there is a place "which the faithful generally designate by the name of the limbo of children," for the souls of those who depart this life with only the guilt of original sin (Pius VI, *Errors of the Synod of Pistoia,* Proposition 26, August 28, 1794).

On the other hand, we also know that, according to God's universal salvific will, somehow he gives all persons the opportunity of reaching heaven. This is authoritatively expressed by the Second Vatican Council in its Dogmatic Constitution on the Church: "Those who, through no fault of their own, do not know the Gospel of Christ or His Church, but who nevertheless seek God with a sincere heart, and, moved by grace, try in their actions to do His will as they know it through the dictates of their conscience—those too can achieve eternal salvation" (*Lumen Gentium,* 16). By implication, their children who die before the age of reason can also be saved.

Saying all of this, one should emphasize how deeply the Church is concerned that children be baptized as soon after birth as possible. "As for the time of Baptism," the Roman ritual states, "the first consideration is the welfare of the child, that it may not be deprived of the benefit of the sacrament." Therefore, "if the child is in danger of death, it is to be baptized without delay."

UNCLEAN. The state of being tainted and in need of purification. It implies the presence of impure elements. This condition of being ceremonially unclean without reference to the purity of one's moral status is unknown among Christians, but current among Moslems, Hindus, Buddhists, and Shintoists. Among Jews, marriage, childbirth, contact with the dead or being in the presence of lepers was thought to contaminate and produce an unclean state. Christ abrogated this feature of the Mosaic law.

UNCONSCIOUS. A person who because of some accident or disability has temporarily or permanently lost the power of mental awareness. Certain sacraments can be validly and fruitfully conferred on an unconscious person provided that, before lapsing into the unconscious condition, the person had at least the implicit willingness to receive the sacrament and the necessary dispositions. Thus an unconscious person can be baptized, sacramentally absolved, and given the anointing of the sick; although in practice these sacraments are administered conditionally in such circumstances, i.e., assuming that the necessary requirements are satisfied.

UNCONSCIOUS MOTIVATION. Impulses for human activity not easily or at all traceable to conscious reasoning or willful deliberation. A person's motives for doing something, or abstaining from something else, for believing this or denying that, may be quite unknown. One may have only an unexplainable urge and feel the urge persisting in spite of conscious reasons to the contrary. One may be influenced by a person seen or a statement heard that shapes his own thought long before the age of reason and quite apart from rational reflection.

UNCREATED GRACE. God himself, insofar as in his love he has predetermined gifts of grace. There are three forms of uncreated grace: the hypostatic union, the divine indwelling, and the beatific vision. In the first of these, God has communicated himself in the Incarnation of Christ's humanity (the grace of union) so intimately that Jesus of Nazareth is a divine person. In the second and third communications, the souls of the justified on earth and of the glorified in heaven are elevated to a share in God's own life. All three are created graces, considered as acts, since they all had a beginning in time. But the gift that is conferred on a creature in these acts is uncreated.

UNCTION. Any anointing with oil with a religious purpose; whether in the actual conferring of a sacrament, as in confirmation and anointing of the sick; or as part of the sacrament's ceremony, as in baptism and holy orders; and in using a sacramental, such as the oil of St. Serapion, the martyr.

(Etym. Latin *unctio*, from *unguere*, to anoint.)

UNDERGROUND CHURCH. A group of persons, generally professed Catholics, who function outside the established church structure. But the term is mainly applied to those who live in places where Catholics, or Christians generally, are persecuted for their profession and sharing of the faith.

UNDERSTANDING. In scholastic philosophy, knowledge that is immediate and undemonstrated; intimate knowledge that penetrates to the essence of that which is known. Understanding is also the intuitive habitual knowledge of the primary speculative principles of reality.

UNIAT CHURCHES. Eastern Christians who profess the same doctrines as the rest of the Roman Catholic Church. Their rites and discipline, however, vary greatly from those of the Latin Rite. Their liturgies originated in Antioch, Alexandria, and Byzantium, and they usually have a married clergy. Nearly all Non-Uniat churches possess corresponding Uniat groups who have reacknowledged their allegiance to the Pope. The expression "Uniat," though found in theological literature, is seldom used by Eastern Catholics. They feel that it implies something less than complete allegiance to the Holy See.

UNICITY OF GOD. The absolute oneness of God. All the creeds of Christendom profess belief in one God, as opposed to polytheism and Manichean dualism, which claim that there is more than one deity. The Church bases God's unicity on his absolute perfection, since there cannot be more than one infinitely perfect God. Moreover, God's absolute oneness is provable from the unity of the world order.

UNIFORMITY. Being the same everywhere. Applied to the Church, uniformity of doctrine in faith and morals must be taught, either in solemn definitions or in her ordinary universal magisterium. Outside of this sphere, there is great pluriformity, according to different cultures and needs of the people. (Etym. Latin *uniformis*, having one form.)

UNIGENITUS. Constitution of Pope Clement XI, published September 8, 1713, in which he condemned one hundred one Jansenist propositions of Pasquier Quesnel (1634–1719), including such doctrines as the irresistibility of grace and that all actions of a sinner, even prayer, are sins.

UNIMPAIRED NATURE. The theoretical

condition in which a person, in addition to one's nature, would possess the preternatural gifts of integrity, i.e., without concupiscence or pain or the prospect of bodily death. In this possible state, one would have been able to reach one's natural destiny more easily and with greater certainty.

UNION. The act of combining the distinct or separate, and also the state of being thus combined. Forms of union are mere composition, mixture, the natural union of body and soul, the union of a substance with its accidents, union or agreement of minds and hearts, union of means to a given end, the union of will with the object it loves, the supernatural union of the soul with God and the hypostatic union of the divine and human natures in Christ.

UNIT. Something that is undivided in itself and distinct from everything else. Something that is one. A metaphysical unit is a simple being; moral unit is a plurality of persons with a single common purpose; organic unit has the unity of a living organism whose parts have specialized functions that act for the good of the whole.

UNITATIS REDINTEGRATIO. Decree on Ecumenism of the Second Vatican Council. It deals with the Catholic principles on ecumenism, the practice of ecumenism, and the Churches and ecclesiastical communities separated from the Roman Apostolic See. A careful distinction is made between spiritual ecumenism, mainly through prayer and the practice of virtue, and practical ecumenism, which actively fosters the reunification of Christianity. Also the faithful are told to recognize various levels of nearness to the Catholic Church, in descending order, the Eastern Orthodox, Anglicans, and Protestants (November 21, 1964).

UNITIVE WAY. The third and final stage of Christian perfection, beyond the purgative and illuminative. Its principal feature is a more or less constant awareness of God's presence, and a habitual disposition of conformity to the will of God. Although commonly regarded as the last stage in the spiritual life, it is recognized that the three traditional levels of progress in holiness are not chronological. They may be present, in greater or less degree, at any point in a person's growth in sanctity.

UNITY. The condition or state of oneness, especially among persons. What ultimately unites people is their common beliefs or convictions, and their common desires and affections. Union is the state of uniting different people. It is their state of mind agreeing on certain ideas and of will attaching its desires or love to certain objects that unify.

UNIVERSAL. Whatever is common to many; or some one thing that is common to many and that can be in many or applied to many. Used in the sense of Catholic, referring to the Church, universal means being everywhere geographically, continuous historically, the same essentially, and available indiscriminately.

UNIVERSAL BISHOP. Applied to the Pope as having truly episcopal power over the whole Church. He is therefore just as much a universal bishop of the entire Church as he is bishop of his diocese of Rome.

UNIVERSAL DOUBT. The state of suspension of positive judgment on any and every truth. Normally it is only a methodical form of doubt; when real, general doubt is pure skepticism.

UNIVERSALISM, BIBLICAL. The anti-nationalist teaching of the Hebrew prophets that God's salvific will included other nations, and not only the people of Israel. This is particularly true of the prophet Jonah.

UNIVERSALISM, DOCTRINAL. The theory that hell is essentially a kind of purgatory in which sins are expiated, so that eventually everyone will be saved. Also called apokatastasis, it was condemned by the Church in A.D. 543, against the Origenists, who claimed that "the punishment of devils and wicked men is temporary and will eventually cease, that is to say, that devils or the ungodly will be completely restored to their original state" (Denzinger 411).

UNIVERSE. All created things considered as forming an orderly unity. It also means all of creation as distinct from God the Creator.

UNIVERSITY OF THE FAITHFUL. An expression of the Second Vatican Council, *universitas fidelium,* declaring that "the whole body [university] of the faithful, whom the holy One has anointed, is incapable of error in belief" (*Constitution on the Church,* II, 12). This means that the faithful of Christ are joined together by their unerring belief in the mysteries of revelation. They are united by their common allegiance to the faith, which is the truth. Truth unites, error divides.

UNJUST AGGRESSOR. An assailant who attacks an innocent person actually and unjustly. Actual aggression is an imminent or practically present assault that cannot be evaded. Unjust aggression is experienced when the assault is at least materially unwarranted, i.e., when the assailant is not morally responsible for the attack. In all cases of unjust aggression it is permitted to use such force as may be necessary to insure self-protection.

UNJUST DAMAGE. Violating the property of another in some unfair manner without deriving any advantage from the harm caused. The obligation to undo the damage caused binds under the following conditions: 1. the act of damage must be unjust in the strict sense; 2. the action must be the real and effective cause of the damage, so that an accidental cause would not require restitution; 3. the harmful action must be formally sinful, i.e., deliberately unjust.

UNLEAVENED BREAD. See AZYMES.

UNMORAL. Condition of a person who has, or seems to have, no consideration for moral issues in his conduct. Also said to be amoral.

UNMOVED MOVER. God as the original and continual cause of motion (change) in creation, while himself remaining unmoved (unchanged).

UNNATURAL. That which is contrary to nature because it is contrary to right reason, hence irrational; or against the dignity of the human being as created to the image of God, hence unworthy; or against the divinely ordained purpose for which a given faculty should be used, hence perverse.

UNNATURAL SINS. Term used to describe those sexual acts from which conception is impossible. When committed alone they are called masturbation; when conception is deliberately frustrated they are some form of onanism; when those engaging in sexual activity are of the same sex, it is sodomy or homosexuality; and if animals are involved it is bestiality.

UNPARDONABLE SIN. Post-biblical term that means blasphemy against the Holy Spirit. When the Pharisees, baffled by a miracle that Jesus had performed, accused him of using the power of the devil to accomplish it, he warned them, "Let anyone speak against the Holy Spirit and he will not be forgiven either in this world or in the next" (Matthew 12:22–32). Also used as a synonym for the sin of despair.

UPPER ROOM, THE. This was the room in which Jesus and his Apostles shared the Last Supper the night before he was crucified. According to Mark it was a large chamber furnished with couches and suitable for a dining room (Mark 14:14–15). It may have been a room erected on the roof, because most homes were one-story structures. Possibly it became a meeting place, because after the Ascension of Jesus, Luke reports that the Apostles and Mary returned to Jerusalem and "went to the upper room where they were staying" (Acts 1:12–14). According to tradition, the house was located near the present Zion Gate and the Armenian quarter.

URBANISTS. Poor Clares, whose primitive rule was mitigated by Pope Urban IV in 1263.

URBI ET ORBI. The Pope's solemn blessing given to his visible audience in Rome and to the invisible audience of the entire world. This public blessing is given quite frequently during jubilee years and on several other important occasions. Pope Pius XI revived this benediction in 1922, after it had been in abeyance for more than fifty years.

URIM AND THUMMIM. Small objects, possibly stones, mentioned several times in the Old Testament but never described or explained. They were worn on the breast of a religious official, possibly designating his status, as he sought divine help (Exodus 28:30). Some believe that they were sacred lots that would evoke advice or instructions from Yahweh (Leviticus 8:9).

URSULINES. The oldest teaching order of religious women in the Catholic Church, founded at Brescia, Italy, by St. Angela Merici in 1525. They were approved by Pope Paul III in 1544 as a society of virgins, dedicated to Christian education but living in their own homes. In 1572, Pope Gregory XIII further approved their community life and simple vows at the request of St. Charles Borromeo. In 1612 the Ursulines of Paris were allowed to take solemn vows, and convents along these lines were soon established elsewhere, following a modified Rule of St. Augustine. In 1900 a congress of Ursulines met in Rome and effected a union of many congregations. These take simple vows, but some independent convents take solemn vows. There are twenty-five pontifical institutes of Ursulines, besides those belonging to the Roman Union.

USURY. Taking of excessive interest for the loan of money is the modern understanding of usury. In essence, however, usury is the acceptance of a premium for the mere use of a thing given in loan. Objectively it is the premium paid for a pure loan. The word has come to mean taking advantage of another who is in need. As such, it is forbidden by the natural law, because it is contrary to commutative justice. In the case of the poor, it is also a sin against charity.

Originally, in Jewish and Christian tradition, usury meant taking any interest for a loan. It was forbidden among the Jews (Exodus 22:25; Leviticus 25:35–37) but was permitted in dealing with Gentiles. Christ, explaining the precept of charity, made no distinction between Hebrew and Gentile and stated that loans must be gratuitous (Luke 6:30; Matthew 5:42). The Catholic Church for centuries reflected this concept of usury and still teaches that, where something is loaned and later returned in kind only, no profit may be made by reason of the contract itself. Concrete circumstances, however, relative to the economic position of the lender and borrower may be involved and change the effects of the contract. Four external circumstances have an economic value and therefore constitute titles to a proportionate compensation over and above the restitution of what was loaned. They are: actual damage, loss of profit, risk to the object loaned, and danger from delay in returning what was lent. Only such titles, external to the loan, when truly present, justify the right to claim and the duty to pay a just rate of interest on money loaned.

Capitalism, with unlimited opportunities for investment, changed the function of money so that it can fructify. Consequently loaning money did involve loss of profit to the lender and further risk of loss from delay in returning the money loaned. By the end of the eighteenth century the distinction between usury and interest was recognized in civil law. The Church also recognized the distinction so that now only exorbitant interest is called usury and considered morally wrong. In the process, however, the Church's basic teaching on the subject did not change. Injustice surrounding money lending was and remains condemned. What changed was the economic system. As this changed, the circumstances under which an injustice is committed changed. The Church necessarily permitted what was no longer unjust. (Etym. Latin *usura,* use of money lent, interest, from *usus,* use.)

USQ. *Usque*—as far as.

UTOPIA. Any imaginary state whose inhabitants live under perfect circumstances; ideal commonwealths described by Plato, Bacon, and St. Thomas More in his book *Utopia;* in an invidious sense, any visionary reform without consideration of man's human weaknesses and defects.

UTRAQUISM. See CALIXTINES.

UTRECHT, SCHISM OF. See OLD CATHOLICS.

UX. *Uxor*—wife.

V

V., VEN., VV. *Venerabilis, Venerabiles*—venerable.

V., VEST. *Vester*—your.

V.A., VIC. AP. *Vicarius apostolicus*—vicar apostolic.

VAC. *Vacat, vacans*—vacant.

VACANCY. An unfilled ecclesiastical position or office. The Holy See is said to be vacant at the death or resignation of the Pope. The college of cardinals summons the conclave to elect a new pope. They have no papal jurisdiction, nor can they perform papal acts. When the death, resignation, translation, or deposition of a bishop creates a vacancy, the government devolves upon the chapter of canons, who within eight days must appoint a vicar capitular. If there is no chapter, the bishop himself appoints an administrator before the vacancy occurs, or the suffragan appoints an administrator afterwards until a new appointment is made.

VAGI. Literally "wanderers," who are persons having no fixed residence or are far from home. Church law provides for their being married anywhere by proper authority, with the approval of a bishop.

VAIN OBSERVANCE. A form of superstition that tries to achieve a certain effect by the use of unsuitable means. Implicit in vain observance is the belief that there are hidden preternatural forces at work in the world which dispense with the need of using ordinary, natural, or supernatural means for obtaining a desired effect. Vain observance also implies the expectation of an infallible result whenever certain words are said or actions performed. There is only a shade of difference between vain observance and divination. In both cases reliance on the evil spirit is involved. But vain observance, unlike divination, is not concerned with obtaining knowledge of the future or of the occult. Its focus is on obtaining some external results, such as making a successful business deal or recovering one's health.

VAL. *Valor*—value.

VALENTINE'S DAY, ST. Traditional lovers' day, going back to the pagan Lupercalia, in mid-February, and the medieval belief that birds began to mate at that time. Eventually this custom and belief became associated with the feast of St. Valentine on February 14, which may refer to any one of three saints by the same name: a priest-physician martyred in Rome in 269; a bishop of Interamna, beheaded at Rome about 273; and a martyr in Africa who was put to death with several companions.

VALENTINIANISM. The Gnostic heresy of Valentinus, who lived in Rome from about A.D. 136 to 165, when he seceded from the Church. The Valentinians claimed that the God of the Old Testament created the visible world. But only the invisible world is real. Christ was a spirit who came to deliver humankind from its bondage to matter, becoming united to the man Jesus at his baptism. Those who followed Valentinus became Gnostics, that is, knowers, destined to enter into a spiritual heaven; Catholics could at best attain to the middle realm of the Old Testament deity; and the rest of humankind, being engrossed in matter, would go into eternal perdition.

VALIDATION. The making valid of a matrimonial contract that had been null and void because of a diriment impediment. A validation requires that the impediment cease or be removed, and that the consent of both parties be renewed. If the impediment is not publicly known, the consent may be renewed in secret. If the impediment is known only to one party, only he or she need renew the consent, provided the other party's consent has persevered. (Etym. Latin *validus*, strong, effective; from *valere*, to be strong.)

VALID FORM. That formula of words or prescribed signs that are required for the valid conferral or production of a sacrament. Thus the valid form for baptism is, "I baptize you in the name of the Father, and of the Son, and of the Holy Spirit." For actually conferring a sacrament, the matter (material or action) must be united with the form.

VALIDITY. Having not only legal force but actually producing the effect intended. Applied to the sacraments, it refers to the conditions of matter, form, and circumstances required for valid administration. In ecclesiastical law it means that certain prescriptions must be fulfilled for the law or contractual agreement to bind or take effect.

VALID MATTER. That which is required, along with the prescribed words, for the valid conferral or production of a sacrament. The valid matter is, therefore, some sense-perceptible material or perceivable action that must be joined with the form, i.e., words or signs, to produce a sacrament. Thus the valid matter in baptism is natural water, that "washes" the person being baptized, by pouring, sprinkling, or immersion.

VALUE. That which makes a thing desirable or considered worthwhile. Value stresses the subjective and relative aspect of the good over the objective and absolute character. It means not so much the inherent excellence of an object as how it stands in one's personal estimation; not so much its built-in perfection as its comparative place in that scale of things called the hierarchy of values. The term *value* commends itself to subjectivist and relativist moral philosophies, in preference to the common *good*. Nevertheless, it is also acceptable to Christians provided it includes the notion of an objective moral standard. (Etym. Latin *valere*, to be worth, be strong.)

VANITY. Or vainglory, an inordinate desire to manifest one's own excellence. It differs from pride, which is the uncontrolled desire for self-esteem, in that vanity primarily seeks to show others what a person has or has achieved. A vain person looks for praise from others and may go to great lengths to obtain it. More commonly, vanity is associated with an exaggerated importance attached to multiple details, especially external appearances, which in no way contain the value attributed to them. It is ostentation in fashion, wealth, or power regarded as an occasion of empty pride. Thus where pride, though sinful, may have some foundation in fact for whatever one prides oneself on being or having done, vanity is the idle effort to obtain recognition or respect for what a person does not have a rightful claim to. Vanity is attributed to shams, which lack substance and are deceitful (like human praise); or to things without solidity and permanence (such as physical beauty); or to means that fail in their purpose (such as vaunting one's own reputation). It is an inflated pride and, as such, is venially sinful.

VASECTOMY. Surgical excision of part of the ducts carrying sperm cells to ejaculation, with the purpose of causing sterilization. If the direct intent of the surgery is to induce sterility, the operation is morally illicit.

VAT. *Vaticanus*—Vatican.

VATICAN. A group of buildings in Rome, clustered around the palace of the Pope. The first to build a residence near the ancient Basilica of St. Peter was Pope Symmachus (reigned 498–514). Through subsequent purchase the popes acquired possession of the entire Vatican Hill. The property now is the largest palace in the world. Only a small part is used for living quarters; most of the buildings serve the purpose of the arts and sciences, and the administration of Church affairs.

VATICAN BASILICA. See BASILICA OF ST. PETER.

VATICAN CHANT. Gregorian melodies revised according to the directives of Pope St. Pius X. "Sacred music," he declared, "should possess in the highest degree the qualities proper to the liturgy. It must be holy, and must therefore exclude all worldliness" (November 22, 1903). The work of restoration was carried out chiefly by the Solesmes monks.

VATICAN CITY. Official name, *Stato della Città del Vaticano*. It is the territorial see of the Papacy, determined by the Lateran Treaty of 1929. Situated within the geographic boundary of Rome, it covers an area of 108.7 acres and includes the Vatican Palace, St. Peter's Basilica, Vatican Radio Station, and numerous other buildings that serve the Pope and the administration of the universal Church. Ultimate authority for Vatican City is vested in the Pope but actually administered by the Pontifical Commis-

sion for the State of Vatican City. In general, the government is based on canon law or, where this does not apply, on existing laws of the city of Rome. It is politically a neutral state and enjoys all the privileges and duties of a sovereign power. The Papal Secretariat maintains diplomatic relations with other nations. Only the citizens of Vatican City owe allegiance to the Pope as temporal ruler.

VATICAN EXTRATERRITORIAL POSSESSIONS. All the property in Rome that is outside the actual confines of Vatican City and that enjoys special privileges since the Lateran Treaty of 1929. More than ten such buildings and their grounds enjoy extraterritorial rights, including the basilicas of the Lateran, St. Paul, St. Mary Major, and the Twelve Apostles; also the Pope's summer residence at Castel Gandolfo.

VATICAN LIBRARY. One of the world's chief depositories of books. The foundation of this famous collection was begun by Pope Martin V (reigned 1417–31), but Pope Nicholas V (reigned 1447–55) is considered its real founder. He acquired the imperial library of Constantinople, scattered by the Turks, and donated it to the Vatican. Pope Sixtus IV (reigned 1471–84) officially established the modern Vatican Library in 1475, and Pope Sixtus V (reigned 1585–90) ordered the construction of new buildings that are still in use. The library is administered by a prefect, writers work on scientifically cataloguing the manuscripts, and assistants catalogue the printed books. The library maintains manuscript repairing, bookbinding and publishing departments, and as a scientific institution for the use of students, it is presently making one of the greatest contributions to human thought.

VATICAN OFFICE OF STATISTICS. It was established by Pope Paul VI in 1967, and its function is to gather and organize such data on the life and personnel of the Church as may assist her pastoral work. The *Annuario Pontificio* is published by the Vatican Central Office of Statistics.

VATICAN PALACE. An irregular complex of many buildings seen beyond the colonnade on the right side of the Basilica of St. Peter's. Today, the residence of the Pope, who, before Gregory XI's return from Avignon in 1377, had lived officially at the Lateran Palace. The original Vatican apartments erected first in the fifth century were used only for the reception of foreign sovereigns visiting Rome. Additions were made to the imposing building begun in 1450 by subsequent pontiffs. Pope Sixtus IV (reigned 1471–84) added the Sistine Chapel in 1473, named after him; Pope Alexander VI (reigned 1492–1503) the Appartamento Borgia; and Innocent VIII (reigned 1484–92) the Belvedere; Julius II (reigned 1503–13) the Logge, and he also laid the foundations for the Vatican Museums. Some of the greatest architects and painters of the times were employed—Bramante, Michelangelo, Raphael, Sangallo, Maderna, Bernini, and others—to make it the largest palace in the world. It has eighty impressive staircases and several thousand rooms, few of which are actually used as papal apartments. Museums, library, picture gallery, collections, Sistine Chapel, galleries, stanzas, loggias also occupy the immense edifice called the Vatican.

VATICAN POLYGLOT PRESS. First planned by Popes Marcellus II and Pius IV, a Vatican printing press was founded by Pope Sixtus V in 1587 for the printing of the Vulgate, the writings of the Fathers, and other Vatican publications. A second press, with various Oriental fonts, was established in 1622 at the Propaganda Fide. The two were merged by Pope St. Pius X in 1908 under the present name and entrusted to the Salesian Fathers.

VATICAN PREFECTURE OF ECONOMIC AFFAIRS. Established by Pope Paul VI in 1967, it directs and co-ordinates all the financial aspects of the work of the Holy See. It sets budgets, controls expenses, and in general makes sure that the numerous enterprises of the Vatican operate on a sound economic basis.

VATICAN PUBLISHING HOUSE. Long associated with the names of Aldo Manunzio and sons, and linked with the Vatican Press, the Editrice Vaticana now handles the numerous publications of the congregations and organs of the Roman Curia. It became an autonomous agency in 1926.

VATICAN SECRET ARCHIVES. Repository of confidential documents of the Holy See, going back to the early centuries. Deterioration of the original papyri, transfers, and political upheavals caused the almost complete loss of the collections earlier than Pope Innocent III. In the fifteenth century the Archives were kept in Castel Sant'Angelo. In 1810, Napoleon ordered the Archives of the Holy See to be transferred to Paris, and though later returned to Rome many documents were lost. The Archives are now housed in a special building off the Piazza of St. Peter's. To the Archives is attached the Vatican School of Palaeography and, since 1968, the School of Archivistry. In 1881, Pope Leo XIII made the Vatican Archives available to consultation by accredited scholars.

VBA. *Verba*—words.

VEIL, BRIDAL. A temporary covering of the head and shoulders of the persons who are getting married. The bridal veil is the best known and dates from ancient times. In some countries it covers both the bride and groom as they proceed to their new home. Also, occasionally it was worn during the time of betrothal. For centuries the custom prevailed of holding a veil over the married couple while they were solemnly blessed. Some rituals prescribe that the veil completely cover the bride and only the shoulders of the groom. Formerly the bridal veil could be flame-colored, yellow, or purple. Today it is usually white and long. (Etym. Latin *velum*, covering.)

VEIL, LITURGICAL. Any one of a variety of symbolic coverings of persons or sacred objects as a sign of reverence, e.g., the veil used to cover the ciborium when it contains the consecrated hosts reserved for Communion.

VEIL, RELIGIOUS. Covering for the head and shoulders worn by women religious. Historically, different veils have signified different roles. The veil of probation, usually white, was given to novices; the veil of profession was given at the pronunciation of vows; the veil of consecration was given consecrated virgins; the veil of continence was given to widows. In the Church's *Order of Religious Profession,* published in 1970, it is assumed that the veil is part of the distinctive garb of religious women. The veiling of virgins consecrated to divine worship and the service of the Church goes back to early patristic times.

VEIL OF PRELATURE. A special head covering once given to abbesses to honor them on having reached their sixtieth year.

VENERABLE. Title given to the Servants of God after the state of their heroic virtue or martyrdom has been proved and a solemn decree to that effect has been signed by the Pope. (Etym. Latin *venerabilis,* from *venerari,* to regard with religious awe.)

VENERATION OF SAINTS. Honor paid to the saints who, by their intercession and example and in their possession of God, minister to human sanctification, helping the faithful grow in Christian virtue. Venerating the saints does not detract from the glory given to God, since whatever good they possess is a gift from his bounty. They reflect the divine perfections, and their supernatural qualities result from the graces Christ merited for them by the Cross. In the language of the Church's liturgy, the saints are venerated as sanctuaries of the Trinity, as adopted children of the Father, brethren of Christ, faithful members of his Mystical Body, and temples of the Holy Spirit.

VENEREAL PLEASURE. The bodily and emotional satisfaction that accompanies any form of sexual activity. (Etym. Latin *venereus,* from *venus,* love, lust.)

VENGEANCE. The infliction of punishment on someone who has done moral wrong. In this sense, only God has the right to avenge wrongdoing. He may delegate this right to those in legitimate authority, as St. Paul declares, speaking of civil rulers, that "the authorities are there to serve God; they carry out God's revenge by punishing wrongdoers" (Romans 13:4). (Etym. Latin *vindicare,* to revenge, vindicate.)

VENIAL SIN. An offense against God which does not deprive the sinner of sanctifying grace. It is called venial (from *venia,* pardon) because the soul still has the vital principle that allows a cure from within, similar to the healing of a sick or diseased body whose source of animation (the soul) is still present to restore the ailing bodily function to health.

Deliberate venial sin is a disease that slackens the spiritual powers, lowers one's resistance to evil, and causes one to deviate from the path that leads to heavenly glory. Variously called "daily sins" or "light sins" or "lesser sins," they are committed under a variety of conditions: when a person transgresses with full or partial knowledge and consent to a divine law that does not oblige seriously; when one violates a law that obliges gravely but either one's knowledge or consent is not complete; or when one disobeys what is an objectively grave precept but due to invincible ignorance a person thinks the obligation is not serious.

The essence of venial sin consists in a certain disorder but does not imply complete aversion from humanity's final destiny. It is an illness of the soul rather than its supernatural death. When people commit a venial sin, they do not decisively set themselves on turning away from God, but from overfondness for some created good fall short of

God. They are like persons who loiter without leaving the way.

VENI CREATOR SPIRITUS. The hymn *Come, Creator Spirit,* most probably written by the Benedictine abbot Rabanus Maurus (776–856). It has for centuries been part of the Divine Office and has been called "the most famous of hymns," sung at the election of popes, consecration of bishops, ordination of priests, at councils, synods, and dedication of churches.

VENI SANCTE SPIRITUS. The *Golden Sequence,* for the Pentecost Eucharistic liturgy. From its opening lines, "Come, Holy Spirit," the hymn sustains the theme of asking for an increase of the seven gifts. Its author was most probably Stephen Langton (d. 1228), Archbishop of Canterbury.

VENITE SEORSUM. Instruction of the Sacred Congregation for Religious and for Secular Institutes on the Contemplative Life and on the Enclosure of Nuns. Besides the doctrinal principles on the contemplative life, the document gives detailed norms on how this life is to be lived by cloistered women religious. Its basic norm is that "papal enclosure is to be regarded as an ascetical regulation particularly consistent with the special vocation of nuns, in that it is a sign, the safeguard, and the characteristic form of their withdrawal from the world" (August 15, 1969).

VERBUM SUPERNUM PRODIENS. The hymn "The Heavenly Word Proceeding Forth" for the Lauds of Corpus Christi. Written by St. Thomas Aquinas, it is translated into every modern language. The fifth and sixth verses are known as the *O Salutaris Hostia,* often sung at Benediction of the Blessed Sacrament.

VERNACULAR IN LITURGY. The use of the common spoken language of the people in the Catholic liturgy. It was authorized on principle by the Second Vatican Council, declaring that "since the use of the vernacular, whether in the Mass, the administration of the sacraments, or in other parts of the liturgy, may frequently be of great advantage to the people, a wider use may be made of it" (*Constitution on the Liturgy,* I, 36). In practice, within ten years of the Council, the vernacular became the norm in the Roman Rite, and the use of Latin the exception. All translations had to be approved by the Holy See. To obviate difficulties about meaning, Rome declared that "a vernacular translation of a sacramental formula . . . must be understood in accordance with the mind of the Church as expressed in the original Latin text" (*Instauratio Liturgica,* January 25, 1974). (Etym. Latin *vernaculus,* domestic; from *verna,* native slave, probably from Etruscan.)

VERONICA'S VEIL. The cloth with which tradition holds that the saintly Veronica wiped the face of Jesus on his way to Calvary. Christ is said to have left the imprint of his face on the veil. It is honored as a treasured relic at St. Peter's in Rome. The episode is commemorated in the sixth station of the cross. Veronica is sometimes identified with the woman whom Christ healed of an issue of blood. (Mark 5:25–32).

VERS. *Versiculus*—versicle.

VERSES, BIBLICAL. Divisions within the chapters of the books of the Bible. The present numeration for the Old Testament was made by Santes Pagnini in his Latin Bible of 1528. The Paris printer Robert Etienne adopted Pagnini's numeration and himself added the numbers of the verses for the New Testament in his edition of 1555.

VERSICLE. A brief exclamatory line preceding a response such as in the Divine Office. It is usually part of a verse.

VESP. *Vesperae*—Vespers.

VESPERS. Evening service of worship. In the new Breviary since Second Vatican Council it has been replaced in the Divine Office by "Evening Prayer."

VESSEL OF HONOR. A title of the Blessed Virgin in the Litany of Loreto. It was given to Mary because she, more than any other human person, deserves to be honored as the one whose body conceived and gave birth to the Son of God.

VESSELS, SACRED. The utensils and receptacles used in liturgical celebrations. In the Latin Rite these are the chalice, paten, ciborium, pyx, capsula, lunette, and monstrance—which come into direct contact with the Blessed Sacrament. Other vessels used in the liturgy are cruets, lavabo dish, thurible, boat, and aspergillum.

VESTIBULE. Originally an entrance courtyard, and later any entrance to a place. Now commonly applied to the anteroom of a church between the outer doors and the church edifice proper. In Catholic churches the vestibule is fairly spacious, depending on the size of the building, and provides room for book or pamphlet racks, bulletin boards, often the holy water fonts, and such notices as provide information to the worshipers either before or after they have attended divine services or engaged in private devotions before the Blessed Sacrament in the church proper.

VESTMENTS. Special garments worn by the clergy, in conformity with Church regulations, at the celebration of the Mass, administration of the sacraments, in procession, when giving blessings, and in general whenever exercising their official priestly duties. The use of vestments goes back to the ritual garb of the priesthood of Aaron. In the Catholic Church, even in catacomb days, priests and bishops were specially, if not always distinctively, garbed when celebrating the liturgy. With the Church's liberation and her emergence into public life, liturgical garments were commonly used to distinguish them from secular dress.

VESTRY. The room or rooms in the front of a church where the sacred vessels and vestments are kept, and where the priest and ministers at the altar vest for liturgical functions. It is also the place where parochial meetings are often held. In the Anglican, or Episcopal, Church the vestry is a body of laymen charged with responsibility for the temporal affairs of the parish. In Catholic tradition the vestry is more commonly called the sacristy.

VETO, ROYAL. The right claimed by some rulers to reject nominees to Catholic episcopal sees that were not acceptable to the civil government. While the Holy See has never recognized the right on principle, it has more than once permitted the exercise of the veto in order to avoid greater evil.

VEXILLA REGIS. The hymn "Abroad the Regal Banners Fly," sung at Vespers from Palm Sunday until Holy Thursday, and on the feast of the Exaltation (or Triumph) of the Holy Cross (September 14). It was also used formerly on Good Friday, when the Blessed Sacrament was taken from the repository to the high altar, and for Vespers on the now suppressed feast of the Finding of the Holy Cross (May 3). Written by Venantius Fortunatus (530–609), it has at least forty translations in English alone.

V.F., VIC. FOR. *Vicarius Foraneus*—vicar forane.

VG. Vulgate.

V.G. *Vicarius Generalis*—vicar-general.

VIA DOLOROSA. The Sorrowful Way. The

route, according to tradition, which Jesus followed walking from Pilate's court to Calvary. It is a steep, narrow street that pilgrims traverse in meditating on the incidents that culminated in the Crucifixion. The Stations of the Cross are marked on buildings along the route to dramatize the events for those who walk in these sacred processions.

VIA MEDIA. A term used by the leaders of the Oxford Movement to identify Anglicanism as the middle road between Popery (Catholicism) and dissent (Protestantism). Although popularized by John Henry Newman and other Tractarians, the expression is already found among seventeenth-century English divines, e.g., George Herbert (1593–1633).

VIATICUM. The reception of Holy Communion when there is probable danger of death. Viaticum should not be deferred too long in sickness lest the dying lose consciousness. It can be given as often as such danger exists, and is required of all the faithful who have reached the age of discretion. No laws of fasting persist either for the recipient or for the priest who must consecrate in order to supply the Host in an emergency. (Etym. Latin *viaticum,* traveling provisions; from *viaticus,* of a road or journey, from *via,* way, road.)

VIC. CAP. *Vicarius capitularis*–vicar capitular.

VICAR. An ecclesiastic who substitutes for another in the exercise of a clerical office and acts in his name and with his authority according to canon law. (Etym. Latin *vicarius,* a substitute; from *vicarius,* substituting, acting for; from *vicis,* change, turn, office.)

VICAR APOSTOLIC. A delegate to a titular see, having episcopal consecration, appointed by the Holy See to govern in territories where the ordinary hierarchy is not established. Vicars apostolic have the same powers as bishops and are generally conceded special privileges because of the extraordinary situation in which they exercise their ministry.

VICAR CAPITULAR. A cleric appointed by the cathedral chapter to administer a vacant episcopal diocese. The bishop's ordinary spiritual and temporal jurisdiction becomes the responsibility of the chapter when a vacancy occurs. But the chapter in turn must elect a vicar to assume this authority within a specified short period of time. When a diocese has no chapter, the board of

consultors or its equivalent elects an administrator.

VICAR FORANE. An experienced priest appointed by a bishop to exercise limited jurisdiction over a specific part of a diocese. He is charged with the care of the sick clergy, presides at conferences, supervises clerical discipline and diocesan property as well as other similar matters.

VICAR FOR RELIGIOUS. A priest appointed by a bishop to act as his representative in dealing with the religious communities in the diocese.

VICAR-GENERAL. A legitimately deputized assistant to a bishop with ordinary jurisdiction over an entire diocese. His term of office expires with the death, resignation, or transfer of the bishop. Unless the size of a diocese or diversity of rites absolutely requires it, there may be only one vicar-general appointed. He should be an experienced priest of excellent moral character. The vicar-general may also be an auxiliary bishop. In view of its importance the office is regulated by definite legislation in the Church's canon law.

VICARIATE OF ROME. The diocese of Rome administered from the Lateran by a cardinal who is Vicar-General of His Holiness. Its jurisdiction is the city of Rome and the part called Agro Romano. Pope Paul IV in 1558 decreed that the Vicar of Rome should be a member of the Sacred College, and Pope Pius XI in 1929 withdrew the Vatican from the jurisdiction of the vicar.

VICAR OF CHRIST. The Pope, visible head of the Church on earth, acting for and in the place of Christ. He possesses supreme ecclesiastical authority in the Catholic Church. This title for the Pope dates from at least the eighth century and gradually replaced the former title, "Vicar of St. Peter." Its biblical basis is Christ's commission of Peter to "feed my lambs, feed my sheep" (John 21:15–17).

VICE. A bad moral habit. Technically a vice is the strong tendency to a gravely sinful act acquired through frequent repetition of the same act. Qualities that characterize a vice are spontaneity, ease, and satisfaction in doing what is morally wrong. (Etym. Latin *vitium,* any sort of defect.)

VICEGERENT. An auxiliary bishop appointed as assistant to the cardinal vicar of the diocese of Rome. He was a papal appointee with equal powers to the vicar in jurisdiction and in episcopal ceremonies. Pope

Pius X (reigned 1903–14) declared the office suppressed as soon as it became vacant during his pontificate. (Etym. Latin *vicis,* in place of + *gerens,* acting.)

VICTIM. A living being offered in sacrifice to God. The sacrifice implies that the victim is actually or equivalently given up as an act of adoration or of expiation to the Divine Majesty. The destruction of the victim is its immolation; the voluntary surrender of the victim is the offering or oblation. Together they constitute the sacrifice.

VICTIMAE PASCHALI. The hymn to the *Paschal Victim,* which is the Easter sequence for the Mass on Easter Sunday and through the octave. Composed by Wipo (d. 1050) of Burgundy (or Swabia), it commemorates Christ's triumphant conquest of death.

VICTIM SOUL. A person specially chosen by God to suffer more than most people during life, and who generously accepts the suffering in union with the Savior and after the example of Christ's own Passion and Death. The motive of a victim soul is a great love of God and the desire to make reparation for the sins of mankind.

VICTORINES. The Canons Regular of the former abbey of St. Victor in Paris. Founded by William of Champeaux in 1113, the abbey became extinct during the French Revolution. It is best known for the number of scholars, mystics, and poets it produced, including Hugh of St. Victor (1096–1141), Richard of St. Victor (d. 1173) and Walter of St. Victor (d. after 1180).

VID. *Vidua*—widow.

VID., VIDEL. *Videlicet*—namely.

VIDI AQUAM. The hymn *I Beheld Water,* sung as antiphon in the Easter season in place of the Asperges. The opening words are based on Ezekiel 47; the verse is Psalm 117:1 (Vulgate).

VIG. *Vigilia*—vigil of a feast.

VIGIL. The day or eve before a more or less prominent feast or solemnity. It was observed as a preparation for the following day with special offices and prayers and formerly with a fast, honoring the particular mystery of religion or the saint to be venerated on the feast day. The Church today observes solemn vigils for Christmas, Easter, and Pentecost. Although the number of such solemn vigils has been reduced since the Second Vatican Council, the Church still wants the notion of vigils to be kept alive in the minds of the faithful. Thus "it is fitting that Bible services on the vigils of great feasts, on certain ferial days of Lent and Advent, on Sundays and feastdays, should also have the same structure as the liturgy of the Word at Mass" (*Inter Oecumenici,* 1964, 38). (Etym. Latin *vigilia,* from *vigil,* alert.)

VIGIL LIGHT. A wax lamp kept burning at a shrine or before a sacred image, generally clustered with similar lamps, and lighted by the faithful as an act of devotion.

VINCENTIAN CANON. The famous threefold test of Catholic orthodoxy expressed by St. Vincent of Lérins (400–50) in his two memoranda (*Commonitoria*): "Care must especially be had that that be held which was believed everywhere [*ubique*], always [*semper*], and by all [*ab omnibus*]." By this triple norm of diffusion, endurance, and universality, a Christian can distinguish religious truth from error.

VINCENTIANS. Members of the Congregation of the Mission founded by St. Vincent de Paul in 1625. Also known as Lazarists from the Place de St. Lazare, which was St. Vincent's headquarters in Paris. The original work of the congregation was the preaching of popular missions and conducting retreats. Later on seminaries were established. Vincentians form a society of common life. They are secular priests living in community under religious vows. Their present apostolate is mission work, conducting seminaries, directing the Daughters and Ladies of Charity, education and spiritual exercises to priests, religious, and the laity.

VINCIBLE IGNORANCE. Lack of knowledge for which a person is morally responsible. It is culpable ignorance because it could be cleared up if the person used sufficient diligence. One is said to be simply (but culpably) ignorant if one fails to make enough effort to learn what should be known; guilt then depends on one's lack of effort to clear up the ignorance. That person is crassly ignorant when the lack of knowledge is not directly willed but rather due to neglect or laziness; as a result the guilt is somewhat lessened, but in grave matters a person would still be gravely responsible. A person has affected ignorance when one deliberately fosters it in order not to be inhibited in what one wants to do; such ignorance is gravely wrong when it concerns serious matters. (Etym. Latin *vincibilis,* easily overcome; *ignorantia,* want of knowledge or information.)

VINDICATION. The defense of a right or claim, especially by public authority whether civil or ecclesiastical. As a form of justice, it is the imposing of a penalty or retribution because of wrong done. (Etym. Latin *vindicare,* to claim, defend, revenge; from *vindex,* claimant, defender, avenger.)

VINE AND THE BRANCHES. An emblem of Christ originating from his own words, "I am the vine; you are the branches. He that abides in me bears much fruit, without me you can do nothing" (John 15:5). This is one of the earliest symbols in Christian art.

VIOL. *Violaceus—*violet.

VIOLATION. Desecration of something holy. A church is violated by the crime of homicide, a criminal shedding of blood, impious and sordid conduct, and (in the Code of 1918) the burial of an infidel or a notorious, excommunicated person. Corpses and graves are violated by stealing from them or putting them to some evil purpose. (Etym. Latin *violare,* from *vis,* force.)

VIOLENCE. Physical or psychological force used to compel one to act against one's choice, or against an inclination to choose in a certain way. Violence may be absolute or relative. Absolute violence demands resistance by all possible means. It destroys free will, and all imputability of the act is then attributed to the violator, if one acts with full freedom of the will. If the victim does not oppose the act with every possible external resistance, or with external resistance internally adheres to the act brought to bear on him or her, violence is called relative. Freedom of the will is not removed but diminished in proportion to the adherence or repugnance present in the mind of the subject.

VIOLET. See PURPLE.

VIRG. *Virgo—*virgin.

VIRGIN. See VIRGINITY.

VIRGIN BIRTH. A popular expression for Christ's conception and birth of a unique mother, Mary. Taught by all the creeds of Christendom, it is an article of faith and a basic norm of Christian orthodoxy.

VIRGINITY. The state of bodily integrity in either sex. This integrity may be physical or moral, and either factual or intentional. Physical virginity is sometimes defined as the absence of any sinfully experienced lustful sensation. But, strictly speaking, a person is physically a virgin unless he or she has had sexual intercourse with a person of the opposite sex. Moral virginity means the absence of any willful consent to venereal pleasure; again, strictly speaking, with a person of the opposite sex. Virginity is factual when, de facto, a person has not in the past sought or indulged in sexual pleasure; it is intentional when a person intends never to experience such pleasure, according to the previous distinctions made. (Etym. Latin *virgo,* maiden, virgin.)

VIRGINITY, VIRTUE OF. A virtue distinct from the virtue of chastity because of its special excellence. Chastity restrains the satisfaction of the sexual appetite, but virginity totally excludes it.

VIRGINITY OF MARY. The revealed dogma that the Mother of Jesus conceived without carnal intercourse, gave birth to Christ without injury to her virginity, and remained a virgin all her life. The Church's faith in Mary's virginal conception of Christ is expressed in all the creeds. Mary's virginal conception was already foretold in the Old Testament by Isaiah in the famous Emmanuel prophecy: "Behold a virgin shall conceive and bear a son and his name shall be called Emmanuel" (Isaiah 7:14). Mary's virginity includes virginity of mind, i.e., constant virginal disposition of soul; virginity of the senses, i.e., freedom from inordinate motions of sexual desire; and virginity of body, or physical integrity. The Church's doctrine refers primarily to her bodily integrity.

VIRGINS, CONSECRATION OF. Solemn dedication of a woman to lifetime virginity. The practice goes back to apostolic times, with a formal rite for the consecration dating from about the year 500. In 1970, Pope Paul VI revised the ritual by which women consecrate their virginity "to Christ and their brethren" without becoming members of a religious institute.

VIRID. *Viridis—*green.

VIRTUAL INTENTION. An intention that was once made and continues to influence the act now being done. But it is not present to the person's consciousness at the moment of performing the act. This kind of intention is sufficient for a human act to be voluntary and therefore morally responsible. (Etym. Latin *virtualis,* from *virtus,* capacity, virtue.) See also ACTUAL INTENTION, HABITUAL INTENTION, INTENTION, INTERPRETATIVE INTENTION.

VIRTUE. A good habit that enables a person to act according to right reason enlightened by faith. Also called an operative good habit, it makes its possessor a good person and his or her actions also good. (Etym. Latin *virtus,* virility, strength of character, manliness.)

VIRTUES. Angels who compose the second choir of the second or intermediate order of angels. They are the ones whom God employs for the performance of stupendous works or extraordinary miracles.

VISIBILITY. That quality of the Church by which she appears externally and can be recognized by the senses. Two kinds of visibility are distinguished. The Church is materially visible in that her members are human beings who can be identified as Catholic Christians. The Church is also formally visible in possessing certain sensibly perceptible properties, notably the required profession of a common faith, the practice of a definite ritual, and obedience to identifiable laws under an authorized hierarchy.

VISION. Supernatural perception of some object that is not visible naturally. A vision is a revelation only when the object seen also discloses some hidden truth or mystery.

VISION OF GOD. See BEATIFIC VISION.

VISITANDINES. The Order of the Visitation of the Blessed Virgin Mary, founded in 1610 by St. Francis de Sales and St. Jane Frances de Chantal. It was established for women who wished a contemplative life but under less austere conditions than those of the older orders, stressing humility, gentleness, and sisterly charity. Originally under simple vows, they became a religious order with strict enclosure in 1618, and thus were approved by Pope Paul V. Houses are relatively autonomous. The best known Visitandine was St. Margaret Mary Alacoque, whose revelations helped to promote the modern devotion to the Sacred Heart. There are also several groups of Visitation Sisters, including a native Japanese community based in Yokohama.

VISITATION, CANONICAL. An official examination by ecclesiastical superiors of persons, communities, institutions, or territories, in regard to matters of faith, worship, morals, or church discipline. Visitations may be either ordinary or extraordinary, and may be authorized by the Holy See, the local ordinary, or general superiors in institutes of Christian perfection.

VISITATION, FEAST OF THE. Annual commemoration of Mary's visit to her kinswoman Elizabeth. First celebrated by the Franciscans in 1263 at the initiative of St. Bonaventure. Then, during the Western Schism, it was extended to the whole Church by Popes Urban VI (reigned 1378–89) and Boniface IX (reigned 1389–1404) to obtain an end to the schism. The feast is now celebrated on May 31.

VITALISM. The philosophy that holds that every living being is composed of an organic body and a vital principle or soul as its substantial form.

VITANDUS. "To be avoided." The most severe form of excommunication, seldom imposed and only then expressly by the Holy See. It means that, as a remedial measure, the faithful are not to associate with the person "except in the case of husband and wife, parents, children, servants, subjects," and in general unless there is some reasonable excusing cause.

VITERBO. Shrine of Our Lady Liberatrix in Italy. Veneration of Mary the Mother of God began here in a special manner in 1320 after Viterbo was delivered from a mysterious and terrifying experience—an unexplained darkness covered the city for four days. The citizens made a fresco painting of Mary and the Divine Child on the wall of a chapel dedicated to St. Anne in the mid-fourteenth century, and for more than a hundred years went there to thank the Virgin. The present edifice was built in 1680 and is still frequented by a great number of pilgrims.

VLADIMIR, OUR LADY OF. A sacred icon of Mary and her Son which has a long and venerable tradition in Russian history. It was probably painted at the beginning of the twelfth century and brought to Kiev in the Ukraine from Constantinople. Then it was taken as a gift to the ruling prince of the city of Vladimir, east of Moscow, where it remained until the time of the invasion of Tamerlane, who was approaching Moscow. The icon was then transferred from Vladimir to Moscow. Tamerlane halted his armies and Moscow was saved (1395). The icon remained in Moscow. On three other occasions, in 1451, 1459, and 1480, the Tatars menaced Moscow, but the city was saved through the intercession of Our Lady of Vladimir. As a sign of gratitude three feasts came to be celebrated in her honor annually, on May 21, June 23, and August 26. At the time of the Russian Revolution, the Communists took the icon from the Cathedral of the Assumption and placed it in the Tretiakov Art Gallery, where it is now on display.

V.M. *Vir magnificus*—great man.

VOCAL PRAYER. The form of prayer that is a "conversation" with God, or the angels and saints, and is formed in words or equivalent symbols of expression. More technically, vocal prayer involves the use of some set formulas, since it is assumed that even when a person prays mentally he necessarily employs some form of at least internal speech. So that in practice the distinction between mental and vocal prayer is more a matter of emphasis, whether one's own unrehearsed sentiments predominate (mental prayer) or a person rather employs verbal expressions that are not, at the time, the immediate product of communication with God (vocal prayer). (Etym. Latin *vocalis*, speaking, talking; from *vox*, voice.)

VOCATION. A call from God to a distinctive state of life, in which the person can reach holiness. The Second Vatican Council made it plain that there is a "Universal call [*vocatio*] to holiness in the Church" (*Lumen Gentium,* 39). (Etym. Latin *vocatio*, a calling, summoning; from *vocare*, to call.)

VOLTO SANTO. Holy face. One of several relics, honored by the faithful as bearing an imprint of the face of Christ. The most famous is Veronica's veil, or simply the Veronica. More widely publicized is the Holy Shroud, preserved at Turin since 1578, believed to be the winding sheet in which the body of Christ was wrapped after the Crucifixion (Matthew 27:59).

VOLUNTARIETY. Will power or the activity of the human will in desiring, choosing, or loving some real or apparent good. On our side, voluntariety is the response of the free will to God's grace and the reason for supernatural merit when the action is morally good and performed in the state of grace. It is also the cause of sin when the will deliberately chooses to do something contrary to the known will of God. Degrees of voluntariety are one of the factors that determine the extent of merit for good actions, and the extent of guilt for sinful actions.

VOLUNTARISM. The doctrine of the primacy of the will. This takes on a variety of forms: 1. that in God his will takes precedence over his intellect, with the result that truth and goodness are what they are because God wants them that way (Duns Scotus); 2. that one's will, including one's freedom, is what makes that person distinctively human (St. Augustine); 3. that the world is the representation of the will, a blind and aimless cosmic power (Schopenhauer); 4. that each person's free will determines for the individual what is morally good or bad (Kant); 5. that what mainly constitutes a human person is his or her lifetime exercise of free will (Existentialism). (Etym. Latin *voluntarius*, at one's pleasure, intentional, freely desired.)

VOLUNTARY DOUBT. An uncertainty of mind totally induced by the will, when a person withholds assent even in the presence of sufficient or prudentially adequate evidence.

VOTE, ECCLESIASTICAL. In order to be valid, a vote cast in an ecclesiastical election, e.g., for a major superior in a religious institute, must be truly free and secret. It is not truly free if an elector is either directly or indirectly led to cast his or her vote through grave fear or deceit for a certain person or for several persons.

VOTIVE CANDLES. Candles burned before some statue or shrine to give honor to Our Lord, Our Lady, or one of the saints. The word "votive" goes back to the ancient custom of lighting candles in fulfillment of some private vow (*votum*).

VOTIVE MASS. A Mass offered in honor of some mystery of the faith, or the Blessed Virgin, or of a saint or all the saints, but not in the liturgical calendar for that day. Votive Masses, with some exceptions, may be offered on any ordinary ferial day in the year, outside of Lent and Advent, and on other days that do not require the Mass of the day to be said. In general, votive Masses may be taken from among those listed as votive in the Roman Missal or from any other Mass of the year. (Etym. Latin *votivus*, from *votum*, vow, vote.)

VOTIVE OFFERING. Any object offered to God or in honor of a saint as an act of appreciation for some favor received, in petition for a favor asked for, and hence the name, in discharge of a vow (*votum*) or promise made. The votive offering may be a sum of money, or a shrine, or sacred vessel, or jewel, or sculpture or anything that reflects the sentiments of the donor as an act of sacrifice.

VOTIVE OFFICE. Formerly the privilege of saying another Divine Office than the one proper for the day. The privilege was abolished in 1911, with the exception of substituting the Office of the Blessed Virgin on Saturdays that were not already important feast days. But even this option has been revoked since the revision of the Liturgy of the Hours after the Second Vatican Council.

VOW. A free, deliberate promise made to God to do something that is good and that is more pleasing to God than its omission would be. The one vowing must realize that a special sin is committed by violating the promise. A vow binds under pain of sin (grave or slight) according to the intention of the one taking the vow. If one vows with regard to grave matter, one is presumed to intend to bind oneself under pain of serious sin. Vows enhance the moral value of human actions on several counts. They unite the soul to God by a new bond of religion, and so the acts included under the vow become also acts of religion. Hence they are more meritorious. By taking a vow, a person surrenders to God the moral freedom of acting otherwise, like the one who not only gives at times the fruit of the tree, but gives up the tree itself. And vows forestall human weakness, since they do not leave matters to the indecision or caprice of the moment. Their very purpose is to invoke divine grace to sustain one's resolution until the vow expires or, in the case of perpetual vows, even until death. (Etym. Latin *vovere,* to pledge, promise.)

VOW OF CHASTITY. The vow by which a person freely gives up the right to marriage, and adds the obligation of the virtue of religion to the duty of abstaining from all voluntary indulgence of sexual pleasure.

VOW OF HOSPITALITY. See HOSPITALITY.

VOW OF OBEDIENCE. The voluntary binding of oneself under oath to obey superiors in a religious institute, or a confessor, or spiritual guide. By this means a person is more permanently and securely united with God's saving will. Speaking of religious, the Second Vatican Council declares: "Moved by the Holy Spirit, they subject themselves in faith to those who hold God's place, their superiors. Through them they are led to serve all their brothers in Christ, just as Christ ministered to his brothers in submission to the Father and laid down his life for the redemption of many. They are thus bound more closely to the Church's service and they endeavor to attain to the measure of the stature of the fullness of Christ" (*Decree on Renewal of Religious Life,* 14). In some institutes of perfection a promise of obedience is taken instead of a formal vow.

VOW OF POVERTY. The vow by which a person freely gives up the ownership, or at least the independent use and administration, of temporal goods.

V. REV. Very Reverend.

V.T. *Vetus Testamentum*—Old Testament.

VULGATE. The Latin translation of the Bible, chiefly the work of St. Jerome, and commissioned by Pope St. Damasus I in 382. In time it became the standard in the Church, but by the sixteenth century several hundred editions were in print, with numerous variants. The Council of Trent declared that the Vulgate "is to be held authentic in public readings, disputations, sermons and exposition" and ordered its careful revision. This decree means that the Vulgate is the official biblical text of the Church. More than once revised, it was the Scripture text used by the First and Second Vatican Councils. (Etym. Latin *vulgata* [editio], "the popular [edition]"; from *vulgatus,* common, popular; from *vulgare,* to make commonly known; from *vulgus,* common people.)

W

WAGE. Just payment for services rendered. It implies at least an implicit contract beforehand between the employer and the one employed. Wages are often treated in the Bible. The first recorded biblical reference is in the bargaining between Laban and his nephew Jacob (Genesis 29:30). Christ used the notion of wages in his teaching, e.g., the vineyard laborers (Matthew 20:1–16). The idea of wages is spiritualized in St. Paul, e.g., "the wage of sin is death"; compared with the reward of virtue, "the present given by God is eternal life in Christ Jesus our Lord" (Romans 6:23).

WAGERING. See BETTING.

WAKE. A watch or vigil. The term was originally applied to the all-night vigil in Anglo-Saxon times before certain major holidays. By the sixteenth century it was used of the holiday itself, and of the fair held to honor a local saint. In some countries, e.g., Ireland, a wake is the watch over the body of the deceased before burial. And more commonly a wake is the period, one or two days before the funeral, when mourners may visit the body of the deceased and offer their condolences to the bereaved. The Church now provides for a liturgical service, if so desired, during the wake. It is called Vigil for the Deceased.

WALDENSES. A sect that arose in France in the twelfth century. Its name is derived from Peter Waldo (Pierre Valdez) of Lyons, who died in 1217. He took a vow of poverty and soon gathered a large following, mainly of persons who were scandalized at the pomp and wealth of the medieval Church. From protests against luxury they attacked Catholic doctrine: rejecting the authority of the Pope, denying Purgatory, claiming that laymen could absolve, and saying that sinful priests could not validly offer Mass or administer sacraments. Condemned by Pope Lucius III in 1184, they became a threat to civil order and were opposed by political rulers. They were among the principal forerunners of the Protestant Reformation and are still organized and active, primarily in Italy, France, Spain, and Switzerland.

WALSINGHAM, OUR LADY OF. The most famous of England's shrines to the Blessed Virgin, near Norfolk in Anglia. As a place of pilgrimage, it dates from the eleventh century, when a noble widow built a replica of the Holy House of Nazareth on English soil in response to her dreams of such a request from the Mother of God. This first chapel, paneled in wood and lighted by candles, was a Marian shrine for four hundred years. A Lady's Chapel was built to enclose the small house, and in the thirteenth century a priory church was added to accommodate the Augustinian canons who serviced the shrine. Thousands began to flock to this shrine by the sea—including kings and the historical great—to revere Mary; it was because of Walsingham that England was titled "Our Lady's Dowry." But in 1538 Walsingham, by royal edict, was totally destroyed. Mary's image was burned and in time the shrine was forgotten except by a few loyal patrons of Mary. Three hundred years passed and all that remained was a legend. However, in the nineteenth century, archaeologists excavating near the site discovered remnants of the holy shrine. Old documents were searched and the Slipper Chapel (on the site of Walsingham) was reborn. In 1897 a new statue duplicating the old, from pictures, was enshrined in the parish church, later to be taken to the restored Slipper Chapel. The famous Lady's Chapel, the rich gold and silver gifts, and the priory are all lacking, but Walsingham's history has been revived. It coincided with John Henry Newman's appearance on the English religious scene. Today pilgrims come from all parts of England, many on foot walking the "penitential mile."

WAR. Conflict of armed force in which one nation or part of a nation seeks to impose its will on another nation or part of a nation. The basic premise of war is that every right is coercible. Thus a state has the right to use force if necessary to defend just rights or to exact reparation for the violation of rights by another state. Another premise is that since no supernational organization exists with the capacity of enforcing its just decisions, with acceptance by all nations, the right of coercibility can be exercised directly by the aggrieved state itself. (Etym. Old High German *werra,* confusion, strife.)

WAR OF AGGRESSION. Unjust military attack on the independence, territory, or any other rights of one nation or part of a nation by another political power.

WASHING OF THE FEET. An action of Christ at the Last Supper (John 13:1–15), when he washed the feet of his disciples to teach them humility as a condition for the practice of charity. This was believed by some early Christians to have been a sacrament of the New Law. As part of the liturgy on Holy Thursday, following the Homily of the Mass, modern popes have performed this ceremony in St. Peter's, washing the feet of a certain number of poor men chosen to participate in the Maundy Thursday liturgy. The ritual is an optional part of the regular Holy Thursday liturgy.

WASHING OF THE HANDS. Liturgical washing of the fingers by a priest before Mass and after Mass, which is not prescribed; and washing the fingers at the Offertory, which is part of the Eucharistic liturgy. It symbolizes the purity of conscience expected of the celebrant at Mass and the respect due to the Eucharistic elements handled during Mass. The hands are also washed by a bishop after using chrism in confirmation and holy orders, and by a priest after using the holy oils at baptism and anointing of the sick.

WASHINGTON, THE NATIONAL SHRINE OF THE IMMACULATE CONCEPTION. Church dedicated to the Immaculate Conception, who was declared patroness of the United States by the Provincial Council of Baltimore in 1846. The project for the shrine was begun in 1914, after Pope St. Pius X approved the plans, which originated with Bishop Shahan, fourth rector of the Catholic University. Pope Benedict XV sent a mosaic of Murillo's *Immaculate Conception* in 1919, in time for the cornerstone laying by Cardinal Gibbons in 1920. Popes Pius XI and XII sent further favors to the shrine, visited by Cardinal Pacelli in 1936, before his elevation to the papacy. The main church was solemnly dedicated in 1959. More than fifty chapels have been installed since the dedication. The campanile houses a fifty-six-bell carillon. With a seating capacity of six thousand persons, the shrine is one of the largest religious buildings in the world. All the American dioceses and numerous religious communities and organizations have contributed to its erection. Over one million persons visit the shrine each year. Pope John Paul II addressed several thousand religious women at the shrine (October 7, 1979) to close his seven-day visit of the United States.

WATER, BLESSED. Besides the ordinary holy water used in the Church's liturgy, there are several other blessings of water approved by the Church. Each has a history of remarkable favors, spiritual and temporal, granted to those who use such water with faith and devotion. Among the best known are water blessed in honor of the Blessed Virgin and St. Torellus, St. Vincent Ferrer, St. Raymond Nonnatus, St. Albert, St. Ignatius Loyola, and St. Vincent de Paul.

WATER, LITURGICAL USE OF. A symbol of exterior and interior purity, water is used in the administration of baptism, to signify the cleansing from sin; at Mass a few drops of water are mingled with the wine to indicate the union of Christ with the faithful and the blood and water that flowed from the side of Christ on Calvary; sprinkling with holy water is practiced before Mass and during Mass on special occasions (e.g., Easter Vigil), at weddings, funerals, and other functions.

WAX. The viscous or heat-sensitive solid substance used for candles and other lamps in church and for liturgical services. For centuries beeswax was to be used in the service of the sanctuary as far as possible. And even now candles made of 51 (or more) per cent beeswax are preferable. But the Church's regulation, since the Second Vatican Council, has been less demanding. According to the directives to episcopal conferences, the materials used are suitable "provided they are generally considered worthy and dignified and properly fulfill a sacred purpose" (*Enchiridion Documentorum Instaurationis Liturgicae,* 1664).

WEALTH. The ownership of a great quantity of material possessions or resources. The Church's teaching on wealth is that: 1. riches of themselves do not help to gain eternal life, but are rather an obstacle to salvation; 2. the rich should have a salutary fear in the light of what Christ said about those who make evil use of their wealth; 3. the practice of charity is a commandment, and all the more pressing as a person has a great deal of this world's goods. The Second Vatican Council added the strong injunction that the more wealthy nations and societies are to share with the less developed peoples of the world (*Constitution on the Church in the Modern World,* Part Two, III, 69).

WEDDING. The ceremony at which a marriage takes place, and the religious or social festivities associated with the ceremony. (Etym. Old English *weddian,* to engage [to do something], marry.)

WEDNESDAY. Named after the Anglo-Saxon god Woden, the fourth day of the week is consecrated by the Church for devotion to St. Joseph.

WESTERN CHURCH. See LATIN CHURCH.

WESTERN SCHISM. Widespread division in Catholic unity caused by rival claims to the Papacy. In the Western Schism (1378–1417) there were two and later three claimants to the Papacy at the same time. The election of Urban VI (1318–89) was challenged *post factum* by thirteen of his cardinal electors, who in 1378 chose Clement VII as Avignon Pope in his stead. After thirty years of fruitless efforts to settle the rift, a council of prelates at Pisa in 1409 sought to depose the Roman and Avignon pontiffs and elected Alexander V. Finally the schism was healed at the Council of Constance (1414–18). Gregory XII, the Roman Pope, resigned; the antipopes Benedict XII of Avignon and John XXIII of Pisa were deposed, and Martin V (1368–1431) was chosen to replace them.

WEXFORD. Shrine of Our Lady's Isle

offshore, in southeastern Ireland. Known as the Church of the Bright Plain since the seventh century, it was the place of a planned massacre by Oliver Cromwell in Reformation times, where many of the faithful were killed while attending High Mass. The shrine was destroyed except for a small statue of Our Lady. A church was rebuilt on the mainland, but the original site remains in ruins, although it has been visited by thousands.

WHEAT AND GRAPES. An emblem of the Eucharist. With the wheat is often represented the Host, of which it is the ingredient, as well as the Chalice of Christ's Blood, to which the substance of the wine from the grapes has been changed. Artistic ingenuity joined with liturgical accuracy finds this symbol used in many forms in ecclesiastical art, going back to early Christian times.

WHITE. The liturgical color for all feasts of the Trinity, Our Lord (except his Cross and Passion), the Blessed Virgin, angels, all saints except martyrs, and on Sundays during Easter Season; also in the celebration of the sacraments that do not imply penance or the remission of sins. White is a symbol of joy, purity, innocence, holiness, and glory. Pope St. Pius V (reigned 1566–72) prescribed that the ordinary papal attire be white.

WHITE CANONS. The Premonstratensians, so called White Canons because of the color of their habit.

WHITE FATHERS. The Society of Missionaries of Africa, founded in Algiers in 1868 by Archbishop Charles Lavigerie (1825–92). Its members are priests and brothers, forming a society of common life, whose principal apostolate is the evangelization of Africa. A community of White Sisters was also founded by Lavigerie in 1869 and reorganized by Pope St. Pius X in 1909.

WHITE FRIARS. Carmelite friars so called because of their white habit and scapular. The term is also applied to Premonstratensians and White Canons.

WHITE LADIES. Popular name of a number of communities of women religious, notably the Sisters of the Presentation of Mary, the Magdalens, and Cistercian nuns.

WHITE MONKS. Cistercian monks, so named white monks because of the color of their habit.

WHITE RUSSIAN BYZANTINES. The Byelorussians, who returned to Roman Catholic unity in the seventeenth century. The liturgical language is Old Slavonic. They have an apostolic visitator residing in Rome.

WHITE SCAPULAR. See SCAPULAR.

WHITE SISTERS. The Society of Missionaries of Africa, founded in Algiers by Archbishop Lavigerie in 1869, and the Congregation of the Daughters of the Holy Ghost, founded in Brittany in 1706.

WHOLE CHRIST. Christ in the fullness of his human and divine natures present in the Holy Eucharist. This means that the same Christ numerically is now present in heaven and in the Blessed Sacrament. There is nothing objectively lacking in the Eucharist of what constitutes Christ. He is there entirely. The only deficiency is the subjective one on the part of the believer, who cannot perceive him with the senses or even reason to his presence, but can only assent on faith that what seems to be bread and wine is really Jesus Christ. Moreover, Christ is present in his entirety in every portion of either species after it is divided. He is also present in his entirety in every spot of either species before it is divided. This does not mean that Christ is present a hundred or a thousand times in a Host (or the chalice) before it is divided, nor that he somehow divides his presence on the thousands of altars of the Catholic world. It is one and the same Christ, wholly present wherever and equally present everywhere.

WHORE (biblical). A woman regularly guilty of adultery or fornication, especially for money. In early biblical times selling daughters into prostitution was not uncommon. It is reprobated in the Old Testament (Leviticus 19:29). Genesis makes it clear that capital punishment was the penalty for whoredom (Genesis 38:24–25).

WIDOW. A woman who does not remarry after the death of her husband. Widows have been the special object of the Church's care since apostolic times (Acts 6). The early Church formed bodies of such consecrated women. St. Paul's teaching is very detailed about widows who are older, while he recommends that younger widows remarry (I Timothy 5:3–16). The Council of Trent declared that objectively widowhood (as celibacy) is more commendable than remarriage (Denzinger 1810). Each case, however, must be judged on its own merits.

WIFE. A woman married to a man. Her duties and privileges are treated at length by St. Paul, who stresses the mutual responsibility of husband and wife (I Corinthians 7; Ephesians 5; Colossians 3). The Second Vatican Council developed these principles of revelation especially in the *Pastoral Constitution on the Church in the Modern World* (47–52).

WILL. The power of the human soul, or of a spiritual being, which tends toward a good or away from an evil recognized by the intellect. It is basically a rational appetite with several functions, namely the ability to intend, choose, desire, hope, consent, hate, love, and enjoy.

WILL OF GOD. In spiritual theology the manifest designs of God for a person's whole life or for any part of that life, which the person is to accept though not naturally appealing, or surrender though naturally desirable, or do whether he or she likes it or not. The will of God can be known to some extent by the light of natural reason, more fully and with greater demands on human generosity through revelation, and most clearly from the teachings of the Church that Christ founded precisely to lead the human race to its final destiny. Moreover, frequent prayer for divine guidance, daily reflection on one's moral conduct, and when necessary the counsel of a prudent adviser are part of God's ordinary providence in showing his will to those who seriously want to serve him as they should.

WILL TO BELIEVE. In Catholic theology the doctrine that in order to assent to God's revealed word a person must receive supernatural grace for the will. The Church calls it "the devout readiness to believe," *pius credulitatis affectus* (Denzinger 375). Also in the psychology of religion the innate tendency of the human will to believe in other people as a precondition for social living. On a higher level the willingness to believe in God beyond all human calculation and with phenomenal results in the achievement of personal sanctity and service of humanity.

WIMPLE. A cloth (generally white) framing the face and drawn into folds under the chin; headdress once worn by laywomen, especially as a protection outdoors. It is now worn by some women religious.

WINDING SHEET. See HOLY SHROUD.

WINE. The fermented juice of the grape, used in the Mass and changed by the words of consecration into the blood of Christ. According to the Church's legislation, "The wine used to celebrate the Eucharist must be made from the fruit of the vine (Luke 22:18), natural and pure, unmixed with anything else . . . The wine must not be allowed to go sour" (*Ordo Missae*, April 6, 1969, numbers 284, 286).

WINEPRESS (biblical). A trough lined with cement or stone in which grapes would be deposited to be converted into wine (Judges 6:11). A hole in the bottom permitted the juice to escape into a vat below. Men trod on the grapes barefooted, holding onto overhead ropes. Winepresses are mentioned in both Old and New Testaments (Matthew 21:33). One of the symbolic predictions of Christ's Passion and Death (Isaiah 63:2).

WINGED LION. An emblem of St. Mark, who wrote especially of the royal dignity of Christ, beginning his Gospel with the account of St. John the Baptist, "the voice of one crying in the wilderness." St. Mark is also the writer of excellence about the Resurrection of Christ, traditionally symbolized by the lion.

WINGED MAN. A symbol assigned to St. Matthew the Evangelist, who opens his Gospel with the genealogy of Christ, "son of David, son of Abraham," stressing Christ's Israelite descent and fulfillment of the Messianic prophecies.

WINGED OX. A symbol of St. Luke the Evangelist, anticipated by Ezekiel. The ox, recognized as the animal of sacrifice, was applied to St. Luke because his Gospel emphasizes the atonement made by Christ's sacrifice of himself on the Cross.

WISDOM. The intellectual virtue concerning the first or highest causes of all things. It is also the actual possession of such knowledge.

WISDOM. Book of the Septuagint Old Testament placed in the Vulgate and the Church's biblical canon. It is called deuterocanonical because, found in the Greek but not the Hebrew, it was not included in the Jewish canon of the Bible, drawn up by the Pharisees at the close of the first century of the Christian era. In Syriac it is called "The Book of the Great Wisdom of Solomon," but the author was more likely an Alexandrian Jew, living toward the beginning of the third century B.C. The book can be divided into two main parts, separated by the famous prayer for wisdom (chapter 19). Part One is an exhortation to rulers to observe justice and wisdom (chapters 1–8). Part Two extols the advantages of wisdom, as seen in the way God dealt with his own people compared with the unwisdom of the idolatrous nations. Wisdom means knowledge that is so perfect it directs the will to obey God's commands. In God wisdom is identified with his Word, a foreshadowing of the revelation of the Trinity.

WISDOM, SEAT OF. An emblem of the Blessed Virgin used symbolically in the Litany of Loreto. She is the Mother of "Christ who is the power of God and the Wisdom of God" (I Corinthians 1). Moreover, she had the fullness of the gift of wisdom.

WITNESS. One who can give evidence based on personal and immediate knowledge of a fact, event, or experience. The Christian concept of witness adds to the popular notion the idea of a religious experience to which a believer testifies by his life, words, and actions, and thus gives inspiration and example to others by his testimony. Implicit in Christian witness is also the element of courage in giving testimony, either because others are not favorably disposed or because they are openly hostile to the message of faith being proposed.

WOLF. A symbol of St. Francis of Assisi (1181–1226). Sharing symbolism with the beast of Gubbio tamed by the saint is the lark, whose song cheered the dying Francis. St. Francis loved all nature as God's creation and so is represented symbolically by birds and beasts as well as by a leaning church which Francis saved from falling by his reforms.

WOMEN, ORDINATION OF. A speculative question that has become highly controversial since the Second Vatican Council, as to whether women could be ordained to the Catholic priesthood and episcopacy. In 1975, Pope Paul VI declared women's ineligibility for the ministerial priesthood (*Acta Apostolicae Sedis,* 67, 265). And in the following year the Sacred Congregation for the Doctrine of the Faith reaffirmed the fact and gave the reasons why this practice has a normative character. "In the fact of conferring priestly ordination only on men, it is a question of unbroken tradition throughout the history of the Church, universal in the East and in the West, and alert to suppress abuses immediately." Having stated the fact, the Holy See went on to clarify this teaching. Since the priesthood is a sacrament, it is a sign that is not only effective but should be intelligible to the faithful: "When Christ's role in the Eucharist is to be expressed sacramentally, there would not be this 'natural resemblance' which must exist between Christ and His minister if the role of Christ were not taken by a man" (Octo-

ber 15, 1976). On his visit to the United States, Pope John Paul II reaffirmed "the Church's traditional decision to call men to the priesthood, and not to call women" (October 4, 1979).

WOMEN'S LIBERATION. The movement in modern times to free women from the discrimination to which they have been subject in civil society and in political legislation. As such, it has two discernible roots, one sociological and the other ideological. On the sociological level is the recognized fact that women in all parts of the world are coming more and more into their own, to find their places alongside of men, making their distinctive contribution in the professions, in education, and in the sciences. The other root is not so much factual as ideological, and stands at variance with Christian principles. It argues from a massive discrimination of women by men, and urges women to revolt against men. The best known proponent of this ideology was Nikolai Lenin (1874–1924), who urged that "the success of a revolution depends upon the degree of participation by women." On these terms, women's liberation is simply part of the larger struggle for the eventual creation of a classless society.

WONDER-WORKING. Applied either to persons or objects, e.g., a shrine or relic, it means the ability to perform miracles. Certain saints, already in their lifetime, e.g., St. Gregory Thaumaturgus (213–70), and others since their death, e.g., St. Anthony of Padua (1195–1231) were outstanding wonder-workers. So, too, such shrines as Our Lady of Lourdes and relics of many saints are outstanding for the authenticated miracles worked through their intercession.

WORD, THE. See LOGOS.

WORD AND DEED. Speech and action as objects of moral responsibility, whether of praise or blame. Between the two, deeds are more important, as testified by Christ (Matthew 7:21).

WORD OF GOD. See LOGOS; PREACHING; REVELATION.

WORDS OF ABSOLUTION. The essential words pronounced by a priest when he absolves a penitent in the sacrament of penance, namely, "I absolve you from your sins, in the name of the Father, and of the Son, and of the Holy Spirit."

WORDS OF INSTITUTION. The words of Christ at the Last Supper, recorded by the synoptic Gospels (Matthew 26:26–29; Mark 14:22–25; Luke 22:19–21); and St. Paul (I

Corinthians 11:23–29). Their essential features are: 1. Christ separately consecrated bread and wine; 2. over the bread he said "This is my body" and over the wine "This is the chalice of my blood"; 3. the elements of bread and wine were thus changed into the living Christ; 4. he empowered the Apostles and their successors to perform the same consecrating action; 5. he bade his followers to partake of the Eucharist; 6. at the Last Supper, Christ offered his life to the Heavenly Father, but the actual death resulting from the sacrifice was to take place on the following day on Calvary.

WORK. Continued exertion directed to some recognized purpose or end. The exertion may be physical or mental, and the purpose may be determined by the one who works or by someone else, who in turn may have his or her own motive for assigning the task. Christianity does not look upon work as demeaning or evil, as though leisure were more worthy of human dignity. Work ennobles a person's character and assimilates one to the Savior. "We believe by faith that through the homage of work offered to God man is associated with the redemptive work of Jesus Christ, whose labor with his hands at Nazareth greatly ennobled the dignity of work. This is the source of every man's duty to work loyally, as well as his right to work; moreover, it is the duty of society to see to it that, according to the prevailing circumstances, all citizens have the opportunity of finding employment" (Second Vatican Council, *Constitution on the Church in the Modern World*, III, 67).

WORLD. The term has two distinct meanings in revelation and Catholic doctrine. It is generally identified with the visible universe, *kosmos*, in the biblical Greek, and *mundus*, in the Latin Vulgate. As such it is the world of creation, made by God, and therefore totally subject to his divine will. But there is also the world of sin, estranged from God as the creation of man's self-will. It is at variance with the divine will and is what Christ meant when he said, "I am not praying for the world" (John 17:9).

WORLDLINESS. The mental attitude of a person who is guided by secular ideas rather than by religious principles, and whose primary concern is for well-being in this life and not in the life to come.

WORLD MIND. A pantheistic theory espoused in Vedanta and Buddhist idealism and later by certain Moslem pantheists against whom St. Thomas Aquinas defended the individuality of each human being's own intellect and personally responsible will. Although variously described, the World Mind philosophy postulates only one spiritual substance in the universe, also called the Absolute. Accordingly, what appears to be a real distinction between God and creation is an illusion. Hence also the name, Non-Dualistic Illusionism, by which the theory of a World Mind is sometimes called.

WORLD SOUL. The pantheistic theory of an intelligent, animating, indwelling principle of the universe. It is conceived either as its organizing or integrating cause, or as the source of its activity, on the analogy of the human soul as the principle of life in a human being. It is familiar in the philosophy of Stoicism, Neo-Platonism, and the immanentism of Giordano Bruno (1548–1600).

WORLD WITHOUT END. The terminal phrase of many prayers, equivalent to "eternal" or "everlasting." In the doxology of the *Gloria Patri* it means that God, who has always existed, is now being praised by a human being who hopes to continue praising God forever in heaven.

WORSHIP. Acknowledgment of another's worth, dignity, or superior position. In religion, worship is given either to God, and then it is adoration, or to the angels and saints, and it is called veneration. Divine worship actually includes three principal acts, namely adoration (or the recognition of God's infinite perfection), prayer or the asking for divine help, and sacrifice or the offering of something precious to God. Worship as veneration also has three principal forms, whereby the angels and saints are honored for their sanctity, asked to intercede before the divine Majesty, and imitated in their love and service of God. (Etym. Old English *weorthscipe*, honor, dignity, reverence: *weorth*, worth + ship.)

WRITTEN WORD. Title of the Bible, originally applied among the Jews only to Ketubim, the Hagiographa or writings. These are the Psalms, Proverbs, Job, Song of Songs, Ruth, Lamentations, Ecclesiastes, Esther, Daniel, Ezra-Nehemiah, and I and II Chronicles.

WRONG. Not right; erroneous. Applied to human actions that deviate from the direction they should be taking, i.e., leading a person to his final, heavenly destiny. Wrong is the same as evil but has the notion of being contrary to the truth, whereas evil is contrary to the good.

WYCLIFISM. A heretical movement founded by John Wyclif (1328–84), parish priest of Lutterworth, Leicestershire, in England. His doctrines were disseminated by the "poor priests" who taught the people that authority to rule depends on moral virtue, the Bible alone contains divine revelation, preaching is more important than the Mass and the sacraments, and the Pope has no primacy of jurisdiction. Condemned posthumously by the Council of Constance, Wyclifism persisted until the Reformation. Also known as Lollardism, it had its main impact in Bohemia, where John Hus used Wyclif's idea as a basis of religious belief and made deep inroads in the Catholic Church in Germany as a prelude to Protestantism.

X Y Z

XC., XCS. *Christus*—Christ (first, middle, and last letters of the Greek name).

YAHWEH. See JEHOVAH.

YEAR, ECCLESIASTICAL. See CALENDAR, CHRISTIAN.

YELLOW. Liturgical color in common use from the twelfth to the sixteenth centuries, and now occasionally worn in France. Yellow occurs elsewhere, however, as a substitute for white or an imitation of gold.

YOKE. A wooden frame used to join two oxen in a team (Deuteronomy 21:3). Metaphorically, it suggested subjection or slavish control and the removal of a yoke, freedom. "When you win your freedom, you shall shake his yoke from your neck" (Genesis 27:40). Christ assured the faithful: "My yoke is easy" (Matthew 11:29).

YULE. A Teutonic term identified with the twelve-day Scandinavian feast of pre-Christian origin celebrating the turn of the year. In Old English it corresponded to the season of December and January. Later, in Anglo-Saxon countries, it was associated with the season of Christmas. Found in such combinations as Yuletide, Yule greetings, generally in contexts where the Christian meaning of Christmas is missing or consciously ignored. (Etym. Middle English *yole, yule,* Old English *geol, geohhol,* originally a twelve-day heathen feast, from common Germanic *jehwla, jejwla.*)

ZACCHAEUS. A wealthy tax collector who was so eager to see Jesus as he passed through Jericho that he climbed a tree to get a better vantage point. He was jubilant when Jesus greeted him and expressed a desire to visit his home. Because of the man's dubious moral reputation, the crowd murmured at this friendly gesture, but it achieved quick results. Zacchaeus promptly promised to give half his property to the poor (Luke 19:1–10). (Etym. Greek *zacchaios;* Hebrew *zakkai,* pure.)

ZACHARIAH. See ZECHARIAH.

ZACHARIAS. See ZECHARIAH.

ZAMBOANGA (shrine). A center of Marian devotion on Mindanao, a southern island of the Philippines. Our Lady's white shrine was part of the fortress wall of the town. Christians would come to pray at this shrine to invoke Mary's help to subdue the fierce hatred of the Moslem Moros who lived near Zamboanga. These natives sent each year a chosen Moro into the Christian crowd that came to celebrate their holy day near the shrine, commissioning him to kill as many Christians as he could, being ready to die himself as a result of his act if captured. The shrine, now a place of special devotion in the Archdiocese of Zamboanga, was erected in 1910.

ZAPOPAN, OUR LADY OF. Marian shrine of Jalisco, ten miles west of Guadalajara, in Mexico. Also known as La Chappareta or The Queen of Jalisco, its main feature is a twelve-inch statue of Mary, brought here by a Franciscan friar in 1530. Some six thousand Indians were converted within a week after a strange light encircled the statue of the Madonna. Numerous miracles are reported, especially during the pilgrimages on August 15 and September 8.

ZEAL. Love in action. The strong emotion of spirit, based on deep affection, that seeks to obtain what is loved or to remove what stands in the way. In religious terms, zeal is manifested by an impelling desire to advance the Kingdom of Christ, sanctify souls, and advance the glory of God by making him better known and loved, and thus more faithfully served. (Etym. Latin *zelus,* eagerness; from Greek *zēlos.*)

ZEALOT. 1. a Jewish member of a radical, violent group bitterly opposed to Roman domination of Palestine. The group was especially active during the century in which Christ lived on earth. The present-day use of the word "zealot," to mean a fanatical enthusiast, derives from this group's name; 2. Simon was one of the Twelve Apostles. He was referred to in the New Testament as Simon the Zealot (Luke 6:15) to distinguish him from Simon Peter. He had probably been a member of the Jewish group until his conversion to Christianity. (Etym. Latin *zelotes;* from Greek *zēlōtēs;* from *zēlos,* zeal.)

ZECHARIAH. A common name in the Bible; between twenty-five to thirty persons are so called. Variant spellings are Zacharias and Zachariah. Three persons are mainly identified with this name: 1. the father of John the Baptist; he was married to Elizabeth, a kinswoman of Mary the Virgin (Luke 1:5). He was rendered speechless when he doubted the message of the angel Gabriel that his wife would conceive in her old age (Luke 1:22). At John's circumcision ceremony Zechariah made a prophecy that Israel's Messiah would soon appear and this newborn son of Elizabeth's would "go before the Lord to prepare the way for him" (Luke 1:59–76); 2. a Jewish martyr, son of Jehoiada, in the Old Testament; he was stoned to death for denouncing the faithlessness of the people (II Chronicles 24:20–22). Jesus referred to him when he spoke of the slaughter of the prophets "from the blood of Abel to the blood of Zechariah" (Luke 11:50–51); 3. a book in the Old Testament named after the eleventh Minor Prophet. This Zechariah was a contemporary of the prophet Haggai. Both wrote in the sixth century B.C.

ZECHARIAH, BOOK OF. Prophetic writing of the Old Testament, containing, for its length, the largest number of predictions about Christ. Three visions concern the foundation of the Messianic kingdom. The fourth makes the promise "to raise my servant Baruch" (3–9b). The fourth through the sixth visions treat of Christ the priest and king. An address stresses the keeping of the commandments, and the motive power of the Messianic prophecies (7–8). The rest of the book is mainly two burdens: one over Syria, Phoenicia, and the Philistines; and the other over Israel. In the first is the prophecy of Palm Sunday (9:9–10), and the purchase of Haceldama for the treason money of Judas, who betrayed Christ. In the second (12) is a promise of the restoration of Jerusalem. The author calls himself "son of Berechiah," but he is most probably not the prophet.

ZEITGEIST. Spirit of the times. Used especially to explain why many people are so skeptical of the supernatural and so demanding that Christian faith and morals conform to the modern mentality.

ZEPHANIAH. Author of the ninth book of the Minor Prophets. The son of Cushi and a descendant of King Hezekiah, he lived in the seventh century B.C. The emphasis in his writing was on the corruption of the people of Judah during the Assyrian rule and the promise of Yahweh's punishment. "Seek integrity, seek humility" was Zephaniah's theme. "You may perhaps find shelter on the day of the anger of Yahweh" (Zephaniah 2:3).

ZION. One of the hills on which Jerusalem stood. Used as a fortress, it was captured by David and renamed the Citadel of David (II Samuel 5:7). It assumed a sacred character when he brought the Ark to Zion. Gradually the name spread until it was applied to all of Jerusalem (II Kings 19:21; Psalms 125, 126). Indeed, increasingly it was used to mean the Jewish faith (Isaiah 33:20); hence, the term Zionism for the modern movement to make Palestine the Jewish homeland. Also spelled Sion.

ZOCE, OUR LADY OF. Marian shrine set on a hill near Shanghai, China. The hill was owned by a General Zo, from whom the place received its name. In 1870 the Chinese, running wild, were ravishing the nearby countryside, and the little Catholic group at Zoce was saved only when a sudden storm dispersed the bandits. The Jesuit priest, Father Della Croce, and his flock attributed their escape to the Blessed Virgin, to whom they had never ceased to pray. In their gratitude they built a small chapel and installed in it a picture of Mary, Help of Christians. The shrine to Our Lady of Zoce became popular. In 1873, a larger church was necessary to accommodate the pilgrims. On the pinnacle of the new church spire, the twenty thousand who came yearly to the shrine could view a heroic size statue of the Virgin Mother and her Son. The City Council of Shanghai, composed of Christians and Buddhists, dedicated China to Mary under the title "Our Lady of Zoce." As late as 1953 over fifteen hundred people received Holy Communion there daily. The present status of the shrine is unknown.

ZUCCHETTO. A small round skullcap worn by prelates in the Catholic Church; white for the Pope, red for cardinals, purple for bishops, and black for abbots.

APPENDIX

THE CREDO
OF THE PEOPLE OF GOD

The Credo of the People of God was proclaimed by Pope Paul VI at the close of the Year of Faith on June 29, 1968. Its purpose was to offer the Christian world, after the Second Vatican Council, a profession of the principal articles of the Catholic faith. It is no mere summary, however, but a carefully assembled synthesis of those revealed truths which today are either most challenged or that especially need to be understood by the faithful. It incorporates all the familiar doctrines of the Nicene Creed but goes beyond them in occasionally updating their verbal expression and showing how these mysteries are to be lived by the Christian believer.

POPE PAUL VI

The Credo of the People of God
as published in *The Acts of the Apostolic See,* August 10, 1968

THE SOLEMN PROFESSION OF FAITH
pronounced by Pope Paul VI at St. Peter's Basilica,
June 30, 1968, at the end of the "Year of Faith," the
nineteenth centenary anniversary of the martyrdom
of Sts. Peter and Paul.

VENERABLE BROTHERS AND BELOVED SONS:

1. With this solemn liturgy we end the celebration of the nineteenth centenary of the martyrdom of the holy Apostles Peter and Paul, and thus close the Year of Faith. We dedicated it to the commemoration of the holy Apostles in order that we might give witness to our steadfast will to *guard the deposit*

of faith from corruption, that deposit which they transmitted to us, and to demonstrate again our intention of relating this same faith to life at this time when the Church must continue her pilgrimage in this world.

2. We feel it our duty to give public thanks to all who responded to our invitation by bestowing on the Year of Faith a splendid completeness through the deepening of their personal adhesion to the Word of God, through the renewal in various gatherings of the Profession of Faith, and through the testimony of a Christian life. To our brothers in the episcopate especially, and to all the faithful of the Holy Catholic Church, we express our appreciation and we grant our blessing.

3. Likewise we deem that we must fulfill the mandate entrusted by Christ to Peter, whose successor we are, the last in merit; namely, to confirm our brothers in the faith. With the awareness, certainly, of our human weakness, yet with all the strength impressed on our spirit by such a command, we shall accordingly make a Profession of Faith, pronounce a formula which begins with the word *Credo, I believe*. Without being strictly speaking a dogmatic definition, it repeats in substance, with some developments called for by the spiritual condition of our time, the Creed of Nicaea, the Creed of the immortal tradition of the Holy Church of God.

4. In making this profession, we are aware of the disquiet which agitates certain groups of men at the present time with regard to the faith. They do not escape the influence of a world being profoundly changed, in which so many truths are being denied outright or made objects of controversy. We see even Catholics allowing themselves to be seized by a kind of passion for change and novelty. The Church, most assuredly, has always the duty to carry on the effort to study more deeply and to present in a manner ever better adapted to successive generations the unfathomable mysteries of God, rich for all in fruits of salvation. But at the same time the greatest care must be taken, while fulfilling the indispensable duty of research, to do no injury to the truths of Christian doctrine. For that would be to give rise, as is unfortunately seen in these days, to disturbance and doubt in many faithful souls.

5. It is supremely important in this respect to recall that, beyond what is observable, analyzed by the work of the sciences, the intellect which God has given us reaches *that which is,* and not merely the subjective expression of the structures and development of consciousness. And, on the other hand, it is important to remember that the task of interpretation—of hermeneutics— is to try to understand and extricate, while respecting the word expressed, the sense conveyed by a text, and not to recreate, in some fashion, this sense in accordance with arbitrary hypotheses.

6. But above all, we place our unshakable confidence in the Holy Spirit, the soul of the Church, and in theological faith upon which rests the life of the Mystical Body. We know that souls await the word of the Vicar of Christ,

and we respond to that expectation with the instructions which we regularly give. But today we are given an opportunity to make a more solemn utterance.

7. On this day which is chosen to close the Year of Faith, on this Feast of the Blessed Apostles Peter and Paul, we have wished to offer to the Living God the homage of a Profession of Faith. And as once at Caesarea Philippi the Apostle Peter spoke on behalf of the Twelve to make a true confession, beyond human opinions, of Christ as Son of the Living God, so today his humble successor, pastor of the universal Church, raises his voice to give, on behalf of all the People of God, a firm witness to the divine truth entrusted to the Church to be announced to all nations.

We have wished our Profession of Faith to be to a high degree complete and explicit, in order that it may respond in a fitting way to the need of light felt by so many faithful souls, and by all those in the world to whatever spiritual family they belong, who are in search of the truth.

Therefore, to the glory of God Most Holy and of Our Lord Jesus Christ, trusting in the aid of the Blessed Virgin Mary and of the Holy Apostles Peter and Paul, for the profit and edification of the Church, in the name of all the pastors and all the faithful, we now pronounce this Profession of Faith, in full communion with you all, beloved brothers and sons.

PROFESSION OF FAITH

8. We believe in one only God, Father, Son and Holy Spirit, Creator of things visible such as this world in which our brief life passes, of things invisible such as the pure spirits which are also called angels, and Creator in each man of his spiritual and immortal soul.

9. We believe that this only God is absolutely one in His infinitely holy essence as also in all His perfections, in His omnipotence, His infinite knowledge, His providence, His will and His love. He is *He Who Is,* as He revealed to Moses; and He is *Love,* as the Apostle John teaches us: so that these two names, Being and Love, express ineffably the same divine reality of Him who has wished to make himself known to us, and who "dwelling in light inaccessible," is in himself above every name, above every thing and above every created intellect. God alone can give us right and full knowledge of this reality by revealing himself as Father, Son and Holy Spirit, in whose eternal life we are by grace called to share, here below in the obscurity of faith and after death in eternal light. The mutual bonds which eternally constitute the Three Persons, who are each one and the same Divine Being, are the blessed inmost life of God thrice holy, infinitely beyond all that we can conceive in human measure. We give thanks, however, to the Divine Goodness that very many believers can testify with us before men to the unity of God, even though they know not the mystery of the Most Holy Trinity.

10. We believe then in God who eternally begets the Son, in the Son, the Word

of God, who is eternally begotten, in the Holy Spirit, the uncreated Person, who proceeds from the Father and the Son as their eternal Love. Thus in the Three Divine Persons, *coaeternae sibi et coaequales,* the life and beatitude of God perfectly One superabound and are consummated in the supreme excellence and glory proper to uncreated Being, and always "there should be venerated unity in the Trinity and Trinity in the unity."

11. We believe in Our Lord Jesus Christ, who is the Son of God. He is the Eternal Word, born of the Father before time began, and consubstantial with the Father, *homoousios to Patri,* and through Him all things were made. He was incarnate of the Virgin Mary by the power of the Holy Spirit, and was made man: equal therefore to the Father according to His divinity, and inferior to the Father according to His humanity, and himself one, not by some impossible confusion of His natures, but by the unity of His person.

12. He dwelt among us, full of grace and truth. He proclaimed and established the Kingdom of God and made us know in himself the Father. He gave us His new commandment to love one another as He loved us. He taught us the way of the Beatitudes of the Gospel: poverty in spirit, meekness, suffering borne with patience, thirst after justice, mercy, purity of heart, will for peace, persecution suffered for justice sake. He suffered under Pontius Pilate, the Lamb of God bearing on himself the sins of the world, and He died for us on the Cross, saving us by His redeeming Blood. He was buried, and, of His own power, rose the third day, raising us by His Resurrection to that sharing in the divine life which is the life of grace. He ascended to heaven, and He will come again, this time in glory, to judge the living and the dead: each according to his merits—those who have responded to the love and piety of God going to eternal life, those who have refused them to the end going to the fire that is not extinguished.
And His Kingdom will have no end.

13. We believe in the Holy Spirit, Who is Lord, and Giver of life, Who is adored and glorified together with the Father and the Son. He spoke to us by the Prophets, He was sent by Christ after His Resurrection and His Ascension to the Father; He illuminates, vivifies, protects and governs the Church; He purifies the Church's members if they do not shun His grace. His action, which penetrates to the inmost of the soul, enables man to respond to the call of Jesus: *Be perfect as your Heavenly Father is perfect.*

14. We believe that Mary is the Mother, who remained ever a Virgin, of the Incarnate Word, our God and Savior Jesus Christ, and that by reason of this singular election, she was, in consideration of the merits of her Son, redeemed in a more eminent manner, preserved from all stain of original sin and filled with the gift of grace more than all other creatures.

15. Joined by a close and indissoluble bond to the Mysteries of the Incarnation and Redemption, the Blessed Virgin, the Immaculate, was at the end of her earthly life raised body and soul to heavenly glory and likened to her risen

Son in anticipation of the future lot of all the just; and We believe that the Blessed Mother of God, the New Eve, Mother of the Church, continues, in heaven her maternal role with regard to Christ's members, co-operating with the birth and growth of divine life in the souls of the redeemed.

16. We believe that in Adam all have sinned, which means that the original offense committed by him caused human nature, common to all men, to fall to a state in which it bears the consequences of that offense, and which is not the state in which it was at first in our first parents, established as they were in holiness and justice, and in which man knew neither evil nor death. It is human nature so fallen, stripped of the grace that clothed it, injured in its own natural powers and subjected to the dominion of death, that is transmitted to all men, and it is in this sense that every man is born in sin. We therefore hold, with the Council of Trent, that original sin is transmitted with human nature, "not by imitation, but by propagation" and that it is thus "in each of us as his own."

17. We believe that Our Lord Jesus Christ, by the Sacrifice of the Cross, redeemed us from original sin and all the personal sins committed by each one of us, so that, in accordance with the word of the Apostle, "where sin abounded, grace did more abound."

18. We believe in one baptism instituted by Our Lord Jesus Christ for the remission of sins. Baptism should be administered even to little children who have not yet been able to be guilty of any personal sin, in order that, though born deprived of supernatural grace, they may be reborn "of water and the Holy Spirit" to the divine life in Christ Jesus.

19. We believe in one, holy, catholic, and apostolic Church, built by Jesus Christ on that rock which is Peter. She is the Mystical Body of Christ; at the same time a visible society instituted with hierarchical organs, and a spiritual community; the Church on earth, the pilgrim People of God here below, and the Church filled with heavenly blessings; the germ and the first fruits of the Kingdom of God, through which the work and the sufferings of Redemption are continued throughout human history, and which looks for its perfect accomplishment beyond time in glory. In the course of time, the Lord Jesus forms His Church by means of the Sacraments emanating from His plenitude. By these she makes her members participants in the mystery of the Death and Resurrection of Christ, in the grace of the Holy Spirit who gives her life and movement. She is therefore holy, though she has sinners in her bosom, because she herself has no other life but that of grace: it is by living by her life that her members are sanctified; it is by removing themselves from her life that they fall into sins and disorders that prevent the radiation of her sanctity. This is why she suffers and does penance for these offenses, of which she has the power to heal her children through the blood of Christ and the gift of the Holy Spirit.

20. Heiress of the divine promises and daughter of Abraham according to the

Spirit, through that Israel whose Scriptures she lovingly guards, and whose patriarchs and prophets she venerates; founded upon the Apostles and handing on from century to century their ever-living word and their powers as pastors in the successor of Peter and the bishops in communion with him; perpetually assisted by the Holy Spirit, she has the charge of guarding, teaching, explaining and spreading the truth which God revealed in a then veiled manner by the Prophets, and fully by the Lord Jesus. We believe *all that is contained in the Word of God written or handed down, and that the Church proposes for belief as divinely revealed, whether by a solemn judgment or by the ordinary and universal magisterium.* We believe in the infallibility enjoyed by the successor of Peter when he teaches ex cathedra as pastor and teacher of all the faithful, and which is assured also to the episcopal body when it exercises with him the supreme magisterium.

21. We believe that the Church founded by Jesus Christ and for which He prayed is indefectibly one in faith, worship and the bond of hierarchical communion. In the bosom of this Church, the rich variety of liturgical rites and the legitimate diversity of theological and spiritual heritages and special disciplines, far from injuring her unity, make it more manifest.

22. Recognizing also the existence, outside the organism of the Church of Christ, of numerous elements of truth and sanctification which belong to her as her own and tend to Catholic unity, and believing in the action of the Holy Spirit who stirs up in the heart of the disciples of Christ love of this unity, we entertain the hope that Christians who are not yet in the full communion of the one only Church will one day be reunited in one flock with one only Shepherd.

23. We believe that the Church is *necessary for salvation, because Christ who is the sole Mediator and Way of salvation, renders himself present for us in His Body which is the Church.* But the divine design of salvation embraces all men; and those *who without fault on their part do not know the Gospel of Christ and His Church, but seek God sincerely, and under the influence of grace endeavor to do His will as recognized through the promptings of their conscience,* they, in a number known only to God, *can obtain salvation.*

24. We believe that the Mass, celebrated by the priest representing the person of Christ by virtue of the power received through the Sacrament of Orders, and offered by him in the name of Christ and the members of His Mystical Body, is in true reality the Sacrifice of Calvary, rendered sacramentally present on our altars. We believe that as the bread and wine consecrated by the Lord at the Last Supper were changed into His Body and His Blood which were to be offered for us on the Cross, likewise the bread and wine consecrated by the priest are changed into the Body and Blood of Christ enthroned gloriously in heaven, and we believe that the mysterious presence of the Lord, under what continues to appear to our sense as before, is a true, real and substantial presence.

25. Christ cannot be thus present in this sacrament except by the change into His Body of the reality itself of the bread and the change into His Blood of the reality itself of the wine, leaving unchanged only the properties of the bread and wine which our senses perceive. This mysterious change is very appropriately called by the Church *transubstantiation*. Every theological explanation which seeks some understanding of this mystery must, in order to be in accord with Catholic faith, maintain that in the reality itself, independently of our mind, the bread and wine have ceased to exist after the Consecration, so that it is the adorable Body and Blood of the Lord Jesus that from then on are really before us under the sacramental species of bread and wine, as the Lord willed it, in order to give himself to us as food and to associate us with the unity of His Mystical Body.

26. The unique and indivisible existence of the Lord glorious in heaven is not multiplied, but is rendered present by the sacrament in the many places on earth where Mass is celebrated. And this existence remains present, after the sacrifice, in the Blessed Sacrament which is, in the tabernacle, the living heart of each of our churches. And it is our very sweet duty to honor and adore in the Blessed Host which our eyes see, the Incarnate Word Whom they cannot see, and Who, without leaving heaven, is made present before us.

27. We confess that the Kingdom of God begun here below in the Church of Christ *is not of this world whose form is passing,* and that its proper growth cannot be confounded with the progress of civilization, of science or of human technology, but that it consists in an ever more profound knowledge of the unfathomable riches of Christ, an ever stronger hope in eternal blessings, an ever more ardent response to the Love of God, and an ever more generous bestowal of grace and holiness among men. But it is this same love which induces the Church to concern herself constantly about the true temporal welfare of men. Without ceasing to recall to her children that *they have not here a lasting dwelling,* she also urges them to contribute, each according to his vocation and his means, to the welfare of their earthly city, to promote justice, peace and brotherhood among men, to give their aid freely to their brothers, especially to the poorest and most unfortunate. The deep solicitude of the Church, the spouse of Christ, for the needs of men, for their joys and hopes, their griefs and efforts, is therefore nothing other than her great desire to be present to them, in order to illuminate them with the light of Christ and to gather them all in Him, their only Savior. This solicitude can never mean that the Church conform herself to the things of this world, or that she lessen the ardor of her expectation of her Lord and of the eternal Kingdom.

28. We believe in the life eternal. We believe that the souls of all those who die in the grace of Christ, whether they must still be purified in Purgatory, or whether from the moment they leave their bodies Jesus takes them to Paradise as He did for the Good Thief, are the People of God in the eternity be-

yond death, which will be finally conquered on the day of the Resurrection when these souls will be reunited with their bodies.

29. We believe that the multitude of those gathered around Jesus and Mary in Paradise forms the Church of Heaven, where in eternal beatitude they see God as He is, and where they also, in different degrees, are associated with the holy angels in the divine rule exercised by Christ in glory, interceding for us and helping our weakness by their brotherly care.

30. We believe in the communion of all the faithful of Christ, those who are pilgrims on earth, the dead who are attaining their purification, and the blessed in heaven, all together forming one Church; and we believe that in this communion the merciful love of God and His saints is ever listening to our prayers, as Jesus told us: Ask and you will receive. Thus it is with faith and in hope that we look forward to the resurrection of the dead, and the life of the world to come.

Blessed be God Thrice Holy. Amen.

Pronounced in front of the Basilica of St. Peter, on June 30, 1968, the sixth year of our pontificate.

POPE PAUL VI

POPES OF THE CATHOLIC CHURCH

The data give first the name of the Pope, for later pontiffs their family names, birthplace or country of origin, date of accession to the papacy, and date of the end of the reign, which is generally the date of death. Double dates include times of election and coronation (installation). A listing of the popes in alphabetical order appears at the end of this chronological list.

1. ST. PETER (Simon Bar-Jona): Bethsaida in Galilee; d. 64 or 67
2. ST. LINUS: Tuscany; 67–76
3. ST. ANACLETUS (CLETUS): Rome; 76–88
4. ST. CLEMENT: Rome; 88–97
5. ST. EVARISTUS: Greece; 97–105
6. ST. ALEXANDER I: Rome; 105–15
7. ST. SIXTUS I: Rome; 115–25
8. ST. TELESPHORUS: Greece; 125–36
9. ST. HYGINUS: Greece; 136–40
10. ST. PIUS I: Aquileia; 140–55
11. ST. ANICETUS: Syria; 155–66
12. ST. SOTER: Campania; 166–75
13. ST. ELEUTHERIUS: Nicopolis in Epirus; 175–89
14. ST. VICTOR I: Africa; 189–99
15. ST. ZEPHYRINUS: Rome; 199–217
16. ST. CALLISTUS I: Rome; 217–22
17. ST. URBAN I: Rome; 222–30
18. ST. PONTIAN: Rome; July 21, 230, to Sept. 28, 235
19. ST. ANTERUS: Greece; Nov. 21, 235, to Jan. 3, 236
20. ST. FABIAN: Rome; Jan. 10, 236, to Jan. 20, 250
21. ST. CORNELIUS: Rome; Mar. 251 to June 253
22. ST. LUCIUS I: Rome; June 25, 253, to Mar. 5, 254
23. ST. STEPHEN I: Rome; May 12, 254, to Aug. 2, 257
24. ST. SIXTUS II: Greece; Aug. 30, 257, to Aug. 6, 258
25. ST. DIONYSIUS: July 22, 259, to Dec. 26, 268
26. ST. FELIX I: Rome; Jan. 5, 269, to Dec. 30, 274
27. ST. EUTYCHIAN: Luni; Jan. 4, 275, to Dec. 7, 283
28. ST. CAIUS: Dalmatia; Dec. 17, 283, to Apr. 22, 296
29. ST. MARCELLINUS: Rome; June 30, 296, to Oct. 25, 304
30. ST. MARCELLUS I: Rome; May 27, 308, or June 26, 308, to Jan. 16, 309
31. ST. EUSEBIUS: Greece; Apr. 18, 309 or 310, to Aug. 17, 309 or 310
32. ST. MELCHIADES (MILTIADES): Africa; July 2, 311, to Jan. 11, 314
33. ST. SYLVESTER I: Rome; Jan. 31, 314, to Dec. 31, 335
34. ST. MARK: Rome; Jan. 18, 336, to Oct. 7, 336

35. ST. JULIUS I: Rome; Feb. 6, 337, to Apr. 12, 352
36. LIBERIUS: Rome; May 17, 352, to Sept. 24, 366
37. ST. DAMASUS I: Spain; Oct. 1, 366, to Dec. 11, 384
38. ST. SIRICIUS: Rome; Dec. 15, or 22 or 29, 384, to Nov. 26, 399
39. ST. ANASTASIUS I: Rome; Nov. 27, 399, to Dec. 19, 401
40. ST. INNOCENT I: Albano; Dec. 22, 401, to Mar. 12, 417
41. ST. ZOZIMUS: Greece; Mar. 18, 417, to Dec. 26, 418
42. ST. BONIFACE I: Rome; Dec. 28 or 29, 418, to Sept. 4, 422
43. ST. CELESTINE I: Campania; Sept. 10, 422, to July 27, 432
44. ST. SIXTUS III: Rome; July 31, 432, to Aug. 19, 440
45. ST. LEO I (the Great): Tuscany; Sept. 29, 440, to Nov. 10, 461
46. ST. HILARY: Sardinia; Nov. 19, 461, to Feb. 29, 468
47. ST. SIMPLICIUS: Tivoli; Mar. 3, 468, to Mar. 10, 483
48. ST. FELIX III (II): Rome; Mar. 13, 483, to Mar. 1, 492
He should be called Felix II, and his successors numbered accordingly.
49. ST. GELASIUS I: Africa; Mar. 1, 492, to Nov. 21, 496
50. ANASTASIUS II: Rome; Nov. 24, 496, to Nov. 19, 498
51. ST. SYMMACHUS: Sardinia; Nov. 22, 498, to July 19, 514
52. ST. HORMISDAS: Frosinone; July 20, 514, to Aug. 6, 523
53. ST. JOHN I, MARTYR: Tuscany; Aug. 13, 523, to May 18, 526
54. ST. FELIX IV (III): Samnium; July 12, 526, to Sept. 22, 530
55. BONIFACE II: Rome; Sept. 22, 530, to Oct. 17, 532
56. JOHN II: Rome; Jan. 2, 533, to May 8, 535
John II was the first pope to change his name; he was originally called Mercury, the name of a pagan deity.
57. ST. AGAPITUS I: Rome; May 13, 535, to Apr. 22, 536
58. ST. SILVERIUS, MARTYR: Campania; June 1 or 8, 536, to Nov. 11, 537 (d. Dec. 2, 537)
59. VIGILIUS: Rome; Mar. 29, 537, to June 7, 555
60. PELAGIUS I: Rome; Apr. 16, 556, to Mar. 4, 561
61. JOHN III: Rome; July 17, 561, to July 13, 574
62. BENEDICT I: Rome; June 2, 575, to July 30, 579
63. PELAGIUS II: Rome; Nov. 26, 579, to Feb. 7, 590
64. ST. GREGORY I (the Great): Rome; Sept. 3, 590, to Mar. 12, 604
65. SABINIAN: Blera in Tuscany; Sept. 13, 604, to Feb. 22, 606
66. BONIFACE III: Rome; Feb. 19, 607, to Nov. 12, 607
67. ST. BONIFACE IV: Abruzzi; Aug. 25, 608, to May 8, 615
68. ST. DEUSDEDIT (ADEODATUS I): Rome; Oct. 19, 615, to Nov. 8, 618
69. BONIFACE V: Naples; Dec. 23, 619, to Oct. 25, 625
70. HONORIUS I: Campania; Oct. 27, 625, to Oct. 12, 638
71. SEVERINUS: Rome; May 28, 640, to Aug. 2, 640
72. JOHN IV: Dalmatia; Dec. 24, 640, to Oct. 12, 642
73. THEODORE I: Greece; Nov. 24, 642, to May 14, 649
74. ST. MARTIN I, MARTYR: Todi; July, 649, to Sept. 16, 655 (in exile from June 17, 653)
His successor, St. Eugene I, was ordained during St. Martin I's exile and, apparently, with the latter's approval.
75. ST. EUGENE I: Rome; Aug. 10, 654, to June 2, 657
76. ST. VITALIAN: Segni; July 30, 657, to Jan. 27, 672
77. ADEODATUS II: Rome; Apr. 11, 672, to June 17, 676
78. DONUS (or DOMNUS): Rome; Nov. 2, 676, to Apr. 11, 678
79. ST. AGATHO: Sicily; June 27, 678, to Jan. 10, 681
80. ST. LEO II: Sicily; Aug. 17, 682, to July 3, 683
81. ST. BENEDICT II: Rome; June 26, 684, to May 8, 685
82. JOHN V: Syria; July 23, 685, to Aug. 2, 686
83. CONON: birthplace unknown; Oct. 21, 686, to Sept. 21, 687
84. ST. SERGIUS I: Syria; Dec. 15, 687, to Sept. 8, 701
85. JOHN VI: Greece; Oct. 30, 701, to Jan. 11, 705
86. JOHN VII: Greece; Mar. 1, 705, to Oct. 18, 707
87. SISINNIUS: Syria; Jan. 15, 708, to Feb. 4, 708
88. CONSTANTINE: Syria; Mar. 25, 708, to Apr. 9, 715
89. ST. GREGORY II: Rome; May 19, 715, to Feb. 11, 731

90. ST. GREGORY III: Syria; Mar. 18, 731, to Nov. 741
91. ST. ZACHARY: Greece; Dec. 10, 741, to Mar. 22, 752
92. STEPHEN II (III): Rome; Mar. 26, 752, to Apr. 26, 757

After the death of St. Zachary, a Roman priest named Stephen was elected but died (four days later) before his consecration as Bishop of Rome, which, according to the canon law of that day, would have marked the beginning of his pontificate. Immediately another man was elected to succeed Zachary as Stephen II. Both Stephens are considered to have been popes.

93. ST. PAUL I: Rome; Apr. (May 29), 757, to June 28, 767
94. STEPHEN III (IV): Sicily; Aug. 1 (7), 768, to Jan. 24, 772
95. ADRIAN I: Rome; Feb. 1 (9), 772, to Dec. 25, 795
96. ST. LEO III: Rome; Dec. 26 (27), 795, to June 12, 816
97. STEPHEN IV (V): Rome; June 22, 816, to Jan. 24, 817
98. ST. PASCHAL I: Rome; Jan. 25, 817, to Feb. 11, 824
99. EUGENE II: Rome; Feb. (May) 824 to Aug. 827
100. VALENTINE: Rome; Aug. 827 to Sept. 827
101. GREGORY IV: Rome; Oct. 827 to Jan. 844
102. SERGIUS II: Rome; Jan. 844 to Jan. 27, 847
103. ST. LEO IV: Rome; Jan. (Apr. 10) 847 to July 17, 855
104. BENEDICT III: Rome; July (Sept. 29) 855 to Apr. 17, 858
105. ST. NICHOLAS I (the Great): Rome; Apr. 24, 858, to Nov. 13, 867
106. ADRIAN II: Rome; Dec. 14, 867, to Dec. 14, 872
107. JOHN VIII: Rome; Dec. 14, 872, to Dec. 16, 882
108. MARINUS I: Gallese; Dec. 16, 882, to May 15, 884
109. ST. ADRIAN III: Rome; May 17, 884, to Sept. 885 (cult confirmed June 2, 1891)
110. STEPHEN V (VI): Rome; Sept. 885 to Sept. 14, 891
111. FORMOSUS: Porto; Oct. 6, 891, to Apr. 4, 896
112. BONIFACE VI: Rome; Apr. 896 to Apr. 896
113. STEPHEN VI (VII): Rome; May 896 to Aug. 897
114. ROMANUS: Gallese; Aug. 897 to Nov. 897
115. THEODORE II: Rome; Dec. 897 to Dec. 897
116. JOHN IX: Tivoli; Jan. 898 to Jan. 900
117. BENEDICT IV: Rome; Jan. (Feb.) 900 to July 903
118. LEO V: Ardea; July 903 to Sept. 903
119. SERGIUS III: Rome; Jan. 29, 904, to Apr. 14, 911
120. ANASTASIUS III: Rome; Apr. 911 to June 913
121. LANDO: Sabina; July 913 to Feb. 914
122. JOHN X: Tossignano (Imola); Mar. 914 to May 928
123. LEO VI: Rome; May 928 to Dec. 928
124. STEPHEN VII (VIII): Rome; Dec. 928 to Feb. 931
125. JOHN XI: Rome; Feb. (Mar.) 931 to Dec. 935
126. LEO VII: Rome; Jan. 3, 936, to July 13, 939
127. STEPHEN VIII (IX): Rome; July 14, 939, to Oct. 942
128. MARINUS II: Rome; Oct. 30, 942, to May 946
129. AGAPITUS II: Rome; May 10, 946, to Dec. 955
130. JOHN XII (Octavius): Tusculum; Dec. 16, 955, to May 14, 964
131. LEO VIII: Rome; Dec. 4 (6), 963, to Mar. 1, 965
132. BENEDICT V: Rome; May 22, 964, to July 4, 966

John XII was deposed Dec. 4, 963, by a Roman council; if the deposition was valid, Leo was the legitimate Pope and Benedict was an antipope.

133. JOHN XIII: Rome; Oct. 1, 965, to Sept. 6, 972
134. BENEDICT VI: Rome; Jan. 19, 973, to June 974
135. BENEDICT VII: Rome; Oct. 974 to July 10, 983
136. JOHN XIV (Peter): Pavia; Dec. 983 to Aug. 20, 984
137. JOHN XV: Rome; Aug. 985 to Mar. 996
138. GREGORY V (Bruno of Carinthia): Saxony; May 3, 996, to Feb. 18, 999
139. SYLVESTER II (Gerbert): Auvergne; Apr. 2, 999, to May 12, 1003
140. JOHN XVII (Siccone): Rome; June 1003 to Dec. 1003
141. JOHN XVIII (Phasianus): Rome; Jan. 1004 to July 1009
142. SERGIUS IV (Peter): Rome; July 31, 1009, to May 12, 1012

The custom of changing one's name on election to the Papacy traditionally dates from the time of Sergius IV. After his time this became a regular practice, with few exceptions; e.g., Adrian VI and Marcellus II.

143. BENEDICT VIII (Theophylactus): Tusculum; May 18, 1012, to Apr. 9, 1024
144. JOHN XIX (Romanus): Tusculum; Apr. (May) 1024 to 1032
145. BENEDICT IX (Theophylactus): Tusculum; 1032 to 1044
146. SYLVESTER III (John): Rome; Jan. 20, 1045, to Feb. 10, 1045
Sylvester III was an antipope if the forcible removal of Benedict IX in 1044 was not legitimate.
147. BENEDICT IX (second time): Apr. 10, 1045, to May 1, 1045
148. GREGORY VI (John Gratian): Rome; May 5, 1045, to Dec. 20, 1046
149. CLEMENT II (Suitger, Lord of Morsleben and Hornburg): Saxony; Dec. 24 (25), 1046, to Oct. 9, 1047
If the triple removal of Benedict IX in 1044, 1046, and 1047 were invalid, Gregory VI and Clement II were antipopes.
150. BENEDICT IX (third time): Nov. 8, 1047, to July 17, 1048 (d. c. 1055)
151. DAMASUS II (Poppo): Bavaria; July 17, 1048, to Aug. 9, 1048
152. ST. LEO IX (Bruno): Alsace; Feb. 12, 1049, to Apr. 19, 1054
153. VICTOR II (Gebhard): Swabia; Apr. 16, 1055, to July 28, 1057
154. STEPHEN IX (X) (Frederick): Lorraine; Aug. 3, 1057, to Mar. 29, 1058
155. NICHOLAS II (Gerard): Burgundy; Jan. 24, 1059, to July 27, 1061
156. ALEXANDER II (Anselmo da Baggio): Milan; Oct. 1, 1061, to Apr. 21, 1073
157. ST. GREGORY VII (Hildebrand): Tuscany; Apr. 22 (June 30), 1073, to May 25, 1085
158. BLESSED VICTOR III (Dauferius, Desiderius): Benevento; May 24, 1086, to Sept. 16, 1087 (cult confirmed July 23, 1887)
159. BLESSED URBAN II (Otto di Lagery): France; Mar. 12, 1088, to July 29, 1099 (cult confirmed July 14, 1881)
160. PASCHAL II (Raniero): Ravenna; Aug. 13 (14), 1099, to Jan. 21, 1118
161. GELASIUS II (Giovanni Caetani): Gaeta; Jan. 24 (Mar. 10), 1118, to Jan. 28, 1119
162. CALLISTUS II (Guido of Burgundy): Burgundy; Feb. 2 (9), 1119, to Dec. 13, 1124
163. HONORIUS II (Lamberto): Fiagnano (Imola); Dec. 15 (21), 1124, to Feb. 13, 1130
164. INNOCENT II (Gregorio Papareschi): Rome; Feb. 14 (23), 1130, to Sept. 24, 1143
165. CELESTINE II (Guido): Città di Castello; Sept. 26 (Oct. 3), 1143, to Mar. 8, 1144
166. LUCIUS II (Gerardo Caccianemici): Bologna; Mar. 12, 1144, to Feb. 15, 1145
167. BLESSED EUGENE III (Bernardo Paganelli di Montemagno): Pisa; Feb. 15 (18), 1145, to July 8, 1153 (cult confirmed Oct. 3, 1872)
168. ANASTASIUS IV (Corrado): Rome; July 12, 1153, to Dec. 3, 1154
169. ADRIAN IV (Nicholas Breakspear): England; Dec. 4 (5), 1154, to Sept. 1, 1159
170. ALEXANDER III (Rolando Bandinelli): Siena; Sept. 7 (20), 1159, to Aug. 30, 1181
171. LUCIUS III (Ubaldo Allucingoli): Lucca; Sept. 1 (6), 1181, to Sept. 25, 1185
172. URBAN III (Uberto Crivelli): Milan; Nov. 25 (Dec. 1), 1185, to Oct. 20, 1187
173. GREGORY VIII (Alberto de Morra): Benevento; Oct. 21 (25), 1187, to Dec. 17, 1187
174. CLEMENT III (Paolo Scolari): Rome; Dec. 19 (20), 1187, to Mar. 1191
175. CELESTINE III (Giacinto Bobone): Rome; Mar. 30 (Apr. 14), 1191, to Jan. 8, 1198
176. INNOCENT III (Lotario dei Conti di Segni): Anagni; Jan. 8 (Feb. 22), 1198, to July 16, 1216
177. HONORIUS III (Cencio Savelli): Rome; July 18 (24), 1216, to Mar. 18, 1227
178. GREGORY IX (Ugolino, Count of Segni): Anagni; Mar. 19 (21), 1227, to Aug. 22, 1241
179. CELESTINE IV (Goffredo Castiglioni): Milan; Oct. 25 (28), 1241, to Nov. 10, 1241
180. INNOCENT IV (Sinibaldo Fieschi): Genoa; June 25 (28), 1243, to Dec. 7, 1254
181. ALEXANDER IV (Rinaldo, Count of Segni): Anagni; Dec. 12 (20), 1254, to May 25, 1261
182. URBAN IV (Jacques Pantaléon): Troyes; Aug. 29 (Sept. 4), 1261, to Oct. 2, 1264
183. CLEMENT IV (Guy Foulques or Guido le Gros): France; Feb. 5 (15), 1265, to Nov. 29, 1268
184. BLESSED GREGORY X (Teobaldo Visconti): Piacenza; Sept. 1, 1271 (Mar. 27, 1272), to Jan. 10, 1276 (cult confirmed Sept. 12, 1713)
185. BLESSED INNOCENT V (Peter of Tarentaise): Savoy; Jan. 21 (Feb. 22), 1276, to June 22, 1276 (cult confirmed Mar. 13, 1898)
186. ADRIAN V (Ottobono Fieschi): Genoa; July 11, 1276, to Aug. 18, 1276
187. JOHN XXI (Petrus Juliani or Petrus Hispanus): Portugal; Sept. 8 (20), 1276, to May 20, 1277

There never was a pope with the title of John XX. This title was dropped to rectify an error in the tenth century when an alleged John XV was mistakenly listed among the popes.

188. NICHOLAS III (Giovanni Gaetano Orsini): Rome; Nov. 25 (Dec. 26), 1277, to Aug. 22, 1280

189. MARTIN IV (Simon de Brie): France; Feb. 22 (Mar. 23), 1281, to Mar. 28, 1285
The names of Marinus I (882–84) and Marinus II (942–46) were mistaken for Martin; because of these two popes and the earlier St. Martin I (649–55) this pope was called Martin IV.

190. HONORIUS IV (Giacomo Savelli): Rome; Apr. 2 (May 20), 1285, to Apr. 3, 1287

191. NICHOLAS IV (Girolamo Masci): Ascoli; Feb. 22, 1288, to Apr. 4, 1292

192. ST. CELESTINE V (Pietro del Murrone): Isernia; July 5 (Aug. 29), 1294, to Dec. 13, 1294

193. BONIFACE VIII (Benedetto Caetani): Anagni; Dec. 24, 1294 (Jan. 23, 1295), to Oct. 11, 1303

194. BLESSED BENEDICT XI (Niccolo Boccasini): Treviso; Oct. 22 (27), 1303, to July 7, 1304 (cult confirmed Apr. 24, 1736)

195. CLEMENT V (Bertrand de Got): France; June 5 (Nov. 14), 1305, to Apr. 20, 1314 (first of the Avignon popes)

196. JOHN XXII (Jacques d'Euse): Cahors; Aug. 7 (Sept. 5), 1316, to Dec. 4, 1334

197. BENEDICT XII (Jacques Fournier): France; Dec. 20, 1334 (Jan. 8, 1335), to Apr. 25, 1342

198. CLEMENT VI (Pierre Roger): France; May 7 (19), 1342, to Dec. 6, 1352

199. INNOCENT VI (Etienne Aubert): France; Dec. 18 (30), 1352, to Sept. 12, 1362

200. BLESSED URBAN V (Guillaume de Grimoard): France; Sept. 28 (Nov. 6), 1362, to Dec. 19, 1370 (cult confirmed Mar. 10, 1870)

201. GREGORY XI (Pierre Roger de Beaufort): France; Dec. 30, 1370 (Jan. 5, 1371), to Mar. 26, 1378 (last of the Avignon popes)

202. URBAN VI (Bartolomeo Prignano): Naples; Apr. 8 (18), 1378, to Oct. 15, 1389

203. BONIFACE IX (Pietro Tomacelli): Naples; Nov. 2 (9), 1389, to Oct. 1, 1404

204. INNOCENT VII (Cosma Migliorati): Sulmona; Oct. 17 (Nov. 11), 1404, to Nov. 6, 1406

205. GREGORY XII (Angelo Correr): Venice; Nov. 30 (Dec. 19), 1406, to July 4, 1415, when he voluntarily resigned from the Western Schism to permit the election of his successor; he died Oct. 18, 1417.

206. MARTIN V (Oddone Colonna): Rome; Nov. 11 (21), 1417, to Feb. 20, 1431

207. EUGENE IV (Gabriele Condulmer): Venice; Mar. 3 (11), 1431, to Feb. 23, 1447

208. NICHOLAS V (Tommaso Parentucelli): Sarzana; Mar. 6 (19), 1447, to Mar. 24, 1455

209. CALLISTUS III (Alfonso Borgia): Jativa (Valencia); Apr. 8 (20), 1455, to Aug. 6, 1458

210. PIUS II (Enea Silvio Piccolomini): Siena; Aug. 19 (Sept. 3), 1458, to Aug. 15, 1464

211. PAUL II (Pietro Barbo): Venice; Aug. 30 (Sept. 16), 1464, to July 26, 1471

212. SIXTUS IV (Francesco della Rovere): Savona; Aug. 9 (25), 1471, to Aug. 12, 1484

213. INNOCENT VIII (Giovanni Battista Cibo): Genoa; Aug. 29 (Sept. 12), 1484, to July 25, 1492

214. ALEXANDER VI (Rodrigo Borgia): Jativa (Valencia); Aug. 11 (26), 1492, to Aug. 18, 1503

215. PIUS III (Francesco Todeschini-Piccolomini): Siena; Sept. 22 (Oct. 18), 1503, to Oct. 18, 1503

216. JULIUS II (Giuliano della Rovere): Savona; Oct. 31 (Nov. 26), 1503, to Feb. 21, 1513

217. LEO X (Giovanni de' Medici): Florence; Mar. 9 (19), 1513, to Dec. 1, 1521

218. ADRIAN VI (Adrian Florensz): Utrecht; Jan. 9 (Aug. 31), 1522, to Sept. 14, 1523

219. CLEMENT VII (Giulio de' Medici): Florence; Nov. 19 (26), 1523, to Sept. 25, 1534

220. PAUL III (Alessandro Farnese): Rome; Oct. 13 (Nov. 3), 1534, to Nov. 10, 1549

221. JULIUS III (Giovanni Maria Ciocchi del Monte): Rome; Feb. 7 (22), 1550, to Mar. 23, 1555

222. MARCELLUS II (Marcello Cervini): Montepulciano; Apr. 9 (10), 1555, to May 1, 1555

223. PAUL IV (Gian Pietro Carafa): Naples; May 23 (26), 1555, to Aug. 18, 1559

224. PIUS IV (Giovan Angelo de' Medici): Milan; Dec. 25, 1559 (Jan. 6, 1560), to Dec. 9, 1565

225. ST. PIUS V (Antonio-Michele Ghislieri): Bosco (Alexandria); Jan. 7 (17), 1566, to May 1, 1572 (beatified April 27, 1672)
226. GREGORY XIII (Ugo Buoncompagni): Bologna; May 13 (25), 1572, to Apr. 10, 1585
227. SIXTUS V (Felice Peretti): Grottammare (Ripatransone); Apr. 24 (May 1), 1585, to Aug. 27, 1590
228. URBAN VII (Giovanni Battista Castagna): Rome; Sept. 15, 1590, to Sept. 27, 1590
229. GREGORY XIV (Niccolo Sfondrati): Cremona; Dec. 5 (8), 1590, to Oct. 16, 1591
230. INNOCENT IX (Giovanni Antonio Facchinetti): Bologna; Oct. 29 (Nov. 3), 1591, to Dec. 30, 1591
231. CLEMENT VIII (Ippolito Aldobrandini): Florence; Jan. 30 (Feb. 9), 1592, to Mar. 3, 1605
232. LEO XI (Alessandro de' Medici): Florence; Apr. 1 (10), 1605, to Apr. 27, 1605
233. PAUL V (Camillo Borghese): Rome; May 16 (29), 1605, to Jan. 28, 1621
234. GREGORY XV (Alessandro Ludovisi): Bologna; Feb. 9 (14), 1621, to July 8, 1623
235. URBAN VIII (Maffeo Barberini): Florence; Aug. 6 (Sept. 29), 1623, to July 29, 1644
236. INNOCENT X (Giovanni Battista Pamfili): Rome; Sept. 15 (Oct. 4), 1644, to Jan. 7, 1655
237. ALEXANDER VII (Fabio Chigi): Siena; Apr. 7 (18), 1655, to May 22, 1667
238. CLEMENT IX (Giulio Rospigliosi): Pistoia; June 20 (26), 1667, to Dec. 9, 1669
239. CLEMENT X (Emilio Altieri): Rome; Apr. 29 (May 11), 1670, to July 22, 1676
240. BLESSED INNOCENT XI (Benedetto Odescalchi): Como; Sept. 21 (Oct. 4), 1676, to Aug. 12, 1689
241. ALEXANDER VIII (Pietro Ottoboni): Venice; Oct. 6 (16), 1689, to Feb. 1, 1691
242. INNOCENT XII (Antonio Pignatelli): Spinazzola; July 12 (15), 1691, to Sept. 27, 1700
243. CLEMENT XI (Giovanni Francesco Albani): Urbino; Nov. 23, 30 (Dec. 8), 1700, to Mar. 19, 1721
244. INNOCENT XIII (Michelangelo dei Conti): Rome; May 8 (18), 1721, to Mar. 7, 1724
245. BENEDICT XIII (Pietro Francesco-Vincenzo Maria-Orsini): Gravina (Bari); May 29 (June 4), 1724, to Feb. 21, 1730
246. CLEMENT XII (Lorenzo Corsini): Florence; July 12 (16), 1730, to Feb. 6, 1740
247. BENEDICT XIV (Prospero Lambertini): Bologna; Aug. 17 (22), 1740, to May 3, 1758
248. CLEMENT XIII (Carlo Rezzonico): Venice; July 6 (16), 1758, to Feb. 2, 1769
249. CLEMENT XIV (Giovanni Vincenzo Antonio-Lorenzo-Ganganelli): Rimini; May 19, 28 (June 4), 1769, to Sept. 22, 1774
250. PIUS VI (Giovanni Angelo Braschi): Cesena; Feb. 15 (22), 1775, to Aug. 29, 1799
251. PIUS VII (Barnaba-Gregorio-Chiaramonti): Cesena; Mar. 14 (21), 1800, to Aug. 20, 1823
252. LEO XII (Annibale della Genga): Genga (Fabriano); Sept. 28 (Oct. 5), 1823, to Feb. 10, 1829
253. PIUS VIII (Francesco Saverio Castiglioni): Cingoli; Mar. 31 (Apr. 5), 1829, to Nov. 30, 1830
254. GREGORY XVI (Bartolomeo Alberto-Mauro-Cappellari): Belluno; Feb. 2 (6), 1831, to June 1, 1846
255. PIUS IX (Giovanni M. Mastai Ferretti): Senigallia; June 16 (21), 1846, to Feb. 7, 1878
256. LEO XIII (Gioacchino Pecci): Carpineto (Anagni); Feb. 20 (Mar. 3), 1878, to July 20, 1903
257. ST. PIUS X (Giuseppe Sarto): Riese (Treviso); Aug. 4 (9), 1903, to Aug. 20, 1914 (beatified June 3, 1951)
258. BENEDICT XV (Giacomo della Chiesa): Genoa; Sept. 3 (6), 1914, to Jan. 22, 1922
259. PIUS XI (Achille Ratti): Desio (Milan); Feb. 6 (12), 1922, to Feb. 10, 1939
260. PIUS XII (Eugenio Pacelli): Rome; Mar. 2 (12), 1939, to Oct. 9, 1958
261. JOHN XXIII (Angelo Giuseppe Roncalli): Sotto il Monte (Bergamo); Oct. 28 (Nov. 4), 1958, to June 3, 1963
262. PAUL VI (Giovanni Battista Montini): Concessio (Brescia); June 21 (30), 1963, to Aug. 6, 1978
263. JOHN PAUL I (Albino Luciani): Forno di Canale (now Canale d'Agordo); Aug. 26 (Sept. 3), 1978, to Sept. 28, 1978
264. JOHN PAUL II (Karol Wojtyla): Wadowice, Poland; Oct. 16 (22), 1978, to ——

POPES LISTED IN ALPHABETICAL ORDER

Numbers in parentheses give the Pope's position in chronological sequence.

Adeodatus II (77)
Adrian I (95)
Adrian II (106)
St. Adrian III (109)
Adrian IV (169)
Adrian V (186)
Adrian VI (218)
St. Agapitus I (57)
Agapitus II (129)
St. Agatho (79)
St. Alexander I (6)
Alexander II (156)
Alexander III (170)
Alexander IV (181)
Alexander VI (214)
Alexander VII (237)
Alexander VIII (241)
St. Anacletus (3)
St. Anastasius I (39)
Anastasius II (50)
Anastasius III (120)
Anastasius IV (168)
St. Anicetus (11)
St. Anterus (19)
Benedict I (62)
St. Benedict II (81)
Benedict III (104)
Benedict IV (117)
Benedict V (132)
Benedict VI (134)
Benedict VII (135)
Benedict VIII (143)
Benedict IX (145, 147, 150)
Bl. Benedict XI (194)
Benedict XII (197)
Benedict XIII (245)
Benedict XIV (247)
Benedict XV (258)
St. Boniface I (42)
Boniface II (55)
Boniface III (66)
St. Boniface IV (67)
Boniface V (69)
Boniface VI (112)
Boniface VIII (193)
Boniface IX (203)
St. Caius (28)
St. Callistus I (16)
Callistus II (162)
Callistus III (209)
St. Celestine I (43)
Celestine II (165)
Celestine III (175)
Celestine IV (179)
St. Celestine V (192)
St. Clement I (4)

Clement II (149)
Clement III (174)
Clement IV (183)
Clement V (195)
Clement VI (198)
Clement VII (219)
Clement VIII (231)
Clement IX (238)
Clement X (239)
Clement XI (243)
Clement XII (246)
Clement XIII (248)
Clement XIV (249)
Conon (83)
Constantine (88)
St. Cornelius (21)
St. Damasus I (37)
Damasus II (151)
St. Deusdedit (68)
St. Dionysius (25)
Donus (or Domnus) (78)
St. Eleutherius (13)
St. Eugene I (75)
Eugene II (99)
Bl. Eugene III (167)
Eugene IV (207)
St. Eusebius (31)
St. Eutychian (27)
St. Evaristus (5)
St. Fabian (20)
St. Felix I (26)
St. Felix III (II) (48)
St. Felix IV (III) (54)
Formosus (111)
St. Gelasius I (49)
Gelasius II (161)
St. Gregory I (64)
    (the Great)
St. Gregory II (89)
St. Gregory III (90)
Gregory IV (101)
Gregory V (138)
Gregory VI (148)
St. Gregory VII (157)
Gregory VIII (173)
Gregory IX (178)
Bl. Gregory X (184)
Gregory XI (201)
Gregory XII (205)
Gregory XIII (226)
Gregory XIV (229)
Gregory XV (234)
Gregory XVI (254)
St. Hilary (46)
Honorius I (70)
Honorius II (163)

Honorius III (177)
Honorius IV (190)
St. Hormisdas (52)
St. Hyginus (9)
St. Innocent I (40)
Innocent II (164)
Innocent III (176)
Innocent IV (180)
Bl. Innocent V (185)
Innocent VI (199)
Innocent VII (204)
Innocent VIII (213)
Innocent IX (230)
Innocent X (236)
Bl. Innocent XI (240)
Innocent XII (242)
Innocent XIII (244)
St. John I (53)
John II (56)
John III (61)
John IV (72)
John V (82)
John VI (85)
John VII (86)
John VIII (107)
John IX (116)
John X (122)
John XI (125)
John XII (130)
John XIII (133)
John XIV (136)
John XV (137)
John XVII (140)
John XVIII (141)
John XIX (144)
John XXI (187)
John XXII (196)
John XXIII (261)
John Paul I (263)
John Paul II (264)
St. Julius I (35)
Julius II (216)
Julius III (221)
Lando (121)
St. Leo I (45)
(the Great)
St. Leo II (80)
St. Leo III (96)
St. Leo IV (103)
Leo V (118)
Leo VI (123)
Leo VII (126)
Leo VIII (131)
St. Leo IX (152)
Leo X (217)
Leo XI (232)
Leo XII (252)
Leo XIII (256)
Liberius (36)
St. Linus (2)
St. Lucius I (22)

Lucius II (166)
Lucius III (171)
St. Marcellinus (29)
St. Marcellus I (30)
Marcellus II (222)
Marinus I (108)
Marinus II (128)
St. Mark (34)
St. Martin I (74)
Martin IV (189)
Martin V (206)
St. Melchiades (32)
St. Nicholas I (105)
(the Great)
Nicholas II (155)
Nicholas III (188)
Nicholas IV (191)
Nicholas V (208)
St. Paschal I (98)
Paschal II (160)
St. Paul I (93)
Paul II (211)
Paul III (220)
Paul IV (223)
Paul V (233)
Paul VI (262)
Pelagius I (60)
Pelagius II (63)
St. Peter (1)
St. Pius I (10)
Pius II (210)
Pius III (215)
Pius IV (224)
St. Pius V (225)
Pius VI (250)
Pius VII (251)
Pius VIII (253)
Pius IX (255)
St. Pius X (257)
Pius XI (259)
Pius XII (260)
St. Pontian (18)
Romanus (114)
Sabinian (65)
St. Sergius I (84)
Sergius II (102)
Sergius III (119)
Sergius IV (142)
Severinus (71)
St. Silverius (58)
St. Simplicius (47)
St. Siricius (38)
Sisinnius (87)
St. Sixtus I (7)
St. Sixtus II (24)
St. Sixtus III (44)
Sixtus IV (212)
Sixtus V (227)
St. Soter (12)
St. Stephen I (23)
Stephen II (III) (92)

Stephen III (IV) (94)
Stephen IV (V) (97)
Stephen V (VI) (110)
Stephen VI (VII) (113)
Stephen VII (VIII) (124)
Stephen VIII (IX) (127)
Stephen IX (X) (154)
St. Sylvester I (33)
Sylvester II (139)
Sylvester III (146)
St. Symmachus (51)
St. Telesphorus (8)
Theodore I (73)
Theodore II (115)
St. Urban I (17)
Bl. Urban II (159)

Urban III (172)
Urban IV (182)
Bl. Urban V (200)
Urban VI (202)
Urban VII (228)
Urban VIII (235)
Valentine (100)
St. Victor I (14)
Victor II (153)
Bl. Victor III (158)
Vigilius (59)
St. Vitalian (76)
St. Zachary (91)
St. Zephyrinus (15)
St. Zozimus (41)

THE ROMAN CALENDAR

The calendar of the Roman Rite of the Catholic Church was thoroughly revised after the Second Vatican Council. Pope Paul VI announced his approval of the reorganization of the liturgical year and calendar in 1969, declaring that the purpose was "no other . . . than to permit the faithful to communicate in a more intense way, through faith, hope and love, in the whole mystery of Christ."

In the ecclesiastical year presented here, all the revisions pertaining to the universal Church have been incorporated. Included also are the saints who are traditionally honored on certain days, either locally or universally, but who are not in the liturgical calendar for the universal Church.

The names of saints who are celebrated liturgically in the universal Church are in capital letters. The names of saints celebrated liturgically but only in certain areas are in lower-case letters and are italicized. The saints who are traditionally honored on certain days but are not liturgically celebrated are in lower-case letters. Names appearing with an asterisk (*) are those of saints from the United States.

KEY

RANKS:
Solemnity   SOL
Feast   FEAST
Memorial   MEM
Optional Memorial   OPT MEM

Abbreviations:

abt.	abbot(s)	m.	martyr(s)
abs.	abbess(es)	mat.	matron(s)
bp.	bishop(s)	pat.	patriarch
cnf.	confessor(s)	p.	pope
dea.	deacon(s)	pr.	priest(s)
dr.	doctor(s)	rel.	religious
evang.	evangelist	v.	virgin(s)
her.	hermit	wd.	widow
k.	king		

JANUARY

1 SOLEMNITY OF MARY, MOTHER OF GOD   **SOL**
Concordius, m.; Felix of Bourger; Almachius or Telemachus, m.; Euphrosyne, v.; Eu-

gendus or Oyend, abt.; William of Saint Benignus, abt.; Fulgentius, bp.; Clarus, abt.; Peter of Atroa, abt.; Odilo, abt.; Franchea, v.

2 BASIL THE GREAT and GREGORY NAZIANZEN, bps., drs. MEM
Macarius of Alexandria; Munchin, bp.; Vincentian; Adalhard or Adelard, abt.; Caspar del Bufalo.

3 Antherus, p. m.; Peter Balsam, m.; Geneviève, v.; Bertilia of Mereuil, wd.

4 *Elizabeth Ann Seton**
Gregory of Langres, bp.; Pharaïldis, v.; Rigobert of Rheims, bp.

5 *John Neumann, bp.**
Apollinaris Syncletica, v.; Syncletica, v.; Simeon Stylites; Convoyon, abt.; Dorotheus the Younger, abt.; Gerlac.

6 EPIPHANY SOL
John of Ribera, bp.; Charles Melchior from Sezze, rel.; Raphaela Maria Porras of the Sacred Heart of Jesus, v.; Wiltrudis, wd.; Erminold, abt.; Guarinus or Guérin, bp.

7 Raymond of Penyafort OPT MEM
Lucian of Antioch, m.; Valentine, bp.; Tillo; Aldric, bp.; Reinold; Canute Lavard; Kentigerna, wd.

8 Apollinaris of Hierapolis, bp.; Lucian of Beauvais, m.; Severinus of Noricum; Severinus of Septempeda, bp.; Erhard, bp.; Gudula, v.; Pega, v.; Wulsin, bp.; Thorfinn, bp.

9 Marciana, v., m.; Julian, Basilissa and Companions, m.; Peter of Sebaste, bp.; Waningus or Vaneng; Adrian of Canterbury, abt.; Berhtwald of Canterbury, abt.

10 Marcian; John the Good, bp.; Agatho, p.; Peter Orseolo; William, bp.

11 Theodosius the Cenobiarch; Salvius or Sauve, bp.

12 Arcadius, m.; Tigirius and Eutropius, m.; Caesaria, v.; Victorian, abt.; Benedict or Benet Biscop, bp.; Antony Pucci, pr.

13 HILARY, bp., dr. OPT MEM
Agrecius or Agritius, bp.; Berno, abt.

14 *Felix Nola, cnf.*
Macrina the Elder, wd.; Barbasymas and Companions, m.; Datius, bp.; Kentigern or Mungo, bp.; Sava, bp.

15 *Paul the First Hermit, cnf.; Maur, abt.;* Macarius the Elder; Isidore of Alexandria; John Calybites; Ita, v.; Bonet or Bonitus, bp.; Ceowulf.

16 *Marcellus I, p.*
Priscilla, mat.; Honoratus, bp.; Fursey, abt.; Henry of Cocket; Berard and Companions, m.

17 ANTHONY, abt. MEM
Speusippus, Eleusippus and Meleusippus, m.; Genulf or Genou, bp.; Julian Sabas, her.; Sabinus of Piacenza, bp.; Richimir, abt.; Sulpicius II or Sulpice.

18 *Prisca, v., m.*
Volusian, bp.; Deicolus or Desle, abt.

19 *Canute or Knute, k., m.*
Germanicus, m.; Nathalan, bp.; Albert of Cashel, bp.; Fillan or Foelan, abt.; Wulstan, bp.; Henry of Uppsala, bp., m.

20 FABIAN, p., m. OPT MEM
SEBASTIAN, m. OPT MEM
Euthymius the Great, abt.; Fechin, abt.

21 AGNES, v., m. MEM
Fructuosus of Tarragona, bp., m.; Patroclus, m.; Epiphanius of Pavia, bp.; Meinrad, m.; Alban Roe, pr., m.

22 VINCENT, dea., m. OPT MEM
Anastasius, m.
Blesilla, wd.; Dominic of Sora, abt.; Berhtwald, bp.; Valerius of Saragossa; Vincent Pallotti, pr.

23 *Emerentiana, v., m.*
Asclas, m.; Agathangelus and Clement, m.; John the Almsgiver, pat.; Ildephonsus, bp.; Bernard or Barnard, bp.; Lufthildis, v.; Maimbod, m.

24 FRANCIS DE SALES, bp., dr. MEM
Babylas, bp., m.; Felician, bp., m., and Messalina, m.; Macedonius.

25 CONVERSION OF PAUL, APOSTLE FEAST
Artemas, m.; Juventinus and Maximinus, m.; Publius, abt.; Apollo, abt.; Praejectus or Prix, bp., m.; Poppo, abt.

26 TIMOTHY AND TITUS, bp.   MEM
    Paula, wd.; Conan, bp.; Alberic, abt.; Eystein, bp.; Margaret of Hungary, v.
27 ANGELA MERICI, v.   OPT MEM
    Julian of Le Mans, bp.; Marius or May, abt.; Vitalian, p.
28 THOMAS AQUINAS, pr., dr.   MEM
    Peter Nolasco, cnf.
    John of Reomay, abt.; Paulinus of Aquileia, bp.; Charlemagne; Amadeus, bp.; Peter Thomas, bp.
29 Sabinian, m.; Gildas the Wise, abt.; Sulpicius "Severus," bp.
30 *Martina, v., m.*
    Barsimaeus, bp.; Bathildis, wd.; Aldegundis, v.; Adelelmus or Aleaume, abt.; Hyacintha Mariscotti, v.
31 JOHN BOSCO, pr.   MEM
    Cyrus and John, m.; Marcella, wd.; Aidan or Maedoc of Ferns, bp.; Adamnan of Coldingham; Ulphia, v.; Eusebius, m.; Nicetas of Novgorod, bp.; Francis Xavier Bianchi.
Sunday after Jan. 6: BAPTISM OF THE LORD   FEAST
Sunday within the octave of Christmas: HOLY FAMILY   FEAST

FEBRUARY

1 Pionius, m.; Brigid or Bride, v.; Sigebert III of Austrasia; John "of the Grating," bp.; Henry Morse, pr., m.
2 PRESENTATION OF THE LORD   FEAST
    Adalbald of Ostrevant, m.; Joan of Lestonnac, wd.
3 BLASE, bp., m.   OPT MEM
  ANSGAR, bp.   OPT MEM
    Laurence of Spoleto, bp.; Ia, v.; Laurence of Canterbury, bp.; Werburga, v.; Anskar, bp.; Margaret "of England," v.; Aelred of Rievaulx, abt.
4 *Andrew Corsini, bp., cnf.*
    Theopilus the Penitent; Phileas, bp., m.; Isidore of Pelusium, abt.; Modan, abt.; Nicholas Studites, abt.; Rembert, bp.; Joan of Valois, mat.; Joseph of Leonessa; John de Britto, m.
5 AGATHA, v., m.   MEM
    Avitus of Vienne, bp.; Bertoul or Bertulf; Indractus and Dominica, m.; Vodalus or Voel; Adelaide of Bellich, v.; The Martyrs of Japan: Peter Baptist, Martin de Aguirre, Francis Blanco, Francis-of-St.-Michael, Philip de las Casas, Gonsalo Garcia, Paul Miki, John Goto, James Kisai, Caius Francis, Francis of Miako, Leo Karasuma, Louis Ibarki, Antony Deynan, and Thomas Kasaki.
6 PAUL MIKI AND COMPANION MARTYRS   MEM
    Mel and Melchu, bp.; Vedast or Vaast, bp.; Amand, bp.; Guarinus, bp.; Hildegund, wd.
7 Adaucus, m.; Theodore of Heraclea, m.; Moses, bp.; Richard, "King"; Luke the Younger.
8 JEROME EMILIANI   OPT MEM
    John of Matha, cnf.
    Nicetius or Nizier of Besançon, bp.; Elfleda, v.; Meingold, m.; Cuthman; Stephen of Muret, abt.
9 *Apollonia, v., m.*
    Nicephorus, m.; Sabinus of Canosa, bp.; Teilo, bp.; Ansbert, bp.; Alto, abt.
10 SCHOLASTICA, v.   MEM
    Soteris, v., m.; Trumwin, bp.; Austreberta, v.; William of Maleval.
11 OUR LADY OF LOURDES   OPT MEM
    Saturninus, Dativus and Companions, m.; Lucius, bp., m.; Lazarus, bp.; Severinus, abt.; Caedmon; Gregory II, p.; Benedict of Aniane, abt.; Paschal I, p.
12 Marina, v.; Julian the Hospitaler; Meletius, bp.; Ethelwald, bp.; Antony Kauleas, bp.; Ludan.
13 Polyeuctus, m.; Martinian the Hermit; Stephen of Rieti, abt.; Modomnoc; Licinius or Lesin, bp.; Ermengild or Ermenilda, wd.; Catherine dei Ricci, v.
14 CYRIL, MONK AND METHODIUS, bp.   MEM
    John Baptist of the Conception (John García), pr.
    Valentine, pr., m.
    Abraham, bp.; Maro, abt.; Auxentius; Conran, bp.; Antonius of Sorrento, abt.; Adolf, bp.
15 Agape, v., m.; Walfrid, abt.; Tanco or Tatto, bp., m.; Sigfrid, bp.

16 Onesimus, m.; Juliana, v., m.; Elias, Jeremy and Companions, m.; Gilbert of Sempringham.

17 SEVEN FOUNDERS OF THE ORDER OF SERVITES — OPT MEM
Theodulus and Julian, m.; Loman, bp.; Fintan of Cloneenagh, abt.; Finan, bp.; Evermod, bp.; Silvin, bp.

18 *Simeon,* bp., m.
Leo and Paregorius, m.; Flavian, bp., m.; Helladius, bp.; Colman of Lindisfarne, bp.; Angilbert, abt.; Theotonius, abt.

19 Mesrop, bp.; Barbatus, bp.; Beatus of Liebana; Boniface of Lausanne, bp.; Conrad of Piacenza.

20 Tyrannio, Zenobius and Companions, m.; Sadoth, bp., m.; Eleutherius of Tournai, bp.; Eucherius of Orleans, bp.; Wulfric.

21 PETER DAMIAN, bp., dr. — OPT MEM
Severian, bp., m.; Germanus of Granfel, m.; George of Amastris, bp.; Robert Southwell, pr., m.

22 CHAIR OF PETER, APOSTLE — FEAST
Thalassius and Limnaeus; Baradates; Margaret of Cortona.

23 POLYCARP, bp., m. — MEM
Serenus the Gardener or Cerneuf of Billom, m.; Alexander Akimetes; Dositheus; Boisil or Boswell, abt.; Milburga and Mildgytha, v.; Willigis, bp.

24 Montanus, Lucius and Companions, m.; Praetextatus or Prix, bp., m.

25 Victorinus and Companions, m.; Caesarius Nazianzen; Ethelbert of Kent; Walburga, v.; Tarasius, bp.; Gerland, bp.

26 Nestor, bp., m.; Alexander of Alexandria, bp.; Porphyry, bp.; Victor or Vittre the Hermit.

27 *Gabriel of Our Lady of Sorrows,* cnf.
Besas, Cronion and Julian, m.; Thalelaeus the Hermit; Leander, bp.; Baldomerus or Galmier; Alnoth; John of Gorze, abt.; Ann Line, m.

28 Proterius, bp., m.; Romanus and Lupicinus, abt.; Hilarus, p.; Oswald of Worcester, bp.

MARCH

1 David or Dewi, bp.; Felix II (III), p.; Albinus or Aubin of Angers, bp.; Swithbert, bp.; Rudesind or Rosendo, bp.

2 Chad or Ceadda, bp.

3 Marinus and Astyrius, m.; Chelidonius and Emeterius, m.; Arthelais, v.; Non or Nonnita; Winwaloe or Guénolé, abt.; Anselm of Nonantola, abt.; Cunegund, wd.; Gervinus, abt.; Aelred of Rievaulx, abt.

4 CASIMIR, cnf. — OPT MEM
Adrian and Companions; Peter of Cava, bp.

5 Adrian and Eubulus, m.; Phocas of Antioch, m.; Eusebius of Cremona; Gerasimus, abt.; Ciaran or Kieran of Saighir, bp.; Piran, abt.; Virgil of Arles, bp.; John Joseph of the Cross.

6 Fridolin, abt.; Cyneburga, Cyneswide and Tibba; Chrodegang, bp.; Balred and Bilfred; Cadroe or Cadroel, abt.; Ollegarius or Oldegar, bp.; Cyril of Constantinople; Colette, v.

7 PERPETUA AND FELICITY, m. — MEM
Paul the Simple; Drausius or Drausin, bp.; Esterwine, abt.; Ardo; Theophylact, bp.

8 JOHN OF GOD, rel. — OPT MEM
Pontius; Philemon and Apollonius, m.; Senan, bp.; Felix of Dunwich, bp.; Julian of Toledo, bp.; Humphrey or Hunfrid, bp.; Duthac, bp.; Veremund, abt.; Stephen of Obazine, abt.

9 FRANCES OF ROME, rel. — OPT MEM
Pacian, bp.; Gregory of Nyssa, bp.; Bosa, bp.; Catherine of Bologna, v.; Dominic Savio.

10 Codratus and Companions, m.; Macarius of Jerusalem, bp.; Simplicius, p.; Kessog, bp., m.; Anastasia Patricia, v.; Droctoveus or Drotté, abt.; Attalas, abt.; Himelin; John Ogilvie, pr., m.

11 Constantine, m.; Sophronius, bp.; Vindician, bp.; Benedict Crispus, bp.; Oengus or Aengus, abt.-bp.; Eulogius of Cordova, m.; Aurea, v.; Teresa Margaret Redi, v.

12 Maximilian of Theveste, m.; Peter, Gorgonius and Dorotheus, m.; Paul Aurelian, bp.; Theophanes the Chronicler, abt.; Alphege of Winchester, bp.; Bernard of Capua, bp.; Fina or Seraphina, v.

13 Euphrasia or Euphraxia, v.; Mochoemoc, abt.; Gerald of Mayo, abt.; Nicephorus of Constantinople, bp.; Ansovinus, bp.; Heldrad, abt.; Roderic and Solomon, m.
14 Leobinus or Lubin, bp.; Eutychius or Eustathius, m.; Matilda, wd.
15 Longinus, m.; Matrona, v., m.; Zachary, p.; Leocritia or Lucretia, v., m.; Louise de Marillac, wd.; Clement Mary Hofbauer.
16 Julian of Antioch, m.; Abraham Kidunia; Finnian Lobhar, abt.; Eusebia, abs.; Gregory Makar, bp.; Heribert, bp.
17 PATRICK, bp.   OPT MEM
Joseph of Arimathea; Agricola, bp.; Gertrude of Nivelles, v.; Paul of Cyprus; The Martyrs of the Serapeum.
18 CYRIL OF JERUSALEM, bp., dr.   OPT MEM
Alexander of Jerusalem, bp., m.; Frigidian or Frediano, bp.; Edward the Martyr; Anselm of Lucca, bp.; Salvator of Horta.
19 JOSEPH, HUSBAND OF MARY   SOL
John of Panaca; Landoald and Companions; Alcmund, m.
20 Photina and Companions, m.; Martin of Braga, bp.; Cuthbert, bp.; Herbert; Wulfram, bp.; The Martyrs of Mar Saba.
21 Serapion, bp.; Enda, abt.
22 Paul of Narbonne and Companions; Basil of Ancyra, m.; Deogratias, bp.; Benvenuto of Osimo, bp.; Nicholas of Flue; Nicholas Owen, m.
23 TURIBIUS DE MONGROVEJO, bp.   OPT MEM
Victorian and Companions, m.; Benedict the Hermit; Ethelwald or Oidilwald the Hermit; Joseph Oriol.
24 Irenaeus of Sirmium, bp., m.; Aldemar, abt.; Catherine of Vadstena, v.; Simon of Trent and William of Norwich.
25 ANNUNCIATION OF THE LORD   SOL
Dismas; Barontius; Hermenland, abt.; Alfwold, bp.; Lucy Filippini, v.; Margaret Clitherow, m.
26 Castulus, m.; Félix of Trier, bp.; Macartan, bp.; Braulio, bp.; Ludger, bp.; Basil the Younger.
27 John of Egypt.
28 Guntramnus; Tutilo.
29 Barachisius and Jonas, m.; Cyril of Heliopolis, m., and Mark, bp.; Armogastes, Archinimus and Saturus, m.; Gundleus and Gwaladys or Gladys; Rupert, bp.; Berthold; Ludolf, bp.
30 Regulus or Rieul, bp.; John Climacus, abt.; Zozimus, bp.; Osburga, v.; Leonardo Murialdo, pr.
31 Balbina, v.; Acacius or Achatius, bp.; Benjamin, m.; Guy of Pomposa, abt.

APRIL

1 Melito, bp.; Walaricus or Valery, abt.; Macarius the Wonder-Worker; Hugh of Grenoble, bp.; Hugh of Bonnevaux, abt.; Gilbert of Caithness, bp.; Catherine of Palma, v.
2 FRANCIS OF PAOLA, her.   OPT MEM
Apphian and Theodosia, m.; Mary of Egypt; Nicetius or Nizier of Lyons, bp.; Ebba the Younger, v.; John Paine, pr., m.
3 Pancras of Taormina, bp., m.; Sixtus or Xystus I, p., m.; Agape, Chionia and Irene, v., m.; Burgundofara or Fare, v.; Nicetas, abt.; Richard Wyche or Richard of Chichester, bp.
4 ISIDORE, bp., dr.   OPT MEM
Agathopus and Theodulus, m.; Tigernach, bp.; Plato, abt.; Benedict the Black.
5 VINCENT FERRER, pr.   OPT MEM
Derfel Gadarn; Ethelburga of Lyminge, mat.; Gerald of Sauve-Majeure, abt.; Albert of Montecorvino, bp.
6 The Martyrs in Persia; Marcellinus, m.; Celestine I, p.; Eutychius, bp.; Prudentius of Troyes, bp.; William of Eskhill, abt.
7 JOHN BAPTISTE DE LA SALLE, pr.   MEM
Hegesippus; Aphraates; George the Younger, bp.; Celsus or Ceallach, bp.; Aybert; Henry Walpole, pr., m.
8 Dionysius of Corinth, bp.; Perpetuus, bp.; Walter of Pontoise, abt.; Julie Billiart, v.

9 Mary of Cleophas, mat.; Waldetrudis or Waudru, wd.; Hugh of Rouen, bp.; Gaucherius, abt.

10 Bademus, abt.; The Martyrs under the Danes; Macarius or Macaire of Ghent; Fulbert, bp.; Paternus of Abdinghof; Michael de Sanctis.

11 STANISLAUS, bp., m.   MEM
   Barsanuphius; Isaac of Spoleto; Godeberta, v.; Guthlac; Gemma Galgani, v.

12 Julius I, p.; Zeno of Verona, bp.; Sabas the Goth, m.; Alferius, abt.

13 MARTIN I, p., m.   OPT MEM
   Hermenegild, m.
   Agathonica, Papylus and Carpus, m.; Martius or Mars, abt.

14 *Tiburtius, Valerius and Maximus*, m.
   Ardalion, m.; Lambert of Lyons, bp.; Bernard of Tiron, abt.; Caradoc; Bénezet; Antony, Eustace and John, m.; Lidwina of Schiedam, v.

15 Basilissa and Anastasia, m.; Padarn or Patern, bp.; Ruadan of Lothra, abt.; Hunna or Huva, mat.

16 Optatus and Companions and Encratis, v., m.; Turibius of Astorga, bp.; Paternus or Pair, bp.; Fructuosus of Braga, bp.; Magnus, m.; Drogo or Druon; Contardo; Joseph Benedict Labre; Bernadette Soubirous, v.

17 Mappalicus and Companions, m.; Innocent of Tortona, bp.; Donnan and Companions, m.; Robert of Chaise-Dieu, abt.; Stephen Harding, abt.

18 Apollonius the Apologist, m.; Laserian, Laisren or Molaisse, bp.; Idesbald, abt.; Galdinus, bp.

19 Leo IX, p.; Expeditus; Ursmar, abt., bp.; Geroldus; Alphege, bp., m.

20 Marcellinus of Embrun, bp.; Marcian or Marian; Caedwalla; Hildegund, v.; Agnes of Montepulciano, v.

21 ANSELM, bp., dr.   OPT MEM
   Simeon Barsabae, bp., and Companions, m.; Anastasius I of Antioch, bp.; Beuno, abt.; Malrubius or Maelrubha, abt.; Conrad of Parzham.

22 Epipodius and Alexander, m.; Leonides, m.; Agapitus I, p.; Theodore of Sykeon, bp.; Opportuna, v., abs.

23 GEORGE, m.   OPT MEM
   Felix, Fortunatus and Achilleus, m.; Ibar, bp.; Gerard of Toul, bp.; Adalbert of Prague, bp., m.

24 FIDELIS OF SIGMARINGEN, pr., m.   OPT MEM
   Mellitus, bp.; Ivo, bp.; Egbert; William Firmatus; Mary Euphrasia Pelletier, v.

25 MARK, EVANGELIST   FEAST
   Anianus, bp.; Heribald, bp.

26 Peter of Braga, bp.; Richarius or Riquier, abt.; Paschasius Radbertus, abt.; Franca of Piacenza, v., abs.; Stephen of Perm, bp.

27 Anthimus, bp.; Asicus or Tassach, bp.; Maughold or Maccul, bp.; Floribert, bp.; Stephen Pechersky, bp.; Zita, v.; Turibius of Lima, bp.; Theodore the Sanctified, abt.

28 PETER CHANEL, pr., m.   OPT MEM
   Vitalis, m.
   Valeria, m.; Pollio, m.; Theodora and Didymus, m.; Cronan of Roscrea, abt.; Pamphilus of Sulmona, bp.; Cyril of Turov, bp.; Louis Mary of Montfort.

29 CATHERINE OF SIENA, v.   MEM
   Peter of Verona
   Wilfrid the Younger, bp.; The Abbots of Cluny: Berno, Odo, Mayeul, Odilo, Hugh, Aymard, and Peter the Venerable; Robert of Molesme, abt.; Joseph Cottolengo.

30 PIUS V, p.   OPT MEM
   Maximus, m.; Eutropius of Saintes, bp., m.; James and Marian, m.; Forannan, abt.; Gualfardus or Wolfhard.

MAY

1 JOSEPH THE WORKER   OPT MEM
  Amator or Amatre, bp.; Brioc or Brieuc, abt.; Sigismund of Burgundy; Marculf or Marcoul, abt.; Theodard of Narbonne, bp.; Peregrine Laziosi.

2 ATHANASIUS, bp., dr.   MEM
  Exsuperius or Hesperus and Zoë, m.; Waldebert, abt.; Ultan, abt.; Wiborada, v., m.; Mafalda or Matilda.

3 PHILIP AND JAMES, APOSTLES   FEAST
Alexander, Eventius and Theodulus, m.
Juvenal, bp.
Timothy and Maura, m.; Philip of Zell.

4 Cyriacus or Judas Quiricus, bp.; Pelagia of Tarsus, v., m.; John Houghton, Robert Lawrence, Augustine Webster, Richard Reynolds, pr., m.; Venerius, bp.; Godehard or Gothard, bp.; Florian, m.

5 Hilary of Arles, bp.; Maurantius, abt.; Mauruntius, abt.; Avertinus; Angelo, m.; Jutta, wd.

6 Evodius, bp.; Edbert, bp.; Petronax, abt.

7 Domitian, bp.; Liuhard, bp.; Serenicus and Serenus; John of Beverley, bp.

8 Victor Maurus, m.; Acacius or Agathus, m.; Gibrian; Desideratus, bp.; Boniface IV, p.; Benedict II, p.; Wiro, Plechlem and Oteger; Peter of Tarentaise, bp.

9 Beatus; Pachomius, abt.; Gerontius, bp.

10 *Antoninus of Florence,* bp., cnf.
Gordian and Epimachus, m.
Calepodius, m.; Alphius, Cyrinus and Philadelphus, m.; Catald and Conleth, bp.; Solangia, v., m.; John of Ávila, pr.

11 Mamertus, bp.; Comgall, abt.; Asaph, bp.; Gengulf or Gengoul; Majolus or Mayeule, abt.; Ansfrid, bp.; Walter of L'Esterp, abt.; Francis di Girolamo; Ignatius of Laconi.

12 NEREUS AND ACHILLES, m.   OPT MEM
PANCRAS, m.   OPT MEM
Epiphanius of Salamis, bp.; Modoaldus, bp.; Rictrudis, wd.; Germanus of Constantinople, bp.; Dominic of the Causeway.

13 Glyceris, v., m.; Mucius or Mocius, m.; Servatius or Servais, bp.; John the Silent; Erconwald, bp.; Euthymius the Illuminator, abt.; Peter Regalatus.

14 MATTHIAS, APOSTLE   FEAST
Pontius, m.; Carthage, Carthach or Mochuda, abt.; Erembert, bp.; Michael Garicoïts; Mary Mazzarello, v.

15 *ISIDORE THE FARMER**
Torquatus and Companions, m.; Isidore of Chios; Hilary of Galeata, abt.; Dympna and Gerebernus, m.; Bertha and Rupert; Hallvard, m.; Isaias of Rostov, bp.; Peter of Lampsacus and Companions, m.

16 *Ubaldus,* bp., cnf.
Peregrine of Auxerre, bp., m.; Possidius, bp.; Germerius, bp.; Brendan, abt.; Domnolus, bp.; Carantoc or Carannog, abt.; Honoratus of Amiens, bp.; Simon Stock; John Nepomucen, m.; Andrew Hubert Fournet.

17 *Paschal Baylon,* cnf.
Madron or Madern; Bruno of Würzburg, bp.

18 JOHN I, p., m.   OPT MEM
Venantius, m.
Theodotus, Thecusa and Companions, m.; Potamon, bp., m.; Eric of Sweden, m.; Felix of Cantalice.

19 *Peter Morrone or Peter Celestine V,* her., p.
Pudentiana and Pudens, m.
Calocerus and Parthenius, m.; Dunstan, bp.; Ivo of Kermartin.

20 BERNARDINO OF SIENA, pr.   OPT MEM
Thalelaeus, m.; Basilla or Basilissa, v., m.; Baudelius, m.; Austregisilus or Outril, bp.; Ethelbert, m.

21 Godric; Andrew Bobola, m.; Theophilus of Corte.

22 Aemilius and Castus, m.; Quiteria, v., m.; Romanus; Julia, m.; Aigulf or Ayoul, bp.; Humility, wd.; Rita, wd.

23 Desiderius or Didier, bp., m.; Guibert; Leonitus of Rostov, bp., m.; Ivo of Chartres, bp.; Euphrosyne of Polotsk, v.; William of Rochester, m.; John Baptist Rossi.

24 Donatian and Rogatian, m.; Vincent of Lérins; David I, King of Scotland; Nicetas of Pereaslav, m.

25 BEDE, pr., dr.   OPT MEM
GREGORY VII, p.   OPT MEM
MARY MAGDALENE DE PAZZI, v.   OPT MEM
Dionysius of Milan, bp.; Zenobius, bp.; Leo or Lyé, abt.; Aldhelm, bp.; Gennandius, bp.; Madeleine Sophie Barat, v.

26 PHILIP NERI, pr.   MEM

Quadratus, bp.; Priscus or Prix and Companions, m.; Lambert of Vence, bp.; Marian of Quito, v.

27 AUGUSTINE OF CANTERBURY, bp. OPT MEM
Restituta of Sora, v., m.; Julius and Companions, m.; Eutropius of Orange, bp.; Melangell or Monacella, v.

28 Senator, bp.; Justus of Urgel, bp.; Germanus or Germain, bp.; William of Gellone; Bernard of Menthon or Montjoux; Ignatius of Rostov, bp.

29 Cyril of Caesarea, m.; Maximinus, bp.; Sisinnius, Martyrius and Alexander, m.; Theodosia, v., m.; William, Stephen, Raymund and Companions, m.

30 Isaac of Constantinople, abt.; Exsuperantius, bp.; Madelgisilus or Mauguille; Walstan; Ferdinand III, King of Castile; Joan of Arc, v.; Eleutherius, p.; Luke Kirby, pr., m.

31 VISITATION FEAST
Petronilla, v., m.
Cantius, Cantianius and Cantianella, m.; Mechtildis of Edelstetten, v.

First Sunday after Pentecost: HOLY TRINITY SOL
Thursday after Holy Trinity: CORPUS CHRISTI SOL
Friday after Second Sunday after Pentecost: SACRED HEART SOL
Saturday after Second Sunday after Pentecost: IMMACULATE HEART OF MARY

JUNE

1 JUSTIN, m. MEM
Pamphilus and Companions, m.; Proculus, "the soldier," and Proculus of Bologna, bp.; Caprasius or Caprais; Wistan; Simeon of Syracuse; Eneco or Iñigo, abt.; Theobald of Alba.

2 MARCELLINUS AND PETER, m. OPT MEM
Erasmus, bp., m.
Pothinus and Companions, m.; Eugenius I, p.; Stephen of Sweden, bp., m.; Nicholas the Pilgrim; Blandina, m.

3 CHARLES LWANGA AND COMPANIONS, m. MEM
Cecilius; Pergentinus and Laurentinus, m.; Lucillian and Companions, m.; Clotilda, wd.; Liphardus and Urbicius, abt.; Kevin or Coegmen, abt.; Genesius of Clermont, bp.; Isaac of Córdova, m.; Morand.

4 *Francis Caracciolo*, cnf.
Quirinus, bp., m.; Metrophanes, bp.; Optatus of Milevis, bp.; Petroc, abt.; Vincentia Gerosa, v.

5 BONIFACE, bp., m. MEM
Dorotheus of Tyre, m.; Sanctius or Sancho, m.

6 NORBERT, bp. OPT MEM
Philip the Deacon; Ceratius or Cérase, bp.; Eustorgius of Milan, bp.; Jarlath, bp.; Gudwal or Gurval; Claud, bp.

7 Paul of Constantinople, bp.; Meriadoc, bp.; Colman of Dromore, bp.; Vulflagius or Wulphy; Willibald, bp.; Gottschalk, m.; Robert of Newminster, abt.; Antony Gianelli, bp.

8 Maximinus of Aix; Médard, bp.; Clodulf or Cloud, bp.; William of York, bp.

9 EPHREM, dea., dr. OPT MEM
Primus and Felician, m.
Columba or Columcille, abt.; Vincent of Agen, m.; Pelagia of Antioch, v., m.; Richard of Andria, bp.

10 Getulius and Companions, m.; Ithamar, bp.; Landericus or Landry, bp.; Bogumilus, bp.

11 BARNABAS, APOSTLE OPT MEM
Felix and Fortunatus, m.; Parisio.

12 *John of Sahagun*, cnf.
Antonina, m.; Onuphrius; Ternan, bp.; Peter of Mount Athos; Leo III, p.; Odulf; Eskil, bp., m.

13 ANTHONY OF PADUA, dr., pr. MEM
Felicula, m.; Aquilina, m.; Triphyllius, bp.

14 Valerius and Rufinus, m.; Dogmael; Methodius I of Constantinople, bp.

15 *Vitus*, m.
Hesychius, m.; Tatian Dulas, m.; Orsiesius, abt.; Landelinus, abt.; Edburga of Winchester, v.; Bardo, bp.; Aleydis or Alice, v.; Germaine of Pibrac, v.

16 Ferreolus and Ferrutio, m.; Cyricus and Julitta, m.; Tychon, bp.; Aurelian, bp.; Benno, bp.; Lutgardis, v.; John Francis Regis.

17 Nicander and Marcian, m.; Bessarion; Hypatius, abt.; Avitus, abt.; Nectan; Hervé or Harvey, abt.; Botulf or Botolph, abt.; Adulf, bp.; Moling, bp.; Rainerius of Pisa; Teresa and Sanchia of Portugal; Emily de Vialar, v.

18 *Mark and Marcellian,* m.
Gregory Barbarigo, bp.; Amandus, bp.; Elizabeth of Schönau, v.

19 ROMUALD, abt.   OPT MEM
Juliana of Falconieri, v.
Gervase and Protase, m.
Deodatus or Dié, bp.; Bruno or Boniface of Querfurt, bp., m.

20 *Silverius,* p.
Goban or Gobain, m.; Bagnus or Bain, bp.; Adalbert of Magdeburg, bp.; John of Matera, abt.

21 ALOYSIUS GONZAGA, rel.   MEM
Eusebius of Samosata, bp.; Alban or Albinus of Mainz, m.; Méen or Mewan, abt.; Engelmund; Leutfridus or Leufroy, abt.; Ralph or Raoul, bp.; John Rigby, m.

22 PAULINUS OF NOLA, bp.   OPT MEM
JOHN FISHER, bp., m., and THOMAS MORE, m.   OPT MEM
Alban, m.; Nicetas of Remesiana, bp.; Eberhard, bp.

23 Agrippina, v., m.; Etheldreda or Audrey, wd.; Lietbertus or Libert, bp.; Joseph Cafasso; Thomas Garnet, pr., m.

24 THE BIRTH OF JOHN THE BAPTIST   SOL
The martyrs under Nero; Simplicius, bp.; Bartholomew of Farne.

25 *William of Vercelli,* abt.
Febronia, v., m.; Gallicanus; Prosper of Aquitaine; Prosper of Reggio, bp.; Maximus of Turin, bp.; Moloc or Luan, bp.; Adalbert of Egmond; Eurosia, v., m.; Gohard, bp., and Companions, m.

26 *John and Paul*
Vigilius, bp., m.; Maxentius, abt.; Salvius or Sauve and Superius; John of the Goths; Pelagius or Pelayo, m.; Anthelm, bp.

27 CYRIL OF ALEXANDRIA, bp., dr.   OPT MEM
Zoilus and Companions, m.; Samson of Constantinople; John of Chinon; George Mtasmindeli of the Black Mountains, abt.; Ladislaus of Hungary; Benvenuto of Gubbio.

28 IRENAEUS, bp., m.   MEM
Plutarch, Potamiaena and Companions, m.; Paul I, p.; Heimrad; Sergius and Germanus of Valaam, abt.; John Southworth, pr., m.

29 PETER AND PAUL, APOSTLES   SOL
Cassius, bp.; Salome and Judith; Emma, wd.

30 FIRST MARTYRS OF THE CHURCH OF ROME   OPT MEM
The Commemoration of Paul, Apostle
Martial, bp.; Bertrand of Le Mans, bp.; Erentrude, v.; Theobald or Thibaud of Provins.

JULY

1 Shenute, abt.; Theodoric or Thierry, abt.; Carilefus or Calais, abt.; Gall of Clermont, bp.; Eparchius or Cybard; Simeon Salus; Serf or Servanus, bp.; Oliver Plunkett, bp., m.

2 *Processus and Martinian,* m.
Monegundis, wd.; Otto of Bamberg, bp.

3 THOMAS, APOSTLE   FEAST
Leo II, p., cnf.
Anatolius, bp.; Irenaeus and Mustiola, m.; Julius and Aaron, m.; Heliodorus, bp.; Anatolius of Constantinople, bp.; Rumold or Rombaut, m.; Bernardino Realino.

4 ELIZABETH OF PORTUGAL   OPT MEM
Bertha, wd.; Andrew of Crete, bp.; Odo of Canterbury, bp.; Ulric of Augsburg, bp.

5 ANTHONY ZACCARIA, pr.   OPT MEM
Athanasius the Athonite, abt.

6 MARIA GORETTI, v., m.   OPT MEM
Romulus of Fiesole, bp., m.; Dominica, v., m.; Sisoes; Goar; Sexburga, wd.; Modwenna, v.; Godelva, m.

7   Pantaenus; Palladius, bp.; Félix of Nantes, bp.; Ethelburga, Ercongota and Sethrida, v.;
    Hedda, bp.
8   Aquila and Prisca; Procopius, m.; Kilian and Companions, m.; Withburga, v.; Adrian
    III, p.; Grimbald; Sunniva and Companions; Raymund of Toulouse.
9   Everild, v.; The Martyrs of Gorkum: Nicholas Pieck, Jerome Weerden, Leonard Vechel,
    Nicholas Janssen, Godfrey van Duynen, John van Oosterwyk, John van Hoornaer, Adrian
    van Hilvarenbeek, James Lacops, Andrew Wouters, Antony van Willehad, and Nicasius
    van Heeze; Veronica Giuliani, v.
10 *Rufina and Secunda, v., m.*
    Amalburga, wd.; Amalburga, v.; Antony and Theodosius of Pechersk, abt.
11 BENEDICT, abt.   MEM
    Drostan, abt.; John of Bergamo, bp.; Hidulf, bp.; Olga, wd.
12 *John Gualbert, abt.*
    Nabor and Felix, m.
    Veronica; Jason, m.; Hermagoras and Fortunatus, m.; John the Iberian, abt.; John Jones,
    pr., m.
13 HENRY THE EMPEROR   OPT MEM
    Silas or Silvanus; Maura and Brigid; Eugenius of Carthage, bp.; Mildred, v.; James of
    Voragine, bp.; Francis Solano.
14 CAMILLUS DE LELLIS, pr.   OPT MEM
    Deusdedit, bp.; Marchelm; Ulric of Zell, abt.
15 BONAVENTURE, bp., dr.   MEM
    James of Nisibis, bp.; Barhadbesaba, m.; Donald; Swithun, bp.; Athanasius of Naples,
    bp.; Edith of Polesworth; Vladimir of Kiev; David of Munktorp, bp.; Pompilio Pirrotti.
16 OUR LADY OF MOUNT CARMEL   OPT MEM
    Athenogenes, bp., m.; Eustathius of Antioch, bp.; Helier, m.; Reineldis, v., m.; Fulrad, abt.
17 Speratus and Companions, the Scillitan Martyrs; Marcellina, v.; Ennodius, bp.; Kenelm;
    Leo IV, p.; Clement of Okhrida and Companions, the Seven Apostles of Bulgaria; Nerses
    Lampronazi, bp.; Mary Magdalen Postel.
18 Pambo; Philastrius, bp.; Arnulf or Arnoul of Metz, bp.; Frederick of Utrecht, bp., m.;
    Bruno of Segni, bp.
19 Justa and Rufina, v., m.; Arsenius; Symmachus, p.; Ambrose Autpert; Macrina the
    Younger, v.; William John Plessington, pr., m.
20 Wilgefortis or Liberta; Joseph Barsabas; Aurelius, bp.; Flavian and Elias, bp.; Vulmar
    or Wulmar, abt.; Ansegisus, abt.
21 LAWRENCE OF BRINDISI, pr., dr.   OPT MEM
    Praxedes, v.
    Victor of Marseilles, m.; Arbogast, bp.
22 MARY MAGDALENE   MEM
    Joseph of Palestine; Wandregisilus or Wandrille, abt.; Philip Evans and John Lloyd, pr., m.
23 BRIDGET, rel.   OPT MEM
    Apollinaris of Ravenna, bp., m.
    Liborius, bp.
    The Three Wise Men; John Cassian, abt.; Romula and her Companions, v.; Anne or
    Susanna, v.
24 *Christina, v., m.*
    Lewina, v., m.; Declan, bp.; Boris and Gleb, m.; Christina the Astonishing, v.; Christina
    of Tyre, v., m.; John Boste, pr., m.
25 JAMES THE APOSTLE   FEAST
    Christopher, m.
    Thea, Valentina and Paul, m.; Magnericus, bp.
26 JOACHIM AND ANN, PARENTS OF MARY   MEM
    Simeon the Armenian; Bartholomea Capitanio, v.
27 *Pantaleon, m.*
    The Seven Sleepers of Ephesus; Aurelius, Natalia, Felix and Companions, m.; Theobald
    of Marly, abt.
28 *Nazarius and Celsus, m.*
    Samson, bp.; Botvid.
29 MARTHA, v.   MEM
    Felix II, p.
    Simplicius, Faustinus and Beatrice, m. *

Lupus or Loup, bp.; Olaf, m.; William Pinchon, bp.
30 PETER CHRYSOLOGUS, bp., dr.   OPT MEM
   Abdon and Sennen, m.
   Julitta, wd., m.
31 IGNATIUS OF LOYOLA, pr.   MEM
   Neot; Helen of Skövde, wd.; Germanus of Auxerre, bp.; Justin De Jacobis, bp.

AUGUST

1 ALPHONSUS LIGUORI, bp., dr.   MEM
  The Holy Machabees, m.
  Faith, Hope, Charity, and their mother, Wisdom, m.; Aled, Almedha, or Eiluned, v., m.;
  Ethelwold, bp.; Peter Julian Eymard, pr.
2 EUSEBIUS OF VERCELLI, bp.   OPT MEM
  Stephen I, p., m.
  Theodota, m.; Thomas of Dover.
3 *The Finding of the Body of Stephen,* protomartyr.
  Waltheof of Walthen, abt.; Nicodemus.
4 JOHN VIANNEY, pr.   MEM
  Ia and Companions, m.; Molua or Lughaidh, abt.
5 DEDICATION OF ST. MARY MAJOR   OPT MEM
  Addai and Mari, bp.; Afra, m.; Nonna, mat.
6 THE TRANSFIGURATION OF OUR LORD   FEAST
  Justus and Pastor, m.; Hormisdas, p.
7 SIXTUS II, p., m., AND COMPANIONS, m.   OPT MEM
  CAJETAN, pr.   OPT MEM
  Donatus, bp., m.
  Claudia, mat.; Dometius the Persian, m.; Victricius, bp.; Albert of Trapani; Donatus of
  Besançon, bp.
8 DOMINIC, pr.   MEM
  Cyriacus, Largus and Smaragdus, m.
  The Fourteen Holy Helpers; Hormisdas, m.; Altman, bp.
9 *Romanus,* m.
  Emygdius, m.; Nathy and Felim, bp.; Oswald of Northumbria, m.
10 LAWRENCE, dea., m.   FEAST
   Philomena or Philumena
11 CLARE, v.   MEM
   Tiburtius
   Susanna
   Alexander the Charcoal-Burner, bp., m.; Equitius, abt.; Blane, bp.; Attracta or Araght, v.;
   Lelia, v.; Gaugericus or Géry, bp.; Gerard of Gallinaro and Companions.
12 Euplus, m.; Murtagh or Muredach, bp.; Porcarius and Companions, m.
13 PONTIAN, p., m., and HIPPOLYTUS, pr., m.   OPT MEM
   Cassian, m.
   Simplician, bp.; Radegund, mat.; Maximus the Confessor, abt.; Benildi (Peter Romançon),
   rel.; Wigbert, abt.; Nerses Klaiëtsi, bp.
14 *Eusebius of Rome,* cnf.
   Marcellus of Apamea, bp., m.; Fachanan, bp.; Athanasia, mat.
15 ASSUMPTION OF MARY   SOL
   Tarsicius, m.; Arnulf or Arnoul of Soissons, bp.
16 STEPHEN OF HUNGARY, KING   OPT MEM
   Arsacius; Armel, abt.; Rock.
17 *Hyacinth,* cnf.
   Mamas, m.; Eusebius, p.; Liberatus and Companions, m.; Clare of Montefalco, v.
18 *Agapitus,* m.
   Florus and Laurus, m.; Helena, wd.; Alipius, bp.
19 JOHN EUDES, pr.   OPT MEM
   Andrew the Tribune, m.; Timothy, Agapius and Thecla, m.; Sixtus or Xystus III, p.;
   Mochta, abt.; Bertulf, abt.; Sebald; Louis of Anjou, bp.
20 BERNARD, abt., dr.   •   MEM
   Amadour; Oswin, m.; Philibert, abt.

21 PIUS X, p. MEM
Luxorius, Cisellus and Camerinus, m.; Bonosus and Maximian, m.; Sidonius Apollinaris, bp.; Abraham of Smolensk, abt.

22 QUEENSHIP OF MARY MEM
Timothy and Symphorianus, m.
Sigfrid, abt.; Andrew of Fiesole; John Kemble and John Wall, pr., m.

23 ROSE OF LIMA, v. OPT MEM
Philip Benizi, cnf.
Claudius, Asterius, Neon, Domnina and Theonilla, m.; Eugene or Eoghan, bp.

24 BARTHOLOMEW, APOSTLE FEAST
The Martyrs of Utica; Audoenus or Ouen, bp.

25 LOUIS IX, KING, cnf. OPT MEM
JOSEPH CALASANZ, pr. OPT MEM
Genesius the Comedian, m.; Genesius of Arles; Patricia, v.; Mennas of Constantinople, bp.; Ebba the Elder, v.; Gregory of Utrecht, abt.; Joan Antide-Thouret, v.; Mary Michaela Desmaisières, v.

26 Joan Elizabeth Bichier des Ages, v.; Teresa of Jesus Jornet Ibars, v.

27 MONICA MEM
Marcellus and Companions, m.; Poemen, abt.; Caesarius of Arles, bp.; Syagrius, bp.; Hugh or Little Hugh of Lincoln; Margaret the Barefooted, wd.; David Lewis, pr., m.

28 AUGUSTINE, bp., dr. MEM
Hermes
Julian of Brioude, m.; Alexander, John III, and Paul IV, bp.; Moses the Black; Edmund Arrowsmith, pr., m.; Joachim of Vedruña, rel.

29 BEHEADING OF JOHN THE BAPTIST, m. MEM
Sabina, m.
Medericus or Merry, abt.

30 *Felix and Adauctus*, m.
Pammachius; Rumon or Ruan; Fantinus, abt.; Margaret Ward, m.

31 *Raymond Nonnatus*, cnf.
Paulinas of Trier, bp.; Aidan of Lindisfarne, bp.

SEPTEMBER

1 *Giles*, abt.
Verena, v.; Lupus or Leu, bp.; Fiacre; Sebbe; Drithelm; Beatrice de Silva Meneses, v.

2 Antoninus of Apamea, m.; Castor, bp.; Agricolus, bp.; William of Roskilde, bp.; Brocard.

3 GREGORY THE GREAT, p., dr. MEM
Phoebe; Macanisius, bp.; Simeon Stylites the Younger; Remaclus, bp.; Aigulf, m.; Hildelitha, v.; Cuthburga, wd.

4 Marcellus and Valerian, m.; Marinus; Boniface I, p.; Ultan of Ardbraccan, bp.; Ida of Herzfeld, wd.; Rosalia, v.; Rose of Viterbo, v.

5 *Lawrence of Justinian*, bp., cnf.
Bertinus, abt.

6 Donatian, Laetus and Companions, bp., m.; Eleutherius, abt.; Chainoaldus or Cagnoald, bp.; Bega or Bee, v.

7 Regina or Reine, v., m.; Sozon, m.; Grimonia, v., m.; John of Nicomedia, m.; Anastasius the Fuller, m.; Cloud or Clodoald; Alcmund and Tilbert, bp.

8 BIRTH OF MARY FEAST
Hadrian, Natalia, m.
Eusebius, Nestabus, Zeno, and Nestor, m.; Disibod; Sergius I, p.; Corbinian, bp.

9 *Peter Claver*, pr.*
Gorgonius
Isaac or Sahak I, bp.; Ciaran or Kieran, abt.; Audomarus or Omer, bp.; Bettelin.

10 *Nicholas of Tolentino*, cnf.
Nemesian and Companions, m.; Menodora, Metrodora, and Nymphodora, v., m.; Pulcheria, v.; Finnian of Moville, bp.; Salvius of Albi, bp.; Theodard, bp.; Aubert, bp.; Ambrose Barlow, pr., m.

11 *Protus and Hyacinth*, m.
Theodora of Alexandria; Paphnutius the Great, bp.; Patiens of Lyons, bp.; Deiniol, bp.; Peter of Chavanon; Bodo, bp.

12 Ailbhe, bp.; Eanswida, v.; Guy of Anderlecht.
13 JOHN CHRYSOSTOM, bp., dr.   MEM
   Maurilius, bp.; Eulogius of Alexandria, bp.; Amatus, abt.; Amatus, bp.
14 TRIUMPH OF THE HOLY CROSS   FEAST
   Maternus, bp.; Notburga, v.
15 OUR LADY OF SORROWS   MEM
   Nicomedes, m.
   Nicetas the Goth, m.; Aichardus or Archard, abt.; Mirin; Catherine of Genoa, wd.
16 CORNELIUS, p., m., and CYPRIAN, bp., m.   MEM
   Euphemia, Lucy and Geminianus, m.
   Abundius, Abundantius, and Companions, m.; Ninian, bp.; Ludmila, m.; Edith of
   Wilton, v.; John Macias, rel.
17 ROBERT BELLARMINE, bp., dr.   OPT MEM
   Stigmata of Francis
   Socrates and Stephen, m.; Satyrus; Lambert of Maestricht, bp., m.; Columba, v., m.;
   Hildegard, v.; Peter Arbues, m.; Francis of Camporosso.
18 *Joseph of Cupertino,* cnf.
   Ferreolus, m.; Methodius of Olympus, bp., m.; Richardis, wd.; Ferreolus of Limoges, bp.
19 JANUARIUS, bp., m.   OPT MEM
   Peleus and Companions, m.; Sequanus or Seine, abt.; Goericus or Abbo, bp.; Theodore
   of Tarsus, bp.; Mary of Cerevellon, v.; Theodore, David, and Constantine; Emily de
   Rodat, v.
20 Vincent Madelgarius, abt.
21 MATTHEW, APOSTLE AND EVANGELIST   FEAST
   Maura of Troyes, v.; Michael of Chernigov and Theodore, m.
22 *Thomas of Villanova,* bp.
   Maurice and Companions, m.
   Phocas the Gardener, m.; Felix III (IV), p.; Salaberga, wd.; Emmeramus, bp.
23 Adamnan, abt.; Martha of Persia, v., m.
24 *Our Lady of Ransom*
   Geremarus or Germer, abt.; Gerard of Csanad, bp., m.; Pacifico of San Severino.
25 Firminus, bp., m.; Cadoc, abt.; Aunacharius or Aunaire, bp.; Finbar, bp.; Coelfrid, abt.;
   Albert of Jerusalem, bp.; Sergius of Radonezh, abt.; Vincent Strambi, bp.
26 COSMOS AND DAMIAN, m.   OPT MEM
   Colman of Lann Elo, abt.; John of Meda; Nilus of Rossano, abt.; Therese Couderc (Marie
   Victoire Couderc), v.
27 VINCENT DE PAUL, pr.   MEM
   Elzear.
28 WENCESLAUS, m.   OPT MEM
   Exsuperius, bp.; Eustochium, v.; Faustus of Riez, bp.; Annemund, bp.; Lioba, v.
29 MICHAEL, GABRIEL, AND RAPHAEL, ARCHANGELS   FEAST
   Rhipsime, Gaiana, and Companions, v., m.; Theodota of Philippolis, m.
30 JEROME, pr., dr.   MEM
   Gregory the Illuminator, bp.; Honorius of Canterbury, bp.; Simon of Crepy.

OCTOBER

1 THERESA OF THE CHILD JESUS, v.   MEM
   Remigius, bp., cnf.
   Romanus the Melodist; Melorus Melar or Mylor, m.; Bavo or Allowin.
2 GUARDIAN ANGELS   MEM
   Eleutherius, m.; Leodegarius or Leger, bp., m.
3 Hesychius; The Two Ewalds, m.; Gerard of Brogne, abt.; Froilan and Attilanus, bp.;
   Thomas of Hereford, bp.
4 FRANCIS OF ASSISI, cnf.   MEM
   Ammon; Petronius, bp.
5 Apollinaris of Valence, bp.; Galla, wd.; Magenulf or Meinulf; Flora of Beaulieu, v.;
   Aymard of Cluny, abt.
6 BRUNO, pr.   OPT MEM
   Faith, v., m.; Nicetas of Constantinople; Mary Frances of Naples, v.

7 OUR LADY OF THE ROSARY MEM
  Mark, p.
  Justina, v., m.; Osyth, v., m.; Artaldus or Arthaud, bp.
8 *Marcellus,* m.
  Simeon; Pelagia the Penitent; Thaïs; Reparata, v., m.; Demetrius, m.; Keyne, v.
9 DENIS, bp., m., RUSTICUS and ELEUTHERIUS, m. OPT MEM
  JOHN LEONARDI, pr. OPT MEM
  Demetrius of Alexandria, bp.; Publia, wd.; Andronicus and Athanasia; Savin; Gislenus or
  Ghislain, abt.; Gunther; Louis Bertrand.
10 *Francis Borgia,* cnf.
  Gereon and Companions, m.; Eulampius and Eulampia, m.; Maharsapor, m.; Cerbonius,
  bp.; Paulinus of York, bp.; Daniel and Companions, m.
11 Andronicus, Tarachus and Probus, m.; Nectarius, bp.; Canice or Kenneth, abt.; Agilbert,
  bp.; Gummarus or Gommaire; Bruno the Great of Cologne, bp.; Alexander Sauli, bp.;
  Maria Desolata (Emmanuela Torres Acosta), v.
12 Maximilian, bp., m.; Felix and Cyprian and Companions; Edwin, m.; Ethelburga of
  Barking, v.; Wilfrid, bp.
13 *Edward the Confessor*
  Faustus, Januarius, and Martial, m.; Comgan, abt.; Gerald of Aurillac; Coloman, m.;
  Maurice of Carnoët, abt.
14 CALLISTUS I, p., m. OPT MEM
  Justus of Lyons, bp.; Manechildis, v.; Angadrisma or Angadrême, v.; Burchard, bp.;
  Dominic Lauricatus.
15 TERESA OF AVILA, v., dr. MEM
  Leonard of Vandoeuvre, abt.; Thecla of Kitzingen, v.; Euthymius the Younger, abt.
16 HEDWIG, rel. OPT MEM
  MARGARET MARY ALACOQUE, v. OPT MEM
  Martinian and Companions and Maxima; Gall; Mommolinus, bp.; Bercharius, abt.; Lull,
  bp.; Anastasius of Cluny; Bertrand of Comminges, bp.; Gerard Majella.
17 IGNATIUS OF ANTIOCH, bp., m. MEM
  John the Dwarf; Anstrudis or Anstrude, v.; Nothelm, bp.; Seraphino; Richard Gwyn, m.
18 LUKE THE EVANGELIST FEAST
  Justus of Beauvais, m.
19 ISAAC JOGUES, pr., m., and COMPANIONS, m.* OPT MEM
  PAUL OF THE CROSS, pr. OPT MEM
  Peter of Alcántara, cnf.
  Ptolemaeus and Lucius, m.; Cleopatra, wd., and Varus, m.; Ethbin; Aquilinus, bp.; Frides-
  wide, v.; Philip Howard, m.
20 Caprasius, m.; Artemius, m.; Acca, bp.; Andrew of Crete, m.; Maria Bertilla (Ann Francis
  Boscardin), v.
21 *Hilarion,* abt.
  Malchus; Fintan or Munnu of Taghmon, abt.; Condedus; John of Bridlington.
22 Abercius, bp.; Philip of Heraclea, bp., and Companions, m.; Mallonius or Mellon, bp.;
  Nunilo and Alodia, v., m.; Donatus of Fiesole, bp.
23 JOHN OF CAPISTRANO, pr. OPT MEM
  Theodoret, m.; Severinus or Seurin, m.; Severinus Boethius, m.; Romanus of Rouen, bp.;
  Ignatius of Constantinople, bp.; Allucio.
24 ANTHONY CLARET, bp. OPT MEM
  Felix of Thibiuca, bp., m.; Proclus, bp.; Aretas and the martyrs of Najran and Elesbaan;
  Senoch, abt.; Martin or Mark; Maglorius or Maelor, bp.; Martin of Vertou, abt.;
  Ebregislus or Evergislus, bp.
25 *Chrysanthus and Daria,* m.
  Crispin and Crispinian, m.; Fronto and George, bp.; Gaudentius, bp.
26 Lucian and Marcian, m.; Rusticus of Narbonne, bp.; Cedd, bp.; Eata, bp.; Bean, bp.
27 Frumentius, bp.; Otteran or Odhran, abt.
28 SIMON AND JUDE, APOSTLES FEAST
  Anastasia and Cyril, m.; Fidelis of Como, m.; Salvius or Saire, Faro, bp.
29 Narcissus of Jerusalem, bp.; Theuderius or Chef, abt.; Colman of Kilmacduagh, bp.;
  Abraham of Rostov, abt.

30 Serapion of Antioch, bp.; Marcellus, m.; Asterius, bp.; Germanus of Capua, bp.; Ethelnoth, bp.; Alphonsus Rodriguez.
31 Quentin or Quintinius, m.; Foillan, abt.; Wolfgang, bp.

NOVEMBER

1 ALL SAINTS   SOL
Caesarius and Julian, m.; Benignus of Dijon, m.; Austremonius or Stremoine, bp.; Mary, v., m.; Maturinus or Mathurin; Marcellus of Paris, bp.; Vigor, bp.; Cadfan, abt.
2 ALL SOULS   OPT MEM
Victorinus, bp., m.; Marcian.
3 MARTIN DE PORRES, rel.   OPT MEM
Winifrid, v., m.; Rumwald; Hubert, bp.; Pirminus, bp.; Amicus; Malachy, bp.
4 CHARLES BORROMEO, bp.   MEM
Vitalis and Agricola, m.
Pierius; John Zedazneli and Companions; Clarus, m.; Joannicus.
5 Elizabeth and Zachary; Galation and Episteme; Bertilla, v.
6 Leonard of Noblac; Melaine, bp.; Illtud or Illtyd, abt.; Winnoc, abt.; Demetrian, bp.; Barlaam of Khutyn, abt.
7 Herculanus, bp., m.; Florentius of Strasbourg, bp.; Willibrord, bp.; Engelbert, bp., m.
8 *The Four Crowned Martyrs*
Cybi or Cuby, abt.; Deusdedit, p.; Tysilio or Suliau, abt.; Willehad, bp.; Godfrey of Amiens, bp.
9 DEDICATION OF ST. JOHN LATERAN   FEAST
Theodore Tiro
Benignus or Benen, bp.; Vitonus or Vanne, bp.
10 LEO THE GREAT, p., dr.   MEM
Andrew Avellino, cnf.
Theoctista, v.; Aedh Mac Bricc, bp.; Justus of Canterbury, bp.
11 MARTIN OF TOURS, bp.   MEM
Menna, m.
Theodore the Studite, abt.; Bartholomew of Grottaferrata, abt.
12 JOSAPHAT, bp., m.   MEM
Nilus the Elder; Emilian Cucullatus, abt.; Machar, bp.; Cunibert, bp.; Cumian, abt.; Livinus, bp., m.; Lebuin or Liafwine or Livinius; Benedict of Benevento and Companions, m.; Astrik or Anastasius, bp.; Cadwallader.
13 *Francis Xavier Cabrini,* v.*
Didacus or Diego, cnf.
Arcadius and Companions, m.; Brice or Britius, bp.; Eugenius of Toledo, bp.; Maxellendis, v., m.; Kilian; Nicholas I, p.; Abbo of Fleury, abt.; Homobonus; Stanislaus Kostka; Nicholas Tavelic, Adeodatus Aribert, Stephen of Cueno and Peter of Narbonne, p., m.
14 Dyfrig, bp.; Laurence O'Toole, bp.
15 ALBERT THE GREAT, bp., dr.   OPT MEM
Abibus, Gurias, and Samonas, m.; Desiderius or Didier, bp.; Malo, bp.; Fintan of Rheinau; Leopold of Austria.
16 MARGARET OF SCOTLAND   OPT MEM
GERTRUDE THE GREAT, v.   OPT MEM
Mechtilde, v.; Eucherius of Lyons, bp.; Afan, bp.; Edmund of Abingdon, bp.; Agnes of Assisi, v.
17 ELIZABETH OF HUNGARY, rel.   MEM
Gregory the Wonderworker, bp., cnf.
Dionysius of Alexandria, bp.; Alphaeus and Zachaeus, m.; Acislus and Victoria, m.; Anianus or Aignan of Orleans, bp.; Gregory of Tours, bp.; Hilda, v.; Hugh of Lincoln, bp.
18 DEDICATION OF THE CHURCHES OF PETER AND PAUL   OPT MEM
Romanus of Antioch, m.; Mawes or Maudez, abt.; Odo of Cluny, abt.
19 Nerses, bp., m.; Barlaam, m.
20 *Félix of Valois,* cnf.
Dasius, m.; Nerses of Sahgerd, bp., and Companions, m.; Maxentia, v., m.; Edmund the Martyr; Bernward, bp.
21 PRESENTATION OF MARY   MEM
Gelasius I, p.; Albert of Louvain, bp., m.

22 CECILIA, v., m.   MEM
    Philemon and Apphia, m.
23 CLEMENT I, p., m.   OPT MEM
    COLUMBANUS, abt.   OPT MEM
    Felicity, m.
    Amphilochius, bp.; Gregory, bp.; Trudo or Trond.
24 *Chrysogonus*, m.
    Colman of Cloyne, bp.; Flora and Mary, v., m.
25 Mercurius, m.; Moses, m.
26 *Silvester*, abt.
    Peter of Alexandria, bp., m.
    Siricius, p.; Basolus or Basle; Conrad of Constance, bp.; Nikon "Metanoeite"; John
    Berchmans; Leonard of Port Maurice.
27 Barlaam and Josaphat; James, Intercisus, m.; Secundinus or Sechnall, bp.; Maximus of
    Riez, bp.; Cungar, abt.; Fergus, bp.; Virgil or Fergal, bp.
28 Stephen the Younger, m.; Simeon Metaphrastes; James of the March; Joseph Pignatelli;
    Catherine Labouré, v.
29 *Saturninus*, m.
    Saturninus or Sernin, bp., m.; Radbod, bp.
30 ANDREW THE APOSTLE   FEAST
    Sapor and Isaac, bp., m.; Cuthbert Mayne, pr., m.
Last Sunday of the liturgical year: CHRIST THE KING   SOL

DECEMBER

1 Ansanus, m.; Agericus or Airy, bp.; Tudwal, bp.; Eligius or Eloi, bp.; Edmund Campion,
    Alexander Briant, and Ralph Sherwin, pr., m.
2 *Viviana* or Bibiana, v., m.
    Chromatius, bp.
3 FRANCIS XAVIER, pr.   MEM
    Lucius; Claudius, Hilaria and Companions, m.; Cassian, m.; Sola.
4 JOHN DAMASCENE, pr., dr.   OPT MEM
    Maruthas, bp.; Anno, bp.; Osmund, bp.; Bernard of Parma, bp.
5 SABAS, abt.
    Crispina, m.; Nicetius of Trier, bp.; Birinus, bp.; Sigramnus or Cyran, abt.; John Almond,
    pr., m.
6 NICHOLAS, bp.   OPT MEM
    Dionysia, Majoricus, and Companions, m.; Abraham of Kratia, bp.
7 AMBROSE, bp., dr.   MEM
    Eutychian, p.; Josepha Rosello, v.
8 IMMACULATE CONCEPTION   SOL
    Romaric, abt.
9 Hipparchus and Companions, m.; the Seven Martyrs of Samosata; Leocadia, v., m.;
    Gorgonia, wd.; Budoc or Beuzec, abt.; Peter Fourier.
10 *Melchiades*, p.
    Mennâs, Hermogenes, and Eugraphus, m.; Eulalia of Merida, v., m.; Gregory III, p.;
    Edmund Gennings, Eustace White, Polydore Plasden, pr., m., and Swithun Wells, m.;
    John Roberts, pr., m.
11 DAMASUS I, p.   OPT MEM
    Barsabas, m.; Fuscian, Victoricus, and Gentian, m.; Daniel the Stylite.
12 JANE FRANCES DE CHANTAL, rel.   OPT MEM
    *Our Lady of Guadalupe**
    Epimachus Alexander and Companions, m.; Finnian of Clonard, bp.; Corentin or Cury,
    bp.; Edburga, v.; Vicelin, bp.
13 LUCY, v., m.   MEM
    Eustratius and Companions, m.; Judoc or Josse; Aubert of Cambrai, bp.; Odilia or
    Ottilia, v.
14 JOHN OF THE CROSS, pr., dr.   MEM
    Spiridion, bp.; Nicasius, bp., and Companions, m.; Venantius Fortunatus, bp.; Dioscorus
    and others, m.

15 Nino, v.; Valerian and other martyrs in Africa; Stephen of Surosh, bp.; Paul of Latros; Mary di Rosa, v.

16 Adelaide, wd.

17 Lazarus; Olympias, wd.; Begga, wd.; Sturmi, abt.; Wivina, v.

18 Rufus and Zozimus, m.; Gatian, bp.; Flannan, bp.; Winebald, abt.

19 Nemesius, m.; Anastasius I, p.

20 Ammon and Companions, m.; Philogonius, bp.; Ursicinus, abt.; Dominic of Silos, abt.

21 PETER CANISIUS, pr., dr.   OPT MEM
Anastasius II of Antioch, bp., m.

22 Chaeremon, Ischyion, and other martyrs

23 JOHN OF KANTY, pr.   OPT MEM
The Ten Martyrs of Crete; Victoria and Anatolia, v., m.; Servulus; Dagobert II of Austrasia; Thorlac, bp.

24 VIGIL OF CHRISTMAS
Gregory of Spoleto, m.; Delphinus, bp.; Tharsilla and Emiliana, v.; Irmina, v., and Adela, wd.

25 CHRISTMAS   SOL
Anastasia of Sirmium, m.
Eugenia, v., m.; The Martyrs of Nicomedia.

26 STEPHEN, THE FIRST MARTYR   FEAST
Archelaus, bp.; Dionysius, p.; Zozimus, p.

27 JOHN, APOSTLE AND EVANGELIST   FEAST
Fabiola, wd.; Nicarete, v.; Theodore and Theophanes; John Stone, pr., m.

28 HOLY INNOCENTS, m.   FEAST
Antony of Lérins

29 THOMAS À BECKET, bp., m.   OPT MEM
Trophimus, bp.; Marcellus Akimetes, abt.; Ebrulf or Evroult, abt.; Peter the Venerable, abt.

30 Sabinus and Companions, m.; Anysia, m.; Anysius, bp.; Egwin, bp.

31 SYLVESTER I, p.   OPT MEM
Columba of Sens, v., m.; Melania the Younger, wd.

Sunday within the octave of Christmas or if there is no Sunday within the octave, Dec. 30:
HOLY FAMILY   FEAST

BYZANTINE CALENDAR

The most widely used calendar, after that of the Roman Rite, is the Byzantine. There are some variants, especially in Slavic countries. But substantially it corresponds to the calendar and martyrology for the Byzantine Rite—Slavonic Usage—which are here given.

SEPTEMBER

1 The Beginning of the "Indiction," i.e., of the Church Year; Simeon, the Elder, the Stylite, and his mother Martha; Synaxis of the Most Holy Mother of God in Missina; Sts. Aithelas, 40 Women of Macedonia and Ammon, Martyrs; Sts. Callistus, Evodius, and Hermogenes, Martyrs; Venerable Josue son of Nave.
2 St. Mammas, Martyr; John of the Fast, Patriarch of Constantinople.
3 St. Anthimus, Priest-Martyr; Theoktistus, Co-Faster of Euthymius the Great.
4 St. Babilas, Priest-Martyr; Three Youths; St. Moses, Prophet and Patriarch; 84 Youths; Sts. Hermione and Eutychia, Martyrs.
5 St. Zachary, Prophet.
6 Commemoration of the miracle by St. Michael the Archangel at Colossa in Chonia; Sts. Eudoxius and with him 1104 Martyrs; Archippus.
7 St. Sozon, Martyr.
8 Nativity of Our Most Holy Mother of God and Ever-Virgin Mary.
9 Sts. and Venerable, Joachim and Anna; St. Severianus, Martyr.
10 Sts. Menodora, Metrodora and Nymphodora, Martyrs.
11 Theodora, of Alexandria, Penitent.
12 St. Autonomus, Priest-Martyr.
13 Commemorating the Restoration of the Church of the Resurrection of Our Lord Jesus Christ; St. Cornelius, Priest-Martyr.
14 Exaltation of the Holy and Vivifying Cross.
15 St. Nicetas, the Great-Martyr.
16 St. Euphemia, the Great, Virgin-Martyr.
17 Sts. Sophia and her Three Daughters, Faith, Hope, and Charity.
18 Eumenius, Bishop of Gortyna.
19 Sts. Trophimus, Sabbatius, and Dorymedont, Martyrs.
20 Sts. Eustace (Placidus), the Great Soldier-Martyr, and his wife, Theopista, and their sons, Agapius and Theopistus, Martyrs.
21 St. Quadratus.
22 St. Phocas, Priest-Martyr; St. Jonas, Prophet; Venerable Jonas, father of St. Theophanes.
23 Conception of St. John the Baptist, the glorious Prophet and Precursor of Our Lord, Jesus Christ.
24 St. Thecla, First Virgin-Martyr.

25 Venerable Euphrosyna.
26 The Death of St. John the Theologian, Apostle and Evangelist.
27 St. Callistratus, Soldier-Martyr.
28 Chariton, Confessor-Martyr.
29 Cyriacus, Hermit.
30 St. Gregory, Priest-Martyr and the Illuminator of Greater Armenia.

OCTOBER

1 Patronage of the Most Holy Queen, Mother of Our God and Ever-Virgin Mary; St. Ananias, Apostle; Roman, the sweet-singer.
2 St. Cyprian, Priest-Martyr; St. Justina, Virgin-Martyr; St. Andreas.
3 St. Dionysius, the Aeropagite, Priest-Martyr; Rusticus and Eleutherius, Athenian converts.
4 St. Hierotheus, Priest-Martyr.
5 St. Charitina, Martyr.
6 St. Thomas, the glorious Apostle.
7 Sts. Sergius and Bacchus, Martyrs.
8 Pelagia and Taisia.
9 St. James, son of Alpheus, Apostle and Brother of St. Matthew, the Apostle and Evangelist; Andronicus and his wife, Athanasia.
10 Sts. Eulampius and his sister, Eulampia, Martyrs.
11 St. Philip, one of Seven Deacons; Theophan, Confessor.
12 Sts. Probus, Tarachus and Andronicus, Martyrs; Cosmas, Bishop of Majuma.
13 Sts. Carpus, Bishop and Papylus, his Deacon, and with them Agathonica, sister of Papylus, and Agathodorus, their servant.
14 Paraskevas; Sts. Nazarius, Gervase, Protase and Celsus, Martyrs; St. Vitalis, Martyr.
15 Euthymius, the New; St. Lucian, Venerable-Martyr.
16 St. Longinus, the Centurion.
17 St. Osee, Prophet; St. Andrew of Crete, Venerable-Martyr.
18 St. Luke, Apostle and Evangelist.
19 St. Joel, Prophet; St. Varus, Martyr; St. Sadoth, Priest-Martyr.
20 St. Artemius, Great Martyr.
21 Hilarion the Great, Hegumen-Abbot.
22 St. Abercius, Bishop of Hieropolis; Sts. Seven Youths of Ephesus.
23 St. James, the Less, Apostle, brother of the Lord, the first Bishop of Jerusalem; Ignatius, Confessor.
24 Sts. Arethas and other Martyrs.
25 Sts. Marcian and Martyrius, Martyrs.
26 St. and Glorious Demetrius, the Great, Martyr.
27 St. Nestor, Martyr; Sts. Capitolina, a Cappadocian lady, with her handmaid; Erotheides, Martyrs.
28 St. Parasceva, Martyr, surnamed "Friday"; Sts. Terentius and Neonila and their Children: Photius, Anicetas, Theodulus, Hierarchus and Eunicius; Stephen of Sabbas.
29 St. Anastasia, Venerable-Martyr; Sts. Abram, Hermit of Edessa and Mary, his niece.
30 Sts. Zenobius and Zenobia, his sister, Martyrs; Venerable Peter, Bishop of Syracuse; Sts. Asterius, Claudius, Neon, Theonilla, Martyrs; Sts. Terentius, Mark, Justus, and Artem, Apostles.
31 Sts. Stachis, Ampliatus, Urban and Narcissus, Apostles; St. Epimachus, Martyr; Maura.

NOVEMBER

1 Sts. Cosmas and Damian, Martyrs; Leontius, Anthimus and Euthropius; Venerable Theodotia.
2 Sts. Acindynus, Pegasius, Aphdonius, Elpidephorus and Anempodistus, Martyrs.
3 Sts. Acepsimas, Bishop; Joseph, Presbyter, and Aithalus, Deacon; Renovation of the Church of St. George the Great-Martyr, in Lydia.
4 Joannicius the Great; Sts. Nicander, Bishop of Myra, and Hermas, Presbyter.
5 Sts. Galacteon and Epistemis; Sts. Patrobas, Hermias, Linus, Gaius and Philologus.
6 Paul, Archbishop of Constantinople.
7 Sts. Hieron and Others with him; Lazarus, wonderworker.

8 Synaxis of St. Michael the Archangel and the Angelic Hosts.
9 Sts. Onesiphorus and Porphyrius, Martyrs; Venerable Theoktista.
10 Sts. Erastus, Olympus, Rodeon, Sosipater, Tertius and Quartus, Apostles.
11 Sts. Mennas, Victor and Vincent, Martyrs; St. Stephenida, Martyr; Theodore Studite, Confessor, Hegumen-Abbot.
12 St. Josaphat, Priest-Martyr; John the "Almoner"; Nilus.
13 St. John the Chrysostom, Archbishop of Constantinople.
14 St. Philip, one of the Twelve.
15 Sts. Gurias, Samonis and Aviva, Martyrs at Edessa.
16 St. Matthew, Apostle and Evangelist.
17 Gregory, Thaumaturgus, i.e., wonderworker.
18 Sts. Plato and Romanus, Martyrs.
19 St. Abdias, Prophet; St. Barlam, Martyr.
20 Gregory of Decapolis; Proclus, Archbishop of Constantinople.
21 Presentation in the Temple of Our Most Holy Queen, Mother of God and Ever-Virgin Mary.
22 Sts. Philemon and Others with him, Apostles; St. Caecilia, Virgin-Martyr.
23 Amphilochius, Bishop of Iconium, and Gregory, Bishop of Agrigentum.
24 St. Catharine, Great Virgin-Martyr; St. Mercurius, Great-Martyr.
25 Clement, Pope of Rome; Peter, Bishop of Alexandria.
26 Alypius, Stylite.
27 St. James the Persian, Great-Martyr; Palladius.
28 St. Stephen "the Younger" Venerable-Martyr; St. Irenarchus, and Seven Women, Martyrs.
29 Sts. Paramon and Philemonus, Martyrs; Bessarion; Venerable Acacius.
30 St. Andrew, the "First-called" Apostle.

DECEMBER

1 St. Nahum, Prophet; St. Filaret, the "Almsgiver" and St. Ananias, Martyr.
2 St. Habacuc, one of the Twelve Lesser Prophets.
3 St. Sophonias, Prophet; Theodulus.
4 St. Barbara, Great Virgin-Martyr; St. John Damascene, Doctor of the Church.
5 St. Sabbas, Hegumen-Abbot.
6 Nicholas, Archbishop of Myra.
7 Ambrose, Bishop of Milan.
8 The Immaculate Conception of Our Most Holy Queen, Mother of God and Ever-Virgin Mary; "The Conception of St. Ann," i.e., when she conceived the Most Holy Mother of God.
9 Patapius, of Thebes.
10 Sts. Mennas, Hermogenes and Eugraphus, Martyrs.
11 Daniel, Stylite.
12 Spiridion, wonderworker.
13 Sts. Eustratius, Auxentius, Eugene, Mardarius and Orestes, Martyrs; St. Lucy, Virgin-Martyr.
14 Sts. Thyrsus, Leucius, Philemon, Appollonius, Arianus, and Callinicus, Martyrs.
15 St. Eleutherius, Priest-Martyr; Paul of Latra.
16 St. Aggeus, Prophet.
17 St. Daniel, and Sts. Three Youths, Ananias, Azarias, and Misael.
18 St. Sebastian and Companion.
19 St. Boniface, Martyr.
20 St. Ignatius, "Theophorus" Priest-Martyr Bishop at Antioch.
21 St. Juliana, Virgin-Martyr.
22 St. Anastasia, Great-Martyr.
23 Sts. Ten Martyrs at Crete.
24 Sts. Eugenia, Venerable-Martyr and her two slaves, Protus and Hyacinth.
25 The Nativity of Our Lord, God and Saviour, Jesus Christ, or "Christmas Day."
26 Synaxis of the Most Holy Mother of God and St. Joseph, her Spouse; St. Euthymius, Priest-Martyr.
27 St. Stephen, Protomartyr, Apostle and Archdeacon; Theodore, brother of St. Theophanes.
28 Sts. 20,000 Martyrs in Nicomedia; St. Domna, Martyr.
29 The Holy Innocents; Marcellus, Hegumen-Abbot.

30 St. Anysia; Venerable Zoticus.
31 Venerable Melania.

JANUARY

1 Feast of Circumcision of Our Lord and Saviour, Jesus Christ; The Feast of St. Basil the Great, Archbishop of Caesarea.
2 Silvester, Pope of Rome.
3 St. Malachias, Prophet; St. Gordius, Martyr.
4 Synaxis of 70 Apostles; Theoktistus, Hegumen-Abbot.
5 Sts. Theopemptus and Theonas, Martyrs; Syncletica, Venerable; St. Micheas, Prophet.
6 Epiphany, or Holy Manifestation of the Divinity of Our Lord and Saviour, Jesus Christ.
7 Synaxis of St. John, the glorious Prophet.
8 George, the Chozebite and Emilian, Confessor; Dominika, of Carthage; Sts. Juliana and Basilissa, Martyrs.
9 St. Polyeucte, Martyr; Eustratius, Venerable.
10 Gregory, Bishop of Nyssa; Dometian, Venerable, Bishop of Melite; Marcian, Presbyter.
11 Theodosius, Hegumen-Abbot.
12 St. Tatiana, Martyr; Eupraxis, Venerable.
13 Sts. Hermylas and Stratonicus, Martyrs.
14 Fathers of Sinai and Raitha.
15 Paul of Thebes and John the "Tent-dweller."
16 Veneration of the Venerable Chains of St. Peter.
17 Anthony, the Great.
18 Athanasius and Cyril, Archbishops of Alexandria.
19 Macarius of Egypt, and Macarius of Alexandria, Monks; St. Euphrosinia, Virgin.
20 Euthymius the Great, Hegumen-Abbot.
21 Maximus, Confessor; St. Neophitus, Martyr; Sts. Eugene, Canidius, Valerian and Aquilas, Martyrs.
22 St. Timothy, Apostle; St. Anastiasius, Venerable-Martyr of Persia.
23 St. Clems, Priest-Martyr; St. Agathangel, Martyr.
24 Xenia.
25 Gregory, the Theologian.
26 Xenophon, his wife, Mary and sons, Arcadius and John; Theodore, Hegumen-Abbot of Monks of Studites, and his brother, Joseph.
27 Translation of the Relics of St. John Chrysostom.
28 Ephraem, "Prophet of Syrians and cithara of Holy Spirit."
29 Translation of the Relics of St. Ignatius, the "Theoforos," Priest-Martyr, Bishop of Antioch; Sts. Roman, James, Philotheus, and St. Aphraates, Martyrs.
30 Feast of the Three Holy Bishops, i.e., Three Cappadocian Fathers; namely, St. Basil the Great, St. Gregory, the Theologian, and St. John, the Chrysostom; St. Hippolytus, Priest-Martyr.
31 Sts. Cyrus and John, Wonderworkers and Unmercenaries.

FEBRUARY

1 St. Tryphon, Martyr.
2 Presentation of Our Lord Jesus Christ in the Temple (Feast of the Purification of the Blessed Virgin Mary or Candlemas Day).
3 St. Simeon, the Venerable-Senex and Theofer.
4 Isidore of Pelusium; St. Jador, Martyr.
5 St. Agatha, Martyr.
6 Bukolus, Bishop of Smyrna.
7 Parthenius, Bishop of Lampsachia; Luke.
8 St. Theodore, the Great-Martyr; St. Zacharias, the Prophet.
9 St. Nicephorus, Martyr.
10 St. Charalampias, Martyr.
11 St. Blase, Priest-Martyr.
12 Meletius, Archbishop of Great Antioch; St. Marina, Virgin.
13 Martinian, Hegumen; St. Zoe and St. Photina, Venerable Women.

14 Auxentius, Hegumen; Cyril, Bishop of Catania.
15 St. Onesimus, Apostle; Paphnutius, Venerable-Hermit in Egypt and his daughter, Euphrosyne.
16 Sts. Pamphilius, Valentine, Paul, Seleucus, Porphyrus, Julian, Theodulus, and the five Martyrs of Egypt, Elias, Jeremias, Isaias, Samuel and Daniel; Flavianus, Archbishop of Constantinople.
17 St. Theodore of Tyre, the Great-Martyr; Memory of St. Mariamna, sister of Philip, the Apostle.
18 Leo the Great, Pope of Rome.
19 St. Archippus, Apostle, a co-worker with St. Paul; Sts. Maxim, Theodot, Isychus and Asklepiodotus, Martyrs.
20 Leo, Bishop of Catania; St. Sadok, Priest-Martyr; St. Agatho, Venerable, Pope of Rome.
21 Timothy, Hermit; Eustacius, Archbishop of Antioch.
22 Finding of the venerable Relics of Sts. Martyrs at Eugenia; Venerable Peter, Monk, and Athanasius, Martyrs.
23 St. Polycarp, Priest-Martyr.
24 First and Second Finding of the Venerable Head of St. John, the Precursor.
25 St. Tharasius, Archbishop of Constantinople.
26 Porphyrius, Archbishop of Gaza; St. Sebastian, Martyr; St. Photina, of Samaria, Martyr.
27 Procopius, venerable Confessor and Monk.
28 Basil, Confessor and co-faster of St. Procopius; Marina, Cyra and Domnicia, Venerable Women.

MARCH

1 St. Eudoxia, Venerable-Martyr.
2 St. Theodotus, Priest-Martyr.
3 St. Eutropius and his bodyguards, Sts. Cleonicus and Basiliscus, Martyrs.
4 Gerasimus, a Hermit; Sts. Paul and his sister Juliana, Martyrs.
5 St. Conon, Martyr.
6 Forty-Two Martyrs at Ammorius: Theodore, Constantin, Callistus, Theophil and others with them.
7 Sts. Priest-Martyrs at Chersonia: Basil, Ephrem, Capito, Eugene, Everius, Missionary Bishops; Venerable Paul, the Simple, in Egypt, a Solitary.
8 Theophylact, Bishop of Nicomedia.
9 Sts. Forty Martyrs at Sebaste in Armenia.
10 Sts. Codratus and companions: Cyprian, Anectus, and Criscent.
11 Sophronius, Patriarch of Jerusalem.
12 Theophan of Syngria; Gregory the Great, Dialogus, Pope of Rome.
13 Translation of Relics of Our Father, Nicephor, Patriarch of Constantinople.
14 Benedict, Abbot; St. Alexander of Pidna, Priest-Martyr.
15 St. Agapius, Martyr and with him six others: Timolaus, two Alexanders, Romel, two Dionisii.
16 Sts. Sabinus and Papas, Martyrs; St. Julian, Martyr; St. Alexander, Priest-Martyr, Pope of Rome.
17 Venerable Father Alexis.
18 Cyril, Archbishop of Jerusalem; Sts. Alexandra, Claudia, Euphrasia and other Martyrs.
19 Sts. Chrysantus and Darias, Martyrs; Thomas, Patriarch of Constantinople.
20 Martyrs of the Monastery of St. Sabbas.
21 Jacob, Bishop and Confessor.
22 St. Basil, Priest-Martyr, Presbyter of the Church in Ancyra; Venerable Isaak, Monk.
23 St. Nicon, Venerable-Martyr and two hundred companions.
24 Zachary, and James, Confessor; Artemius, Bishop of Thessalonica; St. Artemon, Martyr-Presbyter of Laodicea.
25 Annuciation of Our Most Holy Queen, the Mother of God and Ever-Virgin Mary.
26 Synaxis of the Archangel Gabriel.
27 Matrona of Seluna, Martyr.
28 Hilary, Monk and St. Stephen, wonderworker; St. Jonas and his brother, St. Barachisius of Bethasa, Martyrs.
29 Mark, Bishop of Arethusa and Cyril, a Palestinian Deacon.

30 John Climacus, Hegumen-Abbot; Venerable John the Silent, Bishop of Colonia in Armenia.
31 Hypatius, Bishop of Gangra.

APRIL

1 Mary of Egypt.
2 Titus, wonderworker; Sts. Amphianus and Edesius, Martyrs.
3 Nicetas, Confessor and Hegumen-Abbot; St. Theodosia, Virgin-Martyr.
4 Venerable Fathers Joseph and George; St. Platon, Hegumen-Abbot, Studite.
5 Sts. Theodulus and Agathopodus, "The Cretan Martyrs."
6 Eutyches, Archbishop of Constantinople.
7 George, Bishop of Melete; Serapion, an Egyptian Monk and later Bishop of Thumuis.
8 Sts. Herodion, Agavus, Ruphus, Asyncritus, Phlegon, Hermas, et al., Bishop-Martyrs; Celestine, Pope of Rome.
9 St. Eupsychius, Martyr.
10 Sts. Terence, Africanus, Maximus, Pompilius, and a band of 36 Martyrs.
11 St. Antipas, Bishop-Martyr of Pergamus; Pharmuthius.
12 Basil, Bishop of Pharia.
13 St. Artemon, Priest-Martyr, of Laodicea.
14 Martin, Pope of Rome; Sts. Anthony, John, and Eustathius, Martyrs.
15 Sts. Aristarchus, Pudus, and Trophimus, Apostles; St. Sabbas Gothinus, Martyr; Sts. Basilissa and Anastasia, Martyrs.
16 Sts. Agapia, Irene, and Chionia, Martyrs.
17 Simeon of Persia, Martyr; Acacius, Bishop of Melite; St. Agapitus, Pope of Rome.
18 John, a disciple of St. Gregory, Decapolites; Cosmas, Bishop of Chalcedonia; John, Archbishop of Antiochia.
19 John, the ancient Hermit; St. Paphnutius, Martyr.
20 Theodore, surnamed "Trichinas."
21 St. Januarius, Bishop-Martyr, and Sts. Proculus, Sosius and Faustus, Deacons; St. Desiderius, Lector; Sts. Eutyches and Akutionus; St. Theodore from Pergia, Priest-Martyr.
22 Theodore, "Sykcot"; Sts. Nathanael, Luke and Clement, Apostles.
23 Feast of St. George, the glorious Great-Martyr and wonderworker; St. Alexandra, Martyr.
24 St. Sabbas, Martyr.
25 St. Mark, Apostle and Evangelist.
26 St. Basil, Priest-Martyr; Virgin Glaphyra.
27 St. Simeon, Priest-Martyr.
28 Sts. Jason and Sosipater, Apostles; Sts. Masimus, Dadas, Quinctillianus, Martyrs.
29 Sts. Nine Martyrs at Cyzice; Memnon, wonderworker.
30 St. James the Greater, Apostle.

MAY

1 St. Jeremias, Prophet.
2 Athanasius the Great, Patriarch of Alexandria.
3 Theodosius of the Cave, Hegumen-Abbot; Sts. Timothy and Maurus, Martyrs.
4 St. Pelagia, Venerable-Martyr; Venerable-Mother Pelagia.
5 St. Irene, Glorious Martyr.
6 St. and Venerable, Job, the "Patient."
7 Commemoration of the appearance of the Sign of the Cross; St. Acacius, Martyr.
8 St. John, the Apostle and Evangelist; Arsenius the Great.
9 Translation of the Venerable Relics of Our Holy Father, Nicholas, Wonderworker, from Myra to Bari (Italy); St. Christopher, Martyr; St. Isaias, Prophet.
10 St. Simon Zelotes, Apostle.
11 The Holy and equal to the Apostles, Doctors of the Slavs, Our Holy Fathers, Cyril and Methodius.
12 Epiphanius, Bishop in Cyprus, and Germanus, Patriarch of Constantinople.
13 St. Glyceria, Martyr; St. Alexander, Martyr.
14 St. Isidore, Martyr.
15 Pachomius the Great.

16 Theodore, disciple of St. Pachomius; Sts. Vitus, Modestus and Crescentia, Martyrs.
17 St. Andronicus, Apostle and others with him; St. Junia.
18 St. Theodutus of Ancyra in Galatia; Sts. Petrus, Dennis, Andreas, Paul, Christina, Heracleus, Paulinus and Venedimus, Martyrs; Sts. Seven Virgins: Alexandra, Thekusa, Claudia, Falina, Euphrasia, Matrona and Julia.
19 St. Patritius, Bishop-Martyr of Prusa in Bithynia and his companions, Menander and Acatius.
20 St. Thalaleus, Martyr and others.
21 Sts. Constantine the Great, King and Co-Apostle and Helen, his mother.
22 St. Basilisous, Martyr; Commemorating the Second Ecumenical Council Fathers at Constantinople A.D. 381.
23 Michael, Bishop of Synnada at Phrygia.
24 Simeon of the Wonderful Mountain, Stylite.
25 The Third Finding of the Venerable Head of St. John, the Glorious Prophet, Baptist and Precursor of Our Lord.
26 St. Carpus, Apostle.
27 St. Therapontus, Priest-Martyr.
28 Nicetas, Bishop of Chalcedon; St. Helladius, Priest-Martyr; St. Eutyches, Martyr in Miletus.
29 St. Theodosia, Venerable-Virgin-Martyr of Tyre.
30 Isaac, Monk in Dalmatia.
31 St. Hermas, Apostle, Bishop of Philippi; St. Hermeas, Martyr.

JUNE

1 St. Justin, Martyr; Another St. Justin, Martyr and Co-Martyrs.
2 Nicephorus, Patriarch of Constantinople; Alexander, Archbishop of Constantinople.
3 St. Lucillian, Martyr and with him: Claudius, Hypatius, Paul, and Dionysius; St. Paula, Martyr.
4 Metrophanes, Patriarch of Constantinople.
5 St. Dorotheus, Priest-Martyr, Bishop of Tyre.
6 Bessarion, wonderworker; Venerable Hilarion, the "Newer."
7 St. Theodotus, Priest-Martyr, Bishop of Ancyra.
8 Translation of the Relics of St. Theodore the Great-Martyr; Ephrem, Patriarch of Antiochia.
9 Cyril, Archbishop of Alexandria; Sts. Thecla, Martha, and Mary, Martyrs.
10 St. Timothy, Priest-Martyr, Bishop of Prusia; Sts. Alexander and Antonina, Martyrs.
11 Sts. Bartholomew and Barnabas, Apostles.
12 Onufrius the Great, Hermit; Peter of Athon.
13 St. Aquilina, Martyr; St. Trephillus, Bishop of Levkusia in Cyprus.
14 St. Elisseus, Prophet; Methodius, Patriarch of Constantinople.
15 St. Amos, Prophet; Venerable Jerome; Translation of the Relics of Our Father, Theodore "Sykeot."
16 St. Tychon, wonderworker, Bishop of Amathunsa.
17 Sts. Manuel, Sabel and Izmael, Persian Martyrs; Sts. Isaurus, Basil, Innocent, Jeremias, and others.
18 St. Leontius, Martyr.
19 St. Jude, Apostle, brother of St. James the Less; St. Zozimus, Martyr.
20 St. Methodius, Priest-Martyr, Bishop of Patara.
21 St. Julian of Tarsus, Martyr.
22 St. Eusebius, Priest-Martyr, Bishop of Samos; Sts. Galacteon and Juliana, Martyrs.
23 St. Agrippina, Virgin-Martyr.
24 Feast of the Nativity of St. John, the Glorious Prophet, Precursor and the Baptist.
25 St. Febronia, Virgin-Martyr.
26 Venerable David, Hermit.
27 Venerable Sampson, "Father of the Poor."
28 Translation of the Relics of Sts. Cyrus and John, wonderworkers and unmercenary physicians.
29 Feast of Sts. Peter and Paul, prime Apostles.
30 Synaxis of the Holy and most praiseworthy Twelve Apostles.

JULY

1 Sts. Cosmas and Damian, Martyrs.
2 Deposition of the Venerable Vestment of Our Most Holy Queen, Mother of God in the Church of Blachernae; Juvenal, Patriarch of Jerusalem.
3 St. Hyacinthus, Martyr; Anatolius, Patriarch of Constantinople.
4 Andreas, Archbishop of Crete; Martha, mother of St. Simeon of the "Wondermount."
5 Athanasius, Hegumen-Abbot of Mt. Athos; Lampadus, wonderworker of Irenepolis; Martha, mother of the Holy Simeon of the wonderful Mountain.
6 Sisoes the Great, Hermit and Anchoret.
7 Thomas of Malea and Acacius; St. Cyriaca, Martyr.
8 St. Procopius, Great-Martyr.
9 St. Pancratius, Priest-Martyr, Bishop of Taormina; St. Theodore, Bishop of Edessa; and the fasting Ten Thousand Saints.
10 Anthony of the "Kiev-Cave"; Forty-five Martyrs at Nicepolis in Armenia, Mauricius, Daniel, Antonius, and others.
11 St. Euphemia, Martyr; the death of Blessed Olga, Grand Duchess of Kiev.
12 Sts. Proclus and Hilarion, Martyrs; Michael of Malea; St. Mary, Martyr.
13 Synaxis of St. Gabriel, the Archangel; Stephen of Sabbas.
14 St. Aquila, Apostle; Onesimus, Venerable.
15 St. Vladimir the Great, of Apostolic zeal; Sts. Kirykos and his mother, Julitta, Martyrs.
16 St. Athenogenes, Priest-Martyr, with ten of his flock.
17 St. Marina, the Great-Martyr.
18 Sts. Hyacinth and Aemilian, Martyrs.
19 Venerable Macrina, sister of St. Basil.
20 St. Elias of Thesbite, Glorious Prophet.
21 Venerable Simeon, surnamed Salus (fool) and John, his co-faster, Hermits; St. Ezechiel.
22 St. Mary Magdalene, myrrh-bearer and of apostolic zeal; Translation of the Relics of St. Phocas, Priest-Martyr, a Bishop of Sinope.
23 Sts. Trophimus, Theophilus, and others; St. Apollynaris, Priest-Martyr.
24 Sts. Boris and Gleb, Martyrs; St. Christina, Martyr.
25 Dormition of St. Anna, Mother of the Blessed Virgin Mary, Mother of God.
26 Sts. Hermolaus, Priest-Martyr, and two brothers Hermippas and Thermocrates, Martyrs; St. Parasceva, Venerable-Martyr.
27 Pantaleon or Panteleimon, the Great-Martyr; Venerable Anthusa, mother of St. John Chrysostom.
28 Sts. Prochorus, Nicanor, Timon, and Parmenas, Apostles and Deacons; Innocentius, Pope of Rome.
29 St. Callincus, Martyr at Gangrae; Sts. Seraphina, Virgin-Martyr, Theodotia, and her Children.
30 Sts. Silas, Silvanus, Criscentus, Hepenctus, and Andronicus, Apostles; St. John, Soldier-Martyr; St. Julitta, Martyr.
31 St. Eudocimus, Venerable.

AUGUST

1 Procession of the Venerable and Life-giving Cross; Commemoration of the Sts. Seven Machabee Brothers, Martyrs, and their Mother, Solomonia, and their Master, Eleazar.
2 Translation of the Holy Relics of St. Stephen, the First Martyr and Archdeacon, from Jerusalem to Constantinople; St. Stephen, Priest-Martyr, Pope of Rome, and others.
3 Isaacius, Dalmatius, and Faustus.
4 Sts. Seven Youths of Ephesus, Martyrs: Maximilian, Dionisius, Amblichus, Martin, Antonin, John, and Marcell; St. Eudokia, Venerable-Martyr.
5 St. Eusignius, Martyr.
6 The Transfiguration of Our Lord God and Saviour, Jesus Christ.
7 St. Domitius, Venerable-Martyr; St. Pulcheria.
8 St. Aemilian, Confessor, Bishop of Cyzicus; Sts. Eleutherius and Leonidas, Martyrs.
9 St. Matthias, Apostle.
10 St. Lawrence, Archdeacon-Martyr.

11 St. Euplus, Archdeacon-Martyr.
12 Sts. Photius and Anicetus, Martyrs.
13 Maximus, Confessor.
14 St. Michaeas, Prophet; Translation of the Relics of Our Venerable-Father, Theodosius, Hegumen-Abbot of Cave.
15 Dormition (Assumption) of Our Most Holy and Glorious Queen, Mother of God and Ever-Virgin Mary.
16 Translation of the miraculously formed Icon of Our Lord Jesus Christ, from Edessa to Constantinople, called "Veronica's Veil"; St. Diomidius, Martyr.
17 St. Myron, Priest-Martyr; Sts. Paul and Juliana, his sister, Martyrs.
18 Sts. Florus and Laurus, Martyrs.
19 St. Andrew, a Tribune in the Greek army and with his 2,593 soldiers, Martyrs; Sts. Timothy, Agapius, and Thecla, Martyrs.
20 St. Samuel, Prophet; St. Stephen the First, Ap. King of Hungary.
21 St. Thaddeus, Apostle; Sts. Bassa and her children, Theogonius, Agapius, and Pista (Fidelis), Martyrs.
22 St. Agathonicus and with him Zoticus, Theoprepius, Acindynus, and Severianus, Martyrs.
23 St. Lupus, Martyr; St. Iraeneus, Priest-Martyr, Bishop of Lugdun in Galicia, Martyr; Callinicus, Patriarch of Constantinople.
24 St. Eutyches, Priest-Martyr.
25 Return of the Relics of Bartholomew, Apostle; St. Titus, Apostle.
26 Sts. Adrian and Natalia, Martyrs.
27 Poemen, an Egyptian.
28 Moses, an African Negro of Abyssinia styled the "Ethiopian Hermit"; Augustine, Confessor and Bishop of Hippo; St. Anna, daughter of Phanuel.
29 The Beheading of St. John, Glorious Prophet, Precursor and Baptist.
30 Alexander, John, and Paul the New, Patriarchs of Constantinople.
31 Deposition of the Venerable Girdle of the Blessed Virgin Mary, Mother of God.

RELIGIOUS COMMUNITIES AND SECULAR INSTITUTES UNITED STATES AND CANADA

The religious communities of priests, brothers, and women in the United States are listed in alphabetical order according to the initials of the order.

RELIGIOUS COMMUNITIES OF PRIESTS
UNITED STATES

A.A.	Assumptionist Fathers
B.S.	Salvatorian Fathers, Basilian
Cam. O.S.B.	Camaldolese Congregation
C.I.C.M.	Immaculate Heart of Mary Mission Society
C.J.	Josephite Fathers (Belgium)
C.J.M.	Congregation of Jesus and Mary
C.M.	Congregation of the Mission
C.M.	Vincentian Fathers
C.M.F.	Claretian Missionaries
C.M.F.	Missionary Sons of the Immaculate Heart of Mary
C.M.M.	Congregation of Mariannhill Missionaries
C.O.	Oratorian Fathers
C.P.	Congregation of the Passion
C.P.M.	Congregation of the Fathers of Mercy
C.PP.S.	Society of the Precious Blood
C.R.	Congregation of the Resurrection
C.R.	Theatine Fathers
C.R.M.	Adorno Fathers
C.R.S.	Somaschan Fathers
C.R.S.P.	Barnabite Fathers
C.R.S.P.	Clerics Regular of St. Paul
C.S.	Congregation of the Missionaries of St. Charles
C.S.B.	Basilian Fathers
C.S.C.	Priests of the Congregation of Holy Cross
C.S.J.	Pious Congregation of St. Joseph
C.S.P.	Paulist Fathers
C.S.S.	Stigmatine Fathers and Brothers
C.S.Sp.	Congregation of the Holy Ghost and the Immaculate Heart of Mary
C.S.Sp.	Holy Ghost Fathers
C.SS.R.	Redemptorist Fathers
C.S.V.	Clerics of St. Viator
Er. Cam.	Camaldolese, Hermits of Monte Corona
F.D.P.	Sons of Divine Providence

F.M.S.I.	Sons of Mary, Health of the Sick
F.S.C.J.	Sons of the Sacred Heart
F.S.C.J.	Verona Fathers
	Glenmary Home Missioners
	Home Missioners of America
I.C.	Institute of Charity
I.M.C.	Consolata Society for Foreign Missions (Consolata Fathers)
L.C.	Legionaries of Christ
	Monks of the Brotherhood of St. Francis
M.E.P.	Paris Foreign Missions Society
M.H.F.	Saint Joseph's Society for Foreign Missions
M.H.M.	Mill Hill Fathers
M.I.C.	Marian Fathers
M.S.	Missionaries of Our Lady of LaSalette
M.S.C.	Missionaries of the Sacred Heart
M.S.F.	Congregation of the Missionaries of the Holy Family
M.Sp.S.	Missionaries of the Holy Ghost
M.Ss.A.	Missionaries of the Holy Apostles
M.SS.CC.	Missionaries of the Sacred Hearts of Jesus and Mary
M.S.SS.T.	Missionary Servants of the Most Holy Trinity
O.A.R.	Order of the Augustinian Recollects
O.CARM.	Carmelite Fathers
O.CART.	Order of Carthusians
O.C.D.	Discalced Carmelite Fathers
O.C.S.O.	Order of Cistercians of the Strict Observance
O.C.S.O.	Trappists
O.F.M.	Franciscan Fathers
O.F.M.CAP.	Capuchin Fathers
O.F.M.Conv.	Conventual Franciscan Fathers
O.de M.	Order of Our Lady of Mercy
O.M.I.	Oblates of Mary Immaculate
O.M.V.	Oblates of the Virgin Mary
O.P.	Order of Preachers; Dominicans
O.PRAEM.	Canons Regular of Prémontré
O.S.A.	Augustinians
O.S.B.	Benedictine Fathers
O.S.B.	Sylvestrine Benedictines
O.S.B.M.	Order of St. Basil the Great
O.S.C.	Canons Regular of the Order of the Holy Cross
O.S.C.	Crosier Fathers
O.S.CAM.	Order of Saint Camillus
O.S.F.S.	Oblates of St. Francis de Sales
O.S.J.	Oblates of St. Joseph
O.S.M.	Servants of Mary
O.S.M.	Servite Fathers
O.S.P.	Pauline Fathers
O.SS.T.	Order of the Most Holy Trinity
P.I.M.E.	Missionaries of SS. Peter and Paul
P.I.M.E.	Pontifical Institute for Foreign Missions
S.A.	Franciscan Friars of the Atonement
S.A.C.	Pallottine Fathers
S.A.C.	Society of the Catholic Apostolate
S.CH.	Society of Christ
Sch.P.	Piarist Fathers
S.C.J.	Congregation of the Priests of the Sacred Heart of Jesus
S.D.B.	Salesians of St. John Bosco
S.F.	Sons of the Holy Family
S.J.	Society of Jesus; Jesuits
S.D.S.	Salvatorians; Society of the Divine Savior
S.D.V.	Society of the Divine Vocations
S.M.	Brothers of Mary
S.M.	Marianists (Society of Mary)

S.M.	Marist Fathers
S.M.A.	Society of the African Missions
S.M.B.	Society of Bethlehem Missionaries
S.M.M.	Montfort Missionaries
S.O.CIST.	Cistercian Order of Common Observance
s.P.	Servants of the Holy Paraclete
S.P.S.	Saint Patrick's Missionary Society
S.S.	Society of St. Sulpice; Sulpician Fathers
S.S.C.	Saint Columban's Foreign Mission Society
SS.CC.	Fathers of the Sacred Hearts
S.S.E.	Society of Saint Edmund
S.S.J.	Josephite Fathers (Colored Missions)
S.S.J.	Saint Joseph's Society of the Sacred Heart
S.S.P.	Society of Saint Paul
S.S.S.	Congregation of the Blessed Sacrament
S.T.	Missionary Servants of the Most Holy Trinity
S.V.D.	Society of the Divine Word
S.X.	Saint Francis Xavier Foreign Mission Society
T.O.R.	Third Order Regular of St. Francis
W.F.	White Fathers Missionaries of Africa

RELIGIOUS COMMUNITIES OF BROTHERS
UNITED STATES

B.G.S.	Brothers of the Good Shepherd
C.F.A.	Alexian Brothers
C.F.C.	Congregation of Christian Brothers
C.F.M.M.	Brothers of Our Lady of Mercy
C.F.P.	Brothers of the Poor of St. Francis
C.F.X.	Brothers of St. Francis Xavier
C.S.C.	Brothers of the Congregation of Holy Cross
C.S.P.X.	Brothers of St. Pius X
F.C.	Brothers of Charity
F.F.S.C.	Franciscan Brothers of the Holy Cross
F.I.C.	Brothers of Christian Instruction
F.I.C.M.	Brothers of the Immaculate Heart of Mary
F.M.M.	Brothers of Mercy
F.M.S.	The Marist Brothers
F.S.C.	Brothers of the Christian Schools
F.S.E.	Brothers of the Holy Eucharist
F.S.J.	Brothers of St. Joseph
F.S.P.	Brothers of St. Patrick
F.S.R.	Brothers of the Holy Rosary
O.H.	Hospitaller Order of St. John of God
O.S.F.	Franciscan Brothers of Brooklyn
O.S.F.	Franciscan Missionary Brothers of the Sacred Heart of Jesus
O.S.F.	Franciscan Brothers of Christ the King
S.C.	Brothers of the Sacred Heart
S.F.C.	Congregation of the Brothers of Charity of the Immaculate Heart of Mary
S.M.	Brothers of Mary
	Little Brothers of Jesus

RELIGIOUS COMMUNITIES OF WOMEN
UNITED STATES

A.A.	Sisters Auxiliaries of the Apostolate
A.C.J.	Handmaids of the Sacred Heart of Jesus
A.D.	Sisters of the Lamb of God
A.D.S.C.	Sisters Adorers Handmaids of the Blessed Sacrament and of Charity
A.P.	Nuns of the Perpetual Adoration of the Blessed Sacrament

A.P.B.	Sisters Adorers of the Precious Blood
A.R.SS.C.I.	Congregation of the Handmaids of the Sacred Heart of Jesus for Reparation
A.S.C.	Adorers of the Blood of Christ
A.S.C.J.	Apostles of the Sacred Heart of Jesus
AS.S.J.M.	Augustinian Sisters, Servants of Jesus and Mary
B.M.V.A.	Franciscan Sisters of the Blessed Virgin Mary
B.V.M.	Sisters of Charity of the Blessed Virgin Mary
C.A.CH.	Carmelite Sisters of Charity
C.B.S.	Sisters of Bon Secours
C.C.	Carmel Community
C.C.V.I.	Congregation of the Sisters of Charity of the Incarnate Word
C.C.V.I.	Congregation of the Sisters of Charity of the Incarnate Word, Houston, Texas
C.D.P.	Sisters of Divine Providence of San Antonio, Texas
C.D.P.	Sisters of Divine Providence
C.D.P.	Sisters of Divine Providence of Kentucky
C.D.S.	Congregation of Divine Spirit
C.F.P.	Congregation of the Passion and Our Lady of Sorrows
C.H.G.	Sisters of the Holy Ghost
C.I.C.	Sisters of the Immaculate Conception
C.I.J.	Congregation of the Infant Jesus (Nursing Sisters of the Sick Poor)
C.J.C.	Poor Sisters of Jesus Crucified and the Sorrowful Mother
C.L.H.C.	Congregation of Our Lady, Help of the Clergy
C.M.S.T.	Congregation of Carmelite Missionaries of St. Theresa
C.N.D.	Sisters of the Congregation de Notre Dame
C.O.B.	Congregation of the Oblates of Bethany
C.P.	Nuns of the Most Holy Cross and Passion of Our Lord Jesus Christ
C.P.	Sisters of the Cross and Passion
C.PP.S.	Sisters of the Most Precious Blood
C.PP.S.	Sisters of the Precious Blood
C.P.S.	Missionary Sisters of the Precious Blood
C.R.	Sisters of the Resurrection
C.S.	Company of the Savior
C.S.A.	Sisters of Charity of St. Augustine
C.S.A.	Sisters of the Congregation of Saint Agnes
C.S.A.C.	Sisters of the Catholic Apostolate ("Pallottine")
C.S.B.	Congregation of St. Brigid
C.S.C.	Congregation of the Sisters of the Holy Cross
C.S.C.	Sisters of Holy Cross and of the Seven Dolors
C.S.F.N.	Sisters of the Holy Family of Nazareth
C.S.J.	Sisters of St. Joseph of Medaille
C.S.J.	Sisters of St. Joseph of Carondelet
C.S.J.	Sisters of St. Joseph of Chambery
C.S.J.	Sisters of St. Joseph (Lyons, France)
C.S.J.	Sisters of St. Joseph of Peace
C.S.JB.	Sisters of St. John the Baptist
C.S.M.	Sisters of St. Martha
C.S.S.F.	Felician Sisters
C.S.SP.	Sisters of the Holy Spirit
C.S.T.	Carmelite Sisters of St. Therese of the Infant Jesus
C.V.D.	Sisters of Bethany
D.C.	Daughters of Charity of St. Vincent de Paul
D.C.	Daughters of the Cross
D.C.J.	Carmelite Sisters of the Divine Heart of Jesus
D.H.M.	Daughters of the Heart of Mary
D.H.S.	Daughters of the Holy Spirit
D.M.	Daughters of Mary of the Immaculate Conception
D.M.	Daughters of Our Lady of Mercy
D.M.J.	Daughters of Mary and Joseph
D.R.	Sisters of the Divine Redeemer
D.S.F.	Daughters of St. Francis of Assisi
D.S.M.P.	Daughters of St. Mary of Providence

D.S.P.	Pious Society, Daughters of St. Paul
D.W.	Daughters of Wisdom
E.M.S.	Eucharistic Missionary Sisters
F.C.	Daughter of the Cross of Liège
	The Poor Sisters of St. Joseph
F.C.J.	Society of the Sisters, Faithful Companions of Jesus
F.C.S.C.J.	Daughters of The Charity of the Sacred Heart of Jesus
F.D.C.	Daughters of Divine Charity
F.D.N.S.C.	Daughters of Our Lady of the Sacred Heart
F.D.P.	Daughters of Divine Providence
F.H.I.C.	Franciscan Hospitaller Sisters of the Immaculate Conception
F.H.M.	Franciscan Handmaids of the Most Pure Heart of Mary
F.I.	Daughters of Jesus
F.J.	Congregation of the Daughters of Jesus
F.M.A.	Daughters of Mary Help of Christians
F.M.D.C.	Franciscan Missionary Sisters of the Divine Child
F.M.D.M.	Franciscan Missionaries of the Divine Motherhood
F.M.I.	Daughters of Mary Immaculate
F.M.I.	Daughters of Mary Immaculate (Marianist)
F.M.M.	Franciscan Missionaries of Mary
F.M.S.C.	Franciscan Missionary Sisters of the Sacred Heart
F.M.S.J.	Mill Hill Sisters
F.S.E.	The Institute of the Franciscan Sisters of the Eucharist
F.S.I.C.	Franciscan Sisters of the Third Order of Immaculate Conception
F.S.J.	Religious Daughters of St. Joseph
F.S.P.A.	Congregation of the Sisters of the Third Order of St. Francis of Perpetual Adoration
F.S.R.	Franciscan Sisters of Ringwood
F.S.S.E.	Franciscan Sisters of St. Elizabeth
F.S.S.J.	Franciscan Sisters of St. Joseph
G.N.S.H.	Grey Nuns of the Sacred Heart
H.C.G.	Hermanas Catequistas Guadalupanas
H.H.S.	Society of Helpers
H.J.	Hermanas Josefinas
H.M.	Sisters of the Humility of Mary
H.P.B.	Congregation of the Handmaids of the Precious Blood
H.R.S.	Missionary Sisters of Our Lady of the Holy Rosary
H.V.M.	Sisters, Home Visitors of Mary
I.B.V.M.	Institute of the Blessed Virgin Mary (Ladies of Loretto)
I.B.V.M.	Institute of the Blessed Virgin Mary (Loreto Sisters)
I.C.M.	Missionary Sisters of the Immaculate Heart of Mary
I.J.	Sisters of the Infant Jesus
I.H.M.	The California Institute of the Sisters of the Most Holy and Immaculate Heart of the Blessed Virgin Mary
I.H.M.	Sisters of Immaculate Heart of Mary
I.H.M.	Sisters, Servants of the Immaculate Heart of Mary
I.H.M.	Sisters, Servants of the Immaculate Heart of Mary
I.W.B.S.	Congregation of the Incarnate Word of Blessed Sacrament of the Archdiocese of San Antonio
J.C.	Congregation of Jesus Crucified
L.C.M.	Little Company of Mary, Nursing Sisters
L.S.A.	Little Sisters of the Assumption
L.S.I.C.	Little Servant Sisters of the Immaculate Conception
L.S.P.	Little Sisters of the Poor
M.C.	Consolata Missionary Sisters
M.C.	Missionary Catechists of the Sacred Hearts of Jesus and Mary
M.C.	Poor Clare Missionary Sisters (Misioneras Clarisas)
M.C.D.P.	Missionary Catechists of Divine Providence
M.D.	Mothers of the Helpless
M.E.T.	Eucharistic Missionary Sisters of the Little Flower
M.H.S.	Sisters of the Most Holy Sacrament
M.H.S.H.	Mission Helpers of the Sacred Heart

M.J.M.J.	Missionaries of Jesus, Mary and Joseph
M.M.B.	Mercedarian Missionaries of Berriz
M.M.M.	Medical Missionaries of Mary
M.M.O.M.	Missionary Sisters of Our Lady Mercy
M.P.F.	Religious Teachers Filippini
M.P.V.	Religious Venerini Sisters
M.S.	Marist Sisters
M.S.	Marian Sisters Diocese of Lincoln
M.S.B.T.	Missionary Servants of the Most Blessed Trinity
M.S.C.	Congregation of the Marianites of Holy Cross
M.S.C.	Missionary Sisters of the Most Sacred Heart of Jesus of Hiltrup
M.S.C.	Missionary Sisters of the Sacred Heart
M.S.C.	Missionaries of the Sacred Heart of Jesus and Our Lady of Guadalupe
M.S.C.J.	Missionary Society of the Sacred Heart
M.S.M.G.	Missionary Sisters of Mother of God
M.S.S.A.	Missionary Servants of St. Anthony
M.S.S.C.B.	Missionary Sisters of St. Charles Borromeo
M.S.S.J.	Missionary Servants of St. Joseph
M.S.SP.	Mission Sisters of the Holy Spirit
M.SS.S.	Missionary Sisters of the Most Blessed Sacrament
M.S.V.	Missionary Sisters of Verona
N.D.	Notre Dame Sisters
N.D.S.	Congregation of Notre Dame de Sion
O.CARM.	Calced Carmelites
O.CARM.	Carmelite Sisters (Corpus Christi)
O.CARM.	Carmelite Sisters for the Aged and Infirm
O.CARM.	Congregation of Our Lady of Mount Carmel
O.CARM.	Institute of the Sisters of Our Lady of Mt. Carmel
O.C.D.	Discalced Carmelite Nuns
O.C.D.	Carmelite Sisters of the Sacred Heart
O.C.S.O.	Cistercian Nuns of the Strict Observance
O.D.N.	Company of Mary
O.J.S.	Oblate Sisters of Jesus the Priest
O.L.C.R.	Federation of Sisters of Our Lady of Charity
O.L.M.	Sisters of Charity of Our Lady of Mercy
O.L.P.	Missionaries of the Third Order of St. Francis of Our Lady of The Prairies
O.L.S.	Sisters of Our Lady of Sorrows
O.L.V.M.	Our Lady of Victory Missionary Sisters
O.P.	Dominican Nuns of Perpetual Adoration
O.P.	Dominican Sisters
O.P.	Dominican Sisters of Bethany, Congregation of St. Mary Magdalene
O.P.	Dominican Sisters of The Roman Congregation of St. Dominic
O.P.	Dominican Sisters of the Sick Poor
O.P.	Marian Society of Dominican Catechists
O.P.	Poor School Sisters of Penance of the Third Order of St. Dominic
O.P.	Servants of Relief for Incurable Cancer
O.P.	Dominican Sisters of Charity of the Presentation
O.P.	Dominican Nuns of the Perpetual Rosary
O.P.	Dominican Rural Missionaries
O.P.	Eucharistic Missionaries of St. Dominic
O.P.	Religious Missionaries of St. Dominic
O.S.A.	Augustinian Cloistered Nuns
O.S.A.	Sisters of St. Rita
O.S.B.	Benedictine Nuns of the Primitive Observance
O.S.B.	Benedictine Sisters
O.S.B.	Benedictine Sisters of Pontifical Jurisdiction
O.S.B.	Congregation of the Benedictine Sisters of the Perpetual Adoration of Pontifical Jurisdiction
O.S.B.	Missionary Benedictine Sisters
O.S.B.	Olivetan Benedictine Sisters
O.S.B.	Benedictine Sisters Regina Pacis
O.S.B.M.	Sisters of the Order of St. Basil the Great (Pittsburgh Greek Rite)

O.S.B.M.	Sisters of the Order of St. Basil the Great (Ukrainian Greek Rite)
O.S.B.S.	Oblate Sisters of the Blessed Sacrament
O.S.C.	Order of St. Clare—Poor Clares
O.S.F.	Bernardine Sisters of the Third Order of St. Francis
O.S.F.	Congregation of the Sisters of the Third Order of St. Francis, Oldenburg, Ind.
O.S.F.	Congregation of the Third Order of St. Francis of Mary Immaculate
O.S.F.	Franciscan Missionary Sisters for Africa
O.S.F.	Franciscan Missionary Sisters of Our Lady of Sorrows
O.S.F.	Franciscan Sisters, Daughters of the Sacred Hearts of Jesus and Mary
O.S.F.	Franciscan Sisters of Allegany, N. Y.
O.S.F.	Franciscan Sisters of Baltimore
O.S.F.	Franciscan Missionaries of Our Lady
O.S.F.	Franciscan Sisters of Christian Charity
O.S.F.	Franciscan Sisters of Mary Immaculate of the Third Order of St. Francis in Pasto
O.S.F.	Franciscan Sisters of Our Lady of Perpetual Help
O.S.F.	Franciscan Sisters of the Immaculate Conception
O.S.F.	Franciscan Sisters of Little Falls, Minn.
O.S.F.	Franciscan Sisters of the Immaculate Conception and St. Joseph for the Dying
O.S.F.	Franciscan Sisters of the Immaculate Conception of the Order of St. Francis
O.S.F.	Franciscan Sisters of the Sacred Heart
O.S.F.	Hospital Sisters of the Third Order of St. Francis
O.S.F.	Sisters of St. Francis of Philadelphia
O.S.F.	Missionary Franciscan Sisters of the Immaculate Conception
O.S.F.	Sisters of St. Francis of the Perpetual Adoration
O.S.F.	School Sisters of St. Francis
O.S.F.	School Sisters of the Third Order of St. Francis (Savannah, Mo.)
O.S.F.	School Sisters of the Third Order of St. Francis (Pittsburgh, Pa.)
O.S.F.	School Sisters of the Third Order of St. Francis (Panhandle, Texas)
O.S.F.	Servants of the Holy Infancy of Jesus
O.S.F.	Sisters of the Third Order of St. Francis (Bethlehem, Pa.)
O.S.F.	Sisters of Saint Francis of the Providence of God
O.S.F.	Sisters of St. Francis of the Holy Cross
O.S.F.	Sisters of St. Francis of Christ the King
O.S.F.	Sisters of St. Francis of Penance and Christian Charity
O.S.F.	Sisters of St. Francis of the Holy Eucharist
O.S.F.	Sisters of St. Francis of the Congregation of Our Lady of Lourdes
O.S.F.	Sisters of St. Francis of the Holy Family
O.S.F.	Sisters of St. Francis of the Immaculate Conception
O.S.F.	Sisters of St. Francis of the Immaculate Heart of Mary
O.S.F.	Sisters of St. Francis of the Martyr St. George
O.S.F.	Sisters of St. Francis of the Mission of the Immaculate Virgin, Conventuals of the Third Order
O.S.F.	Sisters of the Third Franciscan Order Minor Conventuals
O.S.F.	Sisters of the Third Order of St. Francis (Maryville, Mo.)
O.S.F.	Sisters of the Third Order of St. Francis (Peoria, Ill.)
O.S.F.	Sisters of St. Francis of the Third Order Regular (Williamsville, N. Y.)
O.S.F.	Sisters of the Third Order of St. Francis of Assisi
O.S.F.	Sisters of the Third Order of St. Francis of Penance and Charity
O.S.F.	Sisters of St. Francis, Clinton, Iowa
O.S.F.	Sisters of St. Francis of Millvale, Pa.
O.S.F.	Sisters of the Third Order Regular of St. Francis of the Congregation of Our Lady of Lourdes
O.S.F.	Franciscan Sisters of Chicago
O.S.FR.S.	Oblate Sisters of St. Francis de Sales
O.S.H.J.	Oblate Sisters of the Sacred Heart of Jesus
O.S.M.	Sisters, Servants of Mary
O.S.M.	Servants of Mary
O.S.M.	Servants of Mary (Servite Sisters)
O.S.P.	Oblate Sisters of Providence

O.S.S.	Sacramentine Nuns
O.SS.R.	Oblates of the Most Holy Redeemer
O.SS.R.	Order of the Most Holy Redeemer
O.SS.S.	Brigittine Sisters
O.SS.T.	Sisters of the Most Holy Trinity
O.S.U.	Ursuline Nuns
O.S.U.	Ursuline Nuns, of the Congregation of Paris
O.S.U.	Ursuline Sisters of Mt. Calvary
O.S.U.	Ursuline Sisters (Cork)
P.B.V.M.	Sisters of the Presentation of the B.V.M.
P.B.V.M.	Presentation of the B.V.M. (Mullingar)
P.B.V.M.	Presentation of the B.V.M. (Cork)
P.B.V.M.	Presentation of the B.V.M. (Cashel)
P.C.	Sisters of St. Claire
P.C.J.	Sisters of the Poor Child Jesus
P.C.P.A.	Poor Clares of Perpetual Adoration
P.C.P.A.	Poor Clares of Perpetual Adoration
P.D.D.M.	Sister Disciples of the Divine Master
P.F.M.	Little Franciscan Sisters of Mary
P.H.J.C.	Poor Handmaids of Jesus Christ
P.M.	Sisters of the Presentation of Mary
P.M.C.	Little Missionary Sisters of Charity
P.S.S.F.	Little Sisters of the Holy Family
P.V.M.I.	Parish Visitors of Mary Immaculate
R.A.	Religious of the Assumption
R.A.	Religious of the Apostolate of the Sacred Heart
R.C.	Congregation of Our Lady of the Retreat in the Cenacle
R.C.D.	Sisters of Our Lady of Christian Doctrine
R.C.E.	Religious of Christian Education
R.C.M.	Religious Conceptionist Missionaries
R.D.C.	Sisters of the Divine Compassion
R.E.	Religious of the Eucharist
R.F.	Sisters of St. Philip Neri Missionary Teachers
R.G.S.	Sisters of Our Lady of Charity of the Good Shepherd
R.H.S.J.	Religious Hospitalers of Saint Joseph
R.I.M.	Teaching Sisters of Mary Immaculate (Claretian Missionary Sisters)
R.J.M.	Religious of Jesus-Mary
R.M.S.S.	Religious Mercedarians of the Blessed Sacrament
R.M.S.S.	Sisters of Mercy of the Blessed Sacrament
R.O.D.A.	Sisters Oblates of Divine Love
R.O.D.A.	Sisters Oblates to Divine Love
R.S.C.	Religious Sisters of Charity
R.S.C.J.	Society of the Sacred Heart
R.S.D.	Institute of the Sisters of St. Dorothy
R.S.H.M.	Religious of the Sacred Heart of Mary
R.S.M.	Sisters of Mercy
R.S.M.	Sisters of Mercy of the Union in the United States of America
R.S.M.	Sisters of Mercy (Limerick)
R.S.M.	Sisters of Mercy (Sligo)
R.S.R.	Congregation of Our Lady of the Holy Rosary
R.U.	Ursuline Nuns of the Congregation of Tildonk, Belgium
S.A.	Franciscan Sisters of the Atonement
S.A.	Missionary Sisters of Our Lady of Africa (Sisters of Africa)
S.A.C.	Missionary Sisters of the Catholic Apostolate (Pallottines)
S.A.C.	Sisters of Mary of the Catholic Apostolate
S.A.C.	Sisters of the Holy Guardian Angels
S.A.S.V.	Sisters of the Assumption B.V.M.
S.B.S.	Sisters of Blessed Sacrament for Indians and Colored People
S.C.	Sisters of Charity of Seton Hill, Greensburg, Pa.
S.C.	Sisters of Charity of Cincinnati, Ohio
S.C.	Sisters of Charity of St. Elizabeth, Convent, N. J.
S.C.	Sisters of Charity of St. Vincent de Paul, of New York

S.C.	Sisters of Charity of St. Vincent de Paul, Halifax
S.C.C.	Sisters of Christian Charity
SCH.P.	Sisters of the Pius Schools
S.C.I.C.	Sisters of Charity of the Immaculate Conception of Ivrea
S.C.I.F.	Bethlemita Sisters, Daughters of the Sacred Heart of Jesus
S.C.I.M.	Servants of the Immaculate Heart of Mary (Sisters of the Good Shepherd)
S.C.L.	Sisters of Charity of Leavenworth, Kansas
S.C.M.C.	Sisters of Charity of Our Lady, Mother of the Church
S.C.M.M.	Sisters of Charity of Our Lady, Mother of Mercy
S.C.M.M.	Medical Mission Sisters
S.C.N.	Sisters of Charity of Nazareth
S.C.O.	Sisters of Charity of Ottawa
S.C.Q.	Sisters of Charity of Quebec (Grey Nuns)
S.C.S.C.	Sisters of Mercy of the Holy Cross
S.C.S.H.	Sisters of Charity of St. Hyacinthe (Grey Nuns)
S.C.S.J.A.	Sisters of Charity of St. Joan Antida
S.C.S.L.	Sisters of Charity of St. Louis
S.D.R.	Sisters of Divine Redeemer
S.D.S.	Sisters of the Divine Savior
S.D.S.H.	Sisters of the Society Devoted to the Sacred Heart
S.F.M.G.	Franciscan Missionary Sisters of Assisi
S.F.P.	Franciscan Sisters of the Poor
S.G.M.	Sisters of Charity (Grey Nuns)
S.H.C.J.	Society of the Holy Child Jesus
S.H.F.	Sisters of the Holy Family
S.H.F.	Sisters of the Holy Faith
S.H.G.	Sister-Servants of the Holy Ghost and Mary Immaculate
S.H.J.M.	Sisters of the Sacred Hearts of Jesus and Mary
S.H.R.	Sisters of the Holy Redeemer
S.J.C.	Sisters of St. Joseph of Cluny
S.J.W.	Sisters of St. Joseph the Worker
S.L.	Sisters of Loretto at the Foot of the Cross
S.L.W.	Sisters of the Living Word
S.M.	Sisters Servants of Mary
S.M.	Sisters of Mercy
S.M.	Sisters of Mercy
S.M.	Sisters of Mercy (Clonakilty)
S.M.	Sisters of Mercy (Cashel)
S.M.	Sisters of Mercy (Kells)
S.M.	Sisters of Mercy (Newtownforbes)
S.M.	Sisters of Mercy (Galway)
S.M.	Sisters of Mercy of Meath Community
S.M.D.C.	Misericordia Sisters
	Sisters of Mercy Daughters of Christian Charity
S.M.G.	Sisters Poor Servants of the Mother of God
S.M.HT.J.	Servants of the Most Sacred Heart of Jesus
S.M.I.	Sisters Servants of Mary Immaculate
S.M.I.C.	Missionary Sisters of the Immaculate Conception of the Mother of God
S.M.P.	Sisters of St. Mary of the Presentation
S.M.R.	Society of Mary Reparatrix
S.M.S.H.	Sisters of St. Marthe (of St. Hyacinthe)
S.M.S.M.	Marist Missionary Sisters
S.N.D.	Sisters of Notre Dame
S.N.D.	Sisters of Notre Dame de Namur
S.N.J.M.	Sisters of the Holy Names of Jesus and Mary
S.O.L.M.	Sisters of Our Lady of Mercy
S.P.	Sisters of Providence
S.P.	Sisters of Providence of Saint Mary-of-the-Woods, Indiana
S.P.	Sisters of Providence (Montreal)
S.P.C.	Sisters of St. Paul of Chartres
S.R.C.	Servants of Our Lady, Queen of the Clergy
S.R.C.M.	Sisters of the Reparation of the Congregation of Mary

S.S.A.	Sisters of St. Anne
S.S.A.	Sisters of St. Ann
S.S.C.	Sisters of St. Casimir
S.S.C.	Missionary Sisters of St. Columban
SS.CC.	Sisters of the Sacred Hearts and of Perpetual Adoration
S.S.CH.	Sisters of Ste. Chretienne
S.S.C.J.	Sisters of the Sacred Heart of Jesus of St. Jacut
S.S.C.J.	Servants of the Most Sacred Heart of Jesus
S.S.C.K.	Sister Servants of Christ the King
SS.C.M.	Sisters of Saints Cyril and Methodius
S.S.C.M.	Servants of the Holy Heart of Mary
S.S.E.	Sisters of St. Elizabeth
S.S.F.	Congregation of the Sisters of the Holy Family
S.S.H.J.P.	Servants of the Sacred Heart of Jesus and of the Poor
S.S.J.	Sisters of St. Joseph (Le Puy, France)
S.S.J.	Sisters of St. Joseph of the Third Order of St. Francis
S.S.J.	Sisters of St. Joseph of St. Augustine, Florida
S.S.J.S.M.	Sisters of St. Joseph of St. Mark
S.S.L.	The Congregation of the Sisters of St. Louis, Monaghan
S.S.M.	Sisters of St. Mary of the Third Order of St. Francis
S.S.M.	Sisters of the Sorrowful Mother (Third Order of St. Francis)
S.S.M.I.	Sisters Servants of Mary Immaculate of Mariowka
S.S.M.N.	Sisters of Saint Mary of Namur
S.S.M.O.	Sisters of St. Mary of Oregon
S.S.N.D.	School Sisters of Notre Dame
S.S.P.C.	Missionary Sisters of St. Peter Claver
S.SP.S.	Missionary Sisters, Servants of the Holy Spirit
S.SP.S. de A.P.	Sister Servants of the Holy Spirit of Perpetual Adoration
S.S.S.	Sisters of Social Service
S.S.S.	Sisters of Social Service
S.S.S.	Servants of the Blessed Sacrament
S.S.T.V.	Congregation of Sisters of St. Thomas of Villanova
S.T.J.	Society of St. Teresa of Jesus
S.U.	Society of the Sisters of St. Ursula
S.U.S.C.	Religious of the Holy Union of the Sacred Hearts
S.V.M.	Sisters of the Visitation of the Congregation of the Immaculate Heart of Mary
S.V.Z.	Sisters of Charity of St. Vincent de Paul
V.H.M.	Visitation Nuns
V.I.	Sisters of the Incarnate Word and Blessed Sacrament
V.I.	Congregation of the Incarnate Word and Blessed Sacrament
V.S.C.	Vincentian Sisters of Charity
V.S.C.	Vincentian Sisters of Charity (Bedford, Ohio)
X.M.M.	Xaverian Missionary Society of Mary, Inc.
X.M.S.	Catholic Mission Sisters of St. Francis Xavier

Angelic Sisters of St. Paul
Carmel Community
Community of the Holy Spirit
Daughters of Charity of the Most Precious Blood
Daughters of the Most Holy Saviour
Franciscan Sisters of St. Joseph
Home Mission Sisters of America
Little Sisters of Jesus
Poor Sisters of Nazareth
Sisters of Mercy
Sisters of Mercy (Birr)
Sisters of Mercy (Ardee)
Sisters of Our Lady of Mercy (Wexford)
Sisters of Ste. Jeanne d'Arc
Sisters of the Immaculate Conception of the Blessed Virgin Mary

SECULAR INSTITUTES
UNITED STATES
(Including other Secular Institutes
of Pontifical status in the Catholic Church)

ALLIANCE IN JESUS THROUGH MARY (women)
APOSTLES OF THE SACRED HEART (women)
CARITAS CHRISTI (women)
CATECHISTS OF THE SACRED HEART OF JESUS (women)
CHRIST THE KING (men)
COMPANY OF ST. PAUL (lay people and priests)
COMPANY OF ST. URSULA, DAUGHTERS OF ST. ANGELA MERICI: THE
    ANGELINES (women)
CORDIMARIAN FILIATION: DAUGHTERS OF THE IMMACULATE HEART OF
    MARY (women)
DAUGHTERS OF THE QUEEN OF THE APOSTLES (women)
DAUGHTERS OF THE SACRED HEART (women)
DESALES SECULAR INSTITUTE (women)
DIOCESAN LABORER PRIESTS
FAITHFUL SERVANTS OF JESUS (women)
HANDMAIDS OF DIVINE MERCY (women)
INSTITUTE OF NOTRE DAME DU TRAVAIL (women)
INSTITUTE OF OUR LADY OF LIFE (women)
INSTITUTE OF PRADO (men)
INSTITUTE OF SECULAR MISSIONARIES (women)
INSTITUTE OF THE BLESSED VIRGIN MARY (della Strada) (women)
INSTITUTE OF THE HEART OF JESUS (diocesan priests and lay people)
MISSIONARIES OF THE KINGSHIP OF CHRIST
    Under this title are included three distinct and canonically separate institutes.
    1. WOMEN MISSIONARIES OF THE KINGSHIP OF CHRIST
    2. MEN MISSIONARIES OF THE KINGSHIP OF CHRIST
    3. PRIEST MISSIONARIES OF THE KINGSHIP OF CHRIST
MISSIONARIES OF THE SICK (women)
MISSION OF OUR LADY OF BETHANY (women)
OBLATE MISSIONARIES OF MARY IMMACULATE (women)
OBLATES OF CHRIST THE KING (women)
RURAL PARISH WORKERS OF CHRIST THE KING (women)
SCHOENSTATT SISTERS OF MARY (women)
SECULAR INSTITUTE OF GOSPEL MISSIONARIES (women)
SECULAR INSTITUTE OF PIUS X (priests and laymen)
SERVITUM CHRISTI (women)
SOCIETY OF OUR LADY OF THE WAY (women)
TERESIAN INSTITUTE (women)
VOLUNTAS DEI (secular priests and laymen)
WORKERS OF DIVINE LOVE (women)

RELIGIOUS ORDERS OF PRIESTS
CANADA

AFRICAN MISSIONS (Society of the) (S.M.A.)
ASSUMPTIONIST FATHERS (A.A.)
AUGUSTINIAN FATHERS (O.S.A.)
BASILIAN FATHERS (C.S.B.)
BASILIAN SALVATORIAN FATHERS (B.S.)
BENEDICTINE FATHERS (O.S.B.)
BLESSED SACRAMENT (Congregation of the) (S.S.S.)
CANONS REGULAR OF THE IMMACULATE CONCEPTION (C.R.I.C.)
CAPUCHIN FATHERS (O.F.M.CAP.)
CARMELITE FATHERS (Discalced) (O.C.D.)

CARMELITE FATHERS (O.CARM.)
CISTERCIANS (O.CIST.)
CLARETIAN MISSIONARIES (C.M.F.)
CONSOLATA SOCIETY FOR FOREIGN MISSIONS (I.M.C.)
COMBONIAN MISSIONARIES (VERONA FATHERS) (F.S.C.J.)
DIVINE WORD (Society of the) (S.V.D.)
DOMINICAN FATHERS (O.P.)
EUDISTS (Congregation of Jesus and Mary) (C.J.M.)
FOREIGN MISSIONS SOCIETY (Province of Quebec) (P.M.É.)
FOREIGN MISSIONS SOCIETY (Scarboro Bluffs, Ontario) (S.F.M.)
FRANCISCAN FATHERS (Conventual) (O.F.M.CONV.)
FRANCISCAN FATHERS (O.F.M.)
FRANCISCAN FRIARS OF THE ATONEMENT (S.A.)
HOLY APOSTLES (Society of the) (S.SS.A.)
HOLY CROSS (Congregation of) (C.S.C.)
HOLY GHOST FATHERS (C.S.SP.)
JESUIT FATHERS (S.J.)
LAZARISTS (Congregation of the Mission) (C.M.)
MARIANHILL MISSIONARIES (Congregation of) (C.M.M.)
MARIANISTS (Society of Mary) (S.M.)
MARIST FATHERS (S.M.)
MARY (Company of) (S.M.M.)
OBLATES OF MARY IMMACULATE (O.M.I.)
ORDER OF ST. BASIL THE GREAT IN CANADA (O.S.B.M.) (Ukrainian Rite)
OUR LADY OF LA SALETTE (Missionaries of) (M.S.)
OUR LADY OF SION (Fathers of) (N.D.S.)
PALLOTINE FATHERS (S.A.C.)
PASSION (Congregation of the) (C.P.)
PAULIST FATHERS (C.S.P.)
PREMONTRE (Canons Regular of) (O.PRAEM.)
PRIESTS OF ST. MARY (P.S.M.)
REDEMPTORIST FATHERS (C.SS.R.)
RESURRECTION (Congregation of) (C.R.)
SACERDOTAL FRATERNITY (C.F.S.)
SACRED HEART (Missionaries of the) (M.S.C.)
SACRED HEART OF JESUS (Priests of the) (S.C.J.)
SACRED HEARTS OF JESUS AND MARY (Fathers of the) (SS.CC.)
SAINT CAMILLUS (Order of) (O.S.CAM.)
SAINT EDMUND (Society of) (S.S.E.)
SAINT PAUL (Society of) (S.S.P.)
SAINT VINCENT DE PAUL (Order of) (S.V.) (Priests and Brothers)
SAINT VIATOR (Clerics of) (C.S.V.)
SALESIANS OF ST. JOHN BOSCO (S.D.B.)
SCALABRINIANS (C.S.)
SERVANTS OF MARY (O.S.M.)
SONS OF CHARITY (F.CH.)
SONS OF MARY IMMACULATE (F.M.I.)
STIGMATINE FATHERS (C.S.S.)
SULPICIANS (Sulpician Fathers) (P.S.S.)
TRAPPISTS (Cistercians of the Strict Observance) (O.C.S.O.)
TRINITARIAN FATHERS (Order of the Most Holy Trinity) (O.SS.T.)
WHITE FATHERS (Missionaries of Africa) (W.F.)

SECULAR INSTITUTES

PIUS X SECULAR INSTITUTE
VOLUNTAS DEI INSTITUTE

RELIGIOUS ORDERS OF BROTHERS
CANADA

CHARITY (Brothers of the) (F.C.)
CHRISTIAN BROTHERS (Congregation of) (C.F.C.)
CHRISTIAN INSTRUCTION (Brothers of) (F.I.C.)
CHRISTIAN SCHOOLS (Brothers of the) (F.S.C.)
HOLY CROSS (Brothers of) (C.S.C.)
HOSPITALLER ORDER OF ST. JOHN OF GOD (O.H.)
LITTLE BROTHERS OF THE GOOD SHEPHERD (B.G.S.)
MARIST BROTHERS (F.M.S.)
OUR LADY OF MERCY (Brothers of) (F.D.M.)
PRESENTATION (Brothers of the) (F.P.M.)
SACRED HEART (Brothers of the) (S.C.)
SAINT-GABRIEL (Brothers of) (F.S.G.)
SAINT-LOUIS (Brothers of) (F.S.L.)

RELIGIOUS ORDERS OF WOMEN
CANADA

ADORERS OF THE MOST PRECIOUS BLOOD (Sisters) (A.P.S.)
ADORERS OF THE PRECIOUS BLOOD (London) (R.P.B.)
ANTONIAN SISTERS OF MARY QUEEN OF THE CLERGY (Congregation of) (A.P.S.)
ASSUMPTION (Congregation of the Sisters of the) (R.A.)
ASSUMPTION (Little Sisters of) (P.S.A.)
ASSUMPTION OF THE BLESSED VIRGIN (Sisters of the) (Nicolet) (A.S.V.)
AUGUSTINIAN SISTERS (Mercy of Jesus) (A.M.J.)
BENEDICTINE NUNS (O.S.B.)
BENEDICTINES OF THE PRECIOUS BLOOD (O.S.B.)
BLESSED SACRAMENT (Servants of the) (S.S.S.)
CARMELITE NUNS (Discalced) (O.D.C.)
CARMELITE SISTERS OF THE DIVINE HEART OF JESUS
CHARITY (Halifax, Nova Scotia) (Sisters of) (S.C.)
CHARITY (Quebec) (Sisters of) (S.C.Q.)
CHARITY OF IMMACULATE CONCEPTION (Sisters of) (St. John, New Brunswick)
CHARITY OF OTTAWA (Sisters of)
CHARITY OF ST. LOUIS (Sisters of) (S.C.S.L.)
CHARITY OF ST. MARY (Institute of Sisters of)
CHARITY OF ST. VINCENT DE PAUL (Daughters of) (D.C.S.V.P.)
CHARITY OF THE SACRED HEART OF JESUS (Daughters of)
CHILD JESUS (Religious of the) (R.E.J.)
CHILD JESUS (Religious of the) (S.E.J.)
CHRIST THE KING (Missionary Sisters of) (M.C.R.)
CISTERCIAN NUNS OF THE STRICT OBSERVANCE (O.C.S.O.)
COMPANIONS OF JESUS (Faithful)
CROSS (Daughters of the) (Called Sisters of St. Andrew)
CROSS (Sisters of Our Lady of the) (S.N.D.C.)
DAUGHTERS OF REPARATION OF THE DIVINE HEART (F.R.D.C.)
DISCIPLES OF THE DIVINE MASTER (Sisters)
DOMINICAN CONGREGATION OF ST. CATHERINE OF SIENA (O.P.)
DOMINICAN MISSIONARY ADORERS (O.P.)
DOMINICAN MISSION SISTERS OF NAMUR (O.P.)
DOMINICAN NUNS (O.P.)
DOMINICAN RURAL MISSIONARIES (O.P.)
DOMINICAN SISTERS OF THE ROMAN CONGREGATION OF ST. DOMINIC (O.P.)
DOMINICAN SISTERS OF THE TRINITY (O.P.)
DOMINICANS OF THE HOLY GUARDIAN ANGELS (Congregation of) (O.P.)
FRANCISCAN MISSIONARIES OF MARY (F.M.M.)
FRANCISCAN MISSIONARIES OF THE IMMACULATE CONCEPTION (F.M.I.C.)

FRANCISCAN OBLATES OF ST. JOSEPH (O.F.S.J.)
FRANCISCAN SISTERS OF THE ATONEMENT (S.A.)
FRANCISCANS OF MARY (Little) (P.F.M.)
GOOD SHEPHERD (Congregation of Our Lady of Charity of the)
GOOD SHEPHERD (of Quebec) (Sisters of) (Servants of Immaculate Heart of Mary)
(S.C.I.M.)
GREY NUNS (Sisters of Charity of Montreal General Hospital) (S.G.M.)
GREY NUNS OF SAINT HYACINTHE (S.G.S.H.)
GREY SISTERS OF THE IMMACULATE CONCEPTION (G.S.I.C.)
HEART OF MARY (Daughters of the) (F.C.M.)
HELPERS (Society of) (S.A.)
HOLY APOSTLES (Society of Sisters of)
HOLY CROSS (Sisters of the) (C.S.C.)
HOLY FAMILY (The Little Sisters of the) (P.S.S.F.)
HOLY FAMILY OF BORDEAUX (Sisters of the)
HOLY GHOST (Missionary Sisters of the) (C.S.SP.)
HOLY GHOST (Oblate Sisters of the)
HOLY HEART OF MARY (Servants of) (S.S.C.M.)
HOLY NAMES OF JESUS AND MARY (Sisters of the) (S.N.J.M.)
HOLY REDEEMER (Sisters of the) (O.SS.R.)
HOSPITALLERS OF ST. JOSEPH (Religious) (R.H.S.J.)
HOSPITALLERS REGULAR CANONESSES OF MERCY OF JESUS
IMMACULATE CONCEPTION (Missionary Sisters of the) (M.I.C.)
JESUS (Daughters of) (F.D.J.)
JESUS (Little Sisters of Brother Charles de)
JESUS AND MARY (Religious of) (Sillery, P.Q.) (R.J.M.)
JESUS AND MARY (Servants of) (S.J.M.)
JOAN OF ARC INSTITUTE (Ottawa) (Sisters of) (I.J.A.)
LITTLE MISSIONARIES OF ST. JOSEPH (Otterburne)
LITTLE SISTERS OF THE POOR
LORETTO (Ladies of) (Institute of the Blessed Virgin Mary)
LOVE OF JESUS (Sisters of the) (O.S.B.)
MARIANITES OF HOLY CROSS (Congregation of the) (M.S.C.)
MARIST SISTERS
MARY OF THE ASSUMPTION (Daughters of) (F.M.A.)
MARY HELP OF CHRISTIANS (Institute of the Daughters of) (Salesians of St. John
Bosco) (F.M.A.)
MARY IMMACULATE (Sisters Servants of) (S.S.M.I.)
MARY REPARATRIX (Society of) (S.M.R.)
MERCY (Sisters of) (St. John, Newfoundland) (R.S.M.)
MISERICORDIA SISTERS OF MONTREAL (S.M.)
MISSIONARY SISTERS OF OUR LADY OF THE ANGELS (M.N.D.A.)
MISSIONARY SISTERS OF ST. PETER CLAVER (S.M.S.P.C.)
NOTRE DAME (Congregation of) (C.N.D.)
NOTRE DAME (School Sisters of)
OBLATES OF BETHANY (Congregation of the) (C.O.B.)
OBLATES OF THE SACRED HEART AND MARY IMMACULATE (Missionary)
(M.O.)
OUR LADY, QUEEN OF THE CLERGY (Servants of) (S.R.C.)
OUR LADY OF AFRICA (Missionary Sisters of) (White Sisters) (S.B.A.)
OUR LADY AUXILIATRIX (Sisters of)
OUR LADY OF CHAMBRIAC (Sisters of)
OUR LADY OF CHARITY OF REFUGE (Sisters of)
OUR LADY OF EVRON (Sisters of Charity of) (S.C.E.)
OUR LADY OF GOOD COUNSEL (Institute of Sisters of) (Chicoutimi) (N.D.B.C.)
OUR LADY OF GOOD COUNSEL (Congregation of) (Montreal) (S.B.C.)
OUR LADY OF MISSIONS (Religious of) (R.N.D.M.)
OUR LADY OF PERPETUAL HELP (Congregation of Sisters of) (N.D.P.S.)
OUR LADY OF SION (Sisters of)
OUR LADY OF THE APOSTLES (Missionary Sisters)
OUR LADY OF THE HOLY ROSARY (Congregation of) (R.S.R.)
OUR LADY OF THE SACRED HEART (Sisters of) (N.D.S.C.)

PRESENTATION OF MARY (Sisters of the)
PRESENTATION OF THE BLESSED VIRGIN MARY (Sisters of the) (St. John, Newfoundland)
PROVIDENCE (Sisters of)
PROVIDENCE OF ST. BRIEUC (Daughters of)
PROVIDENCE OF ST. VINCENT DE PAUL (Sisters of) (Kingston) (S.P.)
RECLUSES OF JESUS AND MARY (Missionary)
RESURRECTION (Sisters of the) (S.R.)
SACRED HEART OF JESUS (Sisters of the) (R.S.C.J.)
SACRED HEART OF JESUS (Sisters of the) (S.S.C.J.)
SACRED HEARTS OF JESUS AND MARY (Sisters of the) (SS.CC.J.M.)
SACRED HEARTS OF JESUS AND MARY (Sisters of the)
SACRED HEARTS AND OF PERPETUAL ADORATION (Sisters of the) (SS.CC.)
ST. ANN (Sisters of) (S.S.A.)
SAINT BENEDICT (Sisters of the Order of) (O.S.B.)
SAINTE CHRÉTIENNE (Sisters of) (S.S.CH.)
ST. CLARE'S (Sisters of) (O.S.C.)
SAINT ELIZABETH (Franciscans) (Sisters of) (O.S.E.)
SAINT FRANCIS (Order of) (Felician Sisters)
SAINT FRANCIS OF ASSISI OF LYON (Sisters of) (S.F.A.)
SAINT FRANCIS (The Little Daughters of) (P.F.S.F.)
STE JEANNE D'ARC (Sisters of) (S.J.A.)
SAINT JOSEPH (Hamilton) (Sisters of) (C.S.J.)
SAINT JOSEPH (London) (Sisters of) (C.S.J.)
SAINT JOSEPH OF PEACE (B.C.) (Sisters of)
SAINT JOSEPH (The Little Daughters of) (P.F.S.J.)
SAINT JOSEPH (Pembroke) (Sisters of)
SAINT JOSEPH (Peterborough) (Sisters of)
SAINT JOSEPH (St. Hyacinthe) (Sisters of) (S.J.S.H.)
SAINT JOSEPH (Sault Ste. Marie) (Sisters of)
SAINT JOSEPH (Toronto) (Sisters of)
SAINT JOSEPH OF CLUNY (Sisters of) (S.J.C.)
SAINT JOSEPH OF ST. VALIER (Sisters of) (S.S.J.)
SAINT MARCELLINE (Sisters of) (S.M.)
SAINT MARTHA (Antigonish, N.S.) (Sisters of) (C.S.M.)
SAINT MARTHA (Charlottetown, Prince Edward Island, Nova Scotia) (Sisters of) (C.S.M.)
SAINT MARTHA (Saint Hyacinthe) (Sisters of) (S.M.S.H.)
SAINT MARY OF LEUCA (Daughters of)
SAINT MARY OF NAMUR (Sisters of)
SAINT MARY OF THE PRESENTATION (Daughters of)
SAINT PAUL (Daughters of) (F.S.P.)
SAINT PAUL OF CHARTRES (Sisters of) (S.P.D.C.)
SAVIOUR (Sisters of the) (S.D.S.)
SERVICE (Sisters of) (S.O.S.)
SERVITES OF MARY (Sisters)
SERVITES OF MARY (Compassionate)
SOCIAL SERVICE OF CANADA (Sisters of) (S.S.S.)
SOURIRE (Petites Soeurs de Notre Dame du)
TRINITARIAN SISTERS (O.SS.T.)
URSULINE NUNS (Abbacy Nullius) (O.S.U.)
URSULINE NUNS (Chatham)
URSULINES OF JESUS (of Chavagnes en Paillers, France)
URSULINES OF THE CANADIAN UNION (O.S.U.)
URSULINES OF TILDONCK
VISITATION OF SAINT MARY (Sisters of the) (Visitandines) (V.S.M.)
WHITE SISTERS
WISDOM (Daughters of) (F.D.L.S.)

SECULAR INSTITUTES
CANADA

AUXILIARIES OF CATHOLIC CLERGY (A.C.C.)
DOMINICAN SECULAR INSTITUTE OF ST. CATHERINE OF SIENA
FRANCISCAN AUXILIARIES OF PRIEST AND CATHOLIC ACTION (A.F.)
INSTITUT JEANNE-MANCE (I.J.M.)
INSTITUT NOTRE-DAME DE VIE
MISSIONARIES OF THE ROYALTY OF CHRIST (M.R.C.)
MISSIONARY OBLATES OF MARY IMMACULATE (O.M.I.)
OUR LADY OF THE PROTECTION INSTITUTE (A.N.D.P.)
SERVANTS OF MARY IMMACULATE (S.M.I.)
SOCIAL WORKERS (Les Equipières Sociales)